S0-ARO-797

Government and Not-for-Profit Accounting

Concepts and Practices

Government and Not-for-Profit Accounting

Concepts and Practices

Third Edition

Michael H. Granof
University of Texas, Austin

John Wiley & Sons, Inc.

Acquisitions Editor *Mark Bonadeo*
Editorial Assistant *Brian Kamins*
Associate Editor *Ed Brislin*
Marketing Manager *Steve Herdegen*
Production Editor *Kelly Tavares, Sarah Wolfman-Robichaud*
Managing Editor *Kevin Dodds*
Cover Design *Jennifer Wasson*
Illustration Editor *Michele Chancellor*

This book was set in Janson Text by Leyh Publishing LLC and printed and bound by R.R. Donnelly. The cover was printed by Phoenix Color.

This book is printed on acid-free paper.∞

Granof, Michael H.
Government and not-for-profit accounting : concepts and practices / by Michael H. Granof
p. cm.
Includes index.
ISBN 0-471-23009-X (cloth)
1. Finance, Public—United States—Accounting. 2. Finance, Public—Accounting—Standards—United States. 3. Nonprofit organizations—United States—Accounting. 4. Nonprofit organizations—Accounting—Standards—United States. I. Title.

HJ9801.G7 2004
657'.835—dc22

2003068698

Printed in the United States of America

10 9 8 7 6 5 4 3 2

In Memory of
My mother, Diana S. Granof (a teacher)
My father, David H. Granof (a CPA)

PREFACE

The objectives of this, the third edition of *Government and Not-for-Profit Accounting: Concepts and Practices*, remain unchanged from those of the previous editions. Above all, the text aims to make students aware of the dynamism of government and not-for-profit accounting and of the intellectual challenges that it presents. Government and not-for-profit accounting has changed dramatically in the past decade—far more so than business accounting. Both the Government Accounting Standards Board and the Financial Accounting Standards Board have radically changed the accounting and reporting models of the entities within their purview. The federal government established the Federal Accounting Standards Advisory Board, which developed a new reporting model for both the federal government at-large and its component agencies. Governments at all levels as well as not-for-profit organizations have been expanding the focus of their reporting beyond the traditional financial information to encompass measures of efficiency and effectiveness.

Despite the rapid progress that has been made in improving governmental and not-for-profit accounting and reporting, many key issues remain to be resolved. For the most part, these issues are far less tractable than those encountered by businesses. Businesses have the luxury of directing attention to *profits*—a metric that is relatively easy to define—inasmuch as the overriding objective of businesses is to earn a profit. Governments and not-for-profit entities, by contrast, have broader, much less clear-cut goals. They must determine not only *how* to measure their performance but also *what* to measure. Hence, the accounting profession is almost certain to be dealing with fundamental questions throughout the professional careers of today's students and the pace of rapid change will continue unabated.

Obviously, I intend for this text to inform students of current accounting and reporting standards and practices—those with which they might need to be familiar in their first jobs. More importantly, however, I want to assure that they are aware of the reasons behind them, their strengths and limitations, and possible alternatives. I am more concerned that students are prepared for their last jobs rather than their first. The text aspires to lay the foundation so that the students of today can become the leaders of tomorrow—the members of the standard-setting boards, the partners of CPA firms, the senior managers of government and not-for-profit organizations, and the members of legislative and governing boards.

Courses in government and not-for-profit accounting are just one element of an accounting program and, indeed, of a college education. Therefore, I expect that this text will lead not only to an awareness of the issues of government and not-for-profit accounting, but also to a greater understanding of those in other areas of accounting. Almost all issues addressed in this text—revenue and expense recognition, asset and liability valuation, the scope of the reporting entity, reporting cash flows, and so on—have counterparts in business accounting. By emphasizing concepts, rather than rules and procedures, I hope that students will gain insight into how and why the issues may have been resolved either similarly or differently in the business sector.

Moreover, I trust that this text will contribute to students' ability to read, write, and "think critically." To that end I have made a special point of designing end-of-chapter problems that challenge students not only to apply concepts that are presented in the text, but to justify the approach they have taken and to consider other possible lines of attack.

Needless to say, many students will use this text to prepare for the CPA exam. I have endeavored to cover all topics that are likely to be tested on the exam—an admittedly difficult goal, however, now that the AICPA does not publish past exams. I have also included approximately twenty multiple-choice questions in most chapters as well as several other "CPA-type" questions.

Since the publication of the second edition, standard setting agencies have made several changes to their accounting models—although none as sweeping as those of GASB Statement No. 34, *Basic Financial Statements—and Management's Discussion and Analysis—for State and Local Governments*, which dictated major revisions of that edition. This revision incorporates the new pronouncements. At the same time, I have sought to improve upon the previous edition by clarifying a number of points, adding new exercises and problems, and adding and updating the "In Practice" boxed inserts (newsworthy items illustrative of points addressed in the text).

SPECIAL FEATURES

This edition, like the previous edition, includes illustrations of actual financial statements. The illustrations in the previous edition, however, were the statements incorporated into Statement No. 34 itself. That was because few actual governments had yet adopted the new reporting model. The illustrative statements in this edition are those of Charlotte, North Carolina.

As in the previous edition, each chapter dealing with state and local accounting principles includes a "continuing problem" which asks students to review the comprehensive annual financial report (CAFR) of a city, county, or state with a population over 100,000 and answer questions about it. The questions are applicable to the reports of any major municipal government. However, recognizing the advantages of having all students in a class work from the same report, the text is accompanied by a CD-ROM containing the CAFR of Austin, Texas. This CD-ROM is especially easy to use as it contains "bookmarks" that link to the key sections of the report. Also, the solutions manual contains the "answers" to the continuing problem based on the Austin CAFR.

This text is decidedly oriented more toward concepts than procedures. It is based on the premise that once students have a firm grasp of the theory underlying current practice they can quickly acquire the skills required of professional accountants and auditors. To provide an opportunity for students to get more experience in recording transactions and preparing financial statements than is provided by the numerous problems and exercises in the text, this edition of *Government and Not-for-Profit Accounting* is supplemented by a "practice set." This practice set, however, is much more than a conventional bookkeeping exercise. It is built upon a state-of-the-art computerized fund accounting and reporting program designed by FundBalance, Inc., a leading governmental software developer. Students are presented with files containing beginning balances and related information pertaining to an actual city. They are required to record various types of transactions in individual funds and to make specified end-of-period adjustments, including those required to convert from fund to government-wide statements. The program then prepares a complete set of financial statements, both fund and government-wide, consistent with GASB Statement No. 34 and related pronouncements. With a commitment of only a small amount of additional study time, students are able not only to become familiar with the type of software they are likely to encounter in modern-day governments, but also to gain an overview of the entire accounting cycle and an appreciation of the differences between statements based on the modified accrual basis and those based on the full accrual basis. The practice set was developed by Jan Gillespie of the University of Texas at Austin working closely with Andy Arizala of FundBalance, Inc.

ACKNOWLEDGMENTS

I am especially grateful to Penelope S. Wardlow. Penny, who had a distinguished career with the Government Accounting Standards Board, and I recently published *Core Concepts of Government and Not-for-Profit Accounting*. Many of the insights and ideas that she brought to that book have found their way into this edition and have unquestionably improved it.

Robert Bramlett of the Federal Accounting Standards Advisory Board and Robert W. Kilpatrick of the Office of Management and Budget reviewed and edited the chapters pertaining to federal accounting and budgeting. They not only spared the text of misstatements and assured that it was up-to-date but also helped me to better understand the accounting and budgeting practices and policies of the federal government. Stephen Morgan, City Auditor of Austin, did the same with the chapter directed to auditing and helped lead me through the subtleties of the Single Audit Act and the GAO's "Yellow Book." Roberta Reese of the GASB helped me to better understand the proposed pronouncement on asset impairment.

Ivo Dimitrov and Charity Taber, both former students, carefully read the text and worked the problems. They each proposed numerous worthwhile changes.

I am also indebted to the following reviewers: Barbara Chaney (University of Montana); Rita Hartung Cheng (University of Wisconsin-Milwaukee); Kathryn Hansen (California State, Los Angeles); James Mraz (University of Maryland–Asia); Suzanne Ogilby (California State, Sacramento); Suesan Patton; Sandra Pelfrey (Oakland University, Michigan); Barbara Reider (University of Montana); and William Wrege (Ball State University). Their suggestions were uniformly sound.

M.H.G.
Austin, Texas

CONTENTS

CHAPTER 1

THE GOVERNMENT AND NOT-FOR-PROFIT ENVIRONMENT 1

How Do Governments and Not-for-Profits Compare with Businesses? 2

What Other Characteristics of Governments and Not-for-Profits Have Accounting Implications? 8

How Do Governments Compare with Not-for-Profits? 11

What Is the Purpose of Financial Reporting? 12

Who Are the Users and What Are the Uses of Financial Reports? 13

IN PRACTICE: *Who Receives Annual Reports?* 15

What Are the Objectives of Financial Reporting? 16

IN PRACTICE: *Employees as Statement Users* 17

EXAMPLE: *Clash Among Reporting Objectives* 18

Do Differences in Accounting Principles Really Matter? 21

IN PRACTICE: *Testing the Theory—Do Investors Adjust for Differences in Accounting Principles?* 22

Who Establishes Generally Accepted Accounting Principles? 22

IN PRACTICE: *Assessing the Profitability of a Football Program* 23

IN PRACTICE: *Lessons from Business Scandals* 25

Summary 27

Questions for Review and Discussion 27

Exercises 28

Problems 29

CHAPTER 2

FUND ACCOUNTING 34

What Is a Fund? 35

What Characterizes Funds? 35

EXAMPLE: *Fund Accounting in a School District* 38

How Can Funds Be Combined and Consolidated? 40

What Are the Main Types of Government Funds? 41

What's Notable About Each Type of Governmental Fund? 48

What's Notable About Each Type of Proprietary Fund? 50

What's Notable About Each Type of Fiduciary Fund? 55

What Is Included in a Government's Comprehensive Annual Financial Report (CAFR)? 56

EXAMPLE: *Government-Wide Statement of Activities* 58

How Do the Funds and Annual Reports of Not-for-Profits Differ from Those of Governments? 60

Summary 61

Exercise for Review and Self-Study 64

Questions for Review and Discussion 65

Exercises 65

Problems 68

Solution to Exercise for Review and Self-Study 74

CHAPTER 3

ISSUES OF BUDGETING AND CONTROL 77

What Are the Key Purposes of Budgets? 78

Why Is More than One Type of Budget Necessary? 79

How Are Expenditures and Revenues Classified? 80

Why Are Performance Budgets Necessary? 81

What Are the Key Phases of the Budget Cycle? 83

IN PRACTICE: *Budgeting Cannot Be Divorced from Politics* 85

IN PRACTICE: *Federal Budgetary Legerdemain* 86

IN PRACTICE: *Misestimating Revenues and Expenditures* 87

On What Basis of Accounting Are Budgets Prepared? 87

What Cautions Must Be Taken in Budget-to-Actual Comparisons? 89

IN PRACTICE: *Do Taxpayers Really Want Honest Budgeting?* 89

IN PRACTICE: *Balancing the Budget by Selling Assets to Yourself* 90
How Does Budgeting in Not-for-Profit Organizations Compare with That in Governments? 91
How Do Budgets Enhance Control? 95
What Are the Distinctive Ways Governments Record Their Budgets? 97
EXAMPLE: *Budgetary Entries* 98
How Does Encumbrance Accounting Prevent Overspending? 100
EXAMPLE: *The Encumbrance Cycle—Year 1* 101
EXAMPLE: *The Encumbrance Cycle—Year 2* 103
EXAMPLE: *Impact of Encumbrances on Fund Balance* 103
Are Budgetary and Encumbrance Entries Really Needed? 105
Summary 106
Exercise for Review and Self-Study 107
Questions for Review and Discussion 107
Exercises 108
Problems 111
Solution to Exercise for Review and Self-Study 118

CHAPTER 4

RECOGNIZING REVENUES IN GOVERNMENTAL FUNDS 162

Why and How Do Governments Use the Modified Accrual Basis? 120
What Are the Main Types of Nonexchange Revenues and the Limitations on How and When They Can Be Used? 123
How Should Property Taxes and Other Imposed Nonexchange Revenues Be Accounted For? 124
EXAMPLE: *Property Taxes* 125
EXAMPLE: *Fines* 129
How Should Sales Taxes and Other Derived Tax Revenues Be Accounted For? 130
EXAMPLE: *Sales Taxes* 131
EXAMPLE: *Sales Taxes Collected by State* 132
EXAMPLE: *Income Taxes* 134
How Should Grants and Similar Government Mandated and Voluntary Nonexchange Revenues Be Accounted For? 135
EXAMPLE: *Unrestricted Grant with Time Requirement* 136
EXAMPLE: *Grant with Purpose Restriction* 137
EXAMPLE: *Reimbursement (Eligibility Requirement) Grant* 137
EXAMPLE: *Unrestricted Grant with Contingency Eligibility Requirement* 138
EXAMPLE: *Endowment Gift* 138
EXAMPLE: *Pledges* 138
EXAMPLE: *Donations of Land for Differing Purposes* 139
EXAMPLE: *Food Stamps* 141
EXAMPLE: *On-Behalf Payments* 142
How Should Sales of Capital Assets Be Accounted For? 142
EXAMPLE: *Sales of Capital Assets* 142
How Should Investment Gains and Losses Be Accounted For? 143
EXAMPLE: *Investment Income* 144
How Should Interest and Dividends Be Accounted For? 146
EXAMPLE: *Interest Income* 146
How Should Licenses, Permits, and Other Exchange Transactions Be Accounted For? 147
EXAMPLE: *License Fees* 147
How Should Governments Report Revenues in Their Government-Wide Statements? 148
Summary 149
Exercise for Review and Self-Study 150
Questions for Review and Discussion 151
Exercises 151
Problems 154
Solution to Exercise for Review and Self-Study 160

CHAPTER 5

RECOGNIZING EXPENDITURES IN GOVERNMENTAL FUNDS 162

How Is the Accrual Concept Modified for Expenditures? 163
How Should Wages and Salaries Be Accounted For? 164
EXAMPLE: *Wages and Salaries* 164
IN PRACTICE: *Changing the Pay Date by One Day* 165

How Should Compensated Absences Be Accounted For? 166
EXAMPLE: *Vacation Leave* 166
EXAMPLE: *Sick Leave* 167
EXAMPLE: *Sabbatical Leave* 169
How Should Pensions Be Accounted For? 170
EXAMPLE: *Pension Contributions* 170
How Should Claims and Judgments Be Accounted For? 171
EXAMPLE: *Claims and Judgments* 171
How Should the Acquisition and Use of Materials and Supplies Be Accounted For? 173
EXAMPLE: *Supplies* 173
How Should Repayments Be Accounted For? 175
EXAMPLE: *Prepayments* 175
How Should Capital Assets Be Accounted For? 176
EXAMPLE: *Capital Assets* 177
EXAMPLE: *Installment Notes* 178
EXAMPLE: *Capital Leases* 179
How Should Interest and Principal on Long-Term Debt Be Accounted For? 180
EXAMPLE: *Long-Term Debt* 180
How Should Nonexchange Expenditures Be Accounted For? 183
EXAMPLE: *Unrestricted Grant with Time Requirement* 183
EXAMPLE: *Grant with Purpose Restriction* 183
EXAMPLE: *Reimbursement (Eligibility Requirement) Grant* 183
How Should Interfund Transactions Be Accounted For? 184
EXAMPLE: *Interfund Transfer* 184
EXAMPLE: *Interfund Purchase/Sale* 184
What Constitutes Other Financing Sources and Uses? 186
How Should Revenues, Expenditures, and Other Financing Sources and Uses Be Reported? 187
What Is the Significance of the Current Financial Governmental Fund Statements? An Overview 187
IN PRACTICE: *The Usefulness of Reported Fund Balance* 188
Summary 189
Exercise for Review and Self-Study 189
Questions for Review and Discussion 190
Exercises 191
Problems 194
Solution to Exercise for Review and Self-Study 201

CHAPTER 6

ACCOUNTING FOR CAPITAL PROJECTS AND DEBT SERVICE 203

How Do Governments Account for Capital Projects Funds? 204
EXAMPLE: *Bond Issue Costs* 206
EXAMPLE: *Bond Premiums and Discounts* 206
COMPREHENSIVE EXAMPLE: *Main Types of Transactions Accounted For in Capital Projects Funds* 207
How Do Governments Account for Resources Dedicated to Debt Service? 210
COMPREHENSIVE EXAMPLE: *Main Types of Transactions Accounted For in Debt Service Funds* 212
How Do Governments Handle Special Assessments? 215
IN PRACTICE: *Alleged Abuse of Special Assessments* 217
Accounting for Special Assessments in Proprietary Funds 219
Why Is Arbitrage a Concern of Governments? 221
How Can Governments Benefit from Debt Refundings? 222
EXAMPLE: *Debt Refundings* 223
EXAMPLE: *In-Substance Defeasance* 224
Summary 227
Exercise for Review and Self-Study 227
Questions for Review and Discussion 228
Exercises 228
Problems 232
Solution to Exercise for Review and Self-Study 239

CHAPTER 7

LONG-LIVED ASSETS AND INVESTMENTS IN MARKETABLE SECURITIES 242

What Accounting Practices Do Governments Follow for General Capital Assets? 243

EXAMPLE: *Trade-Ins* 245

Why and How Should Governments Report Infrastructure? 248

IN PRACTICE: *Resolution on Infrastructure of the Government Finance Officers Association* 251

How Should Governments Account for Assets That Are Impaired? 254

EXAMPLE: *Restoration Approach* 255

What Issues Are Critical as to Investments in Marketable Securities and Other Financial Instruments? 256

IN PRACTICE: *Increasing Risk and Courting Disaster* 258

IN PRACTICE: *Report Shows How Governments Can Avoid Fiscal Fiascos* 261

Summary 262

Exercise for Review and Self-Study 262

Questions for Review and Discussion 263

Exercises 263

Problems 266

Solution to Exercise for Review and Self-Study 272

CHAPTER 8

LONG-TERM OBLIGATIONS 273

Why Is Information on Long-Term Debt Important to Statement Users? 274

Can Governments and Not-for-Profits Go Bankrupt? 274

How Do Governments Account for Long-Term Obligations? 275

IN PRACTICE: *Decision Helps Clarify Concept of Municipal Bankruptcy* 276

EXAMPLE: *Accounting for Bonds in Government-Wide Statements* 278

IN PRACTICE: *Valuing a Lottery Prize* 281

What Constitutes a Government's Long-Term Debt? 281

EXAMPLE: *Demand Bonds* 282

EXAMPLE: *Bond Anticipation Notes* 284

EXAMPLE: *Tax Anticipation Notes* 284

EXAMPLE: *Capital Leases* 287

EXAMPLE: *Overlapping Debt* 290

What Other Information Do Users Want to Know about Outstanding Debt? 292

EXAMPLE: *Debt Margin* 293

What Are Bond Ratings and Why Are They Important? 294

IN PRACTICE: *States Misuse Tobacco Settlements to Cover Current Budget Deficits* 296

Summary 296

Exercise for Review and Self-Study 297

Questions for Review and Discussion 297

Exercises 298

Problems 301

Solution to Exercise for Review and Self-Study 307

CHAPTER 9

BUSINESS-TYPE ACTIVITIES 308

What Types of Funds Involve Business-Type Activities? 309

Why Do Governments and Not-for-Profits Engage in Business-Type Activities? 310

Should Business-Type Activities Be Accounted for Differently from Governmental Activities? 311

What Are the Three Basic Statements of Proprietary Fund Accounting? 312

What Accounting Issues Are Unique to Enterprise Funds of Governments? 316

EXAMPLE: *Revenue Bond Proceeds as Restricted Assets* 322

EXAMPLE: *Landfill Costs in an Enterprise Fund* 324

What Are Internal Service Funds and How Are They Accounted For? 325

EXAMPLE: *Internal Service Fund Accounting* 327

IN PRACTICE: *Full Cost Pricing May Encourage Dysfunctional Decisions* 330

What Special Problems Are Created When an Internal Service Fund or the General Fund Accounts for "Self-Insurance"? 331

EXAMPLE: *Insurance Premiums* 333

EXAMPLE: *Self-Insurance in a General Fund* 334

How Are Proprietary Funds Reported? 334

EXAMPLE: *Eliminating Interfund Balances and Transactions* 336

What Do Users Want to Know about Revenue Debt? 337
Summary 338
Exercise for Review and Self-Study 340
Questions for Review and Discussion 340
Exercises 342
Problems 346
Solution to Exercise for Review and Self-Study 352

CHAPTER 10

FIDUCIARY FUNDS AND PERMANENT FUNDS 353

What Is an Endowment? 354
What Are Permanent Funds and How Are They Distinguished from Fiduciary Funds? 355
Should Investment Income Be Reported in an Expendable or a Nonexpendable Fund? 356
EXAMPLE: *Expendable Investment Income* 357
Why Should All Nonexpendable Funds Be Accounted for on a Full Accrual Basis—and Why Aren't They? 357
EXAMPLE: *Charging Depreciation* 358
Should Investment Gains Be Considered Net Additions to Principal or Expendable Income? 359
EXAMPLE: *Investment Gains* 360
EXAMPLE: *Investment Losses* 361
IN PRACTICE: *Disconnect between FASB and Legal Provisions* 363
How Can Institutions Protect against Inflation, Yet Reap the Benefits of Current Income? 363
EXAMPLE: *Fixed Rate of Return Approach* 364
How Are the Main Types of Transactions Recorded in Nonexpendable Trust Funds? 364
EXAMPLE: *Recording Transactions in a Permanent Fund* 364
Why Are Pensions So Important? 368
IN PRACTICE: *Between a Bear Stock Market and Their Own Blunders, Pension Funds Are Hurting* 370
How Does a Defined Contribution Plan Differ from a Defined Benefit Plan? 371
What Is the Relationship between an Employer and Its Pension Trust Fund? 372
What Issues Does a Government Employer Face in Accounting for Its Pensions? 373
EXAMPLE: *Unfunded Actuarial Accrued Liability* 376
EXAMPLE: *Reporting Pension Costs* 376
How Should the Pension Plan Be Accounted For? 378
How Should Postemployment Benefits Other Than Pensions Be Accounted For? 382
What Accounting Issues Do Agency Funds Present? 384
EXAMPLE: *Agency Funds* 384
What Accounting Issues Do Investment Trust Funds Present? 386
Summary 387
Exercise for Review and Self-Study 389
Questions for Review and Discussion 390
Exercises 391
Problems 394
Solution to Exercise for Review and Self-Study 399

CHAPTER 11

ISSUES OF REPORTING, DISCLOSURE, AND FINANCIAL ANALYSIS 400

Why Is the Reporting Entity an Issue for Governments? 401
EXAMPLE: *The Reporting Entity* 401
What Criteria Have Been Established for Government Reporting Entities? 402
EXAMPLE: *Financially Accountable Component Units* 403
EXAMPLE: *Fiscal Dependency* 404
EXAMPLE: *A Closely Affiliated Organization* 408
EXAMPLE: *Summary of Statement No. 14* 408
What Other Elements Make Up the Comprehensive Annual Financial Report? 409
What Are the Reporting Requirements for Colleges, Universities, and Other Special-Purpose Governments? 415
How Can a Government's Fiscal Condition Be Assessed? 421
IN PRACTICE: *States Face Fiscal Crises* 425
Summary 437

Exercise for Review and Self-Study 438
Questions for Review and Discussion 438
Exercises 439
Problems 443
Solution to Exercise for Review and Self-Study 448

CHAPTER 12

OTHER NOT-FOR-PROFIT ORGANIZATIONS 449

Who's in Charge? 450
What Should Be the Form and Content of Financial Statements? 451
EXAMPLE: *Reporting Revenues and Expenses* 453
What Are the Main Types of Contributions, and How Should Pledges Be Accounted for? 459
IN PRACTICE: *Beneficiary Sues to Enforce Pledge* 463
EXAMPLE: *Pledges* 464
When Should Use (Purpose)-Restricted Contributions Be Recognized? 466
EXAMPLE: *Use-Restricted Contributions* 466
Should Contributions of Services Be Recognized? 467
IN PRACTICE: *A Gift with Strings Attached* 468
EXAMPLE: *Service Contributions* 468
Should Receipts of Collection Items Be Recognized as Revenues? 469
IN PRACTICE: *Examples of Contributed Services* 469
When Should Conditional Promises Be Recognized? 470
IN PRACTICE: *When a Contribution Is Not a Contribution* 471
EXAMPLE: *Conditional Promises* 471
How Should "Pass Through" Contributions Be Accounted For? 472
EXAMPLE: *A Federated Fund-Raising Organization* 472
EXAMPLE: *A Foundation That Transfers Assets to a Specified Organization* 472
EXAMPLE: *A Foundation That Supports a Related Organization* 473
When Should Gains and Losses on Investments Be Recognized? 474
EXAMPLE: *Investment Gains* 475
What Are Split Interest Agreements and How Should They Be Accounted For? 476
How Should Depreciation Be Reported? 477
EXAMPLE: *Depreciation* 477
What Issues Does a Not-for-Profit Face in Establishing Its Reporting Entity? 478
COMPREHENSIVE EXAMPLE: *Museum of American Culture* 479
What Unique Issues Do Health Care Providers Face? 484
EXAMPLE: *Patient Care Revenues* 490
EXAMPLE: *Capitation Fee Revenues* 491
IN PRACTICE: *Collection of Errors Adds Up to $21 Million Debacle* 492
EXAMPLE: *Charity Care* 493
EXAMPLE: *Malpractice Claims* 493
EXAMPLE: *Retrospective Premiums* 494
What Unique Issues Do Colleges and Universities Face? 495
IN PRACTICE: *Which Set of Standards Do We Follow?* 496
EXAMPLE: *Tuition and Fee Revenues* 498
EXAMPLE: *Grants* 499
How Can a Not-for-Profit's Fiscal Condition Be Assessed? 500
Traditional Financial Indicators 501
IN PRACTICE: *Outlook Grim for Many Colleges* 503
Summary 504
Exercise for Review and Self-Study 506
Questions for Review and Discussion 509
Exercises 509
Problems 513
Solution to Exercise for Review and Self-Study 520

CHAPTER 13

USING COST INFORMATION TO MANAGE AND CONTROL 521

How Are the Decision Criteria of Governments and Not-for-Profits Similar to Those of Businesses Despite Different Objectives? 522
Why Must Fixed Costs Be Distinguished from Variable Costs? 523
EXAMPLE: *Average Cost* 524

Why Is It Important to Identify Incremental Costs and Benefits? 525
EXAMPLE: *The Foolish Overhaul* 526
EXAMPLE: *The Nuclear Disaster* 526
EXAMPLE: *Allocated Costs* 528
How Can Organizations Assess the Fiscal Benefits of Contracting Out? 529
EXAMPLE: *Contracting Out* 530
IN PRACTICE: *Colleges Are Turning to Private Vendors for More and More Campus Services* 534
IN PRACTICE: *Outsourcing Sometimes Fails to Meet Expectations* 535
IN PRACTICE: *Cities Rethinking Privatization of Utilities* 536
How Should Governments and Not-for-Profits Establish Prices? 537
How Should Governments and Not-for-Profits Establish Costs? 538
IN PRACTICE: *Factors That Should Enter into the Pricing Decisions of a City-Operated Electric Utility* 539
EXAMPLE: *Allocating Cost—Conventional Means* 541
EXAMPLE: *Cost Allocation—Activity-Based Costing* 542
How Should the Costs of Fund-Raising Activities Be Determined? 545
EXAMPLE: *Allocating Charitable Costs* 547
How Can Analyses of Variance Be Used to Control Costs and Evaluate Performance? 548
EXAMPLE: *Standard Costs* 548
Summary 552
Exercise for Review and Self-Study 553
Questions for Review and Discussion 554
Exercises 554
Problems 558
Solution to Exercise for Review and Self-Study 563

CHAPTER 14

MANAGING FOR RESULTS 565

What Role Do Accountants Play in the Management Cycle of Governments and Other Not-for-Profits? 566
How Can the Limits of Traditional Budgets Be Overcome? 568
What Are the Characteristics of Sound Operational Objectives? 570
What Are the Perils of Establishing Operational Objectives? 572
How Do Program Budgets Relate Expenditures to Operational Objectives? 573
IN PRACTICE: *A Classic Case of Reliance on Misspecified Objectives (Two Perspectives of the Vietnam War)* 574
How Should Service Efforts and Accomplishments Be Reported? 580
How Are Capital Expenditures Planned and Budgeted within a Framework of Operational Objectives? 586
EXAMPLE: *Benefits Are Cash Savings* 587
EXAMPLE: *Choosing among Options with Similar Benefits* 588
IN PRACTICE: *September 11 Victim Compensation Fund* 591
Summary 592
Exercise for Review and Self-Study 594
Questions for Review and Discussion 594
Exercises 595
Problems 597
Solution to Exercise for Review and Self-Study 601

CHAPTER 15

AUDITING GOVERNMENTS AND NOT-FOR-PROFIT ORGANIZATIONS 603

How Do Audits of Governments and Not-for-Profits Differ from Those of Businesses? 604
How Has the Yellow Book Influenced Governmental and Not-for-Profit Auditing? 605
What Types of Audits Do Governments Conduct? 605
What Levels of Standards Are Applicable to All Engagements? 606
What Are the Key Differences between Government and Nongovernment Financial Audit Standards? 610
IN PRACTICE: *The Auditors' Dilemma* 612
How Have the Single Audit Act and Other Pronouncements Influenced Auditing? 613
What Approach Do Auditors Take in Performing Single Audits? 614

What Reports Result from Single Audits? 618
What Are Performance Audits? 620
EXAMPLE: *Evidence Gathering* 626
IN PRACTICE: *Findings Must Relate to Program Objectives* 627
What Unique Ethical Issues Do Governmental and Not-for-Profit Accounting and Auditing Present? 628
IN PRACTICE: *Stupid Government Tricks Point to Need for Performance Audits* 629
EXAMPLE: *Ethical Dilemma* 631
Summary 632
Exercise for Review and Self-Study 633
Questions for Review and Discussion 633
Exercises 634
Problems 636
Cases in Ethics 639
Solution to Exercise for Review and Self-Study 641

CHAPTER 16

FEDERAL GOVERNMENT ACCOUNTING 642

Which Agencies Are Responsible for Federal Accounting and Reporting? 644
What Constitutes the Federal Budget? 647
What Are the Form and Content of Government-Wide Federal Statements? 649
Which Entities Should Issue Financial Reports? 650
What Types of Accounts Are Maintained by Federal Entities? 655
What Statements Are Required of Federal Agencies? 656
What Are Other Key Features of the FASAB Model? 662
EXAMPLE: *Subsidized Loan* 670
EXAMPLE: *Loan Guarantees* 670
What Additional Steps Has the Federal Government Taken to Improve Its Fiscal Management? 671
What Are the Key International Trends in Governmental Accounting? 672
IN PRACTICE: *Off-the-Balance Sheet Debt in Great Britain* 674
Summary 675
Exercise for Review and Self-Study 676
Questions for Review and Discussion 676
Exercises 677
Problems 680
Solution to Exercise for Review and Self-Testing 684

GLOSSARY 685

VALUE TABLES 700

INDEX 709

CHAPTER 1

The Government and Not-for-Profit Environment

LEARNING OBJECTIVES

After studying this chapter you should understand:

- The characteristics that distinguish governments and not-for-profit organizations from businesses, and the accounting and reporting implications of these characteristics
- Why other characteristics of governments and not-for-profit entities that do not necessarily distinguish them from businesses may affect accounting and reporting practices
- The features that distinguish governments from not-for-profits
- The overall purpose of financial reporting in the government and not-for-profit sectors
- The information requirements of the main users of the financial reports of governments and not-for-profit entities
- The specific objectives of financial reporting, as established by the Governmental Accounting Standards Board (for state and local governments), the Financial Accounting Standards Board (for not-for-profits), and the Federal Accounting Standards Advisory Board (for the federal government) and the obstacles to achieving these objectives within a set of financial statements prepared on a single basis of accounting
- The extent to which differences in accounting principles affect the decisions based on financial statements and thereby have economic consequences
- The institutional arrangements for establishing accounting standards

Governments and not-for-profit organizations have much in common with businesses. However, the differences between the two environments are sufficiently pronounced that colleges of business have established a separate course in governmental and not-for-profit accounting apart from the usual courses pertaining to accounting functions—financial accounting, managerial accounting, auditing, and information systems.

Every accounting issue or problem that affects governments and not-for-profits has its counterpart in the business sector. But the distinctions between accounting for governments and not-for-profits and accounting for businesses are so marked that the two disciplines warrant specialized textbooks, separate statements of concepts, and separate accounting principles and practices. As we shall see in this text, some of these differences may be justified by substantive distinctions in the two operating environments. Others are the result of long-standing differences in the traditions, composition, and perspective of the standard-setting boards—the Governmental Accounting Standards Board (GASB), for state and local governments; the Federal Accounting Standards Advisory Board (FASAB), for the federal government; and the Financial Accounting Standards Board (FASB), for the private sector, including not-for-profits.

This chapter is divided into eight sections. The first examines the ways in which governments and not-for-profits differ from businesses, and why they require unique accounting principles and practices. The second points out characteristics of governments and not-for-profits that might not distinguish them from businesses but nevertheless have significant implications for accounting and reporting. The third contrasts governments and not-for-profits, emphasizing that although they have much in common, they also differ significantly. The next four sections provide an overview of financial reporting for governments and not-for-profits, highlighting key user groups, their information needs, and the resultant objectives of financial reporting, and address the question of whether differences in accounting practices really matter. The last section spotlights the GASB, the FASB, and the FASAB.

In this text we use the term not-for-profit rather than the equally acceptable nonprofit. Not-for-profit appears to be gaining in popularity, perhaps because it better differentiates entities that don't intend to earn a profit from those that simply fail to do so.

HOW DO GOVERNMENTS AND NOT-FOR-PROFITS COMPARE WITH BUSINESSES?

Governments and not-for-profits differ significantly from businesses in ways that have profound implications for financial reporting. For the most part, governments and not-for-profits provide services targeted to groups of constituents, advocating a political or social cause, or carrying out research or other activities for the betterment of society. The objectives of governments and not-for-profits cannot generally be expressed in dollars and cents, and they are often ambiguous and not easily quantifiable. Moreover, governments and not-for-profits have relationships with the parties providing their resources that are unlike those of businesses.

DIFFERENT MISSIONS

As implied by the designation *not-for-profits*, the goal of governments and similar organizations is something other than earning profit. A key objective of financial reporting is to provide information about an entity's performance during a period. The main objective of a typical business is to earn a profit—to assure that over the life of the enterprise, its owners are returned more cash than they contributed. Accordingly, financial statements that focus on net income are in harmony with the entity's main objective. Specifically, an income statement is a report on how well the entity achieved its goals. To be sure, businesses may have objectives that go beyond "the bottom line." They may seek to promote the welfare of their executives and employees, improve the communities in which they are located, and produce goods that will enhance the quality of life. Financial accounting and reporting, however, are concerned almost exclusively with the goal of maximizing either profits or some variant of it, such as cash flows.

The financial reports of governments and not-for-profits can provide information about an organization's inflows (revenues) and outflows (expenditures) of cash and other resources. As a general rule, an excess of expenditures over revenues, particularly for an extended period of time, signals financial distress or poor managerial performance. However, an excess of revenues over expenditures is not necessarily commendable. An excess of revenues over expenditures may be achieved, for example, merely by reducing the services provided to constituents, which may be at odds with the entity's objectives.

If the financial statements of a government or not-for-profit incorporate only monetary measures, such as dollars and cents, they cannot possibly provide the information necessary to assess the organization's performance. For an organization to report properly on its accomplishments, it must augment its financial statements to include nonfinancial data that relate to its objectives. A school, for example, might include statistics on student achievement, such as test scores or graduation rates. A center for the homeless might present data on the number of people fed or adequately housed.

BUDGETS, NOT THE MARKETPLACE, GOVERN

Governments and not-for-profits are governed mainly by their budgets, not by the marketplace. Through the budgetary process, these organizations control or strongly influence both their revenues and expenditures. The revenues of a government may be determined by legislative fiat, and if they are, the government may not be subject to the forces of competition faced by businesses. Those of the not-for-profits, while they cannot be established by legal mandate, may be obtained from contributions, dues, tuition, or user charges—none of which are comparable to the sales of a business.

EXPENDITURES MAY DRIVE REVENUES

Governments and many not-for-profits establish the level of services that they will provide, calculate their cost, and then set tax rates and other fees to generate the revenues required to pay for them. Colleges and universities, unlike businesses, do not set tuition charges at the highest level that the "market will bear." Instead, they calculate operating costs; estimate contributions, endowment revenues, and other sources of funds; and then set tuition charges at the rate necessary to cover the shortfall. Similarly, fraternities and sororities calculate their expenditures for housing, food, and social activities, and then set dues and other fees accordingly. In sum, expenditures drive revenues.

Although governments and not-for-profits do not participate in competitive markets, they cannot simply raise revenues without regard to their services or increase taxes without limit. Governments may be constrained by political forces. Universities may have to restrict tuition rates to approximately those of peer schools. Further, some not-for-profits such as the United Way or organizations that fund medical research base their expenditures exclusively on their revenues. The more funds they raise, the more they spend.

THE BUDGET, NOT THE ANNUAL REPORT, IS THE MOST SIGNIFICANT FINANCIAL DOCUMENT

For businesses, the annual report is the most significant financial document. A major company's announcement of annual earnings (the preview of the annual report) makes front-page news. By contrast, its annual budget is nothing more than an internal document, seldom made available to investors or the general public.

A government or not-for-profit's release of its annual report is customarily ignored by both organizational insiders and outsiders. Seldom does the report contain surprises, for if revenues and expenditures were markedly different from what were initially budgeted, the entity probably was required to amend the budget during the year.

For governments and not-for-profits, the budget takes center stage—properly so, because the budget is the culmination of the political process. It encapsulates most of the decisions of consequence made by the organization. It determines which constituents give to the entity and which receive; which activities are supported and which are assessed.

Because it is so important, the budget, unlike the annual report, is a source of constituent concern and controversy. Government budget hearings often draw standing-room-only crowds to the legislative chambers. The budget debates of church and synagogue members are frequently marked by fervor more intense than the congregants' worship services.

A government's budget may be backed by the force of law. Government officials are ordinarily prohibited from spending more than what was budgeted. Indeed, they can go to jail for severe violations of budgetary mandates. The budget is not a document to be taken lightly.

In light of the significance of the budget relative to the annual report, it is ironic that the standard-setting agencies focus exclusively on the annual report. Except insofar as governments, such as states, establish rules for the cities or other governments within their jurisdiction, or parent not-for-profits, such as national fraternities, set guidelines for local affiliates, budgetary practices are within the discretion of the individual entity. Neither the GASB nor the FASB or the FASAB has been granted the kind of statutory authority over budgets that they have over annual reports. As a consequence—which shall be made evident in discussions to follow—annual reports are in fact better than budgets at capturing the economic substance of transactions and are far less subject to preparer efforts to artificially boost revenues or reduce expenditures.

BUDGETS DRIVE ACCOUNTING AND FINANCIAL REPORTING

Constituents of an organization want information on the extent of adherence to the budget. They want assurance that the organization has not spent more than was authorized. They want to know whether revenue and expenditure estimates were reliable. The accounting system and the resultant financial reports must be designed to provide that information.

Also, managers need an accounting system that provides them with ongoing data as to whether they are on target to meet budget projections. Even more critically, they need a system that either prevents them from overspending or sets off warning signals when they are about to do so. The budget is a control device, but it requires the support of a complementary accounting and reporting system.

Finally, auditors and other parties concerned with the organization's performance require a basis on which to evaluate accomplishments. As will be discussed in subsequent chapters, state-of-the-art budgets establish that basis by indicating not only how much will be spent on a particular activity, but what the activity will achieve. A post-period assessment can then focus not only on whether the entity met its revenue and expenditure projections but, equally important, on whether it attained what was expected of it. Evaluators can then assess organizational efficiency by comparing inputs (such as dollar expenditures) with outcomes (results). The accounting system should be fashioned so as to facilitate this comparison, assuring that the organization reports and categorizes both revenues and expenditures in a way that is consistent with the budget. Currently, few governments and not-for-profits have established budgetary and accounting systems to measure and report adequately on the nonmonetary aspects of their performance. However, accounting standard-setting authorities have recognized the importance of performance measures and are taking steps either to encourage or to require that the entities under their purview will provide them eventually.

NEED TO ENSURE INTERPERIOD EQUITY

Most governments are required by law, and most not-for-profits are expected by policy, to balance their operating budgets. Balanced operating budgets ensure that, in any particular period, revenues cover expenditures and that, as a group, the entity's constituents pay for what they receive. If organizations fail to balance their budgets—and borrow to cover operating deficits—then the cost of benefits enjoyed by the citizens of today must be borne by those of tomorrow.

The concept that constituents pay for the services that they receive and do not shift the burdens to their children has traditionally been labeled **intergenerational equity.** In recent years, to emphasize that entities should not transfer the costs even to future years, to say nothing of future generations, the term **interperiod equity** has been accepted as more appropriate.

To maintain interperiod equity, the accounting systems of governments and not-for-profits must provide information as to whether this objective is being attained. Table 1-1 compares fiscal practices that promote interperiod equity with those that do not.

The concept of interperiod equity does not suggest that governments should never borrow. The prohibition against debt applies only to operating, not capital,

TABLE 1–1
Fiscal Practices that Promote or Undermine Interperiod Equity

Promote	Undermine
1. Setting aside resources for employee pensions during the years in which the employees provide their services.	1. Paying the pensions of retired employees out of current operating funds.
2. Issuing conventional 30-year bonds to finance the purchase of a new building that is expected to have a useful life of 30 years; repaying the bonds, along with appropriate amounts of interest, over the 30-year period.	2. Financing the purchase of the new building with 30-year zero-coupon bonds that permit the entire amount of principal and interest to be paid upon the maturity of the bonds; making no provision to set aside resources for payment of principal and interest on the bonds until the year they mature.
3. Paying the current-year costs of an administrative staff out of current operating funds.	3. Issuing 30-year bonds to finance the current-year operating costs of an administrative staff.
4. Charging payments of wages and salaries made in the first week of the current fiscal year to the previous fiscal year, that in which the employees actually provided their services.	4. Charging wages and salaries applicable to services provided in the last week of the current fiscal year in the following fiscal year, that in which the payments were made.
5. Charging the cost of supplies as expenditures in the year in which they were used rather than when they were purchased.	5. Charging the cost of supplies as expenditures in the year they were purchased irrespective of the year in which they were used.
6. Recognizing interest on investments in the year in which it is earned, irrespective of when it is received.	6. Recognizing interest in the year in which it is received, irrespective of when it is earned.
7. Setting aside funds each year to pay for an anticipated 20-year renovation of a college dormitory.	7. Paying for an anticipated 20-year renovation of a college dormitory out of current funds in the year the work is performed.

expenditures. A government-constructed highway or university-purchased lab equipment will produce benefits over more than one year. It is only fair, therefore, that they be paid for by incorporating debt service costs into the taxes or tuition charges of the citizens or students who will gain from them.

REVENUE NOT INDICATIVE OF DEMAND FOR GOODS OR SERVICES

For competitive businesses, revenues signal customer demand for goods and services. Holding prices constant, the greater the revenues, the greater the demand—an indication that the entity is satisfying a societal need.

In a government or not-for-profit, revenues may not be linked to constituent demand or satisfaction. An increase in tax revenues, for example, tells nothing about the amount or quality of service provided. Therefore, a conventional statement of revenues and expenditures cannot supply information on demand for services. Supplementary information is required.

NO DIRECT LINK BETWEEN REVENUES AND EXPENSES

Just as the revenues of governments and not-for-profits may not be directly linked to customer demand, so also may they be unrelated to expenditures. The revenues from donations of a not-for-profit entity may increase from one year to the next, but the change may be unaccompanied by a corresponding increase in the quantity, quality, or cost of services provided. Thus, the *matching concept*—financial accounting's central notion that expenditures must be paired with corresponding revenues—may have a different meaning for governments and not-for-profits than for businesses. Businesses attempt to match the costs of specific goods or services with the revenues that they generate. Governments and not-for-profits, however, can sometimes do no more than associate overall revenues with the broad categories of expenditures they are intended to cover.

CAPITAL ASSETS MAY NEITHER PRODUCE REVENUES NOR SAVE COSTS

Unlike businesses, both governments and not-for-profits make significant investments in assets that neither produce revenues nor reduce expenditures. Therefore, the conventional business practices used to value assets may not be applicable.

According to financial theory, the economic value of an asset is the present or discounted value of the cash inflows that it will generate or the cash outflows that it will enable the entity to avoid. Hence, conventional capital budgeting models specify that in evaluating a potential asset acquisition, the business should compare the present value of the asset's expected cash outflows with its inflows.

Many capital assets of governments and not-for-profits cannot be associated with revenues or savings. The highway or bridge being considered by a state or local government will not yield cash benefits—at least not directly to the government. The proposed college library may enrich the intellectual life of the community, but not the college's coffers. In fact, some government and not-for-profit "assets" may be more properly interpreted as liabilities. Inasmuch as they have to be maintained and serviced, they will consume rather than provide resources.

RESOURCES MAY BE RESTRICTED

In contrast to the resources of businesses, many of the assets of government and not-for-profit entities are restricted for particular activities or purposes. As shown in Figure 1-1, for example, a sizable share of one government's revenues may be from other governments and, more than likely, restricted for specific purposes. For example, the federal government may give a state or local government a grant for construction of low-income housing. The award can be used only for low-income housing, not for any other purposes, irrespective of how worthy they might be.

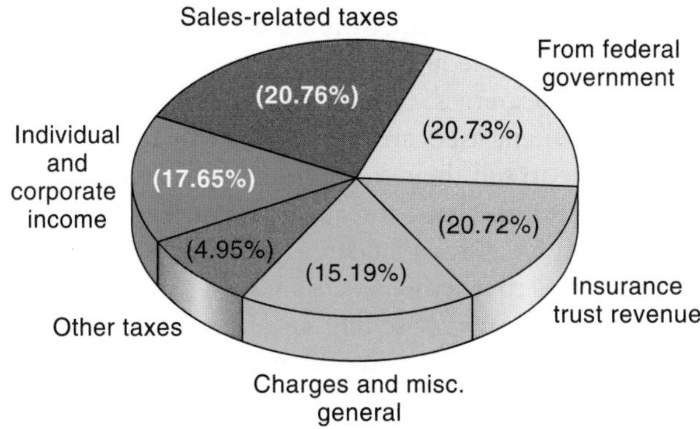

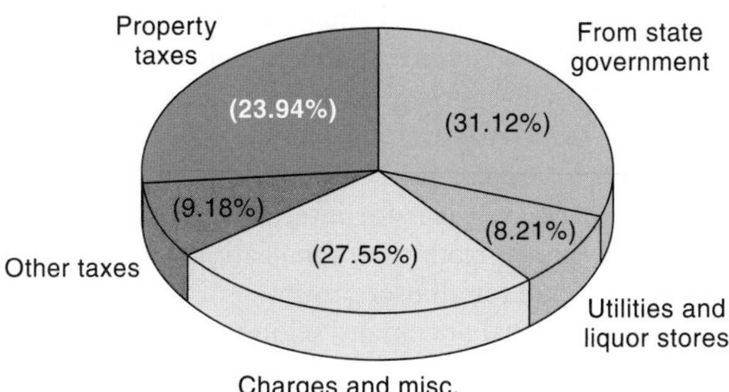

FIGURE 1-1 State and Local Government Revenues by Sources

Source: U.S. Bureau of the Census, United States State and Local Government Finances by Level of Government: 1998–1999.

Taxes and membership dues may also be restricted. A city's hotel tax may be dedicated to financing a local convention center or to promoting tourism. A state's gasoline tax may be targeted by law to highway construction and maintenance. A portion of a not-for-profit cemetery association's fees may have to be set aside for the acquisition of new land.

Both governments and not-for-profits need to assure the parties providing the restricted funds that the money is used properly. At the same time, they must show in their financial reports that the restricted resources are unavailable for purposes other than those specified. Therefore, the financial statements must either segregate the restricted from the unrestricted resources or disclose by some other means that some resources can be used only for specific purposes.

As with budgetary mandates, slipups regarding restrictions carry serious consequences. At the very least they may cause the organization to forfeit past and future awards. Therefore, as with budgets, the organization must design its accounting system so that management is prevented from inadvertently misspending restricted resources. To this end, governments and not-for-profits employ a system of accounting known as **fund accounting.** It is described in Chapter 2.

NO DISTINCT OWNERSHIP INTERESTS

Neither governments nor not-for-profits have defined ownership interests like those of businesses. Typically, the entities cannot be sold or transferred. Should they be dissolved, they involve no stockholders or bondholders who are entitled to receive residual resources.

The most obvious financial reporting implication of this distinction is that the mathematical difference between assets and liabilities cannot sensibly be termed *owners' equity*. Some other term is required.

More substantively, however, the distinction suggests that the financial statements of governments and not-for-profits must be prepared from the perspective of parties other than stockholders. (The main groups of statement users will be identified later in this chapter.) Similarly, for certain entities the distinction implies that there may be less interest in the market values of their resources. Governments cannot typically sell their highways and sewers, and few statement users are interested in their market values. Libraries and museums may be able to sell their collections, but may have to use the funds to acquire similar assets. The market values may be of concern only if the entire institution were to be closed and its assets liquidated. Yet, at the same time, market values may be relevant indicators as to whether assets are being put to their optimum use. For example, a city might be better off selling an office building located downtown and using the proceeds to acquire property in outlying neighborhoods.

LESS DISTINCTION BETWEEN INTERNAL AND EXTERNAL ACCOUNTING AND REPORTING

In the government and not-for-profit arena, the line between external and internal accounting and reporting is less clear-cut than in the business sector. First, in the business sector, external reports focus on profits. Nevertheless, even in businesses, few organizational units are profit centers in which management controls all the key factors that affect profits. Therefore, internal reports present data on other measures of performance, such as total fixed costs or per-unit variable costs.

In the government and not-for-profit arenas, profit is no more an appropriate measure of performance for external parties than it is for internal departments. The relevant performance measures must be drawn from the organizations' unique goals and objectives and are unlikely to be the same for all user groups.

Second, in business the budget is an internal document, seldom made available to external parties. In governments and not-for-profits, it stands as the key fiscal document that is as important to taxpayers, bondholders, and other constituencies as it is to managers.

Third, the distinction between internal and external parties in governments and not-for-profits is more ambiguous than it is in business. Taxpayers and organizational members, for example, cannot be categorized neatly as either insiders or outsiders. Although they are not paid employees (and thus, not traditional "insiders") they may nevertheless have the ultimate say (through either direct vote or elected officers) as to organizational policies.

WHAT OTHER CHARACTERISTICS OF GOVERNMENTS AND NOT-FOR-PROFITS HAVE ACCOUNTING IMPLICATIONS?

Governments and not-for-profits have additional characteristics that do not necessarily distinguish them from businesses but have significant accounting and reporting implications.

MANY DIFFERENT TYPES OF GOVERNMENTS AND NOT-FOR-PROFITS

Approximately 87,500 local governments currently exist in the United States (see Figure 1-2). In common usage, a *municipality* is a village, town, or city. Government specialists, however, use the term to refer also to any other nonfederal government, including school districts, public authorities, and sometimes states.

The number of municipalities may be surprisingly large, but consider how many separate governments have jurisdiction over a typical neighborhood. The neighborhood may be part of a town, several of which comprise a township. The township may be part of a county, which, in turn, may be a subdivision of a state. Further, the

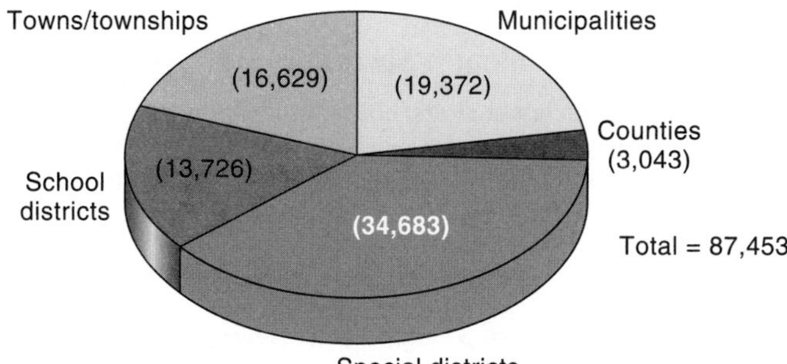

- The average number of local government units per state is 1,751, but Illinois has 6,836, whereas Hawaii has only 20.
- Nine states account for slightly less than half of all local government units in the nation.

FIGURE 1-2 Composition of the Local U.S. Government Units

Source: U.S. Bureau of the Census, *Government Organizations*, 1997 Census of Government, August 1999.

neighborhood school may be administered by an independent school district. The local hospital may be governed by a hospital district, the water and sewage system by a utility authority, and the bus system by a transportation authority. The community college may be financed by a community college district, and the nearby airport may be managed by an independent airport authority.

Each category of government will likely differ from others in the services provided, the type of assets it controls, its taxing and borrowing authority, and the parties to which it is accountable. Moreover, even governments in the same category may vary in the services they provide. New York and Dallas are among the nation's ten largest cities. But New York operates its own school system, whereas Dallas's schools are under the control of an independent school district. San Antonio—Texas's third largest city—provides electric service to its residents, whereas in Houston, the state's largest city, the citizens receive their power from a privately owned utility.

As shown in Table 1-2, not-for-profits are also many in number: nearly one million in the United States. These entities constitute what is sometimes referred to as the *independent sector*.

This diversity limits the suitability of a common accounting model (i.e., set of accounting and reporting principles) for any single, or even for any particular type of, government or not-for-profit entity. Assuming that comparability among entities is a desirable characteristic of financial reporting, standard-setting authorities face a policy question. To what extent should they adopt common standards for all governments and not-for-profits, as opposed to common standards only for entities of the same type? When entities are similar, common standards may promote comparability. When the entities are not, common standards may, like ill-fitting clothes, distort reality. As will be discussed in succeeding chapters, rule-making authorities are heading in the direction of one set of common principles for all not-for-profits and a separate set for all state and local governments.

SHORT-TERM FOCUS OF MANAGERS AND ELECTED OFFICIALS

U.S. managers of both corporations and public enterprises have been accused of sacrificing the long-term welfare of their organizations for short-term benefits—sometimes for their organizations and other times only for themselves. This failing is said to be especially pronounced in governments.

Government officials typically face election every two or four years. In the periods preceding an election, they have powerful incentives both to avoid unpopular measures, such as tax increases, and to make their government look fiscally sound.

TABLE 1–2

Dimensions of the Not-for-Profit ("Independent") Sector

The nonprofit sector in America includes hospitals, museums, schools, homeless shelters, houses of worship, symphony orchestras, research centers, youth groups, and many other organizations in every community across the nation. These charitable groups are sometimes collectively referred to as the "independent sector" to emphasize their unique role in society, distinct from business and government.

Size and Scope

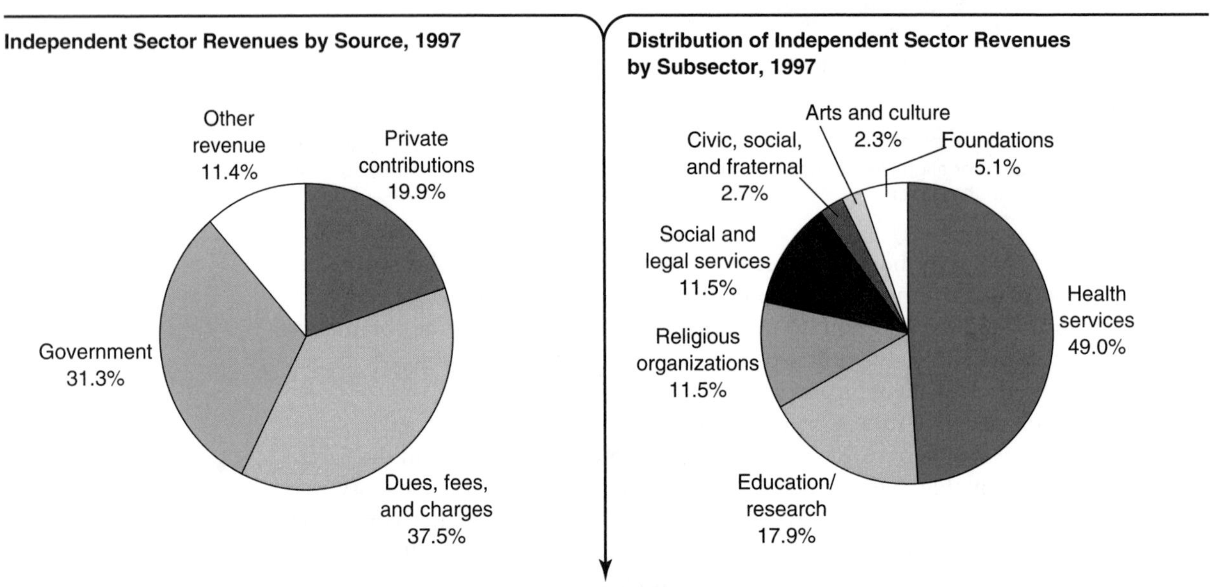

Total 1997 Revenues: $664.8 Billion

Current Highlights

Size and Scope 1997–1998	
Number of independent sector organizations (501(c)(3), 501(c)(4), and religious congregations) (1998)	1.2 million
Total independent sector revenues (1997)	$664.8 billion
Annual contributions from private sources[1] (1997)	$132.1 billion
Percentage of working Americans employed in the independent sector (1998)	7.1%
Percentage of national income attributed to the independent sector (1998)	6.1%
Giving 1998	
Percentage of American households that gave	70.1%
Average annual household contribution	$1,075
Volunteering 1998	
Percentage of Americans who volunteered	55.5%
Number of Americans who volunteered	109.4 million
Total annual hours volunteered	19.9 billion
Value of volunteer time (excluding informal volunteering[2])	$225.9 billion

[1]Contributions from individuals, corporations, foundations, and federated campaigns.

[2]Time not given through organizations.

Source: Nonprofit Almanac In Brief, 2002 (www.independentsector.org/PDFs/inbrief.pdf).

They can use budgetary and accounting techniques to make cosmetic improvements to their entity's budget or annual report. Many of these activities will be described throughout the text.

Standard-setting authorities, the accountants and auditors of individual organizations, and statement users need to be aware that budgets and financial statements can be slanted. They must resist and adjust for any biases. The difficulty they face, however, is that the motives for slanting budgets and statements vary from situation to situation. In some circumstances government officials may artificially overestimate revenues (or underestimate expenditures) so as to avoid cuts in services or increases in taxes. In others, however, they may do the opposite so they can take credit at year-end for managerial effectiveness by presenting better-than-anticipated results.

GOVERNMENTS AND NOT-FOR-PROFITS ENGAGE IN BUSINESS-TYPE ACTIVITIES

Many governments and not-for-profit organizations engage in business-type activities. Cities, for example, operate electric utilities, trash collection services, and golf courses. Colleges and universities operate bookstores, cafeterias, and computer repair services. Environmental organizations publish and sell magazines.

Even if profit maximization is not their overriding objective, these enterprises may, and perhaps should, be managed as if it were. Therefore, both their managers and the parties to whom they are accountable need the same type of financial information that the owners and operators of businesses do. The accounting and reporting practices that are appropriate for the business-type activities of governments and not-for-profits may differ from those that are most suitable for their nonbusiness activities. Thus, the challenge of developing accounting and reporting principles for governments and not-for-profits is made even more formidable by the potential need for more than one set of standards—even for a single organization.

HOW DO GOVERNMENTS COMPARE WITH NOT-FOR-PROFITS?

As explained earlier, governments and not-for-profits share characteristics that distinguish them from businesses. But there are also important differences between governments and not-for-profits. Governments, unlike not-for-profits, have the authority to command resources. They have the power to tax, collect license and other fees, and impose charges. Should a government lack funds to satisfy its obligations or enhance services, it can obtain them by legislative action. From the perspective of accountants or financial analysts, this ability suggests that the actual assets reported on a government's balance sheet may not represent all of the assets under its control. To obtain a comprehensive picture of a government's fiscal health, they must consider not only the resources actually owned by the government, but also those that it has the power to summon.

Suppose, for example, that two towns each report an operating deficit and a high ratio of debt to financial assets. One is a wealthy community with high property values, prosperous industries, little unemployment, and a low tax rate. The other has low property values, little industry, high unemployment, and high tax rates. Clearly, the fiscal capacity of the first town exceeds that of the second. With greater fiscal effort—that is, by increasing tax rates—the first town can readily improve its economic circumstances, whereas the second cannot. This point is further addressed in Chapter 11.

Governments are currently required to include in their annual reports substantial amounts of demographic and economic data about the jurisdictions that they serve.

An ongoing issue, however, is how much disclosure is enough: what types of data are needed by statement users and to what extent are such disclosures within the purview of accounting and financial reporting.

Surprisingly, whether an entity should be categorized as a government or as a not-for-profit is not always obvious, and no definitive criteria exist to distinguish between the two. The homeowners' association of a residential development, for example, may carry out activities similar to that of a government—constructing and maintaining roads, and providing utility and security services. Moreover, it may have the right to assess residents' annual fees. The following characteristics, in addition to the power to tax, are indicative of a government:

- ***It may issue tax-exempt debt.*** Section 103(a) of the Internal Revenue Code exempts the interest on the debt of states, territories, and their political subdivisions from federal taxation. This privilege is a substantial economic benefit to governments because it reduces their borrowing costs. Virtually all local governments qualify as subdivisions of states and territories. Not-for-profits, such as colleges, universities, and hospitals, do not have this opportunity. However, they may be the beneficiaries of it, as governments are permitted to issue tax-exempt debt on their behalf.
- ***Its governing bodies are either popularly elected or are appointed by another government.*** The governing body of a typical government is elected by the citizens within its jurisdiction. The governing boards of other governments, particularly public authorities, may be appointed by the legislature or other public officials of another government.
- ***Another government can unilaterally dissolve it and assume its assets without compensation.*** Under our legal system, governments can arbitrarily seize the assets only of other governments within their jurisdiction—but not those of not-for-profits or businesses.[1]

WHAT IS THE PURPOSE OF FINANCIAL REPORTING?

Having considered the characteristics of government and not-for-profit entities, we now consider the general purposes that financial statements can serve and the groups most likely to use them. We can then address the need for specific objectives of financial reporting and can review the objectives developed by both the GASB and the FASB.

The purposes for which external financial statements—those included in an annual report—are employed vary from user to user and facilitate a combination of functions.[2] For the most part, they should allow users to:

- ***Assess financial condition.*** Users need to analyze past results and current financial condition in order to determine the ability of the entity to meet its obligations and to continue to provide expected services. By establishing trends, users are better able to predict future fiscal developments and to foresee the need for changes in revenue sources, resource allocations, and capital requirements.

[1] These characteristics have been drawn from Martin Ives, "What Is a Government?" *The Government Accountants Journal* 43 (Spring 1994): 25–33. They are similar to those that have been agreed upon by the American Institute of Certified Public Accountants (AICPA) and the Governmental Accounting Standards Board (GASB). See *Audits of State and Local Governmental Units*, AICPA Audit and Accounting Guide (New York: AICPA, 2002), para. 1.12.

[2] These purposes are drawn from GASB Concepts Statement No.1, *Objectives of Financial Reporting* (May 1987).

- ***Compare actual results with the budget.*** In light of the importance of the adopted budget, users want assurance that the entity adhered to it. Significant variations from the budget may signify either poor management or unforeseen circumstances that require an explanation.
- ***Determine compliance with appropriate laws, regulations, and restrictions on the use of the funds.*** Users want evidence that the organization has complied with legal and contractual requirements, such as bond covenants, donor and grantor restrictions, taxing and debt limitations, and applicable laws. Violations can not only have serious financial repercussions, but can jeopardize the entity's viability.
- ***Evaluate efficiency and effectiveness.*** Users want to know whether the entity is achieving its objectives and if so, whether it is doing so efficiently and effectively. Hence, they need to compare accomplishments (outcomes) with service efforts and costs (resource inputs).

WHO ARE THE USERS AND WHAT ARE THE USES OF FINANCIAL REPORTS?

The main users of the financial statements of governments and not-for-profits—like those of the financial statements of businesses—are the parties to whom the organizations are accountable. They include:

- Governing boards
- Investors and creditors
- Taxpayers and citizens; organizational members
- Donors and grantors
- Regulatory and oversight agencies
- Employees and other constituents

General purpose financial statements are targeted mainly at parties external to the organization. As is the case in corporate accounting, reports intended for external groups are inappropriate for many types of managerial decisions. Executives, agency heads, and other managers can, and should, rely on their organization's internal reporting system for the financial information they require. Nevertheless, the information needs of internal and external parties may overlap. Therefore, internal parties, though not intended as principal users of general purpose financial statements, may, in fact, rely on them for a considerable amount of necessary data.

This text focuses primarily on the information needs of external users, and hence is concerned largely with general purpose financial statements. Even so, we also pay special attention to the interests of managers and other internal parties.

GOVERNING BOARDS

Just as the auditors' reports on the financial statements of corporations are generally addressed to their boards of directors, those of governments and not-for-profits are directed to their governing boards. That the governing boards are the prime recipients of the audit reports strongly implies that they are among the principal users of both the auditors' reports themselves and the accompanying financial statements.

A government's governing body is typically an elected or appointed legislature, such as a city council or a board of commissioners. A not-for-profit's governing body is usually a board of trustees or a board of directors.

Governing boards cannot neatly be categorized as either internal or external users. Customarily they are composed of members from outside the management team. However, in almost all organizations, they approve budgets, major purchases, contracts, employment agreements with key executives, and significant operating policies—thereby not only overseeing managers, but also getting involved, sometimes directly, in the decisions they make.

INVESTORS AND CREDITORS

As noted earlier, neither governments nor not-for-profits have owners, and therefore they do not issue shares of stock. Nevertheless, they look to the same financial markets as corporations to satisfy their capital requirements.

As shown in Figure 1-3, in 2002 state and local governments had an estimated $1.8 trillion of bonds outstanding. This compares with $4.0 trillion outstanding for U.S. corporations. The amounts highlight the economic significance of the municipal bond segment. As indicated in Figure 1-4, the main purchasers of this debt are households (e.g., individual investors) and mutual and similar types of investment funds.

Both governments and not-for-profits issue bonds primarily to finance long-term assets. For governments these include buildings, parking garages, office buildings, roads, highways, and utility systems. For not-for-profits they include buildings, other facilities, and equipment.

Investors commonly acquire the bonds of governments and not-for-profits as part of an investment portfolio that also includes corporate securities. Their investment requirements are essentially the same as for similar corporate bonds. They want assurance that the issuing entity will meet its obligations to make scheduled interest and principal payments. In a sense, therefore, the same group of investors constitute the major users of business, government, and not-for-profit financial statements.

Many—probably most—bondholders do not themselves evaluate the bonds they acquire. Instead, they rely on the assessments of bond-rating services and are thereby

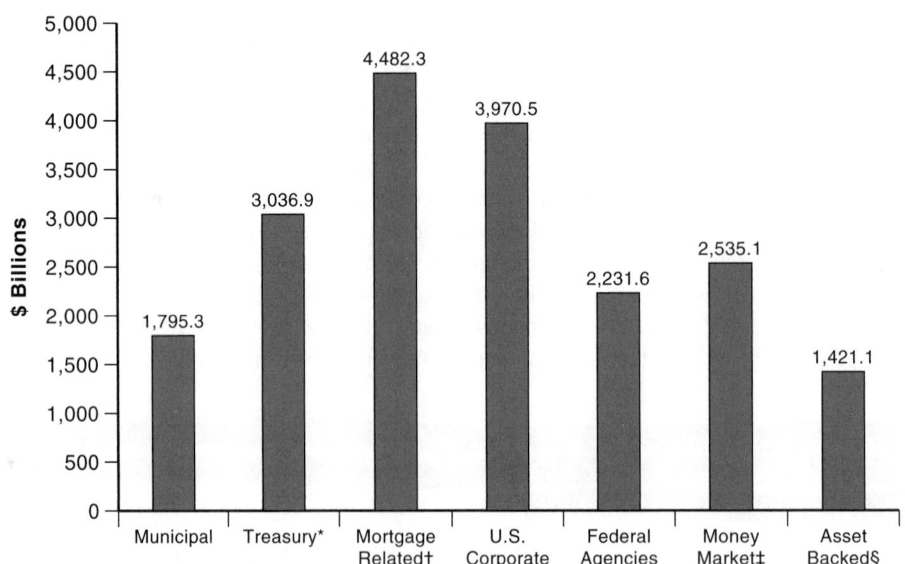

FIGURE 1-3 Outstanding Level of Public and Private Debt—2002

Source: The Bond Market Association.

*Interest bearing marketable public debt.

†Includes GNMA, FNMA, and FHLMC mortgage-backed securities and similar types of debt.

‡Includes commercial paper, bankers acceptances, and large time deposits.

§Includes public and private placements.

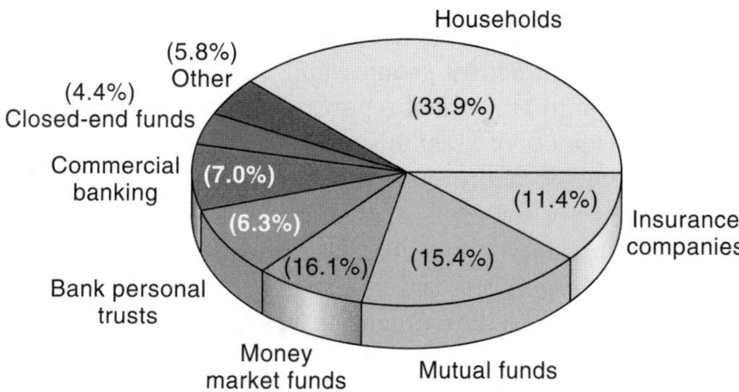

FIGURE 1-4 Holders of Tax-Exempt Debt, 2002
Source: The Bond Market Association (www.bondmarkets.com/cgi-bin/).

only indirect users of financial reports. The three best-known rating services are Standard & Poor's, Moody's, and Fitch IBCA. These services assign to publicly traded bonds a rating (e.g., AAA, AA, A, BBB) reflective of the securities' risk of default.

Governments and not-for-profits also borrow routinely from banks and other financial institutions. The loans may either finance new facilities or cover short-term imbalances between cash receipts and cash disbursements. The lenders and potential lenders use the financial statements of the governments and not-for-profits just as they would those of corporations—to help assess the credit-worthiness of the borrowers.

CITIZENS AND ORGANIZATIONAL MEMBERS

Citizens (or taxpayers) are invariably placed near the top of any list of government financial statement users. In reality, few citizens ever see the annual reports of the governments that have jurisdiction over them. Moreover, a government's release of its annual report is seldom newsworthy. The reports are ordinarily issued at least three months after the close of the government's fiscal year, and, as this text will show, current reporting practices are anything but user friendly. As shown in "In Practice: Who Receives Annual Reports?", most governments do not routinely send their reports to their local newspaper (and few local newspapers have reporters who can understand and interpret the reports).

IN PRACTICE

WHO RECEIVES ANNUAL REPORTS?

A study of 178 U.S. cities with populations of more than 50,000 showed what percentage sent their annual reports to various user groups:

Local newspapers	40%
Insurance companies	42%
Municipal bond dealers	43%
Municipal underwriters	54%
Standard & Poor's bond rating service	69%
Moody's bond rating service	84%
City council members	91%

Source: Rubik Atamian and Gouranga Ganguli, "The Recipients of Municipal Annual Financial Reports: A Nationwide Study," *The Government Accountants Journal*, vol. XXXX, no. 3 (Fall 1991), pp. 3–21.

Do not minimize the significance of citizens as a primary user group. Citizens obtain financial data through a variety of "filters," including civic associations such as the League of Women Voters, political action groups, and newspapers, TV, and radio. Even if they don't pay attention to the annual report, they most definitely take notice, at any time of the year, of instances of fiscal mismanagement or other unforeseen circumstances that will cause unexpected revenue shortfalls or cost overruns.

The extent to which members of not-for-profit organizations are interested in either the statements themselves or data derived from them depends largely on the size of the organization and their involvement in it. A larger percentage of a country club's members can be expected to pay attention to their organization's fiscal affairs—mainly because it bears directly upon their dues and fees—than of broad-based organizations such as the National Geographic Society or the American Automobile Association.

DONORS AND GRANTORS

Few individuals—not even accountants—request financial statements each time they drop their coins into Salvation Army kettles or Muscular Dystrophy Association canisters. But major donors and grantors, such as the United Way, the Ford Foundation, and federal, state, and local governments, are more discriminating in how they part with their resources. They will not only request financial reports and other relevant fiscal information from supplicant associations, but will examine and analyze them with the same care as a banker making a loan.

In addition, individual donors can, and should, obtain financial information about a charity prior to contributing to it. They can inquire as to the organization's allocation of resources, the proportion of its resources directed to substantive programs as opposed to fundraising, and the salaries of the most highly paid executives. Such data will likely be available from the organization itself or from state or local regulatory authorities.

REGULATORY AGENCIES

Local governments are normally obligated to file financial reports with state agencies; charitable organizations may have to file with either state or local authorities; religious and fraternal associations may have to file with their umbrella organizations. The recipients of these reports use them to assure that the entities are spending and receiving resources in accordance with laws, regulations, or policies; to help assess management's performance; to allocate resources; and to exercise general oversight responsibility.

EMPLOYEES AND OTHER CONSTITUENTS

Few employees of governments or not-for-profits spend their off-hours poring over their organization's financial statements. But as noted in the In Practice officers of their unions or employee associations may examine them, looking for ways to free up resources for salary increases or projects in which they have a special interest.

Other constituent or interest groups also use financial reports on an ad hoc basis. Almost certainly, few readers of this text have ever seen the financial statements of the college or university they attend. However, students have been known to use budgets and annual reports to support claims that their college or university need not raise tuition, can afford a new student activities center, or should privatize a money-losing cafeteria or bookstore.

WHAT ARE THE OBJECTIVES OF FINANCIAL REPORTING?

The overall objective of financial reporting is to meet the information needs of statement users. But financial reports cannot possibly satisfy all requirements of all users. Therefore, both the GASB and the FASB have established objectives that

IN PRACTICE

EMPLOYEES AS STATEMENT USERS

Members of the Hotel, Restaurant & Club Employees Union went on strike against New York's prestigious Harvard Club. Citing declining revenues, the club's president was particularly hard-nosed toward the strikers, demanding that the workers begin contributing to the cost of their health plan and, according to *The New York Times*, "surrender the few extra dollars they were paid for doing so-called dirty jobs—unpleasant tasks like cleaning up after vomiting club members."

The union, however, was skeptical when they heard "the Harvard Club crying poverty." They pointed to a management-commissioned audit that had described the club as "relatively prosperous."

Source: Based on Bob Herbert, "Crimson Class," *New York Times*, 11 May 1994.

circumscribe the functions of financial reports. These objectives provide the foundation for their standards. Having agreed on objectives at the outset, the standard-setters should not have to determine the overall purpose of a proposed new standard each time they consider a specific accounting issue.

GASB OBJECTIVES

Taking into account the unique characteristics of governments and their environment, the Governmental Accounting Standards Board established *accountability* as the cornerstone of financial reporting. "Accountability," the GASB says, "requires governments to answer to the citizenry—to justify the raising of public resources and the purposes for which they are used." It "is based on the belief that the citizenry has a 'right to know,' a right to receive openly declared facts that may lead to public debate by the citizens and their elected representatives."

The GASB divided the objective of accountability into three subobjectives:

- ***Interperiod equity.*** "Financial reporting should provide information to determine whether current-year revenues were sufficient to pay for current-year services." It should show whether current-year citizens shifted part of the cost of services they received to future-year taxpayers.
- ***Budgetary and fiscal compliance.*** "Financial reporting should demonstrate whether resources were obtained and used in accordance with the entity's legally adopted budget; it should also demonstrate compliance with other finance-related legal or contractual requirements."
- ***Service efforts costs and accomplishments.*** "Financial reporting should provide information to assist users in assessing the service efforts costs and accomplishments of the governmental entity." This information helps users assess the government's "economy, efficiency, and effectiveness" and "may help form a basis for voting or funding decisions."[3]

The GASB established two additional objectives, each also having three subobjectives. These are set forth in Table 1-3.

The GASB objectives, taken independently, are unquestionably reasonable. But taken together, do they establish the basis for resolving specific issues and establishing specific standards? Consider the simplified example, "Clash Among Reporting Objectives."

[3] GASB Concepts Statement No. 1, *Objectives of Financial Reporting* (May 1987).

TABLE 1–3

Governmental Accounting Standards Board's Additional Objectives of Financial Reporting

Financial reporting should assist users in evaluating the operating results of the governmental entity for the year.

a. Financial reporting should provide information about sources and uses of financial resources. Financial reporting should account for all outflows by function and purpose, all inflows by source and type, and the extent to which inflows meet outflows. Financial reporting should identify material nonrecurring financial transactions.
b. Financial reporting should provide information about how the government entity financed its activities and met its cash requirements.
c. Financial reporting should provide information necessary to determine whether the entity's financial position improved or deteriorated as a result of the year's operations.

Financial reporting should assist users in assessing the level of services that can be provided by the governmental entity and its ability to meet its obligations as they become due.

a. Financial reporting should provide information about the financial position and condition of a governmental entity. Financial reporting should provide information about resources and obligations, both actual and contingent, current and noncurrent. The major financial resources of most governmental entities are derived from the ability to tax and issue debt. As a result, financial reporting should provide information about tax sources, tax limitations, tax burdens, and debt limitations.
b. Financial reporting should provide information about a governmental entity's physical and other nonfinancial resources having useful lives that extend beyond the current year, including information that can be used to assess the service potential of those resources. This information should be presented to help users assess long- and short-term capital needs.
c. Financial reporting should disclose legal or contractual restrictions on resources and risks of potential loss of resources.

Source: GASB Concepts Statement 1, *Objectives of Financial Reporting* (1987).

EXAMPLE *Clash Among Reporting Objectives*

Voters approved the establishment of a county sanitation district and the county provided the new district with $10 million in start-up funds. During its first year of operations the district prepared a cash-based budget and engaged in the following summary transactions, all of which occurred without variance from the budget.

- It purchased sanitation vehicles and other equipment for $10 million cash. The anticipated economic lives of the assets were ten years.
- It billed residents for $9 million, but because bills for the last month of the year were not mailed until early the following year (as planned), it collected only $8.2 million.
- It incurred operating costs, all paid in cash, of $6 million.

Let us prepare a statement of revenues and expenses that would embody accounting standards consistent with the GASB objectives. The distinction between expenses and **expenditures,** a term commonly used in government accounting, is drawn in a subsequent chapter. For now consider them to be the same.

Two problems are readily apparent:

- How should the district report the expense related to the equipment? Should it be the $10 million paid to purchase the equipment, or $1 million, an amount representative of the one-tenth of the assets consumed during the period? The broader question is whether governments should be required to depreciate their assets.
- How much revenue should the district recognize? Should it be the $9 million billed or the $8.2 million collected? More generally, should revenues be recognized on a cash or an accrual basis?

Inasmuch as the district prepared its budget on a cash basis, a statement of revenues and expenses that would fulfill the GASB's subobjective of reporting whether resources were obtained and used in accordance with the entity's legally adopted budget would also have to be on a cash basis. The district would recognize the revenue as the cash is collected; it would record the vehicle-related expense in the period in which the vehicles are acquired and paid for. Thus (in millions):

Revenues from customers		$ 8.2
Operating expenses	$ 6.0	
Vehicle-related costs	10.0	16.0
Excess of revenues over expenses		$(7.8)

As a consequence of preparing statements on a cash basis—the same basis as that on which the budget was prepared—the entire cost of acquiring the long-term assets would fall on the taxpayers of the year of purchase. In the following nine years, the district would report no further expenses related to the purchase or "consumption" of these particular vehicles. The financial statements would thereby allow management to appear far more efficient in those years than in the first year. Additionally, if tax rates were set so that revenues would cover expenses, taxpayers would enjoy a rate decrease. However, since the taxpayers of all ten years will benefit from the assets, the reporting objective of interperiod equity would not be served. On the other hand, the government would be credited with only $8.2 million in revenues, even though it provided $9.0 million in services—another, though opposite, violation of the interperiod equity concept.

By contrast, a statement that would fulfill the interperiod equity subobjective would recognize the $10 million in vehicle costs over the ten years in which they would be used and the $9.0 million in revenues in the years in which the services were provided. Thus:

Revenues from customers		$ 9.0
Operating expenses	$ 6.0	
Vehicle-related costs	1.0	7.0
Excess of revenues over expenses		$ 2.0

But the statement, prepared on a full accrual basis, cannot readily be compared to the adopted budget and therefore cannot, without adjustment, be used to demonstrate budgetary compliance.

As will be apparent throughout this text, the conflict between the two objectives of interperiod equity and budgetary compliance characterizes many of the issues that government accountants, and the GASB in particular, have to face in assuring that financial statements are informative and useful to the parties that rely upon them. In particular, the conflict casts doubt upon whether the objectives can be fulfilled within a single set of financial statements, or whether, as an alternative, two sets—one on a full accrual basis, the other on a budget or near budget basis—might be necessary.

GASB STATEMENT NO. 34: TWO SETS OF FINANCIAL STATEMENTS

Upon its establishment in 1984, the GASB undertook to develop a new model for state and local government reporting. However, owing to numerous controversial issues, it did not issue a final pronouncement (Statement No. 34, *Basic Financial Statements—and Management's Discussion and Analysis—for State and Local Governments*) until June 1999. Statement No. 34 required the most significant changes to the reporting model in sixty years and, in fact, does require that governments prepare the two sets of financial statements cited in the previous paragraph.

Owing to the pervasive reporting changes mandated by Statement No. 34, the GASB established a lengthy phase-in period for the new model. Larger governments had to implement the statement for years beginning June 15, 2001, whereas medium and smaller governments could wait until years beginning June 15, 2002 and 2003 respectively. Since most governments do not issue financial statements until four or more months after the end of their fiscal years, "new model" statements did not begin appearing in large numbers until the end of 2002. Consequently, as this text is being written, governments have had relatively little experience with the new model. As they do, however, it is certain that numerous unforeseen implementation issues will arise and that GASB will be making adjustments to the model for many years to come.

FASB OBJECTIVES

Financial Accounting Standards Board objectives for not-for-profit entities are, for the most part, similar to those of the GASB for governments. They are presented, in summary form, in Table 1-4.

FASB objectives refer only obliquely to budgetary compliance. They provide that information should be useful in "assessing how managers of a nonbusiness organization have discharged their stewardship responsibilities." In elaborating upon this objective, the FASB stresses that external financial statements can "best meet that need by disclosing failure to comply with spending mandates [which presumably are expressed in budgets] that may impinge on an organization's financial performance or on its ability to provide a satisfactory level of services."

SERVICE EFFORTS AND ACCOMPLISHMENTS SEEN AS A LONG-TERM GOAL

GASB and FASB objectives both endorse the notion that financial reporting encompasses information on service efforts and accomplishments. This information cannot easily be expressed in monetary units and has not traditionally been included in financial statements.

TABLE 1-4
Financial Accounting Standards Board's Objectives of Financial Reporting

- Financial reporting by nonbusiness organizations should provide information that is useful to present and potential resource providers and other users in making rational decisions about the allocation of resources to those organizations.
- Financial reporting should provide information to help present and potential resource providers and other users in assessing the services that a nonbusiness organization provides and its ability to continue to provide those services.
- Financial reporting should provide information that is useful to present and potential resource providers and other users in assessing how managers of a nonbusiness organization have discharged their stewardship responsibilities and about other aspects of their performance.
- Financial reporting should provide information about the economic resources, obligations, and net resources of an organization, and the effects of transactions, events, and circumstances that change resources and interests in those resources.
- Financial reporting should provide information about the performance of an organization during a period, periodic measurement of the changes in the amount and nature of the net resources of a nonbusiness organization, and information about the service efforts and accomplishments of an organization.
- Financial reporting should provide information about how an organization obtains and spends cash or other liquid resources, about its borrowing and repayment of borrowing, and about other factors that may affect an organization's liquidity.
- Financial reporting should include explanations and interpretations to help users understand financial information provided.

Source: FASB Statement of Financial Accounting Concepts 4, *Objectives of Financial Reporting by Nonbusiness Organizations* (1980).

Both boards emphasize that the ability to measure accomplishments is still undeveloped. Their discussions of their objectives relating to service efforts and accomplishments make it clear that they see this aspect of performance reporting as a long-term goal rather than an immediate imperative.

DO DIFFERENCES IN ACCOUNTING PRINCIPLES REALLY MATTER?

Financial statements demonstrate what happened to an entity in the past. But they present the evidence from the perspective of the accountant who prepared them. Other accountants may describe the events differently. The underlying accounting principles dictate how the evidence is presented. In this section, we address the issue of whether differences in accounting principles really affect the decisions made on the basis of financial statements.

Just as a witness's explanation of an accident cannot change what actually occurred, neither can an accountant's report on an entity's past transactions change what actually transpired. In the sanitation district example, the district paid $10 million in cash for vehicles, billed its customers $9 million for services, and paid $6 million in operating expenses. Whether the district's financial statements report revenues over expenditures of $2 million, expenditures over revenues of $7.8 million, or any amount in between is irrelevant to the actual event. Moreover, financial statements, no matter how prepared, do not directly affect the economic worth of an entity. At year-end the district's customers owed it $0.2 million, irrespective of whether the district reports a receivable of that amount (as it would under an accrual basis of accounting) or of zero (as it would under a cash basis of accounting).

USER ADJUSTMENTS

Users of financial statements can be indifferent to how an entity's fiscal story is told, as long as they are given adequate information to reconfigure the statements to a preferred form. Research in the corporate sector provides compelling evidence that stockholders are able to see through certain differences in accounting practices and adjust financial statements to take the differences into account. Thus, if one firm reports higher earnings than another solely because it employs more liberal accounting principles, the total market value of its shares may be no greater.

The "efficiency" of the municipal bond market—the extent to which it incorporates all public information in pricing securities—has been investigated much less than that of the corporate stock market. Nevertheless, the available evidence, albeit inconclusive, suggests that investors in tax-exempt bonds, like their stock market counterparts, understand the impact of differences in accounting practices.

ECONOMIC CONSEQUENCES

Accounting principles can—and frequently do—have economic consequences. Important decisions and determinations are made on the basis of financial data as presented and without adjustment.

As stated earlier, budgets are governments' paramount financial documents. Most jurisdictions must present balanced budgets (expenditures cannot exceed revenues) in accord with accounting principles either that they select themselves or that are imposed upon them by higher-order governments. The choice of accounting principles is critical. Whereas one set of accounting principles may result in a balanced budget, another set with identical revenue and expenditure proposals may not.

IN PRACTICE

TESTING THE THEORY—DO INVESTORS ADJUST FOR DIFFERENCES IN ACCOUNTING PRINCIPLES?

In a study to test the efficiency of the municipal bond market, a researcher correlated the market prices of New York City bonds with two sets of accounting measures. The first were drawn from the financial statements as actually issued by New York City during the years just prior to its 1975 fiscal crisis. The second were based on the same financial statements, but adjusted to conform to generally accepted accounting principles (to which, at the time, the city did not adhere). The author found that the bond prices were far more sensitive to the measures based on the adjusted than on the unadjusted statements. This indicates, she reasons, that bondholders were aware of New York's slide toward default despite the misleading financial statements and apparently based their investment decisions on other information.

Source: Virginia E. Soybel, "Municipal Financial Reporting and the General Obligation Bond Market: New York City, 1961–1975," *Journal of Accounting and Public Policy* 11 (Fall 1992): 207–231.

Most governments budget on a cash or near-cash basis. Were they required to budget on a full accrual basis, their balanced budgets might quickly become unbalanced.

Governments may face restrictions on the amount of debt they can incur. The use of one set of accounting principles in defining and measuring debt (for example, not counting a lease as an obligation), might enable them to satisfy the legal limits and thereby be permitted to issue additional bonds. The use of a different set (for example, counting the lease as a liability), might cause them to exceed the limits and be barred from further borrowing.

Other examples abound of how specific reporting practices have economic consequences. Many of these will be discussed again later in the text. To cite three:

- An alumnus makes a generous monetary gift to a university. He stipulates that the funds may be invested in stocks, bonds, and real estate, but only the income from the investment may be used to support university activities. If trading gains from the purchase and sale of the investments were accounted for as income, then the amount available to the university for expenditure would be significantly greater than if the gains were treated as an increase in the original capital.
- A government agrees to keep its pension plan fully funded—that is, to make sufficient annual contributions to assure that the plan's assets equal or exceed the plan's actuarial liabilities. The way in which asset and liability values are established will determine its required annual payments.
- A city establishes a policy that it will contract-out for any services private vendors can provide for less than the city's own departments can. The principles used to establish the cost of internal services will affect the decision to use internal departments or outside vendors.

WHO ESTABLISHES GENERALLY ACCEPTED ACCOUNTING PRINCIPLES?

Generally accepted accounting principles (GAAP) embrace the rules and conventions that guide the form and content of general-purpose financial statements. These principles are expressed mainly in pronouncements of officially designated rule-making authorities and should be consistent with the objectives that they established. However,

IN PRACTICE

ASSESSING THE PROFITABILITY OF A FOOTBALL PROGRAM

The president and other officials of a major university assert that their school's football program is "extremely profitable." As evidence, they cite the program's budget and other financial reports that show impressive positive cash flows.

But would they be equally supportive of the program if "profitability" were calculated differently? For example, how much was the program charged for:

- Wages and salaries of campus police who work overtime on game days
- Costs of players' medical exams and care of injuries
- The marching band
- University overhead (it is a safe assumption that the university president devotes more time to the athletic department than to the accounting department)
- Interest on the debt incurred to build or modernize the football stadium
- The "opportunity" cost of using the prime land on which the stadium is located for football rather than for an alternative purpose

On the other side of the journal, how much credit does the football program receive for the contributions of alumni and others attributable to the goodwill and publicity generated by the football team?

The program's "profitability," and hence all policies that affect it, may be no more objective than the team's ranking in the weekly polls.

in the absence of pronouncements by those authorities, GAAP may also be derived from historical convention and widespread practice.

THE FUNCTION OF THE GASB, THE FASB, AND THE AICPA

Each of the primary standard-setting authorities—GASB for state and local governments, FASAB for the federal government, and FASB for not-for-profits—has been sanctioned by the **American Institute of Certified Public Accountants (AICPA)** to establish accounting principles pursuant to Rule 203 of its Code of Professional Conduct. Rule 203 provides that an auditor should not express an unqualified opinion on financial statements that are in violation of the standards established by the designated authorities. In addition, the AICPA provides accounting guidance on issues not yet addressed by either the GASB or the FASB. Its guidance is incorporated into "industry audit guides" and "statements of position" (SOPs).

Each organization is supported by an advisory council composed of representatives of constituent groups—the Governmental Accounting Standards Advisory Council (GASAC) for the GASB, and the Financial Accounting Standards Advisory Council (FASAC) for the FASB. The boards share facilities in Norwalk, Connecticut. The GASB currently has a full-time chairman and six part-time members; the FASB has seven full-time members, including its chairman.

Established in 1984, the GASB succeeded the **National Council on Governmental Accounting (NCGA)** as the standard-setting body for state and local governments. The NCGA, which was sponsored by the Government Finance Officers Association, was thought to be too unwieldy (twenty-one volunteer members) and inadequately staffed to deal with the complexities of modern government finance.

The FASB, created in 1973, has directed its attention mainly to business enterprises, rather than not-for-profits. However, in 1979 it assumed responsibility for the not-for-profit and other specialized-industry accounting principles that had previously been addressed in the AICPA industry audit guides and SOPs.[4] The not-for-profit organizations dealt with in those AICPA pronouncements included universities, voluntary health and welfare organizations, and hospitals. In 1980, the FASB issued its statement of objectives and standards dealing with the form and content of financial statements, depreciation, revenue recognition from contributions, and valuation of investments, as discussed previously and in Table 1-4.

Until 2002, accounting standard setting for businesses and state and local governments was carried out mainly in the private sector by the FASB, the GASB, and (to a limited extent) the AICPA. Auditing standards were set by the AICPA. As a result of Enron/Andersen and numerous other corporate scandals involving financial accounting and reporting, Congress passed the Sarbanes-Oxley Act of 2002 (Public Law 107-204). This measure established the Public Company Accounting Oversight Board to (1) oversee the audit of public companies that are subject to the securities laws; (2) establish audit report standards and rules; and (3) inspect, investigate, and enforce compliance on the part of registered public accounting firms, their associated persons, and certified public accountants. As this text goes to press, the Public Company Accounting Oversight Board has not yet become fully operational and it is not yet clear how it will exercise its oversight responsibilities. In particular, it has not yet determined what its relationship will be with the FASB and the AICPA. However, per Sarbanes-Oxley the FASB will be funded by fees from SEC registrants. The GASB, by contrast, will have to rely, as it has in the past, from contributions from constituents.

As suggested by the accompanying "In Practice: Lessons from Business Scandals," the lessons of Enron/Andersen may be as applicable to governments and not-for-profits as to businesses.

ENTITIES COMMON TO GOVERNMENT AND NOT-FOR-PROFIT SECTORS

Soon after the GASB was established, it and the FASB and their constituents faced a politically sensitive and potentially divisive issue: Which of the two should set standards for entities, such as colleges and universities, that are common to both the government and the not-for-profit sector? Some constituents of the two boards asserted that there are few conceptual or operational differences between same-type entities in the two sectors to justify different accounting standards and hence separate standard-setting authorities. Others, however, contended that governmental hospitals, utilities, and universities differ fundamentally from their not-for-profit counterparts in that they have different rights, responsibilities, and obligations. For example, governmental entities may have the ability to impose taxes and to issue tax-exempt debt and may be accountable to the citizenry at large rather than to a board of trustees.

The jurisdiction issue was made more complex by concerns over sovereignty. Some managers of the not-for-profit entities maintained that they had little in common with state and local governments and did not want to be within the authority of the GASB. Similarly, state and local government officials refused to yield standard-setting control over any of their component units to the FASB, a board mainly concerned with the private sector.

In 1989, the Financial Accounting Foundation and the constituents of the two boards agreed upon a jurisdictional formula that, in essence, reaffirmed the status quo: the GASB would have authority over all state and local government entities and the FASB would have authority over all other entities. Thus, government colleges and universities (such as the State University of New York) are now within the purview of the GASB; private colleges and universities (such as New York University) are within that of the FASB.

If the GASB or the FASB has not issued a pronouncement on a particular issue, then the organizations under each of their jurisdictions can look to other sources for guidance. These other sources are set forth in two "hierarchies" that were part of the jurisdiction

IN PRACTICE

LESSONS FROM BUSINESS SCANDALS

The corporate accounting and reporting debacles involving Enron, Arthur Andersen, and the numerous other well-known companies and CPA firms rocked the foundation of the accounting profession. The scandals prompted Congress to establish an accounting oversight board, thereby depriving the profession of its long-cherished privilege of self-regulation. They also caused companies and their stockholders to lose billions of dollars and shook global confidence in the U.S. capitalistic economy.

With the notable exception of one prominent accounting and auditing failure involving a large church organization (the Baptist Foundation of Arizona), the scandals did not involve either governments or not-for-profits. Still, key lessons from the businesses can readily be adapted to these types of entities. Notably, for example, governments may be subject to the same pressures to engage in "aggressive" accounting practices as businesses; parties who are aware that revenues or expenditures are being "managed" may have incentives similar to those of their counterparts in business to remain silent about them:

- Elected or appointed officials, like business executives, may attempt to mask operating deficits so as to make their own performance look better and thereby enhance their prospects for reelection or promotion.
- Members of legislative bodies may benefit from revenue and expenditure management so that they can avoid having to raise taxes or making difficult choices as to which programs to cut.
- Citizens may condone aggressive accounting and budgeting because they, too, wish to avoid (at least in the short run) tax increases or spending cuts.
- Investment bankers—those who underwrite the bonds of governments—may turn a blind eye to aggressive accounting because a government that is seemingly healthy is more likely to undertake, and issue debt to support, major capital construction projects.
- "Independent" auditors—those who are most responsible for assuring the integrity of financial statements—may avoid tough confrontations with officials of a government client so as to retain the engagement and accompanying audit fees or sell their client various consulting services.

Sound professional judgment and integrity are no less important in government and business than in private industry. (See Chapter 15 for a discussion and examples of ethical issues facing government and not-for-profit accountants.)

agreement and were adopted by the AICPA in *Statement on Auditing Standards No. 69*, "The Meaning of Present Fairly in Conformity with Generally Accepted Accounting Principles in the Independent Auditor's Report." As shown in Table 1-5, in the column applicable to the GASB, a pronouncement of the FASB that has been specifically adopted by the GASB is of the same standing (the top category) as one issued by the GASB itself. However, a pronouncement of the FASB that has *not* been specifically adopted by the GASB ranks no higher than "other accounting literature" (the lowest category). The FASB hierarchy corresponds to, though is not a mirror image of, that of the GASB.

The influence of the FASB on the accounting practices of governments is greater than might appear from the hierarchies, because governments engage in many business-type activities, such as operating utilities, parking garages, and hospitals. Governments have traditionally accounted for these activities in the same way their private-sector

TABLE 1–5
A Summary of the "Hierarchy" of Generally Accepted Accounting Principles

Governmental Entities	Nongovernmental Entities
a. GASB Statements and Interpretations; AICPA and FASB pronouncements specifically made applicable to state and local governments by the GASB	a. FASB Statements and Interpretations; AICPA Accounting Research Bulletins; Accounting Principles Board Opinions
b. GASB Technical Bulletins; AICPA Industry Audit Guides and Statements of Position if specifically made applicable to governments by the AICPA and cleared (not objected to) by the GASB	b. FASB Technical Bulletins; AICPA Industry Audit Guides and Statements of Position if cleared (not objected to) by the FASB
c. AICPA Practice Bulletins if specifically made applicable to governments by the AICPA; Consensus positions of a GASB Emerging Issues Task Force if and when established	c. AICPA Practice Bulletins if cleared by the FASB; Consensus positions of the FASB Emerging Issues Task Force
d. Implementation guides published by the GASB staff; practices that are widely recognized and prevalent in state and local government	d. Implementation guides published by the FASB staff; AICPA accounting interpretations and implementation guides; practices that are widely recognized and prevalent either generally or in the industry
e. Other accounting literature, including FASB pronouncements not specifically made applicable to state and local governments by the GASB	e. Other accounting literature, including GASB pronouncements

counterparts do and, with only a few exceptions, the GASB has required them to adhere to generally accepted accounting principles as established by the FASB.

FASAB FOR THE FEDERAL GOVERNMENT

Although the U.S. government was constitutionally established in 1789, its accounting and financial reporting system is still in its infancy—a clear case of delayed development. It was not until the republic was more than two centuries old that Congress enacted the Chief Financial Officers Act of 1990. The act acknowledged that the federal government was losing billions of dollars each year through financial mismanagement and that its accounting system was incapable of issuing comprehensive financial statements that could earn the government an unqualified audit opinion. The measure took the first steps toward elevating the federal government to a level of fiscal proficiency taken for granted by businesses and other governments. The act:

- Established a chief financial officer (CFO) for fiscal management, a new position housed within the Office of Management and Budget
- Created corresponding CFO positions in each of the federal departments and agencies
- Mandated that the federal government develop accounting systems capable of providing complete, accurate, and timely financial information
- Required that selected federal agencies prepare annual financial statements and make them subject to audits

The act also led the federal government's "big three" agencies concerned with financial reporting—the Department of the Treasury, the General Accounting Office (GAO),[4] and the Office of Management and Budget—to join forces to create the Federal

[4] As this text goes to press, the GAO is seeking, by way of Congressional legislation, to change its name from the General Accounting Office to the *Government Accountability Office.* This new designation, the GAO officials believe, will better encapsulate the agency's main mission, which is to make the operations of the federal government more efficient and effective. They also hope that it will dispel the common, but ill conceived, image of the agency as the nation's official bean counters.

Accounting Standards Advisory Board (FASAB). This board establishes accounting standards for both the federal government at-large and individual federal agencies.

The FASAB, like the GASB and the FASB, has recommended a statement of objectives and a series of accounting standards and related pronouncements. As a result, there is now a reasonable degree of consistency among the reporting practices of federal agencies.

Because of the unique features of the federal government, federal accounting is addressed in Chapter 16, apart from that pertaining to other governments.

SUMMARY

Governments and not-for-profits need accounting principles and reporting mechanisms that differ from those of businesses. Most important, they have objectives other than profit maximization. Therefore, their performance cannot be assessed by the conventional "bottom line" of businesses. Moreover, they are governed by their budgets rather than by the competitive marketplace.

Other characteristics of governments and not-for-profits also have significant accounting and reporting implications. Governments and not-for-profits are extremely diverse and therefore one set of principles may not fit all entities. Managers tend to have a short-term focus and may strive to delay recognition of expenditures and advance recognition of revenues. Business-type activities may be part of the organization and have to be accounted for differently from governmental activities. The distinction between internal accounting and external accounting is often blurred.

Governments, unlike not-for-profits, have the authority to command resources through taxes and other fees. Therefore, a government's financial wherewithal cannot necessarily be assessed by examining only the resources directly tied to the government itself. Those of its constituents may also have to be taken into account.

The main users of government and not-for-profit financial reports include governing boards, investors and creditors, citizens and organizational members, donors and grantors, regulatory and oversight agencies, and other constituents. Each group may have different information needs.

The GASB and the FASB have developed objectives of financial reporting that stress the importance of providing information that enables users to assess interperiod equity and compliance with budgetary (or spending) mandates. Sometimes these objectives are in conflict in that a basis of accounting that satisfies one objective may not satisfy the other.

Choice of accounting principles has no direct effect on an entity's fiscal history or current status. It might, however, have significant economic consequences if decisions are based on the data as presented.

QUESTIONS FOR REVIEW AND DISCUSSION

1. What is the defining distinction between for-profit businesses and not-for-profit entities, including governments? What are the implications of this distinction for financial reporting?
2. Why is the budget a far more important document in both governments and not-for-profits than in businesses?
3. How and why might the importance of the budget affect generally accepted accounting principles for *external* (general purpose) reports?
4. What is meant by "interperiod equity," and what is its consequence for financial reporting?
5. Why may the "matching concept" be less relevant for governments and not-for-profits than for businesses?
6. What is the significance for financial reporting of the many restrictions that are placed upon a government's resources?
7. Why is it difficult to develop accounting principles that are appropriate for governments within the same category (e.g., cities, counties) and even more difficult to develop them for governments within different categories?
8. What is the significance for financial reporting of a government's power to tax? How does it affect the government's overall fiscal strength?
9. Why has it proven especially difficult to establish accounting principles to satisfy all three elements of GASB's first objective of financial reporting in a single statement of revenue and expenditures or balance sheet?
10. Why are measures of "service efforts and accomplishments" of more concern in government and not-for-profits than in businesses?
11. In what key ways does the FASB influence generally accepted accounting principles for governments?
12. Why is it more difficult to distinguish between internal and external users in governments than in businesses?

EXERCISES

1-1

1. The traditional business model of accounting is inadequate for governments and not-for-profit organizations primarily because businesses differ from governments and not-for-profit organizations in that
   - **a.** They have different missions
   - **b.** They have fewer assets
   - **c.** Their assets are intangible
   - **d.** Taxes are a major expenditure of businesses
2. If businesses are "governed by the marketplace," governments are governed by
   - **a.** Legislative bodies
   - **b.** Taxes
   - **c.** Budgets
   - **d.** State constitutions
3. The primary objective of a not-for-profit organization or a government is to
   - **a.** Maximize revenues
   - **b.** Minimize expenditures
   - **c.** Provide services to constituents
   - **d.** All of the above
4. In governments, in contrast to businesses,
   - **a.** Expenditures are driven mainly by the ability of the entity to raise revenues
   - **b.** The amount of revenues collected is a signal of the demand for services
   - **c.** There may not be a direct relationship between revenues raised and the demand for the entity's services
   - **d.** The amount of expenditures is independent of the amount of revenues collected
5. The organization responsible for setting accounting standards for state and local governments is the
   - **a.** FASB
   - **b.** GASB
   - **c.** FASAB
   - **d.** AICPA
6. The number of governmental units in the United States is approximately
   - **a.** 875
   - **b.** 8,750
   - **c.** 87,500
   - **d.** 875,000
7. Governments differ from businesses in that they
   - **a.** Do not raise capital in the financial markets
   - **b.** Do not engage in transactions in which they "sell" goods or services
   - **c.** Are not required to prepare annual financial reports
   - **d.** Do not issue common stock
8. Interperiod equity refers to a condition whereby
   - **a.** Total tax revenues are approximately the same from year to year
   - **b.** Taxes are distributed fairly among all taxpayers regardless of income level
   - **c.** Current-year revenues are sufficient to pay for current-year services
   - **d.** Current-year revenues cover both operating and capital expenditures
9. Which of the following is *not* one of GASB's financial reporting objectives?
   - **a.** Providing information on the extent to which interperiod equity is achieved
   - **b.** Assuring that budgeted revenues are equal to, or exceed, budgeted expenses
   - **c.** Reporting on budgetary compliance
   - **d.** Providing information on service efforts and accomplishments
10. Which of the following is *not* one of FASB's financial reporting objectives?
    - **a.** Providing information about economic resources, obligations, and net resources
    - **b.** Providing information to help resource providers make rational decisions
    - **c.** Reporting on budgetary compliance
    - **d.** Providing information on service efforts and accomplishments

1-2

1. Rule 203 of the AICPA's Code of Professional Conduct pertains to
   - **a.** CPAs' independence
   - **b.** Authorities designated to establish accounting standards
   - **c.** Standards of competency
   - **d.** Solicitation of new clients by a CPA
2. Which of the following rule-making authorities would establish accounting standards for Stanford University (a private university)?
   - **a.** The AICPA
   - **b.** The FASB
   - **c.** The FASAB

d. The GASB

3. Which of the following rule-making authorities would establish accounting standards for the University of Wisconsin (a public university)?
   a. The AICPA
   b. The FASB
   c. The FASAB
   d. The GASB
4. If the GASB has not issued a pronouncement on a specific issue, which of the following is true with respect to FASB pronouncements?
   a. They would automatically govern
   b. They could be taken into account but would have no higher standing than other accounting literature
   c. They are irrelevant
   d. They could be taken into account by the reporting entity but only if disclosure is made in notes to the financial statements
5. The FASB is to the GASB as
   a. A brother is to a sister
   b. A father is to a son
   c. A son is to a father
   d. An aunt is to a niece
6. Standards promulgated by the FASB are most likely to be adhered to by which of the following governmental units?
   a. A police department
   b. A public school
   c. An electric utility
   d. A department of highways
7. Which of the following practices is most likely to undermine interperiod equity?
   a. Paying for a new school building out of current operating funds
   b. Paying the administrative staff of a school out of current operating funds
   c. Issuing twenty-year bonds to finance construction of a new highway
   d. Recognizing gains and losses on marketable securities as prices increase and decrease
8. The term "independent sector" refers to
   a. States that have opted not to receive federal funds
   b. Not-for-profit organizations
   c. Churches that are unaffiliated with a particular denomination
   d. Universities that are not affiliated with a particular athletic conference
9. Which of the following is not an objective of external financial reporting by either the GASB or the FASB?
   a. To enable the statement user to detect fraud
   b. To disclose legal or contractual restrictions on the use of resources
   c. To provide information about how the organizations meet their cash requirements
   d. To provide information that would enable a user to assess the service potential of long-lived assets
10. Which of the following is the least appropriate use of the external financial statements of a government?
    a. To assess the entity's financial condition
    b. To assess whether the compensation of management is reasonable in relation to that of comparable entities
    c. To compare actual results with the budget
    d. To evaluate the efficiency and effectiveness of the entity in achieving its objectives

PROBLEMS

Continuing Problem

Accompanying this text is a CD-ROM containing the Comprehensive Annual Financial Report (CAFR) of the city of Austin, Texas. A CAFR includes an entity's year-end financial statements; it is not the same as its budget.

Austin's CAFR forms the basis of the "continuing problems" of these chapters. Install the CD-ROM on your computer and practice navigating through the CAFR.

Alternatively you may obtain the CAFR of a different city, town, or county with a population of 100,000 or more. Be sure, however, that the government has adopted the provisions of GASB Statement No. 34. A CAFR can generally be obtained by writing to the government's controller or finance director; most institutions will provide the reports at no charge. An increasing number of governments make their CAFRs available on the Internet.

1-1

Budgeting practices that satisfy cash requirements may not promote interperiod equity.

The Burnet County Road Authority was established as a separate government to maintain county highways. The road authority was granted statutory power to impose property taxes on county residents to cover its costs but it is required to balance its budget, which must be prepared on a cash basis. In its first year of operations it engaged in the following transactions, all of which were consistent with its legally adopted cash-based budget:

1. Purchased $10 million of equipment, all of which had an anticipated useful life of ten years; to finance the acquisition the authority issued $10 million in ten-year term bonds (i.e., bonds that mature in ten years)
2. Incurred wages, salaries, and other operating costs, all paid in cash, of $6 million
3. Paid interest of $0.5 million on the bonds
4. Purchased $0.9 million of additional equipment, paying for it in cash; this equipment had a useful life of only three years
   a. The authority's governing board levies property taxes at rates that will be just sufficient to balance the authority's budget. What is the amount of tax revenue that it will be required to collect?
   b. Assume that in the authority's second year of operations, it incurs the same costs, except that it purchases no new equipment. What amount of tax revenue will it be required to collect?
   c. Make the same assumption as to the tenth year, when it will have to repay the bonds. What amount of tax revenue will it be required to collect?
   d. Comment on the extent to which the authority's budgeting and taxing policies promote interperiod equity. What changes would you recommend?

1-2

Financial statements of a government or not-for-profit organization may not provide sufficient information on which to make a loan decision.

Assume that you are a loan officer of a bank. A local church is seeking a $4 million, twenty-year loan to construct a new classroom building.

Church officers submit a comprehensive financial report that was audited by a reputable CPA firm. In summary form (the actual statement showed details), the church's statement of revenues and expenditures indicated the following (in millions):

Revenues from dues and contributions	$1.8
Revenues from other sources	0.2
Total revenues	$2.0
Less: total expenditures	2.0
Excess of revenues over expenditures	$0.0

The church prepared its financial statements on a near-cash basis, accounting for all capital asset acquisitions as expenditures when acquired.

The church's balance sheet reported assets, mainly cash and investments (at market value), of $0.2 million. In addition, a note to the financial statements indicated that the current market value of its present buildings and equipment is approximately $3 million. The church has no outstanding debt.

1. Is there any information in the financial statements that would make you reluctant to approve the loan? If so, indicate and explain.
2. Is there any other financial information of the type likely to be reported in a conventional annual report that you would like to review prior to making a loan decision? If so, indicate and explain.
3. Is there any other information, of any type, that you would like to review prior to making a loan decision? If so, indicate and explain.
4. Comment on the inherent limitations of the financial statements of this church, or any comparable not-for-profit organization, as a basis for making loan decisions.

1-3

The dual objectives of assessing interperiod equity and assuring budgetary compliance may necessitate different accounting practices.

A city engages in the transactions that follow. For each transaction indicate the amount of revenue or expenditure that it should report in 2004. Assume first that the main objective of the financial statements is to enable users to assess budgetary compliance. Then calculate the amounts assuming that the main objective is to assess interperiod equity. The city prepares its budget on a "modified" cash basis (that is, it expands the definition of cash to include short-term marketable securities), and its fiscal year ends on December 31.

1. Employees earned $128,000 in salaries and wages for the last five days in December 2004. They were paid on January 8, 2005.
2. A consulting actuary calculated that per an accepted actuarial cost method, the city should contribute $225,000 to its firefighters pension fund for benefits earned in 2004. However, the city contributed only $170,000, the amount budgeted at the start of the year.
3. The city acquired three police cars for $35,000 cash each. The vehicles are expected to last for three years.
4. On December 1, 2004, the city invested $99,000 in short-term commercial paper (promissory notes). The notes matured on January 1, 2005. The city received $100,000. The $1,000 difference between the two amounts represents the city's return (interest) on the investment.
5. On January 2, 2004, the city acquired a new $10 million office building, financing it with twenty-five-year serial bonds. The bonds are to be repaid evenly over the period they are outstanding—that is, $400,000 per year. The useful life of the building is twenty-five years.
6. On January 3, 2004, the City acquired another $10 million office building, financing this facility with

twenty-five-year *term* bonds. These bonds will be repaid entirely when they mature on January 1, 2029. The useful life of this building is also twenty-five years.

7. City restaurants are required to pay a $1,200 annual license fee, the proceeds of which the city uses to fund its restaurant inspection program. The license covers the period July 1 through June 30. In 2004 the city collected $120,000 in fees for the license period beginning July 1, 2004.
8. The city borrowed $300,000 in November 2004 to cover a temporary shortage of cash. It expects to repay the loan in February 2005.

1-4

Do conventional financial statements satisfy the objectives of financial reporting?

The financial statements that follow were adapted from those of the University of Arizona. Both the statement of changes in fund balances and the notes to the statements have been omitted. Moreover, the statements show only the combined "totals" columns whereas the actual statements are multicolumned, indicating the various restrictions placed upon the university's resources. Also, a few of the line items have been aggregated, and the dates have been changed.

The University of Arizona Balance Sheet, as of June 30 (in millions)

	2005	2004
Assets		
Cash and investments	$145	$145
Donated land	3	3
Notes and accounts receivable (net of allowances for uncollectibles)	52	47
Inventories and supplies	8	8
Physical properties	995	945
Total assets	$1,203	$1,148
Liabilities and net assets		
Accounts payable	$16	$17
Accrued payroll	12	10
Deferred revenue and deposits	9	8
Funds held for others	11	8
Capitalized lease obligations	36	33
Bonds payable	241	243
Total liabilities	325	319
Net assets	878	829

The University of Arizona Statement of Revenues, Expenses, and Changes in Net Assets for Year-Ending June 30th (in millions)

	2005	2004
Operating revenues		
Tuition and fees	$ 112	$ 111
Grants and contracts	208	194
Sales and services of educational departments	8	6
Sales and services of auxiliary enterprises	69	66
Other	8	6
Total operating revenues	$ 405	$ 383
Operating expenses		
Education and general		
Instruction	$ 182	$ 181
Research	162	155
Public service	26	25
Academic support	51	52
Student services	13	15
Institutional support	36	37
Auxiliary enterprise expenses	76	68
Operation and maintenance of plant	36	34
Scholarships and fellowships	49	46
Total educational and general	$ 631	$ 613
Operating income (loss)	$(226)	$(230)
Nonoperating revenues and expenses		
State appropriations	$ 245	$ 242
Federal appropriations	5	5
Gifts	40	39
Investment and endowment income	8	9
Interest on long-term debt	(23)	(14)
Total nonoperating revenues and expenses	$ 275	$ 281
Increase in net assets	$49	$51
Net assets–beginning of year	829	778
Net assets–end of year	$ 878	$ 829

1. Based on the information included in the financial statements, respond as best you can to the following questions. If you believe the data in the financial statements are inadequate to answer the questions, then tell what additional information you would like and where you would most likely find it.
   a. Were the accomplishments of the university greater or less in 2005 than in 2004?
   b. Did the university achieve its goals more efficiently in 2005 than 2004?

c. Are the university's physical facilities adequate for the next two years? Ten years?

d. Did the university's long-term financial position improve or deteriorate between year-end 2004 and year-end 2005, taking account of the fiscal demands that will be placed upon it in the future?

e. Will the university be able to satisfy its short-term demands for cash?

2. Review the GASB and FASB objectives of financial reporting. Are any of the preceding questions inconsistent with those objectives? Comment on the extent to which conventional financial statements satisfy the GASB and FASB objectives and what additional types of information they will likely have to incorporate in order to satisfy these objectives.

1-5

The jurisdictional overlap among governments may have significant implications for financial reporting.

Suppose that you lived on a street adjoining the college in which you are taking this course.

1. List all the governments (e.g., state, county, town) that have jurisdiction over the residents or property of that street.
2. Indicate why it may be difficult to assess the financial wherewithal of one of those governments without taking into account the others. What are the implications for financial reporting of this jurisdictional overlap?

1-6

Choice of accounting principles may have significant economic consequences.

In preparing its budget proposals, a city's budget committee initially estimated that total revenues would be \$120 million and total expenditures would be \$123 million. In light of the balanced budget requirements that the city has to meet, the committee proposed several measures to either increase revenues or decrease expenditures. They included the following:

1. Delay the payment of \$0.4 million of city bills from the last week of the fiscal year covered by the budget to the first week of the next fiscal year.
2. Change the way property taxes are accounted for in the budget. Currently, property taxes are counted as revenues only if they are expected to be collected during the budget year. New budgetary principles would permit the city to include as revenues all taxes expected to be collected within sixty days of the following fiscal year in addition to those collected during the year. The committee estimates that the change would have a net impact of \$1.2 million.
3. Change the way that supplies are accounted for in the budget. Currently, supplies are recognized as expenditures at the time they are *ordered*. The proposal would delay recognition of the expenditure until they are actually *received*. The committee estimates a net effect of \$0.8 million.
4. Defer indefinitely \$1.5 million of maintenance on city roads.

Except as just noted with respect to supplies, the city currently prepares its budget on a cash basis, even though other bases are also legally permissible. It prepares its year-end financial statements, however, on an accrual basis.

a. Indicate the impact that each of the proposals would have on the city's (1) budget, (2) annual year-end financial statements, (3) "substantive" economic well-being. Be sure to distinguish between direct and indirect consequences.

b. It is sometimes said that choice of accounting principles doesn't matter in that they affect only the way the entity's fiscal "story" is told; they have no impact on the entity's actual fiscal history or current status. Do you agree? Explain.

1-7

Should there be differences in the accounting and reporting systems of governments and businesses that provide the same services?

A town privatized its sanitation department, selling all its plant and equipment to a private corporation. The corporation agreed to hire most of the department's managers and other employees and was given an exclusive franchise, for a limited number of years, to offer the same service as previously provided by the town. When it operated the department, the town charged local residents fees based on the amount of trash collected. It set the scale of fees at a level intended to enable it to break even—to cover all its operating and capital costs, including interest on capital assets.

1. Do you believe that the objectives of financial accounting and *external* reporting of the private sanitation company should be any different from those of the town? Explain.
2. Do you see any differences in the information requirements of the *internal* managers now that they are employed by a private corporation rather than a government? If so, what are they?

1-8

Capital acquisition decisions may be far more complex in not-for-profit organizations than in businesses.

The Chicago Youth Association (CYA) and the Palmer Athletic Club (PAC) are each considering purchasing a van.

The CYA is a not-for-profit organization serving at-risk inner-city youth. It operates a center that provides after-school tutoring, counseling, and supervised athletic activities. It would use the van mainly to drive students from their schools to the center and from the center back to their homes. The CYA estimates that the van would enable it to increase by twenty the number of students it serves at any one time. The CYA is supported entirely by contributions from the United Way and other private sources.

The PAC is a private athletic facility serving the youth of a suburban community. It provides access to athletic facilities and instruction in several sports, including swimming, tennis, and gymnastics. It would use the van for the same purpose as the CYA—to transport students to and from the facility. The PAC estimates that the van would enable it to increase center capacity by twenty customers, each of whom pays weekly fees of $65.

Each organization estimates that the incremental cost of serving the additional twenty clients (including the operating costs of the van) would be $50 per client per week. Each operates fifty weeks per year.

The two vans would each cost $30,000 and have estimated useful lives of three years. Each organization estimates that its cost of capital is 10 percent.

1. Should the PAC acquire the van? Explain and show all computations.
2. Should the CYA acquire the van? Explain and show all computations.
3. Comment on any critical differences between capital budgeting in a business and a not-for-profit organization.

1-9

Financial information that is appropriate for some purposes may be inappropriate for others—just as in business.

A city operates a computer service department. The department maintains and repairs the computers of all other city departments, billing them for each job performed. The billing rates are established so as to cover the repair service's full cost of carrying out its function.

For the latest year available, the department reported the following (all amounts in millions):

Revenues from billing other departments		$8.9
Less: Expenditures		
Wages and salaries	$4.0	
Supplies	2.6	
Other cash expenditures	1.3	
Overhead allocated from other departments	1.0	8.9
Excess of revenues over expenditures		$0.0

The allocated overhead consists mainly of city administrative costs, most of which would remain the same even if the department were to cease operations. However, it also includes $0.3 million in rent. Were the department to be eliminated, the city could move its legal department into the space now occupied by the computer repair service department. The move would save the city $0.2 million, the amount currently paid in rent by the legal department.

A private corporation has offered to provide the same repair service as the computer department for $8.5 million.

1. Based on the limited data provided, should the city accept the offer from the private corporation? Comment on the relevance for this decision of the $8.9 million in total cost—the measure used to establish billing rates.
2. Suppose, instead, that the city did not allocate overhead costs and hence total costs (and billing revenues) were only $7.9 million. Should the city accept the offer? Is the $7.9 million in unallocated costs any more relevant for this decision than the $8.9 million per the allocated statement?

1-10

Year-end financial accounting and reporting can reveal the economic substance of government actions taken mainly to balance the budget.

Public officials, it is often charged, promote measures intended to make the government "look good" in the short-term, but that may be deleterious in the long-term. Assume that the following actions, designed to increase a reported surplus, were approved by a city council:

1. It reduced the city's contributions to the employee "defined benefit" pension plan from the $10 million recommended by the city's actuary to $5 million to finance benefits earned in the current period. Under a defined benefit plan the employer promises employees specified benefits upon their retirement, and the level of benefits is independent of when and how much the employer contributes to the plan over the employees' years of service.
2. It reduced by $1 million the city's cash transfer to a "rainy day" reserve maintained to cover possible future reductions in tax collections attributable to a downturn in the region's economy.
3. It sold securities that had been held as an investment. The securities had been purchased five years earlier at a cost of $2 million. Market value at the time of sale was $5 million.
4. It delayed until the following year $10 million of maintenance on city highways.

Assume that the city's budget is on a cash or near-cash basis. Accordingly, each of these measures would, as the council intended, reduce budgetary expenditures or increase budgetary revenues.

a. Suppose that you were asked to propose accounting principles for external reporting that would capture the true economic nature of these measures—actions that, in substance, did not improve the city's fiscal performance or condition. For each measure, indicate how you would require that it be accounted for and reported.
b. Can you see any disadvantages to the principles that you propose?

CHAPTER 2

Fund Accounting

Learning Objectives

After studying this chapter you should understand:

- The nature of funds, including why they are used and the interrelationship among them
- The basic fund types used by governments—governmental funds, proprietary funds, and fiduciary funds
- The main components of a government's comprehensive annual financial report
- The primary financial statements—both government-wide and fund—issued by governments
- How the fund structures and financial reports of not-for-profits differ from those of governments

In Chapter 1 we set forth some of the key characteristics that distinguish governments and not-for-profits from businesses. We also discussed their implications for accounting and reporting. In particular we noted that governments and not-for-profits use fund accounting. In this chapter we explain the rationale for fund accounting, describe the main types of funds maintained, and examine the relationships among funds.

As noted in Chapter 1, in June 1999 the Governmental Accounting Standards Board (GASB) established a new reporting model for state and local governments. In this chapter we highlight the main distinctions between the new model and that which it has replaced. We also present the key features of the Financial Accounting Standards Board's (FASB) model for not-for-profit entities and show how it differs from government model. A key purpose of our discussion is to emphasize that for purposes of external reporting, funds can be combined and reported in a variety of ways.

WHAT IS A FUND?

Government and other not-for-profit organizations establish their accounting systems on a fund basis. In governmental and not-for-profit accounting, the term "fund" has a different meaning than it does in business accounting. In business accounting, "funds" typically refers either to working capital (current assets less current liabilities) or to selected elements of working capital (such as cash and investments). In governmental and not-for-profit accounting, a fund is a fiscal and accounting entity. Each fund has its own self-balancing set of accounts from which financial statements can be prepared. Governments and not-for-profits customarily use several funds—several fiscal and accounting entities—to account for their resources and activities. For example, a church may use one fund to account for its general operating revenues and expenses, another to account for resources set aside to construct a new building, and a third to account for its religious school.

WHAT CHARACTERIZES FUNDS?

Each fund of a government or not-for-profit can be represented by a variation of the accounting equation that describes a business entity. Rather than

$$\text{assets} = \text{liabilities} + \text{owners' equity}$$

fund accounting uses the equation

$$\text{assets} = \text{liabilities} + \text{fund balance}$$

Remember, governments and not-for-profits may not have owners, so the term owners' equity is replaced by the term **fund balance.** Fund balance, like owners' equity, is a residual—the difference between the fund's assets and the claims against those assets. The fund balance is the amount left to the parties with rights to the assets after all other claims have been liquidated. Fund balance is often referred to as **net assets.** Hence the equation can also be expressed as

$$\text{assets} - \text{liabilities} = \text{net assets (or fund balance)}$$

Because funds can be represented by the basic accounting equation that is used by businesses, they can also be accounted for by the same double-entry system of bookkeeping. Their current status and past performance can be summarized by financial statements similar to those of businesses. For example, the balance sheet of a fund can detail the specific assets, liabilities, and elements of fund balance that underlie the accounting equation as of any point in time. A statement of revenues, expenditures, and other changes in fund balance can explain the reasons for changes in fund balance during a specified period of time.[1] A statement of cash flows can reconcile the changes in cash between the end and the beginning of a period.

USE OF MULTIPLE FUNDS TO ACCOUNT FOR AN ENTITY

Governments and not-for-profits separate resources into funds for reasons that differ considerably from those for which businesses establish subsidiaries. Businesses generally establish subsidiaries to account for their activities by product or region, to isolate certain business risks, and to minimize their tax obligations. Governments and not-for-profits, on the other hand, most commonly separate resources into funds to assure that they adhere to restrictions placed upon them by legislators, grantors, donors or other outside parties. For example, were a university to receive a donation that may be used only for scholarships, it would account for the resources received in a special scholarship fund. Fund accounting promotes both control and accountability over restricted resources. To a lesser extent, governments and not-for-profits establish funds to account for certain activities, often those of a business type, that are different in nature from their usual activities. For example, a government might account for its golf course, which operates similarly to a privately owned course, in a fund separate from that used to account for its general operations. By accounting for these types of activities in their own accounting and fiscal entities, the entities are better able to control the activities' revenues and expenditures and to assess their overall performance.

To appreciate the relationship between the two or more funds used to account for a single entity, one must remember that each fund is a separate accounting entity. Thus, every transaction that affects a fund must be recorded by at least one debit and one credit. Any transaction that affects two or more funds must be accounted for as if it affected two or more independent businesses and must be recorded individually in each fund. Suppose, for example, that a city maintains two funds: a general fund accounts for its unrestricted resources and general operations, and a utility fund accounts for its electric utility that sells electricity to city residents and other government departments. The electric utility bills the other city departments, all of which are accounted for in the general operating fund, for $10,000. The following entries would be appropriate:

Utility fund		
Accounts receivable (from general fund)	$10,000	
Revenue from sale of electricity		$10,000
To record the sale of electricity to general fund		

General fund		
Electricity expenditure	$10,000	
Accounts payable (to utility fund)		$10,000
To record the use of electricity		

BASIS OF ACCOUNTING AND MEASUREMENT FOCUS

Basis of accounting determines *when* transactions and events are recognized. For instance, if an entity adopts the full accrual basis of accounting, a transaction is recognized when it has its substantive economic impact. If, on the other hand, it adopts the cash basis, the transaction is recognized only as cash related to the transaction is

[1]As will be addressed later in the text, in government accounting "expenditures" are distinguished from "expenses." For now, it is sufficient to note that "expenditures" is used in connection with funds that are accounted for on a modified accrual basis, whereas "expenses" is used in connection with those accounted for on a full accrual basis.

received or paid. The **measurement focus** of an entity determines what is being reported upon—which assets and liabilities will be given accounting recognition and reported on the balance sheet. The two concepts obviously are closely related; the selection of one implies the selection of the other. For example, if an entity adopts a cash basis of accounting, then its measurement focus will necessarily be upon cash. Only cash will be reported on its balance sheet. Correspondingly, measurement focus also determines whether net profit (the net increase in all economic resources) or merely the net change in selected resource flows (such as the net increase in current financial resources) is being reported.

If an entity adopts a full accrual basis of accounting, which is required of businesses, then its measurement focus will automatically be upon all economic resources and its balance sheet will report on all assets and liabilities, both current and noncurrent. Increases or decreases in net capital assets and long-term obligations are recognized as revenues or expenses. Capital assets are a government's long-lived (fixed) assets such as land, buildings, equipment, vehicles, roads, bridges, and streetlights. Suppose, for example, an organization purchases a vehicle for $25,000 by giving a note for the entire amount. The following entry (quite familiar to anyone who has studied conventional business accounting) would be appropriate:

Vehicles	$25,000	
Notes payable		$25,000
To record the acquisition of a vehicle		

Inasmuch as governments and not-for-profits may be primarily concerned with the assets needed to satisfy current year obligations, they may adopt a modified accrual basis of accounting and a measurement focus on mainly short-term financial assets and liabilities.[2] Therefore, long-lived assets and long-term liabilities would be excluded from the balance sheet, and net changes in short-term financial assets and liabilities would be recognized as revenues or expenses. For example, if a government borrows $25,000 (issuing a long-term note) and uses the proceeds to purchase a vehicle the following entries would be proper:

Cash	$25,000	
Proceeds from borrowing		$25,000
To record the issuance of a long-term note		
Expenditure for vehicles	$25,000	
Cash		$25,000
To record the purchase of the vehicle		

The government would report neither the vehicle nor the long-term note on its fund balance sheet. Instead, it would record both the increase and subsequent decrease in a financial asset (cash) on the fund's statement of revenues and expenditures or a comparable statement that explains the changes in net financial resources. From an accounting standpoint neither the vehicle nor the related liability would be recognized. The vehicle, in effect, would be written off (expensed) at the time acquired. The proceeds from the note would be recorded as proceeds from borrowing, an increase in fund balance that (like a revenue) would be closed to fund balance.

Governments can report their funds on different bases for different purposes. Thus, for example, to provide a measure of the full cost of services, a government may report its funds on a full accrual basis. To demonstrate compliance with budgetary

[2] Although for purposes of internal management and control not-for-profits may adopt a modified accrual basis of accounting, FASB standards require that they prepare their general-purpose external reports on a full accrual basis.

constraints, it may report them on a modified accrual basis. Businesses, of course, also use two or more bases to account for their operations. They prepare their financial statements on a full accrual basis, their tax returns on a basis specified by the IRS, and their reports to state or federal agencies on a basis defined by the relevant regulatory authority.

Irrespective of whether an entity reports capital assets and long-term liabilities on its fund balance sheets, it must still maintain accounting control over them. Both management and constituents need be concerned with all the entity's resources and obligations—not just those given balance sheet recognition. Therefore, it is incumbent upon the entity to maintain accounting records of all assets and liabilities and to include in its financial statements schedules that not only summarize the assets and liabilities but show the changes during the year.

In the remaining sections of this chapter, we study the financial reports of governments and not-for-profit organizations to observe how they use multiple funds to report their activities. To reinforce the purposes of fund accounting and the relationships among funds we present a simple, highly stylized example, "Fund Accounting in a School District." We use as our illustration a public school district, which accounts for its funds on a modified accrual basis, and hence its measurement focus is on current financial resources. In particular the illustration is intended to emphasize that

- Each fund is, in essence, a separate accounting and fiscal entity.
- Because the funds are not on a full accrual basis, some economic resources and obligations are not recognized on the balance sheet as assets and liabilities (and hence, must be accounted for in off-the-balance-sheet records).

EXAMPLE *Fund Accounting in a School District*

A newly formed public school district accounts for its operations on a modified accrual basis. It maintains three funds:

- ***A general fund.*** This fund accounts for taxes and other unrestricted resources.
- ***A capital projects fund.*** This fund accounts for the proceeds of bonds that are restricted to the construction of buildings and similar assets.
- ***A debt service fund.*** This fund accounts for resources that are to be set aside each year to assure that the district has the wherewithal to make its required payments of interest and principal on its long-term debt. It may be viewed as a savings account (or sinking fund) for resources restricted either by the debt covenants (agreements) or by policies of the district itself.
- ***A special revenue fund.*** This fund accounts for state grants that must be used for specific purposes.

The following is a highly aggregated summary of the district's first year of operations:

1. The district levied \$9.0 million of general property taxes of which it actually collected \$8.8 million. It expects to collect the balance shortly after year-end. These taxes are unrestricted; they can be used for any legitimate educational purpose. Therefore, the district should record them in its general fund.

General fund

Cash	\$8.8	
Property taxes receivable	0.2	
Property tax revenue		\$9.0

To record property taxes

2. The district received a state grant of \$0.2 million to purchase computers. This grant is restricted to a specific purpose and therefore must be recorded in a restricted fund, the special revenue fund.

Special revenue fund		
Cash	\$0.2	
Grant revenue		\$0.2

To record a state grant restricted to the acquisition of computers

3. The district issued \$12.0 million in long-term bonds to construct a school building. The proceeds must be used for the intended purpose and therefore must be recorded in the capital projects fund. Because the district is on a modified accrual basis of accounting, which excludes the recognition of both long-term assets and long-term liabilities, the proceeds are recognized in a revenue-type account—one that will cause fund balance, rather than a liability, to increase. Of course, the district must maintain a record of both its long-lived assets and obligations in capital asset and long-term obligation ledgers or other off-the-balance-sheet lists.

Capital projects fund		
Cash	\$12.0	
Proceeds from borrowing		\$12.0

To record the issuance of bonds

4. The district constructed the school building for \$11.0 million. The construction of the school building must be accounted for as an expenditure rather than a long-lived asset. The asset must be recorded in a supplementary ledger or list.

Capital projects fund		
Construction of building (expenditure)	\$11.0	
Cash		\$11.0

To record the costs of constructing the school building

5. The district incurred \$6.0 million in general operating expenditures of which it actually paid \$5.5 million.

General fund		
General operating expenditures	\$6.0	
Cash		\$5.5
Accounts payable		0.5

To record general operating expenditures

6. Using its state grant, the district purchased computers for \$0.1 million. As with the construction of the building, the district would recognize the acquisition as an expenditure, but record the asset in a supplementary ledger or list.

Special revenue fund		
Acquisition of computers (expenditures)	\$0.1	
Cash		\$0.1

To record the acquisition of computers

7. The district transferred \$1.1 million from the general fund to the debt service fund to make the first payments of both principal and interest that are due in the following year. Broken down into its components, this transaction is straightforward, involving simple entries to each of two funds:

General fund		
Transfer-out to debt service fund	\$1.1	
Cash		\$1.1

To record transfer to the debt service fund

Debt service fund		
Cash	$1.1	
Transfer-in from general fund		$1.1
To record transfer from the general fund		

Tables 2-1 and 2-2 summarize the transactions into balance sheets and statements of revenues and expenditures for the three funds. To emphasize that each fund is a separate accounting and reporting entity, and hence their resources are not interchangeable, combined totals are deliberately omitted.

HOW CAN FUNDS BE COMBINED AND CONSOLIDATED?

As noted in Chapter 1, the new GASB Statement No. 34 model mandates that governments prepare two separate, albeit related, sets of financial statements. The first set, the *government-wide statements*, concentrates on the government as a whole. It *consolidates* all of a government's operations and includes within its measurement focus all of the government's economic resources, including long-lived assets. The statements are presented on a full accrual basis. Tables 2-3 and 2-4 (which will be discussed later in the chapter) illustrate the government-wide statements of Charlotte, North Carolina.

The second set, the *fund financial statements*, views the government as a collection of separate funds. Governmental and business-type funds are reported on separate schedules. The schedule that reports governmental funds includes one column for the general fund, one for each of the other major funds, and one that combines all the nonmajor funds. Although these statements contain "totals" columns, they merely *combine* rather than consolidate the funds. Hence, interfund items (such as receivables and payables or transfers from one fund to another) are not eliminated. These statements focus only on current financial resources and accordingly are on a modified accrual basis. Tables 2-5, 2-6, and 2-7 present Charlotte's fund statements (including a reconciliation schedule, to be discussed later in the chapter) for governmental (as opposed to business) activities. Whereas the government-wide statements better serve the GASB objective of reporting on the extent to which the government achieved interperiod equity, the fund statements are more closely tied to the objective of reporting on budgetary compliance.

Except for funds used to account for business-type activities, governments maintain their funds on a modified accrual basis. Thus, to prepare their government-wide

TABLE 2-1
School District's Fund Balance Sheet (in millions)

	General	Special Revenue	Capital Projects	Debt Service
Assets				
Cash	$2.2	$0.1	$1.0	$1.1
Property taxes receivable	0.2	—	—	—
Totals	$2.4	$0.1	$1.0	$1.1
Liabilities and fund balances				
Accounts payable	$0.5			
Fund balances (net assets)	1.9	$0.1	$1.0	$1.1
Totals	$2.4	$0.1	$1.0	$1.1

TABLE 2-2
School District's Statement of Fund Revenues, Expenditures, and Other Changes in Fund Balances (in millions)

	General	Special Revenue	Capital Projects	Debt Service
Property tax revenue	$ 9.0			
Revenue from state grant		$0.2		
Total revenues	9.0	0.2	—	—
Operating expenditures	6.0			
Construction of building			$ 11.0	
Acquisition of computers		0.1		
Total expenditures	6.0	0.1	11.0	—
Excess of revenues over expenditures	3.0	0.1	(11.0)	—
Other increases and decreases in fund balance				
Transfers in/(out)	(1.1)			$1.1
Proceeds from borrowing			12.0	
Increase in fund balance	$ 1.9	$0.1	$ 1.0	$1.1

statements, they must adjust the individual fund statements so that they are on a full accrual basis. They do not, of course, have to maintain two separate sets of books.

In prescribing how not-for-profits should report to external parties, the FASB takes a considerably different approach from that of the GASB. The FASB permits not-for-profits to consolidate the assets and liabilities of funds into a single balance sheet. However, the *net assets* (assets less liabilities) of the entity must be reported in three categories of restrictiveness: *unrestricted*, *temporarily restricted*, and *permanently restricted* (the characteristics of which will be set forth later in this chapter and discussed in detail in Chapter 12). The FASB also requires that on its statement of activities (similar to a business's income statement) the entity display separately those revenues that are unrestricted, temporarily restricted, and permanently restricted. Assets are considered restricted when **donors** (as opposed to management, boards of governors, or creditors) place constraints on when or how they may be used.

The sections that follow present an overview of the main funds maintained by both governments and not-for-profits and how they are reported. Bear in mind that each fund, like a subsidiary of a corporation, is a separate accounting and fiscal entity for which separate financial statements can be prepared. Just as the financial statements of a corporation can be prepared on different bases (e.g., full accrual, cash, tax, regulatory), so also can those of individual funds (e.g., modified accrual, full accrual). And just as the financial statements of a company's subsidiaries can be combined in different ways (e.g., by region, by product line, by size), so too can those of a government or not-for-profit (e.g., by type, by dollar value, by nature of restrictions).

WHAT ARE THE MAIN TYPES OF GOVERNMENT FUNDS?

In this section we introduce the specific funds governments use to summarize and report upon their activities. First we present a brief overview of the funds structure; then we examine each type of fund in greater detail.

TABLE 2–3
Charlotte, North Carolina

Statement of Net Assets
June 30, 2002 (in thousands)

	Primary Government			Component Unit
	Governmental Activities	Business-type Activities	Total	Auditorium-Coliseum-Convention Center Authority
Assets				
Cash and cash equivalents	$ 455,754	$ 418,273	$ 874,027	$ 12,104
Receivables, net	22,539	47,303	69,842	1,877
Due from primary government	—	—	—	643
Due from other governmental agencies	38,810	26,304	65,114	281
Internal balances	(955)	955	—	—
Inventories	715	2,996	3,711	235
Prepaid items	—	—	—	63
Restricted assets:				
Temporarily restricted—				
Cash and cash equivalents	43,250	112,984	156,234	—
Investments	—	178,254	178,254	—
Permanently restricted—				
Cash and cash equivalents	2,952	—	2,952	—
Receivables	24	—	24	—
Noncurrent accounts receivable	—	15,080	15,080	—
Notes receivable	54,255	—	54,255	—
Deferred charges	446	13,796	14,242	—
Capital assets (Note 4.f.):				
Land	1,741,098	166,876	1,907,974	—
Buildings, improvements, infrastructure and machinery and equipment, net	1,434,392	1,877,311	3,311,703	—
Construction in progress	195,078	412,577	607,655	—
Total assets	3,988,358	3,272,709	7,261,067	15,203
Liabilities				
Accounts payable/claims payable	68,669	19,341	88,010	2,933
Deposits and retainage payable	4,285	6,318	10,603	2,098
Accrued interest payable	6,370	13,728	20,098	—
Due to component unit	643	—	643	—
Unearned revenues	2,337	—	2,337	—
Liabilities payable from restricted assets	1,440	35,809	37,249	—
Noncurrent liabilities (Note 4.i.):				
Due within one year	62,557	42,302	104,859	20
Due after one year	634,205	1,503,886	2,138,091	343
Total Liabilities	780,506	1,621,384	2,401,890	5,394
Net assets				
Invested in capital assets, net of related debt	2,815,150	1,201,756	4,016,906	—
Restricted for:				
Debt service	14,194	55,328	69,522	—
Capital projects	127,162	—	127,162	—
Perpetual care—Nonexpendable	2,976	—	2,976	—
Other purposes	68,039	10,832	78,871	725
Unrestricted	180,331	383,409	563,409	9,084
Total Net Assets	$3,207,852	$1,651,325	$4,859,177	$ 9,809

TABLE 2–4
Charlotte, North Carolina

Statement of Activities
for the Year Ended June 30, 2002 (in thousands)

		Program Revenues			Net (Expense) Revenue and Changes in Net Assets			
					Primary Government			Component Unit
	Expenses	Fees, Fines and Charges for Services	Operating Grants and Contributions	Capital Grants and Contributions	Governmental Activities	Business-type Activities	Total	Auditorium-Coliseum-Convention Center Authority
Activities								
Primary government:								
Governmental—								
Public safety	$ 214,502	$ 26,611	$ 8,393	$ 1,992	$ (177,506)	$ —	$ (177,506)	$ —
Sanitation	35,990	9,318	5	—	(26,667)	—	(26,667)	—
General administration	35,065	9,981	—	—	(25,084)	—	(25,084)	—
Support services	6,104	3,323	—	—	(2,781)	—	(2,781)	—
Engineering and property management	20,187	3,776	—	—	(16,411)	—	(16,411)	—
Streets and highways	42,350	4,166	18,758	681	(18,745)	—	(18,745)	—
Culture and recreation	6,125	—	177	—	(5,948)	—	(5,948)	—
Community planning and development	42,895	8,003	13,822	—	(21,070)	—	(21,070)	—
Interest and other charges	29,942	-	—	—	(29,942)	—	(29,942)	—
Total governmental	433,160	65,178	41,155	2,673	(324,154)	—	(324,154)	—
Business-type—								
Water	63,904	70,406	—	21,952	—	28,454	28,454	—
Sewer	83,243	82,416	—	39,937	—	39,110	39,110	—
Storm water	12,757	23,124	150	2,732	—	13,249	13,249	—
Airport	87,580	91,659	—	17,828	—	21,907	21,907	—
Public transit	63,683	8,972	7,945	19,902	—	(26,864)	(26,864)	—
Total business-type	311,167	276,577	8,095	102,351	—	75,856	75,856	—
Total primary government	$ 744,327	$ 341,755	$ 49,250	$ 105,024	(324,154)	75,856	(248,298)	—
Component Unit:								
Auditorium-Coliseum-Convention Center Authority	$ 28,128	$ 24,477	$ 2,807	$ —	—	—	—	(844)
General revenues:								
Taxes—								
Property					237,125	—	237,125	—
Sales					52,486	—	52,486	—
Sales, levied for Public Transit					-	51,061	51,061	—
Utility franchise					22,009	—	22,009	—
Occupancy					12,972	—	12,972	—
Prepared foods					12,932	—	12,932	—
Licenses					21,331	—	21,331	—
Grants and contributions not restricted to specific programs					262,969	—	262,969	—
Investments earnings					20,852	30,786	51,638	232
Miscellaneous					2,908	564	3,472	—
Transfers					(18,701)	18,701	-	—
Total general revenues and transfers					626,883	101,112	727,995	232
Change in net assets					302,729	176,968	479,697	(612)
Net assets—beginning					2,905,123	1,474,357	4,379,480	10,421
Net assets—ending					$ 3,207,852	$ 1,651,325	$ 4,859,177	$ 9,809

TABLE 2–5
Charlotte, North Carolina

Balance Sheet
Governmental Funds
June 30, 2002 (in thousands)

	General	Debt Service	Capital Projects	Other Govermental Funds	Total Governmental Funds
Assets					
Cash and cash equivalents	$ 99,763	$117,087	$123,435	$ 69,844	$410,129
Receivables, net:					
Property taxes	6,645	1,121	225	21	8,012
Accounts	3,209	—	5,719	578	9,506
Other	—	17	—	511	528
Total receivables	9,854	1,138	5,944	1,110	18,046
Due from other governmental agencies	21,162	2,747	4,933	9,968	38,810
Due from other funds	—	2,300	—	987	3,287
Inventories	715	—	—	—	715
Restricted assets:					
Cash and cash equivalents	—	14,237	29,013	—	43,250
Notes receivable	110	—	18,137	36,008	54,255
Total assets	$131,604	$137,509	$181,462	$117,917	$568,492
Liabilities and fund balances					
Liabilities:					
Accounts payable	$19,651	$314	$10,505	$12,770	$43,240
Deposits and retainage payable	1,472	—	2,034	779	4,285
Due to other funds	1,068	—	2,300	—	3,368
Due to component unit	—	—	—	643	643
Deferred revenues	17,043	1,138	24,081	32,710	74,972
Liabilities payable from restricted assets	—	—	1,440	—	1,440
Total liabilities	39,234	1,452	40,360	46,902	127,948
Fund balances:					
Reserved for—					
State statute	14,316	5,047	—	—	19,363
Convention Center debt service	—	14,194	—	—	14,194
Encumbrances	23,064	—	—	7,195	30,259
Inventories	715	—	—	—	715
Loans	—	—	—	2,737	2,737
Perpetual care	—	—	—	2,976	2,976
Unreserved, reported in—					
General fund	54,275	—	—	—	54,275
Debt service fund	—	116,816	—	—	116,816
Capital projects fund	—	—	141,102	—	141,102
Special revenue funds	—	—	—	58,107	58,107
Total fund balances	92,370	136,057	141,102	71,015	440,544
Total liabilities and fund balances	$131,604	$137,509	$181,462	$117,917	$568,492

Reconciliation of the Governmental Funds Balance Sheet to the Statement of Net Assets

Total fund balances for governmental funds	$ 440,544
Total net assets reported for governmental activities in the statement of net assets is different because:	
Capital assets used in governmental activities are not financial resources and, therefore, are not reported in the funds.	3,370,457
Other long-term assets are not available to pay for current-period expenditures and, therefore, are deferred in the funds.	75,913
Internal service funds are used to charge the costs of insured and uninsured risks of loss as well as employee health and life claims to individual funds. The assets and liabilities of the internal service funds are included in governmental activities in the statement of net assets.	21,366
Long-term liabilities are not due and payable in the current period and therefore are not reported in the funds.	(700,428)
Total net assets of governmental activities	$3,207,852

TABLE 2-6
Charlotte, North Carolina

Statement of Revenues, Expenditures, and Changes in Fund Balances
Governmental Funds
for the Year Ended June 30, 2002 (in thousands)

	General	Debt Service	Capital Projects	Other Governmental Funds	Total Governmental Funds
Revenues					
Property taxes	$189,270	$ 31,548	$ 11,098	$ 1,307	$ 233,223
Other taxes	37,306	12,612	9,572	20,543	80,033
Intergovernmental	43,404	3,029	471	39,541	86,445
Licenses, fees, and fines	32,540	41	9,941	5,307	47,829
Investment earnings	4,925	5,442	6,138	3,627	20,132
Administrative charges	13,832	—	—	—	13,832
Charges for current services	3,802	—	—	—	3,802
Facility fees	—	—	—	230	230
Miscellaneous	4,127	584	545	4,246	9,502
Total revenues	$329,206	$ 53,256	$ 37,765	$ 74,801	$ 495,028
Expenditures					
Current—					
Public Safety	187,048	—	—	16,383	203,431
Sanitation	32,385	—	—	—	32,385
General administration	28,740	—	—	5,023	33,763
Support services	15,548	—	—	—	15,548
Engineering and property management	19,318	—	—	—	19,318
Streets and highways	22,230	—	—	19,258	41,488
Culture and recreation	—	—	—	2,807	2,807
Community planning and development	12,390	—	—	21,125	33,515
Debt service—					
Principal	—	50,500	—	—	50,500
Interest and other charges	—	32,157	—	—	32,157
Capital outlay	—	—	133,542	—	133,542
Total expenditures	$317,659	$ 82,657	$133,542	$ 64,596	$ 598,454
Excess (deficiency) of revenues over (under) expenditures	$ 11,547	$(29,401)	$(95,777)	$ 10,205	$(103,426)
Other financing sources (uses)					
Sales of capital assets	1,035	8,435	6,152	—	15,622
Proceeds from bonds	—	—	73,000	—	73,000
Proceeds from certificates of participation	—	358	36,961	—	37,319
Proceeds from refundings	—	30,738	—	—	30,738
Payments to refunded bond escrow agent	—	(30,738)	—	—	(30,738)
Transfers-in	2,985	37,450	6,573	8,609	55,617
Transfers-out	(23,810)	(293)	(25,288)	(23,827)	(73,218)
Total other financing sources (uses)	$ (19,790)	$ 45,950	$ 97,398	$(15,218)	$ 108,340
Net change in fund balances	$(8,243)	$16,549	$1,621	$(5,013)	$ 4,914
Fund balances—beginning	100,613	119,508	139,481	76,028	435,630
Fund balances—ending	$ 92,370	$136,057	$141,102	$ 71,015	$ 440,544

TABLE 2–7
Charlotte, North Carolina

Reconciliation of the Statement of Revenues, Expenditures, and Changes in Fund Balances Governmental Funds to the Statement of Activities for the Year Ended June 30, 2002

Net change in fund balances—total governmental funds	$ 4,914
The change in net assets reported for governmental activities in the statement of activities is different because:	
Governmental funds report capital outlays as expenditures. However, in the statement of activities the cost of those assets is allocated over their estimated useful lives and reported as depreciation expense. This is the amount by which capital outlays exceeded depreciation in the current period.	119,126
The net effect of various miscellaneous transactions involving capital assets (i.e., sales and donations) is to increase net assets.	226,301
Revenues in the statement of activities that do not provide current financial resources are not reported as revenues in the funds.	12,337
The issuance of long-term debt (e.g., bonds and certificates of participation) provides current financial resources to governmental funds, while the repayment of the principal of long-term debt consumes the current financial resources of governmental funds. Neither transaction has any effect on net assets in the government-wide statements. Also, governmental funds report the effect of issuance costs, premiums, discounts, and similar items when debt is issued, whereas these amounts are deferred and amortized in the statement of activities. This amount is the net effect of these differences in the treatment of long-term debt and related items.	(57,992)
Some expenses reported in the statement of activities do not require the use of current financial resources and therefore are not reported as expenditures in governmental funds.	(2,645)
Internal service funds are used to charge the costs of insured and uninsured risks of loss as well as employee health and life claims to individual funds. The net revenue of certain activities of the internal service funds is reported with governmental activities.	688
Change in net assets of governmental activities.	$302,729

Most general-purpose governments engage in three broad categories of activities:

- ***Governmental*** activities are those financed predominantly through taxes and intergovernmental grants.
- ***Business-type*** activities are those financed predominantly through user charges.
- ***Fiduciary*** activities are those for which the government acts as a trustee or agent for individuals, external organizations, or other governments.

Corresponding roughly to these three kinds of activities, governments classify funds into three broad categories: governmental funds, proprietary funds, and fiduciary funds.

GOVERNMENTAL FUNDS

Governmental funds are maintained to account for governments' operating and financing activities. There are five primary types of governmental funds.

- ***General fund.*** This fund accounts for all resources that are not required to be accounted for in other funds; in essence, it accounts for all unrestricted resources.
- ***Special revenue funds.*** These funds account for revenues that are restricted to specific purposes.
- ***Debt service funds.*** These funds are used to account for resources set aside for the payment of interest and principal on long-term debt.
- ***Capital projects funds.*** These funds are used to account for resources held for the acquisition or construction of major capital facilities.
- ***Permanent funds.*** These funds are used to report resources that are legally restricted in that only earnings, not principal, may be used to support the government's programs.

PROPRIETARY FUNDS

Proprietary funds are used to account for the business-type activities of a government—those that are similar to activities carried out in the private sector. There are two types of proprietary funds:

- ***Enterprise funds.*** These funds are used to account for business-type activities in which the government sells goods or services to the general public.
- ***Internal service funds.*** These funds are used to account for business-type activities in which the customers are other government departments or agencies.

Governmental funds may be characterized as **expendable funds,** in that their resources are received from taxes, fees, or other sources, and then spent. There is no expectation that the funds will be reimbursed for services rendered to constituents or other departments. By contrast, proprietary funds are said to be **nonexpendable** (or **revolving**) funds. The government may make an initial contribution to establish a proprietary fund, but thereafter the fund is expected to "pay its own way" (at least in part) through customer charges.

FIDUCIARY FUNDS

Fiduciary funds are used to account for resources held by the government but that are intended to benefit parties other than the government itself. There are two types of fiduciary funds:

- ***Trust funds.*** These are used to account for assets that the government holds as a trustee (a party that administers property for a beneficiary) for the benefit of parties other than the government itself. They include pension funds (in which the assets are held for the benefit of employees), investment trust funds (established when one government, such as a state, maintains an investment pool for other governments, such as cities, towns or school districts), and private purpose trust funds (in which the assets are held for the benefit of individuals, private organizations, or other governments).
- ***Agency funds.*** These are generally used to account for assets (e.g., taxes collected by one government on behalf of another) that a government holds as an agent (one who acts on behalf of another) temporarily for other parties. The government is mainly responsible for receiving the assets and for distributing them to the parties entitled to them. Agency funds differ from trust funds in

that the government typically holds the assets for a shorter period of time and has only limited responsibility for investing them.

Unlike the other types of funds, fiduciary funds are neither consolidated with, nor even incorporated into, government-wide statements. That is because they benefit only outsiders and a government cannot expect to have use of their resources.

Whereas a government should have only one general fund, it may have any number of the other types of funds. For example, the city may maintain a separate special revenue fund for each revenue source that is restricted. Similarly, it may maintain a separate capital projects fund for each of its major capital projects and a separate debt service fund for each issue of outstanding bonds.

Having provided an overview of the funds structure, we now take a more comprehensive look at each of the main types of funds.

WHAT'S NOTABLE ABOUT EACH TYPE OF GOVERNMENTAL FUND?

THE GENERAL FUND

The general fund is used to account for all resources that are not legally or contractually restricted or arbitrarily set aside for specific activities. All funds are not created equal; the general fund is more equal than the others. In a city or other general-purpose government, it embraces most major governmental functions—police, fire, street maintenance, sanitation, and administration.

Why does one single fund cover so many functions? Recall the rationale for fund accounting. Funds are established mainly to assure that governments adhere to resource restrictions. A government's fund structure rarely mirrors its organizational structure. Funds divide a government into categories of resource restriction, not functional departments or operations. To keep their accounting systems as simple as possible, governments should establish the minimum number of funds to assure legal compliance or efficient administration. Governments finance their general operations mainly with unrestricted resources, such as property taxes. Therefore, they can legally intermingle these resources and can properly account for all activities financed with unrestricted resources in a single fund.

By noting the assets and liabilities reported in a fund, a statement user can draw meaningful inferences as to the fund's measurement focus and basis of accounting. The balance sheet of the general fund in Table 2-5 includes assets other than cash. Were the general fund accounted for on a cash basis, its only asset would be cash. Therefore, the general fund is accounted for on a basis broader than simply cash.

At the same time, however, the balance sheet in Table 2-5 shows neither long-lived assets nor long-term debt. Obviously the city owns police cars, fire equipment, computers, and buildings. Moreover, it probably financed some of its long-lived assets with long-term debt. Were the general fund accounted for on a full accrual basis (full economic resources measurement focus), these assets and liabilities would be reported on the balance sheet. Instead, they have apparently been written off as acquired (and presumably listed in off-the-balance sheet ledgers or other records). Therefore, the general fund is accounted for on a basis between cash and full accrual (i.e., a modified accrual basis) and has a measurement focus between cash and all economic resources (i.e., current financial resources). This basis and measurement focus is discussed in depth beginning in Chapter 4.

SPECIAL REVENUE FUNDS

Special revenue funds are established to account for resources legally restricted to specified purposes. Examples of typical restrictions include:

- Gasoline tax revenues that must be used for highway maintenance
- Lottery fund proceeds that must be used for education
- A state law-enforcement grant that must be used to train police officers
- Private donations that must be used to repair and maintain parks and other recreational facilities

As suggested by the mix of assets and liabilities reported on the balance sheet, special revenue funds, like the general fund and, indeed, like all governmental funds, use a common basis of accounting. Accordingly, almost all of the guidelines pertaining to the general fund set forth in this text can be extended to special revenue funds and other governmental funds.

DEBT SERVICE FUNDS

Debt service funds are similar to special revenue funds in that they are maintained to account for resources restricted to a specific purpose: the payment of principal and interest on long-term debt. Debt service funds have much in common with sinking funds (resources set aside to retire debt) maintained by businesses.

Conspicuously missing from the balance sheet of a debt service fund is the obligation for the debt being serviced. This should come as no surprise. First, the purpose of the debt service fund is to account for the resources being accumulated to service the debt—not the debt itself. Second, as previously noted, the debt service fund is categorized as a governmental fund, like the general fund and special revenue funds, and no governmental fund gives recognition to long-term obligations. The long-term debt, for which resources are being accumulated in a debt service fund, is reported only in the government-wide (full accrual) statements and supplementary schedules.

The one exception to this general rule, that the debt being serviced is excluded from the debt service funds, applies to interest and principal that have matured and are therefore current obligations. They would be reported as matured interest payable or matured bonds payable. But this exception is of only minor practical import. On the day the interest or principal matures, it should be paid and the obligation satisfied. Therefore, on year-end financial statements the liability for interest or principal should be reported only if payment is due but for some reason has been delayed.

Debt service funds derive their resources from other funds (e.g., transfers from the general fund) or from taxes or fees dedicated to debt service. Fund resources are expended to pay principal and interest.

When governments accumulate resources to service their long-term obligations, they commonly invest them in commercial paper, treasury bills, and other financial instruments that, while secure, still provide a reasonable return. Typically, therefore, many debt service fund transactions relate to the purchase and sale of marketable securities and the recognition of investment earnings and related costs.

CAPITAL PROJECTS FUNDS

Capital projects funds, like debt service funds, are categorized as governmental funds and are comparable to special revenue funds. They are maintained to account for the financial resources to be used for the acquisition or construction of major capital facilities. Governments often issue bonds to finance a specific project. The resources received are restricted to that project and must be placed in a restricted fund. Capital projects funds typically derive their resources from the proceeds of bonds. However, they may also receive resources that were initially received by other funds and subsequently earmarked for the acquisition of capital assets.

Just as debt service funds are used to account for the resources accumulated to service a debt—but not the debt itself—so too are capital projects funds used to account for the resources set aside to purchase or construct long-lived assets, but not the assets themselves. The assets, whether in the form of construction in progress or of completed projects, are reported only in the government-wide statements and in supplementary schedules.

Moreover, as with the resources accumulated to service their debts, governments must invest any excess cash awaiting expenditure for capital projects. Therefore, many transactions of typical capital projects funds, like those of debt service funds, relate to investment activities.

PERMANENT FUNDS

Permanent funds are a new type of governmental fund, a creation of the GASB Statement No. 34 reporting model. Permanent funds are a type of trust fund and under the old model were considered fiduciary funds. The new model, however, distinguishes between permanent funds and private purpose trust funds. Permanent funds and private purpose trust funds are similar in that usually only the income, not the principal, may be spent. They differ, though, in that permanent funds benefit the government itself whereas private purpose trust funds (addressed in the section pertaining to fiduciary funds that follows) benefit individuals, private organizations, or other governments.

Suppose, for example, that a government received a donation to support one of its parks. The resources received were to be invested and only the income, not the principal, could be expended. The government would establish a permanent fund to account for and maintain the donation (the principal). As income is earned, the government would transfer it to a special revenue fund, from which it could be used for the intended purpose.

WHAT'S NOTABLE ABOUT EACH TYPE OF PROPRIETARY FUND?

The financial statements of the two types of proprietary funds—the enterprise funds and the internal service funds—are strikingly different from those of the governmental funds. Instead, as shown in Tables 2-8 and 2-9, the statement of net assets (balance sheet) and the statement of revenues, expenses, and changes in net assets (income statement) look decidedly like those of businesses. There are, however, a few exceptions. Thus, for example, the net asset (equity) section of the balance sheet takes the form Assets – Liabilities = Net assets (as opposed to the conventional Assets = Liabilities + Net assets). Further, the net asset section highlights the amount invested in capital assets (capital assets less related debt) instead of showing contributed capital and retained earnings. Most significant, however, is that like the statements of businesses (and unlike the corresponding statements of governmental funds) the statement of net assets reports capital assets and long-term debt and the statement of revenues and expenses includes depreciation.

Proprietary funds are used to account for activities that are operated in a manner similar to private business enterprises and in which a government's intent is to recover costs primarily through user charges. Because one of a government's typical objectives in providing the service is to at least break even, the government officials responsible for the activity require the same types of financial information as their

TABLE 2-8
Charlotte, North Carolina

Statement of Net Assets
Proprietary Funds
June 30, 2002 (in thousands)

	Business-type Activities—Enterprise Funds					Governmental Activities—Internal Service Funds
	Water and Sewer	Storm Water	Airport	Public Transit	Total	
Assets						
Current assets:						
Cash and cash equivalents	$ 91,497	$ 28,846	$178,374	$119,556	$ 418,273	$48,577
Receivables, net—						
Accounts	27,754	4,576	10,157	213	42,700	—
Other	1,599	353	1,789	862	4,603	1,685
Total receivables	29,353	4,929	11,946	1,075	47,303	1,685
Due from other governmental agencies	1,863	234	7,103	17,104	26,304	—
Due from other funds	—	—	—	—	—	81
Inventories	2,086	—	—	910	2,996	—
Total current assets	124,799	34,009	197,423	138,645	494,876	50,343
Noncurrent assets:						
Restricted assets—						
Cash and cash equivalents	25,737	2,963	74,967	9,317	112,984	—
Investments	146,881	—	31,373	—	178,254	—
Total restricted assets	172,618	2,963	106,340	9,317	291,238	—
Accounts receivable	—	—	15,080	—	15,080	—
Deferred charges	5,638	362	7,686	110	13,796	—
Capital assets—						
Land	23,602	—	139,499	3,775	166,876	—
Buildings	10,668	—	485,572	8,330	504,570	—
Improvements other than buildings:						
Water and sewer systems	1,744,916	—	—	—	1,744,916	—
Storm water systems	—	85,598	—	—	85,598	—
Runways	—	—	133,281	—	133,281	—
Other	—	—	28,515	3,848	32,363	—
Total improvements other than buildings	1,744,916	85,598	161,796	3,848	1,996,158	—
Machinery and equipment	16,188	334	9,534	70,716	96,772	228
Construction in progress	275,032	79,226	38,181	20,138	412,577	—
Total capital assets	2,070,406	165,158	834,582	106,807	3,176,953	228
Less accumulated depreciation	413,691	14,789	257,879	33,830	720,189	117
Total capital assets, net	1,656,715	150,369	576,703	72,977	2,456,764	111
Total noncurrent assets	1,834,971	153,694	705,809	82,404	2,776,878	111
Total assets	1,959,770	187,703	903,232	221,049	3,271,754	50,454

(Continues)

TABLE 2-8
Charlotte, North Carolina *(Continued)*

Statement of Net Assets
Proprietary Funds
June 30, 2002 (in thousands)

	Business-type Activities—Enterprise Funds					Governmental Activities—Internal Service Funds
	Water and Sewer	Storm Water	Airport	Public Transit	Total	
Liabilities						
Current liabilities:						
Accounts payable	$ 1,839	$ 1,794	$ 11,627	$ 4,081	$ 19,341	—
Claims payable	—	—	—	—	—	25,429
Deposits and retainage payable	2,704	2,351	1,186	77	6,318	—
Accrued interest payable	12,896	585	183	64	13,728	—
Current maturities of long-term liabilities	35,177	1,892	3,802	1,431	42,302	—
Total current liabilities	52,616	6,622	16,798	5,653	81,689	25,429
Current liabilities payable from restricted assets:						
Accounts payable	8,645	—	1,405	—	10,050	—
Deposits and retainage payable	6,374	—	2,719	—	9,093	—
Accrued interest payable	—	—	7,936	—	7,936	—
Revenue bonds payable	—	—	8,730	—	8,730	—
Total current liabilities payable from restricted assets	15,019	—	20,790	—	35,809	—
Noncurrent liabilities:						
General obligation bonds payable—net of deferred amount on refunding of $12,677	447,757	20,414	6,171	667	475,009	—
Revenue bonds payable—net of deferred amount on refunding of $5,962	529,570	33,852	426,143	—	989,565	—
Other financing agreements	16,878	—	—	10,245	27,123	—
Refundable water and sewer construction deposits	7,501	—	—	—	7,501	—
Due to participants	—	—	—	—	—	2,640
Compensated absences payable	918	152	405	954	2,429	64
Arbitrage payable	13	—	2,246	—	2,259	—
Total noncurrent liabilities	1,002,637	54,418	434,965	11,866	1,503,886	2,704
Total liabilities	1,070,272	61,040	472,553	17,519	1,621,384	28,133
Net assets						
Invested in capital assets, net of related debt	795,484	97,355	238,740	70,177	1,201,756	111
Restricted for:						
Debt service	14,604	2,894	37,830	—	55,328	—
Working capital	—	—	10,832	—	10,832	—
Unrestricted	79,410	26,414	143,277	133,353	382,454	22,210
Total net assets	$ 889,498	$126,663	$430,679	$203,530	$1,650,370	$22,321
Adjustment to reflect the consolidation of internal service fund activities related to enterprise funds.					955	
Net assets of business-type activities					$1,651,325	

TABLE 2-9
Charlotte, North Carolina

Statement of Revenues, Expenses, and Changes in Fund Net Assets
Proprietary Funds
for the Year Ended June 30, 2002 (in thousands)

	Business-type Activities—Enterprise Funds					Governmental Activities—
	Water and Sewer	Storm Water	Airport	Public Transit	Total	Internal Service Funds
Operating revenues						
Charges for services	$141,822	$ 23,124	$ 88,664	$ 8,972	$262,582	$48,971
Capacity fees	9,067	—	—	—	9,067	—
Miscellaneous	1,933	—	2,995	—	4,928	—
Total operating revenues	152,822	23,124	91,659	8,972	276,577	48,971
Operating expenses						
Administration	13,728	778	8,558	10,125	33,189	5,581
Operations and maintenance	53,270	9,143	22,871	42,649	127,933	—
Claims and insurance premiums	—	—	—	—	—	42,389
Other	714	—	4,308	1,426	6,448	—
Depreciation	42,276	1,261	22,441	6,702	72,680	26
Total operating expenses	109,988	11,182	58,178	60,902	240,250	47,996
Operating income (loss)	42,834	11,942	33,481	(51,930)	36,327	975
Nonoperating revenues (expenses)						
Sales tax	—	—	—	51,061	51,061	—
Grant contributions	—	150	—	7,945	8,095	—
Investment earnings	11,449	1,914	11,661	5,762	30,786	1,809
Interest expense and other charges	(37,721)	(1,585)	(20,750)	(479)	(60,535)	—
Non-airline terminal revenue distribution	—	—	(6,498)	—	(6,498)	—
Miscellaneous	562	2	(2,319)	(2,520)	(4,275)	—
Total nonoperating revenues (expenses)	(25,710)	481	(17,906)	61,769	18,634	1,809
Income before contributions and transfers	17,124	12,423	15,575	9,839	54,961	2,784
Capital contributions	61,889	2,732	17,828	19,902	102,351	—
Transfers in	—	—	—	18,701	18,701	—
Transfers out	—	—	—	—	—	(1,100)
Change in net assets	79,013	15,155	33,403	48,442	176,013	1,684
Total net assets—beginning	810,485	111,508	397,276	155,088		20,637
Total net assets—ending	$889,498	$126,663	$430,679	$203,530		$22,321
Adjustment to reflect the consolidation of internal service fund activities related to enterprise funds.					955	
Change in net assets of business-type activities					$176,968	

counterparts in industry. For example, they need data on the full cost (including depreciation) of the services provided so that they are able to establish prices. Outsiders, such as the tax or rate payers, concerned with the activity's performance or fiscal condition, need the same general information as would corporate shareholders. For this reason, proprietary funds are accounted for in essentially the same manner as private businesses. As suggested by their balance sheets, they employ the full accrual basis of accounting and their measurement focus is on all economic resources. This text addresses the issue of which activities should properly be accounted for in proprietary funds, but devotes little attention to specific principles and procedures. Most students, though unaware of it, have been studying proprietary funds since they first matriculated in their accounting principles courses.

ENTERPRISE FUNDS

Governmental activities accounted for in enterprise funds provide services to the public at large. The following are examples of the types of activities that governments may account for in enterprise funds:

- Utilities, such as electric, gas, and water
- Golf courses
- Hospitals
- Mass transportation
- Parking garages
- Airport and harbor facilities
- Housing authorities

Many government enterprises are financed similarly to businesses. Although a government enterprise does not sell stock to the general public, it may issue bonds (called revenue bonds). The principal and interest of the bonds are payable exclusively out of the revenues of the fund itself—not out of the general revenues of the government at large. Therefore, the resources of the fund must be kept intact and cannot be commingled with those of the government's other funds.

INTERNAL SERVICE FUNDS

Departments accounted for in internal service funds provide goods or services to other departments within the same government (or occasionally to other governments). They bill the receiving departments at rates intended to cover the cost of the goods or services. Although there are no specific guidelines as to which intragovernment activities should be accounted for in internal service funds, the following are examples:

- A vehicle repair service that maintains and services the cars and trucks of the police department, fire department, sanitation department, and so forth
- A motor pool that acts as an intragovernment rental car agency
- An electronic data processing department that maintains records and performs computer services for all other departments
- A store that sells office supplies to the other government departments
- A print shop that provides government-wide printing services

Internal service funds are typically established with contributions of resources from the general fund, or some other fund. Thereafter they are expected to be self-sustaining.

Because internal service funds sell their goods and services to other departments, most of their transactions are with other funds. However, internal service fund accounting is relatively straightforward, as long as each fund is seen as a separate accounting entity. When an internal service fund bills another department, it would recognize both a revenue and a receivable. Simultaneously, the fund that accounts for the other department would record both an expenditure and a payable. Most of the other departments to which an internal service fund sells its goods or services are likely to be accounted for in the government's general fund or one of its other enterprise funds. This is primarily because most governmental operations (as opposed to accumulations of resources for specific purposes) are accounted for in those funds. Accordingly, they are shown apart from the enterprise funds and under the caption "Governmental Activities—Internal Service Funds."

WHAT'S NOTABLE ABOUT EACH TYPE OF FIDUCIARY FUND?

Fiduciary funds, in contrast to governmental and proprietary funds, benefit parties other than the government itself. These include employees, other governments, and specific individuals, corporations, or not-for-profit organizations. Accordingly, their activities do not result in revenues or expenses to the government—only in additions or deductions to their own net assets. Although the financial statements of fiduciary funds are included in a government's comprehensive annual financial report, they are not included in the government-wide financial statements.

TRUST FUNDS

Kohler's Dictionary for Accountants defines a trust fund as a "fund held by one person (trustee) for the benefit of another, pursuant to the provisions of a formal trust agreement."[3] Most notably, as indicated by the definition, the resources of trust funds (like those of agency funds, the other type of fiduciary fund) are intended to benefit parties other than the government itself. There are three types of trust funds:

- **Pension trust funds** benefit the government's employees by providing income, disability income, health care insurance, and related forms of remuneration to retirees and their beneficiaries.
- **Investment trust funds,** which are similar to mutual funds, benefit the parties, usually other governments, that have entrusted their resources to the fund.
- **Private purpose trust funds** encompass all trust funds other than pension and investment trust funds. They benefit specific individuals, governments, or businesses. One type of private purpose trust fund is an **escheat** trust fund. Escheat property is the name given to property that reverts to a state when a person dies in the absence of heirs or other legal claimants. It also includes abandoned and unclaimed property, such as balances in bank accounts in which there has been no activity for a specified period of time. Private purpose trust funds may also be used to account for resources held for parties other than the government itself, such as a local not-for-profit historical society or museum.

The resources of trust funds are generally held in financial instruments such as stocks and bonds, and how well they perform in terms of investment earnings is of key concern to beneficiaries and fund managers. Therefore, they are accounted for on a full accrual basis and the measurement focus is on economic resources.

[3] W. W. Cooper and Yuji Ijiri, eds., *Kohler's Dictionary for Accountants*, 6th ed. (Englewood Cliffs, N.J.: Prentice-Hall, 1983), p. 516.

AGENCY FUNDS

Agency funds are used to account for assets held on behalf of other governments, funds, or individuals. Most commonly they are established to maintain control over:

- Taxes collected by one government for the benefit of another
- Special assessments collected to repay debt that the government services but for which it is not responsible
- Refundable deposits
- Pass-through grants—those requiring a government (such as a state) to distribute funds to other parties (such as school districts or individuals) but for which the government has no financial involvement and for which it performs no significant administrative functions such as selecting recipients or monitoring performance

Custodial in nature, agency funds are not used to account for significant governmental operations. Consequently, agency funds are a student's delight—entities of the utmost simplicity. Their balance sheets show only assets (commonly cash and investments) and liabilities (the amounts owing to the beneficiaries). Assets always equal liabilities and hence there are no net assets. Accordingly, governments need not even prepare a statement of changes in net assets.

In summary, governments maintain three main types of funds: governmental, proprietary, and fiduciary. The governmental funds, all of which are accounted for on a modified accrual basis, consist of the general fund, special revenue funds, debt service funds, capital project funds, and permanent funds. The proprietary funds, which are used to account for business-type activities and thus are on a full accrual basis, consist of enterprise funds and internal service funds. The fiduciary funds consist of trust funds and agency funds. The reporting focus of trust funds is on net assets and on the changes in net assets during the period. The reporting focus of agency funds is on their assets and liabilities, the two of which are always equal.

WHAT IS INCLUDED IN A GOVERNMENT'S COMPREHENSIVE ANNUAL FINANCIAL REPORT (CAFR)?

So far we have discussed the basic funds maintained by a government. This section and the one that follows are directed to how governments report on these funds.

The complete annual report, known as a **Comprehensive Annual Financial Report (CAFR),** consists of more than just the basic statements (some of which are illustrated in this chapter). Indeed, the annual reports of states, cities, counties, and other general-purpose governments are notable for their bulk. The reports of medium to large cities may exceed 200 pages, few of which contain pictures or other touches of frivolity. Government accountants are not typically compensated by the page. Why then are the reports so lengthy?

Annual reports are directed to different groups of users, each of which needs different types of information. As previously noted, some users, for example, focus on whether the government's current taxpayers are paying for the cost of services they are receiving. They want to view the government as a whole and want to take into account all the resources received and expended. Others are more concerned with budgetary compliance. They need data that focus on individual funds and are directed to flows of cash and other short-term financial resources. Further, as pointed out in Chapter 1, the fiscal wherewithal of a government cannot be assessed in isolation of the community to which it must provide services and from which it must draw its resources. As a consequence, the CAFR includes statements that combine and report upon the government's activities from both a government-wide and a fund perspective. It also includes the statements of individual funds and an array of statistical data on both the government itself and its jurisdiction.

The CAFR is divided into three main sections:

- ***Introductory section.*** This includes a letter of transmittal and general information as to how the government is organized and who are its key elected and administrative officials. The letter of transmittal (usually from the chief executive or finance officer) presents an overview of financial and economic conditions faced by the government and summarizes recent key financial developments. The introductory section may also include a "Certificate of Achievement for Excellence in Financial Reporting" if the CAFR satisfies the reporting standards of the Government Finance Officers Association, an independent professional organization.
- ***Financial section.*** This is the main body of the CAFR. It contains
  - **Management's discussion and analysis (MD&A)**; similar in nature to the MD&A that is part of the financial statements of businesses, this narrative presents a brief, nontechnical overview of the government's financial performance during the year and its financial position at year-end
  - The basic financial statements (to be discussed in the following paragraphs)
  - Notes to the statements
  - Required supplementary information
  - Combining and individual fund financial statements (if required)

Figure 2-1 illustrates the key elements of this section.

- ***Statistical section.*** This contains current and historical data as to the jurisdiction's demographics, economy, tax rates, outstanding debt, and other information that supplements the basic financial statements. The specific data provided will, of course, differ among different types of governments.

THE FINANCIAL SECTION: AN OVERVIEW

The basic financial statements present information from both a government-wide and a fund perspective. As a consequence, they include up to ten primary statements and a dozen supplementary statements and schedules (depending on the government's

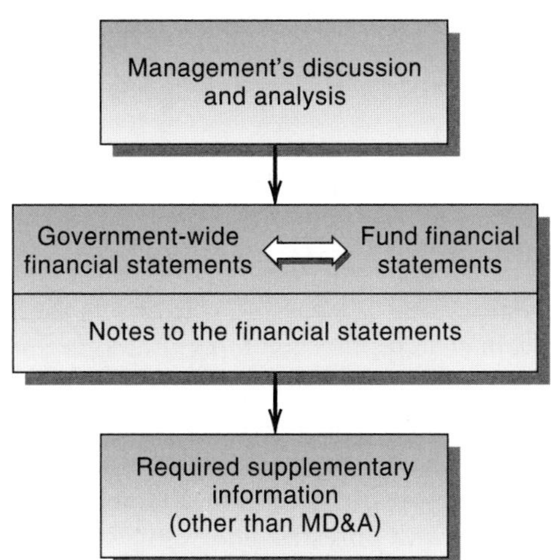

FIGURE 2-1 Minimum Requirements for General Purpose Financial Statements

Source: GASB Statement No. 34, *Basic Financial Statements—and Management's Discussion and Analysis—for State and Local Governments.*

fund structure) that are incorporated into notes and supplementary sections. The government-wide statements are on a full accrual basis. The fund statements are on the basis of accounting required for the specific category of fund—modified accrual basis for governmental funds and full accrual basis for proprietary funds.

Government-Wide Statements

There are just two government-wide statements:

- Statement of net assets (balance sheet)
- Statement of activities (statement of revenues and expenses)

As illustrated in Table 2-3, the statement of net assets is similar to the balance sheet of a business. Unlike that of a business, it has separate columns for governmental and business-type activities, but the totals column consolidates the two types of activities. An additional column presents information on "component units"—entities that are economically intertwined with the government albeit legally separate (and which are discussed in Chapter 11). Moreover, the difference between the government's assets and liabilities is shown as "net assets," rather than "owner's equity" as it would be on the balance sheet of a business.

By contrast, the statement of activities in Table 2-4 bears no resemblance, at least at first glance, to the income statement of a business. Unlike the income statement of a business, the aim of this statement is to show the net cost of each of the government's main functions and programs—the cost that must be covered by taxes and other general revenues. Accordingly, the first column reports total expenses. The next three columns indicate revenues, such as those from charges for services and program-specific grants that help defray the expenses. The next columns (one for government activities, the other for business-type activities) show the differences between the expenses and the revenues, that is, the net cost of the functions and programs. The lower portion of the statement summarizes the taxes and other general revenues of the government at large—those that cannot be associated directly with specific functions and programs and that can be used to cover the net cost of the government's programs. The difference between the net expenses and general revenues is the change in net assets.

The government-wide statements are on a full accrual basis. Therefore, the statement of net assets includes both capital (long-lived) assets and long-term debt. Correspondingly, program and function expenses include charges for depreciation, even though they are not broken out separately. The example "Government-Wide Statement of Activities" illustrates the form and content of a government-wide statement of activities.

EXAMPLE *Government-Wide Statement of Activities*

The government of Charier City performs only two functions: public safety and recreation. Expenses of the public safety function total $100 million. It offsets these expenses, in part, through miscellaneous revenues (e.g., fees for funeral escorts and fun run patrols) of $4 million and receives a state grant of $6 million. Thus, it must cover the remaining balance of $90 million with taxes and other unrestricted revenues. The recreation function incurs $30 million in expenses but collects user fees (for swimming pools, tennis courts, and golf courses) of $8 million and receives a state grant of $9 million. It must cover $13 million with unrestricted revenues. Hence the city as a whole must cover a total of $103 million with unrestricted revenues. In fact, however, the city's revenues total $105 million, and thus the city's net assets increase during the period by $2 million.

The city's government-wide statement of activities is presented in Table 2-10. Although this format may require some getting used to, its virtue is that it highlights more clearly than the conventional statement of revenues and expenditures the net cost to the taxpayers of each of the government's functions.

Fund Statements

The three main categories of funds necessitate three sets of statements, one for each type of fund and each containing a slightly different blend of statements. The following are the basic statements for each fund category.

- ***Governmental funds***—Balance sheet; statement of revenues, expenditures, and changes in fund balances (Tables 2-5 and 2-6).
- ***Proprietary funds***—Balance sheet; statement of revenues, expenses, and changes in net assets (Tables 2-8 and 2-9); statement of cash flows (not illustrated).
- ***Fiduciary funds***—Statement of fiduciary net assets; statement of changes in fiduciary net assets (to be illustrated in Chapter 10).

As shown in Tables 2-5 and 2-6, which illustrate governmental fund statements, separate columns are presented for the general fund and each of Charlotte's "major" funds. Major funds are those in which total assets, revenues, or expenditures/expenses are at least 10 percent of the relevant fund category (governmental or enterprise) and 5 percent of the corresponding total for all governmental and enterprise funds combined. The remaining "nonmajor" funds are combined into the column "other governmental funds." Note that the governmental fund balance sheet includes a reconciliation of total governmental fund balances ($440,544) with the net governmental assets ($3,207,852) per the government-wide statement of net assets. A similar reconciliation (Table 2-7) ties the changes in fund balances per the fund statements ($4,914) with the changes in governmental net assets per the government-wide statements ($302,729).

TABLE 2-10
Charier City
Government-wide Statement of Activities (in millions)

		Program Specific Revenues		
	Total	**Charges for Services**	**Grants and Contributions**	**Net Expense to Be Covered by General Revenues**
Programs				
Public safety	$100	$ 4	$ 6	$ 90
Recreation	30	8	9	13
Total expenses	$130	$12	$15	$103
General revenues				
Property taxes				$ 60
Sales taxes				45
Total revenues				105
Change in net assets				$ 2

Notes to the financial statements include schedules of changes in capital assets and changes in long-term liabilities. Supplementary information may include *combining statements* for the nonmajor funds. The combining statements present each of the nonmajor funds in a separate column. A totals column ties to the "other funds" column of the funds statements.

Supplementary information also includes actual-to-budget comparisons for the general fund as well as other major funds.

The statements of proprietary and fiduciary funds as well as key required schedules and additional statements are discussed in more detail in subsequent chapters.

HOW DO THE FUNDS AND ANNUAL REPORTS OF NOT-FOR-PROFITS DIFFER FROM THOSE OF GOVERNMENTS?

The FASB, the rule-making authority for nongovernment entities, has established standards as to how not-for-profits must aggregate and display their financial information in general-purpose, external financial reports. These standards are substantially different from those of the GASB.

FUND ACCOUNTING AS A CONVENIENCE, NOT A MANDATE

Although the GASB mandates fund-based reporting for governments, the FASB imposes no similar requirement upon not-for-profits. As stressed earlier, fund accounting is an expedient means of control that helps assure that governments or other organizations use resources only for the purposes for which they have been dedicated. But it is not the only means. After all, private businesses also must account for resources that are restricted (e.g., income taxes withheld from employees, sales taxes collected from customers, advance payments on government contracts, proceeds from bond issues that must be spent on specific projects). Yet they do not employ fund accounting.

Unless mandated by law, not-for-profit organizations need not employ fund accounting for purposes of internal accounting and administration. They must, however, comply with FASB requirements for external reporting. But they need only distinguish between resources that are restricted and those that are unrestricted—they do not have to report on separate funds.

Nevertheless, for purposes of internal accounting and control, most not-for-profits do employ fund accounting, and they maintain funds that are comparable to those of governments. All not-for-profits maintain a *current* fund, which is like a government's general fund. Similarly, most maintain one or more *current restricted* funds, which are, in essence, special revenue funds. They may also maintain, as needed, funds to account for resources set aside for the acquisition of long-lived assets and for the repayment of debt. Many colleges and universities categorize all funds having to do with the capital assets and the related debt as **plant funds.** These include an *unexpended* plant fund (similar to a capital projects fund), a *retirement of indebtedness* fund (analogous to a debt service fund), and an *investment in plant* fund (which accounts for both capital assets and related long-term debts).

WHAT IS INCLUDED IN THE FINANCIAL REPORT OF A NOT-FOR-PROFIT ENTITY?

The financial reports of not-for-profit entities more closely resemble those of businesses than of governments. The reports need consist of only three primary statements—a statement of position (balance sheet), a statement of activities (statement of revenues and expenses), and a statement of cash flows. Unlike governments, not-for-profits need not present separate data on each of their major funds or even fund types. Although the FASB imposes some accounting and reporting requirements that are unique to not-for-profits, not-for-profits are generally subject to business standards.

The FASB requires that not-for-profits classify their net assets into three categories based on the restrictions of *donors:*

- Unrestricted
- Temporarily restricted
- Permanently restricted

Temporarily restricted resources are those that must be used for a specific purpose (e.g., to support donor-designated programs or activities) or cannot be spent until some time in the future (e.g., when a donor makes good on a pledge). Permanently restricted resources are typically endowments, only the income from which can be spent.

The FASB permits not-for-profits considerable flexibility as to the form of the primary statements. Tables 2-11 and 2-12 illustrate the statements of position and activities of a private college. In Chapter 12 we consider in detail the form and content of these statements, but we also make occasional comparisons between government and not-for-profit practices in other chapters as well.

SUMMARY

Governments and not-for-profits organize their accounting systems on the basis of funds. Funds are independent fiscal and accounting entities, each with a self-balancing set of accounts. Fund accounting is an effective means of establishing control and accountability over restricted resources.

The fund structure of a government or not-for-profit is typically based on the nature of restrictions, not on the entity's organization chart. Governments classify funds into three broad categories: governmental funds, proprietary funds, and fiduciary funds.

Governments maintain five types of governmental funds to account for their operating and financing activities:

- The **general fund** to account for resources that are not restricted and thereby not reported in any other fund
- **Special revenue** funds to account for resources that must be used for specific purposes as stipulated by legislation or by outside parties, such as grantors or donors
- **Capital projects** funds to account for resources reserved for the construction, acquisition, or improvement of capital assets
- **Debt service** funds to account for resources set aside for the payment of interest and the retirement of debt
- **Permanent** funds to report resources that are legally restricted in that only earnings, not principal, may be used to support the government's programs

Governments maintain two types of proprietary funds to account for their business-type activities:

- **Enterprise** funds to account for activities in which the government sells goods or services to the general public
- **Internal service** funds to account for activities in which the customers are other government departments or agencies

They maintain two types of fiduciary funds to account for resources that they hold for the benefit of parties other than themselves:

- **Trust** funds to account for retirement contributions and investments, for escheat property, and for investment pools
- **Agency** funds to account for resources that they hold as a custodian, such as taxes held for other governments, deposits, and pass-through grants

In June 1999, the GASB established a new reporting model that views an entity from both a government-wide and a funds perspective. The government-wide statements consolidate the entity's governmental funds and proprietary funds into governmental activities and business-type activities, respectively, and report both kinds of activities on a full accrual basis. Hence, the statement of net assets includes both capital assets and long-term debt. Additionally, the statement of changes in net assets incorporates charges for depreciation. The model's fund statements are presented either on a modified accrual basis or on a full accrual basis, depending on whether they are governmental, proprietary, or fiduciary. Fiduciary funds are reported only in the funds statements, not the government-wide statements, since they benefit parties outside of the government and not the government itself.

The complete annual report of a government—its Comprehensive Annual Financial Report (CAFR)—contains far more than basic financial statements. It also includes a letter of transmittal, a management's discussion and analysis (MD&A) that highlights the government's

TABLE 2-11
Hamilton College

Statements of Financial Position
June 30, 2003 and 2002
(dollars in thousands)

Assets	**2003**	**2002**
Cash and cash equivalents	$ 17,647	$ 25,628
Student accounts receivable	167	191
Other accounts receivable	1,184	682
Inventories	413	369
Loans to students	3,678	3,806
Deposits with trustees of debt obligations	66,701	82,572
Collateral received for securities lending	68,686	44,691
Investments	456,052	452,589
Property, plant, and equipment, net	112,014	95,459
Deferred financing costs	2,330	1,844
Other assets	891	827
Total assets	$729,763	$708,658

Liabilities and Net Assets	**2003**	**2002**
Accounts payable	$ 1,834	$ 1,909
Accrued liabilities	3,012	2,322
Deposits and advances	4,476	6,097
Long-term debt	119,525	120,874
Fair value of interest rate swap	2,728	–
Liability under securities lending transactions	68,686	44,691
Annuity and life income obligations	24,008	24,573
Funds held in trust for others	1,695	1,815
Accumulated postretirement benefit obligation	2,344	2,052
Refundable government student loans	1,643	1,768
Total liabilities	$229,951	$206,101
Net assets		
Unrestricted	$305,240	$314,061
Temporarily restricted	81,847	83,167
Permanently restricted	112,725	105,329
Total net assets	$499,812	$502,557
Total liabilities and net assets	$729,763	$708,658

TABLE 2–12
Hamilton College

Statement of Activities
Year Ended June 30, 2003 (with comparative totals for 2002)
(dollars in thousands)

	2003				2002
	Unrestricted	Temporarily Restricted	Permanently Restricted	Total	Total
Operating revenues					
Tuition and fees	$ 54,411			$ 54,411	$ 49,606
Scholarship aid	(16,436)			(16,436)	(15,368)
Net tuition and fees	$ 37,975			$ 37,975	$ 34,238
Auxiliary enterprises	12,938			12,938	12,253
Investment return	5,156	$ 14,762		19,918	16,359
Private gifts and grants	4,988	2,066		7,054	6,096
Government grants and contracts	911	2,040		2,951	2,525
Other income	1,116			1,116	1,312
Net assets released from restrictions	17,224	(17,224)			
Total operating revenues	$ 80,308	$ 1,644		$ 81,952	$ 72,783
Operating expenses					
Instruction	$ 31,575			$ 31,575	$ 28,272
Research	1,250			1,250	1,276
Public service	552			552	548
Academic support	10,622			10,622	9,226
Student services	9,017			9,017	8,165
Institutional support	13,384			13,384	10,063
Auxiliary enterprises	14,556			14,556	13,052
Total operating expenses	$ 80,956			$ 80,956	$ 70,602
Increase in net assets from operating activities	$ (648)	$ 1,644		$ 996	$ 2,181
Nonoperating activities					
Private gifts	$ 1,177	$ 974	$ 5,735	$ 7,886	$ 9,519
Investment return	(7,388)	(476)		(7,864)	(38,553)
Change in annuity and life income obligations		(2,058)		(2,058)	192
Net assets whose restrictions have changed	(41)	(1,404)	1,445		
Fair value of interest rate swap	(2,728)			(2,728)	
Other	807		216	1,023	534
(Decrease) increase in net assets from nonoperating activities	$ (8,173)	$ (2,964)	$ 7,396	$ (3,741)	$(28,308)
Net (decrease) increase in net assets	$ (8,821)	$ (1,320)	$ 7,396	$ (2,745)	$(26,127)
Net assets, beginning of year	314,061	83,167	105,329	502,557	528,684
Net assets, end of year	$305,240	$ 81,847	$112,725	$499,812	$502,557

financial performance during the year and its financial position at year-end, and a wealth of statistical data.

Although the GASB requires that entities within its purview include fund financial statements within their basic financial statements, the FASB does not. Not-for-profits, therefore, employ fund accounting because it enhances internal control, not because it is required for financial reporting. The unique characteristics of the entity and the information needs of its managers, governing board, and constituents dictate its fund structures. For purposes of external reporting, not-for-profits aggregate and present their fund data quite differently than governments. The FASB requires that not-for-profits classify their net assets into three categories: donor unrestricted, donor temporarily restricted, and donor permanently restricted.

EXERCISE FOR REVIEW AND SELF-STUDY

The newly created State Recreation District established the following funds, each of which is a separate fiscal and accounting entity:

- A general fund to account for general operating resources that are unrestricted
- A capital projects fund to account for the proceeds of bonds issued to finance the construction of recreational facilities
- A debt service fund to account for resources set aside to pay principal and interest on the bonds
- An internal service fund to account for the operations of an equipment repair department that will provide services to several departments that are accounted for within the general fund

A summary of the district's first-year transactions follows (all dollar amounts in millions).

1. It levies taxes of $300, of which it collects $250. It expects to collect the remaining $50 shortly after year-end. The taxes are unrestricted as to how they may be used.
2. It incurs $240 in general operating expenditures, of which it pays $170.
3. It issues long-term bonds of $500. The bonds must be used to finance the acquisition of recreational facilities. Accordingly, they are recorded in a restricted fund, the capital projects fund. The capital projects fund is a governmental fund. As such, it is not accounted for on a full accrual basis. It does not recognize long-term debt as an obligation. Therefore, the inflow of resources is accounted for as "bond proceeds," an account that, like a revenue, increases fund balance. The account is classified as "other financing sources" in a statement of revenues, expenditures, and changes in fund balances to distinguish it from operating revenues.
4. The district acquires $400 of recreational facilities using the resources available in the capital projects fund. Just as the capital projects fund recognizes the bond proceeds similarly to a revenue, so too it records the acquisition of the equipment as an expenditure.
5. The bond indenture (agreement) requires that the district periodically set aside funds to repay the principal of the debt. The district transfers $40 from the general fund to the fund specially created to account for resources restricted for debt service. This transaction must be recorded in the two affected independent accounting entities, the general fund and the debt service fund.
6. The repair service, which is accounted for in an internal service fund, acquires $10 of equipment, giving a long-term note in exchange. Internal service funds are proprietary funds and as such are accounted for as if they were businesses. They are accounted for on a full accrual basis; they focus on all economic resources. Hence they recognize both long-term assets and long-term obligations.
7. The repair service bills the district's other departments $15 and collects the full amount in cash. The other departments are all accounted for in the general fund. The service incurs cash operating expenses of $12 and recognizes $2 of depreciation.

    a. Prepare appropriate journal entries to record the transactions in individual funds. Governmental funds are accounted for on a modified accrual basis; proprietary funds on a full accrual basis.

    b. Based on the entries, prepare for the governmental funds a balance sheet and a statement of revenues, expenditures, and changes in fund balances.

    c. Prepare for the one proprietary fund (the internal service fund), a statement of net assets (a balance sheet), and a statement of revenues, expenses, and changes in fund net assets.

    d. Prepare a government-wide statement of net assets (balance sheet) and a government-wide statement of activities (statement of revenues and expenses). These statements should consolidate all funds, including the internal service fund, and should be on a full accrual basis. Assume that the district charged depreciation of $40 on recreational facilities (in addition to the amount charged in the internal service fund). Although internal service funds are categorized as proprietary funds, they typically provide most of their services to governmental activities. Hence, in the government-wide statements they are generally consolidated with the governmental funds rather than with enterprise funds.

QUESTIONS FOR REVIEW AND DISCUSSION

1. Distinguish between funds as the term is used in governmental as contrasted with business accounting.
2. In what way, if any, does the accounting equation as applied in government and not-for-profit accounting differ from that as applied in business accounting?
3. Upon examining the balance sheet of a large city you notice that the total assets of the general fund far exceed those of the combined total of the city's ten separate special revenue funds. Moreover, you observe that there are no funds for public safety, sanitation, health and welfare, and general administration—all important functions of the government. Why do you suppose the city hasn't attempted to "even out" the assets in the funds? Why does it not maintain funds for each of its major functional areas?
4. Why are there generally no capital projects (work in progress or other long-lived assets) in governments' capital projects funds? Why are there generally no long-term debts in debt service funds?
5. The balance sheets of both enterprise funds and internal service funds report long-lived assets and long-term debt. What does that tell you about the funds' measurement focus and basis of accounting? Explain.
6. As will be emphasized later in this text, depreciation is recorded in proprietary funds but not in governmental funds. What is the rationale for recording depreciation in proprietary funds?
7. What are fiduciary funds? What are the two main types and what is the distinction between them?
8. What is permanent about a permanent fund?
9. From what two perspectives must the new-model financial statements be prepared? How do the two differ from each other?
10. What is an agency fund? Why is it the easiest fund for which to account?
11. What is a CAFR? What are its main components?
12. Distinguish among the three categories of restrictiveness into which the net assets of not-for-profit organizations must be separated for purposes of external reporting. By whom must restrictions be imposed for resources to be considered restricted?

EXERCISES

2-1

The following relate to the town of Coupland (dollar amounts in thousands):

• Equipment used in a vehicle repair service that provides service to other departments on a cost-reimbursement basis; the equipment has a ten-year life with no salvage value	$1,400
• Property taxes levied and collected	$6,300
• Hotel taxes (restricted to promotion of tourism collected	$1,200
• Proceeds of bonds to build a parking garage that must be repaid from user charges	$4,000
• Proceeds of general obligation bonds to finance construction of a new city hall; the building, which was completed during the year, has a useful life of thirty years with no salvage value	$9,000
• Proceeds of a federal grant to hire additional police officers	$1,000
• Fees charged to, and collected from, customers by the electric utility	$8,000

Match the fund items below with the amounts that follow. An amount may be selected once, more than once, or not at all.

1. Revenue to be recognized in an enterprise fund
2. Revenue to be recognized in special revenue funds
3. Bonds payable to be recognized in the general fund
4. Bonds payable to be recognized in enterprise funds
5. Depreciation expenditure to be recognized in the general fund
6. Depreciation expense to be recognized in internal service funds
7. Revenue to be recognized in an internal service funds
8. Revenue to be recognized in the general fund
9. Long-lived assets to be recognized in the general fund
10. Long-lived assets to be recognized in internal service funds

a. $0
b. $140
c. $900
d. $1,260
e. $1,040
f. $1,400

g. $2,200
h. $4,000
i. $6,300
j. $8,000
k. $8,500
l. $10,400

2-2

1. Oak Township issued the following bonds during the year:

Bonds to acquire equipment for a vehicle repair service that is accounted for in	
An internal service fund	$3,000,000
Bonds to construct a new city hall	$8,000,000
Bond to improve its water utility, which is accounted for in an enterprise fund	$9,000,000

The amount of debt to be reported in the general fund is
   a. $0
   b. $3,000,000
   c. $8,000,000
   d. $20,000,000
2. Oak Township should report depreciation in which of the following funds:
   a. General fund
   b. Special revenue fund
   c. Internal service fund
   d. Capital projects fund
3. Assuming that Bravo County receives all of its revenues from unrestricted property taxes, it is most likely to account for the activities of its police department in its
   a. Police department fund
   b. Police enterprise fund
   c. Property tax fund
   d. General fund
4. The city of Alpine incurred the following costs during the year in its property tax collection department:

Purchase of computer equipment	$ 10,000
Salaries and wages	$400,000
Purchase of electricity from the city-owned electric utility	$ 40,000
Purchase of supplies, all of which were used during the year	$ 10,000

As a consequence of these transactions, the amount that Alpine should report as expenditures in its general fund is
   a. $400,000
   b. $410,000
   c. $450,000
   d. $460,000
5. Grove City received the following resources during the year:

Property taxes	$50,000,000
A federal grant to acquire police cars	$ 400,000
Hotel taxes, which must be used to promote tourism	$ 3,000,000
Proceeds of bonds issued to improve the city's electric utility	$12,000,000

The amount that the city should most likely report as revenues in its special revenue funds is
   a. $400,000
   b. $3,000,000
   c. $3,400,000
   d. $15,400,000
   e. $65,400,000
6. A city issues $20 million of general obligation bonds to improve its streets and roads. In accordance with the bond covenants it sets aside $1 million to help assure that it is able to meet its first payment of principal and $0.1 million for its first payment of interest. The amount of liability that the city should report in its debt service fund is
   a. $0
   b. $18.9 million
   c. $19 million
   d. $20 million
7. During the year, Brian County collects $12 million of property taxes on behalf of Urton Township. Of this amount it remits $10 million to the township, expecting to remit the balance shortly after the end of its fiscal year. The amount of revenue that the County should report is
   a. $0
   b. $2 million
   c. $10 million
   d. $12 million
8. The City of Round Lake receives a contribution of $20 million. The donor stipulates that the money is to be invested. The principal is to remain intact and the investment proceeds are to be used to support a city-owned nature center. The city should report the contribution in a
   a. Special revenue fund
   b. Permanent fund
   c. Fiduciary fund
   d. Agency fund
9. A city receives a $30 million contribution. The donor stipulates that the money is to be invested. The principal is to remain intact and the investment proceeds are to be used to provide scholarships for the children of city employees. The contribution should be reported as revenue of a
   a. Special revenue fund
   b. Permanent fund
   c. Fiduciary fund
   d. Agency fund
10. The Summerville Preparatory School (a private school) receives a donation of $14 million. The donor stipulates that the entire amount must be used to construct a new athletic field house. The School should classify the donation as
   a. Unrestricted
   b. Temporarily restricted

c. Permanently restricted
d. Semi-restricted

2-3

Measurement focus is closely tied to basis of accounting.

A newly established not-for-profit organization engaged in the following transactions.

1. A donor pledged $1,000,000, giving the organization a legally enforceable ninety-day note for the full amount.
2. The donor paid $300,000 of the amount pledged.
3. The organization purchased a building for $600,000, paying $120,000 and giving a thirty-year mortgage note for the balance. The building has a thirty-year useful life. When appropriate, the organization charges a full year's depreciation in the period of acquisition.
4. It hired employees. By the end of the period they had earned $4,000 in wages, but had not yet been paid.

The organization accounts for its activities in a single fund.

a. Prepare journal entries to record the transactions, making the following alternative assumptions as to the organization's measurement focus:
   - Cash only
   - Cash plus other current financial resources (i.e., cash plus short-term receivables less short-term payables)
   - All economic resources

b. Based on your entries, prepare appropriate statements of revenues and expenses and balance sheets.

2-4

A special district's balance sheet may not capture its economic resources and obligations.

A special district accounts for its general fund (its only fund) on a modified accrual basis. In a particular period it engaged in the following transactions:

- It issued $20 million in long-term bonds.
- It acquired several tracts of land at a total cost of $4 million, paying the entire amount in cash.
- It sold a portion of the land for $1 million, receiving cash for the entire amount. The tract sold had cost $0.8 million.
- It repaid $2 million of the bonds.
- It lost a lawsuit and was ordered to pay $9 million over three years. It made its first cash payment of $3 million.

1. Prepare journal entries to record the transactions in the general fund.
2. Based on your journal entries, prepare a balance sheet and a statement of revenues, expenditures, and other changes in fund balance.
3. Comment on the extent to which the balance sheet captures the district's economic resources and obligations. How can you justify such a balance sheet?
4. Comment on the extent to which the statement of revenues, expenditures, and other financing sources captures the district's cost of services. How can you justify such a statement of revenues, expenditures, and other changes in fund balance?

2-5

Funds are separate fiscal and accounting entities, each with its own self-balancing set of accounts.

The newly established Society for Ethical Teachings maintains two funds—a general fund for operations and a building fund to accumulate resources for a new building. In its first year it engaged in the following transactions:

1. It received cash contributions of $200,000, of which $40,000 were restricted to the acquisition of the new building.
2. It incurred operating costs of $130,000, of which it paid $120,000 in cash.
3. It earned $3,000 of interest (the entire amount received in cash) on resources restricted to the acquisition of the new building.
4. It transferred $17,000 from the operating fund to the new building fund.
5. It paid $12,000 in fees (accounted for as expenses) to an architect to draw up plans for the new building.

   a. Prepare journal entries to record the transactions. Be certain to indicate the fund in which they would be made.
   b. Prepare a statement of revenues, expenses, and other changes in fund balance and a balance sheet. Use a two-column format, one column for each of the funds.

2-6

Typical transactions can often be identified with specific types of funds.

A city maintains the following funds:

1. General
2. Special revenue
3. Capital projects
4. Debt service
5. Enterprise
6. Internal service
7. Permanent (trust)
8. Agency

For each of the following transactions, indicate the fund in which it would most likely be recorded:

a. The city collects $3 million of taxes on behalf of the county in which it is located.
b. It spends $4 million to pave city streets, using the proceeds of a city gasoline tax dedicated for road and highway improvements.
c. It receives a contribution of $5 million. Per the stipulation of the donor, the money is to be invested in

marketable securities and the interest from the securities is to be used to maintain a city park.

d. It collects $800,000 in landing fees at the city-owned airport.

e. It earns $200,000 on investments set aside to make principal payments on the city's outstanding bonds. The bonds were issued to finance improvements to the city's tunnels and bridges.

f. It pays $4 million to a contractor for work on one of these bridges.

g. It pays $80,000 in wages and salaries to police officers.

h. It purchases from an outside supplier $40,000 of stationery that it will "sell" to its various operating departments.

PROBLEMS

Continuing Problem

Review the Comprehensive Annual Financial Report (CAFR) that you obtained.

1. What are three main sections of the report?
2. Review the introductory section of the CAFR.
   - **a.** Was the entity's annual report of the previous year awarded a "certificate of achievement for excellence in financial reporting" by the Government Finance Officers Association? What is the significance of this award?
   - **b.** What are the key issues addressed in the letter of transmittal?
3. Review the financial section.
   - **a.** Did the entity receive an "unqualified" audit opinion? If not, why not?
   - **b.** How can you be sure that the entity has adopted the provisions of GASB Statement No. 34?
   - **c.** Does the report contain management's discussion and analysis (MD&A)? If so, what are the key issues addressed?
   - **d.** Does the report provide a reconciliation between total governmental net assets per the government-wide statement of net assets and total governmental fund balances per the governmental funds balance sheet? If so, what are the main reconciling items?
   - **e.** What are the major governmental funds maintained by the entity? Does the entity's fund structure conform to its organizational structure?
   - **f.** Does the report include "required supplementary information"? If so, what are the main areas addressed?
   - **g.** Does the report include "combining statements"? If so, what is the nature of these statements?
   - **h.** Does the report include other supplemental information? If so, what types of information are in this section of the report?
4. Review the statistical section.
   - **a.** What is the population of the entity being reported on?
   - **b.** Who is the entity's major employer?
   - **c.** What types of information are included in the statistical section?

2-1

Government-wide statements report on assets and liabilities that are denied recognition on funds statements.

Entrepreneurs Consultants, a state agency, was established to provide consulting services to small businesses. It maintains only a single general fund and accounts for its activities on a modified accrual basis.

During its first month of operations, the association engaged in, or was affected by, the following transactions and events:

1. It received an unrestricted grant of $100,000.
2. It purchased five computers at $2,000 each.
3. It paid wages and salaries of $6,000.
4. It borrowed $24,000 from a bank to enable it to purchase an automobile. It gave the bank a long-term note.
5. It purchased the automobile for $24,000.
6. It made its first payment on the note—interest of $200.
7. It destroyed one of its computers in an accident. The computer was not insured.
   - **a.** Prepare journal entries in the general fund to record each of the transactions or other events.
   - **b.** Prepare a balance sheet and a statement of revenues and expenditures for the general fund.
   - **c.** Prepare a government-wide statement of net assets (balance sheet) and statement of activities. These should be on a full accrual basis. Assume that the capital assets have a useful life of five years and that no depreciation is to be charged on the computer that was destroyed.

2-2

Journal entries can be reconstructed from a balance sheet.

The Sherill Utility District was recently established. Its balance sheet, after one year, is presented below. Note the following additional information:

- The general fund received all of its revenue, $150 million, from taxes. It had operating expenditures, excluding transfers to other funds, of $100 million.
- The general fund transferred $20 million to the debt service fund. Of this, $15 million was to repay the principal on bonds outstanding; $5 million was for interest.

- The district issued $130 million in bonds to finance construction of plant and equipment. Of this, it expended $40 million.

1. Prepare journal entries to summarize all transactions in which the district engaged. You need not make closing entries. Do not be concerned as to the specific titles of accounts to be debited or credited (e.g., whether a transfer from one fund to another should be called a "transfer," an "expense," or an "expenditure," or whether proceeds from bonds should be called "bond proceeds" or "revenues").
2. Comment on how the district's government-wide (full accrual) statement of net assets would differ from the balance sheet presented.

Sherill Utility District
Balance Sheet as of End of Year 1
(in millions)

	General Fund	Capital Projects Fund	Debt Service Fund	Totals
Assets				
Cash	$30			$ 30
Investments		$90	$20	110
Total assets	$30	$90	$20	$140
Liabilities and fund balances				
Fund balances	$30	$90	$20	$140

2. Which presentation, the unconsolidated or the consolidated, provides more complete information? Explain. Which presentation might be seen as misleading? Why? What, if any, advantages do you see in this presentation even though it might be less complete and more misleading?

Williamsburg Regional Sewage Treatment Authority
Balance Sheet
October 31, 2004

	General	Capital Projects
Assets		
Cash	$ 751	$ 5,021
Time deposits		16,398
Due on insurance claim	9,499	
Due from general fund		9,000
Due from participants	66,475	4,414
Total assets	$76,725	$34,833
Liabilities and fund equity		
Accounts payable	$17,725	
Due to capital projects fund	9,000	
	$26,725	
Fund balance	50,000	34,833
Total liabilities and fund equity	$76,725	$34,833

2-3

Funds can be "consolidated," but only at the risk of lost or misleading information.

The following balance sheet was adapted from the financial statements of the Williamsburg Regional Sewage Treatment Authority (dates have been changed).

Fund Types

The transactions of the authority are accounted for in the following governmental fund types:

General fund—To account for all revenues and expenditures not required to be accounted for in other funds.

Capital projects fund—To account for financial resources designated to construct or acquire capital facilities and improvements. Such resources are derived principally from other municipal utility districts to which the Williamsburg Regional Sewage Treatment Authority provides certain services.

1. Recast the balance sheets of the two funds into a single *consolidated* balance sheet. Show separately, however, the restricted and the unrestricted portions of the consolidated fund balance account (not each individual asset and liability). Be sure to eliminate interfund payables and receivables.

2-4

The more complete presentation is not always the easiest to understand.

Bertram County maintains a fund accounting system. Nevertheless, its comptroller (who recently retired from a position in private industry) prepared the following balance sheet (in millions):

Assets		
Cash		$600
Investments		1,800
Construction in progress		500
Capital assets		1,200
Total assets		$4,100
Liabilities and fund balance		
Bonds payable		$1,700
Fund balance		
Restricted to capital projects	$ 600	
Restricted to debt service	200	
Unrestricted	1,600	2,400
Total liabilities and fund balance		$4,100

The fund balance reserved for debt service represents entirely *principal* (not interest) on the bonds payable.

1. Recast the balance sheet, as best you can, into separate balance sheets for each of the funds that are apparently maintained by the county. Assume that the county uses a modified accrual basis of accounting that excludes recognition in its funds of both capital assets and long-term debt. Assume also that cash and investments are divided among the funds in proportion to fund balances.
2. In your opinion, which of the two presentations gives the reader a more complete picture of the county's financial status? Why? Which presentation is easier to understand?

2-5

Consolidated balances are not substitutes for individual fund balance sheets.

See the following balance sheet for the town of Paris governmental funds. In addition you learn from other records that the town has capital (capital assets) with a book value (net of depreciation) of $1,450 million and has outstanding long-term bonds of $1,315 million.

1. Recast the balance sheets (taking into account the information on capital assets and long-term debt) in the form of a single consolidated, full accrual, government-wide statement of net assets.
2. Put yourself in the place of an analyst. The town mayor presents you with the government-wide statement of net assets similar to the one you just prepared. She asserts that the town is in excellent fiscal condition as measured by the exceedingly "healthy" balance of net assets. Based on your having seen the combined balance sheet that shows the individual funds, why might you be skeptical of her claim?
3. Comment on why a government-wide consolidated statement of net assets is no substitute for a combined balance sheet that reports upon major funds.

2-6

The nature of a transaction gives a clue as to the type fund in which it should be recorded.

Kendal County engaged in the following transactions. For each, prepare an appropriate journal entry and indicate the type of fund in which it would most likely be recorded:

1. It levied and collected $1 million in taxes dedicated to the repayment of outstanding general obligation bonds.
2. It billed sponsors of a charity bicycle ride $5,000 for providing police patrols during the ride.
3. It recognized $60,000 of cash dividends on investments dedicated to the support of a county arts center.
4. It recognized $70,000 of cash dividends on investments dedicated to scholarships for needy county residents.
5. It incurred $6 million in construction costs to complete a new county jail. The new jail was funded entirely with the proceeds of long-term bonds.
6. It transferred $400,000 of unrestricted funds to an appropriate fund to be invested and eventually used to repay the principal on the long-term jail bonds (entries in two funds required).
7. It recognized depreciation of $100,000 on equipment in a vehicle repair center that services all county departments that have motor vehicles.
8. It collected $30,000 in parking fees at the county-owned garage.
9. It issued $8 million in bonds to improve the city-owned electric utility.
10. It distributed $3 million in taxes collected on behalf of school districts located within the county.

2-7

Transactions affect fund statements differently than they do government-wide statements.

Town of Paris Balance Sheet Governmental Funds (in millions)

	General Fund	Hotel Tax (Special Revenue Fund)	Bridge (Capital Projects) Fund	Bond (Debt Service) Fund	Endowment (Permanent) Fund	Totals
Assets						
Cash	$ 38	$ 20	$ 35	$340	$ 10	$ 443
Investments	105	60	480	136	960	1,741
Due from other funds		120	46	39		205
Total assets	$143	$200	$561	$515	$970	$2,389
Liabilities and fund balances						
Accounts payable	$ 8					$ 8
Due to other funds	205					205
Fund balances	(70)	200	561	515	970	2,176
Total liabilities and fund balances	$143	$200	$561	$515	$970	$2,389

Preston Village engaged in the transactions that follow:

1. It issued $20 million in bonds to purchase a new municipal office building. The proceeds were recorded in a capital projects fund.
2. It acquired the building for $20 million.
3. It recognized, as appropriate, $300,000 of depreciation on municipal vehicles.
4. It transferred $2,060,000 from the general fund to a debt service fund.
5. It paid $60,000 in interest on long-term debt and repaid $2 million of principal on the same long-term debt.
6. It sold for $5 million village land that had been acquired for $4 million. The proceeds were recorded in the general fund.
   a. For each of the transactions, prepare journal entries to record them in appropriate governmental funds (which are accounted for on a modified accrual basis).
   b. Prepare journal entries to reflect how the transactions would be reflected in government-wide statements (which are prepared on a full accrual basis).
   c. How can governments justify preparing two sets of financial statements, each on a different basis?

2-8

Is fund accounting less appropriate for businesses than for not-for-profits?

A newly formed not-for-profit advocacy organization, the Center for Participatory Democracy, requests your advice on setting up its financial accounting and reporting system. Meeting with the director, you learn the following:

- Member dues can be expected to account for approximately 80 percent of the organization's revenues.
- The organization plans to seek grants from private foundations to carry out research projects pertaining to various political causes.
- The center has already received a gift of $100,000. The donor specified that the funds are to be placed in investment-grade securities and that only the income is to be used to support center activities.
- The center leases office space but owns its furniture, fixtures, and office equipment.
- The center has taken out a five-year term loan of $100,000. Although the loan is not due until its term expires, the organization intends to set aside $17,740 each year with the prospect that, properly invested, these payments will provide the necessary $100,000.

1. Do you believe that the center should establish its accounting system on a fund basis? If so, why?
2. Assume you answered "yes" to question 1. What specific fund types do you think the center should set up? Explain.
3. Suppose, alternatively, the center was a privately owned, profit-oriented consulting firm that would provide political advice to its clients. The firm would charge its clients a fixed fee each month, in return for which they would receive periodic newsletters and the opportunity to meet with the firm's partners. In addition, the firm expects to enter into contracts to carry out specific research projects for its clients. Would you now recommend that the firm establish its accounting system on a fund basis (assuming, of course, that it would prepare its external financial reports in accordance with generally accepted accounting principles applicable to businesses)? Explain.

2-9

Business-type financial statements may be appropriate for some, but not all, not-for-profits.

The balance sheet of the Hillcrest Home Care Service, a not-for-profit organization providing assistance to the elderly, is presented here:

Hillcrest Home Care Service
Balance Sheet as of December 31
(in thousands)

Assets	
Current assets	
Cash and cash equivalents	$ 115
Investments	232
Accounts receivable (net of estimated uncollectibles of $60,000)	652
Total current assets	$ 999
Equipment	
Medical and office equipment	75
Vehicles	60
	$ 135
Less accumulated depreciation	(52)
Net equipment	$ 83
Other assets	
Deferred finance charges	15
Total assets	$1,097
Liabilities and fund balances	
Liabilities	
Current maturities of long-term note	$ 18
Accounts payable	50
Accrued vacation costs	346
Estimated third-party payer settlements	35
Total current liabilities	$ 449
Long-term debt less current maturities	110
Total liabilities	$ 559
Fund balances	
Unrestricted	160
Temporarily restricted	273
Permanently restricted	105
Total fund balances	$ 538
Total liabilities and fund balances	$1,097

1. As best you can tell from the balance sheet, what are Hillcrest's measurement focus and basis of accounting? Explain.
2. What is the most likely reason that some assets are classified as temporarily restricted and others as permanently restricted?
3. Suppose you are the independent CPA who audited the financial statements of Hillcrest. The controller of a town, also one of your clients, reviews the financial statements of Hillcrest and observes that they look remarkably like those of private businesses. He wonders why:
   a. The statements of his town are so seemingly complex, consisting of not one, but several, separate fund balance sheets and statements of operations.
   b. The financial report consists of two separate sets of statements, each from a different perspective and on a different basis of accounting.
   c. The statements of his town can't be more like those of Hillcrest.

   What would be your most likely response?

2-10

A hospital's balance sheet tells much about its basis of accounting.

See the following balance sheet of a not-for-profit hospital. The balance sheet is intended to display the hospital's fund structure. Inasmuch as it does not conform to FASB standards, it is inappropriate for external reporting.

1. On what basis of accounting is the general fund maintained? How can you tell?
2. Are the plant replacement and expansion funds on a cash basis of accounting? How can you tell?
3. Why do you suppose that the unrestricted fund assets "whose use is limited [designated] by board for capital improvements" are not reported in a restricted fund?
4. Suppose the hospital were to present its balance sheet in three columns, one each for unrestricted, temporarily restricted, and permanently restricted resources. Which of the funds would most likely be reported in each of the columns?
5. What funds in a government are likely to be most comparable to the specific purpose funds?

2-11

Each fund must account for interfund activity as if it were a separate accounting entity.

The newly formed Buffalo School District engaged in the following transactions and other events during the year:

1. It levied and collected property taxes of $110 million.
2. It issued $30 million in long-term bonds to construct a building. It placed the cash received in a special fund set aside to account for the bond proceeds.
3. During the year it constructed the building at a cost of $25 million. It expects to spend the $5 million balance in the following year. The building has an estimated useful life of twenty-five years.
4. It incurred $70 million in general operating costs, of which it paid $63 million. It expects to pay the balance early the following year.
5. It transferred $12 million from its general fund to a fund established to account for resources set aside to service the debt. Of this, $10 million was for repayment of the debt; $2 million was for interest.
6. From the special fund established to service the debt, it paid $2 million in interest and $6 million in principal.
7. It collected $4 million in hotel taxes restricted to promoting tourism. Since the resources were restricted they were accounted for in a special restricted fund. During the year, the district spent $3 million on promoting tourism.
8. The district established a supplies store to provide supplies to the district's various departments by transferring $4 million from the general fund. It accounted for the store in an internal service (proprietary) fund. During the year the store purchased (and paid for) $2 million in supplies. Of these it "sold" $1 million, at cost (for cash), to departments accounted for in the general fund. During the year these departments used all of the supplies that they had purchased.
   a. Prepare journal entries to record the transactions and other events in appropriate funds. Assume that governmental funds are accounted for on a modified accrual basis and focus only on current financial resources (and thus do not give balance sheet recognition either to capital assets or long-term debts). Proprietary funds are accounted for on a full accrual basis.
   b. Prepare a combined balance sheet—one that has a separate column for each of the governmental funds you established.
   c. Prepare a combined statement of revenues, expenses, and changes in fund balances for all governmental funds. Prepare a separate statement of revenues and expenses and changes in fund balances for any proprietary funds you established.
   d. Prepare a government-wide statement of net assets and a government-wide statement of activities in which all funds are consolidated and are accounted for on a full accrual basis. Be sure to include both long-term assets and liabilities on the statement of net assets and to depreciate the long-term assets. Also, be sure to adjust for any interfund activity. You may find it helpful to redo the journal entries you made in part (a), this time recording the transactions (and not the interfund activity) as if the district accounted for its activities in a single entity and on the full accrual basis.

Central States Rehabilitation Hospital
Balance Sheet as of December 31
(in thousands)

Assets		*Liabilities and Fund Balances*	
	General Fund		
Current assets		***Current liabilities***	
Cash and equivalents	$3,103	Accounts payable	$ 3,200
Patients accounts receivable	15,700	Accrued expenses	3,400
Supplies	1,817	Estimated third-party settlements	2,408
Other current assets	404	Other current liabilities	2,700
Total current assets	$21,024	Total current liabilities	$11,708
Noncurrent assets		***Noncurrent liabilities***	
Assets whose use is limited (designated) by board for capital improvements	$21,000	Estimated cost of malpractice	$4,760
		Long-term debt	34,000
Property, plant, and equipment (net of allowance for depreciation)	42,500		
Other assets	7,300	Fund balance	41,356
Total noncurrent assets	70,800		
Total assets	$91,824	Total liabilities and fund balance	$91,824
	Donor Restricted Funds		
	Specific Purpose Funds		
Cash	$ 389	Accounts payable	$ 205
Investments	250	Deferred grant revenue	80
Grants receivable	613	Fund balance	967
Total assets	$ 1,252	Total liabilities and fund balance	$ 1,252
	Plant Replacement and Expansion Funds		
Cash	$ 25		
Investments	250		
Pledges receivable	110		
Total assets	$ 385	Fund balance	$ 385
	Endowment Funds		
Cash	$ 1,600		
Investments	4,200		
Total assets	$ 5,800	Fund balance	$ 5,800

SOLUTION TO EXERCISE FOR REVIEW AND SELF-STUDY

a. Journal entries

1. General fund

Cash	$250	
Taxes receivable	50	
Tax revenues		$300

To record the levy and collection of taxes

2. General fund

Operating expenditures	$240	
Cash		$170
Accounts payable		70

To record operating expenditures

3. Capital projects fund

Cash	$500	
Bond proceeds		$500

To record proceeds of the bond issue

Although the district does not report the obligation in a fund, it still needs to maintain accounting control over it. Therefore, it must record the obligation in a separate, off-the-balance-sheet balance sheet, ledger, or other "list" of long-term obligations.

4. Capital projects fund

Expenditure—acquisition of facilities	$400	
Cash		$400

To record the acquisition of facilities

From an accounting perspective the facilities are written off when acquired. As with the bonds, the district must maintain a separate, off-the-balance-sheet record of the assets.

5. General fund

Transfer to debt service fund	$40	
Cash		$40

To record the transfer of cash to the debt service fund (the transfer account is similar to an expenditure account)

Debt service fund

Cash	$40	
Transfer from general fund		$40

To record transfer of cash from the general fund

6. Internal service fund

Equipment	$10	
Long-term note		$10

To record acquisition of plant and equipment

Because this is a proprietary fund, and accounted for on a full accrual basis, both the equipment and the note are recognized within the internal service fund itself.

7. Internal service fund

Cash	$15	
Operating revenues		$15

To record operating revenues

Operating expenses	$12	
Cash		$12

To record cash operating expenses

Depreciation expense	$2	
Equipment		$2

To record depreciation (alternatively, the credit could have been made to a contra account, "accumulated depreciation")

The revenues of the internal service fund are expenditures to the general fund.

b. Governmental fund statements

State Recreation District
Statement of Revenues, Expenditures, and Changes In Fund Balances—Governmental Funds, First Year (in millions)

	General Fund	Capital Projects Fund	Debt Service Fund	Total Governmental Funds
Revenues				
Tax revenues	$300			$ 300
Expenditures				
Operating expenditures	255			255
Acquisition of facilities	—	400	—	400
Total expenditures	$255	$ 400	—	$ 655
Excess of revenues over expenditures	$ 45	$(400)	—	$(355)
Other financing sources (uses):				
Bond proceeds		500		500
Transfer to debt service fund	(40)			(40)
Transfer from debt service fund	—	—	40	40
Total other financing Sources and uses	$ (40)	$ 500	$40	$ 500
Net increase in fund balance	$ 5	$ 100	$40	$ 145

State Recreation District
Balance Sheet—Governmental Funds
End of First Year (in millions)

	General Fund	Capital Projects Fund	Debt Service Fund	Total Governmental Funds
Assets				
Cash	$25	$100	$40	$165
Taxes receivable	50	—	—	50
Total assets	$75	$100	$40	$215
Liabilities and fund balances				
Accounts payable	$70			$ 70
Fund balances	5	100	40	145
Total liabilities and fund balances	$75	$100	$40	$215

c. Proprietary fund statements

State Recreation District
Balance Sheet—Proprietary (Internal Service) Fund
End of First Year (in millions)

Assets		
Cash		$3
Equipment	$10	
Less: accumulated depreciation	(2)	8
Total assets		$11
Liabilities and net assets:		
Long-term note		$10
Net assets		1
Total liabilities and net assets		$11

State Recreation District
Statement of Revenues, Expenses, and Changes in Fund Net Assets—Proprietary (Internal Service) Fund
First Year (in millions)

Operating revenues		$15
Less: operating expenses	$12	
depreciation expense	2	14
Change in net assets		$ 1
Total net assets—beginning of year		0
Total net assets—end of year		$ 1

d. Government-wide statements

State Recreation District
Statement of Net Assets
End of First Year (in millions)

Assets		
Cash		$168
Taxes receivable		50
Capital assets	$410	
Less: accumulated depreciation	(42)	368
Total assets		$586
Liabilities		
Accounts payable		$ 70
Long-term notes		10
Bonds payable		500
Total liabilities		580
Net assets:		
Restricted to repayment of debt	$ 40	
Restricted to acquisition of capital assets	100	
Unrestricted	(134)	6
Total liabilities and net assets		$586

State Recreation District
Statement of Activities
First Year (in millions)

Expenses	
Operating	$252
Depreciation	42
Total expenses	$294
General revenues	
Taxes	300
Increase in net assets	$ 6
Net assets—beginning of year	0
Net assets—end of year	$ 6

Explanation of government-wide statements.

Capital assets: The capital assets acquired with resources from both the capital projects fund and the internal service fund

Depreciation and accumulated depreciation: Depreciation of $2 on internal service fund assets and $40 on recreational facility assets

Restricted to payment of debt: Balance in the debt service fund

Restricted to acquisition of capital assets: Balance in capital projects fund

Operating expenditures: Operating expenditures of $255 as reported in the governmental fund statement of revenues and expenditures less the $15 billings from the internal service fund (in effect an intragovernment transfer) plus the $12 of expenses incurred by the internal service fund.

CHAPTER 3

Issues of Budgeting and Control

LEARNING OBJECTIVES

After studying this chapter you should understand:

- The key purposes of budgets
- The need for more than one type of budget
- The various ways of classifying expenditures
- The benefits of performance budgets
- The key phases of the budget cycle
- Why budgets are generally prepared on a cash basis
- The limitations of budget-to-actual comparisons
- How budgets enhance control
- The means by which governments incorporate budgets into their accounting systems
- How an encumbrance system prevents overspending
- The circumstances under which budgetary and encumbrance entries are most beneficial

Budgets are to governments and not-for-profits what the sun is to the solar system. Trying to understand government and not-for-profit accounting without recognizing the centricity of the budget would be like trying to comprehend the earth's seasons while ignoring the sun. As emphasized in Chapter 1, and incorporated into generally accepted accounting principles, **budgets** are the key financial instruments:

> Budgeting is an essential element of the financial planning, control, and evaluation processes of governments. Every governmental unit should prepare a comprehensive budget covering all governmental, proprietary, and fiduciary funds for each annual (or, in some states, biennial) fiscal period.[1]

Governments and not-for-profits are disciplined mainly by their budgets, not by the competitive marketplace. With few exceptions, significant decisions—whether political or managerial—are reflected in their budgets. As also pointed out in Chapter 1, a key objective of financial accounting and reporting is assuring that an entity obtains and uses its resources in accordance with its budget. Budgeting exerts a major influence on accounting and reporting principles and practices.

The main purpose of this chapter is to provide an overview of budgets and the budgeting process, and thereby establish a basis for appreciating the relationship between budgeting and accounting. The first part of this chapter discusses functions of budgets, the different types of budgets, schemes of account classification, budgeting cycles, budgetary bases, and the significance of budget-to-actual comparisons. The second part shows how governments (and, to a lesser extent, other not-for-profits) promote budgetary compliance by integrating the budget into their accounting systems. They do this primarily by preparing journal entries to record both the budget and the goods and services that have been ordered but not yet received.

Although this chapter will describe budgetary procedures and related accounting practices mainly in the context of governments, most of the points can properly be extended to all not-for-profits. For example, whereas the legislatures of governments *appropriate* (a term reserved for governments) funds for expenditure, the boards of directors or trustees of private-sector not-for-profits *authorize* or *approve* outlays—performing essentially the same function. However, the budgets of governments have the force of law, and officials may be subject to severe penalties for violating them. To prevent overspending, governments are required to institute certain accounting controls—such as integrating both the budget and purchase orders into their accounting systems—that are optional for not-for-profits.

WHAT ARE THE KEY PURPOSES OF BUDGETS?

Budgets are intended to carry out at least three broad functions:

- ***Planning.*** In a broad sense, planning comprises *programming* (determining the activities that the entity will undertake), resource *acquisition*, and resource *allocation.* Planning is concerned with specifying the type, quantity, and quality of services that will be provided to constituents; estimating service costs; and determining how to pay for the services.
- ***Controlling and administering.*** Budgets help assure that resources are obtained and expended as planned. Managers use budgets to monitor resource flows and point to the need for operational adjustments. Legislative bodies, such as city

[1] NCGA Statement 1, *Governmental Accounting and Financial Reporting Principles*, para. 77, 1979.

councils or boards of trustees, use budgets to impose spending authority over executives (such as city managers or executive directors), who in turn use them to impose authority over their subordinates (such as department heads).

- ***Reporting and evaluating.*** Budgets lay the foundation for end-of-period reports and evaluations. Budget-to-actual comparisons reveal whether revenue and spending mandates were carried out. More important, when tied to an organization's objectives, budgets can facilitate assessments of efficiency and effectiveness.

WHY IS MORE THAN ONE TYPE OF BUDGET NECESSARY?

The benefits of the budgetary process cannot be fully achieved by a single budget or type of budget. A well-managed government or not-for-profit—just like a well-managed business—should prepare budgets for varying periods of time from multiple perspectives. These include:

- ***Appropriation budgets,*** which are concerned mainly with current operating revenues and expenditures
- ***Capital budgets,*** which focus on the acquisition and construction of long-term assets
- ***Flexible budgets,*** which relate costs to outputs and are thereby intended to help control costs, especially those of business-types activities

In addition, many governments and not-for-profits prepare **performance budgets** (discussed later in this chapter).

APPROPRIATION BUDGETS

A government's *current* or *operating* budget covers its general fund. The operating budget is almost always an **appropriation budget**—one incorporating the legislatively granted expenditure authority, along with the related estimates of revenue. In most jurisdictions the operating budget must, by law, be balanced. Public attention focuses on the budget because it determines the amount of taxes and other revenues that must be generated to cover expenditures. Owing to the importance of appropriation budgets and the influence they have had upon the establishment of accounting principles and practices, this chapter directs attention mainly to this type of budget.

Governments may require that appropriation budgets be developed and approved for special revenue, debt service, or capital projects funds. However, such budgets may be unnecessary if a government has established adequate controls over spending by other means. For example, by accepting a federal grant and creating a special revenue fund to account for it, the government may implicitly approve expenditure of the grant resources. Similarly, by issuing bonds, it may authorize spending for specified capital projects. Still, principles of sound management dictate that a nonappropriation budget—a financial plan not subject to appropriation—be prepared each year for such funds and organizational units. Budgets of some type are almost always necessary if activities are to be effectively planned, controlled, and evaluated.

CAPITAL BUDGETS

Although the accounting cycle is traditionally one year, the budgeting process commonly extends for a considerably longer period. The needs of an organization's constituents must be forecast and planned for years in advance.

A **capital budget,** in contrast to an appropriation budget, typically covers multiple years, often as many as five. It concentrates on the construction and acquisition of long-lived assets such as land, buildings, roads, bridges, and major items of equipment. These assets can be expected to last for many years. Therefore, in the interest of interperiod equity, they will generally be financed with long-term debt rather than taxes of a single year. The capital budget is, in essence, a plan setting forth when specific capital assets will be acquired and how they will be financed.

Capital budgets are closely tied to operating budgets. Each year a government must include current-year capital spending in its operating budget. If the capital projects are financed with debt, however, the capital expenditures will be offset with bond proceeds and will not affect the operating budget's surplus or deficit.

Legislators are sometimes more extravagant with capital than with operating resources. Capital projects, they reason, can be financed with debt rather than taxes, and thus will not affect the surplus or deficit of the general fund, the budget of which must be balanced. Their error is in failing to take into account the additional operating costs associated with new long-term assets. Roads must be repaired, buildings maintained, and equipment tuned up. Further, in future years the debt must be serviced with interest and principal payments made from operating resources.

FLEXIBLE BUDGETS

Enterprise funds, which account for business-type activities, are generally not subject to the same statutory budget requirements as governmental funds. Nevertheless, budgets are as important to enterprise funds as they are to businesses and governmental funds. As a rule, governments should prepare the same types of budgets for enterprise funds as would a private enterprise carrying out similar activities. For certain, they should prepare a series of **flexible budgets,** each of which contains alternative budget estimates based on varying levels of output. Unlike **fixed budgets,** flexible budgets capture the behavior of costs, distinguishing between fixed and variable amounts. Fixed budgets may be appropriate for governmental funds where the expenditures and level of activity are pre-established by legislative authorization. Flexible budgets are especially suited to enterprise funds in which the level of activity depends on customer demand.

HOW ARE EXPENDITURES AND REVENUES CLASSIFIED?

How financial data are presented affects how they are used. Therefore, accountants, public administrators, political scientists, and economists have directed considerable attention to the form and content of budgets. They are aware that the way the budget is prepared and presented can significantly affect the allocation of resources among organizations, programs, and activities.

EXPENDITURES

The Governmental Accounting Standards Board (GASB) advises that "multiple classification of governmental expenditure data is important from both internal and external management control and accountability standpoints" as it "facilitates the aggregation and analysis of data in different ways for different purposes and in manners that cross fund and organizational lines." Suggested classifications include:

- By *fund,* such as the general fund, special revenue funds, and debt service funds
- By *organizational unit,* such as the police department, the fire department, the city council, and the finance office

- By *function* or *program* (a group of activities carried out with the same objective), such as general government, public safety, sanitation, and recreation
- By *activity* (line of work contributing to a function or program), such as highway patrol, burglary investigations, vice patrol
- By *character* (the fiscal period they are presumed to benefit), such as "current expenditures," which benefit the current period, "capital outlays," which benefit the current and future periods, and "debt service," which benefits prior, current, and future periods
- By *object classification* (the types of items purchased or the services obtained), such as salaries, fringe benefits, travel, and repairs[2]

REVENUES

In contrast to expenditures, revenues present less significant issues of classification. Most revenues are not designated for specific purposes (or, if they are, they are reported in separate funds); therefore, their classification is relatively straightforward. The GASB recommends that, in fund statements, revenues be classified first by fund (i.e., the columns on a statement of revenues and expenditures) and then by source (i.e., the rows). Suggested major source classifications include:

- Taxes
- Licenses and permits
- Intergovernmental revenues
- Charges for services
- Fines and forfeits[3]

Most governments divide these classifications into numerous subclassifications, such as property taxes, sales taxes, and hotel taxes.

WHY ARE PERFORMANCE BUDGETS NECESSARY?

The traditional, and most commonly prepared, budget is referred to as an **object classification budget** because it is characterized by the expenditure classification that categorizes objects, such as the type of goods or services to be acquired. Table 3-1 illustrates an excerpt of this type of budget for one department.

The primary virtue of an object classification budget is that it facilitates control. The managers who prepare the budget, and the legislators who pass it, establish rigid spending mandates and thereby direct, in detail, how every dollar should be spent. But this strength may also be a shortcoming:

- By expediting control, an object classification budget discourages planning. It encourages top-level decision makers to focus on specific line items rather than on overall entity objectives, strategies, and measurable performance targets. Thus, for example, the officials of a school district may focus on the need for increased appropriations for salaries, fuel, supplies, and food while failing to consider how the additional outlays will affect the school's primary educational mission.
- It promotes bottom-up rather than top-down budgeting, with each unit presenting its fiscal requirements for approval in the absence of coordinated sets of goals and strategies.

[2] NCGA Statement 1, *Governmental Accounting and Financial Reporting Principles*, para. 111, 1979.

[3] NCGA Statement 1, *Governmental Accounting and Financial Reporting Principles*, para. 110, 1979.

TABLE 3–1
Excerpt from an Object Classification Budget

Expenditure Detail Public Safety

Departmental Summary	**FY 2005 Budget**	**FY 2004 Estimate**	**FY 2003 Actual**
Full-time wages	$1,307,000	$1,348,300	$1,283,147
Part-time wages	26,200	44,000	52,014
Casual wages	27,000	15,000	138
Temporary wages	0	3,800	2,748
Longevity	24,000	21,800	21,257
Overtime	140,500	24,700	27,127
Auto allowance	46,000	44,400	44,700
Retirement	158,000	142,300	135,077
Social Security (FICA)	120,000	106,000	100,385
Group insurance	290,000	290,000	265,515
Worker's compensation	61,300	61,000	54,583
Total personnel	$2,200,000	$2,101,300	$1,986,691
Office supplies & equipment	15,900	14,700	14,302
Postage	23,000	23,500	28,910
Operating supplies & equipment	28,500	29,900	18,915
Fuel & lube	21,200	25,900	17,307
Uniforms & wearing apparel	6,000	4,400	1,461
Health-related supplies	26,800	32,300	19,257
Telephone charges	9,200	8,700	6,420
Electricity charges	9,400	7,300	4,633
Gas charges	3,100	2,700	2,097
Water & sewer charges	3,600	2,500	2,270
Printing costs	9,100	9,600	7,463
Professional services	500	500	150
Advertising costs	3,000	1,300	4,924
Building maintenance	2,000	2,200	0
Vehicular maintenance	27,500	26,500	24,855
Equipment maintenance	2,500	1,980	2,899
Lease & rent	5,100	5,100	1,629
Travel & training	12,900	11,600	8,491
Special services	100,100	83,400	87,482
Hospitality	600	500	753
Fixed assets	0	2,200	2,931
Total operating expenses	$ 310,000	$ 296,760	$ 257,149
Capital outlay	$ 25,000	$ 71,700	$ 61,110
Total expenditures	$2,535,000	$2,469,790	$2,304,950

- It overwhelms top-level decision makers with details. As a consequence, the decision makers are induced to take budgetary shortcuts, such as increasing all expenditures by a fixed percentage.
- By failing to relate specific *inputs* (factors used to provide goods and services) to *outputs* (units of service) or *outcomes* (accomplishments in terms of organizational objectives), it limits post-budget evaluation to whether spending mandates were observed.

Owing to these deficiencies, many governments and not-for-profits have adopted **performance budgets** in place of, or as a supplement to, object classification budgets.

Performance budgets focus on measurable units of efforts, services, and accomplishments. They are formulated so that dollar expenditures are directly associated with anticipated units of outputs or outcomes. Comprehensive performance budgeting systems require managers to specify objectives, consider alternative means of achieving them, establish workload indicators, and perform cost-benefit analyses.

To be sure, other sound managerial approaches can overcome the limitations of object classification budgeting. Performance budgets, however, institutionalize effective decision processes and help assure that they are carried out.

The most common type of performance budgets are **program budgets,** whereby resources and results are identified with programs rather than traditional organizational units, and expenditures are typically categorized by activity rather than by object.

Table 3-2 illustrates an excerpt from a program budget. Program budgeting is discussed in detail in Chapter 14.

WHAT ARE THE KEY PHASES OF THE BUDGET CYCLE?

Budgeting practices in neither governments nor not-for-profits are standardized; they differ from entity to entity. However, irrespective of whether the budget is of object classification or performance type, in most organizations budgeting is a continuous, four-phase process:

- Preparation
- Legislative adoption and executive approval

TABLE 3-2
Excerpt from a Program Budget
Summary of Request

Agency Code: 111	Agency Name: Department of Environmental Quality	Prepared By: John Daily	Date: 08/01/04

Goal/Objectives/Strategy	Expended 2003	Estimated 2004	Budgeted 2005	Requested 2006	Requested 2007
Goal 1: Improve Air Quality in Texas					
Reduce Air Pollutants to Reach Federal Standards by 2008					
Implement EPA's Ozone Policy	$10,500,000	$11,100,000	$11,000,000	$11,125,000	$11,125,000
Promote and Enforce Local Air Quality Programs	250,000	250,000	250,000	250,000	250,000
Reduce Air Toxics Emissions by 40 Percent b/w 2003 and 2009					
Implement Comprehensive Air Toxics Program	4,800,000	5,000,000	5,000,000	5,000,000	5,000,000
By 2009, Analyze 90 Percent of Potential Cases of Toxic Chemical Exposure Through Air Pollution					
Conduct Ongoing Studies of Toxic Chemical Exposure	500,000	500,000	500,000	1,250,000	1,250,000
Total, Goal 1	$16,050,000	$16,850,000	$16,750,000	$17,625,000	$17,625,000
Goal 2: Improve Water Availability and Water Quality					
Increase Compliance to 90 Percent of Regulated Sites by 2009					
Enforce Water Quality Standards	$ 4,200,000	$ 4,200,000	$ 4,000,000	$ 4,000,000	$ 4,000,000
Monitor Maintenance Standards in Water Districts	800,000	800,000	800,000	800,000	800,000
By 2009, Increase by 12 Percent the Amount of Water Available for Beneficial Use					
Negotiate Water Rights with Local and Other Entities	1,400,000	1,400,000	1,500,000	1,190,000	1,125,000
Total, Goal 2	$ 6,400,000	$ 6,400,000	$ 6,300,000	$ 5,990,000	$ 5,925,000

- Execution
- Reporting and auditing

PREPARATION

Budgets are most commonly prepared by an organization's executive branch (e.g., the office of the mayor or executive director) and submitted to the legislative branch (e.g., a city council or board of trustees) for approval. In some jurisdictions, particularly states, the legislature may either prepare its own budget (a legislative budget as opposed to an executive budget) or join with the executive branch in developing a common budget.

Budgeting generally necessitates flows of policies and information to and from all parties involved in the budgetary process. Legislators, for example, will apprise the executive branch as to what they think is politically feasible for revenue measures. Department heads will inform the legislative or executive budget committees as to what they see as their requirements. The committees, in turn, will develop guidelines for funding priorities and establish ranges of funding increases and cuts.

The preparation of a budget requires both forecasts and estimates. Relatively few types of revenues can be determined accurately in advance of the budget period. These types are limited mainly to those that are contractually established (e.g., from lease agreements), have been previously promised (e.g., grants from other governments), or are set by law and affect a known number of parties (e.g., property taxes and special assessments). Most, however, depend on factors that are largely outside the government's control. Most types of tax revenues, for example, are influenced by economic conditions; revenues from fines and fees are affected by the predilections of the citizenry.

Some expenditures are fixed by legislative fiat or can be determined accurately. Examples of these types of expenditures include salaries of key officials (assuming no turnover), grants to other organizations, acquisitions of equipment, payments of interest, and repayments of debt. Others, however, are affected by acts of God or man. Snow removal, parades for championship sports teams, repair of equipment, and purchases of fuel are some examples of unpredictable expenditures.

The literature of public budgeting is replete with descriptions of forecasting models and techniques. Yet, as is made clear in the accompanying description of budgeting at the federal level ("In Practice: Budgeting Cannot Be Divorced from Politics"), the models or techniques are no better than the underlying assumptions. Moreover, as indicated by testimony of a senior White House official, the forecasting techniques are not always as scientific as they might appear (see "In Practice: Federal Budgetary Legerdemain"). As might be expected, and as is evidenced by an actual study, the differences between actual results and budgetary estimates can be substantial (see "In Practice: Misestimating Revenues and Expenditures").

Significant errors in budget estimates, irrespective of direction or cause, thwart the political process and may lead to a distribution of resources that misrepresent what was expressed by voters through their elected representatives. At the very least, as suggested by "In Practice: Budgeting Cannot Be Divorced from Politics," they can make for colorful political contretemps. Insofar as budgets are used by investors or creditors, they may contribute to misguided fiscal decisions and misallocation of resources.

LEGISLATIVE ADOPTION AND EXECUTIVE APPROVAL

When the budget is presented to a legislature for consideration, it is typically turned over to one or more committees for review. In some legislatures, such as the U.S. Congress, the committees that act on revenues are separate from those that recommend expenditures. Moreover, the committees authorizing new programs may be different from those determining the amount to be spent on them. The committees

IN PRACTICE

BUDGETING CANNOT BE DIVORCED FROM POLITICS

Nothing indicates the political ramifications of budgetary projections as does an economic downturn. Consider, for example, the November 2002 gubernatorial election in New York.

According to the *New York Times* (October 17, 2002), state spending was sharply higher than anticipated and state revenues were sharply lower. "While no one disputed the numbers," the *Times* noted, "in the overheated air of a campaign for governor, there was sharp disagreement over whether it came as a surprise."

H. Carl McCall, the Democratic candidate for governor, charged that his Republican opponent, incumbent governor George E. Pataki, "built the budget on a foundation of shaky revenues and backroom deals." Once the election was over, he predicted, the state would have to report a deficit of between $5 billion and $10 billion for the year.

Whereas the governor had predicted that general fund revenue would drop during the year by only 5 percent, in the first six months of the year they were down by 16 percent. Personal income taxes, which are the state's prime revenue source, were projected to decline by only 10 percent, but in fact were down by 23 percent.

The governor, as might be expected, placed the blame for the forecasting errors on events beyond his control—in this case on the events of September 11, 2001 (an all-purpose excuse in the year following the World Trade Center disaster). Moreover, he asserted, the ultimate results may not be as bad as the six-month data would suggest, because taxes are not collected uniformly throughout the year.

typically make recommendations to the legislature as a whole; the legislature may revise their proposals as it deems appropriate.

Upon agreeing to the budget, a legislature officially adopts it by enacting an *appropriation* measure authorizing expenditures. Legislatures differ in the degree of control that they exert over the details of appropriations. Some appropriate lump sums to departments or programs, giving the executive branch the flexibility to allocate the resources among the various object classifications. Others go further, specifying not only the departments or programs, but also the object classifications on which authorized funds can be expended. Then, any subsequent shifts from one classification to another require legislative approval.

Property taxes are commonly *levied* (authorized by the legislature) annually. Most other revenues, such as income and sales taxes, are not authorized each year unless there is to be a change in rates or other provisions.

EXECUTION

The budget is executed (carried out) by an organization's executive branch. In some jurisdictions, expenditures are assigned particular months or quarters by **allotments** or **apportionments.** Both allotments and apportionments are periodic allocations of funds to departments or agencies, usually made by the chief executive's office, to assure that an entire year's appropriation is not dissipated early in the period covered by the budget. They also prevent a department or agency from spending resources that may not be available in the event that actual revenues fall short of budgeted revenues.

As shall be discussed later in this chapter, governments integrate their budgets into their accounting systems. In that way they are able to monitor continually how revenues and expenditures to date compare with the amounts that have been estimated

IN PRACTICE

FEDERAL BUDGETARY LEGERDEMAIN

When you project a federal budget, someone must make crucial economic assumptions. Many federal payments, such as Social Security, are tied to the inflation rate, so first you must decide what that rate is likely to be. Since income taxes depend on corporate profits and thus on Gross National Product (GNP), you need to know how much you can reasonably expect GNP to go up (or possibly even down). Interest payments on federal debt depend on the market interest rate, so you must have some idea of what that rate is likely to be. These numbers, and others, are interrelated: move one, and they all move.

Every forecaster, including the Office of Management and Budget (OMB), the Treasury, and the Congressional Budget Office (CBO), has a complex computer model of government finances and the economy. If you enter one set of numbers, the model will give you a complete, consistent set of output numbers on which the budget is based. But what are the "best" numbers and assumptions to use? That depends in large part on who your boss is. The OMB, in the executive office of the president, tends to generate numbers that will make the president look good—usually low inflation, high real growth, low interest rates, and a shrinking budget deficit.

David Stockman, head of the OMB during a portion of the Reagan administration, in his remarkable book *The Triumph of Politics*, tells how the Reagan administration arrived at its economic input numbers in the spring of 1981. Competing groups of experts were haggling over the numbers. As the deadline approached for locking up the Reagan budget, Stockman called in Murray Weidenbaum, chairman of the Council of Economic Advisers, and made a political deal. If Weidenbaum would agree to a "reasonably high" real growth rate, Stockman would accept whatever inflation rate was consistent with it.

When the "deal" was announced at the final economic meeting, there were grumbles from all of the contending factions. Finally someone turned to Weidenbaum and asked, "What model did this come from, Murray?"

"Weidenbaum," wrote Stockman, "glared at his inquisitor a moment and said, 'It came right out of here.' With that he slapped his belly with both hands. 'My visceral computer.'" And thus were determined the economic assumptions that would shape a $745 billion national budget.

Source: Joseph J. DioGuardi, *Unaccountable Congress: It Doesn't Add Up* (Washington, D.C.: Regnery Gateway, 1992), p.16. Reprinted with permission. DioGuardi claims to be the first *practicing* certified public accountant to be elected to Congress. He served in the House of Representatives (Republican, New York) from 1985 to 1988. In this book he reveals the deceptions used by the federal government to mask spending of billions of dollars.

or authorized. Moreover, to enhance control and facilitate end-of-period budget-to-actual comparisons, they use the same account structure for their budgets as for their actual revenues and expenditures.

Governments, like businesses, should issue interim financial statements to report on their progress in executing their budgets. Per the GASB *Codification:*

> Appropriate interim budgetary reports should be prepared during the fiscal period to facilitate management control and legislative oversight of governmental fund financial operations. Such reports are important both to revenue and expenditure control processes and to facilitate timely planning and budgetary revisions.[4]

[4] *Codification*, Section 2900.103.

IN PRACTICE

MISESTIMATING REVENUES AND EXPENDITURES

A study of 125 U.S. cities having populations more than 100,000 revealed substantial variances between estimated and actual revenues and expenditures.

For all revenues combined, sixty-eight cities (54 percent) overestimated revenues. Twenty-nine (23 percent) overestimated revenues by more than 5 percent and twenty (16 percent) underestimated them by more than 5 percent. Thus, 39 percent of the sample had variations greater than 5 percent.

For all expenditures combined, the average budget variance was considerably larger than for revenues. Eighty-nine cities (71 percent) overestimated expenditures. Of these, sixty-four (51 percent) overestimated expenditures by more than 5 percent. Eleven cities (9 percent) underestimated expenditures by more than 5 percent. Hence, 60 percent of the sample had variances greater than 5 percent.

This study revealed that budget estimates were significantly biased in the direction of conservatism. However, the data were drawn from a single year (1983), one of relative prosperity for local governments. Were the study repeated using data from the late 1980s and early 1990s, a period of economic lethargy, the bias might have been in the opposite direction.

Source: Michael H. Granof and Alan Mayper, "A Focus on Government Budgets," *The CPA Journal* 61 (July 1991): 28–33.

REPORTING AND AUDITING

To complete the budget cycle, information on how the budget was executed must be provided to the analysts and governing officials who must prepare and adopt the subsequent budget. At a minimum, both governments and not-for-profits should include in their annual financial statements or supplementary reports budget-to-actual comparisons for each of the funds for which they have adopted budgets. These comparisons will be discussed later in this chapter.

Performance budgets, unlike traditional object classification budgets, create the basis for evaluating and auditing organizational efficiency and effectiveness. These budgets specify anticipated outputs or outcomes in a quantifiable, measurable form. They thereby provide auditors (both internal and independent) with objective benchmarks by which to gauge organizational accomplishments and to compare them with budgetary expectations. By assessing performance, instead of mere compliance with budgetary spending mandates, auditors can transform the audit from what administrators may perceive as an annoyance into an essential element of the management process. Performance audits are addressed in Chapter 15.

ON WHAT BASIS OF ACCOUNTING ARE BUDGETS PREPARED?

Despite the importance of budgets and the influence of budgeting on financial reporting, both the GASB and the Financial Accounting Standards Board (FASB) establish generally accepted principles only for financial reporting, not for budgeting. Budgetary principles are established either by individual governments or organizations or by the governments or organizations that supervise them (e.g., states may establish the principles for their cities, towns, and districts; national associations may establish principles for their local chapters).

Although it lacks the authority to establish standards for budgeting, the GASB nevertheless recommends that governments prepare their annual budgets for governmental funds on the modified accrual basis—the same basis they are required to use for reporting on the governmental funds in their external financial statements.[5]

The modified accrual basis does not allow for balance sheet recognition of long-term assets and debts. However, it does permit a wide array of transactions and events to be recognized when they have their substantive economic impact, not merely when they result in cash inflows and outflows.

Many governments, however, reject the GASB's advice. They opt to prepare budgets on a cash basis or a slightly modified cash basis.

Governments that budget on a cash basis assign revenues and expenditures to the period in which the government is expected to receive or disburse cash. Some governments modify the cash basis by requiring that **encumbrances** (commitments to purchase goods or services) be accounted for as if they were the equivalent of actual purchases. Others permit certain taxes or other revenues to be recognized in the year in which they are due rather than expected to be collected, as long as they are expected to be collected within a reasonable period of time.

RATIONALE FOR BUDGETING ON THE CASH BASIS

Governments have valid reasons for budgeting on a cash basis. After all, bills must be paid with cash, not receivables or other assets; therefore, the required cash must be on hand in the year the payments have to be made. And goods or services must be paid for in the year of acquisition (or in the periods set forth in a borrowing agreement), not necessarily in the year or years in which the benefits will be received.

Correspondingly, when a government is able to defer payments, it need not have the cash on hand until disbursements are required. Taxpayers are understandably reluctant to part with their dollars so that the government can retain the cash as "savings" until the year needed. Suppose, for example, that government employees are permitted to defer until future years vacations that are earned in a current year. Although the services of the employees unquestionably benefit the period in which the vacations are earned, the government does not need—and the taxpayers might object to providing—the cash for the vacation payments until the employees actually take the vacations. Thus, in the face of a balanced budget requirement, the cash basis of accounting assures that the government receives in taxes and other revenues only what it is required to disburse.

ADVERSE CONSEQUENCES OF THE CASH BASIS

The adverse consequences of the cash basis should not be overlooked. The cash basis may distort the economic impact of a government's planned fiscal activities. A budget that is balanced on a cash basis may be decidedly unbalanced as to economic costs and revenues. It may give the appearance of a budget that has achieved interperiod equity when it really has not.

The cash basis permits a government to balance its budget by taking any number of steps that artificially delay cash disbursements and advance cash receipts. Consider, for example, the quintessential budget-balancing tactic employed by the federal government and a number of states and local governments: changing the date on which employees are paid from the last day of the month to the first of the next month. In the year of the change the government is able to pay its employees for one fewer payroll period than it would otherwise.

On the revenue side, a comparable scheme works equally well: advancing the due date of taxes or fees from early in the following budget year to late in the current year, thereby picking up an extra tax or fee payment in the year of the change. This

[5] *Codification*, Section 1700.116.

tactic, like that of delaying the payday, can be employed only once for each revenue or expenditure. New devices (such as the uncommon ones described in "In Practice: Do Taxpayers Really Want Honest Budgeting?") must continually be developed.

The deleterious consequences of cash basis budgeting are exacerbated by the use of fund accounting. Because each fund is a separate accounting entity, governments can readily transfer resources from a fund that has a budget surplus or that does not require a balanced budget to one that needs extra resources. Some governments budget interfund "loans" for the last day of one fiscal year and repayments for the first day of the next. Others delay, for one day, required payments from the general fund to other funds. Still others sell assets, sometimes to entities that they themselves created and control, and lease them back (as illustrated by "In Practice: Balancing the Budget by Selling Assets to Yourself").

These "one shot" budget balancing techniques would generally not affect revenues and expenditures as reported in the annual financial statements. Governments *must* prepare the external financial reports of their governmental funds on a modified accrual basis. As defined by the GASB, the modified accrual basis requires that short-term loan proceeds, whether from another fund or from an outside source, be accounted for as liabilities rather than revenues. Similarly, most required outlays are reported as expenditures in the period to which they apply, irrespective of when they are actually paid.

Cash basis budgeting complicates financial accounting and reporting. Governments must maintain their accounts to facilitate preparation of two sets of reports—one that demonstrates compliance with the budgetary provisions and one in accordance with GAAP.

WHAT CAUTIONS MUST BE TAKEN IN BUDGET-TO-ACTUAL COMPARISONS?

As emphasized in Chapter 1, a primary objective of government financial reporting is to "demonstrate whether resources were used in accordance with the entities' legally

IN PRACTICE

DO TAXPAYERS REALLY WANT HONEST BUDGETING?

A watchful accountant wrote an op-ed piece in a local newspaper pointing out several budgetary gimmicks, such as advancing the due date of tax payments, that the state comptroller had proposed to balance the budget. He was surprised by the response by a representative of the comptroller's office in the form of a letter to the editor. The taxpayers, he asserted would much prefer the proposed "bookkeeping adjustments" to the alternative—a tax increase.

The comptroller's representative may well be correct. The comptroller, an elected official, is no doubt far more politically astute than the accountant. But one wonders if the taxpayers would be equally willing to acquiesce to the proposed budgetary legerdemain if the question was posed as follows: Do you favor balancing the budget by (1) use of artificial bookkeeping devices that pass the cost of the government services that you enjoy today unto your children and grandchildren or (2) use of accounting that best captures the economic substance of the transactions in which the government engages even if it requires you to pay the full cost of the services that you enjoy today?

IN PRACTICE

BALANCING THE BUDGET BY SELLING ASSETS TO YOURSELF

On April 1, 1991—April Fools Day—New York's Governor Mario Cuomo announced the sale of Attica prison *to the state itself* for over $200 million—all of which was counted as general revenues. The buyer was a state agency that financed the purchase by floating bonds. The bonds were backed by the state and were, therefore, economic obligations of the state. The purchaser immediately leased the prison back to the state under terms specifying that the "rent" payments would be exactly equal to the debt service on the bonds. In essence, the state balanced its operating budget with a loan in the amount of the prison's sale price. The benefits of the loan were reaped by the taxpayers of the year of the transaction; principal and interest will be paid by the taxpayers of the future.

In the previous year, the state sold its Cross Westchester Expressway to the New York Thruway Authority—also to itself—but that transaction was only for $20 million. Following the lead of its neighbor, New Jersey sold a portion of its highway system to a state-owned agency, the New Jersey Turnpike Authority.

One can only marvel at such ingenuity and wonder what these governments will do for an encore. Perhaps, they will repurchase the assets and sell them, at a profit, to the same or another state agency.

adopted budget." Accordingly, generally accepted accounting principles dictate that governments include in their annual reports, as required supplementary information, a comparison of actual results with the budget for each governmental fund for which an annual budget has been adopted.[6]

DIFFERENCES IN HOW ACTUAL RESULTS ARE DETERMINED

Whereas the GASB specifies the principles of accounting to which governments must adhere in reporting on their governmental funds, it is silent on those they can use in preparing their budgets. Unless a government reports its actual results using budgetary principles or its budget using generally accepted accounting principles (GAAP), a comparison between the budget and actual results would not be meaningful. Therefore, per Statement No. 34, the GASB now requires that governments present their budget versus actual comparisons on a *budgetary* basis and include a schedule that reconciles the budgetary and the GAAP amounts.

The differences between legally adopted budgets and the GAAP-based financial statements can be attributed to several factors. Among them are:

- ***Differences in basis of accounting.*** As previously noted, governments often prepare their budgets on a cash or near-cash basis, whereas their financial statements must be prepared on a modified accrual basis.
- ***Differences in timing.*** As shown in its budget, a government may appropriate resources for a particular project rather than for a particular period. For example, in approving resources for a construction project, the government will typically establish the total amount that can be spent. It will not allocate resources to specific years. By contrast, the annual report of the fund in which the project is accounted would have to present the expenditures year by year. Moreover, governments may permit departments to carry over to subsequent years resources not spent in the year for which they were budgeted. Thus, expenditures in a particular year may not have been budgeted in that year.

[6] GASB Concepts Statement 1, *Objectives of Financial Reporting*, para. 77b, 1987.

- ***Differences in perspective.*** Governments may structure their budgets differently from their financial reports. For example, a government may budget on the basis of programs. The programs, however, may be financed by resources accounted for in more than one fund. Thus, the amounts expended in each of the funds cannot be compared to any particular line item in the budget.
- ***Difference in the reporting entity.*** As you will learn in Chapter 11, GAAP requires that a government's reporting entity include organizations that are legally independent of the government yet, in political or economic reality, an integral part of it. For example, a city may create a financing authority—a separate legal entity—to issue bonds on behalf of the city. If the city has political control over the authority (e.g., the mayor appoints the majority of the governing board) or is responsible for its financial affairs (e.g., approves its budget), then GAAP dictates that the authority be reported upon in the city's financial statements. Yet because the authority is a separate legal entity, the city may exclude it from its legally adopted budget.

GOVERNMENTS MUST REPORT BOTH ORIGINAL AND FINAL BUDGETS

Budget-to-actual comparisons may demonstrate either legal compliance or managerial effectiveness in adhering to budget estimates. One of the major improvements of the new GASB model over the old is that the new model requires governments to report their actual results and both their original and final appropriated budgets. Under the old model, governments could report only their amended (final) budget. For some governments, their final budget incorporates changes they authorized only after they were aware of the actual revenues and expenditures of the year. Thus, governments typically reported no significant variance between budgeted and actual amounts.

The GASB encourages, but does not require, governments to present in a separate column the variances (i.e., differences) between actual results and the budget. It recommends that the variances be based on the final rather than the original budget. However, inasmuch as governments must include columns that show both the original budget and the final budget-statement users can readily calculate the differences between actual results and the original budget as well as the changes in the budget that were authorized during the year.[7]

Table 3-3 presents the budget-to-actual comparison of Charlotte's general fund.

HOW DOES BUDGETING IN NOT-FOR-PROFIT ORGANIZATIONS COMPARE WITH THAT IN GOVERNMENTS?

As discussed in Chapter 1, the not-for-profit sector covers organizations that range from those that depend entirely, or almost entirely, on donor contributions (e.g., certain social service organizations) to those that are run much like business (e.g. a university "co-op" bookstore). According, the budgeting process must be custom-designed to suit each particular type of entity.

Not-for-profits differ from governments in at least one critical respect: They lack the authority to tax. Governments can first determine the level of services they wish to provide and then impose the taxes and fees sufficient to provide those services. Non-business types of not-for-profits, by contrast, are limited in their ability

[7] GASB Statement No. 34, *Basic Financial Statements—and Management's Discussion and Analysis—for State and Local Governments*, para. 130 (June 1999); see also GASB Statement No. 41, *Budgetary Comparison Schedules—Perspective Differences* (May 2003).

TABLE 3–3
Charlotte, North Carolina

Statement of Revenues, Expenditures, and Changes in Fund Balance—Budget and Actual General Fund (Non-GAAP Basis)
For the Year Ended June 30, 2002

	Budgeted Amounts		Actual (Budgetary Basis)	Variance with Final Budget Positive (Negative)
	Original	Final		
Revenues				
Taxes—				
Property				
Current year	$182,909	$182,909	$186,551	$3,642
Prior years	3,136	3,136	3,648	512
Interest and penalties	1,352	1,352	1,658	306
Less rebates	(2,031)	(2,031)	(2,587)	(556)
Total property	185,366	185,366	189,270	3,904
Other				
Sales	37,327	37,327	33,435	(3,892)
Occupancy	2,985	2,738	2,228	(510)
Rental car	1,500	1,500	1,643	143
Total other	41,812	41,565	37,306	(4,259)
Total taxes	227,178	226,931	226,576	(355)
Intergovernmental—State of North Carolina				
Utility franchise tax	26,700	16,700	15,251	(1,449)
Inventory tax reimbursement	6,459	6,459	2,491	(3,968)
Intangible tax reimbursement	4,900	4,900	4,530	(370)
Beer and wine	2,400	2,400	—	(2,400)
Other	2,260	2,153	1,526	(627)
Total state of North Carolina	42,719	32,612	23,798	(8,814)
Federal government—Grant income	177	678	505	(173)
Mecklenburg County				
ABC Board contribution	2,192	2,192	1,431	(761)
Law enforcement services	11,673	11,673	12,847	1,174
Other	1,851	2,290	2,087	(203)
Total Mecklenburg County	15,716	16,155	16,365	210
Charlotte–Mecklenburg Board of Education	1,257	1,257	1,332	75
Local municipalities—Service fees	1,396	1,396	1,404	8
Total intergovernmental	61,265	52,098	43,404	(8,694)
Licenses, fees, and fines—				
Business privilege licenses	7,800	7,800	8,686	886
Motor vehicle licenses	1,987	1,987	1,967	(20)
Solid waste fees	8,912	8,912	9,027	115
Cable TV franchise	5,300	5,300	5,638	338
Burglar alarm fines	1,300	1,300	844	(456)
Parking fees	2,880	2,880	2,915	35

(Continues)

TABLE 3–3
Charlotte, North Carolina *(Continued)*

Statement of Revenues, Expenditures, and Changes in Fund Balance—Budget and Actual General Fund (Non-GAAP Basis)
For the Year Ended June 30, 2002

	Original	Final	Actual (Budgetary Basis)	Variance with Final Budget Positive (Negative)
Revenues (continued)				
Other	3,021	3,031	3,463	432
Total licenses, fees, and fines	31,200	31,210	32,540	1,330
Investment earnings	5,100	4,392	4,925	533
Administrative charges—				
Equipment services	$ 14	$ 2,371	$ 2,357	$ (14)
Cost allocation	14,094	14,094	11,475	(2,619)
Total administrative charges	14,108	16,465	13,832	(2,633)
Charges for current services—				
Private street cuts	2,000	2,000	1,920	(80)
Other	3,732	3,755	1,882	(1,873)
Total charges for current services	5,732	5,755	3,802	(1,953)
Miscellaneous	1,966	4,066	4,127	61
Total revenues	346,549	340,917	329,206	(11,711)
Expenditures				
Current—				
Public safety	187,448	188,068	187,820	248
Sanitation	32,596	32,204	31,059	1,145
General administration:				
Finance	7,774	7,774	7,095	679
Human resources	2,286	2,286	2,140	146
City manager	3,871	3,878	3,698	180
Corporate communications	1,790	1,800	1,667	133
City attorney	1,360	1,360	1,350	10
Budget and evaluation	1,166	1,181	1,055	126
City council	1,078	1,092	1,092	—
Retiree health and life insurance	4,250	5,976	5,976	—
Elections office	1,562	1,562	1,548	14
Annexation	—	1,409	1,409	—
Other	1,738	2,761	2,086	675
Total general administration	26,875	31,079	29,116	1,963
Support services	15,433	18,425	15,718	2,707
Engineering and property management	23,888	21,874	19,300	2,574
Streets and highways:				
Transportation	20,574	20,248	18,016	2,232
Street lighting	7,731	6,086	6,086	—
Total streets and highways	28,305	26,334	24,102	2,232

(Continues)

TABLE 3–3
Charlotte, North Carolina *(Continued)*

Statement of Revenues, Expenditures, and Changes in Fund Balance—Budget and Actual General Fund (Non-GAAP Basis)
For the Year Ended June 30, 2002

	Original	Final	Actual (Budgetary Basis)	Variance with Final Budget Positive (Negative)
Expenditures (continued)				
Current (continued)				
Community planning and development:				
Community relations	$ 1,059	$ 1,349	$ 941	$ 408
City–County Planning Commission	4,166	4,169	3,772	397
United Arts Council	2,942	2,942	2,942	—
Convention Visitor's Bureau	3,020	2,314	2,249	65
Other	1,084	2,270	2,042	228
Total community planning and development	12,271	13,044	11,946	1,098
Total expenditures	326,816	331,028	319,061	11,967
Excess of revenues over expenditures	19,733	9,889	10,145	256
Other financing sources (uses)				
Sales of capital assets	1,195	1,195	1,035	(160)
Transfers in—				
Debt service	35	35	35	—
Capital projects	1,476	1,783	1,783	—
Special revenue—Convention Center tax	—	1,050	1,050	—
Permanent—Perpetual care	140	140	117	(23)
Total transfers in	1,651	3,008	2,985	(23)
Transfers out—				
Debt service	16,600	15,868	15,868	—
Special revenue				
Public safety grants	944	3,569	3,471	98
Neighborhood development	4,038	3,571	3,535	36
Employment and training	997	990	936	54
Total transfers out	22,579	23,998	23,810	188
Total other financing sources (uses)	(19,733)	(19,795)	(19,790)	5
Revenues and other sources over (under) expenditures and other uses	$ —	$ (9,906)	(9,645	$ 261
Reconciliation to GAAP basis				
Current year encumbrances			11,273	
Prior year encumbrances			(9,871)	
Net change in fund balance			(8,243)	
Fund balance—beginning			100,613	
Fund balance—ending			$ 92,370	

The notes to the financial statements are an integral part of this statement.

to generate revenues and hence must adjust the level of services they provide to the corresponding level of revenues.

The general approach to budgeting suggested in this chapter for governments is relevant, with some obvious modifications, to not-for-profits. The budget process is the same four-phase process: preparation, adoption (although by a board of directors or trustees rather than a legislature), execution, and reporting and auditing.

Not-for-profits, of course, are not subject to the same types of penalties for violating budgetary mandates as governments are. Nevertheless, reliable estimates of revenues and expenditures are no less important. The consequences of underestimating costs or overestimating revenues are obvious. Not-for-profits, like businesses, are not guaranteed continued existence. The consequences of overestimating costs or underestimating revenues, while not as potentially devastating as the reverse, can also be severe—especially to the organization's intended beneficiaries. A homeless shelter may unnecessarily reduce the number of people that it serves; a church or synagogue can cut back programs that it otherwise could have provided; a private college may defer maintenance only to have to incur greater costs to play catch-up in the future.

HOW DO BUDGETS ENHANCE CONTROL?

Owing to the adverse consequences of violating budgetary mandates, both governments and not-for-profits can build safeguards into their accounting systems that help assure budgetary compliance. These include preparing journal entries both to record the budget and to give recognition to goods and services that have been ordered but not yet received. We begin the discussion by describing the basic books of account maintained by governments and not-for-profits and showing how they accommodate these safeguards.

THE BASIC BOOKS OF ACCOUNT

The basic books of account of both governments and not-for-profits correspond to those of businesses. They consist, either in manual or electronic form, of:

- ***Journals***, in which journal entries are recorded. Most transactions are entered initially in a special journal, such as a property tax cash receipts journal, a parking fines cash receipts journal, a purchases journal, or a cash disbursements journal. Both nonroutine transactions and account totals from special journals are recorded in a general journal.
- ***Ledgers***, in which all balance sheet and operating accounts are maintained. The general ledger consists of control accounts that summarize the balances of the detailed subsidiary accounts that are maintained in subsidiary ledgers.

A city or other general purpose government is likely to maintain hundreds of accounts. For example, the control account, general property taxes, may be subdivided as follows:

General property taxes
  Real property (e.g., land and buildings)
  Personal property
    Tangible personal (e.g., business inventories, machinery, household furnishings, and vehicles)
    Intangible personal (e.g., stocks, bonds, and bank deposits)

In addition, these accounts would be further divided into accounts for each individual taxpayer.

Similarly, one branch of the expenditure tree for police might be structured as follows (with only a small number of the object classification accounts displayed):

Police

Crime control and investigation
- Crime laboratory
  - Salaries
    - Regular
    - Overtime
  - Social Security contributions
  - Rentals
    - Land and buildings
    - Equipment and vehicles
  - Supplies
    - Custodial
    - Fuel
    - Office

BUDGETARY CONTROL FEATURES

As in a ledger for a business, each account consists of columns for debits, for credits, and for the balance (the difference between the two). However, the ledger accounts of governments (and some not-for-profits) incorporate budgetary control features not conventionally found in those of businesses.

The ledger accounts for revenues incorporate an additional debit column, estimated revenues. In this column the government posts the revenue side of an entry (to be described and illustrated in the next section) to record the budget. The difference between the estimated revenues (a debit), actual revenues recognized to date (credits), and any unusual adjustments (debits or credits) equals the amount of budgeted revenues still to be recognized. Thus, for example, the subledger account "Real Property Taxes" might appear as follows (dates and references omitted):

Revenues—Real Property Taxes

Estimated Revenues (Dr.)	Actual Revenues (Cr.)	Adjustments (Dr. or Cr.)	Balance (Dr. or Cr.)
15,000,000	2,300,000		12,700,000
	1,100,000		11,600,000
	500,000		11,100,000

Based on the data shown, the government budgeted real property tax revenue of $15 million and has recognized $3.9 million to date. Therefore, $11.1 million remains to be recognized.

Similarly, the ledger accounts for expenditures incorporate *two* extra columns. One column, appropriations, corresponds to estimated revenues. In this column the government posts a credit for the amount appropriated per the budget. In the second extra column the government posts, as debits, encumbrances—*commitments* to purchase goods or services. The difference between the appropriation (a credit), resources encumbered (debits), actual expenditures to date (also debits), and any unusual adjustments equals the amount of the appropriation that is still uncommitted and is therefore available to be spent (the unencumbered balance). Thus, crime laboratory expenditures might appear as follows:

Expenditures—Crime Laboratory

Appropriations (Cr.)	Encumbrances (Dr.)	Expenditures (Dr.)	Adjustments (Dr. or Cr.)	Unencumbered Balance
300,000		50,000		250,000
		30,000		220,000
	15,000	40,000		165,000

This account indicates that the government appropriated $300,000 for the crime laboratory. To date it has spent $120,000 and has outstanding commitments for goods and services of $15,000. Therefore, it has $165,000 available for future spending.

WHAT ARE THE DISTINCTIVE WAYS GOVERNMENTS RECORD THEIR BUDGETS?

By recording its budget, a government builds into its accounting system a gauge that warns of excesses in spending and deficiencies in collections. This gauge serves only as an *internal* control function. The budgetary entries are reversed at year-end and have no impact on year-end financial statements. To external report users, budgetary entries are irrelevant. Nevertheless, because of their significance in controlling both revenues and costs, students need to be aware of how they affect the accounts.

CREDITING OR DEBITING THE BUDGETED DEFICIT OR SURPLUS DIRECTLY TO FUND BALANCE

Most students initially find budgetary entries counterintuitive and confusing. Mainly, that's because when a government records its budget it *debits* estimated revenues and *credits* appropriations (in effect, estimated expenditures). Most students, of course, are used to crediting revenues and debiting expenditures. The practice of debiting estimated revenues and crediting appropriations makes sense, however, when you understand that each estimated revenue and appropriation account will be tied directly to its related *actual* revenue and *actual* expenditure account. (See "Example: Budgetary Entries" for a case in point.) The resulting differences equal the revenues yet to be recognized and the appropriations still available to be spent. Thus (ignoring encumbrances):

Estimated revenues (Dr.) − Actual revenues (Cr.) = Revenues still to be recognized

and

Appropriations (Cr.) − Actual expenditures (Dr.) = Balance available for expenditure

In a sense, the estimated revenue and appropriations accounts can be thought of as contra accounts to the actual revenue and expenditure accounts.

Moreover, the entries appear to put the cart before the horse. The difference between the debit to estimated revenues and the credit to appropriations is offset by fund balance. Thus, the entity's fund balance may be increased or decreased upon merely *adopting* the budget—that is, wishes and whims—rather than actual transactions. Fortunately, as with other widely used bookkeeping procedures that allow accounts to be temporarily in error (e.g., periodic inventory methods), the entries cause no harm as long as appropriate adjustments are made prior to the preparation of financial statements.

EXAMPLE *Budgetary Entries*

A school district adopts a budget calling for total revenues of $400 million and total expenditures of $390 million. The following entries would record the budget:

(b1)		
Estimated revenues	$400	
Fund balance		$400
To record estimated revenues		

(b2)		
Fund balance	$390	
Appropriations		$390
To record appropriations (estimated expenditures)		

The entries illustrated in this chapter will be made only to control accounts. In reality, corresponding entries would be made to the estimated revenue and appropriation *subaccounts* that support the control accounts. The sum of the debits and credits to the subaccounts should, of course, equal the entries to the respective control accounts.

Suppose that during the year both revenues and expenditures were as estimated and that all transactions were for cash. The transactions would be recorded with standard revenue and expenditure entries (with appropriate entries to the subaccounts as well):

(1)		
Cash	$400	
Revenues		$400
To record revenues		

(2)		
Expenditures	$390	
Cash		$390
To record expenditures		

At year-end, each of the budgeted and actual revenues and expenditures accounts would be *closed* (i.e., reversed) to fund balance. Thus:

(cl 1)		
Appropriations	$390	
Fund balance	10	
Estimated revenues		$400
To close budgetary accounts		

(cl 2)		
Revenues	$400	
Expenditures		$390
Fund balance		10
To close revenues and expenditures		

The net effect of the entries is to increase fund balance by the difference between the actual revenues and expenditures—the same increase as would have been recorded had the budgetary entries not been made.

Suppose alternatively that actual revenues and expenditures differed from what were budgeted—for example, that actual revenues were $420 and actual expenditures were $415. Actual revenues and expenditures would have been recorded as follows:

(1a)		
Cash	$420	
Revenues		$420
To record revenues		

(2a)

	Debit	Credit
Expenditures	$415	
Cash		$415
To record expenditures		

Closing entries would take the same form as illustrated previously:

(cl 1a)

	Debit	Credit
Appropriations	$390	
Fund balance	10	
Estimated revenues		$400
To close budgetary accounts		

(cl 2a)

	Debit	Credit
Revenues	$420	
Expenditures		$415
Fund balance		5
To close revenues and expenditures		

In this situation, as shown in the T-accounts presented in Figure 3-1, year-end fund balance would again be the difference between *actual* revenues and *actual* expenditures. Actual revenues were $420 and actual expenditures were $415. Ending fund balance, after the closing entries have been posted, is thus $5—the same as if the budgetary entries had not been made.

The components of both the budgetary and the closing entries could, of course, have been combined differently. For example, appropriations and expenditures (rather than appropriations and estimated revenues) and revenues and estimated revenues (rather than revenues and expenditures) could have been closed in the same entry. The net impact on fund balance would have been the same.

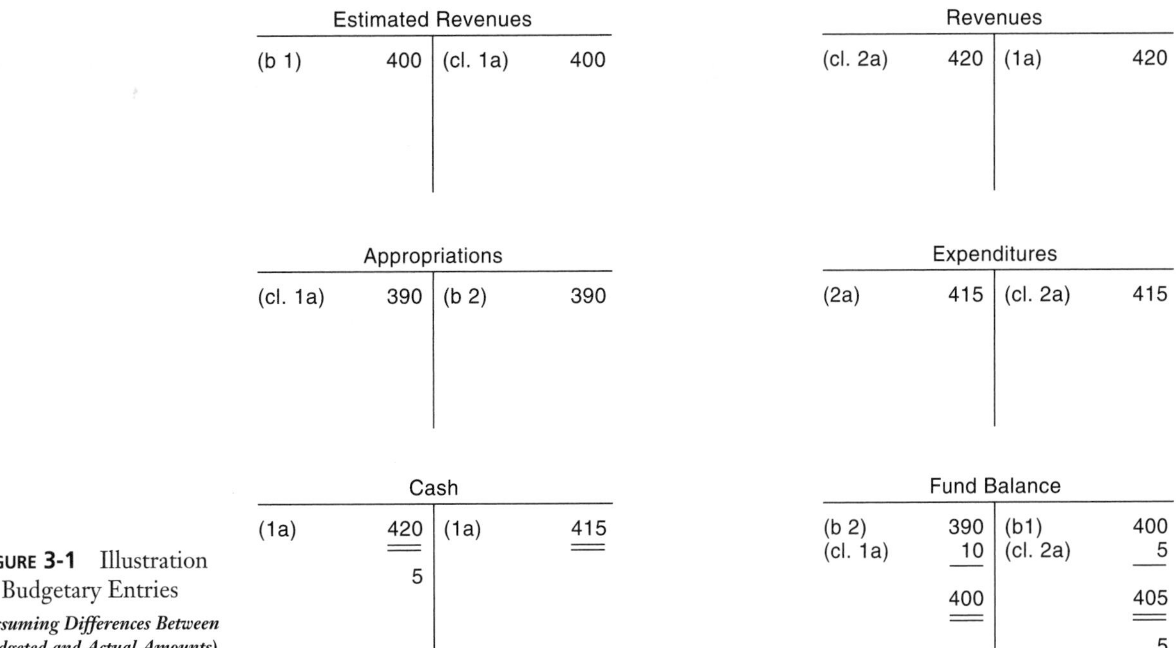

FIGURE 3-1 Illustration of Budgetary Entries

(Assuming Differences Between Budgeted and Actual Amounts)

AN ALTERNATIVE METHOD: CREDITING OR DEBITING THE DIFFERENCE BETWEEN REVENUES AND EXPENDITURES TO "BUDGETARY FUND BALANCE"

Some governments maintain an account called *budgetary fund balance.* In recording the budget they debit or credit this account instead of fund balance. Budgetary fund balance is a temporary account. At year-end, the appropriations and estimated revenues are closed to this account, so that after the closing entries are made its balance is always zero.

Governments prefer (in some cases, must take) this approach so as to avoid contaminating the actual fund balance with appropriations and estimated revenues. The actual fund balance is affected only by authentic revenues and expenditures, which, as in the "Budgetary Entries" example, are closed at year-end, to fund balance. The account reflects only genuine transactions, not forecasts (and in some cases mere hopes) of what will occur during the year.

Thus, when the government adopted the budget, it would make the following entry:

Estimated revenues	$400	
Appropriations		$390
Budgetary fund balance		10

To record estimated revenues and appropriations (estimated expenditures)

At year-end, irrespective of actual revenues and expenditures, the budgetary entry would be reversed:

Budgetary fund balance	$ 10	
Appropriations	390	
Estimated revenues		$400

To close revenues and expenditures

During the year actual revenues and expenditures would be recorded in the normal manner, and at year-end they would be closed to the budgetary fund balance account.

HOW DOES ENCUMBRANCE ACCOUNTING PREVENT OVERSPENDING?

Governments and some not-for-profits record encumbrances to help prevent overspending the budget. The entry to record an encumbrance is usually prepared when a purchase order is issued, a contract is signed, or a commitment is made (e.g., when a university makes faculty and staff appointments for a semester or year). Most organizations do not encumber all anticipated expenditures. Many, for example, do not encumber salaries and wages, expenditures below a specified amount, and expenditures that are adequately controlled by other means.

THE BASIC ENTRIES

The entry to record an encumbrance reduces the budgeted amount available for expenditure (as if the amount had already been spent) and concurrently designates a portion of what would otherwise be *unreserved* fund balance as *reserved for encumbrances* (i.e., for expenditures to which the organization is committed). The entry is reversed as the goods or services are received and expenditures are recorded, as shown in "Example: The Encumbrance Cycle—Year 1."

Whereas both budgetary entries and encumbrances are mainly internal control devices, encumbrances are of slightly greater concern to external parties since they have a minor impact on the basic financial statements. Outstanding commitments at year-end are reported on the entity's fund (not government-wide) *balance sheet* as a reservation of fund balance and accordingly reduce the unreserved portion of fund balance.

EXAMPLE *The Encumbrance Cycle—Year 1*

A state university contracts for repair services that it estimates will cost $5,000. The following entry will reserve the funds to meet the anticipated expenditure:

Encumbrances	$5,000	
Reserve for encumbrances		$5,000
To encumber $5,000 for repair services		

In addition to these control account entries, corresponding entries would be made in the repair-related subaccounts (e.g., encumbrances—electrical contractors).

The reserve for encumbrances account is a balance sheet account—a reservation of fund balance. The encumbrance account, although most definitely *not* an expenditure, is similar to an expenditure in that at year-end any remaining balance is closed to unreserved fund balance. The encumbrance account indicates the net amount that was transferred during the period from unreserved fund balance to fund balance reserved for encumbrances.

The repairs are completed and, as anticipated, the university is billed for $5,000. The repair expenditure must be recorded with the usual entry:

Expenditures	$5,000	
Accounts payable		$5,000
To record repair expenditures		

In addition, the reserve for encumbrance is no longer required. The services have been received and the expenditure has been charged. The reserve must be eliminated by reversing the entry establishing it:

Reserve for encumbrances	$5,000	
Encumbrances		$5,000
To reverse the encumbrance entry upon receipt of services		

At year-end the expenditures would be closed out in standard fashion, thereby reducing fund balance.

Consider two alternative possibilities. Assume first that the contractor *completes* the repairs but bills the university for only $4,800, not the encumbered $5,000. The university must now record an expenditure for the actual amount to be paid:

Expenditure	$4,800	
Accounts payable		$4,800
To record repair expenditures		

As before, it must eliminate the *entire* reserve. With regard to the repairs, the university has no further commitment; it therefore needs no reserve:

Reserve for encumbrances	$5,000	
Encumbrances		$5,000
To reverse the encumbrance entry upon receipt of services		

If the contractor's bill were for more than the encumbered amount, the same approach would be taken. The expenditure would be charged for the amount to be paid; the full amount of the reserve would be eliminated. The university's error in encumbering less than its actual commitment would have no consequences for financial reporting. At worst, it temporarily increased the university's risk of overspending its budget.

As the second possibility, assume that in the current period the contractor completes only 40 percent of the repairs and accordingly bills the university for only $2,000. It expects to fulfill the remainder of its contract in the following period. In this situation, only a part of the encumbrance entry can be reversed; the university still has an outstanding commitment for $3,000. Thus:

Expenditures	$2,000	
Accounts payable		$2,000
To record repair expenditures		
Reserve for encumbrances	$2,000	
Encumbrances		$2,000
To reverse the encumbrance entry upon the contractor's completion of $2,000 of the $5,000 in anticipated services		

At year-end, the expenditures and the encumbrances would be closed to fund balance. (The reserve for encumbrances need not be closed because it is a balance sheet account.) Continuing with the last set of assumptions (expenditures of $2,000; balance in the encumbrances account of $3,000), the following closing entry would be in order:

Fund balance	$5,000	
Expenditures		$2,000
Encumbrances		$3,000
To close expenditures and encumbrances		

As a consequence of these entries, $3,000 of the university's fund balance—the amount committed for completion of the repairs—remains reserved for encumbrances.

ACCOUNTING FOR COMMITMENTS OUTSTANDING AT THE START OF A YEAR

Governments differ in how they budget—and therefore how they account—for commitments outstanding (left over from the prior year). Many governments require that the cost of goods or services be charged against budgeted appropriations of the year in which they are received. In other words, all appropriations lapse at year-end. To satisfy its outstanding commitments, a government must reappropriate the funds for the following year or meet them out of whatever resources are budgeted for the following year within an applicable expenditure classification.

Other governments, either for all or only selected types of commitments (particularly long-term projects), allow appropriations to continue into future years. When the goods or services are received, they are charged against the budget of the year of appropriation.

In the circumstances in which appropriations lapse and the government charges the cost of goods or services against appropriations of the year in which they are received, the accounting for commitments made in a previous year is relatively simple, as is shown in "Example: The Encumbrance Cycle—Year 2." At the start of the new year the government need only restore the encumbrances that were closed at the end of the previous year. This can be accomplished by reversing the closing entry (i.e., debiting encumbrances and crediting fund balance). By restoring the encumbrances, both the reserve for encumbrances (which, as a balance sheet account, was never closed) and the encumbrances would have the same balances as if the closing entries had not been made. Thereafter, the entries to record the fulfillment of the commitments would be the same as if the goods or services were received in the year the encumbrances and the reserve were initially established.

EXAMPLE *The Encumbrance Cycle—Year 2*

At the end of the first year—the start of the second—the university had $3,000 of outstanding commitments for repairs. The following entry would restore the $3,000 of encumbrances for repairs:

Encumbrances	$3,000	
Fund balance		$3,000
To restore encumbrances at the start of the new year		

When the contractor completes the repairs, the university will charge expenditures for the amount billed and reverse the encumbrances and the reserve for encumbrances:

Expenditures	$3,000	
Accounts payable		$3,000
To record repair expenditures		
Reserve for encumbrances	$3,000	
Encumbrances		$3,000
To reverse the encumbrances entry upon the contractor's completion of the remaining $3,000 of repairs[8]		

The next example, "Impact of Encumbrances on Fund Balance," highlights the impact of the encumbrance procedures on fund balance by focusing on a single commitment. Note that over the two-year period the total reduction in fund balance equals the total expenditures.

EXAMPLE *Impact of Encumbrances on Fund Balance*

Year 1

As of January 1, a government's general fund balance sheet shows the following:

Cash	$1,000
Fund balance—unreserved	$1,000

[8] If the appropriation does not lapse and the government charges the cost of goods or services against appropriations of the year in which the commitment was made, then the encumbrance should *not* be restored. Instead, when the commitment is fulfilled, the expenditure should be "dated" to indicate that it is applicable to the previous year. Thus, for example:

Expenditures—Year 1 (prior year)	$3,000	
Accounts payable		$3,000
To record repair expenditures		

These expenditures would then be closed to the previously established reserve for encumbrances:

Reserve for encumbrances	$3,000	
Expenditures—Year 1 (prior year)		$3,000
To close expenditures for the previous year and eliminate the applicable reserve for encumbrances		

During the year, the government orders $1,000 of supplies (which are to be charged as expenditures when received):

	(a)		
Encumbrances		$1,000	
Reserve for encumbrances			$1,000
To encumber $1,000 for supplies on order			

Part of the supplies order costing $800 is received and paid for in cash:

	(b)		
Supplies expenditures		$800	
Cash			$800
To record the receipt of, and payment for, supplies			

	(2)		
Reserve for encumbrances		$800	
Encumbrances			$800
To reverse the encumbrance entry for the portion of the supplies order received			

The government prepares the following year-end closing entries:

	(cl 1)		
Fund balance—unreserved		$1,000	
Encumbrances			$200
Supplies expenditures			800
To close encumbrances and expenditures			

Year 2

The government expects to honor its commitment for the supplies on order, and its budgeting policies dictate that the cost of the supplies on order be charged as expenditures of the year in which they are received. Therefore, at the start of the new year it restores the encumbrances that had been closed at the end of the prior year:

	(d)		
Encumbrances		$200	
Fund balance—unreserved			$200
To restore encumbrances			

It receives, and pays for, the remainder of the supplies. However, the additional charges are only $150, not $200 as encumbered:

	(e)		
Supplies expenditures		$150	
Cash			$150
To record the receipt of, and payment for; supplies			

	(f)		
Reserve for encumbrances		$200	
Encumbrances			$200
To reverse the encumbrance entry for the remainder of the supplies			

It prepares appropriate year-end closing entries:

	(cl 2)		
Fund balance—unreserved		$150	
Supplies expenditures			$150
To close expenditures (Note: the balance in the encumbrances account is zero; it need not be closed.)			

Figure 3-2 summarizes the entries to the accounts. The government began the two-year period with an unreserved fund balance of $1,000. During the two years it incurred expenditures of $950. As shown in the T-account, its unreserved fund balance at the end of the second year is $50—the same as if an encumbrance system were not being employed. The fund's balance sheet at the end of each of the two years and a schedule explaining the change in unreserved fund balance follow:

Balance Sheet

	End of	
	Year 1	**Year 2**
Cash	$200	$50
Fund balance		
Reserve for encumbrances	$200	$ 0
Unreserved	0	50
Total fund balance	$200	$50

Schedule of Changes in Unreserved Fund Balance

	Year 1	**Year 2**	**Total**
Revenues	$ 0	$ 0	$ 0
Expenditures	800	150	950
Excess of revenues over expenditures	(800)	(150)	(950)
Less: Increase/(decrease) in reserve for encumbrances	200	(200)	0
Net change in unreserved fund balance During the year [increase/(decrease)]	(1,000)	50	$ (950)
Add: Beginning of year balance	1,000	0	
End of year balance	$ 0	$ 50	

Note: If the appropriations did not lapse, then the entry to restore the encumbrances would *not* have been made. Instead, when the goods were received, the following entries would be necessary:

Supplies expenditures—year 1	$150	
Cash		$150

To record the receipt of, and payment for, supplies

Reserve for encumbrances	$200	
Supplies expenditures—year 1		$150
Fund balance		50

To close the supplies expenditures for year 1 and eliminate the reserve for encumbrances

ARE BUDGETARY AND ENCUMBRANCE ENTRIES REALLY NEEDED?

Some governments and most not-for-profits do not integrate their budgets into their accounting systems or encumber the cost of goods or services for which they are committed. Under what circumstances should they do so? The general answer is that they should do so when the benefits of added control are worth the costs (in both dollars and inconvenience).

Consistent with this answer, governments are more likely to establish these controls than are other not-for-profits because the penalties for overspending government budgets are likely to be more severe. Similarly, governments are more likely to

Encumbrances

	Dr.		Cr.
(a)	1,000	(c)	800
		(cl. 1)	200
(d)	200	(f)	200

Supplies Expenditures

	Dr.		Cr.
(b)	800	(cl. 1)	800
(e)	150	(cl. 2)	150

Cash

	Dr.		Cr.
Beg. Bal.	1,000	(b)	800
Yr. 1 Bal.	200		
		(e)	150
Yr. 2 Bal.	50		

Reserve for Encumbrances

	Dr.		Cr.
(c)	800	(a)	1,000
		Yr. 1 Bal.	200
(f)	200		
Yr. 2 Bal.	0		

Fund Balance

	Dr.		Cr.
(cl. 1)	1,000	Beg. Bal.	1,000
		Yr. 1 Bal.	0
(cl. 2)	150	(d)	200
		Yr. 2 Bal.	50

FIGURE 3-2 Summary of Budget Entries

implement these mechanisms in their general fund than in some other governmental funds, such as their capital projects funds or their debt service funds, since adequate controls may already be in place in those funds. For example, sufficient controls over the cost of a capital project may be established simply by assuring that the agreed-upon price with the contractor is within the amount of bond proceeds. The expenditures of a debt service fund may be set by the payments of principal and interest spelled out in the bond indentures.

Modern computer systems make it possible for the controls provided by both budgetary entries and encumbrances to be achieved by means other than formal journal entries. For example, a government can simply "load" the budget into its computer. The computer can be programmed to issue a warning whenever actual expenditures and commitments exceed a specified percentage of budgeted expenditures.

SUMMARY

Almost all aspects of management in government and not-for-profit organizations revolve around the entities' budgets. The budget is at the center of planning, controlling, administering, evaluating, and reporting functions.

Budgets can take many forms. Appropriation budgets indicate governments' estimated revenues and authorized expenditures. Capital budgets concentrate on long-lived assets. Flexible budgets, which governments use for enterprise funds, contain alternative budget estimates based on different levels of output. Performance budgets focus on measured units of effort and accomplishment and relate costs to objectives.

Most governments follow a four-phase cycle for budgeting: preparation, legislative adoption and executive approval, execution, and reporting and auditing.

For legislative purposes, most governments prepare cash or near-cash budgets. But these may fail to capture the economic cost of carrying out government activities and are not an adequate basis for planning and assessing results.

To demonstrate that they complied with their budgets, governments are required to include in their annual reports a budget-to-actual comparison on a budget basis (that is, the same basis on which they prepare their budget, usually cash or near-cash). However, the revenues and expenditures from the budget may not be readily comparable to those in GAAP-based statements. Differences may be attributable to basis of accounting (e.g., cash vs. modified accrual), timing (e.g., period over which a project will be completed vs. a single year), perspective (e.g., program vs. object classification), and reporting entity (legal vs. economic). Therefore, governments must both explain and reconcile the differences between budgeted and actual amounts on a GAAP basis.

The accounting systems of governments are similar to businesses in that they use comparable journals and ledgers. However, they differ in that governments include corporate budgetary control features to ensure adherence to spending mandates. In addition, they encumber goods and services on order to prevent themselves from overcommitting available resources.

EXERCISE FOR REVIEW AND SELF-STUDY

To enhance control over both revenues and expenditures, a government health care district incorporates its budget in its accounting system and encumbers all commitments. You have been asked to assist the district in making the entries to record the following transactions:

1. Prior to the start of the year, the governing board adopted a budget in which agency revenues were estimated at $5,600 (all dollar amounts in this exercise are expressed in thousands) and expenditures of $5,550 were appropriated (authorized). Record the budget using only the control (summary) accounts.
2. During the year, the district engaged in the following transactions. Prepare appropriate journal entries.
   - **a.** It collected $5,800 in fees, grants, taxes, and other revenues.
   - **b.** It ordered goods and services for $3,000.
   - **c.** During the year it received and paid for $2,800 of goods and services that had been previously encumbered. It expects to receive the remaining $200 in the following year.
   - **d.** It incurred $2,500 in other expenditures for goods and services that had not been encumbered.
3. Prepare appropriate year-end closing entries.
4. Prepare a balance sheet showing the status of year-end asset and fund balance accounts.
5. Per the policy of the district's board, the cost of all goods and services are to be charged against the budget of the year in which they are received, even if they had been ordered (and encumbered) in a previous year. The next year, to simplify the accounting for the commitments made in the prior year, the district reinstated the encumbrances outstanding at year-end. Prepare the appropriate entry.
6. During the year, the district received the remaining encumbered goods and services. However, the total cost was only $150, rather than $200 as estimated. Prepare the appropriate entries.

QUESTIONS FOR REVIEW AND DISCUSSION

1. Why is it important that governments and not-for-profits coordinate their processes for developing *appropriations* budgets with those for developing *capital* budgets?
2. Why may *flexible* budgets be more important to a government's business-type activities than to its governmental activities?
3. What is the main advantage of an *object classification* budget? What are its limitations? How do *performance* budgets overcome these limitations?
4. Why do most governments and not-for-profits budget on a cash or near-cash basis even though the cash basis does not capture the full economic costs of the activities in which they engage?
5. A political official boasts that the year-end excess of revenues over expenditures was significantly greater than was budgeted. Are "favorable" budget variances necessarily a sign of efficient and effective governmental management? Explain.
6. What are *allotments*? What purpose do they serve?
7. Why may a government's year-end results, reported in accordance with generally accepted accounting principles, not be readily comparable with its legally adopted budget?
8. The variances reported in the "final" budget-to-actual comparisons incorporated in the financial statements of many governments may be of no value in revealing the reliability of budget estimates made at the start of the year. Why? How can you rationalize this limitation of the budget-to-actual comparisons?
9. In what way will budgetary entries and encumbrances affect amounts reported on year-end balance sheets or operating statements?
10. Why do many governments consider it unnecessary to prepare appropriation budgets for, and incorporate budgetary entries into the accounts of, their capital projects funds?

EXERCISES

3-1

1. Appropriation budgets are typically concerned with
   a. The details of appropriated expenditures
   b. Long-term revenues and expenditures
   c. Current operating revenues and expenditures
   d. Capital outlays
2. Which of the following types of budgets would be most likely to include a line item, "purchase of supplies":
   a. Object classification
   b. Performance
   c. Capital
   d. Program
3. Per GASB Statement No. 34, an budget-versus-actual comparison must include columns for the actual results and
   a. The original budget only
   b. The final budget only
   c. Both the original and the final budgets
   d. Both the amended and the final budget
4. Apportionments are made during which phase of the budget cycle:
   a. Preparation
   b. Legislative adoption and executive approval
   c. Execution
   d. Reporting and auditing
5. In adopting and recording the budget a government should
   a. Debit estimated revenues and credit revenues
   b. Credit estimated revenues and debit fund balance
   c. Debit revenues and credit fund balance
   d. Debit estimated revenues and credit fund balance
6. In closing budgetary and expenditure accounts at year-end a government should
   a. Debit appropriations and credit expenditures
   b. Credit appropriations and debit expenditures
   c. Debit expenditures and credit fund balance
   d. Credit appropriations and debit fund balance
7. The prime function of budgetary entries is to
   a. Apportion appropriated expenditures to specific accounts
   b. Help the government monitor revenues and expenditures
   c. Amend the budget during the year
   d. Facilitate the end-of-year budget-to-actual comparisons
8. A government should debit an expenditure account upon
   a. Recording the budget
   b. Approving an apportionment
   c. Ordering supplies
   d. Recording the receipt of an invoice from its telephone service provider
9. If a government records the budget, and actual revenues exceed budgeted revenues, what would be the impact on the end-of-year finance statements?
   a. The difference between actual and budgeted revenues would not be reported on either the balance sheet or the statement of revenues and expenditures
   b. The difference between actual and budgeted revenues would be recorded as a budgetary reserve on the balance sheet
   c. The difference between actual and budgeted revenues would be shown as a revenue contra account on the statement of revenues and expenditures
   d. The actual revenues would be shown on the statement of revenues and expenditures as a deduction from estimated revenues
10. A "cash basis" budget relative to a "modified accrual basis" budget
   a. Better facilitates the preparation of year-end financial statements in accordance with generally accepted accounting principles
   b. Better facilitates the day-to-day management of an organization's cash flows
   c. Limits the opportunities of an entity to balance its budget by arbitrarily delaying cash payments from one period to the next
   d. Better assures that a government will achieve interperiod equity

3-2

1. Upon ordering supplies a government should
   a. Debit encumbrances and credit reserve for encumbrances
   b. Debit reserve for encumbrances and credit encumbrances
   c. Debit expenditures and credit encumbrances
   d. Debit expenditures and credit vouchers payable
2. Upon receiving supplies that had previously been encumbered a government should
   a. Debit reserve for encumbrances and credit encumbrances
   b. Debit fund balance and credit reserve for encumbrances
   c. Debit fund balance and credit expenditures
   d. Debit reserve for encumbrances and credit expenditures
3. Upon closing the books at year-end a government should
   a. Debit fund balance and credit reserve for encumbrances

b. Debit encumbrances and credit reserve for encumbrances
c. Debit fund balance and credit encumbrances
d. Debit reserve for encumbrances and credit encumbrances

4. A government requires that all appropriations lapse at the end of a year. At the end of Year 1 that government has $100,000 of goods and services on order. At the start of Year 2 the government should
   a. Debit fund balance and credit encumbrances
   b. Debit reserve for encumbrances and credit encumbrances
   c. Debit encumbrances and credit reserve for encumbrances
   d. Debit encumbrances and credit fund balance
5. Which of the following accounts would a government be most likely to debit as part of its year-end closing process?
   a. Appropriations, encumbrances, and estimated revenues
   b. Estimated revenues, appropriations, and reserve for encumbrances
   c. Revenues, appropriations, and encumbrances
   d. Revenues, appropriations, and fund balance
6. A government places an order for a particular item of equipment and encumbers $5,500. The item arrives accompanied by an invoice for $5,200. The entries that the government should make should include (but not necessarily be limited to)
   a. A debit to expenditures for $5,200, a debit to fund balance for $300, and a credit to reserve for encumbrances for $5,500
   b. A debit to expenditures for $5,200, a credit to encumbrances for $5,200, and a credit to accounts payable for $5,200
   c. A debit to expenditures for $5,200, a credit to encumbrances for $5,500, and a credit to accounts payable for $5,200
   d. A debit to expenditures for $5,200, a credit to reserve for encumbrances for $5,200, and a credit to accounts payable for $5,200
7. A primary virtue of an object classification budget is that it
   a. Covers a period of more than one year
   b. Facilitates control in that it establishes detailed spending mandates
   c. Shows the impact on the budget of various possible levels of output
   d. Relates inputs to measurable outcomes
8. Per GASB Statement No. 34, governments must
   a. Prepare a general fund budget on a cash basis
   b. Prepare a general fund budget on a modified accrual basis
   c. Prepare a schedule that reconciles any differences between amounts reported on a GAAP basis and a budgetary basis
   d. Prepare a schedule that reconciles any differences between the original budget and the amended budget
9. The amount that a government has available to spend would be indicated by
   a. Encumbrances minus the sum of appropriations, expenditures, and net adjustments
   b. Reserve for encumbrances plus appropriations minus the sum of expenditures and net adjustments
   c. Appropriations plus encumbrances minus the sum of expenditures and net adjustments
   d. Appropriations minus the sum of expenditures, encumbrances, and net adjustments
10. For which of the following funds would a government be least likely to record its annual budget and thereby integrate it into its accounting system:
   a. General fund
   b. Special revenue fund
   c. Capital project fund
   d. Enterprise fund

3-3

A county engages in basic transactions.

Kilbourne County engaged in the following transactions in summary form during its fiscal year. All amounts are in millions.

1. Its commissioners approved a budget for the current fiscal year. It included total revenues of $860 and total appropriations of $850.
2. It ordered office supplies for $20.
3. It incurred the following costs, paying in cash:

Salaries	$610
Repairs	$ 40
Rent	$ 25
Utilities	$ 41
Other operating costs	$119

4. It ordered equipment costing $9.
5. It received the equipment and was billed for $10, rather than $9 as anticipated.
6. It received the previously ordered supplies and was billed for the amount originally estimated. The county reports the receipt of supplies as expenditures; it does not maintain an inventory account for supplies.
7. It earned and collected revenues of $865.
   a. Prepare journal entries as appropriate.
   b. Prepare closing entries as appropriate.
   c. What would have been the difference in the year-end financial statements, if any, had the county not made the budgetary entries?

3-4

Encumbrances are recorded in a capital projects fund similar to a general fund.

Wickliffe County authorized the issuance of bonds and contracted with the USA Construction Company (UCC) to build a new sports complex. During 2004, 2005, and 2006 the county engaged in the transactions that follow. All were recorded in a capital projects fund.

1. In 2004 the county issued $310 million of bonds (and recorded them as "bond proceeds," an account comparable to a revenue).
2. It approved the sports-complex contract for $310 million and encumbered the entire amount.
3. It received from UCC an invoice for construction to date for $114 million, an amount that the county recognized as an expenditure.
4. It paid UCC the amount owed.
5. In 2005 it received from UCC an invoice for an additional $190 million.
6. It paid the amount in full.
7. In 2006 UCC completed the sports facility and billed the county an additional $7 million. The county approved the additional costs, even though the total cost was now $311, $1 million more than initially estimated.
8. The county transferred $1 million from the general fund to the capital projects fund.
9. The county paid the $7 million.
   a. Prepare the journal entries, including closing entries, to record the transactions in the capital projects fund. Assume that expenditures do not have to be appropriated each year. Hence, the county need not reestablish encumbrances at each year subsequent to the first. Instead, it can close the expenditures of the second and third years to reserve for encumbrances rather than fund balance.
   b. What other funds, other than the capital projects fund, or schedules would be affected by the transactions?

3-5

Both budgeted and actual revenues and expenditures are closed to the fund balance.

The budgeted and actual revenues and expenditures of Seaside Township for a recent year (in millions) were as presented in the schedule that follows.

1. Prepare journal entries to record the budget.
2. Prepare journal entries to record the actual revenues and expenditures. Assume all transactions resulted in increases or decreases in cash.
3. Prepare journal entries to close the accounts.
4. Determine the net change in fund balance. Does it equal the net change in actual revenues and expenditures?

	Budget	Actual
Revenues		
Property taxes	$7.5	$7.6
Sales taxes	2.1	2.4
Other revenues	1.6	1.5
Total revenues	$11.2	$11.5
Expenditures:		
Wages and salaries	$6.2	$6.1
Supplies	3.1	3.0
Other expenditures	1.3	1.2
Total expenditures	$10.6	$10.3
Increase in fund balance	$0.6	$1.2

3-6

Encumbrance accounting has no lasting impact on fund balance.

London Township began Year 1 with an unreserved balance of $10 million in its bridge repair fund, a capital projects fund.

At the start of the year, the governing council appropriated $6 million for the repair of two bridges. Shortly thereafter, the town signed contracts with a construction company to perform the repairs at a cost of $3 million per bridge.

During the year the town received and paid bills from the construction company as follows:

- $3.2 million for the repairs on Bridge 1. The company completed the repairs, but owing to design changes approved by the town, the cost was $0.2 million greater than anticipated. The town did not encumber the additional $0.2 million.
- $2.0 million for the repairs, which were not completed, on Bridge 2.

At the start of the following year, the governing council reappropriated the $1 million to complete the repairs on Bridge 2. During that year the town received and paid bills totaling $0.7 million. The construction company completed the repairs, but the final cost was less than anticipated—a total of only $2.7 million.

1. Prepare journal entries to record the events and transactions over the two-year period. Include entries to appropriate, reappropriate, encumber, and reencumber the required funds, to record the payment of the bills, and to close the accounts at the end of each year.
2. Determine the unreserved fund balance at the end of the second year. Is it equal to the initial fund balance less the total cost of the repairs?

3-7

Encumbrances have an impact on unreserved fund balance, but do not affect total fund balance.

At the start of its fiscal year on October 1, Fox County reported the following (all dollar amounts in thousands):

Fund balance:	
Reserved for encumbrances	$200
Unreserved	400
Total fund balance	$600

During the year, the county (all dollar amounts in thousands):

- Estimated that revenues for the year would be $6,300.

- Appropriated $6,500 for operations.
- Ordered goods and services estimated to cost $6,000. Of these, the county received (and used) goods and services that it had estimated would cost $5,000. Actual cost, however, was $5,200.
- Received (and used) all goods that it ordered in the previous year. Actual cost was only $180.
- Recognized actual revenues of $6,400.

1. Prepare a schedule, similar to that illustrated in the text, of changes in unreserved fund balance.
2. Show how the total fund balance (including the reserved and unreserved portions) would be displayed at year-end.
3. Does the total fund balance at the beginning of the year, plus the actual revenues, minus the actual expenditures, equal the total fund balance at the end of the year?

PROBLEMS

Continuing Problem

1. In which section of the Comprehensive Annual Financial Report (CAFR) are the budget-to-actual comparisons of the major funds?
   a. Are the actual amounts on a GAAP or a budgetary basis? Do the statements include a reconciliation of any differences between GAAP and budgetary amounts? If so, what are the largest reconciling items?
   b. Are the reported variances based on the original budget or the end-of-year amended budget?
2. Does the CAFR include budget-to-actual comparisons of *nonmajor* funds? If so, in what section?
3. Does the governmnt encumber goods or services that have been ordered but have not yet been received? How, if at all, are encumbrances reflected on the governmental fund balance sheet? How, if at all, are they reflected on the government-wide statement of net assets?
4. Do encumbrances outstanding at year-end lapse? That is, do the amounts that will be expended in the following year, when the goods or services are received, have to be rebudgeted in the following year? How can you tell?

3-1

Is accrual-based budgeting preferable to cash-based budgeting?

The Disability Research Institute receives its funding mainly from government grants and private contributions. In turn, it supports research and related projects carried out by universities and other nonprofit organizations. Most of its government grants are reimbursement (expenditure driven) awards. That is, the government will reimburse the institute for the funds that it disburses to others.

The institute estimates the following as to the forthcoming year:

- It will be awarded $5,000,000 in government grants, all of which will be paid out to subrecipients during the year. Of this amount, only $4,500,000 will be reimbursed by the government during the year. The balance will be reimbursed in the first six months of the next year. The institute will also receive $200,000 in grant funds that were due from the previous year.
- It will receive $600,000 in pledges from private donors. It expects to collect $450,000 during the year and the balance in the following year. It also expects to collect $80,000 in pledges made the prior year.
- It will purchase new furniture and office equipment at a cost of $80,000. It currently owns its building, which it had purchased for $800,000, and additional furniture and equipment that it acquired for $250,000. The building has a useful life of twenty-five years; the furniture and equipment have a useful life of five years.
- Employees will earn wages and salaries of $340,000, of which they will be paid $320,000 during the forthcoming year and the balance in the next year.
- It will incur other operating costs of $90,000, of which it will pay $70,000 in the forthcoming year and $20,000 in the next year. It will also pay another $10,000 in costs incurred in the previous year.

1. Prepare two budgets, one on a cash basis, the other on a *full* accrual basis. For convenience show both on the same schedule, the cash budget in one column and the accrual in the other.
2. Comment on which budget better shows whether the institute is covering the economic cost of the services that it provides.
3. Which is likely to be more useful to
   a. Institute managers?
   b. Members of the institute's board of trustees?
   c. Bankers from whom the institute seeks a loan?

3-2

Missing data can be derived, and journal entries constructed, from information in the accounts.

The following schedule shows the amounts related to expenditures that a nonprofit welfare organization debited and credited to the indicated accounts during a year (not necessarily the year-end balances), *excluding* closing entries. The organization records its budget, encumbers all of its expenditures, and initially vouchers all payments.

Some information is missing. You are to determine the missing data and construct all entries (in summary form), excluding closing entries, that the organization made during the year.

	Debit	Credit
Cash	$0	$28
Vouchers payable	?	?
Estimated expenditures (Appropriations)	0	55
Encumbrances	?	?
Expenditures	30	0
Reserve for encumbrances	32	50
Fund balance	?	0

3-3

Missing data can be derived, and journal entries constructed, from information in the accounts.

The following schedule shows the amounts related to supplies that a city debited and credited to the indicated accounts during a year (not necessarily the year-end balances), excluding closing entries. The organization records its budget, encumbers all of its expenditures, and initially vouchers all payments. All revenue was collected in cash.

Some information is missing. By reconstructing the entries that the organization made during the year, you are to determine the missing data and construct the journal entries (in summary form), excluding closing entries.

	(in thousands) Debits	Credits
Cash	$117	$?
Estimated revenues	?	0
Revenues	0	?
Vouchers payable	70	54
Appropriations	0	?
Encumbrances	?	58
Expenditures	?	0
Reserve for encumbrances	?	93
Fund balance	115	120

3-4

A city imposes an overhead charge on one of its departments to alleviate its fiscal problems.

A city's visitors' bureau, which promotes tourism and conventions, is funded by an 8 percent local hotel occupancy tax (a tax on the cost of a stay in a hotel). Inasmuch as the visitors' bureau is supported entirely by the occupancy tax, it is accounted for in a restricted fund.

You recently received a call from the director of the visitors' bureau. She complained that the city manager is about to impose an overhead charge of a specified dollar amount on her department. Yet the statute creating the hotel occupancy tax specifies that the revenues can be used only to satisfy "direct expenditures" incurred to promote tourism and bookings at the city's convention center. The manager says that she understands the city is having difficulty balancing its budget, but fails to see how the charge to her department will do much to alleviate the city's fiscal problems.

1. In light of the city's fiscal problems, what is the most likely motivation for the new charge? Will the new overhead charge achieve its objective?
2. What would be the impact of the new charge on the city's annual fund financial statements, prepared in accordance with GAAP (which requires that the city account for its governmental funds on a modified accrual basis)? Would the impact be the same if the city accounted for its governmental funds on a cash basis?
3. What would be the impact of the new charge on the city's government-wide statements in which all governmental funds are consolidated? Would it have an impact on reported net assets?
4. In what way might the charge have a substantive impact on the city's economic condition?
5. Assuming that the city provided accounting, legal, and purchasing services to the visitors' bureau, do you think the charge would be consistent with the statutory requirement that the hotel occupancy tax be used to meet only "direct expenditures" related to tourism and use of the convention center (an issue not addressed in this text)?

3-5

Government activities may be less "profitable" than they appear.

A city prepares its budget in traditional format, classifying expenditures as to fund and object. In 1999, amid considerable controversy, the city authorized the sale of $20 million in bonds to finance construction of a new sports and special events arena. Critics charged that, contrary to the predictions of arena proponents, the arena could not be fiscally self-sustaining.

Five years later, the arena was completed and began to be used. After its first year of operations, its general managers submitted the following condensed statement of revenues and expenses (in millions):

Revenues from ticket sales	$5.7	
Revenues from concessions	2.4	$8.1
Operating expenses	6.6	
Interest on debt	1.2	7.8
Excess of revenues over expenses		$0.3

At the city council meeting at which the report was submitted, the council member who championed the center glowingly boasted that his prophecy was proving correct; the arena was "profitable."

Assume that the following information came to your attention:

- The arena is accounted for in a separate enterprise fund.
- The arena increased the number of overnight visitors to the city. City administrators and economists calculated that the additional visitors generated approximately \$0.1 million in hotel occupancy tax revenues. These taxes are dedicated to promoting tourism in the city. In addition, they estimated that the ticket and concession sales, plus the economic activity generated by the arena, increased general sales tax revenues by \$0.4 million.
- The city had to improve roads, highways, and utilities in the area surrounding the arena. These improvements, which cost \$6 million, were financed with general obligation debt (not reported in the enterprise fund). Principal and interest on the debt, paid out of general funds, were \$0.5 million. The cost of maintaining the facilities was approximately \$0.1.
- On evenings in which events were held in the arena, the city had to increase police protection in the arena's neighborhood. Whereas the arena compensated the police department for police officers who served within the arena itself, those that patrolled outside were paid out of police department funds. The police department estimated its additional costs at \$0.1 million.
- The city provided various administrative services (including legal, accounting, and personnel) to the arena at no charge at an estimated cost of \$0.1 million.
- The city estimates the cost of additional sanitation, fire, and medical services due to events at the center to be approximately \$0.2 million.

1. Would you agree with the council member that the arena was fiscally self-sustaining?
2. In which funds would the additional revenues and expenditures be budgeted and accounted for?
3. Comment on the limitations of both the traditional object classification budget and fund accounting system in assessing the economic costs and benefits of a project such as the sports and special events arena.
4. What changes in the city's budgeting and accounting structure would overcome these limitations? What additional problems might these changes cause?

3-6

To what extent do the unique features of government accounting make a difference on the financial statements?

The transactions that follow relate to the Danville County Comptroller's Department over a two-year period.

Year 1

- The county appropriated \$12,000 for employee education and training.
- The department signed contracts with outside consultants to conduct accounting and auditing workshops. Total cost was \$10,000.
- The consultants conducted the workshops and were paid \$10,000.
- The department ordered books and training materials, which it estimated would cost \$1,800. As of year-end, the materials had not yet been received.

Year 2

- The county appropriated \$13,500 for employee education and training.
- The department received and paid for the books and training materials that it ordered the previous year. Actual cost was only \$1,700. The county's accounting policies require that the books and training materials be charged as an expenditure when they are received (as opposed to being recorded as inventory and charged as an expenditure when used).
- It authorized employees to attend various conferences and training sessions. Estimated cost was \$10,500.
- Employees submitted \$10,800 in reimbursement requests for the conferences and training sessions they attended. The department paid them the requested amounts, and at year-end did not expect to receive any additional reimbursement requests.

1. Prepare all required journal entries that would affect the expenditure subaccount "education and training", including budgetary and closing entries. Assume that all appropriations lapse at year-end (thus, all expenditures in Year 2 would be charged against that year's appropriation of \$13,500 even if the goods and services were ordered in Year 1).
2. Indicate (specifying accounts and dollar amounts) how the transactions would be reported in the county's general fund:
   a. Balance sheet
   b. Statement of revenues and expenditures
3. Suppose, alternatively, that the county did not record its budget and did not encumber its commitments. What would be the difference in the year-end financial statements?
4. Assume instead that appropriations for goods on order at year-end do not lapse. When the goods are received they are charged as expenditures against the budget of the year in which they were encumbered. How would this change affect your entries and the year-end financial statements? How would it affect the amount that

the department had available to spend in Year 2 on goods or services not previously ordered?

3-7

Different budget-to-actual comparisons serve different purposes.

The following information was drawn from a county's general fund budgets and accounts for a particular year (in millions):

	Amended Budget	Original Budget	Actual Results (Budget Basis)
Revenues			
Property taxes	$46.6	$42.5	$53.0
Sales taxes	16.3	13.6	15.1
Licenses and permits	1.1	1.0	1.0
Other	3.2	2.9	3.4
Total revenues	$67.2	$60.0	$72.5
Expenditures			
General government	$18.2	$16.2	$18.1
Public safety	29.2	25.1	28.5
Sanitation	9.7	9.4	9.6
Culture and recreation	8.1	7.8	8.1
Interest	1.4	1.4	1.4
Total expenditures	66.6	59.9	65.7
Excess of revenues over expenditures	$ 0.6	$ 0.1	$ 6.8

You also learn the following:

	Beginning of Year	End of Year
Encumbrances (commitments) outstanding	$2.7	$1.1
Supplies inventories on hand	1.8	1.0
Wages and salaries payable	0.5	0.7
Property taxes expected to be collected within 60 days	1.7	2.5

- For purposes of budgeting, the country recognizes encumbrances as the equivalent of expenditures in the year established; for financial reporting, it recognizes expenditures when the goods or services are received, as required by GAAP.
- For purposes of budgeting, it recognizes supplies expenditures when the supplies are acquired; for financial reporting, it recognizes the expenditure when the supplies are consumed.
- For purposes of budgeting, it recognizes wages and salaries when paid; for financial reporting, it recognizes the expenditures when the employees perform their services.
- For purposes of budgeting, it recognizes as revenues only taxes actually collected during the year; for financial reporting, it recognizes taxes expected to be collected within the first sixty days of the following year.

1. Prepare the following four separate schedules in which you compare the budget to actual results and compute the budget variance. You need present only the *total* revenues, *total* expenditures, and excess of revenues over expenditures.
   a. Actual results on a budget basis to the amended budget
   b. Actual results on a budget basis to the original budget
   c. Actual results as would be reflected in the financial statements to the amended budget restated so that it is on a financial reporting basis
   d. Actual results as would be reflected in the financial statements to the original budget restated so that it is on a financial reporting basis
2. The county executive has boasted that the "better than anticipated results" (based on the comparison of the schedule that appears in the financial statements) are evidence of "sound fiscal management and effective cost controls" on the part of the county administration. Do you agree?
3. Which of the three schedules best demonstrates legal compliance? Explain.
4. Which schedule best demonstrates effective management? Explain.

3-8

Budget variances have to be interpreted with caution.

The data presented below were taken from the books and records of the village of Denaville. All amounts are in millions. The village encumbers all outlays. As it is evident from the data, some goods or services that were ordered and encumbered have not yet been received. City regulations require that all appropriations lapse at year-end.

1. Prepare summary entries to record
   a. The budget
   b. The encumbrance of the goods and services
   c. The receipt of the goods and services (all invoices were paid in cash)
   d. The actual revenues (all cash receipts)
2. Prepare summary entries to close the accounts.
3. What would be the year-end
   a. Fund balance (unreserved)
   b. Reserve for encumbrance balance
4. Prepare a schedule comparing budgeted to actual revenues and expenditures.
5. A citizen reviews the budget-to-actual schedule that you have prepared. She comments on the rather substantial favorable variance between budgeted and actual expenditures and questions why the government did

Village of Denaville

	Estimated/ Appropriated	Amount Encumbered	Amounts Received: Estimated Cost	Actual Cost
Revenues				
Property taxes	$ 7,900			
Sales taxes	3,900			
Licenses	300			
Other	700			
	$12,800			
Expenditures/Appropriations				
General government	$ 3,000	$ 2,600	$ 2,400	$ 2,800
Public safety	6,000	5,900	5,000	4,900
Recreation	1,200	1,200	800	900
Health and sanitation	2,300	2,200	2,200	2,100
	$12,500	$11,900	$10,400	$10,700
Excess of revenues over expenditures/appropriations	300			
Beginning fund balance	1,200			
Estimated ending fund	$ 1,500			

not spend the full amount of money that it appropriated. Briefly explain to her the nature of the variance.

3-9

A city's note to its financial statements provides considerable insight into its budget practices.

Shown next is an excerpt from a note, headed *Budgets*, from the City of Raleigh, North Carolina's annual report for the fiscal year ended June 30.

1. The note distinguishes between the "budget ordinance" and the "more detailed line item budgets."
   a. Provide examples of expenditures that you would expect to see in the budget ordinance.
   b. Provide examples of expenditures that you would expect to see in the line-item budgets.
2. Why do you suspect that budgetary control is not exercised in trust and agency funds?
3. Generally accepted accounting principles require that governments reconcile differences between the entity's budget practices and GAAP in either the financial statements themselves or in accompanying notes. Raleigh's budget-to-actual comparison contained no such reconciliation. Why do you think a reconciliation was also omitted from the notes?
4. Explain how Raleigh's appropriation process would differ between that for its general fund and that for its capital projects fund. How would this difference most likely affect the city's budgetary entries?
5. Since the city had not yet adopted Statement No. 34, it was not required by GAAP to report on the amendments to its budget. Of what use to a statement reader is the note's schedule comparing, by fund, the original and amended budgets?

Note D. Budgets

Budgetary control is exercised in all funds except the trust and agency funds. The budget shown in the financial statements is the budget ordinance as amended at the close of the day of June 30. The City is required by the General Statutes of the State of North Carolina to adopt an annual balanced budget by July 1 of each year. The General Statutes also provided for balanced project ordinances for the life of projects, including both capital and grant activities, which are expected to extend beyond the end of the fiscal year. The City Council officially adopts the annual budget ordinance and all project ordinances and has the authority to amend such ordinances as necessary to recognize new resources or reallocations of budget. At June 30, the effect of such amendments, less eliminating transfers, was as shown on the top of the next page.

All budgets are prepared on the modified accrual basis of accounting as is required by North Carolina law. Appropriations for funds that adopt annual budgets lapse at the end of the budget year. Project budgeted appropriations do not lapse until the completion of the project.

Budget control on expenditures is limited to departmental totals and project totals as specified in the budget ordinances. Administrative control is maintained through the establishment of more detailed line-item budgets, which correspond to the specific object of the expenditure. All budget transfers, both at the ordinance and the

	Original Budget	Total Amendments	Budget June 30
General fund	$145,259,996	$2,965,856	$148,225,852
Special revenue funds	49,087,784	5,034,632	54,122,416
General capital projects funds	135,304,688	4,038,509	139,343,197
Proprietary funds	145,984,461	2,557,523	148,541,984
Internal service funds	845,657	16,640	862,297

line-item levels, are approved by the City Council. The City Manager is authorized to transfer line-item budgeted amounts up to $1,000 within a fund prior to their formal approval by the City Council.

Encumbrances represent commitments related to unperformed contracts for goods or services. Encumbrance accounting—under which purchase orders, contracts, and other commitments for the expenditure of resources are recorded to reserve that portion of the applicable appropriation—is utilized in all funds. Outstanding encumbrances at year-end for which goods or services are received are reclassified to expenditures and accounts payable. All other encumbrances in the annual budgeted funds are reversed at year-end and are either cancelled or are included as reappropriations of fund balance for the subsequent year. Outstanding encumbrances at year-end in funds that are budgeted on a project basis automatically carry forward along with their related appropriations and are not subject to an annual cancellation and reappropriation.

3-10

Different types of funds justify different practices as to budgets and commitments.

Review the budget note to the City of Raleigh's financial statements presented in the previous problem.

Assume that the city engaged in the following transactions in 2004 and 2005:

- In 2004 it signed a service contract with a private security company. The company agreed to provide security services to the city for one year at a cost of $72,000 ($6,000 per month). By year-end the company provided, and the city paid for, services for three months.
- In 2005, the company performed, and the city paid for, the remaining nine months of the contract. However, owing to agreed-upon changes in the services provided by the company, the total charges for 2005 were reduced from $54,000 to $50,000.

1. The city properly budgeted for the services and appropriated the funds consistent with policies set forth in the note. Prepare all budgetary, encumbrance, and expenditure entries relating to the service contract that would be required in 2004 and 2005. In 2004, when the city signed the contract, it appropriated the entire $72,000. Then, at the start of 2005, inasmuch as the city expended only $18,000 in 2004, it reappropriated $54,000.
   a. Assume first that the contract was accounted for in Raleigh's *general fund*.
   b. Assume next that it was accounted for in a *capital projects fund* established for the construction of its Walnut Creek Amphitheatre. The city prepares annual financial statements for capital projects funds, but does not close out its accounts. Moreover, it prepares budgets for the entire project, not for particular periods. The project was started in 2004 and completed in 2005.
2. Justify the city's practice of accounting differently for commitments in the two types of funds.

3-11

Journal entries can be derived from a city's ledger.

Shown on the top of the next page is an excerpt from a city's subsidiary ledger for the first two months of its fiscal year. Missing is the column that explains or references each of the entries.

1. Prepare the journal entries that were most likely made in the account, adding to each a brief note of explanation. Each line of the account records a single transaction (e.g., the receipt of an invoice); however, the entries on January 1 were made before the city engaged in any actual transactions (i.e., with outside parties).
2. The appropriation for consulting fees was intended to last for the entire year. Apparently, the city is spending or committing funds at a faster pace than planned. Can you propose an additional control mechanism to help ensure that the funds are spent evenly throughout the year?

3-12

Speeding up tax collections helps balance a state's appropriations budget.

The following is an excerpt from *Against the Grain*, a series of recommendations by Texas's State Comptroller as to how to "save" $4.5 billion and thereby balance the state's budget:

> Require an Annual August Remittance of One-Half of August's Sales Tax Collections by Monthly Taxpayers. The Legislature should require sales taxpayers to remit half of August's collections during that month.
>
> **Background**
>
> Currently, sales tax payments are remitted either monthly, quarterly, or annually. They also may be prepaid either on a quarterly or on a monthly basis.
>
> Monthly taxpayers, including those who collect taxes on their own purchase or use of taxable items, are required by law to remit to the state all tax collections—less

Fund: General government
Account: Consulting fees

Date	Encumbrances Dr. (Cr.)	Expenditures Dr. (Cr.)	Appropriations Cr. (Dr.)	Available Balance
1/1			$78,000	$78,000
1/1	$7,900			70,100
1/5	(4,000)	$3,000		71,100
1/14		4,500		66,600
2/5	6,000			60,600
2/15	(3,200)	3,400		60,400

any applicable discounts—by the twentieth day of the month following the end of each calendar month. The state's fiscal year ends on August 31.

Recommendation

The Legislature should require all monthly taxpayers to remit one-half of each August's sales tax collections during that month. Specifically, sales taxes collected between August 1 and August 15 would be due with their regular August 20th payment. Monthly taxpayers would remit tax in the usual manner during all other months.

This is not a prepayment plan, but a speeding up of the remittance of actual taxes collected and owed to the state. This would impose an additional burden and would reduce taxpayer cash flow, but should be considered as preferable to a tax increase.

Implications

An annual payment by monthly filers of taxes actually collected during the first fifteen days of August would increase August's collections and decrease September's collections. Although the initial imposition of this proposal might temporarily inconvenience some taxpayers, the prompt payment to the state of some of its sales tax revenues—collected, but not yet remitted—will enhance the revenue stream at a critical time each fiscal year. During the first year of implementation, all months would have normal collection patterns except August, which would be larger than usual, thereby producing a fiscal gain.

Each following year would see smaller than normal (current) collections in September and larger collections in August. These differences would essentially offset each other. It is important to stress that failure to speed up collections each year after implementation would cause a fiscal loss. The gain to the general fund in the year of implementation would be $215 million.

Fiscal Year	Gain to the General Revenue Fund
1994	$215,113,000
1995	$ 0
1996	$ 0
1997	$ 0
1998	$ 0

1. On what basis does the state probably prepare its appropriation budget? Explain.
2. Do you believe the state will be better off, in economic substance, as the result of the proposed change?
3. According to the comptroller (last paragraph), the change would have no impact on revenues of future fiscal years as long as collections are also speeded up in those years. Do you agree? If so, is there any reason not to adopt the proposal?

3-13

Multiple funds provide multiple sources of revenue.

The following is a recommendation from *Against the Grain*, a series of proposals by the State Comptroller of Texas on how the state could enhance revenues and decrease expenditures:

Amend the Lottery Act to Abolish the Lottery Stabilization Fund. The state should amend the Lottery Act to abolish the Lottery Stabilization Fund requirement and use the income to fund critical services.

Background

The State Lottery Act requires the establishment of a Lottery Stabilization Fund. The fund will contain lottery revenue in excess of the Comptroller's Biennial Revenue Estimate. The Lottery Stabilization Fund is then to provide revenue to the General Revenue Fund if the lottery fails to generate monthly revenue as estimated.

In months that lottery revenue exceeds one-twelfth of the annual estimate, the Comptroller is required to deposit $10 million plus the amount of net lottery revenue in excess of the estimate to the Lottery Stabilization Fund. The Act provides only two circumstances under which revenue could be transferred from the Lottery Stabilization Fund to the General Revenue Fund. In months that lottery revenue is less than 90 percent of one-twelfth of the annual estimate, the difference is to be transferred from the Lottery Stabilization Fund to general revenue. The Act also provides for the transfer of one-half of the balance of the Lottery Stabilization Fund to the General Revenue Fund on the first day of every biennium.

In view of the seriousness of the state's fiscal situation, the Legislature should set aside the stabilization fund requirement. The state already maintains a significant "rainy day" fund, and effective revenue forecasting should be adequate to avoid problems with potential future revenue stream instability.

Recommendation

The state should repeal the provision in the State Lottery Act that establishes the Lottery Stabilization Fund. This action would provide additional revenue to the General

Revenue Fund to be used for state programs at the Legislature's discretion.

Implications

Releasing Lottery Stabilization Funds would increase the available revenue for state programs without increasing taxes. General revenue is reduced by at least $10 million in months when lottery revenue exceeds one-twelfth of the annual lottery estimate. In effect, the state is penalized for correctly estimating lottery revenue and operating the lottery efficiently. Repealing the provision that establishes this fund would remove this penalty.

This action would increase general revenue about $65 million per year in the next biennium.

1. Explain briefly how the Comptroller's recommendation would increase general revenue by $65 million per year. In what way would the proposal affect the fiscal well-being of the state?
2. What impact would the Comptroller's recommendation have on the state's budget if the state were to prepare a "consolidated" budget—one in which all funds were combined?
3. With reference to this recommendation, what are the advantages and disadvantages of budgeting on the basis of individual funds as opposed to all funds combined?

SOLUTION TO EXERCISE FOR REVIEW AND SELF-STUDY

1. Estimated revenues	$5,600	
Appropriations		$5,550
Fund balance		50

To record the budget

The budget would specify in detail the revenues anticipated and expenditures appropriated. Hence, the corresponding subledger accounts should be debited and credited for amounts estimated or authorized.

2.

a. Cash	$5,800	
Revenues		$5,800

To record revenues

b. Encumbrances	$3,000	
Reserve for encumbrances		$3,000

To encumber resources reserved to fulfill commitments for goods and services on order

c. Expenditures	$2,800	
Cash		$2,800

To record expenditures

Reserve for encumbrances	$2,800	
Encumbrances		$2,800

To unencumber funds for goods and services already received that have been charged as expenditures

d.Expenditures	$2,500	
Cash		$2,500

To record other expenditures

3. Revenues	$5,800	
Estimated revenues		$5,600
Fund balance		200

To close revenue and estimated revenue accounts

Appropriations	$5,550	
Expenditures		$5,300
Encumbrances		200
Fund balance		50

To close expenditures, encumbrances, and appropriations

The district's closing entries deviate slightly from those illustrated earlier in the text in which the budget accounts were closed in one entry and the actual accounts in another. The end result is the same regardless of the grouping used for the closing entries.

4. The following schedule summarizes the impact of the transactions on fund balance:

Revenues	$5,800
Expenditures	5,300
Increase in total fund balance	500
Less: Encumbrances (Transfer from unreserved to reserved fund balance)	200
Net increase in unrestricted fund balance	$ 300

The following balance sheet shows the status of year-end asset and fund balance accounts:

Cash	$500
Fund balance	
Reserved for encumbrances	$200
Unreserved	300
Total fund balance	$500

5. Encumbrances	$200	
Fund balance		$200

To restore encumbrances of the previous year

6. Expenditures	$150	
Cash		$150

To record expenditures

Reserve for encumbrances	$200	
Encumbrances		$200

To unencumber funds for goods and services already received and charged as expenditures (the entire $200 is reversed, inasmuch as the entire order has been fulfilled; no additional amount need be reserved).

CHAPTER 4

Recognizing Revenues in Governmental Funds

LEARNING OBJECTIVES

After studying this chapter you should understand:

- Why governments focus on current financial resources and use the modified accrual basis to account for their governmental funds
- Why governments focus on all economic resources and use the full accrual basis in their government-wide financial statements
- The key distinctions between the modified and full accrual bases of accounting
- The distinction between exchange and nonexchange transactions
- The main types of nonexchange transactions
- The impact of the "available" criterion on revenue recognition
- How each of the following types of revenues are accounted for:
  - Property taxes
  - Fines
  - Sales taxes
  - Income taxes
  - Grants and donations
  - Investment gains and losses
  - Sales of capital assets
  - Licenses and permits
  - On-behalf payments

We now turn to what are among the most intractable questions of government and not-for-profit accounting: When should revenues and expenditures be recognized, and how should the related assets and liabilities be measured?

In Chapters 4 and 5 we consider revenue and expenditure recognition in governments, while in Chapter 12 we address revenue and expenditure recognition in other not-for-profit entities. Most of the examples in this and the next chapter will implicitly be directed toward governments' general funds. However, the discussion is equally applicable to all *governmental* funds, including special revenues funds, capital projects funds, debt service funds, and permanent funds. In Chapter 9 we examine the same issues as they apply to *proprietary* funds (those that account for business-type activities).

WHY AND HOW DO GOVERNMENTS USE THE MODIFIED ACCRUAL BASIS?

RATIONALE FOR THE MODIFIED ACCRUAL BASIS

The foundation for our discussion of revenue and expenditure recognition was laid in Chapter 1. In that chapter we pointed to two key objectives of financial reporting:

- Indicating the extent to which the entity achieved interperiod equity (i.e., whether current-year revenues were sufficient to pay for current-year services)
- Demonstrating whether the entity obtained and used its resources in accordance with its legally adopted budget

As suggested in Chapter 1, no set of financial statements prepared on a single basis of revenue and expenditure recognition can adequately fulfill both objectives. Therefore, standard setters must choose among three courses of action:

- Adopt principles that fulfill one of the objectives, but not the other
- Adopt principles that compromise the two objectives, fulfilling both to some extent, but neither one adequately
- Develop a reporting model that incorporates more than one basis of revenue and expenditure recognition—either statements that embrace more than one basis of accounting or else two or more sets of statements within the same report

Generally accepted accounting principles as incorporated in the new Governmental Accounting Standards Board (GASB) model reflect the third approach. The government-wide statements consolidate all funds (except fiduciary funds) on a full accrual basis. They thereby demonstrate whether the entity's current-year revenues were sufficient to pay for current year's services. The fund statements, by contrast, present governmental funds on a modified accrual basis (and, for reasons to be explained in Chapter 9, proprietary funds on a full accrual basis).

The modified accrual basis is far more budget oriented than the full accrual basis in that the budgets of most governments focus on either cash or cash plus selected short-term financial resources. However, the budgetary principles of any individual government are determined by applicable state or local laws. Except for governments that elect or are required to budget on a modified accrual basis as defined by GAAP, the revenue and expenditure principles that underlie their fund statements would not necessarily be identical to those of their legally adopted budgets. Hence, as discussed in Chapter 3, schedules that show the variances between budgetary estimates and actual results may have to include a reconciliation that indicates the portion of the variances attributable to differences in accounting principles.

In developing its new model, the GASB opted to retain the modified accrual basis of the old model, rather than a budget basis, for governmental funds statements.

This approach ensures that all governments report on the same basis and thereby facilitates comparisons among entities. Comparisons would have been difficult if each entity reported on its own particular budget basis.

RELATIONSHIP BETWEEN MEASUREMENT FOCUS AND BASIS OF ACCOUNTING

The criteria by which an entity determines when to recognize revenues and expenditures necessarily stem from its measurement focus and its basis of accounting. As pointed out in Chapter 2, *measurement focus* refers to *what* is being reported upon—that is, *which* assets and liabilities are being measured. *Basis of accounting* refers to *when* transactions and other events are recognized. The two concepts obviously are closely linked. If an entity opts to focus on cash, then it will necessarily adopt a *cash basis of accounting*. Correspondingly, if it elects to focus on *all economic resources* (both current and long-term assets and liabilities), then it will adopt a *full accrual basis of accounting*.

Measurement focus and basis of accounting can be viewed as a continuum. As depicted in Figure 4-1, on one end is a cash focus and correspondingly the cash basis of accounting. On the other end is a focus on all economic resources and thus the full accrual basis. Between the two are any number of "modified accrual" (or "modified cash") bases of accounting in which the focus is on resources in addition to cash but not on the full array of economic resources.

If, as is common, a government's budget is on a cash or near-cash basis, then a basis of accounting near the cash end of the continuum best satisfies the reporting objective of demonstrating that resources were obtained in accordance with the legally adopted budget. A basis on the full accrual end of the continuum best fulfills the interperiod equity objective. Any basis between the extremes would compromise the two objectives, satisfying both objectives to some extent, but neither one completely.

OVERVIEW OF THE MODIFIED ACCRUAL BASIS

Per generally accepted practices of today, governmental funds are accounted for on a modified accrual basis. The measurement focus is on **current financial resources.** "Current financial resources" has been interpreted to mean "expendable financial resources"—cash, and other items that can be expected to be transformed into cash in the normal course of operations (less current liabilities). The "other items" include investments and receivables but *not* capital assets.

As is discussed in Chapter 5, inventories and prepaid items are also reported on the balance sheet, even though they do not fall within the conventional view of a financial resource. A frequently cited justification for this apparent inconsistency is that these assets will not ordinarily be transformed into cash (e.g., inventories will be consumed, not sold for cash), but they generally will result in short-term cash savings in that the entity will not have to expend additional cash to acquire them.

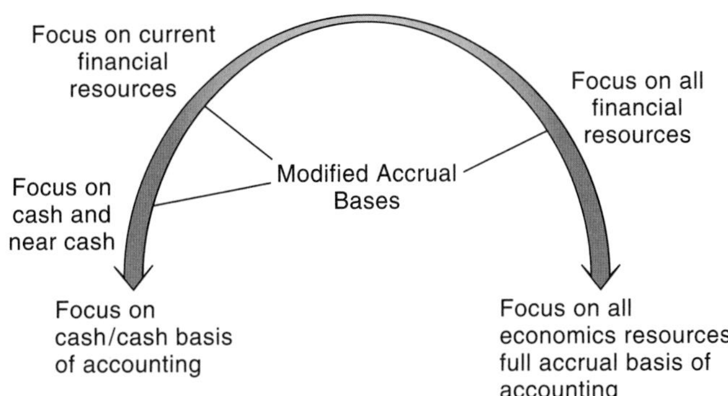

FIGURE 4-1
Measurement Focus and Basis of Accounting

The current claims against financial resources include wages and salaries payable, accounts payable, and deferred credits. They exclude long-term obligations such as the noncurrent portions of bonds payable, and the liabilities for vacation pay, sick leave pay, and legal judgments. Consistent with conventional relationships between balance sheet and operating statement accounts, revenues and expenditures are accompanied by an increase or decrease in net financial resources (as opposed to increases or decreases in net economic resources, as would be true under the full accrual basis).

RECOGNITION OF REVENUE

Accepting the accrual basis of accounting (even if modified) still leaves unresolved the thorny issue of when revenues should be recognized. What key economic event in the revenue generation process should trigger the recognition of revenue and the corresponding increase in net assets? In business accounting, revenues are ordinarily recognized when a firm has exerted a substantial portion of its production and sales effort and the amount of cash to be eventually collected can reasonably be assured and estimated. But standard setters, as well as individual firms, still have to grapple with the problem of when the various types of revenue transactions satisfy these criteria. To enhance consistency of practice, standard setters have established specific guidelines for the recognition of such diverse revenues as those from ordinary sales, sales of real estate, installment sales, interest, loan origination fees, license and royalty fees, and construction contracts.

The revenue-recognition issues facing governments are less tractable than those of businesses. Businesses derive their revenues mainly from exchange transactions—those in which each party gives and receives consideration of equivalent value. Governments (except as they engage in business-type activities) derive their revenues mainly from nonexchange transactions—those in which one party gives or receives value without directly receiving or giving equivalent value in exchange.

GASB Statement No. 33, *Accounting and Financial Reporting for Nonexchange Transactions* (1998) governs the recognition of revenue under both the modified accrual basis (for governmental funds) and the full accrual basis (for proprietary and fiduciary funds and the government-wide statements). The recognition guidelines, to be discussed in the next sections, are the same for both bases. However, when accounted for under the modified accrual basis, revenues are subject to an additional, extremely significant, stipulation. They cannot be recognized until they are both *measurable and available to finance expenditures of the fiscal period.*

MEANING OF, AND RATIONALE FOR, "AVAILABLE TO FINANCE EXPENDITURES OF THE CURRENT PERIOD"

The nonexchange revenues of governments are intrinsically associated with expenditures; they are generated solely to meet expenditures. Budgets are formulated so that each period's estimated revenues are sufficient to cover appropriated expenditures. Expenditures of a current period may either require cash outlays during the period or create liabilities that have to be satisfied shortly after the end of the period. For example, goods or services that a government receives toward the end of one year would ordinarily not have to be paid for until early the next year. *Available*, therefore, means "collected" within the current period or "expected to be collected soon enough thereafter to be used to pay liabilities of the current period."[1]

Business accounting principles dictate that the collection of cash must be reasonably assured before revenue can be recognized. The "available" stipulation assures that, in addition, the cash has been collected or will be collected soon enough to pay the liabilities they are intended to cover.

[1] GASB Statement No. 33, *Accounting and Reporting for Nonexchange Transactions* (December 1998), n. 16.

The liabilities that the revenues may be used to pay are only *current liabilities.* Recall that long-term liabilities are outside of the measurement focus of government funds and hence are not recorded by them. As shall be discussed in the following chapter, under the modified accrual basis of accounting, transactions that result in long-term liabilities are not recorded as expenditures.

How many days after the close of the year must revenues be received to satisfy the criteria of having been received soon enough to pay the liabilities of the current period? With respect to *property taxes*—and only property taxes—existing standards provide that, in the absence of unusual circumstances, revenues should be recognized only if cash is expected to be collected within *sixty (60) days* of year-end.[2]

Because existing standards provide no specific guidance as to time periods for recognition of other revenues, this "sixty-day rule" has become a widely used benchmark for all types of revenues, not just property taxes. However, many governments have established other time periods, such as thirty days, ninety days, or even one year for revenues other than property taxes.

WHAT ARE THE MAIN TYPES OF NONEXCHANGE REVENUES AND THE LIMITATIONS ON HOW AND WHEN THEY CAN BE USED?

GASB Statement No. 33, *Accounting and Financial Reporting for Nonexchange Transactions,* divides nonexchange revenues into four classes:

1. **Imposed nonexchange revenues.** These are assessments imposed on individuals and business entities. The most prominent of these are property taxes and fines.
2. **Derived tax revenues.** These are taxes derived (i.e., that result) from assessments on exchange transactions carried on by taxpayers. They include sales taxes (derived from sales transactions), and income and other taxes on earnings or assets (derived from various income-producing commercial transactions).
3. **Government-mandated nonexchange transactions.** These occur when a government at one level (e.g., the federal or a state government) provides resources to a government at another level (e.g., a local government or school district) and requires the recipient to use the resources for a specific purpose. For example, a state may grant funds to a county stipulating that the resources be used for road improvements. Acceptance and use of the resources are mandatory.
4. **Voluntary nonexchange transactions.** These result from legislative or contractual agreements entered into willingly by two or more parties. They include grants given by one government to another and contributions from individuals (e.g., gifts to public universities). Often the provider imposes eligibility requirements or restrictions as to how the funds may be used. These types of transactions are similar to the government-mandated nonexchange transactions, but differ in that the recipient government is not required to accept the awards. However, if the government accepts the awards it must observe the accompanying requirements as to how they may be spent.

Statement No. 33 establishes standards, discussed in the next sections, for each of the four types of transactions. The standards for government mandated and voluntary nonexchange transactions apply to both revenues and expenditures. Thus payments from one government to another are expected to be accounted for symmetrically.

[2] GASB Interpretation No. 5, *Property Tax Revenue Recognition in Governmental Funds* (November 1997).

The statement also identifies two types of limitations that constrain when or how a government may use the resources it receives in nonexchange transactions:

1. **Time requirements.** These specify the period in which resources must be used or when use may begin. For example, local governments typically levy property taxes designated for a particular fiscal year. Similarly, state governments that grant funds to local school districts may require that the funds be used during the state's fiscal year.
2. **Purpose restrictions.** These specify the purpose for which the resources must be used. For example, certain sales taxes must be used for road improvements, certain property taxes must be used to repay debt, and certain grants or private donations must be used to acquire specific goods or services.

As is noted as the various types of revenues are discussed, governments should not recognize revenue or expenditures on nonexchange transactions until time requirements have been met (e.g., the start of the specific time period in which resources may be used). By contrast, however, they need not delay recognition of revenue until they have satisfied the purpose restrictions. Nevertheless, they must specifically identify resources that are subject to purpose restrictions by reporting a reservation of fund balance in fund financial statements and restricted net assets in government-wide statements. These requirements continue in force until the restricted amounts are spent for the specified purpose.

HOW SHOULD PROPERTY TAXES AND OTHER IMPOSED NONEXCHANGE REVENUES BE ACCOUNTED FOR?

FUNDAMENTALS OF PROPERTY TAXES

Property taxes are the bread and butter of local governments. Although gradually being supplemented by other taxes and fees, they still account for approximately 24 percent of local government revenues (see Figure 1-1 in Chapter 1).

Classified as *ad valorem taxes* (based on value), property taxes are most typically levied against real property (land and buildings). However, many jurisdictions also include within the tax base personal property, such as automobiles, boats, and business inventories, and intangible assets, such as securities and bank deposits.

Property taxes are levied against the *assessed* value of taxable assets. Most jurisdictions are required to assess property at 100 percent of its appraised fair market value. Many, however, assess property as a fraction of appraised value (perhaps in the hope of discouraging taxpayer protests) and then adjust the tax rate upward to offset the reduction in tax base.

Governments establish the property tax rate by dividing the amount of revenue required of the tax by the assessed value of the property subject to tax. For example, if a government needs $400 million in tax revenue and its jurisdiction has $22 billion in taxable property, then the tax rate would be the $400 million in needed revenue divided by the $22 billion in taxable property—1.818 percent, or 18.18 *mils* (dollars per thousand).

In reality the computation is somewhat more complex, as allowances have to be made for discounts, exemptions, and taxes that will be delinquent or uncollectible. Most jurisdictions experience a relatively low rate of bad debts on property taxes, since they are able to impose a **lien** (right to seize and sell) on the taxed property. However, it may take several years before the government is actually able either to collect from a property owner or to seize and sell the property.

Many jurisdictions grant discounts for early payment. For example, taxpayers may be allowed discounts of 3 percent, 2 percent, and 1 percent for paying, respectively, three months, two months, or one month prior to the due date. If they pay after the due date, they are generally subject to both interest and penalties.

Not all property within a jurisdiction is subject to tax. Property held by other governments and religious institutions is ordinarily exempt. In addition, many jurisdictions grant *homestead* exemptions to homeowners on their primary residences. These exemptions include both basic allowances, often of a fixed dollar amount (e.g., $5,000), which are available to all taxpayers, and supplementary amounts to senior citizens or members of other designated classes. Thus, if a residence were assessed at $200,000 but the homeowner were granted a $5,000 exemption, the property's net assessed value would be $195,000. If the tax rate were 18.18 mils, the tax would be $195,000 multiplied by 0.01818, or $3,545.

SIGNIFICANT EVENTS IN THE REVENUE GENERATION PROCESS

Several events in the property tax timeline have potential accounting significance:

- The legislative body levies the tax, establishing the tax rate and estimating the total amount to be collected.
- Administrative departments determine the amount due from the individual property owners, enter the amounts on the *tax roll* (a subsidiary ledger that supports the taxes receivable control account), and send out tax notices (bills) to property owners.
- The taxes are collected, most prior to the due date, some afterward.
- The taxes are due and the government has the right to impose a lien on the property for which taxes have not been paid.

The *stated* due date must be distinguished from the *substantive* due date. Some jurisdictions establish a due date but do not impose interest, penalties, or a lien until a later date. The substantive due date is that date on which interest and penalties begin to accrue or a lien is imposed.

The question facing governments is which of the events is sufficiently significant to warrant revenue recognition, subject (on the fund statements) to the "available" constraint.

In this and subsequent chapters, we spotlight accounting issues by placing them within the context of short examples. We prepare journal entries so as to emphasize the impact of the possible options on both the statement of operations and the balance sheet. In many of the examples, a single entry may be used to summarize what in practice would be many individual entries. The illustrated entry is intended to show the impact of the described events on the year-end financial statements. In most of the examples we assume, for convenience, that the entity's fiscal year ends on December 31, even though the fiscal year of most governments ends on the last day of June, July, August, September, or October.

EXAMPLE *Property Taxes*

In October 2003 a city levies property taxes of $515 million for the year beginning January 1, 2004. During 2004 it collects $410 million. It collects $30 million of the remaining 2004 taxes during each of the first three months of 2005 and estimates that the $15 million balance will be uncollectible.

In addition, in 2004 it collects $20 million in taxes applicable to 2005. Taxes are due on January 31 of each year and the government has the right to impose a lien on the taxed property if it has not received payment by that date.

GASB Standards

Governments should recognize *assets* from property taxes and other imposed nonexchange transactions in the period in which they first have an enforceable claim to the assets or when they first receive the assets, whichever comes first. For property taxes, the date when they have an enforceable claim is specified in the legislation authorizing or imposing the tax and is frequently referred to as the "lien date."

Governments should recognize *revenues* from property taxes *in the period for which the taxes are levied.* As a consequence of this provision, governments must delay recognition of taxes collected in advance until the period for which they have been budgeted, thereby satisfying the relevant time requirement. In addition, in their fund statements, the taxes must be "available"—that is, "collected within the current period or expected to be collected or soon enough thereafter to be used to pay liabilities of the current period. Such time thereafter shall not exceed sixty days."

If property taxes satisfy the criteria for asset recognition before they satisfy those for revenue recognition (e.g., they are collected prior to the period for which they are budgeted or they will not be collected in time to pay liabilities of the current period), then the government should debit an asset (e.g., "cash" or "property taxes receivable") and offset it with a credit to a deferred revenue account (e.g., "taxes collected in advance" or "deferred property tax revenue").

In the property taxes example, therefore, the total amount of revenue to be recognized in 2004 on a modified accrual basis would be $470 million—the $410 million due and collected during the year and applicable to it, plus the $60 million collected in the first sixty days of the next year. The $30 million to be collected after sixty days would be recognized as deferred revenue. These transactions would be summarized in the following entries for 2004:

Property taxes receivable	$515	
Deferred property tax revenue		$500
Allowance for uncollectible property taxes		15
To record the property tax levy for 2004		
Cash	$410	
Property taxes receivable		$410
To record the collection of cash in 2004		
Deferred property tax revenue	$410	
Property tax revenue		$410
To recognize revenue on the taxes collected		
Deferred property tax revenue	$60	
Property tax revenue		$60

To recognize revenue on the taxes to be received in the first 60 days of 2005 (Since this entry would be made as of the year-end, it may appear to recognize only an *estimate* of the tax receipts of the first sixty days of 2005. In reality the government would record its actual collections. Few governments are able to close their books and prepare financial statements within sixty days of year-end. Therefore, by the time they close their books and prepare financial statements, they are able to determine exactly how much revenue from collections subsequent to year-end must be recognized.)

Cash	$20	
Deferred property tax revenue		$20

To record collection of property taxes received in advance of the year to which they are applicable (The taxes collected in advance are intended to cover 2005 expenditures. Hence, they should be recorded in 2005 and thereby matched with the expenditures.)

An equally acceptable means of recording the initial tax levy would be to recognize (credit) revenue rather than *deferred* revenue. Thus, the first entry would be:

Property taxes receivable	$515	
Property tax revenue		$500
Allowance for uncollectible property taxes		15

To record the property tax levy for 2004

As taxes are collected during the year, accounts receivable would be reduced:

Cash	$410	
Property taxes receivable		$410

To record the collection of cash in 2004

Then, at year-end, the government would "back-out" any previously recognized revenue that would not be collected in time to satisfy the sixty-day test. The uncollected amounts would be transferred to *deferred revenue:*

Property tax revenue	$30	
Deferred property tax revenue		$30

To correct accounts for taxes previously recognized as revenue but that will not be collected within 60 days of year-end

This approach requires fewer entries and results in the same year-end balances. However, it causes revenue to be recognized on the basis of the tax levy rather than the collection of cash. Thus, it undermines the budgetary entries, discussed in Chapter 3, that facilitate an ongoing comparison between the budgeted revenues and the results to date.

Irrespective of approach, at year-end overdue taxes receivable should be reclassified as delinquent so they are not intermingled with the current receivables of the following year:

Property taxes receivable—delinquent	$105	
Property taxes receivable		$105

To reclassify uncollected taxes as delinquent

This entry has no impact on revenues, expenditures, or net assets (and hence on fund balance). It provides statement readers with additional information as to the status of property taxes receivable. An increase in delinquent property taxes relative to property tax revenues should serve as warning of a possible economic downturn in the government's jurisdiction or ineffective tax collection practices on the part of the government.

As the delinquent property taxes are collected, they would be recorded as follows:

Cash	$60	
Property taxes receivable—delinquent		$60

To record the tax collections of the first two months of 2005, which had been recognized as revenue of 2004

Cash	$30	
Deferred property tax revenue	30	
Property taxes receivable—delinquent		$30
Property tax revenue (2005)		30

To record the tax collections of the third month of 2005, which had not *been recognized as revenue of 2004*

Despite their powers to enforce their claims against recalcitrant taxpayers, governments are not always able to collect the full amount of tax levies. In some instances, seized property cannot be sold at prices sufficient to cover outstanding balances. In others, the costs of recovery would be inadequate to cover the expected yield, so the governments elect not to exercise all available legal options.

As a government writes off uncollectible taxes, it should offset the reduction in taxes receivable with a corresponding reduction in the allowance for uncollectibles. Thus, if the $15 million of taxes (now classified as delinquent) were written off:

Allowance for uncollectible property taxes	$15	
Property taxes receivable—delinquent		$15

To write off delinquent taxes

This entry has no impact on revenues, expenditures, net assets, or fund balance. The government gave substantive accounting recognition to the potential uncollectible taxes in the period in which it established the allowance for uncollectible taxes.

Governments may accrue interest charges and penalties on delinquent taxes as they impose them. However, on their fund statements they should recognize revenue only when it is measurable and available. Until those criteria are satisfied, they should offset interest and penalties receivable with deferred revenue rather than actual revenue.

DIFFERENCES IN GOVERNMENT-WIDE STATEMENTS

The same general rules of revenue recognition apply to government-wide as to fund statements, with the exception that the "available" criterion does not have to be satisfied. Thus, a government can recognize revenue from property taxes as soon as it either has an enforceable claim to the property taxes or has collected the taxes (whichever comes first)—subject, of course, to the time requirement that the taxes not be recognized prior to the period for which they were budgeted.

In the example, the city could recognize $500 million in revenue—the $410 million actually collected during the year plus the entire $90 million that it expects to collect. The taxes to be recognized as revenue no longer have to be collected within sixty days of year-end. The following entry summarizes the 2004 activity pertaining to the 2004 taxes:

Cash	$410	
Property taxes receivable—delinquent	105	
Property tax revenue		$500
Allowance for uncollectible property taxes		15

To summarize 2004 property tax activity pertaining to 2004 taxes

For most governments, the difference between the amount of property taxes recognized as revenues on the fund statements and the amount on the government-wide statements is relatively small. As long as the ratio of property taxes levied to property taxes collected remains fairly constant, the government-wide gains owing to the year-end accruals of taxes to be collected beyond the sixty-day window will be offset by the losses attributable to the taxes collected in the current year but recognized as revenues in the previous year. However, the differences in the deferred taxes to be reported on the balance sheets will be more pronounced, because the full amount of the deferrals will be reported on the fund statements as additions to liabilities (and hence reductions in fund balances).

It must be emphasized that the government-wide entries in this example and similar examples throughout the text are not ones that a government would actually make. Governments need not maintain two sets of books, one for fund statements and the other for government-wide statements. Instead, they will typically maintain the accounts on a modified accrual basis, appropriate for the funds statements. Then, at year-end, they will make the required adjusting entries using a multi-column worksheet. Thus, for example, since $470 of revenue would be recognized under the modified accrual basis and $500 would be recognized under the full accrual basis, the following entry would be appropriate:

Property tax revenue	$30	
Deferred property tax revenue		$30

To convert from fund to government-wide statements

FINES: KEY DATES AND EVENTS

The other main type of imposed nonexchange revenues is fines. Although the question of when a government "should recognize" its revenues from fines is seldom important in terms of dollar amount, it is nevertheless provocative. Consider, for example, the several dates and events relating to parking tickets and other traffic violations:

- Tickets are issued; from historical experience the government can estimate the percentage of tickets that will actually be paid.
- Violators must either pay or protest the fines by specified dates; if they do not protest, the government has a legal claim to the basic fines plus penalties for late payment.
- For ticketed parties who opt to protest, hearings are scheduled and held; if a party is found guilty, the government now has a legal claim to the basic fine plus penalties for late payment.

EXAMPLE *Fines*

In November 2004 police issued $200,000 in parking tickets. Of the fines assessed $130,000 are paid without protest by the due date of December 31, 2004. Of the balance, $4,000 have been protested and are subject to hearings. The government estimates that an additional $18,000 will trickle in, but will not be available for expenditure in 2004. The balance of $48,000 will be uncollectible.

GASB Standards

The GASB standards direct that both the assets and the revenues from fines, penalties, and most other imposed nonexchange transactions be recognized when the government has an enforceable legal claim to the assets to be received or has collected the cash. Most commonly a government has a legal claim to a fine only after the protest period expires (typically the payment due date) or a court imposes a penalty. However, in the fund statements, revenue recognition is, of course, also subject to the "measurable and available" stipulation.

Hence, in its fund statements the government should recognize as revenue only the $130,000 actually received during the year—the only amount on which the government has a legal claim and which will be collected in time to satisfy liabilities of the current period. The government cannot recognize either an asset or revenue on the $4,000 in tickets under protest inasmuch as it will have an enforceable claim upon the alleged violators only if and when the courts eventually rule in its favor. The following entry would be appropriate:

Cash	$130,000	
Parking tickets receivable (not protested)	66,000	
Revenue from parking fines		$130,000
Deferred revenue from parking fines		18,000
Allowance for uncollectible parking tickets		48,000
To summarize 2004 activity related to November tickets		

DIFFERENCES IN GOVERNMENT-WIDE STATEMENTS

In the government-wide statements, revenue recognition is not subject to the "available" test. Therefore, both the fines that have been collected as well as those expected to be collected and for which the government has an enforceable legal claim may be recognized as revenue:

Cash	$130,000	
Parking tickets receivable (not protested)	66,000	
Revenue from parking fines		$148,000
Allowance for uncollectible parking tickets		48,000
To summarize 2004 activity related to November tickets		

HOW SHOULD SALES TAXES AND OTHER DERIVED TAX REVENUES BE ACCOUNTED FOR?

Sales taxes, along with income taxes, are categorized as *derived tax revenues.* They are derived from exchange transactions, such as the sale of goods or services, or other income-producing commercial transactions.

Sales taxes are imposed on customers who purchase goods or services. The merchant providing the goods or services is responsible for collecting, reporting, and transmitting the taxes. Unlike property taxes, which are government assessed, sales taxes are taxpayer assessed; the tax base is determined by parties other than the beneficiary government. Thus, the government has to wait for, and rely upon, merchant tax returns to become aware of the proceeds to which it is legally entitled.

SIGNIFICANT EVENTS IN THE "EARNINGS PROCESS"

Three significant dates underlie sales tax transactions:

- The date of the sales transaction and the collection of the tax by the merchant
- The date the merchant is required to file the tax return and transmit the taxes (generally the same)

- The date the merchant actually files the return and transmits the taxes

The date of the sale is arguably the most significant of the three dates, since the transaction producing the tax takes place then, the amount of the tax is established, and the liability of the merchant to transmit the tax is created. However, the government is not entitled to the tax until the date the return is to be filed and the tax paid. Moreover, except for unusual circumstances, such as when a merchant files a return but fails to make timely payment, the government does not know what the amount will be until it actually receives the tax.

EXAMPLE *Sales Taxes*

In December 2004 merchants collect $20 million in sales taxes. Of these, $12 million are collected prior to December 15 and must be remitted by February 15, 2005; the remaining $8 million must be remitted by March 15, 2005.

GASB Standards

Current standards, as set forth in GASB Statement No. 33, require that revenues from sales taxes and other derived nonexchange revenues be recognized at the time the underlying exchange transaction takes place. For sales taxes, that would be the date of the sale.

In the fund statements, the sales taxes must also satisfy the "available" test to be recognized as revenue. Neither GASB Statement No. 33 nor other official pronouncements provide guidance as to the length of the period after the close of the fiscal year in which resources must be received to be considered available. As noted previously, the "sixty-day rule" applies only to property taxes, not to other revenues. Hence, governments must exercise their own judgment as to what constitutes "available." At the very least they must assure consistency of practice from one year to the next.

The standards also stipulate that governments should recognize *assets* from derived nonexchange transactions in the period in which the underlying transaction takes place. Thus a government should recognize an asset, "sales taxes receivable," on taxes imposed in the current year even if the taxes will not be collected in time to be available to meet the current liabilities of that year.

Assuming that the government adopts sixty days as the "available" criterion, then it could recognize as revenue of 2004 only the $12 million in taxes that it expects to collect within sixty days of year-end. The $8 million balance must be deferred until 2005:

Sales taxes receivable	$20	
Sales tax revenue		$12
Deferred sales tax revenue		8

To summarize December sales tax activity

Suppose instead that the sales taxes were imposed only on motor fuels and had to be used to construct and maintain roads. Would this purpose restriction affect the recognition of revenue?

Inasmuch as the revenues were now restricted, they should properly be reported in a special revenue fund rather than in the general fund. Special revenue funds, like the general fund, are governmental funds. The GASB rules (and the discussion in this and the following chapter on expenditures) apply uniformly to all governmental funds. Per GASB Statement No. 33, purpose restrictions should not affect the timing of revenue recognition. If the underlying transaction has taken place and the resources are measurable and available, then the government has benefited from an increase in net assets and, according to the GASB, it should recognize this increase.

DIFFERENCES IN GOVERNMENT-WIDE STATEMENTS

The same general principles of revenue recognition apply to both the fund and the government-wide statements, with the exception that under the government-wide (full accrual) statements, the "available" criterion is inapplicable. Hence, in the example, the government should recognize the entire $20 million of taxes derived from the sales of December:

Sales taxes receivable	$20	
Sales tax revenue		$20
To summarize December sales tax activity		

The government-wide statements consolidate the governmental funds, so that if the taxes were subject to a purpose restriction, they would not automatically be shown separately from unrestricted resources. To make the distinction between restricted and unrestricted resources the GASB directs that until the resources are expended for the designated purpose, the resultant net assets (fund balance) should be shown on the government-wide balance sheet as restricted.

SALES TAXES COLLECTED BY ANOTHER GOVERNMENT

Sales taxes are levied by both state and local governments. However, to avoid duplication of effort, most states collect and administer the sales taxes imposed by their local governments. For example, a state may impose a 5 percent sales tax, allowing local governments to add an additional 2 percent on sales within their jurisdictions. The state will collect the entire 7 percent tax, acting as an agent for the local governments with respect to their 2 percent.

The issue facing local governments is whether they can properly recognize revenue as soon as the state satisfies the recognition criteria or whether they must delay recognition until a later date—either when the state notifies them of the amount collected on their behalf or actually transmits the tax to them.

EXAMPLE *Sales Taxes Collected by State*

Assume a slight variation of the previous example. In November and December 2004 merchants collect $20 million in sales taxes. Of these, $5 million are remitted to the state as due, by December 15, 2004; the remaining $15 million are due on January 15, 2005. The state remits the taxes to the city thirty days after it receives them.

GASB Standards

GASB standards do not differentiate between taxes collected by the government itself and those collected by another government on its behalf. The critical date remains the same—that of the underlying sales transaction. Thus, the city should recognize revenue as if it had received the taxes directly, as long as they will be received in time to meet the "available" criterion.

In this example, the city should recognize as revenue of 2004 the entire $20 million in taxes collected by the state in both December 2004 and January 2005, all of which will be received by the city in time to satisfy 2004 obligations:

Sales taxes receivable	$20	
Sales tax revenue		$20
To summarize December sales tax activity		

However, if it were the practice of the state to remit the taxes to the city ninety days after receipt—subsequent to when the city could use them to meet 2004 liabilities—then the city could recognize none of the taxes as 2004 revenue. It would have to report all as deferred revenue.

DIFFERENCES IN GOVERNMENT-WIDE STATEMENTS

Since the GASB standards do not distinguish between taxes collected by the government itself and those collected on its behalf by another government, the city should recognize the entire amount of December taxes, just as if it had collected them itself. The "available" criterion is inapplicable to the government-wide statements, so the date of anticipated collection is irrelevant.

Situations in which a state collects sales tax revenues on behalf of a state must be distinguished from those in which the state imposes the tax but opts to share a designated portion of the tax revenues with local governments within its jurisdiction. In such situations the local government should consider the amount they receive from the state as a grant and should recognize revenue as they would any comparable grants.

INCOME TAXES: THE COLLECTION PROCESS

Almost all states and a few major cities, such as New York, Philadelphia, and Detroit, impose taxes that are based on personal or corporate revenues or income. Some of these states impose what they call a "franchise" tax on businesses, but the tax is nevertheless based, at least in part, on gross revenues or net income.

Income taxes present especially vexatious issues of revenue recognition, owing to their multistage administrative processes. Consider, for example, the following:

- The tax is based on income of either a calendar year or a fiscal year elected by the taxpayer, but such year might not coincide with the government's fiscal year.
- Taxpayers are required to remit tax payments throughout the tax year, either through payroll withholdings or periodic payments of estimated amounts. Within three or four months after the close of the year, they are required to file a tax return in which they inform the government of the actual amount of tax owed. At that time, they are expected to make a final settlement with the government, by either paying additional taxes due or requesting a refund of overpayments. Thus, the taxes received by the government during the year may be more or less than the amount to which they are entitled.
- Governments review all tax returns for reasonableness and select a sample for audit. Moreover, some taxpayers are delinquent on their payments. Thus, taxes continue to trickle in for several years after the due date. Although governments

can reliably estimate the amount of late collections based on historical experience, they may not have a legal claim to the taxes until taxpayers either file their returns or agree to the adjustments resulting from an audit.

EXAMPLE *Income Taxes*

A state is on a June 30 fiscal year. However, income taxes are based on taxpayer income during the calendar year ending December 31. Employers are required to withhold taxes from employees and remit the withheld taxes monthly, and individuals with significant nonsalary earnings are required to make quarterly estimated tax payments By April 15 of the year following the end of the calendar year taxpayers must file a tax return on which they either request a refund of overpayment or pay any remaining tax owed.

In its fiscal year ending June 30, 2004, the state collects $95 billion in income taxes for the calendar years 2003 and 2004. It refunds $15 billion of taxes based on the returns filed by April 15, 2004. As the result of audits of prior-year returns, the state bills taxpayers $10 billion for earlier calendar years; it collects half of this before its fiscal year-end and expects to collect the entire remainder eventually.

GASB Standards

Income taxes are derived from the transactions that produce the income. Therefore, in concept at least, governments should recognize the taxes as revenue in the period in which the income is earned. In practice, however, determining the amount of revenue attributable to income of a particular year is exceedingly difficult inasmuch as the government learns of actual earnings only when a taxpayer files a return or the government conducts its own audit. Moreover, the returns themselves cover a calendar year and therefore do not separate out income earned in each of the fiscal years. Therefore, in an illustration of how income taxes should be accounted for, the GASB suggests that a government base the amount of income to be recognized on the amount of withholding and estimated tax payments received during the year (adjusted for settlements and refunds when tax returns are actually filed)—in essence that they recognize revenue on a cash basis.

In the example the state collects $100 billion in taxes ($95 billion for 2003 and 2004 and $5 billion for prior-year audits) and refunds $15 billion—a net collection of $85 billion. Hence on a cash basis (the pragmatic basis suggested by the GASB) the state would recognize $85 billion in revenue. The GASB does not specifically address how amounts billed—here, the $5 billion still due from audited returns—should be accounted for, but there seems no reason why the state should not recognize them as assets. Thus:

Cash	$85	
Taxes billed but not collected (a receivable)	5	
Revenue from income taxes		$85
Deferred revenue		5

To recognize income taxes for the fiscal year ending June 30

DIFFERENCES IN GOVERNMENT-WIDE STATEMENTS

The general standards for the government-wide full accrual statements are the same, with the exception that all taxes receivable can be recognized as revenue regardless of whether they will be available to meet current-year obligations. Thus, consistent with the general standards (although not specifically addressed by the GASB) the state could recognize as revenue both taxes actually collected and those expected to be collected. Thus (assuming that the collections based on prior-year audits had not yet been recognized as revenue):

Cash	$85	
Taxes billed but not collected (a receivable)	5	
Revenue from income taxes		$90

To recognize income taxes for the fiscal year ending June 30

HOW SHOULD GRANTS AND SIMILAR GOVERNMENT MANDATED AND VOLUNTARY NONEXCHANGE REVENUES BE ACCOUNTED FOR?

State and local governments receive grants and similar forms of financial assistance from both other governments and from private sources. Some grants are mandated by a higher-level government; the lower-level government has no choice but to accept them (as when the federal government requires states to undertake specified environmental clean-up efforts and provides the necessary resources for them to do so). Most, however, are voluntary; the government can choose not to accept the funds if it is unwilling to accept attached conditions or to carry out the specific programs the grant is intended to finance.

Typical intergovernmental grants and similar nonexchange revenues include the following:

- **Restricted grants.** These are payments intended for designated purposes, projects, or activities. The most common form of grants, they are usually made to reimburse specific types of expenditures. They may be either mandated or voluntary.
- **Unrestricted grants.** These are payments that are unrestricted as to purpose, project, or activity.
- **Contingent grants.** These are grants contingent upon a specified occurrence or action on the part of the recipient (e.g., the ability of the recipient to raise resources from other parties).
- **Entitlements.** These are payments, usually from a higher-level government, to which a state or local government is automatically entitled in an amount determined by a specified formula. Entitlements are often designated for a broad functional activity, such as education.
- **Shared revenues.** These are revenues raised by one government, such as a state, but shared on a predetermined basis with other governments, such as cities.
- **Payments in lieu of taxes.** These are amounts paid by one government to another in place of property taxes which it would otherwise be required to pay were it not a government and thereby tax exempt. Such payments constitute an

important source of revenue for governments having within their jurisdiction a substantial amount of facilities of other governments. For example, the federal government, the property of which is tax exempt, may make payments to school districts in which military bases are located to compensate them for educating military dependents.

Examples of voluntary nonexchange revenues from private (i.e., nongovernment sources) include donations to school districts and universities, contributions of land from developers (often tied, at least indirectly, to a project they are undertaking), and gifts of collectible items to museums or cultural centers. Sometimes they take the form of endowments. These are gifts that stipulate that the contribution must be invested, and only the income from the investments can be spent.

GASB Standards

Recipients of grants, irrespective of whether the grants are mandatory or voluntary, should recognize both revenue and related receivables only when all eligibility requirements have been met (subject, of course, in the fund statements to the "availability" criterion). Resources received before the eligibility requirements have been met should be reported as deferred revenue.

Reimbursement grants are generally considered to have an inherent eligibility requirement—the recipient is eligible for the grant only if and when it incurs allowable costs. Hence, recipients typically must recognize revenue from reimbursement grants in the period in which they make the expenditures for which they will be reimbursed.

Endowment contributions that stipulate that only the income from investing the contributions can be spent are subject to infinite time requirements. Does that mean that the recipients can never recognize revenue from the gift? No. The GASB makes an exception to the general rule that revenue from contributions cannot be recognized until all time requirements have been satisfied. Per Statement No. 33, governments can recognize revenue from endowments and similar gifts in which the main benefit to the recipient is from the derived income, not the gift itself, as soon as they receive the gift. Similar rules apply to gifts of historical treasures and art works that the recipient agrees it will hold rather than sell.

EXAMPLE *Unrestricted Grant with Time Requirement*

In October 2004 a school district is notified that, per legislative-approved formulas, the state awarded it $15 million in assistance. The funds, transmitted to the district in December 2004, may be used to supplement teachers' salaries, acquire equipment, and support educational enrichment programs. They can be used only in the year ending December 31, 2005.

The grant is unrestricted. The stipulation that the funds must be used to supplement teachers' salaries, acquire equipment, and support educational enrichment programs is not a purpose restriction. It is a requirement only in form, not in substance;

the state demands nothing of the district that it would otherwise not do. However, the grant is subject to a time requirement—the resources must be used in 2005. Hence the school district must defer recognizing grant revenue until 2005:

Cash	$15	
Deferred grant revenue		$15
To record the receipt of state funds in 2004		

Deferred grant revenue	$15	
Grant revenue		$15
To recognize grant revenue in 2005		

EXAMPLE *Grant with Purpose Restriction*

In October 2004 a school district is notified that, per legislative-approved formulas, the state granted it $15 million to enhance its technological capabilities. The funds, transmitted by the state in December 2004, must be used to acquire computers, but may be spent at any time.

This grant is subject only to a purpose restriction. Purpose restrictions do not affect the timing of revenue recognition; the district should recognize the revenue as soon as the grant is announced. Nevertheless, owing to the purpose restriction the district should record the grant in a special revenue fund, and in its government-wide statements it should report $15 million of its net assets as "restricted to purchase of computers."

Cash	$15	
Grant revenue		$15
To recognize grant revenue (in a special revenue fund) in 2004		

EXAMPLE *Reimbursement (Eligibility Requirement) Grant*

In December 2004 a city is awarded a grant of $400,000 to train social workers. During the year it spends $300,000 in allowable costs, for which it is reimbursed $250,000. It expects to be reimbursed for the $50,000 balance in January 2005 and to expend and be reimbursed for the remaining $100,000 of its grant throughout 2005. The city is subject to an eligibility requirement in that to be eligible for the grant it must first incur allowable costs.

In this example, the government can recognize the grant only as it incurs allowable costs. Thus, in 2004 it can recognize $300,000 in both revenue and increases in assets:

Expenditures to train social workers	$300,000	
Cash (or payables)		$300,000
To record allowable costs		

Cash	$250,000	
Grants receivable	50,000	
Grant revenue		$300,000
To recognize grant revenue		

EXAMPLE *Unrestricted Grant with Contingency Eligibility Requirement*

In January 2004, a private foundation agrees to match all private cash contributions up to $20 million received by a state-owned museum during its 2004–2005 fund drive. In 2004 the museum receives $14 million in private cash contributions.

The museum is eligible for the foundation's matching contribution only insofar as it receives funds from other sources. Thus, in 2004 it can recognize only $14 million of matching foundation revenue:

Grant receivable (foundation)	$14	
Grant revenue (foundation)		$14
To recognize $14 million of a foundation grant		

If the foundation will not actually make its contribution in time for the resources to be available to meet its 2004 current liabilities, then on its modified accrual fund statements the museum should recognize the grant as deferred, rather than realized, revenue.

EXAMPLE *Endowment Gift*

A private citizen donates $1 million to a city to maintain and repair historical monuments. He stipulates that the principal remain intact permanently and that only the income be used for the intended purpose.

Endowments that are intended to support a government's activities and thereby benefit the public are accounted for in a permanent fund, a type of governmental fund. Inasmuch as the gift is intended to provide an ongoing source of income, the city should recognize the $1 million as revenue upon receipt. In its government-wide statements, however, it should show $1 million of its assets as restricted and thereby unavailable for general expenditure.

EXAMPLE *Pledges*

A private citizen pledges $10,000 to a county-operated zoo. The government is confident that the promised donation will actually be made.

Governments should recognize revenue from pledges on the same basis as other grants—that is, as soon as they meet all eligibility requirements. Thus, if a government has to do nothing further to receive a donation (and the resources are probable of collection) it can recognize revenue at the time the pledge is made. However, in its fund statements, consistent with the "available" criterion, it must delay revenue recognition until the resources will be available to meet the current liabilities of the period. In effect, therefore, it would recognize a receivable (offset by deferred revenue) but must wait to recognize the revenue until the period in which the cash is to be received (or will be received within sixty days thereafter).

DIFFERENCES IN GOVERNMENT-WIDE STATEMENTS

The general standards for recognition of grant revenues are the same for full accrual government-wide statements as for modified accrual fund statements. As emphasized with respect to other revenues, however, recognition under the modified accrual basis is subject to the "available" test, whereas under the full accrual basis it is not.

ACCOUNTING FOR GIFTS OF CAPITAL ASSETS

Gifts of capital assets present an especially intriguing accounting issue, mainly because capital assets are not typically reported in governmental funds. Donated capital assets, current standards make clear, should be recorded in either the fund to which they relate if such fund is a proprietary fund or in the schedule of capital assets if such fund is a governmental fund. Are there instances, however, in which donated capital assets can properly be recorded in a governmental fund?

EXAMPLE *Donations of Land for Differing Purposes*

A builder donates two parcels of land to a city. Each has a fair value of $4 million. The city intends to use one as a park and to sell the other.

In current practice, capital assets intended for use cannot be recorded in a governmental fund as assets; correspondingly, donations of capital assets cannot be recognized as revenue. The donated assets should be recorded in the schedule of capital assets. Thus, the land intended as a park would not be recorded in either the general fund or any other governmental fund. It would be recorded only in the schedule of capital assets and in the government-wide statement of net assets.

By contrast, capital assets held for sale are unlike capital assets held for use. From the perspective of the recipient government they are the equivalent of marketable securities or other short-term investments. They are expected to be transformed soon into cash. Arguably, therefore, capital assets intended to be sold should be recorded in governmental funds (such as the general fund or a capital projects fund), and donations of these assets should be recognized as revenues. Nevertheless, the Government Finance Officers Association (the GASB has not yet addressed the issue) recommends that in a governmental fund, such as the general fund, the government report the asset on year-end financial statements only if it has actually been able to sell the asset by the time it issues those statements. If the government sells the asset after year-end but within the availability period (e.g., sixty days) then it would recognize revenue from the gift. Thus, it would make the following entry:

Land held for sale	$4	
Revenue from donations		$4

To record a gift of land that the city sold within the availability period

If, however, it sold the land after the availability period but before it issued the financial statements then it would recognize the land as an asset, but defer the recognition of revenue. Thus:

Land held for sale	$4	
Deferred revenue (from donations)		$4

To record a gift of land that the city sold after the availability period but prior to the issuance of financial statements

If, by contrast, it failed to sell the land by the time it issued the financial statements, then in a government fund it would not recognize the asset and not recognize either revenue or deferred revenue. The rationale for this position is that there is no arm's length transaction with a third party to provide objective evidence of the land's value.[3]

[3] This recommendation is based on Stephen J. Gautier, *Governmental Accounting, Auditing, and Financial Reporting* (Chicago: Government Finance Officers Association., 2001), p. 70.

DIFFERENCES IN GOVERNMENT-WIDE STATEMENTS

The Government Finance Officers Association takes a different (some may contend inconsistent) position with respect to government-wide statements. In government-wide, full accrual statements, it recommends the government should account for the donation of capital assets just as it would a donation of any other type of asset. The government should recognize both the revenue and the property received, irrespective of whether and when the land was sold. If the land is not sold by the time the financial statements are issued, then the government should estimate its value. Presumably, inasmuch as the government-wide statement of net assets, but not a governmental fund balance sheet, already includes other capital assets, the impact of any error in the estimated value of the donated asset would be relatively small.

ACCOUNTING FOR PASS-THROUGH GRANTS

Some types of grants—those for which the recipient is required to distribute the resources to other parties or for which payment is made directly to a third party for the benefit of the recipient—raise the additional question of whether the grant should even be recognized by the recipient government. Suppose, for example, a state receives federal funds earmarked for each of its local school districts. Should the state record the receipt of the funds as a revenue and the disbursement as an expenditure? Or alternatively, should it omit the grant from both its budget and its accounts on the grounds that, with regard to these funds, it is nothing more than an agent of the federal government?

Grants that a government must transfer to, or spend on behalf of, a secondary recipient are referred to as **pass-through grants.** Pass-through grants vary in the extent of responsibility they impose on the primary recipient. For example, a state may receive federal funds over which it has no discretion in determining how, or in what amounts, they can be disbursed. Once it distributes the funds, it has no responsibility for monitoring how they are spent. At the other extreme, a state may be permitted to distribute federal funds within broad guidelines and it will be held accountable for assuring that the funds are used in accordance with federal specifications.

In the past, some governments opted to exclude pass-through funds from both their revenues and expenditures. Perhaps wanting to show that they held the line on spending, they accounted for the funds "off the budget"—often in agency funds in which only assets and liabilities are reported.

To reduce diversity of practice, in 1994 the GASB stated that "as a general rule, cash pass-through grants should be recognized as revenue and expenditures or expenses in governmental, proprietary, or trust funds."[4] Only in those "infrequent cases" in which the government serves as a "cash conduit" may pass-through grants be reported in an agency fund. A government serves as a "cash conduit," the GASB explains, if it "merely transmits grantor-supplied moneys without having 'administrative involvement.'" *Administrative involvement* would be indicated if the government selected the secondary recipients of the funds (even based on grantor-established criteria) or monitored compliance with grant requirements.

ACCOUNTING FOR FOOD STAMPS

Food stamps are a form of pass-through assistance. The federal government gives the stamps to the states, which distribute them in accord with specified guidelines. Until 1994, many governments gave no balance sheet or operating statement recognition

[4] GASB Statement No. 24, *Accounting and Financial Reporting for Certain Grants and Other Financial Assistance*, para. 5, 1994.

to food stamps. Then, in its pronouncement on pass-through grants, the GASB asserted that food stamps received and distributed should be recognized as both a revenue and an expenditure.

EXAMPLE *Food Stamps*

A state receives $100 million in food stamps, of which it distributes $95 million.

GASB Standards

According to the GASB, *state* governments should report both the revenue and the expenditure concurrently, when the stamps are distributed. They should be measured by the stamps' face value.

Moreover, the GASB directed that state governments report food stamps on hand at year-end as an asset (stated at face value). Inasmuch as governments should recognize revenue from food stamps only as the stamps are distributed, not when they are received, the credit offsetting the stamp inventory should be to "deferred revenue."

The following entries summarize the transactions:

Expenditures—food stamps	$95	
Revenues—food stamps		$95
To record the receipt and distribution of food stamps		
Inventory of food stamps	$5	
Deferred revenues—food stamps		$5
To recognize food stamps on-hand at year-end		

States sometimes involve local governments in the food stamp distribution process. Nevertheless, overall administrative responsibility for the program rests with the states. The local governments serve mainly as agents of the state. Although the GASB does not deal with the issue of how local governments should account for their role in the food stamp programs, most governments have not been reporting stamps received and distributed as either revenues or expenditures. They have, however, been recognizing administrative costs as expenditures and administrative fees charged to the state as revenues.

ACCOUNTING FOR ON-BEHALF PAYMENTS

In the multigovernment system of the United States, one government may make payments for employee fringe benefits "on behalf" (for the direct benefit) of another. For example, a state may contribute to a pension plan for school teachers on behalf of the independent school districts that employ the teachers.

The key issue as to **on-behalf payments** is whether, and in what circumstances, the receipient government should recognize the payments as if it had received, and then spent, a cash grant—that is, should it recognize a revenue and an offsetting expenditure, or should it give no recognition at all to the transactions?

As with so many other accounting issues, the challenges of standard setting are compounded by the variety of forms that a transaction can take. Some state on-behalf payments, for example, are made in lieu of pensions or other compensation that the recipient local government would otherwise have been required by state law to provide on its own. Other payments are made by the state to cover programs or activities in which the local government would otherwise not engage. Some accountants believe that recipient governments should recognize only the on-behalf payments that cover costs for which they are legally responsible.

EXAMPLE *On-Behalf Payments*

A state government is responsible for funding the state's teacher retirement system. It contributes $3 million to the system on behalf of an independent school district.

> **GASB Standards**
>
> The GASB ruled, as another part of its grants project, that the recipient government should recognize both a revenue and a corresponding expenditure for *all* on-behalf payments of fringe benefits and salaries. Despite the objections of two of its five members, it required recognition irrespective of whether or not the beneficiary government was legally responsible for the payments.

The school district would make the following entry:

Pension expenditures	$3	
State aid—pensions		$3

To record the on-behalf pension payments made by the state

Correspondingly, the state would also record an expenditure:

State aid to school districts (expenditure)	$3	
Cash		$3

To record the contribution to the pension fund on behalf of an independent school district

A paying government should classify its on-behalf payments in the same manner as similar cash grants to other entities. For example, if it classifies other educational grants as educational expenditures, then it should classify the payments to the pension fund as educational expenditures, not pension expenditures.

HOW SHOULD SALES OF CAPITAL ASSETS BE ACCOUNTED FOR?

Governments sell capital assets for the same reasons businesses do—the services the assets impart can be provided more economically by another means or by replacement assets. The unique accounting problem faced by governments when they sell general capital assets is that the financial resources received are accounted for in a governmental fund, but the assets that are sold are not.

EXAMPLE *Sales of Capital Assets*

On December 31, 2004, a city purchases a new police car for $30,000. On January 2, 2005, the vehicle is damaged in an accident. The vehicle is uninsured; the city is able to sell the nearly demolished vehicle for $5,000.

Current practice requires the following seemingly odd entry:

Cash	$5,000	
Other financing sources—sale of vehicle		$5,000
To record the sale of general capital assets		

"Seemingly odd" because "other financing sources" is reported on a statement of revenues, expenditures, and changes in fund balance (below the revenues and expenditures). Although not exactly a revenue, it is similar to a revenue in that it may be budgeted as a revenue and results in an increase in fund balance.

From an accounting perspective, therefore, the accident that destroyed a $30,000 vehicle left the government $5,000 better off; that is, the governmental fund's assets and fund balance increased by $5,000. This outcome, while bizarre—and not suggestive of appropriate means by which governments should reduce their deficits—is inevitable when the measurement focus of governmental funds excludes capital assets. As indicated in Chapter 2, when governmental fund resources are used to acquire an asset, its cost is written off (charged as an expenditure) as it is paid for. Consequently, the police vehicle, which is clearly evident to most citizens, is invisible to the governmental fund's accountant.

Although this accounting outcome may seem bizarre, business accounting may produce a similar result. The capital assets of businesses are carried at historical cost less depreciation—amounts that may be considerably less than fair market values. Suppose that a vehicle owned by a business was destroyed in an accident and that the vehicle was insured for more than its book value. That accident, too, would cause the business to report a gain owing to the mishap.

Both businesses and governmental funds state their capital assets at amounts bearing little relationship to their economic worth. Whereas businesses carry them at historical cost, less depreciation, governmental funds report them at zero.

Differences in Government-Wide Statements

In their government-wide, full accrual statements, governments would report their capital assets just as businesses would. They would state them at historical cost, less accumulated depreciation. Upon sale of an asset, they would recognize a gain or loss in the amount of the difference between sale proceeds and book value. Hence, in the example, assuming that no depreciation had yet been charged, the government would recognize a loss of $25,000—the difference between cost of $30,000 and sale price of $5,000.

How Should Investment Gains and Losses Be Accounted For?

Investments, whether they are in debt or equity securities, fluctuate in value. Government portfolios generally contain mainly short-term debt securities. Because they are short-term, their values are not greatly influenced by swings in interest rates. Some portfolios, however, also hold longer-term instruments that are considerably more sensitive to changes in interest rates. In recent years, some governments—sometimes in violation of both accepted standards of sound fiscal management and common sense—have speculated in "derivatives" and other instruments that are extremely sensitive to interest rate changes.

Until 1993, both the GASB and the Financial Accounting Standards Board (FASB) directed that governments, not-for-profit organizations, and most businesses within their purview report short-term investments at either historical cost or the lower of historical cost or market value. In that year, the FASB broke with tradition and required businesses to divide their investment portfolios into three categories: trading securities (those that enterprises intend to hold for only a short period of time); held-to-maturity securities (mainly long-term bonds); and available-for-sale securities (other securities, such as stock held for the long term). They must carry their portfolios of both trading securities and available-for-sale securities at "fair" (i.e., market) values.[5] However, the FASB explicitly exempted not-for-profits from the purview of the statement, opting to deal with them in a separate project.

In 1995, as the result of the promised project, the FASB extended its "mark-to-market" directives to not-for-profits.[6] However, inasmuch as the requirement that investments be classified into the three categories was intended mainly to accommodate specialized industries, such as banks and insurance companies, it was omitted from the not-for-profit pronouncement. Instead, the statement requires that all debt and equity securities (except those accounted for by the equity method or those of consolidated subsidiaries) be stated at fair value. Moreover, gains and losses on investments, both realized and unrealized, must be recognized as such and reported in the statement of activities.

The reasons for reporting investments at fair value are as compelling for government organizations as for other not-for-profits and for businesses. Those frequently advanced include the following:

- For virtually all decisions involving investments, fair value is more relevant than historical cost.
- Investments are often held as cash substitutes. They can be liquidated with a phone call to the entity's broker or a quick computer entry.
- Fair values are objective; up-to-the-minute prices are available from computer and telephone information services.
- The performance of investment managers, and their employer governments, is measured by total return—dividends, interest, and changes in fair values. Insofar as government and not-for-profit portfolio managers are expected to achieve specified investment goals, statement users are entitled to the information needed to assess how well the managers have done.
- To be sure, prices that go up can also come down. But financial statements report on performance within specified periods. An increase in the value of a security in a particular year is indicative of sound investment performance in the year it occurs. A subsequent decline in the following year reflects poor performance in that year. Statement users are entitled to this information.

EXAMPLE *Investment Income*

The following table summarizes the 2004 investment activity in a county's general fund (all amounts in thousands):

---

[5] FASB Statement No. 115, *Accounting for Certain Investments in Debt and Equity Securities* (May 1993).

[6] FASB Statement No. 124, *Accounting for Certain Investments Held by Not-for-Profit Organizations* (November 1995).

	Cost	Fair Value on Jan. 1	Purchases	Sales (proceeds)	Fair Value on Dec. 31
Security A	$120	$120			$140
Security B	520	$540			540
Security C	200	200		$250	0
Security D	90		$90		75
	$930	$860	$90	$250	$755

GASB Standards

Following the FASB's lead, in 1997 the GASB determined that governments, like businesses and not-for-profits, should state their investments at fair value. GASB Statement No. 31, *Accounting and Financial Reporting for Certain Investments and for External Investment Pools*, requires that investment income, including changes in fair value, be reported in the operating statement or other statement of activities of all entities and funds.

The GASB made a notable exception for short-term securities that are not subject to the same volatility as long-term instruments. Governments are permitted to report money market investments having a remaining maturity at time of purchase of one year or less at amortized cost rather than market value. These investments include certificates of deposit, commercial paper, and U.S. Treasury obligations.

Per the new pronouncement, the investments should be reported on the county's December 31, 2004, statements at their fair value—$755. The gain or loss to be reported on the county's 2004 operating statements can be determined by subtracting investment inputs from outputs. The inputs are the securities on hand at the start of the year (stated at fair value as of the beginning of the year) plus the purchases during the year. The outputs are the securities on hand at year-end (stated at fair value as of year-end) plus the proceeds from the sale of securities during the year. Thus:

Outputs		
Fair Value, December 31	$755	
Sales	250	$1,005
Inputs		
Fair Value, January 1	$860	
Purchases	90	950
Increase (decrease) in fair value of investments		$55

The following entry would therefore be appropriate:

Investments	$55	
Revenue—increase in fair value of investments		$55
To record the increase in the fair value of the investments		

Many local governments invest what would otherwise be idle cash in investment pools maintained by their states or other governmental units. These investment pools are similar to mutual funds. Each participant purchases shares in the underlying portfolio. Statement No. 31 specifies that governments should state their investments in a pool at the fair value per share of the pool's underlying portfolio. Each period they should recognize the change in fair value as a gain or loss.

HOW SHOULD INTEREST AND DIVIDENDS BE ACCOUNTED FOR?

The GASB has not yet provided specific directives as to when governments should recognize interest and dividends on their investments. However, by recording the changes in fair value governments will automatically accrue interest and dividends as they are earned.

EXAMPLE *Interest Income*

On December 1, a town purchased a $1,000, two-year discount note for $873, a price that reflects an annual yield of approximately 7 percent. As a discount note, the security provides no periodic payments of interest. However, assuming no change in prevailing interest rates or other factors that would also affect fair value, the note's fair value can be expected to increase by approximately $5 the first month. On December 31, if the fair value of the note were $878, the following entry would recognize the $5 of investment income, attributable in economic substance to the interest earned:

Investments	$5	
Revenue—increase in fair value of investments		$5
To record the increase in the fair value of the investments		

If the security were a short-term Treasury note (one year or less), the government would not look to fair value to adjust the security. Instead, it would amortize the initial discount over the life of the note. If, for example, the initial discount on a six-month, 6 percent, $1,000 note were $30, the following entry would recognize one month's interest income:

Discount on note (or investments)	$5	
Revenue—interest income		$5
To record one-month's interest		

The impact of the two approaches on both net assets and change in fund balance is the same. Both would give recognition to the interest earned and the resultant change in the value of the underlying security.

The GASB approach to investments has been extremely controversial and unpopular among many government officials. It is easy to see why: It widens the gap between financial reporting and budgeting. The investment portfolios of many governments are dominated by notes and other securities having a fixed maturity date. If a government holds its securities to maturity, changes in market value have no impact on the cash that is available for expenditure. Yet increases in market value must be reported as revenues (increases in net assets) and decreases must be reported as expenditures (decreases in net assets). Imagine the difficulty of having to explain to members of governing boards why an increase in net assets is only a "paper gain" that cannot really be spent. Or try telling a TV reporter in thirty seconds why a decline in the value of a government's portfolio will have no impact on the amount for which the securities will eventually be sold.

How Should Licenses, Permits, and Other Exchange Transactions Be Accounted For?

Governments issue licenses (or permits) that allow citizens and businesses to carry out regulated activities over a specified period of time. However, the license period may not coincide with the government's fiscal year.

The primary concern relating to licenses is whether the revenue should be recognized when a license is issued and cash is received (usually concurrently) or whether it should be spread out over the period covered by the license. In other words, is the significant economic event the collection of cash or is it the passage of time?

The issue is by no means clear-cut in light of the following characteristics of licenses:

- Some license fees are intended to cover the cost of services provided to the licensee or related to the activity in which the licensee engages. These license fees have the characteristics of exchange transactions. The licensee pays cash and receives value in exchange. For example, the funds generated from restaurant licenses may be used to inspect restaurants, thereby assuring customers that the restaurants meet minimum standards of cleanliness. Similarly, bicycle registration fees may support bicycle safety programs. Other fees, however, may bear little relation to the cost of services provided and may be imposed mainly as a source of general revenues. They are more in the nature of nonexchange revenues.
- Generally, license fees are not refundable. Therefore, unless a license fee is tied to specific services, once the government receives the fee, it has no further obligation, either actual or contingent, to the licensee.

EXAMPLE *License Fees*

In June 2004 a city imposed license fees on barber and beauty shops for the first time. It collected $360,000. The fees are intended to cover the cost of health inspections. The licenses cover the one-year period from July 1 to June 30.

GASB Standards

In Statement No. 33, the GASB acknowledged that license fees and permits are not always pure exchange transactions. They may not be paid voluntarily, and rarely is the amount paid reflective of the fair value of benefits received by the licensee. Still, the GASB maintains that they should be accounted for as if they were true exchange transactions. GASB standards with respect to miscellaneous exchange revenues state simply: "*Miscellaneous Revenues.* Golf and swimming fees, inspection charges, parking fees and parking meter receipts, and the vast multitude of miscellaneous exchange revenues are best recognized when cash is received."[7] The following entry, therefore would summarize the 2004 activity:

[7] NCGA Statement No. 1, *Governmental Accounting and Financial Reporting Principles*, para. 67, 1979.

Cash	$360,000	
Revenue from license fees		$360,000
To summarize 2004 license fee activity		

This current standard was developed prior to the issuance of Statement No. 33 and, in that it recognizes miscellaneous revenues on a cash basis, is inconsistent with the accrual basis of accounting. The accrual basis would require that the fees be recognized over the period covered by the license (as when a business grants a licensee permission to use a patent or trademark). The current standard was developed as a pragmatic approach to recognizing revenues that for most governments are not of major consequence.

The spirit of Statement No. 34, regarding government financial statements, suggests that in government-wide statements exchange revenues should be accounted for on an accrual basis, as they are in businesses. However, mainly because these miscellaneous types of revenue are not of great significance, the GASB has not definitively stated whether in their government-wide statements governments must accrue these revenues (the conceptually sound approach) or may account for them on a cash basis as they do in their fund statements (the pragmatic approach).

HOW SHOULD GOVERNMENTS REPORT REVENUES IN THEIR GOVERNMENT-WIDE STATEMENTS?

A primary objective of the government-wide statement of activities is to show the relative financial burden to the taxpayers of each function—the amount that has to be financed out of general revenues. As indicated in Chapter 2, the government-wide statement of activities reports the net expenses of each of the government's main functions. The net expenses of a function are its expenses less any revenues that can be directly attributable to it. As a consequence, governments must determine which revenues should be classified as program (function) revenues and which as general revenues. "General revenues" is the default classification; all revenues that cannot be classified as program revenues are considered general revenues.

As a rule, revenues from charges or fees imposed upon parties that benefit from specific activities are classified as program revenues. So also are grants from other governments or outside parties that must be used for specific purposes. By contrast, taxes that are imposed upon the reporting government's citizens are considered general revenues, even if they are restricted to specific programs. Thus, for example, a general sales tax would be classified as a general revenue even though it might be dedicated to education or road construction. Interest and other earnings from investments, as well as other nontax revenues, such as grants and contributions, would be counted as general revenues unless explicitly restricted to specific programs.

As illustrated in Chapter 2, Table 2-4, the government-wide statement of activities reports program-specific revenues in three separate columns and in as many rows as there are functions. The three columns are for:

- ***Charges for services.*** These would include fees for services such as garbage collection, licenses and permits, and special assessments for roads or other capital projects.
- ***Program-specific operating grants and contributions.*** These would include federal or state grants for specific operating purposes, such as law enforcement, education, and recreation.

- ***Program-specific capital grants.*** These would include grants for the purchase and construction of long-term assets, such as for buses, jails, and roads.

Some government grants are for multiple purposes. If the amounts can be identified with specific programs (through either the grant application or the grant notification) they should be apportioned appropriately. If they cannot, they should be reported as general revenues.

SUMMARY

To better achieve two primary objectives of financial reporting—to provide information relating to interperiod equity and to demonstrate budgetary compliance—governments prepare two types of financial statements: fund and government wide. The fund statements of governmental funds are on a modified accrual basis; the government-wide statements are on a full accrual basis.

Because the modified accrual statements focus on expendable financial resources, revenues must be available to pay liabilities of the current period before they can be recognized. The GASB has specified that property taxes can be considered "available" if they are collected during the year for which they are intended or within sixty days thereafter. Although the GASB leaves it to the judgment of individual governments to determine an appropriate number of days for other types of revenues, the "sixty-day rule" has become a widely accepted benchmark.

GASB Statement No. 33, *Accounting and Financial Reporting for Nonexchange Transactions*, provides guidance as to which events are most significant in the process of revenue generation and should therefore dictate the timing of revenue recognition. Nonexchange transactions are those in which one party gives or receives value without directly receiving or giving equivalent value in return.

Statement No. 33 is applicable to financial statements prepared on either the full accrual or the modified accrual basis. However, when reporting on the modified accrual basis, governments should recognize revenues only to the extent that they satisfy the "available" criterion. There is no difference between accrual and modified accrual accounting in the timing of recognition of assets, liabilities, or expenditures.

The revenue recognition guidelines set forth by the GASB in Statement No. 33 as well as other pronouncements include the following:

- Property taxes, which are *imposed* revenues, should be recognized as revenues in the period for which they are levied. If they are collected in advance of the period for which they are intended, they should be accounted for as deferred revenues. Governments should recognize revenues from fines and penalties, the other major type of imposed revenues, as soon as they either receive the assets or have an enforceable legal claim to them.
- Revenues that are *derived* from underlying exchange transactions should be recognized when the underlying transactions take place. Thus, sales taxes should be recognized in the period of sale. Income taxes should be recognized in the period in which the income is earned. However, if practical difficulties prevent them from determining when the income has been earned, governments may recognize income tax revenues in the period in which the taxes are collected (taking into account refunds and other adjustments).
- Grants should be recognized when the government has satisfied all eligibility requirements. Grants that cannot be spent until a specific date are considered to be subject to time requirements and therefore should not be recognized until that date. To be eligible for reimbursement grants, governments must first incur the costs for which they are to be reimbursed. Hence, they should recognize receivables and revenues only as they make the related expenditures.
- Revenues from the sale of capital assets and from other exchange transactions are recognized in the period of the exchange. Since governments do not report capital assets in their governmental funds, the book value of the assets is zero. Therefore, in the fund statements, the gain from the sale of a capital asset is equal to the sale proceeds. In the government-wide statements, by contrast, governments account for their capital assets as do businesses. The gain or loss is equal to the difference between the sales proceeds and the adjusted book value (cost less accumulated depreciation).
- Investments must be market-to-market. Changes in the fair value of securities, including those attributable to anticipated receipts of interest and dividends, should be recognized as revenue as they take place.
- Revenues from most licenses and similar exchange transactions (even if not "pure" exchange transactions in that they may not involve exchanges of equal value) are generally recognized as cash is received (even if the benefits will be provided over more than one period), primarily for practical reasons.

Table 4–1 summarizes the principles of revenue and asset recognition as they apply to the main types of revenue producing transactions in governmental funds.

TABLE 4-1

Summary of Asset and Revenue Recognition in Governmental Funds

Imposed nonexchange transactions (Examples: property taxes and fines)	*Revenue*: In the period in which the revenue is intended to be used *Asset*: When the government has an enforceable legal claim or when resources are received, whichever comes first
Derived taxes (Examples: sales taxes, income taxes, hotel taxes, and fuel taxes)	*Revenue*: In the period of the underlying transaction *Asset*: In the period of the underlying transaction or when resources are received, whichever comes first
Government-mandated exchange transactions (Example: a federal grant to pay for a required drug prevention program)	*Revenue*: When all eligibility requirements, including time requirements, have been met *Asset*: When all eligibility requirements have been met, or when resources are received, whichever comes first
Voluntary exchange transactions (Examples: entitlements, federal grants for general education)	Same as for government mandated exchange transactions
Exchange and "exchange-like" transactions (Examples: license fees, permits, and inspection charges)	*Revenue*: When cash is received *Asset*: When cash is received
Investments (Examples: stocks, bonds, notes, shares in investment pools)	*Revenue*: As securities increase in value *Asset*: As securities increase in value (i.e., should be "marked to market")

Note: The above guidelines apply to both the government-wide (full accrual) and governmental fund (modified accrual) statements. However, in the fund (modified accrual) statements, revenues should be recognized no sooner than the period in which the resources to be received are measurable and available to satisfy liabilities of the current period.

EXERCISE FOR REVIEW AND SELF-STUDY

The town of Malvern engages in the following transactions during its fiscal year ending September 30, 2005. All dollar amounts are in thousands. Prepare summary journal entries to reflect their impact on year-end fund financial statements prepared on a modified accrual basis. Base your entries on generally accepted accounting principles now in effect. In addition, indicate how your entries would differ if the statements were government-wide and prepared on a full accrual basis.

1. During fiscal 2005 the town levied property taxes of $154,000, of which it collected $120,000 prior to September 30, 2005, and $5,000 over each of the next six months. It estimated that $4,000 will be uncollectible.
2. On November 20, 2005, it received $12,000 from the state for sales taxes collected on its behalf. The payment was for sales made in September that merchants were required to remit to the state by October 15.
3. In April the town was awarded a state training grant of $400 for the period June 1, 2005, through May 31, 2006. In fiscal 2005 the town received the entire $400 but spent only $320. Although the funds were received in advance, the city would have to return to the state any amounts that were not used to cover allowable training costs.
4. The town requires each vendor who sells in its "farmers' market" to obtain an annual permit. The funds

generated by the sale of these permits are used to maintain the market. The permits, which cover the period from June 1 through May 31, are not refundable. In May 2005 the town issued $36 of permits.

5. On September 1, 2005, with $500 in funds available for temporary investment, the town acquired two-year, 6 percent U.S. Treasury notes. The notes pay interest upon maturity. On September 30, the market value of the notes was $540.

6. Several years earlier the town received a donation of a parcel of land, upon which it expected to build. During fiscal 2005 it opted to sell the land for $135. When acquired by the town, the land had a market value of $119.

QUESTIONS FOR REVIEW AND DISCUSSION

1. Why is a choice of *basis of accounting* unavoidably linked to *measurement focus*?
2. What are the measurement focus and basis of accounting of governmental funds? What is the traditional rationale for this basis of accounting (used in governmental fund statements)—as opposed, for example, to either a full accrual basis or a budgetary basis?
3. What is the difference between an *exchange* and a *nonexchange* transaction?
4. What are the main categories of revenues per GASB Statement No. 33, *Accounting and Financial Reporting for Nonexchange Transactions*?
5. What criteria must be met before revenues can be recognized on a modified accrual basis? What is the rationale for these criteria?
6. What is the general rule for recognizing property taxes as revenues? How would property taxes be accounted for differently in the fund statements as opposed to the government-wide statements?
7. What is the earliest point in the sales tax collection process that revenue may be recognized? How can you justify recognizing revenue on the basis of this event?
8. What special problems do governments face in measuring the income taxes associated with a particular year?
9. Explain the distinction between reimbursement grants and entitlements. How does this distinction affect the way each type of grant is accounted for?
10. A private citizen makes an unrestricted pledge of $5 million to a city's museum. The city is confident that the donor will fulfill her pledge. However, the cash will not be received for at least two years. How will the amount of revenue recognized differ between the fund statements and the government-wide statements? Explain.
11. What are pass-through grants? Under what circumstances must a recipient government report them as both a revenue and an expenditure?
12. A student comments: "A government destroys a recently acquired car, sells the remains for scrap, and its general fund surplus for the year increases. That's ridiculous. Government accounting makes so much less sense than private-sector accounting." Explain why the situation described by the student arises. Does government accounting, in fact, differ so much from business accounting?
13. Until recently governments were not permitted to recognize revenue on increases in the value of investments. What arguments might you present in support of the current position that investments be stated at fair value and that changes in fair value be recognized as either revenues or expenditures?

EXERCISES

4-1

1. Under the modified accrual basis of accounting, revenues cannot be recognized
   - a. Until cash has been collected
   - b. Unless they will be collected within sixty days of year-end
   - c. Until they are subject to accrual
   - d. Until they are measurable and available
2. "Available" (as in "measurable and available") means
   - a. Available to finance expenditures of the current period
   - b. Subject to accrual
   - c. Collectible
   - d. Available for appropriation
3. Property taxes are an example of
   - a. An imposed exchange transaction
   - b. An imposed nonexchange transaction
   - c. A derived transaction
   - d. A government-mandated nonexchange transaction
4. To be considered "available," property taxes must have either been collected during the government's fiscal year or within

a. The time it takes for the government to liquidate its obligations from the prior year
b. Thirty days of year-end
c. Sixty days of year-end
d. The following fiscal year

5. For its fiscal year ending September 30, 2004, Twin City levied $500 million in property taxes. It collected taxes applicable to fiscal 2004 as follows (in millions):

June 1, 2003, through September 30, 2003	$ 20
October 1, 2003, through September 30, 2004	440
October 1, 2004, through November 30, 2004	15
December 2004	4

The city estimates that $10 million of the outstanding balance will be uncollectible. For the fiscal year ending September 30, 2004, how much should Twin City recognize in property tax revenue (in millions) in its general fund?
a. $440
b. $460
c. $475
d. $490

6. Assume the same facts as in the previous example. How much should Twin City recognize in property tax revenue (in millions) in its government-wide statement of activities?
a. $440
b. $460
c. $475
d. $490

7. Central City was awarded two state grants during its fiscal year ending September 30, 2004: a $2 million block grant that can be used to cover any operating expenses incurred during fiscal 2005 and a $1 million grant that can be used any time to acquire equipment for its police department. For the year ending September 30, 2004, Central City should recognize in grant revenue in its funds statements (in millions)
a. $0
b. $1
c. $2
d. $3

8. Assume the same facts as in the previous example. How much should the city recognize in grant revenue in its government-wide statements?
a. $0
b. $1
c. $2
d. $3

9. Assuming that a government will collect its sales taxes in sufficient time to satisfy the "available" criterion, it would ordinarily recognize revenue from sales taxes in its governmental fund statements
a. When the underlying sales transaction takes place
b. On the date the merchant must remit the taxes to the government
c. On the date the merchant must file a tax return
d. When the taxes are received by the government

10. Assuming that a government will collect its sales taxes in sufficient time to satisfy the "available" criterion, it would ordinarily recognize revenue from sales taxes in its government-wide statements
a. When the underlying sales transaction takes place
b. On the date the merchant must remit the taxes to the government
c. On the date the merchant must file a tax return
d. When the taxes are received by the government

4-2

The following relate to Hudson City for its fiscal year ended December 31, 2004.

- On January 31, 2004, the city purchased as an investment for its debt service fund a fifteen-year, 6 percent $1 million bond for $998,000. During the year it received $30,000 in interest. At year-end the market value of the bond was $999,500.
- On December 31, 2003, the Foundation for the Arts pledged to donate $1, up to a maximum of $1 million, for each $3 that the museum is able to collect from other private contributors. The funds are to finance construction of the city-owned art museum. During 2004, the city collected $600,000 and received the matching money from the Foundation. In January and February 2005 it collected an additional $2,400,000 and also received the matching money.
- During the year the city imposed license fees on street vendors. All vendors were required to purchase the licenses by September 30, 2004. The licenses cover the one-year period from October 1, 2004, through September 30, 2005. During 2004 city collected $240,000 in license fees.
- The city sold a fire truck for $40,000 that it had acquired five years earlier for $250,000. At the time of sale the city had charged $225,000 in depreciation.
- The city received a grant of $2 million to partially reimburse costs of training police officers. During the year the city incurred $1,500,000 of allowable costs and received $1,200,000. It expects to incur an additional $500,000 in allowable costs in January 2005 and be reimbursed for all allowable costs by the end of February 2005.

Match the items below with the amounts that follow. An amount may be selected once, more than once, or not at all.

1. Amount of investment income that the city should recognize in its debt service fund
2. Reported value of bonds in government-wide statements at year-end
3. Amount of investment income that the city should recognize in its government-wide statements

4. Contribution revenue from Foundation for the Arts to be recognized in funds statements
5. Contribution revenue from Foundation for the Arts to recognized in government-wide statements
6. Revenue from license fees to be recognized in funds statements
7. Increase in general fund balance owing to sale of fire engine
8. Increase in net assets (government-wide statements) owing to sale of fire engine
9. Revenue in fund statements from police training grant
10. Revenue in government-wide statements from police training grant
    a. $0
    b. $1,500
    c. $3,000
    d. $3,150
    e. $15,000
    f. $40,000
    g. $60,000
    h. $200,000
    i. $225,000
    j. $240,000
    k. $600,000
    l. $998,000
    m. $999,500
    n. $1,000,000
    o. $1,200,000
    p. $1,500,000
    q. $2,000,000

4-3

Property taxes are not necessarily recognized as revenue in the year collected.

The fiscal year of Duchess County ends on December 31. Property taxes are due March 31 of the year they are levied.

1. Prepare journal entries (excluding budgetary and closing entries) to record the following property-tax related transactions in which the county engaged in 2004 and 2005.
    a. On January 15, 2004, the county council levied property taxes of $170 million for the year ending December 31, 2004. Officials estimated that 1 percent would be uncollectible.
    b. During 2004 it collected $120 million.
    c. In January and February 2005, prior to preparing its 2004 financial statements, it collected an additional $45 million in 2004 taxes. It reclassified the $5 million of 2004 taxes not yet collected as delinquent.
    d. In January 2005, the county levied property taxes of $190 million, of which officials estimated 1.1 percent would be uncollectible.
    e. During the remainder of 2005 the county collected $2.5 million more in taxes relating to 2004, $160 million relating to 2005, and $1.9 million (in advance) applicable to 2006.
    f. In December 2005 it wrote off $1 million of 2004 taxes that it determined would be uncollectible.
2. Suppose the county were to prepare government-wide statements and account for property taxes on a full accrual basis of accounting rather than the modified accrual basis. How would your entries differ? Explain.

4-4

Grants are not necessarily recognized as revenue when awarded.

Columbus City was awarded a state grant of $150,000 to assist its adult literacy program. The following were significant events relating to the grant:

- The city, which is on a calendar year, was notified of the award in November 2004.
- During 2005 it expended $30,000 on the literacy program and was reimbursed for $20,000. It expected to receive the balance in January 2006.
- In 2006 it expended the remaining $120,000 and was reimbursed by the state for the $10,000 owing from 2005 and the amount spent in 2006.

1. Prepare journal entries to record the events.
2. Suppose the city received the entire reimbursement in advance, at the time the award was announced in 2004.
3. Suppose alternatively that the state awarded the city an unrestricted grant of $150,000, which the city elected to use to support the adult literacy program. The city received the entire $150,000 in cash at the time the award was announced in 2004. How much revenue should the city recognize in each of the three years? Explain.

4-5

The accounting for contributions may depend on how they will be used.

Green Hills County received the following two contributions during a year:

- A developer (in exchange for exemptions to zoning restrictions) donated several acres of land that the county intended to convert to a park. The land had cost the developer $1.7 million. At the time of the contribution its fair market value was $3.2 million.
- A local resident donated several acres of land to the county with the understanding that the county would sell the land and use the proceeds to fund construction of a county health center. The land had cost the resident $2.5 million. The county sold the land intended for the health center for $3 million thirty days after the end of its fiscal year.

1. Prepare journal entries to record the contributions. Be sure to specify the appropriate fund in which they would likely be made.

2. Comment on and justify any differences in the way you accounted for the two contributions.
3. Comment on how each of the contributions would be reported on the county's government-wide statements.
4. How would your answers differ if the land intended for the health center were not sold by the time year-end financial statements were issued?

4-6

Sales taxes should be recognized when the underlying event takes place.

A state requires "large" merchants (those with sales over a specified dollar amount) to report and remit their sales taxes within fifteen days of the end of each month. It requires "small" merchants to report and remit their taxes within fifteen days of the end of each quarter.

In January 2005, large merchants remitted sales taxes of $400 million owing to sales of December 2004. In February 2005, they remitted $280 million of sales taxes owing to sales of January 2005. In January small merchants remitted sales taxes of $150 million owing to sales of the fourth quarter of 2004.

1. Prepare an appropriate journal entry to indicate the impact of the transactions on the state's fund financial statements for the year ending December 31, 2004.
2. Suppose, instead, that 10 percent of the taxes received by the state were collected on behalf of a city within the state. It is the policy of the state to remit the taxes to the city thirty days after it receives them. Prepare an appropriate journal entry to indicate the impact of the transactions on the city's fund financial statements for the year ending December 31, 2004.
3. Suppose, instead, that it were the policy of the state to remit the taxes to the city ninety days after it receives them. How would your response to part (2) differ? Explain. Would your response be the same with respect to the city's government-wide statements?

4-7

The recognition of revenue from fines does not necessarily reflect the amount "earned" by merely issuing tickets.

In August 2005, the last month of its fiscal year, Spiedrap Township issued $88,000 of tickets for parking and traffic violations. Of these, the township collected $45,000. It expects to collect an additional $20,000 within sixty days of the close of the fiscal year and $3,000 subsequent to that. It will have to write off the balance. The tickets are due, and the protest period expires, on September 15.

1. How much revenue should the township recognize from the tickets issued in August 2005? Explain.
2. How might your answer change with respect to the township's government-wide statements?

4-8

The amount of revenue to be recognized from grants depends on the type of grant.

The following relate to three grants that the town of College Hills received from the state during its fiscal year ending December 31, 2005:

- A cash grant of $200,000 that must be used to repair roads
- $150,000 in cash of a total grant of $200,000 to reimburse the town for actual expenditures incurred in repairing roads; during the year the town incurred $150,000 in allowable repair costs
- A cash entitlement grant of $200,000 that is intended to supplement the town's 2006 budget and must be expended in that year

Prepare journal entries to record the three grants.

PROBLEMS

Continuing Problem

Review the Comprehensive Annual Financial Report (CAFR) that you obtained.

1. What are the main sources of the government's revenues, including those from both governmental and business-type activities?
2. Which of the entity's governmental functions or activities had the greatest amount of directly identifiable revenues?
3. Does the report discuss the accounting basis for recognizing revenues?
4. Does the government's governmental-wide statement of net assets or governmental-fund balance sheet report "deferred revenue?" If so, what is the most likely reason this revenue has been deferred?
5. What is the government's property tax rate?
6. At what percentage of fair market value is real property assessed?
7. When are property taxes due? When do interest and penalties begin to accrue?
8. By what percentage did each of the largest three sources of tax revenue increase over the last ten years?
9. Did the government generate revenue from traffic fines? As best as you can tell, are these revenues reported in the government-wide statements as program revenues (e.g., associated with police or public safety) or as general revenues?

4-1

The general principles of revenue recognition are the same for both governmental and government-wide statements.

For each of the following situations, indicate the amount of revenue that the government should recognize in an appropriate governmental fund as well as on its government-wide statement of activities in its fiscal year ending December 31, 2005. Briefly justify your response, making certain that, as appropriate, you identify the key issue of concern.

1. In October 2004 a state received a federal grant of $300 million (in cash) to assist local law enforcement efforts. The federal government has established specific criteria as to how the funds should be distributed and will monitor the funds to assure that they are used in accordance with grant provisions. The grant is intended to cover any allowable expenditures incurred in the calendar years 2005 through 2008. In 2005 the state incurred $160 million of allowable expenditures.
2. On October 15, 2005, the Pleasant Valley School District invested $1 million in three-year, 6 percent U.S. Treasury notes. The district intends to hold the notes to maturity. The notes will pay interest ($30,000) on April 15 and October 15. On December 31, 2005, the market value of the bills was $1,012,000.
3. In December 2004 a city levied property taxes of $500 million for the calendar year 2005. The taxes are due June 30, 2005. The city collects the taxes as follows:

December 2004	$ 30 million
January 1, 2005 to December 31, 2005	440 million
January 1, 2006 through March 31, 2006 ($8 million per month)	24 million
Total	$ 494 million

It estimates the balance will be uncollectible.

4. In January 2005 a state received $300 million in food stamps of which it distributed $280 million during the year. It expects to distribute the balance in January 2006.
5. In January 2005 a city received a cash gift of $1 million to provide assistance to the families of public safety officers who died in action. Per the wishes of the donor the funds are to be invested and only the income may be expended. In 2005, the endowment generated $50,000 in income, none of which was spent during the year.
6. For the year 2005 the teachers of the Nuvorich School District earned $26 million in pension benefits. In January 2006, the state in which the district is located paid the entire amount into the State Teachers Retirement Fund.

4-2

Nonexchange revenues can be of four types.

The GASB has identified four classes of nonexchange revenues:

- Derived tax
- Imposed
- Government mandated
- Voluntary

For the city in each of the following revenue transactions, identify the class in which the revenue falls and prepare an appropriate fund journal entry for the current year (2005) as necessary. Provide a brief explanation of, or justification for, your entry.

1. In December, the state in which the city is located announced that it would grant the city $20 million to bring certain public facilities into compliance with the state's recently enacted disability laws. As of year-end the city had not yet received the funds and it had not yet expended any funds on the state-mandated facility improvements.
2. The city imposes a $100 tax on each sale of real estate. The tax is collected by the title companies that process the sales and must be forwarded to the state within thirty days of the transaction. In December there were 600 sales of real estate. As of year-end the city had collected $40,000 of the $60,000 that it was owed.
3. In December the state announced that the city's share of state assistance for the calendar year 2006 would be $120 million.
4. The city imposes a tax on all boats owned by residents. The tax is equal to 1 percent of the assessed value of a boat (determined by the city, taking into account the boat's original cost and its age). The tax is payable on the last day of the year prior to the year for which the tax is applicable. In 2005 the city levied $640,000 of 2006 boat taxes, of which it collected $450,000.
5. A local resident sends to the city a copy of her will in which she bequeaths $3 million to the city museum upon her death.
6. The U.S. Department of Justice announces that it will reimburse the city up to $400,000 for the purchase of telecommunications equipment. As of year-end the city had incurred only $200,000 in allowable expenditures.
7. A resident donates $10 million in securities to the city to support a cultural center. Only the income from the securities, not the principal, can be spent.

4-3

Disproportionate assessments lead to inequities.

The town of Blair determines that it requires $22.5 million in property tax revenues to balance its budget.

According to the town's property tax assessor, the town contains taxable property that it assessed at $900 million. However, the town permits discounts for early payment, which generally average about 2 percent of the *amount levied.* Further, the town grants homestead and similar exemptions equal to 3 percent of the property's *assessed value.*

1. Calculate the required tax rate, expressed in mils.

2. A resident's home is assessed at $300,000. He is permitted a homestead exemption of $10,000 and a senior-citizens' exemption of $5,000. What is the resident's required tax payment prior to allowable discounts for early payment?
3. Blair assesses property at 100 percent of its fair market value. Sussex, a nearby town in the same county, assesses property at only 80 percent of fair market value. The county bases its own tax assessments on the assessments of the individual towns. However, the county grants no exemptions or discounts. Its tax rate is 8 mils.
   a. A taxpayer in Sussex owns a home with a market value of $300,000—the same as that of the Blair resident. Compute and compare the amount of county tax that would be paid by each resident.
   b. Comment on why governments find it necessary to "equalize" tax assessments based on assessments of other governments.

4-4

A change to the full accrual basis may have little impact upon reported revenues.

A city levies property taxes of $4 billion in June 2005 for its fiscal year beginning July 1, 2005. The taxes are due by January 31, 2006. The following (in millions) indicates actual and anticipated cash collections relating to the levy:

June 2005	$ 100
July 2005 through June 2006	3,600
July 2006 through August 2006	80
September 2006 through June 2007	150

The city estimates that $30 will eventually have to be refunded, owing to taxpayer appeals as to the assessed valuation of their property, and that $70 will be uncollectible.

1. Prepare a journal entry that summarizes the city's property tax activity for the fiscal year ending June 30, 2006, based on:
   a. the modified accrual basis (i.e., for fund statements)
   b. the full accrual basis (i.e., for government-wide statements)
2. Indicate the differences in amounts that would be reported on both the statement of net assets and the statement of activities on a full accrual basis.
3. Suppose that in the following year the tax levy and pattern of collections were identical to those of the previous year. What would now be the difference in amounts reported on the statement of net assets and the statement of activities on a full accrual basis?

4-5

Derived taxes are derived from underlying transactions.

A state imposes a sales tax of 6 percent. The state's counties are permitted to levy a tax of an additional 2 percent. The state administers the tax for the counties, forwarding the proceeds to the counties fifteen days after they receive the proceeds from the merchants.

The state requires merchants to file a return and transmit collections either monthly, quarterly, or annually, depending on the amount of taxable sales made by the merchant. This problem pertains only to taxes that must be paid quarterly.

Merchants must file their returns and transmit their taxes within one month after the end of a quarter. The quarters are based on the calendar year. Thus, taxes for the quarter ending March 31 are due by April 30; those for the quarter ending June 30 are due by July 31.

The fiscal year of both the state and its counties ends on September 30.

For the quarter ending September 30, 2005, merchants collected and paid (in October) $300 million in taxes. Of these, 80 percent ($240 million) are applicable to the state; 2 percent ($6 million) are applicable to Cayoga County.

1. Prepare journal entries to summarize the state's sales tax activity for its share of taxes for the quarter ending September 30, 2005:
   a. on a modified accrual basis
   b. on a full accrual basis
2. Prepare journal entries to summarize the county's sales tax activity for the quarter ending September 30, 2005:
   a. on a modified accrual basis
   b. on a full accrual basis

   Be concerned only with any entries that would affect the fiscal year ending September 30, 2005.
3. Some critics have charged that current standards (i.e., those of Statement No. 33) allow for premature recognition of sales tax revenue. What do you think is the basis for their position? What arguments can be made in defense of the Statement No. 33 standards?

4-6

The "sixty-day rule" may not be applicable to all types of revenues.

Manor County was awarded a state grant to establish evening athletic programs for at-risk youth. The $3.6 million award, to cover the calendar year 2005, was announced on November 15, 2004.

According to the terms of the grant, the county will be reimbursed for all qualifying costs within thirty days of its filing an appropriate request-for-reimbursement form.

During 2005 the county incurred $300,000 of costs each month. It filed a reimbursement claim shortly after the end of each month and received a reimbursement check approximately forty-five days after the end of the month in which it incurred the costs. Hence, it received twelve checks, the first on March 15, 2005, and the last on February 15, 2006.

The county operates on a fiscal year beginning October 1.

1. Prepare journal entries to summarize the county's grant-related activity for its fiscal year ending September 30, 2005 on a modified accrual basis.

2. Suppose alternatively that the state would reimburse the county for its costs in four installments, the first on June 30, 2005, and the last on March 31, 2006. Do you think that the county, in its fund financial statements, should recognize the reimbursement of December 31, 2005, as revenue of the county's fiscal year ending September 30, 2005? Justify your answer.

4-7

License fees present challenging, although not necessarily consequential, issues of revenue recognition.

Kyle Township charges residents $100 per year to license household pets. As specified in a statute enacted in 2005, residents are required to purchase a license by October 1 of each year; the license covers the period October 1 through September 30.

The license fees are not refundable. The statute authorizing the fees specifically states that the revenues are to be used to support the township's animal control program. The program, which will be carried out throughout the year, is not expected to receive financial support from any other sources.

During the calendar year 2005 (which corresponds to the township's fiscal year), the township collected $36,000 in license fees for the 2005–2006 licensing period.

1. Prepare a journal entry to record the township's receipt of the license fees.
2. Would you consider the license fees to be an exchange or nonexchange revenue? Explain.
3. How do you justify the accounting standard on which your entry is based (especially since the license period overlaps two fiscal years)?

4-8

The distinction between an entitlement and a reimbursement grant is not always obvious.

A city received two state grants in fiscal 2005. The first was an award for a maximum of $800,000, over a two-year period, to reimburse the city for 40 percent of specified costs incurred to operate a job opportunity program. During 2005, the city incurred allowable costs of $1.4 million (paid in cash) on the program. It was reimbursed for $500,000 and anticipates that it will receive the balance of what it is owed for 2005 early in fiscal 2006.

The second was an award of $600,000, also to cover a two-year period, to assist the city in administering a day-care program. Given only to selected cities, the award was based on several criteria, including quality of program and need for assistance. The amount was calculated as a percentage of the funds incurred by the city on the program in the prior year. Although the award must be spent on the day-care program, there are no specific matching requirements. During the year the city received the entire $600,000. It spent $550,000 (in cash) on the program.

1. Prepare entries to summarize the grant activity during 2005.
2. In a few sentences, justify any differences in your approach to the two grants.

4-9

It's not always obvious whether governments should recognize the revenues or expenditures associated with grants and awards.

For each of the following grants and awards, indicate whether the recipient government should recognize revenues and expenditures. In a sentence or two, justify your response.

1. As the result of damaging floods, New York State receives disaster assistance relief that it must distribute in predetermined amounts to specified cities and towns. The governor had appealed to the president to declare the affected areas as being in a "state of emergency," but the state has no responsibility for monitoring how the funds are spent by the localities.
2. Cleveland receives money from the state to distribute to private health and welfare organizations within the city. The organizations applied for the funds directly to the state, but Cleveland is responsible for assuring that the approved programs are audited by independent CPAs.
3. Santa Fe serves as a representative of the state in administering the federal food stamp program. State governments, which participate in the program, receive stamps from the federal government. The federal government establishes eligibility requirements and the scale of benefits. The states, however, are responsible for selecting the recipients and distributing the stamps.

   Some states involve both local governments and private institutions, such as banks and check-cashing outlets, in the administrative process. Under a contract with the state, Santa Fe, for example, checks the eligibility of stamp applicants and distributes the stamps to them. It serves all stamp applicants and recipients who come to its offices, irrespective of whether they are residents of the city. It receives an annual fee for its administrative services.
4. Arlington township is responsible for all costs of operating its volunteer fire department, with one exception. Its volunteer firefighters receive medical insurance through a state program. The state pays 80 percent of their insurance premiums; the firefighters themselves pay the rest. The township has no legal responsibility for providing insurance benefits to its firefighters. The insurance program was adopted by the state mainly to encourage citizens to join the volunteer departments.

4-10

Seemingly minor changes in the terms of a grant can affect the timing of revenue recognition.

The Foundation for Educational Excellence has decided to support the Tri-County School District's series of teacher training workshops intended to improve instruction in mathematics. The Foundation is considering four ways of wording the grant agreement, which would be dated December 1, 2005:

1. The foundation agrees to reimburse the district for all workshop costs up to $200,000.
2. The foundation is pleased to enclose a check for $200,000 to be used exclusively to support a series of teacher training workshops intended to improve instruction in mathematics.
3. The foundation will donate $200,000 to the school district as soon as the district conducts its planned series of teacher training workshops, intended to improve instruction in mathematics.
4. The foundation is pleased to enclose a check for $200,000 to be used exclusively to support a series of teacher training workshops intended to improve instruction in mathematics. The workshops are to be conducted between January 1 and December 31, 2006.

The school district expects to conduct the workshops in 2006.

Explain how the wording of the grant agreement would affect the year in which the school district recognized revenue. Indicate the relevant restriction, contingency, or eligibility requirement (e.g., time requirement; purpose restriction) to which each grant is subject and explain how it bears upon the issue of revenue recognition.

4-11

Policy changes and other measures will have varying effects on reported revenues.

The board of trustees of an independent school district is contemplating several policy changes and other measures, all of which it intends to implement within the fiscal year that ends August 31, 2005. It requests your advice on how the changes would affect the reported general fund revenues. For each of the proposals, indicate the impact on revenues (or accounts comparable to revenues, such as proceeds from sale of capital assets) and provide a brief explanation. Address the impact on both the fund and the government-wide financial statements.

1. Allow a three-month "grace period" for the payment of property taxes. District property taxes for the fiscal year ending August 31 are currently payable in ten installments. The final installment is due on August 31. The proposed change would give taxpayers a three-month grace period before interest and penalties are assessed. The district estimates that the change would affect $2 million in receipts.
2. Sell a parcel of land that the district purchased three years earlier for $450,000. Current market value is $500,000.
3. Request that a donation be advanced from December 2005 to August 2005. An alumnus of a district high school has indicated a willingness to donate to the district laboratory equipment having a fair market value of $400,000 along with real estate having a fair market value of $300,000. The district intends to use the equipment in student labs. It plans to sell the real estate as soon as possible and, in fact, has an acceptable offer from a buyer.
4. Redeem the district's shares in the State School District Temporary Investment Fund, a state-managed investment pool in which school districts can temporarily invest cash. The shares were initially purchased for $98,000. Current redemption value is $101,000.
5. Sell parking permits to students in the semester prior to that for which they are applicable. The district now sells parking permits to students at the beginning of the fall semester. The permits cover the period from September 1 through June 30. To reduce the start-of-year administrative burden upon staff, the district proposes to begin sale of the permits the previous spring. It estimates that in spring 2005 it will sell $6,000 of permits that would otherwise be sold the following September.

4-12

In some types of transactions assets are recognized concurrently with revenues; in others they are not.

In October 2005, the Village of Mason levied $80 million of property taxes for its 2006 fiscal year (which is the same as the calendar year). The taxes are payable 50 percent by December 31, 2005, and 50 percent by June 30, 2006. The village collected $55 million of the 2006 taxes by year-end 2005 and the $25 million balance by the end of 2006. The government has a legally enforceable claim on the taxed property on the first due date—that is, December 31, 2005.

In December 2005, the state announced that the village would receive $3 million in state assistance. The funds were paid in January 2006 and could have been used (per terms of the state legislation) to cover any legitimate village expenditures incurred in 2006.

1. Prepare journal entries to summarize the property tax and grant activity for the fiscal years ending December 31, 2005 and 2006.
2. How would you justify any apparent inconsistencies as to if and when you recognized the taxes receivable as opposed to the grants receivable?

4-13

Unrealized investment gains and losses may be difficult to explain to legislators and constituents.

A government held the securities shown in the following table in one of its investment portfolios. All the securities are either bonds that mature in more than one year or stocks.

1. Ignoring dividends and interest, how much of a gain or loss should the government recognize during the year?
2. What was the government's "realized" gain or loss (sales proceeds less cost) for the year? Which gain or loss—the amount that would have to be reported on

	Beginning Balance		Transactions during the Year		Ending Balance	
	Cost	Fair Value	Purchases	Sales	Cost	Fair Value
A	$100	$100			$100	$120
B	520	540			520	510
C	200	240		250		0
D			330		330	315
	$820	$880	$330	$250	$950	$945

the financial statements as computed in part (1), or the realized gain or loss—would be more indicative of the change in resources available for future expenditure?

3. Suppose that Security B is a long-term bond that the government intends to hold to maturity. What is the most probable reason for the decline in fair value during the year? In what sense is the reported loss indicative of an economic loss?

4-14

Recording investments at fair value may provide a measure of income similar to that if investments were stated at amortized historical cost, but is it consistent with the "measurable and available" criteria?

On August 2, thirty days prior to the end of its August 31 fiscal year, a government issues $3 million of general obligation bonds. The proceeds are being accounted for in a capital projects fund (a governmental fund). To earn a return on the bond proceeds before they have to be spent, the government invests $1 million in each of three financial instruments:

- A sixty-day discount note with a face value of $1,010,000. The note pays no interest. The purchase price of the note is $1 million (a price that provides an annual yield of 6 percent—0.5 percent per month).
- A two-year note that pays interest at an annual rate of 6 percent. Both interest and principal are payable upon the maturity of the note.
- Shares in an investment pool of government debt securities that provides a fixed return of 6 percent per year. The pool pays no dividends; the returns are reflected as an increase in the value of the shares.

1. Assuming no changes in prevailing interest rates between the date of purchase and year-end, what would you expect to be the market value of each of the three investments? Explain.
2. Prepare journal entries, as appropriate, to record investment income and changes in market values as of the year ending August 31.
3. Why might it be said that your entry for the two-year note is inconsistent with the general rule for fund statements that revenues should be recognized only when they are "measurable" and "available"? Why might it also be argued that your entry is perfectly consistent with the rule?

4-15

The reporting of on-behalf payments may have political consequences.

In 2005, the Bakersville Independent School District incurred $12 million in expenditures for teachers' salary and benefits. In that year, the legislature of the state in which the district is located voted to enhance the pension benefits of all teachers in the state. Starting in 2006, the state would contribute to the Teachers' Retirement Fund an amount equal to 2 percent of teachers' salaries. This amount would be in addition to the contributions currently being made by the school districts in the state.

As a result of this measure, the state contributed $240,000 on behalf of teachers in the Bakersville district.

1. How would the state's contribution to the pension fund be accounted for on the books of Bakersville? Prepare a summary journal entry (if required).
2. In the 2007 election for school board, one of the candidates charged that the incumbent board had promised to hold the line on school district spending. Yet despite its promises, the board increased expenditures on teacher compensation by 2 percent. Do you think the school district should be required to report the state's contribution as an expenditure, even though the district did not make the payment and had no say in whether it should be made? Would your response be different if the state had given the district a grant of $240,000 with the requirement that the money be used to increase the district's contribution to the Teacher Retirement Fund?
3. Suppose instead that the state made a contribution of $240,000 to the Teacher Retirement Fund on behalf of the school district. This contribution enabled the district to *reduce* its payment from what it had previously been. Do you think that the district should be required to report the state's contribution as an expenditure?

4-16

The distinction between exchange and nonexchange revenues is not always obvious.

You are the independent auditor of various governments. You have been asked for your advice on how the following transactions should be accounted for and reported. Characteristic of each transaction is ambiguity as to whether it is an exchange or a nonexchange transaction.

For each transaction indicate whether you think it is an exchange or a nonexchange transaction and make a recommendation as to how it should be accounted for (i.e., the amount and timing of revenue recognition). Justify your response. Note: The GASB has not specified the distinction between exchange and nonexchange transactions. Hence, in this problem, you should consider how you think the transaction should be accounted for; you need not be limited by current GASB standards.

1. A government receives from a developer a donation of 1,000 acres of land valued at $4 million. In return, the government permits the developer zoning variances on nearby property.
2. A college of pharmacy receives a grant of $2 million from a drug company to carry out research on a new formulation. The college agrees to submit the results to the company and to publish them only with the company's approval.
3. A city charges a developer an "impact fee" of $15,000 to compensate, in part, for improvements to the infrastructure in the area in which the developer plans to build residential homes. The city will make the improvements when construction on the new homes gets underway.
4. A city charges restaurants a license fee of $2,500. The license covers a period of two years. The fees must be used for health department inspections.
5. The city issues permits for residents to use city tennis courts. The fee is $100 per year—a small fraction of what it would cost to play on comparable private courts and an amount that covers only a small portion of the cost of constructing, maintaining, and operating the courts.

SOLUTION TO EXERCISE FOR REVIEW AND SELF-STUDY

1. Modified accrual basis

Cash	$120,000	
Property taxes receivable	34,000	
Property tax revenue		$130,000
Deferred property tax revenue		20,000
Allowance for uncollectibles		4,000
To record property tax revenue		

Revenue would be recognized on actual collections plus those of the sixty days following the end of the period; hence, $120,000 plus $10,000. The $20,000 of taxes expected to be collected in the following four months would be reported as deferred revenue.

Full accrual basis

Cash	$120,000	
Property taxes receivable	34,000	
Allowance for uncollectibles		$ 4,000
Property tax revenue		150,000
To record property tax revenue		

Revenue would be recognized on all actual and anticipated collections.

2. Modified accrual basis

Sales taxes receivable	$12,000	
Sales tax revenue		$12,000
To record sales taxes		

Sales taxes are derived from sales transactions. The sales transactions took place in September. Therefore, as long as the city received the taxes in time for them to satisfy the "available" criterion it should recognize them in September.

Full accrual basis

The taxes should be recognized in the period of sale irrespective of when they will be received by the city. In this case the entry would be the same.

3. Modified accrual basis

Cash	$80	
Expenditures	320	
Grant revenues		$320
Deferred revenue		80
To record grant expenditures and revenues		

The revenue from this reimbursement grant would be recognized as the related costs are incurred. Hence, only the funds that were expended can be recognized as revenue; the difference between the cash receipts ($400) and the expenditures ($320) must be reported as deferred revenue.

Full accrual basis

The government is eligible for the grant only as it makes the required expenditures. Therefore, as under the modified accrual basis, it would recognize revenue only to the extent of the $320 actually expended.

4. Modified accrual basis

Cash	$36	
Revenue from permits		$36
To recognize revenue from permits		

According to current standards, miscellaneous exchange revenues, such as those from permits, are best recognized as cash is received.

Full accrual basis

The revenue recognition standards—and hence the entry—are the same.

5. Modified accrual basis

Investment in notes	$500	
Cash		$500

To record investments

Investment in notes	$40	
Investment revenue		$40

To record the increase in the fair value of notes

The notes would be stated at fair value and the increase in value would be recognized as revenue.

Full accrual basis

The entries would be the same.

6. Modified accrual basis

Cash	$135	
Proceeds from sale of land		$135

To record the sale of land

When the land was acquired, the city would not have recorded it as a general fund asset, since capital assets are not recognized in governmental funds. Therefore, when the city sells the land it would recognize the entire proceeds as "proceeds from the sale of land"—an "other financing source."

Full accrual basis

Cash	$135	
Donated land		$119
Gain on sale of land (revenue)		16

To record the sale of land

Under the full accrual basis, the donation of land would have been recognized as revenue when the land was received. The increase in market value would be recognized as a gain at time of sale.

CHAPTER 5

Recognizing Expenditures in Governmental Funds

Learning Objectives

After studying this chapter you should understand:

- The modified accrual basis of accounting for expenditures and the rationale for differences between that basis and the full accrual basis
- How each of the following expenditures are accounted for:
  - Wages and salaries
  - Compensated absences
  - Pensions
  - Claims and judgments
  - Acquisition and use of materials and supplies
  - Prepayments
  - Acquisition and use of capital assets
  - Interest and principal on long-term debt
  - Grants
- The different types of interfund activity and how they are reported
- What constitutes other financing sources and uses
- The overall rationale for, and limitations of, the fund statements

In the previous chapter we addressed the question of when revenue should be recognized in governmental funds. We turn now to the other side of the ledger and consider how expenditures should be accounted for.

Like revenues, expenditures can be of two types: *exchange* and *nonexchange*. Our discussion of revenues centered mainly upon nonexchange revenues, as most governmental fund revenues are of that type. By contrast, our discussion of expenditures focuses primarily on exchange expenditures. Most governmental fund expenditures result from exchanges—the acquisition of goods and services for cash or other assets. This is not to say that governments do not engage also in nonexchange transactions. Just as governments receive grants from other governments, they also provide them—to other governments, to private (mainly not-for-profit) organizations and to individuals (e.g., assistance payments). GASB Statement No. 33, *Accounting and Financial Reporting for Nonexchange Transactions*, applies to both nonexchange revenues and nonexchange expenditures. Nonexchange expenditures, per the statement, should be accounted for as the mirror image of nonexchange revenues. Therefore, we need direct only minimal attention to nonexchange expenditures.

Governmental-fund expenditures, like revenues, are accounted for on a modified accrual basis on the fund statements but on full accrual basis on the government-wide statements. As made clear in Statement No. 34, which establishes the standards for the new reporting model, governments should generally look to FASB standards for guidance on when to recognize exchange expenditures on a full accrual basis (just as they do for business-type activities). This chapter, therefore, is devoted mainly to accounting for and reporting expenditures on a modified accrual basis—the area in which governmental accounting is unique. As we did in the previous chapter, however, we also note how the various expenditures would be accounted for differently on the full accrual basis.

HOW IS THE ACCRUAL CONCEPT MODIFIED FOR EXPENDITURES?

THE DISTINCTION BETWEEN EXPENDITURES AND EXPENSES

Under the modified accrual basis of accounting, governmental funds are concerned with **expenditures.** By contrast, proprietary funds, like businesses, focus on **expenses.** Expenditures are narrower in scope than expenses. Whereas expenditures are decreases in net financial resources, expenses are decreases in net economic resources. Expenditures are generally recognized when an asset is acquired; expenses when it is consumed. Thus, for example, funds that are accounted for on a modified accrual basis would report equipment costs as "capital outlays"—expenditures to be recognized at the time of acquisition. By contrast, those that are accounted for on a full accrual basis would report the equipment costs as "depreciation"—expenses to be recognized over the life of the equipment.

THE VIRTUES OF ACCRUAL ACCOUNTING AND THE RATIONALE FOR MODIFICATIONS

As pointed out in the previous chapter, the accrual basis of accounting is generally considered the superior method of accounting for organizations because it captures the substance of events and transactions, not merely the inflows and outflows of cash or near-cash.

We have seen that the accrual concept is applied differently in governmental funds than in businesses or in proprietary funds, which are accounted for as if they were businesses, as well as in government-wide statements. Governmental fund accounting is heavily influenced by governmental budgeting. Owing to the importance of the budget, expenditures are closely tied to cash flows and near-cash flows rather than to flows of economic resources. In addition, governmental funds report only current, not long-term, liabilities. They focus on obligations that must be funded by current, not future, taxpayers.

Although the general principles of accrual accounting apply to governmental funds, there are key differences between how they are applied in governmental funds and how they are applied in businesses. In this chapter we will discuss seven key differences in how expenditures are accrued in governments versus businesses. The differences are consistent with the concept that under the modified accrual basis of accounting, expenditures are decreases in net current financial resources—current assets less current liabilities. But unlike a business's current liabilities, defined as those that must be paid within a year, a government's liabilities are considered current only when they must be liquidated with expendable available financial resources.

In the context of governmental funds, **financial resources** refers to current financial resources—cash and other assets that are expected to be transformed into cash in the normal course of operations. *Net* financial resources refers, then, to financial resources less claims against them.

A government should recognize an expenditure when its net expendable available financial resources are reduced. That is, when it either pays cash for goods or services received or accrues a liability. But when should it *accrue* (i.e., give accounting recognition to) a liability? Under the modified accrual basis a government should, as a general rule, accrue a liability in the period in which it *incurs* (i.e., becomes obligated for) the liability. This general rule, however, does not by itself distinguish the modified accrual basis from the full accrual basis. What does distinguish the two bases are the several exceptions to this general rule set forth by the GASB.[1] These exceptions permit governments to delay recording both a governmental fund liability and its associated expenditure until the period in which the liability must be paid—that is, when payment will reduce expendable available financial resources. Until that period, the government need report the liability only in its government-wide statements (as well as in its schedule of long-term obligations).

HOW SHOULD WAGES AND SALARIES BE ACCOUNTED FOR?

Wages and salaries may be earned in one fiscal year but paid in the next. Most governments pay their employees periodically—on a specified day of a week or month. Whenever the end of a pay period or the pay date does not coincide with the end of the fiscal year, then the government must carry over wages earned in one year until the next. Therefore, the question arises as to whether the wages and salaries should be reported as expenditures in the period earned or in the period paid.

EXAMPLE *Wages and Salaries*

A city pays its employees for the two-week period ending January 4, 2005, on January 9, 2006. The portion of the payroll applicable to December 2005 is $40 million, an amount included in the city's 2005 budget.

[1] See discussion in GASB Interpretation No. 6, *Recognition and Measurement of Certain Liabilities and Expenditures in Governmental Fund Financial Statements* (March 2000).

GASB Standards

The GASB *Codification* does not specifically address wages and salaries. Hence, the general principles of modified accrual accounting apply. Wages and salaries should be recognized in the period in which the employees earn their wages and salaries, as long as the government's obligation will be liquidated with expendable available financial resources.

In the "Wages and Salaries" example, the employees will be paid within days of year-end and with resources budgeted for 2005 expenditures—resources that would generally be assumed to be available and expendable. Thus (ignoring the usual payroll-related taxes, withholdings, and benefits):

Payroll expenditures	$40	
Accrued wages and salaries		$40
To record the December payroll (in 2005)		

In the following year, when the employees are paid, the entry to record the 2005 portion of the payroll would be:

Accrued wages and salaries	$40	
Cash		$40
To record the payment of wages and salaries recognized as 2005 expenditures (in 2006)		

The entries in this chapter designate an **object** classification (such as payroll, insurance, supplies, etc.). Alternatively, they could designate an *organizational unit* (such as police department, fire department, sanitation department) or a *function or program* (such as public safety, general government, culture and recreation). Although the financial statements of most governments report expenditures by organizational unit, function, or program, the expenditures are typically charged initially to an object account.

DIFFERENCES IN GOVERNMENT-WIDE STATEMENTS

Wages and salaries are already recognized on an accrual basis; no change would be required by a shift to a full accrual basis.

IN PRACTICE

CHANGING THE PAY DATE BY ONE DAY

In Texas, like many other cities and states, state government employees receive their monthly paycheck on the first day of the month following that to which it is applicable. They used to receive it a day earlier, on the last of the month. Why the change? In one year the state needed additional funds to balance its budget. What better way than to move the pay date forward by one day, thereby shifting one complete payroll from the current fiscal year to the next? This scheme worked, of course, for budgeting purposes only, since the state budgets on what is essentially a cash basis. For reporting purposes, however, most of the payroll is accounted for in governmental funds, which are on a modified accrual basis. Therefore, the expenditure must be reported in the fiscal year in which the employees earn their wages and salaries, irrespective of the date that the state issues and distributes their checks.

HOW SHOULD COMPENSATED ABSENCES BE ACCOUNTED FOR?

Governments compensate employees for time not worked for a variety of reasons: vacations, holidays, sick leave, sabbatical leave, jury duty, or military reserve. In concept, the accounting issues are similar to those of wages and salaries earned in one period but paid in another. But there are differences as well. Most significantly, compensated absences are earned in one period, but they are often not paid until several periods later. Hence, the liability cannot be considered current. In addition, the amount of compensation to be paid is not always certain. First, some employees may leave the organization before they take all the time off to which they are entitled. Second, the amount of compensation is almost always based on the employee's wage or salary rate in effect when the time off is taken, not when it is earned.

ACCOUNTING FOR VACATIONS

As in the private sector, government employees are almost always granted paid vacation after completing a specified period of service. The number of vacation days generally varies with years of employment. While on vacation, employees are paid at their current wage rate, irrespective of when they earned their vacation. From their perspective, the paycheck they receive for vacation days is usually indistinguishable from that received for working days. Employers, however, usually charge the expenditure to a vacation pay account instead of their standard wages or salary account.

EXAMPLE *Vacation Leave*

City employees earn $8 million in vacation leave. Of this amount, they are paid $6 million in 2005 and defer the balance until future years. The leave *vests* (i.e., employees are legally entitled to it, even if they resign or are discharged) and can be taken any time up to retirement or as additional compensation at the time of retirement.

GASB Standards

GASB standards state that vacation leave and comparable compensated absences should be accrued as a liability as the benefits are earned by the employees if *both* of the following conditions are met:

- The employees' rights to receive compensation are attributable to services already rendered.
- It is probable that the employer will compensate the employees for the benefits through paid time off or some other means, such as cash payments at termination or retirement.

The compensation should be based on the wage or salary rates in effect at the balance sheet date, and employers should adjust for benefits that are expected to lapse.[2] Although this guidance may appear to sanction accrual of vacation pay, there is a catch. GASB standards explain that compensated absence liabilities are normally liquidated with expendable available resources in the periods in which

[2] GASB Statement No. 16, *Accounting for Compensated Absences* (November 1992), para. 7.

the payments to employees are made. Therefore, both the vacation pay expenditures and the related fund liabilities should be recognized in the periods in which the payments are due. Until those periods, the liabilities should be reported only in a schedule of long-term obligations, not on a governmental fund balance sheet.

The following entry, in the general fund or other appropriate governmental fund, would give effect to the GASB standards:

Vacation pay expenditure	$6	
Cash (or wages payable)		$6
To record vacation pay		

The $2 million deferred until future periods should not be recognized as either an expenditure or a liability in the governmental fund. Instead, it should be reported only in a schedule of long-term obligations.

The deferred amount should, of course, be recognized in the general fund as an expenditure in the years the vacations are taken and paid for.

DIFFERENCES IN GOVERNMENT-WIDE STATEMENTS

Consistent with the accrual concept as applied in the FASB model, the government-wide statements provide for balance sheet recognition of long-term liabilities. Accordingly, the "standard" accrual entry would be appropriate:

Vacation pay expense	$8	
Cash (or wages payable)		$6
Accrued vacation pay		2
To record vacation pay		

ACCOUNTING FOR SICK LEAVE

It might appear as if sick leave is a compensated absence with characteristics similar to those of vacation leave and should, therefore, be accounted for in the same way. However, there is at least one critical distinction between the two types of leave. Vacation leave, along with most other types of paid time off, is within the control of the employee or the employer. Separately or together they decide when the employee will take a vacation or a paid holiday. Sick leave, by contrast, is beyond the control of both the employer and the employee.

In the public sector, sick leave most commonly accumulates, but either only a portion or none of it vests. That is, employees can store sick days that they don't take in a particular year until they need it. However, if they resign or are terminated, they are not entitled to compensation for all of their unused leave.

EXAMPLE *Sick Leave*

A city allows employees one day of sick leave a month and permits them to accumulate any sick leave that they do not take. If they terminate after at least ten years of service, they will be paid for unused sick leave up to thirty days. In 2005, employees earned $12 million of sick leave that they did not take during the year. The city estimates that of this amount $8 million will be paid to employees in future years as sick leave, $1 million will be paid to ten-year employees upon their termination, and $3 million will not be paid.

GASB Standards

GASB standards state that sick leave should be recognized as a liability only insofar as "it is probable that the employer will compensate the employees for the benefits through cash payments *conditioned on the employees' termination or retirement ('termination benefits')*" (emphasis added). In other words, sick leave should be recorded only to the extent that it will *not be paid to employees who are sick*. Instead, it should be recorded only when expected to be paid to employees upon their discharge, resignation, or retirement.[3] The standards are grounded in the rationale that sick leave, other than the portion that vests, is contingent upon an employee getting sick. The key economic event, therefore, is not the employee's service, but rather his or her illness.[4]

In the example, therefore, the city would recognize a liability only for the $1 million to be paid in termination benefits.[5] However, as with vacation pay, only the portion of the liability expected to be liquidated with expendable available financial resources may be recorded in a governmental fund. Assuming, therefore, that none of the termination benefits will be paid with funds budgeted for the current year, no entry is required in the general or other governmental fund. The obligation would be recognized only in a schedule of long-term obligations.

DIFFERENCES IN GOVERNMENT-WIDE STATEMENTS

Recognition of sick leave on a full accrual basis would not affect the measurement of the obligation, only where and when it is reported. As with vacation pay both the expense and the obligation would be reported in the government-wide financial statements in the period the sick leave is earned. Thus,

Sick leave termination benefit expense	$1	
Accrued sick leave		$1
To record sick leave termination benefits		

ACCOUNTING FOR SABBATICAL LEAVE

Government entities, mainly colleges, universities, and public schools, may offer employees sabbatical leaves. After a specified term of service, commonly seven years, employees (usually teachers) may be granted a paid leave of either a semester or an academic year.

As with sick leave, sabbatical leaves may appear to be similar to vacations and accounted for as such. Few teachers, however, perceive them as a time for rest and relaxation. Vacations are provided as a fringe benefit in lieu of salaries and wages. They are compensation for service already rendered. Sabbaticals, by comparison, are typically offered to benefit both the employee and the employer in the future, not the past. Employees are commonly required to perform research or public service, to take courses, or to engage in other activities that will enhance their job-related abilities.

The accounting issue relating to sabbaticals is when the employer should first recognize the sabbatical costs. There are three possibilities:

[3] GASB Statement No. 16, *Accounting for Compensated Absences* (November 1992), para. 8.

[4] FASB Statement No. 43, *Accounting for Compensated Absences* (November 1980), draws a similar distinction between sick leave and other types of compensated absences. Whereas employers are required to accrue the costs of other types of compensated absences, they are not required to accrue a liability for nonvesting sick leave.

[5] GASB Statement No. 16, *Accounting for Compensated Absences*, provides detailed guidance as to how government entities should estimate the amounts to be paid upon termination.

- As they are earned by the employee in the period leading up to the leave
- Over the course of the leave
- Over the years to be benefited from the leave (e.g., from the end of one leave until the start of the next)

EXAMPLE *Sabbatical Leave*

A school district grants faculty members a one-year leave after each seven years of service to engage in research, further study, or other authorized activities. In a particular year it paid \$2 million to faculty on leave. In addition, it estimated that faculty "earned" \$2.4 million toward leaves they are likely to take in the future.

GASB Standards

GASB standards prescribe that the accounting for sabbatical leave depends on the purpose of the leave. If the leave is to provide employees with relief from their normal duties so they can perform research, obtain additional training, or engage in other activities that would "enhance the reputation or otherwise benefit the employer," then the sabbatical should be accounted for in the period the leave is taken. No liability should be accrued in advance of the leave. If, however, the leave is for "compensated unrestricted time off," then the government should accrue a liability during the period that the leave is earned.[6]

In the example, the sabbatical leaves are restricted to approved activities. Therefore, they should be accounted for during the period of the leave; the school district need not accrue amounts expected to be paid in the future. Only the amount actually paid to employees on leave should be recorded as an expenditure:

Sabbatical leave expenditure	\$2	
Cash (or salaries payable)		\$2
To record the salaries of faculty on sabbatical		

If, by contrast, the leave were unrestricted as to purpose and a liability must be accrued in advance, then, as with other compensated absences, only the portion expected to be liquidated with expendable available resources would be reported in a governmental fund. The balance of the liability would be recorded in a schedule of long-term obligations.

The accounting for compensated absences, including vacation pay, sick leave, and miscellaneous leave, represents the *first* major difference between how the accrual basis is applied in governmental funds and how it is applied in businesses.

DIFFERENCES IN GOVERNMENT-WIDE STATEMENTS

The switch to the full accrual basis would not affect the criteria as to whether the sabbatical costs should first be recognized prior to, or during, the leave. Assuming, therefore, that the sabbatical leave is for approved activities, and not for unrestricted time off, then both the expenditure and the related liability need not be recognized until the period in which the leave is taken. The entry would be the same as that for the fund statements.

[6] GASB Statement No. 16, *Accounting for Compensated Absences* (November 1992), para. 9.

HOW SHOULD PENSIONS BE ACCOUNTED FOR?

Pensions are sums of money paid to retired or disabled employees owing to their years of employment. Under a typical plan, an employer makes a series of contributions to a special fund over the working lives of its employees. Under some plans the employees also contribute.

Calculating the employer contribution to the plan is necessarily complex and based on a number of estimates such as employee life expectancy, employee turnover, and anticipated earnings of fund investments. The issue of how to compute the required annual contribution and the related question of how to measure and report a pension plan's actuarial liability are addressed in Chapter 10, which deals with fiduciary funds.

In this chapter, we address the relatively straightforward concern of how a *governmental* fund should report the expenditure for its required annual contribution, assuming that the contribution has been properly calculated. In its simplest form, the required annual contribution is the share of the pension costs attributable to a particular period (i.e., the pension benefits earned by the employees in that period). If the government makes its required contribution in full, the amount to be reported as an expenditure is obvious; it would be the amount of the contribution. But what if, owing to budgetary constraints, it pays into the pension fund only a portion, or none, of the required contribution? Should the expenditure be the required contribution, which is indicative of the economic value of the pension benefits provided to the employees? Or should it be merely the actual payment, which is likely to be indicative of the amount budgeted for pension costs?

EXAMPLE *Pension Contributions*

A city is informed by its actuary that it should contribute $55 million to its pension fund, an amount calculated in accordance with generally accepted accounting and actuarial principles. It elects, however, to contribute only $45 million.

GASB Standards

GASB standards for pensions, as set forth in GASB Statement No. 27, *Accounting for Pensions by State and Local Governmental Employers*, are consistent with those for other compensated absences. The expenditure should be the amount that will be liquidated with expendable available financial resources.

Although, in the example, the economic cost of providing employees with pension benefits would be $55 million, the city would report an expenditure of only $45 million. The balance would be disclosed in notes and reflected as a liability in the city's schedule of long-term obligations, but not in a governmental fund. The following entry would be required in the general fund or other appropriate governmental fund:

	Debit	Credit
Pension expenditure	$45	
Cash (or current pension liability)		$45

Pension accounting represents the *second* difference between how the accrual concept is applied in governmental funds and in businesses.

Differences in Government-Wide Statements

In their government-wide statements, governments should report as their pension expense their required annual contribution—the amount representative of the economic cost—not an amount based on the government's predilection to contribute. This approach also conforms to that directed by Statement No. 27 as it applies to proprietary funds, which are currently accounted for on a full accrual basis. Thus:

Pension expense	$55	
Cash (or current pension liability)		$45
Pension liability		10
To record the pension expense and liability		

How Should Claims and Judgments Be Accounted for?

Governments face many types of claims and judgments. Common examples include those arising from:

- Injuries to employees (e.g., workers' compensation)
- Negligence of government employees (e.g., medical malpractice in city hospitals, failure to properly repair streets, auto accidents, wrongful arrests)
- Contractual disputes with suppliers
- Employment practices (e.g., civil rights violations, sexual harassment, wrongful discharge)

As in the private sector, the key accounting questions relating to claims and judgments are when and in what amounts expenditures and liabilities should be reported. These questions arise, first, because of the considerable length of time between when an alleged wrong takes place and when the claim is ultimately resolved and, second, because of the uncertainties as to the likelihood and dollar amount of a required payment.

In governmental funds, the major constraint in accounting for claims and judgments is identical to that faced in accounting for compensated absences. The event causing the claim or judgment usually precedes by one or more years the actual disbursement of financial resources. Yet, the governmental fund balance sheet has no place for long-term obligations.

EXAMPLE *Claims and Judgments*

A county is sued for personal injuries resulting from negligence on the part of a road maintenance crew. The county attorney estimates that the case will ultimately be settled for $400,000, but that the slow pace of the judicial process indicates it will be at least five years until any required payment must be made. Inasmuch as the county uses a discount rate of 10 percent to evaluate all long-term projects, officials determine the "present value" of the eventual payment to be $248,369.

GASB Standards

GASB standards for recognizing the liability for claims and judgments are drawn from FASB Statement No. 5, *Accounting for Contingencies.* A liability for claims and judgments should be recognized when information available before the issuance of financial statements indicates:

- It is probable that an asset has been impaired or a liability has been incurred at the date of the financial statements, *and*
- The amount of the loss can be reasonably estimated.[7]

However, as with compensated absences, only the portion of the total liability that would be paid with available financial resources would be reported in the governmental fund. The balance would be reported in a schedule of long-term obligations. Thus, the expenditure would be reported in the period that the liability is liquidated, not when the offending incident took place or a settlement was agreed upon or imposed. GASB standards require discounting only in limited circumstances, none of which apply here. Therefore, the liability should be recorded at "face" rather than economic value.

In the example, the county estimates its liability to be $400,000, no portion of which is expected to be liquidated with available financial resources. Thus, no entry would be required in the general or other governmental fund. The liability would be reported in the schedule of long-term obligations.

The standards require that in the year the liability is first recognized, the following information be reported either on the face of the governmental fund statements or in explanatory notes:

Expenditures:	
Claims and judgments ($400,000 less $400,000 recorded as long-term obligations)	$0[8]

The accounting for claims and judgments is the *third* difference between governments and businesses in the application of the accrual concept.

DIFFERENCES IN GOVERNMENT-WIDE STATEMENTS

As with compensated absences and pensions, the full accrual basis would require that the expense be recognized at the time the loss liability first satisfies the criteria of FASB Statement No. 5. Thus:

Claims and judgments (expense)	$400,000	
Liability for claims and judgments		$400,000
To record estimated cost of settling lawsuit		

[7]GASB Statement No. 10, *Accounting and Financial Reporting for Risk Financing and Related Insurance Issues* (November 1989), para. 53.

[8] GASB Statement No. 10, *Accounting and Financial Reporting for Risk Financing and Related Insurance Issues* (November 1989), para. 24.

> The practice of presenting claims liabilities at the discounted present value of estimated future cash payments (discounting) is neither mandated nor prohibited. However, claims liabilities associated with structured settlements should be discounted if they represent contractual obligations to pay money on fixed or determinable dates.

A structured settlement is defined as "a means of satisfying a claim liability, consisting of an initial cash payment to meet specific present financial needs combined with a stream of future payments designed to meet future financial needs, generally funded by annuity contracts." Hence, in the example, the settlement is not structured as there is not yet an obligation to pay money on fixed or determinable dates. Therefore, discounting is not required.

HOW SHOULD THE ACQUISITION AND USE OF MATERIALS AND SUPPLIES BE ACCOUNTED FOR?

The acquisition and use of materials and supplies (and the related issue of prepaid expenditures, to be discussed in the next section) present unique accounting problems in governmental funds. Materials and supplies (and prepaid items) are not strictly *expendable available financial resources*, in that they will neither be transformed into cash nor can they be used to satisfy governmental fund obligations. Nevertheless, having supplies on hand obviates the government from needing to purchase the items in the future.

Unlike businesses, governments do not generally acquire inventories with the intention of either reselling them or using them in manufacturing processes. They do, however, maintain inventories of office supplies, road maintenance and construction materials, spare parts, and other materials needed to carry out day-to-day operations.

Among the primary issues pertaining to governmental fund materials and supplies are:

- The timing of the expenditure; specifically, should governmental funds recognize an expenditure when they *acquire*, *pay for*, or *use* the materials and supplies?
- The reporting of the asset; specifically, should inventory be reported as an asset, even though it is not strictly an expendable available financial resource?

EXAMPLE *Supplies*

During the year a city purchases supplies that cost \$3.5 million, pays for \$3.0 million of the supplies, and uses \$3.3 million of them. At the start of the year it had no inventory on hand. Hence, at year-end it has \$0.2 million of supplies available for future use.

GASB Standards

GASB standards permit a choice. Government may recognize inventory items either when purchased (the *purchases* method) or when consumed (the *consumption* method). However, irrespective of which method is used, significant amounts of inventory should be reported on the balance sheet.[9] Governments may *not* account for inventories on a payment (cash) basis.

The Purchases Method

Using the **purchases method,** a government would record the *purchase* of the inventory as an expenditure. Thus, in the example:

Supplies expenditure	\$3.5	
Accounts payable		\$3.5
To record the acquisition of supplies		

Although the accounting is seemingly unambiguous, there's a complexity. Current standards state that significant amounts of inventory must be reported on the balance sheet. Metaphorically, they prescribe that governments must eat their cake yet have it too. By writing off the inventory upon acquisition, governments implicitly deny its

[9] NCGA Statement No. 1, *Governmental Accounting and Financial Reporting Principles* (March 1979), para. 73.

existence. How, then, can governments account for the full amount of the inventory acquired as an expenditure, yet still report the unused inventory as an asset? Simple, according to current standards! Show the inventory as an asset, offset by a fund balance reserve. The following entry would do the trick:

Supplies inventory	$0.2	
Fund balance—reserve for supplies inventory		$0.2
To record the inventory on hand at year-end		

The year-end entry increases reported assets and increases reserved fund balance. It has no impact on either expenditures or unreserved fund balance.

In subsequent years, the supplies inventory and the fund balance reserve would be adjusted to reflect the change in inventory during the year. If, at the conclusion of the following year, inventory on hand were only $150,000, then both supplies inventory and the reserve would be reduced by $50,000 (the difference between the $200,000 on hand at the end of the previous year and the $150,000 on hand at the end of the current year):

Fund balance—reserve for supplies inventory	$0.05	
Supplies inventory		$0.05
To adjust supplies inventory and related reserve to reflect inventory on hand (following year)		

The Consumption Method

Using the consumption method, a government would account for inventory the same as would a business, with one additional, albeit optional, feature—the establishment of an inventory reserve. As it acquires inventory, the government would record it as an asset:

Supplies inventory	$3.5	
Accounts payable		$3.5
To record the acquisition of supplies		

Then, as it uses the inventory, it would record an expenditure and reduce the balance in the inventory account:

Supplies expenditure	$3.3	
Supplies inventory		$3.3
To record the consumption of inventory		

At year-end, the inventory balance would be $0.2 million—the amount of supplies on hand. The reported expenditure would be $3.3 million—the amount of supplies consumed.

Some accountants, however, see the inventory balance as tainted, for it is not an expendable available financial asset in the same way as are cash, investments, and receivables. They contend it should be offset, not by "fund balance—unreserved," but rather by "fund balance—reserve for inventories." Therefore, they would propose the following additional (and discretionary) entry:

Fund balance—unreserved	$0.2	
Fund balance—reserve for inventories		$0.2
To reclassify fund balance to reflect year-end inventory		

The reserve would indicate the portion of fund balance—that relating to the inventories—not available for future appropriation. The balance in the reserve would always equal the balance in inventory. Therefore, each year-end the government would adjust it to reflect any changes in inventory during the year.

Other accountants oppose establishing the reserve, arguing that the reserve adds confusion to an already complicated balance sheet.

In the example, irrespective of whether it uses the purchases or the consumption method, the government would record the payment for the goods purchased with the conventional entry:

Accounts payable	$3.0	
Cash		$3.0
To record payment of amounts owed to suppliers		

Inventory accounting, specifically the option to use the purchases method, is the *fourth* difference in how expenditures are accrued in governments and businesses.

DIFFERENCES IN GOVERNMENT-WIDE STATEMENTS

The purchases method is inconsistent with full accrual accounting. Hence, inventory should be reported on a consumption basis. Thus, the entries would be similar to those illustrated above for the consumption method, with the exception that as the supplies are used supplies *expense* rather than supplies *expenditure* would be debited. There would not, of course, be any need for an inventory reserve.

HOW SHOULD REPAYMENTS BE ACCOUNTED FOR?

Prepaid expenditures are economically comparable to inventories. For example, a government purchases an insurance policy. As with materials and supplies, it will consume a portion in one period and the balance in the following periods. Or, by paying rent in one period, it acquires the right to use property in a subsequent period.

EXAMPLE *Prepayments*

On September 1, 2005, a town purchases a two-year insurance policy for $60,000 (a cost of $2,500 per month).

GASB Standards

GASB standards offer governments the same choice in accounting for prepaid expenditures as they do for inventories: they may use either the purchases or the consumption method. "Expenditures for insurance and similar services extending over more than one accounting period need not be allocated between or among accounting periods," the standards state. Instead, they "may be accounted for as expenditures of the period of acquisition."[10]

In contrast to the standards for inventories, however, the GASB does *not* prescribe that governments using the *purchases* method report material amounts of prepayments on the balance sheet.

[10] NCGA Statement No. 1, *Governmental Accounting and Financial Reporting Principles* (March 1979), para. 73.

If the town were to use the *purchases* method, it would make the following entry in 2005:

Insurance expenditure	$60,000	
Cash (or accounts payable)		$60,000
To record purchase of a two-year insurance policy		

No additional entries would be required either in 2005 or the subsequent two years.

If the town were to use the *consumption* method, then it would make the following entry upon purchasing the insurance policy:

Prepaid insurance	$60,000	
Cash (or accounts payable)		$60,000
To record purchase of a two-year insurance policy		

Then, each month for the next two years (or at year-end by way of a summary entry) it would record both an expenditure and a reduction in the balance of prepaid insurance:

Insurance expenditure	$2,500	
Prepaid insurance		$2,500
To recognize insurance expenditure for one month		

Whereas under the purchases method, the town would recognize the full $60,000 as an expenditure in 2005, under the consumption method it would recognize only $10,000, the economic cost of four months of insurance.

GASB Standards

GASB standards do not distinguish between "current" and "long-term prepayments." Thus, the unused portion of a three-year insurance policy would be reported as an asset—the same as a one-year policy.

The accounting for prepayments, specifically the option to use the purchases method, is the *fifth* difference in the way in which expenditures are accounted for on the full accrual basis by governments as opposed to businesses.

DIFFERENCES IN GOVERNMENT-WIDE STATEMENTS

The use of the purchases method in full accrual government-wide statements is as inappropriate for prepayments as for inventories. Only the consumption method may be used.

HOW SHOULD CAPITAL ASSETS BE ACCOUNTED FOR?

Capital (fixed) assets provide services in periods beyond those in which they are acquired. In that regard, the accounting issues pertaining to capital assets are comparable to those of each of the costs addressed so far in this chapter. A three-year insurance policy benefits a government over the period covered by the policy, irrespective of whether it is paid for before, during, or after the policy period. Similarly, a computer with a three-year useful life benefits the government over the same number of years regardless of the timing of payments.

In businesses, the cost of a capital asset is recorded on the balance sheet when the asset is acquired. Over the asset's productive life, the cost is allocated, through the process of depreciation, to the periods in which it provides its benefits. In that way, the cost of the asset is matched to the revenues that it helps to generate.

Governmental funds could, of course, account for capital assets in the same way as businesses. Many statement users and accountants have suggested that they should. As emphasized earlier, however, governmental accounting aims to provide information as to both the extent to which interperiod equity was achieved and whether resources were used in accordance with the entity's legally adopted budget. Governments must budget and appropriate the resources for capital assets in the periods when they are to be paid for, not those in which they will be used. Therefore, accounting practices in which capital asset expenditures are tied to services rather than to payments may not provide the sought-after budget-related information.

EXAMPLE *Capital Assets*

A village purchases road maintenance equipment for $90,000 and pays for it at the time of acquisition. The equipment is expected to have a useful life of three years.

GASB Standards

"General capital assets" are the capital assets of a government that are not specifically related to activities that are reported in proprietary or fiduciary funds. Most often they result from the expenditure of governmental fund financial resources. As pointed out in previous chapters, GASB standards preclude governments from reporting general capital assets on governmental fund balance sheets or from depreciating them on governmental fund statements of revenues expenditures and changes in fund balance. Instead, governments report them in the period requiring the outflow of expendable available financial resources.

In the example, the following entry would be appropriate when the assets are acquired:

Capital assets—expenditure	$90,000	
Cash		$90,000
To record the acquisition of equipment		

Regardless of the argument as to whether capital assets should, in fact, be depreciated (which is taken up in Chapter 7), note an obvious inconsistency. Assume that the government *rented* equipment for a three-year period, paying the entire rental costs in advance. Then, if the rental equipment agreement qualified as an operating rather than a capital lease, the government would be permitted to account for the prepaid rent using the *consumption* method, thereby spreading the rent expenditure over the life of the rental agreement.

ACQUISITION OF CAPITAL ASSETS FINANCED WITH DEBT

The main accounting issue presented by the acquisition of capital assets with debt arises because the purchase of the asset is not coincident with the repayment of the debt—and hence, in effect, with the outflow of the cash or other expendable resources required to obtain the asset. Thus, it is not obvious when the expenditures associated with the acquisition of the asset and the repayment of the debt should be recorded. For example, should the cost of the asset be recognized at the time of purchase, even in the absence of a cash outflow, or only as the debt is repaid?

When governments issue bonds to acquire assets, they often account for the debt proceeds in a capital projects fund. However, governments may also account for debt proceeds in other governmental funds, such as the general fund or special revenue funds. The debt may take the form of conventional notes, installment notes, or capital leases. The accounting for capital projects funds is discussed in Chapter 6. At this time it should be noted, however, that because capital projects and special revenue funds are governmental funds, the same general principles of accounting apply to them as to the general fund.

EXAMPLE *Installment Notes*

As in the "Capital Assets" example, a village purchases road maintenance equipment for $90,000. This time, however, the equipment is acquired on an installment basis with three annual installments of $36,190—the amount required to liquidate a loan of $90,000 over three periods at an interest rate of 10 percent.

Inasmuch as long-term obligations are not reported in governmental funds, GASB standards require that the proceeds of long-term debt be reflected as "other financing sources" in the recipient fund's operating statement.[11] Thus, were the village to *borrow* $90,000 cash, the following entry would be appropriate in the governmental fund receiving the proceeds:

Cash	$90,000	
Other financing sources—installment note proceeds		$90,000
To record a loan		

Were the government to use the proceeds to acquire a capital asset, the governmental fund entry illustrated in the previous example would be appropriate:

Capital assets—expenditure	$90,000	
Cash		$90,000
To record the acquisition of equipment		

In the example at hand, the government borrowed the purchase price (through the installment note) and acquired the asset, but at the time of acquisition did not actually receive or pay cash. Hence, it could properly make the following combining entry that eliminates the debit and credit to cash:

Capital assets—expenditure	$90,000	
Other financing sources—installment note proceeds		$90,000
To record the acquisition of equipment		

The related accounting question is how the loan repayment should be recorded. Specifically, to what type of account should the payment be charged, since no long-term liability is reported on the governmental fund balance sheet?

Current practice requires that the repayment be charged as an expenditure. Thus, the following entry would recognize the first payment of principal and interest:

Debt service expenditure (note principal)	$27,190	
Debt service expenditure (interest)	9,000	
Cash		$36,190
To record the first payment of installment note interest (10 percent of $90,000) and principal		

[11] NCGA Statement No. 1, *Governmental Accounting and Financial Reporting Principles* (March 1979), para. 108.

Subsequent payments would be recorded in the same way, with only the division of the payment between principal and interest changing from period to period. The equipment would be in a schedule of capital assets and the long-term debt in a schedule of long-term obligations.

The series of entries may be disconcerting in that it results in the asset being recorded as an expenditure twice—once when acquired and again as the loan is repaid. Nonetheless, the double-counting does not cause fund balance to be misstated, because the expenditure recorded upon acquisition of the asset is offset by "other financing sources"—a credit to fund balance that adds back the amount of the charge.

CAPITAL LEASES

A capital lease is the equivalent of a purchase-borrow transaction. In economic substance, the lessee (the party that will use the property) becomes the owner of the leased asset. The lessee treats the lease as a purchase of the asset. It makes periodic payments, each of which represents a partial repayment of the amount "borrowed" (the value of the property at the inception of the lease), plus interest. By contrast, an operating lease is a conventional rental arrangement under which the lessor remains the owner of the property both in legal form and in economic substance. FASB Statement No. 13, *Accounting for Leases,* established criteria to distinguish between operating and capital leases. These criteria have been adopted by the GASB.

EXAMPLE *Capital Leases*

Instead of purchasing the $90,000 of equipment, the village leases it under an arrangement that satisfies the criteria of a capital lease. The term of the lease is three years. The village agrees to make three annual payments of $36,190, an amount that reflects interest at an annual rate of 10 percent.

Current standards specify that capital leases should be accounted for in the same manner as other forms of long-term debt.[12] Thus, in the example, the village would record the lease in the same way as it did the installment purchase, varying only the account descriptions:

Capital assets—expenditure	$90,000	
Other financing sources—capital lease		$90,000
To record the acquisition of equipment under a capital lease		
Debt service expenditure (lease principal)	$27,190	
Debt service expenditure (lease interest)	9,000	
Cash		$36,190
To record the first lease payment consisting of interest (10 percent of $90,000) and principal		

As with the installment note, subsequent payments would necessitate a different division of the payment between principal and interest.

The accounting for capital assets, whether they are acquired for cash or paid for over time, is the *sixth* difference between expenditure accruals in businesses and governments.

[12] *Codification,* Section L20.

DIFFERENCES IN GOVERNMENT-WIDE STATEMENTS

Capital assets are reported on the government-wide statement of net assets (balance sheet) at historical cost, net of accumulated depreciation. The statement of activities (a statement of revenues and expenses) would include a charge for the depreciation of the assets. Correspondingly, the statement of net assets would also report the debt associated with the capital assets. Special rules apply to infrastructure assets. The accounting for capital assets, including infrastructure, is discussed in greater detail in Chapter 7.

HOW SHOULD INTEREST AND PRINCIPAL ON LONG-TERM DEBT BE ACCOUNTED FOR?

Interest on long-term debt is a major expenditure for many governments. Most typically, government debt takes the form of bonds, which pay interest twice per year. Many governments accumulate the resources to pay both the interest and principal on their debts in a debt service fund (a governmental fund). However, the original source of payments is likely to be either general revenues or revenues specially dedicated for debt service. As the scheduled payments from the debt service fund must be made, the government transfers the necessary cash from the general fund or a special revenue fund.

Long-term debts, as previously emphasized, are not recorded as liabilities in governmental funds; they are listed in the schedule of long-term obligations. When bonds or other forms of debt are issued, the increase in (debit to) cash is offset by a credit to "bond proceeds," an operating statement account, rather than to "bonds payable," a balance sheet account. Therefore, when the bonds are repaid the offset to cash cannot be to a liability account. Instead, it must be to an expenditure or a comparable operating statement account.

The key accounting issues with regard to long-term debt interest and principal arise because debt service payments may extend beyond a fiscal year. A six-month interest payment may cover some months in one year and some in another. A principal repayment covers the entire time the debt has been outstanding. Should the expenditures be allocated proportionately among the years (i.e., accrued) or should they be recognized entirely in the year of payment?

Given the virtues of the accrual basis of accounting in capturing the economic substance of events and transactions, the answer may appear obvious: allocate proportionately among the years. But bear in mind that debt service may involve large dollar amounts. Taxpayers obviously prefer to provide resources only as they are required to satisfy current obligations. Most governments budget (appropriate) resources for principal and interest only for the period in which they must make actual payments. They do not set aside resources for payments to be made in the future. Therefore, the goal of reporting on budgetary compliance, in contrast to that of reporting on interperiod equity, would suggest that the expenditures be recognized entirely in the year the payments are due.

EXAMPLE *Long-term Debt*

A state issues $100 million of twenty-year bonds on August 1, 2004, at an annual rate of 6 percent. Interest of $3 million per semiannual period is payable on January 31 and July 31. The bonds are sold for $89.3 million, a price that reflects an annual yield of 7 percent (semiannual yield of 3.5 percent). The first payment of the interest is due on January 31, 2005.

GASB Standards

GASB standards specify that in governmental funds neither interest nor principal on long-term debt should be accrued in advance of the year in which it is due. Both should be accrued only in the period in which they are due. Until then, they are not current liabilities; they will not require the liquidation of expendable available financial resources.

In the example, the government would make *no entry* in 2004 to accrue either interest or principal on the debt. It would not record an interest expenditure until January 31, 2005, when the first interest payment is due. The following entry would then be required in the fund out of which the payment was to be made:

Debt service, interest—expenditure	$3	
Matured interest payable		$3
To record obligation for interest due		

When the bonds mature in July 2024, the government would make a comparable entry to record the obligation for principal:

Debt service, principal—expenditure	$100	
Matured bonds payable		$100
To record obligation for matured bonds payable		

ADVERSE CONSEQUENCES OF FOCUS ON CASH PAYMENTS

Consistent with the standards that neither interest nor principal should be accrued until due, current standards for governmental funds make no provision for recognizing and amortizing bond discounts or premiums. As a result, the reported interest expenditure fails to capture the true economic cost of using borrowed funds. Instead, it indicates merely the required interest coupon payments. In the example, the state borrowed only $89.3 million (the amount of the proceeds), not $100 million (the face value). Its true economic cost of using the borrowed funds in the six months ending January 31, 2005, was $3.1 million ($89.3 million times the effective interest, or yield, rate of 3.5 percent per period), not $3.0 million (the required payment). Nevertheless, as illustrated, the state would record an interest expenditure equal to the $3.0 million required payment.

The failure of current standards to recognize premiums and discounts may not be particularly serious when the difference is small between a bond's coupon rate and yield rate. But when the difference is large, it results in financial statements that seriously distort borrowing costs. Consider an extreme case. A government issues $100 million in twenty-year **zero coupon bonds.** The bonds are sold for $25.26 million, a price that provides an annual yield of about 7 percent. As implied by their name, these bonds pay zero interest each period. Instead, they are sold at a deep discount, in this case a discount of $74.74 million. Upon maturity, the investor, who loaned the government $25.26 million, would receive $100 million. Inasmuch as $25.26 million is the present value of $100 million discounted at a rate of 3.5 percent for forty periods, the bonds provide a return of 3.5 percent (compounded) per semiannual period.

Under current standards for governmental funds the government would record *no* interest or principal costs until the bonds mature. In the period of maturity it would recognize the entire $100 million as a debt service expenditure. Fortunately, users are informed of the economic costs through the government-wide statements in which long-term debt is accounted for on a full accrual basis.

ACCRUAL OF INTEREST AND PRINCIPAL WHEN RESOURCES ARE TRANSFERRED

GASB standards make one exception to the general rule that neither interest nor principal be accrued. If resources to service the debt are transferred to a debt service fund from another governmental fund in a current year for payment of principal and interest due early the next year (within no more than a month) then both the expenditure and related liability *may* be (not *required* to be) recognized in the recipient debt service fund.[13]

Suppose that in the example, in 2004 the general fund transferred to the debt service fund $2.5 million of the $3 million interest payment due on January 31, 2005. The debt service fund would, of course, recognize the cash received as an asset and would record an increase in fund balance. Per the standard, to avoid reporting a misleadingly high fund balance, the debt service fund would be permitted also to accrue the related interest expenditure. Thus:

Debt service, interest—expenditure	$2.5	
Accrued interest payable		$2.5

To accrue interest in the amount of resources received from the general fund

The accounting for interest and principal is the *seventh* difference in the application of the accrual concept.

DIFFERENCES IN GOVERNMENT-WIDE STATEMENTS

Just as long-lived assets must be recorded at cost less accumulated depreciation in the government-wide statements, long-term debt must be reported at face value plus any unamortized premiums or less any unamortized discounts. Interest must be accrued; the timing of cash payments is irrelevant to the period in which the expense is recognized. Thus, the state would record the issuance of the bonds as follows:

Cash	$89.3	
Discount on bonds payable	10.7	
Bonds payable		$100.0

To record the issuance of operating debt

Then as it pays interest, it would record the payment ($3.0 million), the interest expense (the yield rate times the net carrying value of the bonds), and the amortization of the premium or discount (the difference between the two). As of December 31, 2004, the end of the first period, in which no interest was yet paid, the following entry would be appropriate to accrue five months' interest:

Interest expense	$2.6	
Accrued interest payable		$2.5
Discount on bond payable		0.1

To accrue five months' interest (interest expense = 5/6 of the effective interest rate of 3.5 percent times the effective liability of $89.3 million; accrued interest payable = 5/6 of the required payment of $3.0 million; discount on bond payable = the difference between the two, i.e., 5/6 of the total amount of bond discount to be amortized at time of the first interest payment)

Long-term debt is addressed in detail in Chapter 8.

[13] GASB Interpretation No. 6, *Recognition and Measurement of Certain Liabilities and Expenditures in Governmental Fund Financial Statements* (March 2000).

HOW SHOULD NONEXCHANGE EXPENDITURES BE ACCOUNTED FOR?

Chapter 4, "Recognizing Revenues in Governmental Funds," deals primarily with *nonexchange* revenues, as most governmental fund revenues are derived from nonexchange transactions. This chapter, however, is directed mainly to *exchange* expenditures, as relatively few types of government expenditures are associated with nonexchange transactions. Governments, for example, do not typically pay taxes or fines (nonexchange transactions) though they do make grants to other governments (also nonexchange transactions).

GASB Standards

Nonexchange expenditures should generally be recognized symmetrically with their revenue counterparts. Thus, providers of grants should recognize an expenditure when the recipient has satisfied all eligibility requirements, including time requirements.

EXAMPLE *Unrestricted Grant with Time Requirement*

In December 2005, a county's council approves a $300,000 grant to a not-for-profit health clinic. The funds are to be paid in 2006 out of funds budgeted for that year and are intended to support the clinic's activities in 2006.

Inasmuch as the funds are intended to be used in 2006, the grant is subject to a time requirement. The county should not recognize either a liability or an expenditure until then, when the time requirement is satisfied.

EXAMPLE *Grant with Purpose Restriction*

In December 2005, a state department of transportation awards a county $400,000 for road improvements. Payment is made at the time the award is announced. The county is permitted to use the funds upon receipt, but intends to use them in 2006.

Purpose restrictions have no impact on the timing of either expenditure or revenue recognition, nor does the county's intent to use them in a particular year. The state must recognize an expenditure as soon as it makes the award:

Grant expenditure	$400,000	
Cash		$400,000
To record grant expenditure (in 2005)		

EXAMPLE *Reimbursement (Eligibility Requirement) Grant*

In December 2005, a state awards a city $200,000 for the acquisition of an emergency telephone system. The grant is to be paid as the city incurs and documents allowable costs. In 2005 the city submits claims for $150,000, of which the state pays $125,000.

The state expects to pay the $25,000 balance of submitted claims in January 2006 and the $50,000 balance of the grant by June 2006.

The city is eligible for the award only as it incurs and documents allowable costs. In 2005, the city became eligible for $150,000 of the grant—the amount that the state should recognize as an expenditure.

Grant expenditure	$150,000	
Cash		$125,000
Grants payable		25,000
To recognize a reimbursement grant expenditure (in 2005)		

DIFFERENCES IN GOVERNMENT-WIDE STATEMENTS

The standards of GASB Statement No. 33, *Accounting and Financial Reporting for Nonexchange Transactions*, are applicable to both modified and full accrual statements. On the modified, but not the full, accrual statements, revenues must be available for expenditure before they can be recognized. That requirement is not, of course, relevant to expenses. Hence, the grants would be recognized as expenses in the same period in the government-wide as in the fund statements.

HOW SHOULD INTERFUND TRANSACTIONS BE ACCOUNTED FOR?

As stressed in Chapter 2, each of a government's funds is an independent fiscal and accounting entity. When the focus is on individual funds, many types of activity between funds create revenues and expenditures. Yet when the government is viewed as a whole, most of these activities are nothing more than intragovernmental transfers. If certain types of activities were classified as revenues of one fund and expenditures of another, then the revenues and the expenditures of the government as a whole would be overstated.

EXAMPLE *Interfund Transfer*

A government transfers $3 million from its general fund to a debt service fund for payment of interest. When the debt service fund pays the interest, it will record the payment as an expenditure.

Should the general fund record the payment to the debt service fund as an expenditure and the debt service fund record the receipt as a revenue? As independent entities, both funds incur expenditures; the debt service fund also earns revenue. Yet if each fund recognizes an expenditure, the government as a whole would recognize the interest cost as an expenditure twice (once in the general fund when the resources are transferred to the debt service fund and again when the interest is paid out of the debt service fund).

EXAMPLE *Interfund Purchase/Sale*

A government department, which is accounted for in the entity's general fund, acquires $30,000 of supplies from a supply center that is accounted for in an internal service fund.

The internal service fund will report the cost of the supplies "sold" as an expense. Should the general fund also report an expenditure? If it does not, then its reported expenditures—the measure of the cost of general government operations—would be less than if it had purchased the same supplies from outside vendors.

GASB Standards

Statement No. 34 differentiates between two types of interfund activity:

- **Reciprocal interfund activity.** This is the internal equivalent of exchange transactions (those in which the parties receive and surrender consideration of approximately equal value). They include:
  - *Payments for the purchase of goods and services at a price that approximates their external fair value, such as when the general fund acquires goods from an internal service fund.* These transfers should be reported as revenues in the seller fund and expenditures (or expenses) in the purchasing fund.
  - *Loans and repayments of loans.* If the loans are expected to be repaid within a reasonable period of time, the lending fund should report the loan as a receivable and the borrowing fund should report it as a payable. If the loans are not expected to be repaid within a reasonable period of time (and hence are not bona fide loans) then the transaction should be accounted for by the disbursing fund as a nonreciprocal transfer-out and by the receiving fund as a nonreciprocal transfer-in.
- **Nonreciprocal interfund activity.** This is the internal equivalent of nonexchange transactions. They represent transfers of cash for which goods or services of equivalent value have not been received, such as when the general fund transfers cash to a debt service fund for payment of principal or interest on long-term debt or when the general fund transfers cash to a newly established internal service fund for "start-up capital." Insofar as they represent transfers, they should be accounted for as such.

The statement also notes that interfund reimbursements (repayments from a fund responsible for an expenditure to the fund that initially paid for them) should not be reported at all in the financial statements. Thus, for example, if the general fund paid a bill for a cost that was the responsibility of a capital projects fund, the expenditure and the corresponding reduction in cash should be reported only in the capital projects fund—as if the capital projects fund had paid the bill itself. The capital projects fund should not report a transfer-out to the general fund; the general fund should report neither a payment to the vendor nor a transfer-in from the capital projects fund.

In the "Interfund Transfer" example, the payment of interest by the general fund to the debt service fund would be recorded by the general fund as nonreciprocal transfer-out and by the debt service fund as a nonreciprocal transfer-in:

Nonreciprocal transfer-out to debt service fund	$3	
Cash		$3
To record transfer to debt service fund (in general fund)		
Cash	$3	
Nonreciprocal transfer-in from general fund		$3
To record transfer from general fund (in debt service fund)		

In the "Interfund Purchase/Sale" example, by contrast, the payment by the general fund to the internal service fund for supplies would be considered a reciprocal transaction and hence recorded as if it were an exchange transaction:

Supplies expenditure	$30,000	
Cash		$30,000
To record the purchase of supplies (in the general fund)		
Cash	$30,000	
Sales revenue		$30,000
To record the sale of supplies (in the internal service fund)		

DIFFERENCES IN GOVERNMENT-WIDE STATEMENTS

As implied by their title, government-wide statements present revenues and expenses from the perspective of the entity, not individual funds. Reported expenses are generally those of the entity as a whole (divided into columns for governmental and business-type activities), not of individual funds. To avoid double-counting, interfund revenues and expenditures must be eliminated.

Special provisions of GASB Statement No. 34 direct how interfund activity involving internal service funds should be eliminated. Internal service fund residual balances (those remaining after the interfund activity has been eliminated) are included in the governmental activities column because they provide services mainly to governmental funds. These provisions are addressed in Chapter 9 pertaining to business-type activities.

WHAT CONSTITUTES OTHER FINANCING SOURCES AND USES?

Governmental funds receive or use resources from transactions that, under a full accrual basis, would affect long-term assets or liability accounts. For example, if a business issues long-term debt, it would establish a long-term liability. However, the measurement focus of governmental funds excludes both capital assets and long-term liabilities. Therefore, resources received from the issuance of bonds cannot be recorded as liabilities. Although similar to revenues in that they increase fund balance, they lack the characteristics of conventional revenues in that they will need to be repaid. Similarly, the proceeds from the sale of equipment can neither reduce a reported asset nor be interpreted as a revenue.

Generally accepted accounting and reporting standards direct that certain governmental resource flows that would otherwise affect long-term assets or liabilities be classified on statements of revenues, expenditures, and changes in fund balances as other financing sources and uses. The main types of other financing sources and uses are:

- Proceeds of long-term debt
- Proceeds from the sale of capital assets
- Present value of assets and liabilities created by capital leases
- Payments to bond "escrow" agents who maintain accounts for the eventual repayment of long-term obligations
- Nonreciprocal transfers

HOW SHOULD REVENUES, EXPENDITURES, AND OTHER FINANCING SOURCES AND USES BE REPORTED?

In light of the variety of activities and transactions in which the multitude of entities engage, governments need flexibility as to the form and content of their financial statements. At the same time, though, a certain degree of uniformity is required if statement users are to make meaningful comparisons among governments. Therefore, the GASB has set forth only the general framework of the statement of revenues, expenditures, and changes in fund balances.

GASB Standards

Revenues, expenditures, and changes in fund balances should be reported in governmental funds in a statement that takes the following form:

Revenues (detailed)	$100
Expenditures (detailed)	90
Excess of revenues over expenditures	10
Other financing sources and uses, including transfers (detailed)	(5)
Special and extraordinary items (detailed)	8
Net change in fund balance	13
Fund balances beginning of period	11
Fund balances end of period	$ 24

Expenditures would generally be shown by function (e.g., public safety, recreation, administration) rather than by object (e.g., salaries, travel, rent).

The governmental funds statements of revenues, expenditures, and changes in fund balances of Charlotte, North Carolina, were illustrated in Chapter 2, Table 2–6.

WHAT IS THE SIGNIFICANCE OF THE CURRENT FINANCIAL GOVERNMENTAL FUND STATEMENTS? AN OVERVIEW

The ultimate question faced by governmental fund financial statement readers is, "What does it all mean?" A governmental fund balance sheet presents the fund's resources at a particular point in time; its operating statement accounts for the net change in those resources during a particular period of time. All measurements, however, are in accord with generally accepted accounting principles (GAAP).

As made apparent in this and the previous chapter, governmental fund revenues and expenditures are frequently determined on different bases for purposes of budgeting than for financial reporting. Assuming the budget is on a cash or non-cash basis, examples of significant differences include:

- For purposes of budgeting, governments may recognize taxes as revenues only as collected; in accord with GAAP, they must recognize them as revenues only when they are both measurable and available to finance expenditures of the fiscal period.

- For purposes of budgeting, governments may account for wages and salaries on a cash basis; as required by GAAP, they must accrue compensation expenditures as long as the payments will be made with expendable available financial resources.
- For purposes of budgeting, governments may account for supplies and prepayments on a cash basis; as permitted by GAAP, they may use the consumption method.

Consequently, the reported revenues and expenditures, and the resultant surplus or deficit, may not be comparable with corresponding budgeted amounts.

Moreover, the balance sheet may not present a clear picture of either resources available for appropriation or the claims against those resources. It may not reflect taxes and other receivables that the government may be able to use to cover expenditures of the following and future years. Correspondingly, it may not show all of the claims against the fund's resources, such as those for deferred compensation, interest, and legal judgments. At the same time, however, some reported assets, such as prepaid amounts, might not be available for future appropriation. Therefore, the reported fund balance may not be representative of the net resources legally available for future appropriation.

The operating statement also cannot be counted on to reveal the true economic costs of government operations or the economic value of resources that it actually received or to which it became entitled during the year. Because they are based on modified rather than full accrual accounting, governmental fund operating statements fail to recognize both increases and decreases in such assets and liabilities as taxes and grants receivable, inventories and prepayments (if the purchases method is used), buildings and equipment, deferred compensation payable, and bonds payable. Correspondingly, the balance sheet cannot be relied upon to show the true economic value of all the assets available to the government and the claims against them.

The GASB standards of revenue and expenditure recognition satisfy both the inter-period equity and the budgetary compliance objectives of financial reporting, but only to a limited extent. The government-wide statements provide greater information on the economic costs of operations and on the economic value of resources. However, in the absence of other changes in principles, the fund statements will continue to fall short of indicating budget-based revenues and expenditures and the resources that are legally available for appropriation.

The limitations of the fund statements do not, by themselves, imply criticisms of either the statements themselves or the rule-making authorities responsible for them. As suggested in Chapter 1, it is questionable whether a single set of financial statements can satisfy all of the key accounting and reporting objectives. It is for that reason that the complete government reporting model encompasses two sets of financial statements—fund and government-wide.

IN PRACTICE

THE USEFULNESS OF REPORTED FUND BALANCE

A new member of the National Council on Government Accounting (the predecessor of the GASB) attended his first meeting of the standard-setting organization. In a morning session devoted to a proposed pronouncement, the discussion centered around the impact of the recommended standard, both on operating statement surplus or deficit and on fund balance.

At lunch, the new member asked others at his table, all of whom regularly utilized financial statements, what use they made of reported fund balance. All agreed they paid no attention to it. First, they said, the information is several months out of date by the time the financial statements are issued. Second, the reported fund balance fails to indicate the resources that are actually available to them for future appropriation.

SUMMARY

Rulemaking authorities recommend use of the accrual basis to the fullest extent practicable in the government environment. But they have substantially modified the accrual basis from the way it is applied in governmental funds as opposed to businesses, proprietary funds, and government-wide statements.

As pointed out in the previous chapter, for revenues to be recognized in governmental funds not only must a key underlying event take place, but also the resources to be received must be *measurable and available to finance expenditures of the fiscal period.*

In this chapter, we stressed that governmental fund expenditures are defined as "decreases in *net financial resources,*" in contrast to *expenses,* which represent outflows or consumption of *overall net assets.* As a consequence, we identified seven differences in how the accrual concept is applied in governments as opposed to businesses.

We also noted that governmental fund nonexchange transactions (mainly grants) are accounted for symmetrically to nonexchange revenues. Hence, grants are recognized as expenditures when the recipient has met all eligibility requirements and the grantor thereby incurs an obligation. Table 5-1 summarizes the general principles of expenditure and expenses recognition.

EXERCISE FOR REVIEW AND SELF-STUDY

For years beginning January 1, 2005, the City of Arbor Hills will finance its parks and recreation activities with a special property tax levy. Accordingly, it will account for resources related to parks and recreation in a special revenue fund. During 2005 it engaged in the following transactions:

1. The fund received $6 million from the city's special parks and recreation property tax levy.
2. During the year the parks and recreation employees earned $4.5 million in wages and salaries. Of this amount, the city paid $4.1 million in 2005 and is to pay the balance early in 2006.

TABLE 5-1
Summary of Expenditure/Expense Recognition Principles

I. Governmental fund statements are accounted for on an accrual basis.
   A. However, the accrual basis is modified in the following ways as to when *expenditures* are recognized.
      1. Vacations, sick leave, and other compensated absences are not accrued unless they will be liquidated with current financial resources.
      2. The reported pension expenditure includes only the governmental fund's actual contribution for the year, not, as in businesses, an actuarial contribution.
      3. Claims and judgments are reported as expenditures only insofar as they will be paid out of current financial resources.
      4. Inventory (and hence the cost of using supplies) may be accounted for using either a purchases or a consumption method, but any significant amounts of inventory must be reported in the financial statements regardless of the accounting method used.
      5. Prepaid items (and the related costs) may also be accounted for on either a purchases or a consumption basis, but significant amounts of prepayments need not necessarily be reported on the balance sheet.
      6. The costs of capital assets are reported as expenditures when the assets are acquired; capital assets are not depreciated.
      7. Repayment of long-term capital debt is reported as an expenditure as payments are made; interest on the debt is ordinarily not accrued. However, interest and principal *may* be accrued in a debt service fund if resources have been transferred in from another fund to make payments that are due early the next year (within no more than a month).
   B. Liabilities are recognized in governmental fund statements only to the extent that they will be liquidated with current financial resources.
   C. Nonexchange transactions are recognized symetrically to their revenue counterparts. (See Chapter 4.)
II. Government-wide statements are accounted for on a full accrual basis. Hence *expenses* are generally recognized as they are in businesses and in governments' proprietary funds.

3. Parks and recreation employees earned $0.26 million in vacation leave and were paid for $0.20 million. The city estimates that it will pay the entire balance in the future.
4. The employees earned $0.17 million in sick leave but were paid for only $0.14 million. The leave accumulates but does not vest.
5. According to city actuaries, employees earned $0.37 million in pensions. However, the city had budgeted only $0.30 million. During the year it contributed to its pension fund $0.25 million and plans to contribute an additional $0.05 million in early January 2006.
6. During 2005 the city ordered $0.80 million in parks and recreation supplies. Of this amount, it received $0.70 million, used $0.55 million, and paid for $0.50 million. The city uses the *purchases* method to account for supplies inventory.
7. In January 2005 the city purchased $1 million in parks and recreation equipment. It paid $0.20 million in cash and gave an installment note for the balance. The first payment on the note ($0.30 million plus interest of $0.05 million) is due on January 12, 2006.
   a. Prepare journal entries to summarize the transactions that affected the special revenue fund in 2005.
   b. Prepare a statement of revenues, expenditures, and changes in fund balance and a balance sheet for the Parks and Recreation Fund as of December 31, 2005.
   c. Indicate any assets or liabilities that would be reported in the city's schedules of capital assets or long-term obligation as a consequence of the transactions engaged in by the Parks and Recreation Fund.
   d. Comment on how each of the transactions would be reported on the city's government-wide statements.

QUESTIONS FOR REVIEW AND DISCUSSION

1. What is the distinction between *expenditures* and *expenses* as the terms are used in governmental accounting?
2. A government expects to pay its electric bill relating to its current fiscal year sometime in the following year. An official of the government requests your advice as to whether the anticipated payment should be charged as an expenditure of the current or the following year. How would you respond?
3. Under pressure to balance their budgets, governments at all levels have resorted to fiscal gimmicks, such as delaying the wages and salaries of government employees from the last day of the month to the first day of the following month. In the year of the change they thereby had one fewer pay periods. How would the change affect the reported expenditures of a governmental fund under GAAP?
4. Currently accepted accounting standards require that, if specified conditions are satisfied, the costs of compensated absences be accrued as a liability as the benefits are earned by employees. Yet even if a government adheres to these standards it may not necessarily have to record a governmental-fund expenditure indicative of the amount accrued and the liability recognized. How can that be? Explain and justify.
5. A government permits its employees to accumulate all unused vacation days and sick leave. Whereas (in accord with current standards) it may have to "book" a liability for the unused vacation days, it may not have to record an obligation for the unused sick leave. Explain and justify the applicable standards.
6. A government accounts for inventory on the consumption basis. Why do some accountants believe that it should offset the year-end inventory balance with a fund balance reserve when no comparable reserve is required for cash, taxes receivable, or most other assets?
7. A government accounts for inventory on the purchases basis. Why *must* it offset its year-end inventory balance with a fund balance reserve?
8. Many accountants note that for most governments the reported "bottom line" of their financial statements (i.e., revenues less expenditures/expenses and other charges that affect fund balance/net assets) will not greatly differ between their government-wide statements and their fund statements insofar as the expenditures/expenses relate to long-term assets and the long-term liabilities issued to finance those assets. That's because governments typically repay the debt evenly over a period which approximates the economic life of the related asset. Assuming the accountant's assumption as to means of financing to be correct, will the expenditures and related charges affecting fund balance of the governmental fund statements approximate the expenses of the government-wide statements?
9. Governments are not required to accrue interest on long-term debt in governmental funds even if the interest is applicable to a current period and will be due the first day of the following year. Explain and justify the standards that permit this practice.
10. A school district accounts for its pension costs in a governmental fund. In a particular year the district's actuary calculates the district's required contribution for the year to be $18 million. The district, however, had only budgeted $15 million and chooses to contribute only what was budgeted. What should the district report as its pension expenditure for the year? Explain.
11. A city's electric utility transfers $40 million to its general fund. Of this amount, $30 million is a return of the general fund's initial contribution of "start-up capital." The balance is a payment in lieu of property taxes that a private utility operating in the city would have had to

pay. Explain how each element of the transfer would be reported in the general fund's operating statement.

12. True or false? A government's unreserved general fund balance at year-end is ordinarily indicative of the amount that the government has available for appropriation in future years. Explain and provide an example to support your answer.

EXERCISES

5-1

Assume that Nolanville's fiscal year ends on December 31.

1. Nolanville's payroll for one of its departments is $15,000 per week. It pays its employees on the Thursday of the week following that in which the wages and salaries are earned. In 2005, December 31 fell on a Wednesday. For the workweek beginning Monday, December 29, 2005, and ending Friday, January 2, 2006, employees were paid on Thursday, January 8, 2006. For fiscal 2005, what amount should the city recognize as wage and salary expenditure/expense pertaining to the week ending Friday, January 2, 2006, in its fund statements and its government-wide statements?

	Fund Statements	Government-Wide Statements
a.	$ 0	$ 0
b.	$ 9,000	$9,000
c.	$ 0	$9,000
d.	$ 9,000	$ 0

2. In its fund financial statements, the city would recognize the receipt of a new computer (to be used for general administrative purposes) that it had ordered the previous year as an
   a. Encumbrance
   b. Expense
   c. Expenditure
   d. Asset
3. In 2005, city employees earned $1.4 million in sick leave that they did not take during the year. The city estimates that of this amount $0.8 million will actually be paid to employees who take sick leave. Of the balance, $0.1 million will be paid to employees upon their retirement or resignation and $0.5 will not have to be paid (since employees are limited in the number of sick days that they can carry over from one year to the next). The amount that the city should add to a fund-statement liability account as of year-end 2005 is
   a. $0
   b. $0.1 million
   c. $0.8 million
   d. $0.9 million
4. Assume the same facts as in the previous item. The amount that the city should add to a government-wide statement liability account as of year-end 2005 is
   a. $0
   b. $0.1 million
   c. $0.8 million
   d. $0.9 million
5. In 2005 city employees earned $3.6 million in vacation pay that they did not use during the year. The city estimates that of this amount $2.8 will be paid in 2006 (out of amounts budgeted for that year), $0.6 will be paid in subsequent years and the balance of $0.2 will not have to be paid. The amount that the city should add to a fund-statement liability account as of year-end 2005 is
   a. $0
   b. $2.8 million
   c. $3.4 million
   d. $3.6 million
6. Assume the same facts as in the previous item. The amount that the city should add to a government-wide statement liability account as of year-end 2005 is
   a. $0
   b. $2.8 million
   c. $3.4 million
   d. $3.6 million
7. Nolanville starts fiscal 2005 with $25,000 in supplies. During the year it orders $180,000 in supplies, receives $170,000, and uses $190,000. It accounts for inventories on the purchases basis. In its 2005 governmental fund financial statements it should report

	Expenditure	Fund Balance Reserve
a.	$180,000	$ 0
b.	$170,000	$ 5,000
c.	$190,000	$ 0
d.	$190,000	$15,000

8. Assume the same facts as in the previous item. In its 2005 government-wide financial statements it should report

	Expense	Net Asset Reserve
a.	$170,000	$ 0
b.	$170,000	$15,000
c.	$190,000	$ 0
d.	$190,000	$15,000

9. On December 1, 2005, Nolanville issued $10 million of thirty-year, 8 percent bonds for $9.78 million, a price that reflects a semiannual yield of 4.1 percent. Interest ($400,000 per semiannual period) is payable on May 31 and November 30, beginning May 31, 2006. In its 2005 fund and government-wide statements, Nolanville should report an interest expenditure/expense of

	Fund Statements	Government-wide Statements
a.	$0	$ 0
b.	$66,667	$66,667
c.	$66,830	$66,830
d.	$0	$66,830

10. In May 2008, Nolanville repaid $2 million of the bonds that it had issued in 2003. In its 2008 fund and government-wide statements, Nolanville should report an expenditure/expense relating to the repayment of the bonds of

	Fund Statements	Government-wide Statements
a.	$ 0	$ 0
b.	$2 million	$ 0
c.	$ 0	$2 million
d.	$2 million	$2 million

5-2

The Eaton School District engaged in the following transactions during its fiscal year ending August 31, 2005.

- It established a purchasing department, which would be accounted for in a new internal service fund, to purchase supplies and distribute them to operating units. To provide working capital for the new department it transferred $1.7 million from its general fund to the internal service fund.
- During the year, operating departments that are accounted for in the general fund acquired supplies from the internal service fund for which they were billed $300,000. Of this amount the government transferred $200,000 from the general fund to the internal service fund, expecting to transfer the balance in the following fiscal year. The supplies had cost the purchasing department $190,000. During 2005, the operating departments used only $220,000 of the supplies for which they were billed. They had no supplies on hand at the start of the year.
- The school district transferred $150,000 from its general fund to its debt service fund to make its required March 31, 2005, interest payment. This amount was paid from the debt service fund when due. It represented interest on $8 million of bonds that were issued, at par, on September 30, 2004. The next interest payment of $150,000 is due on September 30, 2005. The district also transferred $75,000 from the general fund to the debt service fund to provide for the eventual repayment of principal.
- The district transferred $4.5 million from the general fund to its pension fund (a fiduciary fund) in partial payment of its actuarially required contribution of $5.0 million for the year.
- On August 31, the district acquired school buses at a cost of $900,000. The district gave the supplier installment notes that required the district to make three annual payments of $361,903. The first payment is due in August 2006. The buses have a useful life of ten years, with no salvage value.

Match the items below with the amounts that follow. An amount may be selected once, more than once, or not at all.

1. Amount that the general fund should recognize as supplies expenditure, assuming that inventory is accounted for on a purchases basis.
2. Amount that the district should recognize as a pension expenditure in its general fund
3. Amount that the district should recognize as a pension expense in its government-wide statements
4. Amount that the general fund should recognize as nonreciprocal transfers-out
5. Amount that the district should recognize as total debt service expenditures in its governmental funds.
6. Amount that the government should recognize as total debt service expense in its government-wide statements
7. Amount that the district should recognize as other financing sources in its general fund financial statements
8. Amount that the district should recognize as capital-related expenditures, including depreciation, pertaining to its buses in its governmental fund financial statements (the district recognizes a full year's depreciation on all capital assets in the year of acquisition)
9. Amount that the district should recognize as capital-related expenses, including depreciation, pertaining to its buses in its government-wide financial statements (the district recognizes a full year's depreciation on all capital assets in the year of acquisition)
10. Amount that the district should recognize as fund-balance reserves in its governmental fund statements.

a. $0
b. $75,000
c. $80,000
d. $90,000
e. $137,500
f. $150,000
g. $220,000
h. $275,000
i. $300,000
j. $900,000
k. $1,925,000
l. $4,500,000
m. $5,000,000
n. $8,000,000
o. $8,900,000

5-3

The purchases method differs from the consumption method.

The Boyd School District began a recent fiscal year with $3,000 of supplies in stock. During its fiscal year, it engaged in the following transactions relating to supplies:

- It purchased supplies at a cost of $22,000.

- It paid for $19,000 of the supplies.
- It used $20,000 of the supplies and therefore had $5,000 in supplies inventory at year-end.

The district establishes inventory reserves as appropriate.

1. Record the transactions assuming that the district uses the purchases method.
2. Record the transactions assuming that the district uses the consumption method.
3. Comment on any differences between the two as they would affect:
   a. The district's general fund balance sheet
   b. Its general fund statement of revenues and expenditures

5-4

Inventory transactions can be derived from a limited amount of data.

The following schedule shows the amounts related to supplies that a city debited and credited to the indicated accounts during a year (not necessarily the year-end balances), excluding closing entries. The organization records its budget, encumbers all of its expenditures, and initially vouchers all payments. It accounts for supplies on a purchases basis.

	(in thousands)	
	Debits	***Credits***
Cash	$0	$70
Inventory	—	0
Vouchers payable	—	—
(Appropriations)	0	115
Encumbrances	—	—
Expenditures	58	0
Reserve for encumbrances	58	93
Fund balance	—	0
Reserve for supplies inventory	0	—

1. Some information is missing. By reconstructing the entries that the organization made during the year, you are to determine the missing data. The city began the year with $5,000 of supplies in inventory and ended the year with $6,000.
2. Assume instead that the city accounts for supplies on a consumption basis. Which of the above amounts (assuming that appropriations remained unchanged) would be different? What would be the new value(s)?

5-5

Fund balance, both reserved and unreserved can be computed from a limited amount of information.

The schedule that follows reports the beginning balances and activity during the year in a town's supplies fund (a restricted governmental fund). The government accounts for supplies on a purchases basis (in thousands).

Fund balance (unreserved), January 1		$ 400
Fund balance, reserved for encumbrances, January 1		240
Fund balance, reserved for inventory, January 1		170
Total fund balance, January 1		$ 810
Appropriations (for purchases of supplies)	$3,400	
Estimated revenues	3,200	
Actual revenues	3,300	
Supplies ordered	3,160	
Supplies received	3,360	
Supplies paid-for	2,800	
Supplies used	3,280	

1. Compute the following (and show your computations):
   a. Fund balance, reserved for inventory, December 31
   b. Fund balance, reserved for encumbrances, December 31
   c. Fund balance (unrestricted), December 31
2. How can you justify the continued use of the purchases method when it appears so contrary to everything you learned in classes pertaining to business accounting?

5-6

Irrespective of how capital assets are acquired, they are recorded differently in governmental funds than in businesses.

In a recent year Ives Township acquired six police cars at a total cost of $200,000. The vehicles are expected to have a useful life of four years.

1. Prepare the journal entries that the township would make in its general fund in the year of acquisition for each of the following assumptions:
   a. It paid for the cars in cash at the time of acquisition.
   b. It leased the cars agreeing to make four equal payments of $63,095, starting in the year of acquisition, an amount that represents the annuity required to liquidate a loan of $200,000 at 10 percent interest. The lease would satisfy the criteria necessary to be accounted for as a capital lease.
   c. It issued $200,000 in installment notes to the car dealer, agreeing to repay them in four annual payments of $63,095, starting in the year of acquisition.
2. Comment on how any "off the balance sheet" assets or obligations would be reported in supplementary schedules and the government-wide statements.

5-7

Expenditures for vacations do not necessarily reflect the amounts the employees have earned.

In 2005, employees of Pecos River County earned $5 million in vacation pay. They were paid for $4.2 million but deferred taking the balance of their earned vacations until subsequent years. Also, employees were paid $0.7 million for vacation earned in previous years.

1. Prepare the journal entry in the general fund to reflect the vacation pay earned in 2005.

2. Prepare the journal entry to reflect the payments for vacation days that had been earned in prior years.
3. Comment on how the schedule of long-term obligations would be affected by these transactions.
4. Comment on how the government-wide statements would be affected by these transactions. Specifically, what would be the reported vacation expenses for 2005, and what would be the end of year accrued liability for vacation pay assuming that the beginning of year liability was $0.7 million?

5-8

Obligations for sick leave should not be recognized as liabilities if they are to cover the wages of employees who actually become ill.

Lemon County permits employees to accumulate any sick leave that they do not take. If employees do not use accumulated sick leave, then they will be paid for those days upon retirement or termination (up to a maximum of forty-five days). In 2005 employees earned $4.0 million in sick leave. Of this amount they were paid $3.1 million. The county expects that they will be paid $0.6 million as they take sick days in future years and $0.2 million upon retirement or termination. The balance of $0.1 will not have to be paid.

1. Based on current standards, prepare journal entries in the general fund to reflect the sick leave earned and paid for in 2005. Indicate the amount to be reported in the schedule of long-term obligations and the government-wide statements.
2. What is the rationale for the standards that underlie your entries?

5-9

The manner in which a transfer is accounted for depends on its nature.

Prepare general fund journal entries to record the following cash transfers that a city made from its general fund to other funds. Be sure your entry reflects the nature of the transfer.

1. $4,000,000 to provide start-up capital to a newly established internal service fund that will account for the city's data processing activities
2. $50,000 to pay for data processing services provided by the data processing internal service fund
3. $38,000 to reimburse the capital projects fund for equipment rental costs that it incurred on behalf of activities accounted for in the general fund
4. $300,000 to pay the electric utility fund for four months of electric service
5. $600,000 to enable the debt service fund to make timely payments of principal and interest on outstanding general obligation debt

5-10

Prepayments may be accounted for on a purchases or consumption basis.

During its fiscal year ending June 30, 2004, the Parkville Independent School District enters into a two-year lease for office space covering the period May 1, 2004, through April 30, 2006. Annual rent is $60,000. The lease specifies that the entire rent for each year is to be paid, in advance, on May 1.

1. Prepare journal entries to record the lease payments and the lease expenditures for fiscal years ending June 30, 2004, 2005, and 2006, assuming that the district uses the consumption method.
2. Prepare journal entries to record the lease payments and the lease expenditures for the same years assuming that the district uses the purchases method.

PROBLEMS

Continuing Problem

Review the Comprehensive Annual Financial Report (CAFR) that you obtained.

1. How does the government classify its governmental expenditures, by function or by "object"? Are the classifications approximately the same in both the government-wide and the fund statements?
2. What are the major differences in expenditures/expenses (i.e., reconciling items) as they are reported in the government-wide and the governmental fund statements?
3. On what basis does the government account for its inventories (purchases or consumption)? Does it maintain a reserve for inventories?
4. On what basis does it account for insurance or other prepaid items in its governmental funds? How can you tell?
5. To and from which funds or component units have there been general fund transfers?
6. Explain the nature of any governmental-fund balance sheet reserves related to expenditures.
7. Does the entity report depreciation as an expense in its government-wide statements? If not, why not?

5-1

All paid time off may not be the same.

A city has adopted the following plan as to compensated time off:

- City employees are entitled to a specified number of days each year for holidays and vacation. The number depends on length of service (twenty days for employees with fewer than five years of service, twenty-five days for employees with between five and ten years, thirty days for employees with more than ten years). Employees may accumulate up to forty days, which they can either carry over to future years or be compensated for upon termination.
- Employees are also entitled to seven sick days per year. They may carry over to future years up to sixty sick days. However, upon termination they can be paid for no more than twenty unused days.

During 2005 the city paid employees $4.2 million for holidays and vacations during the year. Of this amount, $0.4 million was for days carried over from previous years. In addition, employees earned $0.5 million in time off that they expect to use, and be paid for, in the future.

The city also paid $1.5 million in sick leave, none of which was paid to employees upon termination. Of this amount, $0.3 million was carried forward from previous years. The city estimates that employees earned an additional $0.8 million in unused sick leave. Of this, $0.5 million will eventually be paid for as time off, $0.2 million will be paid upon termination, and $0.1 million will lapse.

1. Prepare a general fund journal entry to record the holiday and vacation compensation. Indicate the amount of any other liability that would be recorded on both the government-wide statements and the schedule of long-term obligations.
2. Do the same for the sick leave.
3. Justify any differences between the two sets of entries.
4. Suppose additionally that for the first time in 2005 the city offered up to eight weeks of paid maternity leave to eligible employees. In 2005 the city paid $0.2 million to employees on leave. In addition, employees earned an estimated $0.3 million in leave to be taken in the future. Consistent with your previous entries and justifications, explain how (and why) you would account for this leave (which is not specifically addressed by current GASB pronouncements).

5-2

The guidance on sabbatical programs leaves much to the judgment of school officials and their accountants.

The Allendale School District recently signed a contract with its teachers' union. The contract provides that all teachers will receive a one-semester sabbatical leave after seven continuous years of employment. The preamble to the contract provision stresses that the leave is intended for "renewal, additional education, and academic enrichment." It provides examples of the types of activities it is intended to promote: formal post-baccalaureate courses, service with public or nonprofit organizations, and independent study and research.

The contract indicates that the leave is guaranteed to all teachers who satisfy the time in service and other specified criteria. Although teachers must apply for the leave, the district is required to approve it if the criteria are met. If a teacher opts not to take the leave after seven years, then he or she may accumulate it and either take it in the future or receive payment for it upon retirement. Teachers do not have to report to the school officials either on what they plan to accomplish while on leave or what they actually accomplished.

School officials estimate that the new sabbatical provision will add to its annual compensation costs approximately $3,000 per currently employed teacher per year (after taking account of teachers who will never satisfy the leave criteria). The district currently employs 2,500 teachers. The program will be phased in gradually; the first teachers will be eligible to take their leaves in seven years.

Another school district, the Balcones West School District, which is not unionized, adopted a similar sabbatical program the same year. However, the Balcones West program does not guarantee teachers a leave. Instead they must be granted the leave on the basis of an interview and lengthy application, which includes a schedule of planned activities. Teachers who win approval for the leave must agree to work for the district for at least one year subsequent to the leave. If they fail to return to the district, they will be required to reimburse the district for salary and benefits received while on leave. Moreover, they must submit a written report to the district on their accomplishments during the leave.

Balcones West officials estimate that the cost of its leave will be approximately $2,000 per currently employed teacher per year. The district currently employs 1,000 teachers. As with the Allendale district, the program will be phased in gradually and the first teachers will be eligible for leaves in seven years.

Prepare any entries that you would recommend that (1) the Allendale District and (2) the Balcones West District prepare in the first year after adopting their sabbatical programs. Specify the fund in which your entries would be made. Explain and justify your answers, citing relevant accounting standards.

5-3

Inventory transactions can be derived from year-end balances.

The following schedule indicates selected accounts from a city's *preclosing* 2005 and *postclosing* 2004 general fund trial balances:

	December 31, 2005 (Preclosing)	December 31, 2004 (Postclosing)
Expenditures	$315,000	—
Supplies Inventory	81,000	$54,000
Encumbrances	36,000	—
Reserve for Encumbrances	45,000	9,000
Reserve for Supplies	54,000	54,000

All of the amounts shown relate only to supplies. All purchases during the year were paid in cash.

1. Assume that the city uses the consumption method to account for supplies.
   a. Reconstruct all journal entries relating to supplies that were made in 2005.
   b. Make any additional entries that would be required at year-end 2005 to close the accounts.
2. Assume instead that the city uses the purchases method to account for supplies. Assume also that the supplies inventory balance as reported on the preclosing December 31, 2005, balance sheet is $54,000 (not $81,000 as shown in the schedule), even though actual supplies on hand are still $81,000. (This adjustment is necessary because under the purchases method inventory is maintained throughout the year at the beginning of year balance; it is adjusted only at year-end when the closing entries are made.)
   a. Reconstruct all journal entries relating to supplies that were made in 2005.
   b. Make any additional entries that would be required at year-end 2005 to close the accounts.

5-4

Generally accepted modified accrual accounting practices pertaining to inventories may not fulfill the objectives of financial reporting.

The following is an excerpt from a note to the financial statements of the city of Dallas:

The city prepares its annual appropriated General Fund, Debt Service Fund and Proprietary operating funds budgets on a basis (budget basis) which differs from generally accepted accounting principles (GAAP basis) .... The major differences between the budget and GAAP bases are that encumbrances are recorded as the equivalent of expenditures (budget) rather than a reservation of fund balance (GAAP) in the Governmental Funds.

The city accounts for inventories on the purchases basis. One of the city's departments, which is accounted for in the general fund, budgeted $195,000 in supplies expenditures for fiscal 2005. It began the 2005 fiscal year with $30,000 of supplies on hand. It also had $12,000 of supplies on order. During the year it ordered an additional $180,000 of supplies, received (and paid for in cash) $185,000 of supplies, and consumed $178,000 of supplies.

1. Prepare all journal entries, consistent with GAAP, including budgetary and encumbrance entries that the department should make in 2005.
2. Indicate the accounts and amounts related to supplies that the city would report on its year-end statement of revenues, expenditures, and changes in fund balance and balance sheet.
3. By how much did the department over- or underspend its supplies budget (on a budget basis)?
4. Comment on the extent to which the city's statement provides a basis to:
   a. Assess the "true" economic costs associated with supplies
   b. Determine whether the city adhered to budgetary spending mandates
5. Suppose that in the last quarter of the year, department officials realized that the department was about to over-spend its supplies budget. They therefore ceased placing new orders for supplies. However, they imposed no restrictions on the use of supplies and thereby allowed the supplies inventory to decline to near zero.
   a. What impact would these cost-cutting measures have on supplies expenditures as reported in an actual-to-budget comparison (on a budget basis)?
   b. What impact would the year-end measures have on reported supplies expenditures (per GAAP)? Would your response be different if the city accounted for supplies on the consumption basis?

5-5

Can a government sell assets to itself to generate revenue?

A city is having fiscal problems in 2005. It expects to report a deficit in its general fund, the only fund that is statutorily required to be balanced.

To eliminate the anticipated deficit the city opts to "sell" its city hall—to itself—for $5 million. The city establishes a "capital asset financing agency," which will be accounted for in a fund other than the general fund. It structures the transaction as follows:

- The financing agency pays the city $5 million in 2005 in exchange for "ownership" of city hall. The city hall has been carried as general capital asset.
- The agency acquires the necessary cash by issuing twenty-year, 6 percent notes. The notes will be repaid in twenty annual installments of $435,920. The notes are guaranteed by the city at large. Hence, they are ultimately a liability payable from the general fund.
- The agency leases the city hall back to the city at large. Lease payments are to be paid out of general fund resources.

1. Prepare journal entries in the general fund to record the sale and concurrent lease-back of the city hall. The lease-back satisfies the criteria of a capital lease transaction.
2. Prepare journal entries in the general fund to record the first lease payment, which was made in 2005.
3. Will the transaction, in fact, reduce the 2005 anticipated fund deficit? Briefly justify the accounting principles that underlie this type of accounting.

5-6

How an acquisition is financed may dictate the annual reported expenditure.

The Mainor School District is about to establish a thirty-machine computer lab. It is considering six alternative means of acquiring and financing the machines:

1. Buy the machines outright; cost will be $60,000.
2. Buy the machines and finance them with a $60,000, three-year, 10 percent-interest term note. The district

will repay the note and pay the entire interest with a single payment of $79,860 when the note matures.

3. Buy the machines and finance them with a $60,000, three-year, 10 percent-interest, installment note. The district will repay the note (plus interest) in three end-of-year installments of $24,127 each.
4. Lease the equipment under a standard operating lease. The district will make three end-of-year lease payments of $24,127 each.
5. Lease the equipment under an operating lease, but pre-pay the entire rent ($60,000) in advance.
6. Lease the equipment, but structure the lease so that it satisfies the criteria of a capital lease. The district will make three $24,127 end-of-year lease payments.

The district estimates that the equipment has a useful life of three years.

a. Prepare a table in which for each alternative you indicate the net expenditure that the district would record in its general fund in the year of purchase and the following two years. Ignore any expenditures that are offset by "other financing sources." For the fifth option (the operating lease with the rent paid in advance), assume first that the district accounts for prepayments on the purchases basis and then that it accounts for them on the consumption basis.
b. Determine the present value (using a discount rate of 10 percent) of the cash payments under each option.
c. Comment on any incentives that district officials might have either to spread out the payments over the three-year period (either by a lease or borrowing arrangement) or to postpone the full payment until the third year, rather than to pay for the computers entirely in the year of acquisition.
d. Comment on any significant differences in how the six options would be accounted for in government-wide statements instead of governmental fund statements. How would each year's reported expense be determined?

5-7

Accounting practices for interest expenditures may neither reflect actual economic costs nor mirror those for interest revenues.

A town plans to borrow about $10 million and is considering three alternatives. A town official requests your guidance on the economic cost of each of the arrangements and advice as to how they would affect the town's reported expenditures.

1. For each of the town's three alternatives, determine (1) what the town's economic cost would be of using the funds in the year ending December 31, 2005 and (2) what amount of interest expenditure the town would be required to report for the year ending December 31, 2005, in its governmental funds.
   a. The town would issue $10 million of twenty-year, 6 percent coupon bonds on September 1, 2005. The bonds would be issued at par. The town would be required to make its first interest payment of $200,000 on January 1, 2006.
   b. The town would issue $10 million of twenty-year, 6 percent bonds on July 1, 2005. The bonds would be sold for $9,552,293, a price that reflects an annual yield (effective interest rate) of 6.4 percent. The town would be required to make its first interest payment of $300,000 on December 31, 2005.
   c. The town would issue $32,071,355 of twenty-year zero coupon bonds on July 1, 2005. The bonds would be sold for $10 million, an amount that reflects an annual yield of 6 percent. The bonds require no payment of principal or interest until June 30, 2025.
2. Suppose that the town elects the first option and issues $10 million of twenty-year, 6 percent coupon bonds at par on September 1, 2005. The town establishes a debt service fund to account for resources that it sets aside to pay principal and interest on the bonds. On December 31, 2005, the town transfers $200,000 from the general fund to the debt service fund to cover the first interest payment that is due on January 1, 2006.
   a. How would the transfer be reported in the general fund?
   b. How would the transfer be reported in the debt service fund? What options are available to the town to record 2005 interest in the debt service fund?
3. Suppose that the town borrowed $10 million on September 1, 2005, and temporarily invested the proceeds in two-year, 6 percent Treasury notes. The first payment of interest, $200,000, is payable on January 1, 2006.
   a. What would be the town's economic gain from investing the funds in the year ending December 31, 2005? Ignore borrowing costs.
   b. How much investment revenue should the town report for the year ending December 31, 2005? Assume there was no change in prevailing interest rates.

5-8

Not all interfund activities are classified as "transfers."

The following information was abstracted from a note, headed "Interfund Transactions," to the financial statements of Independence, Missouri.

Interfund Charges for Support Services

Interfund charges for support services (which would otherwise be acquired from outsiders) and rent paid to the General Fund during the fiscal year were as follows:

	Interfund Charges	Rent
Tourism fund	$ —	$ 4,372
Power and light fund	1,285,011	230,933
Water fund	522,244	36,883
Sanitary sewer fund	629,442	34,243
Central garage fund	152,330	3,411
	$2,589,027	$309,842

Rent charges, which consist of leased office space and computer charges, are included in other revenue of the general fund.

Payments in Lieu of Taxes

The payments of $5,161,609, $628,371, and $880,637 in the fiscal year by the power and light, sanitary sewer, and water (enterprise) funds, respectively, to the general fund in lieu of taxes represent franchise taxes and real estate taxes on plants in service. The franchise tax rate, established by City ordinance at 9.08 percent for the year, is applied to gross billed operating revenues less amounts written off to arrive at the franchise tax due the General Fund. Real estate taxes are charged at a set amount.

Interfund Operating Transfers

Interfund operating transfers for the fiscal year were as follows:

	Transfer To	Transfer From
General	$ 173,617	$ 944,327
Special revenue		307,772
Debt service	930,000	
Capital projects	440,551	157,918
Enterprise		3,000
Internal service		140,604
Permanent	9,453	
Total operating transfers	$1,553,621	$1,553,621

1. Based on the information provided, prepare four journal entries (for support services, rent, payments in lieu of taxes, and interfund operating transfers) to record the transfers into the general fund. Be sure the account titles you use make clear the nature of the transaction (e.g., revenue, reciprocal transfer, nonreciprocal transfer).
2. Justify any differences in how you classified the interfund transactions.

5-9

Analysts may (depending on account classification) be able to derive information on cash flows from a statement of revenues, expenditures, and changes in fund balance and balance sheets.

Highbridge County imposes a motor fuel tax to finance road maintenance. It therefore accounts for all road maintenance in a special revenue fund. The fund's statement of revenues, expenditures, and changes in fund balance and balance sheet are presented as follows.

Road Maintenance Special Revenue Fund Statement of Revenues, Expenditures, and Changes in Fund Balance Year Ending December 31, 2005 (in thousands)

Motor fuel tax revenues		$710
Expenditures:		
Wage and salaries	$410	
Contribution to pension fund	35	
Supplies	190	
Acquisition of equipment	90	
Legal settlement	3	
Other expenditures	70	798
Excess of revenues over expenditures		(88)
Other financing sources:		
Proceeds of long-term debt		90
Increase in supplies inventory		8
Total other financing sources		98
Excess of revenue and other financing sources over expenditures		10
Fund balance, beginning of year		69
Fund balance, end of year		$ 79

Balance Sheet as of December 31, 2005 (in thousands)

	2005	2004
Assets:		
Cash	$26	$17
Motor fuel taxes receivable	15	11
Prepaid expenditures	18	22
Supplies inventory	40	32
Total assets	$99	$82
Liabilities and fund balances:		
Accounts payable (for supplies)	$6	$4
Accrued wages and salaries	7	9
Claims and judgments payable	3	0
Current obligation to pension fund	4	0
Total liabilities	20	13
Fund balance		
Reserve for encumbrances (supplies)	12	16
Reserve for inventories	40	32
Unreserved	27	21
Total fund balance	79	69
Total liabilities and fund balance	$99	$82

1. The county prepares its budget for the road maintenance special revenue fund on a strict cash basis—no accruals whatsoever. Based on the information in the financial statements, prepare a schedule in which you account for all inflows and outflows of cash. The county reports inventories on a purchases basis. Be sure that your schedule accounts for the entire $9,000 increase in cash during the year.
2. Are you able to determine from the fund statements presented any of the following?
   a. The actual amount of any claims and judgments incurred during the year
   b. The fund's *required* contribution to its pension fund
   c. The interest cost applicable to the long-term debt issued

If not, would this information be reported elsewhere in the financial statements? Explain.

3. Most governments do not classify their expenditures by object classification as in this example. Instead they report them by function, such as general government, public safety, recreation, and so on. However, they present their assets and liabilities in a fashion similar to that in the example. Is it possible, therefore, to derive information on cash flows from the statement of operations and balance sheets? Explain. Why do you think governments report expenditures by function rather than by object classification?

5-10

Fund balance deficits may not be all bad.

The balance sheet and statement of revenues, expenditures, and changes in fund balance for Boulder, Colorado's Permanent Parks and Recreation Fund, a special revenue fund, for the year ending December 31, 2005, follow (dates charged).

Boulder, Colorado
Statement of Revenues, Expenditures, and Changes in Fund Balance
Year Ended December 31, 2005
(in Thousands)

Revenues:	
General property taxes	$ 855
Other taxes—Development excise	663
Development fees	13
Golf expansion fees	138
Interest earnings	42
Lease/rent from land	24
Other	209
Total revenues	$1,944
Expenditures:	
Culture and recreation	1,881
Interest	119
Total expenditures	2,000
Excess (deficiency) of revenues over expenditures	(56)
Other financing uses operating transfers out	(123)
Excess (deficiency) of revenues and other sources over expenditures and other uses	(179)
Fund balance, beginning of year	(367)
Fund balance, end of year	$(546)

Balance Sheet as of December 31, 2005
(in Thousands)

Assets:	
Cash and equivalents	$ 3
Investments at cost or amortized cost	902
General property taxes receivable	938
Accrued interest	8
Other	9
Due from other funds	14
Restricted asset, cash for special purposes	4
Total assets	$1,878
Liabilities:	
Vouchers and accounts payable	$120
Salaries and wages payable	9
Advances from other funds	1,357
Deferred revenue—General property taxes	938
Total liabilities	2,424
Fund equity:	
Reserved for:	
Encumbrances	112
Special purposes	24
Unreserved	(682)
Total fund equity	(546)
Total liabilities and fund equity	$1,878

A note to the financial statements states the following:

Fund Deficits

The Permanent Parks and Recreation Fund has a fund balance deficit of $546,539. This deficit is the result of the Permanent Parks and Recreation Fund expenditures: one-half of the cost of a central irrigation system for city parks and the acquisition of Roper Fields for soccer fields. The cost of the central irrigation system was shared with the Water Utility Fund to improve water conservation. The Permanent Parks and Recreation Fund has funded these projects through interfund loans with December 31, 2005, balances of: Water Utility Fund ($52,870) and Flood Control Utility Fund ($1,274,524).

1. Suppose that you are the chief accountant of the Parks and Recreation Department. A member of the city council accuses you and your department of mismanagement as evidenced by the substantial fund deficit. How would you defend yourself? What is the significance of the fund deficit?
2. Prepare journal entries (as best you can with the information provided) in the Permanent Parks and Recreation Fund to record:
   a. The acquisition of the central irrigation system and the Roper Fields (assuming that the cost of the assets is equal to the December 31, 2005, interfund loan balances even though the acquisition was, in fact, made prior to 2005 and a portion of the balances had already been repaid by December 31, 2005)
   b. The interfund loans
3. A schedule of changes in general capital assets by function and activity indicates the following with respect to parks and recreation (in thousands):

General capital assets as of January 1, 2005	$24,100
Additions, 2005	1,291
Deductions, 2005	(373)
General capital assets as of December 31, 2005	$25,018

How are the additions (which are other than the irrigation system and the soccer fields) and deductions most likely reflected in financial statements of the Permanent Parks and Recreation Fund?

5-11

The amount available for appropriation may not always be obvious from the balance sheet.

A recent general fund balance sheet of Dallas, Texas, showed the following (in thousands):

Assets	
Cash and equivalents	$49,182
Property taxes receivable	5,265
Sales taxes receivable	25,911
Accounts receivable	11,388
Accrued interest	781
Due from other funds	674
Inventories at cost	3,517
Total assets	$96,718
Liabilities	
Accrued payroll	$12,468
Accounts payable	5,712
Accrued vacation and sick leave	5,081
Due to other funds	527
Deferred revenue	9,067
Housing discrimination case settlement	1,894
Other	5,238
Total liabilities	39,987
Fund equity	
Reserved for encumbrances	14,469
Unreserved	
Designated for contingencies	19,670
Undesignated	22,592
Total fund equity	56,731
Total liabilities and fund equity	$96,718

1. Which method, consumption or purchases, does the city use to account for inventories? How can you tell?
2. In the examples in the text, liabilities for accrued vacation and sick pay and for claims and judgments were not recognized in governmental funds. Yet the Dallas general fund balance sheet shows liabilities for both. What is the most probable explanation? (Dallas's schedule of long-term obligations also reports obligations, in substantially greater amounts than is shown in the general fund, both for vacation and sick pay and for the housing discrimination case settlement.)
3. A note to the financial statements states the following:

   Deferred revenues arise when a potential revenue does not meet both the "measurable" and "available" criteria for recognition in the current period. Deferred revenues also arise when resources are received by the government before it has a legal claim to them, as when grant monies are received prior to the incurrence of qualifying expenditures. In subsequent periods, when both revenue recognition criteria are met, or when the city has a legal claim to the resources, the liability for deferred revenue is removed from the general fund balance sheet and revenue is recognized.

   Assume that Dallas prepares its general fund budget on a cash basis (even though, in fact, it budgets on a basis similar to the modified accrual basis). A city official comments: "For next year we expect to budget $600 million in expenditures. Therefore, as long as we collect at least $543 million ($600 million less approximate fund equity of $57 million) in taxes and other revenues we shall end the year with a positive cash balance."

   a. Do you agree with the official? Review each of the assets and liabilities presented on the balance sheet. Indicate which are likely to generate cash (or, with respect to liabilities, require the use of cash) that will be available to meet the city's budgeted expenditures. (For example, taxes receivable, but not inventories, will generate cash that can be used to meet expenditures.) Note also any assets or obligations *not* reported on the balance sheet that might either provide additional cash or require the use of cash.

   b. From the data on the balance sheet, are you able to determine the amount of cash (and claims against it) that will be generated by the reported net assets (i.e., fund balance)? Do you agree with the member of the National Council on Governmental Accounting cited in the "In Practice" in the text that a governmental fund balance sheet fails to provide information on the resources available for future appropriation?

5-12

Nonexchange expenditures are the mirror image of nonexchange revenues.

A state government provided several grants to school districts and local governments during its fiscal year ending August 31.

1. On August 1, 2005, it announced a $2 million grant to a local school district for the purchase of computers. The district can spend the funds upon receipt. On September 15, 2005, the state mailed a check for the

full amount to the district. The district spent $1.5 million on computers during fiscal 2006 (i.e., the year ending August 31, 2006) and expects to spend the remaining $0.5 million in fiscal 2007.

2. On the same date the state announced a $10 million grant to another school district for the acquisition of equipment. However, per the provisions of this grant the state will make payments only upon receiving documentation from the district that it has incurred allowable costs. In fiscal 2006, the district incurred and documented allowable costs of $8 million. Of this, the state paid only $7 million, expecting to reimburse the district for the balance early in fiscal 2007.
3. The state also announced a $5 million grant to a third school district, again for the acquisition of computers. The state will make annual five $1 million payments to the district, starting on September 15, 2006. The district is required to expend the funds in the fiscal year in which they are received.
4. Toward the end of fiscal 2006, it awarded a $500,000 contract to the accounting department of a local university to support a review of the state's cost accounting system. The department intends to carry out the review during 2007 and issue its final report to the state in early 2008. Upon announcing the award, the state made an advance payment of $100,000 to the department. It intends to pay the balance when the department completes the project to the satisfaction of the state.
   a. Prepare the journal entries that the state would make in fiscal 2006 to record the awards in an appropriate governmental fund. Briefly justify the amount of expenditure that you recognized.
   b. What, if any, adjustment to the amount of expenditure recognized would the state have to make in preparing its government-wide statements?
   c. Describe briefly how the recipients would account, in both fund and government-wide statements for the awards.

SOLUTION TO EXERCISE FOR REVIEW AND SELF-STUDY

1. Journal entries (in millions)

a.

Cash	$6.00	
Property tax revenue		$6.00

To record property tax revenues

b. The general rule is that revenues and expenditures are recognized in governmental funds, such as special revenue funds, on an accrual basis. There are exceptions, but wages and salaries are *not* among them.

Wages and salaries—expenditure	$4.50	
Cash		$4.10
Accrued wages and salaries		0.40

To record wages and salaries

c. Vacation leave should be accrued as a liability as long as employees have earned the time off and the employer is expected to compensate employees for it in the future. However, only the portion of the liability expected to be liquidated with expendable available financial resources should be reported as a governmental fund obligation. The balance should be reported as a liability in the schedule of long-term obligations.

Vacation pay expenditure	$0.20	
Cash		$0.20

To record vacation pay

d. Unused sick leave should be accrued only insofar as employers expect to compensate employees for the leave as a termination benefit. In this case, the leave only accumulates, it does not vest. Thus, the city will not have to compensate employees for leave not taken as a termination benefit. It should charge as an expenditure only the amount that was liquidated with expendable financial resources. It need *not* report a liability even in the schedule of long-term obligations.

Sick leave expenditure	$0.14	
Cash		$0.14

To record sick-leave pay

e. Pension costs should be reported as an expenditure only insofar as they were, or will be, liquidated with expendable financial resources (in this case, actual amounts paid plus amounts to be paid early in the following year). The difference between what the city *should* contribute and what it *actually* contributes should be reported as a liability in the schedule of long-term obligations.

Pension expenditure	$0.30	
Cash		$0.25
Current obligation to pension fund		0.05

To record pension contributions

f. Since the city accounts for inventories on the purchases method, it should report as an expenditure only the supplies actually acquired. However, it should give balance sheet recognition to material amounts of inventory on hand at year-end and should establish reserves for both encumbrances and inventories on hand.

Supplies expenditure	$0.70	
Cash		$0.50
Accounts payable		0.20

To record supplies purchased

Encumbrances	$0.10	
Reserve for encumbrances		$0.10

To give recognition to supplies ordered but not yet received

Supplies inventory	$0.15	
Fund balance—reserve for supplies		$0.15

To record the inventory on hand at year-end

g. Capital assets should be recognized as expenditures as acquired. The proceeds of noncurrent debt issued to finance them should be reported as "other financing sources." Interest and principal on long-term debt need not be recognized as expenditures until they are due.

Capital assets—expenditures	$1.00	
Other financing sources—installment note proceeds		$0.8
Cash		0.2

To record the acquisition of equipment

2. Statements

Statement of Revenues, Expenditures, and Changes in Fund Balance Year Ending December 31, 2005

Property tax revenue		$6.00
Expenditures:		
Wages and salaries	$4.50	
Vacation pay	0.20	
Sick leave	0.14	
Pensions	0.30	
Supplies	0.70	
Acquisition of capital assets	1.00	6.84
Excess of revenues over expenditures		(0.84)
Other financing sources:		
Proceeds of installment notes		0.80
Increase in supplies inventory		0.15
Total other financing sources		0.95
Excess of revenues and other financing sources over expenditures		0.11
Fund balance, beginning of year		0.00
Fund balance, end of year		$0.11

Balance Sheet Parks and Recreation Fund As of December 31, 2005

Assets	
Cash	$0.61
Supplies inventory	0.15
Total assets	$0.76
Liabilities and fund balances	
Accounts payable	$0.20
Accrued wages and salaries	0.40
Current obligation to pension fund	0.05
Total liabilities	0.65
Fund balance	
Reserve for encumbrances	0.10
Reserve for inventories	0.15
Unreserved	(0.14)
Total fund balance	0.11
Total liabilities and fund balance	$0.76

Note: The increase in supplies inventory must be reported as an "other financing source" since the addition of the inventory to assets was offset directly by a credit to fund balance (albeit "fund balance—reserve for supplies"). It was not credited to a revenue account and thereby not included among the items that affect the "excess of revenues over expenditures."

3. The following assets or liabilities would be reported in the schedule of capital assets and long-term obligations:

Fixed (capital) assets	
Parks and recreation equipment	$1.00
Long-term obligations	
Obligation for vacation pay	$0.60
Obligation for pensions	0.07
Installment note	0.80

4. *Impact on government-wide statements*
   a. No difference. The taxes would be recognized as revenue.
   b. No difference. Wages and salaries would be accrued—same as on the fund statements.
   c. The entire $0.26 million of vacation pay would be accrued and charged as an expense.
   d. The same measurement rules apply to sick leave on both the full and modified accrual basis. In this case, since the leave would not be paid as a termination benefit (it does not vest), only the $0.14 million paid need be charged as an expense.
   e. The entire $0.37 million earned by employees (the required contribution per the actuaries) would be charged as an expense.
   f. Supplies must be accounted for on a consumption basis. Hence, the $0.55 of supplies used would be charged as an expense.
   g. Capital assets would be capitalized and depreciated. The $0.05 (approximately) of interest for the period must be accrued and charged as an expense.

CHAPTER 6

Accounting for Capital Projects and Debt Service

LEARNING OBJECTIVES

After studying this chapter you should understand:

- Why and how governments use capital projects funds to account for resources accumulated to acquire long-lived assets
- Why and how governments use debt service funds to account for resources accumulated to repay debt principal and interest
- How governments account for special assessments
- What arbitrage is and why it concerns governments
- The nature of debt refundings, the circumstances in which governments can benefit from them, and the manner in which governments account for them

As indicated in previous chapters, both governments and other not-for-profits maintain separate funds (accounting and reporting entities) for resources to be used to acquire long-lived assets and to service debt. Governments classify these funds as *governmental*, as opposed to proprietary. In other not-for-profits, the resources in these funds are categorized as either *unrestricted* or *temporarily restricted*, depending on their source. For the most part, the principles of revenue and expenditure recognition presented in earlier chapters are applicable to these funds. Nevertheless, since these funds are used to account for transactions having unique features and involving sizable amounts of resources, they warrant special consideration.

Our concern in this chapter is with the *resources* to acquire assets and to service debts, not with the assets or debts themselves. In governments, the resources to acquire capital assets, especially those that are financed with debt, are generally accounted for in **capital projects funds.** However, the costs of capital assets may also be accounted for in the general fund or even special revenue funds, particularly if they are relatively low. Since the general and special revenue funds, like the capital projects funds, are governmental funds, the accounting entries and issues are similar. The resources to service debts are typically accounted for in **debt service funds.** Accounting for the assets and liabilities themselves is addressed in Chapters 7 and 8.

Our focus is on each of the funds as independent fiscal and accounting entities. Both funds are governmental and accordingly are accounted for on a modified accrual basis. However, like other governmental funds, when they are consolidated with other funds in government-wide statements, their accounts are adjusted so that they are on a full accrual basis.

First we discuss capital projects and debt service funds. Then we address the related issues of special assessments, arbitrage, and debt refunding.

HOW DO GOVERNMENTS ACCOUNT FOR CAPITAL PROJECTS FUNDS?

Governments establish capital projects funds to account for resources dedicated to the purchase and construction of capital facilities (other than those to be financed by proprietary and trust funds). They may maintain a separate fund for each major project or combine two or more projects in a single fund. Capital facilities include buildings, infrastructure projects (such as roads, bridges, airports, and sewer systems), and plant and equipment.

REASONS FOR MAINTAINING CAPITAL PROJECTS FUNDS

Governments *must* maintain capital projects funds for resources that are *legally restricted* to the acquisition of capital assets. Some governments also maintain capital projects funds for resources they have set aside for capital purposes at their own discretion. Although this practice is permitted, it may mislead statement users into assuming that the resources are legally restricted when they are not.

Major capital projects are most commonly financed with bonds or other forms of long-term debt, but they may also be funded by grants, special tax levies, or assessments. Restrictions on capital project resources usually stem from debt covenants or from legislation authorizing the taxes or assessments. Generally the restrictions are exceedingly specific as to how the resources may be used. For example, the funds may be used only for the construction of a particular bridge or the purchase of a narrowly defined type of equipment.

BASIS OF ACCOUNTING

Capital projects funds are similar to special revenue funds in that their revenues are restricted to special purposes. Accordingly, the principles of revenue and expenditure spelled out in Chapters 4 and 5, which are applicable to all governmental funds, are also appropriate for capital projects funds. Capital projects funds are accounted for on the **modified accrual basis.** In government-wide statements the funds are accounted for on a full accrual basis (as discussed in previous chapters with respect to governmental funds in general) and consolidated with the government's other governmental funds.

BUDGETARY ENTRIES

As pointed out previously, budgetary entries give formal accounting recognition to the budget and enhance control. They help assure that expenditures do not exceed authorizations.

Governments generally budget capital expenditures on the basis of projects rather than periods. Therefore, they may not find it necessary to prepare an annual budget, to make annual budgetary entries, or to include comparisons of actual-to-budget expenditures for the year in their financial statements.

Nevertheless, budgetary accounts are as useful in maximizing control over project expenditures as period expenditures are. Therefore, the GASB requires budgetary account integration in circumstances in which control cannot readily be established by means other than a budget. Integration is essential, for example, "where numerous construction projects are being financed through a capital projects fund or where such projects are being constructed by the government's labor force."[1] On the other hand, when a government can establish control by entering into a fixed-price contract with a single vendor or construction company, then budgetary entries are not necessary.

The budgetary entries for capital projects would follow the pattern illustrated in Chapter 3 for other governmental funds. Budgetary entries are strictly an internal control mechanism; they do not affect year-end financial statements.

REPORTING BOND PROCEEDS AND ISSUE COST

Government long-term obligations can take many forms, the most common of which is bonds. Bonds are formal certificates of indebtedness, most frequently issued by governments for the long-term. The discussion in this section can be generalized to other forms of debt, such as leases and certificates of participation, which often differ from bonds more in legal form than in economic substance.

Governmental funds, including capital projects funds, do not report long-term obligations. Therefore, when the proceeds of bonds or other long-term obligations are received by a capital projects fund, they must be accounted for as "other financing sources."

When governments issue bonds, they seldom receive in cash an amount equal exactly to the bonds' face value. There are at least two sources of the difference between face value and cash received:

- ***Issue costs.*** The bond underwriters (the brokers and dealers who will distribute the securities to other brokers and dealers or sell them directly to investors) charge for their services and will withhold a portion of the gross proceeds as their fees.
- ***Premiums and discounts.*** The bond **coupon rate** (the stated interest rate) is rarely exactly equal to the market rate at the time of sale. Bonds may be printed

[1] *Codification*, Section 1700.119.

with a coupon rate days or weeks prior to the issue date. Market rates fluctuate constantly, and the market rate that will prevail at the time of issue cannot be determined accurately in advance. The exact rate that the bonds will yield is established by issuing the bonds at a price greater or less than face value. A bond sold to yield an interest rate *greater* than the coupon rate will be sold at a *discount*. Because the prevailing rate is greater than the coupon rate, the bond is of less value to an investor than a bond with a comparable face value paying the prevailing rate; hence, the investor will pay less than the face value for it. Conversely, a bond sold to yield an interest rate *less* than the coupon rate will be sold at a *premium*. Because the prevailing rate is less than the coupon rate, the bond is of greater value than a bond with a comparable face value paying the prevailing rate.

Governments should report the underwriting and other issue costs as an expenditure. If the issue costs are not set out separately from premiums and discounts, then the government should estimate them.

EXAMPLE *Bond Issue Costs*

A city issues $10.0 million of bonds at a premium of $0.2 million. It incurs $0.6 million in issue costs, and thereby nets $9.6 million.

The following entry would be appropriate:

Cash	$9.6	
Expenditure—bond issue costs	0.6	
Other financing source—bond proceeds (face value)		$10.0
Other financing source—bond proceeds (bond premium)		0.2
To record the issuance of bonds and related issue costs		

ACCOUNTING FOR BOND PREMIUMS AND DISCOUNTS

Bond premiums and discounts become an accounting issue only insofar as there is uncertainty as to how the "excess" cash will be disposed of and the manner of compensating for any cash deficiency.

EXAMPLE *Bond Premiums and Discounts*

A government authorizes two highway construction projects, Project #1 and Project #2, each to cost no more than $50 million. To finance the projects, it issues two series of bonds, Series #1 and Series #2, each with a face value of $50 million. Both mature in thirty years (sixty semiannual periods) and pay interest at an annual rate of 6 percent (semiannual rate of 3 percent). Owing to prevailing interest rates of 5.9 percent on the issue date, Series #1 is issued for $50,699,000 (a premium of $699,000). However, as a consequence of subsequent increases in prevailing interest rates to 6.1 percent, Series #2 is issued for $49,315,000 (a discount of $685,000).

The initial entries to record both bond issues are straightforward:

Cash	$50,699,000	
Other financing sources—bond proceeds (face value)		$50,000,000
Other financing sources—bond proceeds (bond premium)		699,000
To record the issue of Series #1		

Cash	$49,315,000	
Other financing sources—bond proceeds (bond discount)	685,000	
Other financing sources—bond proceeds (face value)		$50,000,000
To record the issue of Series #2		

Both projects were authorized to cost no more than $50 million. Therefore, the $699,000 premium should not be used to add unauthorized frills to the planned highway. Instead, it should be applied to future interest payments. The bonds were printed with a coupon rate of 6 percent. Owing to favorable market conditions, the government was able to borrow funds at only 5.9 percent. Still, its annual cash interest payments will be $3.0 million (6 percent of $50 million)—not $2,950,000 (5.9 percent of $50 million). The premium of $699,000 can be seen as interest that investors paid the government "up front" to receive "extra" interest of $0.1 million each year over the life of the bonds. Accordingly, the government should transfer the $699,000 to the *debt service fund*—the fund that will be used to accumulate the resources required to pay the interest and principal on the bonds. The following entry would give effect to this policy:

Other financing use—nonreciprocal transfer of bond premium to debt service fund	$699,000	
Due to debt service fund		$699,000
To record the premium payable to the debt service fund		

Accounting for the discount is generally not the mirror image of that for the premium. A bond discount, like a bond premium, adjusts the bond issue price so as to align the coupon rate with the prevailing rate. Because of the unfavorable market conditions, the government had to pay interest at a rate greater than the bond coupon rate. Therefore, it received less than the face value of the bonds, and less than it apparently planned to spend on the capital project. When the bonds are issued at a premium, the capital projects fund can transfer resources to the debt service fund. However, when the bonds are issued at a discount the debt service fund will not have resources available for transfer to the capital projects fund. Therefore, the government has a choice. It can either reduce the scale of the project or make up the deficiency by some other means. If it elects to reduce the scale of the project, then no further journal entries are required. If it opts to fund the shortfall by other means, then the source of the funds will dictate the additional accounting entries. For example, if the government were to appropriate $685,000 of general fund resources, then the following capital projects fund entry would be necessary:

Due from general fund	$685,000	
Other financing sources—nonreciprocal transfer from general fund		$685,000
To record the anticipated transfer from the general fund to compensate for the bond discount		

COMPREHENSIVE EXAMPLE *Main Types of Transactions Accounted For in Capital Projects Funds*

The voters of New City authorize the issuance of $20 million in general obligation bonds to finance the construction of a new highway. The project is expected to cost $30 million (including bond issue costs), with the additional $10 million to be financed with a state grant. Although the grant may be paid in advance, it is intended to reimburse the city for actual costs incurred.

Authorizing the Project and Recording the Budget

The city is required to account for the resources in a fund dedicated exclusively to this project. It elects to adopt a budget and integrate it into its accounts.

Estimated bond proceeds	$20	
Estimated grant revenues	10	
Fund balance		$30
To record estimated revenues and other financing sources		

Fund balance	$30	
Appropriations		$30
To record appropriations (estimated expenditures)		

Issuing the Bonds

The city issues $20 million of bonds. Owing to favorable market conditions, the bonds are sold for $20.2 million. After deducting issue costs of $0.15 million, the sale nets $20.05 million.

Cash	$20.05	
Issues costs (expenditures)	0.15	
Other financing sources—bond proceeds (face value)		$20.00
Other financing sources—bond proceeds (bond premium)		0.20
To record the issuance of bonds		

Transferring the Premium to the Debt Service Fund

The city transfers the premium to the debt service fund.

Other financing use—nonreciprocal transfer of bond premium to debt service fund	$0.05	
Cash		$0.05
To transfer the bond premium, net of issue costs, to the debt service fund		

Encumbering Available Resources

The city signs several construction-related contracts for goods and services to cost $16 million. Capital projects funds, no less than the general fund, can avoid overspending by encumbering fund balance in the amount of purchase orders and similar commitments.

Encumbrances	$16	
Reserve for encumbrances		$16
To encumber $16 million for contracts signed		

Recording Grants

The city receives $8 million of its grant from the state. To be consistent with the approach taken in other governmental funds, the recognition of reimbursement grant revenue should be expenditure driven. Hence, the city should record the advance payment from the state as deferred revenue.

Cash	$8	
Deferred revenue (grants)		$8
To record the advance from the state		

Recording Expenditures

The city receives and pays contractor invoices of $15 million for construction and related services.

Expenditures—construction related	$15	
Cash		$15
To record construction and related expenditures		

Capital projects funds are maintained to account for resources that will be expended on capital projects, not for the capital projects themselves. Therefore, construction outlays are charged as expenditures, not construction in process.

The new model, unlike the one it replaces, requires that infrastructure assets be accounted for similarly to other types of capital assets. As defined by the GASB, infrastructure assets are "long-lived capital assets that normally are stationary in nature and normally can be preserved for a significantly greater number of years than most capital assets." They include roads, bridges, tunnels, drainage systems, water and sewer systems, dams, and lighting systems. They do not, however, include buildings, except those that are an ancillary part of a network of infrastructure assets.[2] Hence the government should report the construction in process in its schedule of capital assets and its government-wide statements.

Upon recording the expenditures in the capital projects fund, the city must reverse the related encumbrance accounts and recognize the revenue that was previously deferred.

Reserve for encumbrances	$15	
Encumbrances		$15
To reverse the encumbrance entry upon receipt of services		

Deferred revenue (grants)	$8	
Revenue from grants		$8
To recognize grant revenue upon incurring allowable costs		

This entry is based on the assumption that the government recognizes grant revenue as soon as it has incurred any costs that the grant is permitted to cover. Hence, it does not divide its costs between those applicable to the bonds and those applicable to the grant.

Recognizing Investment Earnings

The city invests $5 million in U.S. Treasury notes so as to earn a return on temporarily available cash.

Marketable securities	$5	
Cash		$5
To record the purchase of Treasury bills		

As of year-end it has earned $0.15 million in interest, but it does not expect to actually receive the interest until the notes mature. However, the accrued interest is reflected

[2] GASB Statement No. 34, *Basic Financial Statements—and Management's Discussion and Analysis—for State and Local Governments*, para. 19.

in the market price of the notes. As observed in Chapter 4, GASB pronouncements require that appreciation in the fair value of investments be recognized as revenue.

Marketable securities	$0.15	
Investment revenue		$0.15
To recognize appreciation in investments		

Closing the Accounts

If a government needs to prepare an operating statement that shows revenues, expenditures, and similar accounts for the particular year (as it would for general purpose external reporting), then it can readily close these accounts, along with the related budgetary accounts, in the manner illustrated in Chapter 3. Closing the accounts would reduce the balances in these accounts to zero and enable the government to record the revenues and expenditures of the following year. If the budget were for the entire project, not for a particular year, then the government would have to restore the budgetary accounts at the start of the next year in the amount of the balances not yet expended.

However, if the government intends to prepare reports that indicate only cumulative amounts of revenues and expenditures over the life of the project, then there is no need to close the accounts. They can remain open until the project is completed. Then, the accounts can be closed and remaining resources disposed of in accordance with the government's policy or applicable legal or contractual specifications. The transfer of unspent resources to another fund would be classified as a nonreciprocal transfer.

Table 6-1 presents an operating statement and balance sheet for the capital projects fund.

HOW DO GOVERNMENTS ACCOUNT FOR RESOURCES DEDICATED TO DEBT SERVICE?

Debt service funds are maintained to account for resources accumulated to pay interest and principal on long-term debt. Debt service funds do *not* account for the long-term debt itself. Indeed, the only circumstance in which the principal of debt is reported as an obligation is when it has matured but actual payment has been delayed.

REASONS FOR MAINTAINING DEBT SERVICE FUNDS

The GASB *Codification* directs that debt service funds be established when:

- Legally required, or
- Financial resources are being accumulated for principal and interest payments maturing in future years.[3]

Legal mandates to maintain debt service funds are commonly incorporated into agreements associated with the issuance of the debt. Lenders want assurance that the funds will be available to make timely payments of interest and principal. Therefore, they may require that the borrower maintain a specified amount, perhaps one year's interest, in a "reserve" fund—similar to the way a landlord requires a tenant to provide a deposit of one month's rent.

Debt service funds may receive their resources from several sources:

- Transfers from the general fund

[3] *Codification*, Section 1300.107; NCGA Statement No. 1, *Governmental Accounting and Financial Reporting Principles* (1979), para. 73.

TABLE 6–1
Capital Projects Fund—Construction of Highway

Statement of Revenues, Expenditures and Changes in Fund Balance (in Millions)
For the City's Fiscal Year

Revenues	
Grant from state	$ 8.00
Investment revenue	0.15
Total revenues	8.15
Expenditures	
Bond issue costs	0.15
Construction related	15.00
Total expenditures	$15.15
Excess of revenues over expenditures	(7.00)
Other financing sources (uses)	
Proceeds of bonds (including premium)	20.20
Nonreciprocal transfer of premium to debt service fund	(0.05)
Total other financing sources (uses)	20.15
Excess of revenues and net financing sources over expenditures	13.15
Fund balance, beginning of year	0.00
Fund balance, end of year	$13.15

Balance Sheet
As of the End of the City's Fiscal Year

Assets	
Cash	$ 8.00
Marketable securities	5.15
Total assets	$13.15
Fund balance	
Reserved for encumbrances	$ 1.00
Unreserved	12.15
Total fund balance	$13.15

- Special taxes restricted to the payment of debt (e.g., to construct a new high school, a school district may dedicate a portion of its property tax to the repayment of high school bonds)
- Special assessments (charges to an identifiable group of residents who will receive a disproportionate share of the benefits of a project for which long-term debt was issued)

As with capital project funds, governments may be required to maintain several independent debt service funds or may be permitted to combine some or all into common funds.

BASIS OF ACCOUNTING

Like capital projects funds, debt service funds are *governmental* funds, which are accounted for on the modified accrual basis.

As discussed in Chapter 5, GASB standards stipulate that the major exception to the general rule of expenditure accrual relates to unmatured principal and interest on general long-term debt. Until the period in which they must be paid, interest and principal are *not* considered current liabilities of the debt service fund, as they do not require the expenditure of existing fund assets. Moreover, the resources required for payment are unlikely to be appropriated—and transferred to the debt service fund—until the period in which the interest and principal actually must be paid, not before. To accrue the debt service fund expenditure and liability in one period but record the transfer of financial resources for debt service purposes in a later period, it has been argued, would be confusing and would result in overstatement of debt service fund expenditures and liabilities and understatement of the fund balance. The standards make clear, however, that when the general fund appropriates resources for debt service in one year for payment early (within one month) in the next, then the government *may* (but is not required to) accrue the expenditure and related liability in the debt service fund.[4]

In contrast to the manner in which the expenditures for debt service are accounted for, the interest *revenue* on bonds held as investments is, in effect, accrued as earned, since investments must be stated at fair value and interest earned but not yet paid affects fair value.

BUDGETARY ENTRIES

Both budgets and budgetary entries are less needed, and accordingly, less common in debt service funds than in other governmental funds. Insofar as debt service funds receive their resources from other funds, then, overall internal control is established by the budgets in other funds. Moreover, the expenditures of debt service funds are typically limited to payments of principal and interest, the amount and timing of which are established by the terms of the outstanding debt.

However, if the resources of a debt service fund are derived mainly from special taxes or assessments, then an appropriations budget, and suitable accounting entries, may help enhance internal control and demonstrate legal compliance. In many circumstances the decision of whether to adopt an appropriations budget is beyond the control of accountants; it is specified in legislation authorizing the debt or establishing the fund.

COMPREHENSIVE EXAMPLE *Main Types of Transactions Accounted For in Debt Service Funds*

In January 2005, Carver City establishes a debt service fund to account for a serial issue of $100 million of 6 percent bonds sold at a premium of $0.2 million. Principal is to be repaid evenly over a period of twenty years beginning on December 31, 2005. Interest is payable semiannually, beginning June 30, 2005. Of the bond proceeds, $2 million is to be retained in the debt service fund as a reserve for payment of interest and principal.

The debt is to be repaid from a voter-approved addition to the property tax, plus earnings from debt service fund investments. However, any revenue shortage is to be made up by a general fund appropriation. Although the revenues generated by the property tax are expected to increase over time, the city estimates that in 2005 it will collect only $8 million, far less than the required interest and principal payments.

Serial bonds are repaid in installments over the life of the issue, as distinguished from term bonds, which mature on a single specified date. The first installment may be delayed for several years after the serial bonds have been issued, and uniform payments may not be required. The amount of principal repaid with each installment, although established in advance, may vary from year to year. Serial bonds are, in essence, nothing more than a collection of term bonds, each of which matures at a different time.

[4] GASB Interpretation No. 6, *Recognition and Measurement of Certain Liabilities and Expenditures in Governmental Fund Financial Statements* (March 2000), para. 13.

Recording the Budget

The city estimates its revenues and expenditures as reflected in the entry that follows:

Estimated revenues—investments	$ 60,000	
Estimated revenues—property taxes	8,000,000	
Estimated transfer-in—capital projects fund	2,200,000	
Estimated transfer-in—general fund	2,940,000	
Appropriations—interest		$6,000,000
Appropriations—principal		5,000,000
Fund balance		2,200,000
To record the budget		

Transferring-in the Bond Premium and the Amount to Be Held as a Reserve

The bonds are issued and the proceeds are placed in a capital projects fund. The premium of $200,000 and the $2 million to be held in reserve are transferred from the capital projects fund to the debt service fund.

Cash	$2,200,000	
Other financing source—nonreciprocal transfer from the capital projects fund		$2,200,000
To record the transfer-in of the bond premium and the amount to be placed in reserve		

The debt itself would be recorded only in the government-wide statements and in off-the-balance sheet schedules, not in the debt service fund.

Recognizing Investment Earnings

The city purchases as an investment $1 million (face value) long-term U.S. Treasury bonds. Acquired in the secondary market, the bonds pay interest at a rate of 6 percent annually (3 percent each semiannual period) and mature in seven years. They are purchased for $894,369—a price that provides an effective yield of 8 percent annually (4 percent semiannually).

Investment in bonds	$894,369	
Cash		$894,369
To record purchase of bonds as an investment		

As discussed previously, investments will be carried at fair value. Therefore the bond discount need not be reported separately from the bonds.

During the year the city receives two semiannual interest payments of $30,000 (3 percent of $1 million). Meanwhile, the fair value of the bonds increases by $5,775 in the first period and by $6,006 the second period. In the absence of changes in prevailing interest rates, the fair value of the bonds can be expected to increase each period by the amount by which the discount would otherwise be amortized. In that way, their fair value at maturity would be equal to their face value. In this instance, the increases in value can be attributed entirely to the amortization of the discount.

Cash	$30,000	
Investment in bonds	5,775	
Investment revenue		$35,775
To record the first period's interest		

Cash	$30,000	
Investment in bonds	6,006	
Investment revenue		$36,006
To record the second period's interest		

Recognizing Tax Revenue

During the year the city collects $7.5 million of the $8.0 million in dedicated property taxes due during the period. It expects to collect the balance within sixty days of year-end.

Cash	$7,500,000	
Property taxes receivable	500,000	
Property tax revenue		$8,000,000
To record property taxes		

Property taxes are recognized as revenue on the same basis as if recorded in the general fund or any other special revenue fund. Taxes restricted to a specific purpose may be recorded initially in the general fund, especially if, as in this situation, they are part of a larger tax levy. However, it is generally preferable that they be reported directly in the fund to which they are dedicated.

Recording the Transfer from the General Fund

During the year the city, as budgeted, transfers $2,940,000 from the general fund to the debt service fund:

Cash	$2,940,000	
Other financing source— nonreciprocal transfer from the general fund		$2,940,000
To record the transfer from the general fund		

Recording the Payment of Interest and Principal

The city makes its first payment of interest on the $100 million of bonds, as due, on June 30:

Expenditure—debt service, interest	$3,000,000	
Matured interest payable		$3,000,000
To record the obligation for the first payment of interest		
Matured interest payable	$3,000,000	
Cash		$3,000,000
To record the first payment of interest		

Many governments use a bank or other fiscal agent to distribute payments of interest and principal to bondholders. If they do, then any cash transferred to the fiscal agent should be reported as an asset "cash with fiscal agent." "Cash with fiscal agent," along with the liability "matured interest (or principal)," should be reduced as the fiscal agent reports that it made the required payments to the bondholders.

Although the second payment of interest and the first payment of principal are due on December 31, 2005, the city does not actually mail the checks until January 2, 2006. Nevertheless, the expenditure and related obligation must be recognized when the payments are due:

Expenditure—debt service, interest	$3,000,000	
Expenditure—debt service, principal	5,000,000	
Matured interest payable		$3,000,000
Matured bonds payable		5,000,000

To record the obligation for the second payment of interest and the first payment of principal

Closing the Accounts

At year-end, the city would have to close the non-balance sheet accounts:

Appropriations—interest	$6,000,000	
Appropriations—principal	5,000,000	
Other financing source—nonreciprocal transfer from the general fund	2,940,000	
Other financing source—nonreciprocal transfer from the capital projects fund	2,200,000	
Property tax revenue	8,000,000	
Investment revenue	71,781	
Estimated revenues—investments		$ 60,000
Estimated revenues—property taxes		8,000,000
Expenditure—debt service, interest		6,000,000
Expenditure—debt service, principal		5,000,000
Estimated transfer-in—capital projects fund		2,200,000
Estimated transfers-in—general fund		2,940,000
Fund balance		11,781

To close the accounts

Table 6-2 presents a 2005 statement of revenues, expenditures and changes in fund balance and balance sheet for the debt service fund.

HOW DO GOVERNMENTS HANDLE SPECIAL ASSESSMENTS?

Governments sometimes construct capital projects or provide services that primarily benefit a particular group of property owners rather than the general citizenry. To assign the costs to the beneficiaries, they assess (i.e., charge) those taxpayers the entire, or a substantial share, of the cost of the project or services. Generally, the majority of property owners within the area must vote their approval of the particular project or services and of the assessments. They can ordinarily pay the assessments in installments over several years, but must pay interest on unpaid balances.

REASONS FOR SPECIAL ASSESSMENTS

Cities and towns often levy special assessments when taxpayers in areas beyond their jurisdiction either want to be annexed to the city or town or want to benefit from certain of its facilities and services. In some circumstances, the area to be assessed may be designated a special purpose government district (such as a local improvement district) and may be authorized to levy and collect the assessments. In others, the assessments are levied and administered by the city or town itself.

TABLE 6-2
Debt Service Fund

Statement of Revenues, Expenditures, and Changes in Fund Balance
For Year Ending December 31, 2002

Revenues	
Property taxes	$ 8,000,000
Investments	71,781
Total revenues	8,071,781
Expenditures	
Debt service, interest	6,000,000
Debt service, principal	5,000,00
Total expenditures	11,000,000
Excess (deficiency) of revenues over expenditures	(2,928,219)
Other financing sources	
Nonreciprocal transfer from the general fund	2,940,000
Nonreciprocal transfer from the capital projects fund	2,200,000
Total other financing sources	5,140,000
Excess of revenues and other financing sources over expenditures	2,211,781
Fund balance, beginning of year	0
Fund balance, end of year	$ 2,211,781

Balance Sheet as of December 31, 2002

Assets	
Cash	$ 8,805,631
Property taxes receivable	500,000
Investment in bonds	906,150
Total assets	$10,211,781
Liabilities and fund balance	
Matured interest payable	$ 3,000,000
Matured bonds payable	5,000,000
Total liabilities	8,000,000
Fund balance	2,211,781
Total liabilities and fund balance	$10,211,781

Most often, special assessments are levied for infrastructure improvements, such as water and sewer lines, sidewalks, roads, and street lights. They could also be for discrete projects such as parks, tennis courts, swimming pools, and recreation centers.

Special assessments for services are normally levied when a community wants greater services than the government would normally provide. For example, a community that would otherwise be protected by a volunteer fire department may request that it be serviced by a professional fire department. Or, a neighborhood may petition the city to maintain and provide electricity for its street lights (perhaps after the neighborhood installs the lights itself), to provide trash collection service, or to snowplow its roads. Assessments for services present few, if any, unique accounting and reporting problems. They should be accounted for in the fund that best reflects the nature of the assessment and the services to be provided—usually either the general fund, a special revenue fund, or an enterprise fund.

Inasmuch as the enhancements in either infrastructure or services may provide at least some benefits to the citizenry at large (for example, improved roads are not for the exclusive use of the taxpayers who live along them), governments may share in the cost of the improvements. Therefore, the projects may be financed in part by direct government contributions, by general obligation debt, or by revenue debt (debt to be repaid from user fees, such as water and sewer charges).

Governments ensure collectibility of the assessments by attaching liens against the affected properties. Thus, they can foreclose upon delinquent property owners and can prevent the properties from being sold or transferred until the assessments are current.

Like other financing mechanisms, special assessments may be subject to misuse. The accompanying "In Practice: Alleged Abuse of Special Assessments" illustrates an alleged impropriety in the use of service-type assessments.

ACCOUNTING FOR SPECIAL ASSESSMENT PROJECTS AND THE RELATED DEBT

Capital improvement special assessments involve two distinct, albeit overlapping, phases: the construction and financing phase and the debt service phase.

In the first phase, a project is authorized and the property owners are assessed. To finance the project, the government issues long-term debt. It then undertakes construction.

In the second phase, the property owners pay their assessments and the debt is serviced. Whereas the first phase is usually fairly short—the time required to complete the project—the second may extend over many years.

Until the late 1980s, special assessments were accounted for in a special type of fund called a *special assessment fund.* Today, however, special assessments are accounted for just as any other capital projects are. The construction phase is accounted for in a capital projects fund. The debt service phase is accounted for in a debt service fund.

When a government issues debt to finance a special assessment capital project, it should place the proceeds in a capital projects fund. It should account for issue costs,

IN PRACTICE

Alleged Abuse of Special Assessments

A Michigan lawmaker has introduced a bill intended to end what some see as abuses of special assessments. Owing to resistance to property tax hikes, several Michigan towns have established special districts to provide basic services, such as fire and police protection and ambulance transportation. The services are to be financed by assessments against property owners.

The assessments have come under attack because they are based on the state's equalized value of property. This value, established by the state for purposes unrelated to the service district assessments, is generally higher than the taxable value of the property. Under Michigan law, however, property taxes must be based on the taxable value of the property.

Opponents of the practice contend that the assessments are really property taxes and are being used to circumvent the state limitations on property taxes. To curb these assessments they have proposed legislation that would allow special service districts only for infrastructure improvements.

Bond analysts took a dim view of the efforts to end the alleged abuses. They warned that by closing off an important source of revenues, the legislation could negatively affect the credit standing of Michigan municipalities. It would add to their fiscal pressures, making it more difficult for them to repay their obligations and to maintain essential services.

bond premiums and discounts, and construction costs no differently from those relating to other projects.

When the government levies the special assessments, it should recognize them in a debt service fund. Special assessments are imposed nonexchange transactions. They should be recorded as assets in the period in which the government has an enforceable legal claim to the resources that it will receive. In the debt service fund itself, which like other governmental funds is accounted for on a modified accrual basis, they can be recorded as revenues only when available for expenditure. Therefore, when a government levies the special assessments, it should report the assessments receivable as *deferred* revenue. Only as it collects the assessments (or as the assessments become available to meet current year expenditures) should it recognize them as revenues. It should report contributions from the general fund or other sources just as if they were for other types of projects.

The government should account for interest and principal payable on special assessment debt in a debt service fund, no differently from that on debt relating to other projects. Thus, it should recognize expenditures (and a corresponding liability) only when the payment is actually due. It should not accrue either interest or principal.

Accounting for special assessments is illustrated in the exercise for review and self-study at the end of this chapter.

GOVERNMENT OBLIGATIONS AS TO PROPERTY OWNERS' DEBT

The key accounting issue pertaining to special assessments is if, and under what circumstances, a government should report the special assessment debt as its own debt. Special assessment debt is the primary responsibility of the property owners on whom the assessments are levied. In economic substance, though not necessarily legal form, it is usually an obligation of the property owners, not the government. Arguably, therefore, the government need not report the debt on its own financial statements.

In most circumstances, however, the government is linked to the debt in some manner. These ties can be in a variety of arrangements:

- The government itself may issue the debt (as general obligation debt) with the expectation that the special assessments will be sufficient to cover the debt service.
- To help make the debt more marketable, and lower the interest rate, the government may either back the debt with its full faith and credit or guarantee it with some other type of commitment.
- The government may have no legal commitment for the debt, but nevertheless may assume responsibility for it so as to protect its own credit standing.
- The government may agree to share in the cost of the project and thereby to be responsible for a specified proportion of the debt.

GASB Standards

GASB standards require that a government account for the debt as its own as long as it is *obligated in some manner* to assume responsibility for the debt in the event of property owner default. Conditions that would indicate that a government is obligated in some manner for the debt include the following:

- The government is obligated to honor any special assessment deficiencies.
- The government establishes a fund to pay off the debt as it matures, to purchase or redeem it prior to maturity, or to satisfy any commitments or guarantees in the event of default.

- The government explicitly indicates by contract, such as the bond agreement or offering statement, that in the event of default it *may* cover delinquencies, even if it has no legal obligation to do so.
- Legal decisions within the state or previous actions by the government make it probable that the government will assume responsibility for the debt in the event of default.

Put more strongly, the government is *obligated in some manner* unless:

- It is *prohibited* (by constitution, charter, contract, or statute) from assuming the debt in the event of property owner default, *or*
- It is not legally liable for assuming the debt and makes no statement, or gives no indication that it will, or may, honor the debt in the event of default.

If the government is obligated in some manner for the special assessment debt, then it should account for the project as just described. It should record the construction phase in a capital projects fund and the debt service phase in a debt service fund. It should report the capital assets and the special assessment debt as if they were its own—that is, in schedules of capital assets and long-term obligations and in the government-wide statements.

If the government is not obligated for the debt but simply collects the assessments from property owners and forwards them to the bondholders, then it should:

- Report the debt service transactions in an *agency* fund (reflecting the government's role as a mere agent)
- Report construction activities, like other capital improvements, in a capital projects fund
- Report the capital assets in the schedule of capital assets and the government-wide statements
- Disclose in notes to the financial statements the amount of debt and the government's role as an agent of the property owners; it should *not* report the debt in either its schedule of long-term obligations or its government-wide statements[5]

ACCOUNTING FOR SPECIAL ASSESSMENTS IN PROPRIETARY FUNDS

Governments sometimes assess property owners for projects that they would ordinarily account for in proprietary funds. These projects typically involve infrastructure associated with utilities, such as water, sewer, and power lines and related facilities.

If special assessment debt is related to, and expected to be paid from, a proprietary fund, then all transactions related to both the debt and the improvements financed by the debt should be accounted for in a proprietary fund. The government should account for the special assessment revenues and receivables on a full accrual basis and should capitalize improvements financed with the assessments in the same manner as other capital improvements.

In some situations, the governmental entity is not responsible, in any manner, for special assessment debt issued to finance improvements that are accounted for in a

[5] *Codification*, Sections S40.115–S119.

proprietary fund. Instead, the debt is an obligation exclusively of developers, property owners, or other outside parties. If so, then the government should report a "capital contribution" (in a section of its statement of revenues, expenses, and changes in net fund assets that follow "nonoperating revenue") equal to the amount of the property that it capitalized.[6]

DIFFERENCES IN GOVERNMENT-WIDE STATEMENTS

In their government-wide full accrual statements, governments would display neither debt service nor capital projects funds in separate columns, irrespective of whether the funds satisfied the criteria of "major" funds. Instead, they would combine the funds with all other governmental funds in the governmental activities column, and include the related general capital assets and long-term debt. However, inasmuch as the resources of both the capital projects and the debt service funds may be restricted by the bond indentures to asset acquisition or debt service, the nature of the restriction should be clearly conveyed. This can be accomplished by displaying the government's net assets (i.e., its fund balances—assets minus liabilities) in three sections: invested in capital less related debt, restricted, and unrestricted. The invested-in-capital component would include the government's general capital assets, less its capital related debt. The restricted component would show the net assets set aside in capital projects, debt service, and other restricted funds. Thus, for example:

Net assets		
Invested in capital assets, net of related debt		$200
Restricted to:		
Capital projects	$10	
Debt service	5	
Other purposes	3	18
Unrestricted		25
Total net assets		$243

It might appear that the amount shown as restricted to capital projects would exactly equal the combined fund balances (i.e., net assets) of the government's capital projects funds and that the amount shown as restricted to debt service would exactly equal the combined fund balances (i.e., net assets) of its debt service funds. Such is not always the case. As was emphasized in Chapters 4 and 5, the government-wide statements are prepared on a full accrual basis whereas the fund statements are prepared on a modified accrual basis. Thus, revenues of the government-wide statements would be subject to the same standards as applicable to the fund statements with the notable exception that the "available" test would not have to be met. Expenses would also be subject to the same standards, except that the several exceptions—those that transform the full accrual basis into the modified accrual basis—would not apply to the government-wide statements. Thus, in government-wide, but not in fund, statements:

- Interest on long-term debt would be accrued and charged as an expense as a function of time, irrespective of when payment is actually due.
- Discounts and premiums on bonds payable would be amortized over time—just as they currently are on the financial statements of businesses as well as the enterprise funds of governments.

[6] *Codification*, Section S40.121–122.

- Property taxes that are dedicated to debt service would be recognized as revenues in the year for which they are levied, even if they wouldn't be collected within sixty days of year-end.
- The principal of (but not the interest on) special assessments would be recognized as both assets and revenues (as opposed to deferred revenues) in the period in which the government has a legal claim against the resources to be received, irrespective of when the resources will actually be received. At the same time, however, the full amount of the debt incurred to construct the capital assets would be reported as a liability. Similarly, the construction costs would be capitalized as assets as they are incurred.

WHY IS ARBITRAGE A CONCERN OF GOVERNMENTS?

Arbitrage, as it applies to municipalities (i.e., state and local governments), refers to the issuance of debt at relatively low, tax-exempt rates of interest and the investment of the proceeds in taxable securities yielding a higher return. Arbitrage is of major concern to governments and can have important financial and accounting consequences for both capital projects and debt service funds.

The interest paid on debt issued for *public* purposes by state and local governments is not subject to federal taxation. The federal government draws the distinction between public and private purposes so as to prevent governments from providing assistance to private corporations by substituting their own low-interest, tax-exempt debt for that of the companies.

State and local governments can issue bonds for public purposes at lower interest rates than either the federal government or private corporations because, taking into account the required taxes on the taxable bonds, the tax-exempt bonds can provide the investor a return equivalent to that on the taxable bonds. For example, a 6 percent tax-exempt bond provides a return to an investor in a 30 percent tax bracket equal to that of an 8.571 percent taxable bond [6.0% ÷ (1 – 0.30) = 8.571%].

Arbitrage subverts the federal government's rationale for exempting state and local debt from federal taxation—that of indirectly subsidizing state and local governments by enabling them to save on interest costs. At one time it was argued that the federal government did not have the constitutional right either to regulate the issuance of state and local debt or to tax the interest on it. Today the federal government does regulate the issuance of state and local debt, and it is widely believed that a tax on municipal bond interest could withstand constitutional challenges.

Were governments permitted to engage in arbitrage, they could generate virtually unlimited amounts of earnings simply by issuing their own bonds and investing the proceeds in higher-yielding risk-free federal government securities. Using the federal securities as collateral for their own bonds, they could ensure that their own debt also was risk free.

To prevent municipalities from reaping the benefits of arbitrage, the federal government has added restrictions to the Internal Revenue Code and accompanying regulations.

COMPLEXITY OF FEDERAL REGULATIONS

As previously discussed, governments typically spend the proceeds of bonds over the period of project construction. Major projects may take several years to complete. Moreover, governments may transfer a portion of the proceeds from a capital projects fund to a debt service fund, either because the proceeds include a premium or because the debt covenants stipulate that they must maintain a reserve fund to guard against default. Sound fiscal management dictates that proceeds held for anticipated construction costs, for future debt service, or as bondholder-required reserves be invested in interest-earning securities, such as those issued by the U.S. government.

The tax provisions are complex because they must allow for legitimate temporary investment of funds, yet at the same time prevent arbitrage abuse. To achieve this objective the federal government has produced a set of regulations so complex that few governments can administer them without assistance from outside experts. In essence, they are of two types:

- ***Arbitrage restrictions.*** Primarily developed in 1969, these provisions establish a general rule prohibiting arbitrage. But they set forth several exceptions. Issuers are permitted to invest both construction funds and reserve funds for limited periods of time (e.g., 85 percent of the proceeds must be spent within three years).
- ***Arbitrage rebates.*** Instituted as part of the Tax Reform Act of 1986, these regulations require that all arbitrage earnings, again with some exceptions (e.g., the proceeds are spent within six months, or 75 percent of the proceeds are spent on construction within two years), be remitted to the federal government.

Thus, even if a government is permitted to earn arbitrage under the 1969 restrictions, it may nevertheless have to remit it to the federal government under the 1986 rebate requirements.

A government that fails to comply with these mandates can compromise the tax-exempt status of its bonds, thereby subjecting itself to bondholder litigation and political embarrassment.

ACCOUNTING PROBLEMS

The main accounting problems arise because the regulations permit issuers to calculate and remit their required rebates as infrequently as every five years. Moreover, the arbitrage earnings may be measured over multiyear, rather than annual, periods. At the conclusion of any one year, then, the government may be unable to determine its expenditure and related liability for that year. Thus, although the GASB has not yet issued a pronouncement pertaining to arbitrage, it is clear that governments must estimate their rebate obligations and recognize an appropriate expenditure and liability.

In practice, governments take one of two approaches to accounting for the estimated rebates. Some report the rebates as a deduction from interest revenue (a debit) offset by a payable to the U.S. government. Others treat the obligation as if it were a claim or judgment. In the debt service fund or capital projects fund in which the arbitrage is earned, they recognize (as both an expenditure and a liability) only the portion of the obligation to be liquidated with currently available resources. They account for the balance of the obligation as they would other long-term obligations.

HOW CAN GOVERNMENTS BENEFIT FROM DEBT REFUNDINGS?

Governments, as well as other not-for-profits, retire debt prior to maturity for a variety of reasons. For example, if revenues are greater than anticipated they may be able to pay off bonds earlier than planned. Or, they may elect to sell facilities financed by the debt and use the proceeds to liquidate the obligations.

In this section, however, we are concerned with **bond refundings**—the early retirement of existing debt so that it can be replaced with new debt. Governments refund—

that is, **refinance**—their debt to take advantage of more favorable (lower) interest rates, to shorten or lengthen the debt payout period, or to rid themselves of restrictive bond covenants (such as those that prevent them from incurring new debt).

GENERAL RULE AS TO POTENTIAL FOR ECONOMIC GAINS

As a general rule, if a government had to retire outstanding debt by repurchasing it in the open market and paying a price reflective of current interest rates, then there would be no benefit to refunding—even in the face of prevailing interest rates that are substantially lower than those on the existing debt. There would be no economic gain because the premium to retire existing bonds would exactly offset the present value of the future interest savings. A simple example will demonstrate the point.

EXAMPLE *Debt Refundings*

A government has bonds outstanding that pay interest at an annual rate of 8 percent (4 percent per semiannual period). The bonds mature in ten years (twenty periods). In the years since the bonds were issued, annual interest rates on bonds with similar risk characteristics have decreased to 6 percent. Owing to the decline in interest rates, each of the government's bonds ($1,000 face value) is selling in the secondary market for $1,148.78.

The **economic cost** to the government of the debt, assuming that it will remain outstanding until maturity in ten years, is $1,148.78—the same as its market value. "Economic cost" means the present value of all future payments, based on the prevailing interest rate of 6 percent (3 percent per period). Hence, the economic cost is the twenty semiannual interest payments of $40 each and a single principal payment of $1,000:

Present value, at 3 percent, of $1,000 principal (a single sum) to be paid at the end of twenty periods (present value of $1 = $0.55368)	$ 553.68
Present value, at 3 percent, of $40 interest (an annuity) to be paid at the end of each of twenty periods (present value of an annuity of $1 = $14.87748)	595.10
Total economic cost of existing bonds	$1,148.78

Were the government to retire the debt, it would have to pay the market value of $1,148.78. Assuming that it still needs the funds initially borrowed, it would have to issue new bonds to obtain the required $1,148.78. Inasmuch as current market rates have now fallen to 6 percent, it could reduce its semiannual interest payments from $40 to $34.46 (3 percent of $1,148.78). The present value of all future payments on the new debt (based on the prevailing annual interest rates of 6 percent (3 percent per period) would also be $1,148.78:

Present value, at 3 percent, of $1,148.78 principal (a single sum) to be paid at the end of twenty periods (present value of $1 = $0.55368)	$ 636.07
Present value, at 3 percent, of $34.46 interest (an annuity) to be paid at the end of each of twenty periods (present value of an annuity of $1 = $14.87748)	512.68
Total economic cost of new bonds	$1,148.75

The slight discrepancy of three cents is attributable to rounding. It is, of course, no coincidence that the economic cost of the new bonds is the same as their face value. The present value of bonds issued at par is always the same as their face value.

The economic cost of the new bonds is the same as that of the existing bonds. Hence, there is no economic gain to refunding.

REALIZING ECONOMIC GAINS: EXCEPTIONS TO THE GENERAL RULE

There are exceptions, however, to the general rule that there is no benefit to refunding. First, *yield curves* (the relationship between interest rates and time to maturity) may be such that by refunding the existing bonds with new bonds having a different maturity (and thus different prevailing interest rates and prices) the government can obtain true economic savings. Second, bonds are often issued with specified **call prices.** These give the issuer the opportunity to redeem (call) the bonds at a preestablished price, irrespective of the current market price. The call price places a ceiling on the bond's market price. After all, why would an investor pay more for a bond than its call price, knowing that the government could, at its discretion, buy back the bond at the call price? If a government can redeem a bond at a call price less than the economic value of the existing bonds (i.e., what the market price of the bonds would be in the absence of a call provision) then, of course, it could realize an economic saving.

Suppose, in the example, the bonds contained a call provision giving the government the opportunity to redeem the bonds at a price of $1,050. The government refunds the existing debt, issuing $1,050 of new bonds at the prevailing annual interest rate of 6 percent for ten years—an obligation having a present economic value of $1,050. The government would thereby realize an economic gain of $98.78—the existing bonds' economic cost of $1,148.78 less the new bonds' economic cost of $1,050.00.

Most call provisions do not become effective until a specified number of years after the bonds have been outstanding. By delaying the effective date, an issuer is able to assure investors that they will receive their agreed-upon return for the indicated period and thereby enhance the marketability of its bonds.

Even if a call provision is not yet effective, the government can still lock in the savings that would result from a decline in prevailing interest rates. It can do this through a process known as an **in-substance defeasance**—an advance refunding in which the borrower *economically*, although not legally, satisfies its existing obligations. Issuing new debt, the government places in trust sufficient funds to make all required interest payments through the earliest call date and to redeem the debt on that date.

EXAMPLE *In-Substance Defeasance*

A government has outstanding the same ten-year, 8 percent bonds described in the previous example. The call provision permits the government to redeem the bonds at a price of $1,050 per bond, but the earliest call date is five years (ten semiannual periods) in the future. Prevailing interest rates are 6 percent (3 percent per period).

To defease the bonds in substance the government would have to place $1,122.51 with a trustee. This amount, determined as follows, is based on an assumption that the bond proceeds will be invested in securities earning the prevailing annual interest rate of 6 percent (3 percent per period):

Present value, at 3 percent, of the $1,050 (a single sum) required to redeem the bonds after ten periods (present value of $1 = $0.74409)	$ 781.30
Present value, at 3 percent, of the $40 interest to be paid at the end of each of ten periods (present value of an annuity of $1 = $8.53020)	341.21
Total economic cost of redeeming the bonds in five years (ten periods)	$1,122.51

The government would borrow the required $1,122.51 at an annual rate of 6 percent, an obligation that would have an economic cost of $1,122.51. This amount, if invested in securities earning 6 percent, would be just sufficient to make the required ten interest payments of $40 and the single principal payment of $1,050.

Most commonly (though not necessarily) the maturity date of the new bonds would be the same as those on the existing bonds. If so, the government would have the same amount of time to repay the debt as it had originally planned.

The total economic cost of taking no action is that of the existing bonds, determined previously to be $1,148.78. Therefore, the economic saving from defeasing the bond, in substance, is $26.27 per each $1,000 of existing bonds outstanding—$1,148.78 less $1,122.51.

Reporting the In-Substance Defeasance in Governmental Funds

The in-substance defeasance would generally be reported in the debt service fund. The accounting is straightforward:

Cash	$1,122.51	
Other financing source—proceeds of refunding bonds		$1,122.51
To record the issuance of the refunding (the "new") bonds		
Other financing use—payment to trustee	$1,122.51	
Cash		$1,122.51
To record the transfer of cash to the trust responsible for servicing and redeeming the existing bonds		

GASB Standards

Assuming that an in-substance defeasance transaction satisfies certain conditions intended to assure that the government has, in economic substance, no further responsibility for the existing debt, then it may remove the existing bonds from its schedule of long-term obligations and replace them with the new bonds. Among the conditions are:

- The debtor must irrevocably place cash or other assets with an escrow agent in a trust to be used solely for servicing and retiring the debt
- The possibility of the debtor having to make future payments on the debt must be remote
- The assets in the escrow fund must be essentially risk-free, such as U.S. government securities[7]

In addition, the government must detail the transaction in notes to the financial statements, indicating the resultant economic gain or loss.

The more controversial question involves how refundings should be accounted for on a full accrual basis—either in government-wide or proprietary fund statements. The issue arises because on a full accrual basis long-term liabilities are reported on the balance sheet—they are not shunted off to the schedule of long-term obligations. Hence, when a debt is refunded and must be removed from the balance sheet, a gain or loss may have to be recognized.

[7] GASB Statement No. 7, *Advance Refundings Resulting in Defeasance of Debt* (March 1987), para. 4.

RECOGNIZING THE GAIN OR LOSS IN PROPRIETARY FUNDS AND IN GOVERNMENT-WIDE STATEMENTS

Suppose the bonds described in the previous example were issued initially at par and are thereby reported in a proprietary fund at face value of $1,000. Were the bonds to be defeased by placing $1,122.51 in trust, the following entry would be in order to remove the existing debt from the books:

"Loss" (past, present, or future?)	$ 122.51	
Bonds payable	1,000.00	
Cash		$1,122.51

To record the in-substance defeasance of the existing bonds

As demonstrated previously, the government realizes an economic gain by defeasing the debt prior to maturity. Yet because the book value of debt is less than the reacquisition price, it is forced to recognize an "accounting" loss. As implied by the parenthetical question in the entry, the salient accounting issue relates to the disposition of the loss. There are at least three possibilities:

- ***Recognize the loss over the prior years in which the debt has been outstanding.*** The loss is attributable to declines in interest rates (and corresponding increases in bond prices) over those years. Given perfect foresight as to when, and at what amount, it would defease the debt, the issuer would have amortized the anticipated difference between issue price and reacquisition price over those years. However, in reality it is impractical to do that upon defeasance, because several years of previous financial statements would need to be restated.
- ***Recognize the loss at the time of defeasance.*** Accepting that it is impractical to assign the loss to the periods the debt was actually outstanding, this policy would recognize it as soon as feasible. Immediate recognition may be objectionable, however, in that the operating results of that period would be distorted. Not only would the government be required to report a loss when in economic substance it realized a gain, but, as if to compound the fiscal injury, it would be forced to recognize the entire amount in single period.
- ***Defer the loss, and amortize it over future years.*** This approach is grounded on the assumption that the defeasance is merely a substitution of new debt for existing debt with a corresponding adjustment in interest rates.

GASB Standards

The GASB opted for the third method. It requires that the difference between the book value of the existing debt and the reacquisition price be deferred and amortized over the remaining life of the existing debt or the new debt, whichever is shorter.[8] This period of amortization is consistent with an interpretation that the new debt is merely a restructured version of the old. The GASB does not permit the amortization to extend past the maturity date of the existing debt because it sees any debt outstanding beyond that date as essentially a new borrowing for an additional period of time.

By contrast, in a relatively recent standard (Statement No. 125 of 1996), the FASB ruled that a debtor can "derecognize" a liability only if it has either paid the obligation or has been legally released from it. Therefore, the debtor must report on its balance sheet both the debt that it in-substance defeased and the assets set aside to refund it. Correspondingly, it must include on its statement of revenues and expenditures both the interest expense on the defeased debt and the investment revenue on the assets that it has set aside.

[8] GASB Statement No. 23, *Accounting and Financial Reporting for Refundings of Debt Reported by Proprietary Activities* (December 1993), para. 4.

What needs to be emphasized is that the reported gain or loss from defeasance, whether amortized over several periods or recognized as once, may be counter to the economic gain or loss. Entities may be tempted, therefore, to defease debt at an economic loss just so they can report a gain.

SUMMARY

Both government and other not-for-profit organizations maintain special funds to account for resources set aside for the purchase and construction of long-lived assets and for the service of long-term debt. Governments both account for, and report, these resources in capital projects and debt service funds.

Governments account for capital projects and debt service funds on a modified accrual basis. The principles of revenue and expenditure recognition are the same for these funds as for the general fund and special revenue funds. Accordingly, these funds do not report either long-term assets or long-term liabilities, and interest on long-term debt outstanding need not be accrued. The long-term assets and liabilities are accounted for "off the balance sheet."

Special assessments are accounted for just as any other capital projects. The construction phase is accounted for in a capital projects fund, and the debt service phase is accounted for in a debt service fund. Even though the debt issued to finance special assessment projects is often the responsibility of the property owners rather than the government, the government should nevertheless report it as its own if it is obligated for it in some manner (that is, unless the government is prohibited from making payments on the debt or it gives no indication that it will, or may, honor the debt in the event of default). Governments may account for enterprise-related special assessments either in an enterprise fund or in the funds in which they account for other types of assessments.

In their government-wide statements, governments combine their capital projects and debt service funds with their other governmental funds in a governmental funds column. Both revenues and expenses are recognized on a full accrual basis. Accordingly, both long-lived assets and the related long-term debt are reported on the statement of net assets. Interest is charged as an expense as a function of time irrespective of when it will be paid, and bond premiums and discounts are amortized.

Arbitrage, which refers to the issuance of debt at relatively low, tax-exempt interest rates and the investment of the proceeds in taxable securities yielding a higher return, subverts the federal government's rationale for exempting state and local debt from federal taxation. Consequently, the federal government has established complex regulations to deter municipalities from engaging in this practice. These regulations cause accounting problems, mainly because they require governments to rebate their arbitrage earnings and expose the governments to substantial penalties if they violate the regulations.

As a general rule, bond refundings do not bring economic gains to a government, unless the government is able to call the bonds at less than their market value. However, even if the call date is in the future, a government can lock in the economic gains from the future call through an in-substance defeasance—a transaction in which the government sets aside the resources necessary to make all required interest and principal payments on the bonds to be refunded.

In the next two chapters we consider issues associated with long-lived assets and long-term obligations.

EXERCISE FOR REVIEW AND SELF-STUDY

With the approval of neighborhood property owners, the White City council voted to construct sidewalks in a newly annexed neighborhood, assess the property owners for the cost, and issue debt to finance the project.

1. For the 2004 transactions that follow, prepare journal entries in White City's capital projects and debt service funds:
   a. On January 1, 2004, the city council assessed the property owners the estimated cost of $8,000,000. The assessments are payable over a five-year period ($1,600,000 per year) with interest at 6 percent annually (3 percent per semi-annual period) on the unpaid balance. The first installment is due on December 31, 2004.
   b. The city issued $8,000,000 of five-year, 6 percent, serial bonds. The bonds were issued at a premium of $200,000, but the city incurred issuance costs of $150,000. It transferred the premium (net of the issuance costs) to the debt service fund.
   c. It constructed the sidewalks.
   d. It collected the first $1,600,000 installment of the assessments, along with $480,000 in interest.
   e. It made one payment of $240,000 interest on the bonds. The next payment of interest, along with $1,600,000 of principal, is due in January 2005.
2. For the capital projects fund and the debt service fund prepare: (1) statements of revenues, expenditures, and changes in fund balance, and (2) balance sheets.

3. Assume that the city engaged in no other transactions during the year and that the city amortized $15,000 of the bond premium. Prepare two schedules in which you present the revenues, expenses, assets, liabilities, and net assets of the funds as they would affect the government-wide statement of net activity and statement of net assets.
4. The bond agreement permits the city to redeem the $1,600,000 of bonds that are due in January 2009 one year early in (January 2008), at par, without penalty. In January 2006 (with six semiannual periods until the January 2009 maturity date) interest rates decrease to an annual rate of 4 percent and the city has the opportunity to defease the bonds "in substance."
   a. What is the "economic cost" of the $1,600,000 of bonds outstanding as of January 2006, assuming that the city would have to make six additional interest payments of $48,000 (the semiannual coupon rate of 3 percent times $1,600,000) plus a principal payment of $1.6 million? Base your valuation on the prevailing interest rate of 4 percent (2 percent per period).
   b. How much would the city have to place with a trustee in January 2006 so that it would have sufficient resources on hand to retire the bonds in January 2008—i.e., the four required interest payments of $48,000 through January 2008 and the one payment of principal of $1,600,000? Assume the funds placed with the trustee would earn interest at the annual rate of 4 percent (2 percent per period).
   c. Assume the city would borrow the funds to be placed with the trustee by issuing bonds yielding the prevailing rate of 4 percent. What would be the "economic cost" of this new debt? How does it compare with that of the old debt?

QUESTIONS FOR REVIEW AND DISCUSSION

1. Although many governments prepare budgets for both capital projects and debt service funds and integrate them into their accounts, budgetary control over these funds is not as essential as for other governmental funds. Do you agree? Explain. If budgets are prepared for capital projects funds, in what significant way may they differ from those prepared for other funds?
2. When bonds are issued for capital projects, premiums are generally not accounted for as the mirror image of discounts. Why not?
3. It is sometimes said that in debt service funds the accounting for interest revenue is inconsistent with that for interest expenditure. Explain. What is the rationale for this seeming inconsistency?
4. Until recently governments maintained a unique type of fund to account for special assessments. This fund recorded the construction in process, the long-term debt, and the assessments receivable. Explain briefly how governments account for special assessments today.
5. Special assessment debt may be, in economic substance and/or legal form, an obligation of the assessed property owners rather than a government. Should the government, therefore, report it in its statements as if it were its own debt? What are the current standards as to when a government should recognize special assessment debt as its own obligation?
6. How should governments report their capital projects and debt service activities in their government-wide statements?
7. A government issues bonds at a discount. Where would the government report the discount on its (a) fund statements (b) government-wide statements?
8. What is *arbitrage?* Why does the Internal Revenue Service place strict limits on the amount of arbitrage that a municipality can earn?
9. Under what circumstances can a government refund outstanding debt and thereby take advantage of a decline in interest rates?
10. What is meant by an *in-substance defeasance*, and how can a government use it to lower its interest costs? How must it recognize a gain or loss on defeasance if it accounts for the debt in a proprietary fund? How do the GASB standards pertaining to in-substance defeasances differ from those of the FASB?

EXERCISES

6-1

Select the *best* answer.

1. A government opts to set aside $10 million of general fund resources to finance a new city hall. Construction is expected to begin in several years, when the city has been able to accumulate additional resources.
   a. The government *must* account for the $10 million in a capital projects fund and in its government-wide statements it *must* report the $10 million as "restricted."
   b. The government *may* account for the $10 million in a capital projects fund and in its government-wide statements it *may* report the $10 million as "restricted."

c. The government *may not* account for the \$10 million in a capital projects fund and in its government-wide statements it *may not* report the \$10 million as "unrestricted."

d. The government *may* account for the \$10 million in a capital projects fund but in its government-wide statements it *may not* report the \$10 million as "restricted."

2. A government should distinguish underwriting and other issue costs from bond premiums and discounts and should
   a. Report them as expenditures
   b. Add them to the face value of the bond
   c. Report them in a separate account and amortize them over the life of the bond
   d. Deduct them from the bond premiums or add them to the bond discount

3. When a government issues bonds at premiums or discounts and records the proceeds in a capital projects fund, it should
   a. Transfer an amount equal to the premiums from the capital projects fund to a debt service fund, and an amount equal to the discounts from a debt service fund to the capital projects fund
   b. Transfer an amount equal to the premiums from the capital projects fund to a debt service fund, but make no transfer of an amount equal to the discounts from a debt service fund to the capital projects fund
   c. Make no transfers between the capital projects fund and a debt service fund
   d. Transfer an amount equal to the discounts from a debt service fund to the capital projects fund, but make no transfer of an amount equal to the premiums from the capital projects fund to the debt service fund

4. A city holds U.S. Treasury notes as an investment in a capital projects fund. During the year the market value of the notes increases by \$50,000. Of this amount \$14,000 can be attributed to a decline in prevailing interest rates and \$36,000 to interest that has been earned but not yet received. As of year-end, the city should recognize as revenue
   a. \$0
   b. \$14,000
   c. \$36,000
   d. \$50,000

5. Which of the following accounts is least likely to be shown on the balance sheet of a debt service fund?
   a. Bonds payable
   b. Investments (at market value)
   c. Cash
   d. Special assessments receivable

6. Special assessment debt need not be reported on the balance sheet of a city if the debt is to be paid from assessments on property owners and
   a. The city has not guaranteed payment of the debt
   b. The city has guaranteed payment of the debt but the probability of the city having to make good on the guarantee is remote
   c. The city serves only as a collection agency and is not required to include in its budget either receipts from property owners nor payments to bondholders
   d. None of the above

7. In its fund statements a government should recognize revenue from special assessments
   a. Entirely in the year in which the assessment is imposed
   b. In the years in which the assessments are paid
   c. In the years in which the assessments are due
   d. In the years in which the assessments become available for expenditure

8. In the year it imposes a special assessment, a government should recognize in its government-wide statements
   a. The full amount of the assessment as both revenue and an asset
   b. The present value of the assessment as both revenue and an asset
   c. Only the amount of the assessment due in the current year as revenue but the full amount of the assessment as an asset
   d. Only the amount of the assessment due in the current year as both revenue and an asset

9. Under existing federal statutes, *arbitrage* as it applies to state and local governments
   a. Is illegal
   b. Is illegal unless the government can demonstrate a "just cause" for engaging in it
   c. Is legal in some circumstances, but the government may be required to remit arbitrage earnings to the federal government
   d. Is illegal unless there is no more than a 2 percent difference between interest earned and interest paid

10. Bond refundings are most likely to result in an economic gain when
    a. The bonds are subject to arbitrage
    b. There is an inverted yield curve
    c. The bonds were initially issued at a premium
    d. The bonds are subject to a call provision

6-2

Select the *best* answer.

1. Which of the following items is least likely to appear on the balance sheet of a capital projects fund?
   a. Cash
   b. Investments
   c. Construction in process
   d. Reserve for encumbrances

2. The fund balance of a debt service fund is most likely to be incorporated into the reporting entity's government-wide statement of net assets as
   a. Net assets, invested in capital assets, net of related debt
   b. Net assets, restricted
   c. Net assets, unrestricted
   d. Capital assets

3. The repayment of bond principal should be reported in the fund statements of a debt service fund as

a. An expenditure
b. An "other financing use"
c. A reduction of bonds payable
d. A direct charge to fund balance

4. A state issues bonds, at a premium, to finance road construction projects. The premium would affect
   a. "Interest expenditure" as reported in the state's debt service fund
   b. Nonreciprocal transfers-out as reported in the state's general fund
   c. "Capital assets" as reported in the state's government-wide statement of net assets
   d. "Net assets invested in capital assets, net of related debt" in the state's government-wide statement of net assets

5. If a government issues bonds at a discount, the discount should be reported as
   a. A reduction of fund balance in the balance sheet of a capital projects fund
   b. An amortization expenditure in the statement of revenues, expenditures, and changes in fund balance of a capital projects fund in the periods in which the bonds are outstanding
   c. An amortization expense in the government-wide statement of activities in the periods in which the bonds are outstanding
   d. A liability in the government-wide statement of net assets

6. A city issued bonds on July 1. Interest of $600,000 is payable the following January 1. On December 31, the city transfers the required $600,000 from its general fund to its debt service fund. On its December 31 debt service fund statement of revenues, expenditures, and changes in fund balance, the city
   a. Must report interest expenditure of $0
   b. Must report interest expenditure of $600,000
   c. Must report interest expenditure of $500,000
   d. May report interest expenditure of either $0 or $600,000

7. A city issues $10 million of debt that it uses to acquire an office building. In the year that it issues the debt and acquires the building the city neither charges depreciation on the building nor repays any of the debt principal. Assume that the city accounts for all capital acquisitions in a capital projects fund and all payments of interest in a debt service fund. The transaction would
   a. Increase expenditures of the capital projects fund
   b. Increase other financing sources of the debt service fund
   c. Increase fund balance of the capital project fund
   d. Increase expenditures of the debt service fund

8. A city assesses property owners $50 million to extend sewer lines to their neighborhood. By year-end, however, it has not yet begun construction of the new lines and has not yet collected any of the assessments. It accounts for its wastewater services in an enterprise fund. In its year-end enterprise fund financial statements the government should
   a. Recognize the assessments as assessments receivable and deferred revenue
   b. Recognize the assessments as assessments receivable and revenue
   c. Recognize the assessments as assessments receivable and a liability for future construction costs
   d. Not recognize the assessments until they will be available for expenditure

9. A county engages in an in-substance defeasance of its bonds. The transaction results in an economic gain but an accounting loss. In its government-wide statements the county should
   a. Recognize the loss entirely in the year of the defeasance
   b. Amortize the loss over the remaining life of either the existing debt or the new debt
   c. Report the loss as a direct charge to net assets
   d. Not recognize the loss, but instead continue to report the defeased bonds (as well as the new bonds) as liabilities

10. A government issued, at par, $10 million of twenty-year, 6 percent bonds that it accounts for in its electric utility fund The bonds do not contain a call provision. Ten years later prevailing interest rates have fallen to 5 percent. The government is considering whether to purchase the outstanding bonds at their market price and retire them. It would acquire the necessary funds by issuing new ten-year, 5 percent bonds. The transaction would most likely result in
    a. An economic gain but an accounting loss
    b. An economic loss but an accounting gain
    c. An economic gain and an accounting loss
    d. Neither an economic gain or loss but an accounting loss

6-3

Construction and debt transactions can affect more than one fund.

During 2005 Luling Township engaged in the following transactions related to modernizing the bridge over the Luling River. The township accounts for long-term construction projects in a capital projects fund.

- On July 1 it issued ten-year, 4 percent bonds with a face value of $1 million. The bonds were sold for $1,016,510, an amount that provides an annual yield of 3.8 percent (semi-annual rate of 1.9 percent). The city incurred $10,000 in issue costs.
- On August 1 it was awarded a state reimbursement grant of $800,000. During the year it incurred allowable costs of $600,000. Of these it paid $500,000 in cash to various contractors. It received $450,000 from the state, expecting to receive, early in 2006, the $150,000 difference between allowable costs incurred and cash received. Moreover, it expects to receive the balance of the grant later in 2006.
- It invested the bond proceeds in short-term federal securities. During the year it received $8,000 in interest

and at year-end the market value of the securities was $1,000 more than the township had paid for them.

- It transferred the bond premium (net of issue costs) to an appropriate fund.
- It transferred $20,000 from the general fund to an appropriate fund to cover the first payment of bond interest which was due, and paid, on December 31.
- On January 1, the township defeased in substance $400,000 of bonds that had been issued years earlier to construct the bridge. The bonds had been issued at par. To effect the transaction the township issued $405,000 of new bonds, at par, and placed the proceeds in a trust. The old bonds have a coupon rate 5 percent; the new bonds have a coupon rate of 4 percent.

What amount should Luling report in its December 31, 2005, financial statements as:

1. Nonreciprocal transfers-in to its debt service fund
2. Interest expenditure in its debt service fund
3. Interest expense on its government-wide statements (prior to taking into account amortization of the bond premium)
4. Investment revenue in its capital projects fund
5. Bonds payable in its capital project fund
6. Total expenditures in its capital project fund
7. Bond proceeds in its capital project fund
8. Bond proceeds in its debt service fund
9. Loss on defeasance in its debt service fund
10. Grant revenue in its capital project fund
11. Grants receivable in its capital project fund
12. Bonds payable (on issue of July 1 only) in its government-wide statements

Select each response from the amounts that follow. An amount may be selected once, more than once, or not at all.

a. $0
b. $8,000
c. $9,000
d. $16,510
e. $19,314
f. $20,000
g. $26,510
h. $38,627
i. $150,000
j. $200,000
k. $400,000
l. $405,000
m. $500,000
n. $600,000
o. $610,000
p. $1,000,000
q. $1,006,510
r. $1,016,510
s. $1,015,824

6-4

Capital projects funds account for construction expenditures, not for the assets that are being constructed.

The Wickliffe City Council authorizes the restoration of the city library. The project is to be funded by the issuance of bonds, a reimbursement grant from the state, and property taxes.

1. Prepare journal entries in the capital projects fund to reflect the following events and transactions:
   a. The city approves (and gives accounting recognition to) the project's budget of $9,027,000, of which $6,000,000 is to be funded by general obligation bonds, $2,500,000 from the state, and the remaining $527,000 from the general fund. The city estimates that construction costs will be $8,907,000 and bond issue costs $120,000.
   b. The city issues 9 percent, fifteen-year bonds that have a face value of $6,000,000. The bonds are sold for $6,120,000, an amount reflecting a price of $102. The city incurs $115,000 in issue costs; hence, the net proceeds are $6,005,000.
   c. The city transfers the net premium of $5,000 to its debt service fund.
   d. It receives the anticipated $2,500,000 from the state and transfers $527,000 from the general fund.
   e. It signs an agreement with a contractor for $8,890,000.
   f. It pays the contractor $8,890,000 upon completion of the project.
   g. It transfers the remaining cash to the debt service fund.
2. Prepare appropriate closing entries.

6-5

The accounting for bond premiums is not the mirror image of that for bond discounts.

Pacific Independent School District issued $100 million of general obligation bonds to finance the construction of new schools. The bonds were issued at a premium of $0.6 million.

1. Prepare the capital projects fund journal entries to record the issue of the bonds and the transfer of the premium to an appropriate fund.
2. Suppose, instead, that the bonds were issued at a discount of $0.6 million but that the project will still cost $100 million. Prepare the appropriate entries.
   a. Contrast the entries in this part with those in part 1.
   b. Indicate the options available to the school district and state how they would affect the entries required of the district.
   c. Suppose the government chose to finance the balance of the project with general revenues. Prepare the appropriate capital projects fund entry.

6-6

Governments can seldom realize an economic gain by refunding bonds in the absence of call provisions.

A government has outstanding $100 million of twenty-year, 10 percent bonds. They were issued at par and have sixteen years (thirty-two semiannual periods) until they mature. They pay interest semiannually.

1. Suppose current prevailing interest rates had decreased to 8 percent (4 percent per period). What amount would you estimate the bonds were trading at in the open market?
2. Suppose the government elected to purchase the bonds in the market and retire them. To finance the purchase it issued sixteen-year (thirty-two-period) bonds at the prevailing rate of 8 percent (4 percent per period). What would be the "economic cost" (i.e., the present value of anticipated cash flows) of issuing these bonds? Would the government realize an economic gain by retiring the old bonds and issuing the new?
3. Suppose a call provision permitted the government to redeem the bonds at any time for a total of $101 million. Could the government realize an economic gain by recalling the bonds and financing the purchase by issuing $101 million in new, 8 percent, sixteen-year bonds?

6-7

Debt service funds account for resources accumulated to service debt, not the debt itself.

On July 1, a city issued, at par, $100 million in 6 percent, twenty-year general obligation bonds. It established a debt service fund to account for resources set aside to pay interest and principal on the obligations.

In the year it issued the debt, the city engaged in the following transactions involving the debt service fund:

1. It estimated that it would make interest payments of $3 million and have interest earnings of $30,000 from investments. It would transfer from the general fund to the debt service fund $2.97 million to pay interest and $500,000 to provide for the payment of principal when the bonds mature. Further, as required by the bond indentures, it would transfer $1 million of the bond proceeds from the capital projects fund to the debt service fund to be held in reserve until the debt matures.
2. Upon issuing the bonds, the city transferred $1 million of the bond proceeds from the capital projects fund. It invested $977,254 of the funds in twenty-year, 6 percent Treasury bonds that had a face value of $1 million. The bond discount of $22,746 reflected an effective yield rate of 6.2 percent.
3. On December 31, the city received $30,000 interest on the Treasury bonds. This payment represented interest for six months. Correspondingly, the market value of the bonds increased by $294, reflecting the amortization of the discount.
4. On the same day the city transferred $2.97 million from the general fund to pay interest on the bonds that it had issued. It also transferred $500,000 for the eventual repayment of principal.
5. Also on December 31, it made its first interest payment of $3 million to bondholders.
   a. Prepare appropriate journal entries in the debt service fund, including budgetary and closing entries.
   b. The bonds issued by the city pay interest at the rate of 6 percent. The bonds in which the city invested its reserve have an effective yield of 6.2 percent. Why might the difference in rates create a potential liability for the city?

PROBLEMS

Continuing Problem

Review the Comprehensive Annual Financial Report (CAFR) that you obtained.

1. How many capital projects funds does the government maintain? How can you tell? Are any of these major funds? If so, for what purposes are they maintained?
2. How many debt service funds does the government maintain? How can you tell? Are any of these major funds? If so, for what types of obligations are they maintained?
3. Are the capital projects and debt service funds reported upon in the government-wide statement of net assets? If so, how?
4. Select one of the more recently established (and larger) capital projects funds (a major fund, if there is one).
   a. From where did the fund receive most of its resources?
   b. Did the city acquire or construct new capital assets using resources of this fund? If so, in what amount?
   c. Does this fund have any long-term debts associated with it? If so, does the government maintain a debt service fund to account for the resources to service the debt?
5. Did the government issue additional long-term debt to support governmental activities during the year? Did it repay any long-term debt used to support governmental activities? Did it engage in any in-substance defeasances?

6-1

The financial statements of an actual capital projects fund leave it to the report reader to draw inferences as to key transactions.

The accompanying statements of the parks, recreation, and municipal capital improvement bond fund (a capital projects fund) were drawn from a recent annual report (dates changed) of Boulder, Colorado. According to a note in the report (the only one pertaining to the fund), the fund is maintained "to account for bond proceeds to be utilized for the construction and refurbishment of parks and recreation facilities and the refurbishment of other municipal facilities."

1. The variances in expenditures between budget and actual are substantial. What is the most likely explanation?
2. A schedule of long-term debt payable (in the statistical section of the report) indicates that only $7,000 of parks, recreation, and municipal capital improvement bonds were authorized and issued. How do you reconcile that amount with the proceeds from bonds payable reported in the statement of revenues, expenditures, and changes in fund balance?
3. Another schedule of transfers between funds (in the same section) indicates that $131 was transferred to the general fund. What conclusions can you draw as to whether interest on fund investments must be used either to repay the capital improvement bonds or to construct and refurbish city facilities?
4. How much of fund resources did the government spend during the year on capital improvements?
5. How do you explain the absence in the balance sheet of "construction in process"?
6. Why is the entire fund balance "reserved"?

Parks, Recreation, and Municipal Capital Improvement Bond Fund
Balance Sheet December 31, 2003
(in thousands)

Assets	
Receivables	$ 2
Investments	5,874
Total assets	$5,876
Liabilities and fund equity	
Liabilities	
Accrued wages and salaries	$ 4
Construction contracts payable	202
Due to other funds	220
Total liabilities	$ 426
Fund equity	
Reserved for encumbrances	$ 431
Reserved for bond projects	5,019
Total fund equity	$5,450
Total liabilities and fund equity	$5,876

Parks, Recreation, and Municipal Capital Improvement Bond Fund
Statement of Revenues, Expenditures, and Changes in Fund Balance—Budget and Actual
Year Ended December 31, 2003 (in thousands)

	Budget	Actual
Revenues		
Interest earnings	$ 75	$ 131
Exepnditures		
Capital outlay		
General government—facility	1,552	425
Culture and recreation—facility	5,500	1,177
Total expenditures	$7,052	$1,602
Deficiency of revenues over expenditures	$(6,977)	$(1,471)
Other financing sources (uses)		
Proceeds from bonds payable	$7,052	$7,052
Nonreciprocal transfers out	(75)	(131)
Total other financing sources (uses)	$6,977	$6,921
Excess of revenues and other sources over expenditures and other uses	$ 0	5,450
Fund balance, beginning of year		0
Fund balance, end of year		$5,450

6-2

The transaction of a capital projects fund can be derived from its basic financial statements.

Crystal City established a capital projects fund to account for the construction of a new bridge. During the year the fund was established the city issued bonds, signed (and encumbered) $6 million in contracts with various suppliers and contractors and incurred $4.3 million of construction costs. It temporarily invested a portion of the bond proceeds and earned $20,000 in interest, which was received in cash. The accompanying statement of revenues, expenditures, and changes in fund balance and balance sheet were taken from its year-end financial report.

Based on the data in the two statements, as well as that provided in the previous paragraph, prepare journal entries to summarize the transactions in which the fund engaged. You should prepare budgetary entries, but need not prepare closing entries.

Crystal City, Capital Projects Fund
Statement of Revenues, Expenditures, and Changes in Fund Balance—Actual and Budget
Year Ended December 31 (in thousands)

	Actual	Budget
Revenues		
Cash grant from state	$ 2,000	$ 2,000
Interest	20	
Total revenues	$ 2,020	$ 2,000
Expenditures		
Bond issue costs	$ 50	
Construction costs	4,300	5,000
Total expenditures	$ 4,350	$ 5,000
Excess of revenues over expenditures	$ (2,330)	$ (3,000)

Other financing sources (uses)		
Proceeds of bonds	$10,000	$10,000
Proceeds of bonds (premium)	200	
Nonreciprocal cash transfer of bond premium (less issue costs) to debt service fund	(150)	
Increase in reserve for encumbrances	(1,700)	
Total other financing sources (uses)	$ 8,350	$10,000
Excess of revenues and net financing sources over expenditures	$ 6,020	$ 7,000
Fund balance, beginning of year	0	
Fund balance, end of year	$ 6,020	$ 7,000

Crystal City, Capital Projects Fund
Balance Sheet
As of December 31 (in thousands)

Assets	
Cash	$ 5,320
Investments	5,000
Total assets	$10,320
Liabilities	
Accounts payable (to contractors)	$ 2,600
Fund balance	
Reserved for encumbrances	$ 1,700
Unreserved	6,020
Total fund balance	$ 7,720
Total liabilities and fund balance	$10,320

6-3

The transaction of a debt service fund can be derived from its basic financial statements.

Durwin County issued $200 million in long-term debt to fund major improvements to the county's road and transportation systems. The debt is to be serviced from the proceeds of a specially dedicated property tax. The accompanying statement of revenues, expenditures, and changes in fund balance and balance sheet were taken from its year-end financial report.

Based on the data in the two statements prepare journal entries to summarize the transactions in which the firm engaged. You should prepare budgetary entries, but need not prepare closing entries.

Durwin County, Debt Service Fund
Statement of Revenues, Expenditures, and Changes in Fund Balance—Actual and Budget
Year Ended December 31 (in thousands)

	Actual	Budget
Revenues		
Property taxes	$21,520	$20,000
Interest	50	—
Total revenues	$21,570	$20,000
Expenditures		
Principal retirement	$6,000	$6,000
Interest	12,500	12,500
Total expenditures	$18,500	$18,500
Excess of revenues over expenditures	$3,070	$1,500
Other financing sources (uses)		
Nonreciprocal transfer of bond premium from capital projects fund	150	
Excess of revenues and net financing sources over expenditures	$3,220	$1,500
Fund balance, beginning of year	0	0
Fund balance, end of year	$3,220	$1,500

Durwin County, Debt Service Fund
Balance Sheet
As of December 31 (in thousands)

Assets	
Cash	$ 70
Investments	1,000
Property taxes receivable	2,150
Total assets	$3,220
Fund balance	$3,220

6-4

The financial statements of a debt service fund may reveal less information than is apparent.

The balance sheet and a comparative statement (actual to budget) of revenues, expenditures, and changes in fund balance of the City of Boulder, Colorado's general obligation debt service fund (date changed) is presented as follows.

General Obligation Debt Service Fund
Balance Sheet
December 31, 2003 (in thousands)

Assets	
Equity in pooled cash and cash equivalents	$ 18
Cash with fiscal agent	21
Investments, at market value	1,527
Receivables—accrued interest	2
Due from other funds	44
Total assets	$1,612
Liabilities and fund equity	
Liabilities	
Vouchers and accounts payable	$ 1
Fund equity	
Reserved for special purposes	1
Unreserved,	1,610
Total fund equity	$1,611
Total liabilities and fund equity	$1,612

General Obligation Debt Service Fund
Statement of Revenues, Expenditures, and Changes in Fund Balance—Budget and Actual
Year Ended December 31, 2003 (in thousands)

	Budget	Actual
Revenues		
Investment earnings	$ —	$ 151
Expenditures		
Administrative services	25	22
Debt service payments		
Principal	2,592	2,592
Interest	4,088	4,088
Total expenditures	$6,705	$6,702
Excess (deficiency) of revenues over expenditures	$(6,705)	$(6,551)
Other financing sources (uses)		
Nonreciprocal transfers-in	6,292	6,292
Nonreciprocal transfer-out	(10)	(10)
	6,282	6,282
Excess (deficiency) of revenues and other sources over expenditures and other uses	$ (423)	(269)
Fund balance, beginning of year		382
Other nonreciprocal transfer		1,498
Fund balance, end of year		$1,611

1. Of what significance is the *deficiency* of revenues over expenditures? Is it an indication of poor management?
2. The fund reported a smaller deficit than was budgeted. Is this variance a sign of good management? Explain.
3. Can you assess whether the fund will have the fiscal wherewithal to satisfy its obligations of principal and interest as they come due? Explain.
4. The fund reported a nonreciprocal transfer-in of $1,498. The statement of changes in fund balance of a related capital projects fund indicates a nonreciprocal transfer-out of the same amount. What is a likely explanation for the transfer?
5. A schedule of operating transfers indicates that the transfers-in were as follows:

From the general fund	$2,080
From the permanent parks and recreation fund	25
From the transportation fund	15
From the open space fund (to account for the acquisition of greenbelt land)	3,944
From the major maintenance and equipment replacement fund	228
Total	$6,292

The major maintenance and equipment replacement fund is a capital project funds; each of the other funds, other than the general fund, is a special revenue fund. What are the most likely reasons for the transfers?

6-5

The construction and financing phase of a special assessment project is accounted for in a capital projects fund; the debt service phase in a debt service fund (see the next problem).

Upon annexing a recently developed subdivision, a government undertakes to extend sewer lines to the area. Estimated cost is $10.0 million. The project is to be funded with $8.5 million in special assessment bonds and a $1.0 million reimbursement grant from the state. The balance is to be paid by the government out of its general fund. Property owners are to be assessed an amount sufficient to pay both principal and interest on the debt.

During the year, the government engaged in the following transactions, all of which would be recorded in a capital projects fund.

1. It recorded the capital project fund budget. It estimated that it would earn $0.20 million in interest on the temporary investment of bond proceeds, an amount that will reduce the required transfer from the general fund. It estimated that bond issue costs would be $0.18 million.
2. It issued $8.5 million in bonds at a premium of $0.30 million and incurred $0.18 million in issue costs. The premium, net of issue costs, is to be transferred to a newly established debt service fund.
3. It received the $1.0 million grant from the state, recognizing it as deferred revenue until it incurred at least $1.0 million in construction costs.
4. It invested $7.62 million in short-term (less than one year) securities.
5. It issued purchase orders and signed construction contracts for $9.2 million.
6. It sold $5.0 million of its investments for $5.14 million, the excess of selling price over cost representing interest earned. By year-end the investments still on hand had increased in value by $0.06 million, an amount also attributable to interest earned.
7. It received invoices totaling $5.7 million. As permitted by its agreement with its prime contractor, it retained (and recorded as a payable) $0.4 million pending satisfactory completion of the project. It paid the balance of $5.3 million.
8. It transferred $0.12 million to the debt service fund.
9. It updated its accounts, but did not close them inasmuch as the project is not completed and its budget is for the entire project, not for a single period.
   a. Prepare appropriate journal entries for the capital projects fund.
   b. Prepare a statement of revenues, expenditures, and changes in fund balance, in which you compare actual and budgeted amounts.
   c. Prepare a year-end (December 31) balance sheet.

d. Does your balance sheet report the construction in process? If not, where might the construction in process be recorded?

6-6

The debt service phase special assessment bonds are accounted for in a debt service fund.

As stated in the previous problem, a government issued \$8.5 million of special assessment bonds to finance a sewer-extension project. To service the debt, it assessed property owners \$8.5 million. Their obligations are payable over a period of five years, with annual installments due on March 31 of each year. Interest at an annual rate of 8 percent is to be paid on the total balance outstanding as of that date.

The bonds require an annual principal payment of \$1.5 million each year for five years, due on December 31. In addition, interest on the unpaid balance is payable twice each year, on June 30 and December 31 at an annual rate of 8 percent.

The government agreed to make up from its general fund the difference between required debt service payments and revenues.

At the start of the year, the government established a debt service fund. During the year it engaged in the following transactions, all of which would affect that fund.

1. It prepared, and recorded in its accounts, its annual budget. It estimated that it would collect from property owners \$1.3 million in special assessments and \$0.5 million of interest on the unpaid balance of the assessments. In addition, it expected to earn interest of \$0.08 million on temporary investments. It would be required to pay interest of \$0.68 million and make principal payments of \$1.7 million on the outstanding debt. It anticipated transferring \$0.5 million from the general fund to cover the revenue shortage.
2. It recorded the \$8.5 million of assessments receivable, estimating that \$0.2 million would be uncollectible.
3. The special assessments bonds were issued at a premium (net of issue costs) of \$0.12. The government recognized the anticipated transfer of the premium to the debt service fund.
4. During the year the government collected \$2.0 million in assessments and \$0.4 million in interest (with a few property owners paying their entire assessment in the first year). During the first sixty days of the following year it collected an additional \$0.1 million in assessments and \$0.01 in interest, which were due the previous year.
5. It transferred \$0.12 million (the premium) from the capital projects fund.
6. It purchased \$0.8 million of six-month treasury bills as a temporary investment.
7. It made its first interest payment of \$0.34 million.
8. It sold the investments for \$0.85 million, the difference between selling price and cost representing interest earned.
9. It recognized its year-end obligation for interest of \$0.34 million and principal of \$1.7 million, but did not actually make the required payments.
10. It prepared year-end closing entries.
    a. Prepare appropriate journal entries for the debt service fund.
    b. Prepare a statement of revenues, expenditures, and changes in fund balance in which you compare actual and budgeted amounts for the year ending December 31.
    c. Prepare a year-end balance sheet.
    d. Does your balance sheet report the balance of the bonds payable? If not, where might it be recorded?

6-7

The conversion from fund to government-wide statements involves more than summing the funds.

The accompanying combined statement of revenues, expenditures, and fund balance was drawn from the statements of Plant City, Florida, which, of course, included a general and other funds that are not shown. Suppose, however, that these were the only funds maintained by the city.

1. Prepare a government-wide statement of net assets (balance sheet) and a statement of activities. Make the following assumptions:
    - At year-end the city had \$4.39 million in cash and equivalents (its only assets) in its capital projects fund. It had accounts payable and other short-term liabilities in that fund of \$0.71 million. It had neither assets nor liabilities in its debt service fund.
    - At year-end the city had \$28.28 million in general long-term assets ("construction in process and other assets").
    - It would charge depreciation of \$2.1 million for the year. Accumulated depreciation at year-end would be \$10.4 million.
    - It had \$3.12 million in general obligation long-term debt.
    - Interest paid for the year was equal to interest expense.

   You need not reconcile beginning and ending balances of net assets, and the statement of activity can be in the "traditional" format (i.e., with the revenues and expenses shown in rows rather than columns).
2. Comment on the main differences in the revenues, expenditures/expenses, and other financing sources/uses as reported on the fund statements and on the government-wide statements. Would you expect that over the life of the government the cumulative changes in fund balance (net assets) as reported on the two types of statements would be different? Explain.

Plant City
Statement of Revenues, Expenditures and Changes in Fund Balance (in millions)

	Debt Service	Capital Projects
Revenues and other financing sources		
Intergovernmental revenues	$0.30	
Fees and miscellaneous revenues		$2.47
Total revenues and other financing sources	0.30	2.47
Expenditures		
Retirement of principal	$0.16	
Interest	0.14	
Construction costs		$2.17
Total expenditures	0.30	2.17
Excess of revenues and other financing sources over expenditures	$ 0	$0.30
Fund balance, beginning of year	0	3.38
Fund balance, end of year	$ 0	$3.68

6-8

Governments may report substantially different amounts of interest on their government-wide and fund financial statements.

Charter City issued $100 million of 6 percent, twenty-year general obligation bonds on January 1, 2004. The bonds were sold to yield 6.2 percent and hence were issued at a discount of $2.27 million (i.e., at a price of $97.73 million). Interest on the bonds is payable on July 1 and January 1 of each year.

On July 1, 2004, and January 1, 2005, the city made its required interest payments of $3 million each.

1. How much interest expenditure should the city report in its debt service fund statement for its fiscal year ending December 31, 2004? During 2004, the city did not transfer resources to the debt service fund for the interest payment due on January 1, 2005.
2. How much interest expense should the city report on its government-wide statements for the year ending December 31, 2004? (It might be helpful to prepare appropriate journal entries.)
3. On January 1, 2024, the city repaid the bonds. How would the repayment be reflected on the city's (1) fund statements and (2) government-wide statements?

6-9

Special assessment debt may take different forms.

A city agrees to extend water and sewer lines to an outlying community. To cover the cost, the affected property owners agree to special assessments of $12 million. The assessments are to be paid over five years, with interest at the rate of 6 percent per year.

For each of the following situations describe how the city should account for the special assessment debt.

1. The city finances the project by issuing special assessment bonds. The bonds are to be repaid with the special assessment revenues, which the city will account for, as received from property owners, in a debt service fund. The newly constructed lines will be accounted for as general capital assets.
2. The project is financed by bonds issued by a specially created municipal utility district, which is not part of the city's financial reporting entity. Although the city is to construct and own the lines, the utility district is responsible for collecting the assessments and making all required principal and interest payments. The city has no explicit responsibility for the debt but has indicated to the bond underwriters in a letter that it accepts a "moral obligation" to assume the debt in the event the municipal utility district defaults.
3. The project is financed by bonds issued by a specially created municipal utility district, which is not part of the city's financial reporting entity. The city has agreed to collect the assessments and make all required principal and interest payments on behalf of the municipal utility district. The city is constitutionally prohibited from assuming responsibility for this type of debt.
4. The project is carried out, and the bonds are issued, by the city's water and sewer utility, which is accounted for in an enterprise fund.

6-10

A hospital's footnote distinguishes between the book value and the economic value of long-term debt.

The financial report of Montefiore Medical Center, which operates a major New York City hospital, included the following item in a summary of long-term debt outstanding:

(in thousands)	December 31 1993	1992
Revenue bonds payable	$4,178	$4,303

An explanatory note indicated the following:

The proceeds from the 8.625 percent revenue bonds, dated November 1, 1979, issued by the Dormitory Authority of the State of New York, were used by the Medical Center to construct a parking garage. The fair value of these bonds was estimated to be approximately $5.1 million and $5.4 million at December 31, 1993, and 1992, respectively, using a discounted cash flow analysis based on the Medical Center's incremental borrowing rates for similar types of borrowing arrangements. The bonds are payable serially through June 30, 2010, at increasing annual amounts ranging from $130,000 in 1994 to $500,000 in 2010. Bonds may be redeemed before maturity, for which call premiums are 0.5 percent through June 30, 1994, after which call premiums cease. Under the terms of the revenue bonds agreement, certain escrow funds are required to be maintained. At December 31, 1993, escrow assets aggregated approximately $1.2 million, which exceeded minimum escrow requirements.

1. Why would the *fair* value of the bonds, as calculated by the center, be so much greater than their *face* value?
2. The note states that the "bonds are payable *serially*." What does that mean?
3. Assuming that prevailing interest rates remain constant, why would the market price of the bonds be greater before June 30, 1994, than after?
4. Is it likely that the market value of the bonds is as great as the fair value calculated by the center? Explain.

6-11

Bond refundings may result in an economic gain but a book loss. When should the loss be recognized?

Colgate County issued $1 million of thirty-year, 8 percent term bonds to finance improvements to its electric utility plant. The bonds, accounted for in an enterprise fund, were issued at par.

After the bonds were outstanding for ten years, interest rates fell and the county exercised a call provision to redeem the bonds for $1.1 million. The county obtained the necessary cash by issuing $1.1 million in new, twenty-year, 6 percent bonds.

1. Prepare the entry that the county should have made in its enterprise fund to record the issuance of the original debt (the same entry as in business accounting).
2. Prepare the entry that the county should have made to record the interest expense and payment each semiannual period.
3. Prepare the entry that the county would make to record the redemption of the original debt. Be sure your entry is in accord with GASB standards.
4. Did the county incur an *economic* gain or loss by refunding the debt? Of how much?
5. Suppose, instead, that the county could have predicted that it would redeem the debt after it had been outstanding for ten years (twenty periods) for $1.1 million.
   a. What entry should it have made to record the issuance of the bonds?
   b. Over how many periods should the county have amortized the bond discount?
   c. During the ten years that the bonds were outstanding, what would have been the average reported interest expense each semiannual period, taking into account the amortization of the bond discount? (Assume that the county amortizes bond discounts on a straight-line basis. Although straight-line amortization is not conceptually sound, it provides a measure of the average amortization that would result if the more correct compound interest method were used.)
   d. Prepare the journal entry the county would have made to record interest expense each semiannual period.
6. What is the economic nature of the refunding loss that the county would have to report? In what sense is it really a loss? When did it occur?
7. Compare your response to part f with both GASB and FASB standards pertaining to recognizing refunding gains and losses. Why would it not be practical to recognize the loss in the periods in which it actually occurs?

6-12

Debtors may be able to realize an economic gain by defeasing their debt "in substance."

A hospital has outstanding $100 million of bonds that mature in twenty years (forty periods). The debt was issued at par and pays interest at a rate of 6 percent (3 percent per period). Prevailing rates on comparable bonds are now 4 percent (2 percent per period).

1. What would you expect to be the market price of the bonds, assuming that they are freely traded? Would there be an economic benefit for the hospital to refund the existing debt by acquiring it at the market price and replacing it with new, "low-cost" debt?
2. Assume the bonds contain a provision permitting the hospital to call the bonds in another five years (ten periods) at a price of $105 and that any invested funds could earn a return equal to the prevailing interest rate of 4 percent (2 percent per period). What would be the economic saving that the hospital could achieve by defeasing the bonds "in substance"?

6-13

A debt service fund reports both routine principal and interest payments as well as an in-substance defeasance.

The statement at the top of the next page is from an annual report of the City of Fort Worth, Texas. It was accompanied by the notes that follow.

Defeasance of Prior Debt

During the year, the City issued $194,520 of general obligation bonds. The proceeds were used to refund debt obligations with a face value of $181,985. A portion of the proceeds from the issuance of the bonds was placed in an irrevocable escrow account and invested in U.S. obligations that, together with interest earned thereon, would provide an amount to call the bonds on the appropriate call dates. The advance refunding resulted in an economic gain of $4,816.

Arbitrage

The City of Fort Worth frequently issues bonds for capital construction projects. These bonds are subject to the arbitrage regulations. At September 30, the liability for rebate of arbitrage was $560 for general obligation bonds and $51 for enterprise bonds, respectively. These amounts are included in the "Payable to Federal Government" category of the debt service and enterprise funds.

City of Forth Worth

Statement of Revenues, Expenditures, and Changes in Fund Balance
Year Ended September 30 Debt Service Fund (000s omitted)

Revenues	
Revenues from use of money and property	$ 6,170
Expenditures	
Defeasance of certificates of obligation	$ 1,837
Principal retirement	39,842
Interest and service charges	26,659
Total expenditures	$ 68,338
Excess of revenues over (under) expenditures	$ (62,168)
Other financing sources (uses)	
Proceeds from refunding bonds	$190,009
Proceeds from general obligation bonds	9,617
Nonreciprocal transfers-in	55,565
Payment to refunded bond escrow account	(186,860)
Nonreciprocal transfer-out	(1,995)
Total other financing sources	$ 66,336
Excess of revenues and other financing sources over expenditures and other financing uses	$ 4,168
Fund balance, beginning of year	10,401
Fund balance, end of year	$ 14,569

1. Based on your knowledge of debt service funds, what is the most likely source of "revenue from use of money and property"?
2. Explain in your own words the significance of "proceeds from refunding bonds" and "payment to refunded bond escrow account." (Do not attempt to reconcile the amounts in the statement with those in the footnotes; a portion of the bonds refunded was accounted for in a proprietary fund.)
3. The note pertaining to the bond defeasance also indicates that the refunding resulted in an accounting loss of $536, which was reported in the water and sewer fund, an enterprise fund. How is it possible that the city had an economic gain but an accounting loss? Why is a loss reported in an enterprise fund but not this type of debt service fund?
4. What is the most likely source of the nonreciprocal transfer-in? What was its purpose?
5. What is the most likely reason that the city had an obligation to the federal government for arbitrage? Is the liability necessarily an indication of poor management?

SOLUTION TO EXERCISE FOR REVIEW AND SELF-STUDY

1. Journal Entries

a.

Assessments receivable—current	$1,600,000	
Assessments receivable—deferred	6,400,000	
Revenues		$1,600,000
Deferred revenues		6,400,000

To record the assessments (debt service find, the fund that will account for resources used to service the debt)

The first-year assessments may be recognized as revenues as they will be available for current-year expenditure. The balance must be deferred.

b.

Cash	$8,050,000	
Expenditures—bond issue costs	150,000	
Other financing sources—bond proceeds (face value)		$8,000,000
Other financing sources—bond proceeds (bond premium)		200,000

To record the issuance of the bonds (capital projects fund, the fund that will account for resources used to construct the project)

Other financing use—nonreciprocal transfer of bond premium to debt service fund	$50,000	
Cash		$50,000

To record transfer-out of the bond premium to the debt service fund (capital projects fund)

Cash	$50,000	
Other financing sources—nonreciprocal transfer from capital projects fund		$50,000

To record transfer-in of the bond premium to the debt service fund (debt service fund)

Inasmuch as the city issued the debt in its name (and is thereby obligated in some manner for repayment), the bonds would be recorded in the government-wide statements. Like other long-term debts, however, they would not be recognized in the funds statement balance sheet.

c.

Expenditures—construction	$8,000,000	
Cash		$8,000,000

To record construction of the sidewalls (capital projects fund)

Infrastructure assets are accounted for similarly to other capital assets. Therefore the sidewalks should be recorded as an asset in the government-wide statements, but not in the funds statements.

d.

Cash	$2,080,000	
Assessments receivable—current		$1,600,000
Interest revenue		480,000

To record collection of interest (6 percent of $8,000,000) plus the first assessment installment (debt service fund)

e.

Expenditures—interest	$240,000	
Cash		$240,000

To record interest (debt service fund)

As the debt service fund is a governmental fund and thereby accounted for on the modified accrual basis, neither the interest nor the principal due in 2005 need be accrued.

2. *Fund Statements of Revenues, Expenditures, and Changes in Fund Balances* (see table at bottom of the page)
3. *Government-Wide Statement of Activity*

Revenues	
Assessments	$1,600,000
Interest—assessments	480,000
Total revenues	$2,080,000
Expenses	
Bond issue costs	150,000
Interest ($480,000 less $15,000 amortization of bond premium)	465,000
Total expenditures	$ 615,000
Excess of revenues over expenditures	$1,465,000

	Capital Projects	Debt Service
Revenues		
Assessments		$1,600,000
Interest		480,000
Total revenues		$2,080,000
Expenditures		
Bond issue costs	$ 150,000	
Construction	8,000,000	
Interest		$ 240,000
Total expenditures	$8,150,000	$ 240,000
Excess of revenues over expenditures	$(8,150,000)	$1,840,000
Other financing sources or uses		
Bond proceeds—face value	$8,000,000	
Bond proceeds—bond premium	200,000	
Nonreciporcal transfer to/from other funds	(50,000)	$ 50,000
Net other financing sources or uses	$8,150,000	$ 50,000
Increase in fund balance	$ 0	$1,890,000
Fund balance sheets		
Assets		
Cash		$1,890,000
Assessments receivable—deferred		6,400,000
Total assets		$8,290,000
Liabilities and fund balances		
Deferred revenues		$6,400,000
Fund balance		1,890,000
Total liabilities and fund balances		$8,290,000

Government-Wide Balance Sheet

Assets	
Cash	$ 1,890,000
Assessments receivable—deferred	6,400,000
Infrastructure assets (sidewalks)	8,000,000
Total assets	$16,290,000
Liabilities	
Interest payable	240,000
Deferred revenues	6,400,000
Bonds payable (including unamortized premium of $185,000)	8,185,000
Total liabilities	$14,825,000
Net assets	
Invested in capital, net of related debt	$ (185,000)
Restricted to debt service	1,650,000 (a)
Total net assets	1,465,000
Total liabilities and net assets	$16,290,000

(a) This amount is equal to the $1,890,000 balance in the debt service fund less the $240,000 of interest recognized as an expense in the government-wide full accrual statements but not in the modified accrual fund statements.

Note that in the government-wide statements (1) the infrastructure assets are capitalized; (2) the long-term debt, including the bond premium, is reported as a liability; and (3) interest, taking into account amortization of the bond premium, is reported on a full accrual basis.

4. Debt Defeasance

a.

Present value, at 2 percent, of $1,600,000 principal (a single sum) to be paid at the end of six periods (present value of $1 = $0.88797)	$1,420,754
Present value, at 2 percent of $48,000 interest (an annuity) to be paid at the end of each of six periods (present value of an annuity of $1 = $5.60143)	268,869
Total economic cost of "old" bonds	$1,689,623

b.

Present value, at 2 percent, of $1,600,000 principal (a single sum) to be paid at the end of four periods (present value of $1 = $0.92384)	$1,478,153
Present value, at 2 percent of $48,000 interest (an annuity) to be paid at the end of each of four periods (present value of an annuity of $1 = $3.80773)	182,771
Amount that would have to be placed with trustee	$1,660,924

c. The economic cost of the new bonds would be the same as the amount required to be borrowed. Hence, the economic savings is the difference between the old bonds and the new: $1,689,623 minus $1,660,924, or $28,699.

CHAPTER 7

Long-Lived Assets and Investments in Marketable Securities

Learning Objectives

After studying this chapter you should understand:

- Why and how governments account for capital assets in both fund and government-wide statements
- Why and how governments account for transactions involving donated assets, trade-ins, and collectibles
- GASB's controversial provisions regarding infrastructures
- What special problems asset impairments create
- Why investments in marketable securities may be of high risk and thereby present special problems of accounting and reporting

The accounting for both long-lived assets and investments, albeit for different reasons, should be of vital concern to statement users and preparers. Long-lived assets are a key component of many of the services provided by governments and not-for-profits. They include its police cars, administrative buildings, and utility lines and roads. If they are inadequate to meet the demands for services to be delivered in the future, then the organization will either have to reduce its services or come up with the financial resources to enhance the assets. At the same time, existing stocks of capital assets have to be either maintained or replaced, thereby necessitating an ongoing commitment of financial resources. In addition, the constituents of governments and not-for-profits generally want, and are entitled to, assurance that the organization is using its assets efficiently and effectively.

Whereas the previous chapter was concerned with the *resources* that are used to acquire long-lived, "general" assets, this chapter is directed to the assets themselves.

The accounting issues relating to governments, not-for-profits, and businesses are similar, and, in fact, are now, for the first time, being resolved in much the same way. Until the Financial Accounting Standards Board (FASB) issued Statement No. 93, *Recognition of Depreciation by Not-for-Profit Organizations* in 1987, not-for-profits could record their long-lived assets at cost; they did not have to recognize depreciation. Similarly, until 1999 when the Governmental Accounting Standards Board (GASB) issued Statement No. 34, *Basic Financial Statements—and Management's Discussion and Analysis—for State and Local Governments* (the statement that established the new reporting model), governments also were able to report their general capital assets at their undepreciated original cost. Per the new model, as emphasized in previous chapters, governments may not charge depreciation in their modified accrual fund statements, but must do so in their full accrual government-wide statements. As is made apparent in this chapter, key constituents of the GASB strongly oppose the provisions of Statement No. 34, and the accounting for long-lived assets, especially infrastructure assets, remains controversial.

A second part of the chapter addresses marketable securities held for *investment.* Investments are at the opposite end of the liquidity spectrum from capital assets and present contrasting issues of both disclosure and control. They are of critical concern to both governments and other not-for-profits. Unlike long-lived assets, they are subject to significant risks of declines in market values as well as of fraud and mismanagement on the part of both the financial institutions with whom they deal and of their own employees. The entity needs to inform statement users of these risks and to establish policies and procedures to manage and control them.

WHAT ACCOUNTING PRACTICES DO GOVERNMENTS FOLLOW FOR GENERAL CAPITAL ASSETS?

In its *Objectives of Financial Reporting*, the GASB set forth the purpose of capital asset reporting and laid the foundation for the current provisions:

> Financial reporting should provide information about a governmental entity's physical and other nonfinancial resources having useful lives that extend beyond the current year, including information that can be used to assess the service potential of these resources. This information should be presented to help users assess long- and short-term capital needs.[1]

[1] GASB Concepts Statement 1, *Objectives of Financial Reporting* (May 1987), para. 78.

MAINTAINING ACCOUNTING CONTROL OVER CAPITAL ASSETS

General capital assets—capital assets that, by definition, are associated with the government as a whole, rather than with any specific fund—are distinguished from the assets of proprietary funds (enterprise funds and internal service funds) and of fiduciary funds (pension and other trust funds in which land, buildings, and other capital assets are, for the most part, held as investments).

Nonfinancial in character, general capital assets are excluded from governmental funds because the measurement focus of governmental funds is upon financial resources. Therefore, in governmental funds, the costs of capital assets are reported as expenditures when the assets are acquired rather than capitalized as assets and subsequently written off as the assets are consumed.

Prior to the implementation of Statement No. 34, governments recorded their general capital assets in a **general fixed assets account group.** The general fixed asset account group was little more than a list of government-owned assets. It accounted for no assets other than capital assets—no cash, investments, receivables, or the like. The list, however, was in double-entry form, with the assets (debits) offset with an equity-type account, "investment in general fixed assets" (a credit). The list took the double-entry form mainly so that the assets could be displayed as part of the multicolumn combined balance sheet, along with a government's other assets and liabilities. If the list reported only assets, but not the offsetting account "investment in general fixed assets," then the totals of the combined balance sheet would be out of balance.

Statement No. 34 eliminates the requirement that account groups be included on the combined governmental-fund balance sheet. Instead, it mandates that governments provide a schedule showing the activity during the year in capital asset accounts. Accordingly, governments no longer need present capital asset information in account-group format, and the general fixed asset group and its counterpart, the general long-term debt account group, no longer have a place in external reporting.

All governments must maintain records of their capital assets (and the related accumulated depreciation) that are not recorded on the balance sheets of their governmental funds so that they can prepare their government-wide statements and the required schedule of capital asset activity. Some governments continue to maintain account groups for purposes of internal accounting and control. However, others find alternative types of records to be more convenient or less costly, especially since they need not be kept in double-entry format.

The most common classifications for general capital assets include:

- Land
- Buildings
- Equipment
- Improvements other than buildings
- Construction in progress
- Infrastructure

However, "softer" assets, such as library books and recordings, computer software (whether purchased or developed in-house), and intangibles, such as water rights, may also be capitalized.

DIFFERENCES IN GOVERNMENT-WIDE (FULL ACCRUAL) STATEMENTS

Capital assets, including infrastructure, should be reported on the government-wide statement of net assets at historical cost net of accumulated depreciation, if applicable. Accumulated depreciation may be reported on the face of the balance sheet or disclosed in notes. Most assets should be depreciated over their estimated useful lives in a manner that is "rational and systematic" (i.e., using one of the methods commonly used by businesses). However, governments, like businesses, do not have to depreciate inexhaustible assets, such as land, works of art, or historical treasures. Moreover, as is addressed in a section to follow, governments do not have to depreciate infrastructure assets if they can demonstrate that they are preserving the assets in a specified condition.

A government does not have to include a separate line item for depreciation on its government-wide statement of activity (statement of revenues and expenses). Inasmuch as the statement will typically report expenses by function (e.g., public safety, recreation, health) it may aggregate the depreciation charge applicable to each of the functions with other types of expenses.

A government must, however, include in its notes to the financial statements information as to each of its major categories of capital assets. Usually presented in schedule format, this information would include: beginning and ending balances; acquisitions, sales, and retirements; and current period depreciation (including the amount charged to each of the functions reported on the statement of activities). The City of Charlotte's schedules relating to governmental capital assets are presented in Table 7-1.

The sections that follow address issues that are common to both the fund and the government-wide statements.

PLACING VALUE ON CAPITAL ASSETS

When a government acquires an asset, it should follow the same general guidelines used by businesses to determine the costs to be capitalized. Thus, capitalized value should include all costs necessary to bring an asset to a serviceable condition. For purchased assets the capitalized cost should include purchase price (less any discounts, such as those for prompt payment or for favored customers), plus transportation and installation costs. For an asset such as land, it would include legal fees, title fees, appraisal costs, closing costs, and costs of demolishing existing structures that cannot be used (less recoveries from salvage).

For constructed assets it would include direct labor and materials, overhead costs, architect fees, and insurance premiums during the construction phase. However, unlike businesses, governments should *not* capitalize interest on general capital assets that they construct themselves.[2] This is because, per Statement No. 34, interest expense on general long-term liabilities should be treated as an indirect expense, rather than being attributed to specific functions or programs, such as public works.

Governments should report donated assets at their estimated fair value (plus ancillary charges, if any) at the time of acquisition. If the assets are exhaustible, then in their government-wide statements they should depreciate the assets over their remaining useful lives.

ACCOUNTING FOR TRADE-INS

Governments, like businesses, trade in old assets for new.

EXAMPLE *Trade-Ins*

A government trades in an old automobile for a new one. The old automobile had cost $30,000; its fair market value at the time of trade is $12,000. To date the government

[2] GASB Statement No. 37, *Basic Financial Statements—and Management's Discussion and Analysis—for State and Local Governments: Omnibus* (June 2001), an amendment of GASB Statements No. 21 and No. 34, paras. 6 and 7.

TABLE 7–1
Charlotte, North Carolina
Information about Capital Assets (in Thousands)

Capital asset activity for governmental activities for the year ended June 30, 2002, was as follows:

	Beginning Balance	Increases	Decreases	Ending Balance
Governmental activities—				
Capital assets, not being depreciated:				
Land	$1,536,913	$204,185	$ —	$1,741,098
Construction in progress	295,712	119,243	219,877	195,078
Total capital assets, not being depreciated	1,832,625	323,428	219,877	1,936,176
Capital assets, being depreciated:				
Buildings	418,220	57,850	—	476,070
Infrastructure	1,120,762	206,683	20,148	1,307,297
Machinery and equipment	104,695	29,090	12,658	121,127
Total capital assets being depreciated	1,643,677	293,623	32,806	1,904,494
Less accumulated depreciation for:				
Buildings	107,414	11,032	—	118,446
Infrastructure	281,294	4,789	2,493	283,590
Machinery and equipment	62,427	13,847	8,208	68,066
Total accumulated depreciation	451,135	29,668	10,701	470,102
Total capital assets, being depreciated, net	1,192,542	263,955	22,105	1,434,392
Governmental activities capital assets, net	$3,025,167	$587,383	$241,982	$3,370,568

Depreciation expense was charged to activities as follows:

Governmental activities:	
Public safety	$ 8,884
Sanitation	4,377
General administration	1,392
Support services	921
Engineering and property management	1,053
Streets and highways	4,429
Community planning and development	8,586
Capital assets held by the City's internal service funds are charged to the various functions based on the usage of the assets	26
Total depreciation expense—governmental activities	$29,668

has charged $10,000 in depreciation. Therefore the book value of the asset is $20,000. The fair market value of the old automobile is $12,000 whereas that of the new one is $40,000. Hence the government is required to pay an additional $28,000 in cash.

In its general, or other governmental, fund, only the cash aspects of the transaction need be recognized. The acquisition would be reported as an expenditure:

Expenditure—acquisition of equipment	$28,000	
Cash		$28,000
To record the trade-in transaction		

Of course, in the ledger in which it maintains its list of capital assets, the government would have to remove the old asset (along with the accumulated depreciation) and replace it with the new.

In its government-wide statements the government would have to recognize a loss on the transaction—the difference between the amount for which the old automobile was, in effect, sold (its fair market value of $12,000) and its book value ($20,000):

Equipment (new auto)	$40,000	
Loss on trade-in	8,000	
Accumulated depreciation (old auto)	10,000	
Equipment (old auto)		$30,000
Cash		28,000
To record trade-in of old automobile for new		

ACCOUNTING FOR COLLECTIBLES

Like their not-for-profit counterparts, government museums, universities, libraries, and history centers own works of art, rare books, and historical artifacts. These "collectibles" often have considerable monetary value and for some entities may be their most significant assets.

Governments and not-for-profits have generally opposed both capitalizing the collectibles they hold and recognizing as revenue the collectibles they receive as contributions. They contend that the value of such objects, like their beauty, may be in the eye of the beholder, and only the most philistine of accountants would even consider placing a dollar sign beside a "priceless" work of art. Moreover, works of art are not assets that can be associated with future cash receipts or savings. Rather, when retained, they are a drain upon resources because they require ongoing protection. They generate cash only upon sale. To report them as assets, it can be argued, would result in financial statements that are as surrealistic as some of the art itself.

GASB Standards

In its Statement No. 34, the GASB follows the lead of the FASB, which in Statement No. 116, *Accounting for Contributions Received and Contributions Made*, addresses the same issues. Statement No. 34 does not require (but nevertheless encourages) governments to capitalize their art and similar assets as long as they meet the following conditions:

- They are held for public exhibition, education, or research in furtherance of public service, rather than for financial gain
- They are protected, kept unencumbered, cared for, and preserved
- They are subject to an organizational policy that requires the proceeds from sales of collection items to be used to acquire other items for collections

Works of art and other collectibles that do *not* meet these conditions (e.g., a work of art held purely as an investment or acquired for an administrator's office that is not accessible to the public or for research purposes) must be capitalized.

If governments do capitalize their art or historical collections, then they should depreciate the assets that are exhaustible but not those that do not necessarily decline in value with time.

Governments should recognize contributions of collectibles as revenue just as if they had received other assets (i.e., per the guidelines discussed in Chapter 4). However, if the items were to be added to noncapitalized collections, then the governments should offset the revenue with a charge to a program expense rather than to an asset. In contrast, per FASB Statement No. 116, nongovernmental not-for-profits are not allowed to recognize revenue for items contributed to noncapitalized collections.

WHY AND HOW SHOULD GOVERNMENTS REPORT INFRASTRUCTURE?

A government's infrastructure is its capital assets that are immovable and can be preserved for a significantly longer period than most other assets. They are of value only to the government itself. They include roads, sidewalks, drainage systems, bridges, tunnels, and lighting systems. Although many citizens take the nation's infrastructure for granted, public officials, investors, and economists are expressing serious concern over it. In the past forty years, spectacular failures have called attention to the deteriorating condition of much of the country's public physical plant. For example, in the 1970s New York City was forced to close a portion of its West Side Highway, a scenic drive along the Hudson River, because the road had become unsafe and the city was unable to come up with the cash to repair it. In 1982 the residents of Jersey City, New Jersey, had to go without water for three days owing to a breakdown in the city's aqueduct system. Then in 1983, Connecticut's Mianus River Bridge on Interstate 95, the main East Coast highway, collapsed, killing three people. Numerous research studies have confirmed that there is an increasing gap between the nation's infrastructure requirements and its ability to pay for them.

Infrastructure may be a national problem, but it must be solved mainly at the state and local level. After all, most roads and highways (apart from those that are part of the interstate system), bridges, drainage, and water and public power systems are the responsibility of state and local governments.

Governments are accountable for infrastructure assets, and it is difficult to see how the objectives of financial reporting can be fulfilled without comprehensive information regarding not only expenditures for infrastructure but also on the assets' status. For example, data on infrastructure are essential if government financial reports are to achieve the following general goals set forth in the GASB's *Objectives of Financial Reporting:*

- To help users assess the economy, efficiency, and effectiveness with which government used the resources within its command
- To determine whether the entity's financial position improved or deteriorated during the reporting period
- To provide information about a government's physical and other nonfinancial resources having useful lives that extend beyond the current year, including information that can be used to assess the service potential of those resources
- To help users assess long and short-term capital needs

Until the GASB issued Statement No. 34, governments provided virtually no information as to their infrastructure. Except for those assets (such as sewer and power lines) accounted for in proprietary funds, governments charged infrastructure assets as fund expenditures as they constructed them. They neither reported them in a fund balance sheet nor described them in the notes to the financial statements.

Owing to its provisions pertaining to infrastructure, Statement No. 34 has proven to be the most controversial pronouncement that the GASB has ever issued. Indeed, the vehemence of the opposition toward the statement is evidenced by a resolution of the Government Finance Officers Association in which the organization threatened not only to withdraw its financial support of the GASB but also to encourage governments to violate the statement's infrastructure rules (see "In Practice: Resolution on Infrastructure of the Government Finance Officers Association").

GASB Standards

Statement No. 34 requires that, in general, governments account for infrastructure assets just as they do other capital assets. That is, in their fund statements, they should report infrastructure costs as expenditures as they are incurred. In their government-wide statements they should capitalize the costs and depreciate the assets over their estimated useful lives.

Nevertheless, acknowledging the limitations of depreciation as a measure of the cost of using infrastructure assets, the statement permits governments to avoid charging depreciation if they can demonstrate that they incur the costs necessary to preserve the assets in a specified condition. If a government satisfies certain conditions, then it can elect to report as period expenses in its government-wide statements all infrastructure costs relating to eligible assets *except* those that result in additions or improvements. It need not charge depreciation and need not reduce the capitalized cost of the assets with accumulated depreciation.

To use this modified approach on all or some of its infrastructure assets, a government would have to assess periodically (at least every three years) the condition of its infrastructure assets and estimate the annual amount necessary to maintain and preserve the assets at the specified "condition level" (which would be established by the government itself). In addition, it would have to document that the assets are, in fact, being maintained at or above that level.

THE MODIFIED APPROACH COMPARED WITH STANDARD DEPRECIATION

Under the modified approach, preservation costs (outlays that extend the useful life of an asset beyond the originally expected useful life) are expensed as incurred. No depreciation is charged on either the initial cost of acquiring the asset or the subsequent preservation costs. By contrast, under the standard approach both the initial cost and the subsequent preservation costs are capitalized and depreciated over their expected useful life. Suppose, for example, that to preserve a road at a specified condition, a government must repave it every five years at a cost of $200,000. Under the modified approach, the government would report the $200,000 as an expense when incurred. Under the standard approach, it would capitalize the $200,000 and depreciate it over a period of five years. Thus, for this particular road, the modified approach would result in a charge of $200,000 every five years; the standard approach would result in a charge of $40,000 per year plus the depreciation on the initial cost of the road.

If a government elects the modified approach then it must disclose (as "required supplementary information") the assessed condition of the assets and the basis on which it made that assessment. The basis would ordinarily be an engineering measurement scale, such as one that ranks pavements from zero (unsafe) to 100 (perfect). The government must also report, for the latest five years, the estimated cost of maintaining the assets at the specified condition as compared to the amounts actually expensed. Table 7-2 illustrates the type of disclosures that the GASB expects.

Although the modified approach may be at odds with conventional business practice, it is consistent with the theoretical underpinning of depreciation accounting. Properly maintained infrastructure assets may, like land, have infinite useful lives; they need not decline in economic value. Indeed, as evidenced by Roman aqueducts or Chinese great walls, properly cared-for assets can last well beyond the number of years that are of concern to financial statement users.

TABLE 7–2
Infrastructure Note
Condition Rating of a Street System

	Percentage of Lane-Miles in Good or Better Condition		
	2002	**2001**	**2000**
Main arterial	93.2%	91.5%	92.0%
Arterial	85.2%	81.6%	84.3%
Secondary	87.2%	84.5%	86.8%
Overall system	87.0%	85.5%	87.3%

	Percentage of Lane-Miles in Substandard Condition		
	2002	**2001**	**2000**
Main arterial	1.7%	2.6%	3.1%
Arterial	3.5%	6.4%	5.9%
Secondary	2.1%	3.4%	3.8%
Overall system	2.2%	3.6%	3.9%

Comparison of Needed-to-Actual Maintenance/Preservation (in Thousands)

	2002	**2001**	**2000**	**1999**	**1998**
Main arterial:					
Needed	$2,476	$2,342	$2,558	$2,401	$2,145
Actual	2,601	2,552	2,432	2,279	2,271
Arterial:					
Needed	1,485	1,405	1,535	1,441	1,287
Actual	1,560	1,531	1,459	1,367	1,362
Secondary:					
Needed	990	937	1,023	960	858
Actual	1,040	1,021	972	911	908
Overall sysem:					
Needed	4,951	4,684	5,116	4,802	4,290
Actual	5,201	5,104	4,863	4,557	4,541
Difference	250	420	(253)	(245)	251

Note: The condition of road pavement is measured using a pavement management system, which is based on a weighted average of six distress factors found in pavement surfaces. The pavement management system uses a measurement scale that is based on a condition index ranging from zero for a failed pavement to 100 for a pavement in perfect condition. The condition index is used to classify roads in good or better condition (70–100), fair condition (50–69), and substandard condition (less than 50). It is the City's policy to maintain at least 85 percent of its street system at a good or better condition level. No more than 10 percent should be in a substandard condition. Condition assessments are determined every year.

Source: GASB Statement No. 34, Basic Financial Statements—and Management's Discussion and Analysis—for State and Local Governments, p. 277.

RETROACTIVE CAPITALIZATION OF EXISTING INFRA-STRUCTURE

Recognizing the difficulty of establishing the original cost of infrastructure assets (those in place when a government first implements the new model), Statement No. 34 allows governments to retroactively capitalize only those assets acquired after June 30, 1980. It also permits them to estimate their cost by applying a price-level index to the current replacement cost of the assets. Thus, for example, if in 2005 the replacement cost of a road constructed in 1991 were $10 million and a road construction price level index was 90 for 1991 and 120 for 2005, then the road would be recorded at an initial cost of $7.5 million ($10 million times 90/120), less accumulated depreciation if the standard rather than the modified approach were elected. If the road had

IN PRACTICE

RESOLUTION ON INFRASTRUCTURE OF THE GOVERNMENT FINANCE OFFICERS ASSOCIATION

Under current generally accepted accounting principles (GAAP), state and local governments are not required to report the infrastructure assets of the general government in their financial statements. Recently, however, the GASB has proposed to require the presentation of general government infrastructure assets on the face of the statement of position at their historical cost. This amount would subsequently be allocated to the statement of activities over the useful life of the assets in the form of depreciation expense. Alternatively, the GASB is considering the possibility of allowing governments to forgo the depreciation of infrastructure assets (although those assets would still need to be reported on the statement of position), provided that the government had demonstrated that it was preserving or maintaining such assets at an "acceptable" condition level.

GFOA is persuaded that the type of information needed concerning a government's general infrastructure assets is the type of information set forth in the National Advisory Council on State and Local Budgeting's Guidelines. Furthermore, GFOA continues to believe that the budget, rather than the financial statements, is the appropriate setting for infrastructure reporting. The infrastructure reporting requirements proposed by the GASB (i.e., the retroactive reporting of infrastructure assets at their historical cost and the subsequent depreciation of such assets) are potentially costly and provide information of little practical benefit to financial statement users. Furthermore, GFOA adamantly opposes any effort to move financial reporting into the realm of what "ought to be," as would clearly be the case if GASB were to adopt the "preservation/maintenance option" for reporting infrastructure assets. Such an approach not only potentially encroaches upon public policy (which is properly decided by elected officials), but would clearly "tip the scales" in favor of capital expenditures at the expense of other services to citizens.

GFOA Position:

- To affirm GFOA's strong opposition to GASB's proposal to mandate the reporting and depreciation of general infrastructure assets.
- To authorize GFOA's Executive Board to give consideration to withholding GASB funding if the GASB proceeds with its infrastructure reporting proposal.
- To authorize the GFOA Executive Board to consider encouraging governments not to implement the infrastructure provisions of GASB's proposed financial reporting model.
- To allow governments that do not comply with the infrastructure provisions of GASB's proposed financial reporting model to participate in the Certificate of Achievement for Excellence in Financial Reporting Program.

Source: Government Finance Officers Association public policy statement "Infrastructure Reporting," adopted 25 May 1999; available at www.gfoa.org/services/policy/gfoapp1.shtml.

an expected useful life of thirty years, and therefore, should be 50 percent depreciated, its net book value would be $3.75 million (initial cost of $7.5 million less accumulated depreciation of $3.75 million).

NEW INFRASTRUCTURE

All governments are required to capitalize general infrastructure assets acquired or constructed on or after the effective date of Statement No. 34. (Of course they must also continue to capitalize infrastructure accounted for in proprietary funds.)

However, in further acknowledgment of the difficulty of *retroactively* capitalizing general infrastructure assets (i.e., assets already in service), the GASB extended the effective date for retroactive reporting by three years for large and middle-sized governments and permanently exempted small governments.

A CONTROVERSIAL PRONOUNCEMENT

Critics of Statement No. 34 have presented several arguments as to why its infrastructure provisions are flawed:

- Statement users have given no indication that they want or would use data on the historical cost of infrastructure. In fact, a research study presented a sample of statement users, including investors, managers, and legislators, with six types of information that governments could provide: historical cost, replacement cost, constant dollar cost, budget to actual data, financial plans, and engineering information. The users ranked engineering and financial plan information first and second as most useful. They ranked historical cost data dead last.[3]
- A key reason for maintaining accounting control over assets is to prevent fraud or abuse. But infrastructure assets cannot be stolen or misused. Therefore, there is no reason to capitalize them.
- Another important reason for reporting assets is to enable statement users to assess whether the assets have been used efficiently. Governments are not expected to earn a monetary return on infrastructure. Therefore, a comparison between a measure of output (performance) and any monetary value that might be assigned to the assets in the financial statements is not likely to be meaningful.
- A further rationale for reporting assets is to enable statement users to consider alternative uses for them. Infrastructure assets, however, cannot be either sold or moved. They seldom have alternative uses.
- The cost of infrastructure assets constructed in the past is of no significance. Many of a government's infrastructure assets were probably not constructed as part of a single project. Instead they evolved over time. For example, a government does not typically construct a four-lane highway through virgin fields or forests. More likely, the highway began as a footpath and metamorphosed over generations to an unpaved road, a paved road, and a two-line highway.

In brief, it is argued, the information that must be reported on the face of the government-wide statement of net assets facilitates no decisions and therefore, the cost of record keeping and reporting is not worth the benefits.

The GASB, of course, took note of these criticisms in its deliberations. Its position, however, is not that the historical cost of infrastructure is useful for purposes of decision making. Rather, it is that if the government-wide statements are to provide a measure of the cost of services, and thereby to be on a full accrual basis, then the statements cannot ignore the costs associated with a class of assets as significant as infrastructure.

THE QUESTION OF DEFERRED MAINTENANCE

As pointed out earlier in the text, government assets, especially infrastructure, can be seen as liabilities as much as assets. Infrastructure assets must be maintained and, like an individual's car, home, and college-age children, are a continuing drain upon fiscal resources.

Governments can postpone asset upkeep costs, but they cannot avoid them. For some assets, engineers have developed sophisticated maintenance schedules that minimize long-term costs. For example, streets and highways should be resurfaced after a

[3] Relmond P. Van Daniker and Vernon Kwiatkowski, *Infrastructure Assets: An Assessment of User Needs and Recommendations for Financial Reporting* (Norwalk, CT: Governmental Accounting Standards Board, 1986).

specified number of years. If governments delay beyond that period, then the costs to repair the further deterioration will outweigh the financial benefits of having put off the expenditures.

Deferred maintenance costs are defined as "delayed repair, or upkeep, measured by the outlay required to restore a plant or individual asset to full operating characteristics."[4] They could be measured as the amount necessary to bring the assets up to their expected operating condition. Deferred maintenance costs may be interpreted as a potential call upon government resources—an obligation that is being passed on to taxpayers of the future. They are an indication that taxpayers of the past or present have not paid for the maintenance costs applicable to the services received.

In the GASB infrastructure study, at least 84 percent of the academic, investor, legislator, and citizen groups were in favor of including information on deferred maintenance in annual financial reports. Only managers (who would be responsible for providing the data) were less enthusiastic, with only 52 percent advocating inclusion.[5]

Statement No. 34 goes a long way toward providing the information that users want. Governments that do not depreciate their assets must demonstrate that they are, in fact, maintaining their assets at, or above, a specified condition. In addition they must disclose, for a five-year period, their actual maintenance costs as compared to what would be necessary to maintain those assets at the specified condition (see Table 7-2 for an example).

For governments that do depreciate their assets, the depreciation charge may be interpreted as a surrogate for deferred maintenance costs. Accumulated depreciation may be seen as the cumulative deferred maintenance costs—a very rough measure (based on historical costs) of the portion of the asset that has been consumed.

GASB Statement No. 34 elevated the level of government's capital asset reporting and accountability to that of business's. Most notably, it requires that governments capitalize their infrastructure and charge depreciation on exhaustible assets. Prior to the issuance of Statement No. 34, many governments maintained exceedingly lax accounting control over their capital assets, perhaps in part because once acquired, the assets were not reported on fund balance sheets or statements of revenue and expenditure; they had no impact on fund balances.

LIMITATIONS OF INFORMATION REPORTED ABOUT LONG-TERM ASSETS

"Improved" should not be mistaken for "adequate" reporting. In reality, readers can still learn very little from financial statement data on long-term assets—no more than they could from the financial statements of a business. Even the new financial statements fail to facilitate the significant decisions or judgments that statement users are likely to make.

Consider, for example, typical questions relating to capital assets that either city officials or external parties might ask:

- ***Should the city sell an asset and replace it with another?*** For this decision the recorded amount, indicative of the initial cost of the asset, is irrelevant. It is a "sunk cost" and has no bearing on cash flows of the future. By contrast, the current market price of the asset—that for which it could be sold or replaced—is of direct concern.
- ***Are assets being used efficiently?*** As with the previous question, the historical cost of the assets is irrelevant. Suppose that the city owns two parcels of land, which it uses as sports fields. Both have the same market value. It would make no sense to assert that one is being used more efficiently than the other merely because it was acquired earlier and at a lower price.

[4] W. W. Cooper and Y. Ijiri (eds). *Kohler's Dictionary for Accountants*, 6th edition (Englewood Cliffs, N.J.: Prentice-Hall, 1993), p. 155.

[5] Van Daniker and Kwiatkowski, p. 112.

- ***Is the city replacing assets that it sells or retires?*** The comparison between additions and book value of retirements would shed little light on whether the city is maintaining its asset base, since it would relate assets at current prices with those of the past.
- ***Are the city's assets adequately insured?*** The adequacy of insurance must be assessed by comparing the amount of coverage with the cost of replacing the assets.

In recent years, it has become widely acknowledged that the financial statements of businesses, especially those in high-tech industries, fail to capture a firm's intangible assets, such as intellectual capital, internally developed software, marketing skills, and brand names. The most notable evidence of this deficiency is the wide disparity between the book and stock market values of many of our leading companies (e.g., Microsoft and Dell).

Governments, too, have intangible assets and as we advance further into the electronic age, these will become an increasingly large proportion of their total assets. Indeed "e-government" (electronic government) is an ongoing focus of professional conferences and government-oriented journals. Governments use computers not only to account for financial transactions, but also to regulate traffic flow, dispatch emergency personnel, and read utility meters. While some of the software to manage these functions may be purchased off the shelf—and hence accounted for as long-lived assets—much of it is internally generated and hence expensed as developed. The failure of financial statements to recognize the value of these critical assets is likely to become evident.

HOW SHOULD GOVERNMENTS ACCOUNT FOR ASSETS THAT ARE IMPAIRED?

A capital asset is considered impaired when its service utility has declined significantly and unexpectedly. Impairment can be a consequence of physical damage, technological obsolescence, changes in laws or regulations (e.g., those that impose new environmental standards), changes in manner or duration of use, or construction stoppage (e.g., where construction on a building is halted owing to a lack of funding). In business it is conceptually clear when the service utility of an asset has declined: It will no longer provide the cash flows or generate the cash savings expected of it. In governments and not-for-profit organizations, by contrast, capital assets are not associated with cash flows; they are expected to provide services, the value of which is typically not clear. Accordingly, GASB has had to develop an approach to measuring impairment losses that differs significantly from that taken by the FASB.

GASB Standards

Per GASB Statement No. 42, *Accounting and Financial Reporting for Impairment of Capital Assets and for Insurance Recoveries*, governments should test a capital asset for impairment whenever a prominent change in circumstances indicate that its service utility has declined. If it determines that the reduction in service utility is both significant and unexpected, then a portion of the asset's historical cost representing the impairment should be written off. The amount of the impairment may be measured by one of three methods:

- ***Restoration cost approach.*** The amount of impairment is the estimated cost to restore the utility of the asset. However, the cost to restore must be converted to historical cost. This can be done either by deflating the restoration costs using an appropriate cost index or by applying a ratio of restoration cost over replacement value to the carrying value of the asset. This method (illustrated in the example that follows) would be most appropriate for impairments caused by physical damage.

- ***Service units approach.*** The dollar amount of the impairment is determined by first calculating the percentage decline in number of service units (e.g., number of years of expected service or number of units of output) owing to the impairment event or change in circumstances. This percentage is then applied to the carrying value of the asset. This method is appropriate for impairments caused by technological obsolescence, changes in environmental or legal factors, and changes in manner or duration or use.
- ***Deflated depreciated replacement cost approach.*** Under this approach the amount of impairment is determined by subtracting the carrying value of the asset from what would be the current cost of an asset that would provide the current (impaired) level of service. However, the current cost of the replacement asset must be adjusted to reflect the fact that the (1) original asset was not new (and hence the replacement cost must be depreciated by the proportion of the original asset's life that has already been consumed) and (2) the replacement cost is stated in current rather than historical dollars (and hence must be deflated by a ratio of historical costs to current costs). This method is appropriate for impairment caused by changes in manner or duration of use.

EXAMPLE *Restoration Approach*

The carrying value of the Marlin School District's high school was $30 million (cost of $40 million less accumulated depreciation of $10 million). The school is ten years old and has an estimated useful life of forty years.

A fire damaged the school; estimated costs to restore the school to a usable condition are $5 million. The cost to replace the school today would be $55 million.

The impairment loss would be computed as follows:

Historical cost of school	$40,000,000	
Less: Accumulated depreciation	10,000,000	
Carrying value of school	$30,000,000	
Restoration cost expressed in historical, rather than current, dollars		
Restoration cost—current dollars	$5,000,000	
Deflation factor		
Original cost of school (historical dollars)	$40,000,000	
Current replacement cost (current dollars)	÷ 55,000,000	.7273
Deflated restoration cost		$ 3,636,364
Proportion of asset's original historical cost impaired (deflated restoration cost as a percent of historical cost, i.e., $3,636,364/$40,000,000)		9.0909%
Impairment loss (Proportion of asset's original historical value impaired times asset's carrying value (9.0909% of $30,000,000)		$ 2,727,273

The school district would reduce the carrying value of the school as follows:

Carrying value of school	$30,000,000
Less impairment loss	2,727,273
Adjusted carrying value	$27,272,727

The Board concluded that the impairment and the restoration should be viewed as separate events. Hence, should the school district, in fact, repair the building at the cost of $5,000,000 then it would add $5,000,000 to the adjusted value; the new carrying value after restoration would be $32,272,727.

WHAT ISSUES ARE CRITICAL AS TO INVESTMENTS IN MARKETABLE SECURITIES AND OTHER FINANCIAL INSTRUMENTS?

The standards for valuing investments in marketable securities, such as stocks, bonds, and notes, and for recognizing interest, dividends, and gains and losses (both realized and unrealized) have been discussed in previous chapters. However, the concerns of governments, not-for-profits, and their constituents with regard to investments extend beyond issues of accounting. Investments in marketable securities and related financial instruments, such as commodity options, allow organizations to enhance their revenues and, in some cases, to better manage their risks. But they also present special hazards. This section of the chapter discusses the reasons why governments and not-for-profits purchase marketable securities and related financial instruments and identifies some of the perils associated with them.

REASONS FOR PURCHASING MARKETABLE SECURITIES

Both governments and other not-for-profits may have large pools of cash available for investments. The following are among the major sources:

- Governments and not-for-profits periodically receive large amounts of cash—from donations, tax collections, tolls, fees for services, and so forth. A fundamental rule of cash management is the less cash on hand, the better. As long as the cash is not required to meet required expenditures of the same day, it should be placed in short-term—even overnight—securities.
- They maintain reserve funds to repay debts or to save, either for a particular purpose or for a "rainy day."
- They accumulate resources in pension funds.
- They maintain permanent endowments, which are established to generate investment revenues.

Governments' reasons for investing this cash in marketable securities are, for the most part, similar to those of businesses—to earn a return on resources that would otherwise be unproductive.

Many governments invest their funds directly in stocks, bonds, notes, and other financial instruments. Others, especially smaller units, participate in **investment pools** maintained by other governments. For example, most states operate investment pools for their cities, counties, and school districts. These pools enable these units to gain the benefits of increased portfolio size—lower trading costs, greater opportunity to diversify, and shared expenses for sophisticated investment advice.

CAUSES FOR SPECIAL CONCERN

Until recently the investment activities of governments and not-for-profits received relatively little attention from accounting standard-setting authorities. Generally, governments and not-for-profits were satisfied with "conservative securities" that provided steady, if relatively modest, returns. Accordingly, their risks of loss were low.

Now, however, treasurers and other officials responsible for their organizations' investments are under considerable pressure to increase their portfolio yields. In part, the demands can be attributed to the need for their organizations to maintain or enhance services in the face of increasing costs. Also, though, the treasury function has become more professional. No longer can treasurers simply divide their available resources among local banks or friendly brokerage houses. Today, their performance—and consequently, their salary increases and opportunities for advancement—are more likely to be tied to the yields on the portfolios they control. In the face of these incentives it is easy for portfolio managers to ignore a fundamental concept of finance: the greater the returns, the greater the risk.

At the same time, the range of investment "products" offered by Wall Street has increased dramatically. Succumbing to aggressive sales tactics from brokers and dealers, many treasurers purchase securities that they don't understand and that are clearly unsuited to their institutions' investment objectives.

When governments and not-for-profits restricted their portfolios to conventional financial instruments, the accounting issues of asset classification (e.g., current or noncurrent) and valuation (cost or market) and of revenue recognition (upon change in value or only upon sale) were far less complicated than they are today. The new financial instruments are often multifaceted, and extremely difficult to value. In addition, identical types of financial instruments can be held for diametrically opposed purposes (e.g., to increase risk or to decrease risk).

SPECIAL RISKS OF REPURCHASE AGREEMENTS

In the mid 1980s it became clear that existing requirements were inadequate to assure that investors of all types (governments, not-for-profits, and businesses) fully disclosed their investment risks. One main problem centered around repurchase agreements. A **repurchase agreement** (referred to as a "repo") is a short-term investment in which an investor (a lender) transfers cash to a broker-dealer or other financial institution (the "counterparty") in exchange for securities. The broker-dealer or other financial institution promises to repay the cash, plus interest, in exchange for the same (or in some cases different) securities.

Repurchase agreements usually have either short-term (some times overnight) maturities or open-ended maturities in which the interest rates may be changed daily and the agreement may be terminated at any time by either party. To facilitate the transactions, the investor may not actually take custody of the securities (in effect, the collateral) that back its investment. Instead the securities may be retained by the counterparty (perhaps in its trust department) or by its agent. Moreover, the securities may be held in the name of the counterparty rather than the investor.

The major risk to the government (or other investor) from a repurchase transaction is that the counterparty will be unable to repay cash and that either the government will be unable to obtain the securities or the securities will have decreased in value. As might be expected, for some governments that invested in repurchase agreements the risk became the reality.

Governments and other not-for-profits may also enter into **reverse repurchase agreements.** A reverse repurchase agreement—*reverse repo*—is one in which the government or other party is a borrower rather than an investor. The broker-dealer or other financial institution transfers cash to the government in exchange for securities and the government agrees to repay the cash plus interest and return the securities.

SPECIAL RISKS OF DERIVATIVES

The 1980s and 1990s saw many governments and not-for-profits invest in derivatives. A derivative is defined as a security whose value depends on (is *derived* from) that of some underlying asset (such as a share of stock), a reference rate (such as a prevailing interest rate), or an index (such as the Standard & Poor's index of stock prices). Derivatives embrace many types of securities, ranging from the ordinary to the esoteric.

For example, they include ordinary stock options (such as puts and calls), debt instruments that are backed by pools of mortgages, and interest-only or principal-only "strips" (bond-like securities in which the obligations to pay principal and interest are traded separately). Most derivatives are highly volatile instruments and can enable an investor to achieve gains, or cause it to incur losses, greatly out of proportion to the change in the value of the securities or assets to which they are linked.

Ironically, many types of derivatives were developed to *reduce* overall investment risks. Hence, they may have a legitimate place in the portfolios of even the most conservative organizations. However, they were widely misused by some governments and not-for-profits (and businesses) as means of speculation.

The most spectacular of losses were incurred by Orange County, California, in 1994. They were so severe they caused the County to file for bankruptcy. The county had invested not only its own funds in highly speculative instruments (only a small proportion of which were derivatives), but those of an investment pool maintained for school districts and other governments within the county. "In Practice: Increasing Risk and Courting Disaster" highlights the nature of the transactions in which it engaged.

IN PRACTICE

INCREASING RISK AND COURTING DISASTER

"Orange County's disastrous foray into Wall Street's high-rolling world of leverage and derivatives came to a brutal end yesterday when the county and its investment funds filed for bankruptcy under Chapter 9 of the federal Bankruptcy Code."

So began the lead article of the *Wall Street Journal* (December 7, 1994). "It is the largest such filing by a municipality ever," it continued. "The decision affects not only the county's $7 billion in outstanding public debt, but all 180 municipalities and local government agencies that had invested in the county's fund."

How did Orange County get itself into such a mess? Basically, the county's treasurer, Robert Citron, adopted a strategy to provide a super-high return on the investment fund. As any student in Finance 101 knows, however, the only way to increase return is to increase risk. Citron, therefore, opted for a high-stakes gamble not only with the County's money, but also with that of the governments and agencies that had placed their trust in him.

According to a report by the California state auditor (after the collapse, of course), between January 31, 1991, and November 30, 1994, the assets of the investment pool increased from $5.1 billion to $20.6 billion. However, of the total assets on hand on November 30, 1994, the base portfolio was only $7.6 billion. The $13 billion balance was composed of investments acquired mainly as a result of reverse-repo transactions. Thus, the portfolio was leveraged more than 270 percent (2.7 to 1).

As illustrated by the state auditor, here's an example of how the leveraging worked:

1. The county purchased a $1 million treasury bill that paid 6 percent interest and matured in two and a half years. Using the bill as collateral it entered into a 180-day reverse-repo transaction in which it borrowed $980,000 cash, paying interest at the short-term rate of 5 percent.
2. With the $980,000 cash the county purchased a 7 percent, four-year corporate bond. With the bond as collateral, it entered into another reverse-repo transaction, this time borrowing $960,000, again for 180 days at 5 percent.
3. It now used the borrowed $960,000 to acquire a Federal National Mortgage Association security that paid 7.5 percent and matured in five years. It used that security as collateral to borrow an additional $940,000 in still another reverse-repo transaction.

The end result was that the assets increased from $1 million to $3.88 million. The securities acquired provided a return from 6 to 7.5 percent. Correspondingly, the

County incurred $2.88 million in liabilities on which it paid only 5 percent interest. It was thereby able to dramatically enhance its earnings.

The system worked fine, of course, until interest rates increased. When that happened, the value of the assets (all long term) plummeted. At the same time, the spread between the long-term interest earned (rates into which the County was locked) and the short-term interest paid (which increased each time the reverse repos had to be "rolled over") narrowed and eventually turned negative. The result was predictable: catastrophe.

It's easy to place the blame for Orange County's failures on a single aggressive treasurer who wanted to boost his own reputation as a financial wizard. The evidence suggests otherwise. Several months prior to the collapse, *The Bond Buyer*, a leading journal for professional investors, had warned that Citron's "often-praised" investment strategy was "too risky." Also, Citron had been challenged for re-election as treasurer, by John M. W. Moorlach. A certified public accountant, Moorlach centered his campaign around charges that the county would be in serious trouble if interest rates took a turn northward. The *Los Angeles Times* took note of Moorlach's allegations, but endorsed Citron anyway. "His successful stewardship of the county's money has given the supervisors funds for programs they otherwise could not have afforded," it noted in an editorial. "The cloud drawn over Citron increasingly looks like a bum rap. He deserves another term." In other words, the citizens of Orange County knew of the Citron's strategy and the risks that it involved. They re-elected him anyway, thereby putting their stamp of approval on his investment practices.

As might be expected, the resultant bankruptcy took a huge toll, not only on Orange County and its treasurer, but also on the securities dealers with which the county did business and on its independent auditors. While in bankruptcy, Orange County was effectively barred from issuing new bonds, and even when it emerged from bankruptcy it was burdened with a substantial market-imposed interest-rate penalty. Citron himself was sentenced to a year's jail time after pleading guilty to six counts of investments fraud and misappropriation for engaging in various schemes to cover up the county losses and to transfer a portion of the losses from the county to the other investment pool participants.

The Securities and Exchange Commission charged CS First Boston Corporation and two of its former employees with fraud in connection with the Orange County debacle. CS First Boston Corporation served as investment bankers for the county and thereby underwrote some of its bonds. According to the SEC, the firm and its employees "knew, or were reckless in not knowing, significant negative information about the county pools that was misrepresented in or omitted from the official [bond offering] statement." Similarly, the county's bankruptcy trustees sued, and eventually settled with, Merrill Lynch for restitution of a portion of the county's losses, claiming that the firm engaged in the reverse-repo transactions even though it knew, or should have known, that they were not properly authorized.

The trustees also sought, and received, partial recovery from KPMG Peat Marwick, the county's auditors. The firm, they charged, gave the investment portfolio only a cursory review and failed to sound the alarm as to the "enormously risky wager which the treasurer had placed on interest rates."

SUNSHINE AS THE BEST MEANS TO PROMOTE SOUND INVESTMENT PRACTICES

The GASB has no authority to set standards for the investment practices of governments. It can direct only how governments account for and report their investments in their general purpose financial statements. Nevertheless, by requiring governments to make extensive disclosures as to the securities that they hold, the GASB can induce them to invest only in instruments that are appropriately conservative. After all, few governments would want to reveal that they are taking Las Vegas-style risks with taxpayers' money.

Current Disclosure Requirements for Governments

Current standards mandate extensive disclosures as to investment risks. Per GASB Statement No. 40, *Deposit and Investment Risk Disclosures, an Amendment of GASB Statement No. 3* (March 2003), governments should organize these disclosures by investment type (e.g., U.S. Treasuries, corporate bonds, or commercial paper) and should make separate disclosures for governmental activities, business-type activities, major funds, nonmajor funds in the aggregate, and, under certain circumstances, fiduciary funds. Most significantly, they should describe their deposit and investment policies related to the various types of risks they assume. Thus, if a government has a concentration of investments with a single party and there is a risk that the party will default on its obligations to the government, the government should disclose its policies regarding this type of credit risk. If it has investments denominated in foreign currencies it should describe its policies as to foreign investments. In addition, governments should make the following additional disclosures as to specific types of risks:

- ***Credit risks.*** Governments should indicate the credit quality ratings of investments in debt securities as described by nationally recognized rating agencies. Further, they disclose the amount of balances that are subject to "custodial" credit risk. Custodial risk arises when securities are uninsured, are uncollateralized, are not in the name of the government itself, or are not in the physical possession of the government.
- ***Concentration of credit risks.*** Governments should disclose, by amount and issuer, investments in any one issuer that represent five percent or more of total investments of the particular fund or activity for which disclosures are required.
- ***Interest rate risks.*** Governments should disclose information as to how sensitive their investments are to changes in interest rates. They should do this by using one of several methods described and illustrated in the pronouncement and should disclose the terms of investments that are highly sensitive to changes in interest rates.
- ***Foreign currency risks.*** Governments should disclose the U.S. dollar balances of investments subject to these risks organized by currency type and, if applicable, investment type.

Governments must also explain the nature of derivative transactions, indicate the reasons why they were entered into, and include a discussion of its exposure to credit risk (that of the other party defaulting), market risk (that of changes in interest rates or market prices), and legal risk (that of the transaction being determined to be prohibited by law, regulation, or contract). Moreover, they must disclose the significant terms of the transactions and must reveal any violations of legal, regulatory, or contractual provisions by investing in derivatives.[6]

"In Practice: Report Shows How Governments Can Avoid Fiscal Fiascoes" suggests other "best practices" of investment management.

[6] GASB Technical Bulletin No. 94-1, *Disclosures about Derivatives and Similar Debt and Investment Transactions* (December 1994) and Technical Bulletin No. 03-1, *Disclosure Requirements for Derivatives Not Reported at Fair Value on the Statement of Net Assets* (June 2003).

IN PRACTICE

REPORT SHOWS HOW GOVERNMENTS CAN AVOID FISCAL FIASCOS

CalPERS, the California Public Retirement System, is the largest public employee pension fund, and is widely recognized as one of the most progressive and best managed. Yet in a February 2002 press release the system reported $105.2 million in losses in Enron Corporation stocks and bonds. More significantly, however, the release also acknowledged that it had entered into a private partnership with Enron. This was the type of partnership that allegedly was created to both enrich the executives of Enron and to enable Enron to keep debt off its balance sheet. With this investment, however, CalPERS was more fortunate as it was able to realize a $133 million gain prior to Enron's collapse.

The newspapers are rife with stories of how governments of all types and sizes take undue risks so as to eke out an extra percentage point or two of return on their free cash. A report by the Texas state auditor *(Derivative Investments By Texas State Entities, 1995)* detailed major financial losses by eight colleges and universities attributable to their placing either all or a substantial portion of their investment portfolios in high-risk derivative securities. What was common to all of the institutions was that they had barely a clue as to the true nature of their investments. Some apparently thought they were purchasing reasonably safe mortgage-backed securities, when they were, in fact, acquiring highly volatile instruments the value of which was derived from changes in mortgage rates.

The audit report placed blame for the losses squarely on the practice of university officials in permitting brokers and dealers to make the key investment decisions for their institutions. Whereas university officials should be striving to achieve the goals set forth in their investment policies, the report warned, the objective of brokers and dealers "is to earn money through sale of investments." Moreover, officials allowed the brokers and dealers to trade their portfolios, and, at the same time, gave them free reign to price them. Not only, therefore, did the universities purchase inappropriate securities, they typically paid too much for them.

Taking a constructive tone, the audit report made several recommendations to avoid future fiscal fiascos. It urged governments to:

- Strengthen management controls by
  - Developing an investment policy with clearly defined goals and objectives
  - Periodically reviewing the policy to take into account changes in the market
  - Designing a system to ensure active monitoring of investments by senior management and governing board members
- Establish an ethics policy that addresses conflicts of interest and implement a system whereby potential conflicts of interest are documented for governing board members and key employees involved in investment decisions.
- Ensure that personnel possess the necessary qualifications and expertise to make investment decisions consistent with investment policy. Investments should not be made if personnel and management do not fully understand the transactions and related risks. Internal auditors should also be specially trained to evaluate the investment function.
- Make certain that investments are properly analyzed. Use various pricing sources in purchasing securities and have an independent evaluation of the portfolio to ensure that investments are consistent with established risk levels and expected rates of return.

SUMMARY

In their governmental fund statements, which are accounted for on a modified accrual basis, governments report general capital assets as expenditures when they construct or acquire them. The assets are not reported on the balance sheet and therefore governments must maintain "off the balance sheet" records of them.

The accounting model as described in GASB Statement No. 34 requires that in their government-wide statements, governments capitalize capital assets and depreciate them over their economic lives. In notes to the statements they must include a schedule that shows the beginning and ending balances of their capital asset and accumulated depreciation accounts and the changes that took place during the year.

Statement No. 34 mandates that governments account for their infrastructure assets just as they do other capital assets. However, governments are not required to depreciate infrastructure assets if they preserve them at a specified "condition level." If they do so they may report as expenditures the costs of maintaining the assets at that level, but must disclose the actual amounts spent on maintenance as compared with the amounts necessary to maintain the assets at the specified condition level. Recognizing the difficulty of retroactively capitalizing capital assets, the GASB is permitting governments to estimate the cost of assets for which they cannot establish the actual cost.

The new provisions bring governments into line with other not-for-profits and businesses as to how they report capital assets. These provisions result in financial statements that give users more information than they previously received, but still leave them short of what is needed for many fixed-asset related judgments and decisions.

Investments are of concern because of the substantial risk that investors can incur losses through default, declines in value, and even fraud. In recent years, interest in investments has been heightened by major losses caused by purchases of overly speculative securities. These securities included repurchase agreements (a short-term investment in which the investor transfers cash to a broker-dealer or other financial institution in exchange for securities) and derivatives (a security whose value depends on that of some underlying asset such as a share of stock, a reference rate, or an index). The major risk to a government or other investor from a repurchase agreement is that the counterparty will be unable to repay cash and that either the government will be unable to obtain the securities or the securities will decline in value. The major risk from a derivative is that the value of the underlying securities will decline, causing the value of the derivative to decline by a disproportionately greater amount. Through its standards, the GASB requires disclosure of a wide range of investment information.

EXERCISE FOR REVIEW AND SELF-STUDY

In 2005, Oneida County constructs ten miles of a new highway at a cost of $10 million, all of which was raised through the issuance of general obligation bonds. Engineers estimate that the highway will have a fifty-year useful life and that the county will have to incur $0.3 million in costs per year to keep it functioning at a specified level of condition.

1. Prepare an appropriate journal entry to record the initial construction costs in a governmental fund (such as a capital projects fund). Indicate the amount that the government would record in its government-wide financial statements.
2. Prepare a journal entry to reflect how the county would report the road's first-year depreciation in its government-wide statements.
3. Prepare the journal entry to record the $0.3 million in road preservation costs in a governmental fund. Prepare a second entry to reflect the costs in the government-wide statements.
4. Prepare the journal entry to reflect the annual depreciation of the road preservation costs in the government-wide statements. Is it necessary to record depreciation in the governmental fund?
5. Suppose instead that the county opts not to depreciate infrastructure and it makes the requisite periodic condition assessments. It incurs the $0.3 million necessary to preserve the road at the specified condition. Prepare the entry (which would be essentially the same for both the fund and the government-wide statements) to record the costs incurred.
6. Suppose that the road had been constructed ten years ago, and that this year is the first in which the county is required to capitalize the asset on its government-wide statements. A Department of Transportation road construction index is currently at 140; in the year the road was constructed it was 98. Estimated replacement cost in the current year of capitalization is $12 million. At what value should the road be capitalized? How much accumulated depreciation should be recognized?
7. The county reported its courthouse at $4 million (initial cost of $6 million less accumulated depreciation of $2

million). The courthouse had been constructed ten years earlier. Provide an example, if possible, of one decision or assessment to be made (e.g., whether the building should be insured, whether it should be sold, whether it should be renovated) for which this book value would be a relevant consideration for the county. Explain and justify your response telling specifically how the information would be taken into account.

QUESTIONS FOR REVIEW AND DISCUSSION

1. Why are *general* capital assets recorded in an account group, or some other "off the balance sheet" record, rather than a fund?
2. A state incurs interest on funds used while a highway was under construction. How will this interest be accounted for on the state's (a) capital project's fund statements and (b) government-wide statements?
3. How should governments report their long-lived assets in their government-wide financial statements?
4. A city establishes an art museum. What options does it have in accounting for its collection of paintings?
5. Although Statement No. 34 requires that infrastructure assets be accounted for similarly to other capital assets, it allows for a major exception with regard to depreciation. What is that exception?
6. Why have many government officials objected to Statement No. 34's requirement that infrastructure assets be accounted for similarly to other capital assets?
7. Per the provisions of Statement No. 34, governments, in their government-wide statements, must report their capital assets similarly to businesses. Yet the information provided is still inadequate to facilitate the major types of decisions and judgments made by statement users. Do you agree? Explain.
8. What is a repurchase agreement, and what are its special risks to a government that invests in it?
9. What are the differences between market risk, credit risk, and legal risk? Suppose that a local government invests in twenty-year U.S. government bonds. Assess each of the three risks.
10. What are derivatives? Why can they be especially high-risk securities?

EXERCISES

7–1

Select the *best* answer.

1. Which of the following would be least likely to be classified as a city's *general* capital assets?
   a. Roads and bridges
   b. Electric utility lines
   c. Computers used by the police department
   d. Computers used by the department that collects the city's sale tax, which is dedicated to debt service on general obligation bonds
2. A city should not report on its general fund balance sheet an office building constructed over a hundred years ago because
   a. The building would likely be fully depreciated
   b. It would be too difficult to determine the historical cost of the building as measured in current dollars
   c. The measurement focus of the general fund is on current financial resources and the building is not a current financial resource
   d. The building would be considered an infrastructure asset and infrastructure assets are excluded from governmental funds
3. Which of the following costs should *not* be capitalized and reported on a city's government-wide statement of net assets?
   a. Payments to a city artist to design a new city logo
   b. Computer software that the city purchased from outsiders
   c. Paintings acquired for display in the city's art museum
   d. Legal fees incurred in acquiring land to be used for a city park
4. Which of the following collectibles need *not* be capitalized and reported on a city's government-wide statement of net assets?
   a. A statue donated to the city, which it intends to sell and use the proceeds from the sale to fund a children's art center
   b. A series of books that the city intends to place in its library's general circulation collection
   c. An abstract painting that the city purchased to decorate the mayor's office
   d. An early twentieth-century impressionist painting that the city's art museum purchased for its permanent collection
5. Per GASB Statement no. 34, roads and bridges should be capitalized and reported as assets on
   a. Both a government-wide statement net of assets and a general fund balance sheet
   b. Neither a government-wide statement of net assets nor a general fund balance sheet

c. A government-wide statement of net assets but not a general fund balance sheet
d. A general fund balance sheet but not a government-wide statement of net assets

6. Which of the following conditions does a government *not* have to satisfy to use the modified approach to reporting infrastructure assets?
a. It must assess the condition of its infrastructure at least once every three years.
b. It must estimate the annual amount necessary to preserve the assets at a specified condition level.
c. It must document that the assets are, in fact, being preserved at or above the specified condition level.
d. It must use the modified approach for all of its infrastructure assets.

7. Per the modified approach, a government need not
a. Capitalize infrastructure assets
b. Depreciate infrastructure assets
c. Report in its fund statements expenditures to acquire or construct infrastructure assets
d. Record maintenance costs as expenditures

8. A government constructed a bridge twenty years ago but does not have reliable records of the cost. However, the cost to construct a comparable bridge today would be $30 million. A bridge construction index has a value today of 200 and a value for twenty years ago of 80. The bridge has a useful life of sixty years. The government should record the bridge at a value, net of accumulated depreciation, of
a. $8 million
b. $12 million
c. $30 million
d. $75 million

9. Recognizing the difficulty of implementing the provisions of GASB Statement No. 34 pertaining to the *retroactive* capitalization of general infrastructure, the GASB
a. Exempted "small" governments from having to apply them
b. Gave all governments an additional six years from the effective date of Statement No. 34 to apply them
c. Exempted special purpose governments, such as public schools, from having to apply them
d. Permitted governments to capitalize general infrastructure only prospectively—i.e., only those assets constructed or acquired after the statement's implementation date

10. Per GASB Statement No. 34, deferred maintenance costs
a. Must be estimated and reported in notes to the financial statements
b. Must be reported in the government-wide statement of net assets but not in fund statements
c. Must be estimated and reported in the management's discussion and analysis
d. Need not be explicitly measured or reported when capital assets are depreciated

7–2

Select the *best* answer.

1. A government repaves a section of highway every four years at a cost of $2 million to preserve it at a specific condition level. How much should it report in depreciation charges under the modified approach to accounting for infrastructure? The standard approach?

	Modified Approach	*Standard Approach*
a.	$0	$0
b.	$500,000	$500,000
c.	$500,000	$0
d.	$0	$500,000

2. States typically maintain *investment pools* for their towns and counties primarily to
a. Provide the participants with the benefits of increased portfolio size
b. Assure that the participants adhere to all state investment laws and policies
c. Enable the participants to enhance internal and administrative controls over their investments
d. Spread the risk of losses among the participants

3. When a city enters into a repurchase agreement, it will typically
a. Give an investor the opportunity to repurchase equity securities that it will sell to the investor
b. Borrow cash from a bank with the understanding that it will use the cash to repurchase bonds that the city previously issued
c. Sell securities to an investor guaranteeing that it will repurchase them at a higher price
d. Buy securities from a third party with the promise that the third party will repurchase the securities at a higher price

4. A government would typically enter into a reverse repurchase agreement in order to
a. Borrow cash for a short period of time
b. Invest cash overnight or for some other short period of time
c. Diversify its investment portfolio
d. Hedge its investments against fluctuations in interest rates

5. Derivatives are
a. Variable interest-rate bonds, the interest rate on which is derived from (based on) the prime rate of interest
b. Shares of common stock, the value of which is derived from the market value of the underlying assets (typically investments in subsidiaries) of the issuing corporation
c. Investments, the value of which is derived from some underlying asset or reference rate
d. Investment pools, the value of which is derived from the pools' investments

6. Which of the following statements is true with respect to derivatives?
   - **a.** They are highly speculative instruments and therefore are suitable only for governments that are willing to accept a high degree of investment risk.
   - **b.** Their market values are typically less volatile than those of the underlying assets.
   - **c.** GASB standards require that governments explain in their annual reports the reasons why they invested in derivatives.
   - **d.** They need not be reported on governments' financial statements; they need only be disclosed in notes to the financial statements.
7. The risk that a counterparty to a repurchase agreement will be unable to repurchase securities as required is known as
   - **a.** Credit risk
   - **b.** Market value risk
   - **c.** Interest rate risk
   - **d.** Counterparty risk
8. Investments would generally be considered subject to the least credit risk if they are
   - **a.** Registered in the government's name but in the possession of a broker-dealer
   - **b.** Registered in the government's name and in the physical possession of the government itself
   - **c.** Registered in the broker-dealer's name and in the possession of the broker-dealer
   - **d.** Registered in the broker-dealer's name but in the possession of the government itself
9. A city needs to determine whether it should sell its downtown administrative facility and move to an outlying location. The value of the facility that is most relevant to this decision is
   - **a.** Historical cost
   - **b.** Current market value
   - **c.** Historical cost less accumulated depreciation
   - **d.** Assessed value
10. Which of the following costs should not be included in the cost of a highway that a county constructed itself?
    - **a.** Insurance premiums paid while the project was under construction
    - **b.** Interest incurred on debt used to finance the project while it was under construction
    - **c.** Overhead costs of the construction department
    - **d.** Fees paid to consultants to determine the highway's optimum route

7-3

General capital assets are accounted for differently in fund and government-wide financial statements.

A city engaged in the following transactions during a year:

1. It acquired computer equipment at a cost of $40,000.
2. It completed construction of a new jail, incurring $245,000 in new costs. In the previous year the city had incurred $2.5 million in construction costs. The project was accounted for in a capital projects fund.
3. It sold for $16,000 land that it had acquired three years earlier for $28,000.
4. It traded in a four-year-old sanitation department vehicle for a new model. The old vehicle had initially cost $27,000, its carrying value at the time of trade was $17,000, and its market value was $13,000. The city paid an additional $39,000 cash for the new model. The fair value of the new model was $52,000.
   - **a.** Prepare journal entries to reflect the transactions in an appropriate governmental fund (e.g., a general fund or a capital projects fund).
   - **b.** Prepare journal entries to reflect the transactions in the city's government-wide statements.

7-4

Capital assets are accounted for in government-wide statements on a full accrual basis.

The following summarizes the history of the Sharp City Recreation Center.

1. In 1975, the city constructed the building at a cost of $1,500,000. Of this amount, $1,000,000 was financed with bonds and the balance from unrestricted city funds.
2. In the ten years from 1975 through 1984, the city recorded depreciation (as appropriate) based on an estimated useful life of thirty years.
3. In the same period, the city repaid $750,000 of the bonds.
4. In 1985, the city renovated the building at a cost of $3,000,000. The entire amount was financed with unrestricted city funds. The renovation was expected to extend the useful life of the building so that it would last a total of twenty-five more years—that is, until 2010.
5. In the fifteen years from 1985 through 1999, the city recorded depreciation (as appropriate). Depreciation was calculated by dividing the undepreciated balance of the original cost, plus the costs of renovation, over the anticipated remaining life of twenty-five years.
6. In the same period, the city repaid the $250,000 balance of the debt.
7. In 2000, the city demolished the building so that the land on which it is situated could be converted into softball fields.

Prepare the journal entries to summarize the history of the building as it would be reported in the city's government-wide statements.

7-5

Capital assets are accounted for in governmental fund statements on a modified accrual basis.

Refer to the transactions in the previous exercise.

1. Prepare journal entries that the city would make in its governmental funds (e.g., its general fund or a capital projects fund).

2. How would you recommend that the city maintain accounting control over the capital assets themselves—those you did not record as assets in the governmental funds?

7-6

The initial value to be assigned to an asset is not always obvious.

A city acquired general capital assets as follows:

1. It purchased new construction equipment. List price was $400,000, but the city was granted a 10 percent "government discount." The city also incurred $12,000 in transportation costs and paid $4,000 to its own employees to customize the equipment.
2. It received a donation of land to be set aside for a nature preserve. The land had cost the donor $300,000. At the time of the contribution it was valued on the city's tax rolls at $1.7 million. However, independent appraisers estimated its fair market value at $1.9 million.
3. It constructed a new maintenance facility at a cost of $2 million. During the period of construction the city incurred an additional $110,000 in interest on funds borrowed to finance the construction.

Indicate the value that the government should assign to these assets. Justify briefly the value you assigned and, as appropriate, indicate any other acceptable alternatives.

PROBLEMS

Continuing Problem

Review the Comprehensive Annual Financial Report (CAFR) that you obtained.

1. What was the total amount of capital assets used in governmental activities added during the year? What was the amount retired? Where in the CAFR is this information provided?
2. How much depreciation did the government charge in its government-wide statements on capital assets used in governmental activities?
3. Did the government capitalize infrastructure assets acquired during the year? Did it capitalize such assets acquired in prior years?
4. Did the government capitalize collections of art or historical treasures? Did it depreciate such collections?
5. As best as you can tell from the disclosures pertaining to investments, does the entity have any investments that appear to be especially risky? In your judgment, to which risk (e.g., credit risk, interest rate risk, foreign currency risk) is the exposure of the entity the greatest?
6. Does the government own any "unusual" securities such as derivatives? Has it entered into repurchase agreements? If so, does the report contain an explanation of these transactions?

7-1

Entries to record capital assets can be derived from the schedule of changes in capital assets. Assets acquired with federal funds pose an interesting accounting issue (albeit one not addressed in the text).

An Arizona city included the schedule that follows on p. 267 in its financial statements.

1. Prepare entries to reflect the activity relating to improvements and equipment in both the general fund and the government-wide statements, assuming, as appropriate, that all transactions were for cash. The deleted improvements and equipment were sold during the year for $12,000,000.
2. The schedule is based on numbers drawn from an actual city. What percentage of total assets, at historical cost (ignoring accumulated depreciation), represents infrastructure as of year-end? Despite this sizable percentage, which is typical of most cities, what arguments have critics of GASB Statement No. 34 made in support of their contention that governments should not be required to give balance-sheet recognition to infrastructure assets?
3. A note to the schedule states that "The federal government funded a portion of the capital assets and thereby has an interest in them. This interest includes the right to approve the sale of such assets and to require the return to the federal government of a portion of any sales proceeds." Suppose that the government funded 50 percent of a law enforcement center that had a cost of $10 million and accumulated depreciation of $5 million, and thus had a book value of $5 million. During the year the government sold the center for $4 million and per the agreement with the federal government was required to return 50 percent of the sales proceeds to the government. Prepare a government-wide statement entry to record the sale. What reservations might you have with regard to this entry? Do you have any suggestions as to an alternative way to account for federally funded assets?
4. Assume that the land on which the city's administrative offices are constructed was acquired in 1900 for $500. At what value would that land be reported today? Of what significance is that value to statement users?

7-2

Governments must now account for their capital assets, including infrastructure, and they must recognize in their accounts that the assets may not last forever (unless continually preserved).

In the year a road maintenance district was established, it engaged in the transactions that follow involving capital assets (all dollar amounts in thousands). The district maintains only a single governmental fund (a general fund).

	Balance June 30, 2003	Additions	Deletions	Balance June 30, 2004
Land	$100,298,761	$ 8,575,641	$ 2,318,535	$106,555,867
Buildings	173,307,375	11,241,166	3,672,542	180,875,999
Improvements and equipment	122,911,080	24,777,538	10,568,363	137,120,255
Construction work in process	44,449,433	6,209,591	11,769,183	38,889,841
Infrastructure	345,554,452	43,600,000	10,500,280	378,654,172
Total historical cost	$786,521,101	$85,828,295	$36,510,368	$842,096,134
Less accumulated depreciation for:				
Buildings and improvements	26,893,189	1,075,728	2,530,000	25,438,917
Improvements and equipment	49,164,432	12,690,135	4,380,320	57,474,247
Infrastructure	160,550,000	8,638,861	2,100,676	167,088,185
Total accumulated depreciation	$236,607,621	$22,404,724	$9,010,996	$250,001,349
Capital assets, net	$549,913,480	$63,423,571	$27,499,372	$592,094,785

1. Received authority over roads previously "owned" by the county. The estimated replacement cost of the roads was $60,000. On average they have a remaining useful life of forty years.
2. Acquired machinery and equipment for $700, with general fund resources. They have a useful life of ten years.
3. Incurred costs of $3,000 to construct a building. The construction was financed with general obligation bonds. The building has a useful life of thirty years.
4. Acquired equipment having a fair market value of $60 in exchange for $20 cash (from general fund resources) plus used equipment for which the district had paid $50. The used equipment had a fair market value at the time of the trade of $40; depreciation of $25 had previously been recognized.
5. Sold land for $70 that had been acquired for $90.
6. Received a donation of land from one of the towns within the district. The land had cost the town $120, but at the time of the contribution had a fair market value of $500.
7. Incurred $1,200 in road resurfacing costs. The district estimates that its roads must be resurfaced every four years if they are to be preserved in the condition they were in when they were acquired.
8. Recognized depreciation of $100 on its building, $70 on its machinery and equipment, and $1,500 on its roads, in addition to any depreciation relating to the resurfacing costs.
   a. Prepare entries to record the transactions so that they could be reflected in the district's government-wide statements. The district has opted to depreciate its infrastructure assets.
   b. Suppose instead that the district has elected not to depreciate its roads but to record as an expense only the costs necessary to *preserve* the roads in the condition they were in when acquired. How would your entries differ?
   c. If, in fact, the roads have a useful life of forty years, do you think it is sound accounting not to depreciate the roads? Explain.
   d. If, in fact, the preservation costs are sufficient to preserve the roads in the condition they were in when the district acquired them, do you think it is sound accounting to depreciate the roads? Explain.

7-3

Which is the proper value to be assigned to certain donated assets (a question for which answers cannot be found either in GASB pronouncement or in this text)?

A city's road maintenance department received "donations" of two types of assets:

1. From the county in which the city is located it received earth-moving equipment. The equipment had cost the county $800,000 when it was acquired five years earlier. Accounted for in a county proprietary fund, its book value, net of accumulated depreciation, at the time of donation, was $500,000. Its fair market value was $530,000.
2. From the city's own utility fund (a proprietary fund) it received motor vehicles that had cost the city $400,000 when acquired three years earlier. At the time of transfer, the vehicles were recorded on the utility's books at $180,000, net of accumulated depreciation. Their fair market value was $225,000.

a. At what value should the city record in its government-wide financial statements (1) the earth-moving equipment and (2) the motor vehicles?
b. Briefly justify your response, commenting on any apparent inconsistencies in the values assigned to each of the two types of assets.
c. Comment on the significance of the resultant book values for decisions or assessments to be made by statement users.

5. Do you think it is likely that the city was conscientious about removing assets from its general capital assets account as they were taken out of service?
6. This problem is based on financial statements issued prior to the issuance of Statement No. 34. Why, under the provisions of Statement No. 34 would a government's failure to remove from its accounting records assets that it has taken out of service have relatively little significance for financial reporting?

7-4

Governments sometimes add to, but do not delete, their capital assets.

The following totals were drawn from the City of Independence, Missouri, "Schedule of Changes in Capital assets by Function and Activity," included in the city's financial statements for the year ending June 30, 2005 (dates changed):

General capital assets, July 1, 2004	$33,276,151
Additions/transfers in	459,430
Deletions/transfers out	(265,795)
General capital assets, June 30, 2005	$33,469,786

The complete schedule disaggregates the data by function (e.g., general government, public safety, public works, health and welfare, culture, and recreation) and subfunction (e.g., park maintenance, recreation, tourism). Another schedule, "Schedule of General Capital assets by Source," shows the beginning and ending balances of the specific types of assets:

	2005	2004
Land	$ 8,209,380	$ 8,209,380
Buildings	9,293,847	9,292,611
Improvements other than buildings	1,088,307	1,088,307
Office furniture and equipment	4,863,535	4,536,506
Mobile equipment	7,834,277	8,073,945
Other equipment	2,180,440	2,075,402
	$33,469,786	$33,276,151

1. Assume that the assets, excluding land, had an average useful life of twenty years. What percentage of the total assets, excluding land, would you expect to have been retired each year?
2. What percentage of the assets (beginning of year values), excluding land, were actually retired during 2005 (assuming that all deletions/transfers out represent retirements)?
3. What was the average useful life of the assets as implied by this percentage?
4. Assume that the entire $265,795 of the deletions and transfers out applied to the mobile equipment. What would have been the useful life of the equipment as suggested by the percentage of the equipment retired?

7-5

Favorable revenue-to-expenditure ratios may not always be as favorable as they appear.

In the management discussion and analysis accompanying its 2005 financial statements, Tiber County reported that "for the fifth consecutive year revenues exceeded expenditures." However, a note included in required supplementary information disclosed the following:

County Roads and Highways
Comparison of Needed to Actual Maintenance/Preservation Costs
(in thousands)

	Actual	Needed
2005	$3,400	$4,200
2004	3,000	4,000
2003	2,900	3,000
2002	3,100	3,100
2001	2,800	2,700

The county has not been depreciating its infrastructure system but instead taking GASB Statement No. 34's modified approach.

1. What reservations might you have as to the significance of the county's excess of revenues over expenditures in 2005?
2. Suppose that you were the county's independent auditor. What reservation might you have as to the county's reporting practices?
3. Suppose that the county was required to switch from the modified approach to the standard approach. As of year-end 2005 the estimated initial cost of the roads was $100 million and their estimated useful life was forty years.
   a. How would the change from the modified approach to the standard approach affect the county's general fund excess of revenues over expenditures?
   b. How would it affect the county's government-wide excess of revenues over expenses?

7-6

The schedule of capital assets has a significant impact on the reconciliations between fund and government-wide statements.

The schedule that follows pertaining to governmental capital assets was excerpted from the annual report of Urbana, Illinois (dates changed):

	Balance June 30, 2004	Additions	Deletions	Balance June 30, 2005
Land (not depreciated)	$ 2,843,487	$ 128,528	—	$ 2,972,015
Capital assets being depreciated:				
Buildings and improvements	8,956,049	188,399	—	9,144,448
Accumulated depreciation	(1,991,173)	(159,402)	—	(2,150,575)
Buildings and improvements (net)	6,964,876	28,997	—	6,993,873
Equipment	7,760,379	1,123,568	452,194	8,431,753
Accumulated depreciation	(3,775,555)	(904,509)	(452,194)	(4,227,870)
Equipment (net)	3,984,824	219,059	—	4,203,883
Infrastructure	39,983,947	1,918,116	—	41,902,063
Accumulated depreciation	(8,935,986)	(1,204,668)	—	(10,140,654)
Infrastructure (net)	31,047,961	713,448	—	31,761,409
Total, governmental activities	$44,841,148	$1,090,032	—	$45,931,180

A related schedule indicates the following:

Capital outlays	$3,358,611
Depreciation	(2,268,579)
	$1,090,032

1. As required by GASB Statement No. 34, the annual report includes reconciliations between (1) total fund balance, governmental funds (per the funds statements), and net assets of governmental activities (per the government-wide statements) and (2) net change in fund balance, governmental funds (per the funds statements), and change in net assets of governmental activities (per the government-wide statements). In what way would the data provided in the accompanying schedules be incorporated into the two reconciliations? Be specific.
2. The amount deleted from the equipment account ($452,194) exactly equals the amount deleted from the related accumulated depreciation account. Is this merely a coincidence? Would the amounts always be the same?
3. Based simply on the amount of equipment retired, what would you estimate to be the average useful life of the equipment? Is this reasonable?

7-7

There may be legitimate reasons to borrow—even in times of plenty. Expenditures for amortizing debt principal may be a rough surrogate for depreciation, and hence the new depreciation rules may have less impact than is first apparent.

A school district constructs a new high school at a cost of $24 million. It finances the project by issuing thirty-year general obligation serial bonds, payable evenly over the outstanding term ($800,000 per year). District officials estimate that the school will have a useful life of thirty years (with no residual value).

1. Prepare summary entries, in a capital projects fund, to record the issuance of the bonds and construction of the school.
2. Assume that the district repays the bonds out of current revenues. Prepare the entry that it would make each year in its general fund to record the bond principal payments.
3. Assume that the school district must balance its budget; all general fund expenditures must be covered by general fund tax and other revenues. A member of the district's board of trustees pointed out that, owing to an unanticipated increase in property values, the district enjoyed a budget surplus in the previous two years and consequently had accumulated $4 million in "savings." She argued that the district should have borrowed only $20 million and financed the balance out of savings. Further, she contended, since prosperous times were expected to continue for the next several years the district should have issued bonds repayable over ten years rather than thirty. Focusing exclusively on issues of "intergenerational equity," how would you defend the financing arrangement actually entered into by the district?
4. Compare the total amount that the school district would report as expenditures (repayment of principal or depreciation, as applicable) on its general fund statements and its government-wide statements. Suppose that the district were required to balance its budget; expenditures could not exceed revenues. With respect to expenditures relating to the new building, would it matter whether the expenditures were measured on a full or a modified accrual basis? Would your response be the same if the repayment schedule on the bonds differed from the pattern of depreciation (e.g., the bonds were repaid over only ten years or depreciation were charged on an accelerated basis)?

7-8

If governments don't preserve their infrastructure assets they must depreciate them.

In 2004 Bantham County incurred $80 million in costs to construct a new highway. Engineers estimate that the useful life of the highway is twenty years.

1. Prepare the entry that the county should make to record annual depreciation (straight-line method) to facilitate preparation of its government-wide statements.
2. What reservations might you have as to the engineers' estimate of useful life? Why might any estimate of a highway's useful life be suspect?
3. The engineers have determined that in 2005 the county would have to incur $1 million in resurfacing costs every four years to preserve the highway in the same condition as it was when the road was completed. In 2005 the county spent the $1 million to resurface the highway.
   a. Prepare the entries, including the one for first-year depreciation, that the county should make.
   b. Assume instead that as permitted by Statement No. 34, the county opts to report a road preservation charge in lieu of depreciation. Prepare the entry the county should make.
4. Suppose that in 2005 the county added a new lane to a portion of the highway. The cost was $1.5 million. Prepare an appropriate journal entry to facilitate preparation of the government-wide statements regardless of whether the county takes the depreciation or the modified approach.

7-9

Estimating the cost of old infrastructure is one of the most challenging problems facing governments as they implement the new model. Fortunately the GASB permits an alternative to reconstructing old records.

In 1993 a city constructed a park but has inadequate records of its cost. Engineers estimate that in 2005 the cost of replacing that park would be $3 million. They have also determined that the park has a total useful life of thirty years. An appropriate construction price index had a value of 108 in 1993 and 180 in 2005.

1. What value (estimated initial cost less accumulated depreciation) should the city assign to the park?
2. Suppose that the city opted to report only an annual maintenance charge for the park; it would not report a depreciation charge. At what value would it report the park?
3. In your opinion, does the depreciation charge add significant information to the financial statements? Explain and justify your response.

7-10

Similar collectibles may be accounted for quite differently.

The City of Allentown recently received a donation of two items:

1. A letter written in 1820 from James Allen, the town's founder, in which he sets forth his plan for the town's development. Independent appraisers have valued the letter at $24,000.
2. A 1920 painting of the town's city hall. Comparable paintings by the same artist have recently been sold for $4,000.

The town intends to place the letter on public display in its city hall. It plans to sell the painting, using the proceeds to redecorate the city council's meeting chambers.

It is the town's policy to capitalize collectibles only when required by GASB standards to do so.

a. Prepare journal entries, as necessary, to reflect how each of the contributions should be reported on the city's government-wide financial statements. Briefly explain and justify any apparent inconsistencies in the entries.
b. Suppose that the city had purchased each of the items. Would that affect whether or not you capitalized each of the assets?
c. Suppose that when the city accepted the painting it agreed that if it sold the painting it would use the proceeds only to acquire other works of art. Would that affect how you accounted for the painting?
d. Suppose that the city operated a museum. The museum's building, furniture, and fixtures had cost $10 million and, on average, were now midway through their useful life. They had a replacement cost of $12 million. The art collection had a market value of $300 million. Consistent with your response to part (a), what value would you place on the art collection? What value would you place on the building, furniture, and fixtures? Briefly justify your response, commenting specifically on whether you think the resultant balance sheet would provide useful information to statement users.

7-11

Investment notes provide only limited information on investment risks.

Table 7.3 is an excerpt from a note, "Deposits and Investments," included in the annual report of the City of Minneapolis. These statements were issued prior to the implementation date of GASB Statement No. 40, which established new investment reporting requirements. Nevertheless, they highlight the types of custodial risks that governments assume when they invest in securities.

1. By what type of risk are the securities categorized? Which category of risk (1, 2, or 3) is the most risky? Why?
2. What other major risks does the city accept when it invests in securities?
3. Suppose that the U.S. Federal Agency Obligations held by the city have an average maturity of one year whereas the commercial paper has an average maturity of only thirty days. Which investment is likely to be the more risky? Why?
4. Another note indicates that the city may invest in "repurchase agreements." What are repurchase agreements? What are the risks that the city assumes in investing in them?

TABLE 7-3
City of Raleigh, North Carolina
Investment Note

Investments are categorized into three categories of custodial credit risk as follows:

1. Insured or registered, or securities held by the City or its agent in the City's name.
2. Uninsured and unregistered, with securities held by the counterparty's trust department or agent in the City's name.
3. Uninsured and unregistered securities held by the counterparty, or by its trust department or agent but not in the City's name.

Investments at December 31 (in thousands)

	Custodian Credit Risk Category			
	1	2	3	Fair Value
U.S. Treasury obligations	$ 42,632	$ 559	$1,129	$ 44,320
U.S. Federal Agency obligations	110,147	2,046	468	112,661
Municipal bonds	20,263	21,045	—	41,308
Corporate bonds	—	—	476	476
Commercial paper	172,590	—	161	172,751
Common stock	—	—	2,856	2,856
	$345,632	$23,650	$5,090	
Mutual fund				944
Money market				4,203
Insurance annuities—Trustee				680
Guaranteed investment contracts				45,855
Total				$426,054

7-12

Inspired by Orange County, this problem tries to show the risks of investing in seemingly safe securities.

Bear County maintains an investment pool for school districts and other governments within its jurisdiction. Participating governments contribute cash to the pool, which is operated like a mutual fund, and receive in return a proportionate share of all dividends, interest, and gains. They also, of course, must share in any losses.

The governments may withdraw part or all of their funds at any time, receiving their share of the pool's resources. As of year-end 2005, the value of the Bear County investment pool was approximately $1.2 billion.

Governments have been eager to place their funds in the Bear County pool because it has provided historically higher returns than they could earn independently. The individual governments must restrict their investments to short-term, highly liquid securities, inasmuch as they will likely have need for cash within days, weeks, or months. By contrast, the investment pool can invest a substantial portion of its resources in longer-term, higher-yielding securities, since it is unlikely that all of the participating governments will withdraw their funds at the same time.

The county pool places its funds only in U.S. government notes and bonds or securities guaranteed by the U.S. government. Hence, there is virtually no default risk; the county can be certain that it will receive timely payment of principal and interest.

1. Assume that the county invests $1 billion of the $1.2 billion of its pool portfolio in ten-year, 6 percent government bonds (retaining the balance in cash and short-term securities). Shortly after it purchases the bonds, prevailing interest rates on comparable securities increase to 8 percent. What would you expect would be the *market value* of the bonds after the increase in rates? [*Hint:* The bonds pay interest semiannually. Therefore, using a discount rate of 4 percent per period (one-half the prevailing rate of 8 percent) calculate the present value of $1 billion principal to be received in twenty periods. Then, using the same discount rate of 4 percent, determine the present value of the twenty interest payments of $30 million each (based on one-half the coupon rate of 6 percent).]
2. Suppose that the county invests $1 billion in the ten-year, 6 percent bonds just described. However, it also finances the purchase of an additional $1 billion of similar bonds by entering into reverse repurchase agreements. In effect, therefore, it borrows $1 billion, putting up the ten-year bonds as collateral. Inasmuch as

the loan is short-term, the interest rates are only 4 percent—substantially lower than on the long-term bonds.

a. Determine the net percentage return on the $1 billion in the portfolio, taking into account the total interest received on the entire $2 billion and the total interest paid (exclude consideration of the $0.2 billion held in cash and short-term securities).

b. Suppose that long-term interest rates were to increase to 8 percent. What will be the total market value of the portfolio, net of the amount borrowed (and excluding consideration of the $0.2 billion in cash and short-term securities)?

c. In the face of the sharp decline in the market value of the investment portfolio, county officials assured participating governments that they have nothing to be concerned about, since:

- The county intends to hold all bonds to maturity and therefore the fluctuations in market values are not relevant.
- Based on historical experience, the county will have sufficient funds on hand to meet all routine withdrawals.

Assume also that short-term interest rates increased to 7 percent. If you were the treasurer of a participating government, would you be comforted by the statements of the county officials? Explain. Would it make sense for you to withdraw your funds from the pool?

d. Suppose you—and treasurers of other governments—were not comforted and did, in fact, withdraw funds from the pool. What would be the probable consequences to both the pool and the pool participants?

SOLUTION TO EXERCISE FOR REVIEW AND SELF-STUDY

1. Governmental fund

Road construction expenditures	$10	
Cash		$10

To record construction expenditures

The government would record the highway in its government-wide statements at its cost, $10 million.

2.

Depreciation expense	$0.2	
Accumulated depreciation (infrastructure)		$0.2

To record first-year depreciation ($10 million divided by fifty years)

3.

Road preservation expenditures	$0.3	
Cash		$0.3

To record the road preservation costs in a governmental fund

Road preservation costs (asset)	$0.3	
Cash		$0.3

To record road preservation costs (an asset) in the government-wide statements

4.

Depreciation expense	$0.06	
Road preservation costs (asset)		$0.06

To record the depreciation of the road preservation costs in the government-wide statements

It would be unnecessary to depreciate the road preservation costs in the governmental fund. As with other long-lived assets, the costs would be recognized as expenditures as incurred.

5.

Road preservation expense/expenditure	$0.3	
Cash		$0.3

To record first-year preservation costs

6. The road should be recorded at $8.4 million: 98/140 × 12 million. Annual depreciation would be $0.168 million: $8.4 million divided by useful life of fifty years. Accumulated depreciation for the ten years would be $1.68 million.

7. There are few, if any, decisions or assessments for which an asset's historical cost—or even its historical cost less accumulated depreciation—is relevant (excluding, of course, decisions or assessments for which historical costs are specified, as when a bank demands that an organization maintain particular financial ratios that are defined in terms of historical cost book values). Relevant information would include the amount for which the asset could be sold, its replacement value, and the amount required to maintain it in its current condition.

CHAPTER 8

Long-Term Obligations

LEARNING OBJECTIVES

After studying this chapter you should understand:

- Why information on long-term debt is important to statement users
- The significance of bankruptcy in a governmental and not-for-profit context
- Why and how governments account for long-term obligations in both fund and government-wide statements
- The nature of demand bonds, bond anticipation notes, tax anticipation notes, and revenue anticipation notes, and how they should be accounted for and reported
- The reasons governments lease assets, and how leases are accounted for and reported
- Why governments issue revenue bonds
- What is meant by overlapping debt, and how it is computed
- What is meant by conduit debt, and how it is accounted for and reported
- The significance of other types of information that users want about debt, including credit enhancements, debt margin, payout schedules, reserve funds, and key ratios
- The role of rating agencies

This chapter is directed to long-term obligations, including liabilities—such as bonds that are accorded balance sheet recognition—and other commitments such as loan guarantees that may be disclosed only in notes. Liabilities may be interpreted as negative long-lived assets. They present comparable issues of valuation and reporting and, for the most part, are accounted for as mirror images of their asset counterparts, which were discussed in Chapter 7. Governments exclude long-term liabilities from governmental funds but report them in their government-wide statement just as do both businesses and not-for-profits—that is, on a full accrual basis. Long-term liabilities are important to governments and not-for-profits for the same reasons they are to businesses. They represent claims upon the entity's resources; failure to satisfy them can seriously jeopardize the entity's ability to provide the services expected of it.

The first major section of the chapter sets forth the goals of long-term debt reporting. The next section raises the intriguing question of whether governments and not-for-profits can, like businesses, go bankrupt if they fail to meet their obligations. The following section is directed to the "debits and credits" of accounting for long-term debt by governments. The fourth section addresses the issue of what types of obligations should be included within the rubric **long-term debt** for reporting, legal, and analytical purposes. The fifth discusses credit enhancements and other features of debt that are of concern to statement users. The concluding section pertains to bond ratings, a subject common to both governments and not-for-profits.

WHY IS INFORMATION ON LONG-TERM DEBT IMPORTANT TO STATEMENT USERS?

The issues addressed in this chapter are closely tied to a key objective of financial reporting. As stated by the GASB:

> *Financial reporting should provide information about the financial position and condition of a government entity.* Financial reporting should provide information about resources and obligations, both actual and contingent, current and noncurrent. The major financial resources of most governmental entities are derived from the ability to tax and issue debt. As a result, financial reporting should provide information about tax sources, tax limitations, tax burdens and debt limitations.[1]

The FASB has set forth similar objectives for not-for-profits, emphasizing the importance of information on liquidity and cash flows.

Information on long-term debt is especially important to statement users because an entity's failure to make timely payments of interest and principal can have profound repercussions, for both its creditors and itself. Creditors will obviously incur losses. But insofar as governments and not-for-profits rely on debt to fund acquisitions of infrastructure, buildings, and equipment, a loss of credit standing can seriously harm their ability to provide the services expected of them.

CAN GOVERNMENTS AND NOT-FOR-PROFITS GO BANKRUPT?

An entity's failure to satisfy claims against it can produce dire results, including bankruptcy. In such a situation both governments and not-for-profits can seek protection under the Federal Bankruptcy Code—just as individuals and businesses can.

[1] GASB Concepts Statement No. 1 , *Objectives of Financial Reporting* (May 1987), para. 79.

Not-for-profits are covered under the same chapter of the code as businesses; a special section of the code, Chapter 9, is directed to governments.

Whereas bankruptcy filings by major governments may be rare (Orange County being a notable exception), those of smaller units, especially utility districts, are much more common especially in years of economic downturn. In the last few decades some cities—including New York City; Yonkers, New York; Bridgeport, Connecticut; Philadelphia; Washington, D.C.; and Camden, New Jersey—avoided bankruptcy only by being brought under the authority of "financial control boards" by higher-level governments.

As suggested by "In Practice: Decision Helps Clarify Concept of Municipal Bankruptcy," which discusses Bridgeport's attempt to file for bankruptcy, the concept of municipal bankruptcy is elusive. Governments have the power to tax and in return are expected to provide certain essential services. In a sense, their access to resources is limited only by the wealth of their population. Correspondingly, their expenditures can be reduced to zero by cutting back on services. In reality, however, there are practical limits to both their taxing authority and the extent to which they can eliminate services. Raise taxes above a certain level and both residents and businesses flee the jurisdiction, thereby reducing overall revenues. Reduce services below a certain point and the safety and overall well-being of the community are impaired.

When a court declares a government bankrupt, it temporarily transfers control of the government's affairs to an independent trustee. The eventual outcome, with the court's approval, is generally a settlement with creditors and a reorganization, sometimes with the jurisdiction being permanently incorporated into another government.

Bankruptcy represents the ultimate fiscal failure, resulting in almost certain losses to creditors. But creditors can also experience losses, even in the absence of bankruptcy. New York City, for example, responded to its mid-1970s crisis by obtaining creditor agreement to a voluntary debt "restructuring." Even though creditors may have eventually been repaid the full face value of their loans, payments were delayed and interest was reduced. Thus, the economic loss was as real (if not necessarily as great) as if the city had filed for bankruptcy.

HOW DO GOVERNMENTS ACCOUNT FOR LONG-TERM OBLIGATIONS?

General long-term debt has been defined as:

> ... unmatured principal of bonds, warrants, notes, special assessment debt for which the government is obligated in some manner, or other forms of noncurrent or long-term general obligation debt that is not a specific liability of any proprietary fund or fiduciary fund. General long-term debt is not limited to liabilities arising from debt issuances per se, but may also include noncurrent liabilities on capital and operating leases, compensated absences, claims and judgments, pensions, special termination benefits, landfill closure and postclosure care, and other commitments that are not current liabilities properly recorded in governmental funds.[2]

General long-term debt is the obligation of the government at large and is thereby backed by the government's general credit and revenue raising powers. It is distinguished from *revenue* debt, which is secured only by designated revenue streams, such as from utility fees, highway tolls, rents, receipts from student loans, and patient billings.

The long-term debts of governments by no means include *all* their financial obligations—no more than do those of businesses. As a general rule, only debts resulting

[2] *Codification*, Section 1500.103.

IN PRACTICE

DECISION HELPS CLARIFY CONCEPT OF MUNICIPAL BANKRUPTCY

How destitute must a city be before it can qualify for legal protection under the federal Bankruptcy Code? Very, according to a U.S. bankruptcy court ruling rejecting the City of Bridgeport's petition to be considered a debtor under Chapter 9. It must be able to prove not only that it is in deep financial trouble, but that it will be unable to pay its debts in its current fiscal year or, based on an adopted budget, in its next fiscal year.

The Bridgeport decision was in response to the city's attempt to become the first major government in decades to take refuge in the federal Bankruptcy Code. The city's petition was opposed by both the state of Connecticut and the city's own Financial Review Board, which was established in 1988 to fund the government's deficits and restore it to fiscal stability.

Entity Must Be Insolvent

To be considered for bankruptcy under Chapter 9 of the Bankruptcy Code an entity must satisfy several criteria, the most significant of which is that it must be **insolvent.** According to the statute this means:

- It is generally not paying its debts as they become due *or*
- It is unable to pay its debts as they become due.

Up to the time it filed its petition, Bridgeport had not defaulted on its obligation and therefore did not satisfy the first criterion. Hence, the key question in the case revolved around the second criterion, whether it would be "unable to pay its debts as they become due."

The testimony of Bridgeport officials left no doubt that the city's fiscal condition would eliminate it as a contender for the All-American City award:

- The chief of police estimated that the city had 21 percent fewer police officers than is required to provide basic, adequate service. He indicated that some neighborhoods were controlled by drug dealers and pointed out that the detective staff was so overworked that there was almost no investigation of property crime, even though the auto-theft rate was the nation's second highest.
- The director of public works testified that reduced garbage collections created a rodent and arson hazard. Moreover, the city could afford only one street sweeper for its 275 miles of streets.
- Other officials disclosed that the city had to close two of its four senior citizen programs. Branch libraries were open only one day per week, while the main library was open only twenty hours per week.

Interpretation Should Be Prospective

In opposing the city's bankruptcy petition, the state argued that since the city *had been* paying all of its debts, it was *able* to pay those same debts. Therefore, it asserted, the city was not insolvent. The city, by contrast, maintained that the statute required a prospective interpretation—it might not in the future be able to pay its debts. The court held with the city that the insolvency standard is not limited to current debts.

Nevertheless, the court rejected Bridgeport's claim that it would be unable to pay its debts in the future. Pointing to a $16 million proposed budget deficit for fiscal 1991–92, the city argued that the excess of expenditures over revenues was sufficient proof of insolvency. The Court, however, declared that solvency should be assessed in terms of *cash flow*, not the operating budget. Bridgeport, it noted, had substantial cash reserves in a "contingency" fund resulting from a bond sale. This fund could be drawn upon to satisfy current obligations and could be replenished in the future. Therefore, it said, it was apparent that Bridgeport would be able to pay its 1991–92 obligations. "I conclude," the judge said, "that to be found insolvent a city must prove that it will be unable to pay its debts as they become due in its current fiscal year or based on an adopted budget, in its next fiscal year." Bridgeport, the court decided, did not meet that burden of proof.

Source: *Government Accounting and Auditing Update*, October 1991. Reprinted by permission of publisher, RIA Group/Warren, Gorham, Lamont.

from past transactions for which the government *has already received a benefit* are recognized. Reported obligations thereby exclude commitments for payments of interest when the government has not yet enjoyed the use of the borrowed funds, the salary of a city manager that, although contractually guaranteed, has not been earned, future rent payments that are established by noncancellable operating leases, and amounts owing under long-term service contracts when the promised services have not yet been provided.

ACCOUNTING FOR LONG-TERM OBLIGATIONS IN GOVERNMENTAL FUNDS

As previously emphasized, governmental funds focus on financial resources. A long-term obligation does not require current-year appropriation or expenditure of governmental fund financial resources. Therefore, as noted by the National Council of Governmental Accounting (NCGA), "to include it as a governmental fund liability would be misleading and dysfunctional to the current period management control (for example, budgeting) and accountability functions."[3]

When the proceeds of long-term debt are received by **governmental funds,** the debit to cash (or other assets) is offset by "other financing sources—bond proceeds," or some comparable account signifying an inflow of resources, not by a liability. Just as the existence of buildings, vehicles, and other long-term assets is ignored in governmental funds, so also are long-term debts, including the portion of bonds, notes, claims and judgments, and obligations for sick-leave and vacations for which payment is not required out of resources appropriated for the current year. As a consequence, long-term debt includes amounts arising out of operating as well as capital transactions. As emphasized in previous chapters, the expenditures relating to these operating transactions will be charged in the periods in which the resources are appropriated for payment—in effect, when the long-term debts are liquidated—not necessarily in those in which the government reaped the benefits.

Because governments do not report long-term obligations in governmental funds, they must control them "off the balance sheet." Prior to the issuance of GASB Statement No. 34 and the establishment of the new reporting model, governments accounted for, and reported, long-term obligations in a **general long-term debt account group.** In this account group, the liabilities (the credits) were offset by two types of accounts (debits):

1. Amounts to be provided from general government resources to satisfy the obligations
2. Amounts available in the debt service funds to satisfy the obligations

These accounts were by no means assets; they were merely artificial constructs to give symmetry to the account group.

[3] NCGA Statement No. 1, *Governmental Accounting and Financial Reporting Principles* (March 1979), para. 44.

As emphasized in the previous chapter, per Statement No. 34, the general long-term debt account group and the general fixed asset account group are no longer included as part of the general purpose financial statements. Today, therefore, governments may continue to maintain account groups as internal control devices, but may also keep track of their noncurrent assets and liabilities by other means, such as simple lists or asset and liability ledgers.

DIFFERENCES IN GOVERNMENT-WIDE (FULL ACCRUAL) STATEMENTS

In their government-wide statements, governments should account for their general long-term obligations as do businesses. They record debt either at face value or, if the debt is issued at a premium or discount, at the unamortized issue price. They may account for bond issue costs as an adjustment to the premium or discount. Each period they must amortize the premium or discount, offsetting the unamortized premium or discount with a decrease or increase respectively in interest expense.

A bond premium or discount represents the difference between the face value of a bond and the amount for which it is issued. A bond is sold at a premium whenever its specified interest rate (its coupon rate) is greater than interest rates prevailing at the time of issuance (the yield rate). It is sold at a discount whenever the specified rate is less than the prevailing rates. The greater the difference between the coupon rate and the yield rate and the greater the number of years to maturity, the greater the premium or discount.

Just as a government must include a schedule of changes in capital assets in notes to its financial statements, so must it also present a corresponding schedule of changes in long-term obligations. This should incorporate not only debts, such as bonds, notes and leases, but also other liabilities such as compensated absences and claims and judgments. It should show the beginning and ending balances, and the increases and decreases during the year.

As with general capital assets, the GASB recognizes that some governments may not have adequate records to make the adjustments required by Statement No. 34. Therefore, except for deep-discount or zero coupon debt, they may report debt issued prior to the implementation of Statement No. 34 at face value; they need not adjust it for premiums or discounts. The portion of the schedule for Charlotte, North Carolina, pertaining to governmental activities is presented in Table 8-1.

EXAMPLE *Accounting for Bonds in Government-Wide Statements*

A city issues $10 million of 6 percent, twenty-year term bonds at a price of $10,234,930 (i.e., at a premium of $234,930). The issue price provides an effective yield of 5.8 percent per year (2.9 percent per semi-annual period).

The city would recognize the issuance of the bonds as follows in its government-wide statements:

Cash	$10,234,930	
Bonds payable		$10,000,000
Bond premium		234,930
To record the issuance of bonds		

TABLE 8-1
City of Charlotte, North Carolina
Schedule of Changes in Long-Term Liabilities—
Government Activities Only, June 30, 2002

	Beginning Balance	Additions	Reductions	Ending Balance	Due Within One Year
Governmental activities					
General obligation bonds	$313,986	$ 73,095	$23,974	$363,107	$24,823
Less unamortized amount deferred for refundings	—	(246)	(41)	(205)	(82)
Total bonds payable	313,986	72,849	23,933	362,902	24,741
Certificates of participation	291,092	38,059	26,526	302,625	20,754
Less unamortized amount deferred for refundings	—	(1,297)	(121)	(1,176)	(243)
Total certificates of participation	291,092	36,762	26,405	301,449	20,511
Compensated absences	24,175	21,459	19,137	26,497	15,425
Due to participants	4,201	—	1,561	2,640	—
Law enforcement officers' separation allowance	2,563	711	—	3,274	1,880
Total governmental activities	$636,017	$131,781	$71,036	$696,762	$62,557

Upon making its first semi-annual interest payment of $300,000, it would report interest expense of $296,813, which represents the yield rate of 2.9 percent times $10,234,930, the book value of the liability (bonds payable plus bond premium). Thus,

Interest expense	$296,813	
Bond premium	3,187	
Cash		$ 300,000

To record the first semi-annual payment of interest

This entry would reduce the unamortized premium to $231,743, so the interest expense to be reported when the second payment is made would be only $296,721 (2.9 percent of $10,231,743):

Interest expense	$296,721	
Bond premium	3,279	
Cash		$300,000

To record the second semi-annual payment of interest

By contrast, in the city's capital projects fund (or whichever governmental fund received the proceeds of the bond issuance) no liability would be recognized; the cash received would be offset by "Other financing sources—bond proceeds." The periodic interest expenditures in the debt service fund (or whichever governmental fund paid the interest) would be in the amount of the required cash payment—not the cash payment less the amortization of the premium.

LIMITATIONS OF CURRENT STANDARDS: PRESENT VALUES VERSUS MARKET VALUES

Prior to the issuance of Statement No. 34, governments, in their general long-term debt account group, reported obligations, with few exceptions, at face value. Thus, even if a government issued a bond at a substantial discount—and thereby, in effect, borrowed less than the bond's face value—it would nevertheless report the bond at face value. Statement No. 34 requires that governments report their bonds, notes, and comparable long-term obligations at present value.[4] Similarly, GASB Statement No. 10, *Accounting and Financial Reporting for Risk Financing and Related Insurance Issues*, mandates that they also state certain claims and judgments at present value.

[4] Statement No. 34 incorporates the requirements of Accounting Principles Board Opinions No. 12, *Omnibus Opinion—1967*, and No. 21, *Interest on Receivables and Payables.*

Present values, as currently reported, are firmly rooted in historical cost traditions. They represent the future cash flows (both principal and interest) associated with an obligation discounted by a rate established when the obligation was first recorded. This rate is not adjusted over the life of the obligation to take into account changes in prevailing interest rates.

Present values more faithfully capture the economic substance of transactions than face values do. Like the carrying values of capital assets, however, they are based on transactions and prices of the past and are thereby not as decision-useful as *market values.*

Corresponding to market values of assets, market values of obligations point to the amount for which liabilities can be liquidated. Market values of outstanding debt securities are driven mainly by prevailing interest rates but are influenced by other factors, such as the issuer's financial condition. At the same time, however, the issuer's financial condition may be affected by the market value of its debts.

Virtually all decision models relating to bond retirements and refundings incorporate market, not historical, values as their parameters. Suppose, for example, that a hospital issues thirty-year, 4 percent bonds for $10 million (at par). Five years later interest rates increase to 8 percent and as a consequence the market value of the bonds decreases to $5.7 million.

In assessing the fiscal health of the hospital, the market value of $5.7 million may be more relevant than the historical value of $10 million. As of the date that the value is determined, the hospital can liquidate the entire $10 million liability for $5.7 million by purchasing the bonds in the secondary markets. Indeed, in deciding whether it should purchase the bonds, it should compare the cash flows to be received and paid in the future with the $5.7 million to be paid out immediately. It need not take into account the original issue price. That value, the equivalent of a sunk cost, will not affect any future cash flows. Over time, the effectiveness of hospital officials in managing its debt should be assessed, at least in part, by measuring the changes in the market value of outstanding debt. Declining market values might imply that the hospital correctly forecast interest rate trends and was able to lock in low-cost financing prior to interest rate increases. Increasing markets values might suggest that it committed itself to high-cost financing for a longer period than it should have.

The case in favor of reporting liabilities at market values has become increasingly compelling now that both the FASB and the GASB require entities in their purview to report investments at market values. If a government has long-term debt outstanding and, at the same time, holds long-term bonds as an investment, then the market value of both are affected by prevailing interest rates—albeit in opposite directions. It would be both inconsistent and misleading to show changes on one side of the balance sheet while ignoring those on the other.

The primary argument in favor of historical, rather than market price-based, reporting is that the market value information will not be used. This contention is most convincing when the entity has no intention of retiring the debt until it matures, and therefore is not concerned with period-to-period fluctuations. In its Statement No. 115, *Accounting for Certain Investments in Debt and Equity Securities,* the FASB recognized the legitimacy of this point by allowing businesses to report "held-to-maturity" debt securities at cost (or amortized cost), whereas all other investments must be reported at market. However, as noted in Chapter 4, the FASB did not permit not-for-profits to report their held-to-maturity debt securities at cost.

IN PRACTICE

VALUING A LOTTERY PRIZE

An accountant lucky enough to win the state lottery may have the opportunity to strike a blow for truth in government accounting as well as advertising. Lottery prizes are almost always paid out over an extended period of time, commonly twenty years. When presented with the first $3 million installment of a much publicized prize of $60 million, for example, the winner should graciously thank the government official presenting the check. But he or she should also point out that, contrary to the government's advertisements and publicity campaigns, the economic value of the prize (assuming a discount rate of 6 percent) is only $34,409,764—sufficient to provide a comfortable living, but nevertheless only 57 percent of the prize's stated value.

For many governments the issue of valuing the prize liability on their balance sheets never arises. Rather than appropriating funds over the payout period, they satisfy the obligation immediately by setting aside sufficient resources (in this example, $34,409,764) in a trust fund, or purchasing an "annuity" from a private financial institution, to ensure that the required payments are made.

WHAT CONSTITUTES A GOVERNMENT'S LONG-TERM DEBT?

The basic entries required to account for liabilities are, for the most part, unambiguous. However, when an obligation should be characterized as a liability and whether it should be classified as long-term or short-term is much less clear.

The issue of whether an obligation should be reported as a long-term rather than a current liability is especially consequential in governments, because it determines not just in which *section* of a balance sheet, but even on *which* balance sheet, it should be reported. Governments account for short-term liabilities—those expected to be liquidated with currently available assets—within governmental funds. They report long-term liabilities (except for those relating to proprietary and fiduciary funds) only in government-wide statements. Thus, if assets are held constant, short-term debt reduces a government's general fund (or other governmental fund) balance, whereas long-term debt does not.

DEMAND BONDS: CURRENT OR LONG-TERM LIABILITIES

Demand bonds are obligations that permit the holder (the lender) to demand redemption within a specified period of time, usually one to thirty days after giving notice. They are referred to as *put bonds* because the right of redemption is the equivalent of a put (or sell) option. Although demand bonds may have maturity periods of up to thirty years, their redemption date is not only uncertain but is beyond the issuers' control. Issuers cannot classify them with confidence as long-term (i.e., nonfund) obligations because they may have to redeem them at any time. Yet they may be overly conservative in classifying them as short-term obligations, since they may not have to redeem them until maturity.

One apparent resolution to the classification dilemma is for the issuer to estimate the proportion of bonds likely to be called within the short-term (similar to estimating the proportion of receivables that will be uncollectible). It would classify these as governmental fund obligations and the balance as nonfund liabilities. But this solution is specious in that it fails to consider the inherent characteristics of the bonds and the reasons for redemption.

INHERENT CHARACTERISTICS AND REASONS FOR REDEMPTION

Demand bonds are issued to permit the borrower to take advantage of the lower interest rates paid on short-term obligations. If prevailing short-term rates increase, then the bondholders will no longer find them attractive. They will demand redemption so that they can use the funds to purchase higher-yielding bonds. Since the economic conditions motivating redemption are common to all bondholders, the issuer should expect that if some bonds are presented for redemption, they all will be. In substance, therefore, demand bonds, taken by themselves, are short-term, not long-term, instruments, because the lender has made no long-term commitments and has assumed no long-term risks.

Most issuers provide for the possibility of redemption by arranging with a financial institution to convert the bonds to long-term notes. In a contract called a *take-out agreement*, the financial institution promises to lend the issuer sufficient funds to repay the bonds. The payback period on the notes is usually long-term, sometimes ten years or more. Thus, the demand bonds, together with the take-out agreement, can rightfully be viewed as a long-term instrument.

GASB Standards

In a 1984 interpretation, the GASB tied the classification of demand bonds to the take-out agreement. Demand bonds that are exercisable within one year of the balance sheet date, it said, should be reported as *long-term* liabilities only in the government-wide statement of net assets (not in the balance sheet of a governmental fund) as long as the entity has entered into a take-out agreement that satisfies the following criteria:

- It does not expire within one year.
- It is not cancelable by the lender or prospective lender during that year.
- The lender or prospective lender is financially capable of honoring the take-out agreement.[5]

If the demand bonds do not satisfy these criteria, then they should be reported as liabilities of the governmental fund receiving the proceeds. Usually this would be a capital projects fund.

EXAMPLE *Demand Bonds*

A government issues $20 million of demand bonds and obtains an acceptable take-out agreement from a bank. In a governmental fund, it would record the bond proceeds like those from any other long-term obligation:

Cash	$20	
Proceeds from sale of demand bonds		$20

To record the proceeds of the demand bonds (in a capital projects or other fund receiving the bond proceeds)

[5] GASB Interpretation No. 1, *Demand Bonds Issued by State and Local Governmental Entities*, para. 10. The statement does not specify the interest rate to be paid by the borrower on loans resulting from the take-out agreement. Thus, in the event the bonds had to be redeemed the issuer might have to pay a considerably higher interest rate on the new loan than on the old.

If the demand bonds do not qualify as long-term debt because the government did not obtain an acceptable take-out agreement, then the government would record the bonds as a governmental fund liability as if they were current obligations:

Cash	$20	
Bonds payable		$20

To record the proceeds of the demand bonds (in a capital projects or other fund receiving the bond proceeds)

The government would report the demand bonds as a liability in its government-wide statement of net assets irrespective of whether it reports them as a government fund liability. However, if it reports them as governmental fund liability then it would classify them as it does its other short-term debts; otherwise, it would report them along with its other long-term obligations.

BOND ANTICIPATION NOTES

Bond anticipation notes (BANs) present an issue similar to that of demand bonds—should the debt be classified as current (and thereby reported as a governmental fund liability) or as long-term (and reported only in the government-wide statements)? BANs are short-term notes issued by the lender with the expectation that they will soon be replaced by long-term bonds. Governments issue BANs after obtaining necessary voter and legislative authorization to issue long-term bonds. The BANs enable them to postpone issuing the bonds in the hope of obtaining more favorable long-term interest rates or to begin work on construction projects without having to wait until they have cleared the lengthy administrative and legal hurdles to issue the bonds.

If a government can, as planned, refund the BANs with long-term bonds, then the notes are, in essence, long-term obligations; the government will not have to repay them with current financial resources. However, if it is unable to refund them, then it must repay them when due—and must have on hand the requisite cash.

The issue of whether to classify the BANs as short-term or long-term is not as intractable as that of demand bonds. Governments do not typically issue financial statements until at least three months after the close of the fiscal year. By then, they have usually either issued the long-term bonds or consummated an agreement to do so.

GASB Standards

Generally accepted accounting principles provide that a government may recognize BANs as long-term obligations if, by the *date the financial statements are issued*, "all legal steps have been taken to refinance the bond anticipation notes and the intent is supported by an ability to consummate refinancing of the short-term note on a long-term basis."[6] Evidence of this comes through meeting the conditions set forth by the FASB in Statement No. 6, *Classification of Short-Term Obligations Expected to be Refinanced:*

1. The entity has already refinanced the BANs; or
2. It has entered into a financing agreement
   - **a.** that does not expire within one year of the balance sheet date and is non-cancellable by the lender;
   - **b.** that has not been violated as of the balance sheet date; and
   - **c.** is capable of being honored by the lender.

[6] NCGA Interpretation No. 9, *Certain Fund Classifications and Balance Sheet Accounts* (April 1984), para. 12.

EXAMPLE *Bond Anticipation Notes*

A government issues $3 million of ninety-day BANs. Because the government expects to roll them over into long-term bonds, it would record the proceeds in a governmental fund, such as a capital projects fund. It would not recognize a liability in that fund:

Cash	$3	
Proceeds from sale of bond anticipation notes		$3
To record the proceeds of the BANs		

If, however, by the time the financial statements were issued, it were unable to demonstrate the ability to refinance the BANs, then it would "correct" this entry so that the BANs were recorded as a liability rather than as a source of financial resources:

Proceeds from sale of bond anticipation notes	$3	
Bond anticipation notes payable		$3
To reclassify the BANs as a short-term fund obligation		

As with demand bonds, governments would report the obligations as liabilities in their government-wide statements regardless of whether they must also report them as fund liabilities. They must, however, be sure to properly describe and classify them—for example, as BANs or bonds, and as short- or long-term obligations.

TAX ANTICIPATION AND REVENUE ANTICIPATION NOTES

Governments usually do not receive their taxes or other revenues evenly throughout the year. Property taxes, for example, may not be due until three or more months after the start of a fiscal year. To meet cash needs earlier in the year, governments can issue **tax anticipation notes (TANs)** and **revenue anticipation notes (RANs)**—short-term notes payable out of specified streams of revenues.

Like bond anticipation notes, TANs and RANs are a means of borrowing against expected cash proceeds. But unlike bond anticipation notes, they will *not* be converted into long-term instruments. Therefore, they must be accounted for in the funds in which the related revenues will be reported; they cannot be relegated to off-the-balance sheet status.

EXAMPLE *Tax Anticipation Notes*

A government issues $5 million of TANs, backed by property taxes that will be recorded in the general fund. The appropriate general fund entries to record both the issuance and subsequent repayment of the notes are as follows:

Cash	$5	
Tax anticipation notes payable		$5
To record the issuance of a TAN		
Tax anticipation notes payable	$5	
Cash		$5
To record the repayment of a TAN		

CAPITAL LEASES

Capital versus Operating Leases

Governments, like businesses, may enter into both **capital leases** and **operating leases.** Capital leases are, in essence financing arrangements. The **lessee** (the party that will use the asset) "purchases" an asset in exchange for a long-term note. Operating leases are conventional rental agreements, giving the lessee the right to use property for a portion of its useful life. Operating leases are typified by the daily automobile rental and the long-term rental of office space.

GASB Standards

In its Statement No. 13, *Accounting for Leases*, the GASB has adopted the criteria of a FASB Statement, which coincidentally has the same number and title, to distinguish between a capital lease and an operating lease. A capital lease meets *any one* of the following four conditions:

- The lease transfers ownership of the property from the lessor to the lessee by the end of the lease term.
- The lease contains an option permitting the lessee to purchase the property at a bargain price (i.e., an amount substantially less than market value).
- The lease term is equal to or greater than 75 percent of the estimated economic life of the leased property.
- The present value of rental and other minimum lease payments equals or exceeds 90 percent of the fair value of the leased property.

An operating lease does not meet any of these four conditions.

Capital Leases versus Other Long-term Financing Arrangements

A capital lease may be structured like an ordinary mortgage note or a coupon bond. The **lessor** (the lender) may be a manufacturer, retailer, or financing institution. If it were a financing institution it would first purchase the property from the retailer or manufacturer on behalf of, and for lease to, the ultimate user (the purchaser/borrower). The financing institution may even sell shares in the lease (called *certificates of participation*) to investors for whom the shares would be an alternative to bonds or notes. If the lessee is a government, then the shares might be exempt from federal taxation, just as if they were the government's bonds. Assets commonly acquired under capital leases include heavy equipment, communications systems, motor vehicles, and buildings.

Collateral

Capital leases are almost always secured only by the leased assets, not by the issuer's full faith and credit. The leased assets, however, are often inadequate as collateral. First, if seized by the lessor they may have only limited value. If a government were to abrogate its lease, it may do so for the very reason that the property is of less value than anticipated (e.g., it has become technologically obsolete). Second, seizing government property may be extremely costly in terms of bad publicity and public ill will. After all, which local bank or finance company would like to be shown on the six o'-clock news repossessing a city's ambulance or emergency communications equipment?

Nonappropriation and Nonsubstitution Clauses

Government leases characteristically contain a **nonappropriation clause** or **fiscal funding clause.** This provision, by stipulating that the payments for each year must be separately appropriated by the legislative body, permits the government to cancel the lease at the end of each year. However, to mitigate this clause, a lessor might add provisions to the lease agreement that would make it economically impractical for the lessee to cancel. For example, the contract may contain a **nonsubstitution clause** prohibiting the lessee from replacing the leased property with similar property. Thus, the government would be unable to evoke the nonappropriation clause without impairing its ability to maintain essential services. Similarly, it may structure the payments so that they are "front-loaded," thereby making it uneconomical for the government to cancel the lease since it has already paid a substantial portion of its cost.

Rationale for Leasing

Governments enter into *operating leases* for the same reasons as individuals and businesses:

- They need an asset for only a small part of its useful life.
- They wish to avoid risks of ownership, such as declines in market value and technological obsolescence.
- They have neither available cash nor credit to purchase the asset.

But why would governments opt for *capital leases* rather than conventional buy and borrow arrangements? Owing to the nature of the collateral and the inclusion of nonappropriation clauses, capital leases are decidedly less attractive to lenders than comparable full faith and credit instruments. Therefore, they invariably bear higher effective interest rates.

Capital leases may be an effective means of circumventing debt limitations. Restrictions on the amount of debt that state and local governments are permitted to incur were first imposed in the 1840s. During a period of rapid growth between 1820 and 1837, many states financed public works, such as railroads and canals, with general obligation debt. The bond proceeds were invested in the stock of private rail and canal companies, with the expectation that dividends from these companies would be sufficient to service the debt. When the economy collapsed in 1837, many companies failed and governments were forced to default on their bonds.

To ensure fiscal discipline in the future, state governments limited the amount of debt they or their subdivisions could incur. The original limitations were expressed as fixed dollar amounts. Today, however, they are generally set as a percentage of the assessed value of the jurisdiction's property. Alternatively, the limits can be established indirectly through restrictions on tax increases, balanced budget mandates, or requirements that voters approve either all debt or debt above a specified amount.

The extent to which lease obligations are considered as debt, and thereby subject to debt limitations, has been the object of extensive litigation. The outcomes vary by state, but in at least twenty-six states the courts have upheld capital leases as being beyond the purview of debt restrictions. As might be expected, the court decisions have often run counter to prevailing accounting and financial wisdom. For example, in some states the courts have keyed their opinions to the nonappropriation clauses, asserting that because the lease payments are subject to annual authorization the leases lack the characteristics of long-term debts.

Leasing is especially popular in municipalities in which the debt limitations take the form of voter approvals and in which capital leases are not considered to be debts. It is a convenient means of acquiring assets that public officials might consider more essential to the public welfare than the electorate does.

GASB Standards

Per both GASB and FASB standards, capital leases are accounted for as if the reporting entity purchased an asset and issued long-term debt. The classification of the arrangement as a capital or an operating lease and the resultant accounting is independent of its legal status as to debt limitations.

If the lease meets the criteria of a capital lease, then the entity would record both the acquired asset and the incurred debt at the *present value* of the required lease payments—an amount that would ordinarily be equal to the fair market value of the property. The discount rate would be that agreed upon by the lessor and lessee in establishing the lease payments. (The discount rate could also be derived mathematically from the market price of the property and the schedule of lease payments.)

A government would account for the leased asset and the related lease liability just as it would an installment purchase. In a governmental fund, such as the general fund or a capital projects fund, it would debit an expenditure for the acquisition of the asset and credit "other financing sources—capital leases." As it makes each lease payment it would report the outlay as a governmental fund expenditure, dividing it between "debt service expenditure—interest" (the discount rate times the remaining principal balance) and "debt service expenditure—principal."

A government would account for capital leases in its government-wide statements, as well as in its enterprise funds, just as a business would. Consistent with FASB Statement No. 13, it would record both the asset and the corresponding liability as if it had purchased the asset and borrowed the required funds. It would depreciate the asset over the term of the lease (or the economic life of the property if it expects to receive ownership upon the expiration of the lease). As it makes each lease payment it would charge a portion of the payment to interest (the discount rate times the remaining principal balance) and the remainder to principal. Similarly, not-for-profit organizations would be guided by the provisions of FASB Statement No. 13. They too would account for capital **leases** as purchase/borrow transactions.

EXAMPLE *Capital Leases*

A municipality agrees to lease an office building with a remaining economic life of twenty years. The building has a fair market value of $3 million. Based on an interest rate of 6 percent, annual lease payments are set at $261,554 (the amount required to liquidate a $3 million, twenty-year, 6 percent loan in equal annual installments).

The municipality would record the lease as follows in an appropriate governmental fund:

Governmental fund		
Fixed assets expenditure	$3,000,000	
Other financing sources—capital lease		$3,000,000
To record the acquisition of equipment under a capital lease		

Of the first payment of $261,554, $180,000 would be for interest (6 percent of $3 million); the balance of $81,554 would be for principal. Thus:

Governmental fund		
Debt service expenditure (lease principal)	$ 81,554	
Debt service expenditure (lease interest)	180,000	
Cash		$261,554
To record the first lease payment		

In its government-wide statements, the municipality would record the transaction as if it had purchased the building in exchange for an interest-bearing note:

Government-wide statements		
Building held under lease (a long-lived asset)	$3,000,000	
Capital lease obligations		$3,000,000
To record the acquisition of equipment under a capital lease		

As it makes its first lease payment it would record both an interest expense and a reduction in the lease obligation:

Government-wide statements		
Capital lease obligations (lease principal)	$ 81,554	
Interest expense (lease interest)	180,000	
Cash		$261,554
To record the first lease payment		

Correspondingly, it would record annual depreciation:

Government-wide statements		
Depreciation expense	$150,000	
Accumulated depreciation—building held under lease		$150,000
To record the first year's depreciation ($3 million divided by twenty years)		

Both governments and not-for-profits are required to disclose the specifics of their capital and operating lease obligations. The note disclosures of Charlotte, North Carolina, are presented in Table 8-2.

LINKS BETWEEN REVENUE BONDS AND GENERAL OBLIGATION BONDS

Revenue bonds, unlike general obligation (GO) bonds, are backed only by specific revenues, usually from a government's business-type activities. They are generally reported in enterprise funds and are thereby accounted for as if they were issued by a business. Nevertheless, revenue bonds are integrally linked to GO bonds, and the government's debt burden cannot be assessed without taking both into account.

TABLE 8-2
City of Charlotte, North Carolina
Note Disclosure as to Capital Leases
June 30, 2002 (Dollar Amounts in Thousands)

Pursuant to agreements, the City is leasing water and sewer facilities owned by municipalities within Mecklenburg County. These lease agreements continue until the outstanding bonds on these facilities have been retired, at which time title to the facilities will be conveyed to the City. Debt service requirements to maturity are as follows:

Business-type Activities

Year Ended June 30	Principal	Interest
2003	$ 825	$ 735
2004	825	691
2005	825	647
2006	825	603
2007	825	559
2008–2012	4,125	2,130
2013–2017	4,130	1,018
2018–2020	1,345	120
	$ 13,725	$ 6,503

Even if a government is legally responsible for servicing its revenue debt only out of designated revenues, fiscal reality may dictate that it back the bonds with its full faith and credit. Were a government to default on the revenue debt of one of its component units (for example, a utility, convention center, parking garage, or airport), the fiscal community is likely to view the failure as one of the government at large. Thus, the credit standing of the entire government would be severely diminished and the government would either be denied access to the credit markets or would be admitted only by paying a substantial interest penalty.

Governments generally have a choice whether to finance revenue-generating activities with GO or revenue bonds. Because revenue bonds (like capital leases) are not backed by the government's full faith and credit, they almost always bear higher interest rates than comparable GO bonds. Why then would a government issue the more costly revenue bonds? At least two reasons can be cited, both of which point to the interrelationship between the two types of securities:

- Revenue bonds, because they are not obligations of the government at-large, are usually not subject to voter approvals or other forms of voter oversight. Therefore, revenue bonds are another means of circumventing constitutional or legislative constraints on GO borrowing.
- By using revenue bonds, the government can readily incorporate costs of debt service into user fees. Thus, the facilities financed by the bonds will be paid for out of user charges, not taxes or other general revenues. The costs will be shared among the constituents of the government in proportion to benefits received rather than the factors on which other taxes or revenues are based. Revenue bond-financing may be especially appropriate when parties residing outside of the government's property tax jurisdiction are to be the major users of the facilities. These parties might otherwise escape paying for the assets.

In addition, it should be noted that whereas any single incremental issue of revenue bonds is likely to be more costly than a comparable issue of GO bonds, the choice between the two types of debt may not affect the issuer's total borrowing costs. A government's total revenues and other resources available to service its debt are not changed by the type of debt issued. Accordingly its overall risk of default remains the same irrespective of whether it issues GO or revenue bonds. The mix of bonds affects only the distribution of the risk among the bondholders. By issuing revenue bonds, the government shifts a portion of the risk—and the attendant interest costs—to the revenue bondholders, who are in a less secured position than the GO bondholders. Were the government to issue only GO bonds, however, the same risk and interest costs would have to be assumed by the GO bondholders and the interest rates on the GO bonds would then increase.

OVERLAPPING DEBT

Overlapping debt refers to the obligations of property owners within a particular government for their proportionate share of debts of other governments with overlapping geographic boundaries. Concern for overlapping debt arises because the property located in one government's jurisdiction may serve as the tax base for one or more other governments.

Suppose, for example, a town is located within a surrounding county. The taxable property of the town is assessed at $600 million; that of the county (including the town) is assessed at $800 million. The town has outstanding debt of $30 million; the county has outstanding debt of $50 million.

Based on the ratio of the value of the property within the town to that within the entire county, the town supports 75 percent ($600 million/$800 million) of the county's debt. Thus, the town's overlapping debt would be 75 percent of the county's $50 million debt—$37.5 million. The taxable property of the town also supports 100 percent of the town's own direct debt of $30 million. Its combined overlapping and direct debt would be $67.5 million—overlapping debt of $37.5 million plus direct debt of $30 million.

Insofar as property taxes are the mainstay revenue of local governments, financial analysts look to the ratio of assessed value of property to total debt outstanding as a primary measure of ability to sustain both existing and proposed liabilities. They obviously would run the risk of overstating the town's fiscal capacity if they took into account only the town's direct debt and ignored that of the county—which will be repaid from taxes on the same property as that of the town.

The computation of overlapping debt may be more complicated than suggested by the previous illustration since governments may be overlapped by not one, but several, taxing authorities. Moreover, the boundaries of the governments may not be concentric; instead, only a portion of one entity may lie within the geographical boundaries of another. The general principal of computing overlapping debt is the same as in the simple example, however. A government's share of each other entity's debt is determined by the percentage of the other entity's property that is within the government's boundaries.

Because the overlapping debt is not an actual liability of the reporting entity, a government cannot report it on its own statement of net assets or balance sheets. Owing to its analytical significance, however, a government should include a schedule of direct and overlapping debt as supplementary information in the statistical section of its annual report.

EXAMPLE *Overlapping Debt*

The property of a city is located within a total of five governmental units as shown in the following schedule and in Figure 8-1.

	Outstanding Debt	Assessed Valuation of Taxable Property
	(in millions)	
County	$320	$2,000
School district	160	2,000
Library district	12	2,400
Hospital district	40	4,000
City	400	1,800

The city's *direct* debt is $400 million. The city's share of debt of the overlapping jurisdictions is based on the ratio of the assessed value of the city's own property to that of each of the other jurisdictions. Thus:

		Share of City		
	Debt	Proportion	Percent	Amount
		(dollar amounts in millions)		
Direct debt				
City	$400	$1,800/$1,800	100%	$400
Overlapping debt				
County	320	$1,800/$2,000	90%	288
School district	160	$1,800/$2,000	90%	144
Library district	12	$1,800/$2,400	75%	9
Hospital district	40	$1,800/$4,000	45%	18
Total overlapping debt				$459
Total direct and overlapping debt				$859

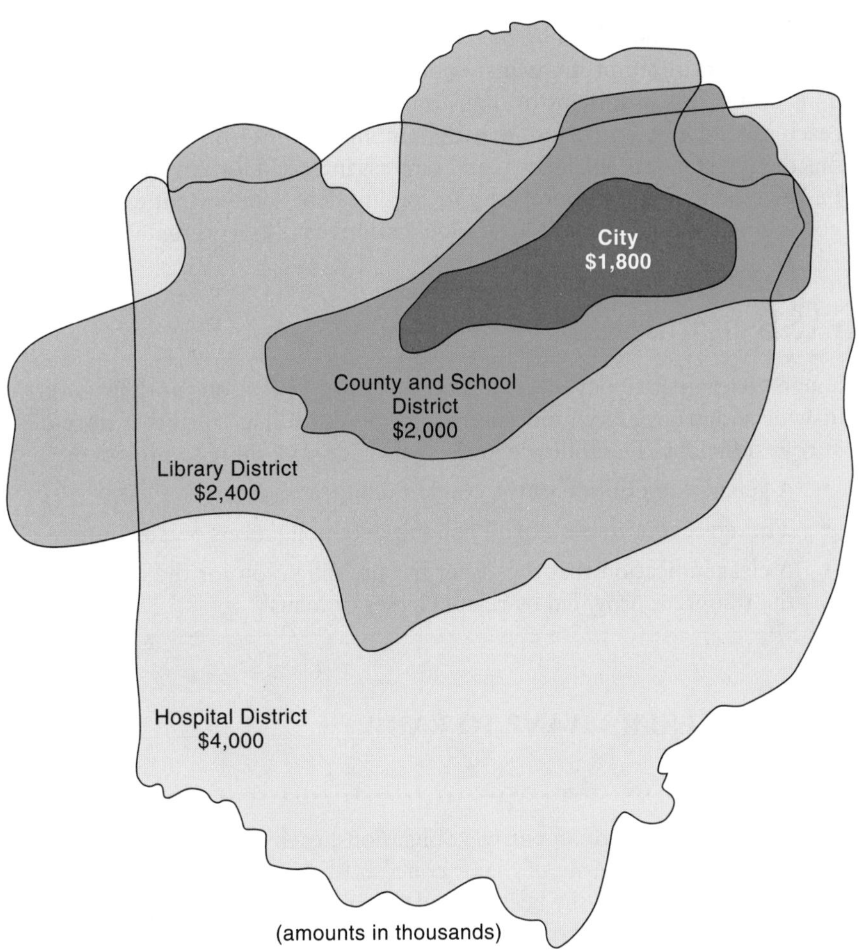

FIGURE 8-1 Diagram of Overlapping Jurisdictions and Assessed Value of Property

The schedule indicates that the city's property (assessed at $1,800 million) supports not only $400 million of the city's own debt but $459 million of the debt of other governments with overlapping geographic boundaries.

CONDUIT DEBT

Conduit debt refers to obligations issued in the name of a government on behalf of a nongovernmental entity, such as a business or not-for-profit organization. The debt is expected to be serviced entirely by the nongovernmental entity and usually takes the form of revenue bonds or certificates of participation. Often the government retains title to the property financed by the obligations and leases it back to the beneficiary. Other times, it simply loans the resources to the beneficiary. The lease or loan payments are typically established so as to match the payments on the debt. The bonds are payable exclusively from the debt payments. Generally the debt is secured by the property financed by the bonds and in the event of default the bondholders have claims only on the property and the lease or loan payments. Therefore, conduit debt is also referred to as **non-commitment debt.**

Conduit debt is a form of government assistance to the beneficiary organizations in that it enables them to obtain financing at lower rates than if they issued the debt themselves. The lower rates can be obtained because interest on debt issued by a government is exempt from federal income taxes, whereas that on debt issued by the beneficiary may be taxable. Bonds that a government issues to attract a private corporation to its jurisdiction are known as **industrial development bonds.** Although the bonds benefit and will be repaid by the corporation, not the government, they nevertheless qualify as tax exempt municipal debt. The federal government imposes strict limitations on the dollar amount of industrial development bonds that can be issued within each state. These limitations constrain municipalities from transferring to corporations the interest-rate subsidies that Congress intended for governments.

The key reporting question relating to conduit debt is the extent to which the issuing government should account for the obligations as if they were its own.

GASB Standards

Although governments may elect to report conduit obligations in their government-wide and proprietary fund statements, the GASB has ruled that **note disclosure** is sufficient. The following information, it said, must be provided:

- A general description of the conduit debt transactions
- The aggregate amount of all conduit debt obligations outstanding
- A clear indication that the issuer has no obligation for the debt beyond the resources provided by related leases or loans[7]

WHAT OTHER INFORMATION DO USERS WANT TO KNOW ABOUT OUTSTANDING DEBT?

The magnitude and nature of an entity's obligations, each with its own unique characteristics and risks, is obviously of major concern to the entity's creditors as well as other statement users. As might be expected, both governments and other not-for-profits devote a substantial portion of their annual financial reports to long-term debt. The disclosures pertaining to long-term debt are far more comprehensive than those relating to long-term assets. They typically include not only technical features of the debt, such as interest rates, payout schedules, and collateral, but also selected financial ratios that incorporate debt.

The economic burden of long-term debt is dependent on the issuer's ability to pay. Ability to pay is tied to a wide range of financial, social, economic, political, and administrative factors, only some of which are reported in financial statements. This section will focus on some of these factors, but will be limited to those tied directly to the debt itself. Broader measures of ability to pay will be considered in Chapter 11, which is directed to financial analysis.

CREDIT ENHANCEMENTS

An issuer can enhance the security of its bonds by replacing its credit standing with that of a more fiscally sound entity. Two such means are by acquiring bond insurance and by obtaining the moral obligation of another issuer to back its debt.

Bond Insurance

Bond and other forms of debt insurance guarantee the timely payment of both interest and principal. Although it is purchased by the bond issuers, it is intended to protect the bondholders.

Written mainly by a small number of specialized companies, the two largest of which are American Municipal Bond Assurance Corp. (AMBAC) and Municipal

[7] GASB Interpretation No. 2, *Disclosure of Conduit Debt Obligations* (August 1995).

Bond Insurance Association (MBIA), bond insurance may appear costly. Premiums range from 0.1 percent to 2.0 percent of principal and interest, depending on the risk. However, municipal bond insurance often results in net savings to the issuer in that the leading bond rating services automatically raise the rating of any covered issue to AAA (the highest). The higher the bond rating, the lower the interest cost.

Moral Obligation Debt

Bonds or notes issued by one entity (usually a state agency) but backed by the promise of another entity (usually the state itself) to make up any debt service deficiencies are referred to as **moral obligation debt.** The obligation is described as "moral" because it is not legally enforceable.

Moral obligation debt is motivated mainly by a state's intent to avoid voter approvals or to circumvent debt limitations. To issue debt that would otherwise be proscribed, a state, with legislative approval, borrows in the name of a state agency, sometimes one formed specifically to issue the debt. To enhance the credit-worthiness of the agency, the state supports the bonds with a promise to cover debt service shortages.

The state does not typically place its full faith and credit behind its pledge. Rather, it promises only to seek future appropriation for any required debt service payments. This promise may be of only dubious value. When New York State issued moral obligation bonds, for example, the promise took the form of a so-called moral makeup clause, wherein the state budget director was required to ask for an appropriation to make up any shortfall in its debt service reserve fund. However, the legislature was not committed to honoring the budget director's request.

Moral obligation bonds obviously are not as secure as the state's general obligation bonds, and rating agencies typically assign them a rating at least one grade below that of the state's general obligation bonds. Still, the rating is likely to be significantly higher than if the bonds were issued by the state agency without the backing of the state.

DEBT MARGIN

As discussed earlier, governments may be limited in the amount of debt that they can incur. The difference between the amount of debt outstanding (computed according to applicable legal provisions, not necessarily as reported on the issuer's balance sheets) and the amount of debt allowed is described as **debt margin.**

EXAMPLE *Debt Margin*

A government's general obligation bond debt is legally limited to 6 percent of the assessed value of taxable property within its jurisdiction. The assessed value of the property is $10 billion and therefore the government can issue a maximum of $600 million in debt. If the government currently has $450 million of debt outstanding, then its legal debt margin is $150 million (25 percent of its limit).

PAYOUT SCHEDULES

Payout schedules can take a variety of forms, ranging from those in which a substantial portion of principal is repaid early in the bond's life to those in which it is paid entirely at the end. A typical payout schedule is one in which 50 percent of the debt is retired in ten years. Often, but by no means always, this is accomplished through a twenty- to twenty-five-year serial bond issue with an equal proportion of the issue maturing each year. Usually lenders see a faster retirement schedule as positive, as long as it does not place too great a fiscal strain upon the issuer. Schedules in which the payout is strung out over thirty to forty years, while not uncommon, are viewed as negative.

Consistent with the concept of interperiod equity addressed in Chapter 1, sound fiscal policy dictates that the payout schedule correspond to the useful life of the property being financed. Indeed, the very rationale for borrowing is that the burden of paying for long-lived assets should be borne by the parties who will use them. When the schedule is shorter than the useful life, then only the early-year users will pay for the assets. When it exceeds the useful life, then parties beyond the period of use will be required to pay for them and, in effect, a portion of the debt will be financing operations rather than capital assets.

RESERVE FUNDS

As discussed in Chapter 6 on debt service funds, lenders commonly stipulate that an issuer maintain a reserve fund to ensure that its keeps current on its principal and interest payments. Usually the amount to be set aside is based on principal and interest payments—for example, the highest year's debt service. A reserve fund can generally be dipped into only for the final year's debt service or in the event that the issuer is otherwise unable to make its required payments. From the perspective of a lender, the reserve fund provides a cushion against difficult fiscal times and thereby makes the bond a more attractive investment.

COMMON RATIOS AND PAST HISTORY

Investors and other statement users look to a variety of bond-related ratios and other data to assess ability to pay and risk of default. The most notable of these include:

- ***Debt service costs as a percentage of total general fund and debt service fund expenditures.*** Similar to the times-interest-earned ratio that is widely used in business, this ratio is usually considered high if it exceeds 20 percent of total general and debt service fund expenditures.
- ***Debt per capita and debt as a percentage of taxable property.*** Both of these ratios are measures of *fiscal capacity.* They relate the bonded debt, not to resources or resource flows within the government, but to the ultimate sources of a government's revenues. As with most ratios involving long-term obligations, debt can be expressed with varying degrees of inclusiveness. For example, debt could be limited to GO debt or could also include revenue debt. Moreover, it could incorporate only the issuer's direct debt or both the direct and overlapping debt.
- ***History.*** As any banker will testify, character dominates all quantifiable measures in capturing a borrower's credit standing. Users want information as to whether past payments were made on time. Whereas the bond community may forgive borrowers for unintentionally missing or being late on payments, it may be less tolerant of an issuer who evades payments through bankruptcy or comparable legal maneuvers.

Ratios pertaining to revenue bonds are discussed in Chapter 9, dealing with business-type activities. The long-term debt of hospitals, universities, and other not-for-profits are often of this type. A more comprehensive discussion of the appropriate use—and limitations—of ratios in analyzing a government's fiscal condition is included in Chapter 11.

WHAT ARE BOND RATINGS AND WHY ARE THEY IMPORTANT?

The leading bond rating agencies, *Standard & Poor's* (S&P), *Moody's Investors Service,* and *Fitch IBCA,* will assign a quality rating to the debt instruments of any issuer (government, not-for-profit, and business) that requests it. Their fees, paid by the issuers, generally range from $2,500 to $80,000.

The agencies base their ratings on a comprehensive review of all factors affecting the issuer's ability to pay. A review would include analyses of the debt instrument itself, the issuer's financial reports and budgets, key demographic data, and a range of economic statistics. It would also incorporate interviews with city officials and assessments of their competence.

The rating services continue to monitor an issuer even after they have assigned an initial rating and expect the issuer to update them continually with current information. A rating generally remains in effect until the issuer's next offering of comparable securities. Sometimes, however, as a result of new developments the agencies will change their initial classification.

The classification bond rating scheme of Moody's Investor Service is presented in Table 8-3.

Debt ratings are of critical concern to both issuers and investors because they affect the debt's marketability and hence its interest rate. In fact, many institutions are legally prohibited from investing in securities classified by a specified rating service as less than "investment grade."

A rating service downgrade, even though it generally does nothing more than spotlight information that was already widely known, can be a traumatic fiscal event

TABLE 8-3
Moody's Investor Service Bond Ratings

Aaa	Bonds that are rated Aaa are judged to be of the best quality. They carry the smallest degree of investment risk and are generally referred to as "gilt edged." Interest payments are protected by a large or by an exceptionally stable margin and principal is secure. While the various protective elements are likely to change, such changes as can be visualized are most unlikely to impair the fundamentally strong position of such issues.
Aa	Bonds that are rated Aa are judged to be of high quality by all standards. Together with the Aaa group they comprise what are generally known as high-grade bonds. They are rated lower than the best bonds because margins of protection may not be as large as in Aaa securities, fluctuation of protective elements may be of greater amplitude, or other elements may be present that make the long-term risk appear somewhat larger than the Aaa securities.
A	Bonds that are rated A possess many favorable investment attributes and are to be considered as upper-medium-grade obligations. Factors giving security to principal and interest are considered adequate, but other elements may suggest a susceptibility to impairment some time in the future.
Baa	Bonds that are rated Baa are considered medium-grade obligations (i.e., they are neither highly protected nor poorly secured). Interest payments and principal security appear adequate for the present, but certain protective elements may be lacking or may be characteristically unreliable over any great length of time. Such bonds lack outstanding investment characteristics and in fact have speculative characteristics as well.
Ba	Bonds that are rated Ba are judged to have speculative elements; their future cannot be considered well assured. Often the protection of interest and principal payments is very moderate, and thereby not well safeguarded during both good and bad times over the future. Uncertainty of position characterizes bonds in this class.
B	Bonds that are rated B generally lack characteristics of the desirable investment. Assurance of interest and principal payments or of maintenance of other terms of the contract over any long period of time may be small.
Caa	Bonds that are rated Caa are of poor standing. Such issues may be in default or there may be elements of danger with respect to principal or interest.
Ca	Bonds that are rated Ca represent obligations that are speculative in a high degree. Such issues are often in default or have other marked shortcomings.
C	Bonds that are rated C are the lowest-rated class of bonds, and issues so rated can be regarded as having extremely poor prospects of ever attaining any real investment standing.

Source: Moody's Investor Service Web site, www.moodys.com (accessed January 2003).

IN PRACTICE

STATES MISUSE TOBACCO SETTLEMENTS TO COVER CURRENT BUDGET DEFICITS

The 1998 settlement with the leading tobacco companies resulted in a commitment by the industry to pay $246 billion to the states over twenty-five years owing to smoking-related deaths and diseases. But instead of tackling the enormous health problems caused by past and continued use of tobacco products, at least eight states are using proceeds from the settlements to plug their current budget deficits. However, using the tobacco funds to meet current-year expenditures not only violates the principles of interperiod equity, but is likely, in the long-run, to result in increased borrowing costs.

Here's why. To generate current revenues, the states are issuing revenue bonds that are backed by the expected future streams of tobacco revenues. Thus, they are, in effect, trading the future revenues for a one-time infusion of cash to meet current operating costs. The tobacco funds to be received over the next twenty-five years will have to be used to pay off the bonds rather than for their intended purpose of providing public health services.

By issuing bonds to cover current costs, the governments are hoisting a red flag signaling that they are relying on "one shot" quick fixes rather than long-term strategies to address their fiscal distress. The credit-evaluating agencies are receiving the message and are downgrading the offending governments' bond ratings. Lower bond ratings translate immediately into higher interest costs.

for an issuer. Almost always it increases the issuer's interest costs, thereby adding to its fiscal anguish.

Despite the significance attached to bond ratings, investors should no more rely solely on them than they should a report of a stock brokerage firm. The rating agencies are fallible and they are neither prophets nor seers. Their ratings are merely opinions, not guarantees. The information on which they base their ratings—all of which is in the public domain—is subject to varying interpretation, and an independent analysis may provide insights in addition to, or at variance with, those of the agencies.

SUMMARY

Long-term obligations represent claims upon the entity's resources, and failure to satisfy them can seriously jeopardize the entity's ability to provide the services expected of it. Hence an analyst interested in a government's fiscal condition must pay careful attention to them.

Whereas bankruptcy filings by major governments are rare, those of small units are more common. Although governments have taxing authority and their access to resources may seem almost unlimited, there are practical limits to the extent of tax increases and service cutbacks. Governments account for their governmental funds on a modified accrual basis and focus on current financial resources. Therefore, they do not give balance sheet recognition either to long-term obligations or to the assets that the obligations finance. By contrast, in their government-wide statements, which are on a full accrual basis and focus on all economic resources, they report both their long-term obligations and capital assets. They record their long-term debts initially at issue price. Thereafter, they amortize any premiums or discounts. In essence, therefore, the book value of an obligation represents the present value of future cash obligations (based on a discount rate established when the bonds were issued). Indeed, in their government-wide statements, governments account for long-term obligations as do both businesses and not-for-profits.

Demand bonds may be reported as long-term debt only if the issuer has entered into a "take-out agreement" ensuring that if the bonds are presented for redemption the debt can be refinanced. Similarly, bond anticipation notes may be reported as long-term debt only if the issuer has already refinanced the notes or has a binding refinancing agreement. In contrast, tax anticipation notes and revenue anticipation notes are not converted into long-term debts, so they cannot be accounted for as long-term obligations.

Leases that meet the criteria of capital leases and are thereby, in essence, financing arrangements are also reported as long-term debt. Capital leasing arrangements are often motivated by an effort to avoid the debt limitations and voter approvals to which conventional general obligation bonds are subject. But whether, in fact, they can be used for that purpose is a matter of state law and judicial decisions.

Revenue bonds and overlapping debt, though not strictly full faith and credit liabilities of the reporting governments, impose financial obligations on their citizens and should be taken into account in assessing the capacity of the government to sustain new and existing debt. In contrast, conduit debt may bear the name of the government issuer, but it may not be an economic obligation because it is expected to be repaid by the beneficiary, not the issuer.

Although the ultimate ability of a government to repay its debt depends on fundamental financial, social, economic, political, and administrative factors, creditors must also be concerned with features of the debt itself: credit enhancements such as moral obligations and bond insurance, debt margin (the difference between allowable debt and outstanding debt), debt payout schedule, reserve fund requirements, and debt rating.

Bond ratings are of critical concern to issuers and investors because they affect the debt instrument's marketability and hence its interest rate. Nevertheless, the ratings are opinions, not guarantees.

EXERCISE FOR REVIEW AND SELF-STUDY

A city agrees to lease an emergency communications system. The term of the lease, which is noncancellable, is ten years. The lease gives the city options to purchase the system at several points during the lease, always at less than expected fair market value. It provides for annual payments of $1,086,944, an amount reflective of an $8 million loan (the fair value of the asset) and interest at a rate of 6 percent.

1. Prepare entries to reflect the lease agreement in the city's (1) general fund statements and (2) government-wide statements.
2. Prepare entries to record the first year's lease payment and depreciation. Assume that the useful life of the equipment is ten years (the same as the lease) and that depreciation will be recorded on a straight-line basis.
3. Suppose, instead, that the city financed the acquisition of the equipment with bonds that could be redeemed at any time at the option of the holder. The bonds pay interest at the rate of 6 percent. At year-end prevailing rates of interest had decreased to 5 percent. The city does *not* have a take-out agreement providing for refinancing if the bonds are presented for payment. How should the city record the debt?
4. The city is permitted to issue a maximum of $30 million of general obligation bonds. It already has $19 million of qualifying debt outstanding. What would be the city's debt margin after issuing $8 million of new debt subject to the limits?
5. The city is served by an independent school district that includes the city as well as nearby towns. The assessed value of taxable property within the city is $600 million; that of the school district is $800 million. The school district has $48 million of debt outstanding. What is the city's overlapping debt with respect to the school district?

QUESTIONS FOR REVIEW AND DISCUSSION

1. What unique issues arise when a government, as opposed to a business, is declared bankrupt?
2. What is the distinction between *general obligation* debt and *revenue* debt? Which one is likely to bear higher interest rates?
3. At what value would a government report bonds payable on its government-wide statements? Why might this value differ from the bonds' face value? Why might it differ from their market value?
4. A government's interest expenditure as reported in its debt service fund differs significantly from its interest expense as reported in its government-wide statements. What is the most likely explanation for the difference?
5. What are *demand* bonds? When can they be reported as long-term, rather than current, obligations?
6. If, under GAAP, capital leases are considered long-term obligations, why, in many jurisdictions, are they not subject to debt limitations?
7. What is *overlapping debt* and why is it of significance to financial analysts and other users of a government's financial statements?
8. What is *conduit debt?* Why are governments required to report it only in notes to their financial statements, not on their balance sheets?
9. What distinguishes *moral obligation* bonds from other types of debt? Why would one government assume a moral obligation for another government's bonds?
10. Why are bond ratings of vital concern to bond issuers?

EXERCISES

8-1

Select the *best* answer.

1. Which of the following is true with respect to bankruptcy?
   a. Per the federal bankruptcy code, a municipality can be declared insolvent but not bankrupt.
   b. Many major cities have avoided bankruptcy by being placed under the control of financial control boards by their state governments.
   c. The concept of bankruptcy does not apply to governments because they have the authority to increase taxes and reduce services.
   d. Municipalities that are declared bankrupt by a court are brought under the control of independent trustees whose primary objective is to ensure that obligations to bondholders are satisfied in full.
2. A government issues $1 million in thirty-year, 6 percent coupon bonds at a discount of $50,000. At what amount would the bonds be reported (net) in the government-wide statement of net assets and governmental fund balance sheet immediately upon issuance?

	Government-Wide	*Fund*
a.	$1,000,000	$1,000,000
b.	950,000	950,000
c.	950,000	0
d.	950,000	1,000,000

3. The government issues the bonds described in question 2. It makes its first semi-annual interest payment of $30,000. How much interest expense/expenditure would it likely have to report in its government-wide and governmental fund statements?

	Government-Wide	*Fund*
a.	$30,000	$30,000
b.	28,500	28,500
c.	28,500	0
d.	28,500	30,000

4. The government makes subsequent interest payments. Reported interest expense/expenditure in the government-wide and governmental fund statements will

	Government-Wide	*Fund*
a.	Increase	Remain the same
b.	Increase	Increase
c.	Remain the same	Remain the same
d.	Decrease	Remain the same

5. Suppose a government issues $1 million in bonds at a premium of $50,000. It temporarily invests the proceeds of $1,050,000 in U.S. Treasury bonds having a face value of $1 million (i.e., at a premium of $50,000). At what value would the government report the bonds payable and the investment in bonds in its government-wide statements subsequent to the date of the transactions?

	Bond Payable	*Investment in Bonds*
a.	Amortized cost	Market value
b.	Market value	Market value
c.	Amortized cost	Amortized cost
d.	Market value	Amortized cost

6. Which of the following is true of demand bonds?
   a. They give the issuer the right to call the bonds at a pre-established price.
   b. They give the issuer the right to demand that the bondholders purchase additional bonds at a pre-established price.
   c. They give the bondholder the right to demand repayment prior to maturity.
   d. They give the bondholder the right of first refusal with respect to any additional bonds sold by the issuer.
7. Demand bonds should be reported as governmental fund liabilities
   a. If the government has not entered into a take-out agreement
   b. If prevailing interest rates are higher than the interest rate on the bonds
   c. If prevailing interest rates are lower than the interest rate on the bonds
   d. If the government, by the time it issues its financial statements, has neither refinanced the bonds nor entered into an agreement to do so
8. A city issues bond anticipation notes on October 21, 2004. It refunds the notes with thirty-year bonds in January 2005. In its financial statements for the year ending December 31, 2004, which are issued in April 2005, it should report the bond anticipation notes as obligations
   a. In both its government-wide statement of net assets and a governmental fund balance sheet
   b. In its government-wide statement of net assets but not its governmental fund balance sheet
   c. In its governmental fund balance sheet but not its government-wide statement of net assets
   d. In neither its governmental fund balance sheet nor its government-wide statement of net assets
9. A city issues revenue anticipation notes on October 21, 2004. It repays the notes in January 2005. In its financial statements for the year ending December 31, 2004, which are issued in April 2005, it should report the revenue anticipation notes as obligations
   a. In both the government-wide statement of net assets and a governmental fund balance sheet

b. In the government-wide statement of net assets but not a governmental fund balance sheet
c. In a governmental fund balance sheet but not the government-wide statement of net assets
d. In neither a governmental fund balance sheet nor the government-wide statement of net assets

10. Which of the following conditions would *not* automatically classify a lease as a capital lease?
   a. Ownership is transferred to the lessee at the end of the lease term.
   b. The term of the lease is 80 percent of the useful life of the property.
   c. The lease contains an option permitting the lessee to purchase the property at a bargain price.
   d. The present value of rental and other minimum lease payments equals or exceeds 50 percent of the fair value of the leased property.

8-2

Select the *best* answer.

1. A town signs a ten-year capital lease by which it acquires equipment with a market value of $1 million. The lease incorporates an implicit interest rate of 8 percent per year. Accordingly, annual lease payments are $149,029. When the town make its *second* annual lease payment, it would report in its government-wide statements
   a. Interest expense of $80,000
   b. Rent expense of $149,029
   c. Interest expense of $74,478
   d. Rent expense of $100,000
2. State courts that have held that capital leases do not qualify as long-term debt subject to debt limitations commonly base their decision on the inclusion in the lease agreement of a
   a. Nonsubstitution clause
   b. Nonappropriation clause
   c. Nonparticipation clause
   d. Forward funding clause
3. Revenue bonds, compared with general obligation bonds, generally
   a. Are paid out of property or sales tax revenues
   b. Bear lower interest rates
   c. Are subject to the same debt limitations
   d. Are not backed by the full faith and credit of the issuing government
4. A town is located within both a school district and a county. The assessed property valuations and bonded debts of the three governments are as follows (in millions):

	Assessed Valuation	Bonded Debts
Town	$ 800	$40
School district	1,600	90
County	2,400	18

   The combined direct and overlapping debt of the town is
   a. $40 million
   b. $51 million
   c. $91 million
   d. $148 million
5. Clifford City has issued $10 million of revenue bonds to help finance a factory for Travis, Inc., a private manufacturing company. The city owns the factory and leases it to the company. The bonds are payable exclusively from the lease payments. In the event the company defaults on its lease payments, the bondholders have claims only on the factory. The city has no obligation for the bonds other than to transmit to the bondholders the lease payments that it receives from the company. In its annual financial statements the city should report the bonds
   a. On its government-wide statement of net assets but not in any fund statements
   b. Only in notes
   c. Only as required supplementary information
   d. Both on its government-wide statement of net assets and in its proprietary funds balance sheet
6. Which of the following is *not* a common reason for issuing revenue bonds rather than general obligation bonds?
   a. To obtain lower interest rates
   b. To incorporate debt service costs into user fees
   c. To avoid debt limitations or voter approvals
   d. To shift a portion of the burden of paying for the project to parties who reside outside the issuer's jurisdiction but nevertheless benefit from the project
7. On December 1, 2005, a city issued $20 million in BANs and $6 million in RANs. By April 15, 2006, the date the city issued its financial statements for the year ending December 31, 2005, the city had neither converted the BANs into long-term bonds nor entered into a refinancing agreement to do so. However, the city repaid the RANs on February 28, 2006. The amount that the city should report as an obligation of its general fund in its December 31, 2005, financial statements is
   a. $0
   b. $6 million
   c. $20 million
   d. $26 million
8. A state agency issues moral obligation debt. This debt
   a. Is probably backed by the full faith and credit of the state
   b. Is probably subject to the same debt limitations as if it had been issued by the state itself
   c. Probably bears a lower interest rate than if there were no moral obligation associated with it
   d. Imposes greater pressure upon the agency to repay the debt than if there were no moral obligation associated with it
9. Certificates of participation have the most in common with
   a. Revenue bonds

b. Pension annuities
c. Participating preferred stock
d. Operating leases

10. A city issues the following bonds:

Revenue bonds to fund improvements to the town-owned electric utility	$50 million
Conduit bonds issued to assist a fast food franchisee to construct a restaurant	$ 7 million

The amount that the city should report as an obligation in its government-wide statement of net assets and its proprietary funds balance sheet is

	Government-Wide	*Proprietary Fund*
a.	$57 million	$57 million
b.	$57 million	$ 0
— c.	$50 million	$50 million
d.	$ 0	$ 0

8-3

Government debts may are reported differently in governmental and government-wide statements.

The Alpine school district engaged in the following transactions in its fiscal year ending August 31, 2005. By law, the district is required to establish a capital projects fund to account for school construction projects and a debt service fund to account for resources legally restricted to the payment of long-term principal and related interest.

On March, 1, it issued $40 million general obligation bonds to finance the construction of new junior high school. The bonds were to mature in twenty years (forty periods) and had a coupon rate of 4 percent per year (2 percent per semi-annual period). They were sold for $38,924,728 (a discount of $1,075,272), a price that reflected an annual yield of 4.2 percent (2.1 percent per period).

On August 31 it made its first interest payment of $800,000.

During the year the builder with whom the district contracted to construct the building completed approximately 10 percent of the building and billed the district for $4 million.

On August 31, the district issued $10 million in bond anticipation notes to finance improvements to its athletic facilities. By the time the district issued its year-end 2005 financial statements in December 2005 it still had not refinanced these notes and had not yet started construction on the facilities.

In June the district issued $2 million in tax anticipation notes. It repaid these notes in September. Interest applicable to the notes for the year ending August 31, 2005, was $25,000, all of which was paid in September when the notes matured.

In August, the district settled a lawsuit with a group of former teachers. Per a structured settlement, the district agreed to make several payments totaling $1,600,000 to the teachers. The district has a policy of recording long-term obligations at present value whenever required or permitted by GAAP. It estimates the present value of this settlement to be $1,350,000.

What amount relating to these transactions should the district report in its August 31, 2005, financial statements as:

1. Interest expenditure in its debt service fund statement of revenues and expenditures
2. Interest expense in its government-wide statement of activities
3. Long-term debt in the capital projects fund balance sheet
4. Current debt in the capital projects fund balance sheet
5. Long-term debt in the debt service fund balance sheet
6. Bonds payable (net of bond discount) in the government-wide statement of net assets
7. Other noncurrent debt in the government-wide statement of net assets
8. Invested in capital assets, net of related debt, in the government-wide statement of net assets
9. Current liabilities in the general fund balance sheet

Select each response from one of the amounts that follow. An amount may be selected once, more than once, or not at all.

a. $(34,942,147)
b. $0
c. $25,000
d. $800,000
e. $817,419
f. $842,419
g. $1,350,000
h. $1,600,000
i. $2,000,000
j. $2,025,000
k. $10,000,000
l. $12,000,000
m. $12.025,000
n. $38,924,728
o. $38,942,147

8-4

Both the reported value of long-term debt and periodic interest charges should be based on unamortized issue price (plus or minus unamortized premiums or discounts) and initial yield.

The City of Fairfield issued $100 million of twenty-year, 6 percent coupon bonds (3 percent per semi-annual period) for $89.32 million. The price reflected a yield of 7 percent (3.5 percent period semi-annual period).

1. Prepare entries to reflect how the following would be reported in the city's government-wide statements:
   a. The issuance of the bond
   b. The first semi-annual payment of interest
   c. The second semi-annual payment of interest
2. Prepare entries to account for the same transactions in an appropriate governmental fund.

8-5

The accounting for BANs depends on events subsequent to year-end.

In anticipation of issuing of long-term bonds, a state issues $200 million of sixty-day BANs to finance highway construction. It expects to roll over the BANs into long-term bonds within sixty days. Its fiscal year ends on May 31.

1. Prepare the appropriate journal entry in a governmental fund (such as a capital projects fund) to record the issuance of the $200 million, sixty-day BANs on May 1, 2005.
2. Prepare the appropriate journal entry, if required, to record the conversion of the BANs to long-term bonds on June 18, 2005.
3. Prepare the appropriate journal entry, if required, to adjust the accounts as of year-end May 31, 2005, assuming that the state was unable to convert the BANs to long-term bonds.
4. Comment on how the BANs would be reported on the government-wide statements as of May 31, 2005, assuming first that they were converted and second that they were not converted.

8-6

Debt is accounted for differently in fund and government-wide statements.

The following transactions affected a city's general fund. Prepare a table in which you indicate for each transaction the expenditure/expense and change in liabilities that the city would report in its (a) general fund and (b) government-wide statements.

1. City employees earned $7.7 million in vacation pay during the year, of which they took only $6.6 million. They may take the balance in the following three years.
2. The employees were paid $0.5 million for vacations that they had earned in previous years.
3. The city settled a claim brought against it during the year by a building contractor. The city agreed to pay $10 million immediately and $10 million at the end of the following year.
4. The city issued $100 million in general obligation bonds at par.
5. It paid $4 million in debt service. Of this, $3 million was for the first payment of interest, the balance for repayment of principal.

8-7

Capital leases create both assets and liabilities.

Pearl City leases an emergency communications system. The term of the lease is ten years, approximately the useful life of the equipment. Based on a sales price of $800,000 and an interest rate of 6 percent, the city agrees to make annual payments of $108,694. Upon the expiration of the lease the equipment will revert to the city.

1. Prepare an appropriate entry in the city's government-wide statements to reflect the signing of the lease.
2. Prepare appropriate entries to record the first payment on the lease. The city charges depreciation using the straight-line method.
3. Will your entries to record the final payment on the lease be the same as the first? Explain.
4. Comment briefly on how the lease transactions would be recorded in the city's general fund or other appropriate governmental fund.

8-8

Not-for-profits account for bonds similarly to businesses.

The Cleveland Historical Society issues $40 million of 6 percent, fifteen-year bonds at a price of $36,321,000 to finance the construction of a new museum. The price reflects an annual yield of 7.0 percent.

1. Prepare the journal entry to record the issuance of the bonds. Indicate the category of funds (e.g., unrestricted, temporarily restricted, permanently restricted) in which the entry would be made.
2. Prepare the journal entry to record the first *semiannual* payment of interest.
3. Prepare the journal entry to record the second *semiannual* payment of interest.

PROBLEMS

Continuing Problem

Review the Comprehensive Annual Financial Report (CAFR) that you obtained.

1. Per the city's schedule of long-term obligations, what is the total long-term obligation for both governmental and business-type activities? Does this amount reconcile with the long-term liabilities as reported on the government-wide statement of net assets?
2. What is the percent of total net bonded debt to assessed value of property? What is the amount of net debt per capita?
3. What is the city's legal debt margin?
4. Does the city have any lease obligations outstanding? Are these accounted for as operating or capital leases?
5. What is the amount of any overlapping debt?
6. Does the city have outstanding any conduit debt?

8-1

Government-wide statements are on a full accrual basis; fund statements are on a modified accrual basis.

The East Eanes School District engaged in or was affected by the following events and transactions during its fiscal year ending June 30, 2005.

1. Teachers and other personnel earned $350,000 in vacations and other compensated absences that they did not take but for which they expect to be paid in the future.
2. The district settled a suit brought by a student, agreeing to pay $3 million by December 31, 2006.
3. The district issued $8 million in GO bonds to finance an addition to its high school. By year-end, it had expended $1 million in construction costs.
4. The district signed a three-year lease for office space. Annual rent is $40,000 per year.
5. It acquired school buses and other vehicles, financing them with an eight-year capital lease. Annual lease payments are $140,000. Had the district purchased the equipment outright, the price would have been $869,371, reflecting an interest rate of 6 percent.
6. The district transferred $500,000, representing the final year's principal payment, to a reserve fund required by the bond indenture.
7. To smooth out cash flows, the district issued ninety-day tax anticipation notes of $950,000.
8. The district paid teachers and other personnel $150,000 for compensated absences earned in previous years.
   a. For each, prepare the entries (as required) to record the transactions in the general fund or whatever other governmental fund seems most appropriate.
   b. Prepare the entries that would be needed to reflect the transactions and events in the district's government-wide statements.

8-2

Governments now report their effective liabilities and interest costs, but do not adjust for changes in market values or rates.

On January 1, a public school district issued $6 million of 6 percent, fifteen-year coupon bonds to finance a new building. The bonds, which require semi-annual payments of interest, were issued for $6,627,909—a price that provides an annual yield of 5 percent (a semi-annual yield of 2.5 percent).

1. Prepare the journal entry that the district would make to reflect the issuance of the bonds on its government-wide statements. Comment on why the net reported liability differs from the face value of the bonds.
2. Prepare the entry that the district would make to reflect the first payment of interest on its government-wide statements. Indicate the value at which the bonds would be reported immediately following the payment. Comment on why the reported interest expense is not equal to the amount paid.
3. Suppose that immediately following the first payment of interest, prevailing interest rates fell to 4 percent. For how much could the district liquidate its obligations by acquiring all outstanding bonds in the open market. [*Hint:* Determine the present value (based on the prevailing interest rate of 2 percent per period) of the remaining twenty-nine coupon payments of $180,000 and the repayment of the $6 million of principal.] Comment on whether this amount would be reported in the district's financial statements (both fund and government-wide). Comment also on why and how this amount might be of interest to statement users.
4. Comment on how the district would report both the liability and interest costs in its fund statements.

8-3

Demand bonds may provide the issuer with the disadvantages, but not the advantages, of long-term debt.

On January 1, 2005, a city issues $2 million in 7 percent demand bonds. Although the bonds have a term of ten years, they contain a "put" option permitting the holder to present the bonds for redemption, at par, any time after December 31, 2006. The bonds pay interest semiannually.

1. Prepare journal entries in the city's general fund or other governmental fund to record the bonds assuming:
   a. The city has entered into a qualifying take-out agreement.
   b. The city has not entered into a qualifying take-out agreement.
2. Suppose that on January 1, 2007, prevailing interest rates for bonds of similar credit risk had fallen to 4 percent. A bondholder needed immediate cash for personal reasons. Assuming that the bonds were publicly traded, do you think the bondholder would redeem his bonds? Do you think that any other bondholders would redeem their bonds? Explain.
3. Suppose, instead, that prevailing interest rates had increased to 9 percent. Do you think that the bondholder needing cash would redeem his bonds? Do you think that the other bondholders would redeem their bonds?
4. Suppose that, since it is not mandated by the applicable GASB pronouncement, the take-out agreement does not specify the interest rate at which the financing institution would provide the funds necessary for the city to redeem its bonds. If prevailing rates had increased to 9 percent, at approximately what rate is it likely the financing institution would loan the city the required funds?
5. Comment on the extent to which the demand bonds provide the city with one of the primary benefits of issuing long-term debt—the guarantee of a fixed interest rate over the life of the bond. To what extent does it burden the city with the corresponding disadvantage—being required to pay no less than the stated rate over the life of the bond (or otherwise retire the bonds at market prices)?

8-4

BANs, TANs, and RANs may sound alike, but they are not necessarily accounted for alike.

In August 2004, voters of Balcones, a medium-sized city, approved a $15 million general obligation bond issue to finance the construction of recreational facilities. In order to begin construction immediately, without waiting to complete the lengthy process of issuing long-term bonds, the city issued $4 million in bond anticipation notes (BANs). The notes matured in March 2005, but the city had the right to prepay them any time prior to maturity.

On February 15, 2005, the city issued $15 million of 6 percent, twenty-year GO bonds. Upon receiving the proceeds it repaid the BANs, along with $80,000 in interest.

1. Prepare a journal entry to indicate how the city should report the BANs in its December 31, 2004, fund, financial statements, assuming that it issued the statements after February 15, 2005.
2. Suppose that the city did not refinance the BANs prior to the date the financial statements were issued. What other evidence must the city present to justify reporting the BANs as long-term obligations? Prepare a journal entry to indicate how the city should report the BANs if it is unable to provide this evidence.
3. Assume, also, that the city experienced a cash flow shortage in November 2004. Anticipating tax collections in January 2005 it issued $2 million in tax anticipation notes (TANs) due February 2005. In February 2005, instead of repaying the notes, it "rolled them over" for an additional six months. In which fund or account group should the city report the TANs? Explain.
4. Assume further that in July 2004 the city was awarded a $1 million reimbursement grant. It expected to receive the grant funds in January 2005. Inasmuch as it expected to incur many of the expenditures covered by the grant in 2004, it issued $1 million in six-month revenue anticipation notes (RANs). As of December 31, the city had not repaid the notes but had secured the written agreement of the lender that they could be extended for an additional six months. How should the city report the RANs on its December 31, 2004, financial statements? Explain.

8-5

For some types of debt, note disclosure is sufficient.

For each of the following items relating to the debt of Marfa City, indicate whether and how the debt would be reported on a balance sheet of one of the city's governmental funds. If it would not be reported, then state whether is would be reported instead on the government-wide statement of net assets or in notes to the financial statements. Insofar as you would need additional information to determine how the debt should be reported, then specify such information and tell how it would affect the determination. Briefly justify your response.

1. The city issues $10 million in thirty-year, 6 percent revenue bonds to enable a local nursing home to construct new facilities. The facilities will be leased to the home for the term of the bonds, and the lease payments will be exactly equal to the debt service on the bonds. At the expiration of the lease, the property will revert to the home. The bonds are backed exclusively by the lease payments from the nursing home.
2. The city issues $20 million in 8 percent BANs, which it expects to refund approximately 9 months after year-end, when, it hopes, long-term interest rates will drop.
3. As part of an annexation agreement, the city constructs roads to an adjacent municipal utility district. The city funds the roads by issuing $15 million in bonds. The bonds are backed exclusively by assessments on the district's property owners. Although the city will collect the assessments and transmit the required payments to the bond trustee, the city is barred by both the state constitution and its own charter from assuming responsibility for the debt in the event of property owner defaults.
4. Ten years ago, the city issued, at par, $15 million in 6 percent, twenty-year GO bonds. After the bonds have been outstanding for six years from the date of issue, they are redeemable at the option of the bondholders. The bonds are rated AAA and are fully insured by a highly reputable bond insurance company. Interest rates on comparable bonds are currently 5 percent.
5. A school district, the boundaries of which are the same as the city, has outstanding $120 million of GO bonds. The school district, which is governed by an independently elected board, is not a component unit of the city. However, both derive their revenues mainly from taxes on the same property and the city serves as the district's property tax collection agent.

8-6

Accountants and lawyers may have differing concepts of debt.

Officials of Danville, determining that the city needed additional administrative space, decided to acquire an available office building. Aware that city voters were unlikely to approve a bond issue to finance the purchase of the building, they decided instead to lease the property.

If the city had purchased the building outright, the acquisition price would have been $5 million. If it had issued general obligation bonds at the prevailing interest rate of 6 percent and elected to service the debt with equal payments over twenty years, then annual interest and principal payments (assuming annual compounding) would have been $435,923.

The city arranged for a financial institution to purchase the building and lease it to the city for twenty years. The lease specified annual payments of $435,923 and gave the city the option to purchase the building for $1 at the expiration of the agreement. The financial institution would sell shares in the lease to the public, just as if the city had issued bonds to acquire the building.

The lease also contained a nonappropriation clause stipulating that the city would make "good faith" efforts to adhere to its payment schedule but that its obligation was limited to amounts that the city council appropriated annually.

1. Prepare a journal entry to reflect acquisition of the building by lease in the city's government-wide statements.

2. Prepare journal entries to record the first lease payment and the first year's depreciation (assuming a twenty-year useful life). Indicate how the entries to record the second lease payment would differ from the first.
3. Suppose you were asked to represent the Danville Taxpayers Association, a group of citizens opposed to the acquisition of the building. The association contended that under the city's charter, the city was required to obtain voter approval for all general obligation debt over $1 million. The lease, it said, was the equivalent of general obligation debt. Therefore, it charged, the lease violated the city's charter and should be voided. What arguments would you make in support of the association's position?
4. Suppose, instead, that you were asked to represent the city. What arguments would you make to support the contention of city officials that the lease is not the equivalent of general obligation debt?

8-7

Overlapping debt can significantly alter key measures of debt capacity.

The following information was taken from the City of Wyoming, Michigan's schedule of direct and overlapping debt.

Name of Government Unit	*Net Debt Outstanding*	*Percentage Applicable to City*
City of Wyoming	$ 22,863,510	100.00%
Kent County	125,653,951	13.40
Kent County Intermediate School District	1,766,795	13.55
Wyoming Public Schools	3,956,922	99.24
Godwin Heights Public Schools	1,338,501	85.96
Kelloggsville Public Schools	2,363,037	61.97
Grandville Public Schools	10,734,809	13.58
Kentwood Public Schools	25,502,958	0.55
Godfrey Lee Public Schools	3,204,362	100.00

1. The schedule does not indicate the origin of the percentages of the debt applicable to the city. What is the most likely way these percentages were derived?
2. Compute the total amount of the City of Wyoming's direct and overlapping debt.
3. Another schedule in the city's annual report indicates that the city's ratio of net direct debt to assessed value of property is 1.861 percent and that net debt per capita is $354.47. The schedule reports that assessed value of property is $1,228,774,900 and that the population is 64,500. What would be the ratio of *total net direct debt and overlapping debt* to assessed value of property? What would be the total net direct and overlapping debt per capita?
4. Why might a statement user be at least as concerned with the ratios that include overlapping debt as with those limited to direct general obligation debt?

8-8

Operating leases, as well as capital leases, represent long-term fiscal commitments.

The following schedule was taken from the notes to the financial statements of Beth County Medical Center, a government hospital. Dates have been changed.

Future minimum payments under capitalized leases and non-cancellable operating leases with initial or remaining terms of one year or more.

	Capitalized leases	**Operating leases**
	(in thousands)	
2004	$ 756	$11,696
2005	560	7,949
2006	415	6,388
2007	242	5,475
2008 and thereafter	116	25,079
Total minimum lease payments	$2,089	$56,587
Less amount representing interest	271	
Present value of minimum payments	$1,818	

1. Where on the medical center's government-wide statement of net assets, if at all, would each of the amounts reported on the schedule, be reflected (or combined with other amounts)?
2. What is the significance of *amount representing interest*?
3. Prepare a journal entry to record the 2004 capital lease payments. Assume that the leases incorporate an interest rate of 6.56 percent (a rate that when used to discount each of the lease payments yields $1,818, the total present value of minimum payments).
4. Prepare a journal entry to record the 2004 operating lease payments.
5. Suppose that the medical center's cost of capital is 6.56 percent and that the $25,079 in operating lease payments for 2008 and thereafter are for a period of five years from 2008 through 2012 (in equal amounts of $5,016). What is the present value of the center's operating lease obligations from 2004 through 2012? [*Hint:* Discount each of the payments at a rate of 6.56 percent. If possible, use the present value functions of

a calculator or a computer spreadsheet program; otherwise, use an interest rate of 7 percent.] Of what significance is this amount to a statement user (i.e., why might it be as important as the actual debt reported on the balance sheet)?

8-9

Entries in both governmental funds and government-wide statements can be reconstructed from a city's schedule of changes in long-term debt.

The table at the bottom of this page was drawn from the City of Ft. Leah's schedule of long-term liabilities (all amounts in thousands).

1. Prepare the entry in the city's general fund to record the transactions affecting compensated absences during the year.
2. Prepare the entries to reflect the compensated absence transactions in the city's government-wide statements.
3. Prepare the entries in the capital projects and debt service funds to record the issuance and retirement of general obligation debt.
4. Prepare the entries to reflect the issuance and retirement of the general obligation debt in the government-wide statements.
5. Pension accounting is discussed in Chapter 10, which deals with fiduciary funds. However, based on what you know about expenditures and obligations in governmental funds, discuss the significance of the $47 million addition to, and $53.5 million reduction in, "net pension obligation."
6. The city recently signed a five-year lease to rent space in an office building. Annual rent was $100,000 per year. Where, if at all, on the schedule would the rent liability appear? Explain.

8-10

Legal debt margins do not typically include all of a government's obligations.

The following was taken from the statistical section of the City of Wyoming, Michigan's, annual report (see also Problem 7).

Computation of Legal Debt Margin for General Obligation Bonds as of June 30

Value of assessed property (excluding certain industrial and commercial properties)		$1,139,255,400
Debt limit—Ten percent of assessed value		113,925,540
Amount of debt applicable to debt limit:		
Total bonded debt	$27,442,000	
Less:		
Assets available for debt service	$1,770,453	
Revenue bonds not subject to debt limitations	2,025,000	
	3,795,453	
Total amount of debt applicable to debt limitations		$ 23,646,547
Legal debt margin		$ 90,278,993

Assume that in its fiscal year ending June 30 the city issued an additional (net of repayments) $30,000,000 of general obligation bonds and $6 million in revenue bonds. It increased its bond reserves (assets available for debt service) by $200,000. Moreover, owing to both a recession and a change in valuing property, the assessed value of its property decreased by 5 percent.

1. What is the maximum the city could issue in general obligation bonds as of June 30?

	Beginning Balance	Additions	Reductions	Ending Balance
Governmental activities				
Bonds and notes payable:				
General obligation debt	$503,341	$ 121	$ 30,179	$473,283
Capital leases	85,423	35		85,458
Special assessment bonds	1,200			1,200
Equipment note	370		27	343
Total bonds and notes payable	$590,334	$ 156	$ 30,206	$560,284
Other liabilities:				
Compensated absences	$125,600	$32,800	$ 29,700	$128,700
Net pension obligation	62,000	47,000	53,500	55,500
Claims and judgments	11,360	4,340	2,000	13,700
Total other liabilities	$198,960	$84,140	$ 85,200	$197,900
Total long-term liabilities	$789,294	$84,296	$115,406	$758,184

2. Suppose the city:
   a. Signed a five-year agreement with a waste disposal firm. The firm agreed to provide services to the city for $50,000 per year. The city could not cancel the contract unless the firm failed to deliver the specified services.
   b. Signed a five-year lease to acquire equipment. The useful life of the equipment was also five years. Annual payments were $50,000 per year and the city had the option to purchase the equipment at the end of its useful life for $1. The lease agreement was based on an interest rate of 8 percent and contained a "nonappropriation clause," which local courts recognized as being decisive with respect to whether the debt was subject to the legal debt margin.

   How would each be reflected in the city's government-wide statement of net assets? If you were writing the legislation establishing debt limits, would you make either leases or service contracts subject to the limits?
3. As indicated in the schedule, and as is typical of most debt limitations, the debt margin does not apply to revenue bonds. What do you think is the reason for this exemption? What argument could you make that revenue bonds should not be exempt?

8-11

Key information as to long-term obligations may be found in a city's comprehensive annual financial report (CAFR) in sections other than the primary financial statements.

This problem is based on a recent annual report of the City of Tucson.

1. The letter of transmittal from the city's finance director reports that the city's bonds were rated AA by Standard & Poor's. What is the significance of an AA rating? (Standard & Poor's ratings are similar to those of Moody's.)
2. Another city of approximately the same size received a bond rating of AAA, even though its overall financial condition by all reasonable measures was substantially weaker than that of Tucson. What would be the most likely explanation of why the city received a higher rating than Tucson, which is financially more sound?
3. A note to the financial statements indicates that the total required general obligation debt service payments over the life of the GO bonds were $370 million. Yet the total reported liability for GO bonds was only $209 million. What is the most likely explanation for the difference? How can you justify reporting the lower amount, when it is the higher amount that will have to be paid?
4. The city's "combined schedule of bonds payable" indicates that GO bonds issued in 1991 bore interest at the rate of 6.4 percent while those issued in the current year carried an interest rate of only 4.95 percent. Why do you suppose the city does not refund (redeem) the 1991 bonds, replacing them with lower-interest obligations?
5. The Arizona constitution limits the amount of debt that a city can have outstanding to 6 percent of the assessed value of its property. The assessed valuation of property in Tucson was $1,818,909,000. Inasmuch as only certain types of debt are covered by the limitations, the city's applicable debt was only $70,998,000, not $209,000,000 as indicated in part (3) of this problem. What was the amount of the city's legal debt margin?
6. In 1991 the assessed value of the property in Tucson was $1,555,216,000 and the city had $110,910,000 in GO debt (and no balances in debt service funds). By 1998 the assessed value of property had increased to $1,818,909,000 and bonded debt had increased to $209,000,000 (with $4,012,000 in debt service funds). Taking into account the amount in the debt service funds, would you say that, other factors being equal, the city's debt burden was greater or less in 1998 than it was in 1991? Explain, making relevant computations.

8-12

This example provides an overview of transactions addressed in this and previous chapters.

Zeff Township assessed property owners $1,000,000 to construct sidewalks. The assessments were payable over a period of ten years in annual installments of $123,290, an amount that reflects interest at a rate of 4 percent.

To fund the improvements the city issued $1,000,000 of ten-year, 4 percent bonds. The bonds were sold to yield interest of 3.8 percent (1.9 percent per period) and were thereby sold at a premium of $16,510 (i.e., at a total of $1,016,510). The township transferred the premium to an appropriate fund. Interest on the bonds is payable semi-annually (i.e., $20,000 each six months).

Inasmuch as the amounts to be received from the property owners are not coincident with the required payments to bondholders, the township will invest all available cash and any assets that remain after the bonds have been repaid will be transferred to the general fund.

In the same year that the township assessed the property owners and issued the notes, it constructed the sidewalks at a cost of $1,000,000. During that year it made one payment of interest on the bonds and collected one installment from the property owners. It invested $119,800 in U.S. Treasury notes—the difference of $103,290 between the assessments received and the interest paid, plus the $16,510 bond premium. It earned $3,000 (cash) interest on these securities.

Assume that the township recognized one full year's interest on the assessments receivable and that it recorded one full year's depreciation (based on a useful life of twenty years) on the sidewalks.

1. Prepare summary journal entries in all appropriate funds.
2. Prepare alternative journal entries to reflect how the transactions would be recorded in the township's government-wide statements.

SOLUTION TO EXERCISE FOR REVIEW AND SELF-STUDY

1. In its general fund statements, the entry would be:

Capital assets expenditures	$8,000,000	
Other financing sources—debt proceeds		$8,000,000

To record the expenditure and offsetting receipt of resources (in the general fund)

In its government-wide statements, it would record both the equipment and the lease obligation:

Equipment held under lease	$8,000,000	
Capital lease obligations		$8,000,000

To record the acquisition of equipment under a capital lease

2. Of the first payment of rent, $480,000 (6 percent of $8 million) represents interest and $606,944 represents principal. The city must record the entire payment as expenditures in its general fund:

Capital lease expenditure—interest	$480,000	
Capital lease expenditure—principal	606,944	
Cash		$1,086,944

To record the first lease payment (in the general fund)

In its government-wide statements it would recognize both interest expense and a reduction of the debt:

Capital lease obligations (lease principal)	$480,000	
Interest expense (lease interest)	606,904	
Cash		$1,086,944

To record the first lease payment

At the same time it would record annual depreciation:

Depreciation expense	$800,000	
Accumulated depreciation—equipment held under lease		$800,000

To record first year's depreciation ($8 million divided by ten years)

3. Since the city does not have a take-out agreement, it cannot record the bonds as long-term obligations—irrespective of whether prevailing interest rates are higher or lower than those of the bonds. It must record the debt as a short-term obligation of the general (or some other governmental) fund. Thus,

Capital assets expenditures	$8,000,000	
Demand bonds payable		$8,000,000

To record the acquisition of the capital asset as financed with demand bonds that do not satisfy the criteria of long-term debt

Both the assets and the debt would be reported on the government-wide statement of net assets. The debt would be classified as short term:

Equipment	$8,000,000	
Demand bonds payable		$8,000,000

To record equipment acquired with demand bonds

4. After issuing the $8 million of new debt, the city would have total debt outstanding of $27 million. Its debt margin would be only $3 million—10 percent of its $30 million limit.

5. Of the taxable property in the school district, 75 percent ($600 million of $800 million) is located within the city. Therefore, the city is responsible for 75 percent of the school district's debt—$36 million.

CHAPTER 9

Business-Type Activities

LEARNING OBJECTIVES

After studying this chapter you should understand:

- What types of funds involve business-type activities
- Why governments and not-for-profits engage in business-type activities
- How governments distinguish between proprietary and governmental activities, and the reasons for and against different accounting practices
- The fundamental principles of proprietary fund accounting
- The unique accounting issues raised by the use of enterprise funds, including those pertaining to capital contributions, restricted assets, and landfills
- The special accounting issues relating to internal service funds
- How governments account for insurance activities
- The special problems of reporting proprietary funds in government-wide statements
- How investors assess revenue debt

Governments and not-for-profits engage in a variety of functions that are similar to those carried out by businesses. They range in size from the small gift shops of churches to multibillion-dollar regional power authorities.

Thus, in this chapter we will look at accounting principles applicable to business accounting. As shall soon be evident, the business-type activities of governments and not-for-profits are accounted for similarly to corresponding enterprises in the private sector. Their financial statements are on a full rather than a modified accrual basis, and their measurement focus is on all economic resources, not merely current financial resources.

We shall direct relatively little attention, therefore, to the general principles (such as those of revenue and expense recognition) of full accrual accounting. Since these are the same as those of businesses, they are covered in other courses dealing with financial accounting.

Instead, our objectives are more specific:

- To consider criteria for distinguishing between business and governmental activities and to raise pertinent questions as to whether and why these activities should be accounted for differently
- To address several selected accounting issues that are unique to government enterprises
- To set forth the purposes, and assess the consequences, of using internal service funds to account for goods and services provided by one government department to another
- To show how business-type activities can be incorporated into government statements
- To present examples of the information needed to assess revenue bonds—the type of debt associated both with a government's business-type activities and with not-for-profit organizations

WHAT TYPES OF FUNDS INVOLVE BUSINESS-TYPE ACTIVITIES?

Governments segregate their business-type activities into *proprietary* funds, of which there are two types:

- ***Enterprise funds*** account for operations in which goods or services are provided to the general public.
- ***Internal service funds*** account for operations in which goods or services are provided by one government department to other departments within the same government or to other governments.

Some of the accounting and reporting issues pertaining to business-type activities are common to enterprise funds and internal service funds. However, each fund has unique features, so at the risk of repetition, we shall devote separate sections to each of the fund types.

Governments account for proprietary funds, both enterprise and internal service, on a full accrual basis. They recognize exchange revenues as earned and *expenses* (rather than expenditures) as incurred, irrespective of when cash is received or paid. They accord balance sheet recognition to both long-lived assets and long-term debt, depreciating the long-lived assets and amortizing any premiums or discounts on long-term debt.

Not-for-profits, in contrast to governments, account for their business-type activities, both internal and external, within their current operating funds. However, the current operating funds of not-for-profits, unlike those of governments, are on a full rather than a modified accrual basis. Therefore, not-for-profits, like governments, account for their business-type operations on a full accrual basis, giving balance sheet recognition to long-lived assets and long-term debt. The resources associated with these activities are generally donor-unrestricted and hence are so classified per the guidelines of Financial Accounting Standards Board (FASB) Statement No. 117, *Financial Statements of Not-for-Profit Organizations.*

WHY DO GOVERNMENTS AND NOT-FOR-PROFITS ENGAGE IN BUSINESS-TYPE ACTIVITIES?

Governments and not-for-profits engage in a wide variety of activities that are also carried out by for-profit businesses. For example:

- Governments provide waste removal, supply electric and other utility services, maintain hospitals (often in competition with stockholder-owned hospitals), and operate swimming pools, tennis courts, and golf courses.
- Universities sell computers, books, and clothing; sponsor professional-like sports team; operate cafeterias and restaurants; and maintain dormitories.
- Churches, synagogues, hospitals, museums, and zoos sell religious artifacts, gifts, posters, and books.
- Girl Scouts sell cookies; Boy Scouts sell candy.

In the United States, prevailing political and economic doctrine dictates that goods and services be provided mainly by the private business sector. Why, then, do governments and not-for-profits engage in activities similar to those carried out by private enterprise? Several reasons can be cited:

- The activities provide resources that would otherwise have to be raised by taxes, contributions, tuition, or other means. Gifts shops, for example, may be major sources of revenue for museums; government-owned utilities may generate cash as well as electricity.
- The activities complement and support the main mission of the entity. Thus, for example, college cafeterias, bookstores, and sports programs are an integral part of a university environment.
- The entity wants control over the activity. Thus, universities operate dormitories not necessarily because they can do so at less cost than a private contractor, but so they can maintain authority over them. Similarly, some cities and counties have rejected proposals to sell their hospitals to private firms so as to keep them entirely within their command.
- The entity can provide the services more cheaply or efficiently than a private firm can. This may be especially true if the government or not-for-profit is not subject to the income, property, or sales taxes that would be charged to private businesses. Public housing authorities, for example, have an inherent cost advantage over private landlords in providing apartments to low-income families in that their properties are not subject to property taxes.
- The entity wants either to subsidize the activity or to assure that the goods or services are available at less than market rates. Thus, a city might maintain a bus service or a public golf course even though it is unprofitable.

In recent years, both governments and not-for-profits have come under attack for operating activities that critics believe should be carried out in the private sector. Opponents of large government have urged the **privatization** of services, claiming that, lacking the profit motive, governments are inherently inefficient. Merchants have charged tax-exempt universities and museums with unfair competition in selling books, computers, and other items at less than prevailing prices.

The issue of whether business-type activities should be carried out by governments and not-for-profits is beyond the scope of this text. But the reasons they carry them out are directly pertinent to the questions of both how to distinguish business-type from governmental activities and how to account for them.

SHOULD BUSINESS-TYPE ACTIVITIES BE ACCOUNTED FOR DIFFERENTLY FROM GOVERNMENTAL ACTIVITIES?

A fundamental question pertaining to business-type activities is whether and why they should be accounted for differently from **governmental activities,** those that are financed predominantly through taxes and intergovernmental grants; in particular, why business-type activities should be accounted for on a full rather than a modified accrual basis of accounting, even in fund statements.

Key reasons cited for using business-type accounting to account for proprietary-fund activities include:

- The full accrual basis of accounting (i.e., a measurement focus upon all economic resources) captures all the resources and obligations, including capital assets and long-term obligations, associated with an activity. It thereby provides a more complete picture of the entity's fiscal status and operating results.
- The measurement focus on all economic resources is more consistent with the objectives of the Governmental Accounting Standards Board (GASB) that financial reporting should provide information to determine whether current-year revenues were sufficient to pay for current-year services and to assist users in assessing service efforts, costs, and accomplishments.
- Full accrual accounting provides information on depreciation, which is an essential cost of operations.
- Business-type accounting facilitates comparisons with similar private enterprises.

At the same time, there are cogent arguments against separate accounting principles for proprietary activities:

- Two separate measurement focuses and bases for accounting within the same set of financial statements are confusing and add complexity to the reporting process.
- As suggested earlier, there are no clear-cut distinctions between business and nonbusiness activities. Despite many similarities, governmental activities cannot—and should not—be compared to activities carried out in the private sector. A government should have sound political and economic reasons—other than merely earning a profit—for conducting a particular activity in the public sector. If it does not, then the activity should be privatized. These reasons, by themselves, should suggest that the activities be assessed by criteria other than profits—the *bottom line* of business-type financial reports.
- Surveys of statement users indicate that information on depreciation is not of high priority to governmental decision makers. They are concerned mainly

with the ability of revenues to cover debt service rather than depreciation. This applies especially to users interested in toll roads, tunnels, and bridges.

Closely tied to the issue of whether proprietary activities should be accounted for using separate accounting principles is whether they should be accounted for and reported in separate funds. A key rationale for fund accounting and reporting in general is that legally restricted resources should be reported apart from those that are unrestricted. To be sure, the resources of some proprietary funds may be contractually dedicated to servicing revenue bonds. The resources of others, especially those accounted for in internal service funds, however, are often not legally restricted. They can be used for all purposes of government and are subject to the claims of general creditors. As will be discussed later in this chapter, governments must present restricted proprietary fund assets (usually owing to revenue bond covenants) separately from those that are unrestricted. Both, however, may be presented within the same fund.

Obviously, there are compelling reasons to account *internally* for each of a government's business-type activities in separate funds. Separate funds facilitate budgeting, planning, and control. However, when resources that are not legally restricted are reported upon apart from unrestricted resources, statement users may have difficulty determining the total resources available for future appropriation or payment to creditors. They may be misled into thinking that unrestricted resources are, in fact, restricted.

In contrast to governments, the financial reports of not-for-profits are guided by the underlying principle that unrestricted resources, even if used to carry out business-type activities, should be reported upon in a common fund. Not-for-profits have traditionally reported upon their business-type activities within their current unrestricted funds, even though they may have maintained separate sets of books for each separate enterprise. This practice has been officially sanctioned by FASB Statement No. 117, *Financial Statements of Not-for-Profit Organizations*, which requires not-for-profits, for purposes of external reporting, to intermingle all resources, irrespective of whether they are associated with business or non-business activities, unless they are *donor* restricted.

Nevertheless, the arguments in favor of reporting upon proprietary activities apart from governmental activities are also persuasive. Up to the point of "information overload," more information is better than less. If managers need separate reports to assess the performance and fiscal status of business-type activities, so too do citizens, investors, and other statement users. Insofar as statement users are concerned with the total amount of unrestricted resources, they can readily add together the resources in unrestricted proprietary funds with those in the general and other unrestricted funds.

WHAT ARE THE THREE BASIC STATEMENTS OF PROPRIETARY FUND ACCOUNTING?

Similar to businesses, governments are required to prepare three basic proprietary fund statements:

- A statement of net assets (balance sheet)
- A statement of revenues, expenses, and changes in fund net assets (income statement)
- A statement of cash flows

Whereas the amounts reported in the individual fund statements of governmental funds are significantly different from those incorporated in the government-wide statements, those of proprietary funds are generally the same. As emphasized previously, the individual proprietary fund statements, like the government-wide statements, are on a full accrual basis of accounting.

THE STATEMENT OF NET ASSETS (BALANCE SHEET)

The GASB grants governments an option comparable to that regarding government-wide statements. That is, they can present the balance sheet in the form *assets less liabilities equal net assets* or *assets equal liabilities plus net assets*. In either case, net assets should be displayed in three broad components:

- Invested in capital assets, net of related debt (i.e., the total capital assets, less the remaining debt used to acquire, construct, or improve these assets)
- Restricted net assets
- Unrestricted net assets

Governments should also segregate the restricted assets themselves (as opposed to the offsetting net assets). Suppose, for example, that a government holds in a separate bank account cash that is restricted to debt service. To classify that cash as a current asset would suggest that it is available for general use. Therefore, the government should report that cash as a restricted asset, apart from its other current assets.

The distinctions between restricted and unrestricted assets, as well as other issues relating to restrictions, are addressed in a subsequent section.

THE STATEMENT OF REVENUES, EXPENSES, AND CHANGES IN FUND NET ASSETS (INCOME STATEMENT)

The statement of revenues, expenses, and changes in fund net assets is comparable to the income statement of a business. It differs, however, in that it is "all inclusive." That is, it reports not only operating revenues and expenses but also capital contributions. Further, it incorporates a reconciliation of beginning and ending net assets. The following summarizes its key elements:

Operating revenues	
Fees and charges	$10,000
Others (detailed)	2,000
Total operating revenues	12,000
Operating expenses	
Wages and salaries	8,000
Others (detailed)	1,500
Total operating expenses	9,500
Operating income (loss)	2,500
Nonoperating revenues and expenses	
State operating grants	2,400
Others (detailed)	500
Total nonoperating revenues and expenses	2,900
Income before other revenues, expenses, gains, losses, and transfers	5,400
Capital contributions and other changes in net assets	
Federal capital grant	800
Others (e.g., additions to permanent and term endowments, special and extraordinary items and transfers)	300
Total capital contributions	1,100
Increase (decrease) in net assets	6,500
Net assets—beginning of period	20,000
Net assets—end of period	$26,500

TABLE 9–1

Classification of Cash Receipts and Disbursements per GASB Statement No. 9, Reporting Cash Flows of Proprietary and Nonexpendable Trust Funds and Governmental Entities That Use Proprietary Fund Accounting

Cash Flows from Operating Activities

Inflows

- Sales of goods or services, including collections of receivables
- Grants for operating activities
- Receipts from interfund services provided by other funds or from interfund reimbursements
- All other cash receipts not defined as capital, financing or investing transactions

Outflows

- Payments to acquire materials for providing services, including payments on accounts payable
- Payments to employees
- Grants to other governments for operating activities
- Payments for taxes, duties, fines, and other fees or penalties
- Payments for interfund services used by other funds, including certain payments in lieu of taxes
- All other cash payments not defined as capital, financing, or investing transactions

Cash Flows from Noncapital Financing Activities

Inflows

- Proceeds from bonds, notes, or other debt instruments not clearly attributable to the acquisition, construction, or improvement of capital assets
- Grants from other governments that are not specifically restricted for capital purposes or are for specific activities considered to be operating activities of the grantor government (e.g., a grant to finance an operating deficit)
- Receipts from other funds except (1) amounts clearly attributable to acquisitions, construction, or improvement of capital assets, (2) interfund services provided, and (3) reimbursements for operating transactions
- Receipts from property and other taxes collected for the governmental enterprise that are not specifically restricted for capital purposes

Outflows

- Repayments of amounts borrowed for noncapital purposes
- Interest payment on amounts borrowed for noncapital purposes
- Grants to other governments except for those specific activities that are considered to be operating activities of the grantor government
- Cash paid to other funds, except for interfund services used

Cash Flows from Capital and Related Financing Activities

Inflows

- Proceeds from issuing bonds, notes, or other debt instruments for the acquisition, construction, or improvement of capital assets
- Capital grants
- Receipts from the sale of capital assets
- Contributions from other funds, governments, or other entities for acquiring, constructing, or improving capital assets
- Special assessments and property taxes to finance capital assets

Outflows

- Payments to acquire, construct, or improve capital assets
- Repayments of capital debt
- Interest on capital debt

(Continues)

TABLE 9-1
Classification of Cash Receipts and Disbursements per GASB Statement No. 9, Reporting Cash Flows of Proprietary and Nonexpendable Trust Funds and Governmental Entities That Use Proprietary Fund Accounting *(Continued)*

Cash Flows from Investing Activities

Inflows
- Receipts from sales of marketable securities
- Interest and dividends received from investments
- Withdrawals from investment pools
- Collections of loans made by the government (except for program loans)

Outflows
- Purchases of marketable securities
- Disbursement for loans (except for program loans)
- Deposits into investment pools

The distinction between operating and nonoperating revenues and expenses is not always clear and is subject to management discretion. In general the classification scheme should follow that adopted for the statement of cash flows (as illustrated in Table 9-1). Issues pertaining to capital contributions will be discussed in a section to follow.

The Statement of Revenues, Expenses, and Changes in Fund Net Assets and the Statement of Net Assets for Charlotte's proprietary funds were presented in Chapter 2 (Table 2-9).

THE STATEMENT OF CASH FLOWS

Governments are required to prepare a statement of cash flows for proprietary funds, but not for governmental funds. There is less need for a statement of cash flows for governmental funds, because governmental funds are accounted for on a modified accrual basis. Therefore, the statement of revenues and expenditures of governmental funds focuses—if not on cash itself—then on resources that are near-cash and are currently available for disbursement.

The preparation of a statement of cash flows can be complex and tedious, but it presents few, if any conceptual problems. In essence, the statement is a summary of an entity's cash account. The issues which both the FASB and the GASB have had to address pertain mainly to transaction classification.

Different Standards for Governments and Businesses

The GASB and FASB standards for statements of cash flows establish differing classification schemes. FASB Statement No. 95 *(Statement of Cash Flows)*, which does not apply to governments, requires that cash transactions be classified into three categories:

- ***Cash flows from operating activities,*** such as receipts from sales of goods and services, interest, and dividends and disbursements for goods and materials, interest and taxes;
- ***Cash flows from financing activities,*** such as proceeds from issuing stocks and bonds and payments for dividends and repayments of loans;
- ***Cash flows from investing activities,*** such as receipts and disbursements from the sale and purchase of marketable securities and long-lived assets.

These categories have obvious limitations if applied to governments. Governments typically characterize their activities as either operating or capital. Capital activities—those involving the acquisition and financing of long-lived assets—are often both budgeted and accounted for apart from operating activities. Yet the FASB classification scheme draws no distinction between the two.

To remedy this deficiency the GASB issued its Statement No. 9 *(Reporting Cash Flows of Proprietary and Nonexpendable Trust Funds and Governmental Entities That Use Proprietary Fund Accounting)*, which provides for a classification scheme with four categories:

- Cash flows from operating activities
- Cash flows from noncapital financing activities
- Cash flows from capital and related financing activities
- Cash flows from investing activities

Table 9-1 sets forth the main transactions included in each category.

The GASB and FASB standards also differ in how interest should be reported. In a significant departure from the precedent of FASB Statement No. 95, the GASB pronouncement requires that government enterprises classify interest paid as financing activities and interest received as investing activities rather than operating activities. Whether interest paid is classified as a capital rather than a noncapital financing activity would depend on how the underlying debt is classified. The GASB maintains that by classifying interest received and disbursed in the same categories as purchases and sales of the underlying securities, governments provide a more complete picture of the cash flows associated with financing and investing activities.

In another very significant departure from FASB Statement No. 95, GASB Statement No. 34 mandates that governments report their cash flows using the direct method. The direct method explicitly reports the operating cash flows in a way that makes clear their source or use (e.g., cash receipts from customers, cash payments to employees). The indirect method, by contrast, reconciles operating cash flows to operating income. Thus, the reporting entity would add to, or subtract from, operating income any differences between cash flows (e.g., cash receipts from customers, cash payments to employees) and the related revenues or expenses (e.g., sales revenues, wage and salary expense). The FASB encourages businesses and not-for-profits to use the direct method but permits them to use the indirect method. But despite the FASB's expressed preference for the direct method, the overwhelming majority of businesses elect to use the indirect method.

Charlotte, North Carolina's Statement of Cash Flows for its proprietary funds is presented in Table 9-2.

WHAT ACCOUNTING ISSUES ARE UNIQUE TO ENTERPRISE FUNDS OF GOVERNMENTS?

Although governments have adopted the business accounting model to account for their enterprise funds, they nevertheless face several unique issues. Two very basic questions pertain to when an activity should be accounted for in an enterprise fund and what principles should govern the accounting for an enterprise fund. Other, more specific, issues relate to budgetary reporting, capital contributions, restricted assets, and landfills.

CRITERIA FOR ESTABLISHING AN ENTERPRISE FUND

Almost all government departments engage in some form of entrepreneurial activity. Accordingly, there is no obvious way to distinguish activities that should be accounted for in enterprise funds, and in the past there has been considerable diversity of practice. To reduce this diversity, the GASB established general criteria as to when a government may, and when it must, account for an activity in an enterprise fund.

TABLE 9-2
Charlotte, North Carolina
Statement of Cash Flows Proprietary Funds
for Year Ended June 30, 2002 (in thousands)

	Business-type Activities—Enterprise Funds					Governmental Activities—
	Water and Sewer	Storm Water	Airport	Public Transit	Total	Internal Service Funds
Cash flows from operating activities						
Receipts from customers	$151,547	$23,724	$ 85,447	$ 8,828	$269,546	$ —
Receipts from participants	—	—	—	—	—	11,053
Payments to suppliers	(32,251)	(7,019)	(20,054)	(24,215)	(83,539)	(4,407)
Internal activity—(payments to) receipts from other funds	(11,255)	(808)	(5,008)	(3,761)	(20,832)	40,144
Payments to employees	(25,839)	(2,512)	(9,352)	(26,298)	(64,001)	(853)
Payments to airlines for non-airline terminal revenue distribution	—	—	(7,802)	—	(7,802)	—
Payments for claims	—	—	—	—	—	(39,279)
Payments for premiums	—	—	—	—	—	(5,494)
Other receipts (payments)	1,004	(394)	(642)	1,043	1,011	—
Net cash provided (used) by operating activities	83,206	12,991	42,589	(44,403)	94,383	1,164
Cash flows from noncapital financing activities						
Operating grants	—	150	—	7,897	8,047	—
Property tax	—	36	—	—	36	—
Sales tax	—	—	—	51,843	51,843	—
Transfers in (out)	—	—	—	18,701	18,701	(1,100)
Net cash provided (used) by noncapital financing activities	—	186	—	78,441	78,627	(1,100)
Cash flows from capital and related financing activities						
Proceeds from capital debt	177,641	—	—	11,840	189,481	—
Water and sewer construction deposits	863	—	—	—	863	—
Acquisition and construction of capital assets	(128,870)	(18,230)	(71,817)	(27,957)	(246,874)	—
Principal paid on capital debt	(31,114)	(1,974)	(18,840)	(775)	(52,703)	—
Interest paid on capital debt	(47,285)	(2,854)	(28,398)	(443)	(78,980)	—
Capital contributions	—	—	11,386	22,606	33,992	—
Net cash provided (used) by capital and related financing activities	(28,765)	(23,058)	(107,669)	5,271	(154,221)	—
Cash flows from investing activities						
Purchase of investments	(146,881)	—	(221,950)	—	(368,831)	—
Proceeds from sale and maturities of investments	105,694	—	252,583	—	358,277	—
Interest received	10,710	1,931	12,793	5,581	31,015	2,249
Net cash provided (used) by investing activities	(30,477)	1,931	43,426	5,581	20,461	2,249
Net increase (decrease) in cash and cash equivalents	23,964	(7,950)	(21,654)	44,890	39,250	2,313
Cash and cash equivalents—beginning of year	93,270	39,759	274,995	83,983	492,007	46,264
Cash and cash equivalents—end of year	$117,234	$31,809	$253,341	$128,873	$531,257	$48,577

GASB Standards

In Statement No. 34, the GASB prescribes that governments *may* account for an activity in an enterprise fund as long as it charges fees to external users for goods and services. They *must* account for an activity in an enterprise fund if the activity satisfies one of the following criteria:

- The activity is financed solely with revenue debt, as opposed to general obligation debt. Whereas general obligation debt is backed by the full faith and credit of the entire government, revenue debt is secured merely by the revenues from a specific activity.
- Laws or regulations require that the activity's costs of providing services (including capital costs) be recovered by fees and charges rather than general purpose taxes or similar charges.
- The pricing policies of the activity establish fees and charges designed to recover its costs, including capital costs (such as depreciation or debt service).[1]

The criteria should be applied to an activity's principal source of revenue—not to insignificant sources. Thus, even if a police department charges fees for escorting funeral processions or for controlling traffic at charitable "fun runs," the activities need not be accounted for in an enterprise fund.

The GASB standards, although much tighter than those that they replaced, still allow governments considerable discretion in determining which of their activities to account for in enterprise funds. Most notably, for example, they state that a government "may" use an enterprise fund to account for any activity for which it charges fees. Thus, governments have the option of using either an enterprise or a governmental fund to account for those activities for which they charge fees but which do not satisfy any of the three mandatory criteria.

ACCOUNTING PRINCIPLES

In general, proprietary funds are accounted for like businesses; they adhere to the pronouncements of the FASB. However, pronouncements issued by the GASB that conflict with FASB pronouncements override the FASB pronouncements. For example, as previously noted, in 1989 the GASB issued Statement No. 9, *Reporting Cash Flows of Proprietary and Nonexpendable Trust Funds and Governmental Entities That Use Proprietary Fund Accounting.* This statement requires proprietary funds to prepare a cash flows statement that differs in significant respects from that mandated by the FASB's Statement No. 95, *Statement of Cash Flows.* Moreover, other FASB statements require disclosures that go beyond those mandated by the GASB for governments' nonbusiness activities.

GASB Standards

To avoid having both to consider the applicability to governments of all future FASB pronouncements and to issue "negative" standards (those which tell governments that they don't have to adhere to an FASB pronouncement) the GASB issued Statement No. 20, *Accounting and Financial Reporting for*

[1] GASB Statement No. 34, *Basic Financial Statements—and Management's Discussion and Analysis—for State and Local Governments* (June 1999), para. 67.

Proprietary Funds and Other Governmental Entities That Use Proprietary Fund Accounting. This statement gives governments an option between two approaches to applying FASB pronouncements:

- ***Option 1.*** A government must apply to its proprietary activities all FASB pronouncements issued on or before November 30, 1989, unless they conflict with, contradict, or are replaced by GASB pronouncements. In addition, they must comply with any post-November 30, 1989, pronouncements that have been specifically adopted by GASB.[2]
- ***Option 2.*** A government must apply to its proprietary activities all FASB pronouncements, irrespective of when they were issued, unless they conflict with, contradict, or are replaced by GASB pronouncements.

Thus, the standard requires all governments, irrespective of which approach they choose to follow, to adhere to all FASB pronouncements issued on or before the 1989 cut-off date (unless those pronouncements have been overridden by specific GASB statements). Then, if they elect the first approach they can adhere to none of the subsequent FASB pronouncements (unless they were specifically adopted by the GASB). By contrast, if they elect the second approach, they must adhere to all of the subsequent FASB pronouncements (unless they specifically conflict with GASB pronouncements). They cannot cherry-pick the most appealing statements and reject the others.

November 30, 1989, is not yet as notable as June 15, 1215 (the signing of the Magna Carta), or July 4, 1776 (the signing of the Declaration of Independence). It owes its significance to what accounting historians of the future will likely see as an equally significant proclamation—the "Jurisdiction Determination of the Board of Trustees of the Financial Accounting Foundation." The key feature of this agreement is a new hierarchy of generally accepted accounting principles, establishing that the GASB has the final standard-setting authority over all government entities, including hospitals, universities, and other proprietary activities. Thus, if the GASB issues a statement that conflicts with one issued by the FASB, the GASB statement must be followed by the entities within its jurisdiction.

As will be noted in the section pertaining to internal service funds, GASB Statement No. 34 modified this standard slightly. Per Statement No. 34, only enterprise funds, not internal service funds, have an option as to whether they will adopt post-November 1989 FASB pronouncements. Internal service funds can adopt them only if they are made specifically applicable by other GASB statements.

THE NEED FOR BUDGETS AND BUDGET-TO-ACTUAL COMPARISONS

Government enterprises are disciplined by the marketplace rather than by their budgets. Both their revenues and expenses, unlike those of governmental funds, are determined by "customer" demand, not by legislative fiat. Principles of sound management dictate that governments, like businesses, prepare annual budgets. However, the budgets of proprietary funds play a decidedly different role from those of governmental funds. Like those of businesses, they facilitate planning, control, and evaluation. They are not, however, the equivalent of either spending authorizations or tax levies. Accordingly, governments neither have to get formal legislative approval for their proprietary fund budgets nor incorporate them into their accounting systems. Moreover, in their annual reports they need not compare the budgeted amounts with actual results.

[2] Per GASB Statement No. 34, para. 17. Option (1) also applies to governmental activities to the extent that a FASB pronouncement is relevant to those activities.

Governments, like businesses, should ordinarily prepare several different types of budgets. For example, they should formulate:

- A cash budget to facilitate cash management and help assure that they will have adequate, but not excessive, cash on hand
- A capital budget to expedite the acquisition of capital assets
- A flexible budget, indicating anticipated fixed and variable costs at different levels of output, to help control costs

CAPITAL CONTRIBUTIONS

Enterprise funds receive capital contributions both from internal (i.e., other funds) and external (e.g., new customers, developers, and other governments) sources. The key accounting and reporting issues pertain to determining how capital contributions should be presented on the financial statements and to distinguishing capital contributions from ordinary revenues.

Consider several examples of different types of nonroutine receipts:

- ***Tap (system development) fees.*** A city charges new customers of an electric or water utility a tap fee to hook up to an existing system. The amount of the fee may exceed the cost of connecting the customer to the system; part may cover the customer's share of the capital cost of the system already in place.
- ***Impact fees.*** A municipal utility district charges developers a fee for anticipated improvements, such as new water and sewer lines, that will be required because of new development. Unlike tap fees, these fees cannot necessarily be associated with specific projects or improvements.
- ***External subsidies.*** A municipal transit authority receives a federal grant both to purchase new busses and to defray operating costs.
- ***Internal subsidies.*** A county hospital receives an annual transfer from the county's general fund based on the number of indigent patients that it serves. The transfer enables the hospital both to cover operating expenses and to acquire new equipment.
- ***Debt forgiveness.*** A state provides a loan to its state-operated liquor stores. The stores have historically been unprofitable, and there is little possibility of the loan ever being repaid.

GASB Standards

Prior to the issuance of Statement No. 34, governments took a "capital maintenance" approach to proprietary fund reporting. That is, contributions of capital assets, permanently restricted financial assets, and other capital contributions were reported as direct additions to fund balance or net assets. They were not counted as revenues and were excluded from the statement of revenues and expenditures; they were balance sheet transactions only. In Statement No. 34, however, the GASB switched to an "all inclusive, net assets" approach. This new approach dictates that the operating statement (statement of revenues, expenses, and changes in net assets) report on all changes in net assets, including capital contributions. Accordingly, as illustrated previously, governments should present capital contributions as revenues on a line following income from operations.

The GASB recognizes that tap fees and similar types of charges may, at least in part, be nonvoluntary capital contributions. Nevertheless, it directs, in

Statement No. 33 pertaining to revenue recognition, that these types of charges (albeit not impact fees since they are not associated with specific projects) should be accounted for as if they were "pure" exchange transactions—hence as ordinary revenues. The GASB does not provide guidance as to whether "mixed" grants, such as those to both acquire capital equipment and to cover operating expenses, should be classified as operating revenues or capital contributions. However, because capital contributions must now be reported on the operating statement rather than as a direct increase in net assets, the distinction between operating revenues and capital contributions is less significant than under the old reporting model.

RESTRICTED ASSETS AND NET ASSETS

Governmental proprietary units are, in key respects, reporting entities within reporting entities. Although accounted for in separate funds, they issue debt and are responsible for servicing it. Accordingly, some of their resources may be restricted. For example:

- Bond proceeds may have to be used for the construction or acquisition of specific assets.
- Resources may have to be set aside for the repayment of bond principal or the payment of interest.
- Customer deposits may have to be segregated from other resources to assure that they are available for return.

To indicate that assets are restricted, governments should report their restricted enterprise-fund assets apart from unrestricted assets. Correspondingly, they should also report any offsetting net assets in a separate equity account.

Governments should include within the restricted category resources that are restricted both by outside parties (such as bondholders and other creditors, grantors, or the laws of higher-level governments) or by themselves (through legislation that limits the use of assets to specified purposes). Restricted resources must be distinguished from resources that are merely "designated" by a government's policy for an intended purpose. Thus, for example, if a government informally sets aside cash for a "rainy day," that cash should not be classified as restricted. To avoid confusion, governments should not report designations of net assets on the face of the balance sheet.

The accounting for restrictions may get a bit complex because some restricted assets are offset not by net assets, but instead by liabilities. Compare, for example, two types of restricted assets relating to debt.

- A government issues bonds and has temporarily invested the proceeds in marketable securities. The marketable securities are restricted assets in that they must be used for the purpose specified in the bond indenture. The securities are offset by a liability, "bonds payable." Hence, the securities and the related bonds have no impact on net assets (assets less liabilities). Therefore, even though the securities are restricted (and should be so classified), it would be inappropriate to categorize any amount of net assets as restricted.
- A government, as required by bond covenants, sets aside cash in a special account restricted to the payment of interest on long-term debt. The interest has not yet been recognized as either an expense or a liability. Accordingly, both the cash and an equal amount of net assets should be classified as restricted.

EXAMPLE *Revenue Bond Proceeds as Restricted Assets*

A government issues $10 million in revenue bonds that are restricted to the construction of plant and equipment. The following entry would be appropriate:

Cash restricted to construction	$10	
Revenue bonds payable		$10
To record the issuance of revenue bonds and to designate the proceeds as restricted		

Inasmuch as the restricted cash is offset by a liability, there is no need to reclassify a portion of unrestricted net assets as restricted.

Subsequently, the government sets aside $2 million cash to pay interest on the debt:

Cash restricted to debt service	$2	
Cash (unrestricted)		$2
To record the designation of cash as restricted		

At the same time, since unrestricted net assets have now been reduced by $2 million the government must reclassify that amount as restricted:

Net assets—unrestricted	$2	
Net assets—restricted		$2
To reclassify a portion of net assets to reflect resources restricted to debt service		

LANDFILL COSTS

One of the most pressing economic and political issues of the foreseeable future will be how to maintain—and pay for—a clean environment. Both governments and private industry will face billions of dollars of costs to dispose of wastes, to prevent additional pollution, and to clean up messes that have been made in the past. Because the magnitude of the costs is so great, and the timing, specific amounts, and distribution of cash outlays are so uncertain, the associated accounting issues are necessarily complex. So far, the GASB has addressed only one aspect of the issues—accounting for landfill costs.[3]

Governments account for landfills in either governmental or enterprise funds, depending mainly on whether they charge usage fees. Since most governments do charge usage fees, they generally account for them in enterprise funds. The GASB standards to be discussed are equally applicable to both enterprise and governmental funds with regard to the calculation of the *amount* of the landfill liability to be reported. But, inasmuch as the two types of funds differ in their measurement focus and basis of accounting, they differ as to *where* the liability should be reported and *when* the related expenditure must be charged.

Landfills provide benefits over the period that they accept waste, often thirty or forty years. However, both state and federal regulations make landfill operators responsible for properly closing their landfills and subsequently caring for and monitoring them. Therefore, an operator must incur sizable costs when it closes the landfill and for an extended period, as long as twenty years, thereafter.

The accounting problems pertaining to closure and postclosure costs are comparable to those of pensions. The benefits are received over the years when the landfill accepts the waste (or, in the case of pensions, when employees provide their services). Although some costs may be incurred prior to the point of closure, most are incurred in the years of closure (retirement) and beyond. Moreover, the actual costs to be incurred are subject to unpredictable factors.

[3] GASB Statement No. 18, *Accounting for Municipal Solid Waste Landfill Closure and Postclosure Care Costs* (August 1993).

GASB Standards

Consistent with the pension accounting principles in both industry and government, the GASB has directed that proprietary funds allocate closure and postclosure costs to the years in which the landfill accepts its waste rather than when they are paid. Therefore, in each year of a landfill's useful life, the government should recognize as both an expense and an increase in a liability an appropriate portion of the estimated total costs for closure and postclosure care.

Total costs would include:

- Cost of equipment expected to be installed and facilities expected to be constructed near or after the date that the landfill stops accepting waste (e.g., gas monitoring and collection systems, storm water management systems, ground water monitoring wells)
- Cost of final cover
- Cost of monitoring and maintaining the landfill during the postclosure period

The amount to be added to a liability account at the end of each year would be based on the percentage of the landfill actually used up to that point. It would equal the percentage of the landfill used during the year times the total estimated costs. At any point during the life of the landfill, the balance in the liability account would equal the sum of the yearly amounts added to the account less any costs incurred.

From a slightly different perspective, the amount to be added to a liability each year—and to be charged as the expense for that year—would be the total amount that should have been recognized as an expense (added to the liability) up to the date of computation, less the amount that has actually been recognized so far. Thus, the amount to be added each year (the current year expense) equals:

$$\frac{\text{Estimated total cost} \times \text{Landfill capacity used to date}}{\text{Total landfill capacity}} - \text{Amounts recognized in the past}$$

Both costs and capacity would be based on *current* conditions at the time of the computation. Each year the government would reestimate both the total landfill capacity and the total closure and postclosure costs, thus taking into account inflation, new regulatory requirements, and technological improvements since the previous computation.

The GASB does *not* deal with the issue of when governments should *finance* closure and postclosure costs. Therefore, a government does not necessarily have to "fund" the costs during the landfill's useful life; it merely has to report both an expense and a liability for them. Moreover, in contrast to the manner in which it would compute its pension liability, it should not take into account the time value of money in making any of its calculations.

The example that follows illustrates how a government would account for a landfill in an enterprise fund (as well as in its government-wide, full accrual statements). If it accounted for the landfill in a governmental fund, only the journal entries, not the total liability or the amount to be added each year, would differ. Inasmuch as governmental funds do not report long-term obligations, the liability for the closure and postclosure costs would be reported only in the government-wide statements, not in the fund itself. Correspondingly, the governmental fund would not report an annual expenditure for the amount added to the liability account. As with other long-term obligations, a fund expenditure would be charged only in the period that the liability is to be liquidated with currently available financial resources. The result, therefore, is that with respect to the expenditure, the government is on a "pay-as-you-go" basis.

EXAMPLE *Landfill Costs in an Enterprise Fund*

At the start of Year 1, a government opens a landfill, which it elects to account for in an enterprise fund. It estimates that total capacity will be 4.5 million cubic feet, that the site will be used for thirty years, and that total closure costs will be $18 million.

Year 1

During Year 1, the government uses 90,000 cubic feet of the landfill. At year-end, it estimates that total capacity will still be 4.5 million cubic feet but that closure related costs will now be $18,036,000. The required expense addition to the liability would be computed as follows:

Total estimated costs	$18,036,000
Proportion of landfill used (90,000/4,500,000)	.02
Required expense (addition to liability)	$ 360,720

Journal Entry

Landfill expense	$360,720	
Liability for landfill costs		$360,720
To record the landfill liability and expense for Year 1		

The end-of-year balance in the liability account would be $360,720.

Year 2

In Year 2, the government uses 120,000 cubic feet of the landfill. At year-end, it estimates that total closure-related costs have increased to $18,526,600 and that landfill capacity has decreased to 4,275,000 cubic feet. Thus:

Total estimated costs	$18,526,600
Proportion of landfill used to date (90,000 + 120,000)/4,275,000	.049122
Amount that should have been added to the liability to date (cumulative expense)	910,079
Less: amount recognized previously	360,720
Required expense (addition to liability)	$ 549,359

Journal Entry

Landfill expense	$549,359	
Liability for landfill costs		$549,359
To record the landfill liability and expense for Year 2		

The end-of-year balance in the liability account would be $360,720 + $549,359 = $910,079.

Year 3

In Year 3, the government uses 135,000 cubic feet of the landfill. At year-end, it estimates that total closure-related costs have increased to $18,840,254 and that landfill capacity has remained at 4,275,000 cubic feet. During the year the government also spends $277,221 on closure-related costs.

Total estimated costs	$18,840,254
Proportion of landfill used to date (90,000 + 120,000 + 135,000)/4,275,000	0.080700
Amount that should have been added to the liability to date (cumulative expense)	1,520,442
Less: amount recognized previously	910,079
Required expense (addition to liability)	$ 610,363

Journal Entry

Landfill expense	$610,363	
Liability for landfill costs		$610,363

To record the landfill liability and expense for Year 3

As the government actually incurs the closure-related costs of $277,221, it would record the payment as follows:

Liability for landfill costs	$277,221	
Cash		$277,221

To record the payment of closure or postclosure costs

It would not matter if these costs were incurred for the acquisition of capital assets (e.g., earth-moving equipment) or for operating purposes (e.g., salaries). When the government incurs the costs, it reduces the previously established liability. It does *not* record as capital assets the equipment and facilities included in the estimate of closure-related costs. The end-of-year balance in the liability account would be $360,720 + $549,359 + $610,363 – $277,221 = $1,243,221.

WHAT ARE INTERNAL SERVICE FUNDS AND HOW ARE THEY ACCOUNTED FOR?

Internal service funds are used to account for governmental units or departments that provide goods or services to other departments or to other governments on a cost reimbursement basis. Like other funds, they are *accounting* rather than organizational entities. Most commonly the accounting entities correspond to related organizational units, such as data processing or vehicle repair centers. Sometimes, however, an internal service fund may be established to account for an activity for which there is no parallel organizational unit. For example, an internal service fund may be used to account for "self-insurance," which may be administered by a finance or accounting department.

REASONS AND BASIS FOR ESTABLISHING

Internal service funds are intended to promote efficiency in the acquisition, distribution, and use of goods and services. The department providing the goods or services is, in effect, a profit center. Therefore, it is expected to keep its costs in line with its revenues and to satisfy the requirements of its "customers." At the same time, the customers are charged for the goods or services that they receive and thereby have incentives to demand only what they can optimally use. In addition, internal service funds are a means of allocating the costs of functions and activities to the departments that are the ultimate beneficiaries.

As with enterprise funds, governments have considerable discretion in establishing internal service funds. Statement No. 34 permits governments to establish internal service funds "to report any activity that provides goods or services to other funds, departments, or agencies of the primary government and its component units, or to other governments, on a cost-reimbursement basis." Only rarely are all the resources assigned to internal service funds legally restricted. Therefore, it would usually be as proper for a government to account for them in its general fund or some other governmental fund as in an internal service fund.

Present practice reflects the absence of specific standards for establishing internal service funds, and the range of activities that some governments account for in internal service funds is far-reaching. Examples include:

- Supplies stores
- Legal, accounting, auditing, and personnel services
- Maintenance and janitorial services
- Insurance
- Capital asset leasing

ACCOUNTING PRINCIPLES

Internal service funds, like enterprise funds, use business-type accounting. Therefore, they follow the FASB model and are subject to standards similar to those of enterprise funds. As noted previously, in accounting for both internal service and enterprise funds, governments must adhere to all FASB pronouncements issued prior to November 30, 1989 (unless they conflict with or have been replaced by a GASB pronouncement). Governments have the option in accounting for their enterprise funds of adopting either all or none of the post–November 30, 1989, pronouncements. However, in accounting for their internal service funds, they do not have the option of adopting the post–November 30, 1989, pronouncements; they can adopt these only if made specifically applicable by other GASB pronouncements. The GASB granted the option for enterprise funds so that their reporting could be comparable to that of similar private-sector enterprises. It felt that this justification did not apply to internal service funds.

Internal service funds derive their revenues from other governmental or proprietary funds. Although they may provide services to a large number of different departments, most of their revenues are generally earned from a small number of funds—typically, the general fund and the enterprise funds. Nevertheless, some internal service funds, particularly those established to account for accounting or data processing activities, may provide services to capital projects, debt service, and other restricted governmental funds.

Per the principles of accrual accounting, the revenues of an internal service fund are recognized when earned, not necessarily when cash is received. Thus, internal service funds ordinarily recognize revenue as they deliver the goods or services. However, they might also recognize revenue uniformly over time—as would be appropriate for a fund that leases assets or underwrites insurance.

The expenses of internal service funds are the costs incurred to produce the goods and services. These, too, are recognized on a full accrual basis. They thereby include both depreciation on capital assets and amortization of bond premiums and discounts. Correspondingly, internal service funds account for, and report on their balance sheets, both capital assets and long-term debt.

Tables 9-3 and 9-4 present the statements of net assets and of revenues, expenses, and changes in net assets of Charlotte, North Carolina's two internal service funds. Note that except for some governmental-specific accounts, the statements could readily be those of a private service business.

The budgets of internal service funds, like those of enterprise funds, seldom require legislative approval, and are almost never incorporated into the funds' accounting system. Like those of enterprise funds, the revenues and expenses are driven by customer demand rather than specific legislative action. Moreover, control over the demand may be

TABLE 9-3
Charlotte, North Carolina
Internal Service Funds Combining Statement of Net Assets
June 30, 2002 (in thousands)

	Risk Management	Employee Health and Life	Total
Assets			
Current assets:			
Cash and cash equivalents	$42,915	$ 5,662	$48,577
Receivables—Other	1,635	50	1,685
Due from other funds	—	81	81
Total current assets	44,550	5,793	50,343
Capital assets:			
Machinery and equipment	228	—	228
Less accumulated depreciation	117	—	117
Total capital assets, net	111	—	111
Total assets	44,661	5,793	50,454
Liabilities			
Current liabilities:			
Claims payable	18,170	7,259	25,429
Noncurrent liabilities:			
Due to participants	2,640	—	2,640
Compensated absences payable	64	—	64
Total noncurrent liabilities	2,704	—	2,704
Total liabilities	20,874	7,259	28,133
Net assets			
Invested in capital assets	111	—	111
Unrestricted	23,676	(1,466)	22,210
Total net assets	$23,787	$(1,466)	$22,321

established by the budgets of the funds receiving the internal service fund's goods or services. Governments should, of course, prepare the same types of budgets (cash, flexible, capital, etc.) as would be expected of any business that provides similar goods or services.

The example that follows highlights the key features of internal service fund accounting.

EXAMPLE *Internal Service Fund Accounting*

Establishment of Fund

A government establishes an internal service fund to account for a new data processing department. It transfers $0.6 million from its general fund to the internal service fund as an initial contribution of capital.

Cash	$0.6	
Nonreciprocal transfer from general fund		$0.6
To record the capital contribution from the general fund		

The general fund would record a corresponding nonreciprocal interfund transfer.

TABLE 9-4
Charlotte, North Carolina
Internal Service Funds Combining Statement of Revenues, Expenses, and Changes in Fund Net Assets, June 30, 2002 (in thousands)

	Risk Management	Employee Health and Life	Total
Operating revenues			
Charges for services—			
Risk management and safety fees	$ 1,553	$ 4,009	$ 5,562
Claims:			
Employer	5,180	27,464	32,644
Employee	—	6,678	6,678
Other	—	295	295
Total claims	5,180	34,437	39,617
Premiums	2,656	1,136	3,792
Total operating revenues	9,389	39,582	48,971
Operating expenses			
Administration	1,572	4,009	5,581
Claims	2,690	35,690	38,380
Insurance premiums	2,873	1,136	4,009
Depreciation	26	—	26
Total operating expenses	7,161	40,835	47,996
Operating income (loss)	2,228	(1,253)	975
Nonoperating revenues			
Investment earnings	1,619	190	1,809
Income (loss) before transfers	3,847	(1,063)	2,784
Transfers out	(1,100)	—	(1,100)
Change in net assets	2,747	(1,063)	1,684
Total net assets—beginning	21,040	(403)	20,637
Total net assets—ending	$23,787	$(1,466)	$22,321

Issuing Long-Term Debt

The government issues $1.0 million in general obligation bonds to support the new department. It intends to service the debt entirely from the revenues of the data processing fund.

Cash	$1.0	
Bonds payable		$1.0
To record the long-term debt		

Even though the bonds are general obligation bonds, they can be recorded as a fund liability as long as the government intends to repay them from the internal service fund.

Acquisition of Capital Assets

The department acquires long-lived assets (buildings, computers, furniture, etc.) for $1.4 million.

Capital assets (specified in detail)	$1.4	
Cash		$1.4
To record the acquisition of capital assets		

Billings to Other Departments

For services rendered during the year, the department bills the utility fund for $0.3 million, and the police department, the fire department, and all other departments accounted for in the general fund for $0.8 million.

Due from general fund	$0.8	
Due from utility fund	0.3	
Operating revenues		$1.1
To record billing to other departments		

Correspondingly, the general fund would report an expenditure, and the utility fund an expense, for the amounts billed. The two funds would recognize expenditures or expenses, rather than intra-governmental transfers, since these transactions qualify as interfund services used—costs that would be characterized as expenditures or expenses if the services were provided by outside vendors.

Depreciation and Other Expenses

The data processing department incurred $0.2 in depreciation and $0.7 in other operating expenses. In addition, it acquired $0.1 in supplies inventory that remained on hand at year-end.

Depreciation expense	$0.2	
Other operating expenses (specified in detail)	0.7	
Supplies inventory	0.1	
Accounts payable		$0.8
Accumulated depreciation		0.2
To record depreciation and other expenses		

Other transactions, such as those involving purchases of investments, the use of materials and supplies, and accrual of interest, would be accounted for in the same manner as they would in a comparable business.

BASIS FOR ESTABLISHING RATES

Internal service funds are used to account for goods and services provided to other governmental units on a cost reimbursement basis. This dictum implies that billing rates should be established so as to cover costs. As any student of management accounting can appreciate, however, cost can have several different meanings: full cost, incremental cost, opportunity cost, and direct cost.

In practice, *cost* has been interpreted to mean full cost. Internal service funds are expected, over time, neither to earn profits nor to incur losses. As a consequence, billing rates should reflect all operating costs, including depreciation, interest, and other indirect costs.

The accumulation of unrestricted net asset surpluses may suggest that billing rates exceed actual costs. However, governments may intentionally establish rates that exceed cost. This enables them to accumulate the resources required either to replace existing assets or to expand the asset base to meet anticipated increases in demand.

Ironically, the practice of establishing billing rates at full cost may subvert a key objective of internal service funds—that the supplying department provides and the receiving department takes an optimal quantity of goods and services. As illustrated in the accompanying "In Practice: Full-Cost Pricing May Encourage Dysfunctional Decisions," full cost prices do not reflect the cost of providing incremental amounts of goods or services. Therefore, they may encourage departments to purchase either more or fewer goods or services than is optimal from the perspective of the government as a whole.

RAMIFICATIONS FOR OTHER FUNDS

The accounting and operating practices of departments accounted for in internal service funds have critical implications not only for the internal service funds themselves but also for the other funds with which they interact.

IN PRACTICE

FULL COST PRICING MAY ENCOURAGE DYSFUNCTIONAL DECISIONS

A city accounts for a vehicle repair unit in an internal service fund and bills departments at full cost. The unit's fixed costs are $80,000 per month; its variable costs are $40 per hour. On average it provides 4,000 hours of service per month. Accordingly, its billing rate is $60 per hour:

Fixed costs per month	$ 80,000
Variable costs (4,000 hours at $40)	160,000
Total costs per month	$240,000
Number of hours	÷ 4,000
Cost per hour	$60

The police department receives a bid of $3,000 from an outside garage to repair one of its vehicles.

The city's repair service calculates that the job will take sixty hours and therefore submits an estimate to the police department of $3,600 (60 hours at $60 per hour). Since the price is greater than $3,000, the police department accepts the outside bid.

Assuming that the repair service had the necessary capacity to carry out the repairs, its fixed costs would have been unaffected by the job for the police department. It would have incurred only the additional variable costs of $2,400 (60 hours at $40).

From the perspective of the city as a whole, the police department's decision to use the outside garage was dysfunctional. The city passed up the opportunity to receive $3,000 of incremental benefits in exchange for incremental costs of $2,400.

Duplicate Reported Expenses

Costs reported by internal service funds are reported twice within the same set of financial statements. They are reported once by the internal service fund providing the goods and services and a second time by the fund that is billed for them. Correspondingly, revenues are also reported twice: once by the fund receiving them from outside parties (as taxes or fees) and again when earned by the internal service fund.

Fortunately, however, as is explained in a section that follows on proprietary fund reporting requirements, the duplications are largely eliminated in the consolidated, government-wide financial statements.

Transfer of Depreciation to Governmental Funds

Governmental funds do not report capital assets; they do not charge depreciation. However, insofar as an internal service fund incorporates depreciation expense into its billing rates, the depreciation charge is transferred, along with all other costs, to the funds that it bills.

The impact on reported expenditures of a governmental fund can be telling. Suppose one government accounts for a motor pool in an internal service fund; another in its general fund. The motor pool of each government serves only other departments that are accounted for in the government's general fund. The general fund of the government maintaining the internal service fund will record the cost of the motor pool vehicles over their useful lives (through the depreciation expense incorporated into the billing rates). That of the other government will record the cost as the vehicles are acquired or paid for.

Detract from Objectivity of Financial Statements

An internal service fund should establish its billing rates so it covers its costs. Yet cost is an elusive concept. It depends on estimates (such as useful life of assets), choices among accounting methods (as to expense recognition, depreciation, inventory), and bases of overhead allocation. Although generally accepted accounting principles may establish broad guidelines for cost determination, they leave considerable latitude for individual companies or governments.

Owing to the leeway permitted governments in establishing costs, neither the billing rates nor the total revenues of an internal service fund can be seen as being objective. And if its revenues are not objective, then neither are its changes in net assets for the year or its total net assets.

The inevitable subjectivity of individual internal service fund financial statements might be of only minor concern to statement users if the impact were limited to the internal service fund statements. But it is not. The revenues of an internal service fund are the expenditures and expenses of other funds. Thus, if the revenues of an internal service fund are subjective, then so also are the expenditures of the general fund and all other funds to which the internal service fund provides goods or services. And if their expenditures are subjective then so too are their annual excess of revenues over expenditures, their fund balances, and their assets or liabilities.

By controlling billing rates, government officials can fine-tune the reported excess of revenues over expenditures of the general fund—the fund most subject to balanced budget requirements and public scrutiny. For example, faced with pressure to hold down general fund expenditures, a government can delay imposing rate increases that would otherwise be warranted. Or, with an eye to maximizing cost recovery under a state or federal grant, it can increase the internal service fund charges to the programs whose costs are eligible for reimbursement.

Obscure Fund Balance Surpluses or Deficits

By adjusting the billing rates, government officials can transfer surpluses or deficits (i.e., positive or negative fund balances) from the general fund to the internal service fund. These surpluses or deficits might be prohibited if they remained in the general fund. Suppose, for example, government officials see a need to set aside resources for the replacement of long-lived assets or for a rainy day. They recognize, however, that if the general fund were to report a surplus, legislators would seek either to increase spending or to reduce taxes.

The officials could achieve their objective by increasing the billing rates of an internal service fund, thereby transferring resources from the general fund to the internal service fund. The reserve would be maintained in the internal service fund rather than the general fund. To be sure, the reserve would be reflected in the net assets of the internal service fund. But the internal service fund may not be as carefully examined as the general fund. Since net assets includes a conglomeration of cumulative earnings for many years and many purposes, the reserve could readily be obscured.

WHAT SPECIAL PROBLEMS ARE CREATED WHEN AN INTERNAL SERVICE FUND OR THE GENERAL FUND ACCOUNTS FOR "SELF-INSURANCE"?

Many governments, seeking ways to reduce costs, elect to "self-insure" all or a portion of their risks, especially those for less than catastrophic losses. Independent insurance companies set premiums at rates that allow them to cover anticipated claims, administrative costs, and capital costs. For the portion of its policy applicable to routine losses, such as from automobile accidents or worker injuries, an insured entity's premiums are almost always based on the entity's own claims history. Self-insurance may provide an opportunity for the government to reduce the portion of the premium that covers the administrative and capital costs.

GASB permits governments to account for their self-insurance activities in either the general fund or an internal service fund.[4] Irrespective of which is used, the insurance

[4] *Codification*, Section C50.124.

"department" (which may be only an accounting entity rather than an organizational unit) operates as if it were an independent insurance company. It periodically bills other departments for premiums, and it pays their claims as losses are incurred.

Self-insurance presents intriguing and controversial issues of accounting. The term **self-insurance** is an oxymoron. The essence of insurance is the transfer of risk to an outsider. When a government self-insures, it retains the risk itself, irrespective of whether it accounts for the activity in an internal service fund or the general fund. Therefore, self-insurance is no insurance.

ACCOUNTING FOR INSURANCE PREMIUMS

The key accounting issues pertain to when, and in what amount, the insured departments should recognize expenditures for premiums paid and the insurance departments should recognize revenues for the insurance premiums received.

Suppose a government accounts for its insurance activities in an internal service fund and all the departments that it insures are accounted for in the general fund. The general fund, therefore, pays annual premiums to the internal service fund.

If the general fund paid these premiums to an outside insurance company, the premiums would be recorded as an expenditure. Consistent with the principles that interfund services used be accounted for as expenditures, it might appear that premiums paid to the internal service fund should also be accounted for as an expenditure.

Payments for self-insurance premiums, however, are different from other types of charges from internal service funds. The general fund does not actually transfer risk to the internal service fund; any losses incurred are a general obligation of the government at-large. Except for the portion of the premiums that covers losses actually incurred, it simply sets aside funds to provide for possible losses in the future. In that regard the transaction is comparable to a transfer of resources to a debt service fund for the future repayment of bonds. Therefore, it has been argued, only the portion of the premium that covers actual losses should be reported as an expenditure in the general fund. The excess should be accounted for as a nonreciprocal transfer. Correspondingly, only the portion of the premium that represents a reimbursement for actual losses should be recognized as a revenue in the internal service fund.

GASB Standards

Rejecting arguments that premium payments are nothing more than nonreciprocal internal transfers, the GASB has held that as long as specified criteria are satisfied, an internal service insurance fund can recognize revenues, and the insured funds (departments) can recognize expenditures, for the full amount of the premiums billed.

An internal service insurance fund, it has ruled, can use any basis to establish its premiums that the government considers appropriate as long as the premiums satisfy either of the following conditions:

- The total charge covers the actual losses incurred by the fund.
- The total charge is based on an actuarial method or historical cost method and adjusted over time so that internal service fund revenues and expenses are approximately equal.

The premiums can also include a provision for expected catastrophe losses.

If the premiums satisfy either of these criteria, then the internal service insurance fund may recognize revenue upon billing the insured funds. Correspondingly, the insured funds may recognize an expenditure. If, however, the premiums exceed the amount that satisfies these criteria, the excess should be reported as a nonreciprocal transfer from the insured funds to the internal service fund. If they are less, the resultant deficit in the internal service fund should be charged back to the insured funds and reported as expenditures in those funds.

Consistent with FASB Statement No. 5, *Accounting for Contingencies*, the internal service insurance fund should recognize its expenses for claims expenses and liabilities when:

- It is probable that an asset has been impaired or a liability incurred.
- The amount of loss can be reasonably estimated.

EXAMPLE *Insurance Premiums*

A government maintains an internal service fund to insure all government vehicles for loss and damage and for liability to third parties. It establishes premiums using actuarial techniques intended to assure that over time the premiums will cover claims, administrative expenses, and catastrophic losses. In a particular year, the internal service fund bills the general fund $260,000 and the utility fund $130,000—a total of $390,000. Of this amount $25,000 is for potential catastrophes. During the year it incurs $360,000 in claims losses, none of which resulted from catastrophes.

The internal service fund would recognize as revenues the entire $390,000 in premiums:

Cash	$390,000	
Revenues—insurance premiums		$390,000
To record premium revenue		

At the same time, the general fund would recognize an expenditure of $260,000 and the utility fund an expense of $130,000.

The internal service fund would also recognize claims expenses for the actual $360,000 of losses:

Expenses—claims	$360,000	
Claims liability (or cash)		$360,000
To record losses incurred		

As a consequence of closing the revenue and expense accounts at year-end, net assets will increase by $30,000. Of this sum, $25,000 is attributable to the premiums for the potential catastrophes. GASB standards direct that this amount should be designated in the notes to the statements as intended for catastrophes.

ACCOUNTING FOR SELF-INSURANCE IN A GENERAL FUND

Although this chapter is directed toward proprietary funds, this section digresses to contrast how self-insurance activities would be accounted for in a general fund rather than an internal service fund.

GASB Standards

The GASB stipulates that when self-insurance activities are accounted for in a general fund, the amount of premium revenue recognized by the general fund should be limited to actual claims expenditures (i.e., those losses that satisfy the criteria of FASB Statement No. 5). Correspondingly, total expenditures and expenses recognized by the general fund and any other insured funds should be limited to the same amounts. Any amounts charged to the other funds (including the general fund itself) in excess of the actual claims should be accounted for as nonreciprocal transfers. The differences in accounting principles are justified, according to the GASB, because the general fund transfers neither risk nor actual resources to either an outside party or to a separate fund.

EXAMPLE *Self-Insurance in a General Fund*

Assume the same facts as in the previous example except that the insurance activities are accounted for in the general fund. The insurance "department" bills other general fund departments for $260,000 in premiums and the utility fund for $130,000, a total of $390,000. As before, the government incurs only $360,000 in actual claims.

The general fund would recognize the claims, as would an internal service fund (except that the general fund would report the claims as an expenditure rather than an expense):

Expenditure—claims	$360,000	
Claims liability (or cash)		$360,000
To record losses incurred		

However, the maximum that the insurance department could recognize as premiums from the other departments would now be $360,000—the amount of the actual claims. Of this, one-third ($130,000/$390,000), or $120,000, would be attributable to the utility fund and two-thirds ($260,000/$390,000), or $240,000, to the other general fund departments. The premiums would be recognized as interfund reimbursements and reported as reductions in expenditures. The $10,000 that the utility fund paid above its share of the allowable premium revenue would be reported as an interfund transfer. Thus, the general fund would record the billings to the utility fund as follows:

Cash	$130,000	
Interfund reimbursements—insurance premiums		$120,000
Nonreciprocal transfer-in (from utility fund)		10,000
To record premiums collected from utility fund		

The utility fund would recognize a premium expense of $120,000 and a nonreciprocal transfer-out of $10,000.

Although the insurance department would also record the billings to the other departments accounted for in the general fund, the entries are not shown here. Because the insurance department is also accounted for in the general fund, there would be no impact on the financial statements. Intrafund revenues and expenditures would net out.

HOW ARE PROPRIETARY FUNDS REPORTED?

ENTERPRISE FUNDS

The reporting of enterprise funds is relatively straightforward. That of internal service funds is more complex.

Government-Wide Statements

The government-wide statement of net assets (balance sheet) contains two columns under the heading "primary government." One is for governmental activities, and the other is for business-type activities. The balances of the various enterprise funds are consolidated and reported in the column for the business-type activities.

The government-wide statement of activities reports on revenues and expenses by functions. The rows listing the functions are divided into separate categories for governmental and business-type activities. As discussed and illustrated in Chapter 2, the statement has one column that indicates the expenses for each function and one or more columns for the revenues (such as fees for goods or services or restricted grants) that are directly associated with the functions. The net expenses (the differences between the expenses and revenues) are shown in one of two columns—one for governmental activities, the other for business-type activities. The net expenses of enterprise funds are, of course, shown in the column for the business-type activities.

The government-wide statements consolidate the government's funds and report on the government as a whole—not as a series of independent funds. Therefore, interfund revenues, expenses, receivables, and payables generally must be eliminated. Suppose, for example, that a city's electric utility sold electricity to departments accounted for in its general fund. At year-end the utility fund had a receivable of $100,000 from the general fund—and correspondingly the general fund had a payable of $100,000 to the utility fund. From the perspective of the government as a whole, both the receivable and the payable would have to be eliminated on the government-wide statement of net assets. The government cannot owe money to itself. Nevertheless, the government-wide statements distinguish between business-type and governmental activities and report them in separate columns. The enterprise fund does have a receivable from the general fund, and the general fund does have a payable to the enterprise fund. These must be shown in the columns for each activity, yet they cannot be shown in the "total" column—that which presents the balances for the government as a whole. How can a government show the receivables and payables in the individual columns but not in the totals column?

GASB Standards

Interfund receivables and payables may be reported either on a single line—with one a positive amount and the other a negative—or on separate lines with the amounts being excluded from the "total" column. Thus, for example, if shown on a single line the amounts might be reported among the assets as follows:

	Governmental Activities	Business-Type Activities	Total
Internal balances	$100,000	($100,000)	—

If shown on two lines (one in the asset section, the other in the liability section) they would be presented as:

	Governmental Activities	Business-Type Activities	Total
Interfund receivable	$100,000		—
Interfund payable		$100,000	—

In concept, the sales of a utility fund and purchases by a general fund should also be eliminated. However, the units accounted for in the general fund are usually but a few of many customers of the utility department, and they acquire electricity that they would have otherwise had to purchase from outside parties. Thus to eliminate the sales and purchases would understate both the operating costs of the governmental activities and the revenues of the business-type activities. Per the GASB, therefore, interfund services provided and used between functions need not be eliminated.

Funds Statements

In the section of the basic financial statements containing the funds statements, the three required statements of proprietary funds (statement of net assets; statement of revenues, expenses, and changes in fund net assets; and statement of cash flows) are presented apart from the statements of governmental funds. The accounts of each major enterprise fund are reported in separate columns. In these statements, each fund is reported as if it were an independent entity. Hence, no eliminations are necessary. Correspondingly, in the statements of the funds that received the services, the interfund activities would be accounted for as if they were transactions with external parties.

INTERNAL SERVICE FUNDS

Government-Wide Statements

The government-wide statements present an overview of the government as a whole and, hence, consolidate the various individual funds. Inasmuch as internal service funds exist to service government units that are accounted for in other funds, interfund receivables, payables, as well as the related revenues and expenses must be eliminated in the consolidation process.

EXAMPLE *Eliminating Interfund Balances and Transactions*

Suppose that a data processing internal service fund provided service to other units, all of which were accounted for within the general fund or other governmental funds. The data processing fund billed the other funds for $10 million, an amount that reflected the "full" cost of providing its services. At year-end it had uncollected receivables of $2 million from the other funds. These transactions would have been reflected in the individual data processing fund and the various governmental funds as follows:

	Data Processing Internal Service Fund	Various Other Governmental Funds	Total
Sales revenues	$10		$10
Expenses	10	$10	20
Accounts receivable	2		2
Accounts payable		2	2

From the perspective of the government as a whole, the cost of providing the data process services was only $10 million—not the total of $20 million that is reported as expenses in the "total" column above. Correspondingly, the government as a whole had zero revenue from the interfund "sales" and no receivables and payables from the amounts that one department owed to another. Therefore, both sales revenues and expenses must be reduced by $10 million, and both the receivables and payables must be reduced by $2 million.

Internal service funds do not exist to earn a profit. As noted earlier, their billings to other departments should reflect actual costs. Accordingly, their revenues should equal their expenses, and both can be eliminated in their entirety in the consolidation process. In fact, even if the rates were not set to equalize revenues and expenses, they should be retroactively adjusted so that the internal service funds just break even. The end result will be that all the costs of operating the internal service funds can be charged back to, and reported as expenditures or expenses by, the funds that were the consumers of the internal service funds' goods and services.

By contrast, the assets and the liabilities other than interfund receivables and payables would not be eliminated in the consolidation process. These include cash, capital assets, and obligations to outsiders. A question arises, therefore, as to whether these assets and liabilities (and the resultant net assets) should be classified as governmental or business-type activities. Internal service funds are, of course, proprietary funds. Nevertheless, they typically provide services mainly to government units that are accounted for in the general fund or other governmental funds.

GASB Standards

The GASB has prescribed that internal service fund balances that are not eliminated in the consolidation process ordinarily should be reported in the statement of net assets (balance sheet) in the governmental activities column, unless the fund provides services predominantly to enterprise funds. If the internal service fund provides services mainly to enterprise funds, then the government should report the balances in the business-type activities column.

The consequence of these standards is that in the government-wide statements the revenues of the internal service fund and the offsetting expenses of the service recipient funds are eliminated in the consolidation process. The expenses of the internal service fund are charged back to the service recipient funds and thereby aggregated with their applicable functional expenses. In the usual situation, that in which the internal service fund provides services mainly to departments accounted for in governmental funds, the internal service fund is considered a governmental fund. Therefore, any receivables from, and payables to, other governmental funds are eliminated in the consolidation process. By contrast, because business-type activities are reported in a separate column, receivables from, and payables to, enterprise funds are not eliminated in the consolidation process. They are included, as appropriate, in either the governmental or business activities column but excluded from the "total" column. Instead, they are reported in a manner similar to that in the earlier illustration in which a utility fund had a receivable from the general fund. At the same time, internal service fund assets and liabilities, such as capital assets and payables to outsiders, that are not eliminated in the consolidation process are reported in the governmental activities column.

Funds Statements

In the funds (as opposed to the government-wide) statements, internal service funds are categorized as *proprietary* funds. In each of the three required proprietary funds statements (statement of net assets; statement of revenues, expenses, and changes in fund net assets; and statement of cash flows), data for all internal service funds are aggregated into a single column. This column is presented alongside those for each of the major enterprise funds. However, even though internal service funds are incorporated into the proprietary fund statements, they appear under a heading "Governmental Activities—Internal Service Funds." Moreover, owing to their different characteristics, the balances in the internal service funds are not combined with those of the enterprise funds into a single "total" column.

WHAT DO USERS WANT TO KNOW ABOUT REVENUE DEBT?

In the previous chapter we highlighted the main types of ratios and other data that investors and other statement users look to in assessing a government's ability to repay its general obligation debt. In this section we do the same as to revenue debt.

Revenue bonds encompass the debt that will be paid from a dedicated revenue stream produced by the assets that the debt financed. These assets typically include utilities, convention centers, stadiums, parking facilities, and similar fee-generating projects. Revenue bonds also incorporate the debt of most not-for-profits, including health care organizations, universities, and museums.

In light of the vast array of entities that issue revenue bonds, it is difficult to generalize as to the data needed by users. The salient fiscal characteristics of a government-operated hospital, for example, may differ considerably from those of a public university. Nevertheless, some types of information are central to the evaluation of any revenue-backed security. Among the types identified by Standard & Poor's, a leading bond rating service, are the following:[5]

- ***Security provisions.*** Revenue bonds are secured by specific fees or taxes. These may include user charges (such as highway tolls, college tuition, and hospital billings) or dedicated taxes (such as a sales tax restricted to debt service or a gasoline tax restricted to highway improvements).
- ***Competition.*** Revenue bonds, unlike general obligation bonds, are often used to support activities that are competitive. For example, hospitals, universities, airports, parking garages, and museums compete with other public and private institutions that provide similar services. Whereas, the general obligation (GO) bonds are backed by the full faith and credit of the government—and thus by its power to tax—revenue bonds are backed only by specified revenues. Competition introduces a credit risk not normally associated with GO bonds.
- ***Service area.*** Projects financed by revenue bonds do not necessarily serve areas that are within predetermined geographic boundaries. For example, a university may attract students from throughout the world. A hospital may compete statewide for patients. The broader the geographic base of a revenue stream, the less likely it is to be affected by local economic downturns.
- ***Revenue-raising flexibility.*** Some user charges can be raised more easily than others. For example, a city may be constitutionally prohibited from increasing a restricted sales tax, whereas a hospital may have considerable flexibility in increasing patient charges. The greater the revenue-raising flexibility, the less the credit risk.

The specific information depends, of course, on the nature of the institution. Table 9-5 outlines the factors that Standard & Poor's deems important in evaluating the revenue debt municipal parking facilities. The list is especially notable for the prominence of nonfinancial factors. It shows that even to assess the ability of the bond issuer to service its debt—the primary concern of a rating service—users must look beyond conventional financial statements.

SUMMARY

Governments account for and report business-type activities in proprietary funds. Activities carried out with outside parties are accounted for in enterprise funds; those with other departments within the government or with other governments are accounted for in internal service funds. Governments (as well as not-for-profits) account for their business-type activities using business-type accounting. They apply a full accrual, all economic resources, model.

Governments and not-for-profits engage in business-type activities for many reasons. Most commonly, the activities provide resources that otherwise would have to be raised through taxes or contributions, or they complement and support the entity's main mission.

As a general rule, governments *may* account for an activity in an enterprise fund if it charges fees to external users for goods and services. However, they *must* account for it in

[5] The information requirements presented in this section were drawn from *Municipal Finance Criteria* (New York: Standard & Poor's Rating Group, 1994).

TABLE 9-5

Factors Focused on (and documents required by) Standard & Poor's in Evaluating the Revenue Bonds of Municipal Parking Facilities

Basic documents
- Official statement
- Bonds resolution or trust indenture
- Five years financial audits
- Consultant's feasibility studies
- Capital programs
- Current budgets

Operational data
- Description of existing facilities
- Service area
- Occupancy rates
- Description of type of use (monthly, daily, or hourly)
- History of rates and rate increases
- Proposed rate schedule
- Rate setting procedure
- Competing facilities (location, number of spaces, and rates)
- Collection and enforcement procedures

Economic data
- Leading employers
- Employment and labor force trends
- Wealth and income indicators
- Retail sales activity
- Building activity

an enterprise fund if it is financed with revenue debt, is required by law to cover its expenses with user charges, or is expected to be self-supporting.

The GASB has established specific guidelines on how to account for landfills. Landfills are often accounted for in enterprise funds, inasmuch as they typically charge user fees. Still, they are sometimes accounted for in governmental funds. Irrespective of fund, however, governments must report the obligation for the estimated costs of closing and monitoring a landfill when it will be taken out of service. The amount of the obligation should be based on the proportionate share of the landfill used to date. As with other long-term obligations, where and how the liability is reported depends on the type of fund with which it is associated. Thus, if the landfill is accounted for in a enterprise fund, the liability will be reported in the fund itself and, of course, in the government-wide statements. If it is accounted for in a governmental fund, it will be reported *only* in the government-wide statements and not in the fund itself.

Internal service funds are established to promote efficiency in the acquisition, distribution, and use of goods and services. Like enterprise funds, they are accounted for on a full accrual basis. Internal service funds bill the funds to which they provide services at rates intended to cover their costs. However, in the absence of standards as to how the costs should be calculated, governments have considerable flexibility in establishing those rates.

By their very nature, internal service funds affect the other funds with which they interact. The consequences of accounting for activities in internal service funds rather than governmental funds are that revenues and costs are counted twice within the same set of financial statements, depreciation charges are incorporated in the expenditures of the funds billed, and surpluses and deficits can be transferred from the funds billed to the internal service funds. These limitations are substantially mitigated, however, in government-wide statements. Government-wide statements present the financial position and results of operations from the perspective of the government as a whole. These statements consolidate the individual funds, and interfund activity and balances are thereby eliminated.

Many governments maintain internal service funds to account for self-insurance. Self-insurance, however, does not result in a transfer of risk to outsiders. Therefore, the GASB has established standards as to the policies by which governments can determine the premium revenue to be recognized by self-insurance funds and the expenditures to be charged by the funds that they insure.

Business-type activities of governments are often supported by revenue bonds, which are backed by specific revenue streams such as dedicated taxes or user charges. The ability of the issuer to maintain these streams can seldom be evaluated by focusing exclusively on factors reported in the financial statements. Users must look to the entire range of elements that affect the entity's operating environment.

EXERCISE FOR REVIEW AND SELF-STUDY

The statement of net assets and statement of revenues, expenses, and changes in fund net assets for the City of Kingsland's proprietary funds are presented on pages 341 and 342.

1. On what basis of accounting (i.e., cash, accrual, modified accrual) are the statements prepared? How can you tell?
2. Is it necessary for the city to adopt a budget comparable to that of a governmental fund for its enterprise funds and to incorporate it into its accounting system by making annual budgetary entries? Explain.
3. The electric utility reports \$116.4 million as "invested in capital assets, net of related debt." Are you able to reconcile that amount with the reported assets and liabilities?
4. The golf course's restricted cash and investments of \$2.389 million are not equal to its restricted net assets of \$2.323. What might account for the difference?
5. Assume that one of the government's internal service funds was for data processing services, for which the golf course was billed \$30,000, all of which was classified as "contractual services" in the golf course fund. How would that amount be reported in the column for internal service fund? How would it be reported in the government-wide financial statements?
6. The internal service fund reported \$2.7 million in depreciation, an amount that the government takes into account in establishing the rates charged to other funds. How would this charge be reflected in the government-wide statements?
7. Suppose that the electric utility charged a customer \$200,000 tap fee to hook into its electric system. The actual cost of the hook-up to the customer was only \$80,000. How would the \$200,000 be reported by the utility fund?
8. Suppose that the electric utility owed \$50,000 to the internal service fund. How would this most likely be reported in the proprietary funds' statement of net assets? How would it be reported in the government-wide statement of net assets?
9. In which column on the government-wide statement of net assets—that for governmental or business-type activities—is it most likely that the assets and liabilities of the internal service funds would be included? Explain.

QUESTIONS FOR REVIEW AND DISCUSSION

1. You are the independent CPA for a medium-sized city. The city manager asks your guidance as to whether, according to generally accepted accounting principles, the municipal golf course should be accounted for in an enterprise fund. What would be your response?
2. How would you compare the accounting for enterprise funds with that of (a) businesses and (b) governmental funds? Summarize the reasons both for and against accounting for enterprise funds differently than governmental funds.
3. Business accounting is governed by the pronouncements of the Financial Accounting Standards Board. Enterprise funds are generally accounted for using the accounting principles applicable to businesses. Must, therefore, a government adhere to all pronouncements of the FASB in accounting for its enterprise funds? Explain.
4. Although proprietary fund accounting is similar to business accounting, there are considerable differences in standards pertaining to the statement of cash flows. What are the main differences?
5. A government accounts for a municipal landfill in an enterprise fund. How will it determine how much to charge as an expense (and add to a liability) each year that the landfill is in use? Suppose, instead, that it accounts for the landfill in a governmental fund. What will be the amount charged as an expenditure?
6. For what types of activities are internal service funds used to account? Provide several examples. Is a government *required* to account for the activities you cite in an internal service fund, or may it account for them instead in its general fund?
7. It is sometimes asserted that the absence of specific principles as to what constitutes "cost" detracts from the objectivity of the financial statements of not only internal service funds but also the general fund. In what sense might this be true?
8. "Self-insurance," it is often said, is an oxymoron. Why? If it is, what are the implications as to whether a government should be permitted to recognize self-insurance premiums as a general fund expenditure when paid to an internal service fund?
9. In what way must a government account for premium revenue differently if it accounts for self-insurance in an internal service fund rather than its general fund?
10. You have been given the responsibility of assigning a bond rating to a municipal parking garage. Indicate the type of information that you would consider essential to your assessment but that is unlikely to be reported on in the facility's financial statements.

City of Kingsland
Statement of Net Assets
Proprietary Funds
December 31, 2005

	Business-type Activities			Governmental Activities—
	Electric Utility	Golf Course	Totals	Internal Service Funds
Assets				
Current assets:				
Cash and cash equivalents	$ 13,466,645	$ 590,669	$ 14,057,314	$ 5,337,758
Investments				274,733
Accounts and notes receivable	5,703,338	5,656	5,708,994	218,133
Due from other governments	66,390		66,390	
Inventories	202,678		202,678	222,925
Total current assets	19,439,051	596,325	20,035,376	6,053,549
Noncurrent assets:				
Restricted cash and investments		2,389,315	2,389,315	
Capital assets:				
Land	1,301,621	28,846,666	30,148,286	
Buildings and equipment	233,023,758	4,834,619	237,858,378	23,554,858
Less accumulated Depreciation	(24,526,257)	(1,258,405)	(25,784,662)	(9,250,775)
Capital assets, net	209,799,122	32,422,880	242,222,002	14,304,083
Total assets	229,238,173	35,408,520	264,646,693	20,357,632
Liabilities				
Current liabilities:				
Accounts payable	715,883	486,405	1,202,288	1,248,912
Due to other funds	280,000		280,000	1,872,621
Compensated absences	180,560	14,123	194,683	380,304
Claims and judgments				2,700,760
Bonds, notes, and loans payable	6,311,374	576,000	6,887,374	398,889
Total current liabilities	7,487,817	1,076,528	8,564,345	6,601,486
Noncurrent liabilities:				
Compensated absences	722,238	56,490	778,728	
Claims and judgments				8,964,640
Bonds, notes, and loans payable	87,122,479	31,270,430	118,392,909	
Total noncurrent liabilities	87,844,717	31,326,920	119,171,637	8,964,640
Total liabilities	95,332,534	32,403,448	127,735,982	15,566,126
Net assets				
Invested in capital assets, net of related debt	116,365,269	576,450	116,941,719	13,905,194
Restricted		2,323,194	2,323,194	
Unrestricted	17,540,370	105,428	17,645,798	(9,113,688)
Total net assets	$133,905,639	$ 3,005,072	$136,910,711	$ 4,791,506

City of Kingsland
Statement of Revenues, Expenses, and Changes Net Assets Proprietary Funds
Year Ended December 31, 2005

	Business-type Activities			Governmental Activities—
	Electric Utility	Golf Course	Totals	Internal Service Funds
Operating revenues:				
Fees and charges	$ 18,127,813	$2,144,417	$ 20,272,230	$24,409,862
Miscellaneous		6,122	6,122	1,706,818
Total operating revenues	18,127,813	2,150,539	20,278,352	26,116,680
Operating expenses:				
Wages and salaries	5,440,894	1,219,757	6,660,651	6,651,450
Contractual services	551,075	153,651	704,726	935,034
Utilities	1,206,571	161,162	1,367,733	343,699
Repairs and maintenance	1,195,704	103,387	1,299,091	3,136,784
Supplies	797,141	27,390	824,531	375,112
Insurance claims and expenses				12,806,858
Depreciation	1,861,024	867,278	2,728,302	2,732,594
Total operating expenses	11,052,409	2,532,625	13,585,034	26,981,531
Operating income (loss)	7,075,404	(382,086)	6,693,318	(864,851)
Nonoperating revenues (expenses):				
Interest and dividends	727,668	234,490	962,158	215,573
Other revenues		167,880	167,880	33,368
Interest expense	(2,561,328)	(1,866,474)	(4,427,802)	(66,586)
Miscellaneous expense		(74,954)	(74,954)	(281,605)
Total nonoperating revenue (expenses)	(1,833,660)	(1,539,058)	(3,372,718)	(99,250)
Net Income (loss) before contributons and transfers	5,241,744	(1,921,144)	3,320,600	(964,101)
Capital contributions	2,633,470		2,633,470	30,061
Transfers-out	(464,000)	(338,254)	(802,254)	(280,053)
Change in net assets	7,411,214	(2,259,398)	5,151,816	(1,214,093)
Total net assets—beginning	126,494,425	5,264,470	131,758,895	6,005,599
Total net assets—ending	$133,905,639	$3,005,072	$136,910,711	$ 4,791,506

11. In government-wide statements enterprise funds are reported differently from internal service funds. Explain and justify.
12. Enterprise funds are also reported differently from internal service funds in the proprietary fund statements of net assets and of revenues, expenses, and changes in net assets. Explain.
13. The balance sheet of an enterprise fund reports an asset "restricted cash and investments" and shows a portion of "net assets" as restricted. Provide an example of the types of restrictions to which the assets of a proprietary fund might be subject. Why might the "restricted cash and investments" not be equal to the portion of "net assets" that is restricted?

EXERCISES

9-1

Select the *best* answer.

1. What basis of accounting do enterprise and internal service funds use?

	Enterprise	*Internal Service*
a.	Modified accrual	Modified accrual
b.	Modified accrual	Full accrual
c.	Full accrual	Modified accrual
d.	Full accrual	Full accrual

2. Which of the following is *not* a GASB-required statement for proprietary funds?
   a. Statement of net assets
   b. Statement of revenues, expenses, and changes in fund net assets
   c. Statement of cash flows
   d. Statement of changes in fund net assets
3. A government need not necessarily account for an activity in an enterprise fund even though it
   a. Charges fees for the activity and those fees are material in amount
   b. Finances the activity solely with revenue debt
   c. Is required by law or policy to recover the cost of the activity by fees
   d. Opts to establish pricing policies so as to recover its costs, including capital costs
4. Except for FASB pronouncements that have been overridden by specific GASB pronouncements, governments, in their enterprise funds, must
   a. Apply all FASB pronouncements, irrespective of when issued
   b. Apply all FASB pronouncements issued prior to November 30, 1989, and either all or none of the pronouncements issued after that date
   c. Apply all FASB pronouncements issued subsequent to November 30, 1989
   d. Apply all FASB pronouncements issued prior to November 30, 1989, and may apply pronouncements of their choosing issued after that date
5. Tap fees should be accounted for as
   a. Capital contributions
   b. Ordinary revenues
   c. A combination of capital contributions and ordinary revenues
   d. Extraordinary items
6. Landfill closure and postclosure costs should be recognized as expenses
   a. In the periods incurred
   b. In the period that the landfill is closed
   c. In the periods that the landfill is in operation
   d. In the period in which the landfill is opened
7. Which of the following would *not* be included in the computation of the amount to be recognized as a landfill closure expense?
   a. The total estimated closure costs
   b. The capacity of the landfill
   c. The proportion of capacity used in prior years
   d. An appropriate discount rate
8. A city maintains a staff of internal auditors. It may properly account for its internal audit costs in an internal service fund only if
   a. It is required to do so by state or city statutes or regulations
   b. The internal audit activity is carried out in a discrete organizational unit
   c. It charges a fee to the city departments for which it provides service
   d. A GASB pronouncement specifies that internal audit activity is eligible for internal service fund accounting
9. A government accounts for its self-insurance activities in an internal service fund. Per GASB guidelines, the premiums charged to other funds
   a. Must, in total and over time, cover the actual losses incurred by the fund
   b. Cannot include a provision for catastrophic losses
   c. Must be competitive with what an independent insurer would charge
   d. Must be at least as great as the losses incurred each year
10. If a government accounts for self-insurance activities in its general fund, then premiums charged in excess of actual claims should be accounted for as
   a. Ordinary revenues
   b. An offset against claims expenditures
   c. An increase in claims reserves
   d. A nonreciprocal transfer-in

9-2

Select the *best* answer.

1. A city's general fund has an outstanding payable to its electric utility, which is accounted for in an enterprise fund. The utility has a corresponding receivable from the general fund. In the city's government-wide statement of net assets, which would be correct?
   a. The payable and the corresponding receivable would be eliminated in the consolidation process and thus not reported.
   b. The payable may be aggregated with payables to an internal service fund and reported as "payables to proprietary funds."
   c. The payable should be reported in the governmental activities column and the receivable in the business-type activities column.
   d. The payable and the receivable would each be reported in the "totals" column, but would not be reported in either the governmental activities column or the business-type activities column.
2. A city's general fund has an outstanding payable to its vehicle repair internal service fund, which has a corresponding receivable from the general fund. In the city's government-wide statements, which would be correct?
   a. The payable and the corresponding receivable would be eliminated in the consolidation process and thus not reported.
   b. The payable may be aggregated with payables to an enterprise fund and reported as "payables to proprietary funds."
   c. The payable would be reported in the governmental activities column and the receivable in the business-type activities column.
   d. The payable and the receivable would each be reported in the "totals" column, but would not be

reported in either the governmental activities column or the business-type activities column.

3. Which of the following projects is a state university most likely to finance with revenue bonds rather than general obligation bonds?
   a. A football stadium
   b. An outdoor swimming pool
   c. An intramural field house
   d. A boathouse for its rowing team
4. In what way would the statement of cash flows of a government-owned electric utility differ from that of a privately owned counterpart?
   a. It would not include a category for operating activities.
   b. It would have separate categories for cash flows from noncapital financing activities and cash flows from capital and related financing activities.
   c. It would not include a category for cash flows from investing activities.
   d. It would include a category for cash flows from other nonoperating activities.
5. A government is considering whether to account for a vehicle repair service in an internal service fund or in its general fund. In a year in which the vehicle repair service did not acquire any capital assets, the amount charged as expenses or expenditures for vehicle repair-related costs would likely
   a. Be the same, irrespective of which fund is used
   b. Be greater if the general fund were used
   c. Be greater if an internal service fund were used
   d. Be the same, irrespective of which fund is used, as long as the internal service fund adopted all FASB pronouncements issued prior to November 30, 1989
6. A school district's internal service fund has cash on hand at year-end of $2 million. On its government-wide financial statements, this amount would be reported as an asset in the
   a. Governmental activities and total columns
   b. Business-type activities and total columns
   c. Total column only
   d. Business-type activities column only
7. In its first year of operations, a self-insurance internal service fund billed the general fund $500,000 for premiums. Of this amount, $75,000 was intended for catastrophes. During the year, the insurance fund paid out $380,000 in claims, none of which was for catastrophes. As a consequence of these transactions, the insurance fund would report on its statement of net assets
   a. Net assets of $120,000
   b. Net assets of $45,000
   c. Reserve for catastrophes of $75,000
   d. Claims reserves of $120,000
8. A city makes an interest payment of $6 million on its utility fund revenue bonds. In the utility fund statement of cash flows, the payment would be reflected as a cash flow from
   a. Operating activities
   b. Noncapital financing activities
   c. Capital and related financing activities
   d. Investing activities
9. A utility fund temporarily invests the proceeds from the issuance of revenue bonds in U.S. Treasury bills and receives interest of $300,000. In the utility fund statement of cash flows, the receipt would be reflected as a cash flow from
   a. Operating activities
   b. Noncapital financing activities
   c. Capital and related financing activities
   d. Investing activities
10. A city's transportation service, which is accounted for in an enterprise fund, has outstanding $10 million in revenue bonds. The bonds are also guaranteed by the city itself. These bonds should be reported as a liability in
    a. Both the governmental fund statements and the proprietary fund statements, as well as both the business-type activities column and the governmental activities column of the government-wide statements
    b. Only the proprietary fund statements and the business-type activities column of the government-wide statements
    c. Only the governmental fund statements and the governmental activities column of the government-wide statements
    d. Only the proprietary fund statements

9-3

Internal service funds are accounted for similarly to businesses.

William County opted to account for its duplication service center in an internal service fund. Previously the center had been accounted for in the county's general fund.

During the first month in which it was accounted for as an internal service fund the center engaged in the following transactions.

1. Five copiers were transferred to the internal service fund from the government's general capital assets. At the time of transfer they had a book value (net of accumulated depreciation) of $70,000.
2. The general fund made an initial cash contribution of $35,000 to the internal service fund.
3. The center borrowed $270,000 from a local bank to finance the purchase of additional equipment and renovation of its facilities. It issued a three-year note.
4. It purchased equipment for $160,000 and paid contractors $100,000 for improvements to its facilities.
5. It billed the county clerk's office $5,000 for printing services, of which the office remitted $2,500.
6. It incurred, and paid in cash, various operating expenses of $9,000.
7. The fund recognized depreciation of $1,500 on its equipment and $900 on the improvements to its facilities.
   a. Prepare journal entries in the internal service fund to record the transactions.

b. Comment on the main differences resulting from the shift from the general fund to an internal service fund in how the center's assets and liabilities would be accounted for and reported.

9-4

Enterprise funds face unique problems in accounting for restricted assets.

The Louisville City bus system engaged in the following transactions.

1. It issued $10,000,000 in 8 percent revenue bonds. It used the proceeds to acquire new buses. The bonds were issued at par.
2. Consistent with a bond covenant, the system set aside 1 percent of the bonds' gross proceeds for repair contingencies. Correspondingly, it designated an equal dollar amount of net assets as restricted to repairs.
3. The bus system accrued nine months' interest ($600,000) at year-end.
4. The bus system incurred $50,000 of repairs costs, paying for them with the cash set aside for repair contingencies.

a. Prepare appropriate journal entries.

b. Comment on how assets set aside for repairs, as required by bond covenants, would be accounted for if the bus system were reported in the government's general fund.

9-5

Internal service fund activities with governmental funds are reported differently than those with proprietary funds.

The following data relate to the City of Spicewood's data processing internal service fund:

Billings to police and fire departments	$800,000
Billings to water utility department	200,000
Year-end receivable from police and fire departments	80,000
Year-end receivable from water utility department	12,000
Net assets other than receivables from other departments	1,300,000

The police and fire departments are accounted for in the general fund. Their activities are classified as "public safety." The water utility department is accounted for in a proprietary fund. The internal service fund establishes billing rates at amounts reflective of the actual costs of providing its services.

Explain how each of the indicated amounts (and the related expenses and payables of the funds receiving the services provided by the data process department) would be reported in the city's government-wide statement of net assets and statement of activities. Be specific.

9-6

Cash flows of a government must be presented in four categories, rather than the three used by businesses.

The following list of cash flows was taken from the statement of cash flows of Grand Junction's internal service fund. All amounts are in thousands.

Cash on hand at beginning of year	$122
Interest from investments	45
Wages and salaries paid	(3,470)
Purchases of supplies	(1,650)
Collections (for services) from other funds	6,380
Interest on long-term debt	(150)
Repayment of loans to other funds	(880)
Purchase of capital assets	(900)
Proceeds of revenue bonds	800
Purchases of investments	(440)
Proceeds from sale of capital assets	23
Proceeds from sale of investments	33
Loans from other funds	600

Recast the list into a statement of cash flows, adding a line for cash on hand at the end of the year.

9-7

The insurance expense recognized by an enterprise fund depends on the type of carrier.

The water and waste-water utility (enterprise) funds of three cities each paid $1 million in casualty insurance premiums.

City A is insured by a small independent insurance company. City B is self-insured and accounts for its insurance activities in an internal service fund. City C is self-insured and accounts for its insurance activities in its general fund.

Each of the insurers collected a total of $10 million in premiums from all of the parties that it insures, including the city utility funds. Of this amount each paid out $8 million in actual claims. The balance was held in reserve for major catastrophes.

Prepare the journal entry that each of the three utility funds should make to record its insurance payment and expense for the year. Comment on any differences.

9-8

Landfill expenses depend on estimates that may change from year to year.

In 2004 Marquette County opened a landfill that was expected to accept waste for four years. The following table indicates estimates that county officials made at the end of each of the four years.

Year	*Total Capacity (millions of cubic feet)*	*Capacity Used This Year (millions of cubic feet)*	*Expected Closure Costs (millions of dollars)*
2004	10	4	$ 8
2005	10	2	9
2006	12	2	10
2007	12	4	10

Determine the total expected closure costs ($10 million) that should be assigned to each of the years that the landfill accepts waste.

PROBLEMS

Continuing Problem

Review the Comprehensive Annual Financial Report (CAFR) that you obtained.

1. Indicate the activities accounted for in both internal service funds and major enterprise funds. Comment on whether any of these activities could also have been accounted for in a general or other governmental fund.
2. How are the internal service fund activities reported in the government-wide statement of net assets? How are they reported in the proprietary funds statement of net assets?
3. Did any of the internal service funds report significant operating surpluses or deficits for the year? Have any accumulated significant net asset balances over the years that were not invested in capital assets?
4. Were any of the government's enterprise funds "profitable" during the year? If so, what has the government done with the "earnings"? Has it transferred them to the general fund?
5. Does the government have revenue bonds outstanding that are related to business-type activities? If so, for what activities?
6. Do the financial statements include a statement of cash flows for proprietary funds? In how many categories are the cash flows presented? Is the statement on a direct or an indirect basis?

9-1

Enterprise funds are accounted for like comparable businesses; nevertheless, they have their quirks.

The Green Hills Water District was established on January 1 to provide water service to a suburban development. It accounts for its operations in a single enterprise fund. During the year it engaged in the following transactions:

1. It issued $6,000,000 of revenue bonds.
2. It purchased, for $4,500,000, the plant and equipment of the private water company that previously served the area.
3. It incurred $500,000 in costs to improve and expand its plant and equipment.
4. It billed customers for $1.8 million, of which it collected $1.5 million.
5. It billed and collected $200,000 in tap connection fees from developers. The actual cost of the hook-ups (paid in cash) was $140,000.
6. It incurred the following operating costs (all paid in cash):
   a. Purchases of water, $850,000
   b. Labor and contract services, $320,000
   c. Interest, $80,000
   d. Supplies and miscellaneous, $60,000
7. It recognized depreciation of $350,000 on its capital assets.
   a. Prepare journal entries to record the transactions.
   b. Prepare a year-end statement of revenues, expenses, and changes in net assets.
   c. Prepare a year-end balance sheet.
   d. In some jurisdictions, water districts may account for their operations entirely in an enterprise fund or in several funds, as if they were full-service governments. If a water district chose the latter, then it would report all revenues and operating expenditures in its general fund and would maintain other funds as appropriate. Describe briefly how the financial statements of the Green Hills Water District would differ if it chose to prepare its financial statements as if it were a full service government. Be specific (note changes in capital assets, long-term debt, etc.).

9-2

The premiums charged by self-insurance funds depend on whether they are accounted for in internal service or governmental funds.

Believing that it is more economical to manage its risks internally, a county elects not to purchase commercial insurance. Instead, it sets aside resources for potential claims in an internal service "self-insurance" fund.

In a recent year, the fund recognized $1.5 million for claims filed during the year. Of these it paid $1.3 million.

Based on the calculations of an independent actuary, the insurance fund billed, and collected, $2.0 million in premiums from the other county departments insured by the fund. Of this amount $1.2 million was billed to departments accounted for in the general fund and $0.8 million to the county utility fund. The total charge for premiums was based on historical experience and included a reasonable provision for future catastrophe losses.

1. Prepare the journal entries in the internal service fund to record:
   a. The claims recognized and paid.
   b. The premiums billed and collected.
2. Suppose instead that the county accounted for self-insurance within its general fund. As in part (1), of the $2.0 million in premiums charged, $1.2 million were billed to the other departments accounted for in the general fund and $0.8 million to the utility department.
   a. Prepare the general fund journal entry to record the claims recognized and paid.

b. Prepare the general fund entry to record the premiums billed and collected from the *utility* fund. (Those billed and collected from the other general fund departments would "net out" against their premium expenditures for purposes of external reporting.)

3. What would be the net expenses (i.e., expenditures less premium revenues) reported by the general fund if the self-insurance were accounted for (1) in the internal service fund and (2) in the general fund? What would be the total expenses charged by the utility fund if the self-insurance were accounted for (1) in the internal service fund and (2) in the general fund? Comment on the rationale for standards that permit such differences.

9-3

The differences in accounting for an activity in an internal service fund rather than the general fund may be striking.

A school district establishes a vehicle-repair shop that provides service to other departments, all of which are accounted for in its general fund. During its first year of operations the shop engages in the following transactions:

- It purchases equipment at a cost of $24 million and issues long-term notes for the purchase price. The useful life of the equipment is eight years, with no residual value.
- It purchases supplies at a cost of $4 million. Of these it uses $3 million. In its *governmental* funds, the district accounts for supplies on a *purchases* basis.
- It incurs $13 million in other operating costs.
- It bills other departments for $19 million.

For purposes of *external* reporting, school district officials are considering two options:

- Account for the vehicle-repair shop in an internal service fund
- Account for the vehicle-repair shop in the general fund

1. For each of the following items indicate the amounts that would be reported in the year-end financial statements of (1) the internal service fund, assuming that the school district selected the first option and (2) the general fund, assuming that it selected the second option.
   a. Billings to other departments (revenues)
   b. Cost of supplies (expense or expenditure)
   c. Expenses or expenditures relating to acquisition or use of equipment
   d. Other operating costs
   e. Equipment (asset)
   f. Accumulated depreciation
   g. Inventory (asset)
   h. Notes payable
   i. Reserve for inventory
2. What would be the total expenses reported in the internal service fund, assuming that the school district selected the first option?
3. What would be the total amount of expenditures reported in the *general fund*, assuming that the school district: (1) selected the first option; (2) selected the second option?
4. What would be the reported revenue and expenses relating to the vehicle-repair shop in the district's government-wide statements? Would it matter whether the district accounted for the shop in an internal service fund or the general fund?

9-4

Internal service funds can be used to reduce general fund expenditures.

A city maintains an internal audit department and accounts for it in its general fund. In the coming year, the department will purchase $300,000 of computer and other office equipment, all of which will be paid for out of current resources (i.e., not with debt).

City officials have given top priority to reducing general fund expenditures. To that end, the city comptroller has proposed accounting for the internal audit department in an internal service fund rather than the general fund.

As envisioned by the comptroller, the audit department would bill each of the units (all of which are accounted for in the general fund) for each audit performed. Fees would be established so that they would cover all audit department costs. The fund would be established by a transfer of $300,000 from the general fund to cover the cost of the new equipment.

The city estimates that for the coming year the audit department's operating costs, excluding any costs relating to the new equipment, will be $1,600,000. The equipment is expected to have a useful life of five years.

1. Assume that the city accepts the comptroller's suggestion. Prepare journal entries in the internal service fund to record:
   a. The transfer-in of the $300,000.
   b. The acquisition of the equipment.
   c. The operating and other costs.
   d. The billings to, and collection of cash from, the general fund.
2. Prepare journal entries in the general fund to record:
   a. The transfer-out of the $300,000.
   b. The billings from, and payment of cash to, the internal service fund.
3. Would the establishment of the internal service fund result in a decrease in overall government costs (e.g., cash outflows)? Would it result in a reduction in reported general fund expenditures? Explain.
4. Suppose that in the following year, the city does not plan to acquire additional capital assets. Comment on whether reported general fund expenditures would be greater if the internal service fund were to be established than if it were not.

9-5

A city's financial statements and related disclosures as to one of its internal service funds raises intriguing questions.

The balance sheet and statement of revenues, expenses, and changes in fund net assets of a medium-sized city's "Support Services" internal service fund are as follows:

Support Services Fund
Balance Sheet

Assets	
Pooled investments and cash	$ 546,463
Prepaid expenses	239,582
Total current assets	786,045
Property plant and equipment	3,587,524
Less accumulated depreciation	(2,007,684)
Net property, plant, and equipment	1,579,840
Total assets	$2,365,885
Liabilities	
Accounts payable	$ 39,034
Accrued payroll	854,956
Accrued compensated absences	291,470
Due to other funds	89,876
Total current liabilities	1,275,336
Bonds payable	1,049,902
Total liabilities	$2,325,238
Net assets	
Invested in capital assets, net of related debt	529,938
Unrestricted	(489,291)
Total net assets	$ 40,647

Statement of Revenues, Expenses, and Changes in Fund Net Assets

Billings to other departments	$20,340,426
Operating expenses	
Operating expenses before depreciation	32,228,281
Depreciation	122,544
Total expenses	32,350,825
Operating income (loss) before transfers	(12,010,399)
Transfers-in	9,083,006
Increase (decrease) in net assets	(2,927,393)
Net assets, beginning of year	2,968,040
Net assets, end of year	$ 40,647

The financial statements provide a limited amount of additional information as to the Support Services Fund:

- The Support Services Fund "includes the activities of the various support service departments."
- The Support Services Fund provides services exclusively to departments accounted for in the general fund.
- The transfer-in was from the general fund.

The city's general fund reported the following (in millions):

Revenues	$196
Expenditures	227
Excess (deficiency) of revenues over expenditures	(31)
Transfer-in	43
Transfers-out	(9)
Net transfers-in	34
Net change in fund balance	3
Fund balance, beginning of year	25
Fund balance, end of year	$ 28

1. The financial statements do not provide additional information as to what constitutes "support services." What are some likely activities that "support services" could include?
2. What is the significance of the internal service fund's balance sheet deficit in "unrestricted net assets"? What concern might it raise as to the proper application of accounting principles?
3. What is the significance of the internal service fund's operating deficit as it relates to the general fund's excess of revenues over expenditures?
4. If you were the city's independent auditor, what changes in the billing practices of the internal service fund might you propose that the city consider?
5. In the city's government-wide statements, how would the revenues and expenses of the internal service fund be reported? Which of the revenues and expenses or expenditures of the internal service fund and the general fund would be eliminated?
6. Suppose that the city accounted for the support services in its general fund, instead of an internal service fund.
   a. Approximately how much more or less would the general fund's net change in fund balance have been?
   b. Which of the internal service fund's expenses would not be reported as general fund expenditures?
   c. Which of the internal service fund's assets and liabilities would not be reported as general fund assets or liabilities?

9-6

The rates to be charged by internal service funds may not be obvious—and can have a significant impact on who pays the costs of government.

A city maintains an internal service fund to account for a maintenance department. The department provides services to all city departments, which, with one exception, are accounted for in the city's general fund. That exception is the department responsible for the city's golf course. It is accounted for in an enterprise fund.

The maintenance department estimates that it provides approximately 20,000 hours of service per year. However, the volume is seasonal. During the "slack season"—four summer months—it provides approximately 1,400 hours of service per month; during the eight other months it provides approximately 1,800 hours of service per month.

The department has determined its fixed costs to be $33,333 per month ($400,000 per year) and its variable costs to be $10 per hour ($200,000 per year, if it provides 20,000 hours of service).

The departments accounted for in the general fund request 17,600 hours of service per year. The department in charge of the golf course requests the remaining 2,400 hours of service per year. However, all of its service is requested during the summer months—600 hours per month. Were it not for the demands of the golf course department, the maintenance unit would otherwise have substantial excess capacity during the slack months, as no other department would require those 600 hours of service per month.

1. Suppose that the maintenance department determines its billing rates on an annual basis, based on total estimated costs for the year.
   a. What would be the cost per hour of service?
   b. How much of the total costs for the year would be billed to the golf course enterprise fund? How much would be billed to the general fund?
2. Suppose, instead, that the maintenance department determines its billing rates on a monthly basis, based on total costs for each month.
   a. What would be the cost per hour of service in the busy months (when it provides 1,800 hours of service)?
   b. What would be the cost per hour of service in the slack months (when it provides only 1,400 hours of service)?
   c. How much of the total annual costs would be billed to the golf course enterprise fund? How much of the total annual costs would be billed to the general fund?
3. If you were in charge of the golf course, why would you argue that both billing policies are unfair?
4. What difference might the choice of policies have on the distribution of costs among the city's tax and fee payers?

9-7

Internal service fund revenues and expenses have to be eliminated in the government-wide statements to avoid "doubling up."

The data in the table below were extracted from a city's fund statements (in millions).

1. Prepare in summary form a government-wide statement of revenues and expenses and a statement of net assets. Although you need not prepare the statement in the format prescribed by the GASB, be sure to have separate columns for governmental and business-type activities and for "totals."
2. GASB Statement No. 34 states that "the effect of interfund services provided and used between functions—for example, the sale of water or electricity from a utility to the general government—should not be eliminated in the statement of activities." What would be the rationale for such a position?

9-8

Financial statements must be adjusted to ensure proper accounting of internal service fund activities.

	General Fund	Utility Fund	Internal Service Fund
Revenues (from outside sources)	$240	$ 64	
Revenues (from other funds)			$16
Total revenues	240	64	16
Expenses/Expenditures (to outsiders)	220	56	16
Expenses/Expenditures (to internal service fund)	12	4	
Total expenses/expenditures	232	60	16
Excess of revenues over expenses/expenditures	$ 8	$ 4	$ 0
Assets (excluding interfund receivables)	$340	$220	$9
Receivables (from other funds)			5
Total assets	340	220	14
Liabilities (to outsiders)	178	180	6
Payables (to internal service fund)	4	1	
Total liabilities	182	181	6
Net assets	$158	$ 39	$ 8

Sun City accounts for its telecommunication services in an internal service fund. In a recent year its records indicated the following:

Billings to units accounted for in governmental funds	$400,000
Billings to units accounted for in proprietary funds	100,000
Year-end accounts receivable from units accounted for in governmental funds	25,000
Year-end accounts receivable from units accounted for in proprietary funds	10,000

Per city policy, the telecommunications department bills other departments for the actual cost of providing its services.

1. Explain how each of the following would be reported in the city's government-wide statement of net assets and statement of activities:
   a. The billings of the internal service fund (and offsetting purchases of services by other funds)
   b. The year-end accounts receivable and payable
2. Explain how each of the following would be reported in the balance sheets and statements of revenues and expenses/expenditures of the individual governmental and proprietary funds to which the internal service fund provided services and of the internal service fund itself.
   a. The billings from the internal service fund
   b. The year-end accounts payable and receivable
3. Internal service funds are classified as proprietary funds. Yet in the government-wide statements their assets and liabilities that have not been eliminated in the consolidation process are reported in the governmental activities column. How can you justify this apparent inconsistency?

9-9

A government's reported landfill closing expense may exceed its required cash payments.

A municipality expects to use a landfill evenly throughout the twenty-five years from January 1, 2004, to December 31, 2028. Upon closing the landfill it estimates that it will incur closing costs of $300,000. Thereafter, it anticipates it will have to monitor the site yearly for the following thirty years at an annual cost of $10,000.

The government intends to pay for the closure and monitoring costs evenly over the twenty-five years that the landfill is in use (2004 through 2028) by making annual cash contributions to a trust fund. The resources of the trust fund will be invested in government securities that can be expected to earn interest at a rate of 5 percent.

1. How much would the municipality need in the trust fund as of December 31, 2028, to satisfy its monitoring obligations for the next thirty years? [*Hint:* What is the present value of an annuity of $10,000 for thirty years?] How much would it need in the fund to pay the closing costs?
2. How much would it have to contribute to the fund during each of the twenty-five years that it adds to the landfill to have a sufficient amount in the fund at the end of 2028 to satisfy its obligations for *both* the closure and the monitoring costs? [*Hint:* The required sum, based on the calculations in part (1), is the equivalent of the future value of a twenty-five-year annuity of unknown amount (x) compounded at a rate of 5 percent.]
3. Per the GASB reporting standards, what amount would the government have to report as its landfill closure and monitoring expenses during each of the twenty-five years (2004 through 2028) irrespective of how much it actually contributes to the trust fund? Assume that the costs were as estimated.
4. If the government were to make the contributions as you calculated in part (2), but charged the expenses that you calculated in part (3), would it be overstating its closure and monitoring expenses? Explain. What might be a factor that mitigates the overstatement of the expenses?

9-10

Landfill costs must be reported as expenses during the periods of use—but only in enterprise funds.

In 2005, a city opens a municipal landfill, which it will account for in an enterprise fund. It estimates capacity to be 6 million cubic feet and usable life to be twenty years. To close the landfill, the municipality expects to incur labor, material, and equipment costs of $3 million. Thereafter, it expects to incur an additional $7 million of costs to monitor and maintain the site.

1. In 2005, the city uses 300,000 feet of the landfill. Prepare the journal entry to record the expense for closure and postclosure costs.
2. In 2006, it again uses 300,000 feet of the landfill. It revises its estimate of available volume to 5.8 million cubic feet and closure and postclosure costs to $10.2 million. Prepare the journal entry to record the expense for closure and postclosure costs.
3. In 2024, the final year of operation, it uses 350,000 feet of the landfill. The actual capacity has proven to be only 5 million cubic feet and closing costs are now estimated to be $15 million. Through the year 2023, the municipality had used 4,650,000 cubic feet and had recorded $14.2 million in closure and postclosure costs. In 2024, it actually incurs $5 million in closure costs, the entire amount of which is paid in cash.
   a. Prepare the journal entry to record the expense for closure and postclosure cost.
   b. Prepare the journal entry to record the actual closure costs paid.

4. Suppose, instead, that the landfill was accounted for in the government's general fund. Indicate how the entries would differ from those in the enterprise fund.

9-11

The operating cash flows of internal service funds can be reconciled with operating income

What follows are the Statement of Revenues, Expenses, and Changes in Unreserved Fund Balance and the Statement of Cash Flows for Tucson, Arizona's fleet services internal service fund.

1. How do you account for the difference between net operating income of $105 and cash from operating activities of $10,789? Prepare a reconciling schedule in which you account for the difference.
2. How would the revenues and expenses of the fund be reported on the city's government-wide statement of activity?
3. How would the revenues and expenses of the fund be reported on the city's statement of revenues, expenses and changes in fund net assets?
4. How would the difference between charges for services and cash received from customers be reflected on the city's government statement of net assets?
5. How would the charges for services most likely be reflected on the city's general fund statement of revenues and expenditures and changes in fund balance?

Fleet Services Fund
Statement of Revenues, Expenses, and Changes in Unreserved Fund Balance (in thousands)

Charges for services	$24,019
Operating expenses	
Wages and salaries	$ 4,609
Contractual services	1,765
Supplies	8,826
Depreciation	8,714
Total operating expenses	23,914
Net operating income	$ 105
Nonoperating revenues (expenses)	
Investment income	$ 498
Interest expense	(182)
Gain from sale of property	751
Capital grants	215
Total nonoperating revenues	$ 1,282
Net income	$ 1,387
Unreserved fund balance—Beginning of year	3,880
Unreserved fund balance—End of year	$ 5,267

Fleet Services Fund
Statement of Cash Flows (in thousands)

Cash flows for operating activities	
Cash received from customers	$24,530
Cash payments to suppliers for goods and services	(9,023)
Cash payments to employees	(4,718)
Net cash provided by operating activities	$10,789
Cash flows from noncapital financing activities	0
Cash flows from capital and related financing activities	
Acquisition or construction of capital assets	$(9,219)
Proceeds from sale of property and equipment	1,914
Principal paid on capital debt	(1,168)
Interest paid on capital debt	(182)
Net cash flows from capital and related financing activities	$(8,655)
Cash flow from investing activities	
Investment income	$467
Net cash flows from investing activities	$467
Net increase in cash and cash equivalents	$2,601
Cash and cash equivalents, beginning of year	5,253
Cash and cash equivalents, end of year	$7,854

9-12

Based on actual circumstances, this minicase illustrates an issue faced by government-operated utilities (one that has not been addressed by standard setters and is not discussed in the text).

The City Electric Utility (CEU), which a city accounts for in its enterprise fund, provides cash rebates to customers who install insulation, storm windows, or energy-saving appliances. The payments are intended to reduce the demand for electricity and thereby enable the CEU to avoid having to add generating capacity.

Like many government-operated utilities, the CEU establishes rates based on a number of factors, of which cost is only one. It is the policy of the city, for example, to make substantial transfers each year from the CEU to its general fund. Utility fees are thereby a form of taxation, and the revenue requirements of the general fund are taken into account in setting the rates.

The CEU controller has raised the question of whether the rebates should be charged as an expense as paid or should be capitalized and charged as an expense over time (i.e., amortized). Moreover, he asks, if the costs should be capitalized and charged as an expense over time, then what should be the basis for determining the length of the amortization period?

Required: Write a brief memo in which you recommend to the controller how the rebates should be accounted for. Be sure to support your position.

SOLUTION TO EXERCISE FOR REVIEW AND SELF-STUDY

1. Capital assets (property, plant, and equipment, with accumulated depreciation) and long-term liabilities appear on the statement of net assets; depreciation expense is shown on the statement of revenues, expenses, and changes in net assets. Thus the statements are based on the full accrual basis of accounting.
2. Both the revenues and the expenses of the enterprise funds are determined by outside demand for the funds' goods and services. Therefore, it is not possible for the city to budget its revenues and expenses as if they could be determined by legislative fiat. Moreover, the revenues of the internal service funds (and hence the level of services to be provided by these funds) are already controlled through the budgets of the departments to which they provide services. For purposes of planning, the city should, of course, prepare budgets for its proprietary funds—just as any private business would. But in the absence of unusual circumstances, the city does not need to incorporate them into its accounting system.
3. Yes. The $116.4 million that is invested in capital assets, net of related debt, is equal to the capital assets, net ($209.8 million) less the bonds, notes, and loans payable (current of $6.3 million and noncurrent of $87.1 million).
4. The difference between reported restricted assets and reported restricted *net* assets would arise if the restricted cash and investments included unspent proceeds of long-term debt. These restricted assets would be offset by bonds payable, rather than by a restriction of net assets.
5. In the fund statements the billings of the internal service fund to the golf course would be reported as a revenue of the internal service funds and as an expense of the golf course. The related costs of providing the service would be reported as an expense of the internal service fund. In the government-wide statements the billings would be reported only as an expense of the golf course. The revenues and expenses of the internal service fund would be eliminated in the consolidation process.
6. The depreciation charges are incorporated into the amounts billed to the funds to which the internal service funds provide services. Therefore, in the government-wide statements they would be incorporated into the expenses of the functions accounted for in those funds.
7. The fees paid by the customers are, in part, a capital contribution to the utility fund. Nevertheless, the GASB directs, in Statement No. 33 pertaining to revenue recognition, that these types of charges should be accounted for as if they were "pure" exchange transactions—hence as ordinary revenues.
8. In the funds statement of net assets, the electric utility would report a payable; the internal service fund a receivable. In the government-wide statement of net assets, the business-type activities would report a payable; the governmental activities would report a receivable.
9. Unless the internal service funds provide services mainly to units accounted for in proprietary funds, their assets and liabilities would be reported in the column for governmental-type activities.

CHAPTER 10

Fiduciary Funds and Permanent Funds

LEARNING OBJECTIVES

After studying this chapter you should understand:

- What an endowment is
- The distinction between permanent funds and fiduciary funds
- How investment gains and losses should be accounted for
- Why all nonexpendable funds should be accounted for on a full accrual basis, and why they are not
- Whether investment gains should be added to principal or expendable income
- How institutions can protect against inflation yet reap the benefits of current income
- How the main types of transactions are accounted for in fiduciary funds
- Why pensions are important
- The distinctions between defined contribution and defined benefit pension plans
- The relationships between an employer and its pension trust fund
- The main issues faced by government employers in accounting for pension plans and how the GASB has resolved them
- How pensions plans are accounted for
- How postemployment health care benefits are accounted for
- The accounting issues presented by agency funds
- The accounting issues presented by investment trust funds

When one thinks of the assets of either governments or not-for-profits, it is natural to conjure up images of highways, buildings, police cars, research laboratories, and so on. In fact, however, governments and not-for-profits represent some of the nation's largest holders of stocks, bonds, and similar securities. Indeed, government pension funds, university endowment funds, and private charitable foundations are among the most powerful and influential of corporate investors.

This chapter is directed to both **fiduciary funds** and **permanent funds.** Fiduciary funds are maintained to account for assets that governments and not-for-profits hold as trustees or agents for individuals, private organizations, or other governmental units. In a general sense the term embraces trust funds, pension funds, and agency funds. "Trust fund" is a generic term for any fund in which one party (a trustee) holds resources for the benefit of another, usually under the terms of a formal agreement.

In Statement No. 34, which established the new reporting model, the Governmental Accounting Standards Board (GASB) distinguished between fiduciary funds and a new type of fund, permanent funds. As is elaborated upon in a subsequent section, permanent funds are to be used to account for *nonexpendable* resources that benefit activities of the government itself (i.e., are held for "public purposes"), rather than outside parties. Fiduciary funds, by contrast, are to be used to account for resources that benefit outside parties, irrespective of whether they are expendable or nonexpendable.

Fiduciary and permanent funds are of critical concern to both statement preparers and statement users not only because they may contain vast amounts of resources, but also because their assets are typically liquid and therefore subject to risk of loss both through fraud and reduction in value. Moreover, the resources may be relied upon by the organizations themselves as well as their employees and other constituents as a main source of income for both the present and the future.

The issues pertaining to fiduciary funds (as broadly defined) are common to not-for-profits as well as governments. Therefore, to avoid duplication in the forthcoming chapter pertaining to not-for-profits, this chapter points out both the similarities and differences in how both types of entities account for them.

WHAT IS AN ENDOWMENT?

The typical *nonexpendable* fiduciary (or trust) fund is used to account for an endowment and is referred to as an endowment fund. An **endowment** is a contribution for which the donor requires that the principal be invested and remain intact; only the income from the investment may be expended. Most endowments stipulate that the principal be preserved in perpetuity. Some, however, referred to as term endowments, permit the principal to be expended after a specified number of years. Depending on the wishes of the donor, the income from an endowment may be either restricted to a specific purpose or unrestricted.

The following are but a few examples of endowments that are maintained by governments and not-for-profits:

- University endowments may take the form of "chairs" or "professorships." Assigned to specific faculty members, they provide salary supplements and support teaching and research. Other type of endowments help to finance scholarships, teaching awards, research, or general operations.
- Private foundations such as the Ford and Carnegie Foundations are, in essence, endowment funds. With billions of dollars in assets, they promote a wide array of educational, social welfare, and scientific activities.

- Public schools sometimes maintain endowments, albeit generally small, to provide ongoing support for specific activities, such as band or science enrichment programs.
- Municipalities establish endowments to account for gifts in support of nature centers, performing arts centers, and parks.
- Churches and synagogues maintain endowments to sponsor lectures, music programs, or youth activities.

Governments and not-for-profits sometimes permit earnings from nonexpendable endowments to accumulate in these funds until they are to be used for their intended purposes. However, it is preferable that these earnings, if they are legally expendable, be transferred to, and accounted for, in an expendable fund, such as a special revenue fund, rather than the unexpendable endowment fund. When organizations report them in the same fund as unexpendable resources they leave the impression that they are unavailable for expenditure, when in fact they are available.

WHAT ARE PERMANENT FUNDS AND HOW ARE THEY DISTINGUISHED FROM FIDUCIARY FUNDS?

PERMANENT FUNDS

Permanent funds are used to account for nonexpendable resources that must be used in support of the reporting government's own programs—those that benefit either the government itself or its citizenry in general. As with other nonexpendable funds, only the income, not the principal, may be spent. The principal must be preserved either in perpetuity or for a specified term. Permanent funds:

- Support government-owned museums, nature centers, or zoos
- Provide for perpetual care of public cemeteries
- Supplement the compensation of public university faculty
- Provide student financial aid
- Fund research at government-owned hospitals

Permanent funds are unique to governments. The Financial Accounting Standards Board (FASB) draws no distinction between endowment resources held for the benefit of an organization's own activities and those held for the benefit of outsiders.

Permanent funds are classified as *governmental* funds, and accordingly the measurement focus is on current financial resources. They are accounted for on a modified accrual basis. Governments report their permanent funds as they do other governmental funds. In government-wide statements they are combined with other governmental funds. In fund statements that combine the various governmental funds, they are shown in a separate column only if they are considered "major" funds. Otherwise they are aggregated with other nonmajor funds. In fund statements that show all governmental funds (i.e., combining statements, which per GASB Statement No. 34 are optional), each permanent fund is displayed in a separate column under the general heading "permanent funds."

FIDUCIARY FUNDS

Fiduciary funds, by contrast, can be either expendable or nonexpendable. They are used to account for resources held in a trustee capacity, for parties other than the government itself. These "outside" parties include employees and their survivors, other governments, and individual citizens and corporations. There are four major types of fiduciary funds:

1. ***Pension (and other employee benefit) trust funds.*** These include both defined benefit and defined contribution plans (discussed later in this chapter).
2. ***Investment trust funds.*** These are used to account for "investment pools"—mutual fund–type arrangements in which a sponsoring government (such as a state or county) holds and invests the cash of other governments (such as the cities and towns within its jurisdiction).
3. ***Private purpose trust funds.*** These are trust funds other than investment pools and pensions in which the resources are held for the benefit of outsiders. Examples include:
   a. Funds used to account for **escheat property**—inactive bank accounts and property of deceased persons that are temporarily held by the state until they are either claimed or revert to the state
   b. Scholarships to benefit a specific narrowly defined class of students (e.g., those with a specified family name)
   c. Endowments held to benefit needy employees or their families (e.g., a fund for children of slain police officers)
4. ***Agency funds.*** These are funds used to account for resources held by an organization in a purely custodial capacity (such as when one government collects taxes on behalf of another).

Fiduciary funds focus on all economic resources and are prepared on a full accrual basis of accounting. Inasmuch as their resources are not assets of the government itself but are held for the benefit of outside parties rather than the government itself, they are excluded from the government-wide statements. However, separate fiduciary fund statements should be reported as part of the fund financial statements, following those of the governmental and proprietary funds.

SHOULD INVESTMENT INCOME BE REPORTED IN AN EXPENDABLE OR A NONEXPENDABLE FUND?

The income from a government's permanent (nonexpendable trust) funds is intended to benefit other funds and must eventually be transferred to them. At issue, however, is whether investment earnings should first be recognized as revenue within the permanent funds and then transferred to the beneficiary funds or whether they should be recorded directly in the beneficiary funds.

The significance of the issue is mainly in whether the income should be reported in the recipient governmental fund as revenue or as a nonreciprocal transfer. If reported as revenue, then it would be incorporated into "excess of revenues over expenditures." If reported as a transfer, however, it would be shown "below the line" and included among "other financing sources." The impact on fund balance is the same; the difference is one of statement-user perception. When investment income is reported as revenue, an organization's ongoing operations may appear to be generating a larger surplus (or incurring a smaller deficit) than if shown as a transfer-in.

GASB Standards

In governments, although the issue is not explicitly addressed in the GASB Codification, it has been common practice to account for all nonexpendable endowment fund income within the nonexpendable fund itself. Periodically (either at the discretion of government officials or as required by law, contract, or donor stipulation) the income (net of investment expenses, if applicable) is transferred to the beneficiary funds. As a consequence, neither all the resources nor the net assets of the nonexpendable fund may in fact be permanently restricted. Some may be available for immediate transfer to another fund.

GASB Statement No. 34, however, directs that in their government-wide statements, governments should report permanent fund investment earnings as specific program revenues if they are restricted to a specific program. If not restricted to a specific program, they should be shown as "investment earnings" within the category of "general revenues" (those that are reported in the lower portion of the statement of activities).

EXAMPLE *Expendable Investment Income*

A city receives a gift of $1 million in securities, the income from which is restricted to the support of its botanical gardens. During its first year the endowment earns $60,000, of which the city transfers $40,000 to a governmental fund restricted to supporting the gardens.

On its year-end permanent fund statement of revenues, expenditures, and changes in fund balances, the city would report investment revenues of $60,000 and transfers-out of $40,000. On its balance sheet it would report a fund balance of $1,020,000.

On its government-wide statement of activities the city would report the entire $60,000 as revenues of the program "Parks and Recreation." On its statement of net assets, in the column for governmental activities, it would categorize the entire $1,060,000 as "restricted net assets."

FASB Standards

Not-for-profit organizations categorize their nonexpendable endowments as "permanently restricted" regardless of whether the resources are held for the benefit of the organization itself or outside parties. Per FASB Statement No. 117, *Financial Statements of Not-for-Profit Organizations*, income from endowment investments should generally be reported directly as revenue that is unrestricted or, if subject to time or purpose restrictions, as temporarily restricted. Income from endowment investments should be reported as revenues that is permanently restricted—and thus in the endowment fund itself—only if, in fact, it is unavailable for expenditure. This would be the case if a donor were to specify that all income for a stated period of time must be added to, and permanently retained in, the endowment principal. Of course, for purposes of internal reporting, an institution may report the endowment income initially in the endowment fund and then transfer it to the beneficiary fund.[1]

WHY SHOULD ALL NONEXPENDABLE FUNDS BE ACCOUNTED FOR ON A FULL ACCRUAL BASIS—AND WHY AREN'T THEY?

Prior to the issuance of GASB Statement No. 34, governments traditionally accounted for all endowments in fiduciary funds whether they were intended to support

[1] FASB Statement No. 117, *Financial Statements of Not-for-Profit Organizations* (June 1993), para. 20.

the activities of the government itself or those of outside parties. The endowments were accounted for on a full accrual basis—and for valid reasons. The full accrual basis helps to assure that the governments do not dissipate their assets by inappropriately basing their distributions on cash flows rather than economic earnings. For governments this means that they apply the same principles as they do in their proprietary funds. Most of the transactions in endowment funds involve investments in stocks, bonds, and similar types of securities. Consistent with the accrual basis of accounting, interest and dividends are recognized as earned, not necessarily when cash is received.

Governments may also invest their resources in nonliquid assets, such as commercial real estate or equity securities of nonpublic corporations. The rationale for using the full accrual basis of accounting can best be demonstrated with an illustration that focuses upon a depreciable asset.

EXAMPLE *Charging Depreciation*

An endowment receives a contribution of a commercial office building having a fair market value of $20 million. The donor stipulates that only the income, not the principal, may be used to carry out the purposes of the gift. The estimated useful life of the building is twenty years (with no residual value). The endowment expects to earn $1 million per year in rent revenue, net of cash operating expenses. Consistent with the wishes of the donor, the endowment will each year distribute all of its reported income, but none of its principal.

If the endowment were not to charge depreciation, then its reported earnings would be $1 million per year—the rent revenue net of cash operating expenses. It would therefore distribute $1 million per year. By contrast, if it were to charge depreciation its reported earnings would be zero per year—net rent revenue of $1 million less depreciation of $1 million ($20 million divided by 20 years).

Irrespective of whether or not the endowment charges depreciation, the economic value of the building at the end of its twenty-year life can be expected to be zero, (i.e., it would generate no additional cash receipts) assuming that the initial estimate of useful life were correct.

The following table compares the consequences of charging, and not charging, depreciation over the period of twenty years (in millions):

	Do Not Depreciate	**Depreciate**
Total assets (building), beginning of period 1	$20	$20
Net cash receipts ($1 million per year)	20	20
Depreciation expense ($1 million per year)	0	20
Net income and hence total cash distributions	20	0
Cash balance, end of period 20	0	20
Market value of building, end of period 20	0	0
Total assets (cash and building), end of period 20	0	20

By charging depreciation, the endowment reduces its reported income—and thus its cash distributions—to reflect the ongoing decline in the value of the building. It thereby preserves the principal at $20 million, consistent with the expectations of the donor. At the end of the twenty-year period, it no longer has a building of value, but has $20 million in other assets; in this example, cash.

By not charging depreciation, the endowment is, in effect, distributing not only its cash earnings, but also a portion of the building. At the end of the twenty-year economic life of the building, it is left with neither a building nor any compensating assets.

Donors may explicitly stipulate that depreciation need not be charged against revenues in determining expendable income. Moreover, in some jurisdictions, in the absence of donor stipulations, the endowment is not required to charge depreciation. Even so, inasmuch as the capital asset is losing economic value over time, sound accounting would dictate that depreciation be charged and that any distributions in excess of net income (after depreciation) be explicitly reported as distributions of principal.

GASB Standards

Consistent with both tradition and the rationale implied by the depreciation example, GASB requires that governments account for their fiduciary funds on a full accrual basis. At the same time, however, it directs that they account for their permanent funds on a modified accrual basis.

Why the discrepancy? The resources held in permanent funds generally benefit governmental activities, such as cemeteries, libraries, museums, parks, and scholarships. For that reason it makes sense to account for them in governmental rather than proprietary funds. If they are to be classified as governmental funds, then, like all other governmental funds, they must be accounted for on a modified, rather than full, accrual basis.

Moreover, the assets accounted for in permanent funds are typically financial assets, mainly marketable securities. Relatively few permanent funds hold depreciable assets. Financial assets are accounted for identically under both the full and modified accrual bases. Interest and dividends are recognized as revenue when they are earned; changes in market values are recognized as they take place. Therefore, in practice, as long as the amount of depreciable assets is not material, the measurement of earnings remains the same whether the funds are accounted for under the full or modified accrual basis of accounting.

SHOULD INVESTMENT GAINS BE CONSIDERED NET ADDITIONS TO PRINCIPAL OR EXPENDABLE INCOME?

The primary accounting issue pertaining to endowments in both governments and not-for-profits relates to whether, in the absence of specific donor or legal stipulations, investment gains and losses, including unrealized appreciation, should be recognized as a component of expendable income or nonexpendable principal. The issue has economic consequences that reach far beyond the content of financial reports; it affects the amount of resources available for operations and is likely to influence the organization's investment policies.

DIFFERING POLICIES OF GOVERNMENTS AND NOT-FOR-PROFITS REGARDING INVESTMENT GAINS

Whether gains on the sale of investments (capital gains) or gains from appreciation should be accounted for as income or as an adjustment to principal is undoubtedly one of the most provocative questions related to permanent and fiduciary funds. But it is as much a legal as an accounting question. If a particular policy is required either by donor stipulation or law, then that policy will dictate accounting practice.

Parties establishing endowments often stipulate that gains from the sale of investments be added to the principal (the "corpus") of the endowment and not incorporated into income. Thus, the gains will not be expendable; they will be available only for reinvestment. However, in the absence of donor stipulations or other applicable legal provisions, the governing board of the recipient institution is generally free to appropriate investment gains for current use.

The widespread practice of accounting for gains as adjustments to endowment principal rather than to income is grounded in the need to protect endowment principal from inflation. In the long term, owing to inflation, the market value of a corporation's common stock can be expected to increase, even in the absence of substantive changes in supply and demand relationships. Thus, when an endowment sells that stock, the gain may represent nothing more than a decrease in the purchasing power of a dollar.

Although it may protect an endowment from inflation, a policy of automatically assigning investment gains to principal rather than income may have the perverse consequence of encouraging institutions to adopt less than optimum investment strategies.

EXAMPLE *Investment Gains*

A university's policies require that all investment gains, both realized and unrealized, be added to endowment principal. The university has to choose between one of two stock portfolios as an investment for a $1 million endowment. The first portfolio contains the common stock of "high-tech" companies that pay either no, or very small, dividends. The returns will be almost entirely from appreciation. The second contains an extremely conservative mix of bonds, preferred stocks, and the common stocks of well-established industrial firms, all of which pay high dividends or interest. The endowment fund managers estimate that the first portfolio will provide a total return of 14 percent per year (almost all appreciation); the second only 6 percent per year (almost all interest and dividends).

Assuming that the university needs the income to be generated by the endowment, it has little choice but to select the second portfolio; the first provides no accessible resources. Yet the first provides the greater returns and—were the university to periodically liquidate a portion of the portfolio—the greater cash flows.

GASB Standards

Current GASB pronouncements do not explicitly address the issue of whether investment gains should be added to endowment principal or should be made available for expenditure. Therefore, in the absence of specific donor or legal stipulations, the gains should be reported as unrestricted net assets, and hence considered expendable.

As discussed in Chapter 4, investments must now be "marked to market" and no distinction is made between realized and unrealized gains and losses. Therefore, unrealized gains, like realized gains, are also unrestricted, and hence expendable, absent donor or legal restrictions.

FASB Standards

The FASB is more precise in permitting entities to expend investment gains, but the resultant practices are the same as those of governments. Statement No. 117, *Financial Statements of Not-for-Profit Organizations*, says: "A statement of activities shall report gains and losses recognized on investments and other assets (or liabilities) as increases or decreases in *unrestricted* net assets unless their use is temporarily or permanently restricted by explicit donor stipulations or by law."

If by donor stipulation or law investment gains were permanently restricted (i.e., not expendable), then they would be reported as additions to *permanently restricted* net assets. If they were expendable, but had to be used for a specific purpose, then they would be reported as additions to *temporarily restricted* net assets.

Not-for-profits, like governments, must state their investments at market. Hence gains from appreciation include those that are unrealized as well as those that are realized.

DIFFERING POLICIES OF GOVERNMENTS AND NOT-FOR-PROFITS AS TO INVESTMENT LOSSES

The issue of accounting for net investment losses—those that reduce the value of an endowment below the amount contributed to it—is especially intriguing, because investment losses are not the mirror image of investment gains. Whereas investment gains can be distributed to other funds, investment losses cannot always be recovered from them.

EXAMPLE *Investment Losses*

At the start of a year, an organization has an endowment fund to which donors had contributed $1 million in securities. In addition, as a result of previous investment gains, it has $10,000 of securities that are restricted to programs specified by the endowment donor. These are reported in a special revenue fund. Thus, the total value of its investment portfolio, all of which is restricted, is $1,010,000. During the year, owing to losses on the sale of securities, the value of the portfolio declines by $25,000 to $985,000.

The key question is whether, in the absence of specific legal requirements or donor stipulations, the organization should reduce the stated value of the principal of its endowment fund to an amount below the $1 million original contribution or whether it should compensate for the loss from other sources, such as restricted or unrestricted net assets.

GASB Standards

Neither the GASB nor its predecessor organizations has yet addressed explicitly the issue of investment losses. However, as noted previously, in the absence of specific provisions to the contrary, most governments report all types of investment income initially in a nonexpendable fund. If they are permitted to appropriate the gains for expenditure, they then transfer resources to an appropriate recipient fund or to outside beneficiaries. Therefore, if all of the losses were applicable to securities held in the nonexpendable fund, they would reduce the fund by the amount of the losses. If some of the losses were applicable to securities held in a restricted fund, then they would reduce the balance in that fund. Thus, in the event of losses, the balance in a nonexpendable fund could be reduced below the amount contributed by the donors and which they expected to be preserved in perpetuity.

In the example, if the $25,000 in losses were uniform across the portfolio then $24,752 [$25,000 × ($1,000,000/$1,010,000)] would be assigned to the nonexpendable fund and $248 [$25,000 × ($10,000/$1,010,000)] to the expendable special revenue fund.

FASB Standards

Per FASB Statement No. 124, *Accounting for Certain Investments Held by Not-for-Profit Organizations*, unless a not-for-profit is required by donor or legal stipulation to do otherwise, it should first charge investment losses (both realized and unrealized) to **temporarily restricted net assets** to the extent that donor-imposed restrictions on previously recognized net appreciation have not yet been met. "Temporarily restricted net assets" is the not-for-profit equivalent of a special revenue fund, the assets of which must be used for a specific purpose.

It should charge any remaining losses to unrestricted net assets, the not-for-profit equivalent of the general fund. If, in a subsequent year, investment gains restore the value of the investments to their original value, then organizations should credit them first to unrestricted net assets (to the extent previously deducted) and then to temporarily restricted net assets.

In the example, therefore, the organization should continue to report the endowment principal at $1 million. It should charge the first $10,000 of the $25,000 loss to temporarily restricted net assets (thereby reducing the balance of those net assets to zero) and the remaining $15,000 to unrestricted net assets. Thus (assuming a beginning-of-year balance in unrestricted assets of zero):

	Unrestricted	Temporarily Restricted	Permanently Restricted	Total
Beginning of year	$ 0	$10,000	$1,000,000	$1,010,000
Investment losses	(15,000)	(10,000)	0	(25,000)
End of year	$15,000	$ 0	$1,000,000	$ 985,000

Suppose, in the example, that in the following year, the organization realizes $27,000 in investment gains, thereby increasing the total value of the portfolio from $985,000 to $1,012,000. The organization would credit to unrestricted net assets the first $15,000—the amount previously deducted from unrestricted assets. It would credit the $12,000 balance to temporarily restricted net assets. Thus:

	Unrestricted	Temporarily Restricted	Permanently Restricted	Total
Beginning of Year	$(15,000)	$ 0	$1,000,000	$ 985,000
Investment Gains	15,000	12,000	0	27,000
End of Year	$ 0	$12,000	$1,000,000	$1,012,000

The end result is intuitively appealing. Since receiving its initial donation of $1 million the organization experienced net investment gains of $12,000 ($10,000–$25,000+$27,000). The entire amount of the net gain is available for expenditure for the donor-specified programs and is thereby classified as temporarily restricted—just as if there had been only a total gain of $12,000 without any losses and subsequent recoveries of the losses.

The FASB guidelines for reporting gains and losses, it must be emphasized, do not necessarily lead to financial statements that are indicative of amounts that are legally available for distribution to endowment beneficiaries or to other funds. This conflict between accounting and legal provisions is addressed in the accompanying "In Practice."

IN PRACTICE

DISCONNECT BETWEEN FASB AND LEGAL PROVISIONS

The FASB requirement that not-for-profit organizations charge realized and unrealized losses first to temporarily restricted net assets and then to unrestricted net assets rather than to permanently restricted assets went relatively unnoticed in the 1990s when the stock market was booming. But it caused considerable consternation among not-for-profit executives and trustees in the early 2000s as the stock market headed downward. Since the market value of many of their permanently restricted endowment funds had declined well below the amounts contributed by donors, not-for-profits were forced to recognize losses in both temporarily and unrestricted funds.

Consider the case of one church-related foundation that maintains numerous endowment funds, the income from which is intended to be distributed to various individual churches and charitable agencies. As the result of unrealized investment losses, it was forced first to write off the net assets of several of its temporarily restricted funds to zero and then to absorb additional losses in its unrestricted fund.

Nevertheless, the foundation's attorneys advised that despite the FASB rules, the foundation could, for legal purposes, charge the investment losses to its permanent funds rather than to the temporarily restricted or unrestricted funds. Hence, it could continue to make distributions from these funds even if, in their financial statements, they had to report zero resources available for distribution. In other words, there was now a significant disconnect between the reported net assets as reported under FASB standards and those that were legally available for distribution.

The foundations executives were concerned that seemingly weak balance sheets prepared in accordance with GAAP would deter creditors from making further loans and deter donors from making further contributions. Much as they protested to their independent auditors, the auditors warned that they could not issue an unqualified opinion on their financial statements unless they abided by the FASB standards.

AGREEMENT ON HOW TO ACCOUNT FOR GAINS OR LOSSES ON EXPENDABLE RESOURCES

Expendable income from an endowment fund that is not immediately needed may be invested temporarily in revenue-producing securities, such as equity or debt securities. Therefore, an organization may reap gains or incur losses on its expendable endowment resources just as it does on its nonexpendable resources.

A question is sometimes raised, therefore, of whether gains or losses on securities purchased with expendable resources are expendable or nonexpendable. This issue, however, can be resolved without debate. Although there may be confusion on the point by accounting students, there are no substantive legal or accounting issues. Expendable resources, whether held in an expendable fund or in an endowment fund awaiting transfer to an expendable fund, are, by definition, expendable. Therefore, the gains on expendable resources are also expendable.

HOW CAN INSTITUTIONS PROTECT AGAINST INFLATION, YET REAP THE BENEFITS OF CURRENT INCOME?

Institutions can readily protect against inflation, yet simultaneously reap the benefits of current income, by taking a *fixed rate of return* (often referred to as a *total return*) approach to the distribution of income. The fixed rate of return approach requires the institution to make available for current expenditure a fixed percentage of its endowment portfolio, irrespective of actual interest and dividends. The fixed (or "spending") rate would be based on long-term estimates of anticipated appreciation, inflation, dividends, and interest.

EXAMPLE *Fixed Rate of Return Approach*

A university expects to earn an annual return of 10 percent on its $1 million portfolio, divided as follows:

Interest and dividends	$ 40,000
Appreciation	60,000
Total return	$100,000

It anticipates an annual inflation rate of 3 percent per year. Thus, it expects its real (inflation-adjusted) return to be only 7 percent (10 percent less 3 percent).

Consistent with the fixed rate of return concept, the university permits annual spending of only 7 percent of its endowment principal—$70,000 the first year. The first-year excess of $30,000 is to be added to the principal and reinvested.

The apparent—and one-time controversial—accounting issue faced by organizations that take a total return approach is whether the fund in which the endowment *income* is reported should recognize as investment revenue the amount *transferred to* it or the amount *actually earned by* the endowment fund. However, under current practice for governments and Statement No. 117 for not-for-profits, the answer is now clear.

A fixed rate of return approach has no special accounting standing. Both governments and not-for-profits should account for investment income, including appreciation, as described in the previous sections.

In the example, therefore, if endowment income does not legally have to be added to principal, then, irrespective of whether the university were public or private, the entire $100,000 should be accounted for as ordinary investment revenue. The university could authorize the expenditure of only $70,000, opting to retain $30,000 as if it were permanently restricted. If it were to do so, however, then it should report the $30,000 in the same fund as other investment earnings. It could "designate" a portion of fund balance as an nonexpendable endowment, but it should make clear that the resources are, in fact, legally expendable.

HOW ARE THE MAIN TYPES OF TRANSACTIONS RECORDED IN NONEXPENDABLE TRUST FUNDS?

Governments account for their permanent funds on a modified accrual basis, whereas they account for other fiduciary funds on a full accrual basis. Not-for-profits, on the other hand, account for all their activities on a full accrual basis. This example presents the main types of transactions affecting a government's permanent fund. However, in the absence of depreciable assets, the accounting would be similar in both a government's private purpose fiduciary funds and a not-for-profit's endowment funds.

EXAMPLE *Recording Transactions in a Permanent Fund*

Establishing the Endowment Fund

A town receives a bequest of $12 million in cash to support its zoo. The donor stipulates that only the income may be expended to support the activities of the zoo. However, any investment gains beyond an amount required to protect the endowment from declines in the value of the dollar may be appropriated for zoo use as if they were ordinary income. The bequest is to be accounted for in a nonexpendable trust fund.

Cash	$12,000,000	
Endowment contributions		$12,000,000
To record the bequest of cash		

Recording the Budget

The town estimates its first year income and prepares a budget.

Budgets are almost never recorded in nonexpendable endowment funds. The distribution of the income to expendable funds is generally governed by donor or legal stipulation, and the actual appropriation of the income for substantive purposes can be more directly and effectively controlled by the budget of the expendable fund to which the income is distributed. Hence, no journal entries are required.

Purchases of Securities

The town purchases common stock for $2 million and bonds having a face value of $10 million. The bonds are twenty-year 9 percent bonds that yield 10 percent and pay interest annually. They are acquired for $9,149,000. Both securities are recorded at cost.

Common stock	$2,000,000	
Bonds	9,149,000	
Cash		$11,149,000
To record the purchase of stocks and bonds		

Interest Revenue

The town collects its first payment of bond interest, $900,000.

Cash	$900,000	
Interest revenue		$900,000
To record collection of the first payment of interest		

The interest to be recognized as revenue is based on the cash received. Inasmuch as the bonds will be stated at fair value, the amortization of the bond discount will be incorporated implicitly into the revenue from appreciation.

Unrealized Appreciation

Owing mainly to decreases in prevailing interest rates, the market value of the bonds increases by $751,000 to $9.9 million. The market value of the stock increases by $200,000 to $2.2 million. The town recognizes the changes in value.

Bonds	$751,000	
Stocks	200,000	
Investment income—appreciation		$951,000
To record appreciation in the value of the securities		

The town sells the bonds for $9.9 million, the amount to which the carrying value of the bonds had been adjusted immediately prior to sale.

Cash	$9,900,000	
Bonds (face value)		$9,900,000
To record the sale of bonds		

Administrative Costs

The town incurs $20,000 of costs in administering the investments.

Administrative expenditures	$20,000	
Cash		$20,000
To record administrative costs		

Closing Revenue and Expenditure Accounts

The town closed its revenue and expenditure accounts, other than investment income—appreciation.

Interest revenue	$900,000	
Administrative expenditures		$ 20,000
Income available for transfer to a special revenue fund		880,000
To close revenue and expenditure accounts		

"Income available for transfer to a special revenue fund" is a temporary account, similar to "income summary" in a business. It is established mainly to show the distributable income in a single account.

Distribution of Investment Gains between Principal and Income

The town determines that the prevailing inflation rate is 4 percent. Per the donor's stipulations, any annual investment gains greater than the inflation rate are expendable. Thus:

Investment income—appreciation (per unrealized appreciation entry)		$951,000
Beginning of year balance in the endowment fund	$12,000,000	
Inflation rate	× 0.04	
Amount to be retained in a nonexpendable fund		(480,000)
Amount of investment income—appreciation available for distribution to an expendable fund		$471,000

The following entry would affect the distribution of the investment gains between principal and income:

Investment income—appreciation	$951,000	
Fund balance		$480,000
Income available for transfer to a special revenue fund		471,000
To close the investment income—appreciation account and distribute the balance between fund balance and income available for transfer		

Transfer to Special Revenu e Fund

The town transfers the distributable income ($880,000 + $471,000) to a special revenue fund (an expendable fund restricted to zoo operations).

Nonreciprocal transfer to zoo operations special revenue fund	$1,351,000	
Cash		$1,351,000
To transfer available income to a special revenue zoo operations fund		

Correspondingly, of course, the expendable zoo fund records a transfer-in of the same amount.

Closing Remaining Accounts

To complete the bookkeeping process, the government closes both the operating transfer and the income available for transfer accounts:

Income available for transfer to a special revenue fund	$1,351,000	
Fund balance		$1,351,000
To close the income available for transfer account		
Fund balance	$1,351,000	
Nonreciprocal transfer to zoo operations special revenue fund		$1,351,000
To close the transfer account		

Table 10-1 presents a summary statement of revenues, expenditures and changes in fund balance and a balance sheet.

TABLE 10-1
Governmental Zoo Funds
Statements of Revenues, Expenditures and Changes in Fund Balances

	Expendable Zoo Fund (Special Revenue)	Nonexpendable Zoo Fund (Permanent)
Revenues		
Contributions		$12,000,000
Interest		900,000
Investment income—appreciation		951,000
Total revenues		13,851,000
Expenditures		
Administrative expenditures		20,000
Excess of revenues over expenditures		13,831,000
Other financing sources (uses)		
Transfer to expendable fund	$1,351,000	(1,351,000)
Net change in fund balances	1,351,000	12,480,000
Beginning fund balance	0	0
Ending fund balance	$1,351,000	$12,480,000

Governmental Zoo Funds
Balance Sheets

	Expendable Zoo Fund (Special Revenue)	Nonexpendable Zoo Fund (Permanent)
Assets		
Cash	$1,351,000	$10,280,000
Common stock		2,200,000
Total assets	$1,351,000	12,480,000
Fund balance	$1,351,000	$12,480,000

In the town's government-wide statements, the expendable income would be shown as program revenue in the same function (e.g., parks and recreation) as that in which the zoo's operating expenditures and any other of its revenues are reported.

Differences If the Endowment Were Maintained as a Private Purpose Trust (Fiduciary) Fund

Suppose instead that the zoo was operated by an independent not-for-profit organization but that the town was nevertheless responsible for administering the zoo endowment fund. In that case the town would account for the endowment as a private purpose fiduciary fund. Inasmuch as the endowment held no long-term depreciable assets, the journal entries would basically be the same.

However, the distributable income of $1,351,000 would be paid to the independent not-for-profit organization rather than being transferred to a special revenue fund of the town. Therefore, the private purpose trust fund would record a *deduction from net assets* ("Benefits") rather than a nonreciprocal transfer-out to another fund of the same government.

Fiduciary funds are one of the three major categories of fund types (along with governmental and proprietary funds). The fund statements of fiduciary funds should be presented in a separate section of the financial statements, immediately following those of proprietary funds. Only two statements need be prepared: a statement of fiduciary net assets and a statement of changes in fiduciary net assets. As their titles imply, these statements focus on net assets and hence their format differs somewhat from that of governmental funds. Table 10-2 shows how the statements of the zoo fund would appear if it were a private purpose trust fund.

As previously emphasized, fiduciary funds benefit outside parties rather than the government itself. Therefore, they are not included in the government's government-wide statements.

Differences If the Endowment Were Maintained by a Not-For-Profit Organization

Were the endowment established for a not-for-profit organization rather than a government, the accounting and reporting would differ in the following respects:

- For purposes of external reporting, the interest income and the appropriate share of the investment gains would be reported in the statement of activities directly as increases in temporarily restricted resources (the equivalent of the government's special revenue fund). The interest income and the investment gains are expendable. Therefore, in contrast to how they would be reported by a government, they would not be reported initially in a permanently restricted (i.e., endowment) fund and then transferred to a nonexpendable fund.
- The investment income would most probably be aggregated and reported on a single line. However, an organization is free to present the details within the statement itself or in a separate schedule.

Table 10-3 illustrates how a not-for-profit organization would likely report on the zoo expendable and nonexpendable funds.

WHY ARE PENSIONS SO IMPORTANT?

A pension is a sum of money paid to retired or disabled employees owing to their years of employment. Although employees earn their pensions—and the employer

TABLE 10-2
Zoo Endowment Fund (Private Purpose Trust)
Statement of Changes in Fiduciary Net Assets

Additions	
Contributions of donor	$12,000,000
Investment earnings:	
Interest	900,000
Investment income—appreciation	951,000
Total investment earnings	1,851,000
Less: administrative expenses	(20,000)
Net investment earnings	1,831,000
Total additions	13,831,000
Deductions	
Benefits	1,351,000
Change in net assets	12,480,000
Net assets—beginning of year	0
Net assets—end of year	$12,480,000

Zoo Endowment Fund (Private Purpose Trust)
Statement of Fiduciary Net Assets

Assets	
Cash	$10,280,000
Common stock	2,200,000
Total assets	12,480,000
Liabilities	0
Net assets	
Held in trust for benefit of zoo	$12,480,000

TABLE 10-3
Not-For-Profit Zoo Funds
Statement of Activities

	Temporarily Restricted	Permanently Restricted
Income from investments including both realized and unrealized gains	$1,351,000	$ 480,000
Contributions to establish nonexpendable fund		12,000,000
Net assets (end of year)	$1,351,000	$12,480,000

Not-For-Profit Zoo Funds
Statement of Financial Position

Assets	
Cash	$11,631,000
Common stock	2,200,000
Total assets	$13,831,000
Net assets	
Temporarily restricted	$1,351,000
Permanently restricted	12,480,000
Total net assets	$13,831,000

benefits from their services—during their years of employment, the actual cash payments do not have to be made to the employees until their years of retirement. Thus, the benefits received and the cash payments may be mismatched by many years.

Both employer obligations for unpaid pensions and the resources set aside for eventual payment can be gargantuan. The assets of CalPERS, the California Public Employees Retirement System, total more than $132 billion; those of the New York State Teachers Retirement System are more than $77 billion. These funds face pressures similar to large mutual funds to maximize earnings while protecting against investment losses.

The road to governmental fiscal failure is paved with inadequately funded pensions. In the years following World War II, New York City substantially expanded its work force. In exchange for smaller increases in direct wages and salaries, the city offered some groups of employees exceedingly generous retirement benefits. In the subsequent years the city failed to contribute adequately to its pension funds, sometimes basing its contributions on outmoded actuarial tables. By the mid-1970s, when many of the employees hired after the war reached retirement age, the required pension outlays consumed so large a portion of the city's current budget that they were a major cause of its fiscal crisis and its resultant forced reorganization. As noted in the accompanying "In Practice," in the early 2000s, owing to the stock market decline, the pension funds of many state and local governments were severely underfunded. The need to make up for the losses thereby added to their fiscal pressures, which had been brought about by a nationwide economic downturn.

IN PRACTICE

BETWEEN A BEAR STOCK MARKET AND THEIR OWN BLUNDERS, PENSION FUNDS ARE HURTING

Whereas in the 1990s state and local governments were reducing their contributions to what were then overfunded pension plans, in the 2000s, officials of many of the same plans were worrying about whether and how they would be able to make the payments to which future retirees were entitled. The cause of both the euphoria of the 1990s and the despair of the 2000s was mainly the same—the vagaries of the stock market.

According to the *Wall Street Journal* (August 16, 2002), by mid 2002 more than half of all public pension funds were underfunded—and some were in dire straits. West Virginia's Teacher Retirement Plan, for example, had assets that were only 21 percent of actuarial liabilities.

Some governments, however, have themselves, in addition to the stock market, to blame for their woes. New Jersey, for example, failed for many years to make its actuarially required contributions to its employee pension fund. In 1997, to eliminate the resultant unfunded obligation, the state issued $2.75 billion in bonds. State officials believed that getting rid of the unfunded obligation in this way was advantageous because the interest rate on the bonds was 7.68 percent and pension investments could potentially yield substantially more. The state could then pocket the difference.

The plan worked just fine while the stock market was booming. Indeed for the first two years the pension fund was generating returns of over 19 percent. But then the market headed southward. Whereas the returns on the pension investments turned negative, the interest rates on the bonds remained fixed. Thus, the state not only had to continue paying the interest on the bonds, but it now had to cover the new unfunded obligation caused by decline in the value of its pension assets.

HOW DOES A DEFINED CONTRIBUTION PLAN DIFFER FROM A DEFINED BENEFIT PLAN?

Employers maintain two types of pension plans. The first, and by far the simpler to account for, is a **defined contribution plan.** Under a defined contribution plan, an employer agrees to make a series of **pension contributions.** Typically, the amount is expressed as a percentage of each employee's salary, and very often the pension fund is totally independent of the employer. For example, a college may contribute eight percent of a faculty member's salary to TIAA-CREF (Teachers Insurance and Annuity Association–College Retirement Equities Fund, an independent not-for-profit retirement plan), provided that the faculty member also contributes a corresponding percentage. TIAA-CREF invests the contributions, and upon retirement the employee can begin to withdraw the funds, plus accumulated earnings. The actual benefits to be received by the employee depend on the fund's investment performance. As implied by the plan's name, the employer defines (specifies) the inputs, its contributions; it makes no guarantees as to the outputs, the payments to be made to its employees when they retire.

Defined contribution plans present few financial or accounting complexities. The employer reports an annual expense for the amount that it is obligated to contribute to the pension fund. Hence, this chapter is concerned mainly with the second type of plan, the **defined benefit pension plan.**

Under a defined benefit plan, the employer specifies the benefits—the actual pension payments—that the employee will receive. Usually the benefits will vary according to length of service and salary. For example, a college might promise to pay faculty members 2.5 percent of their average annual salaries during their last three years of service for each year of employment. Faculty members with thirty years of service who earned an average of $100,000 during the three years prior to retirement would be guaranteed an annual pension of $75,000 (2.5 percent × 30 years × $100,000). In contrast to the defined contribution plan, the employer guarantees the outputs (payments to the retirees), not the inputs (contributions to the pension fund). It is therefore up to the employer to assure that it sets aside sufficient resources each year to make the required payments.

Both funding and accounting decisions relating to defined benefit plans are complex, mainly because of the uncertainties as to the amounts that will have to be paid to the retirees and that will be earned on fund investments. Sound financial policy and the need to report on interperiod equity dictate that the costs of pensions be allocated to the periods in which employees perform their services and earn their pension benefits—not those in which they receive the cash benefits. However, the actual cost cannot be known for certain until the employees receive all the benefits that they have been promised. These will not be known until the employees (and sometimes their spouses if they are also entitled to benefits) have died. The key uncertainties affecting the actual cost of a defined benefit pension plan include:

- Employee life expectancy
- Employee turnover rates (employees usually must accumulate a specified number of work years before qualifying for even minimum benefits and must satisfy other conditions relating to length of employment and age to qualify for full benefits)
- Future wage and salary rates
- The investment returns on pension fund assets

The amount that an employer must provide each year to meet its future **pension obligations** can be calculated actuarially. Actuaries are statisticians who compute insurance risks and premiums.

An **actuarial cost method** is the means of allocating the total cost of expected benefits over the total years of employee service. Actuarial cost methods have much in common with depreciation methods. Whereas a depreciation method allocates the cost of long-lived assets over the periods in which the assets provide service, an actuarial method allocates pension costs over the periods in which employees provide service. Just as depreciation can be allocated in many different patterns (e.g., straight-line or double declining), so too, can pension costs.

WHAT IS THE RELATIONSHIP BETWEEN AN EMPLOYER AND ITS PENSION TRUST FUND?

Assets that have been set aside for pensions are generally legally restricted and are held for the benefit of employees. Therefore, they are accounted for in a trust (fiduciary) fund. Government pension trusts that are organizationally separate from their sponsoring governments are often referred to as **Public Employee Retirement Systems (PERS).**

Some pension plans are established by a single employer and cover only the employer's own employees. Others are established by a sponsoring organization, such as a state or a county for employees of governments within its jurisdiction. Under one type of multiple employer plan (an *agent* multiple employer plan), separate accounts are maintained and actuarial computations are made for each employer. In substance, therefore, each employer has its own plan; the sponsoring agent merely provides administrative and investment services. Under another type of multiple employer plan (a *cost-sharing* multiple employer plan), all employees are placed in a common pool. Their employers share all risks and costs and make contributions at the same rate.

A pension trust fund, whether maintained by the employer itself or an outside party, is an independent legal, financial, and accounting entity. If maintained by the employer, then the employer must include the fund in its financial statements just as it does its other fiduciary funds. If maintained by an outside party, then the employer must disclose information as to its financial condition in notes to its financial statements.

The assets of a pension trust fund consist mainly of cash, securities, and other income-producing assets. Its economic obligations (irrespective of whether and when they are given accounting recognition) are the pension benefits that have been earned by its plan members—both employees already retired and those currently in the work force.

Even if pension trust funds are independent fiscal and accounting entities, they are inexorably linked to their sponsoring employers and the individual funds from which the pension contributions will be received. Under a defined benefit plan, an employer is ultimately liable for the benefits to be paid to retirees. Therefore, the liabilities of the pension trust fund are, in economic substance, those of the employer. Similarly, if the trust fund assets increase or decrease in value, the ultimate benefits or costs revert to the employer in that its future contributions can be greater or less.

In this chapter, we first discuss how employers should account for and report pension costs, obligations, and assets. Our attention is on the funds used to account for the pension contributions, not the pension trust fund. We then turn to issues relating to the pension trust funds.

Our focus in the chapter will be mainly on governments, and more specifically on GASB Statements No. 25, *Financial Reporting for Defined Benefit Pension Plans and Note Disclosures for Defined Contribution Plans,* and No. 27, *Accounting for Pensions by State and*

Local Governmental Employers (both issued in November 1994). We emphasize governments rather than other not-for-profits in this text primarily because pensions tend to be of greater significance to governments than to not-for-profits. Not-for-profits often participate in defined contribution rather than defined benefit plans, and the plans are usually maintained by independent financial institutions. The accounting for pensions of not-for-profits that do maintain defined benefit plans is governed by FASB Statements No. 35, *Accounting and Reporting by Defined Benefit Pension Plans* (March 1980), and No. 87, *Employers' Accounting for Pensions* (December 1985).

WHAT ISSUES DOES A GOVERNMENT EMPLOYER FACE IN ACCOUNTING FOR ITS PENSIONS?

DIFFERENCES FROM PRIVATE-SECTOR STANDARDS

As the GASB carried out its project on pension accounting and reporting, it faced a fundamental question. In light of the similarity between pensions in the private and public sectors, should the GASB simply adopt the FASB's pension pronouncements and apply them to governments? In other words, is there an economic rationale for different principles and practices?

In the view of the GASB, pensions of governments are sufficiently different from those of businesses to justify their own set of accounting standards. Relevant distinctions between businesses and governments include the following:

- In governments, short-term measures of financial condition are less important than in businesses. Businesses, unlike governments, can be bought and sold. In some circumstances the pension plans of businesses can be liquidated, and any excess of plan assets over obligations to current employees and retirees can either be used for other corporate purposes or be distributed to stockholders. Thus, point-in-time values of plan assets and obligations are of critical concern to current and potential investors. Governments, by contrast, can be assumed to have a "perpetual" existence, and it is unlikely that their pension plans will be dissolved.
- In governments, a primary objective of financial accounting is reporting on budgetary compliance. Therefore (as emphasized throughout this text), the need for measures that capture the full economic cost of services must be tempered with the need for those based on the budget.
- Many federal statutes that influenced the development of pension standards for businesses are inapplicable to governments.

THE BASIS FOR DETERMINING THE ANNUAL PENSION COST

In considering possible bases for determining a government's annual pension cost, one must be careful to distinguish between pension *cost* and pension *expenditure*. In governmental funds, an expenditure represents a decrease in net current financial resources. Costs that result in liabilities that will not be liquidated with expendable available financial resources are not recognized as expenditures. Hence, whereas *expenditure* refers to the amount that will be liquidated with financial resources, *cost* measures the full value of economic resources to be sacrificed. As shall be evident later in this chapter, governments are required to disclose their full pension costs, even if they do not recognize the costs as expenditures.

Governments have a choice among several widely accepted actuarial methods to determine the amount that they should contribute to their pension plans each year. The method that they choose, as well as what they actually contribute, are beyond the purview of the GASB. The GASB is empowered only to establish accounting and reporting standards. It has no authority to mandate the funding (contribution) practices of individual governments.

In developing standards on pension cost, the GASB had to choose between two competing approaches. The first dictates that *for purposes of external reporting*, all governments determine their pension costs according to a specified actuarial method and other assumptions. They would have to use these methods and assumptions for reporting purposes even if they use others to establish their actual funding schedule. This approach would permit the GASB to develop principles that capture the full economic costs of pensions and assure that those costs are allocated among periods in what the board considers the most appropriate pattern. Equally important, it would assure that reported pension costs among all governments are comparable.

The second approach allows each government to use the same actuarial methods and assumptions to determine its reported pension cost as it does its actual funding schedule. This approach would assure that a government's budgeted and reported expenditures are comparable to its required contribution per its own actuarial procedures. Moreover, it would reduce the complexity of financial statements, as it would eliminate the need to explain and reconcile differences between what should have been contributed per the government's own actuarial procedures and what should have been contributed per a GASB-specified formula.

The GASB adopted the second approach, but with constraints. It said that a government's *annual pension cost* should be based mainly on its *annual required contribution* (as determined by its own actuaries) as long as the annual required contribution satisfies specified guidelines. The guidelines are intended to give governments reasonable flexibility in their choice of actuarial methods and assumptions but at the same time prohibit those methods and assumptions that are clearly unacceptable (such as the pay-as-you-go method, whereby expenditures are recognized only as payments are made to retirees). The *annual pension cost* is the government's *annual required contribution* subject to certain technical adjustments. These adjustments are required when, in prior years, the government did not contribute the cumulative annual required contributions to the pension plan and thus has a pension obligation. They take into account interest on, and amortization of, the past deficiencies.

Minimum Criteria for Acceptable Annual Required Contribution

The criteria that an employer's *annual required contribution* must satisfy to be considered acceptable include the following:

- The contribution must consist of the employer's *normal cost* plus a provision for amortizing the plan's unfunded actuarial accrued liability. This requirement is discussed in more detail in the section that follows.
- Actuarial assumptions, including those pertaining to mortality, changes in compensation rates, and investment earnings, must be in accordance with standards of the Actuarial Standards Board, the actuarial equivalent of the FASB and the GASB.
- The actuarial value of pension plan assets must be market related. That is, in calculating the employer's annual required contribution, the actuary does not necessarily have to value plan assets at their market price as of a specific date, but rather can look to average values over a period of three to five years. The advantage of using an extended period rather than a point in time is that changes in value can be recognized over several years rather than a single year, thereby dampening year-to-year swings in the annual required contribution.
- Assumptions as to investment earnings rates and future inflation should be based on long-term projections, rather than on those for a single year.

Determination of Normal Cost

The employer's normal cost is the portion of the present value of pension plan benefits that is allocated to a particular year by an actuarial cost method. The GASB requires that normal cost be based on one of six specified actuarial cost methods. These bear such esoteric names as "projected unit credit," "entry age normal," and "frozen entry age normal." The normal cost is computed by actuaries, and the specifics of the various methods are beyond the scope of this text.

Unfunded Actuarial Accrued Liability and Amortization

The plan's unfunded actuarial accrued liability is the excess of the actuarially computed pension liability over the pension plan's assets. For example, if an actuary has determined that a government's current employees and retirees have earned a total of $50 million of pension benefits (computed in accordance with an appropriate actuarial method) and the value of the plan's investments totals $45 million, then the unfunded actuarial accrued liability would be $5 million.

Even if a government has consistently contributed to its pension fund the amounts that were actuarially required, it may still face an unfunded actuarial accrued liability. An unfunded actuarial accrued liability can result from several circumstances. These include:

- ***Transition losses.*** When an employer applies GASB Statement No. 27 for the first time, it may have to recognize a pension liability that previously it did not. This would be the case, for example, if it previously accounted for its plan on a pay-as-you-go basis or on some similar basis that did not meet minimum GASB criteria.
- ***Actuarial losses.*** As a result of changes in actuarial methods or actuarial assumptions, the unfunded pension liability may increase.
- ***Improvements in pension benefits.*** If an employer increases pension benefits, then the plan may have a significant increase in its unfunded actuarial accrued liability. For example, if an employer increases pension benefits from 60 to 65 percent of a final year's salary (and the change is applicable to all employees, including those who are about to retire), then the unfunded actuarial liability would increase.
- ***Special termination benefits.*** By sweetening pension benefits as an incentive for employees to retire early, employers will increase their pension obligations. For example, to trim its work force without having to discharge employees, an employer may reduce the number of years of service employees must accumulate before they can retire with full pension benefits.

While we have set forth the circumstances in terms of increases to the unfunded pension liability, decreases are accounted for in a similar fashion. For example, a change in actuarial methods could result in a gain rather than a loss. If a plan is overfunded, the unfunded liability is negative.

To mitigate possible spikes in pension expenditures, the GASB allows an employer to amortize these components of its unfunded actuarial accrued liability, rather than recognize them in a single period. Each circumstance that contributes to the unfunded liability causes increases in the employer's pension costs. Were the employer required either to fund the increased costs entirely in the year of the change or to report an expenditure equal to the full amount of the additional costs, then its pension contribution or expenditure for that year would be unduly large.

GASB permits employers to amortize the unfunded liability over up to thirty years.

EXAMPLE *Unfunded Actuarial Accrued Liability*

An employer's normal annual pension cost is $40 million. Owing to an improvement in pension benefits, its actuarial pension obligation increases by $15 million. If the employer elects to amortize the additional cost over the maximum of thirty years, then the employer would add $0.5 million to its normal costs each year. Its total annual required contribution would therefore be $40.5 million—the normal cost plus the amortization of the unfunded liability.

The GASB permits such a long amortization period in order to minimize the volatility of employer pension costs. However, critics of the statement, including one member of the GASB who dissented to its issuance, have charged that this range is far too broad and the maximum number of years is too great. The maximum period, they note, is far longer than the remaining working lives of most employees.

REPORTING PENSION COSTS

An employer would generally report its pension costs in the same fund as it charges the related wages and salaries. Owing to a different basis of accounting, the amount of pension expense or expenditure recognized would be determined differently in proprietary as opposed to governmental funds. The pension expense for employees of a utility fund would be accounted for in a proprietary fund, while the pension expenditure for police officers would be accounted for in the general (a governmental) fund.

EXAMPLE *Reporting Pension Costs*

A city maintains a defined benefit plan for its employees. During the year the city contributed $25 million to its pension fund, even though its actuary calculated the annual pension cost, consistent with GASB guidelines, to be $32 million. In prior years the city had always contributed the amount determined by its actuary and therefore did not have a net pension obligation.

In a Proprietary Fund

If the pension costs are to be accounted for in a proprietary fund, and thus on the full accrual basis, then the reported pension expense would be the same as the annual pension cost (which in this situation is the same as the annual required contribution since the employer did not have an outstanding net pension obligation). As discussed previously, the individual employer has considerable flexibility in calculating its pension cost, but it must satisfy the GASB-imposed criteria.

Insofar as the employer contributes its annual required contribution, it need not report a pension liability. However, if it contributes less than what is required, it must account for the difference as a liability, "net pension obligation."

In the example, inasmuch as the annual pension cost ($32 million) as calculated in accord with GASB guidelines exceeds the employer's contribution ($25 million), the following entry would be appropriate:

Pension expense	$32	
Cash		$25
Net pension obligation		7
To record the annual pension contribution and expense		

Had the city in prior years not contributed the annual required contributions, and thus had a beginning of year net pension obligation, then it would have had to modify its *annual pension cost* to provide for interest on, and amortization of, that obligation. Thus, its annual pension cost (the amount to be charged as the pension expense) would differ from its annual required contribution.

In each subsequent year, the net pension obligation would be increased or decreased by the difference between the pension expense (the annual pension cost—i.e., the annual required contribution subject to the adjustments for interest and amortization) and the actual contributions. Were cumulative pension contributions to exceed the cumulative reported expenses, then the excess would be reported as a net pension asset.

In a Governmental Fund

In a governmental fund, which is accounted for on a modified accrual basis, the reported pension expenditure would be the contribution to be liquidated with expendable available financial resources—that is, the amount actually contributed plus contributions expected to be made with current-year resources shortly after the end of the current year. The cumulative difference between the annual pension costs and the amounts reported as the expenditure would be recognized as increases to the net pension obligation—a long-term liability that would be reported, not in the fund itself, but only in the government-wide statements and in notes to the statements. Thus, the pension expenditure would be only the $25 million contributed to the pension fund; the $7 million difference between the annual pension cost and the actual contribution would be accounted for similarly to other long-term liabilities:

Pension expenditure	$25	
Cash		$25
To record the annual pension contribution and expenditure		

In Government-Wide Statements

In their government-wide statements governments report on a full accrual basis, as they do in their proprietary funds. Therefore, irrespective of whether or not the pension costs are applicable to governmental or proprietary funds, the reported pension expense would be the annual pension cost—the actuarial required contribution as determined by the government's actuary subject to adjustment for interest on, and amortization of, the net pension obligation. The cumulative difference between the government's contributions to the plan and its pension expenses would be reported as either a liability or an asset.

LIMITATIONS OF THE INFORMATION REPORTED IN THE BASIC FINANCIAL STATEMENTS

In truth, the pension information disclosed in the body of an employer's financial statements provides relatively little insight into an employer's pension costs and obligations. The following are but a few of its limitations:

- Insofar as employment costs and obligations are divided among several funds, so too are pension expenditures and liabilities. Even in government-wide statements they may be divided between governmental and business-type activities.
- The reported liability (the net pension obligation) does not capture the full economic obligation to current and future pensioners; it is merely the difference between the cumulative pension expense or expenditure (i.e., the annual pension cost) and actual contributions.

- Since employers have considerable flexibility in actuarial methods and assumptions, neither the pension expenditures nor obligations are readily comparable among employers.

To compensate for these limitations the GASB directs that employers provide extensive information about both their pension costs and obligations and the financial condition of the underlying pension plan. The required disclosures include the following:

- A detailed description of the pension plan, including the types of benefits provided
- The employer's funding policy, including employer and employee contribution rates for the current and past two years
- The components of pension cost and the changes in the net pension obligation
- Key assumptions used in determining the pension costs, including actuarial method, inflation rate, projected salary increases, and investment rate
- The actuarial value of plan assets and liabilities for the current and past two years
- Significant ratios, such as the funding ratio (actuarial value of plan assets to actuarial value of plan liabilities) and the ratio of unfunded actuarial accrued liabilities to annual covered payroll for the current and past two years

Table 10-4 indicates Charlotte, North Carolina's disclosures with respect to one of its pension plans.

HOW SHOULD THE PENSION PLAN BE ACCOUNTED FOR?

In this section we shift our attention from the funds that provide the pension contributions to the pension trust fund, a fiduciary fund, that receives them.

The GASB issued Statement No. 25, *Financial Reporting for Defined Benefit Pension Plans and Note Disclosures for Defined Contribution Plans*, concurrently with Statement No. 27, *Accounting for Pensions by State and Local Governmental Employers*. Its objective was to assure that the information provided by both pension plan and employer was consistent.

As seen by the GASB, the main objective in pension plan accounting and reporting is to provide useful information for assessing:

- The stewardship of plan resources and the ongoing ability of the plan to pay benefits when due
- The effect of plan operations and benefit commitments on the contributions required of both employers and employees

Therefore, according to the GASB, the plans should provide information on:

- Plan assets, liabilities, and net assets available for benefits
- Year-to-year changes in plan net assets available for benefits
- The funded status of the plan from a long-term perspective
- The contribution requirements of employers and employees

REPORTING PLAN NET ASSETS

The most fundamental issue faced by the GASB relates to the form and content of the basic financial statements. Specifically, the main question the board had to address was whether or not information as to current plan assets and activities could be combined with actuarial data into the same set of financial statements.

TABLE 10-4
Charlotte, North Carolina, Note Disclosure as to Firefighters' Pension Plan, June 30, 2002

Description

The Charlotte Firefighters' Retirement System (System), a single-employer defined benefit plan, provides retirement, disability, and death benefits to civil service employees of the Charlotte Fire Department. The System issues a publicly available financial report that includes financial statements and required supplementary information. That report may be obtained by writing to Charlotte Firefighters' Retirement System, 428 East Fourth Street, Suite 205, Charlotte, North Carolina 28202.

Basis of Accounting

The financial statements of the System are presented on the accrual basis of accounting. Plan member and City contributions are recognized in the period in which the contributions are due. Benefits and refunds are recognized when due and payable in accordance with the terms of the plan. Interest and dividend income are reported as earned. The net appreciation (depreciation) in the fair value of investments includes realized gains and losses on investments that were both bought and sold during the year.

Method Used to Value Investments

The investments of the System are reported at fair value. Short-term investments are reported at cost, which approximates fair value. Securities traded on a national or international exchange are valued at the last reported sales price at current exchange rates. Mortgages are valued on the basis of future principal and interest payments and are discounted at prevailing interest rates for similar instruments. The fair value of real estate investments is based on independent appraisals. Investments that do not have an established market are reported at estimated fair values.

Contributions

Pursuant to the North Carolina Act (Act) which created the System, the City is required to match the member's contribution. The Act dictates that the member's contribution is equal to the member's compensation multiplied by the sum of the current social security contribution rate plus 5.0 percent. The current rate is 12.65 percent. The Act was established and may be amended by the North Carolina General Assembly.

Annual Pension Cost and Net Pension Obligation

The City's annual pension cost and net pension obligation to the System for the current year were as follows (dollar amounts in thousands):

Annual required contribution	$ 5,062
Interest on net pension obligation	(530)
Adjustment to annual required contribution	492
Annual pension cost	5,024
Contributions made	(5,062)
Decrease in net pension obligation	(38)
Net pension obligation, beginning of year	(6,845)
Net pension obligation, end of year	$(6,883)

The board determined that the two types of information are fundamentally different in character and need to be reported in different ways. Therefore, it decided that the primary financial statements, a balance sheet (statement of net assets available for benefits) and statement of activities (statement of changes in net assets available for benefits), should report only on net plan assets, excluding actuarially determined benefits to current and future retirees. The actuarial obligations and related information should be reported in supplementary schedules and notes.

Because they exclude actuarial liabilities, the statement of net assets available for benefits and the statement of changes in net assets available for benefits do not depend on the estimates and assumptions discussed earlier. Net assets consist mainly of three categories of resources:

- **Receivables.** These are generally short term, primarily contributions actually due on the reporting date from employees and employers, and investment interest and dividends.

- **Investments.** These include the stocks, bonds, and real estate acquired with employer and employee contributions. Pension plan investments, including real estate, should be reported at fair (i.e., market) value.
- **Assets used in plan operations.** These include the buildings, equipment, furniture, and fixtures used in administering the plan. Generally minor in relation to investments, they should be stated at cost less accumulated depreciation.

Charlotte's statements of net assets available for benefits and changes in such net assets for its firefighters' plan is illustrated in Table 10-5. This statement was included in Charlotte's CAFR itself. Hence it differs slightly from corresponding statements in the stand-alone report of the plan itself (e.g., it is titled "statement of *fiduciary* net assets" rather than simply "statement of net assets").

REPORTING AND CALCULATING ACTUARIAL INFORMATION

Per GASB Statement No. 25, pension plans should report their actuarial information in notes to the basic financial statements and in two supplementary schedules.

Schedule of Funding Progress

Whereas the statement of net assets focuses on pension fund resources held in trust to pay benefits, the schedule of funding progress presents the plan's funded status (the actuarial value of plan assets compared with the actuarial accrued liability for benefits earned to date). A minimum of six years is required because, given the long-term nature of public pension plans and the inherent volatility of actuarial calculations, the GASB believes that users are better informed by observing the trend in the funded status (whether it is improving or deteriorating) than by focusing on the results of a single actuarial valuation.

The actuarial value of assets is based on market values but may not be identical to plan assets reported in the statement of net assets. The methods used to calculate it generally spread year-to-year fluctuations in market values over a three- to five-year period, to avoid large single-year effects on the funded status and, therefore, on the employer's contribution rates.

The actuarial accrued liability is the amount of benefits earned by retirees and current employees that are not yet due and payable. The unfunded actuarial accrued liability is the current shortfall between the actuarial assets and liabilities. Sometimes, there is a surplus: actuarial assets exceed the liabilities. Either way, the difference will be reduced through increases or decreases in future employer contribution requirements.

The funded ratio (actuarial value of assets divided by the actuarial accrued liability) is a statistic commonly used to assess a plan's funding progress. If the funding policy is sound and the employer is making its required contributions, the ratio should be increasing over time. Conversely, the ratio of the unfunded actuarial accrued liability to covered payroll should be decreasing over time.

Schedule of Employer Contributions

Perhaps the single most influential factor affecting a plan's funding progress is whether the employer is making its required contributions. Even the most soundly conceived funding policy will fail if the employer does not comply. Thus, this schedule is intended to supplement the schedule of funding progress. For example, if the funded ratio is not increasing, the schedule of employer contributions may show that at least part of the reason is that the employer is contributing less than the required amounts. Conversely, if the ratio is not increasing even though the employer is making its required contributions, then users should look to other factors, such as the investment policy, asset mix, or increases in benefits without corresponding increases in contribution rates.

TABLE 10–5

City of Charlotte, North Carolina, Statement of Fiduciary Net Assets Pension Trust Fund—Firefighters' Retirement, June 30, 2002 (in thousands)

Assets	
Cash and cash equivalents	$ 5,880
Receivables:	
Employer contributions	61
Member contributions	57
Interest and dividends	409
Total receivables	527
Investments:	
Equity securities—stocks	88,898
Fixed income securities—bonds	27,609
Mutual funds	101,244
Total investments	217,751
Capital assets, at cost, net of accumulated depreciation of $68	374
Total assets	224,532
Liabilities	
Accounts payable	520
Net assets	
Held in trust for pension benefits	$224,012

City of Charlotte, North Carolina, Statement of Changes in Fiduciary Net Assets Pension Trust Fund—Firefighters' Retirement, for the Year Ended June 30, 2002 (in thousands)

Additions	
Contributions:	
Member	$ 5,114
Employer	5,062
Total contributions	10,176
Investment loss:	
Net depreciation in fair value of investments	(13,659)
Interest	1,661
Dividends	1,428
	(10,570)
Investment expense	(1,255)
Net investment loss	(11,825)
Total additions (loss)	(1,649)
Deductions	
Benefits	$ 13,605
Refunds	275
Administration	352
Depreciation	12
Total deductions	14,244
Change in net assets	(15,893)
Net assets—beginning	239,905
Net assets—ending	$224,012

GASB Statement No. 25 requires governments to disclose in notes to the required schedules the actuarial methods and assumptions used, significant changes in benefits, and other information that may affect users' interpretation of the reported trend in the plan's funding progress.

Schedules of funding progress and employer contributions of Charlotte's firefighter pension are included in the pension note illustrated in Table 10-6 (see the schedules titled "Trend Information" and "Schedule of Funding Progress"). They differ slightly (e.g., they include data for only three years rather than the required six) from comparable schedules that would be included in the stand-alone report of the plan itself.

HOW SHOULD POSTEMPLOYMENT BENEFITS OTHER THAN PENSIONS BE ACCOUNTED FOR?

Employers commonly offer retirees benefits other than pensions. Primary among them are continued health care benefits (including medical, dental, vision, and hearing benefits) but they may also include life insurance, disability insurance, and nursing-home care.

TABLE 10-6
Charlotte, North Carolina, Note to the Financial Statements June 30, 2002 (in thousands)

Trend Information

Year Ended June 30	Annual Pension Cost (APC)	Percentage of APC Contributed	Net Pension Obligation
2000	$ (15)	N/A	$ (7,848)
2001	5,540	81.90%	(6,845)
2002	5,024	100.76	(6,883)

Schedule of Funding Progress

Actuarial Valuation Date	Actuarial Value of Assets (a)	Actuarial Accrued Liability (AAL) Entry Age (b)	Unfunded AAL (UAAL) (b–a)	Funded Ratio (a/b)	Covered Payroll (c)	UAAL as a Percentage of Covered Payroll [(b–a)/c]
7/1/00	$235,901	$239,784	$3,883	98.38%	$33,080	11.74%
7/1/01	246,614	254,767	8,153	96.80	38,079	21.41
7/1/02	254,013	265,712	11,699	95.60	39,849	29.36

The information presented in the schedule of funding progress above was determined as part of the actuarial valuation. Additional information follows:

Actuarial valuation date	7/1/02
Actuarial cost method	Entry age
Amortization method	Level dollar open
Remaining amortization period	33 years
Asset valuation method	5-year smoothed market
Actuarial assumptions:	
Investment rate of return	7.75%
Projected salary increases	4.75 to 7.75%
Includes inflation at	3.75%
Cost of living adjustments	None

Postemployment health-related benefits present all of the issues associated with ordinary pension benefits—and then some. The ultimate net cost of providing health-related benefits to retirees is subject to the same uncertainties of ordinary pension benefits—mortality rates, investment rates, turnover rates, and so on. In addition, however, the cost will depend on the extent to which retirees claim the benefits (their health after retirement) as well as on medical technology and the institutional and economic structure of health care—factors difficult to predict five years in the future, to say nothing of the potential sixty to eighty years between the start of an employee's career and the end of his or her life. Nevertheless, actuaries have established methods to address these uncertainties.

In light of the similarity between pensions and other postretirement benefits, it is not surprising that the GASB takes the same approach toward the two.[2]

As with pensions, the GASB distinguishes between reporting by the employer and reporting by the plan. The employer must compute an acceptable annual required contribution within parameters that are comparable (except for certain technical adjustments) to those required for pensions. That is, it must apply the standards of the Actuarial Standards Board, must use one of several specified actuarial cost methods, must make reasonable demographic and economic assumptions, and must include in the required contribution amount both the normal cost and a provision for amortizing the various unamortized gains and losses that affect the actuarial liability. As with pensions, the reported expense in proprietary fund and government-wide statements must be based on the annual required contribution, whereas expenditures in governmental funds must be dependent on the actual amount contributed to the benefit plan (with disclosure of the required amount, if different). Similarly, the reported liability or asset in proprietary and government-wide statements should represent the extent to which the required contributions have been paid in. The requirements for disclosures in notes and supplementary schedules are also akin to those for pensions and, therefore, include the actuarial value of plan assets, the actuarial accrued liability, the unfunded liability, and related funding ratios.

The financial reporting framework for the benefit plans also parallels that for pensions. The two basic statements, a statement of plan net assets and a statement of changes in plan net assets, report plan cash, investments, and benefits currently paid or payable to retirees. They exclude actuarially determined benefits that have been earned by current and future retirees but are not currently payable. Required notes and supplementary schedules are also similar to those for pension plans.

In a departure from its approach to pensions, the GASB allows small governments (those with fewer than 100 members in their benefit plans) to simplify their calculations of the annual required contribution and related measures. Instead of applying the

[2] This section is based on two exposure drafts pertaining to postemployment benefits, issued in February 2003. One addresses reporting by the employer; the other, reporting by the plan. Until the proposals in the exposure drafts are adopted and subject to implementation, reporting is governed by GASB Statement No. 12, *Disclosure of Information on Postemployment Benefits Other Than Pension Benefits by State and Local Governmental Employers*, as amended by GASB Statement No. 27, *Accounting for Pensions by State and Local Governmental Employers*, and GASB Statement No. 26, *Financial Reporting for Postemployment Healthcare Plans Administered by Defined Benefit Pension Plans*. Statement No. 12, as amended, permits government employers to account for the benefits on a pay-as-you-go basis and requires only that they provide note disclosures of the key features of the benefits, their accounting and funding policies, and the expenditures/expenses for the benefits recognized for the period. Under Statement No. 26, a pension plan that provides postemployment health care benefits must include two statements: a statement of postemployment health care plan net assets and a statement of changes in postemployment health care plan net assets. Neither the employer nor the plan is required to provide actuarial data relating to the benefits. The exposure drafts propose that governments with total revenues of $100 million implement the new standards for periods beginning after June 15, 2006, with smaller governments being granted a one or two year grace period depending on size. Plans would implement the new standards one year earlier than their respective participating employers.

actuarial assumptions that would satisfy the standards of the Actuarial Standards Board, they may use alternative assumptions that meet specified GASB criteria.

For most governments the currently reported annual cost of providing retiree health care and related benefits is considerably less than that of pensions, because most governments currently finance these benefits on a pay-as-you-go basis. That is, only benefits payable in the current year are reported, not those that have been earned in the current year but will be payable in future years. Under the new standards, however, the reported annual cost (in government-wide and proprietary fund statements) is likely to be substantially greater. Medical costs have been increasing from year to year and the reported amount will now have to include the cost of all benefits earned that year and payable in future years, not just those that are currently payable. Governments that continue to finance only those benefits that are currently due and payable are likely to report large and increasing liabilities for unfunded required contributions per the GASB standards. Moreover, they will be required to disclose the total unfunded liabilities of their postemployment benefit plans. These amounts are likely to be large because many governments have not accumulated assets to offset the actuarial obligations for benefits earned and payable in the future. It remains to be seen whether the requirement to report these potentially large and increasing liabilities will encourage government employers to begin actuarially prefunding postemployment health care benefits, as most currently do for pension benefits.

WHAT ACCOUNTING ISSUES DO AGENCY FUNDS PRESENT?

Agency funds are the other main category of fiduciary funds. Associated mainly with governments, they are used to account for resources held by one entity in a capacity as a trustee or an **agent** (a representative) of another. Agency funds are the simplest of all funds to account for. They are custodial in nature. Assets always equal liabilities. There are no fund balances—and therefore no changes in fund balances—upon which to report. Budgets are unnecessary.

Because agency funds are custodial in nature, they do not carry out operations that affect the governments that administer them. Nevertheless, governments should prepare agency fund balance sheets and statements that show the changes in assets and liabilities. The assets and liabilities should be measured on the modified accrual basis.

The journal entries of an agency fund present few problems. An increase in assets is generally offset with a liability—amounts due to the party on whose behalf the assets are being held.

EXAMPLE *Agency Funds*

To reduce billing and collection costs, a county collects property taxes for the independent school district with which it shares common boundaries. The county bills taxpayers for both itself and the school district on a single invoice. The county maintains an agency fund to account for the school district's taxes. At the start of a year it held \$0.3 million in cash not yet remitted to the school district.

During the year, the county collects \$4.5 million of taxes on behalf of the school district. The following entry would be appropriate in the county's agency fund:

Cash	\$4.5	
Due to school district		\$4.5
To record the collection of taxes		

To enhance administrative control over the collection and distribution of taxes, some governments might record a receivable (e.g., school district taxes receivable) and a corresponding liability (e.g., due to school district) upon being notified of the tax levy by the other government. However, the agent government does not have a legal liability to the other government until it actually collects the taxes, and it is not responsible for losses resulting from uncollectible taxes. To emphasize this point in this example, we avoid recording both the receivable and the liability. Further, since taxpayers will make a single payment for the taxes of both governments, many governments initially account for both their own taxes and those of the other government in a common agency fund. Periodically they apportion the receipts between the other government and itself. To avoid complicating the example, we assume that the government accounts for only the school district taxes in an agency fund.

To earn interest on the funds received, the county invests $4 million in short-term securities.

Investments	$4.0	
Cash		$4.0
To record purchase of short-term securities		

It earns, but does not yet collect, $0.1 million in interest. The interest would be accounted for on an accrual basis. Assuming that by agreement with the school district all investment risks and rewards are those of the district, not the county, the interest would be recognized as due to the school district

Interest receivable	$0.1	
Due to school district		$0.1
To record interest earned		

It sells $2.9 million of the investments.

Cash	$2.9	
Investments		$2.9
To record the sale of investments		

It distributes $3.0 million to the school district.

Due to school district	$3.0	
Cash		$3.0
To record distribution of assets to school district		

At year-end, its balance sheet and statement of changes in assets and liabilities (combined into a single statement) would appear as follows:

Property Tax Collection Agency Fund Statement of Changes in Assets and Liabilities (in millions)

	Beginning Balance	Additions	Deductions	Ending Balance
Assets				
Cash	$0.3	$7.4	$7.0	$0.7
Interest receivable		0.1		0.1
Investments	0.0	4.0	2.9	1.1
Total assets	$0.3	$11.5	$9.9	$1.9
Liabilities				
Due to school district	$0.3	$4.6	$3.0	$1.9

ESTABLISHING AGENCY FUNDS

The challenging—and sometimes controversial—questions relate to when an agency fund should be established. Consider, for example, two issues.

Special Assessments

A government issues debt that is to be serviced entirely from special assessments. The government collects the assessments from the assessed property owners, temporarily invests any funds on hand, and makes the required payments to the bondholders or the bond trustee. Although the government anticipates that it will service the debt entirely from the assessments, it may, to a variety of degrees, be liable for any shortages. For example, it may formally guarantee the debt, it may be required to cover delinquencies until foreclosure proceeds are received from defaulting property owners, or it may explicitly indicate that in the event of default it *may* cover delinquencies even if not legally obligated to do so.

As pointed out in the previous discussion of special assessments (Chapter 6), a government should account for special assessment resources in an agency fund only when it is not obligated for the related debt *in any manner*. "Any manner" would include any indication that it is either legally obligated for the debt or may assume responsibility for it, even if not legally obligated.[3]

Pass-Through Grants

Governments routinely receive grants that they are required to "pass through" to secondary recipients. Although the assets may be used only to benefit the secondary recipients, depending on the terms of the award, the governments may have varying responsibilities for administering the grants. For example, some grants require the government to disburse funds to parties named by the grantor. Others require the government to select the recipients and subsequently monitor their performance. Thus, in some circumstances the government may be a mere agent for the grantor; in others the government may have substantive control over the funds.

Per GASB Statement No. 24, *Accounting and Financial Reporting for Certain Grants and Other Financial Assistance*, a government may account for the proceeds of a pass-through grant in an agency fund only when it serves as a *cash conduit*. It serves as a cash conduit when it merely transmits funds to the recipient without having any administrative involvement in the grant program. Administrative involvement includes monitoring compliance with grant requirements, selecting recipients, or exercising discretion in how the funds are allocated.[4] When a government has administrative involvement, it should account for grant receipts and subsequent outlays as revenues and expenditures or expenses, respectively.

WHAT ACCOUNTING ISSUES DO INVESTMENT TRUST FUNDS PRESENT?

Governments, especially states and counties, may sponsor investment pools as a service to the other governments within their jurisdiction. They operate these pools like mutual funds. Governments are permitted to invest temporarily available cash in these pools and thereby earn a return on their assets without having to incur the costs

[3] GASB Statement No. 6, *Accounting and Financial Reporting for Special Assessments* (January 1987), para. 19.

[4] GASB Statement No. 24, *Accounting and Financial Reporting for Certain Grants and Other Financial Assistance* (June 1994), para. 107.

and risks of either managing an investment portfolio themselves or giving their assets over to private money managers.

Sponsoring governments must account for their investment pools in accord with the provisions of GASB Statement No. 31, *Accounting and Financial Reporting for Certain Investments and for External Investment Pools.* With only a few exceptions, the statement requires governments to account for their investment pool assets just as they do for their own assets. Most notably, therefore, investment pool investments, both equity and debt securities, must be "marked to market." Changes in market values must be recognized as gains and losses as they occur.

The main exception pertains to "2a7-like" pools. These pools derive their description from the Security and Exchange Commission's Rule 2a7 of the Investment Company Act of 1940. This rule permits certain types of mutual funds to report their assets at amortized historical cost rather than market values. The funds to which the rule applies are "money market" funds. These funds invest in securities, such as Treasury bills, notes, and certificates of deposit, that are both safe and have short maturities—typically sixty days or less. Accordingly, they are not subject to major price swings. The GASB, like the SEC, permits 2a7-like external investment pools to report their investments at amortized cost.

Both Statements No. 33 and 34 emphasize that governments should report only the assets held in trust for the outside governments in a fiduciary fund. Insofar as they invest their own assets in the pool, these should be recorded in the fund with which they are associated. Thus, for example, if resources that a sponsoring government invests in its pool came from its own general fund, then both the assets and the resultant income should be reported in the general fund. They should be "backed out" of the fiduciary fund in which the government accounts for the pooled investments.

Governments that maintain external internal investment pools must, of course, prepare stand-alone financial reports for the benefit of the other government participants. These reports should include a statement of net assets and a statement of changes in net assets. They need not prepare a statement of cash flows. The statements should be on the accrual basis of accounting and should include note disclosures as to:

- The fair value and the carrying value (if different from the fair value) for each major category of investments as well as their ranges of interest rates and maturity dates
- The regulatory oversight to which the pool is subject, including an indication of whether it is registered with the SEC as an investment company
- The frequency with which the pool determines the fair value of its investments
- The methods that the pool uses to compute the number of shares to which a participant is entitled when it contributes to the pool and the amount of cash to which it is entitled when it withdraws its fund
- Legally binding guarantees that the pool has provided or obtained to support the value of its shares

SUMMARY

Fiduciary funds are maintained to account for assets that governments and not-for-profits hold as trustees or agents for individuals, private organizations, or other governmental units. These funds can be either expendable or nonexpendable. They are distinguished in government accounting from *permanent funds*, a new type of fund, used to account only for *nonexpendable* resources that benefit activities of the government itself, rather than outside parties.

Nonexpendable trust funds, also called *endowments*, are those in which only income earned from the fund assets can be expended. The principal must be preserved intact. Expendable funds, by contrast, are those in which all resources, regardless of whether principal or income, may be expended. Whereas permanent funds are, by definition, nonexpendable, fiduciary funds can be either expendable or nonexpendable.

Permanent funds are classified as *governmental* funds, and accordingly the measurement focus should be on current financial resources. They should be accounted for on a modified accrual basis. GASB standards do not specify whether the investment income from the fund should be recorded first in the permanent fund and then transferred to a beneficiary fund or should be recorded directly in a beneficiary fund without passing through the permanent fund. However, they do require that in government-wide statements, governments report permanent fund investment earnings as specific program revenues if they are restricted to a specific program. If not restricted to a specific program they should be shown as "investment earnings" within the category of "general revenues."

There are four major types of fiduciary funds:

1. Pension (and other employee benefit) trust funds
2. Investment trust funds, which are used to account for mutual fund–type arrangements where a sponsoring government holds and invests the cash of other governments
3. Private purpose trust funds, such as those for scholarships and escheat property in which resources are held for the benefit of outsiders
4. Agency funds, which are used to account for resources held by an organization in a purely custodial capacity

As a general rule, nonexpendable trust funds should be accounted for on a full accrual basis. The full accrual basis encompasses changes in all resources, not just cash, and thereby helps to assure that a trust does not dissipate its principal through excessive spending. Nevertheless, the GASB requires that permanent funds be accounted for on a modified accrual basis. Permanent funds are intended to benefit governmental activities, and are therefore classified as governmental funds. So as to be consistent with other governmental funds, they must be accounted for on the modified accrual basis. However, inasmuch as permanent funds typically include mainly cash and investments, and not depreciable assets, the results are not significantly different than if they were to be accounted for on a full accrual basis.

One of the most significant issues relating to nonexpendable funds is whether investment (i.e., capital) gains and losses should be considered expendable or unexpendable. This issue, however, is more of a legal and contractual issue than an accounting issue. If a particular policy is required either by law or donor stipulation, then that policy will dictate accounting practice.

The resources of expendable trust funds, by definition, are expendable. Therefore, investment gains are available for expenditure and investment losses decrease the resources available for expenditure.

The fixed rate of return approach requires an institution to make available for current expenditure a fixed percentage of its endowment portfolio. For accounting purposes, however, the actual earnings should be recognized as investment revenue, irrespective of whether they are greater or less than the stated fixed percentage.

Because of their dollar magnitude, pensions are of vital concern to statement preparers and users. Defined contribution plans—which are becoming increasingly popular—are simple to account for because the employer defines the inputs (contributions) and makes no guarantees as to outputs (benefits paid to retirees). Therefore, the reported expenditures are generally the agreed-upon contributions. Defined benefit plans are far more complex because the employer defines the outputs and is required to contribute a sufficient amount to pay the required benefits when its employees retire. But inasmuch as the benefits are subject to uncertainties, the funding and accounting determinations have to be based on estimates and allocations.

Although a government employer and its pension trust fund may each be independent legal and reporting entities, the two are inextricably linked. The government is responsible for assuring that the trust fund has sufficient resources to pay retirees. Ultimately, albeit indirectly, the government benefits from investment and actuarial gains and incurs the cost of corresponding losses.

According to GASB standards, each employer should report as its pension costs its annual required contribution to its pension plan (plus or minus an adjustment for interest and other technical factors) as long as that contribution satisfies certain criteria of reasonableness as to actuarial methods and assumptions. If the government accounts for its pension costs in a governmental fund, then the recognized expenditure should be the portion of the pension cost to be liquidated with expendable available financial resources. The difference between the cumulative annual pension costs and the cumulative contributions should be reported as a liability in the schedule of long-term obligations. If it accounts for its pension costs in a proprietary fund, then the recognized expense should be the annual required pension contribution, and the difference between the cumulative pension cost and the cumulative contributions should be reported as a fund liability.

As a consequence of the GASB standards, the basic financial statements of government employers do not provide information on the pension plan's unfunded actuarial liability to current and future retirees. Governments are required to report these actuarial data in notes and supplementary schedules.

Pension plans include in their basic financial statements information only on net plan assets, excluding actuarial obligations. Like the employers, they must report actuarial information in supplementary schedules and notes. Moreover, like employers, they have broad discretion as to how they determine their actuarial values. However, the actuarial values of the plan must be consistent with those reported by the employers.

Health care and other postemployment benefits present accounting challenges similar to those of pensions. Accordingly, per recently released GASB pronouncements, they should be accounted for and reported in parallel fashion.

Agency funds are the simplest of funds for which to account. They are custodial in nature, so assets must equal liabilities. There are no fund balances, and hence no changes in fund balances to account for and report. The most salient accounting issues relate to the circumstances in which transactions should be reported in agency funds as opposed to other types.

EXERCISE FOR REVIEW AND SELF-STUDY

The following note was taken from the June 30, 2005, financial statements of a state government:

Pension Plan

- ***Plan description.*** The state contributes to the State Employees Pension Plan (SEPP), a single-employer defined benefit pension plan administered by the State Retirement System. SEPP provides retirement, disability, and death benefits to plan members and beneficiaries. Cost-of-living adjustments are provided to members and beneficiaries at the discretion of the state legislature.
- ***Funding policy.*** The contribution requirements of plan members and the state are established and may be amended by the state legislature. Plan members are required to contribute 8.1 percent of their annual covered salary. The state is required to contribute at an actuarially determined rate; the current rate is 12.9 percent of annual covered payroll.
- ***Annual pension cost and net pension obligation.*** The state's annual pension cost and net pension obligation to SEPP for the current year were as follows (dollar amounts in thousands):

Annual pension cost	$206,874
Contributions made	(196,374)
Increase (decrease) in net pension obligation	$ 10,500
Net pension obligation beginning of year	57,332
Net pension obligation end of year	$ 67,832

The annual pension cost for the current year was determined as part of the June 30, 2005, actuarial valuation using the entry age actuarial cost method. The actuarial assumptions included (a) 7.7 percent investment rate of return (net of administrative expenses) and (b) projected salary increases ranging from 6.5 percent to 9.5 percent per year. Both (a) and (b) included an inflation component of 5.4 percent. The unfunded actuarial accrued liability is being amortized over twenty-three years.

Three-Year Trend Information (Dollar Amounts in Thousands)			
Fiscal Year Ending	*Annual Pension Cost (APC)*	*Percentage of APC Contributed*	*Net Pension Obligation*
6/30/03	$179,664	99.1	$56,187
6/30/04	187,559	99.4	57,332
6/30/05	206,874	94.9	67,832

1. This plan is a single employer plan. What is the difference between a single employer plan and a multiple employer plan?
2. Suppose the plan were a defined contribution plan rather than a defined benefit plan. What would be the major difference in how the state's contributions were determined?
3. Suppose the state were to change its actuarial projections of salaries, increasing them by an average of 1 percent. At the same time it would change its assumed investment rate, decreasing it by 1 percent. How would these changes affect the present value of the plan's pension obligation to current employees? How would they affect the annual pension cost for the current year—that is, would they increase it by the full amount of the increase in the obligation? Explain.
4. What does the "net pension obligation" represent? Suppose the wages and salaries of the employees covered by the pension plan are accounted for entirely in the state's general fund. Where would the "net pension obligation" be reported?
5. Suppose, instead, that the wages and salaries of the employees covered by the pension plan are accounted for entirely in an enterprise fund. Where would the "net pension obligation" be reported?
6. Assume the wages and salaries of the employees covered by the pension plan are accounted for entirely in the state's general fund. Prepare the general fund journal entry to record the 2005 pension expenditure.

7. Assume, instead, that the wages and salaries of the employees covered by the pension plan are accounted for entirely in an enterprise fund. Prepare the enterprise fund journal entry to record the 2005 pension expense.
8. What is the significance of the "percent of APC contributed"? How was it derived?
9. What is meant by the "unfunded actuarial accrued liability"? How does it differ from the net pension obligation? Why is it being amortized rather than added to the pension expenditures of the years in which its components were first recognized?
10. As indicated in the note, the annual pension cost was $206,874. This cost increased the plan's unfunded actuarial accrued liability. However, the state contributed only $196,374. How would the contribution of $196,374 affect the unfunded actuarial accrued liability? How would it affect the statement of net assets of the pension *plan?* How would the increase of $206,874 in the actuarial accrued liability affect the statement of net assets of the plan?
11. Suppose that during the year retirees were entitled to $150,000 of current-year benefits. How would the liability be reflected on the statement of net assets of the plan?

QUESTIONS FOR REVIEW AND DISCUSSION

1. What is the distinction, as drawn by the GASB, between a fiduciary fund and a permanent fund?
2. What is the rationale for accounting for nonexpendable endowment funds on a full, rather than a modified, accrual basis? Why is it important that depreciation be charged on long-term assets held as fiduciary fund investments?
3. Why, despite your response to the previous question, does the GASB direct that permanent funds be accounted for on a modified accrual basis?
4. Suppose that you are the independent auditor for a local performing arts association (either government or not-for-profit) that recently received a sizable endowment. The association's president has asked whether gains, both realized and unrealized, from the appreciation of endowment investments should be accounted for as expendable or nonexpendable resources. What should be the primary factors that determine your response? How should GASB or FASB pronouncements influence your recommendation?
5. How should governments report permanent fund and fiduciary fund balances and income in their government-wide statements? Explain.
6. You are the sole contributor to a philanthropic foundation. You must specify whether investment gains should be expendable or nonexpendable. Present the key arguments in favor and against permitting the gains to be expendable.
7. A college has adopted a "fixed rate of return" approach to the distribution of investment income. Each year it transfers 6 percent of its endowment value to expendable funds, irrespective of actual earnings. Suppose that in year one the fund actually earns 8 percent; in year two it earns 4 percent. Assuming the endowment earnings are not restricted to any particular purpose, how much should the college report as unrestricted earnings in each of the two years? How should the difference, if any, between what is transferred and what is reported be classified and accounted for?
8. A not-for-profit organization has an endowment fund that, at the start of the year, has a value of $1 million— the amount initially contributed to establish the fund. Owing to investment losses, the year-end balance decreased to $950,000. In a previous year, the organization had added $30,000 of endowment fund investment gains to temporarily restricted assets. Of this amount, $20,000 has already been spent. How should the $50,000 of investment losses be accounted for? More specifically, what should be the reported value of the endowment fund? In which category of assets should the losses be recognized?
9. Distinguish between a defined benefit plan and a defined contribution plan. Why does a defined benefit plan present far more complex accounting issues than a defined contribution plan?
10. How should an employer determine its annual pension cost? What minimum GASB criteria must it satisfy?
11. Why may a government's reported pension expenditure differ from its annual pension cost?
12. Why do the fundamental financial statements (statement of plan net assets available for benefits and statement of changes in plan net assets available for benefits) of a pension plan provide inadequate information to assess the plan's funding status? Where would a statement user look for more comprehensive information?
13. Why are the problems of accounting for postemployment health care benefits similar to those of accounting for pensions? Why, however, are they even more intractable?
14. Why do the balance sheets of agency funds contain only assets and liabilities, but no fund balances? Why is it often unclear whether the resources relating to a particular activity should be accounted for in an agency fund or a governmental fund?

EXERCISES

10-1

Select the *best* answer. Items 1 though 5 refer to Riverview City.

1. Riverview City received a gift of $1 million. The sum is to be maintained as an endowment, with income used to preserve and improve the city's jogging trails. The $1 million should be reported in
   a. A governmental fund
   b. An agency fund
   c. A fiduciary fund
   d. A proprietary fund
2. Riverview City collected $80 million in property taxes on behalf of the Riverview Independent School District. The $80 million should be reported in
   a. A governmental fund
   b. An agency fund
   c. A fiduciary fund
   d. A proprietary fund
3. The $80 million collected by Riverview City would be reflected in statements of the appropriate fund as an increase in cash and an offsetting increase in
   a. A liability
   b. A reserve
   c. Fund balance
   d. None of the above
4. In the city's government-wide statements the $80 million would be reported as
   a. A liability
   b. A reserve
   c. Net assets
   d. None of the above
5. The city maintains a $1 million endowment to provide financial assistance to needy retired employees and their families. In its government-wide statements, the $1 million would be reported as an asset in the column for
   a. Governmental activities
   b. Business-type activities
   c. Totals, but not in the column for either governmental or business-type activities
   d. None of the above
6. As of year-end, a city's pension plan had $1.5 million in current obligations to retired employees. The city would report this amount as a liability on
   a. The pension trust fund statements only
   b. The pension trust fund statements and the government-wide statements
   c. The government-wide statements only
   d. Neither the pension trust fund statements nor the government-wide statements
7. Depreciation on capital assets would never be reported in which of the following funds?
   a. Fiduciary
   b. Permanent
   c. Internal service
   d. Enterprise
8. Which of the following would *not* be reported on a pension plan's statement of plan net assets?
   a. Long-term investments at fair value
   b. Capital assets used in plan operations at cost less accumulated depreciation
   c. Net assets held in trust for pension benefits
   d. Actuarial accrued liability to current and retired employees
9. A city maintains a $10 million endowment fund to preserve and improve its parks. During the year, the fund had investment gains from the sale of securities of $1 million. These investment gains should be
   a. Added to the endowment principal and thereby not be expendable
   b. Added to the fund that accounts for dividends and interest and thereby be expendable
   c. Either added to the endowment or added to the fund that accounts for dividends and interest, depending on the stipulations of the donor that established the endowment or, absent donor stipulations, on the decision of the endowment's trustees
   d. Added to the endowment to the extent necessary to cover losses due to inflation; the balance would be added to the fund that accounts for dividends and interest
10. In a particular year, the Haynes Independent School District collects $100 million in property taxes. State law requires that property-rich school districts appropriate and contribute 2 percent of all property taxes that they collect to a state pool, which will be divided among property-poor districts. Upon receipt of the taxes, the Haynes district, which the state considers a property-rich district, should account for
    a. $100 million in an agency fund
    b. $98 million in a governmental fund and $2 million in an agency fund
    c. $100 million a governmental fund
    d. $98 million in a governmental fund and $2 million in a fiduciary fund other than an agency fund

10-2

Select the *best* answer.

1. A city's annual required contribution (as distinguished from its pension expenditures) represents the city's

a. Required contribution to a pension trust fund as determined on the accrual basis by an appropriate actuarial method
b. Actual cash contribution to the pension trust fund
c. Required payments to retired employees per the terms of the pension plan
d. Normal cost, as determined by an appropriate actuarial method

2. A city's annual required contribution to a pension trust fund
   a. Must be no less than the actual payments to retirees
   b. Must consist of normal cost plus an amount for amortizing the pension plan's unfunded actuarial accrued liability
   c. Must consist of normal cost plus an amount for amortizing the city's actuarial accrued liability
   d. Is the amount that the city should report as its pension expenditure in a governmental fund

3. Per its actuary, Carlin City's annual required pension contribution for a particular year is $2.5 million. Of this amount, $2 million is applicable to employees whose compensation is accounted for in its general fund and $500,000 is applicable to employees whose compensation is accounted for in a utility (enterprise) fund. For that year, the city contributes to the pension plan $1.8 million from its general fund and $450,000 from its utility fund. How much should the city record as an expenditure in its general fund and an expense in its utility fund?

	General Fund	Utility Fund
a.	$2,000,000	$500,000
b.	$1,800,000	$450,000
c.	$1,800,000	$500,000
d.	$2,000,000	$450,000

4. Assume the same facts as in the previous item. The amount by which the city's total pension liability (net pension obligation) would increase in its government-wide statements is
   a. $0
   b. $50,000
   c. $200,000
   d. $250,000

5. A pension plan's actuarial accrued liability refers to
   a. The difference between the plan's assets and its obligations, computed by an appropriate actuarial method, to current and retired employees
   b. The total amount to be paid to current and retired employees computed by an appropriate actuarial method
   c. The total amount to be paid to current and retired employees, computed by an appropriate actuarial method, that has been earned by those employees to date
   d. The difference between the total amount to be paid to current and retired employees, computed by an appropriate actuarial method, and the amount that has actually been paid to them

6. Which of the following would *not* be reported on the statement of plan net assets of a city's pension plan?
   a. Actuarial accrued liability
   b. Plan investments at fair value
   c. Obligations to retired employees that are past due
   d. Contributions receivable from employers

7. Which of the following is a city *not* required to disclose in its notes or required supplementary information pertaining to its pension trust fund?
   a. Unfunded actuarial accrued liability as a percent of covered payroll
   b. Difference between cost and fair value of plan investments
   c. Percentage of annual required contribution actually contributed
   d. Ratio of plan assets to actuarial accrued liability

8. A city is notified by its actuary that its actuarially determined required contribution to its postemployment health care plan is $800,000. Of this amount, the city contributes only $600,000. The compensation cost of all covered employees is accounted for in the general fund. The city should report an expenditure in its general fund and an expense in its government-wide statements of

	General Fund	Government-Wide
a.	$800,000	$800,000
b.	$800,000	$600,000
c.	$600,000	$800,000
d.	$600,000	$600,000

9. A city maintains a defined contribution plan to which it agrees to contribute 6 percent of employee wages and salaries. During the year, employees earned $10 million in wages and salaries, but the government appropriated and contributed only $500,000 to the plan. The city accounts for the compensation of all employees in the general fund. The amount that the city should report as an expenditure in its general fund and an expense in its government-wide statements is

	General Fund	Government-Wide
a.	$500,000	$500,000
b.	$500,000	$600,000
c.	$600,000	$500,000
d.	$600,000	$600,000

10. A defined benefit plan is one in which
    a. The employer promises specified payments to employees upon their retirement
    b. The specific provisions are defined by the Internal Revenue Code
    c. The specific provisions are defined by the Uniform Code of Retirement Plans
    d. The employee can specify the mix of benefits (e.g., health, pension, insurance) that will be received upon retirement

11. Elton City contributes to a pension plan for its firefighters. The city makes contributions to the pension

trust fund from its general fund. As of year-end, the pension plan owed $2 million to retired employees. The city would report this amount as a liability on

a. Its general fund statements and government-wide statements
b. Its permanent fund statements and government-wide statements
c. Its government-wide statements only
d. Neither its governmental fund statements nor its government-wide statements

12. The funded ratio of a pension plan compares

a. The actuarial value of plan assets to the actuarial accrued liability
b. Employer contributions to the actuarial value of plan liabilities
c. Employer contributions to the unfunded actuarial liability
d. Employer contributions to the annual required contribution

10-3

Fiduciary funds are accounted for differently from permanent funds, even though both may be nonexpendable.

Christopher City received a contribution of $520,000 to provide scholarships to the children of deceased city employees. The donor stipulated that all income, including both realized and unrealized investment gains, should be used to support the beneficiaries.

1. Record journal entries for the following assuming that the gift is to be accounted for in a fiduciary (i.e., nonexpendable trust) fund.
   a. The gift was composed of
      - cash of $20,000
      - Marketable securities with a fair market value of $100,000
      - A building with a fair market value of $400,000 and an estimated useful life of forty years
   b. The city leased the office as office space to Brooks Law Firm. It collected $46,000 in rent and incurred expenses, other than depreciation, of $15,000. The city records depreciation on the straight-line basis.
   c. The city sold $20,000 of the equity securities for $26,000. At year-end the remaining securities had a market value of $97,000.
   d. It earned and received dividends of $5,000.
2. The city closed the fund's revenue and expense accounts and distributed to beneficiaries the total amount available for distribution. It then closed the distribution account. Prepare the entries to make the distribution and close the accounts.
3. Prepare the fund's year-end balance sheet.
4. How would the fund be reported in the city's government-wide statements? Explain.
5. Suppose the trust was established to benefit programs and activities of the city itself. In what type of fund would it be accounted for? What would be the main differences in accounting principles? How would it be reported in the city's government-wide statements?

10-4

Investment gains and losses may have to be accounted for differently in nonexpendable than in expendable funds.

The McCracken County Humane Society (MCHS), which is part of a county's reporting entity, established a permanent fund to provide support for its pet neutering program. As of the start of the year, the fund had a balance of $600,000, composed of both cash and marketable securities.

The program itself, which is accounted for in a special revenue fund, is funded by both direct contributions and the income from the permanent fund. At the start of the year, the special revenue fund had assets (all investments) of $26,000.

The following transactions and events occurred in a recent year.

1. The MCHS conducted a "walk your pet day" fund-raising drive. The event raised $120,000, of which $20,000 was in pledges expected to be collected shortly after year-end.
2. The society acquired food and medicine at a cost of $60,000 (cash). During the year, it used $30,000 of these supplies. The society accounts for supplies on a consumption basis. It incurred other operating costs (all paid in cash) of $85,000.
3. The society earned interest of $45,000 on investments accounted for in the permanent fund.
4. During the year, the market value of the investments held by the permanent fund increased by $30,000. Per the terms of the agreement establishing the endowment, all capital gains, both realized and unrealized, must be added to principal.
5. During the year, the value of investments held by the special revenue fund increased by $3,000.
6. The society transferred cash to the special revenue fund in the amount of the earnings of the permanent fund.
   a. Prepare journal entries to record the events and transactions. Be sure you indicate the fund in which they would be recorded.
   b. In your opinion, should the unrealized gains on the investments held in the special revenue fund be considered expendable or nonexpendable? Explain.
   c. How would the transfer from the permanent fund to the special revenue fund be reported in the government-wide statements?

10-5

Recorded pension expenditures are not always influenced by actuarial computations.

Hayward City maintains a defined benefit pension plan for its employees. In a recent year the city contributed $5 million to its pension fund. However, its annual pension cost as calculated by its actuary was $7 million. The city accounts for the pension contributions in a governmental fund.

1. Record the pension expenditure in the appropriate fund.
2. Suppose in the following year the city contributed $6 million to its pension fund, but its annual pension cost per its actuary was only $5 million. Prepare the appropriate journal entries.
3. In which fund, if any, would the excess of pension cost over pension contribution be recorded?

10-6

Investment losses need not impair the principal of not-for-profits' endowment funds.

In 2005, the Rubin Center for the Arts received a $2 million endowment, the income of which was to be used to support local artists. The center invested the proceeds in securities. In 2005, owing to interest, dividends and changes in market prices, the value of the endowment increased by $120,000. Of this amount, the center spent $80,000 on programs that were consistent with the endowment's restrictions. In 2006, owing to a market downturn, the portfolio incurred net losses of $60,000. In 2007, it had net earnings of $70,000. In neither 2006 nor 2007 did the center use any endowment resources to support its programs.

In the absence of donor specifications and applicable statutes, what would be the balances, at the end of 2005, 2006, and 2007, in the center's (a) permanently restricted endowment fund and (b) related temporarily restricted fund? Indicate also any impact on unrestricted funds.

10-7

Nonexpendable fiduciary funds should be accounted for on a full accrual basis.

The Nebraska Institute of Science (NIS) pools all of its endowment funds so that it can obtain the benefits of a large and diverse investment portfolio. The institute recently acquired a commercial office building as an investment property. The cost was $12 million and its economic life was expected to be fifteen years. Upon acquiring the building, NIS signed a fifteen-year lease with a tenant. The annual rent was $1.3 million, with the tenant responsible for all maintenance and other operating costs.

1. Suppose that the NIS did not charge depreciation and distributed to expendable funds the entire "income" earned on the office building.
   a. What would be the total amount distributed over the fifteen-year life of the building?
   b. Assuming that NIS's estimate of economic life was correct, what would likely be the market value of the building when the lease expired? Would NIS have had available any cash for the acquisition of other assets that would compensate for the decline in value of the building?
2. Suppose NIS charged depreciation and distributed to expendable funds the entire "income" earned on the office building.
   a. What would be the total amount distributed over the fifteen-year life of the building?
   b. Assuming that NIS's estimate of economic life was correct, what would likely be the market value of the building when the lease expired? Would NIS have had available any cash for the acquisition of other assets to compensate for the decline in value of the building?

PROBLEMS

Continuing Problem

Review the Comprehensive Annual Financial Report (CAFR) that you obtained.

1. Does the government maintain any permanent funds? If so, for what purposes?
2. Does the government maintain any fiduciary funds? If so, for what purposes?
3. Does the government contribute to one or more pension plans? Are they defined benefit or defined contribution plans? If they are defined benefit plans, are they single employer (maintained by the government itself) or multiple employer?
4. Does the government report pension expenses or expenditures? If so, in which fund or funds?
5. Does the government report pension liabilities? If so, in which fund or funds?
6. Does the CAFR indicate the actuarial value of plan assets and liabilities? Are the plans over- or underfunded?
7. Does the CAFR contain the financial statements of the pension plans? Does it indicate that the pension plans issue their own reports and that these are publicly available?
8. Does the CAFR indicate that the government provides postretirement benefits? If so, what is the nature of these benefits? How are they reported?

10-1

The accounting for trusts is dependent upon donor stipulations.

To promote computer education, a leading computer manufacturer donates $4 million to the Kerrville Independent School District. The donor stipulates that the district is to establish an endowment, from which income only is expendable. Income is defined to include interest, dividends, and investment gains. All income is to be recorded initially in a nonexpendable permanent fund. Each year the district is to transfer to an expendable endowment fund (i.e., a special revenue fund) all income of the year that exceeds the rate of inflation as measured by the consumer price index times the beginning fund balance. The expendable funds are to be used exclusively to acquire computer-related materials and to provide computer training for teachers.

In the year the contribution was received, the district:

- Purchased bonds having a face value of $3 million for $2,970,000 and common stock of $1 million
- Received $180,000 in interest and recognized an increase of $3,000 in the fair value of the bonds
- Sold $500,000 of the common stock at a gain of $50,000 and used the proceeds to purchase additional common stock
- Transferred expendable income to a newly established special revenue fund (during the year the consumer price index increased by 5 percent)

1. Prepare journal entries, including closing entries, in the nonexpendable permanent fund to record the year's transactions.
2. Prepare a statement of revenues, expenses, and changes in fund balance and a balance sheet for the nonexpendable endowment (permanent) fund.
3. Some donors stipulate that no investment gains are expendable. What is the most probable purpose of that restriction? What is its limitation? In what way is the approach taken by the donor in this example preferable?
4. How would the permanent fund be reported in the district's government-wide statements?

10-2

Investment losses cannot be accounted for as the mirror image of investment gains.

On December 31, 2004, The Child Crisis Center establishes an endowment fund with a $5 million gift of securities. Income from the endowment is to be used exclusively to support a nutrition program. Expendable income is defined in the indenture agreement so as to include all investment gains, both realized and unrealized. Investment gains and losses are to be accounted for as recommended by the FASB.

During 2005, the endowment earns $100,000 in interest and dividends and spends the entire amount on the nutrition program. The value of its securities portfolio increases by $500,000, from $5 million to $5.5 million.

During 2006 the endowment again earns $100,000 in interest and dividends and spends the entire amount on the nutrition program. This year, however, the value of its securities portfolio decreases by $800,000, from $5.5 million to $4.7 million.

During 2007 the endowment continues to earn and spend $100,000 in interest and dividends. This year the portfolio recovers $400,000 of its investment losses and at year-end is worth $5.1 million.

At the start of 2005, the center had a cash balance of $600,000 in an unrestricted fund. Over the three-year period, this balance was unaffected by transactions other than those just described.

1. Prepare a schedule for each of the three years (2005 through 2007) in which you summarize the transactions as they affect permanently restricted, temporarily restricted, and unrestricted net assets.
2. At the beginning of 2006, the year of the loss, the total value of the security portfolio was $5.5 million. Of this amount, the initial $5 million was classified as permanently restricted; the balance as temporarily restricted. Assuming that you adhered to the FASB pronouncement, how much of the loss did you assign to the permanently restricted assets and how much to the temporarily restricted assets? How can you justify this division of the loss?

10-3

Choice of accounting basis may determine whether endowment principal will be preserved.

On January 1, 2005, the JKG Foundation received a $10 million bequest consisting of a commercial warehouse building and $5 million of cash.

The foundation immediately invested the $5 million cash in twenty-year, 7 percent corporate bonds having a face value of $4,485,512. The bonds, which pay interest annually, were purchased to yield 6 percent. The total premium was $514,488, and hence the total purchase price was $5 million. The annual interest payments (7 percent of the face value) are $313,986. In 2005, the fair value of the bonds decreased by $13,986, an amount equivalent to the first year's amortization of the bond premium.

The JKG Foundation leased out the warehouse for $600,000 per year. The useful life of the building is twenty years.

Per the terms of the bequest, income only is available for spending. However, neither the terms nor the applicable law specifies how income is to be determined.

1. Determine the amount available in 2005 for expenditure, assuming that the foundation calculates income:
   a. On a cash basis
   b. On a full accrual basis, recognizing changes in the market value of the securities and depreciating (on a straight-line basis) the warehouse
2. Assume that the foundation spent all of its income. Prepare both a cash-basis and an accrual-basis balance sheet.
3. Is there a difference in fund balance between the two balance sheets? If not, can it be said that one basis of accounting better preserves endowment principal? Explain.

10-4

Expendable trust funds may be different in character than nonexpendable funds.

On January 1, 2005, the balance sheet of a city's funds for the acquisition of library books showed the following (in thousands):

	Permanent (Nonexpendable)	Special Revenue (Expendable)
Cash	$ 1,400	$120
Marketable securities	10,000	160
Total assets	$11,400	$280
Fund balance	$11,400	$280

The endowment was established in 1997 with a contribution of cash, securities, and real estate (a building) having a total market value of $24 million. The endowment agreement stated that income only (excluding both realized and unrealized investment gains, and deducting depreciation on a straight-line basis) could be used to acquire library books.

The building has a useful life of forty years with no expected salvage value. It had a market value of $20 million when acquired.

The following table provides information about cash transactions and other events (excluding depreciation) during 2005 (in thousands):

	Permanent	Special Revenue
Interest and dividends received (in cash)	$ 760	$60
Rent received (in cash)	1,800	
Cash expenditures for building maintenance	400	
Sales price of securities sold	800	20
Book value of securities sold	200	15
Increase during the year in market value of securities on hand at year-end	150	12

As of January 1, 2005, all prior-year earnings of the nonexpendable fund had been transferred to the expendable fund and are therefore available for expenditure.

1. Prepare in good form a schedule in which you calculate the total amount available at December 31, 2005, for the acquisition of books.
2. Did you account for the investment gains in the expendable fund in the same way as in the nonexpendable fund? If not, justify any differences.
3. Why is the building not reported on the balance sheet of the permanent fund? How would the building be reported on the city's government-wide statements?

10-5

Pension expenditures are reported differently in governmental than in proprietary funds.

Pebble City maintains a defined benefit pension plan for its employees. In a recent year, the city's consulting actuary calculated that the city's annual pension cost for the year was $6 million. Its determination was consistent with the GASB-specified parameters. The city records 50 percent of its payroll in its general fund and 50 percent in an enterprise fund.

1. During the year the city contributed the entire $6 million to the pension fund. Prepare the pension journal entries that the city should make to record its pension contribution, expenditure or expense, and obligation (if any) in all applicable funds (excluding the pension plan itself).
2. Assume the city contributed only $5.6 million. Prepare the appropriate journal entries.
3. How can you justify the differences in the reported expenditures/expense between the two funds?

10-6

A pension plan's reported net assets must be distinguished from its actuarial net assets.

The 2005 financial statements of a city's single employer pension plan revealed the following (in thousands):

Total assets, year end	$7,200,000
Total liabilities, year-end	10,000
Annual required employer contributions, 2005	274,000
Actual employer contributions, 2005	250,000
Actuarial value of assets, year end	7,200,000
Actuarial accrued liability	8,450,000

1. Assuming that the city (the employer) accounts for pension fund expenditures in its general fund, prepare all journal entries that the city should make to record its 2005 pension fund expenditure and contribution.
2. What is the amount that the pension plan should report as "net plan assets" for year-end 2005?
3. What is the amount of the plan's unfunded actuarial accrued liability?
4. What is the total amount that the city should report as its government-wide statement liability at year-end 2005 assuming that up until 2005 it has made all annually required contributions? What is the significance of this liability? Is it indicative of the estimated present value of the amount to be paid to current and future retirees? Explain.

10-7

The basic financial statements of a pension plan provide only limited amounts of information as to its economic condition.

The following information relates to the Lincoln County Firefighters' Pension Plan (dollar amounts in millions):

Beginning-of-Year Balances	
Cash and cash equivalents, January 1	$ 67
Marketable securities and other investments at fair value, January 1	3,180
Current liabilities to retirees, January 1	4
Actuarial accrued liability, January 1	3,430
Transactions During the Year	
Contributions received during the year from employers and employees	138
Benefits to which retirees were entitled during the year	120

Benefits actually paid to retirees, including amounts owed from prior year	122
Interest and dividends earned during the year	145
Net appreciation in fair value of marketable securities and other investments (i.e., realized and unrealized gains) during the year	36
Investment and administrative expenses	45
End-of-Year Balances	
Cash on hand, December 31	92
Marketable securities and other investments at fair value, December 31	3,307
Current liabilities to retirees, December 31	2
Actuarial accrued liability, December 31	3,690

1. Prepare a statement of plan net assets available for benefits (balance sheet) as of January 1. You may not have to include all of the data provided.
2. Prepare a statement of changes in plan net assets available for benefits (statement of activities) for the year.
3. Prepare a statement of plan net assets available for benefits (balance sheet) as of December 31.
4. Comment on the significance of the data provided that you did not include in your statements. Where in the plan's financial statements would this information be reported?
5. Determine the amount of the unfunded actuarial accrued liability as of December 31, assuming that the actuarial value of the plan assets is the same as their fair value. (Sometimes actuaries use average values over several years rather than point-in-time values as of the balance sheet date.)

10-8

A pension plan's financial statements provide useful, but limited, information as to the plan's fiscal condition.

The following are Rockville School District Teachers Retirement Plan's statement of plan net assets (balance sheets) for 2005 and 2004, and statement of changes in plan net assets for 2005.

All dollar amounts are in millions.

Statement of Plan Net Assets
As of December 31

	2005	2004
Assets		
Cash	$ 210	$ 440
Due from employer	39	46
Interest and dividends receivable	87	81
Investments in stocks and bonds (at fair value)	9,176	8,831
Total assets	$9,512	$9,398
Less: benefits payable	6	37
Net assets available for benefits	$9,506	$9,361

Statement of Changes in Plan Net Assets
For the Year Ended December 31, 2005

Additions	
Employer contributions	$ 541
Interest and dividends	630
Total additions	$1,171
Deductions	
Net depreciation in value of investments	621
Benefits to which retirees are entitled for year	394
Administrative expenses	11
Total deductions	1,026
Net increase	145
Plan net assets, December 31, 2004	9,361
Plan net assets, December 31, 2005	$9,506

1. Prepare a summary journal entry to record the employer contributions recognized during the year, the cash actually received from the employer during the year, and the change in the contributions receivable from previous years.
2. Prepare a journal entry to record the benefits paid to retirees.
3. Should the net depreciation in value of investments include unrealized as well as net realized losses? Why?
4. Based on the data provided, are you able to determine the obligation of the plan attributable to benefits earned by current and retired employees? Are you able to determine whether the financial health of the plan has improved or deteriorated in 2005? If not, where could you find this information?

10-9

Required supplementary schedules provide the actuarial information necessary to assess a plan's fiscal status.

The following information was reported in a state's Police Officers Pension Plan's schedule of funding progress. Dollar amounts are in millions.

	Valuation Date December 31,	
	2005	2004
Value of assets (a)	$2,411	$2,005
Actuarial accrued liability (b)	$2,902	$2,626
Unfunded actuarial accrued liability (b – a)	$491	$621
Funded ratio (a/b)	83%	76%
Covered payroll (c)	$957	$902
Unfunded actuarial accrued liability as a percent of covered payroll [(b – a)/c]	51%	69%

The plan's schedule of employer contributions indicated that the employers' annual pension cost was $106 million in 2005 and $100 million in 2004. In both years the employers contributed 100 percent of those amounts.

1. Based on the limited data available, do you think that the fiscal health of the plan improved in 2005? Explain, citing the specific factors you took into account and telling why they are significant.
2. Suppose you were asked to prepare a schedule explaining the change in the value of assets. What factors might account for increases and decreases in this amount?
3. Suppose that you were asked to prepare a schedule explaining the change in the actuarial accrued liability. What factors might account for increases and decreases in this amount?
4. What is the total amount that employers should report as pension expenditures in 2005? How much must they add to, or subtract from, their pension liability accounts?

10-10

The major issue relating to agency funds is when they should be established.

Consider each of the following situations. Indicate whether (and why or why not) you think that the government should account for the transactions and resources in an agency fund, a governmental fund, or some other type of fiduciary fund. Not all the situations have been explicitly addressed in the text. Therefore, you may have to generalize from those that have been discussed.

1. A city extended sewer and water lines to a recently annexed community. Per agreement with the community, the improvements are to be paid for entirely by local residents. To finance the improvements, the city issued ten-year notes on behalf of the residents. It assessed the residents for the amount of the debt, plus interest. The city guaranteed the notes and agreed to collect the assessments from the residents and make appropriate payments to the noteholders. However, the city's role is primarily one of an intermediary. The residents, not the city, are expected to service the debt.
2. A state receives a federal law-enforcement grant intended to assist local communities in hiring additional police officers. The federal granting agency selects the cities and counties that are to receive the awards and determines the amounts they are to receive. The federal government, not the state, is responsible for monitoring grant compliance. The state's only responsibility is to write the checks to the cities and counties.
3. A state receives a federal educational grant intended to assist local school districts in hiring additional teachers. The federal granting agency establishes the criteria that the state is to use in determining the school districts to receive the awards and the amounts they are to receive. The district has no discretion in selecting recipients other than to apply the specified criteria.
4. A county collects sales taxes that it distributes among itself and the towns within its jurisdiction. The taxes are levied by the county and are divided among the recipient governments in accordance with a formula set forth in the legislation that authorized the tax.

10-11

The types of transactions affecting an agency fund (although not necessarily the exact amounts) can be derived from its statement of changes in assets and liabilities.

The statement at the bottom of this page is that of the Sewer User Fee Fund of Tucson, Arizona, a fund that "accounts for sewer user fees collected by the city and remitted to Pima County": Dates have been changed.

1. Prepare summary journal entries to record:
   a. The recognition of interest
   b. The receipt of interest
   c. Collection of $30,000 in sewer fees not previously recognized as receivables
   d. Payments to other governments of $45,000
2. Suppose $10,000 of the accounts receivable must be written off as uncollectible. Prepare an appropriate journal entry.

Statement of Changes in Assets and Liabilities (in thousands)

	Balance July 1, 2004	Additions	Deductions	Balance June 30, 2005
Assets				
Cash/deposits/pooled investments	$ 578	$55,227	$55,079	$ 726
Due from other funds	7	439	438	8
Accounts receivable	1,786	28,082	27,971	1,897
Interest receivable	1	31	29	3
Total assets	$2,372	$83,779	$83,517	$2,634
Liabilities				
Accounts payable	$ 2	$27,511	$27,512	$ 1
Due to other governmental agencies	2,370	55,914	55,651	2,633
Total liabilities	$2,372	$83,425	$83,163	$2,634

SOLUTION TO EXERCISE FOR REVIEW AND SELF-STUDY

1. A single employer plan covers the employees of only one employer (in this example, the employees of the state). A multiple employer plan covers the employees of more than one employer (e.g., when a state maintains a plan for the employees of all counties within the state).
2. If the plan were a defined contribution plan, the state would contribute a fixed percentage of employees' wages and salaries. No actuarial computations would be required.
3. If the state increased its projection of salary increases, then it is expecting that the current employees will be entitled to greater pensions upon their retirement. Similarly, if it decreased the assumed investment rate, then the contributions to date would have been inadequate. Hence, the actuarial liability for pension benefits already earned would increase. This change would increase the state's annual pension cost of the current year, but not by the full amount of the increase in the actuarial liability. As indicated in the note, the liability is being amortized over twenty-three years. Hence, the annual pension cost for the current year would increase by only one twenty-third of the total increase in the actuarial liability. In addition, the changes in salary and investment rates would affect the computation of the normal cost. It would thereby have an impact on the annual pension costs of both current and future years.
4. The net pension obligation represents the cumulative difference between what the state should have contributed to the pension plan (the annual pension cost) and what it actually contributed. If wages and salaries, and hence pensions, are accounted for in the general fund, then the net pension obligation (a long-term liability) would be reported only in the state's schedule of long-term obligations and government-wide statements, not in any particular fund.
5. If pensions are accounted for in an enterprise fund, then the net pension obligation would be reported in that fund.
6. The reported pension expenditure would be the actual contribution to the pension fund. The difference between the annual pension cost ($206,874) and the actual contribution ($196,374) would not be reported as a fund liability. Thus:

General Fund

Pension expenditure	$196,374	
Cash		$196,374

To record the annual pension contribution and expenditure

7. The reported pension expense would be the annual pension cost.

Enterprise Fund

Pension expense	$206,874	
Cash		$196,374
Net pension obligation		10,500

To record the annual pension contribution and expense

8. The percent of APC (annual pension cost) contributed represents the percentage of the annual pension cost as computed by the government's actuaries (consistent with the GASB guidelines) that was actually contributed. Thus, for 2005:

Actual contribution	$196,374
Annual pension cost	÷206,874
Percent of annual pension cost contributed	94.9%

9. The unfunded actuarial accrued liability is the excess of the actuarially computed pension liability over the pension plan's assets. By contrast, the net pension obligation is the cumulative difference between what the employer should have contributed to the pension plan (the annual pension cost) and what it actually contributed. The unfunded actuarial accrued liability relates to the pension plan (and thereby indirectly to the employer), whereas the net pension obligation relates directly to, and is reported on the balance sheet of, the employer. The unfunded actuarial accrued liability is being amortized mainly so that changes in the liability, attributable for example to plan improvements, do not affect reported expenditures or expenses entirely in the year in which they take place and thus make the expenditures or expenses appear excessively volatile.
10. The state's contribution of $196,374 would increase the plan's cash and, correspondingly would increase its net assets as reported on the plan's statement of its net assets. The increase in the $206,874 increase in unfunded actuarial accrued liability, however, would have no impact on the plan's statement of net assets. The plan's balance sheet reports only actual liabilities (those currently due to retirees), not actuarial obligations.
11. The amount due retirees would increase liabilities, thereby reducing net assets. Thus:

Retiree benefits	$150,000	
Benefits payable (liability)		$150,000

To record current obligations to retirees

"Retiree benefits" would be closed to net assets.

CHAPTER 11

Issues of Reporting, Disclosure, and Financial Analysis

Learning Objectives

After studying this chapter you should understand:

- Why the make-up of a government's or not-for-profit's reporting entity is an issue
- The criteria that the Governmental Accounting Standards Board (GASB) has established to determine the units that constitute a government's reporting entity
- The various ways of reporting component units
- The reports of public colleges and universities
- The main elements of a government's Comprehensive Annual Financial Report (CAFR)
- The critical factors to be taken into account in assessing a government's financial condition

This chapter, the final chapter that deals mainly with external reporting by governments, presents an overview of the annual financial report. It begins by considering the issue of the reporting entity—what affiliated organizations a primary entity must incorporate into its financial reports. Thereafter it highlights the structure of the annual report and the need for statistical information to supplement the financial statements. It then addresses reporting issues faced by public colleges and universities. It concludes by presenting an approach to assessing a government's financial condition.

WHY IS THE REPORTING ENTITY AN ISSUE FOR GOVERNMENTS?

The composition of the reporting entity has proven one of the least tractable issues facing business, government, and not-for-profit standard setters. As has long been recognized in the business sector, an organization's legal entity may differ from its economic entity. If a company controls another company, then its economic entity comprises the company itself plus its subsidiaries. Yet satisfactory definitions of control have proven illusive, and even the Financial Accounting Standards Board (FASB) has yet to develop standards that meet the challenges of today's complex organizational relationships.

The reporting entity issue in the government sector is delineated in the example that follows and its subsequent variations.

EXAMPLE *The Reporting Entity*

A city operates an electricity-generating facility that supplies power exclusively to its municipal subway system. The facility needs costly capital improvements, but owing to debt limitations the city is unable to borrow the required funds. To circumvent the limitations, the city forms a new unit of government, a public power authority, to which it transfers the generating facility. The facility is to be governed by a board of directors, the members of which will be the same officials that compose the city council. The authority will issue city-backed bonds, which it will repay from revenues earned from the sale of electricity to the city.

In this example, the power authority, though an independent legal entity, is within the economic and political control of the city, no less than if it were another city department. City council members govern the authority, and the city is obligated for its debt. The city is the sole beneficiary of its resources. Therefore, if the city's financial statements were to report on all of its economic assets and liabilities, they would have to encompass the assets and liabilities of the authority.

Consider, however, a continuum of modifications to the example:

- The authority's governing board, rather than being composed of city council members, is appointed by the city's mayor.
- The authority's governing board is independently elected, but the city retains the right to approve the authority's budget.
- The governing board is independently elected, and the city has no right to approve the authority's budget.

In this sequence of variations the city's ability to control the authority is gradually eroded and the economic borders between the city and the authority are made more pronounced. Consequently, with each variation the rationale for including the authority within the city's reporting entity is diminished. But where should standard setters draw the line?

This sequence of variations oversimplifies the problem, however, in that it focuses exclusively on whether the city *controls* the authority. In fact, the extent to which entities are economically intertwined cannot be assessed on the single vector of control. Economic interdependence is also measured by whether one organization shares geographic boundaries with the other, is responsible for its debts, must fund its deficits, can benefit from its surpluses, and is a major source of its revenues. Rule-making authorities have had to develop a multidimensional framework of standards that is appropriate for the over 80,000 U.S. governments, all of which are tied to at least one other government.

The following are but a very small sample of common intergovernmental relationships in the United States:

- Housing authorities established by cities to provide low-cost financing for residents of the cities
- Turnpike commissions established by states to finance and operate toll roads
- Volunteer fire departments partially funded by counties or towns
- Universities that receive state funds but are controlled by independently elected boards of regents

WHAT CRITERIA HAVE BEEN ESTABLISHED FOR GOVERNMENT REPORTING ENTITIES?

The current standards for governments are set forth in GASB Statement No. 14, *The Financial Reporting Entity.* This statement established the criteria for determining the units that should be included in a reporting entity and how they should be reported.

TYPES OF UNITS COMPOSING THE REPORTING ENTITY

Per Statement No. 14, a financial reporting entity should consist of a **primary government** and its **component units.**

A primary government can be a state government, a general purpose local government such as a municipality or a county, or a special purpose state or local government. Statement No. 14 explicitly states that "a primary government is any state government or general purpose local government (municipality or county)." Under the U.S. system of federalism, local governments are subunits of the states in which they are located and are subject to state control. Were the definition of a primary government not to explicitly include general purpose local governments, then virtually all cities, towns, and counties would be component units of their states rather than primary governments.

Special purpose governments include a vast array of authorities and districts, such as school districts, municipal utility districts, and transportation authorities. To qualify as a primary government, a special purpose government must have a separately elected governing body, be legally separate from other primary governments, and be *fiscally independent* of other governments. Fiscally independent implies that the government has the authority, without approval from other governments, to:

- Determine its budget
- Levy taxes and set rates
- Issue bonds

A *component unit* is a legally separate government for which the elected officials of the primary government are financially accountable. A component unit may also be an organization whose exclusion would cause a primary government's statements to be misleading or incomplete because of the nature and relationship between the two. Such a relationship would exist if the potential component unit were created solely to benefit the primary government. For example, to help New York City out of its financial difficulties in the mid-1970s, the State of New York established the Municipal Assistance Corporation (known as "Big MAC"). The function of the corporation was to supervise the city's fiscal affairs and to issue bonds on its behalf. Since the city was financially accountable to the corporation, not the other way around, the corporation would not qualify as a component unit were it not for this "misleading or incomplete" provision.

MEANING OF FINANCIALLY ACCOUNTABLE COMPONENT UNITS

The key criterion as to whether a primary government is financially accountable for another government—thus qualifying the other government as a component unit—is that either (1) the primary government appoints a voting majority of the unit's governing body or (2) a majority of the unit's governing body is composed of primary government officials.

In addition, the relationship between the two governments must satisfy either of two additional criteria:

- The primary government is able to *impose its will* upon the potential component unit. For example:
  - □ It can remove appointed members of the potential component unit's governing board.
  - □ It has the authority to modify or approve the unit's budget.
  - □ It can approve or modify the unit's fee charges.
  - □ It can veto, overrule, or modify decisions of the unit's governing board.
  - □ It can appoint, hire, reassign, or dismiss the unit's managers responsible for day-to-day operations.
- The component unit is able to provide specific financial benefits to, or impose specific financial burdens on, the primary government. For example:
  - □ The primary government is entitled to the potential component unit's financial resources.
  - □ It is legally obligated for, or has assumed the obligation to finance, the unit's deficits or is otherwise obligated to support the unit's operations.
  - □ It is obligated "in some manner" for the unit's debt, whether that obligation is express or implied.

EXAMPLE *Financially Accountable Component Units*

The Jefferson Hospital District was established to furnish medical aid and hospital care to indigent persons residing in Jefferson County. The district is governed by a board of trustees that sets policy for the district and oversees its day-to-day operations. The district is located entirely within Jefferson County and the county's commissioners' court appoints the members of the district's board of trustees. The commissioners' court has the authority to approve the hospital district's budget.

The hospital district is a component unit of the county. It satisfies the two criteria of financial accountability in that:

- The county appoints the voting majority of the district's governing board.
- The county's authority to approve the district's budget gives it the ability to impose its will on the district.

As a general rule, a potential component unit is fiscally accountable to a primary government *only* if the primary government controls the appointment of its governing board. However, Statement No. 14 provides for an exception. Even if its board is independently elected and thereby outside the influence of the primary government, a potential component unit may be considered financially accountable to a primary government if the unit is *fiscally dependent* on the primary government. A unit is fiscally dependent on the primary government if it is unable to determine its own budget, levy taxes or set rates, or issue bonds without approval of the primary government.

EXAMPLE *Fiscal Dependency*

A school district has its own independently elected governing board. Nevertheless, the board of supervisors of the surrounding county must approve the district's budget and tax rates.

The school district is financially accountable to the county because it is financially dependent upon it. Thus, even though the county has no control over the district's governing board, the district would nevertheless satisfy the criteria of a component unit.

WAYS OF REPORTING COMPONENT UNITS

Governments must report the component units in either of two ways:

- ***Discrete presentation:*** reporting one or more units in a single column, apart from the data of the primary government.
- ***Blending:*** combining the unit's transactions and balances as if they were part of the primary government—that is, reporting the unit's special revenue funds, capital projects funds, debt service funds, and permanent funds as if they were corresponding funds of the primary government.

Discrete presentation is the default means of reporting. **Blending** is appropriate only when the relationship between the primary government and the component unit is so close that the two governments, albeit legally separate, are substantively the same. Either of the following two circumstances would indicate that the two units are substantively the same and should be blended:

- The two units are controlled by governing boards having the same members (as would be the case if the members of a city council also served as the component unit's board of directors).
- The component unit provides services solely to the primary government. A common example of this type of relationship is when a financing authority issues debt and acquires property exclusively for lease to the primary government. This criterion is satisfied only when the component unit provides the services to the primary government itself, not to the same citizens who are served by the primary government.

Governments must report component units that satisfy the criteria for blending as if the component units were an integral part of the government. They would incorporate them into both their fund and their government-wide statements. By contrast, they must report all other component units (i.e., those that must be presented discretely) only in their government-wide statements, not in their funds statements. The rationale for this distinction is that, by the very criteria for blending, blended component units are as much a part of the government as the units that it accounts for in its own funds.

Discrete Presentation

In their government-wide statements, governments should report those component units that must be presented discretely to the right of the "totals" columns of the primary government. However, they have several options:

- They may combine all the component units in a single column.
- They may report each component unit in a separate column.
- They may combine component units into any number of columns based on the characteristics of the component units (e.g., all power authorities into one column, all housing authorities into another).

Thus, for example,

Total Primary Government	*Component Unit No. 1*	*Component Unit Nos. 2, 3, 4*

Blending

When a primary government blends one or more component units into its own financial statements, it reports the funds of the component units as if they were its own funds. Thus, it accounts for the component units' special revenue funds as if they were its own special revenue funds, its debt service funds as if they were its own debt service funds, etc. However, owing to the significance of the primary government's general fund, there is an exception. A primary government should report only one general fund. It should report the general funds of its component units as if they were its own special revenue funds. In determining whether they are major or nonmajor special revenue funds, the government should apply the same criteria as it does to its own funds.

Required Disclosures

Irrespective of how it reports its component units, the primary government must disclose detailed information as to each *major* component unit. This information can be shown in one of three places:

- In the government-wide statements themselves (i.e., by presenting the component unit in a separate column)
- In notes to the financial statements
- In combining financial statements (one column for each major component unit) within the government's basic financial statements, presented in a section following the fiduciary funds

Data that must be disclosed include a key statement of net assets and a statement of activities accounts and should be drawn from the totals column of the component unit's own government-wide financial statements. The decision as to whether a component unit is major or nonmajor is made by the government officials and is based on the significance of it's the unit's relationship to the primary government.

Table 11-1 contains excerpts of Charlotte's note on its component units.

TABLE 11-1
Note as to Reporting Entity
June 30, 2002 (dollar amounts in thousands)

The City of Charlotte (City) is a municipal corporation governed by an elected mayor and eleven-member council. The accompanying financial statements present the activities of the City and its two component units, entities for which the City is financially accountable. The Charlotte Firefighters' Retirement System (System) is so intertwined with the City that it is, in substance, the same as the City. Accordingly, the System is blended and reported as if it was part of the City. The Charlotte Auditorium-Coliseum-Convention Center Authority (Authority) is reported in a separate column in the government-wide financial statements to emphasize that it is legally separate from the City. The following table describes the City's component units:

Component Unit	Criteria for Inclusion	Reporting Method	Separate Financial Statements
Charlotte Firefighters' Retirement System	The System provides retirement, disability, and death benefits to civil service employees of the Charlotte Fire Department. These services are exclusively for the City.	Blended	Charlotte Firefighters' Retirement System 428 East Fourth Street, Suite 205 Charlotte, North Carolina 28202
Charlotte Auditorium-Coliseum-Convention Center Authority	A "special district" as defined by state statutes. The City Council appoints the governing board and the City pays outstanding general obligation bonded debt. Net operating proceeds are to be used as directed by City Council.	Discrete	Auditorium-Coliseum-Convention Center Authority 100 Paul Buck Boulevard Post Office Box 669247 Charlotte, North Carolina 28266-9247

The Charlotte Housing Authority (Housing Authority), which is excluded from the City's financial statements, is considered a related organization. The City Council appoints the Housing Authority's governing board; however, the City is not financially accountable for the Housing Authority.

The Charlotte Transit Center, Inc., is a joint venture resulting from an agreement between the City and Bank of America. The corporation was established to build and operate a public transportation terminal known as the Charlotte Transit Center (Center). The Board of Directors is comprised of two members appointed by the City and two members appointed by Bank of America. The City provided the land and Bank of America constructed the building. The Center has two sections, transit and retail. The City funds all expenses related to the transit section and common areas which benefit transit riders and employees. Bank of America funds all expenses related to the retail area which is available for lease to tenants. The City does not have an equity interest but does have an ongoing financial responsibility because the Center's existence depends on continued funding by the City. The City's expenditures related to the transit section are reflected in the Public Transit Enterprise Fund. The financial statements of the Center, which has an August 31 year-end, may be obtained from the following address:

Charlotte Transit Center, Inc.
c/o Lincoln Property Company
100 North Tryon Street, Suite 3350
Charlotte, North Carolina 28202

WAYS OF REPORTING OTHER TYPES OF UNITS

Joint Ventures

Governments sometimes enter into joint ventures with other governments. A **joint venture** is a contractual arrangement, whereby two or more participants agree to carry out a common activity, with each sharing in both its risks and rewards. For example, two cities (e.g., Dallas and Fort Worth) may join together to construct and operate an airport.

If a government has invested in a joint venture and thereby has an equity interest in it (i.e., owns a share of it) then it should account for the investment as an asset. If it made the investment with proprietary fund resources, it would record the asset in a proprietary fund. It would account for gains and losses on the *equity* basis (just as a corporation accounts for unconsolidated subsidiaries in which it has a 20 percent or more interest).

If the government made the investment from a governmental fund, then it would report it as it does other long-lived assets. Since governmental funds are accounted for on a modified accrual basis, it would not report the investment in the fund itself, but only in the schedule of capital assets. Moreover, it would recognize revenue in the governmental fund based on the usual criteria for that fund. Generally, for example, it would recognize revenue from the joint venture as the venture declares dividends that satisfy the "available" criterion. However, in its government-wide statements, the primary government would report its entire interest in the joint venture, measured on an equity basis, and would recognize revenue on a full accrual basis.

Related Organizations

Statement No. 14 defines a **related organization,** as an entity that satisfies the criterion of financial accountability (that is, the primary government appoints a voting majority of its governing board) but neither of the other two criteria (that is, the primary government cannot impose its will upon the organization and there is no potential for the organization to provide specific financial benefits to, or impose specific financial burdens upon, the primary government). For example, a transit authority would qualify as a city's related organization if the city council appoints a majority of the authority's governing board, but the governing board has the power to levy taxes, authorize the issue of debt, set fares, and adopt its own budget. Since a related organization does not qualify as a component unit, it therefore cannot be incorporated into the primary government's basic financial statements. Nevertheless, per Statement No. 14, the primary government should describe each organization to which it is related and indicate the nature of the relationship.

Other Organizations with Special Ties to the Reporting Entity

Governments may be closely tied to entities other than component units and related organizations. These entities may be distinguished from component units and related organizations in that the primary government does not appoint a majority of their governing boards and they are not fiscally dependent on the primary government. Many of these organizations qualify as tax-exempt, not-for-profit organizations under the Internal Revenue Code, Section 501(c)(3), and their purpose is to provide financial and other types of assistance to the government with which they are associated.

One example of an affiliated organization is a state university's development foundation, the main mission of which is to raise funds for the university. Although its officers might work closely with university administrators, the foundation would be governed by an independent board of trustees. The university would have no direct or indirect control over the foundation.

Other examples of entities that might be considered potential affiliated organizations include:

- A state university's football booster club
- A public school's parent–teacher association
- A government hospital's fund-raising foundation

There can be a wide variety of relationships between governments and associated organizations. Consequently, the GASB has found it extraordinarily difficult to define precisely the types of organizations that governments should report upon in their financial statements and to determine how governments should present information about them into their financial statements. Nevertheless, after many preliminary efforts, the GASB issued Statement No. 39, *Determining Whether Certain Organizations Are Component Units.*

In Statement No. 39, the GASB amended Statement No. 14 to require governments to report "certain organizations" as discretely presented component units if they are *legally separate* from the primary government, are *tax-exempt*, and meet *all three* of the following conditions:

1. The economic resources received or held by the separate organization are entirely or almost entirely for the direct benefit of the primary government, its component units, or its constituents.
2. The primary government, or its component units, is entitled to, or has the ability to otherwise access, a majority of the economic resources received or held by the separate organization.
3. The economic resources received or held by an individual organization that the specific primary government, or its component units, is entitled to, or has the ability to otherwise access, are significant to that primary government.

The last provision is expected to exempt most small organizations, such as parent–teacher associations and booster clubs. If an organization does not meet the three criteria, governments should nevertheless report it in accord with Statement No. 14 if its exclusion would render the primary government's financial statements misleading or incomplete.

EXAMPLE *A Closely Affiliated Organization*

A state university cooperative bookstore is incorporated as a Section 501(c)(3) not-for-profit entity. The bookstore is governed by a nine-member board of directors. Four members of the board are elected by university students, four are appointed by the university president, and one (the chair) is elected by the other eight members. The bookstore distributes a portion of its profits as sales rebates to students and faculty customers. It contributes the balance, excluding amounts that it retains for expansion, capital replacement and the like, to the university and to student organizations in support of specific programs and activities. In a recent year it distributed $2 million to the university and the student organizations. The total university budget is $1 billion. In the event that the bookstore should be liquidated, its resources would revert to the university.

The bookstore is legally separate from the university, is tax exempt, its resources (after rebates) are entirely for the benefit of the university and the university is ultimately entitled to the bookstore's resources. However, the resources of the bookstore are not significant to the university and therefore the university need not incorporate the bookstore into its reporting unit.

EXAMPLE *Summary of Statement No. 14*

A legally separate financing authority was created to improve access to low and moderate income housing in a state by providing mortgage loans to homebuyers. The governing board of the authority is appointed by the governor. The authority determines its own budget, holds title to property in its own name, and controls its own day-to-day operations. Mortgage loans are made according to guidelines included in the authority's enabling legislation. The authority is permitted to issue debt, subject to a statutory limitation. All bonds issued to provide mortgage loans are secured by first mortgages on the related properties and are payable from the proceeds of mortgage repayments. In the event that the authority determines that funds will not be sufficient for the payment of the principal and interest on its bonds during the next succeeding state fiscal year, the chairman of the authority certifies to the governor the amount required to pay such principal and interest. The governor is obligated to include these amounts in the state budget. However, the legislature has no obligation to appropriate funds for the authority.[1]

The flowchart in Figure 11-1 can be used to assess whether and, if so how the financing authority should be incorporated into the financial statements of the state:

- Is the financing authority legally separate? Yes.
- Does the state appoint a voting majority of its board? Yes.
- Is the state able to impose its will on the financing authority? There is no evidence that any one of the factors indicative of an ability to impose will are present.
- Is there a financial benefit/burden relationship? Yes, the state is obligated, in "some manner," for the authority's debt. It must include the debt in its budget. Therefore, the agency qualifies as a component unit.
- Are the governing boards of the state and the authority the same? No.
- Does the authority provide services entirely or almost entirely to the state? No. Therefore, the state should report the authority as a component unit, using discrete presentation.

Controversy Surrounding Statement No. 14

The objective of the GASB in promulgating Statement No. 14 was to ensure that a government's financial statements include information on all organizations for which it is accountable. Yet in the eyes of critics, the statement requires governments to cast out nets that are both too wide and too fine, thereby drawing into their reporting entities organizations for which they are only remotely accountable. In the summary example, the state would have to include the financing authority in its reporting entity even if, in reality, it had only a minimum degree of accountability for its activities and obligations. For example, if the governor's appointees to the board served for nonrenewable terms and could not be removed from office except for cause, then the governor may have little ability to influence them. Similarly, if it were highly improbable that the authority would default on its obligations, and, even if it did, it was unlikely that the legislature would appropriate the funds to make up the deficiencies, then the state would bear little financial risk. Nevertheless, the GASB believed that the voting majority criteria, coupled with the other requirements (i.e., imposition of will or financial benefit/burden), provided reasonable assurance that governments would have to include in their reporting entity only other governmental units for which they were legitimately accountable.

In addition, critics have charged that when a government aggregates two or more component units into a single column for discrete presentation, the information loses significance. This is especially true, they note, when the aggregated units engage in totally dissimilar activities (e.g., a power authority and a housing authority).

WHAT OTHER ELEMENTS MAKE UP THE COMPREHENSIVE ANNUAL FINANCIAL REPORT?

In Chapter 2, we briefly summarized the main features of the Comprehensive Annual Financial Report (CAFR). In this chapter, we expand upon the earlier discussion.

[1] Drawn from GASB Implementation Guide (June 1994), a guide to implementing Statement No. 14, *The Financial Reporting Entity* (June 1991).

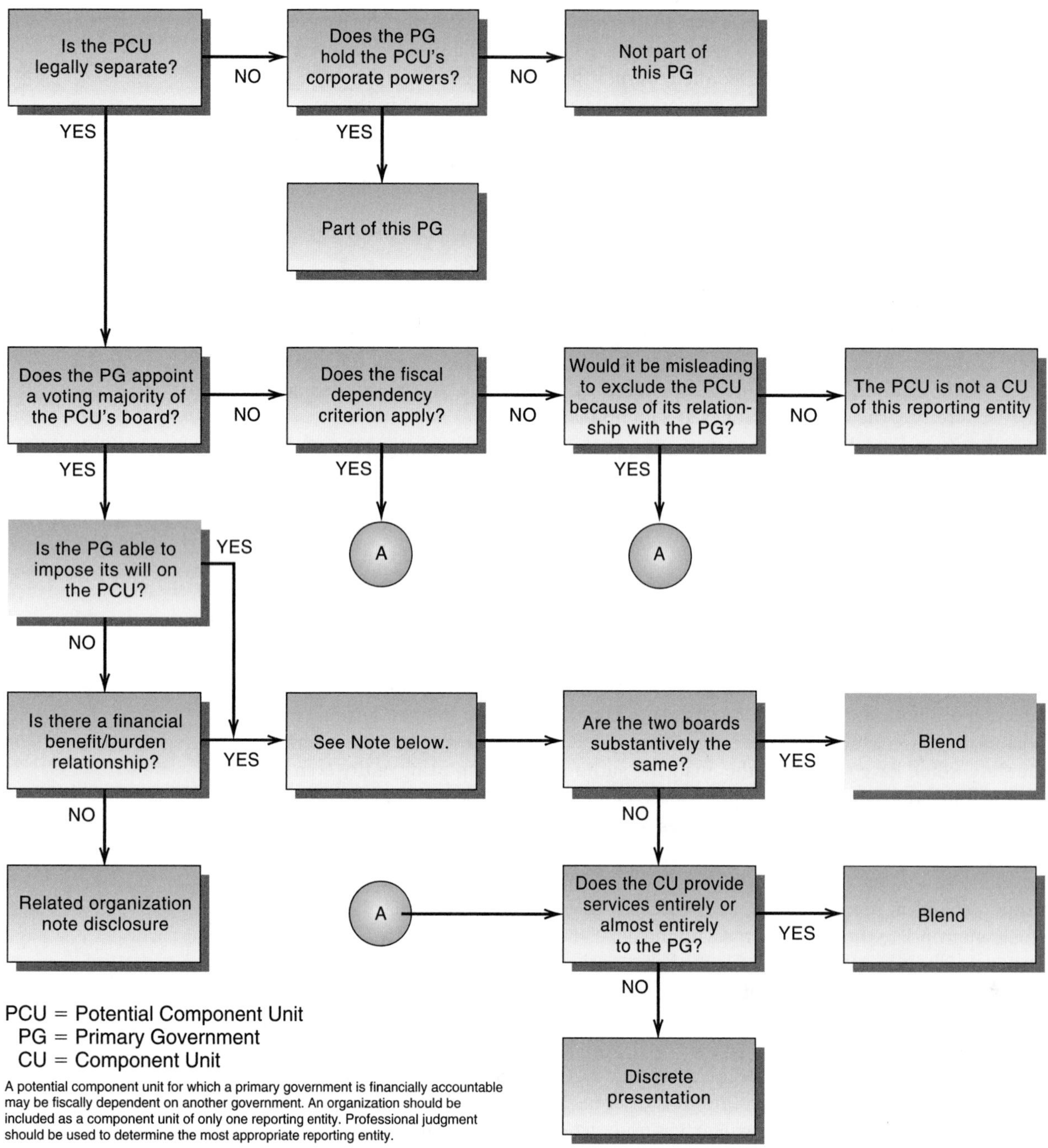

FIGURE 11-1 Flowchart of Reporting Entity Decision Process

Source: *Codification.* Section 2100.901.

As noted in Chapter 2, the CAFR is divided into three main sections:

- Introductory section
- Financial section
- Statistical section

SIGNIFICANT COMPONENTS OF THE INTRODUCTORY SECTION

The introductory section consists of:

- The table of contents
- A letter of transmittal
- Any other material deemed appropriate by management, such as the Government Finance Officers Association's certificate of achievement.

Traditionally, the letter of transmittal, usually from the government's chief financial officer (often cosigned by the city manager or other chief executive officer) and addressed to the governing board and the citizenry, has been the most significant component of the introductory section of the CAFR. This letter has served as a written "state of the government" address, describing local economic conditions, providing an overview of the government's financial status, setting forth major initiatives and summarizing key budgetary and accounting practices. Much of the information that has been included in the letter of transmittal must now be incorporated into the required management's discussion and analysis, an element of the CAFR's financial section. Hence, the role the letter of transmittal will play in the future is uncertain.

The introductory section would generally contain a "certificate of achievement for excellence in the financial reporting," if one has been awarded by the Government Finance Officers Association (GFOA) for the report of the previous year. The certificate of achievement is awarded to governments whose annual reports conform to GFOA standards. The GFOA does not, however, audit the government's books and records and does not therefore vouch for the accuracy of the underlying information. Subsequent to Orange County's 1994 multibillion dollar investment losses, reporters questioned GFOA officials as to how, in light of obvious fiscal mismanagement, the county was awarded a certificate of achievement. The officials painstakingly had to explain that investment losses are by no means necessarily indicative of improper financial reporting and that even if they were, the certificate of achievement is not an endorsement of the underlying data.

IMPORTANT PARTS OF THE FINANCIAL SECTION

The financial section consists of:

- The auditors' report
- The management's discussion and analysis (MD&A)
- The basic financial statements
- Required supplementary information other than the MD&A
- Combining statements, individual statements, and schedules

The Auditors' Report

The auditors' report serves the same general function in financial statements of governments as it does in business: It provides assurance that the statements are presented fairly and are in accordance with generally accepted accounting principles. However, as will be addressed in Chapter 15, audits of governments are considerably more comprehensive than those of businesses.

The typical audit is undertaken to express an opinion on the financial statements taken as a whole. It is not designed to cover all information included in the CAFR. Accordingly, auditors do not always subject statistical data, individual funds (if presented), and supplementary information to the same range of audit procedures as the basic financial statements.

The Management's Discussion and Analysis (MD&A)

Although it may be easy to dismiss the MD&A as little more than a re-embodiment of the letter of transmittal, it has the potential to become one of the most informative elements of the CAFR. As was noted in Chapter 1 and is emphasized again later in this chapter, basic financial statements, no matter how comprehensive and detailed, can never, by themselves, provide adequate information as to a government's financial standing. In large part, this is because a government's fiscal health is as much dependent on the economic environment from which it draws its resources as on the resources already within its control. It is also, however, because the financial statements fail to provide sufficient information on the nature and extent of services that the government will be expected to provide in the future. Governments have long been required to include in the statistical section of the CAFR extensive data on both demographic and economic trends. These data, however, are generally presented in tables. It was left to the statement users to interpret them and place them in perspective.

The MD&A contains a wealth of information and insights not previously available in the CAFR. Equally important, however, it provides government officials the opportunity to present the government's fiscal condition in a way that is understandable to the average citizen.

Table 11-2 highlights the main features of the MD&A as required by the GASB.

The Basic Financial Statements

The basic financial statements, as emphasized throughout this text, are of two main types: government-wide and fund. There are only two government-wide statements:

- The statement of net assets (balance sheet)
- The statement of activities (statement of revenues and expenses)

Fund statements must be prepared for each of the three categories of funds—a total of seven statements:

- Governmental funds
  - ◻ Balance sheet
  - ◻ Statement of revenues, expenditures, and changes in fund balances
- Proprietary funds
  - ◻ Balance sheet
  - ◻ Statement of revenues, expenses, and changes in net assets
  - ◻ Statement of cash flows

TABLE 11-2

Key Types of Information That Must Be Included in the MD&A

- A brief description of the required financial statements
- Condensed financial information derived from government-wide statements
- An analysis of the government's overall financial position and results of operations, including impact of important economic factors
- An analysis of balances and transactions of individual funds
- An analysis of differences between original and final budget amounts and between actual and budgeted amounts
- A description of changes in capital assets and long-term debt during the year
- A discussion of the condition of infrastructure assets
- A description of currently known facts, decisions, or conditions that have, or are expected to have, a material effect on financial position or results of operations

- Fiduciary funds
  - Statement of fiduciary net assets
  - Statement of changes in fiduciary net assets

The statements for the governmental and proprietary fund categories focus only on major funds. Nonmajor funds are aggregated into a single column. Major funds are those in which total assets, revenues, or expenditures/expenses are at least 10 percent of the relevant fund category (governmental or enterprise) and 5 percent of the corresponding total for all governmental and enterprise funds combined. The concept of "major funds" does not apply to the fiduciary funds category. Instead, fiduciary fund statements should present all fiduciary funds aggregated into columns by each fund type: pension (and other employee benefit) trust funds, investment trust funds, private purpose trusts, and agency funds.

As noted previously in the discussion of component units, governments may elect to provide detailed information about their major component units in the form of combining statements. If they choose this option, the combining statements (one column for each unit) should be included after the fund financial statements.

Required notes are considered an essential element of the basic financial statements. Similar to notes to the financial statements of businesses, these describe significant accounting policies and disclose details of various accounts, commitments, and contingencies. Most significantly, per the provisions of Statement No. 34, the notes must include the schedules of capital assets and long-term liabilities. These schedules reconcile, by type of asset and liability, beginning and ending balances and indicate the amount of depreciation allocated to each of the government's main functions. The notes also should include a summary reconciliation of the governmental fund statements to the government-wide statements unless this information is provided at the bottom of the fund statements.

Required Supplementary Information (RSI)

Governments are required to incorporate statistical data and information that supplements the basic financial statements into the financial section of the CAFR schedules. Examples include:

- The budget-to-actual comparisons
- Information about infrastructure condition (for those governments that elect not to depreciate these types of assets)
- Details of pension actuarial valuations

Required supplementary information has much in common with the notes to the basic financial statements. In both sections governments present GASB mandated schedules and data. However, whereas the notes are considered part of the basic financial statements, the required supplementary information is not. As a consequence the RSI may be subject to a lower level of auditor scrutiny than the notes.

Combining Statements, Individual Statements, and Schedules

The combining statements support and supplement the basic statements. The basic fund statements for governmental and proprietary funds have columns for each of the major funds and a single column in which all of the nonmajor funds are aggregated. The combining statements provide the details of the nonmajor funds, one column for each of the funds. The totals columns of the combining statements tie into the amounts reported in the nonmajor funds column of the funds statements. Except for fiduciary funds, GASB Statement No. 34 changed the emphasis of reporting from fund type (e.g., special revenue funds, capital projects funds) to major funds. Therefore, combining statements for nonmajor funds are optional, not required.

Internal service funds, as indicated in Chapter 9 on business-type activities, are presented in the proprietary fund statements in a single column that combines all of a government's funds of that type. Internal service funds do not have to be separately reported in the basic fund statements even if they would otherwise meet the criteria of major funds. Therefore, individual internal service funds may be reported upon in the combining statements.

Governments may also include in this section statements of individual funds necessary to demonstrate compliance with legal and contractual provisions. For example, a government might present a statement of a nonmajor enterprise fund so as to show that it has made proper use of cash or other assets that secure outstanding revenue bonds. Similarly, they may incorporate in this section schedules that tie together data that are dispersed among several statements but which are nevertheless informative when presented together. Thus, a government might present a table that summarizes all its investments, irrespective of the funds in which they are held.

NEED FOR, AND KEY FEATURES OF, THE STATISTICAL SECTION

Statistical data are a necessity because of key limitations of government financial reports. Governments have the power to tax. They can thereby command the resources of their constituents. The fiscal wherewithal of a government cannot be assessed merely by examining the resources actually within the government's control. The resources potentially within its control must also be taken into account.

Both Orange County, California, and Bridgeport, Connecticut, sought the protection of bankruptcy courts in the 1990s. The financial statements of both governments were equally dismal. Yet their overall fiscal conditions were dramatically different. Orange County was one of the wealthiest communities in the country while Bridgeport was one of the poorest. If Orange County defaulted on its debts or reduced public services, it did so not because it lacked access to the necessary resources, but because the citizenry elected not to draw upon them.

In addition, financial statements present key financial indicators, such as fund balances, revenues, and expenditures for only a current year. Single point data are, by themselves, not very useful in assessing a government's fiscal condition. Only by examining trends can an analyst make a reasonable assessment as to where a government has been and where it is heading in the future.

The statistical section supplements the financial statements. As this text goes to press, the GASB Codification specifies fifteen tables and schedules that governments must include in their statistical section. However, in August 2003, the GASB issued an exposure draft of a pronouncement that would modify and supplement the current requirements. Per the proposed pronouncement, a government will have to present in its statistical section five categories of information:

- financial trends that show how its financial position has changed over time;
- revenue capacity data that point to its ability to generate revenue from its own sources;
- debt capacity measures that reflect on its current debt burden and its ability to issue additional debt in the future;
- demographic and economic statistics that shed light on the socioeconomic environment in which it operates and facilitates comparisons with other governments; and
- operating data that help give greater understanding to the dollar amounts reported in the basic financial statements.

Table 11-3 provides specific examples of the data in each category that the GASB will likely require.

TABLE 11-3
Examples of Statistical Information to Be Reported in the Statistical Section of the CAFR

(Generally this information will have to be presented for the most recent ten years.)

Financial trends

- The components of net assets (invested in capital assets net of related debt, restricted, and unrestricted)
- Changes in net assets, including expenses, general revenues, and programmatic revenues

Revenue capacity

- Tax rates, including those for overlapping jurisdictions
- Tax levies and collections
- Value of property by category (e.g., residential, commercial, tax exempt)

Debt capacity

- Ratios of debt by category (general obligation, revenue, leases, loans, certificates of participation) such as debt per capital and debt to total personal income
- Amount of overlapping debt
- Details of debt limitations
- Details of debt that is backed by pledged revenues

Demographic and economic

- Population
- Total and per capita personal income
- Unemployment rate
- Largest employers including number of employees and percentage of total employment that each represents

Operating

- Number of employees by program or function
- Indicators of demand or level of service by function (for example, for police activity these might include number of reported crimes, number of arrests, number of responses to 911 calls)
- Volume, usage, and nature of capital assets by function (for example, for a motor vehicle pool this might include number of vehicles by type, mileage, and percentage of fleet in service)
- Data on pension and post-employment benefit plans

Source: Proposed Statement of the Governmental Accounting Standards Board, *Economic Condition Reporting: The Statistical Section*, an amendment of NCGA Statement 1, August 2003.

WHAT ARE THE REPORTING REQUIREMENTS FOR COLLEGES, UNIVERSITIES, AND OTHER SPECIAL-PURPOSE GOVERNMENTS?

GENERAL REQUIREMENTS

To this point, the text has focused mainly on "general purpose" governments, such as towns, cities, countries, and states. Many (perhaps even most) government units serve only a single, well-defined, purpose. These include universities and special districts that provide utility, health, and educational services. These governments are legal entities in their own right, but may be component units of other governments. Nevertheless, they often are either required to, or elect to, issue their own financial statements.

Broadly speaking, GASB Statement No. 34's reporting guidelines direct that special-purpose governments that issue stand-alone financial statements should prepare the same types of statements as general-purpose governments unless they engage in such a narrow range of activities that a complete set of financial statements would be unwarranted. Thus, special-purpose governments that engage in more than one program or engage in both business- and governmental-type activities must prepare both government-wide and fund statements. They must adhere to the same reporting and disclosure requirements as general-purpose governments.

By contrast, special-purpose governments that engage in only a single governmental (as opposed to proprietary) program (e.g., a park or road district) have an option. First, they may combine their government-wide and fund statements into a single statement. That is, in one column they can present the government-wide full accrual data and in one or more columns (one for each fund) they can present the fund, modified accrual, data. However, in another column, they must show the differences for each line item between the fund and the government-wide data. The differences (the amounts that reconcile the fund financial data to the government-wide data) must be described and explained either on the face of the financial statements or in an accompanying schedule.

As an alternative, special-purpose governments that engage in only a single governmental program may present separate government-wide and fund statements, but may present the government-wide statement of activities in a simpler format than that required for general purpose governments. Thus, for example, instead of the multicolumn statement (with revenues being deducted from expenses) they can show both revenues and expenses in two or more rows within a single column. However, unlike in the conventional income statements of businesses (and in keeping with the spirit of the statement of activities required of general-purpose governments), the program revenues must be deducted from the program expenses. The difference—the net expenses to be covered from other sources—should be followed by contributions to endowments, transfers, and extraordinary items.

Special purpose governments engaged only in business-type activities need present only the statements required for enterprise funds—a balance sheet, statement of revenues and expenses, and a statement of cash flows. They must also, however, present the other key elements of the financial section of a CAFR—an MD&A, notes, and required supplementary information.

REQUIREMENTS FOR COLLEGES AND UNIVERSITIES

U.S. higher education is characterized by diversity unparalleled in other countries. Not only is our system dichotomized between public and private institutions, but colleges and universities range in size from small liberal arts colleges of a few hundred students to multicampus systems of a hundred thousand or more students. As a consequence, standard setting has been beset by controversy, not only over specific accounting and reporting standards but even as to which bodies should have rule-making authority. When the GASB was being established, constituents of private colleges and universities contended that the FASB, not the GASB, should have jurisdiction over all colleges and universities, whereas those of the GASB asserted that GASB should have responsibility for at least government-operated institutions. The issue was resolved by granting the FASB jurisdiction over all not-for-profit (private) colleges and universities and the GASB over all government (public) colleges and universities. Today, therefore, not-for-profit colleges and universities follow the FASB pronouncements pertaining to not-for-profit organizations. These will be discussed in the following chapter. Government colleges and universities must adhere to the same GASB pronouncements as other types of governments.

Accounting and reporting by colleges and universities posed especially thorny issues to the GASB owing to several considerations, some of which are that:

- Public colleges and universities have much in common with their not-for-profit counterparts, so comparability is clearly desirable.

- Most colleges and universities have a long tradition of using an accounting and reporting model designed especially for them. In recent years this model was set forth by the American Institute of Certified Public Accountants. Some institutions, however, most notably community colleges, have used the standard government model.
- Colleges and universities are unique institutions that differ from other governments in how they are funded and managed. For example, although colleges and universities have both restricted funds and auxiliary enterprises, most do not budget by fund. Therefore, statement users may have only limited interest in fund-by-fund information. Auxiliary enterprises are the units of a college or university that carry-out business-type activities and are funded mainly by user charges. They typically include intercollegiate athletics, dormitories, food services, and bookstores.

With these considerations in mind (and after much debate), the GASB decided that colleges and universities should be subject to the same reporting requirements as other special-purpose governments—but with a loophole.[2] The loophole is that most public colleges and universities satisfy Statement No. 34's criteria of entities that engage exclusively in business-type activities. They qualify as business-type enterprises because (per the standards for enterprise fund reporting) "enterprise funds *may* be used to report any activity for which a fee is charged to external users for goods or services."[3] Therefore, public colleges and universities have a choice: they may elect to report as special purpose entities engaging (1) only in business-type activities, (2) only in governmental activities, or (3) in both. Most colleges and universities lobbied the GASB to be able to report as business-type entities, and it is thereby probable that most will opt to report as special-purpose governments engaged only in business-type activities.

As noted earlier, a special-purpose government engaging only in business-type activities need prepare only a statement of net assets, statement of revenues and expenses and a statement of cash flow. They need not present detailed fund statements. The statement of net assets and statement of revenues and expenses would, of course, have to be prepared on a full accrual basis. These statements must include capital assets and depreciation. The University of Virginia's required statement of net assets is illustrated in Table 11-4a. The required statement of revenues, expenses, and changes in net assets is in Table 11-4b and the statement of cash flows is in Table 11-4c.

Statement No. 34 requires all governments that use enterprise fund accounting to present segment information in notes to the financial statements. It defines a segment as any identifiable activity for which revenue bonds have been issued and which thereby has an identifiable revenue stream pledged in support of those bonds. For colleges and universities, segments are likely to include auxiliary enterprises such as dormitories, bookstores, and intercollegiate athletics. Required segment information includes key elements from the statement of net assets, statement of activities, and statement of cash flows.

The statement of revenues and expenses of a government that elects business-type reporting would usually be in object classification format. That is, its reported expenses would be items such as salaries, utilities, and supplies. To supplement this information the GASB encourages (but does not require) colleges and universities to present cost information about their various programs and activities.

[2] GASB Statement No. 35, *Basic Financial Statements—and Management's Discussion and Analysis—for Public Colleges and Universities* (An Amendment of GASB Statement No. 34).

[3] GASB Statement No. 34, para. 67.

TABLE 11-4A
University of Virginia
Statement of Net Assets
As of June 30, 2002 (in thousands)

ASSETS	
Current assets	
Cash and cash equivalents	$ 205,509
Short-term investments	205,096
Accounts receivable, net	155,939
Prepaid expenses	6,940
Inventories	13,246
Notes receivable, net	4,712
Other	3
Total current assets	$ 591,445
Non-current assets	
Restricted cash and cash equivalents	$ 30,171
Endowment investments	1,801,066
Other long-term investments	220,502
Deposit with bond trustee	8,881
Appropriations available for plant	31,927
Notes receivable, net	22,263
Pledges receivable, net	30,529
Capital assets, net	1,198,072
Goodwill	1,983
Other	429
Total non-current assets	$3,345,823
Total assets	$3,937,268
LIABILITIES	
Current liabilities	
Accounts payable and accrued liabilities	$ 122,007
Deferred revenue	57,690
Obligations under securities lending	3,853
Deposits held in custody for others	133,744
Long-term liabilities, current portion	53,151
Advance from Treasurer of Virginia	321
Total current liabilities	$ 370,766
Non-current liabilities	
Long-term debt	$ 318,967
Other non-current liabilities	20,639
Total non-current liabilities	339,606
Total liabilities	$ 710,372
NET ASSETS	
Invested in capital assets, net of related debt	$ 868,783
Restricted:	
Non-expendable	282,440
Expendable	1,201,241
Unrestricted	874,432
Total net assets	$3,226,896

TABLE 11–4B
University of Virginia
Statement of Revenues, Expenses, and Changes in Net Assets
As of June 30, 2002 (in thousands)

REVENUES	
Operating revenues	
Student tuition and fees (net of scholarship allowances of $34,115,874)	$ 177,913
Patient services (net of charity care of $250,689,581)	568,372
Federal grants and contracts	210,624
State and local grants and contracts	7,632
Non-governmental grants and contracts	43,558
Sales and services of educational departments	21,464
Auxiliary enterprises revenue (net of scholarship allowances of $5,398,179)	77,070
Other operating revenues	10,374
Total operating revenues	$1,117,007
EXPENSES	
Operating expenses	
Compensation and benefits	$ 796,959
Supplies and other services	426,501
Student aid	34,156
Utilities	56,227
Depreciation	98,628
Other	22,522
Total operating expenses	$1,434,993
Operating income (loss)	$ (317,986)
NON-OPERATING REVENUES (EXPENSES)	
State appropriations	$ 176,177
Payments from Commonwealth for indigent care	21,195
Gifts	65,016
Investment income	26,975
Interest on capital asset-related debt	(12,038)
Losses on affiliated company sold	(12,113)
Other non-operating revenues (expenses)	(935)
Net non-operating revenues	264,277
Income before other revenues, expenses, gains, or losses	$ (53,709)
Capital appropriations	16,595
Capital grants and gifts	11,509
Additions to permanent endowments	63,701
Total other revenues	$ 91,805
Increase in net assets	$ 38,096
NET ASSETS	
Net assets—beginning of year	$3,188,800
Net assets—end of year	$3,226,896

TABLE 11–4C
University of Virginia
Statement of Cash Flows
As of June 30, 2002 (in thousands)

CASH FLOWS FROM OPERATING ACTIVITIES	
Tuition and fees	$ 176,115
Grants and contracts	265,354
Receipts from patients and third parties	535,901
Sales and services of educational activities	21,339
Sales and services of auxiliary enterprises	76,545
Payments to employees and fringe benefits	(783,610)
Payments to vendors and suppliers	(469,399)
Payments for student aid	(34,165)
Loans issued to students	(6,794)
Collection of loans to students	6,531
Other receipts (payments)	20,502
Net cash used by operating activities	$ (191,681)
CASH FLOWS FROM NON-CAPITAL FINANCING ACTIVITIES	
State appropriations	$ 172,958
Payments from Commonwealth for indigent care	21,195
Additions to true endowments	63,701
Direct lending receipts, including PLUS	52,441
Direct lending payments, including PLUS	(52,441)
Receipts on behalf of agencies	71,244
Payments on behalf of agencies	(65,210)
Non-capital gifts and grants and endowments received	48,219
Other	2,104
Net cash provided by non-capital financing activities	$ 314,211
CASH FLOWS FROM CAPITAL AND RELATED FINANCING ACTIVITIES	
Capital appropriations	$ 10,086
Capital gifts and grants received	14,756
Proceeds from capital debt	4,923
Proceeds from sale of capital assets	3,267
Acquisition and construction of capital assets	(188,184)
Principal paid on capital debt and leases	(19,685)
Interest paid on capital debt and leases	(12,038)
Reduction in deposit with trustee	26,803
Net cash used by capital and related financing activities	$ 160,072
CASH FLOWS FROM INVESTING ACTIVITIES	
Proceeds from sales and maturities of investments	$2,307,116
Interest on investments	57,816
Purchase of investments and related fees	(2,309,543)
Other investment activities	1,566
Net cash provided by investing activities	$ 56,955
Net increase in cash and cash equivalents	$19,413
Cash and cash equivalents, July 1	216,267
Cash and cash equivalents, June 30	$ 235,680

(continued)

TABLE 11-4C
University of Virginia
Statement of Cash Flows
As of June 30, 2002 (in thousands) *(continued)*

Reconciliation of operating losses to net cash used by operating activities	
Operating loss	$(317,986)
Adjustments to reconcile operating loss to net cash used by operating activities:	
Depreciation expense	98,628
Provision for uncollectible loans and write-offs	239
Miscellaneous non-operating income	(315)
Changes in assets and liabilities:	
Receivables, net	(4,660)
Inventories	(778)
Prepaid expenses	(1,028)
Notes receivable, net	(1,218)
Accounts payable and accrued liabilities	17,915
Non-cash adjustment to supplies and services	8,876
Deferred revenue	4,801
Accrued vacation leave—long term	3,876
Accrued vacation leave—current	(31)
Total adjustments	126,305
Net cash used by operating activities	$(191,681)
Non-cash investing, capital, and financing activities	
Assets acquired through assumption of a liability	$ 8,799
Assets acquired through a gift	18,317
Change in fair value of investments	(81,095)
Increase in receivables related to non-operating income	68

HOW CAN A GOVERNMENT'S FISCAL CONDITION BE ASSESSED?

Assessing a government's financial condition (that is, its ability to finance its services and satisfy its obligations on a continuing basis) is a daunting task. Not only is a government's fiscal condition directly dependent upon economic, political, social, and demographic factors within its jurisdiction, it is also intertwined with those of other governments that provide financial aid or serve the same constituents.

Table 11-5 presents one approach to the task. Accountants are unquestionably as well trained as any other group of professionals to perform a comprehensive financial analysis of a government. Nevertheless, they must approach an analysis with humility. As the outline makes clear, financial statements are but one, albeit critical, source of information about governments. Nonfinancial considerations are at least as important as the financial factors, although they may be less subject to quantification as ratios or other numerical measures.

Assessing financial condition in government is especially challenging in light of the small number of bond defaults and bankruptcy filings among general-purpose governments. Yet it is also extremely important, especially (as pointed out in the accompanying "In Practice") in hard fiscal times. In the business sector, the ability of ratios

TABLE 11–5
A City's Fiscal Status: A Comprehensive Analysis

I. General approach
   A. Review the current economic, political, and social environment in which the city operates
   B. Identify and assess the impact of key factors likely to affect the city's economic, political, and social environment in the future (e.g., the next five years)
   C. Assess the city's current status as revealed in its comprehensive annual financial report (taking into account the city's reporting practices and policies)
   D. Forecast the city's fiscal status for the next five years taking into account the previously identified environmental changes and the city's likely response to them
II. Current state of, and trends in, the government's operating environment
   A. Population
      1. Age of population
      2. Income level
      3. Educational and skill level
      4. Other relevant demographic factors
   B. Economic conditions
      1. Wealth and income of citizenry (e.g., per capita net worth and income)
      2. Major industries (and stability)
      3. Unemployment rates
      4. Value of property per capita
      5. Sales tax base
      6. Elasticity of revenues
   C. Political climate
      1. Formal structure of government
      2. Extent of political competition
      3. Competence of government officials
      4. Overall citizen satisfaction with and expectations of government
      5. "Liberal" or "conservative" citizen view as to role of government
      6. Relations with state government and other local governments (e.g., those of surrounding and overlapping entities)
   D. Social conditions
      1. Crime rates
      2. Other measures of social well-being
III. Changes likely to affect the government's operating environment and its finances
   A. Demographics and geographical boundaries
      1. Impact on infrastructure
         a. Highways and streets
         b. Utilities
      2. Impact on operating revenues
      3. Impact on operating expenses
   B. Nature and scope of government services to be performed
   C. Nature and scope of enterprise activities carried out (e.g., future of electric utility)
   D. Political climate (e.g., pro- or anti-growth; pro- or anti-business)
   E. Form and organization of government (e.g., possibility of single-member election districts)
   F. Political attitudes and intergovernmental relationships
      1. Changing views toward the role of government
      2. Relations with legislature
      3. Extent of state and federal assistance
      4. Additional costs imposed by overlapping governments (e.g., school districts)

(Continues)

TABLE 11–5
A City's Fiscal Status: A Comprehensive Analysis *(Continues)*

- G. Technological changes such as increased use of computers, and new means of transmitting electricity
- H. Social changes (e.g., changes in family structure resulting in need for more government facilities to provide care for elderly)
- I. Commerce and industry
    1. Major employers (including stability and likelihood of relocating)
    2. Impact on revenues (e.g., property taxes) and expenditures (e.g., infrastructure improvements)
- J. Wealth and income of population
- K. Other economic changes (e.g., those affecting the electric power and health care industries)

IV. Insight into city's financial condition as revealed by accounting and reporting practices
- A. Overall quality of disclosure
- B. Auditor's opinion
- C. GFOA certificate
- D. Letter of transmittal
- E. Key accounting policies
    1. Reporting entity
    2. Number, type, and character (purpose) of funds
    3. Revenue and expenditure recognition
    4. Accounting changes
- F. Budget- and accounting-related practices
    1. "One-shot" additions to revenues or reductions in expenditures
    2. Unusual budget-balancing transactions (e.g., interfund transfers)
    3. Changes in budget-related practices (such as delaying payments or speeding up tax collections)
    4. Use of "off the balance sheet" debt (e.g., leases, long-term contracts) and of revenue debt
    5. Use of long-term debt to finance operating expenditures
    6. Increased use of short-term debt to cover temporary cash shortages

V. Calculation and interpretation of financial indicators
- A. Fiscal capacity and effort
    1. Per capita revenues from own sources/median family income
    2. Revenue from own sources/total appraised value of property
    3. Total sales subject to tax/total retail sales
    4. Sales and property tax rates
- B. Trends in fund balance
- C. Trends in mix of revenues and expenditures and reasons for trends
- D. Trends in adequacy and stability of revenues
    1. Total revenues/total total expenditures
    2. Intergovernmental revenues/total operating revenues
    3. Property tax revenues/total operating revenues
    4. Restricted revenues/total operating revenues
    5. One-time revenues/total operating revenues
    6. Uncollected property taxes
- E. Trends in spending patterns
    1. Number of employees per capita
    2. Nondiscretionary expenditures/total expenditures
    3. Percentage breakdown of total expenditures by function

(Continues)

TABLE 11–5
A City's Fiscal Status: A Comprehensive Analysis *(Continued)*

- F. Trends in liquidity
  1. Adequacy of fund balance—unreserved fund balance/operating revenues
  2. Adequacy of working capital—cash, short-term investments, and receivables/current liabilities
- G. Trends in burden of debt
  1. Debt margin
  2. Debt service as a percentage of total general fund and debt service expenditures
  3. Debt per capita
  4. Debt as a percentage of taxable property
  5. Maturity structure
- H. Trends in pension and other postemployment benefits
  1. Unfunded pension obligation
     - a. Pension assets compared to actuarial liabilities
     - b. Unfunded liabilities compared to values of property, annual payroll
  2. Percent of annual pension costs actually contributed
- I. Bond ratings
- J. Trends in amounts of new borrowing
- K. Overlapping debt
- L. Trends in capital expenditures
  1. By type
  2. By geographic area
  3. Reasons behind trends
  4. Commitments and planned expenditures per capital improvement program

VI. Fiscal forecasts
- A. Overview of how trends and exogenous variables will affect key fiscal indicators in the next five years (taking into account how city will likely respond to them)
- B. Pro forma financial statements of general and other key funds

VII. Summary and conclusion
- A. Will the city have the financial wherewithal to provide the services expected of it in the next years?
- B. What are the key risks and uncertainties facing the city that might impair the ability of the city to provide these services?
  1. How can the city best manage these risks?
  2. What should be the key concerns of city managers, especially those directly concerned with finances?

and similar indicators to predict fiscal stress can be evaluated statistically by constructing regression or similar models in which the ratio and other indicators are associated with actual failures. In the public sector, owing to the small number of bankruptcies and defaults of general purpose governments, considerably less evidence is available as to which indicators actually point to impending failure. Hence, the indicators to be presented in this section, while widely accepted, have not been statistically validated.

The discussion that follows expands upon the key elements of the outline, concentrating mainly on data that are reported in the CAFR. Although the outline is specific in some respects to cities, the general approach can readily be adapted to special purpose governments, such as school districts, as well as to not-for-profits.

The general approach described in the outline is to first assess the current economic, political, and social environment in which the government operates and then

IN PRACTICE

STATES FACE FISCAL CRISES

At no time is financial analysis more important than when governments are in fiscal despair. And at no time have state and local governments been in more dire fiscal straits than in 2003.

According to a survey by the National Governors Association, nearly every state is in a fiscal crisis. The main cause is a stagnant U.S. economy and the resultant decline in income and sales tax revenues. During the go-go years of the 1990s many state and local governments not only increased spending, but they also cut tax rates. Some states did put money into "rainy day" funds, but few put in enough to cover the downpours that would occur in the 2000s.

In the absence of raising taxes—measures that are understandably unpopular when business and individual have their own economic problems—the only remedy is to cut costs. Cost cuts are not without consequences, however. They can range from the humorous to the harsh:

- The governor of Missouri has ordered every third lightbulb in state offices unscrewed.
- Texas plans to reduce or eliminate health care benefits to 275,000 children.
- Colorado suspended property exemptions for 120,000 elderly homeowners.
- School districts throughout the country are cutting out "frills" such as summer school and art and music classes. They have been laying off teachers and increasing class sizes.

Owing to a convergence of the overall decline in the economy, a meltdown in the financial services industry and the disaster of September 11, 2001, New York City faced its worst fiscal calamity since it barely averted bankruptcy in 1975. Referring to New York, a *New York Times* article (April 20, 2003) noted in its headline, "When Cities Go Broke, the Options Are Few." The article correctly pointed out that there comes a "tipping point" at which city officials face an intractable dilemma. If they raise taxes they run the risk that businesses and citizens will flee to lower tax jurisdictions. If instead, however, they cut services, then they face the possibility that the citizens will take flight because of the decline in the quality of everyday life.

to identify the changes that are likely to occur in the future (for example, the next five years). The accounting information can then be examined within the framework of the current and future available resources and claims upon those resources.

THE CAFR AS AN IMPORTANT, BUT NOT EXCLUSIVE, SOURCE OF INFORMATION

The CAFR is probably the single richest source of data as to a government's fiscal condition. But the data by themselves, are little more than a collection of numbers. They provide a scant basis on which to assess past performance or make predictions as to its future. They are useful only when related to other data in the form of ratios, trends, and comparisons. Although the CAFR reports some of these relationships and trends it is mainly a source of raw data. The burden of analysis and interpretation falls upon individual users.

The CAFR is intended to provide information that is relevant to a wide range of decisions; it is not designed to be the sole source of information for any particular decision. Bond rating agencies, for example, require governments to supplement their CAFRs with additional documents, such as budgets, long-range forecasts and plans, biographical summaries of key officials, and economic reports. Diligent analysts are not bound by documents provided by government officials. They should also look to newspaper and magazine articles, economic reports and forecasts by government agencies, private research services, knowledgeable business people, and community representatives.

EVALUATING THE OPERATING ENVIRONMENT

The ultimate ability of a government to perform the services expected of it and to meet its obligations will be determined not by the resources currently on hand, but by those within the government's command. Thus, the demographic, economic, and social bases of the community that the government serves are of prime importance in assessing the government's financial condition.

Demographic Factors

Population size and composition have a major impact on a community's economic base. The composition of a population is as critical as its size. Factors that are of particular importance include:

- Age (e.g., the elderly require extensive medical care; the young, education)
- Income distribution (e.g., the poor require more social services; the wealthy may demand more recreational and cultural services as well as a higher level of basic services)
- Educational level (e.g., better educated populations make it easier to attract technologically oriented industries; they are also likely to demand higher quality schools for their own children)
- Native born vs. immigrant (e.g., new arrivals to the country require different types of services than native born)

Economic Conditions

The potential of an economy to generate tax and other revenues depends on the composition of its taxpayers. If the leading taxpayers are in a variety of industries rather than concentrated in just a few, the government's revenue stream is less likely to be adversely affected by recessions, technological developments, changes in consumer tastes, or similar factors. In addition, some industries may be riding a wave of expansion, whereas others are caught in an undertow of decline. Some companies, perhaps because of high capital investments or historical ties, are likely to remain in a community. Others, maybe because their facilities are aging or they can reduce operating costs by relocating abroad, may be candidates for early departure. It has long been recognized that textile and clothing manufacturing firms are especially likely to transfer operations to other countries. In recent years, however, it has become apparent that even "white collar" activities, such as insurance claim processing, the "back office" operations of banks and brokerage firms, and the telephone "tech support" functions of computer firms can be carried out overseas.

Political and Leadership Characteristics

The ability of a government to exercise decisive leadership both in planning for the future and in responding to crises adds strength to its fiscal condition. This ability can be influenced by several factors. These include:

- ***Formal structure of the government and the powers that are granted to key officials.*** In some governments, the chief executive officers have the authority to make major spending decisions on their own, without legislative approval. In others, even minor decisions are subject to lengthy administrative or legislative processes.

- ***Degree of political competition.*** In the absence of political competition, as might be evidenced by closely contested elections, the chief executive officer may be able to act swiftly and forcefully irrespective of requirements for formal legislative approval.
- ***Competence and integrity of government officials.*** Bright, experienced, and honest officials are a necessary, if not always a sufficient, condition for fiscal well-being.
- ***Relations with other governments.*** These are affected not only by the power of home rule (the authority to act without the approval of the state or some other government) but also by personal and political relationships among the officials of the various levels of government.
- ***Political climate.*** Politics and economics go hand-in-hand. Albeit a highly subjective factor, a favorable political climate makes it easier for a community to achieve its social, environmental, and educational goals while assuring that the costs are distributed equitably. Moreover, some elected officials may favor an expanded role for government and an increase in the range of services it provides; others may advocate a diminished role and a reduction of its activities.

Social Considerations

Closely tied to demographic considerations are sociological factors such as crime rates, percentage of citizens requiring public assistance, and percentage of residents owning their own homes. These factors affect the extent and level of services that the government will have to provide, as well as its ability to raise revenues.

ASSESSING CHANGES LIKELY TO TAKE PLACE IN THE FUTURE

Analysts are concerned with both the past and the present mainly because they provide the basis for predicting the future. Although analysts are not seers, the essence of financial analysis is forecasting. Therefore, they must attempt to identify the changes that will likely affect the government's environment within the time horizon they are considering. The outline sets forth a few specific factors in addition to those presented in the previous section that must be considered.

Population

Increases in population are often associated with expanding economies and the creation of new businesses. Growth, however, may have its fiscal downside, especially in the short term. As new housing developments are constructed and families, often with young children, move into a community, the government may have to extend infrastructure, construct new schools, and augment social services.

Enterprises

Without question, the nature of services provided by governments is going to change in the next decade. Many governments are going to be under pressure to privatize (outsource) at least some of the functions that they carry out today (an issue to be addressed in more detail in Chapter 13). Perhaps the most fiscally significant of these is electric service. An electric utility may constitute the major portion of a city's revenues, expenses, assets, and liabilities. Until recently, electric utilities were the quintessential example of a regulated monopoly. The 1990s, however, witnessed a decided trend toward both competition and deregulation. The early 2000s, however, were characterized by power shortages in California and other western states. Among the alleged causes were illegal manipulation of the markets by Enron and other energy firms and misguided government regulation. As a consequence, the future of municipal utilities is now quite problematic. Similar developments are also affecting other government activities. In response to the resultant economic uncertainty, many cities are considering selling to private companies not only their utilities, but also their hospitals and sanitation facilities. Further, some governments are outsourcing clerical operations (such as processing welfare payments or payroll checks), internal audit functions, and repair and maintenance services.

Technology

"E-commerce" and related means of transmitting information electronically will almost certainly affect governments in much the same ways that they are transforming private businesses. Activities that some governments still carry out manually (e.g., reading electric and water meters and issuing purchase orders) are being performed electronically by others. The shift to electronics may make governments more efficient and thereby reduce operating costs. But it will also require enormous investments in computer hardware and software.

EXAMINING THE BUDGET AND FINANCIAL STATEMENTS

It goes without saying that the computation of ratio and statistical measures is central to financial analysis. However, key clues to the financial health of a government can be obtained as much from an organization's accounting and reporting practices as from its ratios or the underlying numbers.

The Budget

A government's plans are most explicitly revealed in future-oriented documents, such as its operating and capital budgets and long-term capital improvement plans. As indicated in Chapter 1, governments and not-for-profits are "governed" by their budgets (as opposed to the marketplace). Therefore, the budget is a detailed map of the fiscal path down which the government is proceeding.

Analysts must, of course, test the integrity of the budget by comparing previous budgets with actual results. In addition, they must assess whether the estimated revenues are attainable and the amounts budgeted for nondiscretionary expenditures are reasonable. Further they must make certain that the budget provides for foreseeable changes in population and other changes in conditions as well as for contingencies and unanticipated events.

Budgets are generally on a cash or near cash basis. Consequently, governments are able to engage in any number of measures to increase revenues or decrease expenditures even in the absence of substantive changes in economic resources. For example, as noted in previous chapters, they can delay payments to suppliers or employees, speed up collections from taxpayers, or transfer resources from one fund to another. These and other "one shot" infusions to fund balance may provide compelling evidence of fiscal stress—that the government is unable to balance its budget by legitimate means.

The Financial Statements

Financial statements must adhere to generally accepted accounting principles, which require a full or modified accrual basis. Therefore, governments have far less opportunity to artificially manipulate their reported than their budgeted revenues and expenses. Nevertheless, as observed in previous chapters, they can influence values reported on their financial statements in numerous ways. To cite but a few, they can:

- Account for certain transactions in internal service or proprietary funds rather than the general fund

- Finance capital acquisitions by incurring "off the balance sheet" obligations (such as might be created by operating leases or service contracts) rather than general obligation debt
- Opt for "liberal" accounting practices and policies that recognize revenues sooner rather than later and delay the recognition of expenditures (e.g., shorten the period after year-end during which cash receipts satisfy the "available" criterion for revenue recognition; reduce estimates of uncollectible taxes)
- Make "liberal" actuarial assumptions and estimates in determining the required contribution to pension plans

Analysts should take note of an entity's reporting practices for at least two reasons. First, and more importantly, certain reporting practices (like budget practices) may be a symptom of underlying financial deficiencies. If a government can produce a reported surplus only by stretching the limits of generally accepted accounting principles and taking advantage of available reporting loopholes, then it may be masking a true economic deficit. Second, insofar as analysts are comparing one government with another, they need to be sure that the governments are adhering to similar accounting principles.

CAVEATS REGARDING FINANCIAL INDICATORS

As with financial analysis in the business sector, individual numbers taken by themselves have virtually no significance. They acquire meaning only when related to other numbers, usually in the form of ratios. Ratios, however, must be interpreted with the utmost of caution.

First, there are no reliable "rules of thumb" as to what constitutes an acceptable or an out-of-line ratio. As noted previously, the over 80,000 governments in the United States carry out disparate functions. Even seemingly similar governments, such as cities that may be of similar size and within the same state, may engage in different types of activities. Thus, for example, the total per capita debt of a Texas city such as Austin, which operates an electric utility, should be expected to be significantly greater than that of Dallas, which does not. Nevertheless, both professional associations and government agencies make available extensive databases that enable analysts to make comparisons among similar government units. The Government Finance Officers Association, for example, maintains separate databases for cities, schools, and counties. The Texas Education Agency can provide an interactive CD that permits users to select school districts with similar characteristics (e.g., size, ethnic composition, location) and evaluate them over a wide range of ratios and similar indicators.

Second, governments account for their operations in varying ways. One entity, for example, may account for a particular function in a governmental fund; another in an internal service fund. Hence, ratios involving general fund balances or expenditures may not be directly comparable.

Third, whether a higher or lower ratio is preferable is not always clear. Much depends on the issue that is being addressed and the perspective of the analyst. Consider for example a ratio of total general fund revenues to total general fund expenditures. Seemingly, a high ratio would be preferable to a low one as it indicates that the government is having no difficulty meeting its expenditures and that the cost of providing services is being met by current, not future, taxpayers. That would definitely be true from the perspective of a bondholder who is concerned with the ability of the government to meet a forthcoming interest or principal payment, or a creditor worried about whether receiving payment for goods or services that it provided. On the other hand, a government's relatively high amount of revenues may be attributable to high taxes. Possibly, the government may face either legal or political barriers to additional increases in taxes. The government with the lower ratio might have greater capacity to raise taxes in the future and therefore be the more fiscally sound of the two over the long term. Thus, from the perspective of a state or federal environmental regulator, a low ratio (assuming it does not indicate ongoing deficits) might point to the ability of the government to meet an obligation to monitor and close a landfill several years hence.

Fourth, cities can be expected to have higher or lower ratios depending on their stage of maturity. A high-growth city, for example, may have to rapidly expand its infrastructure, financing it with long-term debt. A mature city, by contrast, may have its infrastructure in place and may have repaid the associated debt years earlier. As a consequence, a city with high debt per capita may in fact have brighter long-term fiscal prospects than one with low.

Fifth, ratios are no better than the underlying numbers. Throughout the text, we have emphasized the limitations of the current accounting model, some of which are inherent in any model that might be developed (e.g., it incorporates "subjective" estimates, allocations, and choices among completing accounting principles; it values most assets at historical, rather than current, costs). Moreover, the underlying accounting principles were developed for "general purpose" financial statements, not for any particular decision on hand. These limitations do not disappear when the numbers are incorporated into ratios.

This is not to imply that ratios have no meaning. They are especially useful in identifying trends and raising pertinent questions. Analysts should never draw conclusions merely because the ratios of one government differ from those of others or have changed over time—no matter how great the difference or the change. But a significant difference or change should cry out for investigation. Only when analysts fully understand the reason behind the difference or change can they discern its implications.

DETERMINING THE SCOPE OF A RATIO

In calculating and interpreting financial indicators, analysts face an immediate issue—one for which there is no obvious resolution. Should ratios and other measures be based on (1) the government-wide statements, (2) the general fund only, or (3) some analyst-selected combination of funds?

Measures based on the government-wide statements capture the totality of the government's resources and do not show which specific assets are restricted and may therefore be used only for specified purposes. On the other hand, over the long term, all resources, whether restricted or not, benefit the government and can be used to provide government services or to satisfy its obligations.

Thus, the answer to the question must depend on why the measure is being calculated and how it will be interpreted. If analysts are interested in determining the total amount of government resources directed to specify functions (e.g., road repair), then it makes sense for them to include expenditures from all funds from which applicable expenditures can be made. Similarly, if they want to take a long-term perspective, then inasmuch as the government-wide statements include depreciation as an expenditure, they will likely give a more relevant measure of on-going costs. By contrast, if the analysts are concerned with the ability of the government to meet its short-term obligations from a specific fund, such as the general fund or an enterprise fund, then they should probably take into account only the resources of that fund.

ASSESSING FISCAL EFFORT

A government's **fiscal effort**—the extent to which it is taking advantage of its fiscal capacity—may be measured by comparing the revenues that it generates from its own sources (i.e., total revenues excluding grants from other governments) with either the wealth or the income of its taxpayers. Income can be captured by measures such as median family income; wealth can be represented by indicators such as total appraised (market) value of property. Thus, fiscal effort equals:

$$\frac{\text{Per capita revenue from own sources}}{\text{Median family income}}$$

or

$$\frac{\text{Revenue from own sources}}{\text{Total appraised value of property}}$$

These ratios increase as the government exerts greater fiscal effort and uses a greater portion of its fiscal capacity. The more it takes of its constituents' resources that are economically or politically available for taxation, the less it will be able to raise taxes in the future.

ASSESSING THE SIGNIFICANCE OF OPERATING DEFICITS

Operating deficits should be to financial analysts what red flags are to bulls. They should draw attention, yet not distract focus away from other, more consequential, targets.

A widely used rule of thumb holds that two consecutive years of operating deficits connotes serious fiscal distress. But operating deficits as a measure of fiscal performance have inherent limitations and must be interpreted with considerable caution.

First, operating deficits (as well as all other accounting measures) result from the application of generally accepted accounting principles. These principles represent compromises among competing objectives and were not developed to facilitate any particular decisions. The resultant accounting revenues and expenditures may not necessarily have been determined on a basis that is most appropriate for the purpose at hand.

Second, operating deficits, whether government-wide or of individual funds, even if over a period of two or more years, do not necessarily signify deteriorating financial condition. If a government has accumulated excessive surpluses in the past, it may elect, quite sensibly, to draw them down by running planned deficits over the following several years.

ANALYZING REVENUE AND EXPENDITURES TRENDS

In governments more revenue is not necessarily preferable to less. Revenues need only—but at the same time must—be sufficient to cover expenditures. A key step in assessing the adequacy of revenues, therefore, is to associate trends in revenues with those in expenditures.

Both revenues and expenditures are closely correlated with size of the constituency. To compare the revenues and expenditures of the same government over time or of one government with another, it is necessary to take into account difference in population. For many analytical purposes, revenues and expenditures are best expressed per capita.

The adequacy of revenues is most obviously indicated by the extent to which revenues exceeds expenditures—that is:

$$\frac{\text{Total revenues}}{\text{Total expenditures}}$$

In the short-term, and from the perspective of a bondholder or other creditor, the higher the ratio the better.

A stable revenue base is generally characterized by the presence of several diverse sources of revenues, so that a decline in one source will not necessarily be contemporaneous with declines in others. Moreover the revenues should be linked to population, so that costs of providing for a larger population are automatically offset by a broader revenue base. For example, a state government that generates its revenue from a mix of property taxes, incomes taxes, sales taxes, user fees, and intergovernmental aid is less likely to suffer from either a recession or a downturn in the price of a single commodity than one that relies primarily upon taxes on the production of oil.

The following ratios spotlight the stability of a government's revenues:

- ***Intergovernmental revenues/Total operating revenues.*** Governments generally want to maximize the amount of resources received from other governments. Failure to take advantage of appropriate intergovernmental grants can rightfully be interpreted as a sign of poor management. But what a granting government gives, it can also take away. Therefore, a high or increasing ratio of intergovernmental revenues to total revenues is a sign of risk and hence is generally considered a negative fiscal characteristic.
- ***Restricted revenues/Total operating revenues.*** Restricted revenues decrease the flexibility of governments to respond to changing conditions and may lead to a misallocation of resources. State gasoline taxes, for example, may be dedicated to highway construction, and thereby be unavailable to meet pressing needs for new schools. Therefore, lower percentages of restricted revenues are preferred to high percentages.
- ***One-time revenues/Total operating revenues.*** By definition, one-time revenues cannot be expected to be ongoing. As suggested earlier in the text, these revenues may result from substantive measures, such as sales of assets, or merely "one shot" technical adjustments, such as changes in the due date of taxes or license fees. Some can be motivated by opportunities to enhance productivity; others by a need to artificially balance the budget. A high proportion of one-time revenues is generally viewed as a decidedly negative characteristic.
- ***Property tax revenues/Total operating revenues.*** Property tax revenues are considered a stable source of revenue; a high ratio of property tax revenues to other, less stable, revenues is a positive attribute.
- ***Uncollected property taxes/Total property taxes levied.*** A high rate of uncollected property taxes may signal an underlying weakness in the economy and hence be a warning of an impending reduction in revenues, not only from property taxes, but from other sources as well.[4]

Expenditures are a measure of the cost of services provided. Changes in per capita expenditures can be the result of several factors, some positive, some negative, and some neutral. For example, increases in expenditures can be attributable to:

- Decreases in productivity or increases in prices (i.e., the government provides the same services but at greater cost)
- Changes in the number, quality, or mix of services owing to favorable economic conditions (e.g., new housing developments or new industries that require a city to enhance its infrastructure)
- Changes in the number, quality, or mix of services owing to unfavorable economic factors (e.g., increases in unemployment that require a city to provide free medical care for a larger number of citizens)
- Factors beyond the control of the government, such as bad weather

Ratios that may be used to identify changes in spending patterns and thereby signal the need for an investigation into the cause of the change include the following:

- ***Number of employees/Population*** or ***Payroll expenditures/Total expenditures.*** Without evidence of corresponding increases in the level or quality of

[4] These and several other ratios presented in this section have been adapted from Sanford M. Groves and Maureen Godsey Valente, *Evaluating Financial Condition: A Handbook for Local Government* (Washington, D.C.: International City Management Association, 1986).

services, increases in payroll costs may be a consequence of decreased productivity.

- ***Expenditures for specific functions/Total expenditures.*** Disproportionate increases in expenditures for specific functions (such as public safety, health and welfare, or recreation) may indicate new policies or circumstances that presage additional increases in the future.
- ***Nondiscretionary expenditures/Total expenditures.*** Governments typically have control over only a limited percentage of their total costs. Others are dictated by contractual agreements (such as leases), debt commitments, and mandates from higher levels of government. The higher the percentage of nondiscretionary expenditures, the less flexibility the government has to reduce (or limit increases in) spending.

As in businesses, analysts can key in on a specific revenue or expenditure by comparing it to the balance sheet account with which it is associated. For example, the extent to which property taxes are being collected on a timely basis can be evaluated by dividing property taxes receivable (or uncollected property taxes) by the total property tax levy for the year.

ASSESSING ABILITY TO MEET SHORT-TERM COMMITMENTS

The balance sheets of governmental funds focus on short-term resources and claims against these resources. Therefore, they provide an indication of a government's near-term ability to perform the services expected of it to fulfill its obligations.

Of all the government-fund balance sheet accounts, fund balance typically draws the greatest attention. In large part, fund balance is so highly visible because it embodies all other balance sheet accounts and in governmental funds is indicative of net available financial resources.

Most governments try to maintain positive fund balance so as to be better able to cope with unforeseen expenditures or revenue shortfalls. The adequacy of fund balance is often measured by the ratio of unreserved fund balance to operating revenues:

$$\frac{\text{Unreserved fund balance}}{\text{Total operating revenues}}$$

Other factors being equal, a trend of decline in the ratio is seen as a sign of deteriorating financial condition. However, the significance of fund balance can easily be overstated. Fund balance is nothing more than the accumulation of annual surpluses and deficits and is therefore subject to the limitations ascribed earlier to operating deficits. If, as is common, the budgetary principles applicable to a particular government differ from the generally accepted accounting principles on which reported fund balance is based, the fund balance may not necessarily denote the resources legally available for expenditure.

Liquidity in governments can be measured just as in businesses—by comparing some or all current assets to current liabilities. Because a government's inventories are not usually for sale and will not be a source of cash, most analysts exclude them from their liquidity ratios. Thus, the current ratio includes only cash, short-term investments (i.e., near cash), and receivables:

$$\frac{\text{Cash, short-term investments, and receivables}}{\text{Current liabilities}}$$

A more rigorous form of the ratio also excludes receivables:

$$\frac{\text{Cash and short-term investments}}{\text{Current liabilities}}$$

ASSESSING ABILITY TO MEET LONG-TERM COMMITMENTS

In this text, key issues in assessing the burden of a government's long-term obligations and the adequacy of its long-term assets have already been addressed in the chapters dealing with long-term debt and general capital assets. As noted in those chapters, an analyst must consider trends in debt per capita, debt as a percentage of taxable property, and debt service costs as a percentage of total general fund and debt service expenditures. Also of special concern are debt margin, overlapping debt, and the ratings assigned to the government's bonds by independent rating services. Moreover, analysts must be wary of a build-up in unfunded pension obligations. This can be detected by examining trends in various pension ratios (e.g., actuarial value of assets divided by actuarial accrued liabilities, and unfunded actuarial accrued liabilities as a percentage of covered payroll). These are reported in the schedule of funding progress, which is included in the required supplementary information section of the CAFR.

Similarly, as noted in earlier chapters, no analysis of a government's fiscal condition can be meaningful if it fails to consider the condition of the entity's capital assets and especially its infrastructure. To be sure, both the government-wide statements and the schedule of changes in long-lived assets (included in notes to the financial statements) provide data on the historical cost of, and the accumulated depreciation applicable to, long-lived assets. As previously emphasized, however, these data tell the analyst nothing about the physical condition of assets and their adequacy for the future. Still, to gain insight into whether a government is properly maintaining its assets, analysts may be able to look to the note disclosures regarding the condition of infrastructure assets and comparison of actual to needed maintenance and preservation costs. These are required by governments that elect the "modified" as opposed to the "depreciation" approach to accounting for infrastructure assets.

Although GASB Statement No. 34 substantially improved disclosures regarding long-lived assets, analysts still cannot count on the CAFR for all relevant information. Analysts must therefore obtain from other sources information on the age, condition, and capacity of infrastructure and assess the demands that infrastructure maintenance and improvement will place on future-year revenues.

Table 11-6 illustrates key ratios based on the financial statements and supplementary information of Charlotte, North Carolina. As noted previously, all of the ratios could have been computed differently using either data from the government-wide statements or from different combinations of funds.

DRAWING CONCLUSIONS

The goal of financial analysis is to draw conclusions regarding the ability of a government to provide the services expected of it in the future. One means of capturing the factors discussed so far is by preparing pro forma financial statements. Based on forecasts of revenues, expenditures, capital outlays, and proceeds from debt, analysts can prepare statements of revenues and expenditures, balance sheets, and statements of cash flow for each year covered by the projections. These will provide evidence as to whether the revenues will be sufficient to cover expenditures and, even more importantly, whether cash inflows will be adequate to cover outflows. They will make apparent the need for increases in inflows or decreases in outflows that were not incorporated into initial projections.

Unless analysts are blessed with the power of prophecy, they are certain to be unable to foresee all events and circumstances that will affect the government in the future. Nevertheless, they must do their best to identify key risks and uncertainties and assess the ability of the government to cope with them. Indeed, one of the advantages of computer spreadsheets is that they enable analysts to examine any number of "what if" situations. These should always include "bad case" and even "worst case" scenarios. Clearly, no government will have the resources to cover all potential calamities, but analysts should look for evidence that the entity is taking no imprudent risks.

TABLE 11-6
Selected Key Ratios Based on the Financial Statements and Supplementary Information of Charlotte, North Carolina

Ratio	Calculation	Source	Interpretation
Fiscal Effort			
Revenue from own sources/ Median family income	(Total governmental funds revenues less total intergovernmental revenues)/ Median family income = (495,028,000 – 86,445,000)/ 56,754 = 7,199.2	Statement of Revenues, Expenditures, and Changes in Fund Balances for Governmental Funds (Table 2-6) and Statistical Section[1]	Lower ratios are better. As the value increases, the government exerts greater fiscal effort and thereby uses a greater portion of its fiscal capacity. That means that it will have less ability to raise taxes in the future.
or			
Revenue from own sources/ Total appraised value of property	(Total governmental funds revenues less total intergovernmental revenues)/ Total appraised value of property = (495,028,000 – 86,445,000)/ 49,967,972,000 = 0.0082	Statistical section[2]	
Adequacy of Revenues (Operating Position)			
Total revenues/ Total expenditures	(Total governmental funds revenues)/ (Total governmental funds expenditures) = 495,028,000/ 598,454,000 = 0.827	Statement of Revenues, Expenditures, and Changes in Fund Balances for Governmental Funds (Table 2-6)	Higher ratios are better. A high value indicates that a government's revenues are adequately covering its expenditures.
Stability of Revenues			
Intergovernmental revenues/ Total operating revenues	(Intergovernmental revenues from General + Debt Service + Other Governmental funds)[3]/(Revenues from General + Debt Service + Other Governmental funds) = (43,404,000 + 3,029,000 + 39,541,000)/(329,206,000 + 53,256,000 + 74,801,000) = 0.188	Statement of Revenues, Expenditures, and Changes in Fund Balances for Governmental Funds (Table 2-6)	This ratio indicates the proportion of revenues received from other governments. Insofar as the other governments may be able to arbitrarily cease to provide the revenues,an increase in the ratio may indicate increased risk and hence decreased fiscal strength. However, at the same time, a decrease in the ratio may point to the government's failure to take advantage of all the grants and other revenues available from other governments.
Restricted revenues/ Total operating revenues	(Total Governmental fund revenues less total General fund revenues)/(Revenues from General + Debt Service + Other Governmental funds) = (495,028,000 – 329,206,000)/(329,206,000 + 53,256,000 + 74,801,000) = 0.363	Statement of Revenues, Expenditures, and Changes in Fund Balances for Governmental Funds (Table 2-6)	Lower ratios are better. Restricted revenues decrease the flexibility of governments to respond to changing conditions and may lead to misallocation of resources.
Property tax revenues/ Total operating revenues	(Property tax revenues from General + Debt Service + Other Governmental funds)[4]/(Revenues from General + Debt Service + Other Governmental funds) = (189,270,000 + 31,548,000 + 1,307,000)/ (329,206,000 + 53,256,000 + 74,801,000) = 0.486	Statement of Revenues, Expenditures, and Changes in Fund Balances for Governmental Funds (Table 2-6)	Higher ratios are better. Property tax revenues are considered a stable source of revenue.
Uncollected property taxes/ Total property taxes levied	(Total tax levy less Current tax collections)/Total tax levy = (237,546,000 – 230,863,000)/ 237,546,000 = 0.028	Statistical section[5]	Lower ratios are better. A high rate of uncollected property taxes may signal an underlying weakness in the economy.

(Continues)

TABLE 11-6
Selected Key Ratios Based on the Financial Statements and Supplementary Information of Charlotte, North Carolina *(Continued)*

Ratio	Calculation	Source	Interpretation
Spending Patterns			
Number of employees/ Population	5,806/579,684 = 0.01	Statistical Section[6]	An increase may suggest that the government is operating less efficiently (a signal of fiscal weakness) or, on the other hand, may indicate that the government is able to increase the level of services that it is providing (a sign of fiscal strength).
Expenditures for specific functions/ Total expenditures	**Public Safety:** 203,431,000/598,454,000 = 0.340 **Sanitation:** 32,385,000/598,454,000 = 0.054 **General Administration:** 33,763,000/598,454,000 = 0.056 **Streets/Highways:** 41,488,000/598,454,000 = 0.069 **Engineering/Property Management:** 19,318,000/598,454,000 = 0.032 **Support Services:** 15,548,000/598,454,000 = 0.026 **Community Planning/Development:** 33,515,000/598,454,000 = 0.056	Statement of Revenues, Expenditures, and Changes in Fund Balances for Governmental Funds (Table 2-6)	An increase in expenditures for a specific function may indicate new policies or circumstances that presage additional increases in the future—perhaps a sign of deteriorating fiscal strength. Or, on the other hand, it could signal merely a change in priorities—a neutral development.
Adequacy of Fund Balance (Operating Position)			
Unreserved fund balance/ Total operating revenues	(Unreserved fund balance from General + Debt Service + Other Governmental funds)[7]/(Revenues from General + Debt Service + Other Governmental funds) = (54,275,000 + 116,816,000 + 58,107,000)/ (329,206,000 + 53,256,000 + 74,801,000) = 0.501	Balance Sheet (Table 2-5); Statement of Revenues, Expenditures, and Changes in Fund Balances for Governmental Funds (Table 2-6)	The higher the ratio, the greater the cushion against future deficits. An increase may be seen as a sign of fiscal strength. However, a larger reserve is not preferable per se. If the reserve is unnecessarily high, then the government may be either spending too little or taxing too much.
Liquidity Position			
Cash, short-term investments and receivables/ Current liabilities	(Cash and cash equivalents + Net Receivables + Due from other governmental agencies)/(Accounts payable + Deposits and retainage payable + Liabilities payable from restricted assets) = (410,129,000 + 18,046,000 + 38,810,000)/(43,240,000 + 4,285,000 + 1,440,000) = 9.537	Balance Sheet (Table 2-5)	A high ratio indicates that the government is able to meet its short-term obligations as they come due—a sign of fiscal strength. However, inasmuch as the numerator encompasses receivables, an increase in the ratio as a result of a receivables build-up could be reflective of an inability to collect taxes or other revenues.

(Continues)

TABLE 11-6
Selected Key Ratios Based on the Financial Statements and Supplementary Information of Charlotte, North Carolina *(Continued)*

Ratio	Calculation	Source	Interpretation
Debt Structure			
Debt service costs/ Total general and debt service fund expenditures	Debt service expenditures (interest + principal)/(Expenditures from General + Debt service fund) = (50,500,000 + 32,157,000)/(317,659,000 + 82,657,000) = 0.206	Statement of Revenues, Expenditures, and Changes in Fund Balances for Governmental Funds (Table 2-6)	Lower ratios are better. A low value suggests the entity is able to pay its debt service requirements when due.
Direct long-term debt/ Total population	Total debt outstanding for governmental activities/Total population = 665,700,000/ 579,684 = 1,148	MD&A[8]	Low ratios are better. That means that the government has the ability to repay its general long-term debt.

[1] Demographic Statistics for the Last Ten Years, Statistical Section, CAFR 2002.

[2] Schedule of Assessed Value of Property for the Last Ten Years, Statistical Section, CAFR 2002.

[3] For consistency, capital projects fund revenues are excluded from the intergovernmental revenues because the denominator includes total operating revenues, which exclude capital project fund revenues.

[4] For consistency, capital projects fund revenues are excluded.

[5] Schedule of Property Tax Levies and Collections for the Last Ten Years, Statistical Section, CAFR 2002.

[6] Miscellaneous Statistics, Statistical Section, CAFR 2002.

[7] For consistency, capital projects fund revenues are excluded.

[8] Schedule of Outstanding Debt, MD&A, CAFR 2002.

SUMMARY

The United States is characterized by many types of governments and relationships among them. Therefore, rule-making authorities have had to develop a multidimensional framework for defining reporting entities.

According to the GASB, a primary government should include a potential component unit in its reporting entity if the unit is financially accountable to it. A potential component unit is financially accountable if the primary government can appoint a majority of its governing board, and it is either able to impose its will on the entity or the unit is able to provide specific financial benefits to, or impose specific financial burdens on, the primary government.

The most significant component of the introductory section of the Comprehensive Annual Financial Report (CAFR) has been the letter of transmittal. This letter is analogous to a state-of-the-government address and reports on the overall fiscal health of the entity. GASB Statement No. 34 now requires that much of the information that has been included in the letter of transmittal be incorporated in the management's discussion and analysis (MD&A).

The financial section of the CAFR consists of the auditor's report, the MD&A, the basic financial statements, required supplementary information, combining statements, individual statements, and schedules. The MD&A, which may prove to be one of the most important elements of the CAFR, explains the basic financial statements, provides an analysis of key transactions and events, and presents information relevant to a government's financial health that is beyond the scope of the basic financial statements.

The basic financial statements consist of the two government-wide statements (the statement of net assets and statement of activities) and the fund statements for each of the three types of funds (governmental, proprietary, and fiduciary). They include also the notes to the financial statements. The governmental and proprietary fund statements present each major fund in a separate column. The fiduciary fund statements present all fiduciary funds aggregated by fund type. The nonmajor funds of each type are aggregated into a single column. The basic financial statements may also include combining statements of major component units.

Required supplementary information encompasses statistical data and information that supplements the basic financial statements. Examples include budget-to-actual comparisons, information about infrastructure condition (if the government elects not to depreciate infrastructure assets), and details of pension valuations.

Governments must present combining statements for all internal service funds, since these funds do not have to be reported individually in the funds statements. They may also present combining statements for nonmajor funds that are aggregated in a single column in the funds statements as well as for nonmajor component units.

The statistical section, which can consist of fifteen types of tables, is valuable because of its supplementary disclosures. The tables provide additional information or insights into the data reported in current or previous financial statements and report on economic conditions within the government's jurisdiction.

Colleges and universities are subject to the same reporting requirements as other special-purpose governments. Most universities will satisfy the criteria of Statement No. 34 that allow them to be accounted for as entities that engage exclusively in business-type activities. Thus, they need prepare only a statement of net assets, a statement of activities (both on a full accrual basis), and a statement of cash flows. They need not prepare the funds statements required of general-purpose governments.

Governments have the power to tax and the obligation to provide services. Hence, the financial wherewithal of a government is tied directly to that of the citizens and businesses within its jurisdiction. The wealth of the community is a key determinant of the resources that can be commanded by the government as well as the services that are expected of it. Therefore, a comprehensive financial analysis of a government involves examining the government in the context of its economic, social, and political environment.

Analysts should first consider the current environment in which a government operates and then try to identify the critical changes that will affect the government. They should review the government's accounting and budgeting practices, looking especially for those that might have been used to obscure fiscal weaknesses. They should then calculate those financial ratios that are widely accepted as being indicative of fiscal health. These include ratios that indicate relationships not only between items reported on the basic financial statements but also between financial statement values and economic and demographic measures.

Ratios are of value mainly in that they highlight out-of-ordinary conditions and are especially useful in "benchmarking" one government against others. Nevertheless, financial analysis is very much an art rather than a mere mechanical process. Analysts must make subjective assessments of a wide range of factors, including competence of government officials, the political climate of the jurisdiction, and the nature of relations with other governments. Most importantly, they must be able to identify the risks faced by the government and its ability to respond to them.

EXERCISE FOR REVIEW AND SELF-STUDY

The suburban town of Evansville experienced considerable growth in the five years between 2000 and 2005. Table 11-7 was drawn from the town's CAFR. Based on the limited information provided, you are to assess whether the town's fiscal condition has improved or deteriorated in that period. You may ignore the impact of inflation and assume that all significant revenues and expenditures are reported in the general fund.

1. Has the town's debt burden increased or decreased between 2000 and 2005?
2. Based on revenues from its own sources, has the government imposed a greater burden upon its constituents? Assess the burden in terms of both population and wealth.
3. Is the town more liquid in 2005 than it was in 2000?
4. Does the town have a proportionately greater general fund balance in 2005 than in 2000?
5. Has there been any change in the mix of revenues from more to less stable revenues?
6. Has the annual burden of debt service increased?
7. Is there any evidence that the growth in population has forced a change in mix of services provided?
8. Propose at least five additional questions (the answers to which would not be obvious from the financial statements) you would raise before you would draw conclusions as to whether the fiscal condition of the town improved between 2000 and 2005.

QUESTIONS FOR REVIEW AND DISCUSSION

1. Per GASB Statement No. 14, what is the key criterion as to whether a government should be included as a *component unit* in the reporting entity of another government?
2. How does *discrete presentation* differ from *blending?* When is each appropriate?
3. What is the primary deficiency of discrete presentation as it must be applied in government-wide statements?
4. What are the three main sections of the Comprehensive Annual Financial Report? What are the main components of the financial section?
5. What is meant by "combining statements"? Why is it especially appropriate to present combining statements for internal service funds?
6. Provide five examples of the type of information to be addressed by management in its discussion and analysis (MD&A).
7. What are the main reporting options available to government colleges and universities? Will they have to prepare funds statements? Explain.

TABLE 11-7
Selected Information from CAFR
2000 versus 2005
(All Dollar Amounts, Including Per Capita Amounts, in Thousands)

	2000		2005	
	Actual	Per Capita	Actual	Per Capita
Population	73,706		95,818	
Total assessed value of property	$1,885,000	$25.57	$2,827,500	$29.51
Total property tax levy	21,560	0.29	32,340	0.34
General fund cash and investments	2,280	0.03	3,457	0.04
General fund total assets	18,201	0.25	19,307	0.20
General fund total liabilities	12,952	0.18	14,388	0.15
General fund reserved fund balance	510	0.01	307	0.00
General fund unreserved fund balance	4,739	0.06	4,612	0.05
General fund total tax revenues	36,764	0.50	56,617	0.64
General fund total expenditures	39,174	0.53	60,328	0.63
General fund debt service expenditures (1)	5,793	0.08	9,633	0.10
General fund revenue from own sources	38,600	0.52	56,550	0.59
General fund total revenues	40,063	0.54	61,697	0.64
General fund intergovernmental revenue	1,463	0.02	5,147	0.05
General fund public safety expenditures	13,654	0.19	24,301	0.25
General fund health and welfare expenditures	2,979	0.04	4,915	0.05
Direct debt	35,849	0.49	72,900	0.76
Overlapping debt	27,159	0.37	47,875	0.50

(1) Includes transfers to debt service fund

8. The text notes that two consecutive years of operating deficits are generally seen by analysts as a sign of serious fiscal distress. Suppose that a government has had several years of *general fund* surpluses. Is this necessarily a sign of financial strength?
9. Notes to the financial statements and required supplementary information (RSI) must both be included in a government's CAFR. What, then, does it matter if information is provided in notes as opposed to RSI?
10. Why might analysts be concerned if a government has an unusually high ratio of intergovernmental revenues to total revenues relative to a comparable government? Why might they be concerned if the same ratio is unusually low?
11. What is meant by fiscal capacity and fiscal effort? Why are they of significance in assessing a government's financial condition?
12. Why do some analysts see the budget of a government as being of no less importance than its CAFR in assessing financial condition?
13. The GASB requires governments to identify their principal taxpayers in their CAFR's statistical section. In what way does this information contribute to an analysis of financial condition?
14. Why are "one shots" and other financial gimmicks of special concern to analysts?

EXERCISES

11-1

Select the *best* answer.

1. New York State has unlimited authority to control and regulate Yonkers as well as all other municipalities within its jurisdiction. Consistent with GASB Statement No. 14:
   a. Both New York State and Yonkers could be considered primary governments.
   b. Only New York State could be considered a primary government.
   c. Yonkers could be considered a primary government only if the state has explicitly passed legislation ceding key fiscal controls to local governments such as Yonkers.
   d. Yonkers could be considered a primary government only if the state opts not to account for Yonkers as a component unit.

2. Which of the following is *not* a power that a municipality must have to be considered fiscally independent of other governments?
   a. To determine its budget
   b. To levy taxes and set rates
   c. To establish debt limitations
   d. To issue bonds
3. Carson City's council appoints a voting majority of the Carson City Housing Authority's governing board. Which of the following additional criteria would *not* be sufficient evidence that Carson City is financially accountable for the Carson City Housing Authority?
   a. The mayor of Carson City must approve the Housing Authority's budget.
   b. Two of the five members of the Housing Authority's governing board are also members of the Carson City council.
   c. Carson City guarantees any debt incurred by the Housing Authority.
   d. The Carson City council can appoint the managing director of the Housing Authority.
4. The Sierra Library District satisfies the criteria to be blended into the financial statements of Sierra County. Which of the following fund types of the two governments would *not* be combined in the blended statements?
   a. Pension trust funds
   b. General funds
   c. Permanent funds
   d. Proprietary funds
5. A primary government could "blend" its financial statements with those of a component unit as long as
   a. The governing boards of the two governments are substantively the same.
   b. There is a financial benefit/burden relationship between the two governments.
   c. The primary government provides services exclusively to the component unit.
   d. The two governments satisfy GASB Statement No. 14 criteria for "economic inseparability."
6. With respect to a *nonmajor* component unit, a government
   a. Must disclose key financial data about the unit in either the financial statements themselves or in notes thereto.
   b. Must, in its combining fund statements, present detailed financial statements of the unit in a separate column.
   c. May, in its government-wide statements, exclude data pertaining to the unit from its component units column.
   d. Is not required to provide even summary financial data of the individual unit.
7. Which of the following is *incorrect* with respect to a joint venture?
   a. It must be reported as a component unit of each government that has an interest of 20 percent or more in the venture.
   b. It may be accounted for in a proprietary fund on the equity basis.
   c. It may be reported in a schedule of capital assets.
   d. It must be accounted for in government-wide statements on an equity basis.
8. A related organization
   a. Must be reported in the combining statements of the government to which it is related, but must not be incorporated into the government-wide statements of that government.
   b. May be reported as a component unit of the reporting government to which it is related if the reporting government elects so.
   c. Must be described in notes to the financial statements of the reporting government to which it is related but must not be incorporated into the financial statements of that government.
   d. May either be described in notes to the financial statements of the reporting government to which it is related or be incorporated into the financial statements of that government.
9. The James City school system, although not a separate legal entity, maintains its own set of financial records. It is administered by a board, the members of which are appointed by the James City mayor. The system receives 70 percent of its funds from city appropriations and the balance from state and federal grants. The James City council has the authority to approve the school system's budget and to veto any decisions of its administering board. James City
   a. Should account for the system as a component unit and blend its financial statements with its own.
   b. Should account for the system as a component unit and report it "discretely."
   c. Should account for, and report, the system as it does other city departments.
   d. Should account for the system as a component unit only if the system does not prepare its own standalone financial statements.
10. If a primary government has several component units, none of which satisfies the criteria for blending, then in its government-wide statements it
   a. Must report governmental component units in one column and business-type component units in another.
   b. Must combine all component units into a single column.
   c. Must present each major component unit in a separate column but may combine all nonmajor component units into a single column.
   d. Must incorporate data of all component units, whether major or nonmajor, into one or more columns.

11-2

Select the *best* answer.

1. Which of the following should *not* be included in the introductory section of a city's CAFR?

a. Management's discussion and analysis
b. Letter of transmittal
c. Government Finance Officers' certificate of achievement
d. Photos of city officials

2. Which of the following should *not* be included in a city's management's discussion and analysis?
   a. Condensed financial information drawn from government-wide statements
   b. A ten-year forecast of sales tax revenues
   c. A discussion of the condition of the city's road system
   d. An explanation of the decrease during the past year in the unrestricted general fund balance
3. A city's general fund budget-to-actual comparisons should be included as part of a CAFR's
   a. Introductory section
   b. Notes to the basic financial statements
   c. Required supplementary information
   d. Statistical section
4. Internal service funds
   a. Should be presented in the governmental fund statements in a single column
   b. Should be presented in the proprietary fund statements in a single column
   c. Should be presented in multiple columns (one for each major fund) in a separate set of fund statements
   d. Need not be reported in the fund statements
5. Which of the following tables would be least likely to be found in the statistical section of a city's CAFR?
   a. General revenues by source—last ten years
   b. Computation of overlapping debt
   c. Property values—last ten years
   d. Salaries of key government officials—last ten years
6. For purposes of external reporting, private colleges and universities
   a. Must adhere to all FASB pronouncements
   b. Must adhere to all GASB pronouncements
   c. Can opt to follow either all FASB or all GASB pronouncements
   d. Must follow all FASB pronouncements issued prior to November 30, 1989, and either all or none of the GASB pronouncements subsequent to that date
7. For purposes of external reporting, a public college or university
   a. Must report as if it were a general purpose government
   b. May report as if it were a comparable private college or university
   c. May report as a special purpose government engaged exclusively in business-type activities
   d. May report in accordance with the AICPA college and university model if it had adhered to that model prior to the issuance of GASB Statement No. 35
8. Which of the following would *not* be reported as required supplementary information?
   a. Management's discussion and analysis
   b. Details of pension actuarial valuations
   c. The condition of infrastructure
   d. The GFOA certificate of achievement (if earned)
9. Which of the following is least likely to be included in the CAFR of New Jersey State University, a public university that reports as a business-type entity?
   a. Government-wide statement of activities
   b. Management's discussion and analysis
   c. Statement of cash flows
   d. Required supplementary information
10. A special purpose government, such as an independent school district, that carries out multiple programs
    a. May opt to report as if it were a single purpose government engaged in only governmental activities
    b. May opt to report as if it were a single purpose government engaged in only business-type activities
    c. Must report as if it were a general purpose government
    d. Must report as if it were a general purpose government, except that it need not prepare government-wide statements

11-3

Governments must apply the criteria of GASB Statement No. 14 in determining whether and how to include an affiliated entity in its reporting entity.

A city is considering whether and how it should include the following affiliated organizations in its reporting entity.

1. Its school system, although not a legally separate government, is managed by a school board elected by city residents. The system is financed with general tax revenues of the city and its budget is incorporated into that of the city at large (and thereby is subject to the same approval and appropriation process as other city expenditures).
2. Its capital asset financing authority is a legally separate government that leases equipment to the city. To finance the equipment, the authority issues bonds that are guaranteed by the city and expected to be paid from the rents received from the city. The authority leases equipment exclusively to the city.
3. Its housing authority, which provides loans to low-income families within the city, is governed by a five-person board appointed by the city's mayor and its debt is guaranteed by the city.
4. Its hospital is owned by the city but managed under contract by a private hospital management firm.
5. Its water purification plant is owned in equal shares by the city and two neighboring counties. The city's interest in the plant was acquired with resources from its water utility (enterprise) fund.
6. Its community college, a separate legal entity, is governed by a board of governors elected by city residents and has its own taxing and budgetary authority.

Based on the very limited information provided, indicate whether and how the city should report the affiliated entities.

11-4

Some component units are presented "discretely"; others are "blended."

A city's reporting entity includes the following component units:

1. A capital projects financing authority purchases capital assets and leases them exclusively to the city. It finances the acquisitions by issuing revenue bonds, which are payable out of the lease payments collected from the city.
2. A housing finance authority is governed by a board, the majority of whose members are appointed by the city council. The board purchases houses and leases them to low-income city residents. It finances the acquisitions by issuing revenue bonds, which are payable out of the lease payments collected from the residents.
3. A housing finance authority is governed by a board, the members of which are also members of the city council. The board purchases houses and leases them to low-income city residents. It finances the acquisitions by issuing revenue bonds, which are payable out of the lease payments collected from the residents.
4. A sanitation authority is governed by a board, the majority of whose members are appointed by the city council. The authority provides trash collection services exclusively to city residents. It finances its capital assets with bonds that are guaranteed by the city. It obtains all of its revenues from user charges.

   a. Based on the limited information provided, indicate whether each of the component units described above should be presented discretely or should be blended. Justify your responses.
   b. Explain what is meant by "blending." How is the general fund of a component unit reported on the primary government's financial statements?

11-5

Ratios can help users assess fiscal condition.

The data that follow were taken from the CAFR of Chaseville, a mid-sized midwestern city with a population of 82,000. All dollar amounts are in thousands.

Total assessed value of property	$2,300,000
Total property tax levy	42,500
General fund cash and investments	3,120
General fund total assets	19,500
General fund total liabilities	16,230
General fund reserved fund balance	780
General fund unreserved fund balance	5,789
General fund total tax revenues	38,756
General fund total expenditures	44,600
General fund debt service expenditures	4,500
General fund revenue from own sources	46,500
General fund total revenues	48,865
General fund intergovernmental revenue	2,003
General fund public safety expenditures	9,321
General fund health and welfare expenditures	4,567
Direct debt	70,000
Overlapping debt	46,486

Indicate and calculate the ratios that would best be used to compare Chaseville with similar cities as to whether

1. It is more dependent upon revenues from other governments.
2. It is directing a greater share of its expenditures toward public safety.
3. It has the necessary liquid resources to be better able to meet its short-term obligations as they come due.
4. It has a greater available general fund balance relative to revenues to meet future needs.
5. Its citizens pay a higher tax rate.
6. Its citizens pay more in taxes per person.
7. It is a wealthier city, in that its citizens own relatively more property.
8. It exerts greater fiscal effort.

11-6

The GASB flowchart can be used to guide decisions as to whether and how to incorporate a potential component unit.

A town's library system is a legally constituted government entity. It is governed by a ten-person board. Six of the members are appointed by the town's council; the other four are selected by the other members of the board. The members serve staggered terms of three years. Once appointed, the members can be removed from office only for illegal activities.

The town provides 95 percent of the library system's resources and thereby can control the total amount spent by the system. However, the governing board adopts the system's budget and the budget need not be approved by the town. The board also controls the day-to-day operations of the system.

Using the flowchart presented in the text, indicate whether and, if so, how the town should incorporate the library system into its own financial statements.

11-7

A government's Comprehensive Annual Financial Report (CAFR) is divided into three main sections.

The statements, schedules, tables, and other types of data that follow are found in the annual report of a typical municipality. For each of these items indicate whether it would be found in:

- the introductory section,
- the financial section, or
- the statistical section.

If the item would be found in the financial section, then specify whether it would be included in:

- the management's discussion and analysis (MD&A)
- the basic financial statements

- required supplementary information other than the MD&A
- combining statements and schedules

1. A balance sheet of nonmajor special revenue funds
2. A certificate of achievement for excellence in financial reporting
3. Data on general revenues, by source, for the past ten years
4. The letter of transmittal
5. The MD&A
6. A government-wide statement of activities
7. The total unfunded actuarial liability of its pension plan for the past three years
8. Data on property tax collections for the past ten years
9. A statement of revenues, expenses, and changes in net assets for the city's utility fund (one of two major fund proprietary funds)
10. A statement comparing budgeted and actual revenues and expenditures for a special revenue fund
11. A statement of cash flows for a nonmajor enterprise fund

PROBLEMS

Continuing Problem

Review the Comprehensive Annual Financial Report (CAFR) that you obtained.

1. Do the notes to the financial statements indicate the component units and other related entities that are included within the reporting entity? Do they indicate any units that are not included? Do they explain why these units are included or excluded?
2. How are the component units presented in the government-wide financial statements?
3. How are they presented in the funds statements?
4. Has the government entered into any joint ventures? If so, how are they reported?
5. What schedules or other information does the government report as "required supplementary information" (RSI)?
6. Does the report contain all of the statistical information presented in Table 11-3?

11-1

Public housing authorities are typical of the related entities toward which GASB Statement No. 14 is directed.

A city established a public housing authority to fund the construction of low-income residential homes within city limits. The authority is governed by a nine-person board of trustees. New trustees are nominated by the board itself, but are formally appointed by the city council. However, the city council has never rejected a board nominee. The trustees have complete responsibility for the day-to-day operations of the authority, but are required to obtain city council endorsement of the authority's annual budget and must submit audited annual financial statements to the council. The authority is permitted to issue its own debt, which is guaranteed by the federal government.

Approximately 90 percent of the authority's day-to-day operating costs are paid by the Housing and Urban Development Department (HUD, a federal agency) and 10 percent by the city.

The sources of the funds used by the authority to perform its functions are as follows:

- Authority-issued bonds (which will be repaid by tenant rents)—60 percent
- Direct federal subsidies—30 percent
- Direct city subsidies—10 percent

1. Should the city include the public housing authority in its reporting entity as a component unit per the provisions of GASB Statement No. 14? If so, how? Explain your response.
2. Suppose the same facts except that the authority did not directly fund the construction of homes. Instead, it lent money to the city's housing department, which in turn lent the funds to home buyers. How, if at all, would your response differ?
3. Suppose, instead, that the city council also served as the authority's board of trustees. How, if at all, would your response differ? Explain.

11-2

State governments face especially difficult issues as to whether to incorporate their "independent" agencies in their reporting entity.

A state established the Mohansic River Power Authority to construct and operate dams and to provide electric power to rural areas. The authority, a state-owned corporation, is governed by an independent board of directors, the ten members of which are appointed by the governor. They can be removed only for criminal misconduct or comparable misdeeds.

The board of directors has complete control over the authority's operations. The authority does not need approval to issue debt, to sign contracts, or to hire managers. Its debt is not guaranteed by the state. Per the authority's charter, any excess of revenues over expenditures is to be used for capital expansion or improvements or to offset future deficits.

Because the authority is a public utility, the rates that it charges its customers must be approved by the state's public utility commission. The public utility commission considers the authority's request for rate adjustments just as if the authority were a private utility.

1. Do you believe that the state should include the authority in its reporting entity? If so, how? Justify your

response, with reference to the GASB criteria. (This problem is based on an actual situation; there is no clear-cut solution.)

2. Suppose, instead, that the governor could remove members of the board at will. Would your answer be the same? Explain.
3. Suppose the members can serve indefinitely on the board, subject to annual reappointment by the governor. Would your answer be the same? Explain.

11-3

Discrete presentation, unlike blending, may combine two or more entities into a single column.

Hawkins Township has two component units that it is required to include in its reporting entity. The first, a housing authority, maintains two funds: a general fund and a special revenue fund. The second, a transportation authority, has but one fund, an enterprise fund. The township itself has only a general fund.

The fund balance sheets, in highly condensed form, of all three entities are shown below (in millions). Also presented, as appropriate, are capital assets and long-term obligations that are not recognized on the fund statements, since the statements are on a modified accrual basis.

Hawkins Township

	General Fund	Capital Assets and Long-term Obligations
Cash and investments	$800	
Capital assets		$140
Less: accumulated depreciation		40
Net capital assets		$100
Total assets	$800	$100
Long-term obligations		$ 30
Fund balance	$800	
Total long-term obligations and fund balances	$800	$ 30

Transportation Authority

Cash and investments	$ 50
Capital assets	800
Less: accumulated depreciation	200
Net capital assets	600
Total assets	$650
Long-term obligations	$200
Fund balance	$450
Total long-term obligations and fund balance	$650

Housing Authority

	General Fund	Special Revenue Fund	Capital Assets and Long-term Obligations
Cash and investments	$10	$5	
Capital assets			$45
Less: accumulated depreciation			20
Net capital assets			$25
Total assets	$10	$5	$25
Long-term obligations			$ 5
Fund balance	$10	$5	
Total long-term obligations and fund balance	$10	$5	$ 5

1. Assume that both component units qualify for discrete presentation. On its government-wide statements, the township elects to combine the two units into a single column.
   a. Prepare a government-wide statement of net assets (on a full accrual basis) that presents both the township and its component units.
   b. Comment on the significance of the column in which the two component units are presented.
2. Suppose instead that the town is required to blend the two component units.
   a. Prepare a government-wide statement of net assets. Be sure to show the transportation authority as a business-type activity.
   b. If the township were to prepare fund statements, how would it report the housing authority's special revenue fund? How would it report its general fund?

11-4

Colleges and universities may report as if they engaged only in business-type activities.

Review the financial statements of the University of Virginia in Table 11-4 of the text.

1. For purposes of internal accounting, the university maintains several funds. Why must the university maintain so many funds? Provide examples of the funds most likely maintained by this (or for that matter any major public university).
2. What is the most likely distinction between the net assets classified as "expendable" and those as "nonexpendable?"
3. Suppose that the university financed the construction of its dormitories by issuing bonds secured by revenues from student room fees. The dormitories are accounted for as an auxiliary enterprise. What information about the auxiliary enterprise would the university have to include in its CAFR? Why?

4. Suppose that the university elected to report as a special-purpose government engaged in both governmental and business-type activities. How would the financial statements differ from those presented? Which set of financial statements would provide more-comprehensive information? Explain.
5. The university attributes some of its revenues to "auxiliary enterprises." What is the most likely distinction between auxiliary enterprises and other academic or service units of the university? Provide examples.
6. The university reports unrestricted net assets of over $874 million. Suppose that a faculty member complained in a letter to the university president that the institution is holding back resources that should properly be used to increase faculty salaries, acquire computers and library books, and improve classroom facilities. What might be an obvious response to the faculty member's complaint?
7. The university reports a significant (over $317 million) operating loss. Why might you argue that such is misleading and, indeed, should be expected?
8. The university's reported operating loss exceeded its operating cash outflow. What was the primary reason for the difference?
9. Do the financial statements provide you with any reason to question whether the university is investing adequately in plant, equipment, and other capital assets?

11-5

The fund balance sheet of a public university can be recast so that it conforms with GAAP.

The fund balance sheet of Sundown State University, a public institution, is presented below. For purposes of external reporting, the university has opted to report as a special purpose entity that engages in business-type activities.

As best the data permit, recast the balance sheet into one that conforms to generally accepted accounting principles.

11-6

Citizens of wealthier cities may not only have a lighter tax burden, but they may also receive more intergovernmental assistance.

The following data were drawn from the CAFRs of two northern Virginia cities (all dollar amounts are in thousands):

	Fairfax	Manassas
Population	20,200	27,856
Value of taxable property	$1,933,472	$1,948,337
Property tax levy	18,664	24,534
Total general fund revenues	38,397	36,092
General fund tax revenues	31,861	29,706
Intergovernmental revenues	5,050	2,351

Sundown State University, Fund Balance Sheet (in thousands)

	Current	Loan	Endowment	Plant	Total
Assets					
Cash and temporary investments	$18,567	$22,108	$29,611	$ 10,853	$ 81,139
Accounts receivable		2,736		45,974	48,710
Inventories	1,990				1,990
Loans to other funds	8,557		6,879		15,436
Land, buildings and equipment, net of accumulated depreciation				283,181	283,181
Total assets	$29,114	$24,844	$36,490	$340,008	$430,456
Liabilities					
Accounts payable	$23,024			$ 1,704	$ 24,728
Loans from other funds		$32		15,404	15,436
Bonds payable		24,505		188,466	212,971
Total liabilities	$23,024	$24,537	$0	$205,574	$253,135
Net assets	$6,090	$307	$36,490	$134,434	$177,321
Fund balances					
Restricted	$ 4,102		$20,346	$134,434	$158,882
Designated by the university	1,002		10,000		11,002
Unrestricted	986	$ 307	6,144	0	7,437
Total fund balance	$ 6,090	$ 307	$36,490	$134,434	$177,321

1. Based on the limited data provided, which city has the greater resources upon which to draw?
2. Which city imposes the greater tax burden on its population based on
   a. Per capita total general fund taxes?
   b. Per capita property taxes?
   c. Tax rate (i.e., property taxes as a percent of property value)?
3. Which city receives a greater amount of assistance from other governments
   a. As a percentage of its total general fund revenues?
   b. Per capita?

11-7

Environmental regulators see the financial forests, but not the trees.

The U.S. Environmental Protection Agency (EPA) requires owners of municipal solid waste landfills to demonstrate that they are financially capable of satisfying the costs of closing and subsequently caring for the landfills that they operate. Per EPA regulations, one way for a local government to demonstrate financial capability is by satisfying certain financial standards. In particular, a government must meet the following four ratio targets:

1. Cash plus marketable securities to total expenditures must be greater than or equal to 0.05
2. Annual debt service to total expenditures must be less than or equal to 0.20
3. Long-term debt issued and outstanding to capital expenditures must be less than or equal to 2.00
4. Current cost estimates for closure, postclosure, corrective action to total revenue must be less than or equal to 0.43

The regulations provide no interpretative guidance except to imply that the ratios are to be based on financial statements prepared in accordance with generally accepted accounting principles.

Suppose you are engaged as a consultant to a state agency that has to administer the regulations. In the course of examining the evidence of financial capability supplied by municipal landfill operators, state officials raised the following questions as to how the ratios should be calculated:

1. Should the ratios be based only on a government's general fund or should they encompass funds in addition to the general fund
2. Assuming the ratios should not be based exclusively on the general fund, should they include proprietary funds (i.e., does use of the term *expenditures* imply that expenses should be excluded)?
3. Should the ratios incorporate restricted as well as unrestricted funds?
4. Should capital expenditures include only those for the year in question, or an average of several years?

   a. Propose answers to these questions that you believe are most consistent with the EPA's objective of assuring financial capability. For each question, recommend an appropriate policy, justify it, and cite any potential limitations.
   b. Suggest at least three additional questions that you believe need to be addressed.

11-8

Changes in mix of revenues and expenditures must be interpreted with care.

The data that follow were drawn from the city of Boulder, Colorado's CAFR. Dates have been changed. They are from two statistical-section schedules showing the mix of revenue and expenditures for a ten-year period. They include amounts only from the general fund, special revenue funds, and debt service funds.

	2004	1995
	(amounts in thousands)	
Revenues		
Sales and use taxes	$41,941	$18,750
General property taxes	9,501	4,900
Other taxes	9,673	3,756
Charges for services	5,004	2,524
Intergovernmental	10,114	6,840
Proceeds from bonds and notes		16,330
Other	8,246	5,692
Total revenues	$84,479	$58,792
Expenditures		
General government and administration	$10,222	$3,975
Public safety	17,466	10,786
Public works	16,472	7,499
Housing and human services	6,195	4,093
Culture and recreation	16,764	9,016
Acquisition of real estate and open spaces	11,315	11,706
Debt service	10,816	2,886
Other	2,323	
Total expenditures	$91,573	$49,961

1. As a consultant for a citizens' association, you have been asked to determine whether there have been significant changes in the way the city acquires and spends its resources. Prepare a schedule in which you compare the mix of revenues and of expenditures of 2004 with that of 1995. Note and comment on any items that might distort a straightforward comparison of revenues and expenditures.
2. Comment on any changes between the two years that you consider significant.
3. Expenditures for debt service increased significantly. What are the most likely reasons for the increase? Is it necessarily a sign of increased financial stress?

11-9

Strong financial statements are not necessarily indicative of strong financial condition.

The following information was taken from the CAFRs of two cities of approximately the same size in the same state.

	Riverside	Lakeview
	(dollar amounts in thousands)	
Population	92,000	96,000
Number of employees	1,050	1,420
Total operating revenues	$120,000	$170,000
Property tax levy	83,000	102,000
Total operating expenditures	112,000	174,000
Cash, investments and receivables	27,000	15,000
Current liabilities	9,000	12,000
Unreserved general fund balance	7,000	1,000
General obligation debt	21,000	32,000
Total appraised value of property	965,000	1,620,000

1. Compare the financial condition of the two cities based on the following indicators:
   a. Per capita operating expenditures
   b. Per capita general obligation debt
   c. Operating surplus (deficit)
   d. Liquid assets/current liabilities
   e. Unreserved general fund balance/total operating revenues
   f. Per capital number of employees
2. Compare the financial condition of the two cities based on the following additional measures:
   a. Operating revenue/total appraised value of property
   b. Property taxes/total appraised value of property
   c. Per capita total appraised value of property
3. What conclusions can be drawn from the two sets of measures? Comment on the apparent discrepancy between them.

11-10

Qualitative factors may be as important as quantitative factors in assessing a government's fiscal health.

You are a CPA in charge of auditing a midsize school district. You recognize that the risk of financial failure is dependent as much on factors not reported in the basic financial statements as on factors that are reported. Accordingly, you conduct a comprehensive analysis of the district. Some of your findings are summarized below. For each, indicate how it might affect the ability of the district to service its outstanding debt and provide the services that its constituents expect.

1. Owing to an influx of new high-tech firms into a nearby community (which is not within the jurisdiction of the school district), the population within the district is increasing by approximately 8 percent per year. Most of the new arrivals are young engineers and other professionals.
2. A developer is constructing a senior citizens' retirement village within the jurisdiction of the school district. The village is expected to increase both the district's population and its land value by approximately 4 percent.
3. During the year the district changed the pay date of its employees. Previously employees were paid on the last day of the month; now they will be paid on the first day of the following month.
4. The district's largest taxpayer, representing 10 percent of its property tax revenues, manufactures blue jeans and other clothing made of denim.
5. The district's superintendent recently resigned in the wake of charges that he falsified student scores on statewide achievement tests.
6. School district elections are hotly contested. The present school board is composed of three members who are committed to "traditional" educational methods and four who are considered "progressives." Board meetings are almost always contentious.
7. Voters of the county in which the school district is located recently approved the largest general obligation bond issue in the county's history.
8. One of two candidates for governor of the state in which the school district is located is a strong advocate of a school voucher plan. The plan would provide financial assistance to students who elect to attend private schools.

11-11

One of the challenges of financial analysis in government is that it is not always obvious whether an increase in a financial ratio is a sign of increasing or decreasing fiscal strength.

Explain the significance of each of the following ratios. For each of the ratios indicate whether an increase can be interpreted as a sign of (1) increasing or (2) decreasing fiscal strength. Where appropriate, show how an increase in the ratio can be interpreted as a sign of either. Explain and justify your response.

1. Cash, short-term investments, and receivables/Current liabilities
2. Revenue from own sources/Median family income
3. Number of employees/Population
4. Property tax revenues/Total operating revenues
5. Nondiscretionary expenditures/Total expenditures
6. Unreserved general fund balance/Total operating revenues
7. Intergovernmental revenues/Total operating revenues
8. Expenditures for public safety/Total expenditures

SOLUTION TO EXERCISE FOR REVIEW AND SELF-STUDY

1. As measured by both per capita direct debt (discussed in Chapter 8) and percentage of total assessed value of property, the debt burden increased substantially. Per capita direct debt increased from $0.49 to $0.76 (all dollar amounts in thousands). Direct debt as a percentage of total assessed value of property increased from 1.90 percent to 2.58 percent:

	2000	2005
Direct debt	$ 35,849	$ 72,900
Total appraised value of property	1,885,000	2,827,500
Direct debt as a percentage of appraised value of property	1.90%	2.58%

Similarly, overlapping debt also increased both per capita and as a percentage of assessed value of property.

2. Based on population, the government is imposing a somewhat greater revenue burden on its constituents in 2005 than in 2000. Per capita revenue from own sources increased from $0.52 to $0.59. Relative to wealth (i.e., assessed value of property), however, it is imposing a slightly lighter burden:

	2000	2005
Total revenue from own sources	$ 38,600	$ 56,550
Total appraised value of property	1,885,000	2,827,500
Revenue from own sources as a percentage of appraised value of property	2.05%	2.00%

3. Liquidity can be measured by the ratio of cash and investments to current liabilities. Based on liabilities of the general fund only (all of which can be assumed to be current), the town is more liquid in 2005 than it was in 2000:

	2000	2005
General fund cash and investments	$ 2,280	$ 3,457
General fund, total liabilities	12,952	14,388
Cash and investments as a percentage of general fund liabilities	17.6%	24.03%

4. Based on a comparison of unreserved general fund balance to total general fund revenues, the town's reserves have been diminished:

	2000	2005
General fund unreserved fund balance	$ 4,739	$ 4,612
General fund, total revenues	40,063	61,697
General fund unreserved fund balance as a percentage of general fund revenues	11.83%	7.48%

5. Property taxes are often considered a stable form of revenue. The percentage of revenue received from property taxes has remained approximately the same:

	2000	2005
Total property tax levy	$21,560	$32,340
General fund, total revenues	40,063	61,697
Property tax levy as a percentage of total general fund revenues	53.82%	52.42%

However, intergovernmental revenues, generally considered more subject to risk, increased:

	2000	2005
General fund intergovernmental revenue	$ 1,463	$ 5,147
General fund, total revenues	40,063	61,697
General fund intergovernmental revenue as a percentage of total general fund revenues	3.65%	8.34%

6. The per capita burden of debt service has increased from $0.08 to $0.10, but debt service as a percentage of general fund expenditures has increased only slightly:

	2000	2005
Total debt service expenditures	$ 5,793	$ 9,633
Total general fund expenditures	39,174	60,328
Debt service as a percentage of total general fund expenditures	14.79%	15.97%

7. Between 2000 and 2005, expenditures for public safety increased substantially relative to other expenditures whereas those for health and welfare increased slightly.

	2000	2005
Public safety expenditures	$13,654	$24,301
Total general fund expenditures	39,174	60,328
Public safety expenditures as a percentage of total general fund expenditures	34.85%	40.28%
Health and welfare expenditures	$ 2,979	$ 4,915
Total general fund expenditures	39,174	60,328
Health and welfare expenditures as a percentage of total general fund expenditures	7.60%	8.15%

8. Additional questions to be raised include the following:
   a. Did the revenues or expenditures of either year include substantial "one shot" transactions?
   b. What changes were there in the mix of industries on which the town relies for its revenues?
   c. What changes were there in the characteristics of the population (e.g., in age, income, and educational distribution)?
   d. What changes were there in per capita income?
   e. What is the condition of the town's infrastructure? Is it adequate for the future?
   f. What are the town's forecasts of revenue and expenditures for the next five years?
   g. How do the ratios and forecasts of this city compare with those of similar cities?

CHAPTER 12

Other Not-for-Profit Organizations

Learning Objectives

After studying this chapter you should understand:

- Which standard-setting authorities are responsible for not-for-profit organizations
- How and why the financial statements of not-for-profits divide all resources into three categories (unrestricted, temporarily restricted, and permanently restricted) based on donor stipulations
- How not-for-profits report cash flows
- How contributions are distinguished from exchange transactions
- The general rules governing the recognition of contributions
- How pledges, both unrestricted and restricted, are accounted for
- When contributions of services should be recognized as revenue
- When collection items should be recognized as revenue
- The special issues pertaining to conditional promises to give
- How pass-through contributions are accounted for
- How and when gains and losses on investments should be recognized
- How fixed assets should be depreciated and reported
- The unique issues of accounting and reporting faced by hospitals
- The unique issues of accounting and reporting faced by universities (both private and governmental)
- What factors should be taken into account in assessing the financial condition of not-for-profits

Governments and not-for-profit organizations confront similar accounting and reporting issues. However, they do not necessarily resolve them alike. Differences in standards can be partly explained—and indeed, justified—by differences in the entities' characteristics and resultant differences in constituents' information needs. For example, not-for-profits lack the authority of law to generate revenues, and they have greater flexibility in administering their budgets. Differences in standards may also be attributed to dissimilarities in the composition and perspectives of the standard-setting authorities. This chapter will first address accounting and reporting issues that affect all not-for-profits in general. Then it shall consider the issues facing two types of specialized entities—hospitals and other health care institutions, and universities.

WHO'S IN CHARGE?

Whereas the Governmental Accounting Standards Board (GASB) has standard-setting jurisdiction over all state and local governments, the Financial Accounting Standards Board (FASB) has jurisdiction over all other not-for-profits, except the federal government. As a consequence, even similar types of organizations may fall within the province of different boards. A state university or city hospital would be under the authority of the GASB, whereas a private university or hospital would be under the jurisdiction of the FASB.

Although the FASB began operations in 1973, it did not establish standards targeted specifically at not-for-profit organizations until 1987, when it issued Statement No. 93, *Recognition of Depreciation by Not-for-Profit Organizations.* Until then, the American Institute of Certified Public Accountants (AICPA) articulated the accounting and reporting practices of not-for-profit organizations through a series of industry audit guides. Individual guides dealt with colleges and universities, hospitals and other health care providers, voluntary health and welfare organizations, and other not-for-profit entities. Separate AICPA committees were responsible for each of these publications, causing inconsistencies in the accounting and reporting guidelines. However, because the FASB pronouncements were now common to all not-for-profits, in 1996 the AICPA eliminated the inconsistencies and consolidated its audit guides into two:

1. ***Health care organizations*** covers hospitals, clinics, health maintenance organizations, nursing homes, and home health organizations.
2. ***Not-for-profit organizations*** covers all other not-for-profits, including colleges and universities.

These guides, which are updated periodically, incorporate the latest FASB pronouncements. However, they also provide guidance as to issues not addressed by FASB.

As will be evident in this chapter, the accounting practices of not-for-profits are more compatible with those of businesses than of governments. Like their GASB counterparts, the FASB and AICPA pronouncements emphasize the superiority of the accrual basis over the cash basis of accounting. But they are far less indulgent of modifications of, and exceptions to, the accrual basis.

External reporting is entirely on the full accrual basis. Irrespective of how not-for-profits maintain their records for purposes of internal management, the modified accrual basis has no place in their publicly issued statements. As a consequence, not-for-profits do not distinguish between expenses and expenditures. They have only expenses.

WHAT SHOULD BE THE FORM AND CONTENT OF FINANCIAL STATEMENTS?

As emphasized in Chapter 2, not-for-profits, like governments, account for their resources in funds, each of which is a separate accounting entity. As in governments, most entities maintain an unrestricted operating (or general) fund, as well as one or more restricted funds. Accordingly, the journal entries to be proposed in this chapter will be made in the individual funds. However, the FASB is not concerned with the specific funds maintained by not-for-profits. Instead, it is interested in how entities report their overall financial position and results of operations. A key issue, therefore, is whether not-for-profits should display separately each of the funds, consolidate them into single column presentation, or aggregate the funds in a way that would combine groups of funds. Although this chapter directs considerable attention to revenue and expense recognition, it will soon become apparent that how funds are combined affects how and when certain types of revenues and expenses are reported.

REPORTING ASSETS AND LIABILITIES

In 1993 the FASB issued Statement No. 117, *Financial Statements of Not-for-Profit Organizations*, which established standards for the form and content of financial statements. The statement provides that not-for-profits must issue three primary financial statements:

- A statement of financial position (balance sheet)
- A statement of activities
- A statement of cash flows

Per Statement No. 117, not-for-profits must classify their net assets into three categories based on the existence or absence of *donor-imposed* restrictions:

- Unrestricted net assets
- Temporarily restricted net assets—mainly resources that must be used either for specific purposes, in specific periods, or when specified events have occurred
- Permanently restricted net assets—ordinarily, endowments with a principal that must remain permanently intact, with only the income available for expenditure

Temporarily restricted net assets can take several forms. Resources that must be used for research, for specific programs, or for acquisition of plant and equipment would be temporarily restricted as to *purpose*. The resources would be released from the restriction when the organization incurred expenses that satisfied the donor's stipulations. A **term endowment** would be temporarily restricted as to *time*. A term endowment is a gift from which only the income is available for expenditure for a specified period of time. Once the period of time has expired, then the principal of the gift is also available for expenditure. Pledges that will not be received until future periods may also be seen as subject to time restrictions. They are unavailable for expenditure until then. An **annuity** would be temporarily restricted pending the occurrence of a *specified event*. An annuity is a gift that provides the donor with income until his or her death. Upon death, the balance of the gift reverts to the donee for either restricted or unrestricted purposes.

Even assets classified as unrestricted are not necessarily free of all restrictions—only those imposed by *donors*. Restrictions imposed by the organization's members, its own governing board, or by outside parties other than donors, such as bondholders and regulatory authorities, do not affect how net assets should be classified.

Statement No. 117 does not detail how net assets must be presented. It merely requires that the balance sheet present six totals: total assets, total liabilities, total net assets, total unrestricted net assets, total temporarily restricted net assets, and total permanently restricted net assets. However, in an illustrative balance sheet, it combines the organization's assets, liabilities, and net assets (i.e., fund balances) from all of its funds and presents them in a single column. Net assets are then broken down into the three required categories of restrictiveness. Information as to the nature and amount of restrictions may be shown on the face of the balance sheet or in notes to the financial statements. If shown on the face of the balance sheet, separate line items may be added to the two categories of restricted net assets (e.g., "restricted to acquisition of plant" or "restricted to scholarships"). As another (but not the only other) possibility, the three categories of assets may be presented in three separate columns, with specific resources as well as net assets assigned to each of the three categories.

The FASB statement also directs that data as to the liquidity of the organization's assets and liabilities be reported either on the face of the financial statements or in the accompanying notes. Most organizations satisfy this requirement by categorizing their assets and liabilities as either current or noncurrent. For not-for-profits (unlike governments), there is little ambiguity as to what constitutes a current asset or liability: The definitions of business accounting control. Per the AICPA's *Accounting Research Bulletin* 43, Chapter 3a, current assets are resources reasonably expected to be realized in cash or sold or consumed during the normal operating cycle of the business. Current liabilities are obligations whose liquidation is expected to require the use of existing resources classified as current assets, or the creation of other current liabilities. Table 12-1 presents the balance sheet of the American Health Association, a voluntary health and welfare organization.

REPORTING REVENUES AND EXPENSES

FASB Statement No. 117 directs that revenues and expenses be reported in a **statement of activities.** Like the balance sheet, the statement of activities should focus on the organization as a whole, rather than on individual funds. Further, it should report the changes in each of the three categories of net assets. The FASB specifies that the statement of activities must break out gains and losses recognized on investments and other assets from revenues and expenses, but otherwise leaves the form and content of the statement to the individual organization. Therefore, as in the balance sheet, organizations can present the information in respect to the three categories of net assets in separate sections of the statement (several rows each for the different categories) or in three separate columns.

As would be expected, the statement instructs that revenues be reported as increases in one of the three categories of net assets, depending on donor-imposed restrictions. However, in a controversial decision, the Board concluded that *all expenses should be reported as decreases in unrestricted net assets.* The Board reasoned that donors restrict only how the contributed resources may be used. They do not control expenses. "Expenses result from the decisions of an organization's managers about the activities to be carried out, and how and when particular resources are to be used," it explained. In other words, donors do not determine the activities in which an organization engages. Their control is limited to dictating the activities for which their contributions will be used to pay.

As a consequence of this requirement, a not-for-profit must make two sets of journal entries whenever it spends restricted resources. The first, in a restricted fund, records the decrease in cash or other assets and the release of the restrictions (a decrease in restricted net assets); the second, in an unrestricted fund, records the expense and the release of the restriction. This entry has no effect on unrestricted net assets, inasmuch as it consists of an expense (a debit) offset by the bookkeeping equivalent of a transfer in (a credit).

EXAMPLE *Reporting Revenues and Expenses*

The Professional Accountants' Association receives a $50,000 contribution to promote "truth in budgeting" among state and local governments. In the same year it spends the funds for the stipulated purpose.

Inasmuch as the contribution is restricted as to purpose, it would be recorded in a temporarily restricted fund:

Cash	$50,000	
Revenue from contributions		$50,000
To record the receipt of a temporarily restricted contribution (restricted fund)		

When the association expends the resources for the stipulated purpose, it would account for the reduction in cash as "resources released from restriction." Thus:

Resources released from restriction	$50,000	
Cash		$50,000
To record the disbursement of cash in satisfaction of contributor restrictions (restricted fund)		

"Resources released from restriction" is comparable to "other financing sources (or uses)," such as nonreciprocal transfers. It would be reported in the statement of activities as negative revenue (a negative revenue rather than an expense because, as indicated, restricted funds do not report expenses).

At the same time, an unrestricted fund would recognize the expense and a corresponding increase in net assets:

Program expense	$50,000	
Resources released from restriction		$50,000
To record an expense and the release of contributor restrictions (unrestricted fund)[1]		

To be sure, the Board's approach adds complexity to the financial reporting process. However, it permits not-for-profits to report all expenses in a single column and thereby make clear the full cost of organizational operations.

[1] In a sense, "resources released from restrictions" can be viewed as a transfer of resources from the restricted fund to the unrestricted fund. Indeed, the same bookkeeping results could be achieved by actually transferring the cash from the restricted to the unrestricted fund:

Resources released from restriction (restricted fund)	$50,000	
Cash		$50,000
To record the transfer-out of cash from a restricted fund to an unrestricted fund (restricted fund)		
Cash	$50,000	
Resources released from restriction (unrestricted fund)		$50,000
To record the transfer-out of cash from a restricted fund to an unrestricted fund (unrestricted fund)		
Program expense	$50,000	
Cash		$50,000
To record an expense (unrestricted fund)		

TABLE 12–1

Voluntary Health and Welfare Organization

American Health Association, Local Affiliate
Statement of Financial Position as of June 30, 2004

Assets	Unrestricted	Temporarily Restricted	Permanently Restricted	Total
Current assets				
Cash and cash equivalents	$ 806,383	$ —	$ —	$ 806,383
Short-term investments	8,884,309	288,073	—	9,172,382
Accrued investment income	192,427	—	—	192,427
Accounts receivable—				
Federated and nonfederated	—	694,382	—	694,382
National center	20,382	—	—	20,382
Bequest receivable	—	286,000	—	286,000
Pledges	84,601	19,000	—	103,601
Other	70,719	—	—	70,719
Educational and campaign material inventory	250,670	—	—	250,670
Prepaid expenses	79,410	—	—	79,410
Total current assets	$10,388,901	$1,287,455	$ —	$11,676,356
Noncurrent assets				
Accounts receivable—				
Pledges, net of discount of $1,000	$ —	$ 19,000	$ —	$ 19,000
Charitable gift annuity—national center	40,500	—	—	40,500
Long-term investments	6,622,538	331,695	2,383,620	9,337,853
Beneficial interest in perpetual trust	—	—	2,767,900	2,767,900
Contributions receivable from charitable remainder trust	—	4,963,216	—	4,963,216
Land, buildings, and equipment, at cost Less accumulated depreciation of $2,344,393	3,921,690	—	—	3,921,690
Total noncurrent assets	$10,584,728	$5,313,911	$5,151,520	$21,050,159
TOTAL ASSETS	$20,973,629	$6,601,366	$5,151,520	$32,726,515
Liabilities and net assets				
Current liabilities				
Payable to the national center				
campaign share	$ 3,181,641	$ 414,241	$ —	$ 3,595,882
purchased material	137,781	—	—	137,781
Accounts payable and accrued expenses	585,896	—	—	585,896
Research awards payable within one year	3,315,845	—	—	3,315,845
Total current liabilities	$ 7,221,163	$ 414,241	$ —	$ 7,635,404
Noncurrent liabilities				
Payable to the national center				
campaign share	$ —	$1,240,804	$ —	$ 1,240,804
Annuity obligation	19,640	—	—	19,640
Research awards payable after one year, net of discount of $50,000	1,983,172	—	—	1,983,172
Post retirement benefit obligation	$ 932,246	—	$ —	$ 932,246
Total noncurrent liabilities	$ 2,935,058	$1,240,804	$ —	$ 4,175,862
Total liabilities	$10,156,221	$1,655,045	$ —	$11,811,266

(Continues)

TABLE 12-1
Voluntary Health and Welfare Organization *(Continued)*

Assets	Unrestricted	Temporarily Restricted	Permanently Restricted	Total
Net assets				
Unrestricted				
Net investment in land, building, and equipment	$ 3,921,690	$ —	$ —	$ 3,921,690
Designated by the governing board for programs and operations for the ensuing fiscal year	6,697,513	—	—	6,697,513
Research designated to future years	177,345	—	—	177,345
Charitable gift annuity—national center	20,860	—	—	20,860
Temporarily restricted				
Land, buildings, and equipment	—	168,953	—	168,953
Research	—	232,759	—	232,759
Public health education	—	354,341	—	354,341
Community services	—	467,856	—	467,856
Charitable remainder trust	—	3,722,412	—	3,722,412
Permanently restricted				
Endowment Funds	—	—	2,383,620	2,383,620
Beneficial interest in perpetual trust	—	—	2,767,900	2,767,900
Total net assets	10,817,408	4,946,321	5,151,520	20,915,249
TOTAL LIABILITIES AND NET ASSETS	$20,973,629	$6,601,366	$5,151,520	$32,726,515

The Board permits an important exception to the requirement that all restricted contributions be classified upon receipt as restricted. It gives not-for-profits the option of reporting restricted contributions as unrestricted if the restriction has been met in the same period as the contribution is made.

Table 12-2 presents the statement of activities of the American Health Association.

To fulfill its stated goal, financial reporting should provide information as to an organization's service efforts (see excerpts from statement of objectives in Table 1-4 of Chapter 1). The FASB mandates that either the statement of activities or the accompanying notes report expenses by *function*—that is, by program services or supporting activities. As a result of this requirement, the statement indicates to users not only the activities on which the organization is spending its resources, but more importantly the proportion of resources that are being directed toward substantive, as opposed to administrative, undertakings.

Voluntary health and welfare organizations must also report expenses by "natural" (i.e., object) classification, such as salaries, rent, electricity, and interest. The dual classification should be presented in matrix form in a separate financial statement. Other not-for-profits are encouraged, but not required, to provide information about expenses by their natural classification. Although the distinction between voluntary health and welfare organizations and other types of not-for-profits is not always clear, voluntary health and welfare organizations are formed to provide services to a community rather than to its own members. Examples include the United Way, Boy and Girl Scouts, the American Heart Association, and most social service agencies.

Table 12-3 illustrates the American Health Association's schedule of expenses. The Association, like almost all not-for-profits that present their expenses in both natural and functional classifications, had to allocate various natural expenses to the

TABLE 12–2
Voluntary Health and Welfare Organization

American Health Association, Local Affiliate,
Statement of Activities for the Year Ended June 30, 2004

	Unrestricted	Temporarily Restricted	Permanently Restricted	Total
Revenue				
Public support				
Received directly				
Contributions	$ 2,603,328	$ 263,759	$ —	$ 2,867,087
Contributed services	85,160	—	—	85,160
Capital campaign	—	9,486	—	9,486
Special events	10,528,221	12,500	—	10,540,721
Special event incentives	(1,802,014)	—	—	(1,802,014)
Net special events	$ 8,726,207	$ 12,500	—	8,738,707
Legacies and bequests	1,327,126	788,844	$270,000	2,385,970
Total received directly	$12,741,821	$ 1,074,589	$270,000	14,086,410
Received indirectly				
Allocated by federated fund-raising organizations	—	694,382	—	694,382
Allocated by unassociated and nonfederated fund-raising organizations	142,472	—	—	142,472
Total received indirectly	$ 142,472	$ 694,382	$ —	836,854
Total public support	$12,884,293	$ 1,768,971	270,000	14,923,264
Other revenue				
Grants from national center	$ 87,180	$ —	$ —	87,180
Program fees	302,530	—	—	302,530
Sales of educational materials	1,106,074	—	—	1,106,074
Membership dues	68,103	—	—	68,103
Investment income	806,041	107,433	—	913,474
Perpetual trust revenue	—	64,732	—	64,732
Gains on sale of long-lived assets	6,468	—	—	6,468
Unrealized gain on perpetual trust contribution	—	—	308,100	308,100
Gains on investment transactions	—	103,544	—	103,544
Miscellaneous revenue	96,296	—	—	96,296
Total other revenue	$ 2,472,692	$ 275,709	308,100	3,056,501
Net assets released from restrictions				
Satisfaction of research restrictions	$ 704,264	$ (704,264)	$ —	—
Satisfaction of program restrictions	118,256	(118,256)	—	—
Satisfaction of equipment acquisition restrictions	20,298	(20,298)	—	—
Satisfaction of geographic restrictions	266,000	(266,000)	—	—
Expiration of time restrictions	513,898	(513,898)	—	—
Total net assets released from restrictions	$ 1,622,716	$(1,622,716)	$ —	—
Total public support and other revenue	$16,979,701	$ 421,964	$578,100	$17,979,765

(Continues)

TABLE 12-2
Voluntary Health and Welfare Organization *(Continued)*

	Unrestricted	Temporarily Restricted	Permanently Restricted	Total
Expenses				
Program services				
Research—to acquire new knowledge through biomedical investigation	$ 3,659,784	$ —	$ —	$ 3,659,784
Public health education—to inform the public about the prevention and treatment of cardiovascular diseases and stroke	3,565,704	—	—	3,565,704
Professional education and training—to improve the knowledge, skills, and techniques of health professionals	971,708	—	—	971,708
Community services—to provide organized training in emergency aid, blood pressure screening, and other community-wide activities	2,050,768	—	—	2,050,768
Total program services	10,247,964	—	—	10,247,964
Supporting services				
Management and general—providing executive direction, financial management, overall planning, and coordination of the association's activities	1,069,084	—	—	1,069,084
Fund-raising—activities to secure vital financial support from the public	2,487,090	—	—	2,487,090
Total supporting services	3,556,174	—	—	3,556,174
Total program and supporting services expenses	13,804,138	—	—	13,804,138
Allocation to the American Health Association, Inc. (national center) for national research and other activities	3,467,527	—	—	3,467,527
Total expenses and allocation to national center	17,271,665	—	—	17,271,665
Change in net assets before Cumulative effect of change in accounting principles	(291,964)	421,964	578,100	708,100
Cumulative effects of changes in accounting principles	(520,508)	3,844,838	2,459,800	5,784,130
Change in net assets	(812,472)	4,266,802	3,037,900	6,492,230
Net assets, beginning of year	11,629,880	679,519	2,113,620	14,423,019
Net assets, end of year	$10,817,408	$4,946,321	$5,151,520	$20,915,249

TABLE 12–3
Voluntary Health and Welfare Organization

American Health Association, Local Affiliate,
Statement of Functional Expenses for the Year Ended June 30, 2004

		Program Services					Supporting Services			
Account Title	Special Event Incentives	Research	Public Health Education	Professional Education and Training	Community Services	Sub Total	Management and General	Fund-Raising	Sub Total	Total
Salaries	$ —	$ 86,541	$1,600,091	$ 158,077	$ 951,992	$ 2,796,701	$ 366,639	$1,109,774	$1,476,413	$ 4,273,114
Payroll taxes	—	6,915	131,026	13,005	78,838	229,784	30,150	90,125	120,275	350,059
Employee benefits	—	9,169	283,924	26,003	171,947	491,043	65,398	194,719	260,117	751,160
Occupancy	—	4,501	146,862	12,827	84,405	248,595	36,220	103,152	139,372	387,967
Telephone	—	2,641	82,012	7,404	55,080	147,137	19,459	58,594	78,053	225,190
Supplies	—	1,015	76,404	5,343	30,400	113,162	20,832	24,382	45,214	158,376
Rental and maintenance of equipment	—	1,952	70,242	3,617	40,394	116,205	18,506	47,729	66,235	182,440
Printing and publication	—	3,900	587,178	549,617	338,437	1,479,132	26,616	338,334	364,950	1,844,082
Postage and shipping	—	4,092	188,810	27,479	64,285	284,666	26,826	194,228	221,054	505,720
Visual aids, films and media	—	47	6,197	2,123	1,581	9,948	10,602	4,755	15,357	25,305
Conferences and meetings	—	24,681	77,137	106,291	55,776	263,885	137,827	44,357	182,184	446,069
Other travel	—	3,559	76,541	14,162	44,183	138,445	62,452	87,244	149,696	288,141
Professional fees	—	85,787	72,449	29,184	32,479	219,899	134,282	62,031	196,313	416,212
Awards and grants	—	3,419,771	—	—	—	3,419,771	—	—	—	3,419,771
Other expenses	—	503	20,979	3,218	12,642	37,342	79,495	27,639	107,134	144,476
Depreciation and amortization	—	4,710	145,852	13,358	88,329	252,249	33,780	100,027	133,807	386,056
Total expenses before allocation to national center	$ —	$3,659,784	$3,565,704	$ 971,708	$2,050,768	$10,247,964	$1,069,084	$2,487,090	$3,556,174	$13,804,138
Allocation to the national center	—	2,285,083	257,928	190,933	187,582	2,921,526	375,167	170,834	546,001	3,467,527
Total functional expenses and allocation to the national center	$ —	$5,944,867	$3,823,632	$1,162,641	$2,238,350	$13,169,490	$1,444,251	$2,657,924	$4,102,175	$17,271,665
Special event incentives	$1,802,014	$ —	$ —	$ —	$ —	$ —	$ —	$ —	$ —	$ 1,802,014
Total functional expenses, allocation to national center, and incentives	$1,802,014	$5,944,867	$3,823,632	$1,162,641	$2,238,350	$13,169,490	$1,444,251	$2,657,924	$4,102,175	$19,073,679

various programs (functions). Thus, for example, the association may have carried out all of its programs in the same building and sometimes with common personnel. Therefore it had to allocate on some reasonable and systematic basis "occupancy" expense, depreciation and amortization, and several other expenses.

REPORTING CASH FLOWS

As discussed in Chapter 9, pertaining to business-type activities, the GASB requires that governments report their cash flows in four categories:

1. Cash flows from operating activities
2. Cash flows from noncapital financing activities
3. Cash flows from capital and related financing activities
4. Cash flows from investing activities

By contrast, the FASB in Statement No. 95, *Statement of Cash Flows,* directs that business classify their cash flows into three categories:

1. Cash flows from operating activities
2. Cash flows from financing activities
3. Cash flows from investing activities

In requiring a statement of cash flows for not-for-profits, the FASB faced a dilemma. On the one hand, many experts, including a task force of the AICPA, asserted that with respect to cash flows the operations of not-for-profits more closely parallel those of governments than of businesses. Not-for-profits, like governments, draw the distinction between cash flows attributable to operations and those that are restricted to capital and comparable long-term purposes, such as permanent endowment funds. Accordingly, the experts contended, the FASB should adopt a four-way classification scheme similar to that established by the GASB. On the other hand, however, by requiring a four-way scheme the FASB would be widening the gulf between business and not-for-profit reporting, thereby countering a trend, and apparent objective, of narrowing it.

Emphasizing the importance of comparability between businesses and not-for-profits, the FASB elected to apply the three-way scheme to not-for-profits. However, recognizing that not-for-profits engage in different types of transactions than businesses, the FASB (in Statement 117) modified Statement No. 95 so that it would be more germane to not-for-profits. For example, it stipulated that cash flows from financing activities should include both contributions restricted to long-term purposes and interest and dividends from investments restricted to long-term purposes. Other contributions and interest and dividends on investments not restricted to long-term purposes should be classified as operating cash flows. Table 12-4 sets forth the main types of cash flows included in each category, and Table 12-5 presents the Statement of Cash Flows of the American Health Association.

In another notable difference between the GASB and FASB approaches to cash flows, the GASB (per Statement No. 34) now mandates that governments use only the direct, as opposed to the indirect, method to report their cash flows. The FASB, however, encourages, but does not require, businesses and not-for-profits to use the direct method.

WHAT ARE THE MAIN TYPES OF CONTRIBUTIONS, AND HOW SHOULD PLEDGES BE ACCOUNTED FOR?

Contributions, a mainstay means of support for many not-for-profits, encompass all *nonreciprocal* receipts of assets or services. A nonreciprocal receipt is one for which the

TABLE 12–4
Classification of Cash Receipts and Disbursements Per FASB Statement No. 95, *Statement of Cash Flows,* as Modified by FASB Statement No. 117, *Financial Statements of Not-for-Profit Organizations*

Cash Flows from Operating Activities

Inflows
- Contributions that are either unrestricted or restricted to short-term purposes
- Sales of goods and services
- Interest and dividends not restricted to either long-term purposes, to acquisition of capital assets, or to additions to endowments

Outflows
- Payments to employees
- Payments for supplies
- Payments of interest
- Payments of taxes
- Grants to other organizations

Cash Flows from Investing Activities

Inflows
- Proceeds from sale of facilities
- Payments received on notes from sale of capital assets
- Receipts from the sale of stocks and bonds

Outflows
- Purchases of stocks and bonds
- Acquisitions of capital assets

Cash Flows from Financing Activities

Inflows
- Contributions restricted for long-term purposes
- Interest and dividends from investments restricted to long-term purposes
- Contributions restricted to the acquisition of capital assets
- Interest and dividends restricted to the acquisition of capital assets
- Contributions to endowments
- Proceeds of borrowing

Outflows
- Repayment of debt
- Lease payments under capital leases

recipient gives nothing in exchange. As defined by the FASB in its 1993 pronouncement, *Accounting for Contributions Received and Contributions Made* (Statement No. 116), contributions include gifts of cash, marketable securities, property and equipment, utilities, supplies, intangible assets (such as patents and copyrights), and the services of professionals and craftsmen.[2]

Contributions also include **unconditional promises**—that is, **pledges**—to give those items in the future. Thus, pledges are regarded as contributions. They exclude, however, **conditional promises** to give these items in the future. A conditional promise depends on a specified future and uncertain event to bind the donor. For example, a university alumnus may pledge funds to construct a new physics laboratory if the university is successful in winning a government research grant.

[2] Para. 5.

TABLE 12–5

Statement of Cash Flows of a Not-for-Profit organization

American Health Association, Local Affiliate, Inc.
Statement of Cash Flows
for the Year Ended June 30, 2004

Cash flows from operating activities	
Change in net assets	$ 6,492,230
Adjustments to reconcile change in net assets to net cash provided by operating activities	
Depreciation and amortization	386,056
Unrealized gain on perpetual trust contributions	(308,100)
Gains on investment transactions	(103,544)
Gain on sale of long-lived assets	(6,468)
Contributions restricted to investment in property	(9,486)
Contributions to endowment funds	(270,000)
Increase in accrued investment income	(57,260)
Increase in federated and nonfederated receivable	(13,516)
Increase in national center receivable	(20,382)
Decrease in other receivable	116,532
Decrease in bequest receivable	314,000
Decrease in pledges receivable	2,812
Decrease in educational and campaign material inventory	78,454
Increase in other assets	(21,255)
Increase in perpetual trust	(2,459,800)
Increase in charitable gift annuity	(40,500)
Increase in charitable remainder trust	(4,963,216)
Increase in payable to national center	1,332,258
Increase in accounts payable and accrued expenses	808,360
Increase in research awards payable	225,508
Increase in annuity obligation	19,640
Decrease in deferred revenue and support	(413,959)
Net cash provided by operating activities	$ 1,088,364
Cash flows from investing activities	
Purchase of equipment	(724,492)
Proceeds from sale of equipment	200,217
Proceeds from maturities of investments	7,730,368
Purchase of investments	(8,216,079
Net cash used in investing activities	$(1,009,986)
Cash flows from financing activities	
Contributions to endowment funds	270,000
Proceeds from contributions restricted to investment in property	9,486
Net cash provided by financing activities	$ 279,486
Net increase in cash and cash equivalents	357,864
Cash and cash equivalents (at beginning of year)	448,519
Cash and cash equivalents (at end of year)	$ 806,383
Supplemental data	
Noncash investing and financing activities—gifts of equipment	$ 30,000

DISTINGUISHING A CONTRIBUTION FROM AN EXCHANGE TRANSACTION

Contributions must be distinguished from exchange transactions. A contribution is a transfer of assets in which the donor does not expect to receive equal value in return. An exchange transaction is a reciprocal transfer in which each party receives and gives up resources of commensurate value. For example, if a private corporation were to give a not-for-profit research foundation funds to study the cause of a disease with the expectation that the results would be published in a scientific journal, the transaction would be considered a contribution. If, on the other hand, it gave the funds with the contractual agreement that it would have the rights to resultant patents, then the transaction would be an exchange transaction.

The difference between the two is not always obvious. When people join the local Friends of the Library Association, do they do so to support the library's scholarly activities or to benefit from the right to attend member-only lectures? Do they join the American Automobile Association to promote auto safety and good roads or to obtain emergency road service and travel directions? Do they join the AARP (formerly known as the American Association of Retired Persons) to advance the interests of senior citizens or to take advantage of low-cost life and auto insurance offers?

Distinguishing between asset transfers and exchange transactions and contributions requires the exercise of judgment. Factors to be taken into account should include the recipient's intent in soliciting the resources, the party that establishes the amount of resources transferred (e.g., the transferor or the transferee), and the penalties assessed if either party fails to deliver what has been promised.

As previously discussed, the classification of resources into the three categories of restrictiveness is based on *donor* stipulation. Hence, only contributions can be so categorized. Exchange transactions are always classified as unrestricted; by definition, the resources received are not subject to donor restrictions. They should be accounted for as ordinary commercial transactions.

ACCOUNTING FOR PLEDGES

The recognition of unrestricted gifts of cash and other assets (that have not been preceded by a pledge) has never been a major issue. Not-for-profits, irrespective of type, have recognized gifts of cash and other assets as revenue upon receipt. Gifts of assets other than cash have been measured at their fair (i.e., market) value.

But when should not-for-profits recognize pledges—promises to make donations of cash or other assets in the future? Organizations generally lack legally enforceable claims against fickle donors. Even if they do have legally enforceable claims, they may be reluctant to act on them because the likely benefit is exceeded by the costs in both goodwill and legal fees. Pledges may be legally enforceable when the organization has acted on a pledge and thereby incurred costs. Suppose, for example, relying on a donor's promise to finance a new building, an organization engages an architect to draw up plans. The donor reneges. The organization may have a valid claim upon the donor for its losses. The accompanying In Practice describes one not-for-profit's effort to enforce a claim against the estate of a deceased benefactor.

More importantly, pledges receivable, albeit assets, are not available for expenditure. They cannot be used to pay employees or suppliers. Recognition of pledges might give the unwarranted impression that the organization has excess spendable funds and thereby has less of a need for further fiscal assistance.

On the other hand, many organizations have sufficient experience to be able to estimate with reliability the percentage of pledges that will be uncollectible and, like merchants, can establish appropriate allowances for uncollectibles. Further, they can borrow against the pledges and spend the proceeds. Arguably, therefore, there is no more justification for a not-for-profit than for a merchant to delay revenue recognition until cash is in hand.

IN PRACTICE

BENEFICIARY SUES TO ENFORCE PLEDGE

Faith Bybee couldn't say no.

The Houston socialite pledged hundreds of thousands of dollars to Dallas, Houston, and San Antonio museums. She also promised $500,000 to the Lady Bird Johnson Wildflower Center in Austin. She wanted to do it all.

She couldn't.

When the 96-year-old Bybee died in 1996, she left behind an estate worth $997,000—far less than what she had promised to her beloved charities. Most groups forgave the unfulfilled pledges. The wildflower center sued.

"We think we were unjustly shut out of her estate, and we just didn't think that was right," said Robert G. Breunig, the group's executive director.

Bybee's executor says the pledge isn't valid and there just isn't enough money to go around. After years of litigation and a failed attempt at mediation, both sides asked a Harris County probate judge Thursday to rule in their favor. No decision was reached, and the case could go before a jury in September.

"It's a sad case, and what's sad about it is that charities don't usually do this," said Bill Ogden, lawyer for Chase Bank of Texas, the estate's executor. "All the money is going to charity anyway."

The Lady Bird Johnson Wildflower Center, supported by Lady Bird Johnson, was established in 1982 in eastern Travis County to preserve and teach about hundreds of species of wildflowers. Among its board members was Bybee, a longtime friend of Mrs. Johnson.

When the group began raising money for a $9.5 million facility, Bybee was among the first to donate. She promised $500,000, to be paid upon her death.

That pledge was revoked in 1992, when Bybee's lawyer sent a certified letter saying the philanthropist could not financially fulfill her promise.

"But just days later, Bybee called the wildflower center's executive director," said Mark Mayfield, the center's lawyer.

"She informed him that her lawyer had no authority to send that letter and that was not her intention," he said.

The new center opened in 1995 in southwest Travis County with officials still expecting Bybee's $500,000. But when Bybee died in 1996, the executor earmarked the majority of her estate for the Bybee Foundation, a charity she and her husband founded to preserve Texas pioneer arts and history. The executor refused to approve the $500,000 pledge to the research center, saying the pledge had been revoked.

"The research center—which has $13 million in property and equipment assets—wasn't hindered by the unfulfilled gift," Ogden said.

"They built a $9.5 million center and never had to borrow a dime," he said. "They didn't rely on Faith's pledge, they didn't need it, and they built the center without it."

"Not true," Breunig said.

"The research center had to borrow from its reserves to complete the project," he said. "They also scaled back the facility, constructing smaller buildings, abandoning plans for trails and eliminating an education building."

"If a judge or jury rules in its favor, the center could add those features," Breunig said.

"But money isn't the main issue," he said.

"This has been an attempt to paint us as the rich bad guys preying on an estate," Breunig said. "The point is that Mrs. Bybee made a pledge. We believe she intended to honor that pledge."

"Unfortunately," Ogden said, "Bybee's heart was bigger than her billfold."

"She wanted to be a person who was recognized," he said. "She didn't want to disappoint her friends."

Postscript: In August 2000, a Harris County judge ruled, without offering a written explanation, that the Wildflower Center could *not* collect the $500,000 pledge.

Source: Andrea Ball, "Wildflower Center Sues over Pledge Unfulfilled," *Austin American-Statesman*, 21 July 2000. Reprinted with permission.

Until the FASB standardized practice, some types of not-for-profits recognized revenue upon receipt of a pledge. Most, however, consistent with their conservative accounting traditions, chose to wait until cash had been collected.

Businesses measure receivables at the present value of anticipated cash flows (except for short-term receivables, those for which the impact of discounting would be immaterial). They adjust the stated amount of a receivable to take into account both anticipated defaults and the time value of money. Prior to the FASB pronouncement on contributions, not-for-profits that recorded pledges reduced their carrying value to take into account anticipated defaults. They did not, however, discount the face value to take into account the time value of money.

EXAMPLE *Pledges*

In November, a public broadcasting station conducts its annual pledge drive and receives telephone pledges of $700,000. By year-end December 31, it collects $400,000 of the pledges.

Based on previous experience, it estimates that $60,000 of the balance will be uncollectible. In addition, it receives a pledge from a local foundation to contribute $100,000 at the end of each of the next three years.

FASB Standards

The FASB, in Statement No. 116, over the vociferous objections of many of its constituent not-for-profit organizations, decided that unrestricted pledges should be reported as revenue in the period received; organizations need not wait until pledges are fulfilled. They should measure the pledges at "the present value of estimated future cash flows using a discount rate commensurate with the risks involved."[3] That is, they should take into account both anticipated bad debts and the time value of money. However, they need not discount pledges to be collected within one year.

To avoid recognizing contributions as revenue before they are available for expenditure, not-for-profits should consider pledges of cash to be received in future periods as subject to time restrictions. The FASB concluded that by promising to make payments in the future, donors implicitly restricted the donated resources to support of future, not current, activities. Hence, the recipient organizations should classify them as temporarily restricted. When the cash is received and available for expenditure, they should release resources from the

[3] Para. 20.

temporarily restricted category and transfer them to the unrestricted category.

The standard allows an option to recognize pledges that are restricted, either as to time or use, as unrestricted if the restriction has been met in the same period as the donation is made.

Thus, in the example, the following entries, in both unrestricted and temporarily restricted funds, would summarize the results of the year's pledge drive:

Pledges receivable	$400,000	
Revenues from contributions		$400,000

To record the pledges of cash to be paid in the current year (in an unrestricted fund)

Cash	$400,000	
Pledges receivable		$400,000

To record the collection of cash (in an unrestricted fund)

These pledges need not be reported as being subject to time restrictions and thereby recorded in a temporarily restricted fund. They fall under the exception that when time restrictions are satisfied within the same year, the revenue may be reported as unrestricted.

Pledges receivable	$300,000	
Pledges receivable—allowance for uncollectibles		$ 60,000
Revenues from contributions		240,000

To record the pledges expected to be collected in future periods (in a temporarily restricted fund)

As the pledges are collected in subsequent years, the resources would be released from the temporarily restricted category and added to the unrestricted category. Thus, if $75,000 were collected:

Resources released from restriction	$75,000	
Pledges receivable		$75,000

To release the resources from restriction upon collection of cash (temporarily restricted fund)

Cash	$75,000	
Resources released from restriction		$75,000

To record the collection of cash (unrestricted fund)

Were the station to determine that 3 percent is an appropriate discount rate, then the present value of the annuity of $100,000 per year for three years would be $282,861. The present value of an annuity of $1 for three periods, discounted at a rate of 3 percent, is $2.8286. Hence, the present value of the annuity of $100,000 is $100,000 × 2.8286. The appropriate discount rate is the prevailing *risk-free* interest rate. The risk-free rate should be used because by establishing an allowance for uncollectibles the organization will have already factored in the risk of loss from bad debts.

Pledges receivable	$282,861	
Revenues from contributions		$282.861

To record a pledge of three annual payments of $100,000, the present value of which, discounted at 3 percent, is $282,861 (temporarily restricted fund)

Each year, as the $100,000 is received, the station would recognize interest at a rate of 3 percent on the net balance of the pledge (the pledge receivable less the remaining discount) and record the excess as a reduction of the pledges receivable. Interest for the first year would be 3 percent of $282,861, or $8,486. Thus, when the first installment is received:

Resources released from restriction	$91,514	
Pledges receivable		$91,514

To release the resources upon collection of cash in the first year (temporarily restricted fund)–$100,000 cash received less interest at a rate of 3 percent on the pledge balance of $282,861 ($91,514 is also the present value of a single payment of $100,000 to be received in three years, discounted at 3 percent)

Cash	$100,000	
Contributions—interest revenue		$8,486
Resources released from restriction		91,514

To record the first year's payment of $100,000 (unrestricted fund)

In the two subsequent years, as the balance in pledges receivable is reduced, greater proportions of the $100,000 would be assigned to principal and lesser proportions to interest. By the end of the third year the balance in the pledges receivable account would be reduced to zero. The interest should be reported as additional contributions.

WHEN SHOULD USE (PURPOSE)-RESTRICTED CONTRIBUTIONS BE RECOGNIZED?

In concept, a not-for-profit's *use (purpose)-restricted contributions* are equivalent to a government's restricted grants. Use-restricted contributions can be used only for donor-specified purposes. Before the FASB issued its pronouncement on contributions, most not-for-profits recognized revenue from restricted grants as they expended the funds for the specified purpose. In that way, they matched the revenues to the expenses to which they were related.

As a consequence of this practice, organizations failed to give timely recognition to transactions that, it could be argued, clearly enhanced their welfare. A restricted gift, no less than an unrestricted gift, provides an economic benefit; it helps the organization to carry out its mission.

EXAMPLE *Use-Restricted Contributions*

In 2005 The Lyric Opera Society receives a $150,000 contribution to fund a production of Gilbert and Sullivan's *H.M.S. Pinafore*, to be performed in 2006.

FASB Standards

Per FASB Statement No. 116, revenue from restricted contributions is accounted for on the same basis as that from unrestricted contributions. Restricted contributions, including pledges, are recognized as revenues in the period received, irrespective of when the resources will be expended.[4] As discussed previously, for reporting purposes, distinctions must be drawn among resources that are unrestricted, temporarily restricted, and permanently restricted.

[4] Paras. 14–20.

Thus, in the example, the Lyric Opera Society would report its gift in a temporarily restricted fund:

Cash	$150,000	
Revenues from contributions		$150,000
To record a temporarily restricted gift (in a temporarily restricted fund)		

When, in 2006, the Society expends the resources, it would record the release of the funds in the restricted fund and the expenditure in its current operating fund:

Resources released from restriction	$150,000	
Cash (or payables)		$150,000
To record the release of restrictions (in the temporarily restricted fund)		

Production expenses	$150,000	
Resources released from restriction		$150,000
To record the expenditure of funds previously restricted (in an unrestricted fund)		

The expenditure of the funds raises a related issue. Suppose the society budgeted an additional $150,000 or more of its own resources to finance the production. When it spent the first $150,000, was it spending its own resources or the donated resources?

Per the FASB, as long as the organization incurs an expense for a purpose for which the restricted resources are available, it should consider the restriction as having been released. The only exception is that if the organization receives resources from two external donors, both of which restrict resources for the same purpose, then it cannot release the two restrictions with the expenditure of the same resources. Thus, if the opera society received $150,000 from Donor A and $150,000 from Donor B, it could not release both restrictions upon spending the first $150,000

The FASB approach is similar to that of the GASB in that pledges subject to use restrictions can be recognized as revenue upon receipt of the pledge. Recall from Chapter 4 that GASB standards permit governments to give immediate recognition to grants or other revenues subject to purpose restrictions. The recipients should not delay recognition until they have satisfied the restrictions.

The accompanying In Practice raises still another issue regarding restricted gifts. It suggests that some gifts may not be as restricted as the donors may have been led to believe.

SHOULD CONTRIBUTIONS OF SERVICES BE RECOGNIZED?

Not-for-profits benefit from the services of volunteers. The services range from professional assistance that would otherwise have to be paid for at commercial rates to those that are part of the normal activities carried out by an organization's members. Consider some examples:

- An advertising agency develops a fund-raising campaign for a not-for-profit welfare agency.
- An attorney provides free legal counsel to a hospital.
- An attorney is a member of the board of directors of a performing arts association and is frequently called upon for legal guidance.

IN PRACTICE

A GIFT WITH STRINGS ATTACHED

Is it really possible to restrict a gift? Yes, but not as easily as it may appear. Resources are fungible and can readily be transferred from one account to another.

Suppose, for example, you contribute $100,000 to your favorite university, stipulating that the gift must be used to support teaching and research in accounting. The chairman of the accounting department would no doubt be delighted by your generosity and sense of priorities. His joy might be short lived, however, if the university president reduced the department's standard budget allocation by $100,000, claiming that the accounting department is now less needy than other departments.

To be sure, donors can add covenants to gift agreements that minimize the likelihood that their wishes will be circumvented. But these are difficult to enforce and many organizations would be unwilling to accept unusual controls upon their administrative prerogatives.

Only by limiting a gift to activities that the organization would not otherwise undertake can a donor be certain that the gift will support the intended activity.

- Nurses are paid considerably less than the prevailing wage by a hospital maintained by a religious order of which they are members.
- Community members perform odd jobs at a local hospital, such as carrying meals to patients, staffing the reception desk, and maintaining the hospital's library and recreation area.

Church members paint the church facilities and construct a children's play center. In each of these examples, the organization receives an economic benefit from the contributed services. Correspondingly, it incurs a cost in that it "consumes" the services provided. Yet it is not obvious whether the values of these contributed services can be reliably measured and, if they can, whether they should be accorded financial statement recognition.

EXAMPLE *Service Contributions*

The Northern New Mexico Clinic, a not-for-profit health care provider, recruits a local contractor to repave its parking lot. Had the contractor billed the clinic at standard rates, the cost would have been $12,000.

FASB Standards

Recognizing the diverse nature of contributed services, the FASB in Statement No. 116 prescribes that they should be recognized only if they are of a *professional nature* and of the type that the *entity would ordinarily have had to pay for* had they not been donated. It establishes two conditions, either of which must be met, for recognition:

- The services create or enhance nonfinancial assets.
- The services require specialized skills, are provided by individuals possessing those skills, and would typically need to be purchased if not

> provided by donation. Services requiring specialized skills, according to the FASB, are those provided by accountants, architects, carpenters, doctors, electricians, lawyers, nurses, plumbers, teachers and other professionals, and craftsmen.[5]

The services received by the Northern New Mexico Clinic in the example satisfy both of these conditions. Hence, the clinic should recognize both a revenue and a corresponding expense:

Repair and maintenance expense	$12,000	
Revenue from contributed services		$12,000
To recognize revenue and the related expense from contributed services		

SHOULD RECEIPTS OF COLLECTION ITEMS BE RECOGNIZED AS REVENUES?

In Chapter 7, pertaining to long-lived assets, we addressed the issue of whether governments should capitalize the "collectibles" that they hold in their museums, universities, libraries, and similar institutions. We noted that the GASB adopted the basic position of the FASB as set forth in FASB Statement No. 116. A notable difference between the FASB and GASB positions, however, is that the GASB requires that

IN PRACTICE

EXAMPLES OF CONTRIBUTED SERVICES

A veterans association conducts an annual fund-raising campaign to solicit contributions from members of the community. In prior years the association's own members made the phone calls. This year, a local telemarketing company agreed to contact the potential donors.

The association should not recognize the contributed services of the firm because neither of the two conditions is met. The services do not create nonfinancial assets. Moreover, they do not require specialized skills, and, based on experience, the association would otherwise not have purchased the services.

A local welfare organization benefits from the services of two CPAs. One is its treasurer, a position that must be filled by a member of its board of directors, all of whom are unpaid. The second, who is not a member of the board, provides ongoing accounting services (e.g., making monthly journal entries, closing the books, and preparing annual financial statements). Were it not for the services of this CPA, the organization would have to engage a part-time bookkeeper or accountant.

The welfare organization should not recognize the services of the treasurer. Although the organization benefits from his professional advice, his services are offered as an unpaid board member, not as a professional accountant. Therefore, neither condition is satisfied.

The other CPA provides services that require special skills and would otherwise have to be purchased. Therefore, the second condition is satisfied and the welfare organization should recognize his contributed services.

[5] Para. 9.

governments recognize the receipt of all collectibles as revenues. If they capitalize the collectibles, they would offset the revenues with a capital asset. If not, they would offset the revenues with an expense. The FASB, by contrast, does not permit not-for-profits to recognize as revenues the receipt of collectibles that they do not capitalize.

FASB Standards

Statement No. 116 encourages not-for-profits to recognize contributions of collectibles as revenues and to capitalize their entire collections. However, it states that entities *need* not (note: not *cannot*) recognize contributions of collectibles as long as the items satisfy all of the following conditions:

- They are held for public exhibition, education, or research in furtherance of public service rather than financial gain.
- They are protected, kept unencumbered, cared for, and preserved.
- They are subject to an organizational policy requiring that proceeds from sales of collection items be used to acquire other items for collections.

If not-for-profits elect not to capitalize their collections, then they must disclose, in notes to the statements, the details of items both purchased and "deaccessed." If they capitalize their collections, they shall recognize contributions of collection items as revenues; if not, they should not recognize them as revenues.[6]

WHEN SHOULD CONDITIONAL PROMISES BE RECOGNIZED?

Donors may promise to contribute to a not-for-profit on condition that a specified event take place or that the entity take specified actions. Conditional promises to give must be distinguished from *restricted* contributions. A restricted gift is one that must be used for a particular purpose. A conditional promise, by contrast, is one in which the donor will provide the resources only if the specified condition is satisfied. The resources to be provided may be either restricted or unrestricted.

In practice, the distinction between a restricted gift and a conditional gift may be ambiguous. A donor may pledge resources that can be used only to support a particular activity, such as a conference. Although the promise is not explicitly conditioned upon the entity holding the conference, the donor is not likely to provide the resources if the conference is not held. Such a restricted gift is not much different from a conditional gift—one in which the donor promises to provide resources to the organization if and when it holds the conference.

A conditional promise unquestionably is an economic benefit to a not-for-profit entity, as long as there is a positive probability that the conditions can be met. Yet, if there is reasonable uncertainty that the conditions will be met, the entity may be premature in recognizing revenue until it has "earned" the right to the contribution by satisfying the conditions.

[6] Paras. 11–13.

IN PRACTICE

WHEN A CONTRIBUTION IS NOT A CONTRIBUTION

Not-for-profit organizations, no less than both businesses and governments, may try to artificially boost their revenues or lower their expenses. "Some United Way organizations, trying to appear more successful and more efficient with their donors' money," *The New York Times* (November 19, 2002) reports, "are counting contributions in ways that make the numbers look more robust—and expenses look smaller." The United Way is by far the largest fund-raising not-for-profit organization in the United States, collecting money on behalf of thousands of national and local charities.

The most serious accusation against the United Way, according to the *Times*, is that two or more affiliates double-count the same dollars. The United Way of Suburban Chicago, for example, is an umbrella organization for fifty-two other United Way organizations in the Chicago area. When the Lake County United Way, which is a United Way organization but one that is not affiliated with the United Way of Suburban Chicago, raised $350,000 from a major employer in the region, both agencies reported the contributions as their own. Each claimed that it had managed the campaign for the company.

Other alleged violations of sound accounting and reporting include the following:

- Counting as contributions funds raised by other fund-raising organizations. Some companies permit fund-raising organizations other than the United Way to manage their employee campaigns. Yet some United Way organizations are counting as their own the contributions raised in those campaigns. United Way defends this practice, contending that even though it didn't actually receive the contributions, it was the United Way's marketing and publicity that generated the contributions.
- Overstating the value of noncash gifts.
- Recognizing as contributions the value of the time of volunteers even though their services don't meet the FASB standards of revenue recognition.

EXAMPLE *Conditional Promises*

The City Symphony is conducting a campaign to provide financing for a new auditorium. In 2005 a private foundation agrees to match 50 percent of all other contributions up to $1 million (that is, each $1 of its gift is conditioned upon the symphony raising $2 from other sources). The following year, 2006, the symphony receives $500,000 in other donations.

FASB Standards

Statement No. 116 stipulates that conditional promises to give shall be recognized when the conditions on which they depend are substantially met.[7]

[7] Para. 22.

In 2006 the symphony in the example satisfied the conditions to receive $250,000 of the foundation's donation:

Pledges receivable	$250,000	
Revenues from contributions		$250,000
To record the fulfillment of conditions necessary to receive the foundation's matching funds		

It would delay recognition of any further contributions from the foundation until it raised additional funds from other parties.

Reimbursement grants generally fall within the category of conditional promises. Either implicitly or explicitly the grantor pledges to reimburse the grantee for allowable costs conditioned upon the grantee incurring those costs and providing suitable documentation of them.

HOW SHOULD "PASS THROUGH" CONTRIBUTIONS BE ACCOUNTED FOR?

In Chapter 4, we raised the issue of how governments should account for "pass through" grants. These are grants that a recipient is required to distribute to other parties—for example, when a state receives a federal grant that it must "pass through" to local governments. The position of the GASB is that the original recipient of the grant should recognize the grant as revenue (and the subsequent distribution as an expenditure) unless the original recipient is nothing more than a "cash conduit"—an entity that has no decision-making authority to select the ultimate beneficiaries.

Not-for-profits face similar issues with regard to contributions. Consider, for example, the following situations:

EXAMPLE *A Federated Fund-Raising Organization*

The United Campaign of Springfield distributes all contributions received to numerous local, regional, and national organizations. These include entities as diverse as local food distribution centers and the Red Cross. Donors are given three choices as to how their contributions may be used:

- They can give without restriction, in which case the distribution of their gifts is left to a committee composed of United Campaign board members.
- They can specify that their gifts be designated for one of several groups of organizations, each of which targets a specific community need (e.g., health care, youth activities, poverty, education, culture).
- They can designate a gift to one or more specific organizations.

EXAMPLE *A Foundation That Transfers Assets to a Specified Organization*

The Foundation for Classical Music, which is governed by an independent board of trustees, was established to benefit a local opera company. The charter of the foundation states that all contributions will be added to the foundation's permanent endowment. Income from the endowment will be transferred to the opera company, subject to the right of the foundation's trustees to redirect funds to other arts-related organizations without donor approvals if and when, in the judgment of the trustees, the opera company becomes self-supporting.

EXAMPLE *A Foundation That Supports a Related Organization*

The Friends of the Museum Foundation, which is governed by a board of trustees selected by the museum's board of governors, was established to stimulate private contributions from the community to assist the museum in acquiring works of art and carrying out various cultural activities. Although all funds collected by the foundation will eventually benefit the museum, the foundation's trustees can choose the timing of transfers from the foundation and the specific purposes for which they will be used.

FASB Standards

In a 1999 pronouncement, *Transfers of Assets to a Not-for-Profit Organization or Charitable Trust That Raises or Holds Contributions for Others* (Statement No. 136) the FASB took a position that is similar in spirit, but different in approach, to that of the GASB. The FASB held that when an organization accepts contributions from a donor and agrees to transfer the assets to, or use them on behalf of, a specific beneficiary, then it should not recognize the donation as revenue (or the subsequent distribution as an expense). Instead it should offset the assets received with a liability—a payable to the ultimate beneficiary. There are, however, two main exceptions:

1. If the donor has explicitly granted the organization **variance power,** then the organization must recognize the contribution as revenue. "Variance power" is the unilateral right to redirect the use of the assets received to another beneficiary. The rationale for this exception is that an organization that has variance power is not merely an agent but has substantive decision-making authority and discretion over how the donation may be used.
2. If the recipient organization and the beneficiary organizations are "financially interrelated," then the recipient organization must recognize the contribution as revenue. Correspondingly, the beneficiary organization must recognize an interest in the net assets of the recipient organization (an asset) and periodically adjust that interest for its share in the change in the net assets of the recipient organization. This type of accounting is similar to the equity method of accounting for an interest in a subsidiary. Organizations are considered to be "financially interrelated" when
   a. One organization has the ability to influence the operating and financial decisions of the other (as when one organization has "considerable" representation on the governing board of the other) *and*
   b. One organization has an ongoing economic interest in the net assets of the other characterized by "residual rights" (as when the beneficiary organization profits from the investment, fund-raising, or operating activities of the recipient organization).

This exception is based on the premise that when two organizations have a close cooperative relationship with each other, the recipient organization is unlikely to have an obligation to transfer its assets to the beneficiary organization at any specific time. Instead, the beneficiary organization is content to leave the resources with the recipient organization knowing that it will have access to the resources whenever it needs them. Typically, however, this exception may in fact be moot. If one of the entities is able to exercise control over the other, then the two will most probably be required to consolidate their financial statements (an issue to be commented on later in this chapter). Then, of course, the contribution would be recognized as revenue by the consolidated entity when received.

In the first of the pass-through examples, the United Campaign would recognize as unrestricted revenue the contributions in which the donors did not designate *specific* beneficiaries. The contributions that could be distributed by the board would be classified as unrestricted. Those donations designated for one of the several groups of organizations would be recorded as "temporarily restricted," inasmuch as they must be used for specified purposes. United Campaign could not, however, recognize as revenue the contributions of the donors who designated specific organizations. The receipt of these contributions would have to be recorded as a liability to those organizations; the United Campaign does not have variance power, and it is not financially affiliated with the beneficiary organizations.

In the second example, the Foundation for Classical Music has been granted variance power; it can redirect endowment income to arts organizations other than the local opera company. Therefore, it can recognize contributions as revenue (permanently restricted since they must be added to a permanent endowment) upon receipt.

In the third example, the Friends of the Museum Foundation and the museum are related organizations. Upon receipt of contributions, the foundation can recognize contributions as revenue (restricted or unrestricted depending on the stipulations of the donors). In the same period, the museum would recognize an asset (e.g., "interest in net assets of museum foundation"), offset by a revenue (e.g., "increase in interest in net assets of museum"). However, assuming that the two entities are so tightly intertwined that they will have to prepare consolidated financial statements, the foundation's interest in the net assets of the museum (and the offsetting increase in the net assets) will be eliminated in the consolidation process.

WHEN SHOULD GAINS AND LOSSES ON INVESTMENTS BE RECOGNIZED?

FASB Standards

As noted in Chapter 4, the FASB, in Statement No. 124, *Accounting for Certain Investments Held by Not-for-Profit Organizations*, prescribed that not-for-profits, like businesses, must report their investments at fair value and recognize the changes in fair value as they occur. They need not, however, classify the investments into the three categories (trading, available-for-sale, and held-to-maturity) as required of businesses. Therefore, even debt securities that are expected to be held to maturity must be stated at fair value. The only exempt securities are investments accounted for under the equity method, investments in consolidated subsidiaries, and investments for which the fair value is not readily determinable. The fair value of an equity security is generally considered to be "readily determinable" if the security is traded on a major exchange or over the counter.

Per Statement No. 124, interest, dividends, and gains and losses from changes in the fair value of securities should be reported on the statement of activities as increases or decreases in *unrestricted* net assets—unless their use is temporarily or permanently restricted by explicit donor stipulation or by law. However, even investment income and gains from restricted assets may be recognized as increases in unrestricted assets if the restrictions are met in the same reporting period and the organization follows the same policy with respect to contributions received.

EXAMPLE *Investment Gains*

In June 2005, the Children's Welfare Association receives a grant of $100,000, which it classifies as temporarily restricted. To earn a return until it needs the funds, the Association invests the proceeds in Treasury notes. As of December 31, 2005, the fair market value of the notes is $103,000. The following entry in an *unrestricted* fund would be appropriate:

Investments	$3,000	
Investment earnings—appreciation in fair value		$3,000
To record the increase in fair value		

The investments would now be divided into the two fund categories:

Unrestricted	$ 3,000
Temporarily restricted	100,000
Total	$103,000

If the securities were subsequently sold for $103,000, entries in both an unrestricted and restricted fund would be needed:

Cash	$100,000	
Investments		$100,000
To record the sale of securities in a temporarily restricted fund		
Cash	$3,000	
Investments		$3,000
To record the sale of securities in an unrestricted fund		

If instead, the $100,000 were not a grant but rather a contribution to an endowment fund, the same approach would be taken with respect to the gains. As discussed in Chapter 10, unless the donor specified that investment gains should be added to principal, earnings from the endowment were restricted to a specified purpose, or the general rules of the FASB were trumped by legal provisions, then the $3,000 in unrealized investment gains would be recognized as unrestricted. Chapter 10 also addresses the issue of how endowment losses should be accounted for. It is strongly suggested, therefore, that the reader review the material in that chapter pertaining to how not-for-profits should account for gains and losses on endowment investments.

The FASB standards for not-for-profits are generally consistent with those of the GASB. Both require that investments be marked-to-market.

CURRENT DISCLOSURE REQUIREMENTS

The toughest investment decision for the managers of some not-for-profits is whether they should place their cash in a checking or a savings account. Others, however, must manage multibillion dollar portfolios. The Ford Foundation, for example, has investments that are worth almost $10 billion; the endowment portfolio of Harvard University is over $6 billion. Many not-for-profits face the same pressures as governments and businesses to maximize their investment returns and as a result may place their funds in sophisticated financial instruments, such as derivatives, and engage in complex transactions, such as interest rate swaps. Financial reporting standards do not address the suitability of particular instruments. Rather, they assure that reporting entities disclose information as to the value of their investments and the nature of the transactions in which they engage. The disclosure requirements are set forth mainly in three FASB statements that, although designed mainly for businesses, also apply to not-for-profits:

- No. 105, *Disclosure of Information about Financial Instruments with Off-Balance-Sheet Risk and Financial Instruments with Concentrations of Credit Risk* (March 1990). Directed mainly at instruments such as interest rate swaps (a transaction in which a party trades a promise of fixed interest payments for variable payments), foreign currency contracts, and futures contracts, the statement mandates that the nature, terms, and risks of these instruments be described.
- No. 107, *Disclosures about the Fair Value of Financial Instruments* (December 1991). This statement requires the disclosure of fair market value for short-term and long-term investments, including derivatives and other nonconventional securities.
- No. 119, *Disclosures about Derivative Financial Instruments and Fair Value of Financial Instruments* (October 1994). Issued after several corporations incurred major losses in derivatives, this statement expands upon Statement No. 107 to require considerably more detail as to an organization's derivative transactions, including dollar amounts, nature, terms, trading gains and losses, and reasons as to why they were undertaken.

WHAT ARE SPLIT INTEREST AGREEMENTS AND HOW SHOULD THEY BE ACCOUNTED FOR?

Split interest agreements are those in which the donor makes a gift to a not-for-profit organization but the organization is not the sole beneficiary. These agreements take many forms, and the accounting is governed by the specific rights and obligations of the recipient organization. One type of split interest agreement is a charitable remainder trust. A donor establishes a trust fund, contributes assets to the fund, and appoints a recipient not-for-profit organization as the trustee. The trust agreement provides that as long as the donor or spouse is alive, a set percentage of the trust assets will be distributed to them. Any additional earnings will remain in the trust. Upon the death of both donor and spouse, the trust assets will revert to the not-for-profit organization.

As a general rule, the not-for-profit organization should recognize revenue from a split interest agreement upon receipt of the assets. Thus, in the case of the charitable remainder trust, the recipient organization should record the assets received at their fair market value. Correspondingly, however, it should recognize a liability to the other beneficiaries. This liability would be measured as the present value of the estimated future payments (based on actuarial tables) to be made to the donor and spouse. The difference between the assets and the liabilities would be recognized as contribution revenue.[8]

HOW SHOULD DEPRECIATION BE REPORTED?

As emphasized in previous chapters, owing to their focus upon budgets, governments do not currently charge depreciation in their governmental funds—only in their government-wide statements and proprietary and fiduciary funds. Not-for-profits, like governments, generally budget on a cash or near-cash basis, and governing boards, managers, and external constituents are vitally concerned with budget-to-actual comparisons. The major challenge faced by managers and governing boards of most not-for-profits is meeting day-to-day cash demands. Inasmuch as depreciation is not a cost that requires cash, they have little or no interest in it; it does not enter into their financial deliberations or decisions.

On the other hand, as important as the budget is to not-for-profits, it does not have the same force of law as it does for governments. Therefore, not-for-profit statement users (particularly outsiders to whom general purpose financial statements are directed) may place greater weight on reporting objectives calling for information on the cost of services than on budgetary compliance. Depreciation represents the cost of consuming assets; in any comparison of service efforts with accomplishments, it may be too significant to ignore.

EXAMPLE *Depreciation*

A not-for-profit job placement service acquires a personal computer for $3,000. It pays for the computer out of a fund restricted to the acquisition of equipment. Estimated useful life is three years.

FASB Standards

The FASB, in its Statement No. 93, *Recognition of Depreciation by Not-for-Profit Organizations*, mandates that not-for-profits "shall recognize the cost of using up the future economic benefits or service potentials of their long-lived tangible assets—depreciation." It requires that they disclose depreciation expense and accumulated depreciation for the period.

The FASB did not indicate the specific funds in which not-for-profits should account for long-lived assets and report depreciation. For purposes of internal control and reporting, some not-for-profits account for long-lived assets, and charge depreciation, in their current operating funds; others maintain special plant funds. However, owing to Statement No. 117, *Financial Statements of Not-for-Profit Organizations*, the fund in which the entity records depreciation has no reporting significance. As discussed previously, Statement No. 117 requires that all expenses be reported as decreases in *unrestricted* net assets. Thus, whether the depreciation is initially recorded in a current operating fund or a plant fund, it would still be reported in the unrestricted column or section of the statement of activities.

[8] For a comprehensive discussion of split interest agreements, see the AICPA Accounting and Auditing Guide *Not-for-Profit Organizations*.

In the example, the following entries would record the acquisition of the computer and first-year depreciation:

Resources released from restriction	$3,000	
Cash		$3,000
To record the release of restricted assets to acquire the computer (in a restricted fund)		
Equipment	$3,000	
Resources released from restriction		$3,000
To record the purchase of the computer (in an unrestricted fund)		
Depreciation expense	$1,000	
Accumulated depreciation		$1,000
To record first year depreciation (in an unrestricted fund)		

An organization may sometimes acquire property, plant and equipment with funds received by a donor who specifies that the assets must be used for a set period of time. Alternatively, even in the absence of such donor restrictions, the organization may adopt a policy whereby if it acquires long-lived assets from restricted funds, it will impose a time restriction that expires over the life of the asset. In such circumstances, it should record the assets in a temporarily restricted fund rather than an unrestricted fund. Then, as it depreciates the assets, it should reduce their value and release the net assets from the restrictions. The depreciation, like all other expenses, should be recorded in an unrestricted fund.

WHAT ISSUES DOES A NOT-FOR-PROFIT FACE IN ESTABLISHING ITS REPORTING ENTITY?

Not-for-profits, no less than governments, can own or be integrally affiliated with either businesses or other not-for-profits. Indeed, these relationships among not-for-profits can be as varied as those among other types of entities. For the most part, however, the relationships manifest three basic (although overlapping) characteristics:

- ***Ownership.*** An organization may own all or part of another entity. For example, a hospital may own another hospital or a physicians' group practice; a college may own a research laboratory.
- ***Control.*** An organization may control another entity by having the power to appoint the majority of its governing board. For example, a health care organization may establish a fund-raising foundation, specifying that the foundation's governing board be composed of the organization's own officers. Alternatively, per affiliation agreements a national fraternal organization may have the authority to establish operating policies and standards for its local chapters; a religious "judicatory," such as an archdiocese, presbytery, or synod, may have certain supervisory powers over local churches that are members of its denomination.
- ***Economic interest.*** An organization may have an economic interest in another entity because the entity holds or utilizes resources on its behalf, the entity produces income or provides services to it, or the organization guarantees the debt of the entity. For example, a professional association may provide 100 percent of the funding for a political action committee that lobbies on its behalf; a legally independent, self-governing, fund-raising foundation may support the activities of a university or hospital.

As this text goes to press, generally accepted accounting principles for related entities are still very much in flux. In 1999, the Financial Accounting Standards Board issued an exposure draft, *Consolidated Financial Statements: Purpose and Policy*, that addressed several key reporting entity issues pertaining to not-for-profits. However, the FASB got side-tracked by more pressing issues (those pertaining to the reporting entity of businesses, for example), and never finalized its recommendations. Accordingly, the primary source of guidance remains the AICPA's 1994 Statement of Position, *Reporting of Related Entities by Not-for-Profit Organizations* (94-3). The overarching theme of that statement is that a not-for-profit should include a related organization in its own reporting entity when it can exercise significant influence over that organization. Its key provisions include the following:

- A not-for-profit organization should consolidate a related not-for-profit organization when it has a controlling *financial* interest through direct or indirect ownership of a majority voting interest.
- It should also consolidate a related not-for-profit organization when it is able to control that entity by having *both* a voting majority on its governing board and an "economic interest" (as discussed above) in that entity. If it has either a voting majority or an economic interest, but not both, then only disclosure of the relationship is required.
- It may consolidate another not-for-profit, but is not required to, when it is able to control the other entity by means other than majority ownership or voting interest, such as a contract or affiliation agreement.

Owing to the myriad of organizational relationships among not-for-profits, there remains a need for further guidance, which the FASB is likely to provide. "Control," however, as pointed out in the discussion relating to the reporting entity of governments, is an illusive concept. It is both multidimensional and not subject to precise measurement. An organization may be able to direct the resources of another entity for its own benefit even in the absence of ownership, an ability to appoint a majority of directors, or specific contractual arrangements. For example, a university's athletic director may have de facto command over the funds collected by the football team's booster club even if the booster club is not owned by the university, is governed by an independently elected board, and has no formal affiliation or contractual agreements with the university. Hence, any future FASB proposals are certain to be controversial.

COMPREHENSIVE EXAMPLE *Museum of American Culture*

This example, which focuses on the Museum of American Culture, synthesizes several of the principles presented so far. We start with the museum's balance sheet as of December 31, 2005 (presented in Table 12-6), account for the transactions in which the museum engaged during 2006 (journalized in the body of the text), and prepare selected financial statements as of December 31, 2006 (presented in Table 12-7).

The museum engages in two main programs: curatorial and exhibits, and education. These are backed by two support functions: fund-raising and administration.

The AICPA's audit and accounting guide, *Not-for-Profit Organizations*, provides the most comprehensive and authoritative accounting guidance for museums. It covers not-for-profit organizations as diverse as colleges and universities, cemetery associations, civic organizations, fraternal associations, labor unions, professional associations, religious organizations, and performing arts organizations. It does not, however, cover health care organizations, which are addressed in a separate guide.

The key transactions in which the museum engaged during the year (in summary form) follow (in thousands).

TABLE 12-6
Museum of American Culture

Statement of Financial Position
December 31, 2005
(in thousands)

Assets	
Current assets	
Cash	$ 120
Investments	4,210
Pledges receivable	165
Less: allowance for uncollectibles	(15)
	150
Supplies inventory	20
Prepaid expenses	50
Total current assets	4,550
Property, plant, and equipment	2,100
Less: accumulated depreciation	(540)
	1,560
Total assets	$6,110
Liabilities	
Current liabilities	
Wages and salaries payable	$ 8
Accounts payable	250
Total liabilities	258
Net assets	
Unrestricted	2,002
Temporarily restricted	850
Permanently restricted (endowments)	3,000
Total net assets	5,852

Accrual of Wages and Salaries

Museum employees earned wages and salaries of $1,045. During the year the museum paid employees $1,039, including $8 from the previous year. At year-end, it owed employees $14, which was slated to be paid in early 2007. Hence, a provision must be made for the wages and salaries earned, but not yet paid.

FASB Statement No. 117, *Financial Statements of Not-for-Profit Organizations*, provides that the statement of activities set forth expenses by *function*. The museum allocated the wages and salaries to its functions as indicated in the following entry:

Wages and salaries—curatorial and exhibits	$780	
Wages and salaries—education	85	
Wages and salaries—fund-raising	50	
Wages and salaries—administration	130	
Cash		$1,039
Accrued wages and salaries payable		6
To record wages and salaries (in an unrestricted fund)		

Other Operating Expenses; Inventory

The museum incurred other operating expenses of $280 ($200 in curatorial and exhibit costs, $30 for education, $10 for fund-raising, and $40 for administration). The expenses are, of course, accounted for on an accrual basis and must also be allocated to the organization's functions.

Consistent with the accrual basis, the museum is required to account for both supplies inventory and prepaid items on the *consumption basis.* During the period, the museum purchased $5 more of supplies than it used and, as a consequence, inventory increased by the same amount. Moreover, it reduced its balances in accounts payable by $3 and in prepaid expenses by $7. It disbursed a total of $281 in cash relating to the operating expenses:

Other operating expenses—curatorial and exhibits	$200	
Other operating expenses—education	30	
Other operating expenses—fund-raising	10	
Other operating expenses—administration	40	
Accounts payable	3	
Inventory	5	
Cash		$281
Prepaid expenses		7

To record other operating expenses (in an unrestricted fund)

Acquisition of Fixed Assets; Long-Term Debt

The museum acquired $20 of new furniture and fixtures in exchange for a long-term note of the same amount. Although for internal purposes many not-for-profits account for both their long-lived assets and related long-term debt in a plant fund (mentioned in Chapter 2), this museum accounts for them in its operating (an unrestricted) fund. For reporting purposes, the results would be the same. The assets are reported in the unrestricted funds along with other unrestricted resources:

Property, plant, and equipment	$20	
Notes payable		$20

To record the acquisition of fixed assets (in an unrestricted fund)

Unlike governments (in their governmental fund statements), not-for-profits must account for interest on the long-term note on the accrual basis.

Depreciation

The museum recognized depreciation of $210. Depreciation, like other expenses, is always recorded in an unrestricted fund:

Depreciation expense—curatorial and exhibits	$160	
Depreciation expense—education	15	
Depreciation expense—fund-raising	5	
Depreciation expense—administration	30	
Allowance for depreciation		$210

To record depreciation (in an unrestricted fund)

Admissions and Memberships

The museum's main operating revenues are derived from admissions and membership fees. In 2006 they totaled $505:

Cash	$505	
Revenues—admissions and memberships		$505
To record revenues from admissions and members (in an unrestricted fund)		

Interest and Dividends

The museum earned $280 in interest and dividends on its investments, most of which are held in an endowment fund. For this particular museum, the endowment income is unrestricted and thereby should be recorded in the operating fund and reported as unrestricted income. Were it restricted to a specific purpose, it would be recorded in a temporarily restricted fund and reported as temporarily restricted income. The endowment principal itself is accounted for in a permanently restricted fund. For internal bookkeeping purposes, many not-for-profits initially account for endowment interest and dividends in the endowment fund and then transfer them to the beneficiary funds. For external reporting purposes, however, the investment income should be reported as revenue of the beneficiary fund:

Cash	$280	
Investment earnings—interest and dividends		$280
To record dividends and interest (in an unrestricted fund)		

Changes in Fair Values

During the year, the fair value of the museum's investments increased by $100. Assuming that there are no explicit legal or donor-imposed restrictions requiring that gains from the appreciation of the endowment portfolios be added to the principal of the endowment, the increase in fair value would be recognized as unrestricted investment earnings—the same as dividends and interest.

Investments	$100	
Investment earnings—appreciation in fair value		$100
To record appreciation in fair value (in an unrestricted fund)		

Revenues and Expenses of Auxiliary Enterprises

The museum operates a gift shop. In 2006 revenues and expenses totaled $470 and $350, respectively.

Governments account for their business-type activities in enterprise funds. These funds are accounted for on the full accrual basis and, for purposes of external reporting, are not combined with governmental funds.

Since not-for-profits account for their general operations on full accrual basis, there is less need to separate their business from their nonbusiness activities. Although it is usually convenient to account for "auxiliary" activities (i.e., business-type activities) in separate funds, for external purposes they are usually reported along with other operations and the resources classified as unrestricted. Many not-for-profits aggregate their auxiliary revenues on one line and their auxiliary expenses on another. Others break out the revenues and expenses by individual, or types of, enterprises. The following summary entry would capture the museum's 2006 auxiliary activities:

Expenses applicable to auxiliary activities	$350	
Cash	120	
Revenues from auxiliary activities		$470
To record the activities of auxiliary activities (in an unrestricted fund)		

Insofar as the revenues and expenses affected accounts other than cash, such as inventory, prepaid expenses, and allowance for depreciation, then those balance sheet accounts, rather than cash, would be debited or credited.

Unrestricted and Time-Restricted Pledges

During the year, the museum conducted a fund-raising campaign. As of year-end it received cash of $338 and pledges for $180.

Contributions, including unconditional promises to pay, should be recognized as revenue upon receipt. However, the pledges outstanding, inasmuch as they are unavailable for expenditure (and thereby subject to time restrictions), should be reflected as an increase in restricted resources.

Cash	$338	
Revenue from unrestricted contributions		$338
To record unrestricted contributions (in an unrestricted fund)		

Pledges receivable (temporarily restricted)	$180	
Revenue from unrestricted contributions		180
To record pledges subject to time restrictions (in a temporarily restricted fund)		

It is assumed that these pledges will be received with a few months of year end and hence it is unnecessary to discount them to take into account the time value of money.

Of these temporarily restricted pledges, the museum estimates that $20 will be uncollectible.

Other operating expenses—fund-raising (uncollectible pledges—unrestricted)	$20	
Resources released from restrictions (unrestricted net assets)		$20
To record the estimated bad debt expense (in an unrestricted fund)		

Resources released from restrictions (temporarily restricted net assets)	$20	
Allowance for uncollectible pledges (temporarily restricted)		$20
To add to the allowance for uncollectible pledges (in a temporarily restricted fund)		

The latter two entries, though potentially confusing, are necessary because the pledges are being recorded as temporarily restricted. Hence the allowance for uncollectibles must also be recorded as temporarily restricted. As emphasized previously, however, not-for-profits must recognize all expenses as unrestricted. Hence the expense for uncollectible pledges (herein aggregated with other operating expenses and allocated to fund-raising) must be recorded in an unrestricted fund. As is required when other temporarily restricted resources are used for their intended purposes, they must be released from their restrictions and, in effect, "transferred" from the temporarily restricted to the unrestricted categories.

During the year, the museum collected $145 of time-restricted pledges receivable outstanding from prior years and wrote off $10 as uncollectible:

Cash	$145	
Resources released from restrictions		$145
To record cash collected on outstanding pledges (in an unrestricted fund)		

Resources released from restriction	$145	
Allowance for uncollectible pledges	10	
Pledges receivable		$155
To release resources from time restrictions and to write-off uncollectible pledges (in a temporarily restricted fund)		

Use-Restricted Contributions

The museum received a $90 contribution from a patron who required that the gift be used to acquire additional works of art. During the year, the museum used the gift, along with $620 of resources that had previously been restricted, to add to its collection.

Because the gift is restricted (and in this instance the museum did not expect to expend it in the current year), it accounted for in a temporarily restricted fund:

Cash	$90	
Revenue from restricted contributions		$90

To record contributions restricted to acquisition of art (in a temporarily restricted fund)

This museum, like most others, elects *not* to capitalize its art collection (as long as it satisfies the FASB conditions that allow for a choice). Therefore, the costs to acquire the new art would be reported as an expense. However, because not-for-profits must report all expenses in an unrestricted fund, the resources must be released from the restricted fund to the current fund:

Resources released from restriction	$710	
Cash		$710

To record the release of restricted resources upon acquiring new art (in temporarily restricted fund)

Acquisition of art—expense	$710	
Resources released from restrictions		$710

To record the acquisition of art (in an unrestricted fund)

To pay for the art, the museum sold $500 of unrestricted investments. There was no gain or loss on sale inasmuch as the museum carried the investments at fair value:

Cash	$500	
Investments		$500

To record the sale of investments (in an unrestricted fund)

Volunteer Services

The museum benefits from the services of volunteer guides. Guides are essential to the operations of the museum and were it not able to attract volunteers, the museum would have to hire them. Nevertheless, the guides do not have to possess specialized skills (those characteristic of craftsmen or professionals), and therefore the museum may not recognize the value of their services as either revenues or expenses.

Table 12-7 summarizes the museum's 2006 transactions in a statement of activity, a year-end balance sheet, a schedule of program and support expenses, and a statement of cash flows.

WHAT UNIQUE ISSUES DO HEALTH CARE PROVIDERS FACE?

Health care in the United States is in the midst of a massive economic reorganization in which the divisions between business, not-for-profit, and government providers are becoming increasingly blurred. Consequently, the accounting distinctions among health care providers in the three sectors are also becoming less significant. Moreover, with the FASB's issuance of Statement No. 117, *Financial Statements of Not-for-Profit Organizations*, the differences in financial reporting between not-for-profit

TABLE 12–7
Museum of American Culture

Statement of Activity
For the Year Ending December 31, 2006 (in thousands)

	Unrestricted	Temporarily Restricted	Permanently Restricted	Total
Support and revenues				
Admissions and memberships	$ 505			$ 505
Investments—dividends and interest	280			280
Investments—appreciation	100			100
Revenue from auxiliary enterprises	470			470
Unrestricted contributions, Including pledges	338	$ 180		518
Restricted contributions	____	90		90
Total support and revenues	$1,693	$ 270		$1,963
Expenses				
Program				
Curatorial and exhibits	$1,140			$1,140
Education	130			130
Support services				
Fund-raising	85			85
Administration	200			200
Acquisition of art	710			710
Expenses of auxiliary enterprises	350			350
Total expenses	$2,615	____		$2,615
Excess (deficiency) of support and revenue over expenses	$ (922)	$ 270		$ (652)
Resources released from restrictions	875	(875)		____
Net (decrease) in fund balances	$ (47)	$(605)		$ (652)
Net assets, beginning of period	2,002	850	3,000	5,852
Net assets, end of period	$1,955	$ 245	$3,000	$5,200

(Continues)

TABLE 12–7
Museum of American Culture *(Continued)*

Statement of Financial Position
December 31, 2006
(in thousands)

Assets	
Current assets	
Cash	$ 68
Investments	3,810
Pledges receivable	190
Less: allowance for uncollectibles	(25)
	165
Supplies inventory	25
Prepaid expenses	43
Total current assets	$4,111
Property, plant, and equipment	$2,120
Less: accumulated depreciation	(750)
	$1,370
Total assets	$5,481
Liabilities	
Current liabilities	
Wages and salaries payable	$ 14
Accounts payable	247
Total current liabilities	$ 261
Note payable	20
Total liabilities	$ 281
Net assets	
Unrestricted	$1,955
Temporarily restricted	245
Permanently restricted (endowments)	3,000
Total net assets	$5,200

TABLE 12–7
Museum of American Culture *(Continued)*

Schedule of Program and Support Expenses
For the Year Ending December 31, 2006
(in thousands)

	Curatorial & Exhibit	Education	Fund-Raising	Administration and Other	Total
Wages and salaries	$ 780	$ 85	$50	$ 130	$1,045
Other operating expenses	200	30	30	40	300
Depreciation	160	15	5	30	210
Acquisition of art				710	710
Auxiliary enterprise				350	350
Total	$1,140	$130	$85	$1,260	$2,615

(Continues)

TABLE 12-7
Museum of American Culture *(Continued)*

Statement of Cash Flows
For the Year Ending December 31, 2006

Cash flows from operating activities	
Contributions	$ 573
Admissions and memberships	505
Interest and dividends	280
Cash from auxiliary enterprises	120
Cash from sale of art	500
Wages and salaries paid	(1,039)
Purchases of art	(710)
Payments for other operating expenses	(281)
Net cash provided by operating activities; net increase (decrease) in cash	$ (52)
Cash on hand, beginning of year	120
Cash on hand, end of year	$ 68
Supplemental data	
Noncash investing and financing activity—acquisition of property, plant, and equipment in exchange for a note payable	$ 20

health care providers and other types of not-for-profit organizations are now only minimal. Therefore, in this section of the text, we limit our discussion to transactions that are either unique, or of special importance, to health care providers.

The accounting and reporting practices of health care organizations have been strongly influenced by the Healthcare Financial Management Association and the American Hospital Association, both of which are industry associations, and the AICPA. Until recently, external financial reporting was governed mainly by AICPA industry audit guides pertaining to hospitals and other types of health care organizations. Now that the FASB is taking an active interest in not-for-profit accounting, many of the guides' directives have been superseded by FASB pronouncements such as Statements No. 116 (contributions) and No. 117 (financial statements). Nevertheless, the AICPA's current industry guide, *Health Care Organizations* (which unlike earlier versions deals with both hospitals and other types of health care providers) is the primary authoritative source for issues not addressed by the FASB.

Health care may be provided by individual practitioners (including physicians, therapists, and counselors), hospitals, outpatient clinics, medical service and retirement institutions, and a wide range of not-for-profit specialty organizations (such as screening clinics, support organizations, and research institutes). Most health care organizations bill their patients (or third-party payers such as insurance companies) for services actually rendered. Health maintenance organizations (HMOs) and related types of health plans provide services to members in return for fixed, periodic payments. These HMOs and health plans may subcontract with hospitals, physicians associations, or other medical groups to provide specialized services in exchange for *capitation* (per person) fees. The capitation fees are generally based on number of persons covered and expected costs to be incurred rather than actual services provided.

To a greater extent than most other not-for-profits, health care organizations must be concerned with their costs. Many other not-for-profits focus mainly on fund-raising; they then adjust the level of services to available revenues. Health care organizations charge for their services. Often the amount of fees charged are limited by competition or pre-established reimbursement rates. Therefore, they must be vitally interested both in determining and controlling the cost of their services.

FUND STRUCTURE

The basic financial statements of not-for-profit health care organizations are similar in all major respects to those of the museum illustrated in the previous section. The balance sheet and statement of activities should distinguish among unrestricted, temporarily restricted, and permanently restricted resources. The statement of activities should classify the revenues as unrestricted, temporarily restricted, and permanently restricted but should report expenses only as decreases in unrestricted resources.

For purposes of internal accounting, hospitals and health organizations typically maintain one or more unrestricted operating funds as well as several temporarily and permanently restricted funds. The general operating funds report both financial resources and property, plant, and equipment. Temporarily restricted funds are established to account for donated resources received for particular purposes. These purposes include specified programs or services (e.g., geriatric care, research, community education) as well as replacement of, or additions to, plant and equipment. In addition, temporarily restricted funds include term endowment funds, annuity funds, life income funds, and other split-interest agreements.

Two points regarding temporarily restricted funds warrant emphasis:

- Temporarily restricted funds related to plant and equipment generally account only for *resources* restricted to the purchase or construction of plant and equipment. They do not usually account for the plant and equipment itself. Plant and equipment is typically reported in the general operating fund. (A notable exception involves plant and equipment acquired by gift. These assets may be subject to restrictions that expire as the asset is depreciated, and hence they may be accounted for in temporarily restricted funds.)
- An organization may opt to establish temporarily restricted funds to account for resources designated by its governing board for specific purposes (e.g., to replace plant and equipment). For purposes of external reporting, however, board-designated resources are *not* considered restricted and should therefore be reported along with other unrestricted operating resources. They may, however, be classified within the unrestricted fund as "assets whose use is limited" (or some similar category).

As with the other not-for-profits, permanently restricted funds encompass mainly ordinary endowments (funds the principal of which must remain intact and only the earnings are expendable).

Like other not-for-profits (as well as governments), health care organizations may maintain numerous funds of each of the three categories. For reporting purposes, however, the funds should be combined by category.

CLASSIFICATIONS OF REVENUES AND EXPENSES

The statement of activities of a health care organization is relatively straightforward. Revenues are displayed by category (often in columns): unrestricted, temporarily restricted, and permanently restricted. They are divided into at least two classifications (usually rows): patient care revenues and other revenues. Patient care revenues include:

- Routine services (such as room, board, and general nursing)
- Other nursing services (such as operating room services)
- Professional services (such as physicians' services, laboratories, and pharmacy)

Other revenues include:

- Contributions
- Educational services
- Miscellaneous sources (such as rental of space, auxiliary enterprises, and fees charged for providing medical records)

In addition, revenues from capitation fees should generally be shown apart from other types of revenues.

Expenses are reported exclusively within the unrestricted category. They may be classified either by function or by object. However, per Statement No. 117, if the expenses are classified by object, then the functional classification must be presented in the notes.

The statement of activities must also indicate resources released from restriction and any transfers between funds. Likely functional and natural (object) classifications of expenditures include the following:

Functional

- Nursing services
- Other professional services
- General services
- Fiscal services
- Administrative services
- Bad debts
- Depreciation
- Interest

Natural

- Salaries and wages
- Employee benefits
- Fees to individuals and organizations
- Supplies and other expense
- Purchased services
- Bad debts
- Depreciation
- Interest

RECOGNIZING FEE-FOR-SERVICE PATIENT-CARE REVENUES

Health care organizations may provide patient services over an extended period of time. Yet patients are often billed only at the conclusion of their stay at the facility.

In reality, most patients pay only a small portion of their bills themselves. Most health care organizations derive most of their revenues from third parties, such as Medicare, Medicaid, Blue Cross, and other insurance companies and health plans. These third parties pay the hospital or other health care provider based on contractual or other predetermined rates. For example, in most circumstances, Medicare reimburses hospitals based on the nature of patients' illnesses. Under its Prospective Payment System, it classifies patient care into diagnosis-related groups and allows a specified rate for each group. In some circumstances, however, it reimburses specified allowable costs. The amounts paid by the third-party payers are almost always less than the provider's "standard" billing rate.

At the time they provide patient care, hospitals and other health care providers cannot always be certain as to the portion of their standard charges that they ultimately will be paid. Usually the amount is known for certain only when they receive payment. In fact, under some "retrospective" payment arrangements, payments are based on total costs incurred during a particular period. Although the third-party payer makes interim payments during the period, a final determination may not be reached until after the end of the period.

Inasmuch as many patients who are uninsured cannot afford the costs of an extended hospital stay or expensive medical procedures, health care providers may face high rates of bad debts. Moreover, unlike businesses, providers often serve patients who they know will be unable to pay the amounts billed.

Owing to the uncertainty of the amounts that they will actually collect for their services, hospitals face salient issues of when and how to report their patient care revenues and value their related receivables.

EXAMPLE *Patient Care Revenues*

During a particular week a hospital records $400,000 in patient charges. The charges applicable to patients that were actually discharged from the hospital (including charges incurred in prior weeks) were $395,000.

The hospital estimates that 80 percent ($320,000) of the charges will be billed to third-party payers, who will, on average, discount the invoiced amounts by 30 percent ($96,000).

The remaining 20 percent ($80,000) of the hospital's charges will be billed to patients who are uninsured. Of this 20 percent, 60 percent ($48,000) will be uncollectible.

AICPA Guidance

According to the AICPA audit guide *Health Care Organizations* (2001 edition), revenue from health care services is usually recorded "when coverage is provided to an enrollee or the service is provided to a patient or resident."[9] Thus, the patient discharge method (at one time a popular basis for revenue recognition) is inappropriate.

Further the guide advises:

> Revenue and the related receivables for health care services are usually recorded in the accounting records on an accrual basis at the provider's *full established rates.* The provision for contractual adjustments [that is, the difference between established rates and third-party-payer payments] and discounts [that is, the difference between established rates and the amount collectible] are recognized on an *accrual basis* and deducted from gross revenue to determine net service revenue. Contractual adjustments, discounts, and an allowance for uncollectibles are recorded to report the receivables for health care services at net realizable value. [emphasis added][10]

Bad debts, as implied in the recommended classification of expenses, should be reported as an expense, not a deduction from revenues.

In the example, the following entries would be consistent with these guidelines:

Patient accounts receivable	$400,000	
Patient revenues		$400,000
To record one week's patient revenues		
Revenue from patient services—estimated contractual adjustments	$96,000	
Patient accounts receivable—allowance for contractual adjustments		$96,000
To establish an allowance for contractual adjustments (30 percent of the $320,000 that will be paid by third parties)		

[9] Para. 10.04.

[10] Para. 5.03.

Bad debt expense	$48,000	
Patient accounts receivable—allowance for bad debts		$48,000
To establish an allowance for bad debts (60 percent of the $80,000 that will be paid directly by patients)		

RECOGNIZING CAPITATION FEE REVENUES

Health care organizations receive capitation fees when they contract either with an individual or with an insurance company or other third-party payer to provide covered services during a specified period of time. Typically an organization receives the payments at the beginning of each month and is obligated to provide the services during the month. Sometimes the organization also assumes the risk of having to refer a patient to other organizations for diagnosis or treatment and to pay for those services.

EXAMPLE *Capitation Fee Revenues*

A physicians group receives $300,000 in capitation fees from the Hartford Insurance Company to provide comprehensive health care to members of the company's health plan. During the month it provides services for which it would bill, at standard rates, $240,000. In addition, it refers patients to hospitals and other health care providers for which it expects to be billed $18,000.

AICPA Guidance

Per the AICPA audit guide, revenue from capitation fees "is earned as a result of agreeing to provide services to qualified beneficiaries and not as a result of actually providing the care."[11]

The physicians group in the example should recognize revenue in the period covered by the capitation fees. Correspondingly, it should establish a liability for any related costs for which it has not yet paid.

Thus:

Cash	$300,000	
Revenue from capitation fees		$300,000
To record capitation fees received		
Patient referrals (expense)	$18,000	
Obligations for patient referrals		$18,000
To record liability for patient referrals		

The amount for which it would have billed at standard rates is therefore irrelevant.

ACCOUNTING FOR AND REPORTING CHARITY CARE

Health care organizations provide uncompensated patient care as a matter of both policy and law. The Hospital Survey and Construction Act of 1946 (Public Law 79-725, usually referred to as the Hill-Burton Act), stipulates that hospitals receiving federal construction funds must provide a certain amount of charitable care. This

[11] Para. 1.22.

IN PRACTICE

COLLECTION OF ERRORS ADDS UP TO $21 MILLION DEBACLE

The following are excerpts from an article published shortly after Austin's municipal hospital, which had previously reported that it was profitable, disclosed that it was in fact facing a major deficit.

Behind the now infamous $21 million shortfall at Brackenridge Hospital is a collection of several problems, not one. They came to light as Richard Lewis, who took over September 1 as the hospital's chief financial officer, began reviewing the closing of the books for the 1993 fiscal year, which ended September 30.

Mostly, the $21 million shortfall centered on accounting for projected income from big institutional payers—the federal government, health maintenance organizations, and preferred provider organizations—that pay only part of the full charge for a patient's medical services. "They booked some $70 million worth of deductions," [city budget official Betty] Dunkerley said. But $70 million wasn't enough: "They made some errors in math; they made some errors in the accounting."

[Dunkerley and Lewis] outline some of what they say are accounting errors at the hospital:

- About $4.1 million involved Medicare "contractual allowances." A contractual allowance, or discount, is the amount of money Medicare and Medicaid, federal health insurance programs, will not pay of a hospital's full bill. Like other hospitals, Brackenridge needs to know how much money it can expect to come in, not just how much it has billed, to project income and plan accurately. "Of the $4.1 million, $1.53 million was money the hospital received from Medicare but was booked twice in the process of accounting for the contractual allowances when the books were closed for the fiscal year," Lewis said.
- About $8.6 million involved patients who were billed at full service rates and only later were identified as Medicaid patients. "When patients are admitted with no insurance," Lewis said, "the hospital assumes none of the bill will ever be paid. But thanks to an aggressive program to recover as much money as possible from Medicaid, Brackenridge often does collect part of the bill charged to such patients."
- $4.5 million resulted when accountants did not book enough discounts given to HMOs and PPOs until the hospital was paid for its service. While awaiting payment, therefore, the accountants were reporting that the full payment—not the discounted payment—would be paid.
- $3.4 million came from reconciling the hospital's general ledger with its more detailed subsidiary ledger, which lists individual patients and their accounts. "I'll just be up front with you," Lewis said. "That was bad accounting."

Source: Bruce Hight, "Collection of Errors Add Up to $21 Million Debacle," *Austin American-Statesman*, 23 January 1994. Reprinted with permission.

care does not result in cash inflows and consequently, it can be argued, should not qualify for recognition either as revenue or as receivables. On the other hand, charity care is conceptually similar to patient care for which third parties will reimburse the hospital or other provider for less than full rates (in the case of charity care, at zero) or patient care in which substantial bad debts are anticipated.

EXAMPLE *Charity Care*

A hospital values care provided to indigent patients at $300,000, based on standard billing rates. However, it anticipates collecting for none of its services.

AICPA Guidance

The AICPA audit guide specifies that gross revenue should *exclude* charity care. However, it also makes clear that health care organizations are obligated to disclose their policies for providing charity care and should indicate the amounts provided based on the provider's "rates, costs, units or service, or other statistics."[12]

The guide recognizes that distinguishing bad debt expense from charity care requires judgment. However, it notes that "charity care represents health care services that are provided but are never expected to result in cash flows," whereas it defines bad debt expense as "the current period charge for actual or expected doubtful accounts resulting from the extension of credit."[13] The key distinction is that an entity provides charity care in the expectation that it will not receive compensation but incurs bad debts by providing service in the hope of at least partial payment.

Thus, in the example, the hospital need not make an entry to record the value of the charitable care. It should, however, explain its policies and report the total value of the care provided in notes to the financial statements.

ACCOUNTING FOR AND REPORTING MALPRACTICE CONTINGENCIES

Malpractice claims have become an accepted, if unwanted, concern of health care organizations and a routine element of their financial reports. Potential losses arising from malpractice claims are obviously consequential, so most entities transfer a portion of their risk to independent insurers. However, even if all or a portion, of the risk is insured, litigation costs can still be daunting. The key accounting and reporting issues relate to when and how much of a loss should be recognized owing to both unsettled claims and claims that have not yet been filed.

EXAMPLE *Malpractice Claims*

A hospital has been charged with negligence in the death of a patient. Although no claim has yet been filed, past experience indicates that the hospital is almost certain to be sued.

FASB Standards

FASB standards for malpractice and other claims are drawn from FASB Statement No. 5, *Accounting for Contingencies*, and are therefore the same as for businesses. They provide that a health care organization should accrue an estimated loss by a charge to operations as soon as both of the following conditions are met:

[12] Paras. 10.03 and 10.20.

[13] Glossary.

- It is probable that an asset has been impaired or a liability has been incurred.
- The amount of the loss can be reasonably estimated.

If either of these conditions are not met, but there is at least a *reasonable possibility* that a loss will be incurred, then the organization should disclose the nature of the contingency and estimate the possible loss or the range of the loss (or state that an estimate cannot be made).

Thus, the cost of a malpractice claim should be accrued when the incident giving rise to the claim occurs, as long as the eventual loss can be reasonably estimated. Obviously, health care organizations face considerable practical difficulties in estimating the amounts for which claims will eventually be settled, particularly those that have not yet been asserted. Nevertheless, the organization can draw upon both its own past experience and industry data. Moreover, it does not have to assess each incident individually. It can group together similar incidents and thereby take advantage of statistical relationships. The total accrued cost should take into account litigation fees but should be reduced by anticipated insurance recoveries.

In the example, the hospital would be required to charge an expense (a loss) in the period of the incident only if it were able to make a reasonable estimate of the amount. If it were unable to estimate the amount, then it would be required to disclose the details of the incident. Assuming that the hospital, was, in fact, able to estimate reasonably that the loss would be $300,000 (after taking into account insurance recoveries), the following entry would be appropriate:

Anticipated legal claims (expense)	$300,000	
Commitments and contingencies (liability)		$300,000
To record the estimated cost of settling a potential malpractice claim		

REPORTING "RETROSPECTIVE INSURANCE PREMIUMS"

Another aspect of the question as to when and how malpractice claims should be reported is that of reporting malpractice insurance expense. Some insurance policies make provisions for "retrospectively rated premiums." These policies require that at the expiration of the policy, the premium costs be adjusted to take into account actual loss experience. Thus, if claims during the period are greater than anticipated, the insured will have to pay an additional premium; if claims are less, then it will receive a refund. As a consequence, the insured does not always know by year end what that year's actual insurance costs will be. These types of policies do not provide true insurance coverage (except, perhaps, for claims above a specified amount), since the insured is being charged for all, or a portion, of actual losses.

EXAMPLE *Retrospective Premiums*

In June 2004 a not-for-profit physicians practice plan entered into an insurance contract for the period July 1, 2004, through June 30, 2005. The basic premium was $120,000 for the year, which the physicians group paid in June 2004. However, the policy also contained a complex formula for premium adjustments upon the termination of the policy. Prior to preparing its financial statements for the year ended December 31, 2004, the practice plan estimated, based on both asserted and unasserted claims, that it would have to pay an additional $10,000 in premiums resulting from incidents in the last six months of 2004.

AICPA Guidance

The AICPA health care audit guide indicates that the insured entity should charge the basic premium as an expense pro rata over the term of the policy. In addition, it should accrue additional premiums or refunds based on the FASB Statement No. 5 criteria for recognition of losses. If it is unable to estimate losses from claims, then it should disclose the contingencies in the notes.[14]

In the example, the following entry would summarize insurance activity for 2004 relating to the policy acquired in June:

Malpractice insurance expense	$70,000	
Prepaid insurance (basic premium for 2005)	60,000	
Cash		$120,000
Commitments and contingencies (liability to insurance company)		10,000

To record 2004 malpractice insurance expense (basic premium of $60,000 for six months plus anticipated claims adjustment of $10,000) and prepaid insurance for 2005 (basic premium of $60,000 for six months)

DIFFERENCES BETWEEN GOVERNMENT AND NOT-FOR-PROFIT HEALTH CARE ORGANIZATIONS

Although government hospitals are within the purview of the GASB and not-for-profit hospitals are under the jurisdiction of the FASB, there are relatively few differences in their accounting practices. Most government health care organizations (the notable exception being those that are financed entirely with nonexchange revenues) are accounted for in enterprise funds. They follow the same practices as comparable business and not-for-profit entities and therefore adhere to the guidance in the AICPA's health care audit guide.

WHAT UNIQUE ISSUES DO COLLEGES AND UNIVERSITIES FACE?

APPLICABLE STANDARDS

Not-for-profit colleges and universities are subject to the same FASB standards as other not-for-profit entities. As noted in the previous chapter, most government colleges and universities can be expected to exercise the GASB Statement No. 34 option that permits them to account for their activities in enterprise funds. Therefore, inasmuch as both government and not-for-profit colleges and universities will account for their activities on a full accrual basis, the differences are likely to be less pronounced than in the past. Nevertheless, the FASB's reporting structure and principles of revenue and expenditure recognition differ in significant ways from those of the GASB. Notably, for example, FASB requires that revenues be classified into three categories of restrictiveness based on donor specification, whereas the GASB draws no distinction between resources restricted by donors and those restricted by other outside parties (such as bondholders).

Although the FASB pronouncements directed toward not-for-profits apply to colleges and universities, they do not address the unique accounting and reporting issues of these entities. In 1973 the AICPA issued an industry audit guide, *Audits of Colleges and Universities*, that dealt exclusively with colleges and universities. It supplemented this guide in 1974 with Statement of Position 74-8, *Financial Accounting and Reporting By Colleges and Universities*. However, the AICPA has now superseded this publication

[14] Para. 8.14.

with its more inclusive industry audit guide, *Not-for-Profit Organizations*, which covers all not-for-profits (except health care organizations). Like the FASB pronouncements, this audit guide does not deal with the specific issues facing colleges and universities.

For guidance on specific questions pertaining to colleges and universities, one can look to the superseded AICPA publications and to the literature of the National Association of College and University Business Officers, which is the leading association of university accounting and financial managers, and to prevalent practice.

The AICPA's *Not-for-Profit Organizations* guide carried forward from the superseded publications a description of what is referred to as the "AICPA model." This model establishes a fund structure, summarized in Table 12-8, that many colleges and universities continue to maintain for purposes of internal accounting and control. However, for purposes of external reporting, colleges and universities must now group their funds into the three categories of restrictiveness established by the FASB in its Statement No. 117.

CLASSIFICATION OF REVENUES AND EXPENSES

FASB Statement No. 117 does not specify how revenues and expenses should be classified. But most colleges and universities, both governmental and private, classify revenues by source and expenses by function. Common categories of revenues include:

- Tuition and fees
- Government appropriations
- Government grants and contracts
- Gifts and private grants
- Endowment income
- Revenues from auxiliary enterprises
- Gains (or losses) on sales of investments

Common categories of expenditures include:

- Education and general
    - Instruction and departmental research
    - Extension and public service
    - Libraries
    - Student services
- Sponsored research
- Operation and maintenance of plant
- General administration
- Expenses of auxiliary enterprises

IN PRACTICE

WHICH SET OF STANDARDS DO WE FOLLOW?

Most colleges and universities are clearly either public or private. Some, however, face an accounting and reporting identity crisis.

Cornell University, for example, consists of both public and private colleges. The public ("statutory") colleges include its School of Industrial and Labor Relations, College of Veterinary Medicine, and College of Agriculture and Life Sciences. The private ("endowed") colleges include its College of Arts and Sciences, School of Management, Law School, and Graduate School.

The college has chosen to adhere to the FASB standards.

TABLE 12–8
AICPA Model Funds Structure (for Internal Accounting and Reporting Only)

Current Operating Funds

The current funds of a university are equivalent to a government's general fund and its special revenue funds. Like a government, a university maintains a single current operating fund plus as many current restricted funds as needed.

Loan Funds

As implied by their title, loan funds account for resources dedicated for student loans. A type of restricted fund, their assets are principally loans receivable and investments. They do not typically have liabilities of consequence, except if the university itself has borrowed the funds that it lends. Fund balances are ordinarily increased by gifts and grants and by investment earnings. They are decreased by administrative costs and by provisions for bad debts.

Endowment Funds

Endowment funds are analogous to a government's permanent funds (i.e., nonexpendable trust funds). They are used most commonly to account for gifts which specify that the donated amount is to be invested and that only the income from the investments may be expended. The donors may either stipulate the purpose for which the income must be expended or leave it to the discretion of the university.

Annuity and Life Income Funds

Annuity and life income funds are special types of endowment funds. They are used to account for split-interest gifts that provide a return to the donor (or a person designated by the donor) for a specified term or for the remainder of his or her life. Thereafter, what remains of the gift will revert to the university. For example, a donor may want to contribute his fortune to a university while he is alive, but still reap all or a portion of the earnings from it. He can accomplish this (and perhaps also be rewarded with advantageous tax treatment) by attaching to his gift the stipulation that he receive either a stated annual sum (an annuity) or a percentage of the investment earnings from his gift (life income) until his death.

Plant Funds

Universities divide their plant funds into four categories:

- *Plant funds—unexpended.* These are the university version of capital projects funds. They are maintained to account for resources reserved for the construction or purchase of plant and equipment. Universities finance the construction of capital projects by issuing bonds, accepting gifts or grants, or by setting aside general operating revenues. To ensure that the resources are used only for their intended purposes, they are accounted for in specially dedicated funds.
- *Plant fund—renewals and replacements.* These are, in essence, additional capital projects funds. The resources in these funds, however, are committed to the renewal and replacement of existing plant and equipment rather than the acquisition of new facilities.
- *Plant funds—retirement of indebtedness.* These funds correspond to a government's debt service funds. Their assets, mostly cash and investments, are held for the retirement of debt and the payment of interest.
- *Plant funds—investment in plant.* These funds report the university's long-term assets, including land, buildings, construction in progress, improvements other than buildings, equipment, and library books.

Plant funds report both assets and related debt. Thus, if proceeds from issuing bonds are initially reported in an unexpended plant fund, then the cash received would be recognized as an asset; the bonds payable as a liability. If the bond money was subsequently used to construct a building, then both the cash and the bonds payable would be removed from the unexpended plant fund. In the investment in plant fund, the new building would be reported as an asset; the related bonds payable as a liability. The excess of plant fund assets over liabilities in each of the categories is generally reported as either "fund balance" or "investment in plant."

Agency Funds

The agency funds of a university are virtually identical to those of a government. They are maintained to account for resources that the institution holds as a custodian or fiscal agent for "outsiders," such as student organizations and employees. The accounting for these funds is as straightforward as for governmental agency funds; the funds have only assets and liabilities, no fund balances.

- Depreciation
- Interest
- Provision for uncollectible student loans

THE MEANING OF "OPERATING INCOME"—A CONTROVERSIAL ISSUE

Approximately 60 percent of not-for-profit colleges and universities distinguish between "operating" and "nonoperating" activities in their statements of activities. The balance do not. Moreover, among the institutions that do distinguish between the two, there is no uniformity as to the classification of the various activities. As a consequence, although the "bottom line" (net increase in net assets) is unaffected by how they report their revenues and expenses, some institutions may appear to be more efficient in their operations than others.

Among the items over which there is the greatest disparity of practice are contributions and bequests, investment gains and losses, and the change in value of split interest agreements (including those which result from changes in actuarial assumptions).[15]

As noted earlier, public colleges are required by GASB Statement No. 34 to present separate subtotals for operating and nonoperating revenues and expenses.

RECOGNIZING TUITION AND FEE REVENUES AND RELATED EXPENSES

The issue of when tuition and fee revenue should be recognized arises mainly because most colleges and universities end their fiscal year in the summer months, their "slow" season. Therefore, summer semesters or quarters may overlap fiscal years. Fall or spring terms, however, generally take place entirely within a single fiscal year.

Several events or transactions could be justified as a point of revenue recognition for tuition and fees:

- As students pay their tuition or fees (i.e., a cash collection basis)
- The start of a semester
- The last date at which refunds can be claimed
- The passage of time (i.e., if a semester overlaps two fiscal years, then the revenue could be allocated between the years based on the number of semester days in each year)

EXAMPLE *Tuition and Fee Revenues*

The fiscal year of a college ends July 31. In June 2005 a college collects $6 million in tuition and fees for its summer semester that begins on June 1 and ends on August 15. It also collects $9 million for the following fall semester, which begins on September 5. Faculty salaries applicable to summer session courses are $500,000. Of this amount, $400,000 is paid in June and July and $100,000 in August.

AICPA Guidance

The 1973 AICPA audit guide, *Audits of Colleges and Universities*, states that "revenues and expenditures of an academic term, such as a summer session, which is conducted over a fiscal year end, should be reported totally within the fiscal year in which the program is predominantly conducted."[16]

[15] See Mary Fischer, Teresa Gordon, Janet Greenlee, and Elizabeth Keating, "What Does 'Operating Income' Really Mean? An Analysis of the Financial Statement of Private Colleges and Universities," *Financial Accountability & Management*, forthcoming.

[16] Page 7.

Thus, in the example, the entire summer semester tuition and fees, as well as the related faculty salaries, should be recognized in the year ending July 31, 2005:

Cash	$6,000,000	
Revenue from tuition and fees		$6,000,000
To record revenue for the summer semester beginning June 1, 2005		

Faculty salaries relating to the summer semester—expense	$500,000	
Cash		$400,000
Deferred faculty salaries relating to the summer semester (liability)		100,000
To record the faculty salaries applicable to the summer semester beginning June 1, 2005		

In this example it is assumed that faculty salaries, but not other operating costs, can be tied directly to summer courses (e.g., that faculty are paid on a "per course" basis). Therefore, the faculty salaries have been matched to the tuition revenues and fees. The other operating costs would be accounted for as "period" costs and expensed as incurred.

The $9 million in tuition and fees applicable to the fall semester should be recognized as revenue in the year ending July 31, 2006, and should therefore be reported as deferred revenue when received in June 2005:

Cash	$9,000,000	
Deferred revenue—fall semester tuition and fees (liability)		$9,000,000
To record tuition and fees applicable to the fall semester beginning September 5, 2005		

Neither FASB pronouncements nor the AICPA not-for-profits audit guide addresses the issue of tuition revenue, so the 1973 AICPA college and university guide remains the most authoritative source of guidance for both government and not-for-profit institutions.

ACCOUNTING FOR AND REPORTING GRANTS

For many colleges and universities, reimbursement grants for research and related activities are a mainstay of financial support. Grantors, especially the federal government, do not expect recipients to earn a "profit" from their grants; they expect the grants merely to cover the costs of the specified research or other activities. Nonetheless, almost all grants provide reimbursement for "indirect costs" or overhead, and Office of Management and Budget rules detail how overhead allowances on federal grants should be computed.[17]

The most controversial accounting issue as to research grants is the same as that discussed in Chapter 4 pertaining to government grants: When should revenue and expenses be recognized, inasmuch as the various stages in the grant process (award, fulfillment of terms, and payment) may occur in different accounting periods?

EXAMPLE *Grants*

In 2005 a private university's accounting department received a $300,000 federal grant to carry out research in government budgeting. Of this amount, $180,000 was to cover faculty salaries and $120,000 was to cover overhead. During 2005 the department began the research and paid faculty members $45,000. It was reimbursed by the federal government for $75,000 (the direct costs incurred plus a proportionate share of the overhead).

[17] Office of Management and Budget Circular A-21, *Cost Principles for Educational Institutions* (rev. August 2000).

FASB Standards

Per FASB Statement No. 116, grants (excluding those that are exchange transactions in which the grantors expect to receive reciprocal value) are a form of contributions and should be accounted for as such.[18] Reimbursement grants are conditioned upon the grantee's incurring qualifying costs. Therefore, they should be accounted for as conditional grants. They should be recognized as revenue only as the grantee incurs qualifying costs.

In the example, the following entries would be appropriate in 2005:

Sponsored research—expense	$45,000	
Cash		$45,000
To record faculty salaries (in an unrestricted fund)		

The overhead costs incurred are not broken out separately because by their very nature they cannot be. They are subsumed in categories such as maintenance, administration, and library costs.

Due from federal government	$75,000	
Government grants and contracts—direct reimbursement (revenue)		$45,000
Government grants and contracts—reimbursement for overhead (revenue)		$30,000
To record the amount due from the federal government for reimbursement of direct and indirect costs (in an unrestricted fund)		

Cash	$75,000	
Due from federal government		$75,000
To record the collection of cash from the federal government (in an unrestricted fund)		

In this illustration, the resources received from the federal government are restricted to specified research. Nevertheless, the transactions are recorded entirely in the unrestricted category because it is assumed that the university will exercise its option to report restricted promises to give as unrestricted if the restriction has been met in the same period as the donation is made.

The exercise for review and self-study further illustrates these practices of non-government colleges and universities. See also Table 2-11 of Chapter 2, which contains excerpts from the financial statements of Hamilton College.

HOW CAN A NOT-FOR-PROFIT'S FISCAL CONDITION BE ASSESSED?

In the previous chapter, we emphasized that the fiscal condition of a government can be assessed only by taking into account a wide range of economic, demographic, and social factors, many of which may not be incorporated in a complete CAFR, let alone the basic financial statements. In a broad sense, the outline in Table 11-5, "A City's Fiscal Status: A Comprehensive Analysis," is as applicable to not-for-profits as it is to governments.

[18] Para. 20.

Every type of organization has unique characteristics, and an analysis must be custom-crafted to take them into account. Some not-for-profits are comparable to businesses, and hence the approach taken in a financial analysis of a business would generally be applicable to them. Thus, for example, insofar as not-for-profit hospitals rely mainly on patient billings for their revenues, the factors that affect the fiscal health of a not-for-profit hospital would generally be similar to those affecting a comparable for-profit institution. Indeed, most not-for-profit hospitals today are in direct competition with stockholder-owned facilities. Likewise, the fiscal dynamics of a not-for-profit country club are not very different from those of a for-profit club.

Other not-for-profits are more like governments in that their revenues are derived mainly from sources other than exchange transactions—grants and contributions. However, they lack at least two characteristic that may make it decidedly more difficult for an outsider to evaluate these not-for-profits. First, they lack the power to tax. To be sure, the tax revenues of governments may always be subject to the uncertainties of the economy and other factors. Nevertheless, within limits, governments can generally either increase taxes or reduce services to tide them over hard times. Not-for-profits, by contrast, may have no guaranteed revenue sources, and even mild perturbations in the overall economy or in the funding policies of grantors can have a profound impact on their fiscal wherewithal. Second, because not-for-profits are private rather than public institutions, their financial reports are not nearly as informative as those of governments, or even publicly traded corporations. For example, the reports do not have to include either a management's discussion and analysis or a detailed statistical section comparable to those of governments.

Still other not-for-profits are hybrids, relying both on exchange and nonexchange revenues. Colleges and universities, for example, are typically funded by a mix of tuition and fees (exchange revenues) and contributions (nonexchange revenues).

TRADITIONAL FINANCIAL INDICATORS

Traditional financial indicators and ratios, most of which are similar to those applicable to both businesses and governments, are also germane to not-for-profits. These include, but are not limited to, those that assess:

- ***Liquidity:*** The quick ratio (cash, short-term investments, and current receivables to current liabilities) and the current ratio (current assets to current liabilities)
- ***Burden of debt:*** Total debt to total assets
- ***Adequacy of available resources:*** Unrestricted net assets (preferably excluding capital assets) divided by expenses. (This ratio provides an indication of the extent to which the organization has "reserves" in case of a temporary imbalance between revenues and expenses.)
- ***Current fiscal performance:*** The extent of operating surpluses or deficits
- ***Reliability of budgetary projections:*** Both the dollar and percentage variances between budgeted revenues and expenses and actual results

INDICATORS OF SPECIAL RELEVANCE TO NOT-FOR-PROFITS

But analysts of not-for-profits must go beyond the traditional financial indicators. Of special concern is how a not-for-profit spends it money. First and foremost, an analyst needs to know how and what proportion of an organization's revenues are directed to its main mission as opposed to its administrative and fund-raising expenses. Organizations that exist mainly to pay the salaries of administrators and fund-raisers are unlikely to be viable over the long-term. Accordingly, the following two ratios are central to any assessment of a not-for-profit entity:

- ***Fund-raising ratio:*** This ratio, which measures fund-raising expense as a percentage of total related revenues, can be expected to vary widely among not-for-profit organizations depending on their nature. Some organizations, especially those that derive most of their revenues from exchange transactions, incur no fund-raising costs. Others, however, including some that border on the fraudulent, spend almost all of their revenues on fund-raising (and salaries of administrators). Per the Better Business Bureau, this ratio should be no greater than 35 percent. Fund-raising activities are often carried out as part of other, more mission oriented, pursuits. Thus, for example, a political advertisement by an environmental group urging citizens to vote in favor of a particular ballot proposition (a mission oriented activity) might also include a plea for donations (a fund-raising activity). Chapter 13, which deals with issues of cost determination, includes a discussion of how joint costs can be allocated between fund-raising and mission-oriented programs.
- ***Program ratio:*** Similar in concept to the fund-raising ratio, this ratio compares expenses devoted to mission-oriented programs to the total of fund-raising and administrative costs. The Better Business Bureau advices that program expenses should be at least 65 percent of *all* expenses (i.e., program, fund-raising, and administrative expenses).

Also of interest to an analysts of a not-for-profit entity is how it obtains its revenues and in particular the stability of its funding sources. The following two ratios are, therefore, of special relevance:

- ***Contributions and grants ratio:*** This ratio indicates revenues from contributions and grants as a percentage of total revenues and thereby encourages the analyst to consider the riskiness of the entity's revenue stream.
- ***Revenue from services ratio:*** Complementing the contributions and grants ratio, this ratio indicates revenues from fees and other charges for goods and services as a percentage of total revenues.

Generally, but not always, contributions and grants are a less reliable source of revenue than those from user charges. Much more significant is the character of the revenues. Thus, for example, a college or research institution that relies on a few major grants from governments or private foundations, for which it must reapply each year, may face greater risks than one that derives its revenues mainly from tuition and fees. On the other hand, however, a college that depends primarily on tuition and fees, but whose student base is narrow, may also face special threats to its fiscal stability. Following the World Trade Center disaster, the U.S. government made it more difficult for overseas students to obtain visas. As a consequence several small colleges that catered to overseas students had either to close their doors or to make major changes in their target population.

Obviously there can be no universal guidelines as to what constitutes acceptable revenue ratios; all depends on the type of institution. Institutions that traditionally charge for their services, such as educational and health care organizations, can be expected to have very different ratios than those that rely primarily on donations. Nevertheless, the ratios can be useful in comparing similar entities and in calling attention to changes in the mix of revenues within the same organization over time. The ratios must, however, be tailored to the specific type of organization being evaluated. Thus, for example, if one is assessing a medical research organization, the contributions and grants and the revenue from services ratios should be disaggregated for key specific sources of revenues, such as grants from the federal government, grants from private foundations, and gifts from individuals.

Ultimately the fiscal health of a not-for-profit depends on a broad range of economic, social, and demographic factors. Tables 12-9 and 12-10 provide an insight into several of them. They outline the key factors that Standard & Poor's takes into account in rating the debt instruments of health care organizations and private colleges and universities.

SOURCES OF INFORMATION ABOUT NOT-FOR-PROFITS

A wealth of information on not-for-profit organizations is readily available through the Internet. Philanthropic Research, Inc., the mission of which is to collect and disseminate information on not-for-profit organizations, maintains an online database known as GuideStar (www.guidestar.org). The site contains extensive financial data on over 850,000 organizations of all types. Most of the data are drawn from the Internal Revenue Service Form 990 filed by organizations. This is the form on which organizations must report on their finances to the federal government, even though they are not required actually to pay taxes. In addition, the site provides a scanned image of the form itself as well as information about the organization's mission, its officers and directors, and its goals and results.

The Better Business Bureau and the National Charities Information Bureau, through their Wise Giving Alliance Web site (www.give.org), also provide fiscal and

IN PRACTICE

OUTLOOK GRIM FOR MANY COLLEGES

In 2002, U.S. colleges and universities issued a record number of bonds, but the fiscal outlook for many of the institutions was grim. In 2002, Moody's Investor Service rated 277 colleges and university bond offerings for a total of $14.1 billon. This compares with 225 issues ($12.9 billion) in the previous year.

According to reports in *The Chronicle of Higher Education* (February 7, 2003, and March 7, 2003), of the colleges that Moody's rates approximately 29 percent had operating deficits in 2002. Moreover, the rating service was classifying an increasing number of their bonds as either "junk" or "below investment grade."

Moody's attributed the problems of these schools in large measure to the overall decline in the economy. Private colleges are often in direct competition with public counterparts but charge $10,000 or more in tuition and fees.

Moreover, the fall in the stock market hurt colleges and universities in two ways. First, as families lost a major part of their wealth, they became less able to afford private school tuition. Hence enrollments declined. Falling enrollments can pack a double whammy. Not only does tuition revenue decrease, but donors may be less willing to give to an institution that appears to be contracting rather than expanding.

Second, the institutions lost a major part of their own endowments. Hence income from investments was reduced.

The most endangered institutions, according to the experts, were small regional private colleges. Especially hard-hit were those that had fewer than 3,000 students, that accepted more than 70 percent of their applicants, and that had total financial resources per student of less than $50,000.

The reports quoted one analyst for a mutual fund that invests in small college bonds as saying that he now favored the securities of "niche" schools, such as those that prepare students for careers in aviation or design. Liberal arts colleges, he observed, were a harder sell.

TABLE 12–9
Factors Focused on by Standard & Poor's in Evaluating the Revenue Bonds of Health Care Organizations

I. Demand and service area characteristics
   A. Trends in volume, such as number of outpatient procedures, number of inpatient and outpatient surgeries, and observation days
   B. Utilization rates
   C. Demographic factors, including age distribution
   D. Economic factors, such as unemployment rates and local wealth levels

II. Institutional characteristics and competitive profile
   A. Size, age, and level of board certification of medical staff
   B. Ability to attract and retain new doctors
   C. Relationships with physicians groups that may provide financial incentives for doctors to remain loyal to the organization

III. Management and administrative factors
   A. Depth and experience of management team and ability to deal effectively with hospital staff, to promote sound budgeting, to control financial and personnel resources, and to provide strong leadership
   B. The strength of management information systems

IV. Financial factors
   A. Trends in revenue growth and profitability
   B. Financial flexibility as indicated by the ratio of fixed to variable costs
   C. Market position
   D. Costs in comparison with competitors
   E. Strength of income statement as indicated by operating margins, debt service coverage, and debt burden
   F. Strength of balance sheet as indicated by days' cash on hand, cash flow to total debt ratio, and debt to capitalization ratio

Source: Drawn from *Public Finance Rating Criteria* (New York City: Standard & Poor's, 1999), pp. 117–119.

related information about hundreds of charitable organizations that solicit contributions. The alliance has established standards that it expects charitable organizations to meet and it reports whether each organization has met them. These standards pertain to fund-raising and administrative costs as a percentage of revenues, on having independent directors on their governing boards and on making publicly available their annual reports.

SUMMARY

The Financial Accounting Standards Board sets accounting standards for not-for-profits other than governments. As might be expected, therefore, not-for-profits, like businesses, are on a full accrual basis of accounting. However, inasmuch as not-for-profits typically derive a substantial portion of their revenues from contributions, many of which are restricted, the form of their financial statements differs from those of businesses, and they must adhere to special guidelines as to revenue and expense recognition.

Per FASB pronouncements, not-for-profits should classify their resources into three categories: unrestricted, temporarily restricted, and permanently restricted. Whether or not resources are restricted is based solely on donor stipulations. Not-for-profits should report all expenses as changes in *unrestricted* resources. By contrast, governments can report expenses in both restricted and unrestricted funds.

Not-for-profits should recognize as revenue all unconditional contributions, including both pledges and restricted donations, when they are received. However, they should recognize conditional contributions only as the conditions are satisfied. Governments, on the other hand, account for

TABLE 12–10
Factors Focused on by Standard & Poor's in Evaluating the Revenue Bonds of Private Colleges and Universities

I. Student demand
  A. Enrollment trends, including the reasons for upward or downward cycles
  B. Flexibility in admissions and programs
    1. The acceptance rate (a college that accepts almost all applicants is more vulnerable to a decline in demand than one that is highly selective and admits only a small percentage)
    2. Geographic diversity (the wider the geographic diversity, the less likely that an economic downturn will affect enrollment)
    3. Student quality (strong student quality, as measured by high school class rank, standardized test scores, and other factors, enhances a school's ability to withstand a decline in enrollment)
    4. Faculty (the higher the percentage of tenured faculty, the less likely that the university's program offerings can change to reflect current demand)
    5. Program offerings (the more specialized the programs, the greater the risk of an enrollment decline owing to changes in the work force)
    6. Competition (schools that are the first choice of its students are less threatened by widespread enrollment declines than those that are their second or third selections)
    7. Attrition (high attrition may be a sign of student dissatisfaction and a precursor to declining demand)

II. Finances
  A. Revenues
    1. Diversification (a diverse revenue base, in which a substantial portion of revenue is from grants, endowment income, dormitories, and other sources in addition to tuition, tends to mitigate shortfalls in any single revenue stream)
    2. Ability to raise revenues through tuition adjustments (low rates in comparison with competitors indicates room for increases)
  B. Expenditures
    1. Ability to reduce expenditures (a high ratio of fixed to variable costs limits flexibility)
    2. Amounts being retained to build up plant and endowment (large amounts of resources being transferred to plant and endowment funds signify the availability of resources that could be redirected to debt service)
  C. Operating results (modest surpluses convey that revenues are sufficient to meet expenditures, but one or two year deficits are not necessarily a problem)
  D. Endowment
    1. Comparison with debt level
    2. Amount per student
    3. Proportion that is unrestricted (the greater the proportion, the greater the flexibility)
  E. Debt (a ratio of maximum annual debt service to unrestricted current fund expenditures; greater than 10 percent generally indicates an excessive debt burden)

III. Management
  A. Ability to foresee and plan for potential challenges
  B. Strategies and policies that appear realistic and attainable
  C. A track record indicative of an ability to deal with new situations and problems
  D. A history of management continuity

IV. Legal provisions
  A. Security pledges (debt secured by enterprise revenues, such as dormitory rentals, is seen as weaker than that backed by general revenues or tuition revenues)
  B. Covenants (provisions requiring the institution to set certain rates and fees at specified levels may enhance the security of the bonds)
  C. Debt service reserve policies (the existence of reserve funds enhances the security of the bonds, especially those that are backed strictly by enterprise revenues)
  D. Credit enhancements such as loan guarantees or bond insurance

Source: Drawn from *Public Finance Rating Criteria* (New York City: Standard & Poor's 1999), pp. 130–133.

their governmental funds on a modified accrual basis. Therefore, they recognize fund revenues, irrespective of source, only when they satisfy the "available" criterion. In their government-wide statements, similarly to not-for-profits, they accrue contributions as soon as all eligibility requirements have been met.

Not-for-profits, according to the FASB, should recognize contributed services only if they are of a professional nature and are of the type that would have to be paid for if not donated. Similar to governments, they are also encouraged, but not required, to recognize and capitalize donations of art objects as long as they are held for public exhibition, are properly cared for, and will not be sold for purposes other than the acquisition of other collectibles. Unlike governments, they should not recognize contributions of collectibles as revenues when they do not capitalize them.

Not-for-profits, like governments, face special problems of accounting for "pass through" grants and contributions. As a general rule, not-for-profits should not recognize as revenue contributions that they have agreed to transfer to other specific beneficiaries. They are permitted to recognize the contributions as revenue only if they have been granted variance power or are financially interrelated with the beneficiary organization.

Most of the accounting practices followed by hospitals are similar to those of other not-for-profits. However, owing to reimbursement arrangements with third parties, bad debts, malpractice claims, charity care, and insurance premiums, they face unique issues as to revenue and expense recognition. Accordingly, the AICPA has provided special accounting and reporting guidance for health care organizations.

Not-for-profit colleges and universities are similar to their public counterparts. Nevertheless, not-for-profit colleges and universities must follow the same accounting and reporting principles as other not-for-profits, whereas public colleges and universities must follow those applicable to other governments. Since most government colleges and universities can be expected to account for their activities in enterprise funds, and thereby are expected to be on a full accrual basis, the differences between the two types of entities will be mainly in the form of their financial statements rather than in principles of revenue and expense recognition.

The fiscal health of not-for-profits can be assessed using traditional financial ratios, such as those that measure liquidity and the burden of debt. Of additional concern to analysts are those that indicate the percentage of contributions that support the main mission of the organizations as opposed to administrative and fund-raising activities. Ultimately, however, the fiscal wherewithal of not-for-profits, like that of governments, depends on a wide range of economic, social, and demographic factors. Therefore, although analysts should view the financial statements as a key source of information, they must also look to other sources.

EXERCISE FOR REVIEW AND SELF-STUDY

The balance sheet and statement of activities of New Hampshire College (adapted from the financial statements of a well known New England college) are presented in Table 12-11. The statements are as of June 30, 2004, and all amounts, both in the statements and in the text that follows, are in thousands.

1. In addition to the tuition and fees reported on the statement of activities (all of which were received in cash), the college received $4,000 in tuition applicable to the 2004 summer semester, which runs from June 15 to August 15. Prepare a summary journal entry to record the tuition and fees collected for the year ended June 30, 2004.
2. Prepare appropriate summary entries to record grant and contract revenues and expenses.
3. Among the college's temporarily restricted funds is a plant fund that accounts for resources reserved for the acquisition of facilities. During the year, the college used $24,000 of fund resources to acquire plant and equipment. Prepare appropriate journal entries to record the acquisition of the plant and equipment.
4. What was the college's "profit" on the inn that it operates? On its student housing and dining?
5. The college accounts for student loans in a temporarily restricted "student loans" fund. What is the amount owed to the college by students? How much interest on student loans did the college earn during the year? Is the interest on the loans available for general purposes, or is it restricted? Explain.
6. Why is endowment income not reported in the permanently restricted funds? How much of the 2004 endowment income must be used for specific purposes? Why are gains on investments reported in the permanently restricted funds?
7. During the year the college received the following pledges:
   - **a.** $2,500 from an alumnus to construct a new wing to its science building
   - **b.** $4,500 to be used for general educational purposes
   - **c.** $5,000 to be used to acquire investment grade securities; only the earnings from these securities may be used to support teaching, research, and other routine activities of the college
   - **d.** Up to $1,000 to be used to match other expected contributions to a scholarship fund in honor of a recently retired faculty member

   Indicate how each of the pledges would be accounted for.
8. Does the college distinguish between operating and nonoperating activities in its statement of activities?

TABLE 12-11
New Hampshire College

Statement of Financial Position
For Year Ending June 30, 2004

	Unrestricted	Temporarily Restricted	Permanently Restricted	Total
Assets				
Current				
Cash and temporary investments	$ 18,567	$ 36,309	$ 29,611	$ 84,487
Grants and contracts receivable		30,200		30,200
Pledges receivable	4,000			4,000
Other receivables	14,772	57	781	15,610
Total current	$ 37,339	$ 66,566	30,392	$ 134,297
Noncurrent				
Student loans receivable		$ 36,954		$ 36,954
Inventories	1,990			1,990
Deferred charges	5,628	6,867		12,495
Investments	24,940	10,525	$796,116	831,581
Land, buildings, and equipment (net of $89,241 accumulated depreciation)	283,181			283,181
Other assets	15,475		6,879	22,354
Total noncurrent	$331,214	$ 54,346	$802,995	$1,188,555
Total assets	$368,553	$120,912	$833,387	$1,322,852
Liabilities				
Current				
Accounts payable	$ 23,024	$ 1,760	$ 1,627	$ 26,411
Deferred revenue	12,672			12,672
Other current liabilities		1,399		1,399
Total current	$ 35,696	$ 3,159	$ 1,627	$ 40,482
Noncurrent				
Notes and bonds payable	188,466	24,505		212,971
Other liabilities		15,436	7,564	23,000
Total noncurrent	$188,466	$ 39,941	$ 7,564	$ 235,971
Total liabilities	$224,162	$ 43,100	$ 9,191	$ 276,453
Net assets	$144,391	$ 77,812	$824,196	$1,046,399

(Continues)

TABLE 12–11
New Hampshire College *(Continued)*

Statement of Activities
For the Year Ending June 30, 2004

	Unrestricted	Temporarily Restricted	Permanently Restricted	Total
Revenues				
Tuition and fees	$110,568			$ 96,662
Grants and contracts		$ 38,914		52,820
Private gifts	16,503	33,868	$20,396	70,767
Endowment income	12,382	18,548		30,930
Other investment income	1,593	3,619		5,212
Departmental sales and service	13,544			13,544
Athletic income	1,308			1,308
Income from museums and other programs	15,713			15,713
Auxiliary enterprises				
Student housing and dining	20,117			20,117
College inn	5,806			5,806
Rentals, recreational, and other facilities	11,871			11,871
Interest on student loans		1,856		1,856
Gains on investments		1,649	73,552	75,201
Total revenues	$209,405	$ 98,454	$93,948	$401,807
Expenses				
Instruction and department research	$ 64,697			$ 64,697
Grants and contracts	47,661			47,661
Libraries, computers, and other academic support	37,406			37,406
Student services	15,677			15,677
General administration	13,326			13,326
Plant operation and maintenance	20,667			20,667
Financial aid	26,616			26,616
Athletics and physical education	6,207			6,207
Auxiliary enterprises				
Student housing and dining	18,999			18,999
College inn	6,564			6,564
Rentals, recreational, and other facilities	11,079			11,079
Interest on debt	6,602			6,602
Depreciation expense	9,381			9,381
Other expenses	8,707			8,707
Total expenses	$293,589	$ 0	$ 0	$293,589
Excess (deficiency) of revenues over expenses	$ (84,184)	$ 98,454	$93,948	$108,218
Resources released from restrictions	124,518	(124,518)		0
Change in net assets	$ 40,334	$(26,064)	$93,948	$108,218

QUESTIONS FOR REVIEW AND DISCUSSION

1. Provide an example of resources that are temporarily restricted as to (a) purpose, (b) time, and (c) occurrence of a specific event. Provide an example of permanently restricted resources.
2. A not-for-profit organization receives a restricted gift. When, and in which type of fund, should it recognize the revenue? When, and in which type of fund, should it recognize the related expense? What is the reason for the apparent inconsistency between the fund type in which the revenues and expenses are reported?
3. Parents of a college junior pledge to donate $1 million to her college upon her expected graduation, one year in the future. When, and in what amount, should the university recognize revenue? The university applies a discount rate of 10 percent to all pledges. Would your response be the same if the parents pledged to donate the funds only if and when the daughter were graduated? Why do many not-for-profits object to the standards pertaining to revenue recognition of pledges?
4. Members of the National Accounting Association, a not-for-profit organization, are charged annual dues of $150. Of this amount, $50 is restricted, per association policy, to covering the cost of the association's journal, which every member receives. In what category of restrictiveness should the association report the portion of revenues associated with the journal? Explain.
5. In what significant way do not-for-profits account for investments differently from businesses?
6. In a recent month a CPA provided ten hours of volunteer time to the Society for the Visually Impaired. He devoted seven hours to maintaining the organization's financial records and three to recording tapes of newspapers and magazine articles. If volunteers had not provided these services, the organization would have had to hire paid personnel. Should the organization give accounting recognition to the CPA's services?
7. A museum received gifts of two valuable paintings. It recorded the value of one as an asset and recognized the corresponding revenue. It gave no accounting recognition to the other. What might be a legitimate explanation for such an apparent inconsistency?
8. Hospitals and other health care organizations provide services knowing that they will collect from third-party payers, such as insurance companies, considerably less than their established billing rates. In addition, they provide services to uninsured patients, aware that they will collect either none or only a small portion of the amounts to be billed. Comment on how these organizations distinguish between charity care, bad debts, and contractual adjustments, and indicate how each affects the amount of revenue from patient care that they should report.
9. What is meant by "retrospective" insurance premiums, and how should they be reported?
10. How do not-for-profits differ from governments in the way they account for business-type activities, such as dining halls, gift shops, and admission fees?
11. What is meant by "variance power"? Suppose that a charitable foundation receives a gift that the donor specifies must be used to support the college education of a particular individual. Of what relevance is "variance power" to how the foundation accounts for the gift?
12. In what significant ways do the FASB standards differ from those of the GASB with respect to the statement of cash flows?
13. Why is the "fund-raising ratio" of key concern to both donors and financial analysts?

EXERCISES

12-1

Select the *best* answer.

1. A *term endowment* is a gift
   a. The principal of which must be returned to the donor after a specified period of time
   b. The principal of which is available for expenditure after a specified period of time
   c. The income from which must be expended within a specified period of time
   d. The income of which must be added to the principal for a specified period of time
2. A not-for-profit organization maintains an endowment of $1 million, the income from which must be used for research into substance abuse. In a particular year, the endowment had income of $60,000, all of which was expended in accord with the donor's specifications. The expense should be reported as a decrease in
   a. Permanently restricted net assets
   b. Temporarily restricted net assets
   c. Unrestricted net assets
   d. Any of the above

3. A private think tank receives a gift of $100,000 that must be used to fund a symposium on federal accounting. When the institution conducts the symposium, which of the following accounts should be debited in a temporarily restricted fund?
   a. Program expense
   b. Deferred revenue
   c. Resources released from restriction
   d. Deferred program expense
4. The statement of cash flows of a not-for-profit should be divided into which of the following categories of cash flows?
   a. Operating activities, noncapital financing activities, capital and related financing activities, investing activities
   b. Operating activities, capital activities, investing activities
   c. Operating activities, financing activities, capital activities
   d. Operating activities, financing activities, investing activities
5. The Senior League, a not-for-profit welfare agency, redeemed a $100,000 bond that it had held as an investment of unrestricted resources. It also received an interest payment of $6,000. In its statement of cash flows the league should report
   a. $106,000 as a cash flow from investing activities
   b. $106,000 as a cash flow from operating activities
   c. $100,000 as a cash flow from investing activities and $6,000 as a cash flow from financing activities
   d. $100,000 as a cash flow from investing activities and $6,000 as a cash flow from operating activities
6. Enrex Corporation gave a not-for-profit research foundation $500,000 to conduct research relating to the development of a new type of battery. Per the terms of the gift, Enrex had the rights to any patents issued as a consequence of the research and could control when and where the research results were published. At the time of receipt of the $500,000, the foundation should recognize
   a. Revenue of $500,000 in a temporarily restricted fund
   b. Revenue of $500,000 in an unrestricted fund
   c. Deferred revenue of $500,000 in a temporarily restricted fund
   d. Deferred revenue of $500,000 in an unrestricted fund
7. Harley Safe-Place, a not-for-profit organization, received an unrestricted pledge of $600,000. The donor promised to make payment within six months (which would be in the organization's next fiscal year). At the time of the pledge, the organization should recognize
   a. Revenue of $600,000 in a temporarily restricted fund
   b. Revenue of $600,000 in an unrestricted fund
   c. Deferred revenue of $600,000 in a temporarily restricted fund
   d. Deferred revenue of $600,000 in an unrestricted fund
8. Walden Institute, a not-for-profit, politically oriented association, was promised a $1 million endowment on condition that it establish a program in entrepreneurial studies and hire a leading scholar to lead it. Upon receiving the pledge the institute should recognize
   a. Zero revenue
   b. Revenue of $1 million in a permanently restricted fund
   c. Revenue of $1 million in a temporarily restricted fund
   d. Deferred revenue of $1 million in a permanently restricted fund
9. Emerson Museum received a cash gift of $7 million. The board of trustees decided that the gift should be used to establish a permanent endowment, the income from which would be used to provide research grants to Impressionist art historians. The museum should report the gift as an increase in
   a. Unrestricted resources
   b. Temporarily restricted resources
   c. Permanently restricted resources
   d. Board-restricted resources
10. The Fellowship Church of America issues $10 million of bonds of which the proceeds must be used to construct new facilities. Included in the bond indenture is a provision that the church must maintain $400,000 in a specially designated bank account to ensure timely payment of principal and interest. Upon receiving the $10 million in bond proceeds and placing the $400,000 in the designated bank account, the church should report
    a. Cash of $9.6 million in an unrestricted fund and $400,000 in a temporarily restricted fund
    b. Cash of $10 million in an unrestricted fund
    c. Cash of $10 million in a temporarily restricted fund
    d. Cash of $9.6 million in a temporarily restricted fund and $400,000 in a permanently restricted fund

12-2

Select the *best* answer.

1. A local chapter of the Society for Protection of the Environment benefited from the voluntary services of two attorneys. One served as a member of the society's board of directors, performing tasks comparable to other directors. During the year he attended twenty hours of meetings. The other drew up a lease agreement with a tenant in a building owned by the society. She spent five hours on the project. The billing rate of both attorneys is $200 per hour. In the year in which the services were provided, the society should recognize revenues from contributed services of
   a. $0
   b. $1,000
   c. $4,000
   d. $5,000
2. The Museum of Contemporary Art received two valuable paintings. The museum has determined that one, with a market value of $7,000, is inappropriate for display and therefore will be sold. The other, with a market

value of $10,000, will be placed on exhibit. The museum has a policy of not capitalizing works of art unless required to do so. In the year that it receives the two paintings, it should recognize contribution revenues of

a. $0
b. $7,000
c. $10,000
d. $17,000

3. The United Way of Lano County distributes all contributions to not-for-profit organizations within its county. Donors have a choice: They can either designate the organization to which their contributions will be given or permit the United Way to distribute their contributions as it deems appropriate. During the current year, the United Way received $1 million of specifically designated contributions and $6 million of undesignated contributions. It should recognize contribution revenue of

a. $0
b. $1 million
c. $6 million
d. $7 million

4. *Variance power* refers to the ability

a. Of a not-for-profit organization to use property for commercial purposes even though it was zoned for residential purposes
b. Of a charitable organization to unilaterally decide to direct the use of donated assets to a beneficiary other than that specified by the donor
c. Of a donor to change the beneficiary of a gift from that which was initially specified
d. Of a not-for-profit organization to alter the terms of any purpose restrictions associated with a contribution that it received

5. The Association for Educational Enrichment receives a contribution of $400,000 that must be used for student scholarships. Prior to granting any scholarships, the association invests the funds received in marketable securities. During the year, the securities pay dividends of $10,000 and increase in market value to $440,000. The association should report

a. Unrestricted investment earnings of $50,000
b. Temporarily restricted investment earnings of $50,000
c. Unrestricted investment earnings of $10,000 and temporarily restricted investment earnings of $40,000
d. Temporarily restricted investment earnings of $10,000

6. Carter Research Center, a not-for-profit entity, acquires $50,000 of laboratory instruments with funds that were donated and restricted to the purchase of equipment. The instruments have a useful life of five years and no salvage value. During each of the five years of the instruments' useful life, the center should recognize depreciation expense of

a. $0
b. $10,000 in a temporarily restricted fund
c. $10,000 in an unrestricted fund
d. $10,000 in either a temporarily restricted fund or an unrestricted fund, depending on which fund is used to account for the instruments

7. With respect to the statement of cash flows

a. Both the FASB and the GASB encourage entities to use the direct method.
b. The GASB, but not the FASB, requires entities to use the direct method.
c. The FASB, but not the GASB, requires entities to use the direct method.
d. Both the FASB and the GASB require entities to use the direct method.

8. The Friends of the Opera, a financially interrelated fund-raising support group for the City Opera Company, receives $100,000 in donations, all of which will eventually be transferred to the City Opera Company. When Friends of the Opera receives the gift

a. Friends of the Opera should recognize revenue of $100,000, and the City Opera company should make no journal entries.
b. Friends of the Opera should recognize a liability of $100,000, and the City Opera Company should recognize a receivable.
c. Friends of the Opera should recognize revenue of $100,000, and the City Opera Company should recognize an increase of $100,000 in its interest in the net assets of Friends of the Opera.
d. Friends of the Opera should recognize a liability of $100,000, and the City Opera Company should make no entry.

9. At the start of the year, the permanent endowment fund of the State Performing Arts Festival Association reported net assets of $1 million. During the year, it earned $40,000 in interest and dividends, but its investments lost $60,000 in market value. The association spent the entire $40,000 of interest and dividends. At year-end the permanent endowment fund should report net assets of

a. $1,000,000
b. $980,000
c. $960,000
d. $940,000

10. The Mountain Research Institute began the year with net assets in its permanent endowment fund of $1 million. During the year it earned $70,000, and the market value of its investments increased by $20,000. However, the institute's policy is to permit earnings to be spent only to the extent that they exceed an amount necessary to cover inflation. The inflation rate for the year was 3 percent. During the year, the institute spent none of the $70,000. At year-end, the permanent endowment fund should report net assets of

a. $1,000,000

b. $1,020,000
c. $1,030,000
d. $1,090,000

12-3

Minor differences in the terms of a contribution may justify major differences in revenue recognition.

Upon meeting with the executive director of the Crime Victims Advocacy Group, the president of a private foundation agreed to contribute, in the following year, $100,000 in support of the group's proposed program to provide legal assistance to victims of violent crimes. Suppose that the foundation's formal letter acknowledging its pledge was worded in three different ways:

1. "We are pleased to pledge $100,000 in support of your group's efforts to assist victims of violent crimes."
2. "We are pleased to pledge $100,000 in support of your group's efforts to develop a new program to provide legal assistance to victims of violent crimes."
3. "We are pleased to pledge $100,000 upon your developing a new program to provide legal assistance to victims of violent crimes."

For each of the three options:

a. Prepare the journal entries that should be made upon receipt of the letter from the foundation. Assume that it was unlikely that the pledge would be fulfilled in the same period as it was made.
b. Prepare the journal entries that should be made to record the expenditure of $100,000 on activities related to the legal assistance program.
c. Prepare the journal entries that should be made upon receipt of the $100,000 check, assuming that it was received shortly after the legal assistance program was established and the group spent the $100,000 on program related activities.
d. Comment on why minor differences in wording might justify major differences in accounting.

Be sure to indicate the type of fund in which your entries would be made.

12-4

Some, but not all, contributions of goods and services are given accounting recognition.

In each of the following scenarios, an organization receives a contribution in kind. Prepare journal entries, as necessary, to give them accounting recognition. For each, tell why you made an entry or why you did not.

1. A local not-for-profit art museum receives advertising for its yearly benefit from radio station WLOU. The airtime would have cost the museum $1,000.
2. Volunteers for "Breakfast on Bikes," a voluntary health and welfare organization, deliver hot meals to the elderly three times a week. Each of the ten volunteers works about six hours per week. All of the volunteers have permanent jobs with pay averaging $16.10 an hour.
3. Lynn Simms, a local CPA, maintains the books and records of her church. Although her normal billing rate is $60 per hour, she accepts no payment from the church. She works on church matters approximately four hours a week.
4. A construction company allows a not-for-profit community association to use its bulldozer at no cost to clear land for a new baseball park. If the association had to rent the bulldozer it would have incurred costs of $1,400.

12-5

Investment gains and losses have to be recognized as they occur—and have to be assigned to the appropriate category of net assets.

During 2004 University Hospital received a contribution of marketable securities that were to be placed in a permanent endowment fund. Neither donor stipulations nor applicable state law requires that capital gains or increases in value be added to the endowment principal. The income from the securities was to be restricted to research in pulmonary diseases. The following schedule indicates the value of the securities as of the date of receipt (labeled "cost"), the fair value at December 31, 2004, and the unrealized gains and losses of the year.

Endowment Portfolio as of December 31, 2004 (in thousands)

	Cost	Fair Value	Unrealized Gain (Loss)
Northwest Industries	$260	$275	$15
Campbell Corp.	317	304	(13)
St. Regis, Inc.	141	171	30
	$718	$750	$32

1. Prepare a journal entry to record the unrealized net gain during the year. Be sure to indicate the type of fund (unrestricted, temporarily restricted, permanently restricted) in which the entry would be made. Assuming no other transactions and no other assets in the relevant funds, show how the investments would be reported on the hospital's year-end 2004 balance sheet.
2. During 2005, the hospital sold Northwest Industries for $280. Prepare appropriate journal entries to record the sale. Credit the gain to the same account in which you credited the unrealized appreciation of 2004.
3. As of December 31, 2005, the market value of Campbell Corp. had increased to $320; that of St. Regis, Inc., to $180. Prepare a journal entry to record the unrealized gain during the year. Show how the hospital would report the investment portfolio on its December 31, 2005, balance sheet. You may combine the cash and securities of each type of fund into a single account.

12-6

The basis for recognizing patient care revenue is not always obvious.

In a particular month Northwest Medical Clinic reported the following:

1. It provided direct care services to patients, billing them $400,000. Of this amount it received $120,000 in cash, but as a consequence of bad debts it expects to collect a total of only $330,000.
2. It provided direct care to patients covered by insurance and who are members of various group health plans for which, at standard rates, it would have billed $650,000. However, owing to contractual arrangements with the payers it actually billed them for, and expects to collect, only $480,000.
3. It provided charity care for which it would have billed, at standard rates, $82,000.
4. It received capitation fees of $1,400,000 from health care plans and provided services to members of those plans for which it would have billed, at standard rates, $1,600,000.

Prepare appropriate journal entries to recognize revenue.

12-7

Contributions of fixed assets may affect more than one type of fund.

Discovery Barn, a not-for-profit science center for children, received a contribution of $30,000 explicitly designated for the acquisition of computers. During the year it acquired $21,000 of computers, which it estimated to have a useful life of three years. It is the policy of the organization to charge an entire year's depreciation in the year of acquisition.

Prepare all required journal entries, being certain to indicate the type of fund in which each entry would be made.

PROBLEMS

12-1

A multifund balance sheet can readily be recast so that it conforms with FASB standards.

A balance sheet of Brown University, issued prior to the effective date of FASB Statement No. 117, is shown on page 514.

Recast the fund balance (net asset) section of the balance sheet so that it presents the fund balances in the three categories required by Statement No. 117. Show the balances in a single column, divided into three sections. Thus, for example, current undesignated funds should be reported in the unrestricted section; current restricted funds in the temporarily restricted section. Make appropriate assumptions as to the type of restriction that applies to each of the balances.

12-2

University plant funds can readily be recast from an AICPA to an FASB presentation.

A university maintains several plant funds as shown in the condensed balance sheets that follow. The fund structure and presentation are consistent with the AICPA college and university reporting model. Although this model has been superseded by FASB Statement No. 117, *Financial Statements of Not-for-Profit Organizations,* it is still used by many colleges and universities for internal purposes.

Plant Funds
(in thousands)

Unexpended plant funds		
Assets		
Cash		$ 9,000
Investments		27,000
Total assets		$ 36,000
Liabilities and fund balances		
Bonds payable		$ 24,000
Fund balance		
Restricted by donors for specified projects	$ 4,000	
Unrestricted	8,000	12,000
Total liabilities and fund balances		$ 36,000
Funds for renewals and replacements		
Assets		
Cash		$ 4,500
Investments		85,100
Total assets		$ 89,600
Liabilities and fund balances		
Fund balance		$ 89,600
Funds for retirement of indebtedness		
Assets		
Cash		$ 21,600
Investments		25,600
Total assets		$ 47,200
Liabilities and fund balances		
Fund balance		$ 47,200
Investment in plant		
Assets		
Construction in process		$ 3,500
Equipment		39,300
Land		12,000
Buildings		127,800
Total plant		182,600
Less accumulated depreciation		(78,200)
Total investment in plant		$104,400

Brown University

Balance Sheet as of June 30, 1992
(in thousands)

	Total	Current Funds	Loan Funds	Endowment Funds	Plant Funds
Assets					
Cash	$110,922	$45,268	$ 590	$ 61,555	$ 3,509
Investments	507,503	9,042		456,126	42,335
Accounts receivable	15,070	14,499	426		145
Notes receivable	26,000		26,000		
Inventories and pre-paid expenses	5,047	5,047			
Land, buildings, and equipment (less accumulated depreciation)	196,897				196,897
Due from (to) other funds		11,338	(3,376)	3,323	(11,285)
Total assets	$861,439	$85,194	$23,640	$521,004	$231,601
Liabilities and fund balances					
Accounts payable—accrued liabilities	$ 29,788	$20,836		$ 6,597	$ 2,355
Deferred revenues	5,424	5,424			
Agency accounts	10,375	10,375			
Bonds payable	88,399				88,399
Total liabilities	$133,986	$36,635		$ 6,597	$ 90,754
Fund balances					
Current funds					
Designated	20,445	20,445			
Restricted	28,114	28,114			
Student loan funds established by gift and grants	23,640		23,640		
Endowment and similar funds					
Unrestricted quasi-endowment funds	59,644			59,644	
Restricted endowment funds	68,352			68,352	
Other endowment funds	369,399			369,399	
Life income funds	17,012			17,012	
Plant funds					
Unexpended	19,452				19,452
Retirement of indebtedness	6,306				6,306
Net investment in plant	115,089				115,089
Total fund balances	$727,453	$48,559	$23,640	$514,407	$140,847
Total liabilities and fund balances	$861,439	$85,194	$23,640	$521,004	$231,601

Liabilities and fund balances	
Notes payable	$ 20,000
Bonds payable	39,000
Capital lease obligations	8,500
Net investment in plant	36,900
Total investment in plant	$104,400

1. Recast the plant funds as they would appear in external reports in accord with Statement No. 117. That is, show how each of the reported amounts would be shown in a balance sheet with one column each for unrestricted and temporarily restricted amounts (there are no permanently restricted amounts). Allocate the cash ($9,000) and investments ($27,000) of the unexpended plant funds to the donor restricted category based on donor restricted fund balance as a proportion of total liabilities and fund balances (e.g., $4,000/$36,000).
2. Comment briefly on the advantages and disadvantages of each presentation.

12-3

Pledges must be distinguished by the extent to which they are restricted.

A private college receives the following pledges of support.

1. As part of its annual fund drive, alumni and friends of the college pledge $8 million. The college estimates that about 15 percent of the pledges will prove uncollectible.

2. A CPA firm promises to establish an endowed chair in the accounting department by donating $500,000. The chair agreement will provide that the funds be used to purchase investment grade securities and that the income from the securities be used to supplement the salary of the chairholder and support his or her academic activities.
3. A private foundation promises to donate $100,000 to be used to support a major revision of the college's accounting curriculum.
4. An alumnus pledges $25,000 to the college's loan fund, which is used to make loans to students requiring financial assistance.
5. The college is seeking support for construction of a new athletic field house. A local real estate investor promises to donate ten acres of land on which a field house could be built if the college is able to raise the funds required to construct the building. The land has a market value of $1 million.

Indicate the category of net assets (unrestricted, temporarily restricted, or permanently restricted) in which each of the contributions should be recorded and the amount of revenue, if any, that should be recognized when the pledge was made. Briefly explain your response.

12-4

A single contribution may affect all three types of funds.

The following events and transactions relate to a single contribution.

1. A high-tech firm pledged to contribute $1 million in the company's common stock to a university's business school if the school would establish a new program in the management of information technology. The securities were to be placed in an endowment fund and the annual dividend earnings were to be used to purchase computer hardware and software.
2. The business school established the program and thereby satisfied the conditions to receive the contribution.
3. The business school received the stock and placed it in an endowment fund.
4. In the first year after receiving the stock, the business school earned $30,000 in cash dividends. They were credited to an appropriate fund.
5. The business school purchased $20,000 of computer equipment.
6. The computer equipment was estimated to have a useful life of four years (no salvage). The school charged one year's depreciation.

Prepare journal entries, as necessary, to record these events and transactions. Be sure to indicate the type of fund (permanently restricted, temporarily restricted, or unrestricted) that would be affected by the entries.

12-5

The distinction between contributed services that warrant financial statement recognition and those that do not is not always clear.

For each of the following situations, indicate whether the organization should recognize the described contributed services as revenue (offset by a corresponding expense). Briefly justify your response or identify key issues.

1. Nellie Wilson, the noted country-western singer, performs a benefit concert for the Save Our Farms Association, a political advocacy group. Wilson, who would normally charge $60,000 per concert, did not accept a fee.
2. Camp Chi-Wan-Da, a summer camp for disadvantaged youth, benefits from the services of four physicians, each of whom spends two weeks at the camp providing medical services to the campers. The doctors receive free room and board but no salary. Camp association standards require that a camp of Chi Wan-Da's size have either a physician on the premises or one on call.
3. The Taconic Music Festival, a performing arts association, needed new practice facilities. The architecture firm of Lloyd Wright designed the facilities for the association without charge, and local merchants provided the building materials. All construction work was carried out by community volunteers, only a few of whom had professional experience in the building trades.
4. A neurologist serves on the board of trustees of the Neurological Disease Foundation, an organization that funds clinical research. He was asked to serve because of his expertise in the area of neurological research and chairs the board's committee that selects grant recipients.
5. Daughters of Charity Hospital draws its nursing staff from members of its religious order. The nurses do not get paid a salary. Instead, they receive free room and board and a living allowance. The total cost to the hospital is approximately 60 percent of what it would have to pay in salary and benefits in the open market. In addition, the hospital benefits from the services of "candy stripers" and other volunteers, who staff the hospital's gift shop, carry meals to patients, and perform a variety of other important functions. Were it not for these volunteers, the hospital would have to hire additional personnel to carry out many of their duties.

12-6

Should exchange transactions be accounted for differently from contributions?

In December 2004, the Consumer Association of America (CAA), a not-for-profit research organization, received a $6 million grant from the Sporting Goods Manufacturers Association (SGMA) to develop a football helmet that will provide better protection against head injuries. The grant was intended to cover $4 million of direct costs and $2 million of overhead costs. The grant contract stipulated that the SGMA would make its payment to the CAA upon receiving invoices from CAA for the actual direct costs incurred. It further required that the research results be reported only to the SGMA and not be made publicly available. Each reimbursement payment for direct costs incurred would also include an appropriate proportion of indirect costs (i.e., an additional $0.50 for each $1 of direct costs).

In 2005 the CAA carried out and completed the research for which it contracted. Direct costs were, as estimated, $4 million. It submitted the necessary invoices and received payment in full.

1. Prepare required journal entries for 2004 and 2005. Be sure to indicate whether each entry should be made to an unrestricted or temporarily restricted fund. You need not, however, record the indirect costs themselves (inasmuch as, by their very nature, they are not tied directly to the grant).
2. Assume instead that in December 2004 the CAA received from the National Sports Association (NSA) a pledge of $6 million. The donation is for research relating to football helmets. The NSA is a not-for-profit agency, and the results of any research will be in the public domain. In January 2005, the CAA received the contribution. Throughout the remainder of 2005 it carried out its football related research (incurring $4 million of direct costs). Prepare the required journal entries for 2004 and 2005 and indicate whether each entry should be made to an unrestricted or temporarily restricted fund.
3. Comment on any differences between the two awards that might justify differences in revenue recognition.
4. Suppose instead that the NSA promised to make its contribution only upon receiving a report that the research had actually been completed. Would your approach have been different? Explain.

12-7

Hospitals and other health care providers face several issues of accounting and reporting.

Doctors Hospital, a private, not-for-profit hospital, engaged the following transactions.

1. It provided patient services with a standard billing rate of $1,200,000 for which it invoiced third-party payers $900,000. Of the balance, $200,000 was billed to individual patients and $100,000 was for charity care. The hospital estimates that third-party payers will, on average, pay only 80 percent of the invoiced amounts and that 40 percent of the amount billed to individual patients will be uncollectible. How much should the hospital report as net revenue?
2. Volunteer nurses provided services that were comparable to those provided by paid nurses. Were the volunteer services provided by the paid nurses, the hospital would have incurred $58,000 in additional compensation and benefit costs. Also, members of the Hospital Auxiliary staffed the reception desk, family waiting rooms, and the gift shop. If the hospital had to hire and pay employees to provide their services (all of which were essential to sound hospital operations), the cost would have been approximately $105,000. How much, relating to these services, should the hospital report as compensation? Explain.
3. The hospital received a $100,000 cash grant to fund, in part, a study of the efficacy of a certain patient-care protocol. During the year, the hospital completed approximately 70 percent of the study, incurring total costs of $120,000. How much of the $100,000 grant should the hospital report as temporarily restricted?
4. The hospital's malpractice insurance policy covers a period that coincides with its fiscal year. During the year the hospital paid premiums of $450,000. It received a retrospective premium adjustment for the prior year of $37,000. However, it estimates that it will have to pay an additional $25,000 as a retrospective adjustment for the current year. How much should it report as an insurance expense for the current year?
5. During the year, the hospital was sued by a patient for $5,600,000. Claims of this type are 80 percent covered by insurance. The hospital has denied culpability and expects that the suit will go to trial. It estimates that if it loses its case, the judgment will likely be between $1,000,000 and $3,000,000. How much should the hospital recognize as a loss (or expense) for the current year?

12-8

For purposes of external reporting, not-for-profits, unlike governments in their governmental funds, do not distinguish between plant and other types of resources.

In 2004, the Northwest Ballet Association (NBA), a not-for-profit performing arts organization, undertook a major capital campaign to fund a new theater, expected to cost $10 million. It was quickly able to raise $6 million, all of which was donor restricted. It borrowed the balance, issuing a five-year, 8 percent term note for $4 million.

During the year, the NBA broke ground on the project and incurred construction costs of $3.4 million. It earned $0.52 million in interest on temporary investments. It incurred and paid $0.32 million in interest on the note. In addition, as required by the note, it placed $0.7 million in a reserve fund (a specially dedicated bank account) for the repayment of the debt.

1. To show how these transactions would be reflected on the NBA's financial statements, prepare a December 31, 2004, statement of financial position and statement of activities. Assume that these were the only transactions in which the organization engaged and that all available cash, except that in the reserve fund, had been invested in short term marketable securities. Be sure to properly classify all resources as to whether they are temporarily restricted or unrestricted.
2. Comment briefly on whether the contributions from donors and the proceeds from the bonds should be reported as restricted or unrestricted.
3. Comment briefly on whether the $0.7 million in the reserve fund should be reported as restricted or unrestricted.

12-9

The cash flow statement for a government hospital would differ from that of a not-for-profit hospital.

The following represent a hospital's inflows and outflows of cash:

- Patient service fees received
- Government grants for operating purposes
- Government grants for specific research programs
- Contribution restricted to construction of a new building
- Salaries and wages
- Supplies
- Interest paid on long-term debt
- Interest paid on short-term operating debt
- Acquisition of fixed assets
- Purchases of marketable securities
- Proceeds from sale of marketable securities
- Interest received from investments
- Dividends received from investments
- Proceeds of long-term debt to finance a new building
- Proceeds of short-term borrowings for operating purposes

1. Categorize the cash inflows and outflows as they would be reported in a statement of cash flows assuming that the hospital is government owned.
2. Do the same, this time assuming that the hospital is a not-for-profit.
3. Why did the GASB opt for a four-way classification, whereas the FASB retained for not-for-profits the three-way classification developed for businesses?

12-10

This example, drawn from the actual financial statements of a major urban not-for-profit hospital, illustrates the main types of transactions (in summary form) in which hospitals engage.

The December 31, 2004, statement of financial position of Mosholu Medical Center, a major urban hospital and research center, is shown on page 518. All amounts are in thousands.

The following transactions and events occurred in 2005 (all dollar amounts in thousands):

1. The hospital provided $705,943 in patient care at standard rates. On average, it expects to collect approximately 75 percent ($529,457) of this amount, owing mainly to discounts allowed third-party payers. Further, it expects that 5 percent of the 75 percent ($26,473) will have to be written off as bad debts.
2. It collected $480,125 in patient accounts and it wrote off $50,000 of bad debts.
3. It also provided $52,000 in charity care which it never expected to collect.
4. It earned $15,040 in investment income, of which $10,080 is unrestricted and $4,960 is temporarily restricted.
5. It purchased plant and equipment of $242, all of which was paid for with restricted resources.
6. It charged depreciation of $29,262.
7. It received unrestricted pledges of $2,070 and temporarily restricted pledges of $120. It collected all of the unrestricted pledges and $100 of the temporarily restricted pledges.
8. It earned other operating revenues (including those from auxiliary enterprises) of $135,000.
9. It incurred $430,650 in wages and salaries, of which it paid $425,000. The balance was accrued. It also incurred $200,000 in other operating expenses (including those of auxiliary enterprises), of which it paid $198,500. The balance was vouchered (and thereby credited to accounts payable).
10. It incurred and paid $210,200 in costs related to restricted contracts and grants (amounts that were not included in any other expense category). It was reimbursed for $206,800 and expects to be reimbursed for the balance in the future. In addition, it received $3,000 in advances on other grants.
11. The other operating expenses include insurance costs. However, under "retrospective" insurance policies, the hospital anticipates having to pay an additional $3,500 in premiums.
    a. Prepare journal entries to record the transactions. Be sure to indicate whether each entry would affect unrestricted, temporarily restricted, or permanently restricted fund types.
    b. Prepare a statement of activities for 2005 and a statement of financial position as of December 31, 2005.

12-11

Is there a sound reason for accounting for contributions to a not-for-profit university differently from a government university?

In January 2005, Kirkland University receives a pledge of $200,000, to be used exclusively to support research in a specialized area of communication disorders. The university's fiscal year ends on July 31.

In December 2005 (the following fiscal year), Kirkland receives the pledged contribution of $200,000 and spends $150,000 on qualifying research.

1. Prepare all required journal entries to reflect the transactions described. Indicate the type of fund in which the entries would be made.
    a. Assume first that Kirkland is a private, not-for-profit university.
    b. Assume instead that Kirkland is a public university and that it elects to be accounted for (a) as a government engaging exclusively in business type activities and (b) as a full service government that accounts for the contribution in a governmental fund.
2. On what grounds, if any, can you justify different principles of accounting for the same transaction depending on type of institution (public or private) or assumption as to type of public institution?

Mosholu Medical Center

Statement of Financial Position as of December 31, 2004

	Unrestricted	Temporarily Restricted	Permanently Restricted
Assets			
Current assets			
Cash	$ 2,449	$ 252	$ 3
Receivables for patient care ($110,465 less allowance for contractual adjustments and doubtful accounts of $45,755)	64,710		
Other receivables	13,059	11,343	
Marketable securities	109,085	61,691	17,133
Other current assets	27,853		
Total current assets	$217,156	$73,286	$17,136
Noncurrent assets			
Property, plant, and equipment ($512,184 less accumulated depreciation of $223,259)	$288,925		
Other assets	11,522		
Total noncurrent assets	$300,447		
Total assets	$517,603	$73,286	$17,136
Liabilities and fund balances			
Current liabilities			
Accounts payable	$ 55,960		
Accrued wages and salaries	56,942		
Total current liabilities	$112,902		
Noncurrent liabilities			
Long-term debt	$292,370		
Deferred revenue and other noncurrent liabilities	96,609	$10,323	
total noncurrent liabilities	$388,979	$10,323	
Total liabilities	$501,881	$10,323	
Net assets	$ 15,722	$62,963	$17,136
Total liabilities and net assets	$517,603	$73,286	$17,136

12-12

A review of the actual statements provides insight into the form and content of not-for-profit college reporting practices.

Review the financial statements of Hamilton College in Chapter 2 and respond to the following questions:

1. What percentage of the college's total revenues (including nonoperating items) is attributable to tuition and fees (net of scholarship aid)?
2. A note to the financial statements indicates that the college's board of trustees designates only a portion of the college's cumulative investment return for support of current operations (both restricted and unrestricted). How much was so designated in 2003? Taking into account that amount, what was the college's net loss on investments for the year?
3. What are likely examples of "auxiliary enterprises"? Taken collectively, were they profitable in 2003?
4. How much of temporarily restricted funds did the college expend during the year?
5. What percentage of the college's total assets is attributable to investments? Of the investments, approximately what percentage is most likely attributable to endowments?
6. A note to the financial statements reports that compensation costs were almost $43 million. Why is that amount not reported on the statement of activities?

12-13

Financial ratios are useful in comparing one not-for-profit to another.

The data that follows at the bottom of this page pertaining to two not-for-profit hospices were taken from GuideStar, an online database (www.guidestar.org) that provides information about not-for-profit organizations. Names and dates have been changed. The forms 990 that are included on the Web site indicate that Pleasant Valley and Ancient Falls had fund-raising expenses of $38,327 and $11,075 respectively.

1. Which of the two is the more likely to be able to satisfy its current liabilities as measured by the quick ratio? Include only cash and receivables.
2. Which has the greater financial resources as measured by the ratio of total expenses to net assets (excluding property, plant, and equipment)?
3. Which spends the greater percentage of its revenues on fund-raising?
4. Which directs a greater portion of its revenues to program services?
5. Based on this limited amount of information, which of the two, in your opinion, is the more fiscally sound?

12-14

Extensive information about local charities can be obtained on the internet.

Visit GuideStar at www.guidestar.org. Select two not-for-profit health and welfare organizations that have a similar mission and are of relatively similar size (e.g., the Parkinson's Disease Foundation and the American Parkinson Disease Association). Suppose that you are an analyst for a foundation and you are concerned with the long-term fiscal viability of the two.

Statement of Activities for the Year Ending December 31, 2004

	Hospice Pleasant Valley	Hospice Ancient Falls
Revenues		
Contributions	$ 841,162	$ 704,529
Government grants	94,830	—
Program services	1,555,450	2,331,263
Investments	3,455	146,318
Other	2,187	—
	$2,497,084	$3,182,110
Expenses		
Program services	$1,881,381	$2,521,516
Administration	444,853	403,425
Other	38,227	74,891
Total expenses	$2,364,461	$2,999,832
Excess of revenues over expenses	$ 132,623	$ 182,278

Statement of Position as of December 31, 2004

	Hospice Pleasant Valley	Hospice Ancient Falls
Assets		
Cash and equivalent	$215,999	$441,229
Accounts receivable	141,570	307,252
Pledges and grants receivable	70,135	6,331
Inventories for sale or use	—	14,250
Investments/securities	13,063	2,417,152
Property, plant, and equipment	269,298	2,656,105
Other	1,295	78,801
Total assets	$711,360	$5,921,120
Liabilities		
Accounts payable	$165,809	$183,483
Noncurrent loans and notes	161,556	—
Other noncurrent obligations	5,319	—
Total liabilities	$332,684	$183,483
Net assets	$378,676	$5,737,637

1. Compare the two as to:
   a. Proportion of resources directed to fund-raising
   b. Proportion of resources directed to program activities
   c. Percentage of revenues from contributions and grants
   d. Percentage of revenues of user charges and other sources
   e. Short-term liquidity
   f. Burden of debt
   g. Adequacy of fiscal resources
   h. Current fiscal performance
2. Comment on which appears to be the more fiscally sound.

SOLUTION TO EXERCISE FOR REVIEW AND SELF-STUDY

1. *Tuition and fees*

Cash	$100,662	
Tuition and fees		$96,662
Deferred revenue		4,000

To record tuition and fees (in an unrestricted fund)

The summer session tuition collected in the fiscal year ended June 30, 2004, would be recognized as revenue in the following fiscal year, inasmuch as the major portion of the summer semester would be carried out in that year.

2. *Grants and contracts*

Grants and contracts receivable	$52,820	
Grants and contracts (revenue)		$52,820

To record revenue from grants and contracts (in a temporarily restricted fund)

Grants and contracts	$47,661	
Resources released from restrictions		$47,661

To record expenses incurred to fulfill grants and contracts, both government and private (in an unrestricted fund)

Resources released from restrictions	$47,661	
Cash		$47,661

To record the payment of cash in connection with the grant and contract expenses (in a temporarily restricted fund)

Note that only some of the grants and contracts must have been reimbursement type. If all were reimbursement type, then the grant and contract expenses would be at least as great as the revenues.

3. *Acquisition of plant and equipment*

Land, buildings, and equipment	$24,000	
Resources released from restrictions		$24,000

To record the acquisition of plant and equipment (in an unrestricted fund)

Resources released from restrictions	$24,000	
Cash		$24,000

To record the payment of cash for the plant and equipment (in a temporarily restricted plant fund)

The resources were recorded initially in a temporarily restricted fund, but as plant and equipment is acquired it must be recorded in an unrestricted fund.

4. *Auxiliary enterprises*

	College Inn	*Housing and Dining*
Revenues	$5,806	$20,117
Expenses	6,564	18,999
Excess of revenues over expenses	$ (758)	$ 1,118

5. *Student loans*

Per amounts reported in the temporarily restricted funds, the college is owed $36,954 in principal and it earned $1,856 in interest. The interest is restricted, most probably for purposes related to student loans, as evidenced by its being reported in a temporarily restricted rather than an unrestricted fund.

6. *Endowment income*

The endowment income (unlike the endowment principal) is available for expenditure by the college and therefore must be reported as revenue of either unrestricted or temporarily restricted funds. The distribution depends on whether the income must be used for specific purposes or is available for general purposes. In 2004, $18,548 of the earnings were restricted, the balance unrestricted. The $73,552 of gains on investments is most likely reported in the permanently restricted funds because, by law or donor stipulation, they must be added to principal, not made available for expenditure.

7. *Pledges*
   a. The pledge of $2,500 to construct the wing to the science building would be reported as revenue and a receivable in a temporarily restricted fund.
   b. The pledge of $4,500 for general purposes could be reported as revenue and a receivable in an unrestricted fund if it were to be fulfilled in the same year as it were made; otherwise it would be reported in a temporarily restricted fund.
   c. The $5,000 to purchase investment grade securities would be reported in an endowment fund (a permanently restricted fund).
   d. The pledge of $1,000 in matching funds is a *conditional contribution* and as such would *not* be reported as revenue and a receivable until the conditions upon which the pledge is contingent (i.e., obtaining the other contributions) are satisfied.
8. No, the college does not distinguish between operating and nonoperating activities.

CHAPTER 13

Using Cost Information to Manage and Control

LEARNING OBJECTIVES

After studying this chapter you should understand:

- The similarities and differences in decision criteria of managers in businesses and in governments and other not-for-profits
- The importance of distinguishing between fixed and variable costs
- Why managers must identify incremental costs and benefits
- How managers can assess the costs and benefits of "contracting out"
- The factors that governments and not-for-profits should take into account in establishing prices of goods and services that they provide
- The application of both conventional costing and activity-based costing to governments and not-for-profits
- The special problems of determining the cost of fund-raising activities
- The application of analysis of variance to governments and not-for-profits

With this chapter, the text takes a turn. In previous chapters, we focused mainly on general purpose financial reports and how they can be used to assess the financial condition of governments and other not-for-profits. Chapters 13 through 15 deal primarily with how financial data and related information can be used to plan, administer, and evaluate these organizations. So far we have covered topics typically categorized as financial accounting and widely associated with external users; now we will cover those classified as managerial accounting and identified with managers and other internal parties. As noted in Chapter 1, however, the boundaries between internal and external accounting are less well defined in government and not-for-profit entities than in businesses. The "outside" constituencies of governments and not-for-profit organizations (such as citizens or members) may play an active role in establishing policies, allocating resources, and assessing accomplishments.

Recall from Chapter 1 that in key respects managing a government or not-for-profit organization is much the same as managing a business. In this chapter we expand upon this point, demonstrating that the managerial accounting concepts applicable to businesses are, for the most part, relevant for governments and not-for-profits. Indeed, the chapter covers few concepts that are not addressed in managerial and cost accounting courses. Here we consider cost accounting in a government and not-for-profit context and emphasize that the material dealt with in those managerial accounting courses is as germane to governments and not-for-profits as to businesses.

As we shall see, conventional, business-type management accounting may be necessary for government and not-for-profit organizations, but it is hardly sufficient. It focuses mainly on maximizing net inflows of cash rather than on achieving the organization's other objectives. In Chapter 14, we consider these other goals.

HOW ARE THE DECISION CRITERIA OF GOVERNMENTS AND NOT-FOR-PROFITS SIMILAR TO THOSE OF BUSINESSES DESPITE DIFFERENT OBJECTIVES?

Although businesses are concerned with maximizing profit, relatively few of their decisions are actually directed toward profits. The typical organizational unit of a business is either a cost center or a revenue center, not a profit center. Hence, its objective is either to minimize costs or to maximize revenues. For example, the foreman in charge of a road maintenance crew for a private contractor may have no influence on revenues; he is held accountable for controlling costs. In that regard, his objective is the same as that of a foreman of a government road maintenance crew.

An overriding theme of this chapter is that managers of governments and not-for-profits, no less than those of businesses, must be aware of the impact of their decisions on **incremental receipts** and disbursements. Incremental receipts and disbursements are those that would be different if one alternative were chosen over another. Only future receipts and disbursements can be affected by a decision. Past benefits and costs are irrelevant unless they affect the future. Similarly, costs that are common to two or more activities are relevant only if they will change as a consequence of a decision.

For some decisions, especially those relating to cost reimbursements, prices of goods and services, and resource allocation, managers may need to focus on the **full cost** of goods or services. Full cost includes a proportionate share of costs that are common to two or more goods or services. This chapter will address issues of allocating overhead and other common costs and also consider the relationship between full cost of goods or services and the fees that should be charged for them. It will pay particular attention to controversies as to when and how charitable organizations should allocate costs between fund-raising and programmatic activities.

A secondary theme of this chapter is that variance analysis is as fundamental to cost control in governments and not-for-profits as in businesses. We shall develop this theme by highlighting the importance of cost standards and flexible budgets.

WHY MUST FIXED COSTS BE DISTINGUISHED FROM VARIABLE COSTS?

Of the many ways in which costs can be classified, the most significant from the perspective of managers is by degree of variability. Information on variability is essential if managers are to determine the effect of their actions on costs to be incurred in the future or are to assess deviations between actual results and amounts that were budgeted.

Fixed costs remain the same over fairly broad ranges of volume. **Variable costs** are those that change in direct proportion to volume. Volume refers to the quantity or output of the activity under consideration. Common measures of output in government and not-for-profit organizations include patients and clients served, students enrolled, miles of road repaired, and number of documents processed.

Fixed costs are *not unchanging*. The costs of heating and air conditioning a medical clinic or an employment service may be highly volatile. Nevertheless, they should be classified as fixed rather than variable, as long as they vary with the outside air temperature, not with the number of patients or clients served.

SIGNIFICANCE OF RELEVANT RANGE

In practice, no costs are completely fixed or variable. They are fixed or variable only within a particular range of output. The salaries of school cafeteria managers, for example, are fixed as long as a school district can serve its population within the same number of schools (assuming one manager per school). Once the district has to add another school, the cost becomes variable. Thus, within a range of zero to 1,000 students (assuming 1,000 to be the capacity of a single school) cafeteria managers' salaries may be fixed; within a range of zero to 5,000 they would be variable, because additional managers would have to be hired as new schools are added.

Similarly, the cost of food in a school cafeteria is variable within small ranges. Each incremental student requires another container of milk, an extra serving of dessert. In practice, however, inasmuch as many items of food cannot be purchased in single units, the addition of one—or even ten—students will not increase total food costs. Thus, within a range of zero to 10 they may be fixed, within a range of zero to 100 they would be variable.

As illustrated in Figure 13-1, both managers' salaries and food costs can be shown graphically as step functions. Within a relevant range (appropriate for a decision at hand) fixed costs can be depicted as a horizontal line, variable costs as an upward sloping line.

Costs behave in a variety of ways, and cost "curves" take an assortment of shapes. For example, old-age survivors and disability insurance (Social Security) taxes are a fixed percentage of each employee's wages and salaries up to a specified ceiling; thereafter, they are zero. By contrast, the lease on a copy machine may specify a fixed monthly charge plus a per-copy charge once a minimum number of copies has been made. This per-copy charge may decrease as the number of copies increase. Graphs of these costs are illustrated in Figure 13-2. For virtually all decisions, including preparation of budgets and evaluation of performance, managers must be explicitly aware of how the costs will behave within the relevant range.

LIMITATIONS OF AVERAGE COST

Average (per unit) cost is arrived at by dividing total costs for a specified number of units of output by the number of units of output.

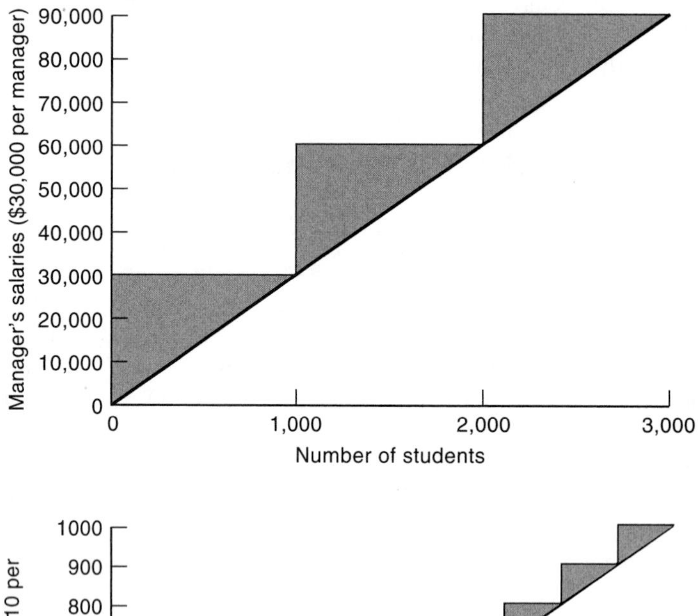

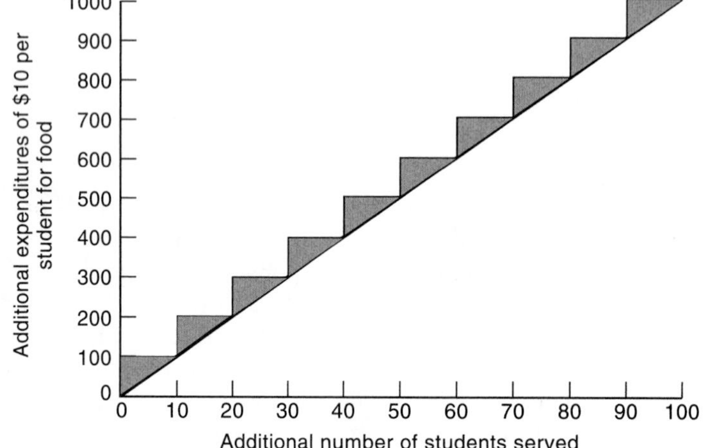

FIGURE 13-1 Graphs Showing Relevant Range

EXAMPLE *Average Cost*

The fixed costs to operate a school cafeteria are $200,000 per year and variable costs are $400 per student. If the cafeteria serves 1,000 students, then the average cost per student is $600:

Fixed costs		$200,000
Variable cost per student	$ 400	
Number of students	× 1,000	400,000
Total costs		$600,000
Number of students		÷ 1,000
Average cost per students		$ 600

There are few types of decisions for which average cost is appropriate and for which a manager would not be better served by disaggregating the average cost into fixed and variable elements. For example, faced with a decision to increase enrollment by thirty students, the average cost of $600 provides little useful information.

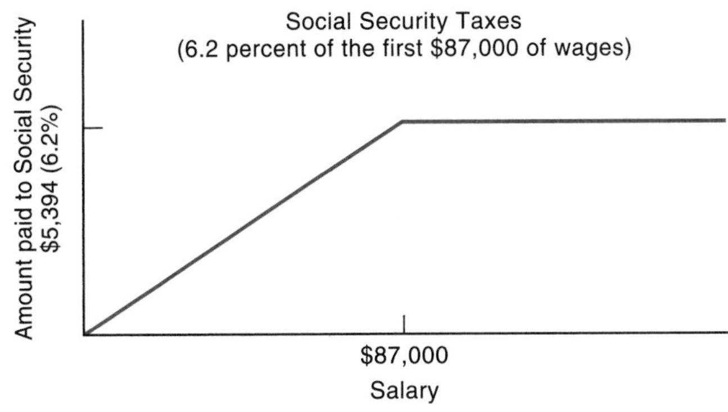

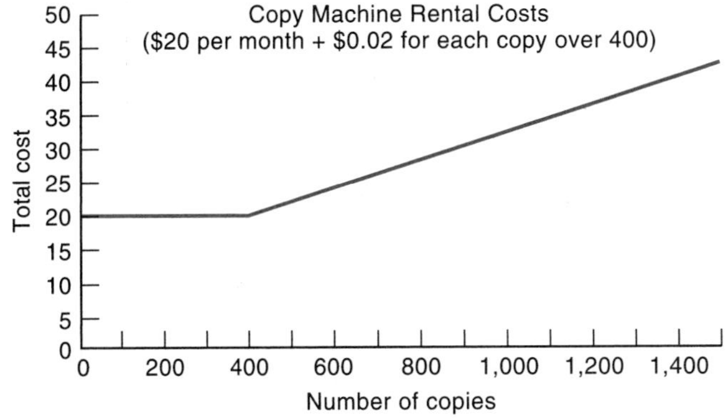

FIGURE 13-2 Graphs of Behavior of Selected Costs

The cost of additional students would not be $600 per student; it would be only the variable costs of $400 per student.

Despite its limitations, average cost is a common—and often misused—expression of cost. It is not unusual for managers of both governments and not-for-profits to argue for an increase in their budgets proportionate to an expected increase in services provided. Thus, if they anticipate a 3 percent increase in services, they will assume that average cost will remain constant and will request a 3 percent increase in appropriations—missing the obvious point that depending on the behavior of costs, the increase in output may require a less than, or greater than, proportionate increase in appropriations.

WHY IS IT IMPORTANT TO IDENTIFY INCREMENTAL COSTS AND BENEFITS?

A financial decision involves a choice between two or more possibilities, both of which ordinarily cause the decision maker to incur costs and to reap benefits. The objective of the decision maker is to select the option that provides the greater net benefit—the margin between benefits and costs.

In any type of organization the benefits must ultimately be tied to the entity's objectives. In governments and not-for-profits the objectives are sometimes less well defined than in business. Fortunately, though, for most decisions managers do not have to specify all the costs and benefits associated with each option. They need only be concerned with the costs and benefits that will differ among the choices. They need not take into account those that will be unaffected by the selection. For many decisions, the costs and benefits that are the least tangible and most difficult to define and quantify will be the same irrespective of the option chosen. Often, in fact, the only differential costs or benefits will be the cash inflows or outflows—the same as in many business decisions. When this is so, the objective of the decision is either to maximize net cash inflow or to minimize net cash outflow. For example, a decision by a mental health clinic as to whether to focus on inpatient or outpatient care may indeed involve costs and benefits that are difficult both to identify and to quantify. But the more common types of decisions—whether to acquire a new software package for its computer, for example—can likely be narrowed to questions of cash flow.

The general concept that only incremental costs and benefits—those that will make a difference—are relevant has at least two corollaries: Sunk costs are irrelevant and allocated costs are irrelevant.

IRRELEVANCE OF SUNK COSTS

Sunk costs need not and should not be incorporated into an analysis of costs and benefits. Sunk costs are costs that have already been incurred. They cannot be recovered, and therefore they do not matter. The examples that follow are intended to highlight this point.

EXAMPLE *The Foolish Overhaul*

A health and welfare organization recently spent $10,000 to repair and overhaul its copy machine. The machine makes copies at a cost of approximately $0.12 per copy, an amount that includes paper, supplies, electricity, and maintenance, all of which are variable costs.

The day after the machine was returned to service, a representative of a copy machine company offered to lease the organization a technologically superior machine at a rate based entirely on number of copies—$0.04 per copy. Additional variable costs, such as paper and toner, would bring the total cost of each copy to $0.10. The period of the lease would be three years—a period that, by coincidence, is the same as the remaining life of the overhauled machine.

The administrator of the agency rejected the offer outright. "We just spent $10,000 to repair the machine," she noted. "Surely, there's no point in abandoning the machine until we can recover our investment in the overhaul."

Is the position of the administrator fiscally sound?

The answer is unequivocally in the negative. The $10,000 overhaul is a sunk cost; it cannot be recovered. The only relevant costs are those to be incurred in the future. With the benefit of hindsight, it is clear that the administrator erred in over-hauling the old machine. The question she faces now is whether to compound the mistake by spending $0.12 to make copies when, by signing the lease, she could reduce the cost to $0.10.

The following example, inspired by an actual nuclear disaster (that fortunately was only fiscal), reinforces the point, albeit from a slightly different perspective, that sunk costs are irrelevant.

EXAMPLE *The Nuclear Disaster*

A midsize city constructed a nuclear power plant at a cost of $3 billion, financing it with thirty-year bonds that required annual debt service, including principal and interest, of $218 million.

The plant took five years longer to construct than was anticipated, and by the time it was completed, it was obvious that the project should never have been undertaken. Owing to new safety and environmental standards and declining prices for conventional fuels, the city would be able to meet its electricity demands more economically by purchasing electricity from independent utilities. In fact, the city estimated that by purchasing electricity from independent utilities it could save $103 million per year in cash outlays (excluding debt service on the nuclear plant bonds).

Unfortunately, the city could not sell the new plant—despite advertisements in national newspapers, there were no interested buyers. Its only options were to abandon the plant or to operate it. If it elected to abandon the plant it would have had to incur approximately $10 million in annual monitoring costs. Moreover, it would have had to continue to service the debt.

City officials estimated that the useful life of the plant would be thirty years, and that all of its cost estimates would be applicable over the life of the plant.

The city council chose to put the plant in service and reject the opportunity to purchase electricity from outside sources. It argued that if it abandoned the plant it would have had to recognize an immediate loss of $3 billion, an amount that would not be compensated for by the annual cash savings of $93 million (the operating savings of $103 million less the $10 million in monitoring costs). Moreover, it could not see paying $218 million per year in principal and interest on an abandoned plant.

Did the city make the fiscally sound decision?

This case has much in common with "The Foolish Overhaul" example. The $3 billion spent to construct the plant is irrelevant to the decision at hand. Whether the plant is retained on the balance sheet or is written off has no impact on future cash flows. Similarly, the $218 million in annual debt service is equally extraneous; it must be paid irrespective of whether the plant is operated or abandoned.

The only relevant costs are those to be incurred in the future, the costs of running the plant or the costs of purchasing electricity from independent utilities. Since purchasing electricity would yield a net annual cash savings of $93 million, as awkward as it might be to abandon a $3 billion plant, it is the proper course of action.

Suppose, instead, that the utility officials estimated that excluding debt service, the annual cost to operate the nuclear facility would be $700 million, determined as follows:

Depreciation on nuclear plant ($3 billion over thirty years)	$100
Cash operating costs	600
Total annual costs	$700

The city could purchase its electricity from outside sources for $620 million (and would incur $10 million annually to monitor the abandoned plant). Should it still take advantage of the apparent cost savings and abandon the plant?

Depreciation is nothing more than an allocation of a cost incurred in the past and, hence, the accounting recognition of a sunk cost. Sunk costs are not relevant, irrespective of how they are reported on the general purpose financial statements. Therefore, in this example, the relevant comparison is between the annual $600 million in cash operating costs to be incurred if the plant is placed in operation and the annual $630 million in electricity purchase and monitoring costs to be incurred if electricity is obtained from outsiders. Therefore, the city should place the plant in service; its annual cash outlays in the future would be $30 million less.

INAPPLICABILITY OF ALLOCATED COSTS

The general rule that only incremental costs should be taken into account applies also to *allocations* of common costs. Allocation is the process of charging costs to the various activities, processes, operations, or products in proportion to benefits received. Common costs are irrelevant to decisions affecting individual activities, processes, operations, or products, except to the extent that they will be either increased or decreased in *total.* Circumstances in which **allocated costs** should be taken into account will be discussed later in this chapter in the section dealing with the pricing of goods and services.

EXAMPLE *Allocated Costs*

The Health-North Rehabilitation Hospital operates a speech clinic to provide therapy for its patients. The clinic is staffed by three therapists, each of whom contracts with the hospital to provide services at a rate of $50 per hour. On average, the therapists bill the hospital for 390 hours per month, a total of $19,500.

The clinic is operated as a profit center and each month is allocated a share of hospital **overhead** (indirect costs) as follows:

Building occupancy costs ($1 per square foot of space; 2,000 feet at $1)	$ 2,000
Administrative costs ($0.20 per dollar of independent contractor costs; $19,500 × $.20)	3,900
Total speech clinic overhead	$ 5,900

Accordingly, the cost per therapy hour is $65.13:

Direct costs per month (390 hours at $50)	$19,500
Allocated overhead	5,900
Total costs per month	$25,400
Number of therapy hours per month	÷ 390
Cost per therapy hour	$ 65.13

Physicians Practice Associates, a local health maintenance organization (HMO), has proposed that the clinic provide outpatient speech therapy to its members. It estimates that it would refer patients for approximately fifty hours of therapy per month. It has offered to pay $58 per hour. Should the hospital accept the offer?

If the hospital accepts the offer, it would receive $2,900 per month in additional revenue (50 hours at $58). Assuming that it would not be required to add either space or administrative personnel, it would incur only $2,500 in additional costs (the $50 per hour to be paid to the speech therapists). Therefore, by accepting the offer, it would increase its monthly cash flow by $400 per month.

Note, however, that the decision criteria of the hospital at large is not necessarily congruent with that of the clinic. If the clinic is being allocated overhead at the $0.20 per dollar paid to the therapists, then for purposes of internal performance evaluation its incremental cost of providing the service is $60 per hour [$50 + ($0.20 × $50)], not merely the direct contract costs of $50. Given a choice, therefore, the clinic would presumably reject the offer, even though it would benefit the hospital as a whole.

Allocated costs are relevant to a decision if they would be changed by it. For example, if by accepting the offer the hospital would incur additional administrative costs of $500 per month—$100 more than the net direct cash inflow—then obviously the HMO's proposal would no longer be to its advantage.

How Can Organizations Assess the Fiscal Benefits of Contracting Out?

In the next two sections we discuss contracting out and pricing—two types of decisions to which the concepts of incremental costs are central. In addressing both these decisions we emphasize that only costs that will actually change need be taken into account. Both sunk costs and allocated costs are irrelevant.

Contracting out—engaging an outside, private-sector firm to provide services that have previously been performed in-house—has been one of the most compelling movements of recent years. When governments contract out they are said to **privatize** the affected activity, and in recent years considerable public attention has been centered upon privatization initiatives at all levels of government. Yet the ideology of contracting out (also referred to as *outsourcing*) has permeated both private corporations and not-for-profit organizations with equal potency.

Decisions to contract out can have consequences that range from the marginal to the momentous—a university's department of accounting may get cheaper and fresher coffee by arranging with an independent service company to supply coffee and to service its coffee machine; an eastern European country may transfigure its economy by selling its major industries to private investors.

Examples abound of services that are being contracted out by governments and not-for-profits:

- A hospital engages an outside cleaning service to replace its own maintenance staff.
- A university contracts with a catering concern to take over its cafeterias and snack bars.
- A county turns over the operation of its jails to a prison-management company.
- A school district contracts with a private bus operator to transport its students.
- A theater company transfers its ticket-sales operations to an independent ticket agency.

A full discussion of the advantages and disadvantages of contracting out is well beyond the scope of this text. Nevertheless, among the most frequently offered reasons for the practice are the following:

- It brings the efficiencies and lower costs that are associated with both competition and specialization.
- It encourages innovation, as the firm providing the service can draw upon the ideas gleaned from a variety of organizations, not just the one to which it provides the service.
- It opens new career paths for the employees that perform the activities. For example, a member of a hospital's small maintenance staff may have scant opportunity to advance in the organization. Yet if employed by a service firm that employs many maintenance workers, that person may have the chance for promotion to supervisory and management positions.

The fiscal aspects of a decision to contract out are mainly additional applications of the general principle that one should select the option that provides the greater incremental benefits (least costs). In practice, however, the decision to contract out may become extraordinarily complex, often requiring an inordinate number of estimates and assumptions.

EXAMPLE *Contracting Out*

A data processing company has offered to assume responsibility for a hospital's accounting and information management functions, currently carried out by the hospital's data-processing department. The company would charge the hospital $1,350,000 each year of a three-year contract.

The hospital has provided the following cost information as to the data-processing department being considered for elimination. It assumes that the costs will remain constant over the three years of the contract:

Salaries, wages, and benefits	$ 730,000
Equipment rental	180,000
Phone and other utilities	56,000
Training, travel, and other miscellaneous costs	80,000
Depreciation of computer software	19,000
Depreciation of computer hardware	320,000
Total direct costs	$1,385,000
Overhead allocated from other departments	$ 176,000
Total departmental costs	$1,561,000

It has also determined the following:

- The hardware could be sold for $400,000.
- Were the data processing department eliminated, hospital overhead could be reduced by $22,000 per year.
- The cost of administering the contract would be $45,000 per year.
- The department was planning to spend approximately $25,000 per year to upgrade its software and $240,000 per year to upgrade its hardware.

Based on this limited amount of information, the analysis, as presented in Table 13-1, should focus on the incremental costs—the changes in the cash flows. Thus the analyst should:

- Identify the differential cash flows associated with each of the two options
- Determine the present value of the cash flows
- Select the option in which the net cash outflows are the least (or the net cash inflows the greatest)

For purposes of the decision at hand, the differential cash flows associated with the option to reject the offer (i.e., to continue to perform the services in-house) include the costs of upgrading both the hardware and the software. They exclude, however, depreciation on previously purchased hardware and software. Depreciation, as pointed out earlier, is an allocation of a sunk cost; it does not require a cash outflow.

The overhead costs assigned to the "reject" alternative include only the $22,000 above what would be incurred if the offer were accepted: The remaining $154,000 in overhead costs are irrelevant in that they would stay the same irrespective of whether the offer were accepted or rejected.

TABLE 13–1
Accept or Reject Offer to Contract Out Accounting and Information Functions

Reject Offer	**Present Value at 6%**	**Year 1**	**Year 2**	**Year 3**
Salaries, wages, and benefits	$1,951,299	$ 730,000	$ 730,000	$ 730,000
Equipment rental	481,142	180,000	180,000	180,000
Phone and utilities	149,689	56,000	56,000	56,000
Training, travel, etc.	213,841	80,000	80,000	80,000
Software upgrades	66,825	25,000	25,000	25,000
Hardware upgrades	641,523	240,000	240,000	240,000
Overhead	58,806	22,000	22,000	22,000
Net outlays	$3,563,125	$1,333,000	$1,333,000	$1,333,000
Accept Offer	**Present Value at 6%**	**Year 1**	**Year 2**	**Year 3**
Payment to contractor	$3,608,566	$1,350,000	$1,350,000	$1,350,000
Cost of administering contract	120,286	45,000	45,000	45,000
Total	$3,728,852	$1,395,000	$1,395,000	$1,395,000
Sale of hardware	(400,000)			
Net outlays	$3,328,852			
Advantages of Contracting Out				
Net outlays if contract is rejected	$3,563,125			
Net outlays if contract is accepted	3,328,852			
Net saving	$ 234,273			

The costs of administering the contract are mainly those of interacting with the contractor and of monitoring its performance. They are included in this example so as to emphasize their importance; in practice, they are often overlooked.

The time value of money must be taken into account in any decision in which all cash flows do not occur simultaneously. Cash to be received or disbursed in the future is worth less than that to be received or disbursed in the present. If the difference in value is likely to be significant then all cash flows must be *discounted* to the present. In the example, cash flows are assumed (for computational convenience) to take place at the end of each period, with the exception that the cash from the sale of the hardware is assumed to be received at the time the contract is signed. Therefore, the cash from the sale of the hardware does not have to be discounted and is included in the present value column rather than in any one of the three contract years. It is assumed that 6 percent is the appropriate discount rate.

As shown in Table 13-1, the present value of the differential net cash outflows if the offer were to be rejected is $3,563,125; if accepted, it is only $3,328,852. Therefore, the offer would result in a net saving of $234,273 and should be accepted.

FINANCIAL COMPLEXITIES

In practice, the decision to contract out is far more complex than suggested by the example and, unfortunately, the complicating factors are often either ignored or assumed away as if they didn't matter. The following are suggestive of some of these.

Time Horizon

The contract period may not be an appropriate length of time over which to assess the contracting out opportunity. Once it elects to contract out, an organization cannot simply return to the status quo without financial penalty. Restoration of a department or function that has been abandoned may be extremely costly. New employees have to be hired; capital assets may have to be purchased. Yet the price of renewing the contract for additional periods (either with the same or new contractors) might be greater than that of the initial contract, especially if, as is common, the contractor agrees to a "low-ball" rate for the initial contract.

Varying the time horizon (e.g., carrying out the analysis over two or more contract periods) can markedly affect the cash flow comparisons. Differences in net cash flows would be particularly great, for example, if there are material nonrecurring proceeds, such as from the sale of assets when the contract is first implemented. Moreover, the greater the number of contract periods over which the analysis is carried out, the less the credibility of the cash flow estimates of the more distant years. At the same time, however, owing to discounting, the more distant the receipts or disbursements, the less their impact on the net present value of the cash flows. Regrettably, there are no agreed-upon guidelines as to the number of contract periods over which to carry out an analysis.

Value of Assets at Conclusion of Period of Analysis

In the example, the hospital forecast that if it continued to operate the data processing department it would upgrade its hardware and software evenly over the three-year period of analysis. However, no assumption was made as to the disposition of assets at the conclusion of the period. Hence, it was implicitly assumed that the assets had no value at that time.

To ensure that the comparison between the two alternatives is properly balanced, it is necessary either to make an explicit assumption as to an asset's salvage value at the expiration of the contract or to extend the analysis until the end of the asset's useful life. Making an explicit assumption will introduce an additional element of arbitrariness into the comparison, whereas extending the analysis may cause the time horizon to be open-ended. If the organization has assets without concurrent useful lives, then assets will continually have to be retired and replaced, and there will never be a clean cut-off date.

Discount Rate

Choice of discount rate can have a dramatic impact on the present value of cash flows and, unless the cash flows are uniform over the period of analysis, may affect the alternatives differently. It is generally agreed that an entity's discount rate should relate to its cost of capital. Yet there is no concurrence as to whether cost of capital should be based on the rate at which an entity can borrow funds (perhaps a tax-exempt rate) or the rate at which it can invest funds (an opportunity cost). Moreover, it is arguable whether the rate should reflect an average cost of capital, taking into account all of the organization's outstanding debt, or only any new funds to be borrowed.

Alternative Use of Resources

When an organization discontinues an activity, it may transfer its assets to other departments. Even though the transfer will not involve a flow of cash, it will provide something of value to the recipient departments. Yet the actual worth of assets to those departments might not be clear, especially if the recipient department would not otherwise have purchased the assets. For example, a department might receive more floor space, which adds to the comfort of its employees but would not actually be needed until the future. Any cash flow assumptions as to the value of the assets would necessarily be arbitrary.

Calculating Reductions in Overhead

By its very nature, overhead cannot be easily traced to specific departments. Therefore, the amount to be saved can seldom be established objectively. Suppose, for example, a pool of overhead costs includes the cost of an entity's internal audit department. If an activity is contracted out the audit department may have the luxury of directing greater attention to audits of remaining activities, but it may not be able to reduce its staff.

NONFINANCIAL ISSUES

As suggested by the three following In Practices, decisions to contract out may have important ramifications that extend far beyond flows of cash, and the results may not always be what were anticipated. Several significant factors should be taken into account.

Impact on Employees and Organizational Morale

Contracting out may permit reductions in the workforce. Layoffs are obviously economically and emotionally traumatic for the discharged workers. But they can also diminish the morale of retained employees who may become fearful of losing their own jobs or see a change in the organizational culture and values with which they have become secure. Alternatively, contracting out can improve the outlook of remaining employees by demonstrating that the organization is responding positively to financial exigencies and that it is taking steps to become more efficient and effective.

Loss of Control and Reduction in Flexibility

When an organization outsources an activity it may sacrifice both control and flexibility. A hospital that contracts out for its maintenance service, for example, may lose its ability to assign personnel to tasks other than those contractually specified, to have employees on the premises except at previously agreed-upon hours, and to provide incentives for above-minimal performance.

Political and Social Values

Constituents of an organization may believe that certain functions are the responsibility of the organization and cannot be abdicated. Governments, for example, have been slow to privatize prisons, mainly because many citizens see incarceration as an inherent obligation of government. Similarly, university efforts to outsource their food services to popular-name franchises have faced opposition from students who see the businesses as commercial intrusions into their pristine academic environment.

Social and Economic Externalities

When an organization, especially a government, contracts out it may incur costs or reap benefits only indirectly tied to the activity that is being outsourced. Suppose, for example, that a city sells its electric utility. The new owner hires some of the city's employees but lays off others. The discharged employees may place added demands upon the city's unemployment, medical, and other social welfare services. On the other hand, the property of the new owner, now that it is in private hands, can be added to the tax rolls and thereby generate property tax revenue.

Decisions to contract out are complex and even seemingly minor changes in estimates and assumptions can alter the outcome of an analysis. Moreover, where individuals stand on particular outsourcing decisions may be strongly influenced by their own political persuasions and how the decision will affect them personally. Accordingly, comparative cost analyses should always be viewed with the utmost skepticism.

IN PRACTICE

Colleges Are Turning to Private Vendors for More and More Campus Services

Many colleges are finding out that if they want something done well, it might be better to hire someone else for the job.

College business officers are signing on with private companies that can provide or manage a variety of campus support services. It's a practice called *outsourcing, privatizing,* or *contracting out,* and it is driven by two goals: saving money, by paying a private company to provide a service at a lower cost; or making money, by having someone run a service, then sharing in the profits that the vendor generates.

The most frequently privatized services are bookstores and food-service operations, says Richard D. Wertz, vice-president for business affairs at the University of South Carolina at Columbia and a consultant on outsourcing. But companies are increasingly being sought to provide campus health, computing, custodial, fund-raising, mail delivery, maintenance, printing, security, and trademark-and-licensing services.

Private colleges have contracted out services for years, but now budget-conscious legislators in many states are pushing all publicly supported institutions to consider the practice.

Even so, outsourcing is moving at a slower pace on the campuses than elsewhere, says William D. Eggers, director of the Privatization Center, a division of the Los Angeles–based Reason Foundation, which assists state governments in privatizing efforts. Colleges, he says, could easily hire private companies to perform as much as 40 percent of their support services.

Some university officials say outsourcing would allow institutions to "buy" expertise and business acumen while improving the level of service.

Clemson University, for example, is seeking a contractor to serve as a chief facilities officer. "The contractor would bring the breadth and depth of a corporate structure to bear on our operations and point out savings well beyond what we would be able to identify ourselves," says Gary A. Ransdell, Clemson's vice-president for administration and advancement.

Privatizing can offer a college the chance to gain new equipment at a company's expense. Under the terms of a contract between Marshall University and Follett College Stores, the company will install more cash registers in the campus bookstore to speed service.

Privatizing also has another benefit, some people believe: It forces university employees to think creatively about ways to save money and improve efficiency.

But privatization also can mean the loss of jobs. Even though difficult economic times have familiarized many colleges with cutbacks, layoffs are still painful on the campuses, which pride themselves on collegiality.

Public employees are "rarely laid off" when services are contracted out, responds Mr. Eggers of the privatization center. A 1989 study of state and county governments by the U.S. Department of Labor—still the definitive work, he says—showed that half of all employees went to work for the company hired by their employers and that most of the others retired or were reassigned.

At George Mason University, most of the employees who have been affected by privatizing have opted for early retirement, were kept on by the contractor, or were retrained and placed elsewhere, says Maurice W. Scherrens, vice president for finance and planning.

One official says the day is coming when there will be almost no limit to what a campus will consider privatizing.

"I think it's only a matter of time before somebody outsources areas of instruction," such as developmental-education programs, says Mr. Davies, the director of Virginia's higher-education council. "There would be people who would say that's horrible. But the essence of creating and maintaining a community is not doing everything yourself."

Source: The Chronicle of Higher Education, July 7, 1995. Excerpted with permission.

IN PRACTICE

Outsourcing Sometimes Fails to Meet Expectations

Professors say the housekeeping at the University of Pennsylvania simply never got better. The trash cans still didn't get emptied and the roofs still leaked, despite the outside supervision of the so-called experts, the Trammell Crow Company.

Penn labor union officials say they knew from the start that the university's outsourcing strategy would never work. The flaws in the approach, they say, are why Penn last month scaled back its closely watched contract with Trammell Crow for operation and maintenance of campus buildings.

Neither explanation is correct, say officials at Penn and at the company. The key factor was that Trammell Crow was asked to do the impossible: maintain buildings that are essentially unmaintainable because they are in such bad repair. Trammell Crow couldn't make any money, and the collaboration was destined to sour.

Penn's experience may offer lessons for other universities that are rushing into outsourcing as a solution to their myriad management problems. Penn officials say they have concluded that outsourcing won't solve a thing if the priorities of the institution are not well defined.

"The approach is usually, 'This is really screwed up. Let's outsource it. Let's make it someone else's problem.' Nine times out of ten, that will fail," says John A. Fry, Penn's executive vice president.

Penn and Trammell Crow, a diversified construction and real-estate company based in Dallas, jointly announced that the company would no longer supervise day-to-day operations and maintenance of on-campus buildings, terminating a contract that was to last ten years. The company will remain in charge of supervising all construction projects on campus and managing the buying, selling, and leasing of all real estate on and off the campus. The renegotiated contract means the annual revenue for Trammell Crow from the Penn contract will be cut from about $18 million to about $11 million. And Trammell Crow will only pay about half of the $30 million it had agreed in 1997 to give to Penn in exchange for exclusive access to the campus.

"The college outsourcing business is growing so quickly—in volume and in scope—that there has been very little time to step back and determine how effective much of it is," says Manuel R. Cunard, executive director of the National Association of College Auxiliary Services.

"Institutions need to be thoughtful, and understand what their mission is," says Mr. Cunard. Outsourcing "might save money in the short run, but in the long run, it potentially can have a negative impact on the educational priorities of the institution."

In recent years, colleges have been exploring every opportunity to outsource any activities that are not at the core of teaching and research. For decades, institutions have had outside companies come in and manage their bookstores and dining operations, but that has now expanded to such things as operating college sports arenas and parking lots, and managing mail delivery and groundskeeping.

There are no readily available estimates of how large the outsourcing business is now in higher education, although the biggest segments of the industry are tracked. Slightly more than a third of all college bookstores are now operated by outside contractors, generating $5.8 billion in sales of course materials. The building of on-campus housing by private companies was a $500 million business last year, and may double this year.

Mr. Cunard's organization has just opened a center to try to track overall figures for outsourcing.

With every passing week, there seems to be another announcement of a college being among the first to outsource an operation. Some recent examples include:

- The University of Miami has contracted with Strategic Distribution, Inc., based in Bensalem, Pennsylvania, to acquire all materials required for maintenance, repair, and operations at its main campus and medical center. The company will purchase such items as electrical parts, janitorial supplies, pipes, fittings and wiring.
- The University of Maryland at College Park has signed a contract with a private company to operate its steam plant and convert it to also generate electricity and chilled water.
- Chatham College has retained a management company to run its library and hire most of the staff.

Source: "How the U. of Pennsylvania Learned that Outsourcing is No Panacea," *The Chronicle of Higher Education*, April 7, 2000.

IN PRACTICE

CITIES RETHINKING PRIVATIZATION OF UTILITIES

In the 1990s, privatization of municipal electric utilities was all the rage. As articulated by one private electric utility executive, "the American way is that everything that can be done should be done by private enterprise. In the end, private enterprise almost always does a better job than government." However, as reported in *The Wall Street Journal* ("As Problems Mount for Utilities, Cities Pull Plug on Deregulation," November 4, 2002), many U.S. cities, as well as European and Latin American countries, are rethinking whether privatization is all that it was supposed to be. Why the second thoughts? *The Wall Street Journal* cited three reasons:

- California's efforts at market deregulation sent electricity prices through the roof in 2000 and 2001. The estimated cost to rate-payers was over $40 billion.
- The scandals involving Enron and other large private utility providers cast doubt on whether trading in the energy markets can be carried out free of market manipulation and can be accounted for honestly.
- As electricity prices eventually turned downward, the fiscal viability of the major energy providers has been cast in doubt.

As a consequence, many municipal officials now believe that governments can do a better job of providing a reliable source of low-cost electricity than their profit-oriented counterparts, which are often located out-of-state and have no stake in the local community. Not only has the trend toward privatization been slowed, but many governments are now looking into ways by which they can buy out investor-owned companies.

HOW SHOULD GOVERNMENTS AND NOT-FOR-PROFITS ESTABLISH PRICES?

Both governments and not-for-profit organizations charge fees for some or all of their services. For businesses the guidelines for establishing prices are relatively unambiguous—charge the price that will maximize net revenues (revenues less the cost of the goods or services). If a business operates in an environment of perfect competition, then that price would be the prevailing market price. At the prevailing market price it will be able to sell all of its available goods. If it sets the price above the prevailing market price, then it can expect to sell none. If it sets the price below market, then it can expect to sell the same amount of goods as if it had charged the market price (the entire amount available) but would realize less revenue.

For governments and not-for-profit organizations, pricing decisions—like most other decisions—are more complex. These entities provide goods or services to achieve objectives other than, or in addition to, profit maximization. Most of the objectives can be grouped into the following five categories:[1]

1. ***To provide revenue.*** User fees and other charges can supplement or substitute for taxes, contributions, and other revenues.
2. ***To ration output.*** User charges help to ration output among the various claimants. In a competitive economy, pricing schemes can be used to assure that the output is acquired by the parties that could use it most efficiently. Thus, the federal government auctions off communication licenses and mineral rights in the expectation that the highest bidders will put them to their most profitable use. Universities establish a scale of rates for different parking lots, so that the most desirable spaces will go to those willing to pay for them. London, in 2003, began charging motorists substantial fees to drive in its center city as a means of rationing the capacity of downtown streets and parking spaces.
3. ***To allocate burdens.*** User fees are a means of allocating the cost of goods or services to the parties that will benefit from them. For example, a local YMCA may fund the construction of a new gym in whole or part by assessing fees to members who elect to use the facility. Governments finance parking garages by operating them as business enterprises.
4. ***To provide demand signals.*** User fees can provide information as to the extent that a service is demanded. They indicate the number of service recipients that value the service at least as much as the fee being charged. They thereby help the organization to determine the quantity of the service to provide and the amount of resources to be directed to it. By experimenting with different fares, a municipal bus system can gauge the value of its service to potential riders.
5. ***To regulate demand.*** Governments may establish a monopoly over a product, such as alcoholic beverages, and then set prices at a level that discourages consumption. Correspondingly, governments or not-for-profits may establish a below-cost price, such as for inoculations against childhood diseases, to encourage consumption.

[1] For an extended discussion of reasons for user charges and the bases on which they are established, see Werner Z. Hirsch, "User Charges," Chap. 3 in *The Economics of State and Local Government* (New York: McGraw-Hill, 1970), and Mary T. Ziebell and Don T. DeCoster, "Pricing Decisions," Chap. 8 in *Management Control Systems in Nonprofit Organizations*, (San Diego: Harcourt Brace Jovanovich, 1991).

The basis on which a user fee is established should, of course, reflect the reason for the fee. Thus, consistent with one or more of the objectives, user fees can range from nominal amounts to amounts greatly in excess of full cost.

Pricing policies can be categorized as being either market- or cost-based. Market-based policies are those in which the prices are influenced mainly by market forces—the relationship between demand and price. Cost-based policies are those in which cost factors dominate. In practice, of course, almost all pricing decisions must take into account both market forces and cost.

Organizations may adopt market-based policies in the interests of "profit" maximization. Taking into account the relationship between price and demand, for example, a not-for-profit may set ticket prices for a fund-raising concert at rates that will generate the greatest revenues. Similarly, a graduate school of business may establish tuition charges for executive development programs at a level reflective of the prevailing rates charged by both professional associations and private business-education companies.

Organizations using cost-based pricing strategies typically use some measure of cost, such as incremental cost or full cost, as a starting point and then decide how much above (or below) that cost they should charge. In Chapter 9, for example, it was noted that internal service funds operate on a cost reimbursement basis and that in practice *cost* is usually interpreted to mean *full cost.*

The problem set forth in the accompanying In Practice, pertaining to the prices to be charged by a municipal electric utility, suggests the multiplicity of variables in addition to the costs that may have to be taken into account in establishing user charges. The text provides no specific solution to the utility pricing problem, mainly because it would require the development of a highly complex econometric model.

HOW SHOULD GOVERNMENTS AND NOT-FOR-PROFITS ESTABLISH COSTS?

ESTABLISHING AND TAKING INTO ACCOUNT FULL COST

Even though most pricing decisions should focus on incremental costs and benefits, the significance of the full cost of goods or services should not be minimized. Indeed, over an extended period of time, full cost is often an approximation of incremental cost. Information on the full cost of a product is an important element of pricing decisions. Even if managers elect not to set a price that covers full cost, they should be aware of the magnitude of any subsidy. Federal agencies are required to establish user fees at either market price or full cost.[2]

Similarly, full cost is an essential ingredient of decisions as to whether activities or programs should be carried out. To be sure, organizations do not have to cover the full cost of *each* product or service that they provide. But they cannot incur losses on *all* products and services. Information as to full cost, therefore, helps managers compare goods and services and establish priorities among them. As implied in a Chapter 1 In Practice, the enthusiasm with which university officials view their institution's football program will likely be influenced by whether revenues cover full cost or only incremental cost. Further, full cost data are helpful in comparing the efficiency with which two or more units provide similar services. For example, if a state highway department needs to establish which of its districts maintains roads at the least cost per mile, it would require data that encompass all costs associated with the maintenance, not merely those that vary with output.

Full costs are especially important to government and not-for-profit organizations that are reimbursed for some of their activities, but not others. The means by

[2] Office of Management and Budget, Circular No. A-25 (revised), *User Charges* (1993).

IN PRACTICE

Factors That Should Enter into the Pricing Decisions of a City-Operated Electric Utility

A city operates an electric utility. The utility provides service not only to all electricity users within its boundaries, but also to neighboring communities. In the jurisdictions in which it operates, the city is a regulated monopoly. Although its rates are subject to approval by a state public utility commission, they are unlikely to be rejected unless they are far out of line with those charged by other power providers within the state.

The rates charged by the utility are considerably in excess of cost. In fact, each year the utility provides approximately 33 percent of the city's general fund revenues. Were it not for the transfer of cash from the utility fund to the general fund, the city would have to increase property tax rates.

The following are but a sample of the factors that the city should properly take into account in setting its utility rates:

- ***Elasticity of demand.*** Even though the city faces no direct competition for electricity within its boundaries, like any monopolist it faces a downward-sloping demand curve; that is, the higher the price, the less quantity it sells. Therefore, the city must consider the elasticity of the demand for its product—the percentage decline in electricity sold associated with percentage increases in price. Indeed, at some point increases in price will cause decreases in total revenues. Moreover, the city faces competition in sales beyond its jurisdiction. If the city sets its price sufficiently high, then the customers outside the city can elect to obtain their power from other sources.
- ***Regressivity of user charges relative to alternative revenue sources.*** Although the burdens of both electric rates and alternative sources of revenue will fall mainly on city residents, they will not be shared in the same proportions. Some revenue sources will be more regressive than others, meaning that wealthier residents pay a lower percentage of their income than poorer citizens do. The regressivity of any particular source of revenue will depend largely on the residents' consumption patterns; for example, how much electricity they use and how much real property they own (and must pay taxes on).
- ***Amount of revenue that could be raised from parties that are exempt from property taxes.*** A sizable portion of property within city limits is exempt from property taxes. This includes federal military bases, state office buildings, and real estate owned by religious organizations. The owners of this property are subject to utility charges, but not property taxes.
- ***Amount of revenue that could be raised from parties outside of the city.*** Electricity users outside of city limits pay utility charges, but not property taxes. Therefore, by increasing utility rates and lowering property taxes, the city is able to transfer a portion of its overall fiscal burden to nonresidents.
- ***Federal income tax savings that will accrue to citizens by shifting from utility charges to property taxes.*** The Internal Revenue Code permits individuals who itemize deductions to deduct local property taxes, but not utility charges. The federal government thereby pays a share of property taxes. The value of this subsidy is especially difficult to measure because it depends on the amount of property taxes paid by the taxpayers, whether or not they itemize their deductions, and the taxpayers' marginal income tax rates.

The optimum property tax rates and user charges would be those that not only minimize the total amount to be paid by city residents, but that also distribute the revenue burden equitably.

which overhead is allocated among activities is a frequent source of controversy. Universities, for example, routinely spar with the federal agencies for which they perform contract research over what constitutes a fair allocation of overhead. In fact, to reduce what it considers excessive overhead charges, the federal government has established an elaborate set of cost accounting standards and disclosure rules for colleges and universities.[3]

To determine the full cost of an **object,** it is necessary to assign to it all relevant costs, both direct and indirect. An object is the unit being measured. It could be an activity, program, or product. For example, the object of a hospital might be a patient served. Alternatively, so as to recognize explicitly that the cost of caring for patients depends on their ailments, it could be the cost of treating a patient with a particular diagnosis. In fact, Medicare uses diagnosis-related groups (DRGs) as its object of reimbursement. For a highway department, the cost object might be a single pothole. For an accounting department it might be an activity, such as processing payroll, or a product, such as a single processed voucher.

The development of cost accounting systems of both governments and not-for-profits has generally lagged far beyond that in industry. Only within the last decade have the federal government and several state governments mandated that their component units provide information on the full cost of programs and activities.

Both the conventional and the more recently developed **activity-based costing (ABC)** means of establishing the full cost of an object are as applicable to governments and not-for-profits as to businesses. Both means of costing are discussed in this section.

The full cost of an object consists of **direct costs**—direct labor and direct materials—and overhead. Direct labor and materials, by definition, can readily be associated with specific units of product. Overhead (indirect) costs are common to more than one object. The conventional and the activity-based costs systems differ only in how they assign the overhead costs to the individual products.

Conventional Approach

Taking the conventional approach, an organization initially assigns all costs to cost centers, some of which are directly associated with the cost object and others of which are only indirectly associated with it. In a governmental or not-for-profit environment, the cost centers directly associated with the cost object are referred to as "mission" or "operating" centers. These correspond to *production centers* in a manufacturing concern. The cost centers that are only indirectly associated with the cost object are called *service* or *support* centers (as they are in manufacturing companies).

The costs of the service centers (overhead costs) are allocated among the various mission centers. They are then combined with the mission centers' own overhead costs and, based on an *overhead charging rate,* absorbed into (or applied to) the cost object. An overhead charging rate is predetermined and is used to apply overhead from the mission departments to the cost object (the units of product or service). It is generally computed by dividing the total overhead by a factor of production, such as direct labor or direct materials. Thus, if a mission department estimates that it will incur $100,000 in overhead cost and utilize 5,000 direct labor hours, its overhead charging rate would be $20 per direct labor hour. If a particular service required thirty direct labor hours, then $600 of overhead costs (i.e., thirty hours at $20 per hour) would be charged to that service.

[3] Office of Management and Budget, Circular No. A-21, *Cost Principles for Educational Institutions* (2003). This circular also extends the applicability of certain Cost Accounting Standards Board (CASB) rules to institutions of higher education that receive federal funds and requires them to file a CASB disclosure statement.

EXAMPLE *Allocating Cost—Conventional Means*

The Urban Legal Clinic provides assistance to low-income residents of a major city. The clinic's legal staff is divided into two departments (mission centers). One is devoted to criminal matters; the other to civil. Ten attorneys are assigned to the criminal department; six to the civil department. The clinic maintains three support centers: an administrative section, a library, and a secretarial pool.

The clinic is funded in part by a government grant that provides reimbursement on a case-by-case basis. Accordingly, it must determine the cost of each case that it handles.

The clinic initially charges all building occupancy, insurance, and a wide array of miscellaneous costs to the administrative section. It allocates the cost of this section to the two mission centers and the two other support centers. The costs are allocated on two different bases. Costs associated with building occupancy ($100,000) are allocated on the basis of percentage of floor space occupied (excluding the space occupied by the administrative section itself). The remaining administrative costs ($300,000) are allocated on the basis of proportionate share of total employees (excluding the employees of the administrative section).

After allocating the administrative costs to the other cost centers, the clinic allocates the costs of the library and the secretarial pool (including the allocated administrative costs) to the two mission centers. The costs of both service centers are allocated on the same basis—proportionate number of employees (although, of course, different bases could also have been used).

As shown in Table 13-2, the criminal department was allocated $338,281 of the $550,000 of total overhead costs. The civil department was assigned $211,719.

TABLE 13-2

Urban Legal Clinic Allocation of Overhead Costs—Conventional Costing

	Mission Centers		Support Centers			
	Criminal	Civil	Administration	Library	Secretarial	Total
Number of employees	10	6	4	1	3	24
% floor space	30.00%	25.00%	20.00%	15.00%	10.00%	100%
% floor space excluding administration	37.50%	31.25%		18.75%	12.50%	100%
% employees excluding administration	50.00%	30.00%		5.00%	15.00%	100%
% of employees in mission centers	62.50%	37.50%				100%
Number of case hours	15,000	8,000	—	—	—	23,000
Costs incurred			$400,000	$60,000	$90,000	$550,000
Allocation of administrative costs:						
Building occupancy cost (% floor space excluding administration)	$ 37,500	$31,250	(100,000)	18,750	12,500	0
Other administrative costs (% employees excluding administration)	150,000	90,000	(300,000)	15,000	45,000	0
Total overhead costs after allocation of administrative costs	$187,500	$121,250	$ 0	$93,750	$147,500	$550,000
Allocation of library costs (% employees in mission centers)	58,594	35,156		(93,750)		0
Allocation of secretarial costs (% employees in mission centers)	92,187	55,313			(147,500)	0
Total allocated overhead	338,281	211,719	$ 0	$ 0	$ 0	$550,000
Number of case hours	÷15,000	÷8,000				
Overhead per hour	$ 22.55	$ 26.46				

Inasmuch as direct labor (attorney's time) is the key component of a case (the cost object), the department applies overhead to each case based on direct labor hours. The department estimates that throughout the year the ten criminal attorneys will charge a total of 15,000 hours to specific cases; the six civil attorneys will charge only 8,000 hours. Therefore, for each hour that a criminal attorney works on a case the clinic will apply $22.55 in overhead ($338,281 divided by 15,000 hours); for each hour that a civil attorney works on a case it will apply $26.46 ($211,719 divided by 8,000 hours).

Suppose, for example, that a criminal attorney spends ninety hours on Case No. 103. The clinic determines that salary and benefits of the attorney are $43 per hour. Moreover, the attorney has incurred $520 in other costs (such as travel, filing fees, long-distance calls, and supplies) that can be directly traced to the case. The total cost to be charged to the case would be $6,420, computed as follows:

Direct labor (attorney salaries and benefits, 90 hours at $43.00)	$3,870
Other direct costs	520
Allocated overhead (90 hours at $22.55)	2,030
Total cost of case	$6,420

Activity-Based Costing

Under activity-based costing, overhead costs are collected in cost pools. Then, rather than being allocated both to other service departments and to production departments, they are assigned directly to the cost objects.

Each of the overhead cost pools should be homogeneous in that the costs should be driven (influenced) by a common factor. The activity pools can cut across departmental lines, and they can include overhead costs of both mission and service centers.

Once overhead costs are collected in cost pools, they are distributed to the cost objects by a *cost driver*, one for each pool. A cost driver is conceptually similar to an overhead charging rate. However, whereas in practice an overhead charging rate is based on direct labor hours or direct materials, cost drivers are more representative of the factors that influence the amount of overhead costs incurred. The following are examples of cost drivers that might be used to assign various types of overhead costs:

Type of Cost (Cost Pool)	*Cost Driver*
Materials handling	Materials requisitions
Maintenance	Maintenance hours
Depreciation on equipment	Machine hours
Payroll processing	Labor hours
Accounts payable processing	Vouchers purchases

Figure 13-3 contrasts conventional and activity-based costing.

EXAMPLE *Cost Allocation—Activity-Based Costing*

Assume the same facts as in Table 13-2, plus the additional information as to the two mission centers (criminal and civil law) presented in Table 13-3, Part I. The legal clinic collects its overhead costs in three pools (administrative, library, and secretarial),

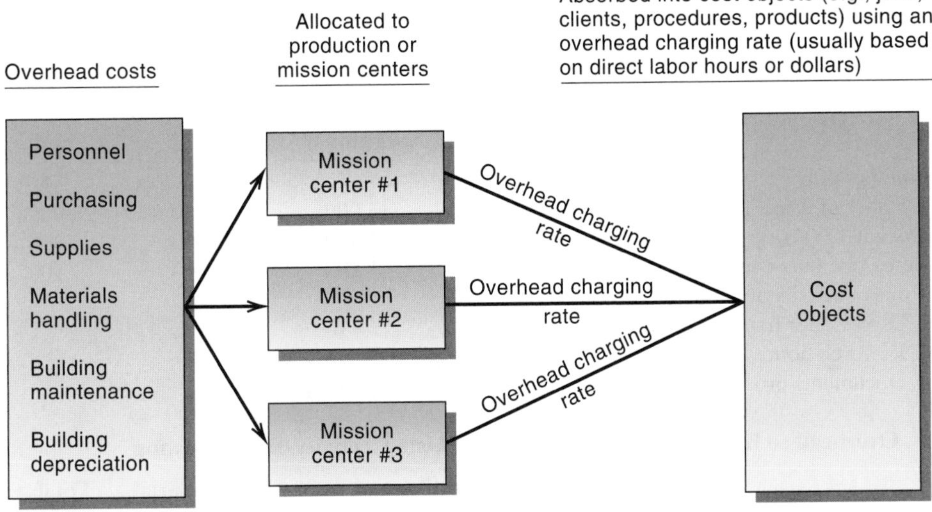

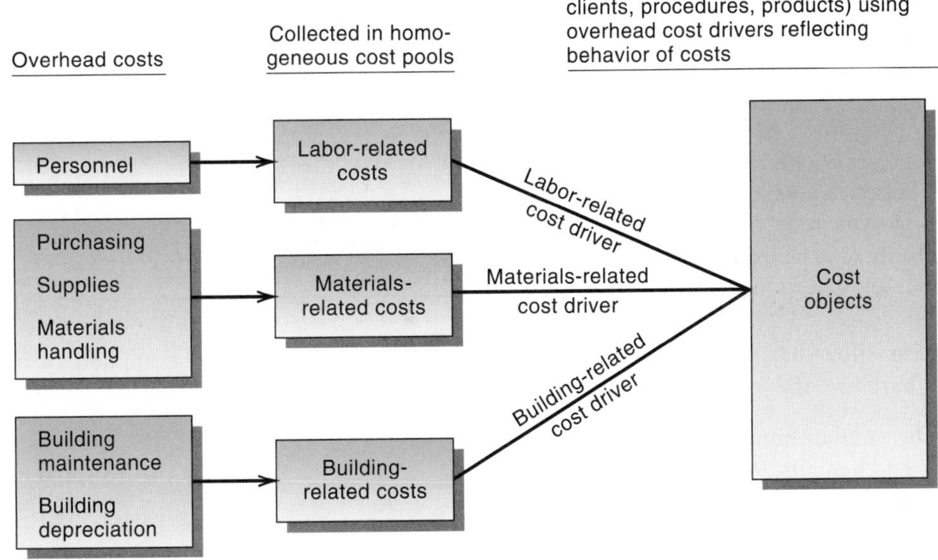

Figure 13-3
Conventional Versus Activity-Based Costing

which happen to coincide with the entity's organizational structure. The clinic selects the following cost drivers to assign these costs to each of its cases:

Cost Pool	*Cost Driver*
Administrative	Direct labor hours
Library	Research hours
Secretarial	Documents processed

Table 13-3, Part II, indicates the costs assigned to each pool, the estimated number of units of activity for a year, and the resultant overhead cost per unit of activity to be applied to each case. It also indicates the units of activity attributable to a particular

TABLE 13-3
Urban Legal Clinic Allocation of Overhead Costs—Activity-Based Costing

I. Additional Information Required for Activity-Based Costing

	Mission Centers		
	Criminal	**Civil**	**Total**
Number of lawyers	10	6	16
Number of direct labor hours	15,000	8,000	23,000
Documents processed for center	4,400	1,400	5,800
Research hours conducted	1,200	300	1,500
Units of activity attributable to case no. 103			
Direct labor hours	90		
Research hours	12		
Documents processed	19		

II. Overhead to Be Assigned to Case No. 103 Using Activity-Based Costing

	Administrative	**Library**	**Secretarial**	**Total**
Costs incurred	$400,000	$60,000	$90,000	
Estimated annual units of activity				
Direct labor hours	÷ 23,000			
Research hours		÷ 1,500		
Documents processed			÷ 5,800	
Cost per unit of activity	$ 17.39	$ 40.00	$ 15.52	
Number of units attributable to case no. 103				
Direct labor hours	× 90			
Research hours		× 12		
Documents processed			× 19	
Overhead to be applied to case no. 103	$ 1,565	$ 480	$ 295	$2,340

case, No. 103, and the amount of overhead that would thereby be applied to it. Therefore, the total to be charged to the case would be $6,730:

Direct labor (attorney salaries and benefits, 90 hours at $43.00)		$3,870
Other direct costs		520
Applied overhead:		
Administrative	$1,565	
Library	480	
Secretarial	295	2,340
Total cost of case		$6,730

Assuming that the estimates incorporated in the overhead charging rate and cost drivers are accurate, both the conventional and the ABC procedures will assure that all overhead costs are assigned to specific cost objects. As is apparent from the examples, however, they will not necessarily distribute the overhead costs among the jobs in the same amounts. Presumably, if the overhead is more strongly influenced by the ABC cost drivers than by the conventional overhead charging rate (the underlying rationale for ABC costing) then the ABC procedures provide the more reliable measure of the resources consumed in providing the goods or services.

The difference in the allocations that result from the two methods may be far from academic. Suppose, that in the example, the legal clinic will be reimbursed for all relevant costs if it wins Case No. 103. If it allocates costs using conventional means then it will be reimbursed $2,030 in overhead costs. If it uses activity-based costing it will be reimbursed $2,340.

HOW SHOULD THE COSTS OF FUND-RAISING ACTIVITIES BE DETERMINED?

As discussed in Chapter 12, contributors, as well as other users of financial statements, want assurance that their donations are being used mainly to support substantive programs and activities rather than merely additional fund-raising or administrative efforts. To be sure, few individuals drop their coins into a charity's canister contingent upon receiving financial statements. However, private foundations, umbrella agencies such the United Way, and major donors almost always demand detailed financial data prior to making a commitment of resources. Moreover, state and local government regulatory authorities established to deter fraud may require that organizations permitted to solicit funds in their jurisdictions furnish information as to how they spend their resources.

Fund-raising activities are often carried out in conjunction with programmatic or administrative activities. Therefore, the costs of the fund-raising activities may not be easily distinguishable from those of the other activities.

Consider, for example the following activities that are intended not only to advance an organization's main mission but also to solicit donations:

- The American Cancer Society takes out newspaper advertisements alerting readers to the seven danger signals of cancer. The ads include a plea for funds, accompanied by a coupon asking for the donor's name, address, and amount of contribution.
- Friends of the Environment conducts a door-to-door campaign seeking signatures on a petition urging a city council not to permit development in a wildlife habitat area. Each person spoken to is asked also to make a financial contribution to aid additional advocacy efforts.
- A hospital mails its annual report, which contains its financial statements and a report on its accomplishments, to trustees, employees, and previous donors. An accompanying letter suggests programs for which additional financial support is needed.
- An organization that seeks to prevent teenage drug abuse conducts a broad-based mail campaign to solicit funds. It includes in each mailing a pamphlet informing teens of ways in which they can "just say no" to their peers.

Each of these situations raises two related questions:

- Should the costs of the activity be apportioned between fund-raising and mission-related programs?
- If so, on what basis should they be apportioned?

In a 1998 Statement of Position (SOP 98-2), *Accounting for Costs of Activities of Not-For-Profit Organizations and State and Local Governmental Entities that Include Fund-Raising*, the AICPA addressed both of these issues.

CRITERIA FOR ALLOCATING A PORTION OF COSTS TO PROGRAM OR MANAGEMENT FUNCTIONS

Left unchecked, many organizations would prefer to assign costs to programmatic rather than to fund-raising efforts. In that way, they would appear to be spending more of their funds fulfilling the purposes for which they were established.

The AICPA directs that not-for-profit organizations classify as fund-raising all costs of activities that include fund-raising as well as programmatic, management, or general functions unless the activities satisfy three broad criteria:

- Purpose
- Audience
- Content

That is, if an activity does satisfy all three criteria, then its costs may be allocated between fund-raising and the other applicable functions. If it does not, then all of its costs must be classified as fund-raising.

Purpose

The purpose criterion is met if the purpose of a joint activity includes accomplishing program or management and general functions. Factors that would indicate such a purpose include:

- The activity calls for specific action by the audience that will help accomplish the entity's mission. For example, if the mission of an organization were to improve individuals' physical health, then an advertisement advising people on specific ways to stop smoking would satisfy the purpose criterion.
- The organization conducts a similar program or management activity separately and on a similar or greater scale. Suppose, for example, an environmental organization takes out a full-page newspaper ad appealing for donations and urging readers to recycle trash. The ad would be consistent with the purpose criterion if the organization ran similar full-page ads that promoted recycling but did not ask for donations.
- Other evidence, such as the measures used to assess the results and accomplishments of the joint activity, the qualifications of the parties carrying it out and organizational mission statements, minutes, or plans make it clear that the activity goes beyond fund-raising.

The purpose criterion is not met if a majority of compensation or fees paid to outside contractors, such as consultants, is based on contributions raised.

Audience

The audience criterion is met if the audience for the materials or activities is selected principally on its need for the program or for its ability to advance program goals in ways other than by financial support. Thus, in the examples presented earlier, the American Cancer Society would satisfy the criterion since its advertisement was directed to a broad segment of society, all the members of which are potential cancer victims. By contrast, the drug abuse organization would not (unless the mailing were specifically targeted at households with teenagers), since most of the recipients of the mailing would unlikely be of the age group toward which the informational pamphlet was aimed.

Content

The content criterion is met if the materials or activities call for specific actions that will help accomplish the entity's mission beyond providing financial support. For example, they might ask the recipients to take actions that would either improve the recipients' own physical, emotional, or spiritual well-being or address a societal need. If the materials or activities are in support of management or general functions, then they should fulfill one or more of the entity's management responsibilities, such as reporting on the organization's accomplishments or financial status.

EXAMPLE *Allocating Charitable Costs*

Facts. The Citizens for Educational Reform conducts a telephone campaign, both to solicit funds and to urge the persons called to write their legislators in favor of increased spending for education. The telephone list was purchased from a fund-raising concern and includes only households with incomes in the top 10 percent of the population.

Conclusion. In the absence of compelling evidence that persons in upper-income households are especially likely to contact their legislators in favor of increased spending for education, the campaign would not satisfy the audience criterion, and hence, all costs of the campaign should be reported as fund-raising costs.

Facts. The Protect our Children Society sends a brochure, along with a request for donations, to all citizens within selected areas of a city that have high crime rates. The brochures recommend ways in which parents can shield their children from criminal activity. The brochures were prepared by an outside consultant whose only compensation will be a percentage of the contributions received.

Conclusion. The mailing does not satisfy the purpose criterion, as the majority of compensation is based on amount of funds raised.

Facts. The Senior Citizens Coalition sends representatives to speak to senior citizens groups about the virtues of physical exercise. After a presentation, the coalition mails to each person that attended a request for a contribution, along with literature advising how to maintain a healthy lifestyle.

Conclusion. The mailing satisfies all three criteria and its costs should be allocated between fund-raising and educational programs.

MEANS OF ALLOCATION

The statement of position allows organizations broad discretion in allocating joint costs between fund-raising and other activities. It specifies only that the method should be "rational and systematic," that it should result in an allocation that is reasonable, and that it should be applied consistently. It further emphasizes that costs need not be allocated when a fund-raising activity is only incidental to a substantive program or management activity (e.g., when a single line in an advertisement otherwise devoted entirely to a programmatic purpose provides an address to which contributions may be sent).

The following three methods are among those that would be considered rational and systematic.

Physical Units Method

The joint costs are allocated on the basis of physical units, such as number of lines, or square inches. Suppose an American Cancer Society newspaper ad costs $10,000. Based on square inches, 80 percent of the ad is directed to information about the disease and 20 percent to an appeal for funds. The organization would allocate $8,000 to its information program and $2,000 to fund-raising.

Relative Direct Costs Method

The joint costs are allocated to each of the component activities based on the identifiable direct costs. Suppose an organization mails to supporters an informational brochure, a flyer asking for a contribution, and a return envelope in which to mail the contribution.

The mission-related brochures cost $90,000, whereas the fund-raising flyers and return envelopes cost $10,000. Direct costs thereby total $100,000, 90 percent of which are directed to informational activities and 10 percent to fund-raising. Common mailing costs, including postage and the outside envelope, cost $15,000. Based on the direct costs, the organization would allocate 90 percent ($13,500) of the common mailing costs to informational activities and 10 percent ($1,500) to fund-raising.

Stand-Alone Costs Method

The joint costs are allocated to each of the components based on what it would have cost to conduct each of the component activities independently. Suppose in the previous example, it would have cost a total of $100,000 to produce the brochures and mail them separately ($90,000 for the brochures and $10,000 for envelopes and postage). It would have cost $18,000 to send and mail the solicitation flyers and return envelopes ($10,000 for the flyers and $8,000 for the outside envelopes and postage). Hence, total costs would have been $118,000. Based on this amount the organization would allocate the $15,000 in common costs as follows:

Informational program	$100,000/118,000 × $15,000 =	$12,712
Fund-raising	$ 18,000/118,000 × $15,000 =	2,288
Total common cost allocated		$15,000

HOW CAN ANALYSES OF VARIANCE BE USED TO CONTROL COSTS AND EVALUATE PERFORMANCE?

Although managers of government and not-for-profit organizations may be aware of the costs incurred in providing goods or services, many are exceedingly lax in compiling cost information in a form that can be used to compare actual costs with budgets and explain the reasons for deviations.

Standard costs and *variable budgets* are at the core of many systems of budgeting, managerial control, and performance evaluation. In private industry they are most commonly associated with manufacturing operations, but they have been adapted, with equal success, to clerical, materials handling, and other support activities. However, they are no less relevant to government and not-for-profit organizations.

As illustrated in the example to follow, the analysis of variances—differences between actual costs incurred and standard costs—is the key not only to identifying less (or greater) than par performance, but to understanding the reasons for it and the particular units that are responsible for it. In this particular example, for instance, the above par performance of one department reporting a favorable variance was attributable not to its own efficiencies but to factors within the control of another department to which it provides services.

A standard cost is a planned or allowable cost per unit of either input or output. Standard costs not only facilitate budgeting, but provide a basis for assessing performance and taking corrective actions, if warranted. Standards can represent ideal levels of performance (goals the organization would like to attain) or merely reasonable expectations based on past performance.

EXAMPLE *Standard Costs*

The College Assistance Association is dedicated to helping low-income high school students get information about college scholarships and loans and apply for them. It also teaches their parents to manage better their finances so as to be able to contribute to their children's college education.

The association fulfills its mission mainly through its counseling service. Students and their parents who avail themselves of the organization's services meet with a counselor for approximately an hour and a half. On the basis of this meeting, the counselor, with the aid of the association's support staff, prepares a written report outlining key recommendations.

In a typical month the association serves 250 clients. Based on both past experience and cost constraints, the association has established a standard time of two hours per client for a counselor's interview and written report. The standard compensation cost per counselor, including benefits, is $20 per hour. However, the actual compensation cost may vary, since not all counselors are paid at the same rate. On average, the counselors collectively provide 500 hours of service per month at a total standard direct cost of $10,000.

The counselors are supported by an administrative staff that establishes appointments and assists in preparing the written reports. The association has determined that its standard fixed administrative costs (including building occupancy costs) are $4,000 per month. In addition, it has found that some overhead costs vary with the number of direct labor (counselor) hours. It has calculated these costs to be $4 per direct labor hour. Hence, it assigns overhead to each client served at a total rate of $12 per direct labor hour:

Fixed administrative overhead cost	$4,000
Variable administrative overhead (500 hours per month at $4)	2,000
Total administrative overhead costs	$6,000
Number of direct labor (counselor) hours per month	÷ 500
Overhead per direct labor hour	$ 12

Thus, standard overhead is $24 per client (2 direct labor hours at $12) and the total standard cost per client is $64:

Direct labor (counselor) costs (2 hours at $20)	$40
Administrative (overhead) costs (2 hours at $12)	24
Total standard cost per client	$64

In a month that the association serves the usual 250 clients, its expected costs would be $16,000 (250 clients at $64).

In the month of June the association served only 220 clients, thirty fewer than normal. The counselors charged 470 hours and actual costs were $14,950:

Direct labor (counselors)		
400 hours at $20	$8,000	
70 hours at $15	1,050	$ 9,050
Overhead		
Fixed	$4,100	
Variable	1,800	5,900
Total actual costs for June		$14,950

Cost per client served was therefore $67.95 ($14,950 divided by 220 clients), $3.95 per client greater than standard. By itself, the magnitude of the variance, however, provides no insight into its significance or the reasons for it.

Direct Labor Usage and Rate Variance

Actual direct labor for the month was, as shown above, $9,050. Standard for 220 clients is $8,800 (220 clients at 2 hours per client at $20 per hour). Hence, direct labor costs were $250 greater than standard.

The direct labor usage (efficiency) and rate variances help explain whether and why direct labor varied from standard. The direct labor *usage* variance focuses on the amount of labor used, assuming that the labor was compensated for at standard rates. Thus:

Direct labor usage (efficiency) variance = (actual labor hours used − standard labor used) × standard wage rate

For June (U = Unfavorable; F = Favorable):

Actual labor hours used	470
Standard labor hours for actual output (220 clients at 2 hours)	440
Excess hours used	30
Standard wage rate per hour	×$ 20
Labor efficiency variance	$600U

The direct labor *rate* variance keys in on the extra costs incurred (or the costs saved) because the actual hours used were compensated at more or less than standard. Thus:

Direct labor rate variance = (actual rate − standard rate) × actual number of hours

Thus:

Actual rate ($9,050 divided by 470 hours)	$19.2553
Standard rate	20.0000
Excess of standard rate over actual rate	$ 0.7447
Actual number of hours	× 470
Labor rate variance	$ 350F

The two variances combined explain the $250 excess of actual over standard cost. The variances clarify that the association was "inefficient" in that it used an excessive number of hours to serve its clients and suggest that a possible cause for the excessive hours was that it employed less experienced (or at least less compensated) personnel.

In governments and not-for-profit organizations, the direct labor variances must be interpreted more guardedly than in a manufacturing concern. In a manufacturing concern the output—the product—is likely to be precisely defined. It either meets specifications or it does not. Products that do not meet the specifications are excluded from the count of number of units produced. In governments and not-for-profits, however, each unit of output, especially if it is a unit of service, may differ qualitatively from others. Thus, the June labor usage variance may be high because the counselors dealt with an unusually high number of especially difficult cases or because they elected to spend more time with their clients, thereby enhancing the quality of service to them.

Overhead Variances

Actual administrative overhead for the month was only $5,900 ($4,100 fixed and $1,800 variable), whereas standard is $6,000. Three overhead variances—the flexible budget variance, the overhead efficiency variance, and the overhead volume variance—shed light on the reasons for the $100 of apparent savings.

The key to understanding—and thereby controlling—overhead is a **flexible budget.** A flexible budget indicates the expected overhead costs that should be incurred at various levels of activity. It explicitly distinguishes between the fixed and the variable portions of overhead. The variable overhead (administrative costs) of the College Assistance Association varies with the number of counselor hours (direct labor). Its flexible budget for overhead would reflect total overhead costs for several levels of input, four of which are as follows:

	Direct Labor Hours			
	440	470	480	Normal 500
Fixed overhead	$4,000	$4,000	$4,000	$4,000
Variable overhead ($4 per direct labor hour)	1,760	1,880	1,920	2,000
Total overhead	$5,760	$5,880	$5,920	$6,000

In June the counselors charged 470 hours. As indicated in the schedule, budgeted overhead for that level is $5,880. Inasmuch as the association incurred $5,900 in administrative costs, it exceeded its flexible budget by $20 (an unfavorable *flexible budget variance*):

	Fixed Overhead	Variable Overhead	Total
Actual costs	$4,100	$1,800	$5,900
Budgeted per flexible budget (470 counselor hours)	4,000	1,880	5,880
Flexible budget variance	$ 100U	$ 80F	$ 20U

The flexible budget variance compares actual overhead with overhead per the flexible budget. The flexible budget takes into account the factors that drive variable overhead. The association's unfavorable variance indicates that costs were greater than budgeted for the actual level of activity. But it does not, by itself, pinpoint responsibility for the variance or even suggest that the variance was within the control of anyone within the association. Additional investigation would be required to determine whether it could be ascribed to inefficiencies (e.g., low productivity) or factors beyond the association's control (e.g., hot weather that boosted air conditioning costs).

The counselors charged 470 hours, but they served only 220 clients. Based on the standard of two hours per client, they should have charged only 440 hours. Inasmuch as variable overhead is a function of direct labor, their extra hours contributed to additional overhead charges. The *overhead efficiency variance* measures the additional overhead costs attributable to the inefficiency in the use of the factor that influences variable overhead. It compares the budgeted overhead costs (per the flexible budget) for the actual input (i.e., direct labor hours) with the budgeted overhead costs for the standard input. Thus:

	Fixed Overhead	Variable Overhead	Total
Budgeted per flexible budget for actual input (470 counselor hours)	$4,000	$1,880	$5,880
Budgeted per flexible budget for standard input (440 counselor hours)	4,000	1,760	5,760
Overhead efficiency variance	$ 0	$ 120U	$ 120U

In June, the counselors served only 220 clients compared with the expected 250 clients. Had they operated at standard efficiency, 220 clients should have required 440 direct labor hours, as opposed to 500 hours had they served 250 clients. Thus, per the flexible budget they should have incurred $240 less costs—that is, the organization had a favorable *volume variance* of $240:

	Fixed Overhead	Variable Overhead	Total
Budgeted per flexible budget for standard input (440 counselor hours)	$4,000	$1,760	$5,760
Budgeted per flexible budget for normal volume of 250 clients (500 counselor hours)	4,000	2,000	6,000
Overhead volume variance	$ 0	$ 240F	$ 240F

The three overhead variances combined account for the total difference between actual and standard overhead at normal volume. They make clear that overall administrative costs were $100 less than standard mainly because the counselors served thirty fewer clients. In fact, had both the counselors and the administrative departments been operating "efficiently," then administrative costs should have been $240 less instead of merely $100 less. However, the counselors spent thirty hours more than standard in serving clients, thereby requiring additional administrative services and causing administrative costs to increase by $120. Further, the administrative department itself incurred $20 more in costs than were budgeted for the services it actually provided. Thus:

Overhead volume variance attributable to fewer than normal clients served by counselors	$ 240F
Overhead efficiency variance attributable to counselors' use of more direct labor hours than standard for the actual number of clients served	120U
Flexible budget variance attributable to greater than standard amount of costs incurred by administrative staff in providing actual amount of service	20U
Net overhead variance	$100F

In recent years many governments and not-for-profits have adopted an activity based costing system. By contrast, however, few carry out the type of variance analysis illustrated here. That is unfortunate. If this type of analysis is appropriate for businesses, then it is no less suitable for governments and not-for-profits when they carry out similar kinds of activities.

SUMMARY

Governments, other not-for-profits, and businesses are typically organized into revenue and cost centers. Their managerial decisions should focus on incremental costs (i.e., those that differ if one alternative is chosen instead of another) because only future receipts and disbursements can be affected by a decision.

Variable costs increase proportionately to changes in volume, whereas fixed costs remain the same. Costs are not intrinsically fixed or variable; they are fixed or variable only within the range that is relevant to the decision at hand. Despite widespread use, the average cost of goods or services is an inadequate measure for most cost-based decisions.

Sunk costs are irrelevant to management decisions. They have already been incurred and have no bearing on the future. Similarly, allocated costs are of concern to managers mainly to the extent that they will differ in total among the decision options. They are irrelevant if only the distribution of the costs among organizational subunits will change.

Contracting out, or outsourcing, can have advantages: efficiencies and lower costs that are associated with competition and specialization, innovation, and enhanced opportunities for employee advancement. Nevertheless, the decision to contract out involves fiscal complexities requiring estimates and assumptions and nonfiscal issues, such as impact on employee and organizational morale and loss of control.

Businesses establish prices to maximize net revenues. Governments and other not-for-profits may have additional objectives, such as rationing output, allocating burdens, providing demand signals, and regulating demand.

Information about full costs helps managers compare goods and services and establish priorities among them. Full costs include direct and overhead costs. There are two approaches to allocating overhead. Under the conventional approach, costs of service centers (overhead costs) are allocated among the various mission (operating) centers, combined with the mission centers' own overhead costs and absorbed in the cost object (based on an overhead charging rate). Under activity-based costing, overhead costs are collected in cost pools (in which costs are influenced by a common factor) that can include the overhead costs of both service and mission centers. The overhead costs are then assigned directly to the cost objects by a cost driver, one for each pool.

Not-for-profit organizations face the problem of how to allocate common costs of fund-raising and program and administrative activities. The AICPA's three general criteria for concluding that a bona fide program or management function has been conducted involve purpose, audience, and content.

Analysis of variance, the differences between actual costs incurred and standard costs, help organizations to understand better the reason for cost overruns and to target responsibility for them.

EXERCISE FOR REVIEW AND SELF-STUDY

The Permits Division of a state's Land Commission processes, on average, 500 permits per month. Each permit takes approximately two hours to complete. The employees who work on the permits are paid on average $22 per hour, including benefits.

The Permits Division is supported by an Administrative Center, which also serves other divisions of the Land Commission. The center has determined that it incurs fixed costs of $20,000 per month and additional costs that vary with the direct labor hours of the divisions to which it provides service. It estimates these variable costs to be $3 per hour. In a typical month it provides service to divisions that accumulate a total of 4,000 direct labor hours. Accordingly, it charges the divisions that it serves $8 for each of their direct labor hours:

Fixed costs	$20,000
Variable costs (4,000 d.l.hrs. at $3)	12,000
Total administrative center costs	$32,000
Estimated number of d.l.hrs. per month	÷ 4,000
Overhead charging rate	$ 8 per d.l.hr.

The standard costs per permit processed by the Permits Division is therefore $60:

Direct labor (2 d.l.hrs. at $22)	$44
Overhead charged by administrative center (2 d.l.hrs at $8)	16
Total standard cost per permit	$60

In the month of April, the Permits Division processed 600 documents. Its staff worked 1,150 direct labor hours and were paid compensation of $27,600, an average of $24 per hour. In addition, the division was charged $9,200 by the Administrative Center (1,150 direct labor hours at $8). Its total costs for the month were therefore $36,800.

The Administrative Center incurred $33,300 in costs. The divisions that it served worked a total of 4,150 direct labor hours. The 150 hours above normal were attributable entirely to the Permits Division.

1. How much in direct labor costs should the Permits Division have incurred to process the 600 permits? Explain the reason for the deviation.
2. How much overhead should the Administrative Center have budgeted for 4,150 hours per a flexible budget? By how much did the Administrative Center exceed this amount?
3. How much should the Administrative Center have budgeted for 4,200 direct labor hours—the total direct labor hours that all the divisions that it serves would have used assuming the Permits Division used the standard 1,200 direct labor hours rather than the 1,150 hours—to process 600 permits? How much did the Administrative Center save because of the efficiency of the Permits Division in processing the permits with only 1,150 direct labor hours?
4. How many additional direct labor hours should the Permits division have been required to work to process 600 permits rather than the normal 500 permits? How much

in additional variable costs should these additional hours have caused the Administrative Center to incur?

5. As just indicated, the Administrative Center budgets $32,000 for a normal month in which 500 permits are processed. In the month of April it incurred $33,300. Do the three overhead variances—volume, efficiency, and flexible budget—account for the entire difference of $1,300?
6. Suppose that a private firm offers to process permits at a cost of $50 per permit. The manager of the Administrative Center estimates that if the offer were accepted, the Center could reduce its fixed costs by $1,000 per month (net of additional costs to administer the contract) and its variable costs by $3 per direct labor hour. Assuming that the Permits Division expects to process 500 permits per month, should the state accept the offer?
7. Suppose the State wants to charge permit applicants just enough "to cover its costs." What is the minimum that it should charge? What is the maximum?

QUESTIONS FOR REVIEW AND DISCUSSION

1. A division head automatically budgets the same amount for fixed costs each month, noting, with seemingly sound logic, that fixed costs are by definition fixed and therefore remain constant. Is this approach reasonable?
2. Why is average cost not relevant for most management decisions?
3. In reality both fixed cost curves and variable cost curves have a similar shape—that of a flight of stairs. Do you agree? If so, what is the difference between the two types of costs?
4. "Obviously, sunk costs need not be taken into account in deciding whether to replace an old machine with a new. But depreciation is not a sunk cost; it is an ongoing cost, just like wages and materials, and therefore too important to be omitted from the decision analysis." Do you agree?
5. A not-for-profit has decided to contract out its food service to an independent catering company. Based on a detailed cost analysis, it calculates that it will save several thousands of dollars over the three-year period of the initial contract with the caterer. What pitfalls do you see in restricting the analysis to only the period covered by the initial contract?
6. The decision of a government to contract out an activity cannot be based exclusively on the cash flows directly associated with that activity or the amount to be paid to the contractor. Indicate three "nonfinancial" (or factors not involving direct cash flows) that should be given consideration.
7. Specify three purposes that user charges serve when imposed by either governments or other not-for-profits.
8. Why is it especially important that not-for-profits dependent on contracts or grants from outside parties develop defensible bases for allocating overhead to the various programs and activities that they conduct?
9. In what significant ways do conventional and ABC cost allocation schemes differ?
10. What special abuse does the AICPA address in its statement of position on the allocation of fund-raising costs? What general criteria does it establish as to when common costs of materials and activities that include a fund-raising appeal can be allocated to programmatic, rather than fund-raising, activities?
11. Why are unfavorable overhead efficiency variances and volume variances unlikely to be the fault of the departments that actually provide the services categorized as overhead?

EXERCISES

13-1

1. For most governments and not-for-profits the costs of heating and air conditioning administrative buildings would most probably be classified as
   a. Direct costs
   b. Variable costs
   c. Fixed costs
   d. Opportunity costs
2. For a not-for-profit medical clinic the costs of nurses' salaries would most probably be classified as
   a. Fixed
   b. Variable
   c. Fixed or variable, depending on the relevant range
   d. Overhead or direct, depending on the relevant range
3. When analysts are assessing whether to replace a new machine with an old one, they should consider annual depreciation on the old machine
   a. A sunk cost and thereby not relevant to the analysis
   b. A direct cost, and thereby one that should be discounted, along with other cash and non-cash expenses
   c. An incremental cost and thereby one to be taken into account only to the extent that it exceeds or is less than depreciation on the new machine

d. A fixed cost and thereby one that is not relevant to the analysis

4. In the decision as to whether to contract out the maintenance of a university's athletic facilities, a service currently being performed by a maintenance department that also cares for both academic and administrative facilities, the salaries of the clerical staff of the maintenance department should be
   a. Reallocated among each of the various other facilities that will continue to be served by the maintenance department
   b. Taken into account only if they will be changed as a result of the decision
   c. Taken into account only if they are considered a direct rather than an overhead cost
   d. Not taken into account inasmuch as clerical salaries are classified as fixed overhead

5. A major European city requires all vehicles that enter its downtown area to purchase a special inner-city driving permit. The primary purpose in requiring the permit and imposing the charge for it is most likely to:
   a. To provide revenue
   b. To ration output
   c. To provide demand signals
   d. To allocate operating cost burdens

6. Full cost
   a. Is irrelevant for virtually all management decisions
   b. Is the most relevant measure of cost for most contracting-out decisions
   c. Excludes fixed overhead
   d. May be indicative of long-term incremental cost

7. Activity-based costing
   a. Is most appropriate for nonmanufacturing activities, such as those carried out by most governments and not-for-profits
   b. Requires that all overhead costs be collected in a common pool and assigned to activities by way of an overhead charging rate
   c. Requires that overhead costs be collected in cost pools and distributed to cost objects by way of cost drivers, one for each cost pool
   d. Is based on the premise that most overhead costs vary primarily with direct labor hours

8. All costs of activities that have a fund-raising component must be classified as fund-raising costs unless it can be demonstrated that they satisfy the criteria dealing with all of the following except
   a. Purpose
   b. Audience
   c. Content
   d. Fiscal viability

9. In allocating joint costs between fund-raising and other activities, a not-for-profit could use all of the following methods except
   a. Physical units
   b. Relative direct cost
   c. Straight-line
   d. Stand-alone costs

10. A negative flexible budget overhead variance would most likely be caused by
   a. Inefficient use of direct labor
   b. Greater than expected number of clients served or other measure of volume
   c. Inefficiencies in the departments responsible for overhead costs
   d. Inefficiencies in the use of the factors that influence variable overhead

11. A negative volume variance would most likely be caused by
   a. Inefficient use of direct labor
   b. Greater than expected number of clients served or other measure of volume
   c. Inefficiencies in the departments responsible for overhead costs
   d. Inefficiencies in the use of the factors that influence variable overhead

12. A negative overhead efficiency variance would most likely be caused by
   a. Inefficient use of direct labor
   b. Greater than expected number of clients served or other measure of volume
   c. Inefficiencies in the departments responsible for overhead costs
   d. Inefficiencies in the use of the factors that influence variable overhead

13-2

The advantages of outsourcing cannot be assessed on the basis of "full" cost.

A state manufactures its own road signs. In a recent year it produced 27,000 signs. Based on the following data, average cost per sign was $3,000:

Direct materials	$27,200,000
Direct labor	20,600,000
Manufacturing overhead:	
Indirect labor	13,500,000
Depreciation	12,800,000
Plant manager & staff	900,000
Pension expense	2,000,000
Costs allocated from other departments	4,000,000
Total costs	$81,000,000
Number of signs	÷ 27,000
Cost per sign	$ 3,000

An independent sign manufacturer has offered to produce the signs for an average of $2,400 per sign.

Were the state to accept the offer:

- It would have to place selected direct-labor employees in other state jobs. Their wages, $2 million, would be approximately $800,000 more than the state would otherwise have to pay to fill those positions.

- Owing to early retirement provisions, it would be able to reduce its pension costs by only $1.5 million per year.
- None of the costs allocated from other departments could be reduced.

1. Which of the costs included in the above computation of average cost are relevant to the state's decision to accept the contract in that they would no longer be incurred? Assume that even if the state were not to accept the offer, it has no plans to replace plant and equipment in the foreseeable future.
2. Based on the limited amount of data, should the state accept the contract? Explain.
3. Why did you include or exclude depreciation expense in your list of relevant costs? Explain. How does that decision bias your analysis?

13-3

Deviations from average cost may not indicate either efficiencies or inefficiencies.

The Children's Health Center serves all residents of Harris County. The center primarily provides immunizations to infant children. During a normal month it serves approximately 450 patients.

Based on prior experience, the center has established a standard time of thirty minutes of medical staff time for each patient visit. The medical staff of the center generally spend a cumulative total of 225 hours per month serving patients. Their average wage or salary rate is $45 per hour. Hence, the standard direct medical staff cost is $10,125 per month (225 hours at $45).

The center has determined that standard fixed administrative costs are $9,000 per month. In addition, some of the administrative costs vary with the number of hours worked by the medical staff. These have been calculated at $10 per direct medical staff hour.

For a typical month, in which the center serves 450 patients using 225 hours of direct medical staff time, total administrative costs are therefore $50 per direct medical staff hour:

Fixed administrative overhead	$ 9,000
Variable administrative overhead (225 hours at $10)	2,250
Total administrative costs	$11,250
Number of direct medical staff hours	÷ 225 hrs
Overhead per direct labor hour	$50.00

1. Based on the data presented, what should be the average cost of serving each patient?
2. Suppose that in a particular month, the center served 500 patients using 260 staff hours. All personnel were paid at the standard rate per hour of $45, so total direct medical costs were $11,700. Total administrative costs were $10,900. Hence, total costs were $22,600 and average cost per patient was $45.20.
   a. How much in additional direct medical staff costs can be attributed to the inefficiency of the medical staff (that is, to the above standard number of hours required to serve the 500 patients) as opposed to the additional number of hours required to serve more than the normal number of patients?
   b. How much less administrative overhead did the center actually incur than what it would expect to incur in a normal month (in which it serves 450 patients)?
   c. How much administrative overhead should the center have incurred for the 260 direct medical staff hours actually used? What is the difference between the actual overhead and what it should have incurred (a flexible budget variance)?
   d. How much administrative overhead should the center have incurred for 250 direct medical staff hours—the standard number of hours to serve 500 patients? What is the difference between what it should have incurred for 260 direct medical staff hours and what it should have incurred for 250 hours (an overhead efficiency variance)?
   e. How much administrative overhead should the center have incurred for a normal volume of 450 patients (225 medical staff hours)? What is the difference between what it should have incurred for 250 hours and what it should have incurred for a normal volume of 450 patients (an overhead volume variance)?
   f. Do the three elements of the administrative overhead variance as just computed sum to the total administrative overhead variance computed in question b?
3. Comment on why average cost is of little use for purposes of pinpointing operational efficiencies or inefficiencies.

13-4

Average costs seldom facilitate appropriate decisions.

Westview College maintains a repair and maintenance division that provides services to other divisions of the college on a cost-reimbursement basis.

The division's annual expenditure budget is $1 million. Approximately 30 percent of its costs ($300,000) are fixed; the balance of $700,000 are variable—$35 per service hour provided. Based on approximately 20,000 hours of service that it provides in a typical year, the fixed costs are $15 per hour. Accordingly it bills at a rate of $50 per hour.

The college permits divisions a choice of obtaining needed services from the repair and maintenance division or from private vendors.

1. Assuming that the policy of the division is to recover all costs, what would be the division's hourly rate for providing service?
2. The food service division needs to have equipment installed. An outside repair firm has agreed to do the job for $4,700 (plus parts and other out-of-pocket costs). The repair and maintenance division has estimated that

the work will require 100 hours, and has therefore bid $5,000 (plus parts and other out-of-pocket costs).

a. What would be the savings to the food service division if it accepted the bid from the outside repair firm?

b. What would be the cost or savings to the college as a whole if the food service division accepted the bid of the outside firm?

3. Suppose that in a typical year the repair and maintenance division provides 4,000 of its 20,000 hours of service to the food service division. The food service division decides that in the future it will "outsource" all of its repair and maintenance needs. As a consequence the repair and maintenance division will have to reduce to 16,000 the number of hours its provides.

a. What will be the impact on the rate that it charges to other divisions of the college, assuming that the repair and maintenance division is unable to reduce its fixed costs?

b. What will be the most likely impact on the decisions of the other divisions of the college as to whether to continue to deal with the repair and maintenance division or to obtain service from outside providers?

13-5

Financial reporting losses are not necessarily economic losses.

The Independent Accountants Association, a not-for-profit organization, has occupied its office building for many years. The building, which was purchased for $4 million, currently has a book value (cost less accumulated depreciation) of $1.8 million.

The association needs more space for the next five years. After that, it plans to sell whatever property it owns in its current city and relocate to another part of the country.

It is considering two options. First, it could keep its current building and rent space in an adjoining building for $200,000 per year for the next five years. It estimates that in five years it would be able to sell its current building for $1 million.

Second, it could sell its current building immediately. It has been offered $1.1 million. It would then purchase a new, more spacious building for $2.5 million. It estimates that the new building would retain its value for the next five years and could be sold then for same $2.5 million.

The association uses an annual discount rate of 8 percent to evaluate all capital investment proposals involving the time value of money.

For some members of the association the decision is clear. They would reject the second option in favor of the first inasmuch as the second would require that the association recognize an immediate loss of $700,000 that would not be compensated for with future gains or savings.

1. Are the members correct in asserting that the association would have to recognize an immediate loss of $700,000? Prepare the required journal entry to record the sale of the building if the association selected the second option.

2. Do you agree that the association should select the first option? Prepare an analysis in which you show which of the two options is the more financially favorable.

13-6

Activity-based costing may result in different overhead allocations than conventional costing.

The University of the Hills computer repair and service division is divided into two mission departments—hardware and software—plus an administrative department. In the past, using conventional costing, the department first allocated the costs of the administrative department to each of the mission departments based on billable labor hours. Then it assigned the allocated administrative costs to the individual jobs—also on the basis of billable labor hours. Recently, however, it switched to activity-based costing. It now collects all administrative (i.e., overhead) costs in three pools and applies them to the cost objects (individual jobs) using appropriate cost drivers. The three pools and the cost drivers are as follows:

Pool	*Cost Driver*
Payroll and general overhead (e.g., space, utilities, maintenance)	Billable labor hours
Purchasing and materials handling	Materials requisitions
Accounting and billing	Number of jobs

The following data relate to the month of November:

	Hardware	*Software*	*Total*
Billable labor hours	1,360	1,040	2,400
Number of jobs	340	300	640
Number of requisitions	360	80	440

Total administrative overhead for the month was collected in cost pools as follows:

Payroll and general	$14,000
Purchasing and materials handling	4,000
Accounting and billing	2,000
Total administrative overhead	$20,000

Job #22, undertaken in November, involved the installation of a new hard drive and miscellaneous other repairs to a computer. A single job, it required four billable hours of labor and three materials requisitions. Direct labor, billed at $30 per hour, was therefore $120; direct materials were $620.

1. Suppose that under conventional costing, the computer and repair service allocated the entire $20,000 in administrative costs to the two mission departments based on billable labor hours. The departments then assigned both the allocated overhead and their own overhead to individual jobs based on billable labor hours. What would be the cost assigned to Job #22?

2. What would be the cost of Job #22 under the new ABC costing procedures?

PROBLEMS

13-1

Variable costs may not always be as variable as they appear.

The Commuter Division of the Metropolitan Transit System (MTS) operates a commuter bus service between a suburban community and the downtown area of a major city.

The division currently operates ten buses, each of which has a practical capacity of 300 passengers (rides per day). As the number of riders increases, the division can schedule more frequent service. However, each time the number of passengers exceeds the maximum capacity of 300, another bus must be added. The additional bus must be scheduled for the same number of daily trips as the others.

The division currently provides service for approximately 2,900 passengers per day. Inasmuch as the division does not operate on weekends or holidays, it bases all monthly calculations on twenty-two operating days per month. Thus the division currently provides 63,800 (2,900 × 22) rides per month.

The division leases, rather than purchases, its buses. Operating costs for a recent month were as follows:

Monthly costs per bus

Lease charges	$ 2,000
Wages of drivers	4,000
Fuel costs	2,400
Variable maintenance and miscellaneous costs	800
Total costs per bus	$ 9,200
Number of buses	× 10
Total direct costs of operating buses	$ 92,000
Administration, general, and fixed maintenance costs	32,000
Total monthly costs	$124,000

The fare for each ride is $2.75; monthly revenues are $175,450 (63,800 rides at $2.75).

1. The division manager anticipates that ridership will increase by 3 percent. He estimated that earnings (revenues less expenses) will also increase by 3 percent. Do you agree? If not, indicate the amount by which you believe earnings will increase.
2. The division's financial manager, only slightly more knowledgeable about accounting, believes that ridership will increase by 5 percent. She has determined that earnings will increase by the difference between the additional revenue and the additional variable costs. She has computed variable costs to be $92,000 divided by average monthly ridership of 63,800—that is $1.44 per rider. Do you agree with her computations? If not, determine the amount by which you believe earnings will change.
3. In light of your computations, do you believe that the division should make an effort to increase ridership by 5 percent, or would it be better off by attempting to restrict ridership to its current level?

13-2

Seemingly unprofitable operations may be worth continuing.

The dean of a leading college of business (a former professor of marketing) has asked a joint student-faculty committee to advise him as to whether to discontinue the school's food service. The food service, which provides sandwiches, salads, snacks, and beverages, is located in a corner of a large student lounge and study area. If the service were discontinued, its space would be used to expand the lounge.

The dean's request to the committee was motivated by the following monthly sales and cost data indicating that the service is a drain on business school finances:

Sales	$56,000
Cost of food and supplies	42,000
Gross margin	$14,000
Other costs	
Wages and salaries	$ 8,200
Depreciation of equipment	1,200
Repairs and maintenance	3,000
Occupancy costs	2,700
Other overhead	1,500
Total other costs	$16,600
Net profit (loss)	$(2,600)

Upon investigation, the committee learned that the occupancy costs were allocated on the basis of square feet. As best they were able to determine, the only savings in occupancy costs were the service to be discontinued would be $400 per month in electricity. "Other overhead" represents an arbitrary assignment of accounting and administrative costs, none of which would clearly be saved if the service were discontinued.

The committee also learned that the food service estimates it will spend, on average, $2,000 per month to replace existing equipment. Were the existing equipment to be sold today, it would yield only a negligible amount.

1. Based on the available data, and taking into account only financial considerations, do you think the food service should be discontinued? Justify your response.
2. Suppose, instead, that the equipment could be sold today for $60,000. The dean has indicated that the funds would be invested in an account that would earn

6 percent interest per year. How would the sale of equipment affect your analysis? Explain.

13-3

Universities sometimes adopt overhead policies that are especially arbitrary and may be dysfunctional.

Wertimer University, like almost all major research universities, permits its component academic departments, bureaus, and research institutes to enter into research contracts with government agencies, corporations, and other outside organizations. Out of the negotiated price, the university unit must pay all direct costs pertaining to the project for which it contracts. In addition, however, the university charges as overhead 60 percent of the direct wage and salary costs that will be incurred in fulfilling the contract.

The university maintains an office of "contract research," the mission of which is to assist the academic departments, bureaus, and research institutes in obtaining and administering contracts. The cost of maintaining the office is approximately $200,000 per year. For the most part, however, the overhead charged to the units undertaking contract research represents costs that are incurred to support the traditional academic functions of the university—buildings and grounds, maintenance, libraries, laboratories, computer facilities, administration, and so on. These costs are fixed; they cannot be identified with any single contract research project.

Most contracts, particularly those with government agencies, are reimbursement-type agreements. A unit gets reimbursed for all costs, including overhead, that it incurs, but earns no "profit." Some contracts, however, are for a negotiated amount that provides for payment in excess of costs incurred. When the unit performing the research enters into such a contract it is permitted to retain the excess of revenues over costs and use it to supplement university budget allocations. The primary motivation for conducting contract research is that it provides funding for projects that faculty and research associates want to conduct but that otherwise would have no financial support.

In recent years the contract value of sponsored research was $40 million annually.

Critically evaluate the university's policy of imposing a charge for overhead.

1. What do you think are the primary purposes of the charge?
2. What effect do you think it has on the motivation of the various units to obtain research contracts?
3. How do you think the 60 percent charge was arrived at?
4. What objections might be raised to the policy?
5. What alternatives to the policy merit consideration?

13-4

Decisions to contract out are often far more complex than they appear.

The National Association of Professional Accountants (NAPA) operates a printing department that prints the professional pronouncements, brochures, catalogs, and most other printed matter that it distributes to members. The NAPA is deliberating whether to discontinue the operation and contract with independent printers for its requirements. The change would be effective January 1, 2005.

The association has compiled the following data with respect to its printing department:

Direct labor	$180,000
Paper and supplies	620,000
Repair and maintenance	30,000
Depreciation of equipment	50,000
Other costs (all cash)	40,000
Allocation of overhead	70,000
Total operating costs	$990,000

- The equipment could be sold today for $200,000. Although the printing department was not planning on acquiring new equipment or replacing existing equipment for several years, the equipment would have to be overhauled in December 2006 at a cost of $50,000.
- The space occupied by the printing department could be converted into office space, thereby saving NAPA $15,000 in rental costs. No other overhead costs would be reduced if the printing operations were discontinued.
- NAPA estimates that the cost of satisfying its printing requirements with independent printers would be approximately $850,000 per year. In addition, the association would have to hire an additional media specialist to make arrangements with and work with the independent printers. The cost would be $50,000 per year.
- The association uses a discount rate of 6 percent to make all capital budgeting and comparable decisions.

1. Should NAPA contract out its printing operations as of January 1, 2005? Assume that the association has a three-year time horizon—i.e., through December 31, 2007. For convenience, assume that all cash flows (except those relating to the initial sale of equipment) occur at year-end.
2. Suppose alternatively that the printing department plans to purchase new equipment at the end of 2006 and that the equipment would have a useful life of seven years. How would that affect your analysis?
3. Suppose you were asked to make the decision as to whether to discontinue the printing operation. What other factors would you want to take into account, or what other questions would you raise?

13-5

A mission center must share blame for budget variances in a service center.

The Tri-County Blood Center, a not-for-profit organization that collects and processes donated blood, has several operating units and overhead cost pools.

Per standards established by the collection department, a technician should be able to draw blood from three donors per hour. During a typical month, the five technicians of the department work a total of 880 direct labor hours and draw 2,640 pints of blood. Technicians are paid at the rate of $12 per hour. Hence, the typical payroll for a month is $10,560.

The overhead costs accumulated in a pool of payroll-related costs, such as benefits and insurance, vary with the direct labor *dollars* of the mission centers that it serves. The accountant in charge of the pool has determined that in an average month it incurs fixed costs of $5,000 and variable costs of $0.15 per direct labor dollar. Over time, the payroll of the several mission departments, including the collection department, averages $30,000 per month. Hence, the budgeted monthly costs of the payroll-related pool are $9,500 [$5,000 + (0.15 × $30,000)].

During September, the collection department drew 2,688 pints of blood. Technicians worked a total of 960 hours, and since some of these hours were compensated at premium rates the wages averaged $12.50 per hour. Total wages were $12,000.

In the same month, the payroll-related cost pool incurred $10,300 of costs. The departments that it serves paid $34,000 in direct labor dollars.

1. Determine the direct cost to the center of the excessive use of labor on the part of the collection department (i.e., the labor efficiency variance). Determine also the cost of having to pay greater than standard wages (the labor rate variance).
2. Determine the total variance of the payroll-related cost pool (i.e., actual costs less those budgeted for a normal month).
   a. Of this variance, how much can be attributed to the additional direct labor dollars (i.e., $34,000 less $30,000) of all the departments that it serves?
   b. Of the variance attributable to the departments served, how much can be attributed to the collection department (i.e., the difference between the total wages paid by the collection department and the standard wages for the normal volume of 2,640 pints)?
   c. Of the variance attributable to the collection department (in letter b), how much is the result of:
      - The forty-eight more than normal number of pints processed?
      - The "inefficiency" of the collection department (i.e., the combined direct labor usage and direct labor rate variances as just calculated)?
   d. Mission departments other than the collection department incurred $2,560 of direct labor costs more than anticipated. What was the impact of these additional costs on the payroll-related cost pool?
   e. Assuming that $600 of the total variance of the payroll-related cost pool (as you might have calculated in part 2a) can be attributed to additional direct labor costs incurred by mission departments, how much of the total variance can be assigned to other factors (such as increases in insurance and other benefit rates)?

13-6

When it comes to classifying costs, it's not only what you say, it's when you say it.

Parents Against Underage Drinking (PAUD) recently paid $50,000 to sponsor a series of commercials on a local television station. Each commercial is one minute in length. In the first forty-five seconds, sports stars plead with teenagers to avoid peer pressure to consume alcoholic beverages. In the remaining fifteen seconds, a celebrity solicits funds for the organization and gives a telephone number to call, and an address to which to send a contribution. The commercials are scheduled to run during *Real World*, a hip MTV program that is popular among the high school set.

1. How much of the cost of the commercials should PAUD allocate to mission-related programs and how much to fund-raising?
   a. Assume first that the allocation is to be based on physical units.
   b. Assume, alternatively, that the allocation is to be based on "stand-alone costs." The cost of a single forty-five-second commercial would be approximately $40,000; that of a fifteen-second commercial would be $20,000.
2. Suppose that the organization elected to run the same series of commercials on reruns of the *Lawrence Welk Show*, a musical variety program that features tunes of the 1950s and appeals primarily to the grandparents of those to whom *Real World* is targeted. The cost is the same $50,000. Would your response be the same? Explain.

13-7

Costs of adding capacity do not necessarily mirror those of reducing it.

A northwestern state operates a program of halfway houses for teenagers who have run away from home or have been delinquent (arrested for minor drug violations, for example). The halfway houses are located throughout the state and teenagers are assigned to a house that is located within or near their county of residence. The houses provide food and lodging. While they are residing at the houses the teenagers are encouraged to meet, both individually and in groups, with trained counselors who help them work out their problems and pave the way for a return to their homes and schools. In addition, the program provides that each teenager receive a thorough physical exam and medical counseling to help control any physical problems that might contribute to their emotional difficulties.

To date the program has been generally successful. More than 75 percent of the teenagers who spend time at the halfway houses return to their homes, improve their grades at school, and abandon their use of drugs.

Each halfway house can serve forty teenagers at a time. The average stay is two months; hence, each house serves approximately 240 teenagers per year (i.e., forty slots each occupied by an average of six different teenagers).

There are currently twenty halfway houses in operation throughout the state. Since the program began each of the houses has always been filled to its prescribed capacity. Indeed, there is a waiting list for admission to each of the houses. As a consequence, the administrators of the program see a need to increase the number of teenagers served. They prefer to increase the number of halfway houses, but as an alternative they would increase the prescribed enrollment at each from forty to a maximum practical capacity of fifty. An increase in the number of teenagers served at existing houses may, of course, decrease the quality of service, but the administrators believe that an increase in the stated capacity of each house would better serve the state than no increase at all.

The cost of operating the entire program is $10,480,000; that of operating each of the twenty houses is $524,000. The cost of maintaining a teenager at the center is, on average, $13,100 a year ($2,184 for a two-month stay). The breakdown of costs is as follows:

Annual Cost of Operating a Halfway House (Based on a capacity of 40)

Rent	$ 24,000
Director	56,000
Counselors (4 at $40,000)	160,000
Kitchen and maintenance employee	32,000
Furniture and fixtures (see Note A)	12,000
Food ($4,000 per teenager per year)	160,000
Supplies and miscellaneous costs ($600 per teenager per year)	24,000
Utilities	6,000
Medical and drugs ($800 per teenager per year)	32,000
Central office costs (see Note B)	18,000
Total costs per center	$524,000

Note A: Total cost of furniture and fixtures is $48,000; useful life is four years. The current stock of furniture will not have to be replaced for at least another two years.

Note B: Central office costs are $360,000. They are divided equally among the twenty centers. Of these costs, $240,000 are fixed; the remainder vary with number of centers ($6,000 per center).

1. Specify the annual costs of increasing the capacity—the incremental cost per place—of each of the existing centers by ten places per center (and thereby serving sixty additional teenagers per center, a total of 1,200 for the twenty centers).
2. Specify the costs of adding 200 places at an additional five centers (a total 1,200 teenagers served). Consider only the costs of the first year.
3. Why might you not recommend the option with the lower cost?
4. Suppose that the state were forced to reduce the scope of the program. The administrator of the program was informed that the budget would be reduced by 15 percent ($1,572,000). How would you recommend the cuts be affected (i.e., by reducing the number of centers or reducing the number of places at each center)? Consider only savings for the first year. Explain and indicate any factors for which information is not provided that you would want to take into consideration.

13-8

Past errors can easily be compounded by the failure to take advantage of new cost-saving opportunities.

Two years ago, the Democratic Ideals Foundation completed the acquisition and installation of a new computer software system. The director of the foundation has determined that the total cost was approximately $200,000 including purchase price, consulting fees, and training costs.

The system is operating as expected and has resulted in the anticipated efficiencies and cost savings. However, a newer system has been developed which would affect even greater efficiencies and cost savings.

The director estimates that the new system would cost $250,000 to acquire and install, including all costs necessary to bring it to proper operating condition.

The director predicts that the new system would have an economic life of four years, approximately the same as the remaining life of the system just installed. He forecasts that it would result in annual cash operating savings of $80,000 per year.

Despite these savings, the director has elected not to acquire the system, basing his decision on the following analysis:

Cost of the new system	
Direct outlay	$250,000
Loss on abandonment of old system (see below)	100,000
Total cost	$350,000
Less: annual savings attributable to new system ($80,000 per year for 4 years)	320,000
Net disadvantage of new system	$ 30,000

The $100,000 loss on the abandonment of the old system was determined as follows:

Cost of purchasing the software (consulting and training costs were charged as expenses as incurred)	$150,000
Less: amortization to date, based on initial expected life of 6 years (two years at $25,000)	50,000
Net loss on abandonment of old system	$100,000

The analysis, he points out, is conservative in that it actually understates the disadvantages of replacing the old system. First, he notes, the cash savings will occur over several years and have not been discounted back to the present. If discounted at a rate of 8 percent, for example, their present value would be only $264,970. Second, he says, owing to arbitrary accounting conventions only the purchase price of the software has been capitalized and is reflected as a loss. The actual loss, were the consulting and training costs to be factored in, would be much greater.

1. Do you agree with the analysis and decision of the director? If not prepare your own analysis.
2. Suppose that when confronted with your analysis the director asserts that the foundation's auditor has warned him that if a system is acquired, the $100,000 loss would have to be recognized in the foundation's financial statements. Why, he wonders, should a management action that is supposedly in the fiscal interests of the organization result in a reported loss? Is he correct that the foundation would have to recognize a loss? If so, how would you respond to his question?

13-9

Choice of allocation basis may be more than academic.

The Port City Municipal League, a voluntary health and welfare organization, carries out four primary programs:

- Job training
- Emergency home repair
- Alcohol and drug abuse
- Activities for youth

Each of the programs is supported by federal, county, and city reimbursement grants. In addition, the league receives private contributions and dues from the United Way, corporations, and league members.

The following schedule provides information relating to the job training program, the three other mission programs, and the league's administrative activities.

	Job Training	Other Mission Programs	Administrative Activities
Direct salaries and benefits	$140,000	$312,000	$148,000
Equipment maintenance and rental	14,000	7,000	6,000
Telephone	2,500	4,000	7,200
Supplies	2,900	15,600	1,100
Contractual services	7,300	220,000	5,000
Other costs	4,600	9,700	14,500
Occupancy costs			27,000
Independent auditor			12,000
Total costs	$171,300	$568,300	$220,800
Square feet occupied	2,000	2,200	3,000
Number of employees (full time equivalent)	5.6	13.0	6.1

Port City, which finances the job training program, reimburses the league for all direct costs, plus a proportionate share of administrative costs. The sponsors of the other programs, by contrast, refuse to reimburse for administrative or other overhead costs.

1. The league currently allocates all administrative costs to the mission programs on the basis of total direct costs—i.e., those that can be identified with a specific program. What would be the total amount that the league should request for reimbursement from Port City for the job training program?
2. Suppose that the league divides its administrative costs into pools and allocates them on the following bases.

Cost Pool	*Basis for Allocation (Cost Driver)*
Salaries and benefits, contractual services, equipment maintenance and rental, and other costs	Direct salary and benefits
Occupancy costs	Square feet
Independent auditor	Total direct costs
Supplies, telephone	Number of employees

The amount of costs in each pool allocated to each of the mission programs is the program's proportionate share of the cost driver (excluding the share associated with administrative activities). Thus, for example, the job training program would be allocated 5.6/(5.6 + 13.0) of the $8,300 of administrative supplies and telephone costs.

What would be the total amount that the league should request for reimbursement from Port City for the job training program under this alternative basis of allocation? Which of the two allocation schemes is more justifiable? Why?

13-10

Activity-based costing systems provide a basis for establishing charges.

The repair and installation division of a municipal utility has two mission departments—one for repairs, the other for installation. The repair division not only maintains equipment of the utility, but also services equipment of its customers. However, if the equipment is owned by the customer, then the utility bills the customer for actual costs incurred.

The division has established three pools of overhead costs and assigns them to particular jobs as follows:

Cost Pool	*Cost Driver*
Accounting, supervision, and administration	Direct labor dollars
Vehicle and equipment related costs (including depreciation and maintenance)	Direct labor hours
Materials and supplies related costs (including warehousing and ordering)	Materials usage

The division has accumulated the following data for what it considers to be an "average" month:

	Repairs and Maintenance	Installation	Overhead
Direct labor hours	1,600	3,000	
Direct labor dollars	$ 32,000	$ 54,000	
Materials used	340,000	900,000	
Accounting, supervision, and administration (total)			$20,000
Vehicle related costs (total)			5,000
Materials related costs			7,000

1. For each of the cost drivers determine the cost per unit that the division should assign to a job.
2. Repair Job No. 103 required 8 hours for which employees were paid a total of $190. It required $2,000 of parts and materials. How much should the utility bill the customer assuming that it intends to recover the full cost of providing the service?

SOLUTION TO EXERCISE FOR REVIEW AND SELF-STUDY

1. To process 600 permits, the division should have incurred only $26,400 in direct labor costs (600 permits at $44) rather than $27,600. The $1,200 excess can be explained by both a labor efficiency variance and a labor rate variance:

Actual labor hours used	1,150
Standard labor hours for actual output (600 documents at 2 hours)	1,200
Excess (fewer) hours used	(50)
Standard wage rate per hour	× $ 22
Labor efficiency variance	$1,100F
Actual rate	$ 24
Standard rate	22
Excess of standard rate over actual rate	$ 2
Actual number of hours	× 1,150
Labor rate variance	$2,300U
Total direct labor variance	$1,200U

2. The Administrative Center should have budgeted (per a flexible budget) $32,450 in overhead for 4,150 hours:

Fixed costs	$20,000
Variable costs (4,150 d.l.hrs. at $3)	12,450
Total budgeted costs per flexible budget	$32,450

Therefore, the flexible budget variance was $850 (unfavorable):

Actual overhead costs	$33,300
Budgeted per flexible budget for actual (4,150) direct labor hours	32,450
Flexible budget variance	$ 850U

3. The Administrative Center should have budgeted (per a flexible budget) $32,600 for 4,200 hours:

Fixed costs	$20,000
Variable costs (4,200 d.l.hrs. at $3)	12,600
Total budgeted costs per flexible budget	$32,600

The Administrative Center thereby saved $150, a favorable overhead efficiency variance, owing to the better-than-standard use of labor by the Permits Division:

Total budgeted costs per flexible budget for actual (4,150) direct labor hours	$32,450
Total budgeted costs per flexible budget for standard (4,200) direct labor hours	32,600
Overhead efficiency variance	$ 150F

4. The Permits division should have been required to work an additional 200 hours (2 hours per permit) to process an additional 100 permits. At $3 variable costs

per hour, the additional hours should have caused the Administrative Center to incur $600 in additional costs—an unfavorable volume variance.

5. Yes:

Volume variance	$ 600U
Efficiency variance	150F
Flexible budget	850U
Total overhead variance	$1,300U

6. If the state accepts the offer, then its costs per month would be $25,000 (500 permits at $50). If it rejects it, then it would have to incur the following incremental costs relating to the permits:

Direct labor costs (500 permits at $44)	$22,000
Adminstrative overhead	
Fixed (additional amount only)	1,000
Variable (500 permits at 2 d.l.hrs at $3)	3,000
Total relevant costs to be incurred if offer is rejected	$26,000

The state could save $1,000 per month in differential costs by accepting the contract and, other factors held constant, should do so.

7. At a minimum the state should seek to recover its *incremental costs.* Thus, it should charge $50 per permit:

Direct labor costs	$44
Variable overhead	6
Total incremental costs	$50

More realistically, it should charge at least $52, an amount that takes into account $1,000 of the fixed costs ($2 per permit if 500 permits are processed) that the Administrative Center could save if it did not have to serve the Permits Division.

As a maximum, it should charge the full cost—$60 per permit.

CHAPTER 14

Managing for Results

LEARNING OBJECTIVES

After studying this chapter you should understand:

- The various roles that accountants can play in the management of governmental and other not-for-profit organizations
- How program budgets overcome the limitations of traditional object-classification budgets
- The need for, and characteristics of, sound operational objectives
- The risks of establishing explicit organizational objectives
- The ways in which program budgets link expenditures to objectives
- The advantages and disadvantages of program budgets
- Why it is important for organizations to develop and report measures of service efforts and accomplishments
- The special problems that governments and not-for-profits face in planning and budgeting their capital expenditures and how they can address them

In Chapter 13 we saw that conventional, business-type management accounting focuses mainly on maximizing net inflow of cash rather than on achieving the organization's other objectives. In this chapter, our emphasis shifts to these other goals of governments and not-for-profits. The central messages of this chapter are that organizations must be managed so as to achieve intended results, and that all phases of the management cycle must be linked to this end.

We first review the management cycle and explain how an organization's operational objectives tie together each of its phases. The role of accountants in each of these phases is described briefly. We then consider several ideal characteristics of operational objectives and show how operational objectives can be incorporated into what are referred to as program budgets. Next we discuss how organizations can report on "service efforts and accomplishments"—in essence, on the extent to which they achieved their objectives. We conclude by showing why and how capital, and capital-related expenditures, no differently from operating expenditures, must be budgeted and planned within the framework of the organization's operational objectives. We address two key steps in the process: benefit–cost analysis and project ranking.

This chapter pertains to topics to which entire courses are directed and as to which there is an extensive body of literature. Nevertheless, as readily will be apparent, the issues raised are not nearly as well defined as those dealt with in earlier chapters and the options for resolving them are not nearly as clear. Indeed, if only a small portion of the subject matter of this chapter is covered on the CPA or other professional exams, part of the reason could well be that there are be no agreed-upon answers to relevant objective-type questions.

WHAT ROLE DO ACCOUNTANTS PLAY IN THE MANAGEMENT CYCLE OF GOVERNMENTS AND OTHER NOT-FOR-PROFITS?

The development, implementation, and assessment of programs in governments and other not-for-profits (herein referred to as "social" programs) have been diagrammed and described in almost as many different ways as there are textbooks and articles on public and not-for-profit administration. The diagram presented in Figure 14-1 divides the process into four phases—none of which are as well defined or as discrete as might be suggested by the four separate boxes. It is intended to emphasize that accountants can play multiple roles in an entity's fiscal management; they need not be confined to their widely accepted roles of statement preparers and auditors.

As social problems within the purview of an entity arise, teams of area specialists develop and analyze potential solutions (Box 1). They collect and analyze budgetary and related financial information, and compare the potential costs and benefits associated with various options. These teams may be composed primarily of organizational managers but, depending on the size and the magnitude of the entity, may also include social scientists, statisticians, economists, and policy, program, and budget analysts. Since much of this data collection and analysis centers around financial information, accountants can make valuable contributions to this phase of the program cycle.

The proposed options are presented to policy makers—the legislature, board of directors, or other governing body (Box 2). The policy makers select among the options, modify them as they see fit, and appropriate the required resources. They also establish the expected goals. Ideally the goals will be set forth explicitly in a budget, appropriations legislation, or other documents, and will take the form of operational objectives that are measurable and quantifiable. Often, however, they are revealed

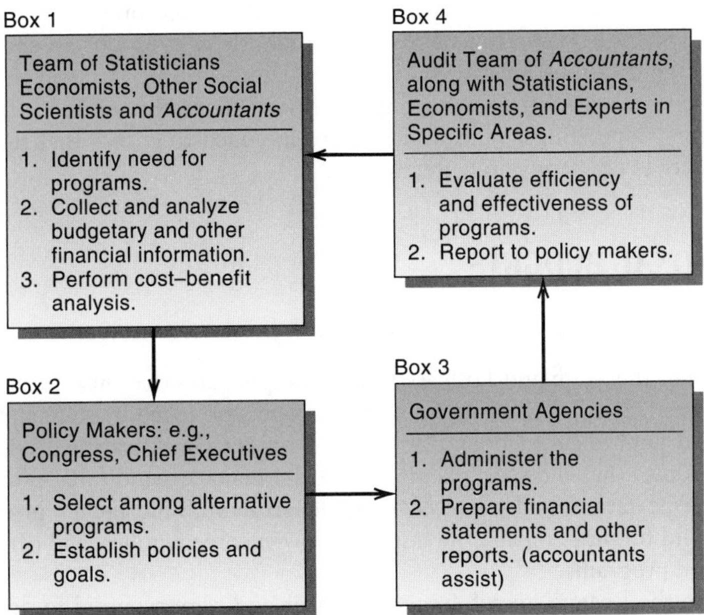

FIGURE 14-1 Management Cycle: Development, Administration, and Evaluation of the Social Programs of Governments and Other Not-For-Profits

only obliquely through written minutes of legislative debates or changes in the appropriations measures as they work their way through the legislative process. Moreover, they are seldom specific. Accountants, as accountants, have no special role to play in this phase of the program cycle (although they are undoubtedly as competent as members of other professions to serve as members of legislatures and other governing boards).

Once adopted, the programs are administered by appropriate agencies and departments (Box 3). These units are responsible for ensuring that the program objectives are achieved. Accountants, of course, are key participants in this phase, actively involved in establishing plans and operating budgets, controlling costs, and preparing financial and other operating reports to officials of both the agency itself and to outside entities charged with monitoring the agency.

Finally, the programs are audited (Box 4). Not only are programs' financial statements attested to (a conventional financial audit), but more importantly, the programs are assessed as to the extent to which they achieved their objectives. Audit teams almost always include accountants, but they may be joined by statisticians, economists, and specialists in the particular programs. The results of the audit are made available not only to the agencies and departments administering the programs, but also to the policy makers and the analysts involved in budgeting and program analysis.

The cycle then repeats. The team involved in budgeting and program analysis must assess the success of the programs, recommend whether they should be continued, and if so, propose an appropriate level of funding. The audit reports, while by no means the only source of information, can be expected to play a prominent role in their analyses.

From one perspective programming/budgeting and auditing are far apart in the cycle and have little in common. Program/budgeting appears to lead the cycle; auditing concludes it. Programming/budgeting looks to the future; auditing at the past.

From another perspective, however, the two phases are next to each other and are functionally similar. The cycle is continuous; it has neither a beginning nor an end. Programming/budgeting decisions must be based on the success of programs in the past; auditing is carried out with an eye to making improvements in the future. Both are linked by the entity's operational objectives and are intended to ensure that the entity fulfills the objectives efficiently and effectively.

HOW CAN THE LIMITS OF TRADITIONAL BUDGETS BE OVERCOME?

The proposed budget of the Highland Hills Assistance League, an urban health and welfare agency, is presented in Table 14-1. Typical of budgets prepared by state and local governments and not-for-profit organizations, this **object classification budget** is backed by schedules that show details of each of the major expenditures—for example, salaries, transportation, and travel costs by department. This agency provides job counseling and training, repairs the homes of low-income families, and carries out youth-oriented programs.

Suppose you were the League's chief executive officer and were required to defend the proposed budget before the board of directors. You were asked:

- Will the requested funds—an increase over the prior year—be sufficient to increase the number of homes repaired? If so, by how many?
- Will they enable the organization to improve its drug prevention program? If so, how will the improvements be measured?
- Will they increase the number of job trainees that obtain well-paying jobs? If so, by how many?
- Will they reduce the community's school drop-out rate? If so, by how much?

Based on the budget alone, it is obvious that you would be unable to respond adequately to the questions. It is equally self-evident that the queries reflect legitimate concerns of the board members and the constituents they represent. By contrast, you would be able to provide data on the amount to be spent on travel, supplies, and rent. These costs should be of concern to the organization's managers. But the organization's members and policy makers are likely to—and should—be more concerned with the relationship between costs and results.

As emphasized throughout this text, the budget is the most significant of financial documents for both governments and not-for-profit organizations. It determines the amount of resources to be received from the various groups of constituents and the programs and activities that the resources will support. Directly or indirectly it affects, or is affected by, virtually all decisions of consequence that a governing body must make. The budget details in financial terms the strategy of the organization to accomplish its mission.

Yet the traditional budget, as illustrated in the exhibit, provides no insight into what the organization's constituents can expect for their contributions. It offers no information as to the extent that the expenditures will advance the entity's mission or better enable it to achieve its objectives.

This chapter is directed mainly to budgeting, performance reporting, and evaluation. These topics are linked with a common thread—the importance of defining the organization's mission, developing broad goals, and establishing operational

TABLE 14-1
Highland Hills Assistance League Proposed Budget

Summary of Support/Revenue and Expenses

	Budgeted	
	FY 2005–06	**FY 2004–05**
Support/Revenue		
Interest on investments/endowments	$ 7,200	$ 7,800
Fund-raising	75,096	75,000
Individual contributions	4,860	19,800
Government grants	1,063,830	800,545
Corporate/foundations	28,848	37,000
United Way	67,009	60,504
Other	13,009	6,504
Total support/revenue	$1,259,852	$1,007,153
Expenses		
Salaries	$ 638,626	$ 464,785
Employee benefits	53,737	42,672
Payroll taxes	55,962	58,012
Professional fees	46,145	38,004
Rent	106,666	105,360
Equipment rental and maintenance	23,166	19,112
Travel and transportation	25,378	22,030
Subcontracting	211,742	317,614
Promotion and printing	13,056	9,840
Specific assistance to individuals	23,100	13,800
Insurance	5,397	6,000
General and administrative	29,100	19,727
Total expenses	$1,232,075	$1,116,956
Surplus/(deficit)	$ 27,777	$ (109,803)

Note how each of the expenses relates to means of carrying out the agency's activities; none is tied to specific objectives. The budget provides no basis for assessing subsequent performance.

objectives. The term **operational objectives** is used herein to signify *specific* sought-after results. Whenever possible, operational objectives should be both quantifiable and measurable. They should be distinguishable from goals, which are more generalized statements of aspirations.

Establishing appropriate objectives is at the heart of budgeting, because if an organization doesn't have a clear idea as to *where* it wants to go, it cannot determine how to get there and when it has arrived. Nevertheless, as shall be stressed in this chapter, the importance of operational objectives is matched by the challenge of establishing them. Virtually no managers of government or not-for-profit organizations deny, or even minimize, the need for operational objectives—but for organizations other than their own. Their own objectives, they may contend, are too intangible to quantify.

WHAT ARE THE CHARACTERISTICS OF SOUND OPERATIONAL OBJECTIVES?

Operational objectives should be central to the functions that compose the management cycle. They should not simply be technical contrivances within the province of budget analysts, accountants, and auditors. Derived from the organization's mission and its goals, they should be the basis for allocating resources, managing day-to-day activities, and distributing rewards and reprimands. Per an often-repeated aphorism, "What we measure is what we manage." This section sets forth ideal characteristics of operational objectives, but at the same time emphasizes that the ideal is not readily attainable.

OPERATIONAL OBJECTIVES SHOULD REPRESENT TRUE ENDS (OUTCOMES), NOT MEANS (OUTPUTS)

Operational objectives should be distinguishable from the means of achieving the organization's broad goals. They should not preclude alternative means of accomplishing the desired results. The "true" goal of a state highway department, for example, might be to enable drivers to reduce travel time from home to work rather than the obvious one of building more miles of highway. Building more miles of highway may be one primary means of reducing travel time, but it may not be the only one. Other means may include synchronizing the timing of traffic signals on existing roads and designating special lanes for buses and other multi-passenger vehicles.

Operational objectives should be doable and measurable. In addition, they should be accomplishable within a specific time or by a specified date.

What might be a means at one level within an organization might be an objective at another. For example, the objective of the highway construction division, a unit within the highway department, might well be to build highways. The measure of its performance might be the number of miles constructed.

The distinction between true ends and means is more of a continuum than a dichotomy. Whereas higher order objectives—those that refer to more abstract statements of intent and are generally referred to as "goals"—are associated with true ends, the more specific, readily measurable actions that entities take to achieve the goals are identified with the means.

In ideal circumstances, operational objectives would capture the true ends rather than the means. But owing to difficulties of measurement, this is often not possible. In a city that is expanding in both population and geographic area, it may not be feasible for a highway department to assess its success in reducing travel time. It may be constrained, therefore, to rely on miles of new highway construction as one of its main operational objectives.

The virtues of focusing on true ends rather than means is a central theme of recent management literature. Organizations, this literature has stressed, should be "mission" rather than "rules" driven. Top management should tell lower-level managers and employees what to accomplish rather than how to accomplish it.[1]

Closely tied to the concepts of ends and means, but connoting more precisely specified consequences, are those of **outcomes** and **outputs.** *Outcomes*, like ends, represent the *results* of an activity. *Outputs*, like means, indicate the quantity or units of service provided by the activity. Outcomes reflect accomplishments and typically include an element of quality—e.g., number of units that satisfy specified criteria.

[1] See, for example, D. Osborne and T. Gaebler, *Reinventing Government: How the Entrepreneurial Spirit is Transforming the Public Sector* (Reading, Mass.: Addison Wesley, 1992), especially Chapter 4, "Mission-Driven Government: Transforming Rules-Driven Organizations," pp. 108–37.

Accordingly, in the ideal organization operational objectives should be expressed as outcomes rather than outputs.

The following are examples of outputs and the outcomes that they may help to effect:

Output	*Outcome*
Number of accounting majors	Number of students passing the CPA exam; number of students in accounting positions after a specified number of years following graduation
Number of criminal investigations carried out	Number of crimes cleared; crime rate
Number of air-quality samples tested	Percentage of population living in areas in which the quality of air meets specified standards; percentage of samples meeting air-quality standards
Number of applicants served by an employment agency	Number of applicants placed in suitable (as specifically defined) jobs
Number of patients served	Percentage of patients cured

OPERATIONAL OBJECTIVES SHOULD BE READILY MEASURABLE, YET CAPTURE THE DESIRED OUTCOME

Operational objectives should be readily measurable. Yet often the true outcome of a program cannot easily be quantified, and certainly not described, by any single metric. The aims of an undergraduate accounting program (like those of most other undergraduate programs) include enhancing students' abilities to read, to write, to reason, and to develop sound moral, ethical, and cultural values. In the eyes of many faculty, these goals are at least as important as the more obvious objectives—enabling students to pass the CPA exam or obtain employment in a professional or managerial capacity. They are far more difficult to measure, however, and therefore less likely to be focused or reported upon.

In the absence of measures indicative of true outcomes, organizations must resort to surrogates. However, the less the similarity of the surrogate to the true outcome, the less its utility, and the greater the danger that it will result in dysfunctional behavior (as discussed in the section that follows on the perils of operational objectives).

OPERATIONAL OBJECTIVES SHOULD BE MEASURABLE WITHIN A PERIOD SUFFICIENTLY SHORT TO TAKE CORRECTIVE ACTION

If operational objectives are to be the basis of performance evaluation, then they should not only capture true outcomes, but do so in a timely manner. An objective of an accounting program may be to produce leaders of the accounting profession. However, it generally takes graduates at least fifteen years to fulfill their leadership potential. Most departments are unable to wait that long to learn whether they need to change their curriculum, replace faculty, or adjust admission standards so as to better achieve their objective. Hence, they are required to rely upon expedients, such as percentage of students who are placed with prestigious employers or who passed the CPA exam.

OPERATIONAL OBJECTIVES SHOULD BE PRECISE

Operational objectives should be precise. They should leave little room for individual interpretation. But the precision should not be at the risk of misspecification.

The objective of a park police unit might be "to reduce the number of assaults in city parks and to arrest the perpetrators"—an apparently well-defined goal. Nevertheless, it leaves open issues that if not properly resolved could undermine that objective:

- Should the number of assaults be based on the number of actual or reported incidents? (If actual incidents, then there is no objective way to determine the number, since some incidents may go unreported. If reported incidents, then the department could best achieve the objective by taking its phone off the hook—or, perhaps more realistically, by not encouraging victims to report the incidents.)
- Should "arrest of perpetrators" be based on arrests of suspects, indictments, or actual convictions? (If based on arrests, then the police could achieve the objective by taking into custody any potential suspects, no matter how low the probability that they are the actual criminals. If based on convictions, however, then the performance of the police unit depends on other city departments, such as the district attorney's office, over which it has no control. If based on indictments, then the problems of the other two indicators are mitigated, but by no means eliminated.)
- Should all assaults be grouped together, or is it preferable to divide them into categories as to degree of severity? (If all assaults are grouped together, then police may have the incentive to concentrate on assaults that are easy to prevent, but not especially severe.)

OPERATIONAL OBJECTIVES GENERALLY MUST BE MULTIPLE

The mission of an organization must generally be expressed through more than one objective. Rarely is a single objective sufficient.

Multiple objectives create special problems of both resource allocation and performance evaluation, since outcomes cannot be assessed on a single scale. A unit or activity that ranks high on one scale may rank low on another. Therefore, the organization may have no obvious way of determining which of its activities or units is the more efficient overall. This limitation may be alleviated to some extent by sophisticated mathematical techniques, such as data envelopment analysis and other types of goal programming, that combine the relative strengths of each unit or activity and create a single "frontier" of efficiency.

WHAT ARE THE PERILS OF ESTABLISHING OPERATIONAL OBJECTIVES?

Despite the importance of operational objectives, many organizations are reluctant to establish them. Operational objectives can have adverse consequences. It is critical that they be understood and dealt with forthrightly.

OPERATIONAL OBJECTIVES MAY FOMENT CONFLICT

By establishing objectives, an organization invariably signals which of its activities are primary and which are secondary. Arguably, in fact, that is one of the main purposes of the process. Implicitly, therefore, organizations distinguish between the individuals or units that are central to achieving their objectives and those that are merely supportive.

Suppose, for example, an academic department of accounting establishes as one of its objectives "increasing the pass rate on the CPA exam." This objective may be perceived as enhancing the stature of the faculty members who teach the courses from which the CPA examination questions are drawn (e.g., intermediate accounting) at the expense of those responsible for those from which they are not (e.g., accounting history). The elevation in status of some employees at the expense of others will almost certainly create organizational tensions.

Similarly, by being too precise as to their objectives, organizations risk alienating their constituents. Recognizing this reality, political parties, for example, often confine their platforms to vague generalities. University presidents, for fear of offending undergraduate students and their parents, may be reluctant to publicize their objective of creating top-flight research programs.

OPERATIONAL OBJECTIVES MAY RESULT IN DYSFUNCTIONAL BEHAVIOR

Objectives are intended to lay the foundation for specific evaluative criteria for the organization as a whole, for the various component units, and ultimately for individual employees. Operating under mandates from governing authorities or top managers to establish objectives, an organization may substitute objectives that are convenient to measure for those that express its true mission. As a consequence, employees may target their efforts toward improving what will be measured rather than what may be ultimately beneficial to the organization and its constituents.

If a stated, but not true, objective of an accounting department is to increase the CPA pass rate, then presumably the department will compile data on exam results. Individual instructors will be under pressure (actual or implied) to ensure that their students perform well on the exams and will therefore emphasize exam-related material to the detriment of topics that may be of greater long-term importance to the students.

A main goal of the U.S. involvement in the Vietnam conflict was to ensure that South Vietnam was governed by a pro-Western, non-Communist government. Success could not be guaranteed, as in conventional wars, by capturing territory. Instead it had to be achieved by winning the support ("the hearts and minds") of the populace. In what has been widely cited as a quintessential case of placing reliance on misspecified objectives, the U.S. military evaluated both progress and the performance of individual units on "body counts"—a criterion easy to measure but not genuinely indicative of the military's ultimate aim. Contrast the two views of this measure as presented in the accompanying In Practice.

HOW DO PROGRAM BUDGETS RELATE EXPENDITURES TO OPERATIONAL OBJECTIVES?

As pointed out in Chapter 3, **performance budgets** explicitly relate expenditures to operational objectives. Accordingly, both governments and not-for-profits use them in place of, or as a supplement to, the traditional object classification budgets. **Program budgets,** the most common type of performance budgets, allocate funds by programs rather than by objects. Thus, the governing board of a city would appropriate funds for public safety programs, fire prevention programs, and health programs, rather than for salaries, equipment, or supplies.

Programs are composed of activities that are directed toward a common goal. They are generally carried out within a single organizational unit, but they may also cut across departments. For example, a drug prevention program may involve a city's police department, health department, and education department. When program budgets were first popularized (in the 1960s), considerable emphasis was placed on the advantages of allocating costs to programs, rather than departments, even when the programs involved two or more departments. In practice, however, budgeting across departments is fraught with managerial pitfalls as it blurs the lines of authority and responsibility over the appropriated resources.

Program budgets can take many forms, each reflective of the specific needs and culture of the specific entity. In this chapter we illustrate **zero-base budgeting (ZBB),** which is one variant of program budgeting. We choose this variant not because it is the most widely used, but because its requirements are precisely delineated. Other budget forms are more organization-specific. ZBB requires entities to make explicit the

IN PRACTICE

A CLASSIC CASE OF RELIANCE ON MISSPECIFIED OBJECTIVES (TWO PERSPECTIVES OF THE VIETNAM WAR)

I. The Soldier's Perspective

The rugged terrain and frequent night attacks made it very hard to place priority on recovering casualties, which helped prevent accurate counts. Because of such difficulties, field commanders were inclined to estimate the enemy's losses without hard evidence. Although most tried to be accurate, for others, body count became a work of creative fiction.... Exaggerated counts never seemed to be questioned higher up. Officers who tried to render accurate body counts had to fight against a current of pressure to produce results—on paper, if not in truth. [This] manipulation of reality affected not only battle news, which was edited and revised until it was acceptable to those higher up, but also friendly casualty reports, pacification reports, food distribution status—anything that lent itself to statistical measurement as a demonstration of progress. [A noted officer] was quoted as saying, "Duplicity was so automatic that lower headquarters began to believe the things they were forwarding to higher headquarters.... Paper graphs and charts became the ultimate reality." This situation was reinforced, as [an observer] points out, by the fact that the unquestioned tallies "were readily rewarded by medals, promotions, and time off from field duty."

Incentives offered to the enlisted personnel were usually the result of increasing pressure from above to produce more kills. [A field officer], for example, claimed that his unit was "constantly under pressure to turn in a body count, and the word was out that companies with the greatest number would get to spend more time at Cocoa Beach. It was an accepted thing to cheat on a body count report—all of us had been guilty of this."

Source: James R. Ebert, *A Life in a Year: The American Infantryman in Vietnam*, 1965–1972 (Novato, Calif.: Presido Press, 1993) pp. 273–74. Reprinted with permission.

II. The Secretary of Defense's Perspective

But I insisted we try to measure progress. As I have emphasized, since my years at Harvard, I had gone by the rule that it is not enough to conceive of an objective and a plan to carry it out; you must monitor the plan to determine whether you are achieving the objective. If you discover you are not, you either revise the plan or change the objective. I was convinced that, while we might not be able to track something as unambiguous as a front line, we could find variables that would indicate our success or failure. So we measured the targets destroyed in the North, the traffic down the Ho Chi Minh Trail, the number of captives, the weapons seized, the enemy body count, and so on.

The body count was a measurement of the adversary's manpower losses; we undertook it because one of [the commanding general's] objectives was to reach a so-called crossover point—we needed to have some idea what they could sustain and what their losses were.

Critics point to use of the body count as an example of my obsession with numbers. "This guy McNamara," they said, "he tries to quantify everything." Obviously, there are things you cannot quantify: honor and beauty, for example. But things you can count, you ought to count. Loss of life is one when you are fighting a war of attrition. We tried to use body counts as a measurement to help us figure out what we should be doing in Vietnam to win the war while putting our troops at the least risk. Every attempt to monitor progress in Vietnam during my tenure as secretary of defense was directed toward those goals, but often the reports were misleading.

Source: Robert S. McNamara with Brian VanDeMark, *In Retrospect: The Tragedy and Lessons of Vietnam* (New York: Random House, 1995) pp. 237–38. Reprinted with permission.

decisions and judgments that other forms allow to leave implied. Accordingly, it is more clearly indicative of the strengths and pitfalls of program budgets in general.

The defining feature of ZBB is its mandate that both current and proposed activities be subject to a common review and priority ranking. As implied by its name, all activities must be evaluated from a base of zero. None, irrespective of how long it has been in existence, is exempt from budgetary review. In this respect, ZBB is distinguished from "incremental" budgeting procedures, in which the emphasis is primarily on requests for initial funding for new activities or added funding for continuing activities. An implicit assumption of incremental budgeting is that in the absence of affirmative measures to the contrary, activities will continue to be funded at no less than their current level.

In the 1970s, ZBB received considerable attention and was adopted by many governments. With great fanfare, President Carter introduced it into the federal government, and states such as Illinois and Texas, as well as many cities and not-for-profits, followed the federal lead. It is currently being promoted by consulting firms (under the name "priority-based budgeting"). Although relatively few organizations use ZBB in its totality, many of its elements are common to the other variants of program budgeting.

FOCUS ON ACTIVITIES

Within programs, expenditures are almost always disaggregated by object and fund. However, so as to tie expenditures more closely to objectives, they should also be broken down by activity and the focus of the budget deliberations should be on the activities rather than the object or the fund. Suppose, for example, the Highland Hills Assistance League (the organization whose object classification budget was presented in Table 14-1) maintains the following programs:

- Employment skills
- Housing rehabilitation
- Teen substance abuse

The following are examples of activities that might comprise the employment skills programs:

- Job-seeking skills (resume-writing, "dress for success," and interviewing skills)
- Computer training
- Electronics training
- Day care (for children of program participants)

THE DECISION PACKAGE

At the heart of program budgeting are the materials that must be presented as part of the budget request. Under zero-base budgeting, the budget request takes the form of a **decision package** that must be presented for each activity. Table 14-2 illustrates a decision package for computer training, one of the activities that comprises the employment skills program of the Highland Hills Assistance League. Illustrative of the type of information that many organizations require be presented as part of program budget requests, it includes the following components:

- The objectives of the activity, expressed in a way that makes clear the desired objectives (e.g., to train unemployed adults for positions requiring word-processing and spreadsheet computer skills)
- Alternative means of accomplishing the same objective (e.g., contract with a proprietary business college) and reasons why the alternatives were rejected
- Consequences of not performing the activity (e.g., program participants will have no marketable skills)

TABLE 14–2
Example of a Program (Zero-Base) Budget Decision Package
Highland Hills Assistance League

Date: September 17, 2006

Prepared by: Joshua Kalman

Fiscal Year Ending: December 31, 2007

Activity Name: Computer training

Program: Employment skills

Activity Objective: To train unemployed adults in word processing and spreadsheet computer applications and place them in positions requiring those skills.

Activity Description: The organization conducts a six-month course in which participants are first taught the basics of using computers and then are given specific training in word processing and spreadsheet programs. The course, which lasts fifteen weeks, meets four days a week for four hours a day. There is one instructor, plus an assistant, for each section of twenty participants. The classroom in which the course is conducted has one computer for each participant. It is open to students on evenings and Saturdays so that they can practice what they have been taught and do "homework" exercises.

Current (2006) Budget

Total cost:		
Salaries and benefits		
Instructor (1)	$38,000	
Assistants (2)	34,000	$72,000
Computers		11,000
Software		1,700
Repairs and maintenance		3,500
Instructional materials		3,100
Other		$ 4,900
Total		$96,200

The amount budgeted for computers assumes that the organization will replace four computers per year.

Current (2006) Workload (Output) Measures: Three sections per year, each with twenty participants

Estimated Outcome: Of the sixty participants that enroll in the program, it is estimated that forty-eight will complete the program, and of these forty-four will obtain jobs requiring the skills they acquired.

Estimated direct agency cost per projected successful outcome will be $96,200/44 = $2,186.

Level 1 Request (No More than 80 Percent of Current Level)

Costs: $75,500

Reduce number of sections to two per year, and the number of participants to forty per year. This will likely reduce the number actually obtaining employment to twenty-nine. Staff will work only thirty-four weeks per year. This cut will not only lessen the extent to which the organization fulfills its mission but will put it at risk of losing key staff members.

The organization will save $10,500 in the instructor's salary and $10,000 in assistants' salaries. In addition, it will save $500 in other costs.

Estimated direct agency cost per projected successful outcome will be $75,500/29 = $2,603.

Level 2 Request (Current level)

Additional Amount, This Level: $20,700

See Current 2006 Budget

Cost: $96,200

Level 3 Request (No More than 5 Percent Above Current Level)

Additional Amount, This Level: $4,200

Cost: $100,400

Increase staff salaries by 5 percent ($3,600) and increase expenditures for software by $600. This will give the staff a deserved salary increase (their first in two years), thereby helping to retain them. The acquisition of the software will enable

(Continues)

TABLE 14–2
Example of a Program (Zero-Base) Budget Decision Package
Highland Hills Assistance League *(Continued)*

the instructors to expose the participants to word processing programs other than the two with which they currently work, thereby making them more marketable and potentially increasing both their starting and long-term salaries.

Estimated direct agency cost per projected successful outcome will be $100,400/44 = $2,281.

Level 4 Request (No More than 20 Percent Above Current Level)

Additional Amount, This Level: $14,600
Cost: $115,000

Acquire four additional computers at $3,000 each, plus one printer at $1,000. This will enable the league to increase the size of each section from twenty to twenty-four, the total number of program participants from sixty to seventy-two, and the estimated number of participants obtaining jobs from forty-four to fifty-three.

Open the classrooms to participants for four additional hours per week (on Sunday) so that students, many of whom work on evenings or Saturdays, can get additional practice. This will require additional wages for assistants of $1,600.

Estimated direct agency cost per projected successful outcome will be $115,000/53 = $2,169.

Alternative Means of Accomplishing This Activity:
Contract with Computronics, Inc. a local proprietary school. The school has offered to provide training similar to that of the league for $3,500 per student. This alternative was rejected because the training is far more costly than what could be provided in-house and less appropriate to the needs of league clientele.

Consequences of Not Performing This Activity:
A primary mission of the league is to improve economic conditions in the Highland Hills neighborhood by assisting low-income residents to obtain employment. Discontinuing this activity would strike at the heart of the organization's ability to fulfill its mission.

- Inputs (such as dollar amounts and number of employees), quantity or units of service provided (*outputs*) and results (*outcomes*) at various levels of funding (e.g., three sections of the course will be offered, resulting in approximately 200 participants per year being qualified for the job market)

Inasmuch as the objectives of an activity may not change from year to year, much of the ongoing effort of program budgeting can be directed toward the last component, that of estimating the inputs, outputs, and outcomes at various levels of funding. In some organizations, budget requests must include estimates for at least four levels of funding—for example, the current level, two levels above the current level, and one level substantially (perhaps 20 percent) below the current level.

Implicit in the requirement for data at the different levels of funding should be the understanding that the entity will apply appropriate cost accounting procedures (such as those discussed in the previous chapter) to relate inputs to outputs and outcomes. Thus, if the managers of an activity aim to increase outcomes by 20 percent, they should not necessarily request a 20 percent increase in funding. Instead, by taking into account the behavior of each of its costs (i.e., the step functions), they should request the amount actually needed—which could be more or less than 20 percent. By budgeting at discrete levels, organizations thereby minimize *slack* (funds that cannot be used to increase outcomes) and maximize resource productivity.

REVIEW AND RANKING

Once the requests for funding have been prepared, they must be reviewed and ranked. Some organizations leave it up to individual units to establish criteria as to how funding proposals should be ranked; others establish uniform guidelines for all their units. It is not uncommon for organizations to ask units to give top priority to activities that will advance a particular phase of its mission—for example, a social service agency, such as the Highland Hills Assistance League, may determine that in a particular year activities involving children should be given funding preference.

Under the ZBB approach, the decision packages for all activities within a program are combined into a table that ranks the funding proposals. As illustrated in Table 14-3, each discrete level of funding is treated as a separate request. Thus, if the program were to be allocated only $75,500, the entire amount would be directed toward the first level of the computer training course. If the program were granted an additional $80,300, it would be applied to the first level of electronic training (an activity for which a decision package, not illustrated, would have been prepared). If it were granted an additional $28,000, it would be used for the first level of day care (another activity for which a decision package, not illustrated, would have been prepared). Only if it were granted an additional $20,700 (a total of $222,500) would the second level of the computer training course be funded.

ZBB presupposes that the governing body responsible for appropriating funds will accept the rankings submitted by the program administrators (although it is generally not required to do so). If it does, then it need only specify the total amount to be allocated to a program. That amount will be a cut-off point. Activities above the cut-off will be funded at the level implied by the table; those below will not be funded.

ZBB requires all activities, both new and ongoing, to be reviewed and included in an explicit ranking table. Other forms of program budget focus mainly on the amounts to be added to a program's funding level and do not require budget requests to be explicitly ranked.

The primary virtue of the comprehensive ranking process is that it forces program administrators to weigh the need for new activities against those of existing activities. Administrators can ensure funds for a proposed activity by ranking it high, but they risk losing support for activities to which they assign a lower priority.

The ranking table makes a further contribution to efficient resource allocation in that, like the underlying decision packages, it specifies discrete funding levels. It emphasizes that resources above one level, but below another, will not necessarily advance the program's objectives. Thus, it encourages the parties responsible for making appropriations to grant spending authority only at the discrete levels.

The main disadvantage of the comprehensive ranking process—and indeed, the reason that many entities have either abandoned or rejected ZBB—is that it requires

TABLE 14-3

Example of a Program (Zero-Base) Budget Ranking Schedule
Highland Hills Assistance League Employment Skills Program

Rank	Activity Name and Level	2007 Request	2007 Cumulative
1	Computer Training (Level 1 of 4)	$75,500	$ 75,500
2	Electronics Training (Level 1 of 4)	80,300	155,800
3	Day Care (Level 1 of 3)	28,000	183,800
4	Job Training Skills (Level 1 of 2)	18,000	201,800
5	Computer Training (Level 2 of 4)	20,700	222,500
6	Day Care (Level 2 of 3)	5,400	227,900
7	Electronics Training (Level 2 of 4)	20,100	248,000
8	Computer Training (Level 3 of 4)	4,200	252,200
9	Electronics Training (Level 3 of 4)	2,400	254,600
10	Computer Training (Level 4 of 4)	14,600	269,200
11	Day Care (Level 3 of 3)	2,800	272,000
12	Electronics Training (Level 4 of 4)	7,900	279,900
13	Job Training Skills (Level 2 of 2)	5,400	285,300

budgetary units to provide information that may never be used in the decision process. If an organization has no intention of reducing the funding for certain basic, often essential, activities, then the effort expended in preparing the decision packages for them is likely to be superfluous. Worse yet, the requirement that some activities be compared and ranked with others—if none are being considered for budget reductions—runs the risk of arousing sentiments of resentment and jealousy among employees associated with the lower-ranked activities.

MAIN ADVANTAGES OF PROGRAM BUDGETING

As implied in the discussion so far, program budgeting has several advantages over conventional object classification budgeting:

- It relates expenditures to objectives. Decision makers are made aware of the specific additional benefits (outcomes) to be derived from additional expenditures.
- It encourages explicit consideration both of alternative means of achieving the same objective and of whether the objective even needs to be achieved.
- It promotes analysis of the behavior of costs and discourages funding at levels other than those that will result in actual increases in results.
- It invites (and in the form of ZBB requires) the periodic review of all programs and activities to ensure that they are consistent with the entity's current objectives. Programs and activities that no longer contribute efficiently and effectively to the entity's mission give way to those that do. Program budgeting may incorporate what are, in essence, "sunset" reviews of all activities, thereby encouraging organizations to discontinue activities that have outlived their usefulness.

PITFALLS OF PROGRAM BUDGETING

Despite its several favorable features, program budgeting runs the risk of adding many pitfalls to the budgetary landscape:

- As noted earlier, organizational objectives may provoke conflict. If activities are explicitly ranked, the rankings may send a formal, and unavoidable, message that some endeavors—and the employees engaged in them—are less important than others.
- Program budgeting encourages governing boards, such as a city council, to establish and make known to the public their funding priorities. This form of candor may run counter to the inclination of both elected and appointed officials to assure each of their different constituencies that their interests—often competing—are of paramount importance.
- It links dollar expenditures with anticipated outcomes. However, even when outcomes can be readily quantifiable, they may not be casually linked to expenditures. The number of students passing the CPA exam may be a desirable (and even readily quantifiable) objective of an accounting department. But increasing the department's budget will not necessarily lead to a measurable increase in the CPA exam pass rate.

  Contemporary forms of program budgeting recognize this limitation and focus mainly on outputs rather than outcomes. Thus, the budget request of an accounting department might be based upon the relationship between dollar expenditures and number of students served in total, or perhaps more specifically, number of places in CPA review classes, rather than on the number of students passing the exam.
- It may require extraordinary efforts to implement initially, but thereafter may be applied perfunctorily. When program budgeting is first instituted, budgetary

units may have to establish objectives and outcome measures, develop new techniques of cost analysis, and adjust their accounting systems to conform to new budgetary classifications. Managers have to learn to prepare budget requests in new formats. Indeed, many of the benefits of program budgeting may be ascribed to the organizational self-examination that it requires at the outset. Once adopted, however, the organizational units can readily call up prior-year budget requests on their word processors and merely change the numbers. The advantages of program budgeting can easily be lost if the budgeting process becomes nothing more than a mechanical exercise.

- It may be imposed by the organization's budgetary generals on their troops and thereby be resented by them. Governmental and not-for-profit folklore is replete with anecdotes of senior managers who attend seminars on new budgetary techniques and order that they be implemented immediately. Program budgeting requires the active participation and support of employees at all levels of the organization. Budget requests must be prepared by the parties responsible for individual activities. If program budgeting is to be successfully instituted, then senior-level managers must first convince the lower-level employees of its benefits.
- It may require easily overlooked "technical" adjustments to computer programs and other elements of the accounting and control systems. The required changes may be costly, may result in organizational confusion, and may delay implementation.
- It may present decision makers, especially in large organizations such as state and federal agencies, with so much information that they are overwhelmed by its sheer volume—and hence likely to ignore much of it.
- It may not live up to the expectations of the participants in the budgetary process and thereby leave them cynical and discouraged. New forms of budgeting are typically promoted as an effort to bring "rationality" to the budget process. But what is rational to one person may be absurd to another. Indeed, to some, *rationality* may imply an increase in resources for activities they favor. No widely reported upon empirical evidence suggests that program budgeting alters budgetary allocations. Budgeting is primarily a political process. Irrespective of the elegance or the logic of budgetary proposals, they are unlikely to turn liberals into conservatives or conservatives into liberals. Program budgeting might be useful in challenging the biases of both liberals and conservatives and encouraging them to look beyond the short-term interests of their immediate constituents. But no budgeting system, by itself, can be expected to diminish the influence of the politically powerful nor enhance that of the politically weak.
- The budgeting recommendations and rankings of program officials may be overridden by the ultimate decision makers. As a result, those who expended great effort in preparing their budget requests, only to have their advice ignored or rejected, may become cynical toward the entire budget process.

HOW SHOULD SERVICE EFFORTS AND ACCOMPLISHMENTS BE REPORTED?

If an organization is to tie its budgets to specific performance objectives, it follows that it should periodically report on the extent to which it has achieved those objectives. It should report upon results (Box 3 of Figure 14-1) and those results should be subject to audit (Box 4).

Leading accounting organizations disagree as to the extent to which information on performance measures should be incorporated into annual general-purpose financial statements or other required supplementary reports that would be publicly available. Some say that measures of performance are necessarily so subjective that they should be outside the scope of financial reporting. There is virtually no disagreement, however, that performance should be assessed and the results reported *within* organizations.

As noted in Chapter 1, the GASB established the following as one of the main objectives of financial reporting: "Financial reporting should provide information to assist users in assessing the service efforts costs and accomplishments of the governmental entity." This information helps users assess the government's "economy, efficiency, and effectiveness" and "may help form a basis for voting or funding decisions."[2]

In furtherance of this objective the GASB has conducted extensive research on **service efforts and accomplishments (SEA) indicators.** Most notably, it commissioned a series of studies on how they can be applied in twelve significant areas of state and local government (such as education, fire protection, and mass transit).[3] These studies led the GASB to issue a concepts statement, *Service Efforts and Accomplishment Reporting,* setting forth the criteria that SEA measures should meet.[4] Moreover, the GASB has a link on its Web page (www.GASB.org) directed to performance measurement. The performance measurement site presents conceptual information on the subject, numerous examples drawn from different types of government units, and links to related Web sites.

Although the concepts statement is intended to lay the foundation for the GASB to develop standards for reporting SEA measures to outsiders, for the most part it is equally relevant to measures that would be used within an organization. More recently the GASB published a monograph, *Reporting Performance Information: Suggested Criteria for Effective Communication* (2003), that sets forth additional characteristics of sound SEA reporting. This section of the text reflects many of the GASB's conclusions and recommendations.

PERFORMANCE MEASURES

Irrespective of whether governments should include SEA measures in their general purpose financial statements, there are compelling reasons as to why they should compile and incorporate performance measures into their management processes:

- Measuring and reporting upon performance promotes higher-order accountability among employees at all levels of the organization. Employees are put on notice explicitly that they are expected to achieve certain objectives—objectives that presumably are consistent with the organization's overall mission. Organizations make statements as to what is important by what they measure and report. Whereas traditional statements signal the significance of budgetary compliance and custodianship of resources, SEA reports stress the importance of achieving organizational objectives.
- SEA measures are consistent with both the purposes of financial reporting (both internal and external) and the nature of government and not-for-profit organizations. Financial reporting is intended to indicate the extent to which an organization achieves its objectives. The main objective of businesses is profit (or cash flow) maximization. Hence, their statements emphasize profitability and cash flow. The main objectives of governments and not-for-profits are to

[2] GASB Concepts Statement 1, *Objectives of Financial Reporting* (1987). *Codification,* para. 77.

[3] For a summary of these studies, see *Service Efforts and Accomplishments Reporting: Its Time Has Come (An Overview),* (Norwalk, Conn.: Governmental Accounting Standards Board, 1990).

[4] Concepts Statement No. 2, 1994.

provide services, advocate a political or social cause, or carry out research or other activities for the betterment of their constituents. Therefore, reports on their accomplishments should be geared to those objectives.

- SEA reporting fosters sound budgeting and administration. As suggested in Figure 14-1, effective budgeting and administration requires information on the results of previous expenditures. Reports on performance indicate whether previously appropriated resources were used efficiently and effectively.

MAIN TYPES OF SEA INDICATORS

The GASB concepts statement divides SEA measures into three categories:

- ***Measures of efforts***—the resources applied to a service (i.e., the *inputs*). Although the primary measure of effort is dollar cost, effort can also be expressed in nonfinancial metrics, such as number of personnel, amount of equipment, and amount of other capital assets (e.g., feet of floor space or amount of land).
- ***Measures of accomplishment***—what was provided and achieved with available inputs. These include both *outputs* and *outcomes* and reflect the organization's operational objectives.
- ***Measures that relate efforts to accomplishment***—the GASB subdivides these measures into two categories: efficiency measures and cost-outcome measures. Efficiency measures relate efforts (inputs) to outputs. Examples include cost per full-time student, cost per passenger-mile, and number of doctors per patient. Cost-outcome measures relate efforts (inputs) to outcomes. Examples include cost per student who passes the bar exam, cost per commuter who arrives at a destination within a specified time, and number of doctors per patient successfully treated.

The GASB concepts statement also emphasizes that these three types of data should be supplemented with explanatory information that can better help users understand the measures presented and put them in proper perspective. The explanatory information can be both quantitative and narrative. The quantitative information can include data on factors beyond the control of the entity, such as on population or the economy. It might include number of students from families below the poverty line or percentage of citizens by age grouping. The narrative information can interpret the data and indicate how the entity is responding to them.

The GASB concepts statement makes no reference to ZBB or other specific systems of program budgeting. It is no coincidence, however, that most variants of program budgeting also require specification of inputs, outputs, and outcomes. Consistent with the theme of this chapter, both budgeting and assessment must be tied to organizational objectives.

Table 14-4 presents an example of SEA indicators of an Aid for Dependent Children program. Table 14-5 presents examples from a police department crime program.

LIMITATIONS

SEA measures also have obvious limitations. Some of these, along with means of overcoming them, are discussed here.

SEA measures, insofar as they are drawn from an entity's objectives, are unlikely to be any more indicative of the entity's true accomplishments than the stated objectives are of the entity's true goals. Moreover, they are silent as to whether the objectives, even if they are indicative of true goals, are really worth achieving and if they genuinely reflect the values of the organization's constituents. As they do in formulating objectives, organizations must be sure not to sacrifice measurement convenience for substance. Also, as suggested in the discussion of objectives, accomplishments can seldom be described by a single measure. Therefore, several measures may have to be provided.

TABLE 14–4
Service Efforts and Accomplishments
Examples of SEA Indicators—
Aid for Dependent Children Program

Inputs

- Administrative cost of program
- Total cost
- Total staff-hours used to operate program

Outputs

- Total number of recipients
- Total amount of assistance provided

Outcomes

- Percentage of applications processed within forty-five days
- Percentage of cases redetermined within six months
- Payment error rates
- Percentage of surveyed who meet predetermined levels of physical health
- Percentage of surveyed who live in adequate housing
- Percentage of grants reduced due to employment of parents
- Percentage of cases not reopened within two years

Efficiency Indicators

- Number of accurate case actions processed per worker
- Administrative cost per case
- Staff-hours per accurate case action

Explanatory Information

- Unemployment rate
- Number of cases per worker
- Percentage of working parent recipients
- Staffing problems

Source: Adapted from S. Wagner, R. E. Brown, and J. B. Tinnin, "Public Assistance Programs" in *Service Efforts and Accomplishments Reporting: Its Time Has Come* (Norwalk, Conn.: Governmental Accounting Standards Board, 1990), p. 217.

SEA data may not provide sufficient information to enable meaningful comparisons among organizations, or units within the same organization, since they do not take into account different operating conditions. Consider the following examples of situations in which misleading inferences can easily be drawn:

- A school district uses results on standardized reading and mathematics tests to assess the performance of elementary schools. The scores, by themselves, provide no information on social, economic, and cultural differences in the composition of the schools' student bodies—differences that almost certainly affect test scores. Not surprisingly, scores of schools in wealthy neighborhoods are almost always higher than those in poor ones.
- A sanitation department measures the efficiency of its several districts as cost per ton of trash collected. The metric fails to take into account district differences in the average distances between homes and in the percentage of the customers that are businesses rather than residences.

Similarly, even comparisons over time within the same organization can be deceptive in the face of changing conditions. A decrease in the ratio of clients to placements at a

TABLE 14-5
Service Efforts and Accomplishments Examples of SEA Indicators— Police Department

Inputs
- Budget expenditures
- Equipment facilities, vehicles
- Number of personnel; hours expended

Outputs
- Hours of patrol
- Responses to calls for service
- Crimes investigated
- Number of arrests

Outcomes
- Deaths and bodily injury resulting from crime
- Value of property lost due to crime
- Crimes committed per 100,000 of population
- Percentage of crimes cleared
- Response time
- Citizen satisfaction

Efficiency Indicators
- Cost per case assigned
- Cost per crime cleared
- Personnel-hours per crime cleared

Explanatory Information
- Population by age
- Unemployment rate
- Percentage of population below poverty line
- Land area
- Number of calls for service

Source: Adapted from A. Drebin and M. Brannon, "Police Department Programs," in *Service Efforts and Accomplishments Reporting: Its Time Has Come* (Norwalk, Conn.: Governmental Accounting Standards Board, 1990), p. 193.

job placement service may be due not to a decline in efficiency but to a downturn in the local economy, a factor beyond the control of the service. The failure of SEA measures, by themselves, to take into account differences in circumstances can be mitigated by supplementing the quantitative data with narrative explanations of factors that influence the measures.

SEA data, especially if presented in numerous and lengthy tables, can be mind-numbing. In some circumstances, charts and graphs can more sharply spotlight organizational or temporal differences. At the same time, however, graphs and charts can easily be used to mislead. For example, on a line graph, changes from one year to the next can be made to appear greater by altering the scales of either the horizontal or vertical axis.

SEA data can easily be under- or over-aggregated. A recent study of performance data in four countries revealed that members of parliament did not use the data to the extent anticipated. The members complained that the reports they received failed to provide the "right" amount of information and that they lacked the time or staff assistance to properly interpret them.[5] Level of detail must be tailored to the user. Governing boards, for example, would ordinarily benefit most from data that are more aggregated and summarized than those provided to department managers.

[5] U.S. General Accounting Office, *Managing for Results: Experiences Abroad Suggest Insights for Federal Management Reforms* (GAO/GAD 95-120), 1995. The four countries were Australia, Canada, New Zealand, and the United Kingdom.

FEDERAL INITIATIVES

In the United States, the federal government is taking a leading role in ensuring that performance measurement is an integral part of governments' management processes. Its initiatives have been driven mainly by the Government Performance and Results Act of 1993. This act seeks to shift the focus of government decision making away from the means by which agencies carry out their activities (such as amount of grant money awarded or number of inspections undertaken) and toward the results of those activities (such as real gains in number of persons employed or number of workplace accidents). It requires federal agencies to develop long-term strategic plans as well as explicit operational objectives and performance measures. In addition, it mandates that the agencies report annually on the extent to which they are meeting their objectives and on the actions needed to achieve or modify any goals that have not been met.

In support of the act, the government established the National Partnership for Reinventing Government (formerly known as the National Performance Review). Per the organization's mission statement, its objective is to "reinvent government to work better, cost less, and get results Americans care about." Since its creation it has studied federal agencies and made hundreds of recommendations as to how they could become more efficient and effective. Equally important, it fashioned means for sharing information among agencies and for rewarding outstanding performance.

Agencies have now had more than a decade's worth of experience in implementing the Government Performance and Results Act. Both the General Accounting Office[6] and the Office of Management and Budget have issued several reports setting forth what federal agencies have accomplished as the result of the act and the challenges that they must still face.[7]

AUDITS OF SEA REPORTS

The role of auditors in attesting to reports on service efforts and accomplishments can be similar to that in expressing an opinion on traditional financial statements. If the service efforts and accomplishments can be measured and reported upon, then the measurements can be verified and the reports attested to. In fact, the AICPA now has separate standards for attesting to nonfinancial assertions. They have formed the basis for auditor opinions on matters as diverse as the circulation of newspapers and the distance traveled by golf balls.[8]

As they are in traditional financial engagements, auditors could be required to assess the adequacy of the information systems used to compile the SEA data, to verify that the data are reliable, and to evaluate whether they are fairly presented. This would require that they review the organization's internal control systems and test selected transactions. The auditing profession has not, as yet, developed guidelines and standards as to what constitutes fair presentation of the data and as to how the data should be examined and the underlying information systems tested. It will, of course, have to do so if auditors are to expand the scope of their engagements to cover SEA data. However, by developing standards as to what constitutes fair presentation, it runs the risk of intruding on the judgments and values of elected officials in determining what aspects of performance are important in their jurisdictions.

---

[6] As noted in footnote 4 in Chapter 1, as this text goes to press, the GAO is seeking, by way of Congressional legislation, to change its name from the General Accounting Office to the *Government Accountability Office*. This new designation, the GAO officials believe, will better encapsulate the agency's main mission, which is to make the operations of the federal government more efficient and effective. They also hope that it will dispel the common, but ill conceived, image of the agency as the nation's official bean counters.

[7] See, e.g., the GAO's *Performance and Accountability Series* (a series of reports that highlights the management challenges and program risks faced by federal agencies) and the OMB's annual *Federal Financial Management Status Report and Five Year Plan*.

[8] See the series of AICPA professional standards, *Statements on Standards for Attestation Engagements*.

Auditors cannot be expected to assess the appropriateness of either the organization's basic objectives or indicators selected to gauge whether they have been achieved. That, as stressed earlier, is the function of legislatures, governing boards, or other policy makers.

Auditing the performance of an entity is far more complex than merely expressing an opinion on organization-prepared SEA reports. "Performance" audits will be discussed in greater detail in Chapter 15.

HOW ARE CAPITAL EXPENDITURES PLANNED AND BUDGETED WITHIN A FRAMEWORK OF OPERATIONAL OBJECTIVES?

Both government and not-for-profit organizations shape their futures through their acquisitions of capital assets. Capital assets may not only be costly, but they may have long lives and have a long-term impact on both operating costs and results. By purchasing or constructing capital assets, organizations make commitments of resources that can generally be revoked only with substantial economic penalty.

In Chapter 1 it was noted that a key difference between businesses and not-for-profits, including governments, is that the latter make significant investments in assets that neither produce revenues nor reduce expenditures. Accordingly, the analysis of proposed outlays may be far more complex and difficult in not-for-profits than in businesses.

In businesses the general approach to determining whether to acquire an asset (or undertake a project) is to compare the cash outflows associated with the asset (the costs) with the cash outflows or savings that it will provide (the benefits). However, cash has a *time value*, and both the outflows and inflows may occur over a number of years. Therefore, to make the inflows and outflows comparable, they must be *discounted* back to the present. This general approach is consistent with the objective of a business—to maximize net cash flows.

Governments and not-for-profits have objectives other than maximizing net cash flows. Accordingly, they must take an approach to capital budgeting that relates the costs of a proposed acquisition to fulfillment of their own unique goals and operational objectives.

DIFFERENCES BETWEEN CAPITAL AND OPERATING EXPENDITURES

It is widely accepted that interperiod equity dictates that capital assets may be financed and paid for differently from operating expenditures. Capital assets provide benefits over more than one year. Hence, it is asserted, they should be paid for by the taxes—and the taxpayers—of more than one year. It therefore may be not only acceptable, but desirable, to finance capital acquisitions with debt rather than with taxes or other operating revenues. To do otherwise would strongly discourage investment in long-term projects, because in the year of acquisition they may necessitate a significant onetime increase in taxes or decreases in other expenditures.

Insofar as capital projects will be financed with debt rather than operating revenues, it is especially important that they be budgeted and planned for separately. The amount of debt that an organization can issue is almost always limited, either by legal debt limitations or fiscal prudence. Accordingly, a project to be financed with debt should compete for funds, not with all other activities, but only with the others that will be financed out of the same pool of resources.

Separate budgeting and planning also enables an organization's managers and constituents to focus more sharply upon capital outlays, narrowing their attention to a subset of all expenditures. In that way they decrease the likelihood of misguided expenditures—mistakes the entity will have to live with for many years.

CAPITAL IMPROVEMENT PROGRAMS AND BUDGETS

Just as an operating budget, when approved, authorizes operating expenditures, a capital budget sanctions capital outlays. Because of their cost, their longevity and the long lead time required for financing as well as purchase or construction, capital expenditures are usually planned for over a period of at least five or six years. An entity's long-term schedule of capital acquisitions is conventionally termed its **capital improvement program (CIP).**

Most entities define capital assets as physical properties (almost always above a specified dollar amount). Capital budgets and improvement programs are commonly associated with infrastructure assets, such as buildings, roads, airports, and utilities, and with major items of equipment, such as emergency communication systems, construction equipment, and mainframe computers. However, some organizations also include within the scope of their capital budgets projects other than physical assets—such as toxic clean-ups—that require major outlays and will provide benefits over many years.

Capital budgeting and programming are generally carried out in two stages. In the first, individual projects are screened to determine whether they should be undertaken at all, assuming that the resources will be available to fund them. As part of this stage, the organization compares alternative means of achieving the same objective (e.g., lease or purchase office space) and selects that which will be the most cost-effective. The essence of this stage is **benefit–cost analysis.** The second stage is that of ranking the projects that pass through the initial screen.

BENEFIT–COST ANALYSIS

Benefit–cost analysis is nothing more than a generic term for any form of expenditure analysis that identifies and quantifies the benefits of a proposal and compares them to its costs. In business, the benefits are cash flows; in government and not-for-profits they should be drawn from the entities' own operational objectives. By requiring that the benefits be explicitly identified and quantified, organizations help ensure that they are consistent with their own operational objectives and overall mission.

Benefit–cost analysis has often been misused and subjected to ridicule as analysts go overboard in attempting to assign numbers to benefits that are not readily quantifiable. However, to the extent that benefits can be quantified, it provides a reasonable means of deciding whether an asset should be acquired or a project should be undertaken and of ranking competing proposals. Benefit–cost analysis may be used to enhance the objectivity of decision making. By no means can it eliminate the role of informed judgment, and it should not be used to give the appearance of mathematical precision when such rigor is unjustifiable.

Benefits Are Cash Savings

As stressed in Chapter 13, many types of not-for-profit decisions are comparable to those in businesses and thus are amenable to business-type analysis. Proposed capital acquisitions may affect mainly the cost of achieving desired outcomes, not their quality or quantity. Therefore, the potential benefits of many capital assets or long-term projects can be expressed as cash savings and can be assessed by standard discounting procedures.

The benefits and costs of a project must always be assessed over its entire life cycle. Some assets may seem relatively cheap to maintain. Over time, however, key parts may have to be replaced, repaired, or overhauled. These costs must be taken into account, especially when selecting among alternatives.

EXAMPLE *Benefits Are Cash Savings*

The Food for the Elderly Center currently relies on a private messenger service to deliver meals to its clients. The cost per year is $40,000. The center is considering acquiring a van and engaging a driver to deliver the meals. The price of the vehicle, to be paid in cash at time of acquisition, is $52,000. Annual estimated operating costs, including insurance, maintenance, repairs, and the wages and benefits of the required part-time driver, are expected to be $24,000. Thus, the center would save $16,000 per year in annual operating costs (the $40,000 cost of the messenger service less the $24,000 in anticipated costs). The estimated useful life of the van is five years. The center uses a discount rate of 10 percent to assess all long-term proposals.

Per the following analysis, the center should accept the proposal:

Annual anticipated cash savings for five years:	$ 16,000
Present value of an annuity of $1 at10 percent for five years	× 3.7908
Present value of annual benefits (annual cash savings)	$ 60,653
Less: cost of vehicle (present value)	52,000
Present value of net cash savings	$ 8,653

The benefits exceed the costs by $8,653.

It is often useful in comparing the benefits of two or more competing options, especially if projects require initial investments of differing amounts, to express the relationship of cost to benefits (net of all post-acquisition costs) as a ratio:

$$\text{Benefit-cost ratio} = \frac{\text{Present value of net annual benefits}}{\text{Initial investment}}$$

Thus, in this example:

$$\frac{\$60{,}653}{\$52{,}000} = 1.1666$$

Having calculated the quantifiable net benefits of an acquisition, the organization's managers must then weigh them against factors that cannot easily be reduced to numbers. In this example, these might include the potential for improvement (or deterioration) in the quality of delivery service and the risks of unanticipated repair costs.

Of course, as anyone who has studied capital expenditure analysis in other contexts is aware, the computations can be far more complex than is suggested by the example. The example, however, is intended merely to demonstrate that a systematic, discounted cash-flow approach to capital expenditure analysis is as applicable to governments and not-for-profits as to businesses.

Benefits Are the Same among Options

Benefit–cost analysis, including present value techniques, is obviously easier to apply when, as in the previous example, the benefits are mainly cash savings rather than gains that are less tangible. But it can also be utilized in circumstances, of which there are many, in which an organization has to select among two or more options, each of will provide the same benefits. For if the benefits are the same, they need not be taken into account.

EXAMPLE *Choosing among Options with Similar Benefits*

City Transit, a public authority, is required by its charter to make its services available to mobility-impaired city residents. It is considering three options:

- Install special equipment on selected buses to enable wheelchair-bound passengers to board the vehicles. Installation costs would be $10 million, to be incurred in the current year. Thereafter, maintenance and repair costs would be covered by state and federal grants.

- Purchase and operate a fleet of special transit vans. The initial cost would be $2.5 million. Estimated maintenance, repair, and other operating costs, including the wages of drivers, would be $1.8 million.
- Distribute vouchers to eligible passengers enabling them to use private taxis for a specified number of rides per month. Estimated cost would be $2.4 million per year.

The economic life of both the special equipment and the vans is expected to be five years and is therefore a reasonable period over which to assess the three options. The authority uses a discount rate of 10 percent to evaluate all capital proposals. The following analysis compares the three options:

	Cash Outflow (thousands)	Present Value of an Annuity of $1 at 10%	Present Value of Cash Flow (thousands)
Option #1, Special Equipment			
Period 0	$10,000	$1.0000	$10,000
Option #2, Acquisition of Vans			
Period 0	$ 2,500	$1.0000	$ 2,500
Periods 1–5	1,800	3.7908	6,823
Total			$ 9,323
Option #3, Taxis			
Periods 1–5	$ 2,400	$3.7908	$ 9,098

Based on the present value of the costs and assuming the benefits of all three options to be the same, the authority would select the third options, that of giving taxi vouchers to eligible passengers. It would result in the cash outflows with the least present value.

This example is intended mainly to demonstrate the applicability of present value analysis to circumstances in which the benefits of the options cannot be expressed in monetary units but nevertheless are similar. But it can also be used to highlight two inherent limitations of present value analysis.

First, present value analysis may be sensitive to the choice of discount rate. The following analysis replicates the previous one, except that it incorporates a discount rate of 6 percent rather than 10 percent. Note that the order of preference of the three options is reversed. The installation of special equipment is now the least costly.

	Cash Outflow (thousands)	Present Value of an Annuity of $1 at 6%	Present Value of Cash Flow (thousands)
Option #1, Special Equipment			
Period 0	$10,000	$1.0000	$10,000
Option #2, Acquisition of Vans			
Period 0	$ 2,500	$1.0000	$ 2,500
Periods 1–5	1,800	4.2124	7,582
Total			$10,082
Option #3, Taxis			
Periods 1–5	$ 2,400	$4.2124	$10,110

Second, even though the benefits of the options may be similar, they are unlikely to be identical. In the illustration, for example, transportation by taxi as opposed to public buses embodies a very different set of advantages and disadvantages (both physical and psychological) for the affected passengers. Thus, the analysis, which compares only present value of dollar outflows, may fail to take into account costs and benefits that are difficult even to describe, let alone measure—factors that, especially in a political environment, are crucial to an ultimate decision.

Benefits Differ among Options

Because of their very purpose, governments and not-for-profit organizations undertake projects that are intended to extend the length, or enhance the quality, of human lives. Moreover, they must make decisions in which the benefits of available options will not be the same.

Benefit–cost analysis requires that costs be compared with benefits. Since they can be compared only when expressed in common terms, organizations must come to grips with the monetary value of human life or various aspects of the quality of human life.

Although it is never easy—nor analytically satisfactory—to place a dollar value on human lives or happiness, both governments and not-for-profit organizations (and their constituents) must constantly do so, either implicitly or explicitly. A decision to purchase an additional ambulance involves a tacit comparison of the cost of the ambulance with the value of the human lives it might save or suffering it might reduce.

One widely used approach to placing an economic value on human life is grounded on future earning capacity. Estimated future earnings of the individuals affected by a proposed program are discounted back to the present. Courts, for example, generally base wrongful death damages on the victim's anticipated earnings. Thus, the life of a twenty-five-year-old medical student is considered far more valuable than that of a fifty-year-old homemaker. Similarly, as described in the accompanying In Practice, the U.S. government was required to determine the economic value of the victims of the September 11 disaster as measured by lost income. An obvious objection to these approaches is that they place no value on dimensions of human existence other than earning power—e.g., that of noncompensatory services, such as housekeeping, and of the emotional support, love, and affection that people provide to others.

Monetization of costs and benefits not only facilities analysis, but serves as a reminder that as long as resources are limited, human life cannot be considered "priceless." Nevertheless, it runs the same risk as quantifying an organization's objectives and accomplishments—that of misspecifying the true benefits of a proposal and of thereby promoting decisions that are inconsistent with the true goals of the organization and the values of its constituents. As observed earlier, merely because an outcome can be measured does not make it meaningful.

RANKING PROPOSED CAPITAL ACQUISITIONS

Ranking assets or projects is never easy. Since all general obligation debt is issued in the name of a government or organization, not its subunits, projects from all divisions must be combined into a common ordering. For obvious reasons, there are no clear-cut criteria that are suitable for comparing projects as diverse as highways and jails. Nevertheless, institutions attempt to discern common denominators. For example, one state government (Massachusetts) assigns general rankings as follows:

1. Needed for legal compliance (e.g., court mandated)
2. Needed to preserve an existing facility

IN PRACTICE

SEPTEMBER 11 VICTIM COMPENSATION FUND

How much is a life worth? Per federal law (49 U.S.C. 40101) the estates of those who perished in the September 11, 2001, World Trade Center disaster are entitled to compensation for economic losses. The following is a summary of the how the September 11 Victim Compensation Fund of 2001 computes the amount of the loss:

1. Establish the victim's age and income
2. Determine after-tax income by applying appropriate federal, state, and local tax rates
3. Add the value of employer-provided benefits
4. Determine the remaining number of years of workforce participation using generally accepted actuarial tables
5. Project income and benefits through the victim's expected work-life using growth rates that incorporate an annual inflationary or cost-of-living component, as well as an annual real overall productivity adjustment
6. Adjust the projected income and benefits to take into account adverse contingencies such as unemployment (e.g., using a discount factor of 3 percent)
7. Based on Bureau of Labor Statistics data on average annual expenditures and characteristics, subtract from the projected income and benefits the victim's share of household expenditures or consumption as a percentage of income
8. Calculate the present value of the projected income and benefits using a discount rate based on mid- to long-term treasury securities

Source: Adapted from information on the Web site (www.usdoj.gov/victimcompensation/index.html) of the September 11th Victim Compensation Fund of 2001, administered by the U.S. Department of Justice.

3. Needed to promote operational efficiency
4. Needed to promote additions to capital stock[9]

Others establish systems that require each program to be scored on a variety of criteria. For a government, these may include:

- Benefit–cost ratio
- Impact on the economy, including number of jobs and sales to be generated (both directly and indirectly)
- Impact on the government's costs and revenues to the extent they are incorporated in the benefit–cost ratio
- Proportion of population that will benefit
- Effect on environment
- Extent of inconvenience and disruptions during construction
- Effect on health and safety

If a government or not-for-profit has established the total amount of costs it is willing to incur for capital expenditures, then, as with ZBB, it will undertake all projects the cumulative sum of which is less than the determined maximum. But as with operating

[9] John L. Mikesell, *Fiscal Administration, Analysis and Applications for the Public Sector*, 4th ed., (Belmont, Calif.: Wadsworth, 1995), p. 225.

expenditures, the process of ranking is seldom as objective as might appear from benefit–cost ratios or other numerical scores assigned to projects. Capital budgeting, no less than operating budgeting, is a political process in which various constituencies and interest groups vie for available resources. In the end, therefore, many organizations make at least some of their capital budgeting decisions the old-fashioned way—by subjective (albeit, hopefully, informed) judgment.

THE DOWNSIDE OF EVALUATING CAPITAL SPENDING SEPARATELY FROM OPERATIONAL SPENDING

As noted earlier, capital budgets and improvement programs enable an organization's managers and constituents to sharpen their focus upon capital outlays. The downside, however, is that they run the risk of failing to account for the operating and maintenance costs associated with the newly acquired assets.

As was noted in Chapter 1, many government and not-for-profit assets have more of the characteristics of liabilities than of assets. They provide no cash inflow, yet they must be serviced and maintained. The cost of a capital asset—that which is incorporated in a capital budget—is comparable to the hospital bill for a newborn child. It may be just the tip of a fiscal iceberg. Roads and highways are not only in need of ongoing repair, they must be patrolled by police. University buildings must be heated and air-conditioned. Indeed, when proponents of major capital projects, such as sports arenas and convention centers, assure voters that the ventures will "pay for themselves" through lease payments, fees, and added sales tax revenues, they often fail to make mention of the added operating costs, such as for police, fire protection, and administration.

The risk of overlooking operating and maintenance costs can be minimized by explicitly incorporating into the benefit–cost analysis of all proposed projects an itemization of anticipated additional operating costs. Moreover, procedures can be established so that when the capital budget is approved, the additional operating costs are automatically added to the operating budget. Similarly, when a not-for-profit, such as a university, accepts donations for a building or other capital project, sound (and widely accepted) policy dictates that it solicit additional funds to establish an operating endowment. Such endowment should be of sufficient amount to yield the cash required for the annual upkeep of the asset.

Table 14-6 presents an excerpt from a city's capital budget. Note that the impact on operating expenditures is highlighted.

SUMMARY

Accountants have a role to play in all phases of the management cycle in governments and not-for-profits: programming and budgeting, appropriating funds, administering, auditing, and assessing.

Operational objectives should be the basis for allocating resources, managing day-to-day activities, and distributing rewards and reprimands. Ideally, operational objectives should represent true ends, capture outcomes, be measurable within a sufficiently short period, and be precise. However, in practice, owing to measurement difficulties, many entities express their objectives as outputs rather than outcomes. Moreover, most organizations find that they require multiple objectives to express fully their missions.

Organizations face significant obstacles in establishing operational objectives that facilitate, rather than detract from, their ability to accomplish their missions. In some cases organizations are not clear as to the results they want to achieve or are unable to distinguish results from the means of accomplishing them. In others, the objectives provoke conflict among employees and other constituents or encourage dysfunctional behavior.

Traditional budgets provide no information about the extent to which expenditures advance an entity's mission or enable it to achieve its objectives. By contrast, program budgeting helps to ensure that all expenditures are justified in relation to organizational objectives. It encourages consideration of alternative ways of achieving the same objective and of whether the objective is even appropriate for the organization. Further, it helps to ensure that the behavior of costs is explicitly taken into account and that programs or

TABLE 14-6
An Excerpt from a Capital Budget Emphasizing Impact of Additional Operating Costs

New County Jail

Project Description: A new 576-bed prison facility will be constructed in the same vicinity as the current facility, which is more than forty years old. The new prison will house state prisoners. The old prison—which has 256 beds but houses fewer than thirty county prisoners today—will then be remodeled as an annex for the county jail.

	Prior	FY 05	FY 06	Total
Financing method				
Direct revenue				
grants	$447,000	$7,500,000		$7,947,000
PAA Fund		185,000		185,000
Other CIP fund sources				
balance forward		389,602	$3,309,700	—
GF CIP reallocation	9,700			9,700
Total	$456,700	$8,074,602	$3,309,700	$8,141,700
Project cost				
Land				
Land improvements		$120,000		$120,000
ROW/Easements				
Legal				
Arch/Eng/CM	$67,098	379,902		447,000
Demolition				
Utility relocation		100,000		100,000
Road construction		85,000		85,000
General construction		4,080,000	2,800,000	6,880,000
Landscaping			9,700	9,700
Public art element				
Furnishing/Equipment			500,000	500,000
Administrative				
Total	$67,098	$4,764,902	$3,309,700	$8,141,700
Balance	$389,602	$3,309,700	$ 0	$ 0

Benefit to the Community: The Consolidated Government uses inmate labor extensively to offset operating costs in such areas as parks maintenance and waste management. The new prison will add 320 inmates to our "labor pool." Additionally, the old facility will be converted into a county jail annex, providing inexpensive additional beds for county inmates.

Impact on Operating Budget: Using state-of-the-art design methods and theory devised to optimize human resource requirements, the new prison should reduce the operating deficit by increasing revenue potential by increasing the number of prisoners (for which the City receives a per diem). Associated operating costs are expected to increase at a slower rate relative to operating revenues. These actions are expected to decrease the FY '05 projected $430,000 operating deficit by half in future years. The additional inmate labor provided will help to offset anticipated parks' maintenance costs increases due to sales tax-supported projects.

activities that have outlived their usefulness are replaced with those that would do more to advance the organization's mission.

Although, ideally, program budgets should link costs to outcomes, in reality increases in costs cannot always be causally associated with improvements in outcomes. Therefore, many entities have found it more practical to tie costs to outputs rather than to outcomes.

If governments and other not-for-profits are to budget so as to achieve specific performance objectives, it follows that they should report on the extent to which they have achieved those objectives. That is, they must provide information about their service efforts and accomplishments. This information should encompass inputs, outputs, and outcomes. SEA reporting is consistent with the GASB's objectives of reporting, and it promotes higher-order accountability, sound budgeting, and forward-looking administration.

Governments and not-for-profits shape their destiny through the acquisition of capital assets, which are not only costly but have long lives. Therefore, the acquisition of capital assets requires commitments that can generally be revoked only with substantial economic penalty. Capital budgeting is usually carried out in two steps: screening (of which benefit–cost analysis is a key aspect) and ranking.

Benefit–cost analysis is a generic term for procedures in which the benefits of a project are compared with its costs. It is a means of ensuring that as many benefits and costs as feasible are explicitly identified and quantified. For many decisions the benefits are cost savings. For others, the benefits remain constant irrespective of the means of achieving them. In both these situations the standard discounted cash flow models that are widely used in business can be used to assess whether a project should be undertaken. In other situations, those in which the costs and benefits are intangible, such as number of lives lost or saved, the costs or benefits may be expressed in dollar terms so as to facilitate comparisons.

One of the disadvantages of evaluating capital expenditures apart from operating expenditures is that it is easy to overlook the operating costs associated with newly acquired assets. To ensure that these costs are taken into account, organizations should develop procedures that automatically incorporate estimated operating costs in the capital expenditure analysis and correspondingly add them to the expenditures of the operating budget.

EXERCISE FOR REVIEW AND SELF-STUDY

The subway system of a major U.S. city has several overall goals. These include:

- Serving a broad segment of society
- Providing on-time service
- Providing frequent service
- Ensuring passenger safety
- Ensuring that the environment in which passengers travel, including trains and stations, are clean and pleasant

a. For each of these goals propose at least two operational objectives.

b. Suppose that the system is to report on its service efforts and accomplishments. Propose at least two *input*, *output*, *outcome*, and *efficiency* indicators relating to the goal that trains and stations are clean and pleasant.

c. The system is considering improving safety at selected stations by installing TV cameras, emergency call boxes, and more modern lights and by making minor structural changes at selected stations. It estimates the cost to be $400,000 per station. In addition, it forecasts that it would be required to spend approximately $30,000 per year to monitor, maintain, and repair the new equipment. It estimates that the useful life of the equipment would be ten years. The system assesses all proposed capital expenditures using a discount rate of 12 percent. It estimates that the improvements would reduce crime by 10 percent.

1. Based on this limited amount of information, is it possible to determine whether the expenditure is economically advantageous?

2. Suppose that as an alternative to the physical improvements the system is considering adding police patrols to the stations.The cost of the additional police would be approximately $110,000 per year. Assuming that both options would have the same impact on passenger safety, which of the two would you recommend?

3. If the system were to approve the capital outlays, what changes would have to be made to its *operating* budget?

QUESTIONS FOR REVIEW AND DISCUSSION

1. Indicate four significant criteria that "operational objectives" should satisfy.
2. Why may an organization foment conflict merely by establishing specific objectives?
3. In what key way do program budgets more directly link expenditures to organizational goals than do conventional object classification budgets?
4. What are the key elements of program budgets as exemplified by a zero-base budget decision package for an activity?
5. The ultimate aim of governmental and not-for-profit organizations is to produce *outcomes.* Yet in preparing program budgets, many organizations link expenditures to *outputs* rather than outcomes. Why?
6. Why is it more important for governments and not-for-profit organizations than for businesses to report on service efforts and accomplishments?
7. What are the three main categories of SEA indicators?

8. Describe at least three limitations, both actual and potential, of SEA indicators and tell how they might be overcome.
9. Why is it advantageous to budget for capital outlays apart from operating expenditures?
10. What are the advantages of "monetizing" the value of human lives (often said to be "priceless") in assessing the costs and benefits of a proposed project or activity? What is the most widely used basis for valuing human lives? What are the limitations of this basis?

EXERCISES

14-1

1. Which of the following is likely to be a line item in a fire department's program budget but not its object classification budget?
   a. Administrative salaries
   b. Travel to conferences and training
   c. Safety inspections
   d. Acquisition of new equipment
2. Number of safety inspections performed by the Coast Guard would most likely be considered a
   a. Input measure
   b. Output measure
   c. Outcome measure
   d. Efficiency measure
3. Outcomes are frequently distinguished from outputs in that outcomes
   a. Are more likely to have a quality dimension associated with them
   b. Are more precise than outputs
   c. Are more likely to foment conflict among employees
   d. Cannot generally be quantified
4. Which of the following is not necessarily a desirable characteristic of outcome measures?
   a. They should be precise
   b. They should be long-term
   c. They should be quantifiable
   d. They should be measurable with a period sufficiently short to take corrective action
5. Which of the following is not characteristic of zero-base budgeting?
   a. It starts with the assumption that all activities within a program should be granted a zero increase unless evidence to the contrary is presented
   b. All activities, both new and proposed, within a program are subject to review and ranking
   c. It requires proposed funding increases to be tied to increases in outputs or outcomes
   d. It requires assessment of the consequences of funding activities at various levels
6. Per GASB pronouncements, information on "service efforts and accomplishments"
   a. Should be reported in the "management's discussion and analysis"
   b. Should be reported in the notes to the financial statements
   c. Should be reported as "required supplementary information"
   d. Need not be reported
7. The Government Performance and Results Act (1993) mandates that
   a. Federal agencies develop and report explicit operational objectives and performance measures
   b. Federal agencies meet specified Office of Management and Budget performance standards
   c. The federal government report measures of service efforts and accomplishment in its comprehensive annual report
   d. The General Accounting Office incorporate a "results" audit as part of its annual financial examination of federal agencies
8. A primary disadvantage of preparing separate operating and capital budgets is
   a. The distinction between a capital and an operating expenditure is often not clear
   b. It increases the risk of violating the principle of "interperiod equity"
   c. It risks overlooking the impact of capital expenditures on operating expenditures
   d. It leads organizations to favor operating expenditures, which have an immediate pay-off over capital expenditures, which have a long-term pay-off
9. In selecting between two projects, both of which will provide the same noncash benefits (e.g. increasing firefighter response time)
   a. It is preferable to use the thirty-year Treasury rate as a discount rate
   b. It would be inappropriate to use present-value analysis
   c. It is necessary to express the benefits in dollars, so that they can be compared to the costs
   d. It is appropriate to select the project with the smallest net discounted cash outflow (costs)
10. In selecting between two projects, both of which will provide different noncash benefits (e.g. increasing firefighter response time or improving a fire prevention program)
    a. It is necessary (albeit difficult) to express the benefits in common terms (such as dollars), so that they can be compared to the costs
    b. It would be inappropriate to use present-value analysis

c. The dollar value of a human life should be based on the "human value" tables of the American Actuarial Society
d. The focus of analysis should be mainly upon costs, inasmuch as there is no reliable measure of benefits.

14-2

Programs budget more closely tie expenditures to organizational objectives.

The "object classification" budget of a police department includes the following expense categories:

Salaries
Employee benefits
Supplies
Equipment
Vehicle maintenance, gas, etc.
Dues and subscriptions

Based on your lay knowledge of the operations of a police department, indicate five or six categories that would likely appear if the budget were recast in program format.

14-3

Organizations should consider desired outputs as well as outcomes.

For each of the following organizations, propose at least one measure of outputs and two of outcomes.

1. The admissions office of a selective private college
2. The sales tax division of a city government
3. A private foundation that provides college scholarships to economically disadvantaged students
4. A municipal housing authority that makes loans to low-income families so as to encourage home ownership
5. The Parkinson Disease Information Service, a not-for-profit organization that provides information to Parkinson patients and their families

14-4

Average costs generally contribute little to the budget process.

The Pleasant Valley School District, which leases its buses from a private transportation company, has determined that the direct costs of operating a bus (including rental fees, driver, and fuel) is $40,000 per year. The district currently operates thirty buses, each of which provides service to ninety children—hence, to a total of 2,700 children. The district also incurs $350,000 per year in fixed costs relating to transportation.

1. Calculate the average cost per child of providing bus transportation.
2. The district expects that next year it will have to provide transportation for an additional 300 children—a total of 3,000.
   a. Based on average cost, how much additional cost should the district budget?
   b. How much additional costs do you think the district should budget?
3. Suppose that the district expects that it will have to provide transportation for another sixty children in addition to the 300—a total of 360. How much more should it budget for the additional sixty children?

14-5

Conventional capital budgeting techniques are a useful starting point for investment decisions.

The Metropolitan Housing Authority is charged with providing housing to low-income residents. The authority is currently assessing two options, each of which would provide homes for 100 families.

Under the first option the authority would construct an apartment building at a cost of $8 million. Tenants would rent their apartments from the authority at subsidized rates. The authority estimates that its net annual cash operating costs (after taking into account the rent paid by the tenants) would be $300,000 per year. The expected useful life of the building would be twenty years.

Under the second option, the authority would make direct cash assistance payments to the tenants and they would arrange for their own housing. The expected annual payment to each family would be $12,000 per year—a total of $1,200,000 per year for 100 families.

The authority evaluates all capital projects using a discount rate of 8 percent.

1. Based on the limited information provided, which option would be the more cost-effective?
2. What other financial or nonfinancial factors should the authority consider in selecting between the two options?

14-6

Benefit–cost ratios may be useful in assessing the benefits of capital investments.

Antonio County is assessing whether it should build a new correctional facility for nonviolent offenders. Currently offenders are housed in the county jail at a cost per inmate of approximately $52,000 per year.

The new facility would cost $4 million to construct. However, inasmuch as inmates would be housed in dormitories rather than cells and the need for supervision would be reduced, the cost per inmate could be reduced to $43,000 per year.

The county estimates that if the new facility were constructed, it could accommodate 100 inmates who would otherwise be housed in the jail.

The county assesses all capital projects using a discount rate of 8 percent and uses a time horizon of ten years to evaluate proposals, such as that for the new facility, for which useful lives are indeterminate.

1. Determine the present value of the net savings that would result from undertaking the proposed project.
2. Calculate a benefit–cost ratio. Based on the limited amount of data provided, should the project be undertaken? Explain.

PROBLEMS

14-1

Object classification budgets can be recast to "program-type" budgets in which expenditures are tied to objectives.

The "object classification" budget of a fire department includes the following expense categories:

- Salaries
- Employee benefits
- Supplies
- Equipment
- Station maintenance, utilities, etc.
- Vehicle maintenance, gas, etc.
- Dues and subscriptions

Based on your lay knowledge of the operations of a fire department, indicate three categories that the department's budget might include if it were recast in "program" format. For each category indicate the following:

a. An appropriate operational objective
b. Possible measures of inputs, outputs, and outcomes

14-2

Inputs, outputs, and outcomes are not always readily distinguishable.

The following are selected measures of service efforts and accomplishments that might be appropriate for a university. For each, indicate whether it is an *input*, *output*, or *outcome* and state the objective with which it would most likely be associated. If it could be more than one, explain why. (For example, number and amount of research grants could be either an input or outcome associated with the objective of increasing the quality and quantity of research. Research grants are given as a reward for past research accomplishments and are therefore an outcome of a successful research program. At the same time, they facilitate research to be conducted in the future and are thereby an input.)

1. Tuition revenues
2. Number of students enrolled
3. Number and percentage of students passing the CPA exam
4. Number of articles published by faculty in specified "top tier" journals
5. Scholastic Aptitude Test scores
6. Graduate Record Exam scores
7. Revenues generated by a football program

14-3

Budgets—whether zero-base or any other type—should relate costs to objectives and take into account the actual behavior of costs.

Vision for Kids, a clinic funded by the Community Health Plan, a not-for-profit agency, provides eye examinations, eye glasses, and eye-related medical care for children from low-income families. Children are referred to it by school nurses and teachers, physicians, and social workers on the basis of poor performance on a vision screening test.

In its current year, Vision for Kids expects to serve 6,200 children. It will give each child an examination and, if needed, issue a pair of glasses. On average, one pair of glasses is issued for each child, since only children who failed the screening test are referred to the clinic, and some children lose or break their glasses after they have been issued.

The total budget for the current year is $942,000, broken down as follows:

Director	$ 75,000
Ophthalmologist (one full-time)	140,000
Optometrists (2 at 70,000)	140,000
Secretaries (2 at $30,000)	60,000
Technician	35,000
Nurses (2 at $40,000)	80,000
Glasses (6,200 at $60)	372,000
Drugs and other supplies	15,000
Other operating costs	25,000
	$942,000

Vision for Kids' ability to serve patients is limited by available funds. Were the resources available, it could easily serve twice as many patients. It receives all funds from its parent organization.

The ophthalmologist examines only those children referred to him by one of the optometrists. He is currently examining and treating the maximum number of patients in the available time (approximately 1,300—one out of every four children served by the center). The director estimates, however, that the organization would be able to hire an additional ophthalmologist on a one-quarter-time basis for $30,000 per year.

The director has also determined the following:

- An additional secretary would have to be added when the number of patients reaches 8,000.
- The currently employed ophthalmologist and two optometrists would not accept less than full-time employment. In light of their extensive experience, it would be uneconomical in the long-run to reduce their appointments to less than full time and replace them with part-time personnel (except, of course as a last resort). By contrast, one of the nurses has indicated a willingness to drop down to either three-quarter time or half-time status.

- Additional nurses and ophthalmologists can be added in quarter-time increments. Optometrists can be added only in half-time increments.
- Each optometrist can handle 3,200 patients per year; additional optometrists can be hired on a one-half time basis for $30,000.
- Each nurse can also serve 3,200 patients; nurses can be hired on a quarter-time basis for $10,000.
- The technician can handle at least 10,000 additional patients.
- Variable cost per patient is $64, determined as follows:

Glasses	$60
Drugs and other supplies	2
Other operating costs	2
Total variable costs	$64

The staff has submitted requests for many small items of equipment totaling $50,000 in costs. Although this equipment would not enable the clinic to serve additional patients, it would improve their care.

Prepare a zero-base decision package to be submitted to Vision for Kids' parent organization. Consider Vision for Kids to be an activity that is part of a children's health care program. Funding should be requested at the following levels, in addition to the current level:

- 90 percent ($847,800) of the current level
- 105 percent ($989,100) of the current level
- 120 percent ($1,130,400)

These percentage levels, however, should be interpreted only as approximations. If a major increase in efficiency (e.g., cost per unit of outcome) could be effected by operating at a level slightly greater or less than those specified, then the request should be at that level. Similarly, if all funds up to the stated level could not be used productively, then a lesser amount should be requested.

Based on your own judgment provide output and outcome measures, alternative means of carrying out the activity, and consequences of not performing the activity.

14-4

Successful outcomes may not necessarily be indicative of effective performance, especially when considered in isolation of factors beyond an organization's control.

The Education Agency of one of the nation's most populous states evaluates public elementary schools on the basis of the following inputs and outcomes:

Outcomes

- Total campus attendance
- Average student scores on standardized tests in math, reading, and writing

Inputs

- Total number of students enrolled
- Average teacher salary
- Average teacher experience
- Total number of teachers employed in regular education
- Total number of teachers employed in special education
- Average instructional expenditure per student
- Total number of economically disadvantaged students
- Total number of limited English proficiency students

The inputs and outcomes are factored together to obtain outcomes an overall performance rating.

a. Comment on these criteria as a basis for evaluating the performance of elementary schools.

b. Can you propose a means of improving upon these criteria?

14-5

Program-type budgets may not be as management friendly as they may initially appear—especially when the program and organizational structures are incongruent.

A public school district recently converted its budget from an object to a program format. The district is organized into three instructional divisions: elementary school (kindergarten through grade 6); middle school (grades 7 and 8); and high school (grades 9 through 12). In addition, it maintains support divisions for transportation, food services, and administration.

The district's two elementary schools are each organized in a traditional manner. They are headed by a principal and, depending on size, two or three vice-principals. There are up to six classes for each grade; the teachers assigned to a grade form the equivalent of a department.

Each elementary class is within the charge of a single teacher. He or she teaches all the main subjects (reading, science, mathematics, etc.). However, specialist teachers may provide instruction in areas such as computers and physical education.

Under the previous object classification format, all appropriations were broken down by school and, if appropriate, by grade. The main expenditure categories included the following:

- Administrator salaries
- Teacher salaries
- Aide salaries
- Support personnel salaries
- Supplies
- Computer and audio visual equipment
- Library books

Under the new format, the elementary school division has two major programs: basic education and support. These are subdivided into the following activities:

Basic Education

- Reading
- Mathematics

- Social studies
- Science
- Music
- Art
- Computer literacy
- Physical education

Support

- Administration
- Library
- Computers and visual aids

Teacher salaries and other costs that cut across programs and activities are allocated to programs and activities on an appropriate basis, such as percentage of classroom hours spent on a subject (for teacher salaries) or amount of usage (for computers and audio equipment).

The district has set forth specific objectives for each activity. For example, the primary objective for "reading" is "to ensure that at least 90 percent of students are reading at or above grade level as measured by [a specified standardized test]." The primary objective for each of the other academic activities is similar.

1. Suppose that you are a member of the district's governing board.
   a. Owing to an increase in district population, two first-grade classes will have to be added. Which of the two budget formats (if either) would better permit you to direct additional resources to the first grade?
   b. You are concerned that sixth graders are not reading as well as you think they should. You attribute their deficiencies to teachers spending too much time on "frivolous" subjects such as music and art rather than on reading. Which of the two budget formats (if either) would permit you to redistribute resources so that more time is spent on reading?
   c. Comment on why the program and activity structure of the district's elementary schools, although closely tied to the schools' educational objectives may not facilitate allocation of resources.
2. Suppose that the district's high school is organized by subject. There is a history department, a mathematics department, a biology department, etc. Would it be more fitting in the high school than in the elementary schools to have a program structure that is tied to academic subject-matter? Why?

14-6

Capital budgeting decisions depend on specification of objectives.

To enhance security in Riverside Park, a city is considering whether it should install a high-tech security system. The system would not only reduce the cost of police patrols but would also deter crime.

The city has received offers from two contractors who have proposed competing systems. System A would cost $4 million; System B would cost $6 million. The city estimates that by reducing the cost of police patrols, System A would save $150,000 per year and System B $260,000 per year.

The city uses a discount rate of 10 percent to evaluate all capital outlays. It determines that each of the systems would have an economic life of five years.

1. Considering the cost as the initial investment and the benefits as the present value of the cash savings from reduced police patrols, which of the two systems would cost the least in relation to benefits. Based only on this criterion, should that system be acquired?
2. Suppose that the city estimates that System A is likely to deter forty violent crimes per year and that System B is likely to deter fifty violent crimes per year. Which of the two would cost the least (considering cost as the initial investment less the present value of savings from reduced police patrols) in relation to benefits?
3. Suppose further that consultants engaged by the city have placed a dollar cost upon violent crime. Taking into account victims' medical bills and lost wages, they estimate the present value of net outflows owing to a violent crime to be $90,000 per victim. Considering the costs as the initial investment and the benefits as the present value of the cash savings (including those from both reduced police patrols and crimes deterred), which of the two systems would cost the least in relation to benefits? Based only on this criterion, should that system be acquired?

14-7

Capital expenditures cannot be assessed in isolation of operating expenditures.

A city is weighing the costs and benefits of a new convention center. The center would be accounted for in an enterprise fund. It would cost $20 million and would be funded from the proceeds of twenty-year revenue bonds. Officials estimate that the center would generate $3.5 million each year in rental and other fees and would cost $1.6 million (excluding interest) to operate.

1. Based on this limited amount of information, should the city construct the convention center? Assume that the term of the bonds is indicative of the center's useful life and that the city's cost of capital is 6 percent.
2. Suppose that city officials estimate that the center would generate an additional $150,000 in general sales taxes and $200,000 in hotel occupancy taxes that are dedicated to promotion of tourism. However, the center would cost the city an additional $250,000 to provide police, fire, and other services in connection with center events. Further, the city utility department (accounted for in an enterprise fund) would have to extend utility lines to the center at an initial cost of $1.7 million and would have to incur annual costs of $50,000 to maintain and repair these lines. None of these operating and utility costs would be charged to the convention center.

Taking into account these costs and revenues, should the city construct the convention center?

3. Assuming that the city were to construct the convention center, what would be the annual impact on revenues and expenses/expenditures (excluding interest and other financing costs) of the following funds?
   a. Convention center fund
   b. General fund
   c. Hotel occupancy tax fund
   d. Utility fund

14-8

Conventional capital budgeting techniques can be applied to nonconventional assessments.

The Mount Eden Medical Center is considering establishing a screening program for a virulent form of cancer. If the program were established, the center would have to acquire equipment that would cost $8.2 million. Thereafter, the center would incur operating costs of $400,000 per year. The equipment has a useful life of four years.

The center estimates that it would screen 3,000 high-risk patients per year. It calculates that 0.2 percent (six) of these will test positive. With proper treatment, at minimal cost, these patients would be spared the disease. Experts have determined that if they were not screened and, as a consequence developed the disease, they would incur at least $300,000 per year in medical costs, for a period of two years, before succumbing to it. The disease would cut short their working lives by an average of ten years, during which time they would have earned an average of $28,000 per year.

The center uses an interest rate of 10 percent to assess all long-term projects.

1. What would be the *annual* net benefits of the program, taking into account the operating costs (excluding the cost of the equipment), the present value of the medical costs, and the present value of lost earnings?
2. Does the present value of the annual net benefits exceed the cost of the equipment? Based exclusively on this criterion, should the program be established? What reservations would you have as to the significance of your analysis?
3. Assume that the center has decided to establish the screening program. However, the screening could be carried out with equal reliability by physician examinations coupled with laboratory tests rather than with the special equipment. The annual cost, however, would be $3 million. Should the center acquire the equipment or carry out the screening with physician examinations and laboratory tests? Base your analysis on a period of four years, the life of the equipment. Do you have the same reservations about this analysis as you did the previous one?

14-9

Misspecified objectives and performance measures can have dysfunctional consequences.

The Granite Falls Detention Center is a boot camp for criminal offenders aged eighteen to twenty-five. "Campers" spend one year at the camp, during which time they take vocational courses (mainly in the construction trades), engage in vigorous physical exercise, and receive psychological counseling. Upon completion of the program, they are returned to their hometowns. They fulfill the remainder of any sentence on parole instead of in prison. The overall mission of the center is to prevent recidivism—to ensure that, once released, the campers commit no further criminal acts and become productive members of society.

A unit of the state prison system, the center has a limited capacity, which is far less than the number of offenders who would qualify for it. Offenders who are not admitted to the camp are sentenced instead to conventional jails or prisons.

Campers are subject to strict discipline, similar to that in a military training facility. Those who violate camp rules, or fail to make satisfactory progress in courses and other activities, are subject to transfer to prison.

The center is a budgeted program of the state prison system.

In a recent budget, the prison system set forth the objective of the detention center as follows:

To provide programs of vocational training, physical exercise and psychological counseling for youthful offenders with the aim of preventing them from committing criminal acts after their release and of enabling them to become productive members of society.

At the end of each year the center submitted a report of its performance. Outcome measures included the following:

- Percentage of campers released to society (as opposed to being transferred to other prison facilities)
- Number of campers completing vocational courses
- Number of hours of psychological counseling provided

1. Comment on the program's objective and its outcome measures. Do you believe that they provide a basis on which to assess the program's performance?
2. Indicate ways in which employees of the center could enhance the center's performance as measured by the outcome measures yet which would not be consistent with the center's overall mission.
3. Suppose that the center included as one of its outcome measures "percentage of campers that did not commit a crime within five years." Comment on the virtues and deficiencies of this measure.

14-10

Indiscriminate comparisons of SEA data can be more misleading than enlightening.

The city manager of Midfield summoned the city's sanitation commissioner. He had compared the service efforts and accomplishments data for the sanitation department with those for Lowville, a nearby city of comparable size and population. Midfield fared poorly on virtually all measures. The city manager wanted an explanation.

Both cities used SEA measures that were recommended in a GASB research report (cited in this chapter). These included the following:

Inputs

- Expenditures in current and constant dollars
- Number of personnel
- Number of vehicles

Outputs

- Number of customers served
- Tons of waste collected

Outcomes

- Percentage of scheduled collections missed
- Percentage of scheduled collections not completed on schedule
- Percentage of streets rated acceptably clean
- Average customer satisfaction rating
- Number of customer complaints

Efficiency

- Cost per ton of solid waste collected
- Cost per customer served
- Tons of solid waste collected per employee

It is generally acknowledged that comparisons of SEA measures must be supplemented with explanations as to possible differences in operating conditions.

1. Suppose that you were Midfield's sanitation commissioner. List at least seven factors, each of which is likely to be beyond your control, that might explain the apparently poor performance of your department. Specify one or more outcome or efficiency indicators that they would affect.
2. Suppose instead that the city manager had compared the sanitation department's performance of the current year with that of the previous year and noted a deterioration in several of the measures. List at least three factors, each of which is likely to be beyond your control, that might account for the apparent deterioration in performance. Assume that there have been no major changes in the city's population or its policies as to frequency of collection or other factors affecting customer service.

SOLUTION TO EXERCISE FOR REVIEW AND SELF-STUDY

1. Examples of operational objectives

Serving a Broad Segment of Society

- A subway station is located within one-half mile of 90 percent of city residences and places of employment.
- 85 percent of the population can commute between their homes and offices in less than one hour.

Providing On-Time Service

- 90 percent of the trains arrive at stations within two minutes of scheduled time.
- No more than 1 percent of trains are subject to major delays (greater than twenty minutes).

Providing Frequent Service

- During rush hours trains are scheduled no more than six minutes apart.
- During off-peak hours trains are scheduled no more than twenty minutes apart.

Assuring that Passengers are Safe

- There are no more than six reported violent crimes per 1,000,000 passenger trips.
- There are no more than three accidents per 1,000,000 miles.

Assuring that the Environment in Which Passengers Travel, Including Trains and Stations, Are Clean and Pleasant.

- At least 80 percent of passengers surveyed are satisfied with the conditions of trains and stations.
- 95 percent of trains departing from the terminal are rated 4 or better (on a scale of 1 to 5) by system inspectors.

2. Examples of service effort and accomplishment indicators

Inputs

- Dollar cost of cleaning trains and stations
- Number of employees engaged in refurbishing trains

Outputs

- Number of trains repainted each year
- Number of cars cleaned
- Number of stations cleaned

Outcomes

- Percentage of cars meeting specified standards (e.g., no broken doors, adequate lights, no torn seats)
- Number of passenger complaints about unsatisfactory conditions

Efficiency (Inputs to Outputs or Outcomes)

- Cost per car cleaned
- Number of maintenance employees per cars meeting specified standards

3. Capital outlays

   a. The net economic benefit of expenditures to enhance safety can be determined by comparing the cost of the improvements to the economic savings that will result from fewer crimes. Although it is possible to estimate the dollar costs of crimes (e.g., the lost wages of the victims) the reliability, and hence the utility, of such estimates are, at best, problematic.

   b. If the system must choose between two alternatives, each providing approximately the same benefits, then the merits of each option can be determined using conventional capital budget analysis. Thus, over a ten-year period, using a discount rate of 12 percent:

Present Value of Costs of Hiring Additional Police

Cost per year	$110,000
Present value of an annuity of $1, 10 periods, 12 percent	× 5.6502
Net present value	$621,522

Present Value of Capital Improvements

Maintenance and monitoring cost per year	$30,000
Present value of an annuity of $1, 10 periods, 12 percent	× 5.6502
Present value of maintenance and monitoring costs per year	169,506
Present value of initial outlays	400,000
Net present value	$569,506

The cost of the capital improvements is less than that of hiring police; hence, they should be undertaken.

   c. The operating budget should account for the operating costs associated with the newly acquired assets. Procedures can be established so when the capital budget is approved, the additional operating costs are added automatically to the operating budget.

CHAPTER 15

Auditing Governments and Not-for-Profit Organizations

Learning Objectives

After studying this chapter you should understand:

- The primary differences between auditing in the government and not-for-profit sectors and in the business sector
- How the Yellow Book has influenced governmental and not-for-profit auditing
- The types of audits that governments conduct
- The standards to which government audits must comply
- How the Single Audit Act and supporting regulations have influenced auditing
- The reports that auditors must prepare as part of a single audit
- The unique characteristics of performance audits
- The key elements of performance audits
- The unique ethical issues facing governmental and not-for-profit accountants and auditors

The theme of the previous chapter is that government and not-for-profit organizations must be managed to achieve their objectives. By extension, therefore, their performance must also be evaluated as to whether they achieved these objectives. In this chapter we consider how governments and not-for-profits organizations are audited—how their accomplishments are attested to and reported upon.

Whereas in the development of financial auditing standards and practices the independent public accounting profession has played the leadership role, in the areas of reporting on compliance and assessing performance, the government and not-for-profit sectors have been at the forefront of progress. The advances in compliance and performance auditing can be attributed mainly to the federal government, especially to the leadership of the **General Accounting Office (GAO)**[1] and the requirements of the Single Audit Act. The federal government provides financial assistance, either directly or indirectly through the states, to almost all general-purpose local governments, most colleges and universities, and a substantial portion of not-for-profit entities. As a condition of awarding financial assistance, it requires that the entities submit financial statements that are audited in accord with federally specified standards. The federal government is thereby able to influence the auditing standards applicable to entities as disparate as major state governments and small-town soup kitchens. In addition, inasmuch as the internal audit departments of more progressive corporations began to focus on performance audits as early as the 1960s, the Institute of Internal Auditors, the professional association of internal auditors, has also made substantial contributions to promoting performance auditing and to developing appropriate concepts and practices.

Auditing is a discipline in its own right, and therefore comprehensive coverage is well beyond the scope of this text. The objective of this chapter is to shed light on some of the unique features of government and not-for-profit auditing and to show how federal requirements have affected both state and local governments and not-for-profits. The chapter first discusses the unique features of auditing in the government and not-for-profit sectors. It then addresses the two primary types of audits—financial audits and performance audits. A final section deals with ethical issues facing auditors and accountants—a topic only tangentially related to the main thrust of the chapter, but nevertheless of special concern to government accountants and auditors.

HOW DO AUDITS OF GOVERNMENTS AND NOT-FOR-PROFITS DIFFER FROM THOSE OF BUSINESSES?

An **audit** is defined in general-purpose dictionaries as an examination of records or accounts to check their accuracy. Business-sector financial audits are characterized by the attest function. **Attest** means "to affirm to be correct, true, or genuine; corroborate." The attest function adds credibility to the assertions of others—in the case of an independent financial audit, to an entity's financial data as presented by management.

In the government and not-for-profit sectors, auditing extends beyond the attest function. Auditors not only attest to the data reported in financial statements. They also make, and report upon, their own independent evaluations as to whether auditees have complied with appropriate laws, regulations, and terms of grants. Further, they assess whether the auditees have achieved their objectives and carried out their missions efficiently and effectively.

[1] As noted in footnote 4 in Chapter 1, as this text goes to press, the GAO is seeking, by way of Congressional legislation, to change its name from the General Accounting Office to the *Government Accountability Office*. This new designation, the GAO officials believe, will better encapsulate the agency's main mission, which is to make the operations of the federal government more efficient and effective. They also hope that it will dispel the common, but ill conceived, image of the agency as the nation's official bean counters.

How Has the Yellow Book Influenced Governmental and Not-for-Profit Auditing?

In 1972, the U.S. General Accounting Office (GAO) issued the first edition of *Government Auditing Standards (Standards for Audit of Governmental Organizations, Programs, Activities, and Functions)*, commonly referred to (because of the color of its cover) as the **Yellow Book.** The GAO, an agency of Congress, is responsible for auditing all federal agencies and programs. In addition, it is accountable, along with the Department of the Treasury and the **Office of Management and Budget (OMB),** for prescribing the accounting standards and practices of federal agencies. It is headed by the **Comptroller General of the United States,** who is appointed by the president, with the advice and consent of the Senate, for a term of fifteen years.

Government Auditing Standards was issued to elevate the practice of auditing by both federal agencies and state and local governments. The GAO has no direct authority over state and local governments, but by publishing—and publicizing—the standards, it exerts its influence through the force of persuasion and example.

Federal legislation now requires that the **inspectors general** (the chief auditors) of all federal agencies apply the Yellow Book to their own audits. In addition, they must also ensure that all audits for which they are responsible, mainly those of entities to which their agencies provide funds, satisfy the GAO standards. Thus, for example, if a federal department were to make an award to a state or local government or to a not-for-profit organization, then that organization's auditors, even if an independent CPA firm, must adhere to the GAO standards.

When it initially established government auditing standards, the GAO incorporated into them the relevant standards of the American Institute of Certified Public Accountants (AICPA). Since then, the AICPA has also adopted many, but not all, of the GAO standards as they apply to government audits. Hence, while there are no inconsistencies between the GAO and the AICPA standards, the GAO standards impose extra requirements. Until 2002, the AICPA had primary responsibility for promulgating the audit standards that had to be followed by all CPAs. However, owing to accounting scandals involving Enron and numerous other major corporations, Congress (by way of the Sarbanes-Oxley bill) created the **Public Company Accounting Oversight Board** to which it assigned the authority to establish auditing standards for *public corporations* (that is, those corporations the shares of which are publicly traded). As this text went to press, the AICPA is expected to retain the responsibility for setting auditing standards for governments and not-for-profit entities.

What Types of Audits Do Governments Conduct?

The most recent edition of *Government Auditing Standards* (2003) characterizes government audits into three categories:

- Financial audits
- Attestation engagements
- Performance audits

Financial audits determine whether an entity's financial statements are presented fairly in accordance with generally accepted accounting principles. They may also have related objectives, such as ensuring that the entity has complied with laws and regulations that may have a material effect on the financial statements, providing special reports on selected accounts or items of a financial statement, issuing letters for underwriters or other parties, and reviewing interim financial data.

Attestation engagements cover a broader scope of engagements than financial audits. They involve examining, reviewing, or performing agreed-upon procedures as to various types of management assertions. For example, subjects of attestation engagements might include:

- An entity's internal accounting or administrative controls
- Compliance with rules, regulations or terms of contracts
- Prospective or pro forma financial statements
- Costs of contracts

Performance audits, often referred to as **operational audits,** may be intended to achieve a variety of different objectives. These include:

- Measuring the extent to which a program is achieving its goals and objectives and determining whether the entity is using its resources in the most effective and economical manner
- Determining whether its internal controls are effective in relation to managements goals and objectives
- Verifying that the organization is complying with the terms of laws, grants, and contracts in that its programs are serving the appropriate population and delivering the intended services
- Providing guidance as to how the organization can improve in the future; that is, providing information on "best practices," analyzing alternatives to existing programs, and assessing budgeting proposals

The GAO standards note that the objectives of these three types of engagements may sometimes overlap. Therefore, in determining which set of standards to follow, auditors must take into account users' needs and the auditors' skills, experience, and knowledge.

WHAT LEVELS OF STANDARDS ARE APPLICABLE TO ALL ENGAGEMENTS?

Financial audits and other attestation engagements of all entities, irrespective of whether governmental or nongovernmental, that are carried out by independent CPAs must first satisfy AICPA standards, known as **generally accepted auditing standards (GAAS),** except those that are explicitly excluded from governmental standards. These standards focus mainly on audits of an entity's financial statements. They result in reports in which the auditors express an opinion as to whether the statements are fairly presented in accordance with generally accepted *accounting* standards—those established or recognized by the Governmental Accounting Standards Board (GASB), the Financial Accounting Standards Board (FASB), or the Federal Accounting Standards Advisory Board (FASAB).

Agencies that provide funds to governments or not-for-profit entities may stipulate that the audit they require be conducted in accord with a second set of standards, that set forth in *Government Auditing Standards* (the Yellow Book).

Government Auditing Standards constitute what are known as **generally accepted government auditing standards (GAGAS).**

Audits of governments or not-for-profit entities that are subject to the Single Audit Act must satisfy a third, additional level of standards—those of the Single Audit Act and its supporting circulars.

The diagram in Figure 15-1 shows the types of reports required at each of the three levels of audit, and thereby implies the differences in the scope of the examinations required at each level.

The Yellow Book standards for financial audits are modeled after the ten basic "generally accepted auditing standards" of the AICPA. These ten standards were first developed in 1939, but have subsequently been augmented by numerous detailed requirements, most of which are set forth in the AICPA's eighty-plus statements on auditing standards (SASs). Like the AICPA standards, the government auditing standards are divided into three categories:

- General standards
- Field work standards
- Reporting standards

The general standards apply to all engagements. Separate field work and reporting standards have been developed for each of the three categories of engagement.

The GAO has modified and supplemented the basic AICPA standards with both additional standards and additional guidance as to how they should be interpreted and implemented. Table 15-1 sets forth the resultant standards, excluding the interpretative and implementation guidance. The discussion that follows highlights some of the key features of the GAO standards and the differences between the two sets of standards.

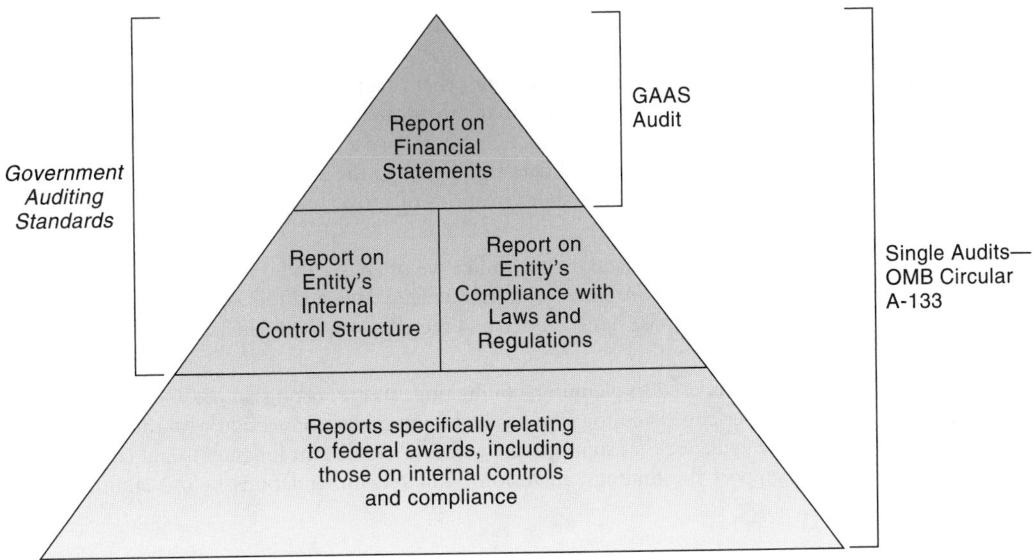

FIGURE 15-1 Levels of Reporting in Governmental Single Audits: Generally Accepted Auditing Standards (GAAS) Audit versus Government Auditing Standards Audit versus Single Audit

Source: Adapted from *Audits of State and Local Governmental Units* (New York: American Institute of Certified Public Accountants, 1996), p. 181.

TABLE 15–1
Government Auditing Standards for Financial Audits

General Standards

1. ***Independence.*** In all matters relating to the audit work, the audit organization and the individual auditor, whether government or public, should be free both in fact and appearance from personal, external, and organizational impairments to independence.
2. ***Professional judgment.*** Professional judgment should be used in planning and performing audits and attestation engagement and in reporting the results.
3. ***Competence.*** The staff assigned to perform the audit or attestation engagement should collectively possess adequate professional competence for the tasks required.
4. ***Quality control.*** Each audit organization performing audits and/or attestation engagements in accordance with generally accepted government auditing standards (GAGAS) should have an appropriate internal quality control system in place and should undergo an external peer review.

Field Work Standards

1. ***AICPA Standards.*** For financial audits, GAGAS incorporate the American Institute of Certified Public Accountants' (AICPA) three generally accepted standards of field work, which are:
   (a) The work is to be adequately planned, and assistants, if any, are to be properly supervised.
   (b) A sufficient understanding of the internal control structure is to be obtained to plan the audit and to determine the nature, timing, and extent of tests to be performed.
   (c) Sufficient competent evidential matter is to be obtained through inspection, observation, inquiries, and confirmations to afford a reasonable basis for an opinion regarding the financial statements under audits.
2. ***Auditor communication.*** Auditors should communicate information to the auditee, the individuals contracting for or requesting the audit services, and the audit committee regarding the nature and extent of planned testing and reporting on compliance with laws and regulations and internal control over financial reporting.
3. ***Results of previous audits and attest engagements.*** Auditors should consider the results of previous audits and attestation engagements and follow up on known significant findings and recommendations that directly relate to the objectives of the audit being undertaken.
4. ***Detecting material misstatements.*** Auditors should design the audit to provide reasonable assurance of detecting material misstatements resulting from violations of provisions of contracts or grant agreements that have a direct and material effect on the determination of financial statement amounts or other financial data significant to the audit objectives. If specific information comes to the auditors' attention that provides evidence concerning the existence of possible violations of provisions of contracts or grant agreements that could have a material indirect effect on the determination of financial statement amounts or other financial data significant to the audit objectives, auditors should apply audit procedures specifically directed to ascertain whether violations of provisions of contracts or grant agreements have occurred or are likely to have occurred.

   Auditors should be alert to situations or transactions that could be indicative of abuse, and if indications of abuse exist that could significantly affect the financial statement amounts or other financial data, auditors should apply audit procedures specifically directed to ascertain whether abuse has occurred and the effect on the financial statement amounts or other financial data.
5. ***Audit documentation.*** Audit documentation related to planning, conducting, and reporting on the audit should contain sufficient information to enable an experienced auditor who has had no previous connection with the audit to ascertain from the audit documentation the evidence that supports the auditors' significant judgments and conclusions. Audit documentation should contain support for findings, inclusions, and recommendations before auditors issue their report.

(Continues)

TABLE 15-1
Government Auditing Standards
Financial Audits *(Continued)*

Reporting Standards

1. ***AICPA Standards.*** For financial audits, generally accepted government auditing standards (GAGAS) incorporate the American Institute of Certified Public Accountants' (AICPA) four generally accepted standards of reporting, which are:
   (a) The report should state whether the financial statements are presented in accordance with generally accepted accounting principles.
   (b) The report shall identify those circumstances in which such principles have not been consistently observed in the current period in relation to the preceding period.
   (c) Informative disclosures in the financial statements are to be regarded as reasonably adequate unless otherwise stated in the report.
   (d) The report shall either contain an expression of opinion regarding the financial statements, taken as a whole, or an assertion to the effect that an opinion cannot be expressed. When an overall opinion cannot be expressed, the reasons should be stated. In all cases where an auditor's name is associated with financial statements, the report should contain a clear-cut indication of the character of the auditor's work, if any, and the degree of responsibility the auditor is taking.
2. ***Compliance with GAGAS.*** Audit reports should state that the audit was made in accordance with GAGAS.
3. ***Reporting on internal control and compliance.*** When providing an opinion or a disclaimer on financial statements, auditors should include in their report on the financial statements either a (1) description of the scope of the auditors' testing of internal control over financial reporting and compliance with laws, regulations, and provisions of contracts or grant agreements and the results of those tests or an opinion, if sufficient work was performed or (2) reference to the separate report(s) containing that information. If auditors report separately, the opinion or disclaimer should contain a reference to the separate report containing this information and state that the separate report is an integral part of the audit and should be considered in assessing the results of the audit.
4. ***Reporting deficiencies in internal control, illegal acts and noncompliance.*** For financial audits, including audits of financial statements in which the auditor provides an opinion or disclaimer, auditors should report, as applicable to the objectives of the audit, (1) deficiencies in internal control considered to be reportable conditions as defined in AICPA standards, (2) all instances of fraud and illegal acts unless clearly inconsequential, and (3) significant violations of provisions of contracts or grant agreements and abuse. In some circumstances, auditors should report fraud, illegal acts, violations of provisions of contracts or grant agreements, and abuse directly to parties external to the audited entity.
5. ***Reporting views of responsible officials.*** If the auditors' report discloses deficiencies in internal control, fraud, illegal acts, violations of provisions of contracts or grant agreements, or abuse, auditors should obtain and report the views of responsible officials concerning the findings, conclusions, and recommendations, as well as planned corrective actions.
6. ***Reporting privileged and confidential information.*** If certain pertinent information is prohibited from general disclosure, the audit report should state the nature of the information omitted and the requirement that makes the omission necessary.
7. ***Report issuance and distribution.*** Government auditors should submit audit reports to the appropriate officials of the audited entity and to appropriate officials of the organizations requiring or arranging for the audits, including external funding organizations such as legislative bodies, unless legal restrictions prevent it. Auditors should also send copies of the reports to other officials who have legal oversight authority or who may be responsible for acting on audit findings and recommendations and to others authorized to receive such reports. Unless the report is restricted by law or regulation, or contains privileged and confidential information, auditors should clarify that copies are made available for public inspection. Nongovernment auditors should clarify report distribution responsibilities with the party contracting for the audit and follow the agreements reached.

Source: *Government Auditing Standards,* 2003 Revision (Washington, D.C.: Comptroller General of the United States).

WHAT ARE THE KEY DIFFERENCES BETWEEN GOVERNMENT AND NONGOVERNMENT FINANCIAL AUDIT STANDARDS?

GENERAL STANDARDS

The general standards pertain to the qualifications of the auditors, the independence of both the individual auditors and the audit organization, the auditors' exercise of due professional care, and the need for quality control. Although the first three GAO standards (as set forth in Table 15-1) are similar to those of the AICPA, the implementation guidelines differ in that they are tailored specifically to government audits.

Independence

The Enron and related scandals raised salient questions as to whether auditors were sufficiently independent of their clients to render objective financial statement opinions. Of primary concern was the opportunity for auditors to earn fees for nonaudit consulting and tax services. Critics of the profession charged that auditors could not be expected to take a hard line against violations of accounting principles while at the same time trying to sell their clients these additional services.

The GAO was out in front of other government and private-sector agencies in tightening standards relating to auditor independence. In a 2002 amendment to its 1994 Yellow Book, the GAO promulgated an extensive set of new guidelines. These were subsequently incorporated into the 2003 revision of the Yellow Book. The new independence standards with respect to nonaudit services are based on two overarching principles:

- Auditors should not perform management functions or make management decisions
- Auditors should not audit their own work or provide nonaudit services in situations where the amounts or services involved are significant/material to the subject matter of the audit

The new standards permit audit organizations to perform nonaudit services but only insofar as they do not violate the two fundamental principles. Thus, for example, the standard allows auditors to assist in preparing draft financial statements based on a client's trial balance, but prohibits them from maintaining the underlying records. Similarly, auditors may advise a client on the best commercial accounting software package to acquire and can assist in installing it. They cannot, however, do all the installation work except for "pushing the button."

The GAO standard on independence also addresses relationships that are unique to governments. In the private sector, auditors cannot be considered independent if employed by the entity they are to audit. However, most government audit agencies are part of the government that they have been established to audit. Therefore, the GAO advises that an audit organization of a government can be considered independent with respect to *external* parties as long as it meets one of the following conditions:

- It is from a different branch (e.g., legislative, executive) of the government than the particular units that it is to examine or assigned to a different level of government (e.g. a federal auditor may audit a state program)
- It is headed by an auditor who is elected by the citizens of the government's jurisdiction or who is elected or appointed by a legislative body and accountable to that legislative body

The audit organization can also be considered independent as long as there are sufficient safeguards that prevent the audited entity from unduly interfering in the work of the auditors.

The audit organization can be considered independent with respect to *internal* management of a government entity as long as it is accountable, and reports the audit results, to either the head or deputy head of the entity and is located organizationally outside the line or staff management functions of the audited entity.

Continuing Professional Education

The standards' interpretative guidelines require that to meet the test of professional competence, auditors must be knowledgeable of government auditing standards and accounting principles. Auditors who perform government audits must complete at least eighty hours of continuing professional education (CPE) every two years, of which twenty-four hours must be related directly to the government environment and to government auditing. The requirement for twenty-four hours of specialized government education goes beyond the CPE standards of both the AICPA and state CPA licensing boards, which make no demands as to specific industry content. It applies to all auditors who participate in government engagements (including those of not-for-profits receiving federal assistance)—even if the engagements constitute only a small part of the auditors' overall practice.

Peer Review

The GAO standards require that each audit organization have "an appropriate internal quality control system in place and undergo an external quality control review." To satisfy this standard the organization must undergo a "peer review" by an independent audit organization at least once every three years. Although peer reviews were not required by the AICPA's general standards, Sarbanes-Oxley now mandates them for CPA firms whose audit clients include more than a hundred corporations that issue publicly traded securities.

STANDARDS OF FIELD WORK

The standards of field work are intended to ensure that audits are properly planned and supervised, that the auditees' internal control structures are properly reviewed, and that auditors obtain sufficient evidential matter.

Compliance

Both the AICPA and the GAO standards require auditors to design their engagements to provide "reasonable assurance" of detecting fraud and material misstatements resulting from illegal acts or similar irregularities, such as intentional omissions or fabrications. Because governments and not-for-profits are accountable to the parties from which they receive grants or have contracts, the GAO standards also require auditors to design their audits to provide reasonable assurance of detecting noncompliance with the terms of *contracts or grant agreements.*

Working Papers

Audits of governments and of not-for-profits receiving government funds are often undertaken by independent CPAs or by auditors from one government agency for the benefit of another. Therefore, they may be subject to more frequent and careful quality reviews than those of businesses. Whereas both the AICPA and the GAO standards require that auditors document their audit work in "working papers," the

GAO standard is more rigorous. Unlike the AICPA standard, it explicitly says that the working papers must contain sufficient information to convince an auditor having no previous connection with the audit that the evidence supports the auditor's conclusions and judgments.

STANDARDS OF REPORTING

The standards of reporting establish the form and content of auditors' opinions on financial statements and on any other required reports.

Compliance and Internal Controls

The AICPA standards of reporting require that auditors explain, in general terms, the nature of their examination. They do not, however, require that the auditors explicitly describe their tests of compliance or their assessments of internal controls.

In light of the importance governments place on both compliance and internal controls, the GAO adds a standard stipulating that auditors must explicitly describe (either in their reports on the financial statements or in separate reports) the scope of their compliance and internal control testing. They must also indicate any irregularities, illegal acts, and other instances of material noncompliance that they found. To put the violations in perspective, the auditors should also indicate the number of infractions and their dollar amount.

The standard makes no distinction between instances of fraud that are material and those that are not. It requires auditors to report all instances except for those that are "clearly inconsequential." In some circumstances, especially if management fails to take appropriate corrective measures, the auditors may also have to notify legal authorities such as federal inspectors general or state attorneys general.

Public Inspection

Under AICPA standards, auditors are not required to disclose in their audit report either deficiencies in internal control or instances of illegal acts, irregularities, or noncompliance unless they materially affect the financial statements. Usually auditors inform management of their nonmaterial findings in a "management letter," which the entity need not make public.

Under the GAO standards, auditor reports on internal control and compliance are part of the complete audit report. Unless restricted by law or regulation, they must be made available for public inspection.

IN PRACTICE

THE AUDITORS' DILEMMA

The requirement that the complete audit report, including details of all deficiencies in internal controls or instances of noncompliance, be made public may place independent CPAs that audit governments in uncomfortable circumstances.

Opponents of the officials responsible for reported irregularities may seize upon the auditors' report to score political points. The officials may respond by questioning the validity of the auditors' findings.

How should the auditors react? Should they defend their findings and thereby jeopardize their relationship with their client? Or should they agree with their client and thereby jeopardize their own reputation?

How Have the Single Audit Act and Other Pronouncements Influenced Auditing?

In the 1960s, the federal government greatly increased the number, funding, and complexity of its assistance programs. These programs, which were directed to a wide range of activities including education, health and welfare, job training, and transportation, were typically funded by the federal government but administered by the states. However, the federal agencies in charge of the programs were responsible for auditing them.

As a result of congressional disclosures of severe deficiencies in federal audit practices, the OMB urged that federal agencies rely more on CPA firms and other independent auditors than on their own "in-house" auditors. Nevertheless, federal agencies were interested mainly in whether grant recipients complied with the applicable laws, regulations, and grant provisions. Independent auditors, adhering to then-current standards, focused on financial statements and thereby did not provide the compliance assurances needed by the agencies. Hence, the agencies continued to perform their own audits.

Further, many grant recipients, especially local governments, received funds from several federal agencies and were subject to audits from each. Although each audit team directed its attention primarily to the grants from its own agency, they all had to review common books and records, accounting systems, and internal controls. The result was both costly duplication of audit effort and inadequate audit coverage of the entity as a whole.

In 1979, the OMB issued a directive calling for organization-wide **single audits** to be performed by CPAs or other independent auditors.[2] The directive did not preclude federal agencies from conducting their own examinations, but instructed them to build on the independent audits.

To give legislative sanction to the directive, Congress enacted the **Single Audit Act of 1984.** Amended in 1996 to make it easier to administer, the act applies to both direct and indirect recipients of federal assistance and requires that organizations receiving more than $300,000 in federal assistance under more than one program be subject to a single audit.

The objectives of a single audit are to ensure that:

- The financial statements of the entity as a whole can be relied upon
- The entity is adhering to the common set of federal laws and regulations that apply to all recipients of federal aid
- The entity is satisfying the laws, regulations, and provisions that apply to each specific federal award

Whereas prior to the act a recipient of federal funds had to submit audit reports to each agency from which it received funds, now a recipient has to deal with only a single agency. That agency, referred to as the **cognizant agency,** is responsible for ensuring that all audit standards are met and for coordinating the special audit requirements of each of the individual agencies providing funds. The cognizant agency is typically the agency that provides the greatest portion of federal funds to the recipient.

The OMB is primarily responsible for administering the Single Audit Act. It issues circulars that provide detailed guidance as to how the single audit is to be performed. Periodically updated, they address matters such as the nature and scope of

---

[2] Attachment P, "Audit Requirements" to OMB Circular A-102, Uniform Administrative Requirements for Grants-in-Aid to State and Local Governments.

internal control reviews, the extent of compliance testing, and the form and content of reports. Until recently, one circular addressed audits of governments and another those of not-for-profits. OMB has now combined these into a single circular, A-133, *Audits of States, Local Governments and Non-Profit Organizations.*

OMB has augmented the guidance of Circular A-133 with a "Compliance Supplement" that details major compliance requirements and key audit procedures. It has also published ***Uniform Administrative Requirements for Grants and Cooperative Agreements to State and Local Governments*** (referred to as the "**Common Rule,**") a detailed compendium of additional rules and regulations.

The Single Audit Act specifies that single audits be conducted in accord with the GAO's *Government Auditing Standards.* However, it requires that federal recipients be subject only to financial audits, not to performance audits. Therefore, the sections of *Government Auditing Standards* on performance audits need not be applied.

To provide additional guidance on single and other government-related audits, the AICPA issued Statement on Auditing Standards (SAS) No. 74, *Compliance Auditing Considerations in Audits of Governmental Entities and Other Recipients of Governmental Financial Assistance.* By issuing this statement, the AICPA established that CPAs who conduct audits of financial assistance but fail to meet the federal audit requirements also fail to adhere to AICPA standards.

The AICPA also issued Statement of Position (SOP) 98-3, *Audits of States, Local Governments, and Not-for-Profit Organizations Receiving Federal Awards,* that provides auditor guidance on implementing the Single Audit Act and Circular A-133.

WHAT APPROACH DO AUDITORS TAKE IN PERFORMING SINGLE AUDITS?

A single audit has two main components:

- An audit of the financial statements conducted under generally accepted government auditing standards
- An audit of federal financial awards

Per Circular A-133, these two types of audits should culminate in at least four types of reports (which are commented on in greater detail in the following section):

- Opinions as to whether the financial statements are fairly presented in accord with generally accepted accounting principles and as to whether a schedule of expenditures of federal awards is fairly presented
- A report on compliance and on internal controls relating to the financial statements
- An opinion as to whether the organization complied with the requirements of major programs
- A schedule of findings and **questioned costs;** questioned costs are those that are not subject to federal reimbursement because they are in violation of laws or provisions pertaining to a grant, are not supported by adequate documentation, or appear to be unreasonable or imprudent

Although single audits incorporate a conventional financial audit, they are characterized by their focus upon compliance with laws and requirements applicable to federally funded programs. Therefore, this section on single audits will focus mainly on the compliance component of single audits.

IDENTIFYING MAJOR PROGRAMS: A RISK-BASED APPROACH

The Single Audit Act distinguishes between major and nonmajor programs, and requires a substantially higher level of auditing of major programs. Circular A-133 directs that in distinguishing between major and nonmajor programs auditors focus on potential losses owing to noncompliance. As a general rule, major programs are those that make up a relatively large proportion of the total federal awards received by an entity and for which there is a high risk of noncompliance.

To determine whether a program is relatively large, the auditor must apply a sliding scale based on the percentage that federal funds received by the program bears to total federal funds received by the entire entity. If an entity receives less than $100 million in federal awards, then any program on which it expends more than 3 percent of the total would be considered large. On the other hand, if it receives more than $10 billion in federal awards, then only programs on which it expends more than 0.15 percent of the total would be considered large.

To determine whether a program is high risk, auditors must exercise professional judgment. Examples of factors that would point to a high risk of noncompliance include:

- Weakness in internal control over federal programs, taking into account competence and experience of personnel, systems for recording transactions, and effectiveness of management oversight
- Significant portions of federal funds being passed through to subrecipients without effective systems of monitoring whether subrecipients comply with applicable laws and grant requirements
- Newly installed computer systems that have not been adequately tested
- Absence of recent audits
- Complex compliance requirements
- Relatively new program

Circular A-133 provides a detailed set of guidelines as to how size and risk must be combined to establish whether a program is major and thereby subject to comprehensive auditing.

KEY PROCEDURES

Once the auditors have identified the major programs, their audit procedures follow a pattern similar in many respects to that of a financial engagement.[3]

- ***Identify the applicable compliance requirements.*** **Compliance requirements** include those that are specific to the program itself and those that are applicable to all federal awards. The compliance supplement to Circular A-133 describes fourteen types of requirements that apply to all federal awards. These are presented in Table 15-2. Tests for compliance with these general requirements may seem far afield from conventional audit procedures. In practice, however, auditors are not expected to assume the role of detectives or law-enforcement investigators and their tests may be comparable to those used to assess internal and administrative controls. For example, with regard to a proscribed activity, such as political lobbying, auditors might examine personnel and payroll records to identify employees whose responsibilities or activities include partisan political activity. They would then review the accounts to make certain that neither the salaries of these employees nor related costs were improperly charged to a federally assisted program.

[3] This discussion of key procedures is drawn from AICPA Statement of Position 98-3 (March 17, 1998, with conforming changes as of May 1, 2002), *Audits of States, Local Governments, and Not-for-Profit Organizations Receiving Federal Awards.*

TABLE 15–2
General Compliance Requirements for Federal Programs

- ***Allowable activities.*** Federal funds must be used only for activities that are within the scope of the grant or contract; they must not be used for activities that are specifically prohibited by the grant, contract, or laws and regulations.
- ***Allowable costs/cost principles.*** Entities that receive federal funds may be reimbursed only for certain allowable costs (e.g., those that are reasonable and necessary for the performance and administration of the award); they may not be reimbursed for certain explicitly proscribed costs (e.g., those for political activities). Moreover, in calculating allowable costs, federal funds recipients must follow accounting principles that are detailed in various OMB circulars directed to cost accounting.
- ***Cash management.*** Per the Federal Cash Management Improvement Act, recipients of federal funds must maintain systems that minimize the time between the receipt and the disbursements of cash.
- ***Davis-Bacon Act.*** The Davis-Bacon Act requires that the wages of laborers and mechanics employed by contractors of federally funded projects be paid at rates no lower than those prevailing in their region.
- ***Eligibility.*** Each federal program has its own unique requirements as to parties that are eligible to participate in the program or to receive program benefits.
- ***Equipment and real property management.*** Entities that acquire equipment and real estate with federal funds must maintain proper inventory records, adequately maintain and safeguard the property, and properly sell or dispose of it.
- ***Matching level of effort and earmarking.*** Under certain programs, participants must match federal funds received with their own funds or must provide a level of service specified in the grant or contract. Under others, a portion of the funds must be earmarked for (i.e., directed to) specified activities or subrecipients.
- ***Period of availability of federal funds.*** Federal awards usually specify the time period during which the funds must be used. Only costs incurred during that period may be charged against the award.
- ***Procurement, suspension, and debarment.*** Federal funds recipients must adhere to federal purchasing guidelines that are spelled out in various OMB circulars. Moreover, they are prohibited from procuring goods or services from vendors that have been suspended or debarred from contracting with the federal government.
- ***Program income.*** Program income must be deducted from allowable costs or accounted for in other ways permitted by the federal government. Program income is revenue that an award recipient generates as a direct result of the grant. It would include, for example, fees or charges for services performed and rents received from property acquired with federal funds.
- ***Real property acquisition and location assistance.*** When federal funds recipients acquire property and thereby displace businesses and households they must follow specified procedures to ensure that the parties having to relocate receive fair compensation and adequate relocation assistance.
- ***Reporting.*** Federal funds recipients must periodically report, using standard OMB-authorized forms, the status of funds received and disbursed.
- ***Subrecipient monitoring.*** An award recipient that passes funds through to other entities may be responsible for monitoring the subrecipients to assure that they adhere to applicable federal laws and regulations.
- ***Special tests and provisions.*** Each program has unique provisions and thereby requires auditors to perform special audit procedures. These provisions and tests are found in the laws, regulations, and contract or grant agreements pertaining to the program.

Source: OMB Circular A-133, Compliance Supplement, March 2003.

The specific compliance requirements are set forth in the rules and regulations of each federal program or contract. In general, they relate to matters such as:

- □ The individuals or groups that are eligible to participate in the program or to receive financial assistance
- □ The types of goods or services that may be acquired
- □ The percentage of its own funds that an entity must contribute to a program
- □ Any special reports that the organization must submit to the sponsoring agency

- ***Plan the engagement.*** The auditors must develop a strategy to understand the events, transactions, and practices that will have a significant impact upon compliance and to ensure that their tests of transactions and other procedures are sufficient to detect material noncompliance. In planning their engagement, auditors must give paramount consideration to the various risks associated with an audit. These include:
  - ***Inherent risk.*** The risk that material noncompliance could occur assuming that no internal controls have been established to prevent it
  - ***Control risk.*** The risk that material noncompliance that could occur would not be prevented by the entity's internal controls
  - ***Fraud risk.*** The risk that intentional material noncompliance could occur
  - ***Detection risk.*** The risk that the auditors will be unable to detect noncompliance that does occur
- ***Assess the internal control structure related to compliance requirements.*** Circular A-133 explicitly requires the auditor to assess, test, and report upon the controls over compliance requirements. The auditor's tests of the controls should be adequate to assure a low level of control risk (e.g., the risk that the internal controls fail to prevent noncompliance).
- ***Obtain sufficient evidence,*** including tests of transactions and other audit procedures, as to whether the entity has complied with relevant requirements. The compliance supplement suggests several audit procedures that can form the basis of an audit program. However, every entity is unique and, therefore, the tests must be custom-tailored to the engagement at hand. Needless to say, auditors are not expected to test every transaction. They must rely on the same type of statistical sampling techniques that they do in conventional financial audits.
- ***Consider subsequent events.*** Auditors must take into account relevant information that comes to their attention after the end of the audit period but before they issue their report. This information is typically contained in reports of regulatory agencies or other auditors that identify instances of noncompliance.
- ***Evaluate and report on noncompliance.*** Having detected instances of noncompliance (referred to as "findings") auditors must assess how (and to whom) they will report the violations and how the instances of noncompliance will influence the opinions that they must express. Compliance violations may require that the entity return funds to the granting agencies and may result in fines and other financial penalties. Hence they are likely to have an impact on the auditors' opinion not only on compliance, but also on the financial statements.
- ***Perform follow-up procedures.*** Circular A-133 requires auditors to follow-up on findings and recommendations from both their current audit and from those of previous audits (even if by other auditors). Correspondingly, it requires the auditee to develop a plan for appropriate corrective actions. To follow up on audit findings and recommendations, auditors should discuss with management the measures they have taken, review decisions of the federal agencies with respect to actions they have taken, and test transactions of the type that were previous resulted in noncompliance.

These procedures are by no means discrete; they are intertwined. The auditors' study of the entity's internal controls, for example, strongly influences their assessment of risks and thereby affects the extent of testing. At the same time, however, the results of transactions tests bears heavily on the auditors' evaluation of internal controls.

WHAT REPORTS RESULT FROM SINGLE AUDITS?

As noted in the previous section, auditors are expected to produce four types of reports as part of their single audit.

OPINION ON THE FINANCIAL STATEMENTS AND ON THE SCHEDULE OF EXPENDITURES OF FEDERAL AWARDS

Auditors may combine in a single report their opinions on the basic financial statements and the schedule of expenditures of federal awards. The section of the report pertaining to the financial statements is that required for any audit conducted in accord with *Government Auditing Standards* (i.e., one that is not necessarily a single audit). It includes a brief description of the audit work and the standard opinion as to whether the information in the statements is fairly presented.

The **Schedule of Expenditures of Federal Awards** is a listing of total expenditures made by the organization under each federal program from which it received funding. Its main purpose is to enable the federal grantor agencies to coordinate their audit efforts and assure adequate audit coverage. Per relevant OMB directives, the schedule must identify each program by its number as listed in the Catalog of Federal Domestic Assistance (CFDA). It must include expenditures to be reimbursed both directly from the federal government and indirectly through other governments (i.e., "pass through" awards). The schedule should indicate whether programs are major or nonmajor and may include optional information as to matching contributions, the total amount of the program awards, and the time periods that are covered by them.

Table 15-3 illustrates a Schedule of Expenditures of Federal Awards. The auditors' responsibility for this schedule is to ensure that the information presented is materially complete and accurate and that the expenditures are properly categorized. In their report the auditors should express an opinion as to whether the information in the schedule is fairly stated in relation to the basic statements taken as a whole.

REPORT ON COMPLIANCE AND ON INTERNAL CONTROL OVER FINANCIAL REPORTING

The report on compliance and internal control over financial reporting, like the opinion on the financial statements, is directed toward the basic financial statements rather than the laws and provisions pertaining to federal awards. It is based on the audit requirements of *Government Auditing Standards* rather than those of Circular A-133. As such, it is intended to provide assurance that the auditee has committed no violations of laws and provisions *that could have a material impact on the financial statements*. It does not report on compliance violations that do not have a material impact on the financial statements.

In their report the auditors should state that they conducted their audit in accordance with *Government Auditing Standards*, and that they have therefore performed tests of compliance with applicable laws and provisions that could have a direct and material effect on the financial statements. They should indicate whether they detected any compliance violations and, if they have, they should refer the reader to the schedule of findings and questioned costs in which the violations would be set forth. They should note, however, that the objective of this phase of the audit (that on financial statements) is not to express an opinion on compliance per se, and hence they do not do so.

In a section of the report pertaining to internal controls, the auditors should assert that in planning and performing the audit they have considered the entity's internal control over financial reporting. They should emphasize that they assessed the controls only for the purpose of expressing an opinion on the financial statements,

TABLE 15-3
Urban Assistance Federation
Schedule of Expenditures of Federal Awards for Year Ended December 31, 2004

Grantor/Pass-Through Grantor/Program Title	Federal CFDA Number	Grant Award Number	Expenditures
U.S. Department of Housing and Urban Development			
Passed through City Housing Department			
Community Development Block Grant			
Programs Emergency Home Repair			
11/07/04–10/31/05	15.649*	I C420.1	$487,198
U.S. Department of Labor			
Passed through the State Empolyment Commission			
Willard-Feyser 7(b) Program			
1/1/04–2/28/05	18.927*	1-027-70	152,188
Passed through the County Private Industry Council			
Project Exceed (III-A)			
5/1/04–9/30/04	18.971*	II A36.98	38,899
U.S. Department of Education			
Passed through the State Commission on Alcohol and Drug Abuse			
Drug Free Schools and Communities			
9/1/03–8/31/04	92.604*	12-016-841	87,625
9/1/04–8/31/05	92.604*	12-016-941	73,357
Total Federal Awards			$839,267

*Denotes a major program.

not on the adequacy of the controls themselves. They should then indicate whether they detected any material weaknesses in the controls and, as with compliance violations, point the reader to the schedule of findings and questioned costs.

REPORT ON COMPLIANCE WITH REQUIREMENTS OF MAJOR PROGRAMS

The report on compliance with major program requirements, along with the schedule of findings and questioned costs, are the centerpieces of the Circular A-133 provisions. In this report the auditors should state that they have audited the entity's compliance with the requirements that are applicable to each of its major programs and explain briefly the nature of their examination. They should then express an opinion as to whether the auditee complied "in all material respects" with those requirements. They should define what is meant by "reportable conditions," and if the auditors detected any they should note that reportable conditions were detected and define what constitutes reportable conditions. They should then refer the reader to the schedule of findings and questioned costs, in which these conditions would be described.

SCHEDULE OF FINDINGS AND QUESTIONED COSTS

The schedule of findings and questioned costs is perhaps the most distinctive—and often the most informative—of the auditors' reports. In the first section of this report, the auditors should first summarize the results of their audit. They should indicate, for example, the type of opinions (e.g., qualified, adverse) they expressed on the financial statements and on compliance with major programs, and whether the audit disclosed material weaknesses in internal control or reportable conditions.

In the second section, the auditors should describe in detail any reportable conditions relating to the *financial statements.* These would include weaknesses in internal controls, material violations of the provisions of contract or grant agreements, and all (except for those that are clearly inconsequential) instances of fraud and illegal acts. In presenting this information, however, the auditors must put it into perspective, noting, for example, the number of questioned transactions and their dollar value in relation to the entire universe of transactions.

In the third section, the auditors should set forth their findings pertaining to the major programs. These include:

- Reportable conditions over internal control
- Material noncompliance with provisions of laws, regulations, contracts, or grant agreements
- Known questioned costs that are above a specified amount (currently $10,000)
- The circumstances as to why the auditors' report on compliance is other than unqualified
- Instances of known fraud

The report should be forward-looking in that it should be in sufficient detail as to allow the audited entity to prepare a plan of corrective action. It should also include the auditors' recommendations as to how the violations could be prevented in the future.

WHAT ARE PERFORMANCE AUDITS?

Financial audits are intended to ensure that financial statements are fairly presented and that the organization has complied with applicable laws and regulations. Performance audits, by contrast, focus on organizational accomplishments. Inasmuch as the goals of a government or not-for-profit are seldom limited to profitability or other financial measures, the auditors may have to assess organizational performance on a wide range of nonfinancial dimensions, each of which relates to an entity's individual objectives.

Performance audits are most commonly carried out by "internal" audit departments—organizations that may be independent of the various agencies or departments that they examine, but not separate from the government or other entity at large. They are not typically required by creditors, regulatory agencies, or other outside parties. Therefore, the accounting profession, other than the GAO, has not developed a detailed set of standards for performance audits comparable to those for financial audits.

The GAO standards for performance audits have had a substantial influence on practice mainly because audit departments have elected voluntarily to adhere to them. These standards correspond to the standards for financial audits in that they are divided into the same three sections: general, field work, and reporting. The general standards are common to both financial and performance audits; the field work and reporting standards are similar in many respects to their financial counterparts, but also have features (the most significant of which will be pointed out in this section) that are unique.

KEY DIFFERENCES BETWEEN FINANCIAL AND PERFORMANCE AUDITS

Attest Function versus Independent Assessment

Performance audits differ conceptually from financial audits. In carrying out financial audits the auditors *attest* to the fairness of the assertions of management. These assertions are primarily incorporated in the entity's financial statements and for the most part relate to constructs, such as revenues, expenditures, assets and liabilities, that are well defined and subject to accepted accounting standards of measurement.

In performance audits, the auditors make independent assessments as to whether an entity is operating economically and efficiently, and is achieving anticipated results. But the constructs to be measured and the standards of measurement, especially those relating to outcomes, are far less clear and precise than those associated with financial audits.

Pointing to this difference in concept, some auditors contend that they should limit their role to testing management's assertions as to performance. Management should be expected to issue a report that sets forth the extent to which the entity achieved its operational objectives. Auditors would then examine management's assertions and express an opinion as to whether they are fairly presented. If management has not established operational objectives and measured whether they have been achieved, then no performance audit would be possible—no more than a financial audit could be conducted if an entity has not accounted for its financial activities and prepared financial statements.

Focus: Organization at Large versus Specific Programs

Financial statement audits focus on the organization as a whole. An entity's statements of activities (or income statement) and balance sheet summarize virtually every transaction in which the entity has engaged. Auditors do not, of course, verify each of these transactions. Nevertheless, each is within the population from which they draw their samples.

Performance audits are almost always carried out on a specific program or activity, not on the organization in its entirety. Unless the entity is extremely limited in its aims, determining whether the organization as a whole is carrying out its mission is generally infeasible. Imagine, for example, attempting to assess the performance of a major university or metropolitan health care center. As long as their various programs have different objectives, are targeted toward different segments of the population, and are conducted by different employees, little is accomplished by performing a single, unified assessment of the complete entity.

This is not to say, however, that the particular program or activity cannot affect the entire organization. Thus, for example, a performance audit can focus on organization-wide safety or environmental programs, or on various internal control systems that cut across departmental lines.

Timing: Routine versus Occasional

Financial audits are typically conducted annually. They are routine elements of an organization's operating cycle.

Performance audits, however, are conducted irregularly. Unlike financial audits they need not coincide with the issuance of the entity's annual financial statements.

Audit organizations have limited resources and generally cannot afford to expend them on audits of the same programs year after year. Instead, they target programs that will likely yield the greatest benefits (such as cost savings or improvements in results) per dollar of audit cost. Their prime selection criteria are the dollar magnitude of the program and the probability of significant audit findings. Therefore, they may examine large, high-risk programs with some frequency (perhaps even annually) but small, low-risk programs only occasionally.

Evidence: Well Delineated versus Broad

The evidence examined in financial audits is relatively well delineated and limited to a few major categories: These include:

- Books and records that are created by the organization itself, such as journals and ledgers, schedules, canceled checks, purchase orders, and receiving reports
- Documents prepared by outside parties, such as invoices, contracts, and notes
- Physical assets, such as inventories and capital assets

- Letters of confirmation or assurance from creditors, debtors, banks, and attorneys

Performance audits are characterized by a broader range of evidence, much of which may be engagement-specific. Depending on the objectives of a program, the auditors may have to review—in addition to financial data—economic and demographic statistics, engineering reports, and medical records.

Auditor Knowledge: Financial versus Program

Financial audits are performed mainly by specialists in accounting—CPAs or others with similar educational and experiential backgrounds. For some engagements, nonaccountants with expertise in areas such as computers, statistical sampling, or specific industries (e.g., jewelry appraisers or geologists) may be brought in as consultants to address certain phases of the examination. They generally play only supporting roles.

Owing to the wider range of evidence that must be examined, performance audits may require more program-specific knowledge and fewer traditional accounting skills. Thus, the GAO and many other government audit organizations have on their staff economists, engineers, health care specialists, and statisticians. At the same time, however, "generalists"—those with MBA degrees or masters in public administration or policy—make valuable additions to an audit team. Often, in fact, the contributions of accountants are not so much their knowledge of accounting per se, but rather their ability to define a problem and resolve it in a logical and orderly manner.

MANNER OF CONDUCTING

In light of the dissimilarities among programs, each performance audit is unique. Consequently, no generic audit program can readily be tailored to specific engagements. Therefore, the following discussion is necessarily general and may not be applicable to all types of performance audits. Table 15-4 lists the GAO's field work and reporting standards for performance audits. Each standard is backed by extensive explanations and implementation guidance.

Selecting the Audit Target

As indicated previously, audit organizations target for examination the programs for which the potential for cost savings or impact on citizens are the greatest—those in which expenditures or risk of inefficiencies, ineffectiveness, or noncompliance is substantial. The extent to which risk is substantial is a matter of auditor judgment. However, the following are examples of factors that add to a program's exposure:

- Recently installed and untested computer systems
- Past inefficiencies as revealed in previous audits
- Ineffective administration or poor results as reflected in reports to supervisory agencies or higher levels of management
- Opportunities or incentives for illegal activities
- Adverse press reports or tips from employees or other knowledgeable parties

Some audit organizations are required either by law or political necessity to perform audits upon the request of members of legislative or other governing bodies to which they are responsible. The GAO, for example, reports to Congress and therefore responds to requests, if reasonable, from its members. The audit departments of municipalities may be similarly responsive to suggestions from members of city councils.

Perhaps most importantly, audit organizations may have to rely on intangible factors to detect programs of high risk. Experienced auditors tend to develop long-term relations with personnel of the departments that they have examined in the past. Often they become as knowledgeable of departments' operations as its most senior

TABLE 15-4
Government Auditing Standards for Performance Audits

Field Work Standards for Performance Audits

1. ***Planning.*** Work is to be adequately planned.
2. ***Supervision.*** Staff are to be properly supervised.
3. ***Evidence.*** Sufficient, competent, and relevant evidence is to be obtained to afford a reasonable basis for the auditors' findings and conclusions.
4. ***Documentation.*** Auditors should prepare and maintain audit documentation. Audit documentation related to planning, conducting, and reporting on the audit should contain sufficient information to enable an experienced auditor, who has had no previous connection with the audit, to ascertain from the audit documentation the evidence that supports the auditors' significant judgments and conclusions. Audit documentation should contain support for findings, conclusions, and recommendations before auditors issue their report.

Reporting Standards for Performance Audits

1. ***Communication.*** Auditors should prepare audit reports communicating the results of each audit.
2. ***Contents.*** The audit report should include the objectives, scope, and methodology; the audit results, including findings, conclusions, and recommendations, as appropriate; a reference to compliance with generally accepted government auditing standards; the views of responsible officials; and, if applicable, the nature of any privileged and confidential information omitted.
3. ***Quality.*** The report should be timely, complete, accurate, objective, convincing, clear, and as concise as the subject permits.
4. ***Issuance and distribution.*** Government auditors should submit audit reports to the appropriate officials of the audited entity and to the appropriate officials of the organizations requiring or arranging for the audits, including external funding organizations, such as legislative bodies, unless legal restrictions prevent it. Auditors should also send copies of the reports to other officials who have legal oversight authority or who may be responsible for acting on audit findings and recommendations and to others authorized to receive such reports. Unless the report is restricted by law or regulation, or contains privileged or confidential information, auditors should clarify that copies are made available for public inspection. Nongovernment auditors should clarify report distribution responsibilities with the party contracting for the audit and follow the agreements reached.

Source: *Government Auditing Standards*, 2003 Revision (Washington, D.C.: Comptroller General of the United States).

managers. Further, like streetwise detectives, they develop an intuitive sense as to where the entity hides its skeletons.

Establishing Scope and Purpose

Auditors must begin their engagement by establishing the scope and purpose of the audit. Since an organization's programs and objectives may be ill-defined and overlap, the auditors must delineate specifically the activities and outcomes to be addressed.

Auditors can best establish the scope and purpose of an engagement by taking a preliminary survey, the aim of which is to gain an understanding of the entity's mission, personnel, history, and operating procedures. The survey might include:

- Interviews with key executives as to what they see as the mission of the program and its strengths and weaknesses
- A review of the legislation that established the program
- A review of other laws, governing board resolutions, contracts, and administrative regulations to which the organization is subject
- An examination of reports from previous audits (These audits may have been performed by the same or a different audit organization. The importance of these reports as a source of information cannot be overemphasized. Often they

spell out deficiencies that existed in the past and provide a map that marks out the entity's problem areas.)

- A review of the entity's financial statements, as well as related schedules that indicate the sources and uses of entity resources
- A search for literature (such as the GASB studies on service efforts and accomplishments) that set forth potentially applicable performance measures and standards of economy and efficiency
- A review of management controls
- A search for newspaper articles, press reports, transcripts of legislative hearings, and other literature that might provide insight into the organization's strengths and weaknesses
- Explicit consideration of the organization's vulnerabilities to fraud and mismanagement and the "things that might go wrong"

Discerning the Objectives of the Programs

If the objectives of a program are clearly spelled out, are outcome oriented, and are both quantifiable and measurable, then the program is readily auditable. The auditors have either to measure the outcomes themselves or to verify the measurements of management or others.

In Chapter 14 we stressed that well-defined operational objectives are central to sound management. Yet auditors cannot always expect managers to have established a clear statement—written, or even oral—as to the intended outcomes of their programs. The absence of clearly articulated objectives should itself be a "reportable" audit finding. Nevertheless, if a program is to be audited for performance, then the auditors may themselves have to discern its objectives. Auditors can take several steps to determine a program's objectives:

- Examine the legislation that created the program or authorized funds for it; governing bodies can greatly facilitate audits by explicitly incorporating program objectives into their authorization or appropriation measures, but often they do not
- Study the "legislative history" of the program, including committee reports, various versions of the authorization bills as they passed through the legislative process, statements of the bills' sponsors, and transcripts of committee and floor debates
- Review budgets, especially if they are in a program format
- Read internal performance reports and memos
- Interview program managers and other key personnel

Scheduling Disbursements or Other Populations

As in a financial engagement, auditors will likely have to rely on sampling; they may not be able to review all activities within a program and seldom can test all transactions. To determine which activities and transactions to test, the auditors must be aware of the nature and amount of disbursements. Therefore, they should schedule all outlays, summarizing them as appropriate.

However, depending on the objective of the audit, disbursements might not be the proper population from which to select a test sample. For example, to test whether participants in a job training program satisfied admissions criteria, the auditors would want to obtain a list of either program participants or program applicants.

Assessing Management Controls

The GAO's Yellow Book, in elaborating upon the field work standard pertaining to adequate planning, indicates that that auditors obtain an understanding of internal controls that are relevant to the audit objectives. These controls encompass the policies and procedures intended to ensure that:

- Programs meet their objectives
- The data regarding the programs are valid and reliable
- The organization has complied with all laws, regulations, and contractual provisions
- Resources are properly safeguarded

The specific controls to be assessed and the means of reviewing them will depend on the objectives of the audit and the nature of the program. Controls that ensure that a program meets its objectives may be of a different type from those intended to safeguard assets or assure compliance. In general, however, the procedures that auditors follow to gain an understanding of financial controls are equally applicable to the other types of controls. They include:

- Making inquiries of employees
- Flowcharting appropriate systems
- Reviewing and inspecting policy manuals and other documents records
- Preparing and administering questionnaires

Preparing a Written Audit Plan

To satisfy the standard that work be adequately planned, auditors must prepare a written plan (i.e., an audit program) that sets forth audit goals, procedures, staff assignments, and anticipated reports. Based on the preliminary survey, review of controls, and other beginning steps, the plan should always be seen as tentative, subject to change as additional insights into the entity are obtained during the evidence-gathering process.

Gathering Evidence

The overall objectives of performance audits are typically twofold: to provide information on the extent to which a program achieved its objectives and to explain the reasons for its successes or failures.

In gathering evidence as to program outcomes, auditors must either make their own observations and measurements or rely on those of others—i.e., either the auditee or third parties. If they intend to rely on those of others, then they must either test the data or assure its reliability by other means.

The specific evidence to be gathered stems directly from the program's objectives. For example, if the objective of a computer-training program were to obtain employment for participants, then the auditors would need to obtain appropriate placement data. If it were to improve high school graduation rates, then they would require data on the percentage of students graduating.

The reasons as to why a program failed to achieve its objectives can generally be attributed to one of three fundamental causes. Taken together the three imply the auditors' approach to identifying a program's shortcomings:

- ***Shortcoming:*** The program's policies and procedures were poorly designed and, therefore, even if properly executed, would not lead to success.

Auditor approach: The auditors should examine the policies and procedures, including controls, noting any logical or conceptual flaws.

- *Shortcoming:* The program's policies and procedures (including those for supervision and review), while properly designed, were not properly executed.

  Auditor approach: The auditors should test the policies and procedures to gauge the extent to which they were being followed.

- *Shortcoming:* The program was inherently flawed owing to incorrect assumptions or failure to take into account significant factors that would affect its success. For example, a computer training program may have been based on the assumption that if participants learned certain skills, they would be able to find employment. In fact, there may be no demand for those skills in the community served. Hence, even if the policies and procedures were properly executed the program was destined to be unsuccessful.

  Auditor approach: The auditors should identify the conditions that would have been necessary for its success and assess whether they were satisfied.

The following example is illustrative of the auditors' approach to evidence gathering.

EXAMPLE *Evidence Gathering*

A northwest city is becoming a center for the manufacture of silicon chips and other computer-related products. To encourage unemployed young adults (ages twenty to thirty) to undertake technical training in skills needed by local businesses (as well as firms that it would like to attract), the city has established a $5 million revolving loan fund. The fund is used to make low-interest loans of up to $20,000 to eligible candidates so that they can enroll in suitable programs offered by local community colleges and proprietary schools. The loans are repayable over five years, starting when the candidate completes the program. The city makes approximately 150 loans per year. The loan program, which is administered by a specially created educational loan authority, is now in its sixth year of operation.

An audit team assigned to review the loan program has completed its preliminary survey and the other basic steps necessary to prepare an audit plan. It has determined that the program's operating policies and procedures (e.g., qualifications for loan recipients) are consistent with its objectives.

The following are examples of the audit procedures that the audit team should consider:

1. Obtain from the loan authority a schedule indicating all loans made during the period.
2. Select a sample of loans and for each obtain the applicant's loan file.
   a. Verify that the recipient met all specified qualifications and that all appropriate approval guidelines were followed.
   b. Verify that the file contains documents, such as school transcripts, showing that the candidate enrolled in an approved program and made required progress.
   c. Verify the loan recipient's payment history, ensuring that the authority properly pursued all delinquencies.
   d. Make certain that the file contains up-to-date records of the loan recipient's employment history subsequent to completing the training program. Confirm its accuracy by corresponding with the employers.
3. Obtain the authority's summary statistics and supporting schedules as to loans made, recipients successfully completing approved training programs, and participant employment experience.

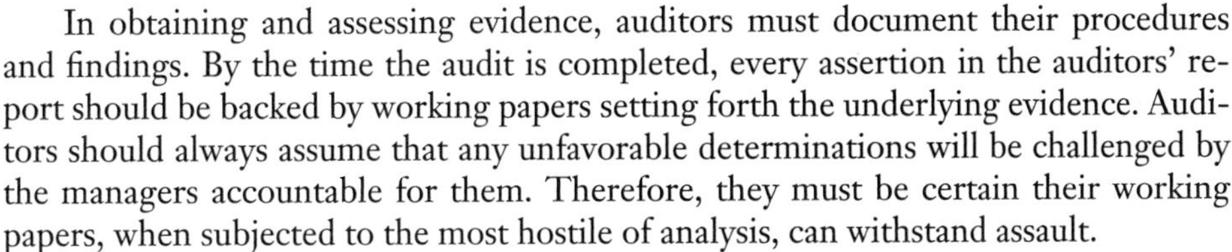

a. Reconcile the supporting schedules to the summary statistics.
b. Test the accuracy of the supporting schedules by tracing a sample of the information on the schedule to the loan files of individual recipients.

In obtaining and assessing evidence, auditors must document their procedures and findings. By the time the audit is completed, every assertion in the auditors' report should be backed by working papers setting forth the underlying evidence. Auditors should always assume that any unfavorable determinations will be challenged by the managers accountable for them. Therefore, they must be certain their working papers, when subjected to the most hostile of analysis, can withstand assault.

Reporting the Results of the Audit

The GAO reporting standards specify that auditors should prepare timely written reports of each engagement. Auditors' reports on financial statement engagements generally constitute only a few standardized paragraphs in which the auditors explain the scope and nature of their engagement and attest to information included in the statements. Those on performance audits, however, set forth data and findings as generated by the auditors, not merely the auditors' opinion on the assertion of others. Therefore, the auditor's reports are often fifty to one hundred pages long.

Per the GAO standards, the reports should include:

- An explanation of the audit's objectives and of its scope and methodology.
- The significant auditing findings and the auditors' conclusions. The findings should relate to the objectives of the engagement. The report should not only indicate the quantitative measures of performance, but also, if the program did not meet expectations, the reasons as to why. It should back any general assertions with specific examples. As noted by the GAO,

> Conclusions should be clearly stated, not implied. The strength of the auditors' conclusions depends on the persuasiveness of the evidence supporting the findings

IN PRACTICE

FINDINGS MUST RELATE TO PROGRAM OBJECTIVES

Upon auditing a federal housing program, the GAO reported that the agency in charge failed to fulfill the program's objectives. The purpose of the program, as established by Congress, was to prevent "middle class" housing from deteriorating into slums. One aspect of the program required the agency to lend funds to homeowners so that they could improve their properties and ensure that they were in compliance with building codes. The GAO charged that the agency directed program funds to areas that were in far worse condition than permitted by the criteria specified in the enabling legislation.

A program official was critical of the GAO report. He claimed that the areas that his department focused on were in far greater need of assistance than those that satisfied the legislative criteria. "The auditors are just a bunch of bean-counters," he said. "They know nothing about the realities of housing."

The GAO auditors rejected the program official's complaints. If the official thinks that the program was misguided and that resources could have been better spent otherwise, they said, he should take his complaint to Congress. "It's our job to inform the members of Congress that the program, as they established it, is not achieving its goals."

> and the soundness of the logic used to formulate the conclusions. Conclusions are stronger if they set up the report's recommendations and convince the knowledgeable user of the report that action is necessary.[4]

- Recommendations as to how to correct problems and improve operations. To be most useful, audits should be as much concerned with the future as with the past. They should be at least as constructive as they are critical.
- An indication of all significant instances of illegal acts or noncompliance with regulations and contractual provisions.
- A description of any significant deficiencies in management controls.
- A description of any noteworthy accomplishments. This type of information not only adds balance to the report and takes the sharp edge off the report's critical comments, but provides suggestions that can be applied to other areas within the same organization or to outside organizations.

The GAO standards also require that the auditors include in the report the views of officials responsible for the program as to the auditors' conclusions and recommendations. To enable them to comment, the auditors should present the officials with a preliminary version of the report and solicit their written response as to why they agree or disagree with the report and what corrective measures, if any, they plan.

If the auditors agree that the objections of the officials are valid, then they can modify their report before issuing a final version. However, if the auditors do not believe that the officials' concerns are legitimate, they can include in their report their reasons why they believe they are invalid—and, in effect, have the last word.

Per the GAO standards, reports on governmental performance audits, like those on governmental financial audits, should be made public, unless their distribution is limited by law or regulation. Some government agencies, such as the GAO, now promote wide distribution of their reports by making them available on the Internet.[5]

Although it is difficult to predict the future of accounting and auditing, it is almost certain that performance auditing will play an increasingly prominent role. As both governments and not-for-profits place greater emphasis on achieving their objectives, it is inevitable that increasing attention will be paid to reports as to the extent that they accomplished what was expected of them.

WHAT UNIQUE ETHICAL ISSUES DO GOVERNMENTAL AND NOT-FOR-PROFIT ACCOUNTING AND AUDITING PRESENT?

A unit on professional ethics is traditionally incorporated into university-level courses in auditing. The discussion is often divided into two parts. The first addresses philosophical principles of ethical behavior. The second concerns the AICPA's Code of Conduct. The Code of Conduct is mainly a series of practices established by the AICPA to advance the interests of both the accounting profession and the constituents that it serves. The code contains rules relating to independence, integrity, advertising, contingent fees, and form of practice organization.

The scandals involving Enron and numerous other companies brought a sense of urgency to developing special courses in ethics as well to integrating discussions of ethics into all business courses. Often overlooked was that employees of governments and not-for-profit entities may face ethical quandaries that are no less taxing than

[4] *Government Auditing Standards*, 2003 Revision (Washington, D.C.: Comptroller General of the United States), para. 8.27.

[5] The GAO's home page is at www.gao.gov/.

IN PRACTICE

Stupid Government Tricks Point to Need for Performance Audits

"David Letterman hasn't staged any contests for stupid government tricks, but if he ever does, Nassau County could have some contenders for the top 10." So begins a *New York Times* article that demonstrates clearly the importance of performance audits that focus on whether an entity is using its resources in the most efficient and effective manner. The "stupid government tricks" identified by the *Times* include:

- The county's emergency communication system was almost shut down because, owing to bureaucratic snafus, it failed to pay its phone bill on time
- 1,200 new desktop computers grew obsolete in unopened boxes for three years while staff used clunkers from years past
- Social service agencies paid hundreds of millions of dollars in Medicare claims without checking for errors or verifying recipient eligibility
- For two or three years the county paid for 1,400 phone lines that were not even hooked up to telephones
- The county failed to maintain an inventory of its extensive real estate holdings
- It seized 1,600 cars from drunk drivers, but got around to selling only 200 of them; it permitted the rest to rust in storage facilities that cost $1,000 per day

Source: Bruce Lambert, "Unused Computers, Unpaid 911 Bills: Nassau Tallies Waste," *New York Times* (January 2, 2003).

those of their private sector counterparts and are subject to similar types of pressures to violate both their own personal ethical norms as well as those of society at large.

This section of the text is not intended to duplicate the materials ordinarily addressed in auditing courses—almost all of which are relevant to CPAs carrying out independent audits of governments and not-for-profit organizations. Neither is it intended to resolve any particular ethical issues. Instead, its purposes are to highlight the characteristics of governments that may justify a special perspective on ethical questions, to set forth an approach to resolving ethical dilemmas (one not unique to the governmental environment), and to illustrate how that approach can be applied to ethical dilemmas. The end-of-chapter material includes ten mini-cases that are illustrative of "real world" ethical predicaments faced by government as well as not-for-profit accountants and auditors.

CHARACTERISTICS OF GOVERNMENTS THAT JUSTIFY A SPECIAL PERSPECTIVE ON ETHICAL QUESTIONS

Governments (and to a lesser extent many not-for-profits) have characteristics that present their employees with ethical decisions different from those faced by employees of businesses. These include the following:

- ***Public expectations.*** The public holds employees of governments to a higher standard of conduct than those of businesses. Whereas it may accept that private companies—and hence, their employees—act in their own self-interest, it expects government employees to put the welfare of the public above that of themselves.
- ***Guardians of public funds.*** Government accountants are guardians of public funds and are accountable to the public as to how they use them. Although corporate managers are accountable to stockholders, the public has far more rigorous standards than investors of what constitutes proper use of resources and is far less tolerant of frivolous expenditures. For example, investors may tolerate lavish entertainment, personal use of company jets, and palatial offices

as acceptable management perks. The public, however, permits few government officials the same luxuries.

- ***Activities carried out in open view.*** Virtually all government activities are carried out in broad daylight. Public officials are answerable to the public for almost all their actions. Under federal and state "open records" statutes, relatively few types of documents, not even internal memos and correspondence, are immune from public scrutiny. "No comment—that's proprietary information," in response to a reporter's question may be accepted from corporate executives, but it is seldom countenanced from government officials.
- ***Special powers.*** Governments have powers that businesses do not. For example, they may compel citizens to disclose personal information, such as earnings and holdings of personal property. Moreover, many citizens attach a legitimacy to requests for data from government officials that they would view with suspicion if they came from private businesses. Therefore, government officials have a particular obligation to maintain the confidentially of information that is not in the public domain and not to exceed the limits of their authority in their dealings with the public.
- ***Conflicting loyalties.*** Government workers are not only government employees, but they are also citizens to whom the government is accountable. Government decisions may be made in a highly charged political atmosphere and may involve the most basic of human values. The government may be led by officials of a political party different from that of an individual employee. Hence, individual employees may be faced with a conflict between loyalty to their organization and their superiors and to their own political and moral values.

ANALYZING ETHICAL DILEMMAS

A *dilemma*, by definition, is a situation that requires a choice between two equally balanced alternatives; a predicament that seemingly defies a satisfactory solution. Few ethical dilemmas can be resolved without an individual selecting among, or compromising between, competing ethical values. There is almost never a single "correct" course of action. Nevertheless, by identifying and analyzing the factors relevant to the issue at hand, the individual can better develop available options and understand their consequences.

The following questions are indicative of an approach (merely one of several possibilities) that can be taken to resolve ethical dilemmas:

1. What are the relevant facts? (Although many situations are seemingly complex, there may be only a small number of facts that are genuinely germane.)
2. Who are the major parties affected and what are their interests in how the dilemma is resolved?
3. What are the ethical values that are in question? How do they rank in importance? Examples of these values include:
   a. Honesty and integrity
   b. Loyalty and obligations to colleagues
   c. Responsibilities to family
   d. Obligation to make full and fair disclosures to appropriate parties
   e. Loyalty and other obligations to one's employer
   f. Responsibilities as a citizen
   g. Pursuit of excellence
4. What are the alternative courses of action?
5. What are the consequences of each course of action? Which values would have to be sacrificed or compromised?

The following example illustrates how these questions may be applied to a specific ethical dilemma.

EXAMPLE *Ethical Dilemma*

James Klavan is a city's assistant comptroller. Within the last year, the comptroller established an enterprise fund to account for the operation of the city's golf course. Previously the course had been accounted for in the general fund. Generally accepted accounting principles permit a government flexibility as to the types of funds in which it should account for activities financed by user charges. There is no question that under those principles golf-course operations can be accounted for in either a governmental fund or an enterprise fund. The main reason for the change was to shift expenses out of the general fund and thereby help to eliminate a general fund deficit. Were it not for the accounting change, the general fund deficit would have to be offset by increased taxes or reductions in services. However, if the reasons for the change were made public, city officials would unquestionably be charged by political opponents with fiscal gimmickry.

The city comptroller was approached by a reporter covering the publication of the city's annual report. Owing to time constraints, the comptroller referred him to Klavan, his assistant. In the course of an interview, the reporter (who couldn't distinguish a debit from a credit) asked Klavan to explain the change and indicate its significance. Klavan is uncertain as to how to respond.

1. Relevant facts
   a. The comptroller established an enterprise fund so as to reduce the reported general fund deficit.
   b. Klavan is aware of the reason for the change and is asked by a reporter for an explanation of its significance.
   c. Although the change is permissible under generally accepted accounting principles, it was made to eliminate a general fund deficit and thereby avert either increases in taxes or reductions in services.
   d. Disclosure of the true reason for the change would embarrass both Klavan's immediate superior and the city administration.
2. Major parties affected (other than Klavan)
   a. The comptroller, who stands to be embarrassed if the reason for the change were made public
   b. The reporter, who presumably expects a full and fair explanation of the change
   c. The citizenry, who might be misled by the change (yet might nevertheless support it if it would avert a tax increase or service reduction)
3. Ethical values in conflict
   a. Loyalty to colleagues and employer (both the comptroller and the city administration)
   b. Honesty (to reporter)
   c. Obligation to make full and fair disclosures to appropriate parties
   d. Responsibilities as a citizen (either to prevent the city from misleading its citizens or, by contrast, to facilitate a means of averting tax increases)
4. Possible courses of action available to Klavan
   a. Explain the change to the reporter, but obfuscate the reason for it
   b. Explain the change and reveal the underlying reason for it
   c. Delay responding to the reporter, and tell the comptroller that he will not meet with the reporter unless the comptroller explicitly gives him permission to reveal the reason for the change

5. Consequences of actions
   a. If Klavan explains the change to the reporter without revealing the reasons for it, he will not be providing full disclosure and will thereby be intentionally misleading. Moreover, he will be allowing his employer (both the comptroller and the city administration) to deceive the citizenry.
   b. If he explains the change and reveals the underlying reason for it, he will embarrass both the comptroller and the city (and thereby place his career with the city at risk).
   c. If he confronts the comptroller and indicates that he will meet with the reporter only if granted permission to reveal the underlying reason for the change, then he will place the comptroller in an uncomfortable position (by suggesting that the comptroller is being deceitful) and thereby jeopardize his relationship with the comptroller and consequently his career with the city.

To be sure, there may be other courses of action available to Klavan. Indeed, the key to resolving most ethical dilemmas is to develop options beyond those that are obvious. There are, unfortunately, no "textbook" solutions.

SUMMARY

In the area of government and not-for-profit auditing the influence of the federal government has been paramount. It has had its impact mainly through the GAO's Yellow Book, *Government Auditing Standards (Standards for Audit of Governmental Organizations, Programs, Activities, and Functions)* and through the Single Audit Act.

The Yellow Book establishes generally accepted government auditing standards (GAGAS), which, owing to the Single Audit Act, must now be adhered to in virtually all audits of both governments and not-for-profit organizations that receive federal financial assistance. Although the standards cover both financial statement audits and performance audits, the Single Audit Act requires only financial audits. Like the auditing standards of the AICPA after which they are modeled, they are grouped into three categories: general standards, standards of field work, and standards of reporting.

The primary difference between financial audits as carried out in a government or not-for-profit entity, as opposed to a business, is the greater influence placed upon ensuring compliance with laws, regulations, and contractual requirements. The GAO standards, for example, require that audit reports include an explicit description of compliance tests and an indication of compliance violations.

Legislative actions, now codified in the Single Audit Act, direct that recipients of federal aid be subject to a single independent financial audit even though they may receive funds from many agencies. Single audits comprise two elements: an audit of financial statements, conducted in accord with *Government Auditing Standards*, and an audit of federal financial awards that follows the provisions of OMB Circular A-133.

The Single Audit Act requires that in their audits of federal financial awards, the auditors take a risk-based approach by which they devote their audit effort mainly to major, as opposed to nonmajor, programs. Major programs are those that make up a relatively large proportion of the total federal awards received by the entity and for which there is a high risk of noncompliance. Moreover, in planning their engagement the auditors must take into account the various audit risks that they face (i.e., inherent risk, control risk, fraud risk, and detection risk).

An audit of federal financial awards should assure that the entity has complied not only with applicable laws and regulations but also with both general and program-specific provisions. The general requirements, of which there are fourteen, are common to all federal awards. These include provisions that promote effective cash management, ensure that entities are reimbursed only for allowable costs, and prohibit the use of federal funds to engage in political activity. The program-specific provisions are typically directed to issues of eligibility, types of goods or services that may be acquired with federal funds, and the percentage of federal funds that the entity itself must match.

The single audit is expected to culminate in four reports: (1) an opinion on the financial statements and the schedule of expenditures of federal awards; (2) a report on compliance and on internal control over financial reporting; (3) a report on compliance with requirements of major programs; and (4) a schedule of findings and questioned costs.

Performance audits differ in concept from financial audits in that the auditors do not merely *attest* to assertions of management. Rather, they make their own assessments as to the extent that an entity or program has achieved its objectives. The key to carrying out a performance audit (consistent with the theme of the previous chapter) is in identifying the operational objectives of the target program or activity. If these objectives are quantifiable and measurable, then the auditors have either to make the appropriate measurements or to verify those of others. Hence, performance audits can be as objective as traditional financial engagements.

As emphasized throughout this text, both governments and not-for-profits have objectives other than profit maximization. Accordingly, the conventional operating statements that highlight revenues and expenditures provide little indication of how well an entity is fulfilling its mission. These statements must be supplemented by reports on service efforts and accomplishments that focus on the entity's actual objectives. Correspondingly, audits that merely attest to the fairness of the conventional statements are of only limited value to the constituents of the entity. Performance audits are therefore an important supplement to conventional financial audits. They are unquestionably the wave of the future.

Although government accountants and auditors face ethical dilemmas similar to those in the private sector, they must resolve them in face of the following unique characteristics of government employees: public expectations, status as guardians of public funds, the open environment in which they function, special powers they may have, and conflicting loyalties. Unfortunately, there are no textbook answers to ethical problems; the key to a satisfactory resolution is the development of options beyond the obvious.

EXERCISE FOR REVIEW AND SELF-STUDY

You are the partner of the CPA firm that has been engaged to perform the annual audit of the Euless School District. The district receives approximately \$1.5 million per year in federal assistance. This includes \$500,000 in annual grants to conduct an experimental high school science enrichment program. The program has now been in existence for three years.

1. You assign one of the firm's managers to be in charge of the audit's field work. The manager recently returned from a two-week professional education course in estate and gift taxation. She took the course to satisfy her state's biannual eighty-hour CPE requirement. She took no other CPE courses in the past two years. Why might her appointment be in violation of *Government Auditing Standards*?
2. The audit manager who was eventually assigned to the engagement inquired as to whether the firm had on hand the most recent version of Circular A-133 and the "Common Rule." What are these documents, and why are they likely to be relevant to the financial audit of a local independent school district?
3. Soon after the audit staff began the engagement, the school district's chief financial officer called to complain that the auditors were making inquiries of the district's employees as to the political activities of district administrators. These matters, he asserted, were clearly beyond the scope of a financial engagement. How would you respond to his objection?
4. After your firm completed the financial audit of the district, the school board requested that it conduct a performance audit of the science enrichment program. In what critical way would the performance audit differ conceptually from the financial engagement?
5. Suppose the objectives of the program were not spelled out in the federal legislation that authorized the program. Moreover, the school district had never prepared a written "statement of objectives." What steps would you take to establish the program's objectives?
6. Suppose you are able to establish that a primary objective of the program is to encourage students to enter vocational fields related to science. The grant funds may be used to pay for teachers' training, curriculum development projects, equipment and texts, and extracurricular activities related to science.
   - **a.** What would be the purpose of preparing a schedule showing how the grant funds were disbursed?
   - **b.** How would you recommend the auditors gain an understanding of the internal controls over program expenditures?
   - **c.** Inasmuch as the program has been in existence for only three years, how might you assess whether the program has fulfilled its objective?

QUESTIONS FOR REVIEW AND DISCUSSION

1. What is the Yellow Book, and why has it influenced audits both of state and local governments and of not-for-profit organizations?
2. In what significant way do financial audits in government and not-for-profit organizations differ from those carried on in businesses?
3. The State Auditor of Missouri is an elected official. In auditing the financial statements of the University of Missouri, what special problems relating to independence would he or she face that a private CPA firm would not? Would he or she be in violation of the GAO standards? Explain, indicating how the GAO standards

deal with the apparent conflicts of interest faced by state and local government audit departments.

4. In what way do the GAO standards impose more rigorous continuing professional education requirements than those of the AICPA?
5. In what way do the reporting standards of the GAO differ from those of the AICPA as to (a) public dissemination of the reports and (b) tests of compliance and internal controls?
6. What is a single audit? What deficiencies in previous practice was the Single Audit Act intended to correct?
7. What are the two main components of a single audit?
8. What are "general" compliance requirements? Provide several examples.
9. What types of matters do "specific" requirements address?
10. It is sometimes said that performance audits are not "true" audits in that they are conceptually different from traditional financial audits. In what way are they conceptually different?
11. What are the four main types of reports required of a single audit?
12. In what ways can it be said that a single audit is "risk based"?
13. In what other significant ways do performance audits differ from financial audits?
14. What are the general criteria that audit organizations use in selecting programs and activities for performance audits?
15. What steps might auditors take to discern the objectives of a program or activity?
16. What are the key features of a performance audit report?

EXERCISES

15-1

1. *Government Auditing Standards* must be adhered to in all financial audits of
   a. State and local governments
   b. Federal agencies
   c. Federally chartered banks
   d. All of the above
2. "Generally accepted government auditing standards" (GAGAS) refers to standards incorporated in
   a. The Yellow Book
   b. The Yellow Book, and OMB Circular A-133
   c. The Yellow Book and the AICPA's Professional Standards
   d. The Yellow Book, OMB Circular A-133m and the AICPA's Professional Standards
3. *Government Auditing Standards* characterizes government engagements into which of the following three categories
   a. Financial audits, compliance audits, and performance audits
   b. Financial audits, operational audits, and performance audits
   c. Financial audits, attest engagements, and performance audits
   d. Financial audits, efficiency and effectiveness audits, and compliance audits
4. The Yellow Book's general standards apply
   a. Only to financial audits
   b. Only to financial audits and other attest engagements
   c. To all three types of engagements
   d. To all professional engagements relating to accounting
5. Per the GAO's independence standards, auditors are not permitted
   a. To perform any consulting services for an audit client
   b. To audit any client who has any senior level employees who had previously worked for the audit organization in the past five years
   c. To perform any management functions for an audit client
   d. To assist an audit client in preparing financial statements from underlying records
6. Per the GAO standards, auditors
   a. Must design their audit to provide reasonable assurance of detecting noncompliance with the terms of contracts or grant agreements
   b. Are not responsible for detecting noncompliance with the terms of contracts or grant agreements but must report such noncompliance if they become aware of it
   c. Must design their audit so that "it is more likely than not" they will detect noncompliance with terms of contracts or grant agreements
   d. Are responsible for detecting noncompliance with the terms of contracts or grant agreements only insofar as such noncompliance will have a material impact on the financial statements
7. Per the GAO standards, auditors must note in their audit report
   a. Only instances of fraud that are material in relation to either the financial statements or to the grants and contracts that they affect
   b. Only those instances of fraud that will have a material impact on the financial statements
   c. All instances of fraud excect those that are clearly inconsequential
   d. Only those instances of fraud that have not been disclosed in the management discussion and analysis
8. Per the GAO standards, an auditor's working papers must

a. Be made public unless they contain information that would be harmful to national security
b. Contain sufficient information to convince an auditor having no previous connection with the audit that the evidence supports the auditor's conclusions and judgments
c. Be retained by the auditor for a period of no less than ten years
d. Include documentation that the individual auditors on the engagement have satisfied the standards' continuing professional education requirements

9. The GAO reporting standards differ from those of the AICPA in that the GAO standards require the auditors to explicitly comment on their testing of
a. Financial transactions
b. Internal control and compliance
c. Efficiency and effectiveness
d. Government-wide statements

10. If the auditors' report discloses deficiencies in internal control, fraud, illegal acts, violations of provisions of contracts or grant agreements, or abuse, the auditors should
a. Notify the federal department designated as the cognizant agency
b. Notify all federal agencies the funds of which were subject to the violations
c. Include in the notes to the financial statements a schedule detailing the violations and indicating their impact on the financial statements
d. Obtain and report the views of responsible officials concerning the findings

15-2

1. A key determinant as to whether, under the Circular A-133, a program is considered major or nonmajor is
a. The overall size of the program as measured by total revenues, regardless of source
b. The overall size of the program as measured by total assets
c. The amount of federal aid received
d. Its score on the OMB risk assessment scale

2. "General" compliance requirements are set forth in
a. The Yellow Book
b. The Single Audit Act
c. The compliance supplement to Circular A-133
d. The AICPA's generally accepted auditing standards

3. The risk that material noncompliance could occur assuming that no internal controls have been established to prevent it is referred to as
a. Inherent risk
b. Control risk
c. Fraud risk
d. Detection risk

4. Per Circular A-133, the Schedule of Expenditures of Federal Awards
a. Must be explicitly tested and reported upon by the auditors
b. Should serve to help auditors to determine the scope of their audit work but need not be explicitly tested
c. Must be tested but need be reported upon by the auditors only if the tests reveal material errors
d. Must be explicitly tested and reported upon by the auditors only if the total of federal awards is material relative to total expenditures

5. Which of the following would *not* be reported upon in the Schedule of Findings and Questioned Costs?
a. Reportable conditions related to internal control
b. Material noncompliance with provisions of laws, regulations, contracts, or grant agreements
c. Material examples of inefficiency and ineffectiveness in carrying out federally funded programs
d. Federally reimbursed expenditures that are not adequately documented

6. The requirement for a report on compliance and internal control over financial reporting is set forth in the
a. AICPA's Professional Standards
b. GAO's Government Auditing Standards
c. Single Audit Act
d. OBM Circular A-133

7. The GAO standards pertaining to performance audits
a. Mandate that programs be audited annually
b. Mandate that programs be audited whenever information comes to the attention of the auditor indicating a need for a performance audit
c. Mandate that a complete audit include both a financial audit and a performance audit
d. Do not specify when and how often a program must be audited

8. Performance audits differ from financial audits in that
a. The GAO's "general standards" do not apply to performance audits
b. In conducting performance audits, the auditors do not necessarily attest to assertions of management
c. The auditors need not issue a formal report setting forth their findings
d. The main focus should be on activities that satisfy the criteria of Circular A-133 as "major programs"

9. In discerning the objectives of a program to be audited, the auditors should give the greatest credibility to
a. The legislation creating the program
b. The organization's program budget
c. The organization's mission statement and strategic plan
d. Comments by the mid-level employees who actually implement the program

10. In reporting the results of a performance audit, it would be inappropriate for the auditors to
a. Conjecture as to the reasons for the program's failure to achieve desired results
b. Include the auditors' response to management's objections to the auditors' findings
c. Provide recommendations as to how the program can be improved
d. Criticize management for failing to establish appropriate goals and objectives

PROBLEMS

15-1

The Yellow Book standards relating to financial audits apply to independent CPA firms as well as government audit departments.

The following descriptions relate to an independent CPA firm that includes among its audit clients municipalities, school districts, and not-for-profit organizations, all of which receive federal financial assistance. Each description presents a possible violation of *Government Auditing Standards* (summarized in Table 15-1). For each description indicate the specific standard at issue and tell why there might be violation.

1. Each year the managing partner appoints a committee of three of its partners to evaluate the quality of the work performed by the firm. The firm is not otherwise reviewed by independent parties.
2. When the firm conducts a financial examination, its primary objective is to determine whether the auditee's financial system is properly designed, the system is operating as intended, and the resultant financial records can be relied upon. Accordingly, the department does not test explicitly for fraud or other illegal activities.
3. The firm has a formal program of continuing professional education. To eliminate the need to pay for the staff to attend outside courses, it brings in outside experts to conduct forty hours per year of training. Each year the training is directed to a specific area. This year's area was changes in the federal tax code; last year's was "how to market the firm."
4. The firm periodically assigns members of its staff on a temporary basis to government and not-for-profit audit clients. The staff members typically serve as financial consultants or as acting financial administrators.
5. The firm may not test compliance with certain federal grant provisions if the grant was examined by the client's internal auditors and no violations were detected.
6. In its single audit of a client's federally assisted program, the firm detected numerous instances of noncompliance with applicable federal regulations. Inasmuch as none of the violations were either serious or material, the firm reported them to the client in its "management letter" but did not mention them in its compliance report to federal officials.
7. As part of all financial audits of federal funds recipients, the auditors carefully assess the adequacy of internal controls. They do not, however, prepare a specific report on internal controls or address them in the standard audit report.

15-2

Even programs involving relatively subjective judgments can readily be audited.

A Department of Housing and Urban Development (HUD) program is aimed at conserving and rehabilitating blighted but salvageable urban areas. One element of the program provides that HUD will make rehabilitation grants and low-interest loans to property owners to help them finance the repairs needed to bring their properties into compliance with housing codes.

When Congress authorized the program it did not establish specific criteria as to what constitutes a "blighted but salvageable" area; it left that up to HUD.

A preliminary survey by the GAO has indicated that HUD is directing funds to areas that were far too deteriorated for conservation and rehabilitation to work.

Suppose that you are assigned to the engagement. Outline an approach that you would take to support (or reject) the findings of the preliminary survey.

15-3

Compliance testing may require auditor ingenuity.

The CPA firm of which you are a manager has placed you in charge of the audit of the Thornburg School District. The district receives substantial financial support from the State Education Agency. The state requires aid recipients to have annual single audits conducted by independent CPA firms. The firms are responsible for verifying that recipients have complied with the provisions of all financial awards from the state.

From your preliminary survey you learn that the district received an award of $3 million to provide free hot lunches to elementary schoolchildren of low-income families. The award specifies that only children from families with incomes under $30,000 are eligible to participate in the program. The state requires districts to determine eligibility, but it provides no guidance as to how they are to do so.

Based only on this limited information, it is obviously not possible to develop a specific audit program to assure that the district has complied with the eligibility provisions. However, before you even meet with district officials to discuss the audit, you wish to have a preliminary strategy in mind.

1. As best you can from the limited amount of information provided, design a strategy to test compliance with the eligibility provisions.
2. Suppose that the audit was being conducted under the federal Single Audit Act and the auditors were required to adhere to all of its reporting provisions. As part of your examination you found that twenty-five students out of 350 in the program failed to meet the eligibility requirements. Assuming that the auditors consider the amounts involved as indicative of a weakness in internal controls, how, if at all, should that finding affect your report on the program?

15-4

A performance audit of investment activities must ascertain whether common-sense controls (not explicitly discussed in this chapter) have been established.

The director of the internal audit department of a midsize city received a memo from a member of the city council that included the following:

> I am certain that you have followed recent press reports of the losses incurred by city and state governments on their investment portfolios. Many of these losses can be attributed to pressures to boost investment returns. These pressures encouraged the investment officers to acquire derivatives and other high-risk securities, which are clearly inappropriate for governments. I am extremely concerned that our city might also be vulnerable to major losses.
>
> The city currently has investments (including those of our retirement funds, bond reserves, and endowments) totaling more than $800 million. These are managed by our Office of Investments (a subunit of the Treasury Department). The mission of the office as set forth in the enabling legislation is "to invest prudently the available resources of the city so as to maximize the return to the city."
>
> I note that whereas our independent CPAs have reviewed the city's investment portfolio as part of their annual financial audit, your department has never conducted a performance audit of the office. I urge, therefore, that you do so as soon as feasible. I think it especially important that you report on the extent to which the office has in place the administrative controls, policies, and practices necessary to assure that it is accomplishing its mission.

1. In light of widely accepted criteria for selecting audit targets, do you find it surprising that the internal audit department has never conducted a performance audit of the Office of Investments? Explain, citing relevant criteria.
2. Suppose you are placed in charge of the engagement. Draft a memo to the head of the internal audit department in which you outline the approach you would take in carrying it out. Be as specific as possible, providing examples of the types of administrative controls that you would expect to find in place. Indicate how you would assess whether the Office of Investments is "maximizing the return to the city."

15-5

The key to auditing the effectiveness of a social program is in establishing its objectives.

The Office of Economic Opportunity (OEO) designed "special impact programs" to reduce unemployment, dependency, and community tensions in urban areas with large concentrations of low-income residents and in rural areas having substantial migration to such urban areas. The purpose of these experimental programs, which combine business, community, and manpower development, is to offer poor people an opportunity to become self-supporting through the free enterprise system. The programs are intended to create training and job opportunities, improve the living environment, and encourage development of local entrepreneurial skills.

One area chosen to participate in several special impact programs was Bedford-Stuyvesant. The Bedford-Stuyvesant program was the first and largest such program to be sponsored by the federal government. It has received more than $960 million in federal funds from its inception through the current year. Another $250 million was obtained from private sources, such as the Ford Foundation and the Astor Foundation.

Bedford-Stuyvesant is a five-square-mile area with a population of 350,000 to 400,000 in New York City's borough of Brooklyn. The area has serious problems of unemployment, underemployment, and inadequate housing.

Bedford-Stuyvesant's problems are deep-seated and have resisted rapid solution. They stem primarily from the lack of jobs in the area and from the fact that local residents, to a considerable degree, lack the education and training required for the jobs available elsewhere in the city. Unemployment and underemployment, in turn, reduce buying power, which has a depressing effect on the area's economy.

The magnitude of the Bedford-Stuyvesant problems are indicated by the following data disclosed by the U.S. census:

- Of the total civilian labor force, 8.9 percent are unemployed, compared with unemployment rates of 7.1 percent for New York City and 6.8 percent for the New York Standard Metropolitan Statistical Area (SMSA).
- Per capita income is 66 percent that of New York City and 51 percent that of the SMSA.
- Families below the poverty level make up 24.8 percent of the population, compared with 11.4 percent in New York City and 9.2 percent in the SMSA.
- Families receiving public assistance make up 25.4 percent of the population, compared with 9.6 percent in New York City and 7.5 percent in the SMSA.

A number of factors aggravate the area's economic problems and make them more difficult to solve. Some of these are:

- A reluctance of industry to move into New York City
- A net outflow of industry from New York City
- High city taxes and a high crime rate
- A dearth of local residents possessing business managerial experience

The area's housing problems result from the widespread deterioration of existing housing and are, in part, a byproduct of below-average income levels resulting from unemployment and underemployment. They are aggravated by a shortage of mortgage capital for residential housing associated with a lack of confidence in the area on the part of financial institutions.

One of the special impact programs that Bedford-Stuyvesant participates in is intended to stimulate the private economy by providing funds to local businesses, both new and existing. Under this program, begun five years ago, the sponsors propose to create jobs and stimulate business ownership by local residents. At first, investments in local businesses were made only in the form of loans. Later, the sponsors adopted a policy of making equity investments in selected companies to obtain for the sponsors a voice in management. Equity investments totaling about $2.5 million were made in four companies.

Loans are to be repaid in installments over periods of up to ten years, usually with a moratorium on repayment for six months or longer. Repayment is to be made in cash or by applying subsidies allowed by the sponsors for providing on-the-job training to unskilled workers. Loans made during the first two years of the program were interest-free. Later, the sponsors revised the policy to one of charging below-market interest rates. Rates charged are now from 3 to 6.5 percent. This policy change was made to (1) emphasize to borrowers their obligations to repay the loans and (2) help the sponsors monitor borrowers' progress toward profitability.

Prospective borrowers learn of the program through information disseminated at neighborhood centers, advertisements on radio and television and in a local newspaper, and word of mouth. Those who wish to apply for loans are required to complete application forms providing information relating to their education, business and work experience, and personal financial condition and references. The sponsors set up a management assistance division that employed consultants to supplement its internal marketing assistance efforts and to provide management, accounting, marketing, legal, and other help to borrowers.

The sponsors proposed to create at least 1,700 jobs during the first four years of the loan program by making loans to seventy-three new and existing businesses.

Required

Put yourself in the position of the GAO manager in charge of all audits pertaining to the Office of Economic Opportunity. Your staff has undertaken a preliminary survey of the Bedford-Stuyvesant program and the above information was extracted from its report on the survey.

The New York City field office has been assigned the job of conducting the detailed performance audit of the special impact program just described. Prepare a memo to the New York City field office in which you indicate, in as great detail as is possible from the information provided, the specific steps its staff should perform in conducting an evaluation of the effectiveness of the program.

This problem is based on an actual GAO audit. It was written by the author of this text and was previously published in Jack C. Robertson, Auditing, *8th ed., (Chicago: Irwin, 1996). Reprinted with permission of McGraw Hill-Irwin.*

15-6

Performance audits are often far removed from financial audits, but even seemingly unauditable programs can be evaluated.

The president of a major state university has a problem. A group of alumni are complaining that the university's athletic program is an embarrassment to the university and are demanding that the athletic director be fired. In response, the president has promised an intensive "audit" of the all aspects of the department's performance.

The university has never explicitly established formal goals for the athletic department. Nevertheless, five years prior to this crisis, at the press conference announcing his appointment, the athletic director (with characteristic exuberance and hyperbole) made the following statements:

1. We intend to win national championships in all major sports.
2. Every one of our athletes will be graduated in five years.
3. The student body will once again be proud of its teams, showing its support by attending our games.
4. We will be "number one" as measured by TV appearances and revenues.

Although these comments are obviously visions, rather than operational objectives, they do imply performance indicators that can be objectively assessed.

Suppose that you are placed in charge of the president's promised audit of the athletic department. For each of the four visions, propose objective indicators that could be used to assess the department's performance. Recognizing that you will be unable to make definitive judgments as to whether the department's performance was satisfactory or not, tell what information you would want to provide the president and the university's board of trustees so that they can make an informed judgment as to the quality of the department's performance.

15-7

Assessment of the procurement process may be a central element in an operations audit.

The chairman of a state legislature's finance committee has charged that the Division of Taxation's computer systems are in chaos and, as a consequence, the state is failing to collect hundreds of millions in income taxes to which it is entitled. According to the chairman, the system was improperly designed and many of its component computers, software programs, and peripheral items of equipment have failed to perform as promised.

The overall system had been designed three years earlier by an outside consulting firm. The component computers, software programs, and peripheral items of equipment were purchased by the state from numerous different vendors.

The chairman has charged that the new system, costing $50 million, was a fiscal disaster and demanded that the State Auditor determine the reasons for the failure.

Suppose that you are a senior-level auditor in the State Auditor's Office. You are asked by the State Auditor to head a team to assess whether, in fact, the systems are not working as intended and, if not, why not and who is responsible.

1. Indicate in general terms how you might determine what was intended of the system.
2. Assume that you concluded that the system was not operating as intended. Indicate your general approach to discerning the reason for the failures and to pinpointing responsibility.

15-8

Even when objectives are clearly stated, the reasons they have not been met may not be easy to discern.

The City on the Lake Convention Center was constructed at a cost of $250 million with the aim of attracting visitors to the area. Taxpayers were assured that the convention center would be self-supporting: that convention-center revenues would be sufficient to cover all expenses, including debt service. Yet in its first five years of operation the center consistently reported operating deficits.

In a recent report to the city council, the convention center manager attributed the deficits to the center's inability to attract sufficient conventions and other events. Whereas convention planners had projected that the center would have events scheduled for at least 250 days during the year, it had so far averaged only 180 days—far fewer than the break-even point.

As the city auditor, you have been requested by the city council to conduct a performance audit to learn why the center has been unable to attract the projected number of conventions and other events and to make recommendations for appropriate changes so that the projections can be met.
Required: Propose, in general terms, an approach to fulfilling the mandate of the city council.

CASES IN ETHICS

15-1: Conflicting Responsibilities

Kevin Watkins is a manager of a CPA firm. At the recommendation of the partner-in-charge he applied, and was accepted, for membership on the Accounting Standards Committee of the Government Finance Officers Association. Committee members are selected on their individual qualifications. In appointing members the association tries to ensure that they are drawn from all major constituent groups, but members do not represent their employers.

The committee has under consideration a resolution urging municipalities to develop measures of service efforts and accomplishment and to report upon them in their annual reports. It is divided on the resolution, but Watkins is convinced of its merits. The partner in charge of Watkins's CPA firm, however, is strongly opposed to it, noting that obtaining the required information would impose a substantial net cost upon the firm.

A voice vote on the resolution is scheduled for the next meeting.

15-2: Audit Failure

In a management letter following its year-end audit of the North Country Hospital, the not-for-profit hospital's independent audit firm questioned the adequacy of the hospital's accounts receivable allowance for contractual adjustments. It noted that owing to contractual changes, the discounts given to insurance companies and HMOs were increasing, and it urged that the hospital carefully review the collectibility of its receivables. It asserted that audit tests revealed numerous required adjustments and as a consequence the hospital reduced its receivable balance by 7 percent. Nevertheless, the firm warned, additional write-downs would likely be required in the future. The firm had issued an unqualified opinion on the financial statements.

Several months following the audit, the hospital announced that operating losses for the then-current year would far exceed expectations, owing to a 30 percent write-down of accounts receivable. The required write-down was greatly in excess of the allowance for contractual adjustments.

The partner in charge of the engagement was asked by a reporter, who was unaware of the management letter, why the audit of the previous year failed to detect the overstatement of receivables.

15-3: Charity Begins with the Auditor

In June 2005, Jason King completed his audit of a 2004 grant that a city made to Field of Dreams, a private, not-for-profit organization that sponsors recreational programs for disadvantaged teens. In the course of his testing, King discovered that material disbursements that were made in 2005 were charged as 2004 expenditures. The program director acknowledged the 2004 overcharges, pointing out that the organization faced a temporary cash shortage in 2004. By charging the 2005 disbursements as 2004 expenditures, he was able to obtain early reimbursement and thereby avoid a fiscal crisis. He assured King that no dishonesty was intended; he was simply shifting funds from one year to another. Indeed, King was able to verify that the organization did not request reimbursement for the same charges in 2005.

The Field of Dreams grant was a pass-through grant in that the federal government provided the funds. Were this discrepancy set forth as a "reportable condition" in King's single audit report, it is almost certain that the organization would be ineligible for federal awards in the future.

Over the course of several years, King has become familiar with the organization's programs and considers them to be of uncommon value to the community.

15-4: Undisclosed Losses

The Office of the Treasurer maintains an investment pool for several quasi-independent governments, such as housing authorities and development boards, affiliated with a city. Michelle Ruiz, a senior manager in the treasurer's office, recently became aware that the treasurer has been investing pool funds in risky derivatives and has been leveraging the funds by financing the purchase of long-term securities with short-term loans. Because of a sustained rise in interest rates over the past year, the market value of the portfolio is considerably below the contributions of pool participants. If the pool participants were to learn of the losses, it is virtually certain that some would withdraw from the fund immediately, thereby prompting an overall run on the pool.

As long as the losses are kept quiet, it is more than probable that the interest rates will soon decline and that the portfolio will recover its value. Indeed, within the last week the Federal Reserve Board announced a reduction in interest rates and the value of the portfolio rebounded slightly. By contrast, a run on the pool would assure that virtually all participants incur substantial losses.

Shortly after Ruiz learns of the losses, she is making a presentation to the media as to the operations of the pool. During a question and answer session she is asked how the pool has performed over the last several years. She explains (truthfully) that over the long-term investment returns have been well above average. She is uncertain, however, as to whether she should add anything as to its short-term results.

15-5: Politically Uncomfortable Conclusion

In verifying the capital asset records of the electric utility department, Jean Hanson, staff auditor of a city's internal audit department, noted that several trucks and pieces of equipment were out of service and apparently unrepairable. Therefore, they should have been written off. She described and documented her conclusions in her working papers.

When she discussed her findings with the manager in charge of the engagement, the manager indicated that she was aware of the problem since it had been raised in previous years. Moreover, she had already discussed it with the internal auditor (the head of the department) and both had agreed that this was not the year to make the required write-off. A large write-off would cause considerable embarrassment to the city manager, the mayor, and members of the city council, all of whom had recently defended the electric utility department against charges that it was mismanaged. Further, the budget of the internal audit department was coming up for consideration before the city council.

Jean Hanson had reason to believe that the working paper in which she described her findings was removed from the audit binder.

15-6: Managing Earnings

Henry Green is the assistant to a county's comptroller. During the year he becomes aware of several accounting and budgeting practices that, taken together, clearly establish a pattern that the county is attempting to turn both budget and reporting deficits into surpluses. Green takes his concerns to the comptroller, who informs him that (1) although the practices may be considered by many to be "aggressive" they are, in fact, in accord with generally accepted accounting principles and have been approved by the county's independent auditors and (2) they have been discussed with and approved by the county executive. Indeed the county executive has encouraged the comptroller to do everything that is both legal and in accord with GAAP to enhance revenues and reduce expenditures.

15-7: Split Bids

As business officer of a school district, Charles Bidright is required to sign off on all purchase orders over $1,000. Under state law and district policy all orders over $5,000 must be put out for bid. Government agencies are required to accept the low bid unless there are specific and compelling reasons not to.

Bidright recently received five purchase orders totaling $20,000 for computer components. Each was for under $5,000. All had been approved by the district superintendent. It was clear to Bidright, however, that the components were part of a single system and therefore should have been combined into a single purchase order and put out for bid.

Bidright contacted the superintendent and explained to him the state law and district policy. The superintendent indicated that he understood the policy but that in this instance he wanted to purchase the equipment from a particular merchant because he knew from past experience that the quality of service provided by this merchant far outweighed any additional merchandise cost that the district was likely to incur. Bidright had no doubt that the superintendent's explanation was legitimate and that the superintendent had no business or personal relationship with the merchant from whom he wanted to purchase the equipment. At the same time, the district superintendent's reason for rejecting the low bid would not have met the legal criteria for so doing.

15-8: Opulent Convention

Five (of ten) members of a town council returned from the three-day national convention of town council members in Las Vegas and submitted their expenses for reimbursement. The bills they presented indicated that they had stayed in luxurious suites, had lavish dinners with extraordinarily expensive wines, and spent freely in night clubs. Although the town has no specific policy on allowable travel costs, William Hamilton, business officer, knew illegitimate expenses when he saw them and these were clearly beyond the bounds of propriety. He expressed his concerns to the town manager (who is appointed by the council), who advised, "Forget it, I have bigger battles that I want to fight with the council."

15-9: Balancing the Budget the Easy Way

State law requires that school district budgets be balanced. After having worked for weeks to reduce expenditures to the minimum that would be educationally acceptable and politically feasible, the school board and the superintendent found the budget still $3 million short of balance. Facing the deadline as to when the budget must be approved, the superintendent (with the school board president at his side) said to Henry Wilson, business officer, "You know, I just took another look at those attendance estimates and I now believe that they were a bit too conservative. Go ahead and increase the estimates by another 600 students and that should just about give us the $3 million additional state aid that we need to get that budget in balance." State aid is based on actual, not estimated, student attendance. Wilson, who has to prepare the budget, is unaware of any evidence that would support a modification of the estimates he had been working with for the past several weeks.

15-10: Pay to Play

Merrill Sachs is an accountant with the treasurer's office of a midsize city. The city is about to issue $50 million in general obligation bonds to construct a new office complex. The treasurer has recommended that the city negotiate the sale of the bonds with a single investment banking firm rather than opening the offering for bids. He cites several advantages to the negotiated sale, all of which have been validated to some extent by reputable experts.

Sachs has evidence that for an offering of the size contemplated by the city and by a government with the characteristics of the city, an auctioned sale would be preferable. More significantly, she is convinced (although she cannot prove) that the treasurer selected the investment banking firm under pressure from the mayor and city council members. This firm was by far the largest contributor to their election campaigns.

SOLUTION TO EXERCISE FOR REVIEW AND SELF-STUDY

1. The appointment of the manager would be in violation of *Government Auditing Standards* because she has not completed the requisite 24 hours of continuing professional education in areas directly related to the governmental environment.
2. The school district receives federal financial assistance and thereby would likely be subject to a single audit. Circular A-133, *Audits of States, Local Governments and Non-Profit Organizations*, provides detailed guidance as to how audits of government organizations, including school districts, should be performed. The "Common Rule," *Administrative Requirements for Grants and Cooperative Agreements for State and Local Governments*, details various OMB rules and regulations.
3. The auditors were correct in making inquiries as to political activities. As part of a single audit, the auditors must test for violations of general compliance requirements, one of which prohibits federal funds from being used to promote political activity.
4. A performance audit is conceptually different from a financial audit in that in a financial audit the auditors *attest* to the assertions of management as set forth in management-prepared financial statements. In performance audits, the auditors make, and report upon, their own, independent assessments of organizational performance.
5. The steps the auditors might undertake to discern the objectives of the program might include the following:
   - Review the legislative history of the program
   - Review the district's budgets, especially those related directly to the program
   - Examine school board minutes
   - Review internal memos
   - Interview school board members and district administrators and teachers
6.
   a. By scheduling the disbursements, the auditors would have a starting point from which to determine whether the outlays were in compliance with the terms of the program and whether they were for purposes consistent with its objectives.
   b. The auditors can gain an understanding of the internal controls by interviewing personnel involved in the program, preparing and administering internal control questionnaires, flowcharting relevant systems, and reviewing applicable policies.
   c. If the program has been in existence only three years, then it would clearly be impossible to make definitive judgments as to its success in encouraging students to enter science-related fields. Nevertheless, the auditors can first determine the number of students participating in the program (i.e., taking extra science classes or engaging in science-related extracurricular activities). If this number is small, then it is unlikely that the program is achieving its objective. Similarly, they can identify any curriculum changes as a consequence of the program. The absence of significant improvements would suggest that the program is having only limited impact. Further, they can establish the percentage of students that are enrolled in university science-related programs and compare this percentage with those of past years or with those of control groups—students possessing similar characteristics (academic, economic, cultural) who have not participated in the program.

CHAPTER 16

Federal Government Accounting

Learning Objectives

After studying this chapter you should understand:

- The unique characteristics of the federal government that necessitate special accounting and reporting practices
- The roles of the main agencies responsible for federal accounting and reporting
- The key objectives of federal financial reporting
- The concept of a unified budget
- The types of accounts maintained by the federal government
- What constitutes a federal reporting entity
- The form and content of government-wide financial reports
- The form and content of agency financial reports
- The main accounting issues addressed by the Federal Accounting Standards Advisory Board (FASAB)
- The recent efforts by the federal government to improve its fiscal management
- Recent trends in international accounting

The federal government is unique among U.S. institutions—and so, also, are its accounting and reporting concerns. Although obviously distinguishable by its size (expenditures for fiscal year 2008 are expected to exceed $2.7 trillion), it also is differentiated by:

- The range of its activities (e.g., defense, Social Security, and managing the money supply)
- The diversity of its resources (e.g., national parks and monuments, stores of gold bullion, and military hardware)
- The nature of its obligations (e.g., Social Security benefits, loan guarantees, and commitments to carry out social programs)
- The extent of its powers (e.g., to tax, to print currency, and to regulate commerce)

In this chapter we provide an overview of the federal accounting structure and the special accounting and reporting issues that it faces. First, we consider the roles played by the key agencies responsible for establishing and administering the federal accounting and reporting system. We follow by describing the federal budget and its relationship to federal accounts and reports. We then present the key features of the accounting and reporting model specified by the Federal Accounting Standards Advisory Board (FASAB). We set forth the main accounting issues addressed by the FASAB and indicate how they have been resolved. We also describe federal initiatives to supplement the agency financial statements with reports on service efforts and accomplishments. We conclude by addressing recent trends in the international arena.

Thomas Jefferson believed that every American "should be able to comprehend [the nation's finances], to investigate abuses, and consequently to control them." Reflecting that view, the U.S. Constitution mandates that the federal government periodically issue financial reports. Article I, Section IX states:

> No money shall be drawn from the Treasury, but in consequence of appropriations made by law; and a regular statement and account of the receipts and expenditures of all public money shall be published from time to time.

The Constitution left Congress and the executive branch to determine the form and content of the reports and to implement and administer the underlying accounting system. Had the founding fathers been able to foresee the nation's accounting and reporting system two hundred years after they ratified the Constitution, they might well have been more specific in establishing accounting and reporting requirements. As of 2004, the federal accounting and reporting system is still inadequate for an organization of the government's size and complexity. Owing to bookkeeping practices that it would never accept from the citizens and corporations that it taxes or regulates, the federal government is even now unable to issue financial statements on which independent auditors can issue an unqualified opinion. According to the General Accounting Office (GAO), the financial systems of key agencies, such as the Defense Department and the Internal Revenue Service, are in such disarray that the amounts of unaccounted-for assets and improperly recorded transactions run into billions of dollars.

Fortunately, major improvements are underway. The Chief Financial Officers Act of 1990 (CFO Act), the Government Performance and Results Act of 1993, and the Federal Financial Management Improvement Act of 1996 are intended to modernize the government's planning, budgeting, and information systems, and the FASAB's comprehensive model of accounting and reporting will facilitate the preparation of auditable, government-wide, financial statements. The GAO reports that even agencies with inadequate accounting and fiscal controls are making significant progress in upgrading their systems, and the Office of Management and Budget (OMB) now receives annual "performance and accountability" reports from all federal agencies.

WHICH AGENCIES ARE RESPONSIBLE FOR FEDERAL ACCOUNTING AND REPORTING?

Federal accounting historically has been decentralized among the government's various agencies and departments, with each agency and department having its own accounting system and preparing their own reports. Currently, however, the three federal agencies with oversight responsibility for financial management—the Department of the Treasury, the Office of Management and Budget, and the General Accounting Office—are taking major strides toward coordinating the accounting systems and reporting practices of the individual agencies.

DEPARTMENT OF THE TREASURY

Per the United States Code (31 U.S.C. § 321), the Department of the Treasury is responsible for a broad range of financial functions. These include managing the public debt, collecting receipts and making disbursements, minting coins and printing currency, managing the government's gold supply, and regulating the nation's banking system. The department's divisions include the Internal Revenue Service, the Alcohol and Tobacco Tax and Trade Bureau, the U.S. Mint, the Office of the Comptroller of the Currency, and the Office of Thrift Supervision.

Another of its units, the Financial Management Service (FMS), is the government's central collection and disbursing agent. As such, it is responsible for taking in revenue from the IRS, Customs, and other agencies and writing most of the government's checks. It is also in charge of the government's main accounting functions, such as overseeing the central accounting and reporting systems, keeping track of monetary assets and liabilities, and issuing financial reports. The FMS also works with the individual federal agencies to bring greater uniformity to their accounting and reporting practices.

OFFICE OF MANAGEMENT AND BUDGET

The Office of Management and Budget (OMB) assists the president in preparing the federal budget and supervises the executive branch agencies in implementing it. Because it has the authority to make budgetary recommendations to the president, the OMB is one of the most powerful agencies in the federal government. The OMB not only recommends overall funding priorities and assesses competing demands for resources, it also reviews each federal agency's spending plans and evaluates the effectiveness of its programs.

In addition, the OMB oversees and coordinates the administration's procurement, financial management, information, and regulatory policies. It has the authority to prescribe the form and content of financial statements and other administrative reports pursuant to the CFO Act, a power that it exercises by issuing bulletins and circulars that establish reporting, cost accounting, auditing, and procurement standards.

The OMB has the further responsibility of *apportioning* federal appropriations. First, Congress (either with the approval of the president or by overriding his veto) appropriates the total amount that can be spent by each agency. Then, OMB grants the agency its apportionments. **Apportionments** are shares of the total appropriation that are available to be spent. The total appropriation is most commonly apportioned by specific time periods (such as quarters), but alternatively by programs, activities, or projects. The apportionment process helps to assure that an agency does not dissipate its resources prior to year-end and it gives the executive branch added control over its spending.

The OMB's responsibilities for fiscal management were substantially expanded by the CFO Act (31 U.S.C. § 501). Asserting billions of dollars were lost each year because of fiscal ineptitude, the bill aimed to build a modern fiscal management structure. To this end, it established both a new position of **Chief Financial Officer (CFO) of the United States** and corresponding CFO positions within each federal agency and department. Officially designated as "Deputy Director for Management," and reporting to the head of the OMB, the CFO of the United States is responsible for:

- Providing overall direction and leadership to the executive branch on financial management matters by monitoring the establishment and operation of financial policies and systems throughout the federal government
- Reviewing agency budget requests for financial management systems
- Monitoring the execution of the federal budget, including timely performance reports
- Advising agency heads as to matters relating to the qualifications and selection of agency CFOs
- Chairing the Chief Financial Officer's Council, another organization established by the new law

In addition, the act charged the agency CFOs with:

- Developing and maintaining integrated accounting systems that comply with applicable accounting standards
- Submitting annual reports to the OMB that describe and analyze the status of financial management in their agencies
- Monitoring the financial execution of their agencies' budgets

The CFO Act also mandated that federal agencies submit their annual reports for independent audit. These audits may be carried out either by their inspectors general or by independent external auditors. Further, it required the OMB to prepare an annual report setting forth its accomplishments in the area of fiscal management and, as appropriate, recommending improvements.

GENERAL ACCOUNTING OFFICE

The **General Accounting Office (GAO)** was created in 1921 (during the administration of President Harding) by the Budget and Accounting Act (31 U.S.C.S. § 702). Until then, all federal audit and accounting functions were within the domain of the Treasury Department. The act specified that the GAO was to be "independent of the executive departments and under the control and direction of the Comptroller General of the United States." Subsequently, the Reorganization Act of 1945 made clear that the GAO was part of the legislative branch.[1]

The GAO (the watchdog of Congress) is most closely identified with its role as the government's auditor, conducting both financial and performance examinations of federal organizations and programs. But it carries out other activities as well. For example, it handles legal services, including:

- Providing advice to Congress on legal issues involving government programs and activities
- Assisting in drafting legislation and reviewing legislative proposals before the Congress

[1] For a comprehensive history of the GAO see Frederick C. Mosher, *The GAO: The Quest for Accountability in American Government* (Boulder, Colo.: Westview Press, 1979).

- Reviewing and reporting to the Congress on proposed rescissions and deferrals of government funds
- Resolving bid protests that challenge government contract awards
- Assisting government agencies in interpreting the laws governing the expenditure of public funds
- Adjudicating claims for and against the government
- Conducting special investigations into criminal and civil misconduct, referring the results of its investigations to the Department of Justice and other law enforcement authorities when warranted

The GAO also deals with accounting and information management policy. The GAO ensures that the Congress has available for its use current, accurate, and complete financial management data. To do this, the GAO:

- Participates with OMB and Treasury in prescribing accounting principles and standards for the executive branch
- Advises other federal agencies on fiscal and related policies and procedures
- Prescribes standards for auditing and evaluating government programs

In addition, the Comptroller General, the Secretary of the Treasury, and the Director of the Office of Management and Budget develop standardized information and data processing systems. These include standard terminology, definitions, classifications, and codes for fiscal, budgetary, and program-related data and information.[2]

FEDERAL ACCOUNTING STANDARDS ADVISORY BOARD

Established in 1990, the Federal Accounting Standards Advisory Board is responsible for promulgating federal accounting standards. In 1999 the American Institute of CPAs, in accordance with **Rule 203** of its Code of Ethics, granted the FASAB exclusive authority to establish generally accepted accounting principles (GAAP) for federal entities, thereby giving it status comparable to that of the Governmental Accounting Standards Board (GASB) and the Financial Accounting Standards Board (FASB).

The FASAB is titled "advisory" because technically both the OMB and the GAO have the authority to dictate accounting practices for federal agencies. Although in practice the FASAB is no less independent than the FASB or the GASB, it must nevertheless submit for review each proposed standard to the Treasury, the GAO, and the OMB—three principal agencies through whose combined effort the board was established. If anyone of them objects, then the standard is returned to the board for reconsideration.

The FASAB is composed of ten members:

- Two from the legislative branch of the federal government (one each from the GAO and the Congressional Budget Office, the office responsible for calculating the budgetary impact of proposed legislation for Congress)
- Two from the executive branch (one each from OMB and Treasury)
- Six, including the chair, who are "public members" (i.e., not employees of the federal government)

The mission of the FASAB is to establish accounting standards "after considering the financial and budgetary information needs of congressional oversight groups, executive agencies, and the needs of other users of federal financial information."[3] Hence,

[2] Primary source: The GAO's Web site, www.gao.gov.

[3] Mission statement as approved by the Board and the Secretary of the Treasury, the Director of the OMB, and the Comptroller General of the United States.

its constituents encompass parties both within and outside of the federal government. Unlike the GASB or the FASB, the FASAB is not concerned primarily with accounting reports that will be used by capital market participants to assess stocks and bonds. Also unlike those two boards, however, the general area of "managerial cost accounting" is within its purview.

Standard setting for the federal government is especially challenging because key users have sharply contrasting information requirements. For example, economists request statistics on national income and product accounts so as to obtain a "macro" view of the economy. Budget analysts, however, need data on the various federal appropriation, apportionment, and cash flow accounts so that they can monitor the budgetary process. Oversight agencies want information on financial position, results of operations, and costs of services. Moreover, as will be discussed, the federal budget can include different combinations of costs and revenues depending on the purpose for which it is to be used. Upon its establishment, the FASAB set out to develop, from the ground up, a fundamental model of accounting for both the federal government as a whole and its separate components. By the mid-1990s, it had largely accomplished that objective, having recommended standards that encompass a wide range of resources, obligations, and transactions. Since then it has been fine-tuning its basic model and by 2003 had issued twenty-five standards, plus three statements of concepts and several technical bulletins.

As one of its early projects (following the precedent of both the FASB and the GASB) the FASAB established a set of financial reporting objectives. These are summarized in Table 16-1. They were intended to lay the foundation for resolving specific accounting issues, the key ones of which are discussed in this chapter.

WHAT CONSTITUTES THE FEDERAL BUDGET?

Upon seeing or hearing mention of the federal budget, a knowledgeable observer can rightfully ask, "What constitutes the federal budget?" Federal operations are accounted for in four types of funds: a general fund, special funds, trust funds, and revolving funds. Because federal operations are so vast and information requirements of users so varied, the OMB tabulates receipts and outlays in different ways, some of which may include only selected fund types.

THE FOUR TYPES OF FEDERAL FUNDS

Like its counterpart in municipalities, the federal government's **general fund** accounts for the resources, mainly from income taxes, that are not restricted for specific purposes. These resources are used to pay for national defense, interest on the public debt, and most social programs (excluding large-dollar programs such as Social Security, Medicare, and unemployment compensation, which are accounted for in trust funds). The general fund includes both capital and operating expenditures. However, the federal budget distinguishes between the two in that the capital expenditures are concentrated in particular budget accounts or identified separately in accounts that include both types of expenditures.

Special funds, like the special revenue funds of municipalities, are maintained to account for resources that are designated for specific programs or activities. Typically financed by dedicated fees, these include the National Wildlife Refuge Fund and the Land and Water Conservation Fund.

Trust funds are also used to account for resources restricted for specific purposes. The largest of the trust funds are the Old-Age and Survivors Insurance Fund (which along with the Disability Insurance Trust Fund constitutes the Social Security

TABLE 16–1
Summary of Objectives of Federal Financial Reporting

- ***Budgetary Integrity.*** Federal financial reporting should assist in fulfilling the government's duty to be publicly accountable for monies raised through taxes and other means and for their expenditure in accordance with the government's legally adopted budget and related laws and regulations. It should enable the reader to determine:
  - How budgetary resources have been obtained and used and whether the acquisition and use were in accordance with the enacted budget
  - The status of budgetary resources
  - How budgetary reporting relates to other information on the costs of programs
- ***Operating Performance.*** Federal reporting should assist report users in evaluating the service efforts, costs, and accomplishments of the reporting entity, the manner in which these efforts and accomplishments have been financed, and the management of the entity's assets and liabilities. It should enable the reader to determine:
  - The costs of providing specific programs and activities and the composition of, and changes in, these costs
  - The efforts and accomplishments associated with federal programs and the changes over time and in relation to costs
  - The efficiency and effectiveness of the government's management of its assets and liabilities
- ***Stewardship.*** Federal financial reporting should assist report users in assessing the impact on the country of the government's operations and investments for the period and show how, as a result, the government's and the nation's financial conditions have changed and may change in the future. It should enable the reader to determine:
  - Whether the government's financial position improved or deteriorated over the period
  - Whether future budgetary resources will likely be sufficient to sustain public services and to meet obligations as they come due
  - Whether government operations have contributed to the nation's current and future well-being
- ***Systems and Control.*** Federal financial reporting should assist report users in understanding whether financial management systems and internal accounting and administrative controls are adequate to ensure that:
  - Transactions are executed in accordance with budgetary and financial laws and the other requirements, are consistent with the purposes authorized, and are recorded in accordance with federal accounting standards
  - Assets are properly safeguarded to deter fraud, waste, and abuse
  - Performance measurement information is adequately supported

Source: Statement of Federal Financial Accounting Concepts No. 1, *Objectives of Federal Financial Reporting* (September 1993).

program), the Supplementary Medical Insurance Fund and the Hospital Insurance Trust Fund (which constitute Medicare), and various government employee retirement funds. Trust funds are conceptually different in the federal government than in other governments or not-for-profits. In the federal sector they are simply any funds that are designated by law as trust funds and have earmarked receipts. Like special funds, they are similar to special revenue funds. They are not funds in which only the income, not the principal, can be expended.

Revolving funds, comparable to a municipality's enterprise funds, account for the federal government's business-type activities. The most significant of these is the U.S. Postal Service. The activities accounted for in revolving funds generate their own receipts, and therefore the sponsoring agencies are authorized by law to expend their resources without annual Congressional appropriation.

THE UNIFIED BUDGET

In 1968 (for fiscal year 1969) the government adopted the practice of preparing a **unified federal budget** that encompasses all four types of funds. The objective was to capture in a single tabulation the impact of federal activities on the national economy. In addition the unified budget was intended to provide a comprehensive measure of the cost of the government's programs that officials could use in establishing spending priorities.

Ironically, through a series of laws enacted in 1983, 1985, and 1990, Congress excluded Social Security receipts and disbursements from the official calculation of the budget, according them special "off-budget" standing. The aim of Congress was to remove Social Security from the constraints to which on-budget expenditures are subject. Accordingly, when the various mandatory spending caps are applied, Social Security receipts and outlays are not taken into account.

The treatment of Social Security is one of the most confusing aspects of the federal budget. Social Security represents one fifth or more of federal revenues and expenditures and is therefore of critical importance in assessing the federal budget's economic effect. As a consequence, budget policy makers tend to emphasize aggregate budget data, including Social Security, and most references to the federal budget incorporate the off-budget Social Security accounts. As one former member of the FASAB cogently explained, "The fact is that, in the document that everyone refers to as the budget, Social Security surpluses serve to reduce what everyone refers to as the budget deficit or increase what everyone refers to as the budget surplus."

In recent years, cash receipts to the Social Security fund have exceeded cash disbursements, thereby increasing aggregate budget surpluses or decreasing aggregate budget deficits. This excess of receipts over disbursements is projected to continue through 2017. Thereafter, however, as baby boomers retire, in the absence of changes to the structure of contributions or benefits, the relationship will reverse and Social Security will have a negative impact on budgetary surpluses or deficits.

Postal Service receipts and outlays are accounted for similarly to those of Social Security, mainly so as to accord the service the flexibility to manage its operations more like a business than a traditional government agency. Hence, while officially part of the unified budget, they are considered "off budget" with respect to certain spending limitations.

WHAT ARE THE FORM AND CONTENT OF GOVERNMENT-WIDE FEDERAL STATEMENTS?

For its fiscal year ending September 30, 1997, the federal government issued, for the first time, an "official" comprehensive financial report that covered all of its activities and was subjected to audit. This report, known as the *Financial Report of the United States Government*, must be distinguished from the *United States Government Annual Report*. The *Financial Report* features statements that are on a full accrual basis. The *Annual Report*, by contrast, presents budgetary results (receipts and disbursements) and thereby focuses on cash, other monetary assets, and monetary liabilities.

As required by the FASAB, the federal government's annual *Financial Report* should be divided into six main sections:

1. A brief letter of transmittal and management's discussion and analysis. The MD&A is similar in form and content to that required of municipalities by

GASB Statement No. 34, though it is more expansive. The FASAB standards invite the preparer to include performance and forward-looking information. The information should include separate segments that address:
   a. Mission and organizational structure
   b. Performance goals, objectives, and results
   c. Financial statements
   d. Systems, controls, and legal compliance
2. The report of the auditors (the GAO).
3. Five basic financial statements
   a. A statement of operations and changes in net position
   b. A statement of net cost
   c. A balance sheet
   d. A statement that reconciles the net operating revenue or cost with the unified budget surplus or deficit and
   e. A statement that reconciles the change in the government's cash position with the unified budget surplus or deficit
4. "Stewardship" information on assets that, for reasons to be discussed in following sections, are not accorded balance sheet recognition.
5. Notes to the financial statements.
6. Supplemental information. Unaudited, this includes data as diverse as the cost of deferred maintenance, unobligated budget authority and the effective income tax rates on both individuals and corporations.

Table 16-2 displays the 2002 basic government-wide statements, the most recent available at press time. Owing to deficiencies in the federal financial management systems, the GAO auditors were unable to express an opinion on these statements (as they were in each of the previous five years).[4]

WHICH ENTITIES SHOULD ISSUE FINANCIAL REPORTS?

One of the fundamental questions facing the FASAB when it was established was what types of federal entities should be required to issue financial reports. The issue exists because the federal government can be viewed from different perspectives. Reports drawn from each of the perspectives may be consistent with one or more objectives of reporting, but not others.[5]

The first perspective is that of organizations. At the top level, the federal government comprises mainly agencies and cabinet level departments. These are subdivided into thousands of smaller units, which bear titles such as bureaus, agencies, services, administrations, and corporations. Some of these units are too small, or lack sufficient independent authority, to be appropriate reporting entities. On the other hand, the top-level organizations may administer thousands of programs, many of which may be only tangentially related. Financial statements of these organizations, if they aggregate all their subunits, would provide little information that is of value to users.

The second perspective is that of the budget accounts, with each account representing a specifically authorized expenditure. Congress has wide discretion in

[4] The annual report of the U.S. government can be found on the Web site of the GAO. The report itself includes explanations of the basic financial statements. The GAO's "opinion" details the deficiencies in the government's accounting and control systems and sets forth the future fiscal challenges facing the federal government.

[5] This discussion is based on the Statement of Federal Accounting Concepts No. 2, *Entity and Display* (June 1995).

TABLE 16-2A
United States Government
Statements of Operations and Changes in Net Position
for the Years Ended September 30, 2002 and September 30, 2001
(in billions of dollars)

	2002	2001
Revenue		
Individual income tax and tax withholdings	$ 1,538.6	$ 1,663.6
Corporation income taxes	143.7	147.9
Unemployment taxes	26.2	26.7
Excise taxes	67.9	67.3
Estate and gift taxes	26.4	28.3
Customs duties	18.3	18.7
Other taxes and receipts	49.3	48.9
Miscellaneous earned revenues	7.3	12.3
Total revenue	$ 1,877.7	$ 2,013.7
Less net cost of government operations	$ 2,259.7	$ 2,545.8
Unreconciled transactions affecting the change in net position	17.1	17.3
Net operating cost	$ (364.9)	$ (514.8)
Net position, beginning of period	$(6,458.8)	$(5,945.4)
Prior period adjustments	3.5	1.4
Net operating cost	(364.9)	(514.8)
Net position, end of period	$(6,820.2)	$(6,458.8)

TABLE 16-2B
United States Government
Statements of Net Cost for the Years Ended September 30, 2002
and September 30, 2001 (in billions of dollars)

	2002			2001		
	Gross Cost	Earned Revenue	Net Cost	Gross Cost	Earned Revenue	Net Cost
Department of Agriculture	$ 80.5	$ 9.6	$ 70.9	$ 83.5	$ 11.1	$ 72.4
Department of Commerce	7.4	1.2	6.2	7.4	1.2	6.2
Department of Defense	420.4	13.9	406.5	776.8	12.6	764.2
Department of Education	49.9	4.8	45.1	39.9	4.1	35.8
Department of Energy	(3.0)	4.8	(7.8)	27.0	5.2	21.8
Department of Health & Human Services	499.9	27.0	472.9	459.2	24.7	434.5
Department of Housing & Urban Development	36.3	2.2	34.1	34.5	2.4	32.1
Department of Interior	15.0	0.7	14.3	11.7	0.3	11.4
Department of Justice	29.5	2.3	27.2	26.5	2.3	24.2
Department of Labor	64.7	—	64.7	42.3	—	42.3
Department of State	10.9	0.9	10.0	10.0	1.0	9.0
Department of Transportation	65.4	1.6	63.8	63.6	0.3	63.3
Department of the Treasury	66.0	3.6	62.4	60.0	4.4	55.6
Interest on debt held by the public	175.4	—	175.4	217.7	—	217.7
Department of Veterans Affairs	218.4	2.6	215.8	196.0	2.7	193.3
U.S. Agency for International Development	8.0	—	8.0	7.1	0.1	7.0
Environmental Protection Agency	8.2	0.5	7.7	8.4	0.5	7.9
Federal Emergency Management Agency	6.2	1.8	4.4	6.3	1.6	4.7
General Services Administration	(0.1)	0.3	(0.4)	0.1	0.3	(0.2)
National Aeronautics & Space Administration	14.7	0.1	14.6	9.2	0.1	9.1

(Continued)

TABLE 16–2B
United States Government
Statements of Net Cost for the Years Ended September 30, 2002 and September 30, 2001 (in billions of dollars) *(Contined)*

	2002			2001		
	Gross Cost	Earned Revenue	Net Cost	Gross Cost	Earned Revenue	Net Cost
National Science Foundation	4.2	—	4.2	3.7	—	3.7
U.S. Nuclear Regulatory Commission	0.6	0.4	0.2	0.6	0.4	0.2
Office of Personnel Management	0.2	—	0.2	0.2	—	0.2
Small Business Administration	1.3	0.5	0.8	0.8	0.2	0.6
Social Security Administration	492.9	0.3	492.6	465.3	0.3	465.0
Export–Import Bank of the United States	(1.2)	0.3	(1.5)	0.8	0.3	0.5
Federal Communications Commission	6.8	1.1	5.7	14.9	6.7	8.2
Federal Deposit Insurance Corporation	1.8	0.7	1.1	3.1	0.5	2.6
National Credit Union Administration	0.2	0.5	(0.3)	0.3	0.4	(0.1)
Pension Benefit Guaranty Corporation	12.7	0.9	11.8	2.3	0.8	1.5
Railroad Retirement Board	9.3	—	9.3	9.0	—	9.0
Tennessee Valley Authority	7.9	6.8	1.1	11.8	6.9	4.9
United States Postal Service	83.1	66.4	16.7	86.2	65.6	20.6
All other entities	22.8	0.8	22.0	19.6	3.0	16.6
Total	$2,416.3	$156.6	$2,259.7	$2,705.8	$160.0	$2,545.8

TABLE 16–2C
United States Government
Balance Sheets as of September 30, 2002 and September 30, 2001 (in billions of dollars)

	2002	2001
Assets		
Cash and other monetary assets	$ 141.6	$ 108.0
Accounts receivable, net	32.0	34.2
Loans receivable, net	219.2	208.9
Taxes receivable, net	21.4	21.1
Inventories and related property, net	192.2	183.8
Property, plant, and equipment, net	324.7	306.7
Other assets	65.4	63.4
Total assets	$ 996.5	$ 926.1
Liabilities		
Accounts payable	$ 55.8	$ 56.2
Federal debt securities held by the public and accrued interest	3,573.2	3,359.3
Federal employee and veteran benefits payable	3,589.4	3,360.8
Environmental and disposal liabilities	273.0	306.8
Benefits due and payable	95.3	86.0
Loan guarantee liabilities	28.1	27.7
Other liabilities	201.9	188.1
Total liabilities	$7,816.7	$7,384.9
Commitments and contingencies		
Net Position	(6,820.2)	(6,458.8)
Total liabilities and net position	$ 996.5	$ 926.1

TABLE 16-2D
United States Government
Reconciliations of Net Operating Cost and Unified Budget Surplus (or Deficit) for the Years Ended September 30, 2002 and September 30, 2001 (in billions of dollars)

	2002	2001
Net operating cost	$(364.9)	$(514.8)
Components of net operating cost not part of the budget surplus (or deficit)		
Increase in liability for military employee benefits		
Increase in military pension liabilities	$ 21.7	$ 17.8
Increase in military health liabilities	11.1	388.6
(Decrease)/increase in other military benefits	(0.4)	0.4
Increase in liability for military employee benefits	$ 32.4	$ 406.8
Increase in liability for veterans compensation and burial benefits		
Increase in liability for veterans	$ 147.7	$ 115.2
Increase in liability for survivors	9.0	24.1
Increase in liability for burial benefits	0.6	—
Increase in liability for veterans compensation	$ 157.3	$ 139.3
Increase in liability for civilian employee benefits		
Increase in civilian pension liabilities	$ 16.9	$ 41.0
Increase in civilian health liabilities	16.2	7.2
Increase in other civilian benefits	5.8	1.9
Increase in liability for civilian employee benefits	$ 38.9	$ 50.1
Decrease in environmental liabilities		
(Decrease)/increase in energy's environmental liabilities	$ (28.7)	$ 4.1
(Decrease)/increase in all others' environmental liabilities	(5.1)	1.6
(Decrease)/increase in environmental liabilities	$ (33.8)	$ 5.7
Depreciation expense	$ 20.5	$ 21.4
Increase in benefits due and payable	9.3	8.1
Increase/(decrease) in taxes receivable	(0.3)	2.2
Increase in other liabilities	13.8	13.1
Premium on early buyback of public debt	3.8	10.7
Seigniorage and sale of gold	(1.0)	(1.3)
(Decrease)/increase in accounts payable	(0.4)	9.4[1]
Components of the budget surplus (or deficit) not part of net operating cost		
Capital fixed assets		
Department of Defense	(18.1)	(11.1)
Civilian agencies	(22.8)	(23.3)
Total capitalized fixed assets	$ (40.9)	$ (34.4)
Decrease in accounts receivable	$ 2.2	$ (1.9)
(Increase)/decrease in inventory	(8.4)	1.4
Increase in other assets	(2.0)	(3.7)
Principal repayments of precredit reform loans	8.2	19.9
Net amount of all other differences	1.0	(6.4)[1]
Other		
Prior period adjustments	$ 6.6	$ 1.4[1]
Unified budget deficit (or surplus)	$(157.7)	$ 127.0

[1]Restated.

TABLE 16-2E
United States Government
Statements of Changes in Cash Balance from Unified Budget and Other Activities for the Years Ended September 30, 2002 and September 30, 2001 (in billions of dollars)

		2002			2001	
Budget receipts—actual		$ 1,853.3			$ 1,990.9	
Budget outlays—actual		(2,011.0)			(1,863.9)	
Unified budget (deficit) or surplus			$(157.7)			$127.0
Adjustments for non-cash outlays included in the budget						
Interest accrued by Treasury on debt held by the public		$ (152.0)			$ (171.0)	
Subsidy expense		4.9			0.7	
Items affecting the cash balance not included in the budget						
Net transactions from financing activity						
Repayment of debt held by the public	$3,570.2			$2,620.7		
Borrowings from the public	(3,791.0)			(2,530.6)		
Total		(220.8)			90.1	
Net transactions from monetary activity						
Increase in special drawing rights	0.8			1.6		
Increase in other monetary assets	14.3			8.2		
Increase/(decrease) in loans to the IMF	2.5			4.7		
Total		17.6			14.5	
Net transactions from other activities						
Net direct loan activity	$ 13.7			$ 18.5		
Interest paid by Treasury on debt held by the public	158.6			175.8		
Premium on early buyback of public debt	3.8			10.7		
Net guaranteed loan activity	(2.3)			4.1		
Increase/(decrease) in other assets	(.9)			1.6		
Increase in deposit fund balances	(.4)			(4.1)		
Decrease/(increase) in other liabilities	3.4			(4.1)		
Seigniorage and other equity	(1.0)			(1.3)		
Revisions to the prior budget results	1.0			—		
Total		175.9			201.2	
Disposition of (deficit) or surplus			(174.4)			135.5
Increase/(decrease) in operating cash balance			$ 16.7			$ (8.5)
Operating cash						
Operating cash balance beginning of period			44.2			52.7
Operating cash balance end of period			$ 60.9			$ 44.2

appropriating resources. Depending on the degree of control it elects to exercise over a department or program, it may appropriate resources in many small amounts or a few large amounts. Budget accounts do not necessarily coincide with a department's or an agency's organizational structure and may cut across programmatic lines. Hence, reports on either individual budget accounts or aggregations of budget accounts may also provide information that is only of limited use.

One reason that budget accounts do not always correspond to organizational lines is that different congressional committees have jurisdiction over programs that cut across agency boundaries. Inasmuch as individual committees are generally reluctant to surrender responsibility and authority to other committees, these peculiarities have proven difficult to correct. A resultant adverse consequence is that program goals may be both vague and internally inconsistent.

The third perspective is that of programs and activities. As just noted, however, the budget accounts do not coincide with programs and activities. Some programs and activities are financed from more than one budget account and, conversely, some budget accounts finance more than one program or activity. Thus, reports formulated along the lines of programs or activities may not provide information on budgetary integrity.

Acknowledging the limitations of each of the perspectives, the FASAB established three criteria for a "component" to be considered a reporting entity:

- There is a management responsible for controlling and deploying the component's outputs and outcomes and for executing its budget. It is held accountable for its performance.
- The component is of sufficient size and significance that its financial statements would provide a meaningful representation of its operations and financial condition.
- Users are interested in the information to be reported in its financial statements and could use it to make resource allocation and related decisions.

These criteria allow the federal government considerable flexibility in constituting reporting entities. The board notes that most top-level departments and agencies would satisfy the three criteria and therefore should be considered primary reporting entities. However, because of the breadth of these organizations, subunit statements may be more useful than those of the primary entity. The board points out that many departments and agencies divide the budget accounts for which they are responsible into responsibility centers. These responsibility centers (the equivalent of cost centers, profit centers, or activity centers) may reflect the mission of the reporting entity, its organizational structure, and budget accounts and funding authorities. Accordingly, they too may satisfy the three criteria, and thereby also constitute appropriate reporting entities.

WHAT TYPES OF ACCOUNTS ARE MAINTAINED BY FEDERAL ENTITIES?

Federal departments, bureaus, agencies, and other types of units maintain dual systems of accounts:

- ***Budget accounts*** ensure that the entity complies with budgetary mandates, does not overspend its appropriations, and is able to fulfill uniform budgetary reporting requirements.

- ***Proprietary accounts*** provide the information for the financial statements based on FASAB standards and are intended to provide an economic, rather than a budgetary, measure of operations and resources. (The term *proprietary* does not, however, imply business activities as when used in a municipal context.)

The budget accounts are comparable to both the budgetary accounts and the encumbrance accounts established by municipalities. Entries are made to record apportionments, allotments (a part of an apportionment that an agency is permitted to expend during a specified time period), commitments (reservations of funds prior to an order), and obligations (encumbrances).

The **proprietary accounts** are similar to conventional revenue, expense, asset, liability, and equity accounts. The accounts that are unique to the federal government are mainly in the equity (referred to as "net position") section of the balance sheet. Thus, for example, "unexpended appropriations" represent the portion of net assets made available by Congress, but not yet expended. "Cumulative results of operations" (the equivalent of retained earnings) indicate the net assets from operations in both the current and previous years.

WHAT STATEMENTS ARE REQUIRED OF FEDERAL AGENCIES?

The FASAB reporting model for individual federal agencies is similar to that of the federal government at large. Like the financial report of the government at large, agency statements should contain a discussion and analysis by management, the auditor's report, the basic financial statements, information on stewardship assets, investments and responsibilities, notes to the financial statements, and other required supplementary information.

The 2002 statements of the Social Security Administration are illustrated in Table 16-3.

The basic financial statements of agencies and other entities consist of either five or six basic statements depending on the entity's mission. They are as follows.

BALANCE SHEET (OR STATEMENT OF FINANCIAL POSITION)

The balance sheet shows the entity's assets, liabilities, and net position. The assets would include the entity's fund balance with the Treasury. This balance can be used only for the purposes for which the funds were appropriated. Net position is the residual difference between assets and liabilities. It is generally composed of unexpended appropriations (amounts not yet obligated or expended) plus the cumulative difference, over the years, between the entity's revenues and other sources of funding and its expenses.

Conspicuously missing from the balance sheet of the Social Security Administration is a cash balance. Most federal agencies do not have substantial cash accounts. What would otherwise be a cash balance is subsumed within the fund balance with the Treasury.

The balance sheet is on a full accrual basis and accordingly reports long-lived assets. However, as is discussed in the following section, owing to their special nature, certain types of long-lived assets are not given balance sheet recognition. These include parklands, historic sites and national monuments. Such assets are considered **stewardship assets** and are reported in a section of the report that supplements the basic financial statements.

TABLE 16–3
Financial Statements of the Social Security Administration
Consolidated Balance Sheets as of September 30, 2002 and September 30, 2001
(in millions of dollars)

	2002	2001 Restated
Assets		
Intragovernmental		
Fund balance with Treasury	$ 2,098	$ 4,058
Investments (U.S. government securities)	1,329,045	1,169,956
Interest receivable, net	20,262	18,476
Accounts receivable, net	751	1,218
Total intragovernmental	$1,352,156	$1,193,708
Accounts receivable, net	$ 5,692	$ 4,464
Property, plant, and equipment, net	690	565
Other	4	2
Total assets	$1,358,542	$1,198,739
Liabilities		
Intragovernmental		
Accrued railroad retirement interchange	$ 3,713	$ 3,673
Other	7,148	5,984
Total intragovernmental	$ 10,861	$ 9,657
Benefits due and payable	$ 47,684	$ 43,187
Accounts payable	494	289
Other	1,142	1,112
Total	$ 60,181	$ 54,245
Net position		
Unexpended appropriations	$ 794	$ 3,528
Cumulative results of operations	1,297,567	1,140,966
Total net position	$1,298,361	$1,144,494
Total liabilities and net position	$1,358,542	$1,198,739

Consolidated Statements of Net Cost for the Years Ended September 30, 2002 and September 30, 2001 (in millions of dollars)

	2002	2001
Old Age and Survivors' Insurance (OASI) Program		
Benefit payments	$385,777	$369,142
Operating expenses	2,299	2,169
Total cost of OASI program	$388,076	$371,311
Less: exchange revenues	8	7
Net Cost of OASI Program	$388,068	$371,304

(Continued)

Consolidated Statements of Net Cost for the Years Ended September 30, 2002 and September 30, 2001 (in millions of dollars) *(Continued)*

	2002	2001
Disability Insurance (DI) Program		
Benefit payments	$ 66,964	$ 59,207
Operating expenses	1,953	1,749
Total cost of DI program	$ 68,917	$ 60,956
Less: exchange revenues	7	6
Net Cost of DI Program	$ 68,910	$ 60,950
Supplemental Security Income (SSI) Program		
Benefit payments	$ 30,239	$ 27,733
Operating expenses	2,788	2,261
Total cost of SSI program	$ 33,027	$ 29,994
Less: exchange revenues	278	253
Net Cost of SSI Program	$ 32,749	$ 29,741
Other		
Benefit payments	$ 458	$ 484
Operating expenses	1,251	1,151
Total cost of other	$ 1,709	$ 1,635
Less: exchange revenues	10	13
Net Cost of Other	$ 1,699	$ 1,622
Total Costs	$491,729	$463,896
Less: Total Exchange Revenue	303	279
Net Cost of Operations	$491,426	$463,617

Consolidated Statements of Changes in Net Position for the Years Ended September 30, 2002 and September 30, 2001 (in millions of dollars)

	2002		2001 Restated	
	Cumulative Results of Operations	Unexpended Appropriations	Cumulative Results of Operations	Unexpended Appropriations
Net Position, Beginning Balance	$1,140,966	$ 3,528	$ 982,733	$ 399
Prior period adjustments	0	0	(5,083)	0
Beginning balances, as adjusted	$1,140,966	$ 3,528	$ 977,650	$ 399
Budgetary Financing Sources (Other than Exchange Revenues)				
Appropriations received		$ 46,400		$ 46,191
Other adjustments	$ (8)	(12)		(5)
Appropriations used	49,122	(49,122)	$ 43,057	(43,057)
Tax revenues	537,733		528,194	
Interest revenues	78,614		70,922	
Transfers—in/out				
Trust fund draws and other—in	1,138		1,747	
Trust fund draws and other—out	(15,323)		(13,520)	
Railroad retirement interchange	(3,686)		(3,859)	

(Continued)

Consolidated Statements of Changes in Net Position for the Years Ended September 30, 2002 and September 30, 2001 (in millions of dollars) *(Continued)*

	2002		2001 Restated	
	Cumulative Results of Operations	Unexpended Appropriations	Cumulative Results of Operations	Unexpended Appropriations
Net transfers—in/out	$ (17,871)		$ (15,632)	
Other budgetary financing sources	81		77	
Other Financing Sources				
Other revenue	5		0	
Imputed financing sources	351		315	
Total Financing Sources	$ 648,027	$ (2,734)	$ 626,933	$ 3,129
Net Cost of Operations	$ 491,426		$ 463,617	
Ending Balances	$1,297,567	$ 794	$1,140,966	$ 3,528

Consolidated Statements of Budgetary Resources for the Years Ended September 30, 2002 and September 30, 2001 (in millions of dollars)

	2002	2001 Restated
Budgetary Resources Made Available		
Budget Authority:		
Appropriations received	$ 661,470	$ 643,047
Net transfers (+/–)	(0)	109
Unobligated Balances:		
Beginning of period	2,842	456
Spending Authority from Offsetting Collections		
Earned		
Collected	3,866	3,509
Change in receivable	1	(236)
Change in obligations		
Advance received	0	(2)
Without advance	0	(3)
Transfers from trust funds		
Collected	7,581	7,166
Anticipated	139	(51)
Subtotal	$ 11,587	$ 10,383
Recoveries of Prior Year Obligations	229	214
Temporarily Not Available Pursuant to Public Law	(154,054)	(154,003)
Permanently Not Available	(11)	(22)
Total Budgetary Resources	$ 522,063	$ 500,184
Status of Budgetary Resources		
Obligations Incurred		
Direct	$ 517,284	$ 493,987
Reimbursable	3,758	3,186
Subtotal	$ 521,042	$ 497,173
Unobligated Balances		
Apportioned	846	2,856
Unobligated Balances—Not Available	175	155
Total Status of Budgetary Resources	$ 522,063	$ 500,184

(Continued)

Consolidated Statements of Budgetary Resources for the Years Ended September 30, 2002 and September 30, 2001 (in millions of dollars) *(Continued)*

	2002	2001 Restated
Relationship of Obligations to Outlays:		
Obligated Balances—Beginning of the Period	$ 51,442	$ 43,073
Obligated Balance—End of the Period		
Accounts receivable	(1,707)	(1,566)
Undelivered orders	1,031	1,476
Accounts payable	56,975	51,532
Outlays:		
Disbursements	515,815	487,484
Collections	(11,446)	(10,675)
Subtotal	$ 504,369	$ 476,809
Less: Offsetting Receipts	15,761	14,310
Net Outlays	$ 488,608	$ 462,499

Consolidated Statements of Financing for the Years Ended September 30, 2002 and September 30, 2001 (in millions of dollars)

	2002	2001 Restated
Resources Used to Finance Activities		
Budgetary Resources Obligated		
Obligations incurred	$521,042	$497,173
Less: offsetting collections	(11,816)	(10,597)
Obligations net of offsetting collections	$509,226	$486,576
Less: offsetting receipts	(15,761)	(14,310)
Net obligations	$493,465	$472,266
Other Resources		
Imputed financing	351	315
Other	(267)	(160)
Net other resources used to finance activities	$ 84	$ 155
Total resources used to finance activities	$493,549	$472,421
Resources Not Part of the Net Cost of Operations		
Change in undelivered orders	$ 445	$ (361)
Resources that fund capitalized costs	(120)	(220)
Resources that fund expenses recognized in prior periods	(1,649)	(283)
Budgetary offsetting collections and receipts that do not affect net cost of operations	15,761	14,310
Other resources or adjustments to net obligated resources that do not affect net cost of operations	(16,444)	(22,585)
Total resources not part of the net cost of operations	$ (2,007)	$ (9,139)
Total resources used to finance the net cost of operations	$491,542	$463,282
Components of the Net Cost of Operations That Will Not Require or Generate Resources in the Current Period		
Components Requiring or Generating Resources in Future Periods		
Increase in annual leave	18	11
Other	71	39
Total components of net cost of operations that will require or generate resources in future periods	$ 89	$ 50

(Continued)

Consolidated Statements of Financing for the Years Ended September 30, 2002 and September 30, 2001 (in millions of dollars) *(Continued)*

	2002	2001 Restated
Components Not Requiring or Generating Resources		
Depreciation and amortization	$ 141	$ 138
Other	(346)	147
Total components of net cost of operations that will not require or generate resources	$ (205)	$ 285
Total components of net cost of operations that will not require or generate resources in the current period	$ (116)	$ 335
Net Cost of Operations	$491,426	$463,617

STATEMENT OF NET COST

The **statement of net cost,** probably the most significant of the six statements, reports on program operating costs and revenues. Similar to the government-wide statement of activities required by GASB Statement No. 34, it presents earned revenues (i.e., those from exchange transactions) as a deduction from costs, thereby highlighting the amount that must be paid from taxes and other financing sources. By focusing on the net cost to the government of individual programs, it provides decision makers a basis on which to compare program inputs with results and thereby assess agency performance. Like the balance sheet, the statement is on a full accrual basis. Hence, the reported expenses capture the full cost of operating a program, including depreciation, not merely the cash disbursements of a particular year.

STATEMENT OF CHANGES IN NET POSITION

The **statement of changes in net position** summarizes all entity transactions other than those, such as earned revenues and expenses, reported in the statement of net cost. It explains how the entity financed its net costs. It includes prior period adjustments and amounts received from appropriations, dedicated taxes, borrowings, and other financing sources. It also reports "imputed financing"—costs incurred by the federal agency that are paid for by another federal entity. In the case of the Social Security Administration, these imputed costs are pensions and other post-employment benefits.

As shown in Table 16-3, the statement of changes in net position links the statement of net costs to the balance sheet. The next to last line of the statement shows the net cost of operations, per the statement of net cost. The last line (including the unexpended appropriations) ties to the year-end total net position, per the balance sheet.

STATEMENT OF BUDGETARY RESOURCES

The **statement of budgetary resources,** which is prepared on a budgetary rather than an accrual basis, reports on the amounts available from both current and prior year appropriations and the entity's cash outlays, newly incurred obligations (the federal equivalent of encumbrances), and obligations of prior years that have been liquidated. The amounts in this report will be incorporated in the Treasury's cash-oriented *Annual Report.* As shown in Table 16-3, the first part of the statement shows the source of budgetary resources (mainly the spending authorized by the federal budget and unobligated balances from prior years). The second shows how these resources were used (obligated during the year, not obligated and thus available for future expenditure, and not obligated but unavailable for future expenditures). The sources of the budgetary resources must, of course, equal the uses. The third part of the statement reconciles the obligations incurred (per the second part of the statement) with the actual outlays.

STATEMENT OF FINANCING

The **statement of financing** links the statement of budgetary resources to the statement of net cost. It reconciles the agency's obligations incurred on a budgetary basis (per budget accounts) with the net cost of operations on a full accrual basis (proprietary accounts). The main differences between the two amounts can be attributed to resources that are not included in the budget, such as donations and exchange revenues, and to the expenses recognized on different bases (e.g., on a budgetary basis plant and equipment are recognized as expenses when acquired; on a full accrual basis they are recognized as expenses over their useful lives).

As shown in its statement of financing in Table 16-3, the Social Security Administration incurred obligations (costs) on a budgetary basis of $521,042 (an amount also reported on the second part of the statement of budgetary resources). Owing to various adjustments and differences between budgetary-basis accounting and full accrual accounting, the net cost of operations on a full accrual basis was $491,426—the "bottom line" of both the statement of financing and the statement of net cost.

STATEMENT OF CUSTODIAL ACTIVITIES

The **statement of custodial activities,** similar to that of an agency fund, is required only of an entity, such as the Internal Revenue Service and the Customs Service, whose *primary mission* is to collect funds to be turned over to the Treasury or other organizations. It shows the resources collected and their disposition (i.e., the amounts transferred to other agencies and the amounts not yet transferred). As a consequence, its bottom line should always be zero. The Social Security Administration is not required to prepare the statement of custodial activities, and therefore it is not included in Table 16-3.

WHAT ARE OTHER KEY FEATURES OF THE FASAB MODEL?

Not surprisingly the issues being dealt with by the FASAB are similar to those being addressed by the GASB and, in a broad sense, the FASB. They deal with the recognition of revenue and expenses and correspondingly with the valuation of assets and liabilities.

BASIS FOR RECOGNIZING REVENUES

The FASAB distinguishes between two types of revenues:

- ***Exchange*** (or earned) ***revenues*** arise from sales transactions in which each party receives benefits and incurs costs.
- ***Nonexchange revenues*** materialize when the government commands resources but gives nothing in exchange (at least not directly). Nonexchange revenues include taxes, duties, fines, and penalties.[6]

Exchange revenues, the FASAB asserts, should be recognized according to conventional business-type principles—that is, when goods or services are provided to the public or to another governmental entity. Thus, for example:

- Revenues from services should be recognized as an agency performs the services.
- Revenues from long-term contracts should be recognized on a percentage of completion basis. If a contract is expected to result in a loss, the loss should be spread over the contract in proportion to the share of estimated total costs incurred in each period. This provision is contrary to the principles of both the FASB and the GASB (as articulated in the FASB's Statement No. 5 and adopted by the GASB) that losses should be recognized when it is probable that an asset

[6] Statement of Federal Financial Accounting Standards No. 7, *Accounting for Revenues and Other Financing Sources* (April 1996).

has been impaired or a liability incurred and the amount of the loss can be reasonably estimated.

- Revenues from goods sold should be recognized upon delivery of the goods to the customer.

Recognizing the importance of both cash and accrual information, the FASAB requires that nonexchange revenues be reported on *both* an accrual and a cash basis. Under this unusual approach, an entity would report the actual amount collected and add to (or subtract from) it an "accrual adjustment." Thus, for example, if an entity were entitled to $200 million in taxes, but collected only $180 million, it would report its revenues as follows (in millions):

Cash collections	$180
Accrual adjustment	20
Total revenues	$200

Correspondingly, the entity would recognize a receivable of $20 million for the taxes to which the government has a legally enforceable claim but has not yet collected.

The accrual adjustment would be negative (subtracted from the cash collections) when the cash collections exceed the revenues earned. For example, if taxes applicable to a period were $300 million but collections were $320 million, then the required accrual adjustment of $20 million would be subtracted from the collections. At the same time, the entity would reduce its taxes receivable by $20 million.

According to the FASAB, a federal entity should accrue revenues "when a specifically identifiable, legally enforceable claim to resources arises, to the extent that collection is probable and the amount is measurable." Thus, for example:

- ***Income taxes*** should be recognized when assessed by the taxpayer (as indicated by a cash payment or a filed tax return) or by the result of audits, investigations, or litigation. The government should not recognize as revenues amounts that it estimates it will receive as the result of audits to be conducted in the future.
- ***Fines and penalties*** may be accrued (1) upon the expiration of the period during which the offender may contest a court summons, (2) when the offender pays the fine before a court date, or (3) when the court imposes a fine.
- ***Donations*** (as to a federal museum, presidential library, or memorial) should be recognized when the entity has a legally enforceable claim to the donated resources, collection is "more likely than not," and the amount is measurable.

ACCOUNTING FOR PLANT AND EQUIPMENT

The federal government controls over a trillion dollars in long-lived assets, some of which are unlike assets owned by businesses or other levels of government. They include military weapons (acquired in the hope that they will never have to be used), national parks and monuments (that produce little or no revenue but are in constant need of maintenance and repair), and conventional assets, such as office buildings and equipment. Recognizing that their diversity necessitates different approaches to accounting and reporting, the FASB groups the assets into two broad categories: general and stewardship. Stewardship assets are then further divided into two subcategories: land and heritage assets.

General Assets

General assets are comparable to those of a business, so the FASAB recommends that they be accounted for similarly. That is, they should be capitalized and (with the exception of land) depreciated over their useful lives. This category consists of assets that:

- Are used to produce goods or services or to support the mission of the entity and can be used for alternative purposes (that is by other federal programs, state or local governments, or nongovernmental entities)
- Are used in business-type activities
- Are used by entities in activities whose costs can be compared to other entities (e.g., costs of federal hospitals that can be compared to other hospitals)[7]

Military Assets

Military assets, such as aircraft, ships, vehicles, tanks and extraordinarily complex and costly weapons systems, pose special accounting issues. In times of peace these assets have useful lives that are as estimatable as general assets. However, when used for the purpose for which they were designed—to fight wars—their anticipated useful lives become considerably shorter and less certain.

Prior to May 2003, recognizing the special characteristics of military hardware, the FASAB directed that what it referred to as "national defense property, plant and equipment" should be accounted for as "other stewardship assets." That is, acquisition costs should be expensed as incurred, not capitalized. Details as to the number, changes during the year, and condition of assets in various categories should be disclosed in a stewardship report accompanying the basic financial statements. Then, however, the board took a different tack. Focusing on the need to provide information to facilitate annual performance assessment, the board stipulated that the cost of military assets should be capitalized and depreciated over their expected useful lives. That is, they should be accounted for like general assets.[8]

The board recognized that its general directive to capitalize and depreciate military assets leaves unresolved several thorny implementation issues. For, example, it is not clear to what extent the various cost elements of research, testing, development, and evaluation of complex weapon systems should be expensed, rather than capitalized. Similarly, further guidance will have to be provided as to how the costs of modifying and modernizing existing assets should be accounted for.

Space Assets

Assets used in the government's space program have characteristics similar to traditional military assets. Nevertheless, even prior to its decision mandating capitalization of military assets, the FASAB prescribed that these assets be accounted for as general assets. Space assets continue to be capitalized and depreciated.[9]

Stewardship Assets

Land

This category encompasses land other that in the general category. It includes mainly national forests, national parks, and the federal government's vast holdings of undeveloped acreage.

In that it is neither used in government operations nor held for sale, stewardship land need not be capitalized and therefore should not be reported on an entity's balance

[7] Statement of Federal Financial Accounting Standards No. 6, *Accounting for Property Plant and Equipment* (June 1996).

[8] Statement of Federal Financial Accounting Standards No. 23, *Eliminating the Category National Defense Property, Plant and Equipment* (May 2003).

[9] Statement of Federal Financial Accounting Standards No. 11, *Amendments to Accounting for Property, Plant and Equipment: Definitional Changes* (October 1998).

sheet. Instead, it should be expensed as acquired. In periods subsequent to acquisition the entity should provide in a "stewardship report" salient information as to the amount of land owned, how it is being used, and its condition.[10]

Heritage Assets

Heritage assets have value because of their historical, natural, cultural, educational, or artistic significance. They include museums, monuments, and historical sites.

Some heritage assets may have the characteristics of both operational and true heritage assets. The government holds some heritage assets, such as the Washington Monument, purely for their cultural, architectural, or aesthetic qualities. It holds others, such as the Eisenhower Executive Office Building in Washington, D.C. (an operating administrative complex), for both its historical and functional attributes. To reduce the subjectivity that would be required in having agencies either allocate a portion of an asset's cost to one category or another or in having them determine whether an asset was primarily operational or heritage, the FASAB stipulated that all multi-use heritage assets be capitalized as **general property, plant, and equipment** and depreciated over their useful lives. Heritage assets that have only historical, artistic, or cultural significance should be accounted for as stewardship assets. They should not be capitalized; they too should be reported upon in the stewardship report.[11]

ACCOUNTING FOR HUMAN CAPITAL

One of the most intriguing questions facing the federal government is whether investments in **human capital** should be accorded the same accounting recognition as those in physical capital. As defined by the FASAB, investments in "human capital" are the outlays for the education and training of the public (excluding federal civilian and military employees) intended to increase the nation's productive capacity.

Government agencies undertake educational and training programs to benefit the future, not the present. Arguably, therefore, consistent with the concepts of both matching and interperiod equity, the costs of these programs should be capitalized as incurred and subsequently amortized over the periods to be benefited. Moreover, accounting principles permitting agencies to capitalize outlays for physical assets, but not human "assets," might bias allocation decisions in favor of the physical assets. The reported expenses for the physical assets would be reported over the life of the assets; those for the human assets would have to be recognized as the costs were incurred.

On the other hand, the long-term benefits of educational and training programs are far less identifiable and measurable than those of physical assets. Determinations of the length of the benefit period would necessarily require arbitrary assumptions.

Faced with obvious practical difficulties, the FASAB (like both the FASB and the GASB) rejects the notion of capitalizing investments in human capital. Instead (unlike both the FASB and the GASB) it mandates supplemental disclosure in the financial report. Minimal reporting, it says, should include the annual investment made for the past five years and a narrative description of the major human capital programs.[12]

---

[10] Statement of Federal Financial Accounting Standards No. 8, *Supplementary Stewardship Reporting* (May 1996). Per Statement No. 8, disclosures pertaining to both stewardship land and heritage assets were reported as "required supplementary stewardship information." However, in an August 2003 exposure draft the board proposed that such disclosures be reclassified as "basic financial information" and thus included in the notes to the financial statements. This change would highlight the significance of the information and would reduce the possibility that statement readers would infer that, because it was classified as "supplementary," it was of less importance than other elements of a governmental annual report.

[11] Statement of Federal Financial Accounting Standards No. 16, *Amendments to Accounting for Property, Plant and Equipment: Measurement and Reporting for Multi-Use Heritage Assets* (July 1999).

[12] Statement of Federal Financial Accounting Standards No. 8, *Supplementary Stewardship Reporting* (May 1996).

DETERMINING INVENTORIES AND COST OF GOODS SOLD

In a statement that may appear more unconventional that it in fact is, the FASAB offers federal entities an option in accounting for inventories that are *held for sale*. They can value inventories held for sale at either of:

- Historical cost, as calculated by either the first-in, first-out (FIFO) or the weighted average method
- Latest acquisition cost, based on each item's last invoice price[13]

If an entity chooses the latter option, then it should show on its balance sheet both the latest acquisition cost and the historical cost, with the difference between the two presented as an allowance for unrealized holding gains or losses. Thus, for example (in millions):

Inventory at latest acquisition cost	$120
Allowance for unrealized holding gains	(20)
Inventory at historical cost	$100

Similarly, cost of goods sold should be based on acquisition prices, but the operating statement should incorporate an adjustment equal to the change during the period in the allowance for unrealized holding gains. As a result, the "bottom line" of the operating statement would be the same as if the cost of goods sold were based on historical cost. Assume, for example, that at the beginning of a year inventory was as shown above. At year-end it was as follows (in millions):

Inventory at latest acquisition cost	$160
Allowance for unrealized holding gains	(35)
Inventory at historical cost	$125

Thus, the allowance for unrealized holding gains increased by $15 million. If sales for the year were $950 million and purchases $800 million an operating statement would reflect the following:

Sales		$950
Cost of goods sold		
Beginning inventory at beginning-of-the-period latest acquisition cost	$120	
Less: allowance for unrealized holding gains at the beginning of the period	(20)	
Plus: purchases	800	
Cost of goods available for sale	900	
Less: ending inventory at end-of-the-period latest acquisition cost	(160)	
Plus: allowance for unrealized holding gains at the end of the period	35	
Cost of goods sold		775
Net results		$175

In contrast to the guidelines for inventories held for sale, those for other types of inventories, such as operating materials and supplies and stockpile materials (e.g., strategic materials held for national defense or national emergencies), call for conventional valuation—that is, at historical cost.

---

[13] Statement of Federal Financial Accounting Standards No. 3, *Accounting for Inventory and Related Property* (October 1993).

Although this approach to inventory valuation is seemingly quite progressive, it was adopted mainly to resolve a practical problem—the Department of Defense maintains many of its records on the basis of latest acquisition cost.

RECOGNIZING LIABILITIES AND RELATED EXPENSES

Of all the accounting and reporting issues facing the federal government, those pertaining to liabilities are probably the least tractable and the most controversial.[14] As explained by the FASAB, government liabilities are attributable to *events*. "Events" encompass both "transactions" and other "happenings of consequence" involving the government.

Transactions can be of two types:

- ***Exchange transactions***, in which each party gives and receives something of value (e.g., when the government purchases goods or services).
- ***Nonexchange transactions***, in which the government provides something of value without directly receiving something of value in return—for example, when the government incurs an obligation under a grant or entitlement program. An entitlement program is one that provides benefits to parties if they satisfy certain conditions (such as being unemployed or having an income below a specified amount). Once the program is authorized, no further congressional action is needed to appropriate the funds to sustain it. Thus, the cost to the government is never certain; it depends on the number of parties satisfying the conditions.

Happenings of consequence can also be classified into two categories:

- ***Government-related events*** represent mainly accidents for which the government is responsible and required by law to reimburse the injured parties for damages.
- ***Government-acknowledged events*** are occurrences for which the government is not responsible but elects, as a matter of policy, to provide relief to the victims. They include primarily natural disasters, such as hurricanes and earthquakes.

Neither exchange transactions nor government-related events pose issues unique to governments. Therefore, consistent with the principles of accrual accounting, the FASAB prescribes that federal entities recognize both a liability and related expense resulting from an exchange transaction when an exchange takes place (e.g., when the government receives the contracted-for goods or services). They should recognize a liability and related expense for a government-related event as soon as the event occurs and the anticipated outflows of resources are both probable and measurable.

Nonexchange transactions and government-acknowledged events raise the difficult question of recognition because they stem from the government's use of its sovereign power and there may be no well-defined event or transaction that establishes the obligation. For example, Congress authorizes financial assistance to parties satisfying specified conditions. It thereby commits the federal government to a future outflow of resources. Yet until the parties demonstrate that they have met the specified conditions, the government does not yet have an obligation either of an established amount or to identifiable parties. The commitment may extend over an unspecified number of years and the ultimate amount to be paid may depend on economic and social conditions well into the future. Further, the government can unilaterally cancel or change the program at any time.

[14] This discussion is based on Statement of Federal Financial Accounting Standards No. 5, *Accounting for Liabilities of the Federal Government* (September 1995).

To help assure consistency among a broad spectrum of events and transactions, the FASAB directs that federal entities recognize liabilities for:

- ***Nonexchange transactions when due.*** Thus, government agencies need recognize liabilities for grants and entitlements only as payments are due.
- ***Government-acknowledged events*** when the government formally *acknowledges* financial responsibility for the event and an amount is *due and payable* as a result. Thus, the government need recognize liabilities for disaster relief only when it has authorized specific grants to specific individuals, or contractors have actually provided their goods or services.

REPORTING THE OBLIGATIONS FOR SOCIAL INSURANCE PROGRAMS

The liabilities that the FASAB had to address that were far and away the most contentious were those stemming from social insurance programs in general and Social Security and Medicare in particular. These programs have no direct counterpart in either the private or municipal government sectors of our economy.

The accounting controversy over social insurance programs stems largely from the different ways in which these programs can be interpreted. Social Security, for example, can be seen as either a government sponsored pension plan (involving mainly exchange transactions) or as a government-managed income redistribution program (involving mainly nonexchange transactions). It is a pension program in that both employees and employers contribute to a fund over the course of the employees working lives in anticipation of the employees receiving a lifetime stipend upon retirement. It is an income redistribution program in that the government taxes both employees and employers, dedicating the tax to program beneficiaries. The tax rate is not calculated on any generally accepted actuarial basis, and the payments that beneficiaries receive upon retirement are not actuarially tied to the taxes that they or their employers paid.

In its Statement No. 17, *Accounting for Social Insurance* (1999), the FASAB specified that both the federal government at large and the individual agencies that administer social insurance programs should account for social insurance costs as if they were nonexchange transactions. That is, the reporting entities need recognize a liability (and related expenditure) for payments to beneficiaries or service providers only when the payments are actually due. Therefore, they need not record on their balance sheet the actuarial value of the benefits earned by program participants.

The FASAB acknowledges that of prime interest to anyone concerned with social insurance programs are their long-term sustainability and their impact on the overall fiscal condition of the federal government. Indeed, these have been a focal point of turn-of-the-century political and economic discourse. Consequently, the FASAB requires extensive disclosure of information such as the following:

- Long-range cash flow projections in nominal dollars and as a percentage of both the payroll that is subject to the tax earmarked for the program and the Gross Domestic Product
- Long-range projection of the ratio of contributors to beneficiaries (commonly called the "dependency ratio")
- A statement presenting the actuarial present values of future benefits, contributions, and tax income

Moreover, recognizing the centrality of information of Social Security to the long-term fiscal health of the federal government, the FASAB, in Statement No. 25, *Reclassification of Stewardship Responsibilities and Eliminating the Current Services Assessment* (2003), indicated that effective fiscal year 2005 the "statement of social insurance," a required schedule containing key statistical information on the program, should be considered a "basic" financial statement and thereby subject to the same degree of auditing as the balance sheet and other basic statements.

Closely tied to the issue of the amounts to be "booked" as liabilities and expenditures is that of how the required disclosures should be calculated. In a nutshell, the questions the FASAB faced were (1) which participants should be taken into account in making projections and measuring the actuarial benefits and obligations; and (2) over how long a period should the projections be made and the actuarial present value calculated.

Private employers report as their actuarial liability the amount that their current employees and retirees have earned but have not yet been paid. For the federal government a similar approach—i.e., reporting what current participants in the insurance programs and retirees have earned—may not be entirely adequate. Social Security and Medicare are not voluntary programs. Everyone must join, and everyone can expect to receive benefits. Therefore, the federal government's obligation for benefits extends not only to current participants or even current U.S. citizens, but to the unborn children of both U.S. citizens and future immigrants to the United States.

After considerable debate, the FASAB stipulated that federal reporting entities should include in their projections and actuarial calculations current participants, current retirees, and all those who are expected to become plan participants during the projection period. The length of the projection period may vary from program to program but should be sufficiently long to illustrate long-term sustainability. For Social Security, this has usually been considered to be seventy-five years.

RECOGNIZING THE COST OF SUBSIDIZED DIRECT LOANS AND LOAN GUARANTEES

As part of their social, educational, and commercial programs, federal entities make low-interest direct loans and guarantee loans made by banks and other institutions. The low-interest loans provide a direct benefit to the borrowers by providing funds at less than the rate they would otherwise have to pay. The guarantees virtually eliminate credit risks to the lenders and thereby enable them to provide funds to the borrowers at reduced interest rates. The targeted beneficiaries of these loan programs include farmers, veterans, students, and small businesses.

Prior to the Federal Credit Reform Act of 1990, agencies were not required to explicitly recognize the costs of making the low-interest loans. Instead, they simply reported less interest revenue than they would have had they charged prevailing interest rates. Correspondingly, they recognized the costs of the loan guarantees only as they reimbursed the lenders upon borrower defaults.

The Federal Credit Reform Act of 1990 requires that the president's budget reflect the long-term costs in the year in which the direct loans and the guarantees are made. To enhance conformity between budgeting and accounting practices, the FASAB directed that the same principles apply to annual financial reports.[15] According to the FASAB, when a government makes a subsidized direct loan, it should recognize as an asset the **present value** of its estimated net cash receipts, including both interest and repayment of principal. It should report an expense equal to the difference between the face value of the loan and the present value of the estimated net cash receipts. Present value should be based on the interest rate of marketable Treasury securities with similar terms to maturity as the cash flows.

[15] Statement of Federal Financial Accounting Standards No. 2, Accounting for Direct Loans and Loan Guarantees (July 1993), as modified by Standard No. 18, Amendments to Accounting Standards for Direct Loans and Loan Guarantees in Statement of Federal Financial Accounting Standards No. 2 (May 2000), and Standard No. 19, Technical Amendments to Accounting Standards for Direct Loans and Loan Guarantees in Statement of Federal Financial Accounting Standards No. 2 (March 2002).

EXAMPLE *Subsidized Loan*

A government agency makes a three-year, 6 percent, direct loan of $1,000 at a time when prevailing Treasury rates on short and intermediate term securities are 10 percent. The loan is to be repaid in three annual installments of $374 (the amount required to amortize a $1,000, 6 percent loan over three years—$1,000 divided by 2.66730, the present value of an annuity of $1 for three periods).

Inasmuch as the present value of three payments of $374, discounted at 10 percent, is only $930 ($374 times 2.4869, the present value of an annuity of $1 for three periods) the agency should recognize an expense of $70 (the difference between the loan's $1,000 face value and the $930 present value of the payments). The following entry would therefore be appropriate when the loan is made:

Loan receivable	$930	
Loan subsidy (expense)	70	
Cash		$1,000
To record a direct loan		

In subsequent periods, the agency should recognize revenue of 10 percent of the balance of the loan receivable, and correspondingly reduce the balance of the loan receivable by the difference between the revenue recognized and the cash received. Thus, in the first year:

Cash	$374	
Loan receivable		$281
Interest revenue (10 percent of $930)		93
To record the first payment from the borrower		

The actual entries recommended by the FASAB are slightly more complex. Per the FASAB guidance, when recording the initial loan the agency should debit the face value of the loan ($1,000 in the example), offsetting it with a contra account, "subsidy allowance" ($70). Thereafter, upon receipt of each payment, the agency should amortize the subsidy allowance until it is equal to zero after the final payment. (The reported loan subsidy expense, interest revenue, and net loan receivable would be the same as in the example, however.) Moreover, each year the agency should reestimate the present value of its anticipated cash flows (taking into account updated information on both potential defaults and changes in the prevailing interest rate) and adjust its accounts to reflect the new calculations.

When a government guarantees loans, it should also recognize both an expense and an obligation in the amount of the present value of its anticipated payments to the lender. Then, each year the government should reassess the present value of the anticipated payments and recognize the change in value as either an increase or decrease in its loan guarantee liability, offset by either a debit or credit to loan guarantee expense.

EXAMPLE *Loan Guarantees*

At the start of Year 1 an agency guarantees $100 million of student loans. The following schedule indicates the agency's estimates of the payments (all at year-end) that it will have to make to lenders owing to defaults and the present value of those payments. The agency applies a discount rate of 8 percent.

End of Year	Amount (in Millions)	Present Value of $1	Net Present Value
1	$2,100,000	0.92593	$1,944,453
2	1,500,000	0.85734	1,286,010
3	1,000,000	0.79383	793,830
Total			$4,024,293

Upon guaranteeing the loans, the agency would make the following entry:

Interest expense	$4,024,293	
Liability for loan guarantees		$4,024,293

To record expense of guaranteeing loans (which, per the FASAB, should be classified as "interest expense")

Suppose that during the first year the agency pays lenders $2.1 million, as estimated, to fulfill its guarantees. Its new estimate of the present value of the anticipated payments, measured as of the end of Year 1, is now as follows:

End of Year	Amount (in Millions)	Present Value of $1	New Present Value
2	$1,500,000	0.92593	$1,388,895
3	1,000,000	0.85734	857,340
Total			$2,246,235

The following entry would be appropriate to record the cash payment of $2.1 million and the adjustment of the liability:

Liability for loan guarantees	$1,778,058	
Interest expense	321,942	
Cash		$2,100,000

To record payment of $2,100,000 and adjust the balance on the remaining liability for the difference between $4,024,293 and $2,246,235 (the interest expense represents 8 percent of the beginning of year balance of $4,024,293)

If the agency revises its estimate of the second- or third-year payments, then to compute the loan guarantee expense in Year 1 and the liability at year-end, it would incorporate the net present value of the addition (or reduction) in expected payments. Thus, if the agency estimates that the Year 3 payment would now be $1.3 million, then it would substitute $1.3 million for $1 million in this computation. If interest rates decreased to 6 percent, it would use that rate in discounting the cash flows.

WHAT ADDITIONAL STEPS HAS THE FEDERAL GOVERNMENT TAKEN TO IMPROVE ITS FISCAL MANAGEMENT?

Recognizing the limitations of traditional accounting systems that focus exclusively on financial metrics (as discussed in earlier chapters), Congress enacted the Government Performance and Results Act of 1993, which requires federal agencies to develop strategic plans, operational objectives, and measures of performance and to report on the extent to which it met its objectives.

As detailed in the Act, as part of its annual budget request to the OMB, each agency must prepare and submit a performance plan that includes:

- Objective, quantifiable, and measurable goals that define the agency's anticipated level of performance
- A description of the operational processes, skills, technology, and "human capital" required to meet the performance goals
- A basis for comparing actual results to the goals
- The means of verifying and validating actual performance

In addition it must also submit a report that:

- Reviews success in achieving the performance goals of the previous fiscal year
- Evaluates the performance plan for the current fiscal year relative to the previous year's results
- Explains any deviations from its goals, indicating why a goal was not met, describing plans for achieving the goal, and, if the goals were impractical or infeasible, spelling out why and recommending corrective steps

The act also requires agencies to develop "strategic plans" that cover five-year periods. The plans should set forth the agencies' missions, goals, and objectives and the means to achieve them.

In 2003, the GAO, as it does every year, issued a performance and accountability report on all cabinet-level departments and selected major agencies. It found that for the most part the units were making significant progress in improving their management processes. Yet, it emphasized, in almost all departments and agencies "significant challenges remain."[16]

WHAT ARE THE KEY INTERNATIONAL TRENDS IN GOVERNMENTAL ACCOUNTING?

Over the last several decades, accounting practitioners as well as students have directed considerable attention to the "international" aspects of business accounting. Initially, owing to the prevalence of international trade and cross-border investment, their concerns were mainly with understanding the accounting and reporting systems of other countries. More recently, however, they have focused on efforts on "harmonizing"—making uniform—business accounting standards throughout the world.

By contrast, far less attention has been paid to the international aspects of governmental accounting. In large measure, governmental accounting standards have been strongly influenced by the institutional characteristics of individual countries. Accordingly, the practices of one country have not been as readily transferable to others. Further, governments—particularly local governments—have typically generated their resources within their own country, so there has been less need for them to present financial statement to outsiders. In addition, even though national governments may have sought funds from sources beyond their borders, the lenders apparently have been willing to base their credit analyses mainly on broad economic, social, and political indicators rather than on financial statements prepared in accordance with generally accepted accounting principles.

[16] See the GAO's *2003 Performance and Accountability Series and High Risk Series*, a collection of twenty-nine reports pertaining to specific federal units or activities and to the government as a whole.

This is now changing. Governments themselves increasingly engage in international exchanges. At both the national and local levels they use nondomestic contractors to construct major infrastructure projects, they purchase goods and services from international corporations, and they sell securities in the international credit markets. In the 1960s, for example, foreign holdings of the U.S. federal debt were less than 5 percent. In 2002 they were 32 percent—$1,134.1 *billion*.[17] Moreover, owing perhaps to major defaults by national governments and losses on projects that they financed, lenders are demanding more and better fiscal data.

Credit-rating agencies, such as Moody's and Standard & Poor's, have responded to the demand for improved information by rating the bonds of governments, both national and local, outside of the United States just as they do those within. Indeed, the factors that they take into account are similar to those they use domestically. Hence they assess factors that are generally reported upon in financial statements as well as those that bear only indirectly on the entity's fiscal condition. Examples include:

- The diversity, performance, and prospects of each member state's national economy
- Intergovernmental fiscal and financial arrangements
- Trends in fiscal balances
- Debt burdens, pension obligations, and contingent liabilities
- Tax competitiveness within [a regional] and worldwide context, along with tax-raising flexibility
- Liquidity and debt management[18]

AN INTERNATIONAL STANDARD-SETTING AGENCY

As might be expected, no standard-setting organization has the authority to establish accounting standards for governments other than those within its own country. Nevertheless, the Public Sector Committee (PSC) of the International Federation of Accountants (IFAC) is developing a set of standards, which, although it lacks the force of law, is intended to improve both the quality and comparability of financial reporting. As suggested by the accompanying "In Practice," there is as much need in other countries as in the United States for rigorous accounting standards.

The IFAC is a worldwide organization dedicated to improving accounting in both the public and private sectors. The PSC is its sub-group concerned with the "public sector"—that is, national, regional, and local governments as well as their related agencies, boards, commissions, and enterprises.

As of 2003, the PSC has issued twenty standards in addition to studies, implementation guides, and occasional papers. In these documents the PSC makes clear that regardless of historical tradition, public sector accounting should be on a full accrual, not a cash, basis. This position is manifest in all of its pronouncements. Thus, for example, per the standards:

- Property, plant, and equipment, including infrastructure (but excluding heritage assets) should be capitalized and depreciated.
- Revenue from exchange transactions should be recognized when the revenue can be measured reliably, it is probable that the entity will realize an economic

[17] Office of Management and Budget, *Analytical Perspectives, Budget of the United States Government, Fiscal Year 2004*, Table 13-6, "Foreign Holdings of Federal Debt," p. 311.

[18] *A Ratings Roadmap for EU Candidate Countries*, Standard & Poor's (Nov 19, 2002), per its Web site, www2.standardandpoors.com/.

IN PRACTICE

OFF-THE-BALANCE SHEET DEBT IN GREAT BRITAIN

The use of accounting gimmicks is by no means confined to the United States. According to a report in the London Times (The Times On Line, July 7, 2003), British Treasury officials are running £100 billion of off-balance sheet liabilities. The debts take the form of Private Finance Initiative (PFI) contracts to build hospitals, prisons, and schools. Under these arrangements, the government contracts with a private consortium, usually composed of large construction firms, to build a project and to own and manage it. The contracts are usually long-term, often up to thirty years. During that time, the government leases the project from the private consortium. The lease payments cover the costs of the project, interest on the implicit loan, and applicable management fees. The PFIs, however, are interpreted as service contracts rather than borrowing transactions and, like service contracts in the United States, are not subject to the usual limitations on debts. As one critic charged, "It is a scam to get around artificial restrictions on public sector borrowing. But a debt is still a debt, even if it's off balance sheet."

Opponents of PFIs note that these contracts not only obfuscate the true amount of government debt but are costing the taxpayers millions of pounds. That's because the private contractors are the ones who must borrow the funds to finance construction. Their credit ratings are considerably lower than that of the government and hence their interest costs are considerably higher. But it is the government—and the taxpayers—that must eventually pay these higher costs.

benefit, and both the stage of completion of the transaction and the costs incurred can be measured reliably.

- Inventories intended for sale should be recognized as an expense in the period in which related revenues are recognized. If there is no related revenue then the expense should be recognized when the goods are distributed or a related service is rendered (i.e., on a consumption rather than a purchases basis).
- Borrowing costs should be recognized as an expense as "incurred" (i.e., not necessarily when cash is disbursed).

The PSC requires that governments present four basic financial statements:

- A statement of financial position (a balance sheet)
- A statement of financial performance (an operating statement)
- A statement of change in net assets/equity (a statement that accounts for all changes in net assets/equity)
- A cash flow statement

Notably, the PSC model does not require the presentation of information on individual funds. Like both the FASB and the FASAB, the PSC views funds and fund accounting as elements of internal control, not as a focal point of external reporting.

The PSC's efforts to promote full accrual accounting are consistent with trends that have been evident in the United States. Its model is similar to both the government-wide model of the Government Accounting Standards Board and that of the FASAB.

SUMMARY

The U.S. Constitution left it to Congress and the executive branch to determine the form and content of financial reports and to implement and administer the underlying accounting systems of the government. Unfortunately, despite significant ongoing improvements, the systems established over the years are still inadequate for an organization of the size and complexity of the federal government.

The three federal agencies with oversight responsibility for financial management are making major strides in coordinating the accounting systems and reporting practices of individual agencies. The Department of the Treasury has a broad range of functions, including managing the public debt and acting as a central collecting and disbursing agent. The Office of Management and Budget, a part of the executive branch and one of the most powerful agencies in the federal government, helps prepare and supervise the federal budget and reviews and evaluates agency programs. The General Accounting Office, a part of the legislative branch, performs an array of functions but is most closely identified with its role as the government's auditor—the watchdog of Congress.

The Federal Accounting Standards Advisory Board, which was established in 1990, is responsible for promulgating accounting standards for the government as a whole as well as its separate components. Since its inception it has developed a comprehensive accounting model as well as detailed standards that address specific types of transactions.

The federal government's unified budget is intended to show the impact of federal activities on the national economy. It encompasses four types of funds—the general fund, special funds, trust funds, and revolving funds. Ironically, the receipts and disbursements of both Social Security and the Postal Service, despite their major impact on the fiscal welfare of both the government and the nation at large, are excluded from unified budget calculations relating to spending caps. Nevertheless, they are included in receipts and outlays that are commonly at the center of most political and economic discussions.

Budget accounts ensure that a federal entity complies with budgetary mandates, does not overspend appropriations, and is able to fulfill reporting requirements. Proprietary accounts, which are based on FASAB standards, provide an economic rather than a budgetary measure of the government's operations and resources.

The FASAB established three criteria for a component to be considered a reporting entity: There is a management responsible for controlling resources and accountable for performance; the component is of significant size so that its financial statements provide a meaningful representation of its operations and financial condition; and users are interested in the information to be reported and could use it to make resource allocation and related decisions.

The FASAB's comprehensive reporting model helps ensure that the financial statements of the government at-large as well as its component units focus on all economic resources and are on a full accrual basis. Key recommendations of the FASAB include the following:

- Exchange revenues should be recognized when goods or services are provided to the public or to another governmental agency. Nonexchange revenues should be recognized on both an accrual and a cash basis. That is, an entity should report the actual cash collections and add or subtract from them an "accrual adjustment" representing the difference between amounts accrued and amounts collected. Revenues should be accrued when the government has a legal claim upon the resources and collection of cash is both probable and measurable.
- General property plant and equipment, multi-use heritage assets, and military assets should be capitalized and depreciated. By contrast, stewardship assets and "pure" heritage assets should be expensed as acquired and described in a stewardship report.
- Inventories held for sale may be valued at latest acquisition price; other types of inventories should be valued at historical cost.
- Investments in human capital should not be capitalized but should be disclosed in notes to the financial statements.
- Liabilities for nonexchange transactions should be recognized when due; those for government-acknowledged events should be recognized when the government formally acknowledges financial responsibility and an amount is due and payable.
- Liabilities, and related expenses, for both loan guarantees and subsidized loans should be recognized at the time the loans are made.

The Government Performance and Results Act is intended to further improve federal accounting and fiscal management. It requires that agencies establish specific goals and objectives and report annually on the extent to which they achieve them.

Recent years have witnessed increased interest in harmonizing international standards and enhancing their quality. These efforts have been spearheaded by the Public Sector Committee of the International Federation of Accountants. This committee is developing a model for governments at all levels that, consistent with trends in the United States, is full accrual-based.

EXERCISE FOR REVIEW AND SELF-STUDY

Congress recently authorized the establishment of the Wilderness Lands Preservation Commission. The Commission satisfies the FASAB criteria for an independent reporting entity.

1. For its first year of operations, the Commission received an appropriation of $100 million. Of this amount, it spent only $80 million. Assuming that the appropriation does not lapse, how would the unspent $20 million be reported on the Commission's year-end balance sheet?
2. To educate the public as to the importance of wildlife preservation, the Commission received a legally binding pledge of $2 million from a private foundation. Of this amount only $0.5 million was received during the year. The balance is expected to be received in the following year. How much of the pledge should be recognized as revenue in the year it was made?
3. The Commission operates a gift shop in which it sells wildlife-related posters, books, and educational materials. In it first year, it had sales of $900,000. It purchased merchandise for $1,000,000, of which it sold $750,000. Based on the latest acquisition cost, the year-end inventory had a value of $300,000. Prepare a summary statement of operations for the gift shop, assuming that the Commission shows the impact of changes in the inventory's latest acquisition cost.
4. One of the Commission's main functions is to encourage landowners to take specified conservation measures. To assist them in covering their costs, the Commission lends them the required funds at below-market rates. During its first year of operations, the Commission lent one landowner $400,000. The landowner was required to repay the loan in three annual payments of $144,139, an amount that reflects an interest rate of 4 percent. At the time of the loan the prevailing rate on three-year Treasury securities was 8 percent. How should the Commission account for the cost of the loan?
5. In the course of the year, the Commission acquired the following assets:
   a. Buildings for $5 million (to provide office space)
   b. Land for $1 million (on which to construct an office building)
   c. Land for $40 million (acquired as a wildlife refuge)

   How should each of these assets be accounted for?
6. Per regulations established by the Commission, landowners in specified areas near designated wildlife refuges are not permitted to kill or trap animals of prey. In return, the Commission reimburses landowners for the value of any livestock killed by the animals. Toward the end of the year, one farmer submitted a claim to the Commission for $12,000. As of year-end, the Commission verified that the claim was legitimate, but had not yet authorized payment. What journal entry, if any, should the Commission make to record the claim?

QUESTIONS FOR REVIEW AND DISCUSSION

1. What is the primary role of the Treasury Department's Financial Management Service?
2. The Office of Management and Budget is responsible for granting agencies *apportionments*. What are apportionments?
3. Why is the FASAB named an *advisory* board? What is the relationship between the FASAB and the GAO, the Treasury Department and the OMB?
4. What are the four main objectives of federal financial reporting as established by the FASAB?
5. What is meant by the *unified* budget? Why are Social Security receipts and disbursements said to be "off budget"?
6. Why may it be unclear as to whether a particular program or sub-unit of an agency or department is an appropriate independent reporting entity?
7. What are the six basic statements that an agency may have to prepare to be in compliance with FASAB standards?
8. In what significant way is the FASAB's approach to inventory accounting different from that of both the GASB and the FASB?
9. Into what two categories does the FASAB divide government assets? How are each of the four accounted for?
10. What is meant by investments in *human capital*? In what way are investments in human capital accounted for differently from investments in *physical capital*?
11. Why does it matter whether Social Security is considered a pension plan or an entitlement program? How does the FASAB direct that Social Security be reported? What unique issue does the federal government face in calculating the actuarial value of its Social Security obligation that a private corporation would not face in calculating the corresponding obligation of its pension plan?
12. If an agency makes a loan at a below-market rate, what would be the nature of any expense recognized at the time of the loan? If it guaranteed a loan made by others, what would be the nature of any expense recognized at the time of the guarantee?

EXERCISES

16-1

1. The federal government's annual financial statements are issued by
   a. The Department of the Treasury
   b. The Office of Management and Budget
   c. The Department of Commerce
   d. The General Accounting Office
2. The General Accounting Office is part of which of the following branch of government?
   a. The executive branch
   b. The legislative branch
   c. The judicial branch
   d. None of the above; it is an independent agency
3. The Chief Financial Officer of the United States reports directly to
   a. The Comptroller General
   b. The President
   c. The Majority Leader
   d. The head of the OMB
4. The unified budget includes
   a. Both Social Security and Postal Service accounts
   b. Social Security accounts but not Postal Service accounts
   c. Postal Service accounts but not Social Security accounts
   d. Neither Social Security nor Postal Service accounts
5. Which of the following is *not* a required element of federal government-wide statements?
   a. Management's discussion and analysis
   b. Descriptions of stewardship assets
   c. A schedule comparing actual to anticipated nonmonetary performance measures
   d. A statement that shows, by major department or agency, the net cost of operations
6. An federal entity should be considered a reporting entity and thereby must issue annual reports if it
   a. Is listed in the OMB's Catalog of Federal Agencies
   b. Is a cabinet-level department or equivalent
   c. Satisfies the three nonquantitative criteria established by the FASAB
   d. Meets OMB minimum revenue requirements
7. In the federal government, "proprietary accounts" are those that
   a. Provide the data required to prepare accrual basis financial statements
   b. Provide the data required to prepare budget-basis financial statements
   c. Are used to account for business-type activities
   d. Are used to account for classified information that cannot be made public for security reasons
8. Which of the following statements reconciles an agency's obligations incurred on a budgetary basis with the net cost of operations on a full accrual basis?
   a. Statement of net cost
   b. Statement of financing
   c. Statement of changes in financial position
   d. Statement of budgetary resources
9. Which of the following is an example of an "exchange" revenue?
   a. Proceeds from the sale of goods or services
   b. Transfers from another agency
   c. An increase in an OMB allotment
   d. Collections of taxes on liquor sales
10. The federal government should recognize revenue from income taxes
    a. As taxpayers earn their income
    b. As taxpayers report on their tax returns the amount of their tax or make periodic cash payments
    c. As soon as it is able to make a reasonable estimate of the amount that it will collect
    d. On the date the taxes are due

16-2

1. Military hardware should be accounted for as
   a. Stewardship assets
   b. Heritage assets
   c. National defense assets
   d. General assets
2. The Executive Office Building has historical significance yet is also used as functioning office space. The cost of the building should be
   a. Depreciated, like that of other general assets
   b. Not accorded balance sheet recognition
   c. Allocated between general assets and heritage assets
   d. Reported on the balance sheet but not depreciated
3. The cost of constructing and renovating the Washington Monument should be
   a. Reported on the balance sheet and depreciated
   b. Not accorded balance sheet recognition
   c. Reported on the balance sheet at a symbolic amount (e.g., $1)
   d. Reported on the balance sheet but not depreciated
4. In a particular year Congress establishes a program that entitles all senior citizens to reimbursements for eye examinations.
   a. The estimated actuarial cost of the program for a period of seventy-five years should be reported as a

liability and corresponding expenditure in the year Congress authorized the program

b. The cost of the program should be reported as a liability and corresponding expense as the payments are due to the senior citizens

c. The cost of the program should be reported as an expense as the payments are made to the senior citizens

d. The cost of the program should be reported as a liability and corresponding expense as the OMB issues an allotment authorizing the agency to make the required disbursements

5. A hurricane strikes the Florida coast and, as required by law, the federal government provides financial assistance to parties who suffer property losses. The federal government should recognize the assistance payments as expenditures in the period in which

   a. The hurricane occurred
   b. The department in charge of the program authorizes the payments
   c. The Treasury Department issues the checks
   d. The department in charge of the program acknowledges that it is responsible for providing assistance to the hurricane victims

6. The actuarial liability for Social Security that the federal government discloses in its financial statements is based on a projection of

   a. One year
   b. Ten years
   c. Seventy-five years
   d. A perpetuity

7. The federal government should recognize the expenses associated with a subsidized loan program

   a. In the period in which it establishes the program
   b. In the periods that it makes the loans
   c. In the periods in which the loan recipients disburse the funds that they borrow
   d. Over the periods the loans are outstanding

8. In the period in which it guarantees a loan, the federal government should recognize a liability in the amount of

   a. Zero, assuming that there are no defaults in that period
   b. The total amount of the loans that it guarantees
   c. The amount that it expects to pay owing to borrower defaults
   d. The present value of the amount that it expect to pay owing to borrower defaults

9. The Government Performance and Results Act of 1993 mandates that

   a. Each federal agency submit a performance plan to OMB
   b. All federal funds recipients be subject to an annual performance audit
   c. Each federal agency be subject to an annual performance audit
   d. Each federal agency prepare its budget using zero-base budgeting or a comparable form of performance budgeting

10. The accounting standards established by the Public Sector Committee of the International Federation of Accountants

   a. Must be adhered to by all national governments whose debt is traded in international markets
   b. Must be adhered to by all national governments that are signatories to the United Nations International Commerce Treaty
   c. Must be adhered to by members of the European Economic Community
   d. Represent recommended "best practices" and are for guidance only

16-3

The financial statements of the federal government are unique.

The left-hand column of the following table describes each of six financial statements that the FASAB recommends agencies prepare. The right-hand column indicates the names of the six statements. Match the description in the left-hand column with the correct title in the right-hand column.

a. Summarizes all entity transactions other than those, such as earned revenues and expenses, reported in the statement of net cost; explains how the entity financed its net costs; includes amounts received from appropriations, dedicated taxes, borrowings and other financing sources.	1. Statement of budgetary resources
b. Shows the resources collected and disbursed; required only of entities, such as the Internal Revenue Service and the Customs Service, that collect funds to be turned over to the Treasury or other organizations.	2. Statement of custodial activities
c. Shows the entity's assets, liabilities, and net position, including fund balance with the Treasury.	3. Statement of financing
d. In essence an operating statement; shows operating costs and revenues.	4. Statement of changes in net position
e. Reconciles the statement of budgetary resources to the statement of net cost.	5. Statement of net cost
f. Prepared on a budget basis; shows amount available for appropriation, cash outlays and newly incurred obligations.	6. Balance sheet

16-4

Nonexchange, as opposed to exchange, revenues present the more difficult issues of accounting recognition.

In 2005 the federal government, through its various government agencies, engaged in the following transactions involving revenues.

1. It rented land to a tenant. It signed a three-year lease requiring monthly payments of $2,000. In 2005, the year in which the lease was signed, the tenant occupied the land for six months but paid an entire year's rent (i.e., $24,000).
2. It signed two contracts to provide engineering services to a foreign government. Each contract was for $50 million. During the year, the federal agency completed 100 percent of one contract and 60 percent of the other. It collected the entire $100 million in cash.
3. It assessed fines of $100,000 each on two firms for polluting waterways. One offender paid the fine; the other notified the government that it would contest the fine in court.
4. It accepted from a private foundation a pledge of $120,000 to fund an exhibit in a government museum. During the year the foundation paid $40,000 of its pledge, promising to pay the balance in the following year. The pledge does not constitute an enforceable legal agreement.
5. As the result of an audit, it assessed a company $250,000 in income taxes for 2003. In their audit report, the auditors estimated that audits of subsequent years would yield an additional $150,000.

Prepare journal entries to record the transactions. Comment briefly on the amount of revenue recognized.

16-5

Low-interest loans constitute a subsidy and hence an expense.

The Business Development Corporation (BDC), a federal agency, makes loans to high-tech companies that satisfy specified criteria. The loans are intended to encourage research and development and are made at rates substantially below market.

In 2005 the BDC made a loan of $100,000 to Interface Networks, Inc. The interest rate was 6 percent and the loan was payable over a three-year period in equal installments of $37,411. At the time of the loan, prevailing Treasury interest rates for loans of comparable maturities were 10 percent.

1. What was the amount of the loan subsidy?
2. How and when should the agency recognize the value of the subsidy? Explain.
3. Prepare a journal entry to record the loan and recognize the subsidy.

16-6

Different types of assets are accounted for in different ways.

The government purchased or constructed the following assets:

1. A monument to honor the sailors who served in the U.S. Coast Guard
2. Land to be incorporated into a national forest
3. Oil to be held in reserve to cover temporary shortages
4. An office building for the General Accounting Office
5. Oil to be used in a government-owned utility that generates and sells electric power
6. Operating room equipment for a Veterans Administration hospital
7. A navy fighter plane
8. A historical building that is being used—and will continue to be used—to house federal offices

For each, indicate whether it should be:

a. Capitalized and depreciated (or amortized) over its useful life
b. Capitalized but not depreciated (or amortized)
c. Expensed as acquired, and described in the stewardship statement
d. Reported either at historical cost (based on either the FIFO or the weighted average methods) or at latest acquisition cost
e. Reported only at historical cost

16-7

Certain types of government inventories may be accounted for at latest acquisition prices.

The statement of net cost of a federal agency included the following (in millions):

Sales		$405
Cost of goods sold		
Beginning inventory at beginning-of-the-period latest acquisition cost	$ 54	
Less: allowance for unrealized holding gains at the beginning of the period	(21)	
Plus: purchases	360	
Cost of goods available for sale	393	
Less: ending inventory at end-of-the-period latest acquisition cost	(72)	
Plus: allowance for unrealized holding gains at the end of the period	35	
Cost of goods sold		356
Net results		$ 49

1. What was the value of the beginning-of-year inventory stated at historical cost?
2. What was the value of the end-of-year inventory stated at historical cost?
3. What would be the cost of goods sold stated at latest acquisition cost?
4. Show how end-of-year inventory would be presented on the balance sheet.

PROBLEMS

16-1

Federal agency financial statements were illustrated but not discussed in detail in this chapter. Nevertheless, despite some unusual terminology, they are readily understandable.

Examine the following financial statements, which are condensed versions of those of a federal agency responsible for collecting taxes and duties and transferring them to the Treasury.

Statement of Custodial Activity for Year Ended September 30 (in millions)

Tax revenues for others	
Collections	$4,900
Increase in taxes receivable	200
Total revenues for others	$5,100
Disposition of revenues	
Amounts transferred to the treasury	$4,800
Increase in amounts to be transferred	300
Total disposition of revenues	$5,100
Net custodial activity	$ 0

Statement of Net Cost for Year Ended September 30 (in millions)

Personnel costs	$ 300
Other costs	500
Net cost of operations	$ 800

Statement of Net Changes in Net Position for Year Ended September 30 (in millions)

Financing sources—appropriations used	$ 775
Less: net cost of operations	800
Net results of operations	$ (25)
Increase in unexpended appropriations	125
Increase in net position	$ 100
Net position, beginning of year	450
Net position, end of year	$ 550

Balance Sheet as of September 30 (in millions)

Assets	
Fund balance with treasury	$ 125
Taxes receivable	615
Plant, equipment, and other assets (net of accumulated depreciation)	285
Total assets	$1,025
Liabilities	
Custodial liability	$ 450
Other liabilities	25
Total liabilities	$ 475
Net position	
Unexpended appropriations	$ 125
Cumulative results of operations	425
Total net position	$ 550
Total liabilities and net position	$1,025

Statement of Budgetary Resources for Year Ended September 30 (in millions)

Budgetary resources made available	
Current appropriations	$ 900
Status of budgetary resources	
Obligations incurred	$ 775
Unobligated balance not available (expired allotments)	125
Total, status of budgetary resources	$ 900
Outlays	
Obligations incurred	$ 775
Add: obligated fund balance and accounts payable, beginning of year	70
Deduct: obligated fund balance and accounts payable, end of year	(60)
Total outlays	$ 785

Statement of Financing for Year Ended September 30 (in millions)

Obligations and nonbudgetary resources	
Obligations incurred	$ 775
Increase in goods and services ordered but not yet received	(5)
Costs capitalized on the balance sheet and not expensed	
Acquisition of capital assets	(10)
Expenses that do not require budgetary resources	
Depreciation	40
Net cost of operations	$ 800

1. How much did the agency actually collect in taxes? How much did it submit to the Treasury? How much

did it owe the Treasury at year-end for both taxes collected and taxes receivable? How much did it owe at the beginning of the year?

2. How much did it cost the agency to carry out its activities during the year?
3. Of its operating costs, how much was financed by federally appropriated funds?
4. What was the total amount that the agency was appropriated during the year? What was the balance that was not used? Is this amount available for immediate use by the agency? If not, why not? Did the agency have a balance in unexpended appropriations at the start of the year? How can you tell?
5. What was the total amount of goods and services ordered by the agency during the year? How much of goods or services was received (including amounts ordered in the previous year but received in the current year)? How much was paid for?
6. Per the statement of financing, the agency ordered $775 of goods and services (obligations incurred), but the net cost of operations per both the statement of financing and the statement of net cost is $800. How can the net cost of operations exceed the amount of goods and services ordered? Explain and account for the differences.

16-2

Veterans benefits (not discussed in this chapter) present especially challenging issues of accounting.

The federal government's consolidated financial statements contained the following excerpt from a note entitled "Veterans' compensation and pension":

> The Department of Veterans Affairs (VA) has a liability to veterans or their dependents for compensation benefits (if the veteran was disabled or died from military service-connected causes) or pension benefits for war veterans (if the veteran was disabled or died from non-service-connected causes).

The note also indicates that the actuarial value of the compensation benefits as of year-end was $235.2 billion and that for pension and burial benefits was $44.3 billion.

In addition, the VA offers medical benefits to veterans. These are provided through VA hospitals, but only to the extent that required facilities are available (except for veterans with service-connected disabilities, who are automatically entitled to medical services). The government makes no guarantees as to level of care and Congress decides annually how adequately the facilities will be funded.

Although this chapter did not address veterans benefits, it did raise the related question of whether the government should report a liability for the actuarial value of anticipated Social Security benefits and correspondingly recognize an expense for the benefits as they are "earned" by the beneficiaries.

Suppose that you are a member of the FASAB. Do you think that the VA should recognize a liability (and a corresponding expense) for each of the following benefits during the years in which the veterans perform their military service (or are injured or die)? Or alternatively, do you think that the liability (and related expense) for the benefits should be recognized only when the payments are actually due or the medical services are actually provided?

1. Payments to be made to veterans or their families as a consequence of disability or death from service-connected causes.
2. Pension benefits attributable to non-service-connected causes. (The actual amount of the benefits is tied mainly to need, rather than to length of service, compensation, or rank. These benefits are in addition to the traditional pension benefits available to career military personnel.)
3. Medical benefits to be provided at VA facilities. (The VA makes no promises to veterans as to the availability or level of care. Congress decides annually on the level of funding.)

Be sure to present your response in the context of FASAB-established principles or issues under consideration as discussed in the text.

16-3

The primary statements of a federal agency can be constructed from the proprietary and budget accounts.

The following balances, in trial balance form, were drawn from the year-end ledgers of the Federal Lending Agency (a fictitious entity) following the agency's first year of operations. Some of the accounts are aggregations of those that would typically be maintained by a federal entity. Budgetary (as opposed to proprietary) accounts are marked with an asterisk.

	Debit	Credit
	(in millions)	
Various expenses	$ 219	
Miscellaneous revenues		$ 93
Appropriations used		412
Fund balance with the treasury	1,140	
Loans receivable	126	
Equipment	80	
Allowance for depreciation		16
Accounts payable and other liabilities		256
Unexpended appropriations		788
Cumulative results of operation, beginning of year	0	
Current appropriations	1,200*	
Borrowing authority	160*	
Obligations incurred		640*
Funds available for commitment		720*
	$2,925	$2,925

1. Following the formats illustrated in the text, prepare the following statements:
   a. A statement of net cost
   b. A statement of changes in net position
   c. A balance sheet
   d. A statement of budgetary resources (omitting the section on outlays)
2. Review the amounts on the financial statements.
   a. Do the cumulative results of operations per the balance sheet agree with the cumulative results of operations per the statement of changes in net position?
   b. Are the unexpended appropriations per the balance sheet equal to the appropriations received per the statement of budgetary resources less the appropriations used per the statement of changes in net position?

16-4

Federal revenues may be accounted for and reported in an unusual manner.

A federal environmental agency engaged in the following transactions during a particular year.

1. It billed corporations for which it provided services $160 million. Of this it collected $140 million.
2. It levied $150 million in fines and penalties against corporations. Of this, $90 million was collected in cash. Of the balance, the protest period has expired on $35 million, which the agency expects to collect in the following year. The remaining $25 million is in dispute and court dates have not yet been set.
3. It collected an additional $20 million in fines and penalties that had been assessed by federal courts in the previous period.
4. It received cash donations of $3 million and pledges of an additional $2 million. The agency's counsel advises that the pledges are not legally enforceable.
   a. Prepare journal entries to record the revenues and collections.
   b. Show how the revenues and related receivables would be reported on the agency's balance sheet and statement of net cost (i.e., an operating statement).

16-5

Loan guarantee costs should be reported mainly in the year the guarantees are made.

To help middle-income students finance the cost of their university educations, the Student Loan Authority guarantees student loans made by private banks. By guaranteeing the loans, the agency enables the banks to make the loans at rates far lower than they would without the guarantees.

In 2004, the agency guaranteed $120 million of loans. It estimates that, owing to student defaults, it will have to fulfill its guarantees as follows (in millions):

Year	Amount
2005	$0.5
2006	1.2
2007	2.0
2008	1.8

1. Prepare the entry that the agency should make in 2004, the year it guarantees the loans. The agency applies a discount rate of 6 percent. It assumes that all guarantee payments will be made at the end of the indicated years.
2. Prepare the entry that it should make at the end of 2005, assuming that it fulfills its guarantees, as estimated, of $0.5 million.

16-6

The reported value of inventory depends on its type.

The Department of Agriculture maintains an educational division that sells publications to the general public.

In a recent year, the division reported publication sales of $3,850,000. At the start of the year, it had inventory on hand that had cost $620,000. Based on latest invoice prices, however, the inventory would be valued at $650,000. During the year, it purchased publications for $3,500,000 and sold publications that had cost $3,335,000. Its year-end inventory was $770,000 at cost and $830,000 at latest acquisition cost.

1. Show how the division would report its beginning and ending inventory on a comparative balance sheet, assuming that it values inventory at latest acquisition cost.
2. Prepare an operating statement for the year, assuming no operating costs other than cost of goods sold.
3. Suppose, instead, that the inventory maintained by the division was in agricultural commodities held for use in a natural disaster. Indicate the main difference in how it would be accounted for.

16-7

When should the costs of subsidized loan programs be recognized?

In 2005, Congress established a small business direct loan program. The program provides that qualifying businesses can obtain loans at a rate 5 percent below that prevailing on Treasury securities of comparable maturity. The program was to be in effect for a period of twelve years. Its total cost was estimated at $1.3 billion.

In 2006, the Small Business Administration, which administers the program, loaned the S & D Produce Company $100,000 for ten years at a rate of 5 percent. At the time, the prevailing Treasury rate was 10 percent. The loan was to be repaid in ten annual installments of $12,950.

1. What journal entry should the Small Business Administration make in 2005 when Congress authorized the program? Explain and justify your response.
2. What journal entry should it make in 2006 when it loaned the S & D Produce Company $100,000? Explain and justify your response.
3. What journal entries should it make in 2007 and 2008 upon collection of the first two loan repayments?

16-8

Federal expenditures raise unique issues of recognition

In 2005 the federal government was affected by the following transactions and events. For each, indicate the amount that it should recognize as an expense during 2005. Cite the FASAB principle upon which you rely.

1. The government ordered ten military aircraft from a manufacturer at a cost of $40 million each. During the year it received five and paid for two. Their expected useful life is ten years.
2. In response to extraordinary floods, Congress appropriated $2.4 billion in disaster relief. Some of the aid was targeted for infrastructure repair. During the year, the government contracted with a construction firm to repair a bridge at an agreed-upon price of $1.2 million. The contractor completed a portion of the job, billing the government for $600,000.
3. As part of the same flood-relief program, the government authorized direct grants to individuals and businesses. During the year, it approved grants totaling $400 million, of which it actually paid $240 million. It expected to pay the balance in the following year.
4. To assist workers laid off as the result of a recently passed free-trade agreement, Congress approved an employee relief act. The act provides that eligible employees would receive direct payments of $500 per month for up to twelve months. The cost of the program over its lifetime is expected to be $380 million. During the year, 25,000 laid-off workers applied, and were certified as eligible for benefits. They were paid a total of $50 million.
5. During the year the employees of one government agency earned pension benefits having an actuarial present value of $30 million. The government made actual payments of $23 million to employees who had previously retired from that agency.

16-9

Federal long-lived assets have unique characteristics justifying unique accounting practices.

For each of the following assets acquired by federal departments and agencies, indicate how the government should report the asset. If it is to be reported on the government's balance sheets, then state whether it should be amortized or depreciated. Justify your response by specifying the category into which the asset would fall.

1. The U.S. Coast Guard purchases for $3 million a mainframe computer to be used to enhance nonmilitary navigation systems.
2. The Department of Defense purchases a mainframe computer for $6 million. The computer is specially designed to be used on board a guided-missile cruiser to target missiles.
3. The Department of Agriculture acquires for $20 million products that it intends to resell. At year-end, based on latest acquisition costs, the market value of these goods has increased to $21 million.
4. The Department of Interior constructs a monument, at a cost of $7 million, honoring the military personnel who served in the Gulf War.
5. The Department of Interior purchases land in Bethesda, Maryland, for $6 million. It expects to construct an office complex on the land.
6. The Department of the Interior purchases land in East Glacier, Montana, for $130 million. The land will be incorporated into Glacier National Park.
7. NASA incurs $24 million to improve facilities at its Johnson Space Center. The facilities are to be used both as a training center for astronauts and other personnel and as a museum for visitors.

16-10

Federal statements may understate both assets and liabilities.

Review the government-wide statements as presented in Table 16-2 of the text.

1. What was the amount of the government's deficit for the year? What was the amount of its net position?
2. What three departments incurred the largest amount of expenses (gross)?
3. What was the government's main source of revenues?
4. The government's balance sheet excludes a significant amount of both assets and liabilities. What government-owned assets are omitted from the balance sheet? What liabilities are omitted?
5. Suppose that the federal government would change the paydays of certain employees from the last day of each month to the first day of the next (a classic means of decreasing budgetary expenditures for a particular year). Would that gimmick reduce the net cost of operations as reported in the statement of net cost?
6. The statement of net cost indicates the gross cost of the Social Security program to be $492.9 billion. No "earned revenues" are attributed to the program. Where in the financial statements is it most likely that the related revenues (i.e., payroll taxes) are reported? What justification is there for not reporting these revenues as earned revenues of the Social Security program?

SOLUTION TO EXERCISE FOR REVIEW AND SELF-TESTING

1. The unexpended appropriation would be shown on the Commission's balance sheet as "Fund Balance with the Treasury." It would also be included in the equity (net position) account "Unexpended Appropriations."
2. Donations should be recognized upon the receipt of a legally binding pledge. Hence, the entire $2 million should be recognized as revenue.
3. The sales and cost of goods sold would be reported as follows:

Sales		$900,000
Cost of goods sold		
beginning inventory at beginning-of-the-period latest acquisition cost	$ 0	
Less: allowance for unrealized holding gains at the beginning of the period	(0)	
Plus: purchases	1,000,000	
Cost of goods available for sale	$1,000,000	
Less: ending inventory at end-of-the-period latest acquisition cost	(300,000)	
Plus: allowance for unrealized holding gains at the end of the period	50,000	
Cost of goods sold		750,000
Net results		$150,000

4. The cost of subsidizing the loan is the difference between the loan's face value ($400,000) and the present value of the anticipated receipts (three payments of $144,139 discounted at 8 percent). The present value of the three payments is $371,461 ($144,139 times 2.5771, the present value of an annuity of $1 for three periods discounted at 8 percent). The difference is $28,539. The Commission should recognize this amount as an expense of the period in which it makes the loan.
5. The assets should be accounted for as follows:
   a. Buildings are general assets and should be capitalized and depreciated over their useful lives.
   b. The land to be used for an office building is also a general asset and should therefore be capitalized (but not, of course, depreciated).
   c. The land to be used as a wildlife refuge is a stewardship asset. It should be expensed when acquired and in that year and subsequent years described in a stewardship report.
6. The Commission's obligation is the consequence of a "government-acknowledged event"—an occurrence for which the government is not responsible but elects, as a matter of policy, to provide relief to the victims. The government should recognize a liability and corresponding expense for such an event when it formally acknowledges financial responsibility and an amount is due and payable. Thus, the Commission need not recognize any liability or expense for the damages until an amount is due and payable.

GLOSSARY

2a7-like investment pool A government external investment pool that operates similarly to investment companies subject to the Security and Exchange Commission's Rule 2a7 of the Investment Company Act of 1940. These companies invest in securities, such as Treasury bills, notes, and certificates of deposit, that are both safe and have short-maturities—typically sixty days or less—and hence are not subject to major price swings.

A

account group An accounting entity with a set of accounts that is self-balancing and is used to account for a government's general fixed assets or general long-term obligations. Account groups are distinguished from funds in that they are not used to account for sources, uses, and balances of expendable available financial resources. Account groups were an integral part of the "old" accounting model; they are no longer needed under the model prescribed by GASB Statement No. 34.

ABC *See* **activity-based costing.**

accrual basis A method of accounting that recognizes revenues when earned and expenses when incurred regardless of when cash is received or paid.

accrued expenses Expenses that have been incurred and recorded, but have not yet been paid.

accrued revenue Revenue that has been earned and recorded, but not yet received.

activity A line of work contributing to a function or program.

activity-based costing (ABC) A method of costing where overhead costs are collected in cost pools and distributed to particular products or services using cost drivers. *See* **cost driver.**

actuarial accrued liability A government's pension obligation as determined by an appropriate actuarial cost method.

actuarial cost method A means of allocating the total cost of expected pension benefits over the total years of employee service.

ad valorem property taxes Property taxes based on the value of the property.

advance refunding Issuance of debt to retire outstanding bonds or other debt instruments prior to their maturity or call date.

affiliated organization A legally independent entity directly tied to a primary government. May be distinguished from both a component unit and a related organization (as defined in GASB Statement No. 14, *The Financial Reporting Entity*) in that the primary government does not appoint a majority of its governing board and it is not fiscally dependent upon the primary government.

agency fund A fund used to account for assets that a government holds temporarily for other parties (e.g., for taxes collected on their behalf).

agent A party that acts on behalf of another. For example, a government that collects taxes for another government.

allocated costs Costs that cannot be associated directly with specific products or services, but are assigned to them according to a predetermined formula or algorithm.

allot To divide a budgetary appropriation into amounts that may be encumbered or expended during an allotment period (e.g., a government may choose to allot its annual budget to twelve monthly periods), or for specified programs or activities.

allotments Periodic allocations of funds to departments or agencies to assure that an entire year's appropriation is not expended early in the period covered by the budget or expended for certain programs or activities to the detriment of others.

American Institute of Certified Public Accountants (AICPA) A professional organization for certified public accountants (CPAs) that is responsible for establishing auditing and related professional standards.

amortization (1) The process of allocating the cost of an intangible asset over its useful life. (2) The reduction of debt by regular payments of principal and interest sufficient to retire the debt by maturity.

annual pension cost A measure of a government's cost of maintaining or participating in a defined benefit pension plan. Per GASB Statement No. 27, the annual pension cost is the annual required contribution subject to adjustments that take into account interest on, and amortization of, any net pension obligations.

annual report The financial report of a business, government, or not-for-profit entity. Typically consists of a balance sheet, operating statement, statement of changes in equity, a statement of cash flows, and other supplementary information.

annual required contribution (ARC) An employer's annual required contribution to a defined benefit pension plan as determined in accordance with specified GASB parameters.

annuity A series of equal payments over a specified number of equal time periods.

annuity fund An endowment fund to account for gifts that provide fixed payments to the donor (or a person designated by the donor) for a specified term or for the remainder of his or her life. Thereafter, what remains of the gift will typically revert to the recipient organization.

apportionment The shares of a total federal appropriation that the Office of Management and Budget permits an agency to spend within a particular time period (such as a quarter) or for designated programs, activities, or projects.

appropriation An amount authorized by a legislative body for a department or to make expenditures and incur liabilities for a specified purpose.

appropriations budget The legislatively approved budget that grants expenditure authority to departments and other governmental units in accordance with applicable laws.

arbitrage The concurrent purchase and sale of the same or an equivalent security in order to profit from differences in interest rates. Generally, as it relates to state and local governments, the issuance of debt at relatively low, tax-exempt, rates of interest and the investment of the proceeds in taxable securities yielding a higher rate of return.

assess To value property for the purpose of property taxes.

attest To affirm to be correct, true, or genuine; corroborate. The attest function (i.e., an audit) adds credibility to the assertions of others; in the case of a financial audit, credibility is added to an entity's financial data as presented by management.

attestation engagements Services provided by audit organizations that cover a broader scope than financial statements audits. They involve performing agreed-upon procedures as to various types of management assertions or types of transactions or processes that do no necessarily have a direct impact on the financial statements. These might include: an entity's internal accounting or administrative controls; compliance with rules, regulations, or terms of contracts; prospective or pro-forma financial statements; and costs of contracts.

audit A systematic investigation or review to corroborate the assertions of others or to determine whether operations have conformed to prescribed criteria or standards. An examination of records to check their accuracy.

auxiliary enterprises Units of colleges, universities, or other not-for-profit entities that charge for the services they provide and whose activities are conducted on a business-type basis. Examples include intercollegiate athletics, bookstores, and dining facilities.

B

basis of accounting The means of determining the timing of revenue and expenditure recognition. *See also* **cash basis** and **accrual basis.**

benefit-cost analysis A generic term for any form of expenditure analysis that identifies and quantifies the benefits of a proposal and compares them to its costs.

bequest To give property by will.

betterment An addition or modification to a capital asset that either enhances its useful life or increases its productivity. Contrasted with maintenance.

blending One of two methods of reporting components units required by GASB Statement No. 14, *The Financial Reporting Entity* (*see* **discrete presentation** for a description of the other method). This method combines a component unit's transactions and balances with the data of the primary government as if the component unit were a part of that government.

bond A written promise to pay a specified sum of money (its face value) at one or more specified times in the future along with periodic interest. Bonds are a form of notes payable but are characterized by longer periods of maturity and more formal documentation.

bond anticipation notes (BANs) Short-term interest-bearing notes issued by a lender in the expectation that they will soon be replaced by long-term bonds.

bond discount At issue date, the excess of a bond's stated (par) value over the bond's initial sales (issue) price. Bonds are issued at a discount so that the return to investors will be equal to the prevailing market interest rate, even though the prevailing market interest rate may be higher than the interest rate stated on the bond (the coupon rate). At later dates, bond discount is the excess of a bond's stated value over the bond's initial price plus the portion of the discount already amortized.

bond premium The same as bond discount except that the bond's initial sales price exceeds the bond's stated (par) value.

bond rating agencies Companies, the leading ones being Standard & Poor's (S&P), Moody's Investors Service, and Fitch IBCA, that evaluate bonds or other securities based on the likelihood that the issuer will not default on payments of principal or interest.

bond refunding The issuance of new bonds to replace bonds already outstanding, usually with the intent of reducing debt service costs.

book value The value of an asset or liability as reported on financial statements; distinguished from market value.

budget A plan of financial operations embodying an estimate of proposed expenditures for a given period and the proposed means of financing them.

budgetary accounts Accounts used to enter a formally adopted annual operating budget into the general ledger so as to enhance management control over revenues and expenditures.

budgetary control The control or management of a government or enterprise in accordance with an approved budget to keep expenditures within the limitations of available appropriations and available revenues.

business-type activities Activities engaged in by a government or not-for-profit entity that are similar in nature to those carried out by businesses; activities that are financed in whole or in part by fees charged to external parties for goods or services.

C

CAFR *See* **Comprehensive Annual Financial Report.**

call price A predetermined price at which the issuer of bonds may redeem (call) the bonds irrespective of the current market price.

callable bond A bond that permits the issuer to redeem the obligation at a specified price before the stated maturity date.

capital assets Long-term assets, such as buildings, equipment, and infrastructure, intended to be held or used in operations; sometimes referred to as "fixed" assets.

capital budget A plan of proposed capital outlays, such as for infrastructure, buildings, equipment and other long-lived assets, and of the means of financing them.

capital debt Long-term debt issued to finance capital assets.

capital expenditures Expenditures to acquire or construct capital assets.

capital improvement program (CIP) A plan for the acquisition of capital assets over several (typically five) years.

capital lease A lease which is essentially an installment purchase and meets the criteria of FASB Statement No. 13, *Accounting for Leases.* The lessee ("purchaser") records the acquired property as an asset and correspondingly recognizes the present value of the agreed upon lease payments as a liability.

capital projects fund A fund to account for financial resources set aside for the acquisition or construction of major capital facilities.

capitation fee A fee, paid by an insurance company or other third-party payor to a health care organization, that is based on number of persons covered rather than on actual services provided.

cash basis A method of accounting in which revenues and expenses are recognized and recorded when received, not necessarily when earned.

cash equivalents Short-term, highly liquid investments that can readily be converted into fixed amounts of cash.

cash flow statement A financial statement that details the inflows and outflows of cash.

certificate of participation (COP) A long-term debt instrument that, although similar in economic substance to a bond, is secured by a long-term capital lease.

Chief Financial Officer of the United States The Deputy Director for Management, a position created by the Chief Financial Officers Act of 1990. He or she is responsible for providing overall direction and leadership in the establishment of sound federal financial practices.

Codification of the Government Accounting Standards Board *Governmental Accounting and Financial Reporting Standards*, a compendium of GASB promulgated accounting principles, including those adopted from predecessor standard-setting organizations.

cognizant agency Under the Single Audit Act, a federal agency responsible for coordinating the special requirements of each federal agency that provides funds to the auditee and assuring that all audit standards are met; typically the federal agency providing the greatest amount of funds to the auditee.

collateral Assets pledged to secure deposits, investments, or loans.

collectibles Works of art, rare books, and historical artifacts.

combined statements The five basic statements that constitute General Purpose Financial Statements (GPFS) under the "old" model. They include the (1) combined balance sheet all fund types and account groups; (2) combined statement of revenues, expenditures, and changes in fund balances—all governmental fund types; (3) combined statement of revenues, expenditures, and changes in fund balances—budget and actual for general and special revenues funds (and other governmental fund types for which annual budgets have been legally adopted); (4) combined statement of revenues, expenses, and changes in retained earnings—all proprietary funds; and (5) combined statement of changes in financial position—all proprietary fund types.

combining statements Financial statements that provide the details of individual funds (e.g., nonmajor funds or internal service funds) that might be combined in higher level statements. A statement in which each fund is displayed in a separate column and in which a "totals" column ties into amounts reported in another statement.

Common Rule *See* **Uniform Administrative Requirements for Grants and Cooperative Agreements to State and Local Governments.**

compensated absences Absences, such as vacations, illness, and holidays, for which it is expected employees will be paid. The term does not encompass severance or termination pay, post-retirement benefits, deferred compensation, or other long-term fringe benefits, such as group insurance and long-term disability pay.

compliance audit An audit designed to provide reasonable assurance that an auditee has complied with applicable laws, regulations and contractual agreements.

compliance requirements A set of fourteen requirements that involve policies and practices to which all federal funds recipients must adhere. Examples are those pertaining to cash management, allowable costs, eligibility, and subrecipient monitoring.

component unit Per GASB Statement No. 14, *The Financial Reporting Entity*, a legally separate government for which the elected officials of a primary government are financially accountable, can impose their will, or there is the potential for the organization to provide special financial benefits to, or impose specific financial burdens on, the primary government.

Comprehensive Annual Financial Report (CAFR) The official annual report of a state or local government. It includes introductory materials (such as a letter of transmittal and auditors report) financial statements (and supporting notes and supplementary schedules) and statistical data.

Comptroller General of the United States The head of the General Accounting Office (GAO).

conditional promise A promise to donate an asset or provide a service in the future that is contingent on a specified future event.

conduit debt Obligations issued in the name of a government on behalf of a nongovernmental entity. The debt is expected to be serviced entirely by the nongovernmental unit.

consolidated statements Statements in which two or more funds are combined so that they are reported as if they were a single economic entity.

constant dollar cost The cost of goods or services in dollars that have been adjusted to take into account changes in the general level of prices (i.e., inflation).

consumption method A method of accounting for inventories and prepaid costs, such as rent, in which goods or services are recorded as expenditures or expenses when used rather than when purchased; differentiated from the purchases method.

contingent grants Grants contingent upon a specified occurrence or action on the part of the recipient (e.g., the ability of the recipient to raise resources from other parties).

contingent liability An obligation that must be paid only if certain events occur (such as when a government guarantees the debt of another party and that party defaults on the guaranteed obligation).

contracting out Engaging an outside, private-sector firm to provide services that have previously been performed in-house; also known as outsourcing or privatizing.

contributed capital The permanent capital of a proprietary fund, generally resulting from transfers from other funds, or from grants or customer fees restricted to capital acquisition or construction. Per GASB Statement No. 34, contributed capital is no longer reported separately from other net assets.

control account An account in the general ledger in which is recorded the aggregate of debit and credit postings to a number of related accounts called subsidiary accounts.

cost accounting The method of accounting that provides for the assembling and recording of all the elements of cost incurred to accomplish a purpose, to carry on an activity or operation, or to complete a unit of work or a specific job.

cost-benefit analysis *See* **benefit-cost analysis**.

cost driver A basis for allocating overhead to particular products or services that is conceptually similar to an overhead charging rate. However, whereas in practice an overhead charging rate is based on broadly representative factors (such as direct labor dollars, direct labor hours, or direct materials) that influence the amount of overhead costs incurred, a cost driver is more specifically indicative of the factors affecting overhead. Examples include materials requisitions, machine hours, and maintenance costs.

coupon rate The stated interest rate on the face of a bond; a bond's nominal interest rate.

credit risk The risk that a party to a contract, such as a borrower, will be unable to make its contractually required payments.

current assets In business and not-for-profit accounting, cash and other resources that are expected to be converted into cash during the normal operating cycle of the entity or within one year, whichever is longer. In government accounting, the assets that are available to meet the cost of operations or satisfy liabilities of the current year.

current financial resources In government accounting, the cash or other assets that will be converted into cash soon enough thereafter to satisfy the obligations of the current period.

current fund The general or main operating fund of a not-for-profit organization.

current liabilities In business and not-for-profit accounting, financial obligations that are reasonably expected to be paid using current assets or by creating other current liabilities within one year or the entity's operating cycle, whichever is longer. In governmental accounting, obligations that are expected to be met from funds appropriated for the current period.

custodial risk The risk that if a financial institution fails a depositor will be unable to recover its deposit in, or securities held by, that institution. Also, the risk that an investor or lender will be unable to recover collateral held by an outside party.

D

debt limit The maximum amount of debt that an entity is permitted to incur by constitutional provision or statute.

debt margin The difference between the amount of debt outstanding computed according to applicable legal provisions and the maximum amount of debt that can legally be issued.

debt refunding *See* **bond refunding.**

debt service fund A fund to account for financial resources set aside for the payment of interest and principal on long-term debt; a sinking fund.

decision package The key element of a zero-base budget in which the entity indicates the objectives of the activity for which funding is proposed, alternative means of accomplishing the same objectives; consequences of not performing the activity, and inputs, outputs, and outcomes at various levels of funding.

defeasance A transaction that annuls or voids a liability or other contractual arrangement. *See* **in-substance defeasance.**

deferred maintenance costs The costs that an entity avoided in a current year or past years by failing to perform required routine maintenance and repairs, but that will have to be incurred in the future.

deferred revenue Receipts of cash or other assets for which asset recognition criteria have been met, but for which revenue recognition criteria have not been met. For example, taxes received in the period prior to that in which they are due.

deficit (1) The excess of liabilities and reserved equity of a fund over its assets. (2) The excess of expenditures over revenues during an accounting period; or in the case of proprietary funds, the excess of expenses over revenues.

defined benefit pension plan A pension plan that specifies the pension benefits to be paid to retirees, usually as a function of factors such as age, years of service, and compensation.

defined contribution pension plan A pension plan that specifies the amount of contributions to an individual's retirement account instead of the amount of benefits the individual is to receive. Under a defined contribution pension plan, the benefits a participant will receive depend on the amount contributed to the participant's account and the returns earned on investments of those contributions.

demand bonds Long-term debt instruments with demand ("put") provisions that require the issuer to repurchase the bonds, upon notice from the bondholder, at a specified price that is usually equal to the principal plus accrued interest. To ensure their ability to redeem the bonds, issuers of demand bonds frequently enter into standby liquidity agreements ("takeout" agreements) with banks or other financial institutions.

depreciation The systematic and rational allocation of the cost of tangible noncurrent operating assets over the periods benefited by the use of the assets.

derivative A financial asset whose value is derived from the shift in the price of an underlying asset, such as a bond, or an index of asset values, such as the Standard & Poors' index of 500 stocks, or an index of interest rates.

derived tax revenues Tax revenues that are based on exchange transactions between parties other than the taxing government. Examples include sales taxes and income taxes.

diagnosis-related groups (DRGs) Under Medicare, a classification scheme of patient conditions used for purposes of reimbursement. Hospitals or other health-care providers receive fixed amounts based on the diagnosis of patients' conditions rather than on the amounts they actually spend to treat the patients.

direct costs Costs such as for labor and materials, directly associated with specific products or activities of an organization. Distinguished from indirect (overhead) costs.

direct debt Debt of a government unit itself, as opposed to that of governments with overlapping boundaries.

discrete presentation One of two methods of reporting component units required by GASB Statement No. 14, *The Financial Reporting Entity* (*see* **blending** for description of the other method). This method reports the component unit in a single column separate from the data of the primary government (as if the unit were another fund). For example, a state government might report its state-owned power authorities in a single column.

donated assets Assets, other than cash, donated to an organization.

donated services Services provided for no charge to an organization by individual volunteers or businesses.

donor-imposed restriction A stipulation by one who contributes to a not-for-profit organization that a contribution must be used for a purpose more specific than indicated by the organization's general goals.

due from (to) other funds An asset (liability) account used to indicate amounts owed to (by) one fund by (to) another.

E

economic cost The full cost of goods or services, as opposed to that which might be recognized for financial accounting. For example, the full amount of compensation to be paid by a government, including that of pensions and compensated absences, rather than merely the amount paid to the employees in a current period.

economic gain (loss) In the context of an advance refunding, the difference between the present value of the old debt service requirements and the present value of the new debt service requirements, discounted at the effective interest rate and adjusted for additional cash paid.

encumbrances Commitments to purchase goods or services.

endowment A sum of cash, investments, or other assets, generally received as gift, of which only the income, not the principal, may be expended.

enterprise fund A proprietary fund established to account for operations financed and operated in a manner similar to a private business (e.g., water, gas and electric utilities; airports; parking garages; and transit systems). Per GASB Statement No. 34, an enterprise fund may be used to account for any activity for which a fee is charged to external users for goods or services. It must be used to account for an activity financed with revenue debt, when laws or regulations require that an activity's costs be recovered with fees and charges or when pricing policies dictate that fees and charges be established to cover the activity's costs.

entitlements Payments, usually from a higher-level government, to which a state or local government or an individual is entitled as a matter of law in an amount determined by a specified formula.

equity transfer *See* **residual equity transfer.**

escheat property Private property that has reverted to a government owing to lack of heirs or claimants or because of a breach of a condition.

escheat trust fund A fiduciary fund used to account for escheat property.

exchange revenues Revenues that arise from sales transactions in which each party receives benefits and incurs costs.

exchange transaction A sales-type transaction in which goods and services are exchanged for consideration of approximately equal value.

exchange-like transaction *See* **quasi-external transactions.**

expendable funds Governmental funds whose resources are received from taxes, fees, or other sources and may be expended ("spent"); the governmental as opposed to the proprietary funds of a government.

expendable trust funds Funds used to account for assets over which the entity acts as a trustee; distinguished from nonexpendable trust funds in that both principal and income may be spent.

expenditures Decreases in net financial resources under the modified accrual basis of accounting.

expenses Decreases in overall net assets from delivering services or producing goods under the full accrual basis.

exposure draft A preliminary version of a standard-setting authority's official pronouncement, issued as means of obtaining public comment.

external report A report issued for use by parties outside the reporting entity, such as citizens, investors, and creditors, as opposed to inside parties, such as managers.

external subsidy An amount of money, generally a grant, received by a governmental entity from a nongovernmental source.

extraordinary items Transactions or other events that are both unusual in nature and infrequent in occurrence. Per GASB Statement No. 34, these items, unlike *special items*, are outside the control of management. *See also* **special items.**

F

face value As applied to securities, the amount indicated on the face of a bond that will have to be paid at maturity.

FASAB *See* **Federal Accounting Standards Advisory Board.**

FASB *See* **Financial Accounting Standards Board.**

Federal Accounting Standards Advisory Board (FASAB) The federal board charged with establishing federal accounting standards.

federal funds The federal government's general fund, special funds and most revolving funds.

fiduciary activities Per GASB Statement No. 34, a government's activities for which the government acts as a trustee or agent for individuals, external organizations, or other governments.

fiduciary funds The trust and agency funds used to account for assets held by a government unit in a trustee capacity or as an agent for individuals, private organizations, other government units, or other funds.

Financial Accounting Standards Board (FASB) The organization responsible for establishing external accounting and reporting standards for all nongovernmental entities, including not-for-profit organizations.

financial audit An examination or review made to determine whether financial statements or related financial reports conform to generally accepted accounting principles or other prescribed criteria.

financial resources Cash, investments and receivables, and other assets that can be expected to be transformed into cash in the normal course of operations. Financial resources minus the current claims against them equals net financial resources.

financial related audits In the context of federal auditing, these determine whether financial reports, including those on specific funds or accounts, are either fairly presented or presented in accordance with stated criteria, and whether the entity has complied with specific financial-related requirements, such as those set forth in laws and regulations, grants, and contracts.

financial statement audits Examinations that determine whether an entity's financial statements are presented fairly in accordance with generally accepted accounting principles and whether the entity has complied with laws and regulations that may have a material effect on the financial statements.

fiscal capacity The economic base that the government can draw upon for the resources necessary to provide the goods or services expected of it.

fiscal effort The extent to which a government is taking advantage of its fiscal capacity. Generally measured by comparing the revenues that the government generates from its own sources (i.e., total revenue excluding grants from other governments) with either the wealth or income of its taxpayers.

fiscal funding clause A clause in a lease agreement providing that the lease is cancelable if the legislature or other funding authority does not appropriate the funds necessary for the government unit to fulfill its obligations under the lease agreement.

fiscal period (year) Any period at the end of which a government determines its financial position and the results of its operations; also accounting period.

fixed assets Long-lived tangible assets, such as buildings, equipment, improvements other than buildings and land.

fixed assets account group *See* **general fixed assets account group**.

fixed budget A budget in which costs and revenues are fixed—i.e., not subject to change as a result of increases or decreases in the volume of goods or services to be provided.

fixed costs Costs of goods or services that do not vary with the volume of goods or services provided (e.g., rent, interest, executive salaries, and air-conditioning costs).

flexible budget A budget in which dollar amounts vary according to the volume of goods or services to be provided.

full cost The cost of goods or services that includes both direct and indirect (overhead) costs.

full faith and credit A government's pledge, usually incorporated into bond indentures, to back a bond issue with its full taxing authority.

functional classification Expenditures that are grouped according to the purpose for which they are made, such as public safety, general administration, or recreation.

fund A fiscal and accounting entity with a self-balancing set of accounts used to account for resources, and claims against them, that are segregated in accord with legal or contractual restrictions or to carry out specific activities.

fund accounting An accounting system in which an entity's resources are divided among two or more accounting entities known as funds.

fund balance The net assets (assets minus liabilities) of a fund.

fund financial statements Financial statements of a government required by GASB Statement No. 34 that report on one or more funds. Governmental fund statements are on a modified accrual basis; business-type fund statements are on a full accrual basis.

funded pension plan A pension plan in which contributions are made and assets are accumulated to pay benefits to potential recipients before cash payments to recipients actually are required; as opposed to a pay-as-you-go plan.

funded ratio The ratio, associated with pension plans, of the actuarial value of assets to the actuarially accrued liabilities.

funding policy In the context of pension plans, the policy that determines the amounts and timing of contributions to be made by plan employees, employers, and any other parties to accumulate the resources required to pay retirees their specified benefits.

fund type A fund category. In government accounting, any one of several categories into which all funds are classified. These include general, special revenue, debt service, capital projects, permanent, enterprise, internal service, and agency.

G

GASB *See* **Governmental Accounting Standards Board.**

General Accounting Office (GAO) The congressional agency responsible for conducting financial and performance audits of federal agencies, programs, and activities and for carrying out other accounting and finance-related activities of the federal government.

general capital assets Capital assets that are not assets of any particular fund, but of the government unit as a whole. Most often these assets arise from the expenditure of the financial resources of governmental (as opposed to proprietary or fiduciary) funds.

general fixed assets account group (GFAAG) Under the "old" model, a group or list of accounts in which the general fixed (capital) assets of a governmental unit are recorded.

general fund A fund used to account for unrestricted resources. The fund that accounts for all resources that are not required to be accounted for in other funds.

general journal A journal in which all entries are recorded, excluding those recorded in special journals.

general ledger A record containing the accounts needed to reflect an entity's financial position and results of operations.

general long-term debt account group (GLTDAG) Under the "old" model, a self-balancing group of accounts established to account for the unmatured general long-term debt of a government. The GLTDAG was also used to report the portion of liabilities, such as for claims, judgments, compensated absences, and unfunded pension contributions of governmental funds and expendable trust funds, that was not expected to be liquidated through the use of expendable available financial resources.

general obligation debt Debt that is secured by the full faith and credit of the issuing body.

generally accepted accounting principles (GAAP) Uniform minimum standards and guidelines for financial accounting and reporting that govern the form and content of financial statements. They encompass the conventions, rules, and procedures necessary to define accepted accounting practice at a particular time.

generally accepted auditing standards (GAAS) Standards established by the AICPA for the conduct and reporting of financial audits.

generally accepted government auditing standards (GAGAS) Standards established by the GAO in its publication *Standards for Audit of Governmental Organizations, Programs, Activities and Functions* (the Yellow Book) for the conduct and reporting of both financial and performance audits.

general property, plant, and equipment A classification of assets in the federal government that represents property plant and equipment used for general purposes; distinguished from stewardship assets.

general purpose financial statements (GPFS) Per the "old" model, the five combined financial statements that, together with accompanying notes, constitute the minimum level of financial reporting needed for fair presentation in conformity with GAAP.

government-assessed taxes Taxes, such as property taxes, assessed by the government in which the government determines the amount owed. Distinguished from taxpayer-assessed taxes, such as income taxes, in which the parties other than the government determine the amount owed.

government-wide statements Statements required by GASB Statement No. 34 that report on all of a government's activities (both governmental and business-type) and are on full accrual basis. These statements are distinguished from *fund* financial statements.

governmental accounting The composite activity of analyzing, recording, summarizing, reporting, and interpreting the financial transactions of governments.

Governmental Accounting Standards Board (GASB) The authoritative accounting and financial reporting standard-setting body for government entities.

governmental activities Activities of a government that are financed predominantly through taxes and intergovernmental grants; distinguished from business-type activities.

government-mandated nonexchange transactions Transactions that occur when a government at one level (e.g., the federal or a state government) provides resources to a government at another level (e.g., a local government or school district) and requires that the recipient use the resources for a specific purpose. For example, a state may grant funds to a county stipulating that the resources be used for road improvements. Acceptance and use of the resources are mandatory.

Government Accounting Standards (Standards for Audit of Government Organizations, Programs, Activities and Functions) The auditing standards of the GAO; the Yellow Book.

Government Auditing Standards (GAS) *See* **generally accepted government auditing standards (GAGAS).**

Government Finance Officers Association (GFOA) An association of state and local governments and officials and other individuals interested in state and local government finance.

governmental funds Funds used to account for the acquisition, use, and balances of expendable financial resources and the related current liabilities, except those accounted for in proprietary funds and fiduciary funds; the five governmental fund types are general, special revenue, debt service, capital projects, and permanent.

grant A contribution from one party to another to be used or expended for a specified purpose, activity, or facility; ordinarily distinguished from an exchange transaction in that the grantor does not receive compensation in return for the resources contributed.

H

Health Maintenance Organization (HMO) An organization that provides health care on a prepaid basis (i.e., patients or their employers pay a fixed annual fee regardless of actual services rendered by the organization).

heritage assets As defined by the Federal Accounting Standards Advisory Board, assets that have value because of their historical, cultural, educational, or artistic significance.

historical cost The purchase price or construction cost plus any additional costs incurred in placing an asset in its intended location, condition, and purpose, less accumulated depreciation or amortization.

human capital As defined by the FASAB, outlays for education and training of the public intended to increase the nation's productive capacity.

I

impact fees Fees charged to developers by a governmental entity for costs of anticipated improvements, such as sidewalks and parks, that will be necessary as a result of a development.

impaired asset A capital asset whose service utility has declined significantly and unexpectedly as a consequence of physical damage, technological obsolescence, changes in the laws, or financial reversals and whose book value may thereby have to be reduced.

imposed nonexchange revenues Assessments imposed on individuals and business entities, the most prominent of which are property taxes and fines.

income The excess of an enterprise's revenue over its expenses.

independent sector The sector of the economy that is composed of not-for-profit organizations (as opposed to governmental and business entities).

indirect costs Costs that are related to an activity or object but cannot be directly traced to that activity; overhead costs; distinguished from direct costs.

industrial development bonds Bonds issued by governmental units at low interest rates to encourage private development in their area. Repayment of the debt is expected to be the responsibility of the beneficiary of the bond.

infrastructure assets Public domain fixed assets such as roads, bridges, curbs, gutters, streets and sidewalks, drainage systems, lighting systems, and similar assets that are immovable and of value only to the government unit.

inputs The resources applied to a service, such as dollar cost, number of labor hours, and amount of material.

in-substance defeasance An advance refunding (retirement of bonds) in which the government places sufficient resources in a trust account to cover all required principal and interest payments on the defeased debt. Although the government is not legally released from being the primary obligor on the refunded bonds, the possibility of it having to make additional payments is considered remote.

intangible asset An asset that has a future benefit, but cannot be physically seen—e.g., a patent or copyright.

interest rate risk The risk that a change in interest rates will adversely affect the value of an investment.

interfund transfers *See* **reciprocal interfund activity** and **nonreciprocal interfund activity.**

intergenerational equity *See* **interperiod equity.**

internal service funds Funds used to account for business-type activities in which the customers are other government departments or agencies.

incremental receipts (disbursements) Receipts (disbursements) that differ if one alternative course of action were chosen over another.

interperiod equity The extent to which current-year revenues are sufficient to pay for current-year services (as opposed to whether the costs of current-year services are being shifted to future years or were paid in past years).

insolvent The condition of being unable to meet debts or discharge liabilities owing to a deficiency of available financial resources.

inspectors general The heads of the internal audit departments of federal agencies.

issue costs Costs incurred to issue bonds, such as amounts paid to underwriters, attorneys, accountants, and printers.

investment in plant fund A fund (no longer reported on financial statements) maintained mainly by colleges and universities and other not-for-profits to account for the entity's fixed assets and the liabilities incurred to acquire those assets; comparable to a government's "old model" general fixed assets and general long-term debt account groups.

investment pools Fiscal entities established to invest the resources of two or more funds or independent entities; comparable to a mutual fund.

investment trust funds Funds maintained by a government to account for investment pools maintained for other governments.

J

joint venture A contractual arrangement whereby two or more participants agree to carry out a common activity, with each sharing in both risks and rewards.

journal A book of original entry in which transactions or events are recorded.

L

lessee The entity that rents an asset from the asset's owner, the lessor.

lessor The owner of rental property who transfers the right to use the property for a specified fee and for a specified period of time, to the user, the lessee.

levy To impose or collect a tax.

lien A claim that a government has on property, most commonly owing to a failure of the owner to pay property taxes.

life income fund An endowment fund to account for gifts that provide a return to the donor (or a person designated by the donor) for the remainder of his or her life. Thereafter, what remains of the gift will typically revert to the recipient entity.

liquidity The ability of an entity to meet its financial obligations as they come due.

loan fund A fund used to account for resources that will provide loans to a designated class of beneficiaries, such as students or small businesses.

long-term debt In government, obligations that are not expected to be paid with currently available financial resources. In not-for-profits, obligations that are not expected to be paid in cash or other operating assets within one year or the entity's normal operating cycle.

M

maintenance The upkeep of a capital asset to preserve its expected useful life or level of productivity. Contrasted with a betterment, which increases expected useful life or enhances productivity.

major fund In the context of GASB standards, a fund whose revenues, expenditures/expenses, assets, or liabilities (excluding extraordinary items) are at least 10 percent of corresponding totals for all governmental or enterprise funds and at least 5 percent of the aggregate amount for all governmental and enterprise funds. Also may be any other fund that the government considers to be of particular importance to statement users.

management's discussion and analysis A component of an annual report in which management provides an analysis of the entity's financial activities.

matching concept The principle that expenses or expenditures should be recognized in the same accounting period as related revenues.

measurement focus The accounting convention that determines which assets and liabilities are included on an entity's balance sheet and which will thereby affect the determination of revenues and expenses (or expenditures) to be reported on the entity's operating statement.

Measurement focus determines what is being measured—e.g., net profits or flows of financial resources.

modified accrual basis The accrual basis of accounting adapted to the governmental fund-type measurement focus. Revenues are recognized in the period in which they become available and measurable. Some expenditures are recognized on a accrual basis; others on a cash basis.

moral obligation debt Bonds or notes issued by one entity (usually a state agency), but backed by the implied (not legally binding) promise of another entity (usually the state itself) to make up any debt service deficiencies.

municipality A city or town or other area incorporated for self-government. Also, in its broadest sense, any state or local government, including states, counties, cities, towns, and special districts.

municipal bond A bond issued by a municipality.

N

National Council on Governmental Accounting (NCGA) The governmental accounting standard setting authority that preceded the GASB.

natural classification Expenditures that are grouped according to an object, such as salaries and wages.

net assets The residual of assets minus liabilities.

net pension obligation (NPO) The cumulative difference between an employer's annual pension costs (determined per the requirements of applicable accounting and actuarial standards) and the employer's contribution to the pension plan.

nominal interest rate The contractual interest rate shown on the face of a bond and used to compute the amount of interest to be paid; in contrast to the effective interest rate.

nonappropriation budget A financial plan for an organization, program, activity, or function approved in a manner authorized by constitution, charter, statute, or ordinance but not subject to appropriation and, therefore, outside the boundaries of an appropriated budget.

nonappropriation clause *See* **fiscal funding clause.**

nonexchange revenues Revenues that materialize when a government commands resources but gives nothing in exchange (at least not directly). Examples include taxes, duties, fines, and penalties.

nonexchange transaction A transaction in which one party provides resources to another without getting consideration of approximately equal value in return; includes voluntary nonexchange transactions, such as contributions and grants and imposed nonexchange transactions, such as taxes, duties, and fines.

noncommitment debt *See* **conduit debt.**

nonexpendable funds Proprietary funds that "pay their own way" through customer charges. Contrasted with expendable funds, the resources of which are provided by taxes, fees, or other revenues and are expected to be spent each year.

nonexpendable trust funds Endowment funds, the principal of which must be maintained intact; only the income of which can be expended.

nonmajor fund In the context of GASB standards, any fund that is not considered a major fund. *See* **major fund.**

nonoperating expenditures/expenses Expenditures/expenses not related directly to a fund's or entity's primary activities.

nonoperating revenues Revenues not directly related to a fund's or entity's primary activities.

nonreciprocal interfund activity (transfers) Per GASB Statement No. 34, the internal equivalent of nonexchange transactions; transfers of cash for which goods or services of equivalent value have not been received, such as when the general fund transfers cash to a debt service fund for payment of principal or interest on long-term debt or when the general fund transfers cash to a newly established internal service fund for start-up capital.

nonreciprocal receipt A contribution for which the recipient gives nothing in exchange. Per FASB 116, *Accounting for Contributions Received and Contributions Made*, contributions may be made in cash, marketable securities, property and equipment, utilities, supplies, intangible assets, and the services of professionals and craftsmen.

nonsubstitution clause A provision often incorporated into governments' capital lease agreements that prohibits the leasee (the government) from replacing the leased property with similar property in the event that it cancels the lease.

normal cost With respect to pensions, the portion of the present value of pension plan benefits that is allocated to a particular year by an appropriate actuarial cost method.

not-for-profit organization An entity that conducts operations for the benefit of its users without a profit motive.

note disclosures Information disclosed in the notes to the financial statements.

O

object An item in an expenditure classification that relates to the type of goods or services obtained rather than to the purpose of the expenditure or the nature of the activity that it supports. Examples include wages and salaries, supplies, and contractual services.

object classification budget A budget that details revenues and expenditures by object, rather than, for example, program or nature of activity.

off-balance-sheet financing Obligations, such as those from operating leases, that do not satisfy the accounting criteria of reportable liabilities and are therefore not disclosed on an entity's balance sheet.

Office of Management and Budget (OMB) The executive branch agency of the federal government that assists the president in preparing the federal budget and supervises the executive branch agencies in implementing it. It also oversees and coordinates federal procurement, financial management, information and regulatory policies. It further has authority to prescribe the form and content of federal agency financial statements and related reports and to establish requirements pertaining to single audits.

on-behalf payments Payments made by one government for the benefit of another. For example, pension contributions paid by a state for employees of a school district.

operating debt Debt issued to cover general operating, as opposed to capital, expenditures.

operating expenditures/expenses Expenditures/expenses related directly to a fund's or entity's primary activities.

operating lease A rental agreement permitting an entity to use an asset for a specified period of time, but does not meet the criteria, set forth in FASB Statement No. 13, *Accounting for Leases*, of a capital lease.

operating revenues Revenues related directly to a fund's or entity's primary activities.

operating statement A statement that shows an entity's revenues, expenditures/expenses and transfers over a specified period of time. *See also* **statement of activities.**

operational audit *See* **performance auditing.**

operational objectives Specific sought-after results of a program or activity. The objectives should be quantifiable, measurable, and distinguishable from broad, nonspecific statements of purpose.

opportunity cost The economic gains that are forgone by choosing one course of action over an alternative.

other financing sources/uses An operating statement classification presenting financial inflows and outflows other than revenues and expenditures. Examples include transfers in/out and proceeds of long-term debt.

outcomes The results (accomplishments) of a service, generally measured so as to take into account the quality of performance.

outputs The quantity, or units of service, provided by an activity.

overhead Indirect costs; those elements of cost necessary in the production of a good or service that are not directly traceable to the product or service, such as rent, heat, light, supplies, management, and supervision.

overlapping debt The proportionate share that property within the reporting government must bear of the debts of all other governments located wholly or in part within its geographic boundaries.

P

pass-through grants Grants that a government must transfer to, or spend on behalf of, a secondary recipient. For example, a federal education grant that a state must distribute to local school districts.

pay-as-you-go-basis In the context of pension accounting and risk management, the failure to finance retirement obligations or anticipated losses on a current basis using an acceptable actuarial funding method.

payments in lieu of taxes Amounts paid by one government in place of property taxes they are not required to pay. Generally occurs when a jurisdiction contains a substantial amount of facilities of other governments; for example, when the federal government makes payments to a local school district in lieu of property taxes it would be required to pay on a military base within the district if federal property were not tax-exempt.

PCAOB *See* **Public Company Accounting Oversight Board.**

pension Sums of money paid periodically (usually monthly) to a retired or disabled employee (or a surviving spouse) owing to his or her years of employment.

pension contribution The amount paid into a pension plan by an employer (or employee), pursuant to the terms of the plan, state law, actuarial calculations, or some other basis for determination.

pension obligation The portion of the actuarial present value of total projected benefits estimated to be payable in the future as a result of employee service to date.

pension trust fund A trust fund used to account for the assets accumulated by a pension plan. Pension trust funds, like nonexpendable trust funds, are accounted for on an accrual basis.

per capita debt The amount of a government's debt divided by its population.

performance auditing A systematic process of objectively obtaining and evaluating evidence regarding the performance of an organization, program, function, or activity in terms of its economy and efficiency of operations and its effectiveness in achieving desired results.

performance budget A budget that focuses on measurable units of efforts and accomplishments and associates dollar expenditures directly with anticipated units of outputs or outcomes.

permanent funds Per GASB Statement No. 34, trust funds in which the beneficiary is the government itself rather than outside parties. Permanent funds are categorized and accounted for as governmental funds.

permanently restricted net assets Endowments of which the principal must permanently remain intact. Only the income is available for expenditure. In the context of not-for-profit financial statements, one of the three main categories into which resources must be classified.

PERS *See* **Public Employee Retirement System.**

plant fund A fund, generally maintained by colleges and universities and other not-for-profit organizations (but no longer explicitly reported on their external financial statements), to account for fixed assets and the resources set aside to acquire or replace fixed assets. As used by colleges and universities, plant funds may be of four types: unexpended plant fund, renewal and replacement fund, retirement of indebtedness fund, and investment in plant fund.

pledge A promise by a donor to make a donation of cash or assets in the future.

present value The amount that a buyer is willing to pay for one or a series of payments to be received in the future. Computed by discounting the future cash flows at an appropriate rate of interest and for an appropriate period of time.

primary government Per GASB Statement No. 14, *The Financial Reporting Entity*, a state government, a general-purpose local government, such as a municipality or a county, or a special-purpose government, such as a school district, that has a separately elected governing body, is legally separate from other primary governments, and is fiscally independent of other governments.

private purpose trust fund A fund maintained by a government to account for assets held for the benefit of outside parties—e.g., individuals, private organizations, or other governments.

privatization *See* **contracting out.**

pro-forma statements Projected financial statements of an organization for future periods.

program A series of related activities intended to fulfill a common objective.

program audit An audit to determine the extent to which an organization is achieving desired results or benefits and whether the entity has complied with significant laws and regulations applicable to its programs. *See also* **performance auditing.**

program budget A budget in which resources and results are identified with programs rather than traditional organizational units. *See also* **performance budget.**

proprietary accounts In the context of federal accounting, the accounts that provide the information necessary to prepare financial statements based on FASAB standards rather than to demonstrate budgetary compliance.

propriety fund Income determination funds that are used to account for a government's business-type activities; enterprise and internal service funds that are accounted for on a business-type basis.

Public Company Accounting Oversight Board (PCAOB) A private-sector, non-profit corporation, created by the Sarbanes-Oxley Act of 2002, to oversee the audits of public companies in order to protect the interests of investors and further the public interest in the preparation of informative, fair, and independent audit reports.

Public Employee Retirement System (PERS) A pension plan maintained for government employees.

purchases method A method of accounting for inventories and prepaid costs, such as rent, in which goods or services are recorded as expenses or expenditures when purchased, rather than when consumed. Differentiated from the consumption method.

purpose restrictions Stipulations, usually as part of a grant, as to the purpose for which the resources must be used.

put bonds *See* **demand bonds.**

Q

qualified opinion An audit opinion stating that "except for" the effect of the matter to which the qualification relates, the financial statements present fairly the financial position, results of operations and (when applicable), changes in financial position in conformity with GAAP. Generally expressed when auditors cannot obtain adequate information to express an unqualified opinion, there are significant uncertainties as to the value of assets or liabilities, or there are material departures from generally accepted accounting principles.

quasi-endowment fund A fund maintained to account for assets to be retained and invested as if they were contractually required endowments—for example, earnings (and only the earnings) from investments acquired with the resources are to be used for a specified purpose.

quasi-external transactions Interfund transactions that would be treated as revenues, expenditures, or expenses if they involved organizations external to the government unit (e.g., payments in lieu of taxes from an enterprise fund to the general fund; internal service fund billings to departments; routine employer contributions to a pension trust fund, and routine service charges for inspection, engineering, utilities or similar services). These transactions should be accounted for as revenues, expenditures, or expenses in the funds involved. Under the new GASB model, these transactions are referred to as "exchange-like" transactions.

questioned costs Costs identified by auditors of federal assistance programs that appear to be in violation of laws, regulations, or contractual provisions and are thereby ineligible for reimbursement.

R

reciprocal interfund activity Per GASB Statement No. 34, the internal equivalent of exchange transactions (those in which the parties receive and surrender consideration of approximately equal value). Examples include payments for the purchase of goods and services, and loans and repayments of loans.

redemption value In the context of investment pools and mutual funds, the amount that the pool or fund will pay per share to an investor electing to withdraw its funds. Generally based on the current market value of the underlying securities.

refinance To replace existing debt with new debt, generally to take advantage of lower interest rates, or to shorten or lengthen the debt payout period.

refundings *See* **bond refunding.**

related organization Per GASB Statement No. 14, *The Financial Reporting Entity*, an entity that satisfies the criteria of financial accountability, but not other necessary criteria and therefore does not qualify as a component unit.

relevant range The range of output that is relevant for the particular decision at hand. The span of output in which the behavior of fixed and variable costs is assumed to remain constant.

renewal and replacement fund A plant fund used mainly by colleges and universities and other not-for-profit entities to account (internally) for resources set aside to restore and replace existing buildings, equipment, and other fixed assets.

replacement cost The cost of acquiring or constructing an asset today that is identical to or has the same service potential as an asset already owned. An indicator of an asset's current value.

reporting entity The organizational unit covered by a set of financial statements. In government, the oversight unit and all of its component units, if any, that are combined in the financial statements per the requirements of GASB Statement No. 14, *The Financial Reporting Entity*, or FASAB Concepts Statement No. 4, *Entity and Display*.

repurchase agreement ("repo") An investment instrument in which an investor (buyer-lender) transfers cash to a broker-dealer or financial institution (seller-borrower). The broker-dealer or financial institution transfers securities to the investor and promises to repay the cash plus interest in exchange for the same securities or for different securities. Contrast with a reverse repurchase agreement.

required supplementary information (RSI) Statements, schedules, statistical data, or other information not included in, but required to supplement, the basic financial statements. Per GASB Statement No. 34 it includes management's discussion and analysis, budget to actual comparisons, information about infrastructure, and details of actuarial pension valuations.

reserve for encumbrances A segregation of fund equity in the amount of encumbrances (commitments to purchase goods or services).

reserved fund balance That portion of fund balance that either represents resources that are not of a type that can be appropriated (e.g., reserves for inventory) or that are legally segregated for a specific future use (reserves for encumbrances).

residual equity transfers Under the "old" model, nonrecurring or nonroutine transfers of equity between funds (e.g., the contribution of capital by the general fund to an enterprise fund or internal service fund, and the subsequent return of all or part of such contributions to the general fund).

restricted grants Payments intended for specified purposes, projects, or activities.

retirement of indebtedness fund A fund maintained by colleges and universities and other not-for-profits (but not explicitly reported on their financial statements) that is comparable to a debt service fund and used to account for resources set aside for the retirement of indebtedness.

revenue anticipation notes (RANS) Short-term notes, issued in anticipation of the collection of revenues, that will not be converted into long-term instruments.

revenue The inflow of net resources owing to the production and delivery of goods or services or from transactions (e.g., taxes, contributions) involving an entity's primary activities.

revenue debt Bonds and other obligations whose principal and interest are payable exclusively from earnings of a specific enterprise, such as an electric utility, toll road, or dormitory, and are thereby not backed by the full faith and credit of the issuer. Contrast with general obligation debt.

reverse repurchase agreement ("reverse repo") A borrowing instrument by which a borrower (seller) receives cash from a broker-dealer or financial institution (buyer-lender); in exchange the borrower (seller) transfers securities to the broker-dealer or financial institution and promises to repay the cash plus interest in exchange for the same or different securities. Contrast with a repurchase agreement.

revolving funds Funds used to account for business-type enterprises; *See also* **expendable funds.**

Rule 203 (of the American Institute of Certified Public Accountants' Code of Professional Conduct) The provision that auditors should not express an unqualified opinion on financial statements that are in violation of the standards established by organizations designated by the AICPA's Council.

S

Schedule of Expenditures of Federal Awards A listing made by an organization of total expenditures under each federal program from which it receives funding.

SEA *See* **service efforts and accomplishments indicators.**

self-insurance The retention of a risk by an entity, as opposed to the transfer of the risk to an independent third party through the purchase of an insurance policy.

serial bonds Bonds that mature in a series of installments at future dates—e.g., a portion of a bond issue matures in five years, a portion in six, a portion in seven, and so on.

service assessments Special assessments for operating activities, such as street cleaning or fire protection, as opposed to capital assets and infrastructure.

service efforts and accomplishments (SEA) indicators Measures of an entity's inputs, outputs, outcomes, and efficiency in carrying out its activities.

shared revenues Revenues levied by one government, such as a state, but shared on a predetermined basis with other governments, such as cities.

short-term debt Obligations that are expected to be paid within one year or the entity's operating cycle.

single audit An audit by a single audit organization intended to meet the needs of more than one regulatory agency or funds provider; an audit performed in accordance with the Single Audit Act and supporting Office of Management and Budget (OMB) circulars.

Single Audit Act of 1984 A federal act mandating that recipients of federal financial assistance meeting specified criteria be subject to organization-wide single audits.

sinking fund A fund to account for financial resources set aside for the payment of interest and principal on long-term debt.

special assessment A compulsory levy on certain properties to defray all or part of the cost of a specific capital improvement or service deemed to benefit primarily those properties or their owners.

special assessment bonds Bonds payable from the proceeds of special assessments.

special items Transactions or other events within the control of management that are significant and either unusual in nature or infrequent in occurrence. *See also* **extraordinary items.**

special-purpose governments Governments that serve only a single, well-defined purpose, such as universities, utility districts, and library districts.

special revenue fund A fund used to account for the proceeds of specific revenue sources that are legally restricted to expenditure for specific purposes.

special termination benefit Improvement to a pension plan or other incentive provided by employers to encourage employees to retire early.

statement of activities One of the two government-wide statements required by GASB Statement No. 34 (the other being the statement of net assets). An operating statement that consolidates separately the revenues, expenses and other items of a government's governmental and business-activities.

statement of budgetary resources In federal accounting, an operating statement prepared on a budgetary basis.

statement of cash flows The statement that provides information about the cash inflows (receipts) and outflows (payments) of an entity during a period of time.

statement of changes in net position In federal accounting, a statement summarizing all agency transactions other than those reported in the statement of net cost.

statement of custodial activities In federal accounting, a statement showing resources collected and disbursed. Required only of agencies such as the Internal Revenue Service and Customs Service, that collect funds to be turned over to the Treasury or other agencies.

statement of financial position A balance sheet.

statement of financing In federal accounting, a statement that reconciles the statement of budgetary resources to the statement of net cost.

statement of net assets One of the two government-wide statements required by GASB Statement No. 34 (the other being the statement of activities). In essence a balance sheet that displays the consolidated assets, liabilities and net assets of governmental and business-type activities (separate by type).

statement of net cost In federal accounting, an operating statement that shows an agency's operating costs and revenues and highlights the net costs that must be paid from taxes or other financing sources.

statement of revenues and expenditures The operating statement of a governmental fund that presents increases (revenues and other financing sources) and decreases (expenditures and other financing uses) in net current financial resources.

stewardship assets In federal accounting, assets that the federal government owns but does not use to produce goods or services and which are not accorded balance sheet recognition. Includes, for example, national parks and forests, undeveloped acreage, and heritage assets.

sunk costs Costs that have already been incurred and cannot be recovered.

suspense account An account carrying charges or credits temporarily pending the determination of the proper account or accounts to which they are to be posted.

T

take-out agreement An agreement between an issuer of demand bonds and a financial institution per which the financial institution will provide funding for the issuer in the event that bondholders demand redemption of their bonds.

tangible asset An asset used in the normal operations of an organization that can be physically seen.

tap fees Fees charged by a governmental utility to new customers to hook up to its system.

tax anticipation notes (TANs) Short-term notes, not expected to be converted into long-term debts, issued in anticipation of future collection of taxes.

tax lien *See* **lien.**

taxpayer-assessed taxes Taxes, such as sales and income taxes determined by parties other than the government. Distinguished from government-assessed taxes, such as property taxes.

temporarily restricted net assets Resources that must be used either for a specified purpose or when specified events have occurred. In the context of not-for-profit financial statements, one of the three main categories into which resources must be classified.

term bonds Bonds that mature in one lump sum at a specified future date.

term endowment An endowment (trust) in which the principal may be expended after a specified number of years.

third-party payor With respect to health care, the insurance company or party other than the patient that pays for services.

time requirements Stipulations, usually as part of a grant, as to the time period in which resources must be used or when use may begin.

transfers *See* **reciprocal interfund activity** and **nonreciprocal interfund activity.**

trustee A party that administers property for a beneficiary.

trust funds Funds used to account for assets over which the entity acts as a trustee or that must be invested and the income only, not the principal, may be expended. In federal accounting the term refers to any fund that is designated by law as a trust fund and has earmarked receipts.

U

unconditional promise A pledge or promise to give an asset or provide a service in the future that is not dependent on a certain event occurring.

unearned income *See* **deferred revenue.**

unfunded actuarial accrued liability The excess of a pension plan's actuarial accrued liability over the actuarial value of its assets.

unified federal budget The budget that encompasses all programs and transactions and is intended to capture the impact of all federal activities on the national economy.

Uniform Administrative Requirements for Grants and Cooperative Agreements to State and Local Governments (the Common Rule) A detailed compendium of administrative rules and regulations that supplements the Single Audit Act and related circulars.

unqualified opinion An auditor's opinion stating that the financial statements present fairly the financial position, results of operations, and (when applicable) changes in financial position in conformity with GAAP.

unrestricted grants Grants that are unrestricted as to purpose, project, or activity.

unrestricted net assets Assets that are not restricted as to when and how they can be used. In the context of not-for-profit financial statements, one of the three main categories into which resources must be classified.

user charge A charge for the use of a service, such as for parking or trash collections, as opposed to a tax that is unrelated to services received.

V

variable costs Costs that change in direct proportion to volume.

variance power The right of a not-for-profit organization to unilaterally redirect contributed assets to a beneficiary other than that specified by the donor.

vested benefit A benefit for which an employer has an obligation to make payment even if an employee is terminated. Thus, the benefit is not contingent on an employee's future service.

voluntary health and welfare organization A not-for-profit organization formed to provide services to a community, rather than to its own members. Examples include the United Way,the American Heart Association, and most social service agencies.

voluntary nonexchange transactions Transactions that result from legislative or contractual agreements entered into willingly by two or more parties. They include grants given by one government to another and contributions from individuals (e.g., gifts to public universities).

voucher A written document that supports a payment and provides evidence of its propriety.

Y

Yellow Book *See* **Government Accounting Standards (Standards for Audit of Government Organizations, Programs, Activities, and Functions).**

yield rate The actual (effective), as distinguished from the nominal (coupon or stated), rate of return on a bond or other investment.

Z

zero-base budgeting A form of program budgeting characterized by its requirement that all activities, both existing and proposed, be evaluated and ranked.

zero coupon bond A bond with a stated annual interest rate of zero. It provides a return to investors in that it is issued at a price considerably less than the bond's face value and sufficiently low so that the difference between face value and issue price will equal a return comparable to that on conventional bonds.

VALUE TABLES

TABLE I
Future Value of 1 (Future Value of a Single Sum)

$$FV_{n,i} = (1 + i)^n$$

(n) Periods	2%	2½%	3%	4%	5%	6%
1	1.02000	1.02500	1.03000	1.04000	1.05000	1.06000
2	1.04040	1.05063	1.06090	1.08160	1.10250	1.12360
3	1.06121	1.07689	1.09273	1.12486	1.15763	1.19102
4	1.08243	1.10381	1.12551	1.16986	1.21551	1.26248
5	1.10408	1.13141	1.15927	1.21665	1.27628	1.33823
6	1.12616	1.15969	1.19405	1.26532	1.34010	1.41852
7	1.14869	1.18869	1.22987	1.31593	1.40710	1.50363
8	1.17166	1.21840	1.26677	1.36857	1.47746	1.59385
9	1.19509	1.24886	1.30477	1.42331	1.55133	1.68948
10	1.21899	1.28008	1.34392	1.48024	1.62889	1.79085
11	1.24337	1.31209	1.38423	1.53945	1.71034	1.89830
12	1.26824	1.34489	1.42576	1.60103	1.79586	2.01220
13	1.29361	1.37851	1.46853	1.66507	1.88565	2.13293
14	1.31948	1.41297	1.51259	1.73168	1.97993	2.26090
15	1.34587	1.44830	1.55797	1.80094	2.07893	2.39656
16	1.37279	1.48451	1.60471	1.87298	2.18287	2.54035
17	1.40024	1.52162	1.65285	1.94790	2.29202	2.69277
18	1.42825	1.55966	1.70243	2.02582	2.40662	2.85434
19	1.45681	1.59865	1.75351	2.10685	2.52695	3.02560
20	1.48595	1.63862	1.80611	2.19112	2.65330	3.20714
21	1.51567	1.67958	1.86029	2.27877	2.78596	3.39956
22	1.54598	1.72157	1.91610	2.36992	2.92526	3.60354
23	1.57690	1.76461	1.97359	2.46472	3.07152	3.81975
24	1.60844	1.80873	2.03279	2.56330	3.22510	4.04893
25	1.64061	1.85394	2.09378	2.66584	3.38635	4.29187
26	1.67342	1.90029	2.15659	2.77247	3.55567	4.54938
27	1.70689	1.94780	2.22129	2.88337	3.73346	4.82235
28	1.74102	1.99650	2.28793	2.99870	3.92013	5.11169
29	1.77584	2.04641	2.35657	3.11865	4.11614	5.41839
30	1.81136	2.09757	2.42726	3.24340	4.32194	5.74349
31	1.84759	2.15001	2.50008	3.37313	4.53804	6.08810
32	1.88454	2.20376	2.57508	3.50806	4.76494	6.45339
33	1.92223	2.25885	2.65234	3.64838	5.00319	6.84059
34	1.96068	2.31532	2.73191	3.79432	5.25335	7.25103
35	1.99989	2.37321	2.81386	3.94609	5.51602	7.68609
36	2.03989	2.43254	2.89828	4.10393	5.79182	8.14725
37	2.08069	2.49335	2.98523	4.26809	6.08141	8.63609
38	2.12230	2.55568	3.07478	4.43881	6.38548	9.15425
39	2.16474	2.61957	3.16703	4.61637	6.70475	9.70351
40	2.20804	2.68506	3.26204	4.80102	7.03999	10.28572

(Continues)

TABLE I (Continued)
Future Value of 1 (Future Value of a Single Sum)

$FV_{n,i} = (1 + i)^n$

8%	9%	10%	11%	12%	15%	(n) Periods
1.08000	1.09000	1.10000	1.11000	1.12000	1.15000	1
1.16640	1.18810	1.21000	1.23210	1.25440	1.32250	2
1.25971	1.29503	1.33100	1.36763	1.40493	1.52088	3
1.36049	1.41158	1.46410	1.51807	1.57352	1.74901	4
1.46933	1.53862	1.61051	1.68506	1.76234	2.01136	5
1.58687	1.67710	1.77156	1.87041	1.97382	2.31306	6
1.71382	1.82804	1.94872	2.07616	2.21068	2.66002	7
1.85093	1.99256	2.14359	2.30454	2.47596	3.05902	8
1.99900	2.17189	2.35795	2.55803	2.77308	3.51788	9
2.15892	2.36736	2.59374	2.83942	3.10585	4.04556	10
2.33164	2.58043	2.85312	3.15176	3.47855	4.65239	11
2.51817	2.81267	3.13843	3.49845	3.89598	5.35025	12
2.71962	3.06581	3.45227	3.88328	4.36349	6.15279	13
2.93719	3.34173	3.79750	4.31044	4.88711	7.07571	14
3.17217	3.64248	4.17725	4.78459	5.47357	8.13706	15
3.42594	3.97031	4.59497	5.31089	6.13039	9.35762	16
3.70002	4.32763	5.05447	5.89509	6.86604	10.76126	17
3.99602	4.71712	5.55992	6.54355	7.68997	12.37545	18
4.31570	5.14166	6.11591	7.26334	8.61276	14.23177	19
4.66096	5.60441	6.72750	8.06231	9.64629	16.36654	20
5.03383	6.10881	7.40025	8.94917	10.80385	18.82152	21
5.43654	6.65860	8.14028	9.93357	12.10031	21.64475	22
5.87146	7.25787	8.95430	11.02627	13.55235	24.89146	23
6.34118	7.91108	9.84973	12.23916	15.17863	28.62518	24
6.84847	8.62308	10.83471	13.58546	17.00000	32.91895	25
7.39635	9.39916	11.91818	15.07986	19.04007	37.85680	26
7.98806	10.24508	13.10999	16.73865	21.32488	43.53532	27
8.62711	11.16714	14.42099	18.57990	23.88387	50.06561	28
9.31727	12.17218	15.86309	20.62369	26.74993	57.57545	29
10.06266	13.26768	17.44940	22.89230	29.95992	66.21177	30
10.86767	14.46177	19.19434	25.41045	33.55511	76.14354	31
11.73708	15.76333	21.11378	28.20560	37.58173	87.56507	32
12.67605	17.18203	23.22515	31.30821	42.09153	100.69983	33
13.69013	18.72841	25.54767	34.75212	47.14252	115.80480	34
14.78534	20.41397	28.10244	38.57485	52.79962	133.17552	35
15.96817	22.25123	30.91268	42.81808	59.13557	153.15185	36
17.24563	24.25384	34.00395	47.52807	66.23184	176.12463	37
18.62528	26.43668	37.40434	52.75616	74.17966	202.54332	38
20.11530	28.81598	41.14479	58.55934	83.08122	232.92482	39
21.72452	31.40942	45.25926	65.00087	93.05097	267.86355	40

TABLE II
Present Value of 1 (Present Value of a Single Sum)

$$PV - OA_{n,i} = \frac{1}{(1+i)^n} = (1+i)^{-n}$$

(n) Periods	2%	2½%	3%	4%	5%	6%
1	.98039	.97561	.97087	.96154	.95238	.94340
2	.96117	.95181	.94260	.92456	.90703	.89000
3	.94232	.92860	.91514	.88900	.86384	.83962
4	.92385	.90595	.88849	.85480	.82270	.79209
5	.90573	.88385	.86261	.82193	.78353	.74726
6	.88797	.86230	.83748	.79031	.74622	.70496
7	.87056	.84127	.81309	.75992	.71068	.66506
8	.85349	.82075	.78941	.73069	.67684	.62741
9	.83676	.80073	.76642	.70259	.64461	.59190
10	.82035	.78120	.74409	.67556	.61391	.55839
11	.80426	.76214	.72242	.64958	.58468	.52679
12	.78849	.74356	.70138	.62460	.55684	.49697
13	.77303	.72542	.68095	.60057	.53032	.46884
14	.75788	.70773	.66112	.57748	.50507	.44230
15	.74301	.69047	.64186	.55526	.48102	.41727
16	.72845	.67362	.62317	.53391	.45811	.39365
17	.71416	.65720	.60502	.51337	.43630	.37136
18	.70016	.64117	.58739	.49363	.41552	.35034
19	.68643	.62553	.57029	.47464	.39573	.33051
20	.67297	.61027	.55368	.45639	.37689	.31180
21	.65978	.59539	.53755	.43883	.35894	.29416
22	.64684	.58086	.52189	.42196	.34185	.27751
23	.63416	.56670	.50669	.40573	.32557	.26180
24	.62172	.55288	.49193	.39012	.31007	.24698
25	.60953	.53939	.47761	.37512	.29530	.23300
26	.59758	.52623	.46369	.36069	.28124	.21981
27	.58586	.51340	.45019	.34682	.26785	.20737
28	.57437	.50088	.43708	.33348	.25509	.19563
29	.56311	.48866	.42435	.32065	.24295	.18456
30	.55207	.47674	.41199	.30832	.23138	.17411
31	.54125	.46511	.39999	.29646	.22036	.16425
32	.53063	.45377	.38834	.28506	.20987	.15496
33	.52023	.44270	.37703	.27409	.19987	.14619
34	.51003	.43191	.36604	.26355	.19035	.13791
35	.50003	.42137	.35538	.25342	.18129	.13011
36	.49022	.41109	.34503	.24367	.17266	.12274
37	.48061	.40107	.33498	.23430	.16444	.11579
38	.47119	.39128	.32523	.22529	.15661	.10924
39	.46195	.38174	.31575	.21662	.14915	.10306
40	.45289	.37243	.30656	.20829	.14205	.09722

(Continues)

TABLE II (Continued)
Present Value of 1 (Present Value of a Single Sum)

$$PV - OA_{n,i} = \frac{1}{(1 + i)^n} = (1 + i)^{-n}$$

8%	9%	10%	11%	12%	15%	(n) Periods
.92593	.91743	.90909	.90090	.89286	.86957	1
.85734	.84168	.82645	.81162	.79719	.75614	2
.79383	.77218	.75132	.73119	.71178	.65752	3
.73503	.70843	.68301	.65873	.63552	.57175	4
.68058	.64993	.62092	.59345	.56743	.49718	5
.63017	.59627	.56447	.53464	.50663	.43233	6
.58349	.54703	.51316	.48166	.45235	.37594	7
.54027	.50187	.46651	.43393	.40388	.32690	8
.50025	.46043	.42410	.39092	.36061	.28426	9
.46319	.42241	.38554	.35218	.32197	.24719	10
.42888	.38753	.35049	.31728	.28748	.21494	11
.39711	.35554	.31863	.28584	.25668	.18691	12
.36770	.32618	.28966	.25751	.22917	.16253	13
.34046	.29925	.26333	.23199	.20462	.14133	14
.31524	.27454	.23939	.20900	.18270	.12289	15
.29189	.25187	.21763	.18829	.16312	.10687	16
.27027	.23107	.19785	.16963	.14564	.09293	17
.25025	.21199	.17986	.15282	.13004	.08081	18
.23171	.19449	.16351	.13768	.11611	.07027	19
.21455	.17843	.14864	.12403	.10367	.06110	20
.19866	.16370	.13513	.11174	.09256	.05313	21
.18394	.15018	.12285	.10067	.08264	.04620	22
.17032	.13778	.11168	.09069	.07379	.04017	23
.15770	.12641	.10153	.08170	.06588	.03493	24
.14602	.11597	.09230	.07361	.05882	.03038	25
.13520	.10639	.08391	.06631	.05252	.02642	26
.12519	.09761	.07628	.05974	.04689	.02297	27
.11591	.08955	.06934	.05382	.04187	.01997	28
.10733	.08216	.06304	.04849	.03738	.01737	29
.09938	.07537	.05731	.04368	.03338	.01510	30
.09202	.06915	.05210	.03935	.02980	.01313	31
.08520	.06344	.04736	.03545	.02661	.01142	32
.07889	.05820	.04306	.03194	.02376	.00993	33
.07305	.05340	.03914	.02878	.02121	.00864	34
.06763	.04899	.03558	.02592	.01894	.00751	35
.06262	.04494	.03235	.02335	.01691	.00653	36
.05799	.04123	.02941	.02104	.01510	.00568	37
.05369	.03783	.02674	.01896	.01348	.00494	38
.04971	.03470	.02430	.01708	.01204	.00429	39
.04603	.03184	.02210	.01538	.01075	.00373	40

TABLE III
Future Value of an Ordinary Annuity of 1

$$FV-OA_{n,i} = \frac{(1+i)^n - 1}{i}$$

(n) Periods	2%	2½%	3%	4%	5%	6%
1	1.00000	1.00000	1.00000	1.00000	1.00000	1.00000
2	2.02000	2.02500	2.03000	2.04000	2.05000	2.06000
3	3.06040	3.07563	3.09090	3.12160	3.15250	3.18360
4	4.12161	4.15252	4.18363	4.24646	4.31013	4.37462
5	5.20404	5.25633	5.30914	5.41632	5.52563	5.63709
6	6.30812	6.38774	6.46841	6.63298	6.80191	6.97532
7	7.43428	7.54743	7.66246	7.89829	8.14201	8.39384
8	8.58297	8.73612	8.89234	9.21423	9.54911	9.89747
9	9.75463	9.95452	10.15911	10.58280	10.02656	11.49132
10	10.94972	11.20338	11.46338	12.00611	12.57789	13.18079
11	12.16872	12.48347	12.80780	13.48635	14.20679	14.97164
12	13.41209	13.79555	14.19203	15.02581	15.91713	16.86994
13	14.68033	15.14044	15.61779	16.62684	17.71298	18.88214
14	15.97394	16.51895	17.08632	18.29191	19.59863	21.01507
15	17.29342	17.93193	18.59891	20.02359	21.57856	23.27597
16	18.63929	19.38022	20.15688	21.82453	23.65749	25.67253
17	20.01207	20.86473	21.76159	23.69751	25.84037	28.21288
18	21.41231	22.38635	23.41444	25.64541	28.13238	30.90565
19	22.84056	23.94601	25.11687	27.67123	30.53900	33.75999
20	24.29737	25.54466	26.87037	29.77808	33.06595	36.78559
21	25.78332	27.18327	28.67649	31.96920	35.71925	39.99273
22	27.29898	28.86286	30.53678	34.24797	38.50521	43.39229
23	28.84496	30.58443	32.45288	36.61789	41.43048	46.99583
24	30.42186	32.34904	34.42647	39.08260	44.50200	50.81558
25	32.03030	34.15776	36.45926	41.64591	47.72710	54.86451
26	33.67091	36.01171	38.55304	44.31174	51.11345	59.15638
27	35.34432	37.91200	40.70963	47.08421	54.66913	63.70577
28	37.05121	39.85980	42.93092	49.96758	58.40258	68.52811
29	38.79223	41.85630	45.21885	52.96629	62.32271	73.63980
30	40.56808	43.90270	47.57542	56.08494	66.43885	79.05819
31	42.37944	46.00027	50.00268	59.32834	70.76079	84.80168
32	44.22703	48.15028	52.50276	62.70147	75.29883	90.88978
33	46.11157	50.35403	55.07784	66.20953	80.06377	97.34316
34	48.03380	52.61289	57.73018	69.85791	85.06696	104.18376
35	49.99448	54.92821	60.46208	73.65222	90.32031	111.43478
36	51.99437	57.30141	63.27594	77.59831	95.53632	119.12087
37	54.03425	59.73395	66.17422	81.70225	101.62814	127.26812
38	56.11494	62.22730	69.15945	85.97034	107.70955	135.90421
39	58.23724	64.78298	72.23423	90.40915	114.09502	145.05846
40	60.40198	67.40255	75.40126	95.02552	120.79977	154.76197

(Continues)

TABLE III (Continued)
Future Value of an Ordinary Annuity of 1

$$FV - OA_{n,i} = \frac{(1+i)^n - 1}{i}$$

8%	9%	10%	11%	12%	15%	(n) Periods
1.00000	1.00000	1.00000	1.00000	1.00000	1.00000	1
2.08000	2.09000	2.10000	2.11000	2.12000	2.15000	2
3.24640	3.27810	3.31000	3.34210	3.37440	3.47250	3
4.50611	4.57313	4.64100	4.70973	4.77933	4.99338	4
5.86660	5.98471	6.10510	6.22780	6.35285	6.74238	5
7.33592	7.52334	7.71561	7.91286	8.11519	8.75374	6
8.92280	9.20044	9.48717	9.78327	10.08901	11.06680	7
10.63663	11.02847	11.43589	11.85943	12.29969	13.72682	8
12.48756	13.02104	13.57948	14.16397	14.77566	16.78584	9
14.48656	15.19293	15.93743	16.72201	17.54874	20.30372	10
16.64549	17.56029	18.53117	19.56143	20.65458	24.34928	11
18.97713	20.14072	21.38428	22.71319	24.13313	29.00167	12
21.49530	22.95339	24.52271	26.21164	28.02911	34.35192	13
24.21492	26.01919	27.97498	30.09492	32.39260	40.50471	14
27.15211	29.36092	31.77248	34.40536	37.27972	47.58041	15
30.32428	33.00340	35.94973	39.18995	42.75328	55.71747	16
33.75023	36.97371	40.54470	44.50084	48.88367	65.07509	17
37.45024	41.30134	45.59917	50.39593	55.74972	75.83636	18
41.44026	46.01846	51.15909	56.93949	63.43968	88.21181	19
45.76196	51.16012	57.27500	64.20283	72.05244	102.44358	20
50.42292	56.76453	64.00250	72.26514	81.69874	118.81012	21
55.45676	62.87334	71.40275	81.21431	92.50258	137.63164	22
60.89330	69.53194	79.54302	91.14788	104.60289	159.27638	23
66.76476	76.78981	88.49733	102.17415	118.15524	184.16784	24
73.10594	84.70090	98.34706	114.41331	133.33387	212.79302	25
79.95442	93.32398	109.18177	127.99877	150.33393	245.71197	26
87.35077	102.72314	121.09994	143.07864	169.37401	283.56877	27
95.33883	112.96822	134.20994	159.81729	190.37401	327.10408	28
103.96594	124.13536	148.63093	178.39719	214.58275	377.16969	29
113.28321	136.30754	164.49402	199.02088	241.33268	434.74515	30
123.34587	149.57522	181.94343	221.9137	271.29261	500.95692	31
134.21354	164.03699	201.13777	247.32362	304.84772	577.10046	32
145.95062	179.80032	222.25154	275.52922	342.42945	644.66553	33
158.62667	196.98234	245.47670	306.83744	384.52098	765.36535	34
172.31680	215.71076	271.02437	341.58955	431.66350	881.17016	35
187.10215	236.12472	299.12681	380.16441	484.46312	1014.34568	36
203.07032	258.37595	330.03949	422.98249	543.59869	1167.49753	37
220.31595	282.62978	364.04343	470.51056	609.83053	1343.62216	38
238.94122	309.06646	401.44778	523.26673	684.01020	1546.16549	39
259.05652	337.88245	442.59256	581.82607	767.09142	1779.09031	40

TABLE IV
Present Value of an Ordinary Annuity of 1

$$PV-OA_{n,i} = \frac{1 - \frac{1}{(1+i)^n}}{i}$$

(n) Periods	2%	2½%	3%	4%	5%	6%
1	.98039	.97561	.97087	.96154	.95238	.94340
2	1.94156	1.92742	1.91347	1.88609	1.85941	1.83339
3	2.88388	2.85602	2.82861	2.77509	2.72325	2.67301
4	3.80773	3.76197	3.71710	3.62990	3.54595	3.46511
5	4.71346	4.64583	4.57971	4.45182	4.32948	4.21236
6	5.60143	5.50813	5.41719	5.24214	5.07569	4.91732
7	6.47199	6.34939	6.23028	6.00205	5.78637	5.58238
8	7.32548	7.17014	7.01969	6.73274	6.46321	6.20979
9	8.16224	7.97087	7.78611	7.43533	7.10782	6.80169
10	8.98259	8.75206	8.53020	8.11090	7.72173	7.36009
11	9.78685	9.51421	9.25262	8.76048	8.30641	7.88687
12	10.57534	10.25776	9.95400	9.38507	8.86325	8.38384
13	11.34837	10.98319	10.63496	9.98565	9.39357	8.85268
14	12.10625	11.69091	11.29607	10.56312	9.89864	9.29498
15	12.84926	12.38138	11.93794	11.11839	10.379966	9.71225
16	13.57771	13.05500	12.56110	11.65230	10.83777	10.10590
17	14.29187	13.71220	13.16612	12.16567	11.27407	10.47726
18	14.99203	14.35336	13.75351	12.65930	11.68959	10.82760
19	15.67846	14.97889	14.32380	13.13394	12.08532	11.15812
20	16.35143	15.58916	14.87747	13.59033	12.46221	11.46992
21	17.01121	16.18455	15.41502	14.02916	12.82115	11.76408
22	17.65805	16.76541	15.93692	14.45112	13.16300	12.04158
23	18.29220	17.33211	16.44361	14.85684	13.48857	12.30338
24	18.91393	17.88499	16.93554	15.24696	13.79864	12.55036
25	19.52346	18.42438	17.41315	15.62208	14.09394	12.78336
26	20.12104	18.95061	17.87684	15.98277	14.37519	13.00317
27	20.70690	19.46401	18.32703	16.32959	14.64303	13.21053
28	21.28127	19.96489	18.76411	16.66306	14.89813	13.40618
29	21.84438	20.45355	19.18845	16.98371	15.14107	13.59072
30	22.39646	20.93029	19.60044	17.29203	15.37245	13.76483
31	22.93770	21.39541	20.00043	17.58849	15.59281	13.92909
32	23.46833	21.84918	20.38877	17.87355	15.80268	14.08404
33	23.98856	22.29188	20.76579	18.14765	16.00255	14.23023
34	24.49859	22.72379	21.13184	18.41120	16.19290	14.36814
35	24.99862	23.14516	21.48722	18.66461	16.37419	14.49825
36	25.48884	23.55625	21.83225	18.90828	16.54685	14.62099
37	25.96945	23.95732	22.16724	19.14258	16.71129	14.73678
38	26.44064	24.34860	22.49246	19.36786	16.86789	14.84602
39	26.90259	24.73034	22.80822	19.58448	17.01704	14.94907
40	27.35548	25.10278	23.11477	19.79277	17.15909	15.04630

(Continues)

TABLE IV (Continued)
Present Value of an Ordinary Annuity of 1

$$PV - OA_{n,i} = \frac{1 - \dfrac{1}{(1+i)^n}}{i}$$

8%	9%	10%	11%	12%	15%	(n) Periods
.92593	.91743	.90909	.90090	.89286	.86957	1
1.78326	1.75911	1.73554	1.71252	1.69005	1.62571	2
2.57710	2.53130	2.48685	2.44371	2.40183	2.28323	3
3.31213	3.23972	3.16986	3.10245	3.03735	2.85498	4
3.99271	3.88965	3.79079	3.69590	3.60478	3.35216	5
4.62288	4.48592	4.35526	4.23054	4.11141	3.78448	6
5.20637	5.03295	4.86842	4.71220	4.56376	4.16042	7
5.74664	5.53482	5.33493	5.14612	4.96764	4.48732	8
6.24689	5.99525	5.75902	5.53705	5.32825	4.77158	9
6.71008	6.41766	6.14457	5.88923	5.65022	5.01877	10
7.13896	6.80519	6.49506	6.20652	5.93770	5.23371	11
7.53608	7.16073	6.81369	6.49236	6.19437	5.42962	12
7.90378	7.48690	7.10336	6.74987	6.42355	5.58315	13
8.24424	7.78615	7.36669	6.98187	6.62817	5.72448	14
8.55948	8.06069	7.60608	7.19087	6.81086	5.84737	15
8.85137	8.31256	7.82371	7.37916	6.97399	5.95424	16
9.12164	8.54363	8.02155	7.54879	7.11963	6.04716	17
9.37189	8.75563	8.20141	7.70162	7.24967	6.12797	18
9.60360	8.95012	8.36492	7.83929	7.36578	6.19823	19
9.81815	9.12855	8.51356	7.96333	7.46944	6.25933	20
10.01680	9.29224	8.64869	8.07507	7.56200	6.31246	21
10.20074	9.44243	8.77154	8.17574	7.64465	6.35866	22
10.37106	9.58021	8.88322	8.26643	7.71843	6.39884	23
10.52876	9.70661	8.98474	8.34814	7.78432	6.43377	24
10.67478	9.82258	9.07704	8.42174	7.84314	6.46415	25
10.80998	9.92897	9.16095	8.48806	7.89566	6.49056	26
10.93516	10.02658	9.23722	8.54780	7.94255	6.51353	27
11.05108	10.11613	9.30657	8.60162	7.98442	6.53351	28
11.15841	10.19828	9.36961	8.65011	8.02181	6.55088	29
11.25778	10.27365	9.42691	8.69379	8.05518	6.56598	30
11.34980	10.34280	9.47901	8.73315	8.08499	6.57911	31
11.43500	10.40624	9.52638	8.76860	8.11159	6.59053	32
11.51389	10.46444	9.56943	8.80054	8.13535	6.60046	33
11.58693	10.51784	9.60858	8.82932	8.15656	6.60910	34
11.65457	10.56682	9.64416	8.85524	8.17550	6.61661	35
11.71719	10.61176	9.67651	8.87859	8.19241	6.62314	36
11.75518	10.65299	9.70592	8.89963	8.20751	6.62882	37
11.82887	10.69082	9.73265	8.91859	8.22099	6.63375	38
11.87858	10.72552	9.75697	8.93567	8.23303	6.63805	39
11.92461	10.75736	9.77905	8.95105	8.24378	6.64178	40

INDEX

A

absenses. *see* compensated absenses

accounting
- agency fund, 47, 56, 384–86
- arbitrage and government, 221–22
- basic books of, 95–100
- budgeting and basis of, 87–91, 120–23, 163–64
- business scandal and, 23–25
- capital asset, 243–47
- capital project fund, 204–10
- debt refinancing, 222–27
- debt service fund, 210–15
- educational institution, 495–500
- ethics, 628–32
- expenditures and basis of, 163–64
- federal government structure for, 643–47
- GAAP and, 22–23
- health care, 484–95
- internal service fund, 325–29
- international trends in governmental, 672–74
- investment trust fund, 386–87
- long-term obligations, 277–79
- methods and reporting, 2–8
- pension fund, 373–77, 378–82
- principles, 21–22, 318–19
- proprietary fund, 309–18
- restricted asset, 321–22
- revenue and basis of, 120–23
- special assessment fund, 217–21
- standard-setting and principles, 23–27
- *see also* basis of accounting; encumbrance accounting; fund accounting; Governmental Accounting Standards Board (GASB); managerial accounting

accrual accounting
- budgeting process and, 87–91
- capital project funds, 205
- fund accounting and, 36–40
- government expenditures and, 163–64
- government revenues and, 120–23
- internal service funds and, 326–29
- nonexpendable funds and, 357–59

activity-based costing (ABC), 540, 542–45, 552

ad valorem taxes, 124

agency funds, 47, 56, 384–86

allocated costs, 527–28, 541–45

American Institute of Certified Public Accounts (AICPA)
- auditing, performance, 585–86
- educational institution accounting, 495–500
- ethics, accounting and auditing, 628–32
- FASAB and the, 646–47
- financial reporting and, 12 n.1
- fund-raising costs and, 546
- generally accepted accounting practices (GAAP), 606–07
- government auditing and, 605
- health care accounting, 487, 490–91, 493, 495
- not-for-profit accounting, 450, 479
- standard-setting and the, 23–27

analyses of variance, cost, 523, 548–52

annual reports
- budgeting process and, 87
- financial reporting and, 4
- financial reporting and the CAFR, 56–60, 409–15
- municipal, 15
- not-for-profits versus government, 60–61
- *see also* budgets; financial statements

annuity, 451

apportionments, 85–86

appropriations, 79, 85, 644
- *see also* expenditures; Office of Management and Budget (OMB)

arbitrage, 221–22

assessed value, property, 124

assessments
- agency funds and special, 386
- capital project financing with, 204–10
- government fiscal, 421–37
- governmental funds and special, 215–21

assets
- accounting for capital, 139–43, 176–79, 243–47, 328
- accounting for federal, 663–71
- capital budgets and, 79–80
- collectibles as, 247, 470–72
- deferred maintenance of, 252–53
- financial statements and reporting, 253–54
- fund accounting, 35–36
- generation and revenues, 6, 126
- government reporting of, 656–71
- governmental funds as, 41–48
- impaired, 254–56
- infrastructure as capital, 248–49
- intangible, 254
- market value versus present value, 280
- measurement focus, 121–23
- not-for-profit reporting of, 451–59, 481
- operational objectives and capital, 586–92
- pension fund, 372–75, 378–82
- project ranking of, 590–92
- restricted, 321–22
- retroactive capitalization of, 250–51

attestation engagements, 605–06

auditing
- budgeting process and, 87
- CAFR, 411

Chief Financial Officers Act of 1990, 26, 645
compliance and performance, 604
ethics and, 628–32
General Accounting Office (GAO), 645
governing boards and, 13–14
government, 605–06
management cycle, 567
performance measurement, 580–84
performance versus financial, 620–28
reports, types of, 618–20
service efforts and accomplishments, 585–86
single audits, 614–20
standards and oversight, 23–27, 606–12
average costs, 523–25

B
balance sheet
example of not-for-profit, 454–55
federal reporting and the, 656–61
governmental funds, 433
proprietary fund accounting, 312–13
bankruptcy, 261, 274–77
basis of accounting
budgeting process and, 87–91
capital project funds, 205
debt service funds, 211–12
expenditures and, 163–64
fund accounting and, 36–40
not-for-profit organization, 450
revenues and, 120–23
see also accounting
benefit-cost analysis, 566, 587–90
board of directors. *see* governing boards
board of trustees. *see* governing boards
bonds
accounting principles and, 22
anticipation notes, 283–84
capital project financing with, 204–10
conduit debt and, 291–92
debt refunding and, 222–27
demand, 281–83
discounts and premiums, 181–82
general obligation, 288–89
industrial development, 291–92
insurance, 292–93
payout schedules, 293–94
ratings, 14–15, 292–96
restricted assets as, 321–22
revenue, 288–89, 309, 338
books of account, 95–100
see also accounting
borrowing. *see* debt; deficits
Budget and Accounting Act of 1921, 645
budgets
accounting principles and, 21–22
analyses of variance, cost, 548
assessing fiscal condition by, 428
basis of accounting and, 87–91, 120–23, 163–64
benefit–cost analysis in, 587–90, 592
capital projects and, 205, 587
compliance and control of, 95–97, 105–06
entry recording, 97–100
FASB reporting and, 20–21
federal, 643, 647–49
financial reporting and, 12–13, 187–88
fund accounting and, 80–81, 319–20
GASB reporting and, 17–18
government versus not-for-profit, 91–95
internal service funds and, 326–29
management cycle in, 567
operational objectives, 3–8, 568–75
phases and process of, 83–87
traditional object classification, 568–69
types of, 78–80
zero-base, 573–79
business
activity of government and not-for-profits, 11, 309–12, 522
auditing, 604
basis of accounting and, 36–40, 163–64
cash flow reporting by, 459
comparison with not-for-profit organizations, 2–8
conduit debt and, 291–92
depreciation, 243
franchise tax, 133
scandal and oversight, 23–25, 605, 610–11

C
capital assets. *see* assets
capital budgets, 79–80, 587, 592
capital contributions, 320–21
capital improvement program (CIP), 587
capital leases, 284–88
capital projects funds
arbitrage and, 221–22
debt financing and, 178–79
government, 47–50, 204–10
capitation fees, 487, 491
case studies. *see* examples; in practice
cash basis of accounting, 36–40, 87–91, 121–23
cash flow
accounting and reporting, 3
fund accounting and, 35–36
not-for-profit reporting of, 459
proprietary fund accounting, 312–17
Catalog of Federal Domestic Assistance, 618–19
charitable groups. *see* 501(c) corporations; independent sector; not-for-profit organizations
charitable remainder trust, 476–77
Chief Financial Officers Act of 1990, 26, 643–45
citizens and taxpayers, financial reports and, 13–16
claims and judgments, 171–72, 172 n.8
collectibles, accounting for, 247, 469–70
colleges and universities, 415–21, 495–505

compensated absenses, 166–69, 168 n.4
compliance
  auditing and reports on, 614–20
  budget controls and, 95–97, 105–06
  FASB reporting and, 20–21
  financial reporting and, 12–13, 56–60
  GASB objectives and, 17–18
  performance auditing and, 604
comprehensive annual financial report (CAFR)
  assessing fiscal condition by, 421–37, 500–501
  elements of the, 409–15
  government funds and, 56–60
Comptroller General of the United States, 605
Congressional Budget Office (CBO), 86, 646
constituencies, financial reports and, 13–16
contracting out, 529–36
contributions
  accounting for, 247
  assessing fiscal condition by, 500–504
  collectibles as, 469–70
  conditional promises as, 470–72
  full cost determination in, 545–48
  not-for-profit accounting for, 459–62, 484
  pass-through, 472–74
  split interest agreements as, 476–77
  use-restricted, 466–67
  voluntary services as, 468–70
  see also nonexchange revenues; revenues
cost accounting
  allocated costs, 527–28, 541–45
  analyses of variance in, 548–52
  average costs, 523–25
  contracting out issues in, 531–33
  fixed vs. variable costs, 523–24
  full cost determination in, 540
  fund-raising costs, 547–48
  incremental costs, 522, 525–28
  sunk costs, 526–27
  see also accounting; managerial accounting
county government, 402–03
  see also government entities
creditors and investors, financial reports and, 13–15
credits, ledger accounts, 96–100
  see also revenues

D
debits, 96–100
  see also expenses; liabilities
debt
  accounting principles and, 21–22
  bond market rating and, 294–96
  capital asset financing with, 177–80
  capital budgets and, 79–80
  conduit, 291–92
  government and tax-exempt, 14–15
  interest and principal on, 180–82
  internal service funds and, 328
  long-term, 275–79, 281–92
  margins, 293
  moral obligation, 293
  not-for-profit accounting for, 481
  operating deficits and, 5–6
  operational objectives and, 586
  overlapping, 289–91
  refunding, 222–27
  restricted asset accounting and, 321–22
  revenue, 337–38
  tax-exempt, 12, 14–15
  see also liabilities
debt margins, 293
debt service funds
  accounting for, 207–10
  arbitrage and, 221–22
  costs and expenditures, 294
  government, 47–50, 204
defeasance, in-substance, 224–25
deferred maintenance, 252–53
deficits, 5–6, 331, 431
demand bonds, 281–83
depreciation
  capital assets, 243–45
  deferred maintenance and, 253
  fund accounting and, 358
  infrastructure, 249
  internal service funds and, 329
  not-for-profit accounting for, 477–78, 481
derivatives, 257–59
derived tax revenues, 130–35
direct costs, 540
disbursements, 522
disclosure
  debt, 292
  not-for-profit organization, 503–04
  requirements, 259–61, 476
discounts and premiums, bond, 181–82, 205–07
dividends. *see* interest and dividends
donations. *see* contributions; nonexchange revenues
donors and grantors
  contributions from, 462
  educational institution accounting and, 499–500
  endowments and annuities, 451
  financial reports and, 13, 16, 545
  fund accounting and, 61
  pass-through funds and, 472–74
  split interest agreements and, 476–77
  use-restricted contributions and, 466–67
duties. *see* nonexchange revenues

E
educational institutions, 415–21, 495–505
employees, financial reports and, 13–17
encumbrance accounting, 88, 96, 100–106
endowment funds, 451
  see also fiduciary funds; nonexchange revenues; revenues

enterprise funds
capital contributions and, 320–21
fund accounting and, 47, 316, 318
government business activity and, 54, 309–12
reporting requirements, 334–37
types of budgets and, 80
waste disposal costs and, 322–25
see also proprietary funds
entitlements, 135
environmental issues, 322–25
equity
accountability in interperiod, 17–18
budgeting and interperiod, 80
capital assets and, 586
financial reporting and, 120–21
fiscal practices of interperiod, 5–6
misuse of, 296
owner's, 7–8
ethics, accounting and auditing, 628–32
examples
agency funds, 384–85
analyses of cost variance, 548–52
average cost calculation, 524–25
benefit–cost analysis, 587–91
bonds, 206–07, 282–83, 284
bonds, government accounting for, 278–79
budgetary entries, 98–99
capital assets, 139–43, 177–80, 245–47, 255–56
capital project funds, 207–10
claims and judgments, 171–72
contracting out, 530–31
contributions, 466–67, 468–69, 471–72
debt, 180–81, 212–15, 223–25, 290–93
depreciation, 358, 477–78
educational institution, 498–500
encumbrance cycle, 101–05
enterprise funds, 324–25
ethics, accounting and auditing, 631–32
financial reporting, 403–04, 408–09
fines as revenue, 129–30
food stamps, 141
fund accounting, 38–40, 364–68
fund-raising costs, 547
government reporting entities, 401–02
grants and other nonexchange revenue, 136–40
health care, 490–91, 493–95
income taxes, 134–35
incremental costs, 526–28
inflation, 364
interest and dividend income, 146–47
internal service fund accounting, 327–29, 336
intragovernmental transfers, 184–86
investment gains and losses, 144–45, 357, 361–62, 475
leasing, 287–88
license fees and permits, 147–48
nonexchange expenditures, 183–84
not-for-profit accounting, 453, 479–84
objectives reporting, 18–19
on-behalf payments, 142
pass-through funds, 472–74
pension funds, 170–71, 376–77
performance audits, 626–27
pledges, 464–66
prepayments, 175–76
property taxes as revenue, 125–29
restricted assets, 322
revenues and expenses, 58–59
sabbatical leave, 168–69
sales taxes, 131–33
self-insurance, 333–34
sick leave, 167–68
subsidies and loan guarantees, 670–71
supplies and materials, 173–75
tax anticipation notes, 284
vacation leave, 166–67
wages and salaries, 164–65
see also in practice
exchange expenditures, 163
exchange revenues, 662–63
see also revenue
exemptions, taxation, 124–25
expenditures. *see* expenses
expenses
accounting and reporting, 3–8, 21–22, 187–88
budgeting process and, 83–87
capital asset financing as, 177–80
claims and judgments as, 171–72
classification of, 80–81
compensated absenses as, 166–69
educational institution reporting of, 496–97
financial reporting and the CAFR, 56–60
financing sources and, 186–88
fund accounting and, 35–36
government reporting of, 120–23, 656–71
governmental funds as, 41–48
health care reporting of, 488–89
independent sector, 10
interest and principal as, 180–82
intragovernmental transfers as, 184–86
ledger accounts, 95–100
nonexchange, 163, 183–84
not-for-profit reporting of, 452–59, 481
operational objectives and, 573–75
pensions as, 170–71
prepaid, 175–76
supplies and materials as, 173–75
wages and salaries as, 164–65
external users, 8, 13, 21–22, 97–100

F

Federal Accounting Standards Advisory Board (FASAB)
accounting practices of, 1–2
budgeting and, 87–91
federal accounting standards and, 662–71

financial reporting and, 12–13, 643
functions of, 23–27, 646–47
Federal Credit Reform Act of 1990, 669
Federal Financial Management Improvement Act of 1996, 643
fiduciary funds
asset accounting and, 354–55
basis of accounting and, 120
depreciation, 358
financial reporting and the CAFR, 59–60
investment returns and, 359–63
types of, 47–48, 55–56, 355–56
see also agency funds
Financial Accounting Foundation, 24, 319
Financial Accounting Standards Board (FASB)
AICPA and, 646
compensated absenses, 168 n.4
contributions, 466–70, 471–73
depreciation, 243–45, 477–78
educational institution accounting, 495–500
financial reporting and, 20–21
functions of, 1–2, 23–27
fund accounting and, 40–41
health care accounting, 493–94
internal service funds, 326–29
investment gains and losses, 357, 360–63, 474–75
investment income, 143–47
not-for-profit accounting and, 450, 478–84
pledges and, 464–66
reporting requirements, 60–61, 274
financial audits, 605–06
financial statements
accounting principles and, 21–22
assessing fiscal condition by, 500–504
auditing and, 605–06, 618–20
basis of accounting and government, 120–23
budgeting process and interim, 85–87
business activity in governmental, 309–12
business scandal and, 23–25, 605
CAFR reporting in, 56–60, 409–15
educational institution, 496–505
fund accounting and, 40–41
GAAP and, 22–23
government proprietary fund, 312–16
health care accounting, 488
internal service funds and, 329–31
not-for-profit, 451–59, 456–58
objectives of, 16–21
pension cost reporting in, 377–82
proprietary fund, 334–37
purpose and use, 12–16, 187–88
see also annual reports; government financial statements
fines, revenue recognition of, 123, 129–30
see also nonexchange revenues
fiscal condition, assessing government, 421–37
Fitch IBCA, bond market rating, 15, 294–96
501(c) corporations, 10
see also not-for-profit organizations
fixed assets. *see* assets
fixed budgets, 80
fixed costs, 523
flexible budgets, 80
food stamps, 140–41
forecasting, 79–80, 83–87
fund accounting
arbitrage and, 221–22
assets and revenue recognition in, 150
basis of accounting, 120–23, 357–59, 364–68
business activity and, 309–12
capital assets and, 243–47
capital project, 204–10
defined, 35–38
federal budget and, 647–49
financial reporting and the CAFR, 56–60
governmental, 47–50, 277–79
health care, 484–95
not-for-profits vs. government, 60–61, 450–53
reserve funds and, 294
users and uses of, 6–7
see also accounting; governmental funds; nonexchange revenues
fund balance, 97–100
fund financial statements, 40–41
fund-raising. *see* contributions; nonexchange revenues

G
General Accounting Office (GAO), 585 n.6, 604–05, 643–46
general funds
federal budget, 647
governmental, 47–48
not-for-profit accounting and, 451–53
operating budgets and, 79
self-insurance and, 331–34
see also governmental funds
generally accepted accounting principles (GAAP)
auditing, 606
basis of accounting and, 120–23
budgets and financial reporting, 87–91, 187–88
creation of, 22–23
FASAB and, 646–47
financing sources and, 186–88
infrastructure assets and, 251
international trends in, 672–74
not-for-profit accounting and, 478–84
summary of, 26
generally accepted auditing standards (GAAS), 606–07
generally accepted government auditing standards (GAGAS), 607–09
gifts. *see* nonexchange revenues
governing boards, 13–14, 83–87, 566–68
see also legislatures
Government Auditing Standards (GAS), 605, 618, 623
government entities

analyses of costs and performance, 548–52
assessment, financial, 421–37, 500–504
auditing standards for, 606–12
bankruptcy, 274–77
basis of accounting and, 36–40
budget process of, 83–87, 89–91
business accounting in, 309–12
business comparison to, 2–8, 522, 604–05
CAFR, 409–15
capital asset management in, 243–47
cash flow reporting by, 459
debt, 274, 281–92
depreciation, 243–45
ethics and, 629–30
federal budget and, 647–49
financial reporting and, 56–60, 401–09, 656–62
fund accounting and, 35–38, 184–86
GASB objectives and, 17–20
infrastructure assets of, 248–49
intergovernmental grants and, 135–38
international trends in evaluating, 672–74
investment returns, 143–47, 359–63
management cycle in, 566–68
managerial accounting in, 522–28
marketable securities in, 256–61
municipalities as, 8–9
nonexchange revenues and, 123–25
not-for-profit comparison to, 11–12, 24–26, 60–61, 91–95
on-behalf payments of, 141–42
pricing and cost determination by, 537–45
privatization, 529–36
proprietary funds, 334–37, 655–56
self-insurance and, 331–34
service efforts and accomplishments in, 581–84
special purpose, 415–21
zero-base budgeting in, 575
see also municipalities; U. S. Government
Government Finance Officers Association (GFOA), 248, 251, 411, 429
government financial statements
accounting and reporting structure, 643–47, 649–55
assessing fiscal condition by, 421–37
assets and revenue recognition in, 150
capital assets in, 140, 143, 180, 220–21, 244–45
claims and judgments, 172
compensated absenses in, 167–70
credit enhancements in, 292–94
expense reporting in, 186
fines as revenue in, 130
fund accounting and, 40–41
grant revenue in, 138, 184
international trends in, 672–74
long-term debt in, 182, 278
materials and supplies in, 175–76
pension contributions in, 171
reporting requirements for, 401–03, 656–71
revenue reporting in, 128–30, 148–49, 186
service efforts and accomplishments in, 581–84
special purpose, 415–21
taxes as revenue in, 132–33, 135
wages and salaries in, 165
see also financial statements
Government Performance and Results Act of 1993, 643, 671–72
Governmental Accounting Standards Board (GASB)
accounting practices of, 1–2
AICPA and, 646
basis of accounting, 120–23, 359
bond anticipation notes, 283–84
budgeting and, 87–91
capital assets, 177, 254–55
claims and judgments, 172, 172 n.8
contributions, 320–21
debt accounting, 181, 218–19
defeasance, in-substance, 225–26
demand bonds, 282
depreciation, 243–45
derived tax revenues, 131–32, 134–35
disclosure, 259–61, 292
educational institution accounting, 495–500
enterprise fund accounting, 318
environmental issues, 323
financial reporting and, 12–13, 16–20, 187–88, 408–09
food stamps, 141
functions of, 23–27
fund accounting and, 40–41, 80–81
infrastructure accounting, 249, 251–52
intergovernmental transfers, 185
inventory accounting, 173
investments and, 143–47, 259–61, 356–57, 360–61
leasing, 285–87
license fees and permits, 147–48
nonexchange expenditures, 183–84
nonexchange revenues and, 126, 136
not-for-profit accounting and, 450
on-behalf payments, 142
pension funds, 170–71, 373
performance measurement, 581
prepayments, 175–76
proprietary fund accounting, 312–16, 318–19, 335, 337
reporting requirements, 60–61, 274
revenue recognition, 129–30
sabbatical leave, 168–69
self-insurance, 331–33
sick leave, 167–68
vacation leave, 166–67
wages and salaries, 164–65
see also accounting
governmental funds
assets and revenue recognition in, 150
budgeting process and, 87–91, 187–88
categories of, 46–50
expenditures and accounting for, 163–64

federal budget and, 647–49
financial reporting in, 59–60, 334–37
intergovernmental transfers in, 184–86
other financing sources in, 186–88
pension costs in, 377
permanent funds as, 354–55
types of, 41–46
see also fund accounting; general funds
grantors and donors, 13, 16, 545
grants
accounting for, 183–84
capital project financing with, 204–10
educational institution accounting for, 499–500
pass-through funds as, 386
see also contributions; nonexchange revenues

H
health care providers
accounting and reporting by, 450–59, 484, 487
assessment, financial, 500–504
capitation fees, 491
charity care, 491–93
fee-for-service revenue, 489–91
government versus not-for-profit, 495
malpractice, 493–95
Hill-Burton Act, 491
human capital, accounting for, 665

I
in practice
auditing, 612, 627, 629
bankruptcy, 276–77
budgets, 85–90
business scandal, 25
contracting out, 534–36
contributions, 468–70, 471
educational institutions, 496, 503
financial reporting, 15, 17, 22–23, 188
government fiscal condition, 425
government investment risks, 258–59, 261
health care accounting, 492
infrastructure assets, 251
internal service funds, 330
international accounting standards, 674
interperiod equity violations, 296
investment returns, 363
long-term obligations, 281
operational objectives, 574
pension funds, 370
pledges, 463–64
politics and budgeting, 85
pricing and full cost determination, 539
special assessments, 217
wages and salaries, 165
see also examples
income, business objectives and, 3
income statement, 3–4, 312–15
income taxes, 133–35, 662–63
see also taxation
incremental costs. *see* cost accounting
independent sector, 9–10
see also not-for-profit organizations
indirect costs, 540
industrial development bonds, 291–92
inflation, 360, 363–64
infrastructure, accounting for, 248–53
in-substance defeasance, 224–25
intangible assets, accounting for, 254
see also assets
interest and dividends
bond discounts and premiums, 181–82, 205–07
debt and, 180–82, 223–25
government accounting for, 146–47
not-for-profit accounting for, 482
intergenerational equity. *see* equity
Internal Revenue Service (IRS), 503, 643–44
internal service funds
accounting for, 319, 325–29
reporting requirements, 334–37
self-insurance and, 331–34
uses of, 47, 54–55, 309–12
see also proprietary funds
internal users, 8, 13–16, 97–100
international accounting standards, 672–74
International Federation of Accountants (IFAC), 673–74
interperiod equity. *see* equity
inventory accounting, 173–75, 481, 666–67
investment
gains and losses from, 359–63, 474–76, 482
income from, 143–47
inflation and, 363–64
market value versus present value, 279–81
marketable securities as, 243, 256–61
investment trust funds, 386–87
investors and creditors, financial reports and, 13–15

J
Jefferson, Thomas, 643
journals and ledgers, 95–100

L
landfill costs, 322–25
leasing, 179–80, 284–88
ledgers and journals, 95–100
legislation
Budget and Accounting Act of 1921, 645
Chief Financial Officers Act of 1990, 26, 643–45
Federal Credit Reform Act of 1990, 669
Federal Financial Management Improvement Act of 1996, 643
Government Performance and Results Act of 1993, 585, 643, 671–72
Hill-Burton Act, 491
Hospital Survey and Construction Act of 1946, 491

Investment Company Act of 1940, 387
Reorganization Act of 1945, 645
Sarbanes-Oxley Act of 2002, 24, 605
Single Audit Act of 1984, 604, 607
Tax Reform Act of 1986, 222
see also U. S. Government
legislatures, 83–87, 566–68
see also governing boards
liabilities
assessing fiscal, 433–34
basis of accounting and government, 121–23
compensated absenses as, 166–69
fund accounting, 35–36
government, 41–48, 164, 171–76, 656–71
long-term obligations as, 274, 293–94
long-term versus current, 281–92
market value versus present value, 279–81
not-for-profit reporting of, 6, 451–59
pension contributions as, 170–71
see also debt
license fees and permits, 147–48
liens, 124–25
loan guarantees and subsidies, 274, 669–71
local government, 402–03
see also government entities
long-term debt. *see* debt
long-term obligations. *see* debt; liabilities

M
management
cycle for social programs, 566–68
discussion and analysis (MD&A), 56–60, 411–13
financial reports and organizational, 13–16
operational objectives and budget, 569–75
service efforts and accomplishments (SEA), 581–84
managerial accounting
accountants role in, 566–68
analyses of costs and performance, 548–52
auditing and, 606
business objectives and, 522
contracting out and, 529–36
FASAB and, 647
fixed versus variable costs, 523–25
full cost determination and, 538–45
fund-raising costs and, 545–48
incremental costs and benefits, 525–28
pricing policies and, 537–38
market value, 7–8, 124, 279–81
measurement focus, basis of accounting and, 121–23
Medicare, 492, 540, 668–69
modeling, budget, 86
modified accrual accounting. *see* accrual accounting
Moody's Investor Service, bond market rating, 15, 294–96
moral obligation debt, 293
municipalities, 8–9
see also government entities

N
National Council on Governmental Accounting (NCGA), 23, 188, 277
natural expenses, 455, 459
net assets. *see* assets
nonappropriation budgets, 79
nonexchange expenditures, 163, 183–84
see also expenditures
nonexchange revenues
accounting for, 124–25, 135–38, 163, 545
federal accounting standards and, 662–63
pass-through funds as, 140–41
pledges as, 462–66, 483
types and limitations of, 123–24
voluntary, 123, 136
see also contributions; revenues
non-profit, defined, 2
not-for-profit organizations
analyses of costs and performance, 548–52
assessment, financial, 500–504
auditing standards for, 606–12
bankruptcy, 274–77
basis of accounting and, 36–40
budget process of, 83–87, 95
business accounting in, 309–11
business comparison to, 2–8
cash flow reporting by, 459
characteristics of, 478–84
comparison to businesses, 522, 604–05
comparison to government entities, 24–26, 60–61, 91–95
debt and, 274, 291–92
depreciation, 243
financial reporting, 415–21
fund accounting and, 35–38
fund-raising costs and, 545–48
government entities comparison to, 11–12
information on, 503–04
investment returns, 143–47, 359–63
management cycle in, 566–68
managerial accounting, 522–28
marketable securities in, 256–61
outsourcing by, 529–36
pricing and cost determination by, 537–45
restricted funds, 204
see also educational institutions; health care providers; independent sector

O
object classification budgets, 81–83
objectives
benefit-cost analysis and operational, 587–90
capital assets and operational, 586–92
FASB reporting, 20–21
federal financial reporting, 647–48, 671–72
financial reporting, 3, 12–13, 16–17
GASB reporting, 17–20

operational, 569–75
performance measurement of, 580–84
project ranking and, 590–92
zero-base budgeting and operational, 575–79
Office of Management and Budget (OMB), 86, 605, 613–14, 644–45
on-behalf payments, 141–42
operating costs. *see* expenses
operating fund. *see* general funds
operating leases, 284–88
operational audits, 605–06
outsourcing, 529–36
overhead costs, 540, 542–45, 548–52
oversight agencies. *see* regulatory agencies
overspending. *see* expenditures
owner's equity, 7–8, 35–36

P

pass-through funds, 140–41, 386, 472–74
penalties. *see* nonexchange revenues
pension funds
accounting, 378–82
contributions, 170–71
determining costs to, 373–77
government trust funds and, 372–73
importance of, 368–70
plans, types of, 371–72
post-employment benefits and, 382–84
see also fiduciary funds
performance
FASB reporting and, 20–21
financial reporting and, 12–13, 671–72
GASB reporting and entity, 17–18
indicators and measurement of, 580–84
international trends in evaluating, 672–74
measuring budget, 78–80
measuring federal government, 585
measuring objectives and, 2–8
performance audits, 605–06, 620–28
performance budgets
budgeting process and, 79, 87
operational objectives and, 573–75
use of, 81–83
see also budgets; program budgets
permanent funds, 47, 50, 354–55, 364–68
pledges. *see* contributions; nonexchange revenues
politics
assessing fiscal condition and, 426–27
budgeting process and, 83–87, 89–90
international accounting standards and, 672–74
oversight and jurisdictional, 24–26
revenue constraints and, 3–8
premiums and discounts, bond, 181–82, 205–07
primary government, 402–03
see also government entities
privatization, 311, 529–36
profits, 2–3, 11
program budgets, 573–75, 579–80
see also budgets; performance budgets
project ranking, 566, 577–79, 590–92
property taxes, 123, 124–29
see also taxation
proprietary funds
accounting, basis of, 163–64
accounting statements for, 312–16
debt refinancing in, 226–27
federal, 655–56
financial reporting and the CAFR, 59–60
government business activity and, 309–12
governmental funds versus, 204
pension costs in, 376–77
reporting requirements, 334–37
special assessment accounting in, 219–21
uses of, 47, 50–55
Public Company Accounting Oversight Board, 24
public debt. *see* debt

R

ranking, project, 566, 577–79, 590–92
receipts, incremental, 522
refinancing, government, 222–27
regulation, 12–13, 222
see also legislation; U. S. Government
regulatory agencies, 4, 13, 16, 22–27
see also oversight agencies
religious organizations, 10, 25, 125
see also independent sector
Reorganization Act of 1945, 645
repayments, 175–76
repurchase agreements, 257
reserve funds, 294, 331
restricted assets. *see* assets
restricted fund accounting, 204, 451
restricted resources. *see* fund accounting
retirement plans, 382–84
see also pension funds
revenue
accounting and reporting, 3–8, 21–22, 187–88
assessing fiscal condition by, 431–33
budgeting process and, 83–87
CAFR and reporting, 56–60
classification of, 80–81
contributions as, 320–21
debt, 275
derived, 130–35
educational institution reporting of, 496–97
fund accounting and, 35–36
government reporting of, 120–23, 148–49, 656–71
governmental funds as, 41–48
health care reporting of, 488–91
independent sector, 10
ledger accounts and, 95–100
license fees and permits as, 147–48
nonexchange, 123–24

not-for-profit reporting of, 452–59
permanent fund earnings as, 356–57
pricing policies and, 537–38
property taxes as, 126
revenue anticipation notes, 284
"sixty-day rule", 123, 131
see also nonexchange revenue
revenue bonds, 288–89, 309, 338
revenue debt, 337–38
revolving funds, federal budget, 648–49

S
sabbatical leave. *see* compensated absenses
salaries and wages, 164–65
see also compensated absenses
sales taxes, 130–33
Sarbanes-Oxley Act of 2002, 24, 605
scandal
auditing standards and, 610–11
ethics and, accounting and auditing, 628–32
oversight and business, 23–25, 605
Schedule of Expenditures of Federal Awards, 618–19
securities, marketable, 243, 256–61, 321–22
see also investment
self-insurance, 331–34
service contributions. *see* contributions; volunteering
shared revenue, 135
see also nonexchange revenues
short-term obligations. *see* liabilities
sick leave. *see* compensated absenses
Single Audit Act of 1984, 604, 607, 613–14
single audits, performing, 614–20
social programs, 566–68, 668–71
Social Security Administration, 649, 668–69
special assessments. *see* assessments
special funds, federal budget, 647
special purpose government, 402–03, 415–21, 495–505
see also government entities
special revenue funds, 47, 49
spending. *see* expenditures
Standard & Poor's, 15, 294–96, 338
standard costs, 548–52
standards. *see* American Institute of Certified Public Accounts (AICPA); Financial Accounting Standards Board (FASB); Governmental Accounting Standards Board (GASB)
state government, 402–03
see also government entities
statements. *see* financial statements
stockholders. *see* external users
subsidies and loan guarantees, 274, 669–71
sunk costs, 526–27
supplies and materials. *see* inventory accounting

T
taxation
arbitrage and, 221–22
authority of government, 11–12
capital project financing with, 204–10
income taxes and, 133–35
intergovernmental payments in lieu of, 135–36
overlapping debt and, 289–91
revenue recognition of, 123–24
sales taxes and, 130–33
tax anticipation notes, 284
see also Internal Revenue Service (IRS); nonexchange revenues; property taxes; revenues
tax-exempt debt, 12, 14–15, 221, 291–92
taxpayers and citizens, financial reports and, 13–16
trust funds
endowments and, 354
federal budget and, 647–48
investment issues with, 386–87
permanent funds as, 356
split interest agreements and, 476–77
uses of, 47, 55
see also fiduciary funds

U
U. S. Constitution, 643
U. S. Department of Defense, 643
U. S. Department of the Treasury, 643–44
U. S. Government
accounting and reporting structure, 643–47
Annual Report of the, 649–50, 650 n.4
auditing standards and the, 605
financial oversight and the, 26–27
Financial Report of the, 649–55
Social Security Administration, 649, 656–71
see also government entities; legislation
unified federal budget, 649
universities and colleges, 415–21, 495–505

V
vacation. *see* compensated absenses
variable costs, 523
voluntary organizations, reporting by, 455
volunteering, 10, 468–70, 484

W
wages and salaries, 164–65, 376, 480
see also compensated absenses
waste disposal, 322–25

Z
zero-base budgeting (ZBB), 573–79